P9-EEL-768

Guide to Gale Literary Criticism Series

When you need to review criticism of literary works, these are the Gale series to use:

If the author's death date is:	You should turn to:
After Dec. 31, 1959 (or author is still living)	*CONTEMPORARY LITERARY CRITICISM* for example: Jorge Luis Borges, Anthony Burgess, William Faulkner, Mary Gordon, Ernest Hemingway, Iris Murdoch
1900 through 1959	*TWENTIETH-CENTURY LITERARY CRITICISM* for example: Willa Cather, F. Scott Fitzgerald, Henry James, Mark Twain, Virginia Woolf
1800 through 1899	*NINETEENTH-CENTURY LITERATURE CRITICISM* for example: Fedor Dostoevski, Nathaniel Hawthorne, George Sand, William Wordsworth
1400 through 1799	***LITERATURE CRITICISM FROM 1400 TO 1800 (excluding Shakespeare)*** for example: Anne Bradstreet, Daniel Defoe, Alexander Pope, François Rabelais, Jonathan Swift, Phillis Wheatley
	SHAKESPEAREAN CRITICISM Shakespeare's plays and poetry
Antiquity through 1399	*CLASSICAL AND MEDIEVAL LITERATURE CRITICISM* for example: Dante, Homer, Plato, Sophocles, Vergil, the Beowulf Poet

---

Gale also publishes related criticism series:

CHILDREN'S LITERATURE REVIEW

This series covers authors of all eras who have written for the preschool through high school audience.

SHORT STORY CRITICISM

This series covers the major short fiction writers of all nationalities and periods of literary history.

ISSN 0895-9439

Volume 3

Short Story Criticism

Excerpts from Criticism of the Works of Short Fiction Writers

8136

Sheila Fitzgerald
Editor

Thomas Votteler
Associate Editor

DETROIT • NEW YORK • FORT LAUDERDALE • LONDON

STAFF

835 Penobscot Bldg.
Detroit, MI 48226-4094

Library of Congress Catalog Card Number 88-641014
ISBN 0-8103-2552-7
ISSN 0895-9439

Printed in the United States of America

Contents

Preface vii

Acknowledgments ix

Authors to Be Featured in *SSC,* Volumes 4 and 5 xiii

Additional Authors to Appear in Future Volumes xv

Djuna Barnes
1892-1982 1

Elizabeth Bowen
1899-1973 28

Paul Bowles
1910- 57

Italo Calvino
1923-1985 87

Arthur C. Clarke
1917- 122

Nathaniel Hawthorne
1804-1864 152

James Joyce
1882-1941 198

H. P. Lovecraft
1890-1937 254

Paule Marshall
1929- 297

Alice Munro
1931- 319

Isaac Bashevis Singer
1904- 351

Dylan Thomas
1914-1953 391

Literature Criticism Series Cumulative Author Index 417

SSC Cumulative Nationality Index 465

SSC Cumulative Title Index 467

Preface

Short Story Criticism (SSC) presents significant passages from criticism of the world's greatest short story writers and provides supplementary materials—biographical and bibliographical—to guide the interested student to a greater understanding of the authors of short fiction. This series was developed in response to suggestions from librarians serving high school, college, and public library patrons who had noted an increasing number of requests for critical material on short story writers. Although major short story writers are covered in such Gale literary criticism series as *Contemporary Literary Criticism (CLC), Twentieth-Century Literary Criticism (TCLC), Nineteenth-Century Literature Criticism (NCLC),* and *Literature Criticism from 1400 to 1800 (LC),* librarians perceived the need for a series devoted solely to writers of the short story genre. A survey conducted in September 1986 provided the editors with fuller information on the needs of library patrons, and, with these criteria in mind, the scope of *SSC* was defined.

The Scope of the Work

SSC is designed to serve as an introduction to the major writers of the short story genre and to the major commentators on those writers. The major short story writers of all eras and nationalities, from Washington Irving and Guy de Maupassant, whom many critics consider the creators of the modern short story, to such contemporary practitioners as Eudora Welty and Donald Barthelme will be covered in the series. Since these authors have inspired a great deal of relevant critical material, *SSC* is necessarily selective, and the editors have chosen the most important published criticism to aid students in their study of short story writers.

Each author entry is intended to provide a comprehensive overview of major criticism on an author. Twelve to fifteen authors will be included in each volume (compared with approximately 30 authors in a *CLC* volume of similar size) so that more attention may be given to an author. Each author entry presents a historical survey of the critical response to that author's work: some early criticism is presented to indicate initial reaction, later criticism is selected to represent any rise or decline in the author's reputation, and current analyses provide students with a modern view. The length of an author entry is intended to reflect the amount of critical attention the author has received from critics writing in English and from foreign critics in translation. Critical articles and books that have not been translated into English are excluded. Every attempt has been made to identify and include excerpts from the seminal essays on each author's work. In order to provide these important critical pieces, the editors will sometimes reprint essays that have appeared in previous volumes of Gale's literary criticism series. Such duplication, however, never exceeds twenty to twenty-five percent of the author entry.

The Organization of the Book

The author entry consists of the following elements: author heading, biographical and critical introduction, a list of principal works, excerpts of criticism (each preceded by an explanatory note and followed by a bibliographical citation), and an additional bibliography for further reading.

- The **author heading** consists of the author's full name, followed by birth and death dates. The unbracketed portion of the name denotes the form under which the author most commonly wrote. If the author wrote consistently under a pseudonym, the pseudonym will be listed in the author heading and the real name given in parentheses on the first line of the biographical and critical introduction. Also located at the beginning of the introduction to the author entry are any name variations under which the author wrote, including transliterated forms for authors whose languages use nonroman alphabets. Uncertainty as to a birth or death date is indicated by a question mark.

- The **biographical and critical introduction** contains background information designed to introduce the reader to an author and to the critical debates surrounding his or her work. Parenthetical material following the introductions provides references to biographical and critical reference series published by Gale, including *CLC, TCLC, NCLC,* and *LC, Children's Literature Review, Contemporary Authors, Dictionary of Literary Biography,* and *Something about the Author.*

- *SSC* entries include **portraits of the author.** Many entries also contain illustrations of materials pertinent to an author's career, including holographs of manuscript pages, title pages, dust jackets, letters, or representations of important people, places, and events in the author's life.

- The list of **principal works** is chronological by date of first publication and lists the most important works by the author. The first section comprises the short story collections, novellas, and novella collections. The second section gives information on other major works by the author. For foreign authors where there are both foreign language collections and English translations, the editors have provided original foreign language publication information and have selected what are considered the best and most complete English language editions of the short fiction.

- **Criticism** is arranged chronologically in each author entry to provide a useful perspective on changes in critical evaluation over the years. All short story, novella, and collection titles by the author featured in the entry are printed in boldface type to enable the user to ascertain without difficulty the works discussed. Also for purposes of easier identification, the critic's name and the publication date of the essay are given at the beginning of each piece of criticism. Unsigned criticism is preceded by the title of the journal in which it appeared. When an anonymous essay is later attributed to a critic, the critic's name appears in brackets at the beginning of the excerpt and the bibliographical citation.

- Critical essays are prefaced with **explanatory notes** as an additional aid to students using *SSC.* The explanatory notes provide several types of useful information, including: the reputation of a critic, the importance of a work of criticism, the specific type of criticism (biographical, psychoanalytic, structuralist, etc.), and a synopsis of the criticism.

- A complete **bibliographical citation,** designed to facilitate location of the original essay or book by the interested reader, follows each piece of criticism.

- The **additional bibliography** appearing at the end of each author entry suggests further reading on the author. In some cases it includes essays for which the editors could not obtain reprint rights.

Cumulative Indexes

Each volume of *SSC* includes a cumulative index to authors listing all the authors who have appeared in *SSC, CLC, TCLC, NCLC,* and *LC,* as well as cross-references to the Gale series *Children's Literature Review, Authors in the News, Contemporary Authors, Contemporary Authors Autobiography Series, Dictionary of Literary Biography, Something about the Author, Something about the Author Autobiography Series,* and *Yesterday's Authors of Books for Children.* Users will welcome this cumulated author index as a useful tool for locating an author within the literary criticism series.

Each volume of *SSC* also includes a cumulative title index. This index lists all short story, novella, and collection titles contained in the series in alphabetical order. Titles of short story collections, novellas, and novella collections are printed in italics, while all individual short stories are printed in roman type with quotation marks. Titles are followed by the corresponding volume and page numbers where commentary on the work may be located. In cases where the same title is used by different authors, the author's surname is given in parentheses after the title, e.g., *Collected Short Stories* (Welty), *Collected Short Stories* (Faulkner). For foreign titles, a cross-reference is given to the translated English title in the index.

Suggestions Are Welcome

Readers who wish to suggest authors to appear in future volumes, or who have other suggestions, are cordially invited to contact the editors, either by letter or by calling Gale's toll-free number: 1-800-347-GALE.

Acknowledgments

The editors wish to thank the copyright holders of the excerpted criticism included in this volume, the permissions managers of many book and magazine publishing companies for assisting us in securing reprint rights, and Anthony Bogucki for assistance with copyright research. We are also grateful to the staffs of the Detroit Public Library, the Library of Congress, the University of Detroit Library, the University of Michigan Library, and the Wayne State University Library for making their resources available to us. Following is a list of the copyright holders who have granted us permission to reprint material in this volume of *SSC*. Every effort has been made to trace copyright, but if omissions have been made, please let us know.

COPYRIGHTED EXCERPTS IN *SSC,* VOLUME 3, WERE REPRINTED FROM THE FOLLOWING PERIODICALS:

The American Book Review, v. 2, May-June, 1980. © 1980 by *The American Book Review*. Reprinted by permission of the publisher.—***The American Spectator,*** v. 21, September, 1988. Copyright © *The American Spectator* 1988. Reprinted by permission of the publisher.—***Arizona Quarterly,*** v. 21, Spring, 1965. Copyright © 1965 by *Arizona Quarterly*. Reprinted by permission of the publisher.—***Book World—The Washington Post,*** September 7, 1969 for "Global Pillage and the Chateau d' If" by Paul West. © 1969 Postrib Corp. Reprinted by courtesy of *The Washington Post* and the author.—***Callaloo,*** v. 6, Spring-Summer, 1983 for "Early Short Fiction by Paule Marshall" by Dorothy L. Denniston. Copyright © 1983 by Charles H. Rowell. All rights reserved. Reprinted by permission of the author.—***Chicago Review,*** v. 31, Spring, 1980. Copyright © 1980 by *Chicago Review*.—***Chicago Sunday Tribune Magazine of Books,*** February 16, 1958 for "Engaging Adventure Tales" by Fritz Leiber. Copyright © 1958, renewed 1986 by The Chicago Tribune Company. Reprinted by permission of the author.—***The Christian Science Monitor,*** December 24, 1953. Copyright 1953, renewed 1981 by The Christian Science Publishing Society. All rights reserved. Reprinted by permission from *The Christian Science Monitor.*/ April 9, 1982 for "Nobel Laureate's Superb Stories" by Bruce Allen. Copyright 1982 by the author. Reprinted by permission of the author.—***CLA Journal,*** v. XVI, September, 1972. Copyright, 1972 by The College Language Association. Used by permission of The College Language Association.—***Claremont Quarterly,*** v. 11, Autumn, 1963 for "The Shadow of the Past: Hawthorne's Historical Tales" by Robert H. Fossum. Copyright, Claremont Graduate School and University Center, 1963. Reprinted by permission of the author.—***Criticism,*** v. XV, Spring, 1973 for "Passage through 'The Dead' " by John Wilson Foster. Copyright, 1973, Wayne State University Press. Reprinted by permission of the publisher and the author.—***Critique: Studies in Modern Fiction,*** v. VIII, Spring-Summer, 1966; v. XI, 1969; v. XXI, 1979; v. XXV, Summer, 1984; v. XXVII, Fall, 1985. Copyright © 1966, 1969, 1979, 1984, 1985 Helen Dwight Reid Educational Foundation. All reprinted with permission of the Helen Dwight Reid Educational Foundation, published by Heldref Publications, 4000 Albemarle Street, N. W., Washington, DC 20016.—***Crypt of Cthulhu,*** v. 4, August 1, 1985 for "The Prophet from Providence" by Dirk W. Mosig; v. 5, November 1, 1985 for "H. P. Lovecraft and the Cthulhu Mythos" by Robert M. Price; v. 7, June 23, 1988 for "The Cosmic Connection" by Mike Ashley. Copyright © 1985, 1988. All reprinted by permission of the respective authors.—***Essays in Literature,*** v. XI, Fall, 1984. Copyright 1984 by Western Illinois University. Reprinted by permission of the publisher.—***Extrapolation,*** v. 30, Spring, 1989. Copyright 1989 by The Kent State University Press. Reprinted by permission of the publisher.—***Forum for Modern Language Studies,*** v. VI, October, 1970 for "Fantasy, Alienation and the 'Racconti' of Italo Calvino" by J. R. Woodhouse. Copyright © 1970 by *Forum for Modern Language Studies* and the author. Reprinted by permission of the publisher and the author.—***James Joyce Quarterly,*** v. 4, Fall, 1966. Copyright, 1966, The University of Tulsa. Reprinted by permission of the publisher.—***Journal of the Short Story in English,*** n. 8, Spring, 1987. © Université d' Angers, 1987.—***The University of Kansas City Review,*** v. XXXIII, Summer, 1967 for "Two Portraits of the Artist: James Joyce's 'Young Man'; Dylan Thomas's 'Young Dog' " by Warren French. Copyright University of Kansas City, 1967. Reprinted by permission of the publisher and the author.—***London Review of Books,*** v. 7, March 7, 1985 for "Return of the Native" by Hugh Barnes; v. 8, April 17, 1986 for "The Slap" by Michael Wilding. Both appear here by permission of the *London Review of Books* and the respective authors./ v. 9, February 5, 1987. Appears here by permission of the *London Review of Books*.—***Los Angeles Times Book Review,*** May 1, 1988. Copyright, 1988, *Los Angeles Times*. Reprinted by permission of the publisher.—***MELUS,*** v. 5, Spring, 1978; v. 12, Summer, 1985. Copyright, MELUS, The Society for the Study of Multi- Ethnic Literature of the United States, 1978, 1985. Both reprinted by permission of the publisher.—***Midstream,*** v. XX, August-September, 1974 for "True Feathers" by Sylvia Rothchild; v. XXII, May, 1976 for "I. B. Singer: The Good of Stories" by Alvin H. Rosenfeld. Copyright © 1974, 1976 by The Theodor Herzl Foundation, Inc. Both reprinted by permission of the publisher and the respective authors.—***Modern Fiction Studies,*** v. 22, Autumn, 1976; v. 24, Summer, 1978. Copyright © 1976, 1978 by Purdue Research Foundation, West Lafayette, IN

47097. All rights reserved. Both reprinted with permission.—***The Nathaniel Hawthorne Journal,*** 1976. Copyright © 1976 by Bruccoli Clark Publishers, Inc. Reprinted by permission of the publisher.—***The Nation,*** New York, v. 205, September 4, 1967. Copyright 1967 *The Nation* magazine/ The Nation Company, Inc. Reprinted by permission of the publisher.—***Negro American Literature Forum,*** v. 9, Fall, 1975. Copyright © Indiana State University 1975. Reprinted with the permission of Indiana State University.—***The New Criterion,*** v. IV, December, 1985 for "Italo Calvino 1923-1985" by James Gardner. Copyright © 1985 by The Foundation for Cultural Review. Reprinted by permission of the author.—***The New England Quarterly,*** v. XXX, March, 1957. Copyright 1957, renewed 1985 by *The New England Quarterly*. Reprinted by permission of the publisher.—***The New Republic,*** v. 157, September 2, 1967. © 1967 The New Republic, Inc. Reprinted by permission of *The New Republic*.—***New Statesman,*** v. LXIII, May 18, 1962. © 1962 Statesman & Nation Publishing Co. Ltd. Reprinted by permission of the publisher.—***New York Herald Tribune Books,*** November 24, 1929. Copyright 1929, renewed 1957 I.H.T. Corporation. Reprinted by permission of the publisher.—***The New York Review of Books,*** v. XI, November 21, 1968; v. XXIV, May 12, 1977; v. XXXI, December 6, 1984. Copyright © 1968, 1977, 1984 Nyrev, Inc. All reprinted with permission from *The New York Review of Books*.—***The New York Times Book Review,*** January 6, 1924. Copyright 1924 by The New York Times Company. Reprinted by permission of the publisher./ July 15, 1956; October 11, 1959; October 1, 1961; August 5, 1962; October 12, 1969; February 7, 1971; April 10, 1977; September 16, 1979; September 30, 1979; October 28, 1979; March 21, 1982; June 30, 1985; September 29, 1985; September 14, 1986; October 23, 1988. Copyright © 1956, 1959, 1961, 1962, 1969, 1971, 1977, 1979, 1982, 1985, 1986, 1988 by The New York Times Company. All reprinted by permission of the publisher.—***The New Yorker,*** v. XXX, January 22, 1955 for "A Singer and a Spectre" by Anthony West. Copyright 1955, renewed 1983 by The New Yorker Magazine, Inc. Reprinted by permission of the Wallace Literary Agency, Inc./ v. LXI, November 18, 1985 for "States of Mind" by John Updike. © 1985 by the author. Reprinted by permission of the publisher.—***The North American Review,*** v. 252, November, 1967. Copyright © 1967 by the University of Northern Iowa. Reprinted by permission from *The North American Review*.—***Novel: A Forum on Fiction,*** v. 7, Winter, 1974. Copyright © *Novel: A Forum on Fiction,* 1974. Reprinted by permission of the publisher.—***The Ontario Review,*** n. 12, Spring-Summer, 1980. Copyright © 1980 by The Ontario Review, Inc. Reprinted by permission of the publisher.—***Papers on Language & Literature,*** v. 20, Winter, 1984. Copyright © 1984 by the Board of Trustees, Southern Illinois University at Edwardsville. Reprinted by permission of the publisher.—***Partisan Review,*** v. XXXV, Winter, 1968. Copyright © 1968 by *Partisan Review*. Reprinted by permission of the publisher.—***Perspective,*** v. 14, Spring, 1965 for "Elizabeth Bowen: Imagination as Therapy" by George Greene. © Perspective, Inc. Reprinted by permission of the author.—***Perspectives on Contemporary Literature,*** v. 5, 1979. Copyright © 1979 by The University Press of Kentucky. Reprinted by permission of the publisher.—***Queen's Quarterly,*** v. 93, Summer, 1986 for "The Plots of Life: The Realism of Alice Munro" by George Woodcock. Copyright © 1986 by the author. Reprinted by permission of the author.—***The Review of Contemporary Fiction,*** v. 2, Fall, 1982 for "Paul Bowles: 'Do Not Appropriate My Object' " by Linda S. Wells. Copyright, 1982, by John O'Brien. Reprinted by permission of the author.—***Revue belge de philologie et d'histoire,*** v. LIX, 1981. Reprinted by permission of the publisher.—***Room of One's Own,*** v. 4, 1979 for "Who Do You Think You Are?: A Review-Interview with Alice Munro" by Carole Gerson. © 1979 by the authors. Reprinted by permission of Carole Gerson and Alice Munro.—***San Jose Studies,*** v. XII, Spring, 1986 for " 'The Time of Friendship': The Short Fiction of Paul Bowles" by John Ditsky. © San Jose State University Foundation, 1986. Reprinted by permission of the publisher and the author.—***Saturday Review,*** v. XLIV, September 16, 1961. © 1961 *Saturday Review* magazine.—***The Saturday Review of Literature,*** v. XXXIII, December 23, 1950. Copyright 1950, renewed 1978 by *Saturday Review* magazine.—***The Sewanee Review,*** v. LVIII, Winter, 1950; v. LX, Autumn, 1952. Copyright 1950, renewed 1977; copyright 1952, renewed 1980 by The University of the South. Both reprinted by permission of the editor of *The Sewanee Review*./ v. LXXIII, Winter, 1965. © 1965 by The University of the South. Reprinted by permission of the editor of *The Sewanee Review*.—***The Short Story Review,*** v. 6, Winter, 1989. Copyright, *Short Story Review,* 1989. Reprinted by permission of the publisher.—***The Southern Review,*** Louisiana State University, n.s. v. V, Winter, 1969 for "Djuna Barnes's Short Stories: An Estrangement of the Heart" by Suzanne C. Ferguson; n.s. v. VII, April, 1970 for "Singer and Hawthorne: A Prevalence of Satan" by Elaine Gottlieb. Copyright, 1969, 1970, by the respective authors. Both reprinted by permission of the respective authors.—***Studies in Canadian Literature,*** v. 5, 1980 for " 'Dull, Simple, Amazing and Unfathomable': Paradox and Double Vision in Alice Munro's Fiction' " by Helen Hoy; v. 8, 1983 for " 'The Other Side of Dailiness': The Paradox of Photography in Alice Munro's Fiction" by Lorraine M. York. Copyright by the respective authors. Both reprinted by permission of the editors.—***Studies in Short Fiction,*** v. X, Fall, 1973; v. 14, Spring, 1977; v. 15, Summer, 1978; v. 19, Fall, 1982. Copyright 1973, 1977, 1978, 1982 by Newberry College. All reprinted by permission of the publisher.—***Time,*** New York, v. 114, August 27, 1979. Copyright 1979 Time Inc. All rights reserved. Reprinted by permission from *Time*.—***The Times Literary Supplement,*** n. 3367, September 8, 1966; n. 3451, April 18, 1968; n. 4058, January 9, 1981; n. 4164, January 21, 1983; n. 4196, September 2, 1983; n. 4239, June 29, 1984; n. 4279, April 5, 1985. © Times Newspapers Ltd. (London) 1966, 1968, 1981, 1983, 1984, 1985. All reproduced from *The Times Literary Supplement* by permission.—***Twentieth Century Literature,*** v. 32, Fall & Winter, 1986. Copyright 1986, Hofstra University Press. Reprinted by permission of the publisher.—***The Village Voice,*** v. XXIX, May 15, 1984 for a review of "Reena and Other Stories" by Adam Gussow. Copyright © News Group Publications, Inc., 1984. Reprinted by permission of *The Village Voice* and the author.—***World Literature Written in English,*** v. 11, April, 1972 for "Unconsummated Relationships: Isolation and Rejection in Alice Munro's Stories" by H. Dahlie. © copyright 1972 *WLWE-World Literature Written in English*. Reprinted by permission of the publisher and the author.

COPYRIGHTED EXCERPTS IN *SSC,* VOLUME 3, WERE REPRINTED FROM THE FOLLOWING BOOKS:

Ackerman, John. From ***Dylan Thomas: His Life and Work.*** Oxford University Press, London, 1964. Copyright © 1964 John Ackerman. Reprinted by permission of Jonathan Clowes Ltd., London, on behalf of John Ackerman.—Austin, Allan E. From ***Elizabeth Bowen.*** Twayne, 1971. Copyright 1971 by Twayne Publishers. All rights reserved. Reprinted with the permission of Twayne Publishers, Inc., a division of G. K. Hall & Co., Boston.—Beachcroft, T. O. From ***The Modest Art: A Survey of the Short Story in English.*** Oxford University Press, London, 1968. © Oxford University Press, 1968. Reprinted by permission of Curtis Brown Ltd., London.—Blackmur, R. P. From an afterword to ***The Celestial Railroad and Other Stories.*** By Nathaniel Hawthorne. New American Library, 1963. Afterword Copyright © 1963 by The New American Library of World Literature, Inc. All rights reserved. Reprinted by arrangement with New American Library, a Division of Penguin Books USA Inc., New York, NY.—Borges, Jorge Luis. From ***Other Inquisitions: 1937-1952.*** Translated by Ruth L. C. Simms. University of Texas Press, 1964. Copyright © 1964 by University of Texas Press. Reprinted by permission of the publisher.—Bowen, Elizabeth. From " 'The Demon Lover': Preface to the American Edition," in ***The Mulberry Tree: Writings of Elizabeth Bowen.*** Edited by Hermione Lee. Virago Press, 1986. Copyright 1959 by Elizabeth Bowen. Collection copyright © 1986 by Curtis Brown Ltd., London, Literary Executors of the Estate of Elizabeth Bowen. Reprinted by permission of Virago Press.—Bowen, Elizabeth. From "Preface to Stories by Elizabeth Bowen," in ***The Mulberry Tree: Writings of Elizabeth Bowen.*** Edited by Hermione Lee. Virago Press, 1986. Copyright 1959 by Elizabeth Bowen. Collection copyright © 1986 by Curtis Brown Ltd., London, Literary Executors of the Estate of Elizabeth Bowen. Reprinted by permission of Virago Press.—Brigg, Peter. From "Three Styles of Arthur C. Clarke: The Projector, the Wit, and the Mystic," in ***Arthur C. Clarke.*** Edited by Joseph D. Olander and Martin Harry Greenberg. Taplinger Publishing Company, 1977. Copyright © 1977 by Joseph D. Olander and Martin Harry Greenberg. All rights reserved. Reprinted by permission of the publisher.—Buchen, Irving H. From ***Issac Bashevis Singer and the Eternal Past.*** New York University Press, 1968. © 1968 by New York University. Reprinted by permission of the publisher.—Burgess, Anthony. From ***Re Joyce.*** Norton, 1965. Published in England as ***Here Comes Everybody: An Introduction to James Joyce for the Ordinary Reader.*** Faber, 1965. Copyright © 1965 by Anthony Burgess. Reprinted by permission of W. W. Norton & Company, Inc. In Canada by the author.—Burleson, Donald R. From ***H. P. Lovecraft: A Critical Study.*** Greenwood Press, 1983. Copyright © 1983 by Donald R. Burleson. All rights reserved. Reprinted by permission of Greenwood Press, Inc., Westport, CT.—Cannon, Peter. From ***H. P. Lovecraft.*** Twayne, 1989. Copyright 1989 by Twayne Publishers. All rights reserved. Reprinted with the permission of Twayne Publishers, a division of G. K. Hall & Co., Boston.—Clareson, Thomas D. From "The Cosmic Loneliness of Arthur C. Clarke," in ***Arthur C. Clarke.*** Edited by Joseph D. Olander and Martin Harry Greenberg. Taplinger Publishing Company, 1977. Copyright © 1977 by Joseph D. Olander and Martin Harry Greenberg. All rights reserved. Reprinted by permission of the publisher.—Collier, Eugenia. From "The Closing of the Circle: Movement from Division to Wholeness in Paule Marshall's Fiction," in ***Black Women Writers (1950-1980): A Critical Evaluation.*** Edited by Mari Evans. Anchor Books, 1984. Copyright © 1984 by Mari Evans. All rights reserved. Reprinted by permission of Doubleday, a division of Bantam, Doubleday, Dell Publishing Group, Inc.—Daiches, David. From ***The Novel and the Modern World.*** Revised edition. University of Chicago Press, 1960. © 1960 by The University of Chicago. Reprinted by permission of the publisher and the author.—Derleth, August. From "H. P. Lovecraft and His Work," in ***The Dunwich Horror and Others: The Best Supernatural Stories.*** By H. P. Lovecraft, edited by August Derleth. Arkham House, 1963. Copyright, 1963 by August Derleth. Reprinted by permission of Arkham House Publishers, Inc., and Scott Meredith Literary Agency, Inc.—Doubleday, Neal Frank. From ***Hawthorne's Early Tales: A Critical Study.*** Duke University Press, 1972. Copyright © 1972 by Duke University Press, Durham, NC. Reprinted by permission of the publisher.—Eisinger, Chester E. From ***Fiction of the Forties.*** University of Chicago Press, 1963. © 1963 by Chester E. Eisinger. Reprinted by permission of The University of Chicago Press.—Gittleman, Edwin. From "Dybbukianism: The Meaning of Method in Singer's Short Stories," in ***Contemporary American-Jewish Literature: Critical Essays.*** Edited by Irving Malin. Indiana University Press, 1973. Copyright © 1973 by Indiana University Press. All rights reserved. Reprinted by permission of the publisher.—Gittleman, Sol. From ***From Shtetl to Suburbia: The Family in Jewish Literary Imagination.*** Beacon Press, 1978. Copyright © 1978 by Sol Gittleman. All rights reserved. Reprinted by permission of Beacon Press.—Hollow, John. From ***Against the Night, the Stars: The Science Fiction of Arthur C. Clarke.*** Harcourt Brace Jovanovich, 1983. Copyright © 1983, 1976 by John Hollow. Reprinted by permission of Harcourt Brace Jovanovich, Inc.—Howe, Irving. From an introduction to ***Selected Short Stories of Issac Bashevis Singer.*** Edited by Irving Howe. The Modern Library, 1966. Copyright © 1966 by Random House, Inc. All rights reserved. Reprinted by permission of Random House, Inc.—Hyman, Stanley Edgar. From ***Standards: A Chronicle of Books for Our Time.*** Horizon Press, 1966. © 1966 by Stanley Edgar Hyman. Reprinted by permission of the Literary Estate of Stanley Edgar Hyman.—Joshi, S. T. From ***H. P. Lovecraft.*** Starmont House, 1982. Copyright © 1982 by Starmont House. All rights reserved. Reprinted by permission of the publisher.—Joyce, James. From a letter in ***Letters of James Joyce, Vol. II.*** Edited by Richard Ellmann. Faber & Faber, 1966. © 1966 by F. Lionel Monro, as Administrator of the Estate of James Joyce. All rights reserved. Reprinted by permission of Faber & Faber Ltd.—Kannenstine, Louis F. From ***The Art of Djuna Barnes: Duality and Damnation.*** New York University Press, 1977. Copyright © 1977 by New York University. Reprinted by permission of the publisher.—Kazin, Alfred. From ***Contemporaries.*** Little, Brown and Company, 1962. Copyright © 1962 by Alfred Kazin. Reprinted by permission of the author.—Korg, Jacob. From ***Dylan Thomas.*** Twayne, 1965. Copyright 1965 by Twayne Publishers. All rights reserved. Reprinted with the permission of Twayne Publishers, a division of G. K. Hall & Co., Boston.—Leiber, Fritz. From "A Literary Copernicus," in ***Something About Cats.*** Edited by August Derleth. Arkham House, 1949. Copyright 1949 by August Derleth. Renewed 1977 by April Derleth Smith and Walden Derleth.

Reprinted by permission of the author.—Levy, Maurice. From ***Lovecraft: A Study in the Fantastic.*** Translated by S. T. Joshi. Wayne State University Press, 1988. Originally published as ***Lovecraft on du Fantastique.*** Bourgois, 1985. Copyright © 1985 by Christian Bourgois Editeur. Reprinted by permission of Christian Bourgois Editeur.—Lovecraft, H. P. From ***Marginalia.*** Edited by August Derleth and Donald Wandrei. Arkham House, 1944. Copyright 1944, renewed 1972 by August Derleth and Donald Wandrei. All rights reserved. Reprinted by permission of Arkham House Publishers, Inc., and Scott Meredith Literary Agency, Inc.—Macy, John. From ***The Critical Game.*** Boni and Liveright, Publishers, 1922. Copyright 1922 by Boni & Liveright. Renewed 1950 by John Macy. Reprinted by permission of Liveright Publishing Corporation.—Martin, Terence. From "The Method of Hawthorne's Tales," in ***Hawthorne Centenary Essays.*** Edited by Roy Harvey Pearce. Ohio State University Press, 1964. Copyright © 1964 by the Ohio State University Press. All rights reserved. Reprinted by permission of Roy Harvey Pearce.—Messerli, Douglas. From "The Newspaper Tales of Djuna Barnes," in ***Smoke and Other Early Stories.*** By Djuna Barnes, edited by Douglas Messerli. Sun & Moon Press, 1982. © Sun & Moon Press, 1982. Reprinted by permission of the publisher.—Moskowitz, Sam. From ***Seekers of Tomorrow: Masters of Science Fiction.*** World Publishing Co., 1966. Copyright © 1966, 1964, 1963, 1962, 1961 by Sam Moskowitz. Reprinted by permission of the author.—Munro, Alice. From an interview in ***Eleven Canadian Novelists Interviewed by Graeme Gibson.*** Toronto: House of Anansi Press, 1972. Copyright © Graeme Gibson. Reprinted by permission of the publisher.—O'Faolain, Sean. From ***The Vanishing Hero: Studies in Novelists of the Twenties.*** Eyre & Spottiswoode, 1956. Copyright © 1956, 1957, 1984, 1985 by Sean O'Faolain. All rights reserved. Reprinted by permission of Sean O'Faolain & Curtis Brown Associates, Ltd. In Canada by A. P. Watt Ltd. on behalf of Sean O'Faolain.—Pacifici, Sergio. From ***A Guide to Contemporary Italian Literature: From Futurism to Neorealism.*** The World Publishing Company, 1962. Copyright © 1962 by Harper & Row, Publishers, Inc. All rights reserved. Reprinted by permission of Harper & Row, Publishers, Inc.—Pattee, Fred Lewis. From ***The Development of the American Short Story: An Historical Survey.*** Harper & Brothers, 1923. Copyright 1923 by Harper & Row, Publishers, Inc. Renewed 1951 by Fred Lewis Pattee. Reprinted by permission of Harper & Row, Publishers, Inc.—Peden, William. From ***The American Short Story: Continuity and Change, 1940-1975.*** Second edition. Houghton Mifflin, 1975. Copyright © 1964, 1975 by William Peden. All rights reserved. Reprinted by permission of Houghton Mifflin Company.—Plumb, Cheryl J. From ***Fancy's Craft: Art and Identity in the Early Works of Djuna Barnes.*** Susquehanna University Press, 1986. © 1986 by Cheryl J. Plumb. Reprinted by permission of the publisher.—Poirier, W. Richard. From "Paul Bowles's 'Under the Sky'," in ***Stories: British and American.*** Edited by Jack Barry Ludwig and W. Richard Poirier. Houghton Mifflin, 1953. Copyright 1953 by Jack Barry Ludwig and W. Richard Poirier. Renewed 1981 by Jack Barry Ludwig. All rights reserved.—Pound, Ezra. From ***The Selected Letters of Ezra Pound: 1907-1941.*** Edited by D. D. Paige. New Directions, 1971. Copyright 1950 by Ezra Pound. Renewed 1978 by D. D. Paige. Reprinted by permission of New Directions Publishing Corp. for the Literary Estate of Ezra Pound.—Pratt, Annis. From ***Dylan Thomas' Early Prose: A Study in Creative Mythology.*** University of Pittsburgh Press, 1970. Copyright © 1970, University of Pittsburgh Press. All rights reserved. Reprinted by permission of the publisher.—Scott, James B. From ***Djuna Barnes.*** Twayne, 1976. Copyright 1976 by Twayne Publishers. All rights reserved. Reprinted with the permission of Twayne Publishers, a division of G. K. Hall & Co., Boston.—Siegel, Paul N. From "Gimpel and the Archetype of the Wise Fool," in ***The Achievement of Issac Bashevis Singer.*** Edited by Marcia Allentuck. Southern Illinois University Press, 1969. Copyright © 1969, by Southern Illinois University Press. All rights reserved. Reprinted by permission of the publisher.—Slusser, George Edgar. From ***The Space Odysseys of Arthur C. Clarke.*** The Borgo Press, 1978. Copyright © 1978 by George Edgar Slusser. All rights reserved. Reprinted by permission of the publisher.—St. Armand, Barton Levi. From ***The Roots of Horror in the Fiction of H. P. Lovecraft.*** Dragon Press, 1977. © 1977, Barton Levi St. Armand. All rights reserved. Reprinted by permission of the publisher.—Torchiana, Donald T. From ***Backgrounds for Joyce's Dubliners.*** Allen & Unwin, 1986. © Donald T. Torchiana, 1986. All rights reserved. Reprinted by permission of Unwin Hyman Ltd.—Wilson, Angus. From an introduction to ***The Collected Stories of Elizabeth Bowen.*** Knopf, 1981. Copyright © 1981 by Curtis Brown Limited, Literary Executors of the Estate of the Late Elizabeth Bowen. All rights reserved. Reprinted by permission of Alfred A. Knopf, Inc.—Wilson, Edmund. From ***Classics and Commercials: A Literary Chronicle of the Forties.*** Farrar, Straus and Company, 1950. Copyright 1950 by Edmund Wilson. Renewed 1977 by Elena Wilson. All rights reserved. Reprinted by permission of Farrar, Straus and Giroux, Inc.

PERMISSION TO REPRINT PHOTOGRAPHS APPEARING IN *SSC,* VOLUME 3, WAS RECEIVED FROM THE FOLLOWING SOURCES:

Berenice Abbott/Commerce Graphics Ltd, Inc.: **p. 1;** Special Collections, University of Maryland College Park Libraries: **p. 10;** Photo from ***The Amazon Letters,*** by George Wickes. Courtesy of the author: **p. 14;** Jack Manning/NYT Pictures: **p. 21;** The Granger Collection, New York: **pp. 28, 198, 391;** Photograph by Cherie Nutting, courtesy of Paul Bowles: **p. 57;** © Jerry Bauer: **pp. 87, 319, 351;** Photograph by Rohan De Silva, courtesy of Arthur C. Clarke: **p. 122;** © 1968 Metro-Goldwyn-Mayer Inc.: **p.131;** Photograph by David C. Bishop: **p. 141;** The Bettmann Archive, Inc.: **p. 152;** Mary Evans Picture Library: **p. 172;** John Flower: **p. 205;** Courtesy of Elizabeth T. Layton: **pp. 230, 246;** Photograph by Rhoda Nathans: **p. 297;** Reproduced by permission of the Trustees for the copyrights of Dylan Thomas: **p. 397;** J.M. Dent & Sons Ltd.: **p. 405;** Photograph by Bill Brandt: **p. 409.**

Authors to Be Featured in *SSC*, Volumes 4 and 5

Jorge Luis Borges, 1899-1986. (Argentinian short story writer, essayist, poet, translator, critic, biographer, travel writer, novelist, and scriptwriter)—Considered the foremost contemporary Spanish-language fiction writer, Borges is noted as the author of esoteric short stories that blend fantasy and realism while addressing complex philosophical questions. Such stories as "The Library of Babel" and "Tlön, Uqbar, Orbis Tertius" explore time, infinity, identity, and memory in innovative fictional forms.

Kay Boyle, b. 1902. (American novelist, short story writer, poet, essayist, and translator)—An eminent author of the American expatriate movement of the 1920s, Boyle is noted for her intriguing and innovative prose style. Her stories often reflect an ardent commitment to social activism and convey an impassioned concern with the individual's search for love and understanding.

Pearl S. Buck, 1892-1973. (American novelist, short story writer, dramatist, essayist, editor, biographer, autobiographer, translator, and author of children's books)—Best known for her Pulitzer Prize-winning novel, *The Good Earth,* Buck is distinguished as the first American woman to have received the Nobel Prize in Literature. Critics applaud Buck's astute descriptions of setting and character in both her novels and her short stories.

Nikolai Gogol, 1809-1852. (Russian novelist, dramatist, short story writer, essayist, critic, and poet)—Gogol is regarded as a progenitor of the modern short story and a seminal influence on Russian literature. In such celebrated stories as "The Overcoat" and "The Nose," Gogol employed grotesque humor, fantastical symbolism, and flamboyant language to satirize Russian bureaucracy and to depict humanity as impotent, alienated, and frustrated.

O. Henry, 1862-1910. (American short story writer and novelist)—A major figure in the history of the short story, Henry is renowned for his poignant caricatures of life in early twentieth-century New York City. Considered a master of the "suprise ending," Henry is perhaps most readily recognized for such widely anthologized stories as "The Gift of the Magi" and "The Last Leaf."

Zora Neale Hurston, 1891-1960. (American novelist, folklorst, short story writer, essayist, dramatist, and autobiographer)—Remembered especially for her novel *Their Eyes Were Watching God,* Hurston wrote short stories that are acclaimed for their vivid use of southern black folklore, dialect, and idiom.

Franz Kafka, 1883-1924. (Czechoslovakian-born German short story writer and novelist)—Frequently identified as a genius who gave literary form to the disorder of the modern world, Kafka's prophetic and profoundly enigmatic stories often describe modern human degradation and cruelty. His well-known and widely-studied short story "The Metamorphosis" is regarded as a masterpiece of the genre.

D. H. Lawrence, 1885-1930. (English novelist, short story writer, poet, essayist, critic, dramatist, and memoirist)—One of the most original and controversial English writers of the twentieth century, Lawrence explored human nature through frank discussions of sex, psychology, and religion in an age when such topics were not openly discussed. Universally recognized for his achievements in the novel form, Lawrence was also a highly esteemed short story writer whose tales often focused on experiences from his working-class youth in England's industrial midlands.

Jack London, 1876-1916. (American novelist, short story writer, essayist, journalist, autobiographer, and dramatist)—The author of the novels *The Call of the Wild* and *The Sea Wolf,* London is also praised for his short stories, including "To Build a Fire" and "Batard." The exciting plots and simple, vigorous style displayed in London's tales have won them a wide audience and the status of American classics.

Frank O'Connor, 1903-1966. (Irish short story writer, novelist, essayist, and critic)—O'Connor is one of Ireland's major literary figures. His stories are widely read and cherished for their realistic and humorously sensitive portrayals of Irish life.

Katherine Anne Porter, 1890-1980. (American short story and novella writer, novelist, and critic)—Acknowledged as one of the finest American short story writers of the twentieth century, Porter displayed her gift for precise imagery and detail in such works of short fiction as *Noon Wine* and *Pale Horse, Pale Rider.*

Alice Walker, b. 1944. (American novelist, short story writer, and essayist)—Author of the Pulitzer Prize-winning novel *The Color Purple,* Walker is known for her powerfully expressive fiction that depicts the striving of black women for spiritual wholeness. Her short story collections *In Love and Trouble* and *You Can't Keep a Good Woman Down* have extended her reputation as a gifted writer and convey her intense allegiance to political and social concerns.

Additional Authors to Appear in Future Volumes

Agnon, Shmuel Yosef 1888-1970
Aiken, Conrad 1889-1973
Aldiss, Brian 1925-
Aleichem, Sholom 1859-1916
Andersen, Hans Christian 1805-1875
Asimov, Isaac 1920-
Atherton, Gertrude 1857-1948
Babel, Isaac 1894-1941?
Baldwin, James 1924-1987
Balzac, Honoré de 1799-1850
Barth, John 1930-
Beattie, Ann 1947-
Beerbohm, Max 1872-1956
Bellow, Saul 1915-
Benét, Stephen Vincent 1898-1943
Bierce, Ambrose 1842-1914?
Boccaccio, Giovanni 1313?-1375
Böll, Heinrich 1917-1985
Brentano, Clemens 1778-1842
Bunin, Ivan 1870-1953
Cable, George Washington 1844-1925
Caldwell, Erskine 1903-
Calisher, Hortense 1911-
Camus, Albert 1913-1960
Carter, Angela 1940-
Carver, Raymond 1938-1988
Cassill, R. V. 1919-
Cervantes 1547-1616
Chandler, Raymond 1888-1959
Chaucer, Geoffrey 1345-1400
Chopin, Kate 1851-1904
Conrad, Joseph 1857-1924
Coover, Robert 1932-
Cortázar, Julio 1914-1984
Crane, Stephen 1871-1900
Dahl, Roald 1916-
Dante Alighieri 1265-1321
Davenport, Guy 1927-
de la Mare, Walter 1873-1956
Dick, Philip K. 1928-1982
Dinesen, Isak (ps. of Karen Blixen) 1885-1962
Disch, Thomas M. 1940-
Doyle, Arthur Conan 1859-1930
Elkin, Stanley 1930-
Ellison, Harlan 1934-
Fast, Howard 1914-
Fitzgerald, F. Scott 1896-1940
Flaubert, Gustave 1821-1880
Forster, E. M. 1879-1970
France, Anatole (ps. of Anatole-François Thibault) 1844-1924
Friedman, Bruce J. 1930-
Gaines, Ernest J. 1933-
Gallant, Mavis 1922-
Galsworthy, John 1867-1933
García-Márquez, Gabriel 1928-
Gardner, John 1933-1982
Garland, Hamlin 1860-1940
Gass, William H. 1924-
Gide, André 1869-1951
Gilchrist, Ellen 1935-
Golding, William 1911-
Gordimer, Nadine 1923-
Gordon, Caroline 1845-1981
Grau, Shirley Ann 1929-
Greene, Graham 1904-
Grimm, Jakob Ludwig 1785-1863
Grimm, Wilhelm Karl 1786-1859
Hammett, Dashiell 1894-1961
Harris, Joel Chandler 1848-1908
Harte, Bret 1836-1902
Heinlein, Robert A. 1907-
Hesse, Herman 1877-1962
Hoffmann, E. T. A. 1776-1822
Hughes, Langston 1902-1967
Jackson, Shirley 1919-1965
James, Henry 1843-1916
James, M. R. 1862-1936
Jewett, Sarah Orne 1844-1909
Jhabvala, Ruth Prawer 1927-
Juvenal A.D. 60?-130?
King, Stephen 1947-
Kipling, Rudyard 1865-1936
Knowles, John 1926-1979
Lardner, Ring 1885-1933
Laurence, Margaret 1926-1987
Lavin, Mary 1912-
LeFanu, Joseph Sheridan 1814-1873
LeGuin, Ursula K. 1929-
Lessing, Doris 1919-
Machado de Assis, Joaquim Maria 1839-1908
Malamud, Bernard 1914-1986
Mann, Thomas 1875-1955
Mansfield, Katherine 1888-1923
Mason, Bobbie Ann 1940-
Masters, Edgar Lee 1869?-1950
McCullers, Carson 1917-1967
Maugham, W. Somerset 1874-1965
Mérimée, Prosper 1803-1870
Mishima, Yukio 1925-1970
Oates, Joyce Carol 1938-
O'Brien, Edna 1936-
O'Faolain, Sean 1900-
O'Flaherty, Liam 1896-1984
Olsen, Tillie 1913-
Ozick, Cynthia 1928-
Paley, Grace 1922-
Pasternak, Boris 1890-1960
Pavese, Cesare 1908-1950
Perelman, S. J. 1904-1976
Pritchett, V. S. 1900-
Robbe-Grillet, Alain 1922-
Roth, Philip 1933-
Saki (ps. of H. H. Munro) 1870-1916
Saroyan, William 1908-1981
Schwartz, Delmore 1913-1966
Scott, Sir Walter 1771-1832
Solzhenitsyn, Alexander 1918-
Spark, Muriel 1918-
Stafford, Jean 1915-1979
Stead, Christina 1902-1983
Stein, Gertrude 1874-1946
Steinbeck, John 1902-1983
Stevenson, Robert Louis 1850-1894
Sturgeon, Theodore 1918-1985
Tagore, Rabindranath 1861-1941
Taylor, Peter 1917-
Thackeray, William Makepeace 1811-1863
Tolstoy, Leo 1828-1910
Turgenev, Ivan 1818-1883
Twain, Mark (ps. of Samuel Langhorne Clemens) 1835-1901
Updike, John 1932-
Vonnegut, Kurt, Jr. 1922-
Warren, Robert Penn 1905-
Wells, H. G. 1866-1946
West, Nathanael 1904-1940
Wharton, Edith 1862-1937
White, E. B. 1899-1986
Zola, Émile 1840-1902

Djuna (Chappell) Barnes

1892-1982

(Also wrote under the pseudonym Lydia Steptoe) American novelist, short story writer, dramatist, poet, and journalist.

An experimental writer associated with the early modernists, Barnes combined elements of Surrealism, Gothicism, black humor, and poetry to depict the hopelessness of modern life. Her literary reputation rests largely on *Nightwood,* a novel of sexual and spiritual alienation that T. S. Eliot praised for its "quality of horror and doom very nearly related to that of Elizabethan tragedy." Critics point to a similar quality in Barnes's short fiction, which ranges from terse urban stories written during her early days as a journalist in New York City to later, more baroque tales. While eclipsed by *Nightwood* and her verse drama *The Antiphon,* Barnes's short story collections *Spillway* and *Smoke, and Other Early Stories* have won attention for their language and themes and the important record they provide of her artistic growth. Although Barnes has never received widespread recognition, an appreciative following of writers, readers, and critics has sustained both popular and academic interest in her work.

Barnes was born in Cornwall-on-Hudson, New York, to an English mother and an idealistic, domineering father who mistrusted society and eventually moved the family to a self-supporting farm on Long Island. Educated at home by her father and her paternal grandmother, an author and suffragist, Barnes was infused with a knowledge of art, music, and literature as a young girl. She studied formally only briefly at the Pratt Institute and Art Students' League in New York City and by age twenty-one had gained a job writing and illustrating features and interviews for the *Brooklyn Eagle.* Her first poems were accepted by *Harper's Weekly* in 1913, and during the next two decades she published stories, poems, and plays in newspapers as well as such popular and artistic magazines as *Charm, Smart Set, Vanity Fair,* the *Dial,* and the *Transatlantic Review.* She became involved in theater as an actor and reviewer, and three of her one-act plays were performed by Eugene O'Neill's Provincetown Players during the 1919-1920 season. Barnes also played a leading role among the bohemia thriving at the time in Greenwich Village, becoming notorious for her mordant humor, inspired conversation, and striking appearance. Her first published volume, *The Book of Repulsive Women,* was self-illustrated with sinuous pen-and-ink drawings reminiscent of Aubrey Beardsley's sketches, and for many years Barnes was known as much for her artwork as for her writing.

In 1920 Barnes moved to Paris, where she became acquainted with such celebrated expatriates as Ezra Pound, Gertrude Stein, and James Joyce, whose stream-of-consciousness technique influenced her prose style, notably in her novel *Ryder.* Barnes was a regular visitor at the salon of Natalie Clifford Barney, whose lesbian circle she caricatured in drawings and Elizabethan verse in her *Ladies' Almanack,* a sly panegyric to a fictional saint based on Barney. Barnes's troubled love affair with American sculptor Thelma Wood dominated much of her decade in Paris and provided the inspiration for *Nightwood.* A dark poetic account of an anguished lesbian misalliance which Barnes labored over for five years, *Nightwood* was published with an admiring preface by T. S. Eliot and commanded the praise of many writers and critics. After moving throughout Europe during the 1930s, Barnes returned to New York before the outbreak of World War II. Apart from *The Antiphon,* a Jacobean-styled family tragedy, she published little, eschewing the interviews and literary memoirs that kept many of her contemporaries in the public eye. She lived her last forty years in a small flat in Greenwich Village as a self-described "recluse, a form of Trappist," visited by such friends as Eliot, Henry Miller, Dag Hammarskjöld, and E. E. Cummings.

Barnes first collected her short stories in 1923 in *A Book,* which also included plays, poems, and drawings. This volume was reprinted six years later, with the addition of three stories, as *A Night among the Horses.* In 1962, Barnes extensively revised ten of the stories for the volume *Spillway,* which critics generally regard as her definitive short fiction collection. Like her full-length works, many of the *Spillway* stories are marked by black humor, decadent and sometimes obscure characters, a keen sense of the absurdity of existence, and a Gothic tone of menace and foreboding. Commentators note Barnes's use of doll and animal images to depict modern man and woman as less-than-human creatures trapped midway between salvation and damnation. In "A Night among the

Horses," for example, a wealthy woman with "a battery for a heart and the body of a toy" attempts to possess her unwilling stableman. Aligned with his animal charges in his simplicity and dignity, the stableman perceives that the woman wants to transform him into "a thing, half standing, half crouching, like those figures under the roofs of historic buildings, the halt position of the damned." By the story's end, he has become a grotesque creature who can live neither in society nor in a natural, animal state; during an attempt to escape from the woman's mechanistic world, he is trampled to death by his beloved horses.

"The halt position of the damned" is a phrase critics often cite in describing Barnes's alienated, depersonalized characters. In addition to qualities of bestiality and mechanization, commentators point to decadence as a mark of damnation among her protagonists, a condition exemplified by Madame Erling von Bartmann, the central figure of "Aller et retour." En route to visit her daughter in the south of France, Madame is engulfed by images of sex, religion, and death: gaudy postcards of bathing beauties displayed near tawdry funeral wreaths, a prostitute plucking a robin, and foul odors, which "neither pleased nor displeased" her. She later urges her meek daughter to delve fully into the horrors and beauties of life, but the girl becomes engaged to a dull, secure man. "Ah, how unnecessary," Madame von Bartmann remarks at the end of the story as she heads back toward Paris, resuming, critics note, the meaningless cycle of comings and goings suggested by the story's title. Other characters in *Spillway* include Moydia, the *"tragique"* young poseur in "The Grande Malade"; Julie Anspacher, the tubercular lover in the title story; and Katrina Silverstaff of "The Doctors," who fails to find any spiritual or metaphysical justification of life. According to critics, the latter two stories express most powerfully the seductive desire to find beauty and meaning in death, a theme underlying much of Barnes's work.

Fourteen of Barnes's earliest short stories, all originally published in New York newspapers and previously uncollected, appeared in 1982 in *Smoke, and Other Early Stories.* Critics note that these pieces diverge from Barnes's later short fiction in their reportorial tone and journalistic style of exposition, their flat, stereotyped, urban characters, and their surprise, twist endings. The publication of this volume is indicative of the heightened interest in Barnes that emerged during the 1970s and 1980s, when she attracted readers not only for her innovative talent but for her inherent feminist sensibility. In addition to *Smoke, and Other Stories,* a biography of Barnes as well as the first extensive critical studies of her works were published during these decades. As observers often note, Barnes herself has become something of a legend for her association with many of the century's greatest artists and her bold insistence on personal and artistic freedom.

Although Barnes's short fiction is faulted by some critics as mannered, obscure, and melodramatic, others assert that it is superior to her longer works in its economy of language and form. Commentators generally agree that while *Nightwood* has become Barnes's best-known work, her short stories occupy a significant place in a distinctive body of work. Kenneth Rexroth wrote: "Djuna Barnes may be considered a late born voice of the *fin de siècle* literary Decadence, but she is also an early born prophet of the black comedy, theatre of cruelty, and literature of total alienation of the later years of the century, the period of decadence and disintegration of Western Civilization, the time of permanent Apocalypse."

(See also *Contemporary Literary Criticism,* Vols. 3, 4, 8, 11, 29; *Contemporary Authors,* Vols. 9-12, rev. ed., Vol. 107 [obituary]; *Contemporary Authors New Revision Series,* Vol. 16; and *Dictionary of Literary Biography,* Vols. 4, 9, 45.)

PRINCIPAL WORKS

SHORT FICTION

A Book 1923; published in an enlarged edition as *A Night among the Horses,* 1929
Spillway 1962
Smoke, and Other Early Stories 1982

OTHER MAJOR WORKS

The Book of Repulsive Women: 8 Rhythms and 5 Drawings (poetry and drawings) 1915
Ryder (novel) 1928
Ladies' Almanack (poetry) 1928
Nightwood (novel) 1936
The Antiphon (verse drama) 1958
Selected Works of Djuna Barnes: Spillway, The Antiphon, Nightwood (short stories, verse drama, novel) 1962

THE LITTLE REVIEW (essay date 1920)

[*The following is an anonymous letter to the* Little Review, *the avant-garde journal in which Barnes published a number of her early stories. The letter-writer admonishes Barnes not to waste her literary gifts on "effects for mere effects' sake," a criticism that later critics echoed.*]

To Djuna Barnes:

I was much pleased to receive the *Little Review.* And I immediately read your picture of degeneracy, entitled **"Oscar."** I am happy to note that it in no wise reminds me of that other Oscar (Wilde) who was worth while—very much worth while—in spite of his errors.

I have read it through a second time and now feel sure that I read it the first time. If I should read it a third time—I think I should read it a fourth and even a fifth time. So I will *not.* I am satisfied already, and desire to *sleep* to-night, without keeping company with all those Barn-shadows with which you so forcefully enshroud your picture.

Of course it *is* a picture—not a study—of some of that morbidity which is so prevalent during these days of the Overwrought, or Kubikul Insanity of the world. But it will do no real lasting good, and will not help you to Arrive in that Field of Real Endeavor, to which you should aspire—and perhaps will some day, finally, enter.

Your longing to be "original," strange, compelling, is only too crudely evident in your prose work; and by the same token, that is why you may never hope to Achieve the Worth While, so long as you allow yourself to be thus held down by, what I may term, your lower self. There is a *big better self*—the *real Djuna*—asleep now, but to awaken, sometime.

This is evidenced by the real power in the things you write, in the remarkable atmosphere of your work, in the fine power of imagination which I find here and there in the things I have read, of yours, in this same **"Oscar,"** and in the few poems I have come across in some of the magazines. Your poetry is much the best thing you do—better artistry, as a rule. Your prose is crude, unpolished, erratic. You should stop trying for effects for mere effects' sake, and allow the effect to come naturally, as it surely will, when you forget *Djuna,* and become the writer you *may* become, if you will only see the necessity for the suppression of mere vulgar eccentricity—in the desire to surprise—so that you may write of things as they, balanced, *are.*

Why do you not *wake* up to the *twist* of the little Bohemia you are in, and *drop* that warp—taking up the *thread* of the *things in life that count and which must be helped along?* Then, you might become of some real worth in life's long, hard battle—and *help,* where you now simply waste your time and your gift. (pp. 72-3)

"Batrachian," in The Little Review, *Vol. VII, No. 1, May-June, 1920, pp. 72-3.*

FLOYD DELL (essay date 1924)

[*An American novelist, dramatist, and critic, Dell was first associated with the Chicago Renaissance writers, then moved in 1914 to New York, where he edited the socialist journals the* Masses *and the* Liberator. *During the 1920s he was part of the bohemia of Greenwich Village, where he became a good friend of Barnes and one of the first well-known critics of her work. In the following excerpt from a review of* A Book, *Dell discusses what he perceives as the unintelligibility of Barnes's writing and offers reasons for it.*]

In the details of Djuna Barnes's stories [in ***A Book***] there is a great deal of fine observation, clearly as well as beautifully phrased. It is the larger outlines of her stories that are obscure. This is perhaps because she sees in detail what the rest of us see, but feels about life as a whole differently from the rest of us. Each of her stories seems to be leading impressively up to an inevitable end; but the inevitable never happens. Perhaps it would seem to her too obvious. What happens is almost always brutally irrelevant to what has gone before.

Doubtless life seems like that to her. "Anything," says one of her heroines, "is a reason for using a pistol, unless one is waiting for the obvious, and the obvious has never been sufficient reason."

But to evade the obvious thus consistently is to embrace the oblivious. By this method, fiction is reduced to just such a meaningless chaos of accident as life itself appears to sensitive and troubled minds. But we are accustomed, in fiction, to find life's chaos thought out and arranged in some fairly orderly and intelligible pattern: that, indeed, is supposed to be one of the purposes of art, and the chief difference between art and life.

But Djuna Barnes is one of those writers, of a recent school, who defiantly refuse to find any sort of significance in the rank welter of life. Or so it would seem; the plain fact is that these stories are on the whole meaningless; the ascription of a highly philosophical intention to their meaninglessness is a mere critical guess.

There remains, of course, the possibility, in this as in other similar cases, that such meaninglessness is a deliberate and possibly mischievous affectation. . . . After all, if one's sense of life is so profoundly different from that of most people as to be self-condemned to unintelligibility, there is no reason why one should not get a little fun out of it by mystifying the bourgeois. Literature depends so essentially on a community of interest between writers and readers, and the stray writer who fails to feel such a bond is so decidedly out of luck that even reprisals in the form of practical jokes must be forgiven. (pp. 14-15)

The whole book, when one has ceased to ponder its unintelligibilities, leaves a sense of the writer's deep temperamental sympathy with the simple and mindless lives of the beasts: it is in dealing with these lives, and with the lives of men and women in moods which approach such simplicity and mindlessness, that she attains a momentary but genuine power. (p. 15)

Floyd Dell, "Irrelevant," in The Nation, *New York, Vol. CXVIII, No. 3052, January 2, 1924, pp. 14-15.*

THE NEW YORK TIMES BOOK REVIEW **(essay date 1924)**

[*In the following assessment of* A Book, *the reviewer praises Barnes's short stories as insightful "portraits of souls in the melée."*]

This miscellany of stories, sketches, plays, poems and pictures [in ***A Book***], the product of a gregarious, cosmopolitan mind, endeavors to limn many of the casual episodes of our American life against the background of a Continental structure. Undoubtedly American in tradition and feeling, but with sufficient acquaintance with European standards, and particularly with European literary expression, the author has achieved a remarkable tour de force in interpreting the American mind and behavior in its most individual aspiration and in the style of a French analyst. Mind, passion, introspection, behavior, are not differentiated by geographical limitation. In a sense, there is no American character. Universality of human thought and endeavor has simply specific modes of expression.

The author contents herself with a negative philosophy, but while her people are sophisticated and dulled, and her scenes for the most part sordid, she does not share that atmosphere. She is merely a candid, heart-searching soul picturing life, whether it be on the east side or in a barnyard on the plains. The thing that interests her is the undercurrent of heart throbs which a phlegmatic world never senses. Even when her characters, in their most tragic moments, suddenly slant into casuality she is not affecting a cynical pose or resorting to a mere literary trick to thrill jaded readers. The purpose is clear and logical, and the style graphic, keen and discerning. This discernment is not unworthy of a Balzac and the artistry not unbecoming to a de Maupassant. . . .

The author's philosophy is hardly optimistic, probably due to severe experience in an unfeeling world. . . . Even in her bizarre charcoal pictures the author has tried to catch some scintillation of the mind lost in the maze, all awry with the intricate adjustment to a world to which there seems no key. If she is unable to tell us what it is all about she has accomplished quite as much as the sages. They have defined values and offered choices. She is wise just to give us portraits of souls in the mêlée and of incidents honest in enactment.

"Literary Pot-Pourri," in The New York Times Book Review, *January 6, 1924, p. 14.*

KENNETH BURKE (essay date 1924)

[*An American critic, novelist, poet, and translator, Burke is esteemed for his philosophical literary criticism. Among the earliest of the New Critics, he has strongly influenced twentieth-century criticism with such works as* Permanence and Change: An Anatomy of Purpose *(1935) and* Language as Symbolic Action: Essays in Life, Literature, and Method *(1966). An early acquaintance and important admirer of Barnes's work, Burke here praises her stories in* A Book *for their truthfulness and vigor.*]

Some considerable time past, when reviewing a book in *The Dial,* I had occasion to speak of immersion-in-life with a somewhat categorical disapproval. Since then, this has lain on the conscience. For though I still feel that the book belittled was an inferior one, and inferior precisely because of its patient and dutiful immersion in life, it has seemed that the category itself should be revised. For in art a category can be degraded or justified by the individual instance exemplifying it.

The reading of Miss Barnes' [***A Book***] makes the revision imperative. The author of these stories, plays, poems, and drawings is undoubtedly immersed—and to such an extent that if you have the modern interest in the mechanics of writing you must wonder how eager her preoccupations must have been to have made her miss so much. Yet her pages have a force, an ingenuity, which rises purely from the intensity of her message.

Miss Barnes seems to have seized upon the form nearest to hand, the one-acter, and to have shaped all her subjects to this simple mould. To wit: there is a situation, this situation is followed by a general jog-trot of plot for so long, and then, with only two or three hundred words to go, the author seizes a knife or a pistol, or stages an incestuous kiss, or something similar—in short, unwinds the rest of her plot with a snap, and the story is over.

If one is looking for an astute and concentrated method of writing, then, one will not find it in any of Miss Barnes' paragraphs. There are no interior designs, no "functioning" sentences. The occasional shame-faced attempts at an epigram are nearly always painful. So that we must situate the appeal of this book precisely in the vigour of her attitudes, in her immersion. Nor are these attitudes themselves unimpeachable. A great deal is weak Russian, a great deal is old stuff; Miss Barnes' vamps, for instance, are almost as pat as movie vamps.

I spoke of a force or ingenuity rising purely from the intensity of her message. The opening of her story **"Oscar"** is a good example of what I mean. It begins with four descriptions: a place, a woman, a man, another man. *A priori* it should be safe to say that a story should not begin with such a Walter Scott sameness. Yet these very pages have a swift stride. Of one of the men:

> He smelled very strongly of horses, and was proud of it. He pretended a fondness for all that goes under hide or hair, but a collie bitch, known for her gentleness, snapped at him and bit him. He invariably carried a leather thong, braided at the base for a handle, and would stand for hours talking, with his legs apart, whirling this contrived whip, and, looking out of the corner of his eyes would pull his moustache, waiting to see which of the ladies would draw in her feet.

The other descriptions are equally firm. The effect is probably gained by the fact that the descriptions themselves are plots. (pp. 460-61)

In ***A Book*** the will to tragedy is maintained with a sureness which is very rarely met with in contemporary writing. And if the author does not convince us that her stories carry very far beyond themselves, she does make us feel that this little corner of experience she is dealing with is handled with the adequate reactions. By which I mean that we can accept the fatalities of her stories, and perhaps even feel that the last bit of plot unwinding with its snap really belonged to the texture of her subject. (p. 461)

Kenneth Burke, "Immersion," in The Dial, *Vol. 76, May, 1924, pp. 460-61.*

EZRA POUND (letter date 1937)

[*Pound, an American poet and critic, is regarded as one of the most innovative and influential figures in twentieth-century Anglo-American poetry. His* Cantos, *published throughout his life, is among the most ambitious poetic cycles of the century, and his series of satirical poems* Hugh Selwyn Maubery *(1920) is ranked with T. S. Eliot's* The Waste Land *(1922) as a significant attack on the decadence of modern culture. Pound knew Barnes during her early years in Paris, where he tried briefly to court her: "Waal, she werent none too cuddly, I can tell you that," he commented. While he praised her early work, he felt that Eliot and others later exaggerated her importance, and in the letter to Eliot excerpted below he offers a limerick mocking her prose style. "Whale" refers to Ford Madox Ford, who published Barnes's work in his journal, the* Transatlantic Review.]

There once wuzza lady named Djuna
Who wrote rather like a baboon. Her
Blubbery prose had no fingers or toes;
And we wish Whale had found this out sooner.

This exaggerates as far to the one side as you blokes to the other. I except *Ladies' Almanack,* which wuz lively.

Ezra Pound, in a letter to T. S. Eliot in January, 1937, in his The Letters of Ezra Pound: 1907-1941, *edited by D. D. Paige, Harcourt Brace Jovanovich, 1950, p. 286.*

ROBERT TAUBMAN (essay date 1962)

[*In the following review of* Spillway, *Taubman characterizes Barnes's attempts at spiritual horror as mannered and ineffectual.*]

In spite of generous opportunities, little has been made of fear as a subject for literature since *The Waste Land.* Adroit substitutes - books we merely use to frighten ourselves - are more manageable for writers and evidently welcomed by readers. And for all her affinity with the ethos of *The Waste Land,* an adroit substitute is just what Miss Djuna Barnes provides. . . . [Readers] of *Nightwood* will have their own views about what the publishers call her 'terrifying imaginative power'. ***Spillway,*** a collection of stories, in fact does nothing to clarify Miss Barnes's dubious reputation. Looking back to *Nightwood,* which appeared in 1936, one can see a kind of magnificence here and there as of the trappings of a Handel opera, and a certain mythopoeic interest in the characters (her Dr O'Connor, for instance, surely has a bearing on the Unidentified Guest in Mr Eliot's *Cocktail Party*?). In the present bits and pieces this is all dislocated and one notices the pasteboard, the indulgence, in effects like [the following from the story **"The Passion"**]:

> Every afternoon at four-thirty, excepting Thursdays, a smart carriage moved with measured excellence through the Bois, drawn by two bays in shining patent leather blinkers, embellished with silver R's, the docked tails rising proudly above well-stitched cruppers.

In this mannered context, full of dexterous international reference (Princess Frederica Rholinghausen is up there, 'erect, in the dead centre of a medallioned cushion'), disproportionate emotions all at once slop over, with an oddly Victorian, vatic effect that was better calculated in Lewis Carroll's verse. She writes, for instance:

> 'And I do not permit you to suffer while I am in the room.' Slowly and precisely she began unfastening her brooch. 'I dislike all spiritual decay.'
>
> 'Oh, Oh!' he said under his breath.

Or someone says, 'It was all dotted *suisse,* with a very tight bodice, and into this bodice, just between the breasts, was embroidered, in very fine twist, a slain lamb. It might, you see, mean everything and it might mean nothing. . . .' And this is exactly how Miss Barnes's gestures in the direction of spiritual horror strike one. The effect of mystification doesn't come only from that blunted, encumbered style, but from writing out of really incoherent experience. (pp. 717-18)

Robert Taubman, "Djunaesque," in New Statesman, *Vol. LXIII, No. 1627, May 18, 1962, pp. 717-18.*

STANLEY EDGAR HYMAN (essay date 1966)

[Hyman was an American critic and editor. The author of numerous critical studies and collections, he is best known as a book reviewer for the New Leader *magazine during the 1960s. Here Hyman assesses the short fiction included in* Spillway *and cites "A Night among the Horses" as the only wholly successful story in the collection.]*

Nine of the 16 stories that Miss Barnes has published in earlier volumes are included [in ***Selected Works of Djuna Barnes***], as a collection entitled ***Spillway.*** The only omission I regret is **"The Nigger,"** that devastating squint at Southern race relations. Otherwise the stories are a good representation. The commonest tone is of scarcely controlled hysteria: "I tried to put my arms around her, but she struck them down crying "Silence!' " The events are gothic and melodramatic: a woman with an idiot child takes to her bed and joins it in idiocy; a gentle tailor strangles a rabbit to please his fiancée.

Some of the images and metaphors are poetic in the best sense: "A great war painting hung over the bed; the painting and the bed ran together in encounter; the huge rumps of the stallions reined into the pillows"; "The waiting room was empty, dark and damp, like an acre risen from the sea"; a woman's bony knees under a skirt are "two sharp points, like the corners of a candy box." A few touches are beautifully effective. Moydia, in **"The Grande Malade,"** wears a tight bodice on which, "just between the breasts, was embroidered, in very fine twist, a slain lamb." When her fiancé dies suddenly, Moydia becomes *"tragique,"* and her sister comments, as the point of the story, "She sugars her tea from far too great a height." When the little tailor has strangled his rabbit, he stands shaking, "his heart wringing wet."

Only one of the stories, however, seems to me successful as a whole. That is **"A Night among the Horses,"** which begins magnificently with a man in evening dress, carrying top hat and stick, creeping through the underbrush of a great estate. Horses thunder by him, "their legs rising and falling like savage needles taking purposeless stitches." He is the horses' groom, dressed as a gentleman to be the consort of his employer, a lady who laughs showing "nostrils scarlet to the pit," and twits him for being "girlish" when he asks what she wants of him. He suddenly perceives her as a praying mantis, flees into the shrubbery, and is trampled to death by his horses, who fail to recognize him in the strange costume. It is a superb story of "debased lady, debased ostler, on the wings of vertigo," a serious and tragic *Lady Chatterley.* (pp. 58-9)

Stanley Edgar Hyman, "The Wash of the World," in his Standards: A Chronicle of Books for Our Time, *Horizon Press, 1966, pp. 58-62.*

SUZANNE C. FERGUSON (essay date 1969)

[In this, the first extensive critical essay devoted to Barnes's short fiction, Ferguson asserts that Barnes expressed her artistic vision more clearly in her short stories than in her novels and that the best of them are "remarkable examples of the genre."]

[The stories included in ***Selected Works of Djuna Barnes***], along with perhaps two or three not reissued, are striking not only as they reveal the development of the themes, characters, and techniques of Miss Barnes's most famous work, *Nightwood,* but as masterpieces of the kind of short story that, however severely limited in its vision, nonetheless presents with ferocious clarity those moments of recognition and illumination in which fallen man perceives his damnation. Moreover, they create in a special and powerful way the feeling of disestablishment and disintegration in the society and the individual so deeply experienced by Miss Barnes's generation.

Her world is a world of displaced persons—of an Armenian country boy on the lower east side of Manhattan, of Russian emigrés in Paris, Berlin, Spain, or New York, of Scandinavians or English in American farmland. They have abandoned national, racial, and ethical traditions; their human contacts are laceration. They lack even the integrity in isolation that comforts the characters of Hemingway or the early Faulkner, for they are estranged against themselves. Their aborted and ineffectual attempts to find meaning, order, or love are the subjects of the stories. Technique, as well as subject, marks the stories as extraordinary. Readers who find the verbal pyrotechnics of *Nightwood,* or of the 1927 novel, *Ryder,* or of *The Antiphon* too often merely talky and falsely rhetorical will discover in most of the stories a fusing of experience and idea. Economy is especially characteristic of the revised versions collected in the ***Selected Works,*** where verbal fat has been pared away, and objects, persons, and actions flash out with chilling precision. This is not to say, of course, that the stories are easy to read; on the contrary, like those of Katherine Mansfield and Katherine Anne Porter—which technically many of them resemble—they retain their meaning in a very dense texture, where each detail is significant and essential to the whole. And in spite of *Nightwood's* relatively wide circulation they are generally unknown today. (pp. 26-7)

The rambling form of [*Nightwood*]—called fugal or symphonic by its admirers—in which the focus moves from one to another of the main characters, resting for a third of its bulk on the homosexual gynecologist, O'Connor, whose only experience is vicarious, in conjunction with the lavish symbolic settings, has invited comparison with Joyce's *Ulysses*. . . . [Although] Miss Barnes adopts some of Joyce's devices, her sense of organic function, or form, in a long work is simply insufficient to assimilate them. Instead of a carefully unfolded epiphany she presents a chain reaction of firecrackers popping, helter-skelter, in a dozen directions. Still, the encomiums of [T. S. Eliot in his laudatory introduction to *Nightwood*] are not wholly unfounded. In parts of *Nightwood,* and even in some passages of *Ryder,* she exhibits truly remarkable gifts of imaginative projection and language. If her eloquence is occasionally specious, it is also at times powerful and accurate. Eliot saw in *Nightwood's* pervading burden of evil "a quality of horror and doom very nearly related to that of Elizabethan tragedy"; more like, I should say, the vision of the Jacobean decadence: Ford, Tourneur, and some of Webster.

In the short stories, where there is less temptation to empty bombast, the vision of depersonalization, of loss of identity, of "horror and doom," comes through with greater clarity. Because the vision is not so extreme as in *Nightwood,* the characters are generally not so extremely psychopathic; repulsive as many of them are, they still retain enough of common humanity to awaken pity, if not full sympathy. The groom who is ironically trampled by his own horses in **"A Night among the Horses,"** for example, is foolish, even contemptible, yet he has the dignity not only of a victim but of one who can distinguish persons from things—a quality not shared by his persecutor. Taken up by his master's daughter, a "small fiery woman with a battery for a heart and the body of a toy, who ran everything, who purred, saturated with impudence, with a mechanical buzz that ticked away her humanity," he loses his simple identity even as she tells him: "You simply can't go on being a groom forever. . . . I'll make a gentleman out of you. I'll step you up from being a 'thing'." She does not "step him up," but debases him. As he contemplates the possibility of marriage—she, it is plain, does not—he correctly perceives its consequences; "he'd be neither what he was nor what he had been; he'd be a thing, half standing, half crouching, like those figures under the roofs of historic buildings, the halt position of the damned."

Half drunk at a masked ball, where he is the only one in evening clothes though she has insultingly invited him to come dressed as a hostler, he makes his break for freedom, first drawing a magic circle about her in the rosin of the dance floor with his cane. Fleeing to the pasture, he slips between the fence rails determined to capture and mount one of his horses, then escape. "He was no longer afraid. He stood up, waving his hat and cane and shouting. They did not seem to know him. . . ." Panicking, the horses run him down while he sobs "I *can* do it, damn everything, I can get on with it; I can make my mark!"

In a typically muted ending, the narrator continues:

> The upraised hooves of the first horse missed him, the second did not. Presently the horses drew apart, nibbling and swishing their tails, avoiding a patch of tall grass.

The grotesque mummery of the courtship is matched by the gruesome irony of death. The mistress, Freda Buckler, who "darted and bobbled about too much, and always with the mindless intensity of a mechanical toy kicking and raking about the floor," has indeed made him a thing—literally as well as figuratively. The horses, mindless too, instinctive, purposeless, perceive the monstrosity she has created and destroy it, but only by accident.

In addition to the bizarre and destructive relationship of man and woman, echoed in other stories and in *Nightwood,* **"A Night among the Horses"** introduces two interrelated motifs of estrangement that appear again and again in the writings of Djuna Barnes: the symbols of the doll and the mindless, peaceful animal.

Of the two, the doll is least ambiguous, for it is one of the manifestations of human beings with the soul removed. Lifeless, mechanical, grotesque, the dolls buzz along spreading misery to those who mistake them for persons. Freda Buckler, Moydia of **"The Grande Malade,"** Addie in **"The Rabbit,"** the idiot child of **"Cassation,"** and Robin Vote, Jenny Petherbridge, and Frau Mann in *Nightwood* are all character-

Self-portrait by Barnes, 1914.

istically dolls. The sexlessness of the doll, as is evident in the activities of Miss Barnes's doll-women, is no warranty that the doll will not participate in sexual experience, but merely that the experience will not be meaningful.

Naturally enough, many of the doll-women also keep dolls and play with them. The lesbian Dusie, in [**"Dusie"**], which is ultimately worked into *Nightwood,* plays with dolls at the home of her lover, Mme. K———. The context of her play is especially relevant:

> When she was ill it was sorrowful to see her, she suffered such shallow pain, as if her body were in the toils of a feeble and remorseless agony. Then she would lie over, her knees up, her head down, laughing and crying and saying, do you love me? to every woman, and every woman answered that they loved her. But it did not change her, and suddenly she would shout: Get out get out of my room! Something in her grew and died for her alone.
>
> When they were gone, thrown out, she would sit up in bed and amuse herself with the dolls they had brought her, wooden animals and tin soldiers, and again she would cast them from her with cunning energy.

Her play and her life are sickeningly the same. (pp. 27-30)

Animals and animal imagery are not so simply evil, and the ambivalence with which Miss Barnes treats her beasts (of whatever genus) indicates perhaps the most profound tension in all her writing. For although reviewers and commentators on all her books dwell upon her "sympathy with the beasts" [see excerpt by Floyd Dell dated 1924] and her yearning to be absorbed into their simple world, this half-truth distorts more than it makes clear. While it is obvious in **"A Night among the Horses"** that the horses are a more noble choice of life than their mistress, it is also obvious that their life is an impossible life for the man. Trying to join them he is only monstrous.

A more subtle and extended treatment of the problem occurs in **"The Rabbit,"** in which the bovine Armenian, Amietiev, "timid," "gentle," though he has always felt a kinship with the cows and ducks of his farm and has taken pleasure in contemplation of them, is goaded into killing "something" by the avaricious and cruel Addie. He strangles a rabbit stolen from a butcher shop near the inherited Manhattan tailoring business for which he left Armenia; prior to his decision to kill for Addie—to be masculine, heroic for her—he always found the butcher shop, with its rows of calves' heads, quarters of beef, and hanging carcasses of ducks "horribly sad; the colours were a very harvest of death." He does not wish to kill, yet he can think of no other way to be a hero. "He thought about this a long time, and finally came to the inevitable conclusion. All heroes were men who killed or got killed. Well, that was impossible; if he were killed he might as well have stayed in the country and never laid eyes on Addie—therefore he must kill—but what?" So he steals the rabbit; in reality, of course, absurd, but the vitality of the writing almost brings it off:

> Something moved in the box, breathing and kicking away from him; he uttered a cry, more grunt than cry, and the something in the box struck back with hard drumming fright.
>
> The tailor bent forward, hands out, then he shoved them in between the slats of the box opening, shutting them tight! tight! tighter! The terrible, the really terrible thing, the creature did not squeal, wail, cry: it panted, as if the wind were blunt; it thrashed its life, the frightful scuffling of the overwhelmed, in the last trifling enormity.

When Addie returns and looks in the box, she begins to laugh "harsh, back-bending laughter. 'Take it or leave it,' he shouted, and she stopped, her mouth open." She accepts the magnitude of his deed, and is in fact frightened by the change in him. In the early version of the story the final effect is blurred, equivocal. She pushes him out of the shop, where, dazed, "he looked up into the air, sniffing it and smiling. 'Come,' she said, 'we are going to have your boots shined.' " The implication is that he has entered her world and is at home there for the first time. The rabbit was after all only a rabbit. In the ***Selected Works*** version, however, when Amietiev emerges from the shop, he has forgotten her. "He was shaking, his head straight up, his heart wringing wet." Like Freda Buckler, Addie has ruined her man; no longer a happy beast, he is not able to enter the world on the other side of beasthood; his "harvest of death" is his own death. (pp. 30-2)

This symbolism of animals and dolls, recurrent as it is in Miss Barnes's stories and novels, directs attention to her constant concern with the idea that becoming human is paradoxically all but impossible for people. This idea is also developed in other contexts. In the brilliant **"Aller et Retour,"** the vigorous Russian widow, Erling von Bartmann, returns from Paris to her daughter in Nice after the death of Herr von Bartmann, deserted by her seven years before. The character is fully drawn in the opening pages, which record her journey, by train, with stopover in Marseilles. Even her casual attention in the marketplace of Marseilles is occupied with sex and death, which come to surround her like an aura: a whore plucking a robin, postcards of mermaids and women bathing on display beside funeral wreaths. She enters a church, but her prayer is only to herself:

> She turned the stones of her rings out and put her hands together, the light shining between the little fingers; raising them she prayed, with all her vigorous understanding, to God, for a common redemption.
>
> She got up, peering about her, angry that there were no candles burning to the *Magnifique*—feeling the stuff of the altar-cloth.

Finding her daughter, Richter—"her father had wanted a boy"—grown up in body but still a child in mind, she prepares to stay home "for quite a while." After dinner, after playing Schubert waltzes "with effervescence" on the piano, she speaks to Richter about life.

> "[Life] is filthy; it is also frightful. There is everything in it: murder, pain, beauty, disease—death. . . . You must know *everything,* and then *begin.* . . . Man is rotten from the start. . . . Rotten with virtue and with vice. He is strangled by the two and made nothing; and God is the light the mortal insect kindled, to turn to, and to die by." [critic's ellipses]

And so on. Then, in the darkness,

> "Are you thinking?" she said.
> "No," the child answered.
> "Then *think,*" Madame von Bartmann said loudly, turning to the child. Think everything, good, bad, indifferent; everything, and *do* everything, everything! Try to know what you are before you die."

A few days afterward Richter asks her mother's permission to announce her engagement to a government clerk chosen by her father. When the mother has ascertained that he has sufficient money, there appears "a look of pain and relief on Madame von Bartmann's face," and she directs Richter to invite Mr. Teal to dinner. Mr. Teal is hilariously true to type:

> "I shall do my best to make your daughter happy. I am a man of staid habits, no longer too young," he smiled. "I have a house on the outskirts of Nice. My income is assured—a little left me by my mother. My sister is my housekeeper, she is a maiden lady, but very cheerful and very good." He paused, holding a glass of wine to the light. "We hope to have children—Richter will be occupied. As she is delicate we shall travel, to Vichy, once a year. I have two very fine horses and a carriage with sound springs. She will drive in the afternoons, when she is indisposed—though I hope she will find her greatest happiness at home."

Two months later, her daughter married, Mme. von Bartmann is on her way back to Paris, saying to herself, simply, " 'Ah, how unnecessary.' " The irony cuts both ways, of course, for although it is clear that Richter will never become a person, it is equally clear that for all her knowledge and wise counsel, Mme. von Bartmann is not a person, either. And considering the world Djuna Barnes has made for her, she is probably fortunate not to be.

The outrageous comedy of plot and character in **"Aller et Retour,"** combined with its simplicity and technical proficiency, result inevitably in a tour de force. In **"Spillway"**—titled more pompously **"Beyond the End"** in the 1923 volume—Miss Barnes's world view is presented in a more complex and psychologically realistic form. If not the best of the stories, it is at any rate the one having the most immediate appeal, partly because its realism is moving where the caricature of **"Aller et Retour"** is merely amusing, and partly because the fundamental problem of inner estrangement is so fully and effectively articulated.

The story of Julie Anspacher's return home, uncured, after five years at a tuberculosis sanitorium, it is set in a farmland apparently meant to be Scandinavian, in any case a place of well water and windlasses. The time is probably in the last years of the nineteenth century; one wonders if Mann's *Tristan* (1902) provided the *donnée.*

Mrs. Anspacher brings with her a daughter, not her husband's ("he was slightly surprised"). . . . Expecting to die, fearing death, "filled with fever and lust" Julie bore the child; its father died, but Julie, contrary to her anticipation, did not. Despite her own illness, neither did the child. And so Julie has come home, she says, because "a thing should make a design; torment should have some meaning. I did not want to go beyond you, or to have anything beyond you—that was not the idea, not the idea at all." She hopes, knowing it is in vain, that he will have some understanding of her problem. She attempts to explain further:

> "I thought, Paytor may know—"
> "Know what?"
> "Division. I thought, he will be able to divide me against myself. Personally I don't feel divided; I seem to be a sane and balanced whole, but hopelessly mixed. So I said to myself, Paytor will see where the design divides and departs, though all the time I was making no bargain, I wasn't thinking of any system—well, in other words, I wanted to be set *wrong.* Do you understand?"

He doesn't, perhaps excusably, but as they talk on he begins to believe that he will understand "sometime later" and will then be able to help her. He leaves, and she hears him practicing with a pistol in his shooting loft.

Alone in the darkening downstairs, Julie hears the brook coming down the mountain; "she thought, water in the hand has no voice, but it really roars coming over the falls. It sings over small stones in brooks, but it only tastes of water when it's caught, struggling and running away in the hands." The passage culminates the imagery of water in the story; and like the rain that impinges on the earth in [James Joyce's] "Araby," its symbolic function is basically traditional. Julie herself associates the brook with memories of her childhood; by extension, it is life—her own and life in general. When it is flowing it has a voice, as life has meaning, audible but unintelligible. For Paytor, who is strong and whose family is all long-lived, the stream flows and sings unnoticed, but for Julie, whose life is perpetually ending, there is no song. "I am lost," she says, "in still water." When Paytor had asked her about her religion, she had replied that religion is "to carry me away, beyond," and she demands more than mere release, the spillway of the title. Even her habitual fight with death is only a determination to be "certain of something else first." Given time, she thinks she may find it.

Cold, feeling for her coat in the darkness, she tries to think:

> "All his family . . . long lives . . . and me too, me too," she murmured. She became dizzy. "It's because I must get down on my knees. But it isn't low enough," she contradicted herself, "But if I put my head down, way down—down, down, down, down . . ." She heard a shot. "He has quick warm blood—" Her forehead had not quite touched the boards, now it touched them, but she got up immediately, stumbling over her dress.

This is the end of the story: ironic, hopeless. Not only has she been denied the understanding she seeks; she has killed Paytor, who in spite of or perhaps because of his strength and logic has come to his conclusion "instantly," as is usual with him, but this time he has not been able to face the "fight to destroy" it.

The beginning of an answer to Julie's question, a provisional understanding—no matter how minimal—between her and Paytor, is quite out of the question. Julie's protestation that she loves Paytor is as meaningless as Mme. von Bartmann's prayer. This is the horror of Miss Barnes's world. That Julie cannot comprehend what we like to call the meaning of life and death is not entirely unbearable; where even *human* love is possible, men can endure without such comprehension. But in a world where religion is no more than release and love only a spillway, life itself is finally stopped off. The terrors of *Nightwood* are its last convulsion. The essential kindness, even good will, of both Julie and Paytor intensifies the horror; in the early version, **"Beyond the End,"** Paytor is merely a typical figure: the self-centered, imperceptive husband, one more than a little culpable in Julie's despair. The humanization of Paytor in **"Spillway"** hones the ironic edge much finer. If Paytor is not unkind, Julie's predicament cannot be simply a reaction to his boorishness or apathy; it must spring entirely from within herself. The total but involuntary estrangement of each human being from all others becomes more and more Miss Barnes's obsession, as her revisions of the early stories show.

In **"The Doctors,"** to me the most powerful of the stories, the threads of Katrina Silverstaff's quest for life in death and Rodkin's pitiful attempt to emerge into life twine and unravel without ever touching, insulated by the ironic fates that govern Djuna Barnes's universe. The story is typical of her writing in the vigorous conception of striking characters and situations, fully visualized scenes, and tense, even epigrammatic pointing of individual phrases, not to mention the unremitting pressure of nameless evil that seems to surround and imprison it with hydraulic force. It is typical, too, in the dissociation of its characters from their own pasts; the doctors Silverstaff, Otto and Katrina, are German Jews living on Second Avenue "in the early twenties" (they eat in a Hungarian grill); Rodkin is apparently from nowhere—in the first version of the story "[he] might have been of any nationality in the world." The story is more extensively reworked than any of the others, testifying not only to Miss Barnes's continued interest in it, but to the real difficulty of embodying such a subject in a short story. Like the boy in Aiken's "Silent Snow, Secret Snow," Katrina can be diagnosed as schizophrenic, yet such classification is in itself meaningless. Both authors are concerned with the peculiar qualities of the individual experience, and the perspective this experience imposes upon the "normal." Moreover, Katrina's problem, like Julie Anspacher's, is essentially philosophical and religious. Here the attempt to establish a relationship to the "not-I" is clearly and desperately an attempt to reach God—or something acceptably like God. While the story is still not wholly satisfactory, its inexorable pessimism is haunting and depressingly persuasive.

While her husband Otto is a medical doctor, Katrina is a metaphysical one, though she is presented as treating animals and birds from the office she shares with her husband. "Both had started out for a doctorate in gynecology. Otto Silverstaff made it, as they say, but Katrina lost her way somewhere in vivisection, behaving as though she were aware of an impudence. . . . She never recovered her gaiety." She is not incapable, not squeamish, but she loses track of the purely medical; something complex, "an impudence," has entered her mind. And so she is introverted, abstracted, "incomprehensible" to her husband, a kind, liberal man devoted to medicine and entirely outside her, though "inordinately pleased" with her. They have two children, a girl and a boy, one nine, the other eight, when the action takes place.

Katrina is given to announcing that " 'We have fashioned ourselves against the Day of Judgment' . . . at the oddest moments seemingly without relevance to anything at all." And one day, for no apparent reason, she opens the door to an itinerant Bible peddler named Rodkin (who had, he said, "just missed it last year when he was selling Carlyle's *French Revolution*"). Rodkin is slight, pale, fair, "so colourless as to seem ghostly." He is led like a somnambulist through an extraordinary encounter with Katrina, who says she "must have religion become out of the reach of the few; I mean out of reach for a few; something impossible again. . . . at the moment religion is claimed by too many." She insists that she needs not his help, but *hindrance;* he is to be "only the means," and she is to be his mistress. " 'But,' she added, 'do not intrude. Tomorrow you will come to see me, that is enough; that is all'."

When he arrives, however, embarrassed and sheepish, "She sent word by the maid that she did not need him." It is not until the third time he calls that she is "in."

> She was quiet, almost gentle, as if she was preparing him for a disappointment, and he listened. "I have deliberately removed remorse from the forbidden; I hope you understand."
> He said "Yes" and understood nothing.
> She continued inexorably: "There will be no thorns for you.
> You will miss the thorns but do not presume to show it in my presence." Seeing his terror, she added: "And I do not permit you to suffer while I am in the room: Slowly and precisely she began unfastening her brooch. "I dislike all spiritual decay."
> "Oh, oh!" he said under his breath.
> "It is the will," she said, "that must attain complete estrangement."
> Without expecting to, he barked out, "I expect so."

The fantastic spiritual vivisection that Katrina performs upon herself and her action is among other things a complete reversal, an overturning, of Christ's symbolic action in his passion and sacrifice; it is willful, desperate denial of all that is human. She will cut away remorse, conscience, repentance, the will itself, and the leftover parts may flutter as they please on the operating table. She has chosen Rodkin as her means to death—"some people drink poison, some take the knife, others drown, I take you"—because she instinctively recognizes him as one of the living dead.

She wants no more to destroy him than Julie wants to destroy Paytor, but once he is let in on her predicament, his destruction is inevitable. His participation with her in her undertaking begins to call him into life. He wants to suffer, though she has forbidden him; he wants to follow her; and when his night with her is over, he feels that he has almost become "somebody." When she refuses to speak to him, he becomes nobody again. Leaving, he cries, "You are taking everything away. I can't feel—I don't suffer, nothing you know—I can't—." When he returns to look at the house a few days later he finds "a single length of crêpe" hung on the door. He becomes a drunkard, a nuisance, "and once, when he saw Doctor Otto Silverstaff sitting alone in a corner [of a café] with his two children, he laughed a loud laugh and burst into tears."

The nightmare world of Katrina Silverstaff is only partly the world of her deranged mind; there is just enough realistic circumstantial detail surrounding her—the seed cakes she carries home for tea, the barges hauling bright bricks to the islands, the furnishings of the office and the waiting room, the daughter's ballet lessons, the cigarette she lights for Rodkin—to retain a focus, however inverted and distorted, on the real world. Somewhere in vivisection, Katrina must have seen the overwhelming impudence, the overwhelming irony of existence. Her response is an overwhelming insult: the only way left to approach God. It is not very far from here to *Nightwood.*

Although most of the stories do not extend to the compass of **"Spillway"** and **"The Doctors,"** they all explore the estrangement and terror of life without love, and since none of the characters can accept traditional responses and relationships instead of love, only emptiness is left. Some die by a fiat of will, like Katrina Silverstaff. Others, like the Russian sisters of **"The Grande Malade,"** "move on." The world developed by Djuna Barnes is a very full fictional realization of the desolate, depersonalized images of T. S. Eliot's *Preludes.* What is missing, significantly, is "The notion of some infinitely gentle / Infinitely suffering thing." Suffering there is in plenty, gentleness, in nothing.

Most of the stories are told by a noncommital omniscient narrator who shows herself only in the quality of her descriptions; she tells nothing directly; even summary is accomplished by skillful accumulation of details. In the few stories with a first-person narrator—**"Cassation," "The Grande Malade," "Dusie,"**—the narrator's detachment has the added horror of coming from one involved in the action. Shocking, remote, the stories nonetheless have all the power a unified vision and superbly controlled prose can give. When they fail it is often merely from overstrain.

Unlike the novels and the long play, where the writing, as Alfred Kazin observed in his review of *Nightwood,* "has occasionally . . . an intensity that is only verbal: long after the idea or emotion has been exhausted, the tone is sustained," the stories maintain correspondence between matter and manner. Along with the novels, they have their being outside society and historical milieu, and indeed the vacuum that surrounds them is responsible for not a little of their impact. While we may feel that Miss Barnes's conception of man is narrow and at times even shallow, the evidence of much contemporary history compels us to admit its appalling veracity. These stories, long out of print and out of sight, deserve a wider appreciation, not only as representative work of the modernist period, but as remarkable examples of their genre. Like the best stories by the best writers of her generation, the best stories of Djuna Barnes—I should pick **"Spillway," "The Doctors," "Aller et Retour,"** possibly one or two more—expand our ideas of what the short story can do, and in this way expand our awareness of life. (pp. 32-41)

Suzanne C. Ferguson, "Djuna Barnes's Short Stories: An Estrangement of the Heart," in The Southern Review, *Louisiana State University,* n.s. *Vol. V, No. 1, Winter, 1969, pp. 26-41.*

JAMES B. SCOTT (essay date 1976)

[*Scott is the author of the first full-length study of Barnes, excerpted below. Here the critic discusses the short stories, describing them as marked by "reverse naturalism," in which realism is employed to affirm the unnaturalness of life.*]

In her treatment of life's meaning, we see the difference between naturalism of the kind Miss Barnes writes and existentialism. Despite the hard realism of naturalism, its determinism and its pessimistic outlook about man's ability to shape the world to his will, naturalistic writing nevertheless insists that human life can be rationally understood. Life is frequently tragic and painful, it is true; but the purpose of the naturalist is to show, nevertheless, *how* and *why* life is tragic and painful. The naturalist believes, that is, in the capability of logic and reason to understand life, even though he or his characters may be powerless to alter its hard realities.

Existentialism, on the other hand, posits not only that life is frequently tragic and painful but that life is also irrational. Some existentialists, like Jean Paul Sartre and Bertrand Russell, endow man with free will and urge him to make sensible patterns of his own within the larger frame of a meaningless universe. Miss Barnes sees life and the perpetuation of life as a mistake; indeed, the mistake is to be alive, and then by procreation, to compound that error and produce more tragedy and pain. She finds death, then, to be an affirmation and a triumph. Tragedy is not dying; rather, it is living. The meaninglessness and irrationality of life, she indicates, can be understood; for, put most simply—and paradoxically—the meaninglessness of life lies precisely in its meaning.

The term inverted naturalism describes, therefore, writing which is essentially positive even though the usual associations between life and hope versus death and despair (or tragedy) have been reversed. To describe Miss Barnes as an existentialist would be to suggest that she sees life as ultimately beyond understanding; but to do so is not accurate since she sees life as meaningless but as quite understandable. In the deepest sense, her stories can be said to show *how* and *why* death can be the only real affirmation in a meaningless universe. (p. 24)

Miss Barnes's stories move with the inevitable determinism of the naturalist toward their conclusions, but the conclusions are frequently enigmatic or ambiguous. Some of her characters know more at this point than they knew at the beginning of the events the story recounts, and others do not. The stories, that is, ultimately concern themselves with enlightening the reader rather than the characters. Madame La Tosca in **"A Boy Asks a Question of a Lady"** knows as much about puberty's mysteries at the start of the story as she does at the end, and the boy is not really enlightened by his encounter with her. John, the hostler in **"A Night among the Horses,"** dies in confusion; and he cannot be said to have made as much sense of his own life as the reader is invited to do. The concluding action of the stories may be as dramatic as the trampling to death of John in **"A Night among the Horses"** or as slight a gesture as old Rabb's lifting her eyes a bit higher after Hardaway's death in **"The Nigger"** or as Moydia's new fashion in **"The Grande Malade"** of sugaring her tea from a greater height, now that she has become "tragique."

A drawing by Barnes from her Book of Repulsive Women.

Obviously, the degree of finality of the concluding action serves as an index of the seriousness of the writing, and even the seriousness of the loss, when death concludes the story. The devices used to conclude the stories resemble James Joyce's epiphanies, but Miss Barnes's are fused with the conventional dramatic climax. The stories end in an action, or a gesture, the force of which is aimed at the reader and invites the reader's understanding. The epiphany, as Joyce conceived it, was a moment of illumination for the reader, which might or might not be shared by the character. For Joyce, it was not necessarily the most dramatic moment of his story; and it did not have to occur at the end of the narration, although it frequently did. Wherever it occurred, it was the moment when the forces of the story came into sharpest focus; and at that moment the reader could see most clearly what the various details had been pointing to from the beginning.

In Barnes's stories, the enlightenment tends to occur at the very end, often in the last sentence, and has some form of action or gesture which is intended to evoke in the reader one or more possibilities for grasping the significance of the events of the story. (pp. 25-6)

Although some lightness and Barnes's characteristic droll humor appear in **"A Boy Asks a Question of a Lady,"** man's mortality is central in this slight story. The boy of the title, Brandt Wilson, is fourteen and is evidently still innocent about the mysteries of puberty. Brandt's brother, who is two years older, has undergone changes which Brandt cannot understand. When he enters the bedroom of the widely known actress Carmen La Tosca by stepping through her window, he poses his problem, evidently supposing that a famous woman of the world would know the answers. While Carmen lies indolently in bed, the youth stands embarrassed before her. Carmen, who has played both male and female roles on stage, may have a feeling for both forms of sexual identity; but, since she is aware of Brandt's innocence, she tells him nothing that will hurry its loss.

Beneath her civilized appearance is Carmen's knowledge that she is an animal; her wisdom accrues from her use of nature as a basis for her moral and philosophical standards. Life, Carmen can see, is but a short trip from birth to the grave—a bit of time in the sun; and all one can do is enjoy life while one has it. She grasps Brandt's problem at once, telling him that everyone suffers life equally, and not to think of his brother's changes any more. Death, she observes, is the end of everything; and she offers him an adage: "A little evil day by day, that makes everything grow." Carmen administers to Brandt a parting physical touch, emblematic, perhaps, of the wisdom she has imparted to him. Brandt can tell about that touch when he tells the story of how he went to visit the great actress in her bedroom. But Carmen knows, as Brandt will when he is a man, that her touch merely reflected her slight and passing interest in him: her sympathy. Essentially each person must live his life alone. (pp. 28-9)

Beauty in death is surely the primary quality that **"No-Man's-Mare"** seeks to convey, for the story presents the naturalist's attitude toward death poetically, through images of natural beauty. In this story, Pauvla Agrippa, the wife and mother who has just died, was young and beautiful; moreover, she wanted to die. Since her baby does not understand that his mother is dead, the infant suffers no loss; and her husband's loss is mitigated by his knowledge that his life will gradually reestablish itself and continue. The story carefully avoids developing the reader's sympathy for Pauvla, for she needed none. The problem for this fishing community (supposedly located at Cape Cod) is to transport Pauvla's body from the promontory on which the village is located to the headlands. Pauvla's sister Tasha reminds the men that the previously uncaptured wild horse known as No-Man's-Mare might be caught and used since it is getting very feeble. The horse is captured, and Pauvla's body tied to its back with fishnet. The funeral procession begins walking along the beach, but after a few steps the horse turns abruptly toward the sea and plunges in it. When a wave washes over the swimming horse, Pauvla's yellow hair can be seen floating behind. When another wave washes over the horse, Pauvla's arms, now freed, appear to be swimming; but the third wave erases both horse and body from sight. Tasha, previously unreconciled to her sister's death, now finds comfort in praying to the sea.

No-Man's-Mare provides the focus of the story. An aging, dying force of nature, her nimbleness in escaping captors and her unwillingness to be touched indicate her natural purity in contrast to which man seems a defilement. The horse is also used as an index to human rapport with nature; for Pauvla has lately approached closely enough to see that the mare has a film over one eye; evidently it is aging rapidly and going blind. Since three children have recently managed to pat the horse, she can be approached as she weakens into death. These approaches establish an implied relationship between the children, the horse, and Pauvla. The children, innocent because of their youth, are still close to nature; but Pauvla, who is not innocent, has a natural quality that approximates innocence: her attitude toward death. For death too is a part of nature, perhaps the only indisputable part; and Pauvla has entered into a deep, almost mystic sympathy with the principle of death. She is fit for the role of the beautiful woman who will be given a unique burial, one that is both poetic and symbolically meaningful; for her burial at sea is emblematic in the story of unending change and of the process of dissolution. (pp. 38-9)

We are reminded by **"No-Man's-Mare"** of the child's fairy tale with its linear plot and by its tendency to present the bizarre and the monstrous as offhandedly as if they were completely natural. We do not question in a fairy tale the presence of giants, ogres, or mermaids. In **"No-Man's-Mare,"** we read of a funeral procession that is wrested away from men by an aged and dying horse that provides a burial at sea; and such a natural funeral is far more satisfactory than any undertaker could produce. As for the people's success in putting a dead woman's body on a horse that they could never capture until this day, Barnes makes no attempt to justify this coincidence; the action is simply a fact of the story. We have also the child's-tale formula, traditionally magical, in the coming of the third sea wave which obliterates all traces of Pauvla and the mare; and we have reconciliation with nature in Tasha's praying to the sea (after unsuccessfully praying to other things) and of finding comfort "this time".

The title **"The Nigger,"** of Barnes' one story about race relations in the South, calls attention to the disdain many southerners feel for Negroes and thus hints at the theme. Rabb, an aged Negress, is watching John Hardaway, her master, die. Rabb, who had been John's "mammy," shows every concern for her dying master's welfare. John will not have the Negress present when he dies; he will not allow her to eat in his presence, although she has been with him for many hours; but he needs her, and is entirely dependent upon her. Implied during the prolonged dying of John Hardaway is the tenor of a lifetime of interrelationships with the Negro; they were never once conducted on a human equal-to-equal level. The story is characterized by a sense of waiting and by a lurking sensuality which death itself seems to bring into the room.

A contrapuntal effect is achieved between the two characters by a number of means. As John's mind wanders, Rabb crouches in the corner, waiting and watching; when Hardaway is hungry, he calls for broth and Rabb feeds him. Hardaway will not have the Negress eat in his presence because of his "southern gentleman" code; and, when she comes out of the corner to fix herself some soup, he forbids her to eat; yet rather than leave him, Rabb chooses to go hungry. Rabb's soup and Hardaway's broth exist in tentative identification, since food is a necessity and it undercuts the more arbitrary master-servant relationship. Added to this device is the contrast between the powerlessness of Hardaway who is too weak to move and Rabb's crouching posture in the corner. As John nears death, Rabb approaches his bed and ends by standing over him at her full height. Contrapuntally arranged are the white man's hatred and the black woman's sympathy. Rabb herself functions in two distinct ways: just as she is a "good" Negro, solicitous of her master's welfare, so she is also the dark shadow of death crouching in the corner; but, when she is ordered to leave the room, she silently refuses. As she approaches and stands taller and taller by the bedside, so does death more and more closely approach Hardaway; and it ends by towering above him.

The movement of the story is toward Rabb's getting to eat soup in her master's presence; toward the final erectness of the black woman in contrast to the white man's final supineness; toward a consummation of these two disjunct yet interrelated lives. At the moment of death, Rabb leans down to force one last breath of life and death into John's failing body. At this instant, his eyes momentarily open as he expires. Hardaway's final "Ah!" amounts to human consummation at the last possible moment, to a final absolution. The last knowledge Hardaway has of this life is that desperate breath imparted to him by the despised Negro. That one breath vanquishes his entire former life, for implied in it is the racial lie which he has lived and which, even given the opportunity, he could never rightfully live again. Rabb runs her tongue over her lips and raises her eyes; a heightened dignity is now hers. When Rabb gets to eat her soup, we see a final wisdom. Having done all that was to be done, she resumes her own life as it had been before John's illness. The reader admires Rabb; he so despises Hardaway that his death, far from being tragic, seems an improvement.

The theme of Barnes's story **"Indian Summer"** reminds us of Edgar Allan Poe's view that the death of a beautiful woman was "the most poetical topic in the world." . . . (pp. 39-41)

Where death to Poe was a mysterious country whose very borders were in doubt, to Miss Barnes death appears preferable to any condition of life. As the author, Miss Barnes controls the tone of the work; and, if she refuses to mourn, and if the dead character is shown to have preferred death, the reader who feels the loss of life distorts the intention of the story. In **"Indian Summer,"** the death of the beautiful woman occurs but in a social milieu far different from that of **"No-Man's-Mare";** and again the author deliberately resists any temptation to see death as tragic.

Madame Boliver of **"Indian Summer"** has lived an unfulfilled existence for fifty-three years. Plain to the point of ugliness, she has been the tolerated old maid who has lived vicariously through her relatives. Suddenly she bursts into late-blooming beauty; she starts to dress well and to acquire imaginative magazines and rare *objects d'art.* Her home becomes a fashionable salon that attracts students, politicians, and intellectuals. Before this development, she had been ignored; now she finds herself proposed to by men of wealth and position. She accepts a suitor, Petkoff, a thirty-year-old Russian; and she is in the midst of her joyous wedding preparations when she is stricken with illness and subsequently dies. The plot, by any expected human standard, seems tragic; but the story ends not only with Petkoff cursing his misfortune while ludicrously lighting a cigarette at one of the four holy candles surrounding the dead body but with the authorial drollery that in death Madame is more beautiful than ever before. The author's control of the tone throughout the story subverts the reader's ability to extend compassion where it is not sought.

Petkoff is probably the most masculine of Barnes' male characters. Unlike Golwein of **"The Robin's House,"** he is not given to philosophical vaporizings; indeed, he is a man of action, not of words. While he is politely tolerant of his fiancée's talkative acquaintances, he does not feel compelled to join their conversations. Even his entrance into the marital state has been carefully considered; for, as a businessman just getting started in America, he is well aware that falling in love and paying court to a woman cause his own affairs to suffer from neglect. He weighs all considerations carefully before proposing; but, once decided, he sweeps away all competition with ease. A comic figure who takes himself seriously, Petkoff does not fit into a stereotyped characterization; he is drawn too realistically. His lighting a cigarette at one of the holy candles has both serious and comic aspects. He has made a heavy emotional investment and lost, and his "Damn it!" is just selfish enough to remind us that love is more a personal than a shared estate. Petkoff is not thinking so much of Madame Boliver's loss of life as he is of his own of madame. Thus Petkoff embodies in his behavior a truth larger than his own realization but one that expresses the author's view of death. (pp. 41-2)

James B. Scott, in his Djuna Barnes, *Twayne Publishers, 1976, 152 p.*

LOUIS F. KANNENSTINE (essay date 1977)

[In the following excerpt from his book-length critical study of Barnes, Kannenstine surveys the short stories, emphasizing the unifying artistic vision that shapes the collection Spillway *and placing it within the context of Barnes's other works.]*

Those carefully revised and sharpened [stories] that form . . . ***Spillway*** hold together almost as chapters of a planned whole. In view of its resemblance to a story sequence in which each distinct part, through interrelated or recurring symbols and literary techniques, contributes to a central purpose or vision, a . . . similarity to James Joyce may be noted. Both ***Spillway*** and *Dubliners* convey a whole rather than a fragmented impression. Both deal with the suppressed life of a particular culture and the moments in which it spills over into daily experience. In *Dubliners,* Joyce is specifically concerned with Ireland's frozen political, social, and historical position and the consequent repression of spirit. Miss Barnes's locale shifts and is less specific, but it no less concretely incorporates the dead forms that remain in a twentieth-century wasteland after the severance of all historical and spiritual connections, leaving a terrible restlessness underneath. Similar polar types appear in the books of each writer: in Djuna Barnes's case, peasants and continental aristocrats, in Joyce's the common men and the elite of Dublin. And of course each is the sole short story collection in the two authors' bodies of work. (p. 57)

An examination of the stories allows a reader to discover nearly all of the techniques, ideas, and motifs that are basic in Miss Barnes's work. The early examples quite closely parallel her work in other genres, while the late ***Spillway*** stands as a volume with a high degree of unity, built almost as if intentionally as a story sequence which would suffer from the removal or displacement of any of its members. Placed at the beginning of ***Selected Works,*** also of 1962, and preceding *Nightwood* in the volume, it serves as an ideal means of approaching that novel. Neville Braybrooke writes that many of the stories in ***Spillway*** act as bridges between *Nightwood* and *The Antiphon* because "they are part of the same imaginative landscape, relayed at the same order of intensity [see Additional Bibliography]. They are also a strong link between the early work and the mature work, bridging the gap between *Ryder* (and *Ladies Almanack*) and *Nightwood.* By the very fact of their revision, they are at once the creations of the developing and the mature artist.

Defining the particular quality of these stories would require relating them to Miss Barnes's work in other genres. In the first place, they have none of the rhetorical excess of either the novels of 1928 or the earlier *Book of Repulsive Women* and the Lydia Steptoe vein of literary sketch, although from the last follow the stories that are narrated by a precocious and perverse "little girl." The affinity of the majority is rather to some of the more stylistically restrained articles and essays and, in certain cases, to the lyrical-bucolic poems. Like those, the stories demonstrate the author's ability to observe and render the natural world, the world outside, with a certain degree of objectivity. In their mode of narration, excepting only the two stories in ***Spillway*** told in the first person by the girl, they hold to an omniscient third-person voice that has no patience with verbal decoration or gratuitous fancy. Pointedly economical, concise both in exposition and metaphor, the narrative voice delivers a terse, often epigrammatic, often either elliptical or involuted, version of common speech. The verbal condensation results in something both elusive and concrete, as will readily appear in quoted passages.

As might be expected, the stories are not confined to any conventional approach to plot. Much different in manner from *Ryder* and *Ladies Almanack,* they are no less of a departure from the great storytelling tradition. In fact, Miss Barnes's least successful stories are those few that do depend upon the elaboration of a plot. For instance, in *Vanity Fair* at the end of the twenties, she attempted a few light ironic tales of European aristocracy somewhat in the manner of de Maupassant or Schnitzler. The results, however, lacked their primary interest in character, and the irony remained merely on the surface, plot-bound. In one of these, **"The First of April,"** two longtime lovers are persuaded by their respective spouses to terminate the affair on the grounds that they have become visibly old and ridiculous. The parting messages that Baron Otto Lowenhaven and Contessa Mafalda Beonetti wire each other are indeed received, but, irresistibly reunited in Rome, the lovers thank each other for not wiring, feigning unbroken trust. In **"The Letter That Was Never Mailed,"** the Baron Anzengruber and the Vicomte Virevaude, friends since childhood, share a "wild, lyric, rococo" infatuation with Vava Hajos, a Viennese dancer, and their rivalry reaches a comparable ironic dénouement. Rather more successful is **"A Duel without Seconds,"** which has to do with repeated thefts at society affairs given over the years by the Baron and Baroness Otterly-Hansclever. Its measure of success, however, comes from the fact that it creates a precise sense of faded, impoverished nobility that remains after the mechanics of its anecdotal plot are forgotten.

Although this milieu is present in parts of ***Spillway,*** the *Vanity Fair* stories relate more closely to Miss Barnes's formulaic one-act drawing room dramas of the twenties than to the majority of her stories. Equally atypical is a much later story, **"The Perfect Murder."** Written in 1942 and published in the *Harvard Advocate,* it concerns a Professor Anatol Profax, whose field is dialectology and whose special interest is in the effect of environment on speech ("The inarticulate had proved particularly satisfactory; they were rather more racial than individual."). Love to him is love of sound, and ridiculously he conceives himself a man of violent passions: "Certainly at some time in his life he must have curbed an emotion, crushed a desire, trampled a weakness." In any case, in his tabulations he has yet to find someone who defies classification.

One day on the streets of New York, he observes a circus poster depicting "the one True and Only Elephant Woman." Shortly he stumbles into a woman who claims that she had just died from a fall from a trapeze and come back: " 'I'm devoted to coming back, it's so agonizing.' " She announces herself as a *Trauma,* saying that she is sometimes the elephant girl, sometimes the trapeze artist, sometimes a milliner, and sometimes hungry. Her speech is a string of nonsense statements, epigrams, and non sequiturs. She calls herself " 'as aboveboard as the Devil,' " and " 'the purest abomination imaginable.' " Perverse and irrational, she walks the streets with the train of her velvet dress dragging cigarette butts and theater ticket stubs in the dust. They proceed to his rooms and agree to marry, but later. (pp. 57-61)

Those who would argue the influence of surrealism upon Miss Barnes could find no better support than this story, with its juxtaposition of incongruous elements and its management of dream as reality. **"The Perfect Murder,"** different though its style may be, relates to the earlier stories directly through its theme of the subjugation of logic by the great force of the irrational, of the suppressed life of the imagination. True knowledge, Miss Barnes repeatedly implies, is intuitive and cuts through rational philosophies. Human language, especially ordinary discourse, is powerless to express it. If language is to achieve a higher synthesis of experience, it must be restored to its living sense through the image. In effect, Miss Barnes is after the same thing as Professor Profax, who hopes to recapture "that great band of sound that had escaped the human throat for over two thousand years":

> No theories for or against; no words of praise or of blame, only a vast, terrible lamentation which would echo like the "Baum!" of the Malabar Caves. For after all what does man say when it comes right down to it? "I love, I fear, I hunger, I die." Like the cycles of Purgatory and Damnation.

The satiric approach of **"The Perfect Murder"** is unique in Miss Barnes's short stories. Its schematic method mocks itself, the end result of a reaction against the sort of mechanical plotting attempted in the *Vanity Fair* tales. While the ***Spill-***

way stories and their early versions react against the conventional plot, however, most of them do have affinities to certain types of narrative fiction or drama. One story involving the tortured relations between a lady and her ostler [**"A Night among the Horses"**] shows the conscious influence of Strindberg. More often, Miss Barnes's way of fleshing out small situations in her mordant, spare prose recalls some of the Russian short stories of the late nineteenth and early twentieth centuries. The naturalism of Chekhov in particular comes to mind. But there also appears a quality that is more difficult to define. Natalie Clifford Barney may have come the nearest to capturing it when she commented, in connection with passages of Miss Barnes's prose that she was introducing in translation, "Ses pensées ne vont jamais jusqu'à la pensée. Ce sont des bribes de sensations, miriors brisées à la joie de vivre ou l'on se coupe." It is in this sense that the stories may be called experimental. They amount to an attempt to get in touch with "the Undercurrents," ignored in journalistic writing, by capturing "fragments of sensations," the very elements that the literary naturalists might have suppressed in expectation of conclusive action, the effective climax of character development in time. They suggest the way which the silent moving picture found to pick and isolate significant details from the stream of sequential action and, by the technique of montage, transcend the frequently mundane requirements of story and dramatic structure. By ordering such fragments, not to reinforce some abstract idea or promote some sequence of events, but to render in a concise image or turn of speech the tentativeness of being, they cohere rather independently of the reader's preconceptions. One can begin to get a sense of how Miss Barnes manages the refractive elements of experience from a look at two of the stories in ***A Book*** that were excluded from ***Spillway.***

In **"The Nigger,"** a Southern gentleman who has lived well and scornfully, who "hated negroes with that hate a master calls love," is dying in the presence of Rabb, the nigger. She had served John Hardaway's mother also at her deathbed, and had tried to do something for her. "But the thing she was trying to touch lay in some hidden corner of Mrs. Hardaway, as a cat hides away under a bed, and Rabb had done nothing after all." The son wishes to tell Rabb something, but only whispers, " 'Keep your place.' " When he is near the point of death, Rabb assists him by placing her mouth to his and breathing one powerful and deadly breath into him. Like the stories in ***Spillway,*** this tale builds upon the indirect, stressing the unsaid and the implied. Between Hardaway and Rabb there has been no communication, yet a feeling of quite frightening intimacy is conveyed. The final result is ambiguity, for their relationship cannot be defined in familiar terms.

Equally elusive and marked by fragments of sensations is **"Mother,"** which returns to Miss Barnes's familiar drab, somewhat seedy urban milieu which is in keeping with the physical descriptions of the characters. Lydia Passova, the pawn shop mistress, is "excessively tall," and "her eyes were small, and not well focused. The left was slightly distended from the long use of a magnifying glass." As for her lover, he is "a little nervous fellow . . . a roundfaced youth with a deep soft cleft in his chin, on which grew two separate tufts of yellow hair. His eyes were wide and pale, and his eyeteeth prominent." Less garish than the women in *The Book of Repulsive Women,* these characters—and there are many of them in Miss Barnes's stories—have a powerful aura of waste about them, a sense of having been bypassed by life and condemned to a semi-isolated existence of unfulfilled or inarticulate love. So, although her lover astonishes himself by thinking Lydia Passova a great woman,

> He never knew where she had come from, what her life had been if she had or had not been married, if she had or had not known lovers; all that she would say was, "Well, you are with me, does that tell you nothing?" and he had to answer, "No, it tells me nothing."

Their relationship even seems to rest directly upon its obscurity as the basis of its endurance. Eventually she dies, and he beholds that she is an old woman: "He felt as one feels who has become conscious of passion for the first time, in the presence of a relative." That night he weeps in bed with knees drawn up.

A sense of elusiveness is gained here by moving around the outer edges of a human relationship. Most of the stories in ***A Book*** and its reprint, ***A Night among the Horses,*** deal obliquely with experience. They make the reader a furtive observer of something that he cannot logically understand, that he finds himself in the middle of and yet not of. Insinuative rather than explicative, Miss Barnes's method is perhaps most effective in **"Aller et Retour,"** the story that opens ***Spillway.***

Barnes and Natalie Barney in Nice, France, circa 1928-30.

Perhaps the best known of all her stories, **"Aller et Retour"** was remembered by Graham Greene as it had first appeared in *Transatlantic Review* as "an impressive story with a cruel, visual wit and dialogue curiously precise and suggestive, like the imagery of a Jacobean dramatist." [A footnote cites the source of the quote as *The Catholic Tablet* 14 (November 1936): 678-79.] The opening one-sentence paragraph, as if in rebuttal of Gertrude Stein's pronouncement, "A Sentence is not emotional a paragraph is," forecasts the directness and precision that are to follow: "The train travelling from Marseilles to Nice had on board a woman of great strength." Her journey itself, following the death of her estranged husband, is from Paris to Nice, back to a daughter she has not seen for seven years. The opening description places an unusual emphasis upon her dress, her jewels, which hint of her self-contained demeanor. She surveys the passing countryside through a lorgnette, having tried with difficulty to read a few sentences of *Madame Bovary.* "A middle-aged and rather absurd Madame Bovary," Graham Greene calls Madame Erling von Bartmann herself.

There is a two and a half day pause in Marseille. Madame von Bartmann walks the dirty streets holding up her skirt in a way that is described as at once careful and absent. As foul odors reach her, "she looked neither pleased nor displeased." From her aloofness, what she observes seems both charged with significance and oddly disconnected:

> A gross woman, with wide set legs, sprawled in the doorway to a single room, gorged with a high-posted rusting iron bed. The woman was holding a robin loosely in one huge plucking hand. The air was full of floating feathers, falling and rising about girls with bare shoulders, blinking under coarse dark bangs. . . .
> At a ship-chandler's she stopped, smelling the tang of tarred rope. She took down several coloured postcards showing women in the act of bathing; of happy mariners leaning above full-busted sirens with sly cogged eyes. . . . A window, fly-specked dusty and cracked, displayed, terrace upon terrace, white and magenta funeral wreaths, wired in beads, flanked by images of the Bleeding Heart, embossed in tin, with edgings of beaten flame, the whole beached on a surf of metal lace.
> (pp. 61-5)

Upon arrival in Nice, Madame von Bartmann announces to Richter, her daughter, that she plans to stay for quite a while. Between the two, all is hesitation. The girl is reticent, embarrassingly immature, and the mother's resentment clearly stands between them. " 'A queer, mad fellow,' " she says of Herr von Bartmann.

That evening, however, Madame von Bartmann attempts to speak to her daughter. Her words pour out in a barely interrupted monologue. Life, she begins, is filthy and frightful. " 'There is everything in it: murder, pain, beauty, disease—death.' " She tells her daughter she knows nothing, and continues:

> "You must know *everything,* and *then* begin. You must have a great understanding, or accomplish a fall. Horses hurry you away from danger; trains bring you back. Paintings give the heart a mortal pang—they hung over a man you loved and perhaps murdered in his bed. Flowers hearse up the heart because a child was buried in them. Music incites to the terror of repetition. The cross-roads are where lovers vow, and taverns are for thieves. Contemplation leads to prejudice; and beds are fields where babies fight a losing battle."
> (pp. 65-6)

This remarkable passage, marking the peak of intensity in the story, is described by Jack Hirschman [in his unpublished Ph.D. dissertation on Barnes] as a "rhythmical and rhetorical elaboration" evoking a poetic response, and then just avoiding the poetically pretentious by virtue of the universal statements framing it. Likewise, the dissociated images that accumulate in montage in the Marseilles passage might have appeared merely esoteric without the verbal extension they are given here. When Richter asks her mother if there had been anything nice in Marseilles, Madame von Bartmann smiles and replies, " 'The Bleeding Heart—sailors—,' " recalling instantaneously the whole poetic tableau of pain and eroticism that she had beheld earlier.

What follows is abrupt. A few days later Richter shyly reveals her engagement to a government clerk that had been prearranged by the father. . . . Two months later, the wedding having taken place, Madame von Bartmann boards the trainback to Paris. " 'Ah, how unnecessary' " is all she says to herself in conclusion. (pp. 66-7)

Here there is an interplay between two orders of experience which relates to a comment of Miss Barnes in her theatre article, "The Dear Dead Days":

> I had written that there are only two kinds of loneliness: love and imagination. I said that only two classes knew love, the high and the low; the high because of their fancy, and the low because of their need. The middle classes dabbled in that simple intrigue which takes itself out in what I called the "home condition"; they never suffer the agony, or discover the ecstasy of the "emotional return." By this was meant that no associations displace their caution; they could, in other words, scarcely be betrayed because their little sardine of love has been decorously sandwitched (sic) between forethought and afterthought.

Hence the inability of Madame von Bartmann to touch her daughter. Richter is vacant, while her mother is overflowing. . . . Here it would seem in order to question Suzanne Ferguson's claim that for all her knowledge, "Mme. von Bartmann is not a person, either" [see excerpt dated 1969]. The strength with which Miss Barnes initially endows her heroine is not in doubt, but there is a gap here between particular orders of being, on a level beyond the individual characters. Like Sophia in *Ryder,* Madame von Bartmann is one of Miss Barnes's women who have come to some terms with the mortal agony. The end note of unnecessity, in her terms of coping, has to be not flippant, but profound. The title itself, recalling the repeated "going to and coming from" pattern in *Ryder,* is a forecast of the irony of her experience.

Two languages play in counterpoint throughout. One is the language of plain narrative, though extremely concise and highly charged, which is capable of lending credibility to the social comedy in the situation. The other is a compact metaphorical poetic construction, a series of striking images reflecting the terror of the impossibility of being with an impact comparable to the final exclamation of horror in Conrad's *Heart of Darkness.* In their particular ways, each of Miss Barnes's stories is involved with what happens when what is dark and suppressed spills out into the deceptive world of daily events and rational motives.

"Cassation," the next story in ***Spillway,*** contains a significant extension of this theme. Originally titled **"A Little Girl Tells a Story to a Lady,"** it is the monologue of a young girl in a café, addressed to a silent lady who is again the presumed interlocutor in **"The Grande Malade,"** formerly called **"The Little Girl Continues"** when it appeared in *This Quarter* in 1925, its only publication prior to ***Spillway.*** A third of these stories, **"Dusie,"** appeared in *Americana Esoterica,* an anthology of 1927, but was never reprinted. The narrator is again one of Miss Barnes's young girls on the verge of womanhood, part innocent yet insouciantly and intuitively involved in adult perversity and sophistication. (pp. 67-9)

The story that Katya tells a lady [in ***"Cassation"***] is a bizarre one indeed. . . . In a Berlin café, Katya observes a magnificent woman, " '. . . savage with jewels, and something purposeful and dramatic came in with her, as if she were the centre of a whirlpool, and her clothes a temporary debris.' " With her is a small, oddly fragile man, her broken husband who remains in the background throughout, but whose presence, once established, hangs in the atmosphere like a ghost. Eventually the woman, Gaya, takes the girl to her home, where, in an expensive but disorderly and melancholy bedroom, a child of about three lies in the center of a tall, massive bed making a thin buzzing noise like a fly. The bed is disheveled and "devastated," and over it hangs a great painting of foreign battle, in which warriors on horseback seem to be charging the battlefield of the bed. The reader is directly thrust into the same landscape that Madame von Bartmann had created through her distilled experience. The woman tells Katya that she will stay here, forgetting her ambitions for the theater, her passion for the dance, everything.

During the course of a year, the girl becomes a *"religieuse"* of a sort, embracing, as she says, " 'a religion, Madame, that was empty of need, therefore it was not holy perhaps, and not as it should have been in its manner.' " As for Gaya's religion, it involves the philosophy that " 'one should be like all people *and* oneself, then . . . one was both ruined and powerful.' " (pp. 69-70)

The weird, seemingly catatonic child is a perfect symbol for Gaya's alienation from herself and from life. As Katya says, " 'It was beautiful in the corrupt way of idiot children; a sacred beast without a taker, tainted with innocence and waste time; honey-haired and failing, like those dwarf angels on holy prints and valentines.' " Indeed, the child's name is Valentine, a touch which is in part Miss Barnes's way of heaping on the decadence again, but which also recalls in oblique fashion the image of the Bleeding Heart. Along with the helpless husband Ludwig, the three, in a configuration anticipating the Volkbeins in *Nightwood,* embody the historical cassation that Miss Barnes had dealt with in *Ryder.* Even Katya too is corrupt with "innocence and waste time." In the course of her narrative, she repeatedly disgresses into the charm of the seasons in Germany, a leitmotif acting in witty counterpoint to the theme of seasonless horror in nothingness, and pointing up her rootlessness, her distance from life, in a word, her estrangement. (pp. 70-1)

In **"The Grande Malade,"** Miss Barnes slips into parody, a parody which is double-edged. First the story satirizes the café view of life with its italics and its inclusion of everything in quotation marks, which is also meant to involve immediately the tone of certain writings of Raymond Radiguet and Jean Cocteau with which it was infected in the epoch. Secondly, Lydia Steptoe is seeing herself clearly, perhaps for the first time, in a mirror. In context, however, the story can be taken (and is taken on the first reading) as perfectly serious. Moydia is estranged from life and from her own emotions. Her malady is obviously chronic. Her early sophistication is its symptom, and as it is obviously incurable, all she can do is move on. In her internationalism, she is everywhere and nowhere, perpetually going to and coming from, her own "aller et retour" deprived of necessity.

The next story, **"A Night among the Horses,"** was anticipated thematically by **"Renunciation,"** published in 1918 in *Smart Set* but uncollected. In **"Renunciation,"** a man tires of his rootlessness and returns to New York twenty-five years after running away from his wife and home. Feeling strange that he, a Pole, should be there, Skirl Pavet stops in a church to pray. He ends, however, by acknowledging the sweetness and power of sin. Hating the sordidness of the city and the commonness of the restaurant that his wife operates, he had fled to the country and open fields, to love in far-off places. In the story's present time, he renounces his freedom for the sake of what is familiar and unvarying and his. In the end, having hoped to return to his inner self, he is dimly aware that he belongs nowhere. Like Pavet, the groom in **"A Night among the Horses"** is caught between alternate possibilities and states of being, but in a situation much more complex.

While a story like **"Aller et Retour"** depended for its impact upon reaching a level of verbal intensity, **"A Night among the Horses"** succeeds through the purposefulness and compactness of its more traditional narrative form. Opening with the spectacle of a man in full evening dress creeping through the underbrush at the edge of a pasture as the sound of horses' hooves approaches, the story proceeds to work up to this moment in flashback. The relationship between John, the ostler, and Freda Buckler, the mistress of the house, is pure torment. In "a game without any pleasure," she lashes at him with objects of culture, with the very promise of stepping him up " 'from being a "thing".' " But he vigorously insists that he likes being common, and lashes out at her with his whip. His violence pleases her in turn, and her cruelty consists of debasing him further by the very prospect of making him a gentleman. (pp. 72-3)

Finally she tells him to come to her common-dress masked ball in his customary clothes, to serve as "whipper-in." Perversely, he appears in evening dress, with top hat and cane. As his mistress dances with him, he sees her as a praying mantis. At that point he steps back, with a primitive gesture draws a circle around her in the rosin, and flees. Back running among his horses, where he feels he belongs again, he attempts to mount one of them, fails, and is trampled to death. (p. 73)

[Existence] appears in Miss Barnes's terms as an incessant struggle, not to understand, but to "stand everything" beyond the end of rational comprehension or understanding. Only Madame von Bartmann in the stories discussed to this point is a woman of great strength, although there is a reverse sort of integrity in Katrina Silverstaff's managing of her own fate, however grim and final that may be. Julie Anspacher, Gaya, the ostler, Amietiev: all are truly caught in the "halt position of the damned," and the stories gain their compressed power in dramatizing the restlessness of their condition. Katya's reference to her sister's restlessness, comparing it to " 'a story that has no beginning and no end, only a passion like flash lightning,' " sums up the quality of intensity that the best of the stories possess. They take characters out of the ordinary routines of their lives and focus upon highly charged situations in which their suppressed dread and passions can no longer remain unbidden and so pour out into the spillways of their lives. Then all is risk and chaos, against which reason is no effective agent.

The venting of repressed emotion calls for a dramatic shift in tone and style. The world these characters inhabit may be rendered in plain language, but the inner life expresses itself with an anguished eloquence. Usually the common language Miss Barnes employs, with its sharp terms of tangible perception, makes her passages of numinous, poetic prose stand out all the more prominently. In **"Aller et Retour,"** for example, Madame von Bartmann's journey remains in the foreground; the emotional drama is treated almost as a secondary factor, much as in the early lyrics the lover's anguish is almost incidental upon the pastoral surface. The effect is not unlike W. H. Auden's use, in "Musée des Beaux Arts," of Breughel's *Icarus* to suggest something of the human position of suffering. At the story's core, however, is a distilled vision of suffering that takes on heightened significance as a result of the mundanity surrounding it. A metaphorical poetic precision then plays against a concrete precision which is applied to the prosaic, and the reader is suspended between dualities along with the characters before him. (pp. 81-2)

[It is] the vision of a lost Eden, of innocence and unity out of time, that lies behind each of Djuna Barnes's short stories. The gap, the vacancy that Gaya suffers in extremity is experienced by all the characters wherever they may be. For Miss Barnes's twentieth-century wasteland is a purgatory where all suffer the middle condition, being at home neither here nor there, being neither one thing nor the other, all fashioned against the Day of Judgement. The groom, the tailor, the doctor, the aristocrat: theirs is a collective damnation, which is a radical physical and spiritual dislocation. Being is a terrible state of tentativeness or suspension, never resolved but certainly terminating in death, ending in the mystery that initiated it. The remarkable thing about the stories is the immediacy and concentration that they gain by abandoning all frills and moving directly in style and content toward a central vision. (p. 85)

Louis F. Kannenstine, in his The Art of Djuna Barnes: Duality and Damnation, *New York University Press, 1977, 194 p.*

DOUGLAS MESSERLI (essay date 1982)

[*The following excerpt is from an introduction to* Smoke, and Other Early Stories. *Messerli here surveys Barnes's early newspaper pieces and discusses how journalistic style influenced and shaped her early fiction.*]

[The various writings collected in ***Smoke, and Other Early Stories***] were begun in 1913, when, at the age of 21, Barnes hired on as a feature writer for the Brooklyn *Daily Eagle.* In the next six years—in the *Eagle,* the New York *Press, Telegraph, World* and other City newspapers—she published more than one hundred feature articles and interviews on celebrities of the day, among them such disparate personages as Lillian Russell, Florenz Ziegfeld, David Belasco, "Mother" Jones, Billy Sunday, and Alfred Stieglitz. This prodigious output is made to seem even more extraordinary by the fact that, beginning in 1916, Barnes contributed to the *New York Morning Telegraph Sunday Magazine* a series of twenty-five dramas and fictions. Eleven of these fictions plus three others that had appeared earlier in *All Story Cavalier Weekly* and *The Trend* make up [***Smoke, and Other Early Stories***].

Readers today may find it difficult to imagine how the mass audience of a newspaper that in its later years marketed itself as New York's "racing sheet," would or even *could* have responded to fictions so peculiar as these, with their radical metaphors (". . .Paprika had a moribund mother under the counterpane, a chaperone who never spoke or moved, since she was paralyzed, but who was a pretty good one at that, being a white exclamation point this side of error."); their oracular observations ("When a woman decides to lie down and play 'possum, she always selects with fearful care her hosiery, her petticoats and her shoes."); and their artificial dialogue ("He walks like a cat. I do not like it. . . . A little dusty cat, with a gray nose from prowling in among what people call great facts. Why, will you tell me, have all great things to be dusted? Cathedrals and books and windmills?"). Several of these tales are so startlingly eccentric that, even in a century characterized by its literary experimentation, it is difficult to place them in the Modernist context.

The fact that these tales first appeared in a newspaper, accordingly, today may seem as odd as if one were to encounter the work of Thomas Pynchon or Kathy Acker in the pages of the New York *Post.* But in 1916, the American newspaper was a remarkably eclectic forum, and fiction and drama were standard features. Although today we retain some of the remnants of that eclecticism in our style and entertainment sections that feature everything from political memoirs to medical advice, the newspapers of Barnes' day often imported the very language of popular entertainment into the news items of the front pages. Hence, Barnes' audience may have been more prepared for the sensationalized metaphors, authorial intrusions, and theatrical dialogue of her stories than we are, encountering them now in our narrower and often more academic literary context. And it is clear that just as her audience may have been primed by the journalistic context in which these tales were presented, Barnes herself adopted certain narrative conventions from the reportorial journalism of her day. Of particular importance are the several ways in which the presentational devices of journalism are manifested in these fictions through Barnes' approaches to character, voice, and plot.

Throughout her writing career, Barnes has employed her figures as emblems, caricatures, and stereotypes that have their roots in the character typologies of the literature of the seventeenth and eighteenth centuries. But in these early newspaper works this method of characterization may have been less a conscious decision of Barnes to draw on previous literary traditions than it was a convention of her medium. Despite the increasing popularity of psychologically "rounded" characterizations in fiction as established by Henry James, Knut Hamsun, Marcel Proust, and others, the American newspaper feature-writing of the second decade of this century had not relinquished entirely the character types used by writers such as Theodore Dreiser and Emile Zola. For instance, Barnes wrote of such types in several of her articles in the *Daily Eagle* and for the same paper she made a series of twenty-four drawings titled "Types Found in Odd Corners Round About Brooklyn," which included sketches of stock figures such as the "Newsboy," the "Society Matron," and the "Vagrant." The characters of Barnes' newspaper tales, in turn, are grounded in Naturalism to the extent that they reflect ideas of environment and heredity that had been assimilated into journalistic thought. In **"Smoke"** the mother fears that instead of her husband having inherited "iron" in his veins, "there's a little blood." In **"A Sprinkle of Comedy"** a father unsuccessfully attempts to prevent his son from repeating his own past. In **"The Coward,"** the very fact that Varra Kolveed has had a reputation all her life for courage, leads her to accomplish a courageous act. Throughout, these fictions are imbued with a sense of inevitability, are inhabited by figures that seemingly are determined by their genetic and environmental inheritances. Less than a total commitment to Naturalism, Barnes' characterizations nonetheless reveal her appropriation of the popular psychological and sociological notions of her day. When one reads of her "terrorists," "cowards," and "revolutionists," in short, one must understand them as participating in the milieu of popular newspaper stereotypes, as sharing in the landscape of the headline "killer," "judge," and "cop."

For similar reasons, Barnes felt no obligation in her stories to maintain the objective point of view—that realist convention of authorial exclusion which by mid-century had metamorphosed into dogma. As a feature writer Barnes could make no pretense that she was not the source of what she reported; and, as a fiction writer Barnes apparently saw no reason to abandon such a rhetorical approach, particularly since her informational asides often contributed to the sense of the inevitability of events. In **"The Jest of Jests,"** in fact, Barnes begins with the traditional journalese naming of "who," "where," "what," and "when," which pervades the story with a sense of authorial control:

> The name of the heroine of this story is the Madelonette. Why never seemed to matter any more than that the hero should have been called the Physician when he had never so much as seen a case of measles in his life.
> The place of climax is Long Beach, but you will not understand until you reach the very end, though I might as well warn you that it was there the Madelonette and the Physician fell into each other's arms, much to the consternation of the "regulars" on the boardwalk.

Although this fiction is the most determinist-oriented of her short works, nearly all the stories of this collection, through informational asides, directions to the reader, and other narrational manipulations, expose the *author* as the source of the story, as the apparent agent of a series of shared events. Even Barnes' use of the oracular voice, which might appear out of place in reportage, shares something in common with the editorial page; just as editorials often proclaim a knowledge of the general good in order to support a specific cause, so Barnes' tales lay claim to a knowledge of basic human behavior in order to support her specific narrative descriptions. In **"A Sprinkle of Comedy,"** for example, Barnes observes:

> This man's [Roger's] friends were of the type that in an instant descend from "friend" into a "gang." It takes circumstance alone to make them either friend, lover, enemy, thief, brawler, what-not. It may be a hand on the shoulder, a word whispered in the ear, a certain combination of apparently unimportant incidents.

Through such commentaries and interruptions, Barnes makes it clear that she is the sole reporter/author of the tale she tells. Almost as if to demonstrate that the media often causes the events it reports, Barnes continually reminds her reader that without her "report," without her creation of these figures, there would be no story.

These tales, moreover, are structured in a manner similar to a news report. Beginning with an introductory paragraph or two in which location, characters, and action are established, the stories generally proceed in chronological order. Seldom do they demonstrate any of the literary techniques—radical shifts in time and place, stops in narrative action, and displacement of character—which distinguish what Joseph Frank has described as the "spatial structure" of Barnes' later work. Rather, in these early fictions there is a clear connection between cause and effect. Coherent with its thematics of determinism, the structure of most of these tales is almost ploddingly grounded in the logical order of events.

For all this, few of these stories end in real dramatic closure. Although the destinies of the characters are determined, most of these tales are not resolved. In **"Who Is This Tom Scarlett?"** for example, the reader certainly suspects that Tom will be assimilated into the "gravy-spilling bourgeoise," but the story ends abruptly and it is uncertain whether the character will even survive. Although Varra Kolveed of **"The Coward"** proves her courage, the reader has no clear idea of what that means in terms of her life; is she arrested?; how does her confession affect Monk, the man who she detests? The reader of **"What Do You See, Madam?"** is frustrated completely in his desire to learn what happens to the central character, Mamie Saloam. The lives of these figures, just as the lives of those described on the front pages of the newspaper, may be determined, but are left incomplete. As in the news report, the event—the murder, the capture, the trial, whatever—does not represent a denouement as much as it does a necessary place to stop. Accordingly, in Barnes' tales, as in the reports of the front-page criminals and disaster victims, incident prevails over both character and theme. History is unimportant except for how it relates to the action; although the characters' destinies are sealed, the reader is seldom permitted to experience the results.

To comprehend the significance of this emphasis on action in process, one need only compare these short works with those of Joyce's *The Dubliners* of two years earlier—the prototype, it is often argued, of the Modern short story. In fictions such as "Araby" and "A Little Cloud" action is relatively unimportant; in each of these stories, in fact, the plot is almost nonexistent. . . . [The] focus of Joyce's short fictions is the characters and their psychology. The incidents merely serve as symbols of their conditions. The closing of the bazaar [in "Araby"], the crying of the child [in "A Little Cloud"], are less significant as events than they are as images of the worlds which the characters inhabit. In Joyce's stories, in short, plot is no longer animus, but is revelation.

In Barnes' more journalistic approach, on the other hand, nearly everything revolves around plot. If the characters seem sketchy, it is because they, rather than their actions, are the images of the condition of their kind. And it is only through their actions that significant meaning can occur. Indeed, Barnes sets up circumstances for her characters to insure that they act. In **"A Night in the Woods,"** for example, Barnes stages the scene for the imprisonment of her figures in the most incidental of manners:

> And then the crash comes. A man and his wife somewhere on the border of the town die suddenly, and the cause has been traced back to poison found

> in a loaf of bread. As Jennie and Trenchard are the only bakers in the town they are immediately pounced upon by the marshall, and both of them landed securely in . . . jail.

What matters most for Barnes is not that they are imprisoned or even whether they will succeed in their attempt to escape, but *that they must attempt to escape.* The author has placed them in prison so that they can act, so that they will run. Once again, the reader cannot be certain of the result. In this fiction as in most of the tales of ***Smoke, and Other Early Stories,*** it is action which reveals the living beings of which her figures are merely emblems. Tragedy, for Barnes, is inaction as demonstrated in the title story, in which the younger generation forgets how to act.

In short, the very qualities which help to make these tales seem so eccentric—the use of flat, stereotyped characters, the narrational intrusions, and the emphasis on unresolved narrative action—may have as much to do with where or when Barnes published them as with any decision to write peculiar or obscure fictions. At the same time, it is also clear that Barnes was not completely naive in her use of journalistic techniques. Her adaption of reportorial procedures to fiction was not an end in itself. For underlying her focus on action and her use of character typologies, the oracular voice, and narrative intrusions is Barnes' deeper commitment to an exploration of the moral condition of humankind. And in this concern she far transcends her newspaper model.

In Barnes' later works she became fascinated by—almost obsessed with—the role of human beings in the metaphysical structure of the universe. Particularly in *Nightwood* and *The Antiphon,* one readily can observe her preoccupation with a metaphysical structure that bears resemblances to the Great Chain of Being, the structure, reified in the eighteenth century, in which man is positioned between salvation and damnation, is caught halfway between the angels and the beasts. In Barnes' late writings characters are positioned along a spectrum of their relationship to these two extremes. Kenneth Burke's linguistic analysis of Barnes' *Nightwood* hints that Barnes represents her characters in that work, for example, through verbal constructions which reveal the posturings of their bodies in conjunction with their metaphysical conditions: through "standing," "bending," "bowing," "crouching," "kneeling," and "lying." Although such images often appear in these early tales (in **"The Coward"** Varra is characterized as positioning herself in bed "furtively, with a crouching movement"; the wife of Pilaat in **"The Terrorists"** is described as wearing heavy boots "that seemed to be drawing her down."), in 1916 Barnes had not yet developed such conceits fully. It is apparent in this early work, nonetheless, that Barnes' disinterest in particularized character and her emphasis on action point to the later preoccupation with moral conditions.

Each of Barnes' approaches to character, voice, and plot, in fact, reinforce one another in pushing her tales toward abstraction. A highly stereotyped character inevitably must be presented as acting in a more exaggerated, theatrical manner; and an authorial focus on action more clearly reveals character behavior, which, in turn, profiles the type. Barnes' persistent intrusions and her oracular statements can be understood, moreover, as drawing character away from the particular, as an attempt to generalize the specific. And, ultimately, such a conjunction of techniques directs these tales toward a revelation of moral values. Witnessing man become type through action, the reader is encouraged to place and judge Barnes' figures. And in that context, the catchwords of these early stories—"freedom," "cowardice," "terror," "sensitivity," and "beauty"—suddenly take on new meaning.

In the light of Barnes' interest in these values in a time of increasing moral relativity, it becomes evident why Barnes never adapted much to the Modernist way of thinking and writing of life. In relation to the literature of her close firends, T. S. Eliot and James Joyce, Barnes' writing may always appear as an anomaly. This early fiction, accordingly, cannot be properly evaluated by Modern "normative realist" standards. Barnes' is a private vision, a moralistic vision that is perhaps more at home in our own time, when fiction writing has been increasingly influenced by moral satirists such as Donald Barthelme, Steve Katz, Harry Matthews, Russell Banks, and Gilbert Sorrentino. And although Barnes' early tales are not major works of literature—Barnes, herself, has dismissed them as juvenilia—they are important, I believe, in the context of our current literary concerns. Perhaps today, more than any period since their first appearance, we can readily share the pleasures of these short tales. (pp. 8-19)

Douglas Messerli, "The Newspaper Tales of Djuna Barnes," in Smoke and Other Early Stories *by Djuna Barnes, edited by Douglas Messerli, Sun & Moon Press, 1982, pp. 7-19.*

VALENTINE CUNNINGHAM (essay date 1983)

[*Cunningham reviews Barnes's early pieces collected in* Smoke, and Other Early Stories, *comparing them in their terseness and sensitivity to the works of Raymond Chandler and O. Henry.*]

Here [in ***Smoke, and Other Early Stories***] are fourteen stories, startlingly strange, cranky even, but also as raw and exciting as swigs of poteen. Culled from the dingier nooks of forgotten New York newspaper archives they inaugurate in arresting fashion the Sun and Moon Press's brave project to light up for us the murky early career of Djuna (*Nightwood*) Barnes. . . .

What in their compelling way these stories do is to mythicize cosmopolis, in its most audacious and grotesque modern manifestation, as the urbs of New York, New York. Even the tiny clutch of these fictions that are about Europe and country people, or about a century other than our own, read like modern New York fiction in potential: as if all earlier times and all other places were to be lived only as shadows of that coming Molochian real. Characteristically, when the Polish farmer Pontos marries off his daughter Theeg—she of the inherited silver eyelashes, the visions of mother earth, the crippled feet: a ritualized object in helpless little boots, on a litter littered with cakes and wine—the farmer does so in a story entitled **"The Head of Babylon".** For What Djuna Barnes goes after relentlessly, even among those indeterminate Polish fields, are the flawed enticements offered by Old Testament Daniel's image of apocalyptic Babylon—its head and breast of precious metals, its feet of clay. In other words she is infatuated by those Babylonian *frissons* of dread and delight which she is not alone in siting in the New York she knew.

The denizens of Djuna Barnes's "modern Babylon" are the poor employed of lower Manhattan, the sellers and buyers of lottery tickets, people only too familiar with early morning ferry-boats, who rely for love upon chance encounters on the stairs and in the street, who share back sinks, look out onto "interminable ranges" of tenements, inhabit "the odor of second-hand clothes", and who all seem to have bedridden female relatives propping up the bedclothes in the corners of their cramped rooms ("Her only family tie was a hard and uncompromising knot, a crippled mother, who hooped out the under side of a rose strewn coverlet, a living trellis"). Thinned by toil, lost among the nearly anonymous multitudes, these people have only stubs of names left, names whose former European polysyllables have been cut right back: Tash, Spave, Glaub, Shrive, Freece, Karl, Monk, Swart, Doik, Race. Against such blunted existences, the types some people have become, or the nicknames they've earned—Lilac Jane, Paprika Johnson, The Terrible Peacock, The Physician—begin to look like triumphs, even if rather grim triumphs, of assertive personality. . . .

Like Conrad, and, for that matter, like Brecht, Djuna Barnes recognizes that giving and owning up to nicknames, typing and self-typing, are necessary strategies of modern, urban knowledge and self-knowledge, and so of survival.

"She will make a great thing of it", the "great peasant father" suggests, stupidly confident as he waves goodbye to his just-married daughter in **"The Head of Babylon".** His wife's recognition that some effort might be needed rings rather truer: "You will find it difficult. You will have to invent a way of living." Inventing a way of living involves, for Djuna Barnes's people, inventing a way of naming. For Djuna Barnes herself, registering the New York way of living meant inventing a new way of writing.

The result is stickily obtrusive, a ripe and cheesy style that strives to be toughly and carelessly knowing—and, of course, is strikingly anticipatory of Raymond Chandler at his most wiseguy. This writing and these people, the implication is, must know their way around, must command experience, be street-wise, if they're to stand any chance at all of getting by. The burden of such ranging wisdom is frequently carried by similes; Djuna Barnes's case is no exception. A suitor has "a breaking voice like a ferryboat coming in from Staten Island"; the moon shines through hair "like butter through mosquito netting"; a woman is "rigged out with a complexion like creamed coffee stood overnight". Similes such as these flaunt their knowingness with obvious flash and clamourousness (and how much, and how oddly, exclamation marks get into this writing's life: beneath Lilac Jane's earrings, "as the periods beneath double exclamation points, floated a pair of green boots"; Paprika's paralysed mother is "a white exclamation point this side of error"; "Some women as they grow old . . . go down life's pages an exclamation point."). But for all their exclamatory showiness the similes are in the end as much revelations of pathos as of insight and power. For even at a brief glance one is struck by how they command urban life mainly from below, locally and domestically; what they illustrate most is the knowledge of the politically helpless ones, the socially enfeebled, the poor (what price, in fact, a shrewdness about dirty coffee cups, prole-laden ferries, and unrefrigerated butter?).

Which is presumably why it turns out that however brave or self-sacrificing, wised-up or merely neighbourly people may contrive to be, they never evade what one of these stories calls "The Jest of Jests"—the perpetually hollow laugh of the city, its ironically galling traps and reversals. . . .

In these tales, Babylon demands heroism of its citizens, while at the same time not letting them get too far on the strength of it. Such downbeat conclusions, and such strong and simple ironies as those of Djuna Barnes, are not uncommon in short stories, especially in New York short stories. One thinks continually of O. Henry. But no one tackled such ironies more steelily—with a steeliness that can risk occasional plunges even into O. Henryish mawkishness—than did the very youthful Miss Barnes.

Valentine Cunningham, "Cosmopolis from Below," in The Times Literary Supplement, *No. 4164, January 21, 1983, p. 50.*

CHERYL J. PLUMB (essay date 1986)

[*In the following excerpt from her full-length critical study of Barnes's early works, Plumb traces elements of modernist literary technique in Barnes's short fiction and characterizes her stories as portraying the individual's separation from nature and middle-class society.*]

In [her] short fiction, Barnes increasingly exploited indirect presentation and ambiguous meaning, becoming, as she did so, a more consciously modern artist. The difference in her fictional technique is apparent if we compare the uncollected fiction with the stories she chose to collect in ***Selected Works of Djuna Barnes.*** In the best of the collected fiction Barnes demonstrates an almost enigmatic reticence. She is a presenter of scenes and characters, yet silent as to significance; however, her earliest uncollected fiction reveals very different practices.

A preliminary observation about the kind of fiction Barnes was interested in can be made by comparing her earliest newspaper tales to those she produced three to four years later. Many of the early stories, properly called "tales" by Douglas Messerli [see excerpt dated 1982], have a complicated plot whose aim is to produce the unexpected twist or concluding surprise. (p. 51)

Very quickly Barnes moved away from these practices. Many of the stories published between 1917 and 1923 in the *Telegraph* and *The Little Review* are examples of Barnes's transition from the newspaper tales with their manipulated plots to stories that exploited external events or images to reflect inner conditions. More modern in technique, the transition stories are characterized by authorial restraint; plot is of minor interest. The surprise conclusions of her early stories are replaced by Barnes's growing preference for an ambiguous or an abruptly opaque conclusion.

"The Coward" (August 1917) is a good example of Barnes's transition, of her increasing use of what might be termed symbolic methods. Her concern in this story focuses on "decay," specifically, Varra's recognition of the meaning of her own actions. The plot is simple. Varra has a reputation for courage and is proud of that reputation. Her fiancé Karl declares that he loves her "for her bravery more than anything else." Nevertheless, the reputation also causes Varra some "anxiety"; she feels that she has to continue to prove herself. Suddenly, her fiancé Karl and his friend Monk are arrested for stealing jewels. To save Karl, Varra decides to claim that she stole the jewels. On the first day of the trial she approaches the judge to confess, but faints. However, a day later after Karl has been sentenced, she marches up to the judge and confesses.

Ironically, her confession, which is too late to save Karl, will save Monk whom she hates and who has implicated Karl. The story concludes: "She had forgotten Karl, she had forgotten Monk. She looked at the black curtains with their heavy tassels." The detail seems irrelevant; however, this conclusion implies that Varra has confessed to save her reputation for courage. Two details suggest, moreover, that she recognizes the futility of her attempt to salvage her self-esteem, though others may be deceived by her confession. First, consider her concentration on the dark curtains after she has confessed. On the first day in court Varra associated the curtains with judges, "like something that would finally fall into the cup of life and lie there, black and horrible and menacing, spoiling it at the lips, as mother spoils the beauty of wine, the malignity of vinegar." The curtains, like judges, suggest Varra's conscience that indicts her for her pride. It is not courage that motivates her confession, or even love for Karl, but the need to preserve her self-esteem. Her focus on the curtains in the conclusion, therefore, implies that her self-esteem is not recaptured; she recognizes the deceitfulness of her motive.

The second detail that establishes Varra's recognition of the deceitfulness of her motive is the parallel established between Monk and Varra. Monk has been described as ugly; he is jaunty with a touch of bravado which Varra dislikes "because she sensed in this same bravado her own bravery. . . . The difference lay in this: he was trying to produce an illusion and Varra was trying not to disillusion." By the end of the story Varra realizes that she has confessed to create the illusion of bravery. The key to this realization rests in Varra's recognition that she is ugly. After she has confessed, she looks into a mirror and confirms that she is indeed ugly, ugliness here implying a moral rather than a physical condition. Like Monk after all, she is trying to maintain an illusion. The denouement is implied but complete. (pp. 52-3)

Stories like **"The Coward"** and many that Barnes published in the following years demonstrate that she had taken the step to writing modern stories in which "revelation" is primary, action secondary. The cause of this transition from plot-centered fiction to symbolic fiction is a matter of conjecture. Joyce's *Dubliners* had been published in 1914, and Barnes's 1922 interview of Joyce revealed her absorption in Joyce's work between 1914 and 1917. . . . (p. 54)

Aside from the disappearance of authorial comment from fiction, the modern short story, as Horst Ruthrof points out, has tended to limit its focus, often excluding "enveloping experience in favor of a few items of consciousness." Considerations of space, time, and process are limited to "focus directly on pointed experience." This elimination of everything but the essential situation suggests that the isolation of characters

Barnes in 1971.

that readers experience in Barnes's fiction is an aspect of her technique rather than a failure of characterization. Varra, for example, is not isolated from her community; in many ways she is typical, the average woman, yet Barnes's singleness of purpose in raising the issue of her moral courage sets Varra apart from daily existence.

In focusing on the motives of a single character, Barnes establishes her area of concern to be the problem of the human race rather than the "social problem of the moment." Her use of the pointed experience and symbols to convey inner states and meaning identify even an early story like **"The Coward"** as modern. Though **"The Coward"** was not collected by Barnes, it represents a new direction from the early tales that Barnes referred to as "juvenalia." As a transition work, it is similar in style to the stories of ***A Book,*** in which the authorial intrusion and mechanical plots of the uncollected tales are replaced by contradiction and reticence. The surprise twist conclusions of the tales are replaced by conclusions that are ambiguous and abrupt—almost flat. Nevertheless, in ***A Book*** Barnes's themes reveal the familiar antagonism to middle-class complacency and her concern for the individual.

The winnowing process that led to ***Spillway*** of 1962 establishes what Barnes considered the best of her fiction. In this collection, an edition of the best stories of ***A Night among the Horses,*** her themes inform structure and character; Barnes exploits indirect statement through the opposition of values, usually represented by two characters. In a 1924 *Dial* review Kenneth Burke had observed the motivating force of Barnes's fiction in her descriptions of her characters: "the descriptions themselves are plots" [see excerpt dated 1924]. Increasingly, in these stories, the surface complexity derives from prose that is contradictory and ambiguous, and from abrupt and truncated conclusions. The reader is involved in perceiving, beneath an often contradictory prose surface, latent themes that explore the limitation of material existence and the response of the superior sensibility.

In ***Selected Works*** Barnes collected only those stories in which themes related to individual integrity and human mortality are most powerful in directing characters and in structuring incident, yet most inconspicuous. Specifically, she deleted many of the stories of ***A Book*** and ***A Night among the Horses*** that treated death directly, for example, **"No-Man's-Mare," "Indian Summer," "Mother,"** and **"The Nigger."** Despite the omission of many stories treating death from Barnes's definitive collection, her preoccupation with death is still apparent. Nevertheless, in the stories that remain death is part of the framework of life. Barnes does not focus on the nature of death—its deceit, or unfairness, or its release. Instead, death is a fact that motivates the need for conscious living rather than evasion. Its presence is the essential condition of human existence. Against this fact human beings in Barnes's fictional world shape their passage.

The following three stories are representative of the best of Barnes's mature fiction. In **"A Night among the Horses," "The Rabbit,"** and **"The Valet,"** Barnes reflects a materialistic view of reality but emphasizes also the value of consciousness. **"A Night among the Horses"** (December 1918) relates John's struggle to "know what he is." The issue is the effect of materialistic values on the human spirit, a theme that has occupied Barnes in the journalistic features and in many of the one-acts. This story is usually interpreted as a contest between John and Freda, whose destructive social world contrasts with the harmony of John's natural world. However, the imagery demonstrates that both worlds are hostile. Tangled vines and images of oblivion dominate the natural world. At one point John, peering through "thickly tangled branches," sees "standing against the darkness, a grove of white birch shimmering like teeth in a skull." Similarly, the world of the horses is threatening, not idyllic; "The soft menacing sound deepened as heat deepens; the horses, head-on, roared by him, their legs rising and falling like savage needles taking purposeless stitches." The horses are also described as "galloping about as though in their own ballroom," blurring further the distinction between the social and the animal world: the indoor ballroom and that of the horses.

Another passage illustrates the separation between man and nature: "A frog puffed forth its croaking unmemoried cry; the man struggled for breath, the air was heavy and hot, as though he were nested in a pit of astonishment." Abstract and concrete, the phrase "nested in the pit of astonishment" suggests a birth image, or metaphorically, man's consciousness of his separation from nature. There is ease in the frog's cry, which contrasts with the man's struggle to breathe. Thus, the subject of the story, established implicitly through symbols and parallel themes, is man's desire to make a mark—not to be "unmemoried."

Freda seems to offer this opportunity. She proposes to step John "up from being a 'thing,' " to make him a gentleman. Like Addie of **"The Rabbit,"** Freda is doll-like and mechanical: "that small fiery woman with a battery for a heart and the body of a toy, who ran everything, who purred, saturated with impudence, with a mechanical buzz that ticked away her humanity." Her description identifies her not only with material reality but also with the horse/animal imagery that pervades the story. She is described as "a little beast," "a preying mantis," and like a horse, "She almost whinnied as she circled on her heels."

John greets her proposal at first with comic indignation: "He blew down his mustache. Freda, with that aggravating floating yellow veil! He told her it was 'aggravating,' he told her that it was 'shameless,' and stood for nothing but temptation. He puffed out his cheeks, blowing at her as she passed." Indeed, the yellow veil is a temptation; moreover, John's desire to be something other than an ostler is what has given Freda the control over him that she possess. He tells her, "I *could* stop you, all over, if I wanted to." *If he wanted to* suggests he is willing to enter the world she offers. His characterization of her confirms his ambition and the source of it:

> The kind of woman who can't tell the truth; truth ran out and away from her as though her veins were pipettes stuck in by the devil; and drinking, he swelled, and pride had him, it floated him off.

The language suggests a kind of "fall," for the "he" referred to is certainly not the devil; it is John, and his pride makes him vulnerable to Freda. In the final scene of the story John has just left the party after drawing a circle on the floor around Freda, as if to break his enchantment. Having crawled through the underbrush to the field where the horses are kept, he moves into the field, thinking to take one of them and escape. When they sweep past him, he is horrified, and hollers, "Bitch," blaming Freda for making him a thing they fail to recognize. Though he seems to have rejected his desire to be something by rejecting Freda, his final lines confirm his ambition. Lying in the field, he sobs, "I can do it, damn everything, I can get on with it; I can make my mark!" The horses trample him as they again circle the field. With the abrupt conclusion Barnes suggests the impossibility of returning to a state of innocence. John can no longer be a simple ostler. His fear of what he will be after Freda is through with him is justified.

By pointing, in the title, **"A Night among the Horses,"** to the ballroom imagery associated with the social and natural worlds, Barnes draws together the ballroom and the field, signifying the spiritual darkness that pervades both. They are not opposites: they are one. Both worlds are deceptive, both destructive. While Barnes appears to exploit a context between John and Freda, she in fact questions the basic human motivation to make a mark, to achieve something. That effort appears futile in the world of nature, which is hostile or at best indifferent to man and in which human consciousness perceives man as apart from nature—yet equally futile is the material and limited social world of Freda Buckler. Barnes exposes a false dilemma in this story, for life is not a choice between pastoral simplicity and social values, including progress and ambition. Rather the abrupt ending implies that mortality itself is the limiting factor of life.

Another early story, **"The Rabbit,"** published in October of 1917, is similar in many ways to **"A Night among the Horses,"** though this story focuses more directly on Rugo's decay: his coming to conscious realization of his situation. (pp. 54-7)

Rugo's "expulsion" from an Edenic pastoral world occurs almost without his awareness of it. At the beginning of the story Hugo lives in the country, peacefully happy with his animals and farm work. His misfortune arrives in the shape of an inheritance that his people urge him to take, for it "might 'educate' him, make him into an 'executive,' a 'boss,' a man of the world." He acquiesces, almost unconsciously, neither affirming nor resisting, though his rural life has been a constant source of pleasure: "The world lived here and moved, and its incidental placing of him where he could profit by it was the thing that amazed and satisfied him." Once in the city, however, he visualizes himself "sewing, up on a table, as though he had died and had to work it out." Metaphorically, his work is punishment, suggesting the biblical parallel of Adam's fall and expulsion from Eden.

Rugo is attracted to a small Italian girl whose willingness to degrade him seems her primary trait. Addie is described as a "sly baggage" and "neither as nice as he thought, nor as young"; she has a "crouching tongue." Rugo confuses this girl with all of the madonnas he has seen on calendars. Thus, he is hurt by her charges that he is nothing, and he is determined in his simple-minded way to prove his worth. He does so by taking a live rabbit from the butcher across the street and strangling it.

What in paraphrase invites a smile of incredulity from the reader and in the course of the narration a short-lived guffaw from Addie is portrayed effectively in Barnes's prose as a trauma for Rugo: "The terrible, the really terrible thing, the creature did not squeal, wail, cry: it panted, as if the wind were blunt; it thrashed its life, the frightful scruffling of the overwhelmed, in the last trifling enormity."

Before he settled on the rabbit, nearly in a mood of distraction and desperation, Rugo had looked again at Addie, and this time she did not remind him of a calendar madonna:

> He looked at her in sorrow. The cruel passing twist of the mouth—(everything about her was fleeting), the perishing thin arms, the small cage of the ribs, the too long hair, the hands turning on the wrists, the sliding narrow feet, and the faint mournful sharp odour of lemons that puffed from her swinging skirt, moved him away from her; grief in all his being snuffed him out.

Rugo no longer sees Addie as he once had; he has lost an innocence of perception. Rugo's killing the rabbit is a symbolic gesture, his acknowledgment of a difference within—no longer done to win Addie, for he tells her to "take it or leave it." The act signals the death of a part of Rugo, but also a birth—the thrashing quality evoked applies equally well to death and birth—referring here specifically to Rugo's growing awareness of Addie's character. After he has killed the rabbit, Addie becomes fearful, for he seems different. She asks, as he leaves the room, "Where are you going?" The story concludes: "He did not seem to know where he was, he had forgotten her. He was shaking, his head straight up, his heart wringing wet."

Barnes gives the reader little to draw on in terms of the identity of the new Rugo. There is the lingering irony of the advice of Rugo's people, who have hoped he would become "a man of the world." Perhaps he has, but the price has been a trusting quality and gentleness of character. Yet there is value in seeing the Addies of the world clearly, though the world also may seem impoverished as a result. What is certain is that Rugo at the end of the story is not the same man who "let Armenia slip through his fingers." For Rugo consciousness is not achieved without the loss of illusions. Whether the change in Rugo is good or bad is likely to be the wrong question. It is both. Barnes refuses to reinforce either implication, for she seems interested primarily in creating the metaphor of coming to consciousness with its attendant struggle.

In both **"A Night among the Horses"** and **"The Rabbit"** Barnes portrays a materialistic world. In **"A Night among the Horses"** both social and natural worlds seem equally destructive. In **"The Rabbit"** a natural Edenic world is lost, and Rugo is condemned to a social world that is destructive, though its final effect on Rugo is ambiguous: his experience represents both a loss and a gain. In **"The Valet"** Barnes examines human limitations against the background of nature, which is identified with fruitfulness but also with death. However, through the character of the valet, Vanka, Barnes symbolizes the artist's work, which transcends the natural world and may achieve lasting value. (pp. 58-9)

[**"The Valet"**] depends almost entirely on contradictory suggestions and a shift of focus, via the title, to Vanka. Though the title asserts the importance of Vanka, the valet, the narrative traces the decline of Louis-Georges whose character is subtly criticized. He makes a show of knowing: he pretends to know about his racing stock but unwittingly reveals a hearty, friendly ignorance. He farms but knows little about it; he plans but his "fierce pride," coupled with lack of knowledge and execution, suggests that he follows rather than orders nature. His death is presented as part of the order of nature. It is slow, described as a "foundering" or ripening: "Louis-Georges ripened into death."

Further criticism of his character is the result of what appear to be extraneous characters in the story. There are two women who are sisters; one has a child and a nagging sense of guilt: "In her youth Leah had evidently done something for which she now prayed at intervals, usually before a wooden Christ hanging from a beam in the barn. . . ." Barnes refers to the subject a second time after the death of Louis-Georges when Vanka observes:

> Of course Leah had made a scene, hardly to be wondered at, considering. She had brought her baby in, dropping him beside the body, giving her first order: "You can play together, now, for a minute."
> Vanka had not interfered. The child had been too frightened to disturb the arranged excellence of Louis-Georges' leavetaking, and both the child and the mother soon left the room in stolid calm.

The scene and its reporting are curious. Why is it "hardly to be wondered at"? Is the reader to understand that the child may have been Louis-Georges's or merely that Louis-Georges has taken in Leah and her child? One situation works to the credit of Louis-George, the other does not. The passages, and Louis-Georges's relationship to Vera Sovna, whom the neighbors believe to be "something" to Louis-Georges, seem intended to raise questions about Louis-Georges's character, questions that are unresolved.

The conclusion of the story is characteristically enigmatic. After Louis-Georges's death, Vanka prepares the body and returns to his room, feeling that he "had left something undone. . . . He loved service and order; he loved Louis-George who had made service necessary and order desirable." Vanka's feeling of uneasiness is interrupted when Vera Sovna climbs the vine to his window. She enters the room, exclaiming, "Most fortunate man, most elected Vanka! He let you touch him, close, close, near the skin, near the heart. . . . You knew him, all of him, for years. Tell me—tell me, what was he like?."

Recovering from his astonishment at the intensity and the nature of her outburst, Vanka calms her: "I will tell you, if you are still, if you will sit down, if you are quiet," and then he continues, "His arms were too long, but you know that, you could see that, but beautiful; and his back, his spine, tapering, slender, full of breeding—." Figuratively, Vanka assumes, with his telling, the role of artist, creating from the physical traits of Louis-George the character of the aristocratic gentleman.

The word *breeding,* though, disrupts our participation in Vanka's recreation, for we recall Louis-Georges's bluff ribaldry, praising the "breeding" of his racing stock: "There's more breeding in the rump of one of these, than any butt in the stalls of Westminister." The quiet irony of "breeding" and its related uses—one opening, the other closing the story—plus the subtle rumors concerning the character of Louis-Georges, alert us to Vanka's efforts. Vanka, as artist, interprets and transforms external reality into something timeless. The loss both Vanka and Vera experience is transformed by Vanka's creation of order: art is the channel in this story whereby excessive emotion is released, creating an image of Louis-Georges which is superior to the Louis-Georges who has "ripened into death." The image of Louis-Georges that Vanka creates is partially a deception, of course. However, the deception achieves its own triumph over mutability, and thereby its truth. In memorializing, art defeats time as life cannot; art, therefore, though a lie, is also a superior reality—a concept common to symbolist thought.

All three of these early stories (1917-19), **"A Night among the Horses," "The Rabbit,"** and **"The Valet,"** demonstrate naturalistic conceptions of the external world. The social and natural worlds are important backgrounds against which characters define themselves, but the use of natural or social backgrounds does not make these stories naturalistic. In *The Symbolist Movement* Balakian describes a significant difference between naturalist and symbolist concerns. Naturalists, she points out, concern themselves with social and hereditary forces, but symbolists are "concerned with man's mental reactions to and reconciliations with the natural order of the cosmos. . . ." What distinguishes Barnes's stories from the naturalistic tradition, then, is her emphasis on the process by which inner, perhaps unconscious feelings come into an individual's consciousness. Barnes focuses on the birth of the individual's consciousness of the human condition, including death, and the reactions of a character to this awareness. Her concern is with man's sense of his place in the flow of time. In **"A Night among the Horses,"** John wavers between acceptance and rejection of Freda's world, which is the social world: he enters that world or faces the oblivion of the natural world. In **"The Rabbit"** Rugo's loss of innocence touches the mythic theme of expulsion, with the ambiguous gain of the knowledge of good and evil and death. In **"The Valet,"** art is seen as something that triumphs over the oblivion of nature.

These stories, representative of Barnes's maturing style, present the problem of coming to consciousness and the price of consciousness in losing a stable, predictable system of life and values. All three indicate Barnes's interest in the human response to the human condition. In none of them does she invoke the sentimental desire for a return to a settled world; she does not look back with nostalgia. Her emphasis is on conscious realization of the nature of the human condition and an awareness of mortality. Her characters enact their separation from nature and from middle-class society.

By creating distance between readers and characters through contradictory or ambiguous actions and through difficult and ambiguous prose, Barnes prohibits a reader's emotional identification with characters, demanding instead the distance of an observor. As a result, readers discern the idea beneath the experience of Barnes's characters. Barnes perfects these techniques in the following group of stories in which the structuring idea has all but disappeared beneath details that are exquisitely arranged in prose that conceals as it reveals.

All of the following stories are the result of Barnes's Paris years, with the exception of **"Spillway,"** which appeared in December 1919 as **"Beyond the End."** Like the magazine journalism and plays, these stories focus on women. **"Aller et Retour," "Spillway," "Cassation," "The Grande Malade,"** and **"The Passion"** offer more complexity than the stories previously discussed. This is true because so *little* seems to happen; indeterminate language and pointed experience create double meanings. Barnes's aim in these stories is to reveal the qualities that motivate her fictional heroines. Though the main characters in the previous group had often seemed victims, the main characters in the stories that follow are, as Scott noted, "fighters." Even though Scott emphasizes the determinism of Barnes's characters, his evaluation that "the best of them" maintain "an amazing fidelity to their own lights" is an intriguing insight, for it hints at something other than determinism in the makeup of Barnes's characters. At the center of each story is a limited number of characters, usually two. These characters do not change. What happens is that the reader gains an insight through their interaction. (pp. 59-62)

The nature of the artist and her relationship to the external world is the subject of **"Cassation," "The Grande Malade,"** and **"The Passion."** In **"Cassation"** Barnes presents not a judgment on detachment and innocence or suffering and madness, but a symbolic representation of the human condition that gives rise to both. (p. 67)

When Katya meets Gaya, she gives up her ambition to be a dancer, goes to live with Gaya, and becomes "a religieuse." She is treated like a child with overtones of a lover. Katya describes the relationship: "I loved her very much because there was nothing between us but this strange preparation for sleep," a preparation that mirrors in part the role Gaya has devised for Katya as companion to her child Valentine. (p. 68)

Gaya, burdened by too much thought, eventually ends in denial of all meaning, all reality, asserting only the existence of a perceiving "I," which, lacking external reality, is only *vacancy.* The philosophical problem, of course, is that she cannot accept lack of purpose and meaninglessness without a bitter sense of betrayal and loss. Therefore, in her identification with Valentine, Gaya reverts to a less human level, denying consciousness and individuality. As the title of the story indicates, Gaya breaks, or annuls, the terms of human life. Gaya identifies completely with that aspect of self which represents physical being, metaphorically rejecting both consciousness and external reality. Her love is self-consuming, turned in upon itself. In her inability to separate her identity from the daughter as physical being, the self, Gaya rejects as she turns inward, Katya, the surrogate daughter who represents both individuality and perception of external reality. Katya, however, moves beyond her withdrawal, which has begun in spring, and ends also a year later in the spring. She moves once again into the external world.

Katya emerges from her year as "a religieuse" making no judgments, simply reporting her experience. Katya, who refuses to deny everything to become Valentine's companion, is preserved by her acceptance of meaninglessness; in effect she separates the ego from the extremity of suffering that destroys Gaya. She is restless, a seeker. On a realistic level, the events have a nightmare quality that is particularly troubling in view of the noncommittal quality of Katya's narration. Troubling events are reported flatly and without emotion, as if they are commonplace. The "innocent ingenuousness" of Katya invites condemnation, as she seems to float through the world unaffected by misfortune. Yet however unnerving, Katya's retelling of the story to an unidentified "Madame" attests to its importance for her. Her "confession" to a nameless "Madame" is in itself an effort of contact, a move not to separation but to understanding. Katya represents articulation as an implement of control, or at least acceptance. As narrator of the story, she suggests the artist. Seen from Katya's perspective, the alternatives are despair because of human limitation or an escape into art and artifice where external reality may be transcended; suffering may become art. And one's passion may again be life and love. One has, after all, to live. This theme is continued in **"The Grande Malade,"** a companion to **"Cassation."** Again, Katya and the listening Madame supply the form of the narrative. **"The Grande Malade"** is singularly translucent—that is, the action is clear, but the meaning remains elusive. (pp. 68-9)

[Readers] who condemn the superficiality of Katya and Moydia overlook the values of the decadent tradition and Barnes's early relation to it and neglect important differences between the two sisters. In an early feature for *Bruno's Weekly,* Barnes had shown a humorous approval of decadent values:

> How much do we owe to those of us who can flutter and find decorative joy in fluttering away this small alloted hour. . . .
> The public—or in other words that part of ourselves that we are ashamed of—always turns up the lip when a dilettante is mentioned, all in a patriotic attempt to remain faithful to that little home in the fifties with its wax flowers, it narrow rockers and its localisms, and above all, to that mother whose advice was always as correct as it was harmful.

The dilettante, she continued, "is always about to pass through that incomparable hour, the hour before and the hour after the supper that may prove the last. And so it is that he . . . has discovered that little something that makes the difference between him and the you, who have ordered supplies home for the week." Barnes's comment suggests her approval of the cultivation of sensibility at the expense of prudential wisdom that sacrifices pleasure and beauty for material needs.

Thus, the extravagence and artificiality of Katya and Moydia, which is consistent with the decadent tradition, is a rebellion against meaningless and mundane reality. Only the superior soul had the sensitivity and imagination to live beautifully. Nevertheless, as she had done in her earlier journalism, Barnes allows readers also to smile at the spirited exaggerations of the two sisters. (p. 70)

In a study of the French poetic tradition, Wallace Fowlie points out an aspect of Baudelaire's aesthetic that is relevant to Katya and Moydia's rootlessness. Fowlie refers to the tradition of the "voyou," the restless adventurer, poet, clown, who is a seeker involved in "quest for what is unseizable, unreal, absurd." Fowlie further describes the voyou:

> The voyou and his brother the clown teach us that true fantasy does not exist and that joy in its purest state is not human. All fantasy is composed of seriousness and all joy borders on sorrow. The voyou is the human being in whom the two worlds of joy and sorrow are confused. . . .
> The voyou is the man who escapes from everything that normally holds back other men: studies, family, civic duties, religious duties. The voyou is the adventurer of space, of non-passable roads, of the immense freedom of cities and fields.

The poet's departure is therefore a flight, an evasion, a seizure of the unreal.

As decadents, Moydia and Katya may be seen, not just as superficial social butterflies, but more pertinently as seekers of knowledge in the role of voyou. Significantly, Moydia comments: "It's because we are so extravagant that we do not reach justice . . . we reach poetry" (Barnes's ellipsis).

Generally, those who read the story as a chronicle of postwar malaise ignore differences between the sisters. Throughout the narration, Katya is reserved, accepting yet vaguely critical of her sister. Katya "lives more slowly"; she relates that "only women listen to me, but men adore Moydia. To her they do not listen, they look." When Moydia finally has a lover, "she laughed and cried, lying face down, and whimpering, 'Isn't it *wonderful!*' "

Katya observes without conviction, "And perhaps it was indeed wonderful, Madame." In this way their life is questioned, causing uncertainty for the reader. How *are* we to view their lives? If Katya's narration reveals reservations about Moydia's life, her participation in the decadent pose is nevertheless unqualified. She is very much part of the "well-planned life" in her dancing and in her desire for high-topped boots that recall her past and her father.

Katya's difference, however, is important. She is skeptical yet accepting, a participant but also an observer. Together they fit Fowlie's description of the clown/voyou. Moydia is the actor, poseur, charlatan, clown; Katya represents the opposite side, the silent observer, the poet who both participates and remains alone, in exile. Katya in observing and reporting becomes the artist, just as Vanka had, though here her voice is not memorializing, except in a very broad sense. Her voice, rather, is that of one who seeks to explain, to render intelligible life and its identity with death, that is, Moydia and her lover, who is "beastly with finis." The artist therefore is both part of life but also always an observer who creates a reality that is superior to life while also reflecting it. Seen from this perspective, the sisters are dual aspects of a single person.

The title reinforces this suggestion, for **"The Grande Malade"** alludes to a sick person, the great, or perhaps, the grown-up sick person. The title probably does not refer to Moydia's lover, the obvious choice, for *Grande* is feminine. Even though the feminine may be appropriate for the gay lover, as Moydia's lover, he has been referred to as "he" throughout the story. Therefore, the sick person may be either Moydia or Katya, or presumably both of them, as they portray tendencies within a single being. They represent, as "The Love Song of J. Alfred Prufrock" does, the objectification of two elements within a single person, perhaps that of the unspeaking Madame. One element experiences, the other observes and creates. From this perspective the action of the story is the acceptance of death and the necessity to create beautiful and well-planned lives. Whether the sisters succeed or not, the search itself is important. This theme, almost unnoticed beneath the surface, structures incident and character, giving both depth and complexity to the story.

With greater restraint and subtletey, Barnes handles the same theme, the symbolic encounter of imagination and external reality, in **"The Passion,"** published in 1924 in *Transition* II. The story, whose progression of precise details creates a static effect, focuses on the life of the princess Frederica Rholinghausen. The omniscient narrator introduces readers to the princess through the ritual of her carriage rides through the park—daily except on Thursdays, when she receives guests. The opening establishes the ordered nature of her life and its slow retreat into a narrower and narrower center as she ages.

The princess herself is an admirable presence whose primary trait is her acceptance of mortality:

> At times, raising her eyeglasses at the uncompromising moment, she had surprisingly the air of a *gallant*, a *bon-vivant*—but there was a wash of blue in her flesh that spoke of the acceptance of mortality. She never spoke of the spirit.

Her Thursday visitors include solicitous aunts and an indifferent nephew whose actions suggest that a scrupulous interest in an inheritance motivates his visits. The other visitor, the important one, in terms of the subtle confrontation of values that the story relates, is Kurt Anders, who has visited the princess on the second Thursday of the month for thirty years. The description of Anders and the depiction of the relationship between Anders and the princess is developed through the balance of what "gossips" say and the narrator's countering assertion of the truth.

Anders is one who courts gossip and reputation in the world. A common figure in Barnes's fiction, he is known by gossips to have disappointed his family; he has associated with the "scion of the house of Valois," who is known as a modern but "could not keep away from museums or wax work, particularly the roped-off sections housing royal equipages." Anders has a sexual reputation with both men and women, but the narrator counters the romance of rumor with a view of the truth: "Anders enjoyed the manoeuvre, the perfected 'leap,' the trick pulled off, and the general sane weather." Anders spends his time walking in the park.

The same pattern of supposition is developed regarding the relationship of Anders and the princess. Some argue that the princess is the only real passion of his life, others that the princess's selfishness has prevented their union, yet others that they were "as good as husband and wife." The pattern of gossip and the return to purported reality at the narrator's observation is again repeated: "All of this was nonsense. They were pages in an old volume, brought together by the closing of the book."

The tone of the story supports this conclusion. The atmosphere describing their Thursdays suggests the warmth and longevity of a pleasant relationship. Anders speaks of autumn, cathedral architecture, drama, etchings, and "he would walk up and down before her until she noticed the pockets of his coat into which he had stuck small flowers." He talks of the "uses of the fool in Shakespeare": to this the princess, referring obliquely perhaps to Anders, comments on "the impracticability of maintaining tradition now that every man was his own fool."

Only in the last visit is there any suggestion of difficulty. The "strain" announced by the narrator involves opposed concepts of love. Anders claims that "walking straight up to dreadfulness . . . is love." The princess counters: "The last attendant on an old woman is always an 'incurable.' " She then adds "with mordant acerbity," "But—if a little light man with a beard had said 'I love you,' I should have believed in God." The story concludes, "Shortly after, she did not live."

Apparently, the comment is directed to Anders, but in what sense can he be considered an incurable? Or his own fool, if the echo of the princess's comment carries that far? The remarks of the princess hint at her recognition that Anders has a reputation for "passionate risk" which he does not possess. Her comments seem to imply that Anders is willing to deceive himself, to believe in illusions. As his own fool, he lacks the sanitive influence recognized as one of the roles of the Shakespearean fool. Her observation affirms both her awareness of his emptiness, that is, his lightness, and yet reveals her love for him. Though her love has existed over the years, she recognizes his unsuitability in his posing and his worldliness. Her response is exile, but, unlike that of Lydia Passova in **"Mother"** (***A Book***), the exile of the princess seems an affirmation of mutually contradictory claims: those of Anders and the world, which are disappointing, and those of the imagination. (pp. 70-3)

Two views of love are thus opposed: Anders's view, which, because of its romantic and desperate nature, remains unfulfilled, and that of the princess, whose statement implies that love is an earthly manifestation of God. In this sense she characterizes love as a spiritualizing force. Her concept of love is implied in the title of the story, **"The Passion,"** which points to a paradox common to Barnes's work: passion is equally love and suffering. They are woven inextricably. In declaring that had she been told that Anders loved her she would have believed in God, the princess asserts the transcendent value of human love. The princess, however, lacking the experience of that kind of love, is admirable in the absolute accuracy of her perceptions and in her imaginative capacity to live without denying the reality of physical human nature. We are told, "Now it is said that the old cannot approach the grave without fearful apprehension or religious rite. The princess did." Not Madame von Bartmann, but the princess is one of Barnes's finest women. She embodies a strength of character and imagination that Barnes herself must have found worthy.

In the necessary silence Barnes set out the "abundant inadequacies of life"; she exploited brief situations, extravagant characters, and elusive prose to suggest both the desire for meaning and purpose and the difficulty of securing that desire. Yet the sturdiness of spirit of Julie and the princess is a compliment to human consciousness and a contrast to the enervating fatalism of Madame von Bartmann and Gaya; Katya and Moydia testify also to the desire for life and meaning. As in the journalism and drama, conscious living is the necessary condition of human life; yet in her world of fiction Barnes recognized also that consciousness itself was a fragile and painful proposition and that meaning was elusive. This is what she lamented, not consciousness itself. (p. 74)

Cheryl J. Plumb, in her Fancy's Craft: Art and Identity in the Early Works of Djuna Barnes, *Susquehanna University Press, 1986, 118 p.*

ADDITIONAL BIBLIOGRAPHY

Baird, James. "Djuna Barnes and Surrealism: 'Backward Grief.'" In *Individual and Community: Variations on a Theme in American Fiction,* edited by Kenneth H. Baldwin and David K. Kirby, pp. 160-81. Durham, N.C.: Duke University Press, 1975.

Discusses aspects of surrealism in the work of Barnes. Centering on *Nightwood* and *Ryder,* the critic touches upon the short stories, treating them mainly as prototypes of the longer works.

Beach, Sylvia. *Shakespeare and Company.* New York: Harcourt, Brace and Co., 1956, 230 p.

Memoir by a central figure in the literary scene in Paris in the 1920s. The book contains reminiscences and anecdotes about Barnes and her circle.

Bodenheim, Maxwell. "Djuna Barnes and W. Carlos Williams." *Chicago Literary Times* 1, No. 9 (1 July 1923): 10.

Appreciative brief sketch of Barnes and her short stories by her acquaintance Bodenheim, who was a poet and notorious figure in Greenwich Village.

Braybrooke, Neville. "Creatures of the Night." *Time and Tide* 43, No. 21 (24 May 1962): 30-1.

A review of *Spillway* noting the poetic language of the stories.

Field, Andrew. *Djuna: The Life and Times of Djuna Barnes.* New York: G. P. Putnam's Sons, 1983, 287 p.

A noncritical biography.

Fuchs, Miriam. "Djuna Barnes: 'Spillway into Nightmare.'" *The Hollins Critic* XVIII, No. 3 (June 1981): 1-6, 8-9.

Traces the theme of detachment in several stories from *Spillway,* focusing on the collection's title story and on "Cassation."

Gildzen, Alex, ed. *A Festschrift for Djuna Barnes on Her 80th Birthday.* Kent, Ohio: Kent State University Libraries, 1972, 18 p.

Collection of tributes to Barnes in the form of prose, poems, reminiscences, and commentary. Contributors include Kay Boyle, Anaïs Nin, Lawrence Durrell, Richard Eberhart, and Thomas McGuane.

Griffin, Barbara J. "Two Experimental Writers: Djuna Barnes and Anaïs Nin." In *American Women Writers: Bibliographical Essays,* edited by Maurice Duke, Jackson R. Bryer, and M. Thomas Inge, pp. 136-66. Westport, Conn.: Greenwood Press, 1983.

General bibliographical essay highlighting major pieces of Barnes criticism and biography and assessing the future of Barnes's critical reputation.

Hardwick, Elizabeth. "The Fate of the Gifted." *The Times Literary Supplement* No. 4201 (7 October 1983): 1071-72.

A review of *Smoke, and Other Stories* and Field's biography (see citation above) that includes a biographical-critical overview centering on *Nightwood.*

Messerli, Douglas. *Djuna Barnes: A Bibliography.* N.p., David Lewis, 1975, 131 p.

Primary and secondary bibliography including works in foreign languages and unpublished theses.

"Letters: Djuna Barnes." *New York Times Book Review.* (17 July 1983): 23.

Two letters from acquaintances of Barnes charging that Field's biography (see citation above) is factually incorrect. The writers stress especially that in her later years Barnes was not the hermit that Field portrays her to have been.

Raymont, Henry. "From the Avant-Garde of the Thirties: Djuna Barnes." *New York Times* (24 May 1971):

A profile of Barnes at age 79 in which she describes herself as "a recluse, a form of Trappist."

Rexroth, Kenneth. "Djuna Barnes." In *Contemporary Novelists,* edited by James Vinson, pp. 81-3. New York: St. Martin's Press, 1976.

Brief critical overview focusing on Barnes's novels and including incisive commentary on her general literary characteristics.

Williamson, Alan. "The Divided Image: The Quest for Identity in the Works of Djuna Barnes." *Critique: Studies in Modern Fiction* VII, No. 1 (Spring 1964): 58-74.

Explores dualism in Barnes's works, centering on *Nightwood.* While the short fiction is not discussed specifically, Williamson treats thematic concerns applicable to all of Barnes's work.

Elizabeth (Dorothea Cole) Bowen

1899-1973

Anglo-Irish novelist, short story writer, essayist, and critic.

Noted for her subtle, evocative novels and short stories, Bowen is compared with such novelists of sensibility as Jane Austen, Henry James, and Virginia Woolf. She is perhaps best known for her novel *The Death of the Heart,* and critics point to that phrase as an apt summation of Bowen's recurrent theme: the inevitable disillusionment inherent in human relationships, particularly as innocent characters make the painful passage to experience. Critics praise Bowen for her descriptive, finely pitched style, and they often compare her with Katherine Mansfield for her extreme sensitivity to perceptions of light, atmosphere, color, and sound. Like Mansfield, Bowen is considered expert at presenting the emotional dynamics of a situation and then swiftly illuminating their significance, particularly within the prescribed bounds of the short story. While Bowen is generally acclaimed as both a novelist and short fiction writer, some critics deem her stories superior to her novels; Bowen herself once commented: "I feel happiest, in the sense of poetic truth, in the short story."

Born in Dublin, Bowen was of Anglo-Irish stock, descended on her mother's side from the Duke of Wellington and on her father's from a Welsh family who had come to Ireland before the seventeenth century. Bowen's Court, the family estate in county Cork lovingly described in Bowen's memoir of the same name, was deeded to a paternal ancestor in 1653 for his service in Oliver Cromwell's campaign against the Irish. As Bowen recounted in her radiant childhood memoir, *Seven Winters,* the first seven years of her life were divided between a Dublin townhouse and Bowen's Court, where the family spent each summer. This tranquil pattern was broken, however, when her father was hospitalized for mental illness, and she and her mother moved to England to stay with relatives while he recovered. In 1912, as the family began preparations to reunite, Bowen's mother was diagnosed with cancer; her death soon afterward left Elizabeth in the care of what she called "a committee of aunts" from her mother's large family. She was educated at Downe House, a boarding school in Kent, England, and at the London Council School of Art, which she left after two terms in 1919.

It was during this period, when she was living on her own in London, that Bowen began to write seriously. Her first short story collection, *Encounters,* appeared in 1923, the year of her marriage to Alan Charles Cameron. Their move in 1926 to Oxford opened Bowen to a stimulating literary circle that included the critics C. M. Bowra and Lord David Cecil; by 1929 she had published two more volumes of short stories and two novels, establishing a rate of production she would maintain much of her life. During the 1930s Bowen began to associate with Virginia Woolf and the Bloomsbury circle in London, where she and Cameron moved in 1935. Her experiences living and working as an air-raid warden in the besieged city during World War II inspired what many critics consider her finest short story collection, *The Demon Lover,* which explores war's insidious effects on the human psyche. In 1952, the year of her husband's death, Bowen moved to Bowen's Court, which she had inherited in 1930. Renowned as a talented hostess with a passion for lively parties, Bowen frequently entertained such literary notables as Sean O'Faolain and Cyril Connolly. Bowen sold her family estate in 1959 and returned to England, where, apart from frequent worldwide travel and reading tours, she remained until her death from lung cancer at age 73.

Critics note that in her short stories as in her novels, Bowen is most often concerned with the theme of innocence versus experience. In stories such as "The Good Girl," a typical Bowen protagonist—young, female, and inexperienced—has her naivete shattered by an unscrupulous man in an ill-fated romance. While Bowen's victims of experience are most often young adults, in such stories as "The Tommy Crans" and "Tears, Idle Tears," she focuses on children who are disillusioned by the adult world. Bowen's innocents can also be middle-aged, like the title character of "Mrs. Moysey," who tries unsuccessfully to insulate herself from reality by staying in bed and eating bonbons, or the Evers sisters in "The Easter Egg Party," whose carefully controlled universe is shattered by a girl who wildly rebels against their attempts to draw her under their protective dome.

As Bowen lived through the wars and social upheaval of the first half of the twentieth century, she often explored their effect on characters. In "Summer Night," for instance, Aunt

Fran becomes convinced that the pernicious morals of a war-torn society have encroached upon her own family. Her niece is unfaithful to her husband, and even her small grandniece behaves incorrigibly, exhibiting a nascent sexuality that appalls Aunt Fran. The older woman feels "stranded" in the modern world, "like some object on a spool that has run dry." A similar unease and loss of identity is suffered by Mrs. Watson in "Attractive Modern Homes," who becomes alienated and detached after moving to a modern housing development, and by the protagonist of "Foothold," who conjures up a ghost to assuage her sense of loneliness in her marriage.

Among Bowen's many artistic responses to a mutable world, however, her stories written during World War II are considered her finest. In *The Demon Lover,* composed between spring 1941 and late 1944, she introduced to her short fiction a hallucinatory tone and supernatural themes in order to convey war's effect on the human mind. In "The Mysterious Kôr," which is often cited among Bowen's greatest stories, wartime London becomes a mysterious, terrifying nether-city through the moon's transforming light. Mrs. Drover, in the collection's title piece, becomes dislocated in time, slipping from World War II back to World War I, where she waits feverishly for the arrival of her long-dead fiancé. In this, as in other pieces in *The Demon Lover,* Bowen employs a disturbing ambiguity, preventing the reader from knowing whether stories depict supernatural states, or illusions created by the characters' neurotic and overburdened psyches.

While acclaimed in her lifetime for both her short stories and novels, Bowen has since her death slipped somewhat from critical attention. Some critics suggest that her romanticism, wit, and sensitivity to both language and feeling have gone out of style; others assert that her writing is flawed by a too-facile style and narrow range of characters. Nonetheless, Bowen is revered by many for the radiance of style and subtlety of expression evidenced perhaps most assuredly in her short stories. In the minds of many readers and critics, they take their place among the twentieth-century's most distinguished works of short fiction.

(See also *Contemporary Literary Criticism,* Vols. 1, 3, 6, 11, 15, 22; *Contemporary Authors,* Vols. 17-20, Vols. 41-44, rev. ed. [obituary]; *Contemporary Authors Permanent Series,* Vol. 2; and *Dictionary of Literary Biography,* Vol. 15.)

PRINCIPAL WORKS

SHORT FICTION

Encounters 1923; revised edition, 1949
Ann Lee's, and Other Stories 1928
Joining Charles, and Other Stories 1929
The Cat Jumps, and Other Stories 1934
Look at All Those Roses 1941
The Demon Lover, and Other Stories 1945; also published as *Ivy Gripped the Steps, and Other Stories* 1946
Selected Stories 1946
Early Stories 1951
Stories 1959
A Day in the Dark, and Other Stories 1965
Elizabeth Bowen's Irish Stories 1978
The Collected Stories of Elizabeth Bowen 1981

OTHER MAJOR WORKS

The Hotel (novel) 1927
The Last September (novel) 1929
Friends and Relations (novel) 1931
To the North (novel) 1932
The House in Paris (novel) 1935
The Death of the Heart (novel) 1938
Bowen's Court (memoir) 1942
Seven Winters (memoir) 1942; also published as *Seven Winters: Memories of a Dublin Childhood,* 1943
The Heat of the Day (novel) 1949
Collected Impressions (essays) 1950
The Shelbourne: A Centre of Dublin Life for More Than a Century (nonfiction) 1951; also published as *The Shelbourne Hotel,* 1951
A World of Love (novel) 1955
After-Thoughts: Pieces about Writing (criticism) 1962
The Little Girls (novel) 1963
Eva Trout; or, Changing Scenes (novel) 1968
Pictures and Conversations (essays and interviews) 1975
The Mulberry Tree: Writings of Elizabeth Bowen (essays, criticism, and interviews) 1986

THE SPECTATOR **(essay date 1923)**

[*In the following excerpt from a favorable review of* Encounters, *the critic compares Bowen with Katherine Mansfield in the subtlety of her stories, "where every detail is subdued to the general effect."*]

Its alluring title [***Encounters***] sufficiently advertises the character of this, Miss Bowen's first volume of short stories. One hopes that it will be followed by many more, equally mature in conception and finished in workmanship. For Miss Bowen is the most notable newcomer to that company which, in the death of Katherine Mansfield, lost perhaps its most brilliant light. Her stories bear, indeed they almost challenge, comparison with Miss Mansfield's. Like hers, Miss Bowen's encounters are bloodless; they will disappoint those who like to see differences settled by an appeal to arms. Like hers, they are concerned with ordinary people, not criminals or lunatics. It is not the conflict of wills or even the clash of raw personalities that Miss Bowen describes, but the contact and reaction of temperaments, scarred, as often as not, with tender spots, sore places, old wounds, the marks of former encounters. The occasions and incidents are slight enough in themselves: a harassed business-man eating breakfast at a boardinghouse with tiresome people; a sensitive schoolmistress intimidated by the sinister maturity of three giggling schoolgirls to whom she had tried to explain the significance and poetry of daffodils; often, just the exits and entrances of tired, selfish, disappointed people.

Such fragile subjects need delicate handling and a nice sense of proportion or they will become like scenes from a madhouse, or at best a series of *tours de force.* Many writers could present more violent juxtapositions, many could find more searching turns of phrase and suggest a scene more vividly, but they would be likely to start with a preconceived standard of intensity to which every situation and theme, however unsuitable to tragic treatment, would be made to conform. They plume themselves, one would think, on being able to wring tragedy from the fall of a pin; to magnify, by an ingenious manipulation of value and perspective, its mild declension into an epic impact. Miss Bowen's stories are free from this violent seasoning. Her dislike of exaggeration, the gravity and simplicity of her style, her restraint and her carefulness never to tear a passion to tatters, preserve the identity of each story and allow its particular quality to emerge. In work where every detail is subdued to the general effect it is hard to find a passage that will do justice to the high standard of Miss Bowen's achievement:

> The white-walled drawing-room . . . smelt very strongly of varnish, and seemed to Herbert emptier than a drawing-room ought to be. The chairs and sofas had retreated into corners, they lacked frilliness; there was something just as startled and staccato about the room as there was about Cicely and Richard. Poor Mother and Dear Father eyed one another apprehensively from opposite walls; the very tick of the clock was hardly regular.

Miss Bowen declines nearly all the artificial aids to storywriting, the element of suspense, the dramatic situation, the cumulative effect, almost—but not quite—the "clever" dialogue. Yet her stories are not mere "slices of life." Their unemphatic position, midway between past and future, and looking, Janus-like, to each, gives them a setting and an atmosphere without which they might seem flimsy and unstable. Imponderability is perhaps their danger as it is their charm. They have no ballast of "copy," no evidence of nature-worship, no feats of irrelevant observation. One does not regret these. But perhaps Miss Bowen will increase the volume of the note she strikes. It could not easily be sweeter or clearer. (pp. 91-2)

A review of "Encounters," in The Spectator, *Vol. 131, No. 4960, July 21, 1923, pp. 91-2.*

FLORENCE HAXTON BRITTEN (essay date 1929)

[*In this review of* Joining Charles, *Britten praises Bowen's precise craftsmanship and skillful use of detail in her stories.*]

Several of these exquisite short stories [in ***Joining Charles***] might almost have come from the pen of Katherine Mansfield. There is the same inevitability of physical detail, and the touch is as light. In Miss Mansfield's world, however, suffused as it is with emotional significances, a flower is never a mere flower: it is the one blossom capable of setting up in her, and in turn in her reader, a sense of emotional appropriateness, of waves of feeling perfectly attuned. . . .

With Miss Bowen the case is a little different. Hers is a freer world, with more material substance and body. (It falls, in fact, about half way between Katherine Mansfield's and David Garnett's at its less fantastic). And she moves through it with inspired precision. There is not a breath of carelessness in any of these stories. She uses the furniture of life with a sharp instinct for its appropriateness: chooses the precise trick of physical appearance, speech, scene to establish a fragile relationship between the figures in her stories and the terms of their life. The result has a strange, cool potency.

"Joining Charles" is a tender story of a young wife left for a few weeks happily in care of her husband's family while he goes off to Lyons to prepare a place for her. The day for joining him comes and she leaves reluctantly to return to the man whom she subtly fears. The whole family share her fancied eagerness to be off to the Charles whom they adore—and she sets off, perforce, forlornly, leaving behind the only home she has ever known, and acutely aware that she has enjoyed it under what must, to one of her delicate sensibilities, seem false pretenses. The story is beautifully accomplished: a fragment of life set down with dignity, grace and comprehension. Yet not a line of it as I have briefly sketched it is baldly there, in words. It is, instead, an idea that comes gradually floating into being, in terms of a chill early morning, a family's affectionate concern, of packing, a traveler's breakfast, a moment by the open fire. . . . Out of which comes, unspoken, a reality and a beauty that is beyond words.

The range of Miss Bowen's stories is wide, and several of them are founded on an extravagant whim, or horror, or mystery. But, having espoused an eccentric theme, she handles it as though it were completely quiet and commonplace. **"Telling"** is a little masterpiece of horror, some fifteen pages long, with not a word wasted nor a movement muffled. **"The Jungle"**—mistakenly second in the volume, if arrangement has any meaning—is a mildly erotic story of an English school girl. **"Shoes: An International Episode,"** an idly satirical account of an English couple honeymooning on the Continent, is reminiscent of *The Hotel.* In **"The Working Party"** a proud young wife goes on serving tea to her guests after a servant has died on the stairs and still lies there, his dead body trapping her footsteps as she passes to and fro. In **"Dead Mabelle"** a white-collar youth is driven to suicidal gesture by his infatuation for a sort of feminine Valentino of the British cinema. And **"Mrs. Moysey"**—well, if Mrs. Moysey's secret vice had been *brandied* chocolates, I could have understood it all better.

The best story in the volume—technically, and for its fragility and fineness—is **"The Dancing Mistress."** It is like exquisite glass—hard, cool and beautiful.

I have watched Miss Bowen, as one would watch a prestidigitator, to see how she accomplishes her magic. She proffers you objective details, one after another, quietly. And shortly, upon the slight bodies of these trivial details—and even more between the interstices—life and character grow up. She has an uncanny delicacy in gauging, not so much *le mot juste*—though she writes with an even-handed precision that is richly satisfying—as the exact detail that will touch off that sense of significance for which the imaginative perpetually hunger. And that—even when achieved with a cool heart—is magic.

Florence Haxton Britten, "Fragments of Life," in New York Herald Tribune Books, *November 24, 1929, p. 4.*

HENRY REED (essay date 1945)

[*Reed was a British poet, playwright, translator, and critic, whose works include the poetry volume* A Map of Verona *(1946) and numerous radio plays and adaptations. The following is from his very favorable review of* The Demon Lover, *in which he praises Bowen for her excellent evocation of atmosphere.*]

In her new collection of stories [***The Demon Lover***] it is frequently obvious that [Elizabeth Bowen] shares James's preoccupation with style; she has that kind of exact awareness of all she wishes to say, which makes her know precisely where a sentence needs to be a little distorted, or where an unusual word needs to be used. She has as well that gift which prose can share with poetry: the ability to concentrate the emotions of a scene, or a sequence of thoughts, or even a moral, into an unforgettable sentence or phrase with a beauty of expression extra to the sense:

> The newly-arrived clock, chopping off each second to fall and perish, recalled how many seconds had gone to make up her years, how many of these had been either null or bitter, how many had been void before the void claimed them.

Or again, about the present day:

> He thought, with nothing left but our brute courage, we shall be nothing but brutes.

Her short stories possess the qualities of her novels, but inevitably the atmosphere in her short stories is richer and more concentrated. The more elaborate of them suggest the climaxes or the elements of novels, but in a necessarily muted or diminished form; it is their atmosphere which moulds them, and which at times perhaps even brings them into existence. A perfect example of this is the first story in the book, **"In the Square."** Little happens in it, but enough strands are gathered together to give a sense of tension, climax and relief. And the relief is achieved mainly by atmospheric means. The story is about a few people living on in a partially bombed house in a ravaged London square. The principal feeling one has about them is their terrible independence of each other; all of them have mysterious, irregular relationships, unhappy and furtive. One has a feeling that what remains in the house, that reluctant proximity of the unconnected, is not what a house is meant to enclose. This is what war has done: to houses, to people. It is a true enough observation; but what startles one is the fact that one suddenly becomes aware that the early evening is spectacularly merging into late; the time of day is changing and a shift in the emotions of all the characters is coinciding with this. A mere observation has become a story quivering with subtle, dramatic life.

The war, and the subtly degrading effect of the war, hold these stories together as a collection. They have great variety and many attractions. One thinks particularly of their comedy and their dialogue; the story called **"Careless Talk"** is a brilliantly literal interpretation of that official phrase; **"Mysterious Kôr"** has a wonderful conversation draped round evocations from a poem by—Rider Haggard; the woman in **"Ivy Gripped the Steps"** is a strong enough figure for a novel. But it is probably those stories which involve the supernatural that are most striking. **"The Demon Lover"** itself, a ghost story of the traditional kind, is horrible enough, though not of Miss Bowen's best. In some of the others—**"Pink May"** and **"The Inherited Clock,"** for example—the ghostliness is blown into existence by, or from, something real; and always, even when the boundary into the abnormal is passed, the normal still accompanies us.

The finest story in the book, and the most ambitious, is called **"The Happy Autumn Fields."** It begins in the past—perhaps seventy or eighty years ago. Various members of a large family are taking a late afternoon walk across the fields of their estate; at a moment of particularly painful emotion for one of the characters, Sarah, the story breaks off, and we are switched to the present: to a partly bombed house where a woman called Mary is waking from the scene we have just read about; it is not the first dream about that epoch she has had, though her real link with it is tenuous; nevertheless her dream has become obsessive, stronger and more attractive than her own life. The scene changes to the old family again, and we find that that afternoon in the fields Sarah has had a black-out which has projected her for a moment into a world nameless and horrible—our own, we gather. The final scene is back in the bombed house, with Mary sorrowing over the irrecoverable day from the past which has blown into and out of her life:

> I am left with a fragment torn out of a day, a day I don't even know where or when; and now how am I to help laying that like a pattern against the poor stuff of everything else?—Alternatively, I am a person drained by a dream. I cannot forget the climate of those hours. Or life at that pitch, eventful—not happy, no, but strung like a harp. . . . '

It is, like "The Turn of the Screw," a story which provokes interpretation and commentary; but since it is, in a serious sense, a discovery, there remains about it something of its own, at once inexplicable and profoundly satisfying. No living writer has, I think, produced a finer collection of stories than this. (pp. 302-03)

Henry Reed, in a review of "The Demon Lover," in The New Statesman & Nation, *Vol. XXX, No. 767, November 3, 1945, pp. 302-03.*

ELIZABETH BOWEN (essay date 1946)

[The following excerpt is from Bowen's postscript to the first U.S. edition of The Demon Lover, *published in 1946. The author here describes how the atmosphere in England during World War II contributed greatly to the creation of the stories, and she discusses the role of hallucination in them.]*

The stories in . . . ***The Demon Lover,*** were written in wartime London—between the spring of 1941 and the late autumn of 1944. They were written for the magazines or papers in which they originally appeared. During these last years, I did not always write a story when I was asked for one; but I did not write any story that I was not asked for. For, at the same time, I have been writing a novel; and sometimes I did not want to imperil its continuity.

Does this suggest that these stories have been in any way forced or unwilling work? If so, that is not the case. Actually, the stimulus of being asked for a story, and the compulsion created by having promised to write one were both good—I mean, they acted as releases. Each time I sat down to write a story I opened a door; and the pressure against the other side of that door must, I found, have been very great, for things—ideas, images, emotions—came through with force and rapidity, sometimes violence. I do not say that these stories wrote themselves—aesthetically or intellectually speaking, I found the writing of some of them very difficult—but I was never in a moment's doubt as to *what* I was to write. The stories had their own momentum, which I had to control. The acts in them had an authority which I could not question. Odd enough in their way—and now some seem very odd—they were flying particles of something enormous and inchoate that had been going on. They were sparks from experience—an experience not necessarily my own.

During the war I lived, both as a civilian and as a writer, with every pore open; I lived so many lives, and, still more, lived among the packed repercussions of so many thousands of other lives, all under stress, that I see now it would have been impossible to have been writing only one book. I want my novel, which deals with this same time, to be comprehensive. But a novel must have form; and, for the form's sake, one is always having to make relentless exclusions. Had it not been for my from-time-to-time promises to write stories, much that had been pressing against the door might have remained pressing against the door in vain.

I do not feel I 'invented' anything written [in the stories]. It seems to me that during the war in England the overcharged sub-consciousnesses of everybody overflowed and merged. It is because the general subconsciousness saturates these stories that they have an authority nothing to do with me.

These are all wartime, none of them *war,* stories. There are no accounts of war action even as I knew it—for instance, air raids. Only one character (in **"Mysterious Kôr"**) is a soldier; and he only appears as a homeless wanderer round a city. These are, more, studies of climate, war-climate, and of the strange growths it raised. I see war (or should I say feel war?) more as a territory than as a page of history: of its impersonal active historic side I have, I find, not written. Arguably, writers are always slightly abnormal people: certainly, in so-called 'normal' times my sense of the abnormal has been very acute. In war, this feeling of slight differentiation was suspended: I felt one with, and just like, everyone else. Sometimes I hardly knew where I stopped and everyone else began. The violent destruction of solid things, the explosion of the illusion that prestige, power and permanence attach to bulk and weight, left all of us, equally, heady and disembodied. Walls went down; and we felt, if not knew, each other. We all lived in a state of lucid abnormality.

Till the proofs of ***The Demon Lover*** came, I had not re-read these stories since they were, singly, written. Reading the stories straight through as a collection, I am most struck by what they have in common. This integrates them and gives them a cumulative and collective meaning that no one of them, taken singly, has by itself. ***The Demon Lover*** is an organic whole: not merely a collection but somehow—for better or worse—a book. Also, the order in which the stories stand—an order come at, I may say, casually—seems itself to have a meaning, or to add a meaning, I did not foresee. We begin with a hostess who has not learned how with grace to open her own front door; we end with a pair of lovers with no place in which to sleep in each other's arms. In the first story, a well-to-do house in a polite square gives the impression of having been organically dislocated by shock; in the last, a pure abstract empty timeless city rises out of a little girl's troubled mind. Through the stories—in the order in which they are here placed—I find a rising tide of hallucination. (pp. 94-6)

The search for indestructible landmarks in a destructible world led many down strange paths. The attachment to these when they had been found produced small worlds-within-worlds of hallucination—in most cases, saving hallucination. Writers followed the paths they saw or felt people treading, and depicted those little dear saving illusory worlds. I have done both in the ***The Demon Lover*** stories.

You may say that these resistance-fantasies are in themselves frightening. I can only say that one counteracts fear by fear, stress by stress. In **"The Happy Autumn Fields,"** a woman is projected from flying-bombed London, with its day-and-night eeriness, into the key emotional crisis of a Victorian girlhood. In **"Ivy Gripped the Steps,"** a man in his early forties peers through the rusted fortifications and down the dusty empty perspectives of a seaside town at the Edwardian episode that long ago crippled his faculty for love. In **"The Inherited Clock,"** a girl is led to find the key to her own neurosis inside a timepiece. The past, in all these cases, discharges its load of feeling into the anaesthetized and bewildered present. It is the 'I' that is sought—and retrieved, at the cost of no little pain. And, the ghosts—definite in **"Green Holly,"** questionable (for are they subjective purely?) in **"Pink May," "The Cheery Soul"** and **"The Demon Lover"**: what part do they play? They are the certainties. The bodiless foolish wanton, the puritan 'other' presence, the tipsy cook with her religion of English fare, the ruthless young soldier lover unheard of since 1916: hostile or not, they rally, they fill the vacuum for the uncertain 'I.' (pp. 97-8)

I cannot answer for much that is in these stories, except to say that I know they are all true—true to the general life that was in me at the time. Taken singly, they are disjected snapshots—snapshots taken from close up, too close up, in the middle of the *mêlée* of a battle. You cannot *render,* you can only embrace—if it means embracing to suffocation point—something vast that is happening right on top of you. Painters have painted, and photographers who were artists have photographed, the tottering lacelike architecture of ruins, dark mass-movements of people, and the untimely brilliance of flaming skies. I cannot paint or photograph like this—I have isolated; I have made for the particular, spot-lighting faces or cutting out gestures that are not even the faces or gestures of great sufferers. This is how I am, how I feel, whether in war or peace time; and only as I am and feel can I write. As I said at the start, though I criticize these stories now, afterwards, intellectually, I cannot criticize their content. They are the particular. But through the particular, in wartime, I felt the high-voltage current of the general pass. (p. 99)

Elizabeth Bowen, "The Demon Lover," in her The Mulberry Tree: Writings of Elizabeth Bowen, *edited by Hermione Lee, 1986. Reprint by Harcourt Brace Jovanovich, 1987, pp. 94-9.*

LOTUS SNOW (essay date 1950)

[*Snow explores Bowen's depiction of her characters' search for personal identity in the short stories included in* The Demon Lover, Joining Charles, The Cat Jumps, *and* Look at All Those Roses.]

All twelve stories contained in ***The Demon Lover*** express the means by which the personal life is salvaged from the depersonalization of war [as described by Bowen in her preface to the American edition of ***The Demon Lover***; see excerpt dated 1946]. In three of them illusions supply a sense of self, as in the attempts of Britishers to maintain the conventions of polite society, or in the plight of homeless young lovers, who create the abstraction of the pure and timeless city Kor. In four of the stories ghosts provide for the characters a sense of the certainty of themselves, as in the title story. **"The Demon Lover"** recounts the hallucination of a London matron who believes that a youthful lover, killed in World War I, has returned to claim her; belief in his existence kindles in her a sense of personal reality. In the remaining five stories the past is ransacked for the provision of an acceptable self. Amidst the bombing of London, a woman identifies herself with a Victorian ancestress amidst an emotional crisis; a girl discovers the source of her childhood neurosis inside a clock; a man examines the boyhood experience which paralyzed his faculty to love. Each of the stories, thus, is a psychological study of an attempt to find the personal life. Illusions, ghosts, past selves provide the certainties of the personal. "Hostile or not," Miss Bowen describes them, "they rally, they fill the vacuum for the uncertain 'I.' " (p. 300)

To fulfill the uncertain "I," the greatest number of the people of the short stories turn to love in one or another of its forms. The adolescent girl, the prototype for the heroines of [Miss Bowen's] novels, gropes for her selfhood in adoration of a school-girl companion [in **"The Jungle"**]; in protectiveness toward her improvident elders [in **"The Tommy Crans"**]; or in a sense of belongingness afforded her by a governess [in **"Reduced"**]. Grown to young womanhood, she looks for her self-importance in the love of either her husband or her lover. Again, the little boy in **"Tears, Idle Tears"** manages to overcome the ignominy of constant crying through the friendliness of a girl on a park bench. The young man, Oswald, in **"Love,"** protects the elderly and demented daughter of his former employer from institutionalization by persuading her that he and she are in hiding because he has committed a murder.

Only six people in the books of short stories, ***Joining Charles, The Cat Jumps,*** and ***Look at All Those Roses,*** assert themselves through hate. Yet they are a noteworthy six, for they proclaim, as do the antagonists of the novels, that hate is love corrupted. Among the children distorted into such negativism, the most provocative is Geraldine of **"The Little Girl's Room."** Cloyed with opportunities for self-expression, Geraldine nightly evokes in her pale-pink bedroom "The Enemies." Only their malevolence stimulates her *amour-propre.* Equally poignant is the lonely woman of **"A Queer Heart."** Dying, she confesses that she has sustained herself since early childhood upon a sense of the favoritism shown by life to her younger sister. Finally, the most desperate case of survival by hatred is Terry in the story **"Telling."** Sent home from school, from Cambridge, from Ceylon, Terry demonstrates that he can do one thing well: he cleanly kills the girl who said she believed he could do something and then laughed.

As in ***The Demon Lover,*** a number of Miss Bowen's earlier people resort to illusion to gain a sense of their own consequence. In five of these studies, curiously incomplete stories, their turning-points indistinguishably muffled, illusion is treated with a painful sense of its barrenness. Only two stories successfully convey the power of illusion to provide a way to live. One is **"The Cassowary."** A younger sister is engaged to a medical missionary who has disappeared two years before the story begins. Should he return, she plans to release him, for in his final letter he had declared himself in love with her older sister. Suddenly he does return. He returns and summons the older sister to London to marry him. The younger sister resents him bitterly. But it is not the loss of him she resents: it is the loss of the distinction of her "widowhood." The other story [**"Mrs. Moysey"**] is named for its heroine. . . . Her good nature, a series of climactic episodes demonstrates, is not the product of private tippling, as the villagers believe, but of a simple admiration for chocolates and the picture-boxes in which they come.

The most acute psychological studies, however, are constituted by those stories in which illusion has crossed the line of sanity and become aberration. Characters invent ghosts to assure themselves of themselves. One such instance is Myra Wing of **"The Apple Tree."** As an adolescent at boarding-school, Myra rejected a friend who was despised by all the school; as a result, the other child hanged herself in an apple tree in the school orchard. Myra nightly re-lives the scene of the hanging, until, years later, a friend exorcises child, apples, and tree by remaining with Myra during their appearance. Cured, Myra disappears "into happiness and sublime nonentity," Miss Bowen remarks significantly.

In a final group of stories no means of establishing the uncertain "I" has been discovered by the characters: they are people in transition, people between worlds. **"The Disinherited,"** the most fully developed story of this group, places in conflict Davina Archworth, an emotionally dislocated modern, and Prothero, her aunt's chauffeur and a criminal. Both "enemies of society," they live as they can, Davina on her aunt, Prothero through a nightly letter, written in Steinesque prose, to the mistress he has killed. Conflict arises when Davina borrows money from Prothero, feeding her pride on the sale of her kisses to a man who boasts enigmatically of his emotional freedom. In the eventual realization that he is no freer than she, Davina decides to borrow the money from her aunt to pay him:

> She saw that events led nowhere, crisis was an illusion, and that passions of momentary violent reality were struck off like sparks from the spirit, only to die. One could precipitate nothing. One is empowered to live fully: occasion does not offer.
>
> (pp. 300-02)

The survey of Miss Bowen's achievement indicates that she has treated the theme of the uncertain "I" most successfully in her short stories and in her last two novels. In the short stories she writes of the world of feeling: her people find a sense of personal identity through the subjective experiences of love, hate, illusion. In *The Death of the Heart* and *The Heat of the Day* she relates the world of feeling to the social background of her characters: people find their ways to live according to the temper of the twentieth century. In the five preceding novels, however, Miss Bowen deals with the world of feeling, yet attributes not to feeling but to society the difficulty of the search for personal identity. The indictment of society does not, therefore, ring true. (p. 309)

Lotus Snow, "The Uncertain 'I': A Study of Elizabeth Bowen's Fiction," in Western Humanities Review, *Vol. IV, No. 4, Autumn, 1950, pp. 299-310.*

SEAN O'FAOLAIN (essay date 1951)

[O'Faolain is considered one of Ireland's most distinguished men of letters. The author of numerous novels, biographies, and books of criticism, he is best known for his short stories, which are collected in such volumes as The Man Who Invented Sin, and Other Stories *(1948) and* Foreign Affairs, and Other Stories *(1976). O'Faolain was also a longtime friend of Bowen. In the following excerpt from O'Faolain's acclaimed critical study of the short story genre, he gives a detailed evaluation and appreciation of Bowen's techniques of characterization, language, and construction in "Her Table Spread."]*

"The Good Girl" is a characteristic [Elizabeth Bowen] story, among her best twelve. It is witty, malicious, intelligent, satirical, amusing. Uncle Porgie, who is not really an uncle, is Rolls-Royceing in Italy with his niece Monica, who is not his niece, and the lovely Dagmar who is not Monica's aunt though Captain Montparnesi is polite enough to pretend to think so. (We are left in no doubt as to Uncle Porgie's relations with Dagmar.) The Captain proposes to Monica who, rather helplessly, for she is a bit of a goose, permits an attachment, if not an engagement. One night she stays out late in his company—to the horror of Uncle Porgie, Dagmar and the proprietors of the hotel. Ladies and gentlemen do not do *this* sort of thing. Is not the hotel fully appointed? The gallant Captain disappears, having found that Monica is not an heiress. The 'good girl' is whirled off to Rome, very exhausted with Virtue, her own especially, and sadly sensible that it is her doom.

Now, the methods Miss Bowen employs to outline her characters—no short-story writer can do more—are of the swiftest. Monica has charm as well as virtue, we gather:

> Uncle Porgie, lifting his glass to twinkle in the pink lamplight, paid Monica tribute: "She's a damn pretty girl and a good girl, too!" Yet, all the time under the table he had been pursuing Dagmar's foot.

It is almost a statement. She is a good girl whom one admires while playing footy with some other girl. That disposes of two characters. Captain Montparnesi is outlined brutally. He proposes, he kisses Monica's hands, she asks for time to think (she would), and when she has walked away:—'Captain Montparnesi brought his pocket-book from against his heart and made some calculations.' No more need be said.

The story can now proceed to display its wit and malice at its ease, and further minor elaborations of character may be picked up on the way, or not, according as the reader is alert or merely passing the time. Thus when Monica finishes reading a book on Leonardo da Vinci (poor child) she takes a walking stick and the hotel-dog (poor child) and walks down to the lake (poor child): if you do not bother to note the little stabs you will not murmur 'poor child.' At the end of her walk

> she found mud-flats, washing, stark damp reeds, no one about. The lake was intended for distant scenery. She spoke Italian to a child who ran away, then she walked up again. On the terrace she had come upon Captain Montparnesi, engaged in sadness. He patted the dog. "I love dogs," he said: "it is almost a passion with me."

Naturally, he being a solitary man . . . and so on, with poor Monica gulping it all in. Or one may appreciate her natural resentment at Dagmar's smooth progress through the bewildering narrows of passion where she alone is lost; or Uncle Porgie's kindness in giving her a pair of coral ear-rings, since a good girl must have some compensations; or we may be amused by Captain Montparnesi's solemn family-council. But, whatever one does or does not find amusing and illuminating, one cannot fail to observe that this entire comedy creates its illusion with a minimum of characterisation. (pp. 165-66)

[Bowen's **"Her Table Spread"**] compresses into the usual modern length of three thousand words material for which Turgenev would have needed twice or three times the space. The scene is Ireland, a castle on the coast, a rainy summer night, the candle-lit dinner table, a friendly party which includes the unromantic Mr. Alban from London, whom the heiress Valeria Cuffe is vaguely expected to marry. In the bay there is a British destroyer whose ambience, all the more romantic by its nearness combined with its inaccessibility, emotionally disturbs them all. Valeria is especially affected. She is a very romantic young lady indeed who has, apparently, dreamed much of 'the Navy' and of marrying one Mr. Garrett who had visited them the previous Easter, when another destroyer was anchored in the estuary. Mr. Alban plays Mendelssohn, and then a Viennese waltz, while Valeria, now quite overbalanced, rushes out into the wet bushes to look at the misty portholes, and hug her dreams under the leaves in the moist night-air, and wave a mad lantern out to the rain-pocked sea. Her uncle and poor, abandoned, self-pitying, civilian Mr. Alban go in agitation to the boat-house to search for her. There is a bottle of whisky in the boat and a bat in the rafters, and the uncle talks of marriage and the parlour-maid. The Irish are, it is evident to Mr. Alban from London, just as dotty as people say. He flies from the bat and the bottle, and runs into Valeria, now beside herself, crying joyously that Mr. Garrett has landed; indeed Mr. Alban *is* Mr. Garrett. It becomes a moment when even Mr. Alban is unmanned and manned, a fleeting mad moment of sheer abandonment to the excitement of the dark, wet summer's night, the creaking satin and the bare shoulders of the woman, a moment of rampant Celtic emotion. . . . The story concludes, or rather exhausts itself:

> Perhaps it was best for them all that early, when next day first lightened the rain, the destroyer steamed out—below the extinguished Castle where Valeria lay with her arms wide, past the boat-house where Mr. Rossiter lay insensible and the bat hung masked in its wings—down the estuary to the open sea.

The compression of this story is in such enormous degree due to the suggestive style (e.g. a word like 'extinguished' above, saves a whole phrase; or the word 'lightened,' which gives a double sense of brightness and diminution) that we should keep this most difficult part of the analysis for [a discussion of language]. When we try to separate construction from situation the subtle management of the tale likewise resists dissection. I have long wondered whether the situation, the group, the place, or the atmosphere may have been felt first by the author; and whether Valeria came first, or Mr. Alban, and felt that nobody would ever know, least of all the author; for the story has such thirst and urge that it looks as if it had sprung from Jove's forehead fully armed, complete when first conceived. When I asked Miss Bowen this question she said that she saw a castle like this and wanted at once to write 'something' about it; only a somewhat odd and rather dotty girl seemed to fit the mood of the place. The 'mood'? But whose mood? We are back at the indefinable; a writer's own personality seeing things in her own unique way.

One may appreciate the cohesion of **"Her Table Spread"** by trying to imagine the story as Turgenev might have written it: the lonely girl (*a*), the remote place (*b*), the timid suitor (*c*), the anxious aunt (*d*), the Navy arriving (*e*)—step by step, leaf laid on delicate leaf, lyric note on lyric note. Here all occurs together. The three unities of Place, Time and Character weld everything like a handgrip. For Place we keep to the castle dining-room, with a slight extension in lamplight to the garden (and for Mr. Alban and Mr. Rossiter a slightly wider but brief extension to the boathouse), all but Mr. Rossiter coming back to the dining-room for the climax. For Time, all occurs within about an hour, possibly two, except for the epilogue I have quoted, which passes to the following dawn. For character Alban is the focus. I cannot explain how much skill all this involves without a digression to what, for convenience, I call the technique of the camera-angle.

By camera-angle I mean the technique by which the writer of short-stories 'sights' his characters one by one without creating an uncomfortable feeling that we are wandering all over the caste; and without breaking the form of the story. As we read a short-story by Maupassant, or Chekov, or O. Henry, or Frank O'Connor, or Liam O'Flaherty, or A. E. Coppard—and as I mention the names a score or more of their stories pass quickly before me—we do not notice how the mental camera moves, withdraws to a distance to enclose a larger view, slips deftly from one character to another, while all the time holding one main direction of which these are only variations. This mobility as to the detail combined with the rigidity of the general direction is one of the great technical pleasures of the modern short-story. (pp. 202-04)

This matter of the angle is paramount. It is a way of answering the question, 'What is the story about?' without being too obvious in the answer. So, I remember reading a story somewhere about a daughter which was really a story about the father, as did not appear until the last few lines. Or, in that story of Chekov's *Gooseberries,* the story was ostensibly about one man, and was so, but when we close the book we find that the narrator, the brother of the subject of the tale, has also unconsciously been revealing himself. (p. 207)

Having explained what I mean by camera-angle we can now come back to **"Her Table Spread,"** and observe how Elizabeth Bowen, while presenting a number of characters, has kept her Unity of Character. I have said that Alban is the focus. The story opens with him. 'Alban had few opinions on the subject of marriage . . .' When the other characters steal into the story we may still feel that it is he who is observing them; some reaction from him is indicated in each paragraph to convey this impression of his pervasiveness. The fourth paragraph breaks into conversation, and the atmosphere of excitement is gradually released. Conversation is every writer's favourite way of escaping from his centre to his circumference. Everybody may share it. All overhear. The writer vanishes. And Mr. Alban may see as well as hear. They have been speaking of the Navy's visit last Easter:

> Will they remember? Valeria's bust was almost on the table. But with a rustle Mrs. Treve pressed Valeria's toe. For the dining-room also looked out across the estuary, and the great girl had not once taken her eyes from the window. Perhaps it was unfortunate that Mr. Alban should have coincided with the destroyer. Perhaps it was unfortunate for Mr. Alban too. For he saw now he was less than half the feast . . .

That rustle of Mrs. Treve's skirt is delicate. He could have heard that. One may presume that he looked up and saw Valeria staring out of the window. The next two sentences belong to anybody. Mrs. Treve's thought? Guessed at by Mr. Alban? They are interesting sentences, technically, because they illustrate how a writer may, having slipped his camera across a scene which includes the main character, quietly pick up other characters on the way. There is, as it were, an elastic bond of thought that ties us to the main character; we may stray from him quite a distance.

There is a nice example of this gentle truancy in the paragraph which follows; the reader will observe the sentence where we slip from Alban to their thoughts of him, and, later, where the writer slips in her own comment on him. (Valeria has meanwhile skipped out into the garden.)

> In the drawing-room, empty of Valeria, the standard-lamps had been lit. Through their ballet-skirt shades, rose and lemon, they gave out a deep welcoming light. Alban, at the ladies' invitation, undraped the piano. He played, but they could see he was not pleased. It was obvious he had always been a civilian, and when he had taken his place on the piano-stool—which he twirled around three times rather fussily—his dinner-jacket wrinkled across his shoulders. It was sad they should feel indifferent, for he came from London. Mendelssohn was exasperating to them—they opened all four windows to let the music downhill. They preferred not to draw the curtains; the air, though damp, being pleasant tonight, they said.

To be sure, we do *not,* in reading for pleasure, observe anything very technical here. It would be obtrusive technique if we did. Indeed, it would not be technique at all since the function of technique is to create illusion, not to break illusion by poking its nose through it. There are hints and suggestions in that paragraph which we will quite unwittingly take; for example, they do not listen well—they get up in the middle of the music to open windows; they speak of the weather. There is more to it than that. They are troubled by Valeria's behaviour and seek to excuse it. 'The air is damp, but it's pleasant,' they said. It is natural for Valeria to have wished to stroll in it. This is true short-story writing; beautiful suggestibility all through.

The camera has stayed long enough away from Alban, so the next sentence returns full-face. 'The piano was damp but Alban played all his heart out . . .' etc. 'The piano was damp.' What compression of suggestion there! This is genuine poetic realism. Damp. The wet night. Neglect all round. The untended castle. And poor Alban playing his civilian heart out on the damp keys while they chatter. More general conversation allows the camera to wander again and this time the atmosphere becomes hysterical, and floating away on it, in the middle of a waltz played by Mr. Alban (still, doubtless, brooding on himself, on her, on everything), Valeria is given the stage, racing past the window with her mad lantern. This is the most daring part of the story, and it comes off. She has robbed the stage from Alban and done it triumphantly. After two pages in which she and her crazy romantic dreams hold all our interest we return to Alban. He and the uncle go down to the boat-house in the rain after her and there is some secret drinking and maudlin chatter about marriage. When he flies from the boat-house he and she will rush into one another in the darkness, and she will take him into her dream and he will, in his woe and excitement, respond to her wild fancy and the climax will mount and topple. That moment is an emotional *tour de force.*

Not until we are thinking back on the story, perhaps days after, do we realise that it all began and ended with Mr. Alban, and yet was called **"Her Table Spread."** It had been a story about a *girl's* romance all the time.

Naturally, Elizabeth Bowen was probably unaware of her own cleverness in all this; long practice, a gift of emotional combustibility, a great gift of words, an eye of a hawk, a special sympathy for the Valeria type—in one form or another Valeria turns up in all Miss Bowen's novels—combined to cast this perfectly fashioned story as freely and as unconsciously and as perfectly and as successfully as a fisherman casts his invisible line. (pp. 207-10)

Here is the opening of **["Her Table Spread"]**. . . . What individual words in the opening passage strike us by their suggestiveness?:

> Alban had few opinions on the subject of marriage; his attitude to women was negative but in particular he was not attracted to Miss Cuffe. Coming down early for dinner, red satin dress cut low, she attacked the silence with loud laughter before he had spoken. He recollected having heard that she was abnormal—at twenty-five, of statuesque development, still detained in childhood . . .

For me the word 'red' seems deliberately chosen. It may, lightly, suggest Miss Cuffe's dramatic taste in dress. The word 'attacked' (the silence) suggests her strident personality; the word 'recollected' implies that Alban is disturbed, thinks back, perks up, is suddenly alert. The word 'detained' in childhood has ominous undertones as applied to this slightly batty lady. It suggests the dog-house.

This language of undertones is Miss Bowen's specialty. Thus, when Miss Cuffe becomes 'preoccupied' with attempts at gravity we may see her as looking even more vacant in her efforts to look less flighty. When Mr. Alban begins to feel miserable by this 'indifferent shore' the adjective has a treble meaning—heedless, not so hopeless, quite hopeless. When Miss Cuffe proposes a row in the bay, rain or no rain, and the ladies 'produced indignation' we may feel that even these dotty Irish ladies are not wholly averse to the idea which they condemn; they have to force their indignation.

As the excitement mounts the language becomes more and more charged and less and less literal. Mr. Alban's state of mind is proposed metaphorically.

> Wandering among the apples and amphoras of an art school he had blundered into the life room; woman revolved gravely. "Hell," he said to the steps, mounting, his mind blank to the outcome.

Words now begin to extend freely, quite dilated.

> Behind, through the windows, lamps spread great skirts of light, and Mars and Mercury, unable to contain themselves, stooped from their pedestals. . . . Close by Valeria's fingers creaked on her warm wet satin. She laughed like a princess, magnificently justified. Their unseen faces were all three lovely, and, in the silence after the laughter, such a strong tenderness reached him that, standing there in full manhood, he was for a moment not exiled. For the moment, without moving or speaking, he stood, in the dark, in a flame, as though all three said, "My darling . . ."

Elsewhere in the story 'a smothered island' gives an immediate bosky effect without labouring for the picture. We see, or do not see, an 'extinguished Castle.' The striking image of 'The bat hung masked in its wings' is a sentence which gives the clue: this is the language of poetry magnificently taken over by prose. 'La poésie ne consiste pas,' says Saint Beuve. 'à tout dire mais à tout faire rêver.'

It is difficult to find a label for this modern use of English. Some of it is frankly neologistic. Some almost catachresis, or extravagant metaphor: cf. our now-common use of the word to 'jockey'; Miss Bowen's 'attacked' the silence. Most of it is what is technically known as radiation of meaning, which is not only legitimate but the normal process of dilating language in poetry.

> By a succession of radiations the development of meaning may become almost infinitely complex. No dictionary can ever register a tithe of them, for, so long as language is alive, every speaker is constantly making new specialised amplifications of its words. . . . The limits of the definition must always be vague and even within these limits there is always scope for variety. If the speaker does not transgress these limits in a given instance we understand his meaning. . . . He has given us a conventional sign or symbol of his idea. Our interpretation of the sign will depend partly on the context, partly on what we know of the speaker, partly on the associations which we ourselves attach to the word . . . [In a footnote, the critic attributes the quote to Greenough and Kittredge, *Words and Their Ways in English* (1926).]

All these three elements are at work in the witty phrase 'detained in childhood,' with its radiated meanings: that Miss Cuffe has got stuck (in the queue), is engaged (in the nursery), has not been allowed to proceed (by Nursey), or is already in the Big House.

It may be said that such use of language does not make for clarity; it does not. Neither does it make pictures; it is impressionistic, in letters a special feminine strength or weakness. It makes stringent demands on the wit and the intelligence lest it become just too, too clever or an end in itself, or 'transgress the limits.' Yet in this language some of the wittiest things in English have been written and without it we should not have had the romantic music of such as Carlyle or Browne. Its value for the writer of short-stories is at least indisputable in one respect: so alert a language helps to make short-stories shorter. (pp. 229-31)

Sean O'Faolain, in his The Short Story, *1948. Reprint by The Devin-Adair Company, 1951, 370 p.*

SEAN O'FAOLAIN (essay date 1956)

[*In the following excerpt, O'Faolain asserts that Bowen's writing is influenced by her Anglo-Irishness and its accompanying sense of exile. The critic also considers Bowen's relationship to Gustave Flaubert and discusses Bowen as a romantic in an anti-romantic age.*]

Elizabeth Bowen is detached by birth from that society she describes. She is an Irishwoman, at least one sea apart from English traditions. She descends from that sturdy and creative sub-race we call the Anglo-Irish. At least a part of her literary loyalties are with that long and honourable pedigree that goes back through Shaw, Joyce, George Moore, Somerville and Ross, Yeats, Wilde, Goldsmith, Sheridan, Burke, Swift and Berkeley to the forced marriage of two races, two islands. (p. 169)

The effects of this detachment seem to be mainly two. Malice would naturally be more free, and the play of sentiment more indulgent. It is a nice ambivalence. No English writer can have quite the same liberty. (p. 170)

Miss Bowen is indebted to another influence besides her race and her exile to stiffen her own natural, shrewd intelligence, her own natural integrity as an observer. This is the early influence of Flaubert. And when we recall the romantic-realist conflict within Flaubert we may see another reason for thinking of Elizabeth Bowen as a bifrontine writer. The conflict in her work is, in fact, not dissimilar. She wavers between two methods of approach.

The essence of her way of seeing life is that, like the singer who was supposed to be able to break a champagne glass by singing at it, she exposes the brittleness of romance by soliciting it ruthlessly. Time, for her characters, is very far removed from Faulkner's continuum, or Hemingway's feeling for events enclosed-at-both-ends. It is a brittle moment, snatched from fate. Happiness in her novels is rapt away, shop-lifted, and always dearly paid for. God is the shop-walker who makes her characters pay, and we vulgar citizens, the run-of-the-mill of ordinary people, decent fathers of families, impatient of all youthful aberrations cannot deny His justice.

Happiness may even have to be snatched between the moments. She pursues these golden if elusive hours on behalf of her heroines. So, in *The Last September* Francie Montmorency found that during her honeymoon time had been "loose-textured, had had a shining undertone, happiness glittered between the moments". In *To the North* when Cecilia returns to her flat and looks about her at the unfamiliar-familiar . . . "Life here, still not quite her own, kept for those few moments unknown tranquillity." Happiness is thus interleaved in the book of life. It is a bonus, a wad of dollars smuggled through the customs of life. But to go after this happiness too hard is, one is led to feel, to wrench from life something that it can only give arbitrarily like a Fairy Godmother. One is not therefore surprised to discover that there is nothing of the Hemingwayan will in her characters. They may seem wilful; they are, in practice, the passive recipients of fate. All they receive from fate is passion, and this receipt is like a soldier's calling-to-the-colours. Her characters are conscripted by passion into action. Once in action they fight well, but what Arnold said of the Celt may be said of them: they go into battle and they always fall. It is true that they may also and for long have desired passion, but the desire is never so powerful as the impulse of chance. Her characters are all played upon.

There is a short story in her second book, ***Ann Lee's,*** written before she had published her first novel, which neatly illustrates this fateful element in all her later work. It is called **"The Parrot"**. A young girl, Eleanor Fitch, is a companion to an old lady, Mrs Willesden, in whose life nothing ever happens. One morning Eleanor accidentally lets her old lady's parrot fly away. She pursues the gaudy bird in its wayward flight from garden to garden until it pauses in the garden of a Mr Lennicott, a novelist of doubtful repute according to Mrs Willesden. Palpitating, Eleanor enters the garden of this fabulous person, enters his house, meets him in his dressing-gown, has the great adventure of capturing the multi-coloured bird with his assistance. When Lennicott kindly wishes to detain her, offering her fruit, she refuses. "Nobody had ever reached out for her like that so eagerly; she did not want to go back to that house of shut-out sunshine and great furniture where the parrot was royally carried from room to room on trays, and where she was nothing." Eleanor goes back unscathed to her dull routine, thinking: "How world overlapped with world; visible each from the other, yet never to be one."

Now, I have a profound suspicion of that technique of criticism which elucidates the interior meaning of stories, and the secret meanings of an author's mind, by his unconscious use of symbols, but whether this brilliant and far-faring bird luring a potential Proserpine from garden to garden to the haunts of Pluto is or is not—and I think it is—in the full tradition of Flaubertian symbolism (the blueness of Emma Bovary's dream-curtains suggesting the Virgin; and such-like symbols) one may fairly use this fable as a symbol of one of Miss Bowen's favoured types: the dreaming but recusant girl. Longing but vigilant, troubled by her own eagerness, she will, one fine day, follow the bright bird of her dreams into the woods of life and suffer the fate of Proserpine, or worse. There is an atmosphere of ancient fable behind all of Miss Bowen's fiction. Her persons are recognisable temperaments rather than composed characters. Flaubert merely overlays the fabulous. Her characters are the modern, sophisticated, naturalistic novelist's versions of primitive urges. One feels that if she had lived three hundred and fifty years ago when passions rode freely and fiercely she would have described the dreams that drove Ophelia, Juliet and Desdemona to love and to death. (pp. 171-73)

Elizabeth Bowen is a romantic up against the despotism of reality. So many other Irish writers are. The metallic brilliance, even the occasional jarring brassiness and jauntiness of her style is, in an admirable sense, a fake, a deceptive cocoon wrapped about the central precious, tender thing. One could imagine a hare settling into her form, a sticky little leveret between her paws, or perhaps a lioness growling over her young. It is the growl of *Ich grolle nicht,* the Flaubertian coldness imposed on Irish feeling, and the theme is so heartbreaking that it would be embarrassing if she were not tight-lipped about those heroines who just do not know what o'clock it is once love enters their unwary lives. She writes of romantic heroines in an age that has made the two words pejorative. The underlying assumptions here are very much of the Twenties. The conflicts are no longer clear enough to justify bold affirmations, positive statements of loyalty, straight fights or declared aims or ends. Miss Bowen's heroines are, after all, always defeated. In Mauriac's phrase their beauty is borrowed from despair. Not, as we have seen, that she is anti-heroic, but that she must state coldly that heroism, the absolute aim, does not stand a chance in modern society, even while she still insists passionately that it is always worth while to try. She has not assumed that we must therefore reject tradition, but she is plainly unenthusiastic about it. She does not assume that violence is the only possible alternative in fiction to thought. She does not assume that the intellect must be abdicated by the modern novelist. She hovers patiently over her subjects. But the prime technical characteristic of her work, as of other modern women writers, such as Virginia Woolf, is that she fills the vacuum which the general disintegration of belief has created in life by the pursuit of sensibility. It is a highly sophisticated pursuit. Sometimes it is over-conscious and overdone.

Her sensibility can be witty; it can also be catty, even brassy, too smart like an over-clever *décor* for a ballet. I do not mind that it is, to my taste, on occasion vulgar, though not quite in the sense in which her young girls are vulgar. She has defended, or at least pleaded, for sympathy with vulgarity, and are there not times when good taste is itself a little vulgar? One thinks of the ghastly good taste of Mr Charles Morgan. But what one means by finding this kind of good taste rather vulgar is that it is bloodless, and that one longs occasionally for a good, warm, passionate howl like an Italian mother baying over her dead child. This sort of earthiness is outside the range of any English-trained writer. When Elizabeth Bowen is dealing with elemental things she skirts around them with too much elegance. There are certain things she will not deign to describe. The actual falling in love of her people is one. (pp. 187-88)

The one place where she is really earthy is when she is being humorous, and would, many times over, that she were humorous more often, for when she is being humorous she is also most human. Louie in *The Heat of the Day* is not only good fun but real; down to earth; far more so than Robert, Harrison and Stella pirouetting about each other exhaustingly. Yet, to take a fair measure of the humanity (as against the elegance) of her sensibilities, one may compare them with the sensibilities of Virginia Woolf whose antennae are as sensitive as remote radar, but who reacts not so much to human beings as to things and "states of mind". Miss Bowen is also responsive to things and states of mind, but she responds chiefly, and warmly, to her own favoured types of people. "Things," Mrs Woolf characteristically makes Terence Hewitt say in *The Voyage Out,* "things I feel come to me like lights. I want to combine them. Have you ever seen fireworks that make figures? I want to make figures." That also, to my taste, is a form of vulgarity through elegance. Miss Bowen would never be quite so refined. She wants to make people not figures, to put them into conflict with society, and her explorations of their feelings are never just an exploitation of her own.

Her outer-imposed limitations do, nevertheless, obtrude themselves. *The Death of the Heart* was, indeed, a firm and passionately felt protest against the modern desiccation of feeling, but one could not help noting that it offered no moral approach to the problem: meaning that it intimated no norm to set against the subnormal. But can one reasonably blame Miss Bowen for this? We are brought back by this longing for a norm to the death of the traditional Hero, that symbol of the norm in all traditional literature. She, too, can only present us with the martyr in place of the Hero, the representative not of the norm but of the disease. Greene's alternative is God. Miss Bowen is too deeply rooted in the great, central humanist tradition of European culture to take refuge in hereafters. What she directs our eyes towards is the malady of our times that breaks the dreaming and gallant few. It is what her master Flaubert did with Emma Bovary, more ruthlessly. She has described the dilemma of our times honestly, beautifully and at times movingly. To have done so much, and done it so well, is to have done a great deal. (pp. 189-90)

Sean O'Faolain, "Elizabeth Bowen; or, Romance Does Not Pay," in his The Vanishing Hero: Studies in Novelists of the Twenties, *Eyre & Spottiswoode, 1956, pp. 167-90.*

ELIZABETH BOWEN (essay date 1959)

[*The following originally appeared in the preface to* Stories by Elizabeth Bowen *in 1959. Bowen here reflects on the art of the short story and discusses the sources of inspiration for her short fiction.*]

Total impersonality in story-writing is, for me certainly, impossible—so much so that it would be a waste of time to wonder whether it would be desirable. And I doubt, actually, whether for any writer it is either desirable or possible, for this reason: the short story is linked with poetry, and that, we know, cannot but bear a signature. The tale without lyricism or passion desiccates into little more than a document. The poet, and in his wake the short-story writer, is using his own, unique susceptibility to experience: in a sense, the susceptibility is the experience. The susceptibility, equally, *is* the writer, who therefore cannot be absent from what he writes. The short story is at an advantage over the novel, and can claim its nearer kinship to poetry, because it must be more concentrated, can be more visionary, and is not weighed down (as the novel is bound to be) by facts, explanation, or analysis. I do not mean to say that the short story is by any means exempt from the laws of narrative: it must observe them, but on its own terms. Fewer characters, fewer scenes, and above all fewer happenings are necessary; shape and action are framed for simplification. As against that, there are dangers and can be penalties: essentially, at no point in the story must the electrical-imaginative current be found to fail. Novels legitimately have "slack" passages, which serve, like intermissions, to ease off the reader between crisis and crisis. But the short story revolves round one crisis only—one might call it, almost, a crisis in itself. There (ideally) ought to be nothing in such a story which can weaken, detract from, or blur the central, single effect.

This, I recognize, has been one idea I have kept before myself. In short-story writing it has been my main aim, and at least as an aim it has been continuous. I state it, though without deluding myself that I have realized it, succeeded in it, in any one story. . . . To return to the matter of the personal, I repeat that one cannot wholly eliminate oneself, for a second, and also sufficient, reason: any fiction (and surely poetry, too?) is bound to be transposed autobiography. (True, it may be this at so many removes as to defeat ordinary recognition.) I can, and indeed if I would not I still must, relate any and every story I have written to something that happened to me in my own life. But here I am speaking of happenings in a broad sense—to behold, and react, is where I am concerned a happening; speculations, unaccountable stirs of interest, longings, attractions, apprehensions without knowable cause—these are happenings also. When I reread a story, I relive the moment from which it sprang. A scene burned itself into me, a building magnetized me, a mood or season of Nature's penetrated me, history suddenly appeared to me in some tiny act, or a face had begun to haunt me before I glanced at it.

On the whole, places more often than faces have sparked off stories. To be honest, the scenes have been with me before the characters—it could have seemed to me, even, once or twice, as though the former had summoned the latter up. I do not feel, necessarily, that this is wrong: a story must come to life in its own order. Also, I reassert what I said when discussing the art of Katherine Mansfield: I do not feel that the short story can be, or should be, used for the analysis or development of character. The full, full-length portrait is fitter work for the novelist; in the short story, treatment must be dramatic—we are dealing with man, or woman or child, in relation to a particular crisis or mood or moment, and to that only. Though (and as to this, law is stern) the crisis must be one in which such-and-such a character would be likely to be involved, or, still more, would be likely to precipitate; the mood must be one to which such-and-such a character would be likely to be prone, or still more, to heighten; the moment should essentially be the one which would, on the given character, act most strongly. Once a story truly germinates in my mind, the inevitable actors in it take form—and not only this, but they also take hold, to the point of remaining after the tale is told. I give, as examples, four stories in this selection: **"The Storm," "Her Table Spread," "Ivy Gripped the Steps,"**

"Mysterious Kôr." Each of these arose out of an intensified, all but spellbound beholding, on my part, of the scene in question—a fountain-filled Italian garden in livid, pre-thundery light; a shabbily fanciful Irish castle overlooking an estuary; an ivy-strangled house in a formerly suave residential avenue; or weird moonlight over bomb-pitted London. Each time I felt: "Yes, this affects me—but it would affect 'X' more. Under what circumstances; for what reason? And who *is* 'X'?" In each case, the "X" I pondered upon became the key character in the resultant story. . . . It could seem to me that stories, with their *dramatis personae,* pre-exist, only wait to be come upon. I know I do not invent them; I discover them. Though that does not mean that they are easily told. On me devolves the onus of narration.

Fantasy . . . another important element. One may of course say that any story (from any pen) is the exercise or working out of a fantasy—that any author of fiction, to write at all, must have recourse to his or her dreaming faculty. But in Elizabeth Bowen stories, it may be found, fantasy is often present twice over; part as it is of the fabric of the actual plot, or governor of the behaviour of the characters. Looking through this selection I have made, I find fantasy strongly represented. Critics may possibly say, too much so? Yet these, I still maintain, are my better stories. If I were a short-story writer only, I might well seem to be out of balance. But recall, more than half of my life is under the steadying influence of the novel, with its calmer, stricter, more orthodox demands: into the novel goes such taste as I have for rational behaviour and social portraiture. The short story, as I see it to be, allows for what is crazy about humanity: obstinacies, inordinate heroisms, "immortal longings." (pp. 128-30)

Elizabeth Bowen, "Stories by Elizabeth Bowen," in her The Mulberry Tree: Writings of Elizabeth Bowen, *edited by Hermione Lee, 1986. Reprint by Harcourt Brace Jovanovich, 1987, pp. 126-30.*

HARRY STRICKHAUSEN (essay date 1965)

[*Strickhausen briefly surveys the characteristics of Bowen's short fiction and the authors who influenced her.*]

Certainly most of Miss Bowen's most completely realized work is in the form of the stories. ***Stories,*** which contains eighteen of the more than eighty that she has written, is a clear illustration of the development of her art. In the earlier stories (such as **"The Storm"**) setting is more important than character; in others (such as **"Summer Night"**) they are equally important. **"The Storm,"** from her second collection, ***Ann Lee's,*** is a story in which the past is only dimly inferred; the crisis of the present is all that matters. A man and a woman, separated for a few moments, independently see ghosts. The character is only what he perceives, is not further delineated. Here is the time before the storm:

> The air was warm and tense, stretched so taut that it quivered. Breathing had become an affair of consciousness, and movement they both felt to be impossible. Behind the terrace, the doorways of the Villa grew solid with darkness, the high façade loomed. Colour faded everywhere, the hills grew livid; forms assumed a menacing distinctness, blade-like against the architecture of the clouds.

And here, eight pages and only a few moments later, is the storm itself:

> The wind caught the Villa full in the face, one stinging challenge like the lash of a gauntlet. Elegant, rococo, with an air of balance delicately perilous, it yet struck down deep into the rock, deep as a fortress. It braced itself, and now the assailing forces of the wind came singing between the pillars of the parapet.

It is immediately apparent that the style, as well as the movement of the wind, is "Elegant, rococo." But the point of the above quotations is that the landscape is the principal actor, that the characters are acted upon. We learn of them through the setting. In **"Summer Night,"** from ***Look at All Those Roses,*** they emerge fully, not as "impatiently jerked-at marionettes," and character and setting act upon each other. In that story there are nine abruptly divided scenes of mostly simultaneous action, some of which take place miles apart. The ways of using time constitute a distinct contribution by Miss Bowen to the form of the short story. In her uses of atmosphere and approaches to characters in settings she may well have influenced such different writers as Jean Stafford, Truman Capote, and—in these and also in her explorations of fantasy—William Goyen, who has taken these elements much further than Miss Bowen has.

Miss Bowen's traditions and purposes are clear. There is plenty of evidence in her fiction that she has read, with care and love, Jane Austen, James, Flaubert, Proust, Forster, and Virginia Woolf. Her limitations are also clear, as precisely marked as a map. But if her range is narrow, limited to characters of the same social class and of roughly the same type and sensibility, her central theme, that of the difficulty of love, is a great one and is handled in many different ways throughout her work. The variety within limitations is immense. Hers is a narrow and honest world, a walled garden, deceptively beautiful, where belladonna flourishes alongside the dahlias. Her world is a difficult one in which characters move passively, subjected to forces that they cannot control. When they attempt to control these forces they are made most miserable. Yet no future critic of Elizabeth Bowen can afford to ignore a point which is just becoming apparent, that, in her most recent novels (*A World of Love* and *The Little Girls*), these forces ultimately work out to *good.* One may best define the progress of her work by saying that her situations have become more difficult and the responses of her central characters more complicated and subtle. And as her craft has increased, her depth of psychological understanding has become more evident. But of course this is not an exactly linear progress. When Miss Bowen's work fails, as it still does sometimes, it is unreal and contrived, the surface too elaborate and the dialogue totally irrelevant, work which may be consigned to the frantic, primarily feminine following which values all of Miss Bowen's work equally and for reasons all its own. But when it is fine, as in *A World of Love* and elsewhere, it is a work of rich sensitivity and great integrity and introduces us to a time and place which we believe in and remember. (pp. 164-65)

Harry Strickhausen, "Elizabeth Bowen and Reality," in The Sewanee Review, *Vol. LXXIII, No. 1, Winter, 1965, pp. 158-65.*

GEORGE BRANDON SAUL (essay date 1965)

[*An American critic, poet, and children's author, Saul has written widely on Irish authors and has served as a contributing editor of the* Journal of Irish Literature. *The following excerpt is from his derogatory critical overview of Bowen's short stories to date.*]

One of the unhappy feelings hard to shake off in reflecting on the short stories of the Irishwoman Elizabeth Bowen is that of their essentially un-Irish quality and character: in fact, occasional prolixity seems almost the only thing possibly suggestive of Irish roots, and that implies merely negative identification. Even Miss Bowen's theorizing (see the preface to her ***Early Stories***)—"a story, if it is to *be* a story, must have a psychological turning-point"—is in a sense un-Irish: the racial inclination is basically toward telling a story and letting psychology worry about itself. Not that "psychological turning-points" can't be frequently recognized or deduced; only that the storyteller doesn't proceed as if he were framing things to oblige a theory. So to me Seán O'Faoláin's assertion in *The Vanishing Hero*—"There is an atmosphere of ancient fable behind all of Miss Bowen's fiction" [see excerpt dated 1956]—is, at least so far as the short stories are concerned, merely flattery. There is behind Miss Bowen's later short stories (which represent only a fraction of her output) Katherine Mansfield; and perhaps behind her earlier, at least by her own intimation in the preface just mentioned, Richard Middleton and E. M. Forster. Certainly there is not the remotest hint of the traditions of the *filid*—or even the "shanachies"; there is no suggestion of the Celtically ambient. (p. 53)

[Why] the lack of racial tincture?—One can only guess. Of course, like many another Irish writer, Miss Bowen is not of purely Irish ancestry, the first Bowen to settle in Ireland having been a Welsh colonel under Cromwell who was rewarded for his service with Irish property. This helps to explain the "land-owning Protestant outlook and Unionist politics" of the Bowen family, remarked in *Seven Winters.* But one suspects that the Dublin-born girl's assimilation to English tradition was sealed by her having been educated and reared in England after the age of seven, and having remained resident there for the most part thenceforth. (p. 54)

In reissuing her early stories in 1951, Miss Bowen went to a surprising degree of sympathetic prefatory analysis of contents for one who—with more pertinence than perhaps really intended—at the same time ventured, "for the student writer they may have the value of cautionary tales." Does one normally issue prentice work as a lesson to students?

In any event, Miss Bowen calls ***Encounters*** "a mixture of precocity and naïvety" in markedly "synthetic language," its "strong point" "visual clarity," with occasionally "an uncorrupted attempt to say something not said before," showing "susceptibility . . . to places, moments, objects, and times of year." At the same time, she admits "harshness" in presenting her characters and "touches of little-girlish smarty unkindness."

The stories of ***Ann Lee's,*** including the first to touch on her "native Irish scene," Miss Bowen counts free from "naïvety" but still harsh in character-handling, although better in "scene-setting," dialogue, and control of action, and possessed of "more texture, fullness, or . . . body." But she admits to a good deal of "prettiness" and "priggishness," confessing that at time of composition she still "liked places and objects better than people."

One isn't inclined to argue. Indeed, there is something downright unpleasant about the tone of ***Encounters,*** a sharpness unjustified by acute insight or even acidulous divination in presenting its studies of peculiarly British futility (**"Requiescat"**), helplessness (**"All Saints"**), and triviality (**"The New House," "Lunch"**). In **"The Lover,"** a middle-aged man anticipates an "upholstered happiness" with his Doris; in **"Mrs. Windermere,"** a meddling woman gets cruel picturization; in **"Coming Home,"** a child is presented for, it would seem, purely the sake of exposing a capacity for morbidity and self-centeredness. Even when situation seems valid, as in **"The Return,"** the way of handling it is bald, abrupt, and unconvincing. And the mere English permits such phraseology as "among the wooliness." In brief, this is a book one would not have missed had he missed it.

Ann Lee's—despite one or two gratuitous jabs at what the author conceives of as "American" language and shoes (*v.* **"Recent Photograph"**), with a touch of the pathetically traditional British snobbery—is a slightly better book than its predecessor, though one can only speculate on why the Mr. Richardson of the title story forced himself on the hat shop proprietor's attention, and on how and why she got rid of him as quickly as she did. And one can hardly be unaware of certain almost shocking absurdities—as when, a lady's paid companion having lied about recapturing an escaped parrot *alone,* one is assured, "It was like the crowing of the cock" (doubtless a reference certain "critics" would relish); or when one finds **"The Visitor"** putting thoughts too patently incredible for even a child's extravagance into the brooding of a little boy taken by friends while his mother is dying: not wanting anyone to come tell him of her death, the boy purportedly thinks, "It would be as though they saw me see her being killed"!

This volume, again, is marred by a curiously gratuitous sarcasm, as in the opening of **"The Contessina,"** aside from the flippancy with which murder and suicide are treated in the opening paragraph of **"Recent Photograph."** Most of the tales lack significant body; they evaporate quickly after being read. And more than one has a superficial, and essentially pointless, verbosity: cp., *e.g.,* **"The Back Drawing-Room,"** vitiated by a tiresome prelude and an ineffective conclusion. One reflects, as in the case of the earlier work, that the author finds no character whom she really likes, that people one and all are to be mocked for futility and dull, nagging stupidity. How, then, could there have been any keys to sympathetic revelation?—Nevertheless, there are some hopeful patches, as when Miss Phelps (**"The Secession"**) "felt herself transparent . . . and knew that her transparency must be darkened visibly by a hurrying shoal of thoughts."

Joining Charles at length brings us, in its eleven stories, some genuinely remarkable work. At least five of the tales are exceptional; and of these, two—the title story and **"Foothold"**—are superlative. The volume as a whole is more subtle than its predecessors in its swift touches of analysis of human relationships; and for once the author does not let hatred or sardonic inclination ruin the flavor of her character-presentation. Further, she gives us frequently the memorably simple phase—as in "the rainy light" (one thinks of Yeats's "windy light").

Probably the finest story here is the initial one: a perceptive and sensitively told one of Louise Ray's dread at leaving for Lyons to join her innately contemptible but superficially perfect husband, Charles. But the ghost story **"Foothold"** is almost equally effective; and **"Mrs. Moysey"**—the tragicomedy of a widow sadly missuspected, **"Telling"**—the almost unbearable tale of a gently insane boy murderer, and **"The Working Party"**—concerned with a young farm wife who, entertaining a huge "working party" of women, finally goes to pieces after trying to ignore a dead workman on her kitchen stairs—are all warrant of a talent far greater than heretofore indicated.

The Cat Jumps, in turn, unhappily returns us to ambiguous responses. Of its twelve stories, five are either trivial or suggestive of the author's early acerbity; the seven better pieces—**"The Tommy Crans," "The Cat Jumps," "The Last Night in the Old Home," "The Disinherited," "Her Table Spread," "The Needlecase,"** and **"The Apple Tree"**—are reprinted among the nineteen of ***Look at All Those Roses,*** which nevertheless recalls emphatically the old question: Doesn't Miss Bowen know any rationally pleasant, wholehearted, approvable people?—Doesn't she really like anybody?—She seems so determined not to be sentimental that she becomes brittle; and time and again she seems in effect merely to be saying, "Here's a situation: make of it what you wish." Even her faculty for suggesting the malign, especially in a nocturnal atmosphere, seems a trifle artificial, factitious.

But one reads—and finds **"The Cat Jumps"** a fairly successful pseudo-horror story, with an inlaid satire on people with "light, bright, shadowless, thoroughly disinfected minds" that whispers "Saki"; **"A Queer Heart,"** with one of the rare characters the author presents with the insight and affectionate humor stirred by apparent approval and love; and **"Love"**—a fine piece concerned with an impoverished young hotel-keeper on an Irish shore and the mentally unbalanced, formerly rich girl he protects in his own way. And one comes on a description of Irish landscape, in the opening paragraphs of **"Summer Night,"** which, almost suggestive of D. H. Lawrence's subtler apprehensions, proves the book is not wholly lacking in lyrical moments, though such moments are almost never stimulated by character. Why, then, one's general feeling of disappointment?

Perhaps an answer to this question may be intimated by further queries: Is there something too painfully cute in comparing a house **("The Needlecase")** to "a disheartened edition of Mansfield Park"?—in asserting **("The Last Night in the Old Home")** "A straw from some packing-case blew past his feet in the dark, which was melodramatic"?—in speaking **("Tears, Idle Tears")** of "diaphanous willows whose weeping was not shocking"?—in postulating a perception so exquisitely delicate as to pretend **("A Love Story"**: the title suggestive of a stupid pretense) that "In the immense tiled fireplace a fire burned with a visible silent roar"?—in conceiving of life as largely an indeterminate series of unresolved scene-settings in frustration and infidelity?—in readings of life of the quality of the following: "There is something about an abject person that rouses cruelty in the kindest breast" **("Tears, Idle Tears")**, or the absurd "She was a true enough artist to have false taste . . ." **("No. 16")**?

Incidentally, one wonders more than once in reading this volume whether the author has forgotten about that "psychological turning-point" she professes a story should have.

The preface to ***Ivy Gripped the Steps,*** the American edition of ***The Demon Lover,*** tells us that its stories were written for specific magazines or papers on request, "in wartime London—between the spring of 1941 and the late autumn of 1944," but were not "forced" [see excerpt dated 1945]." However stimulated, the tales include four of Miss Bowen's best, as well as matter suggestive of the semi-psychopathic, the futile, or the merely trivial, with proposed intimation not always leading beyond vagueness.

As best, one reader should have to name **"The Demon Lover,"** baptized from an old ballad, a masterpiece of horror; **"Pink May,"** the deft picture of a woman blaming a jealous, pitying ghost for her personal tragedy; **"Mysterious Kôr,"** a piece which really has no action, but suggests admirably a state, or condition, and which presents a memorable picture of blacked-out London in full moonlight; and **"Ivy Gripped the Steps"**—another study in futility, but one in which the intimations seem more lucid than usual.

Even so, this volume written against a background of wartime England would not lose if its brittle characters were eliminated, together with its elements of the self-consciously sophisticated (cp. the girl's happiness over having "forgotten" the bungalow of her childhood in **"Songs My Father Sang Me"**) and the merely extraneous. Nor is it fortunate in the apparent shadow of Katherine Mansfield, earlier intimated and suggested by the indirect approach, the concern with attenuated perception and pastel implication, the tendency to read consequence into the essentially trivial. Unquestionably, too, the book is emphatically suggestive of the self-consciously professional—and perhaps that is largely the trouble.

Indeed, perhaps that is the real trouble with the vast majority of Miss Bowen's stories—that and the fact that the unloved is almost never the completely understood and that somehow the author too often seems to use her themes merely as finger-exercises, her material without respecting it. (pp. 54-9)

George Brandon Saul, "The Short Stories of Elizabeth Bowen," in Arizona Quarterly, *Vol. 21, No. 1, Spring, 1965, pp. 53-9.*

GEORGE GREENE (essay date 1965)

[*Greene offers a brief discussion of Bowen's stories written during wartime and their portraits of youth in conflict.*]

The best of Miss Bowen's early stories . . . focus on youthful distress. In **"The Tommy Crans,"** for example, a small girl and boy meet at her birthday party, and the growing attraction they feel over the years is blighted by the girl's compulsion to help the frivolous couple who have adopted her. When Nancy sells her gold watch because her benefactors need money, both children have already begun to suspect the deceit of the world. They ask themselves "how one could penetrate far into life without despair." It is impossible to adjust to the tricks which experience dictates. " '. . . I don't see how we are ever to live; we seem to know everything. Surely there should be something for us we don't know?' "

Those stories which grow out of the war against Fascism reply to Nancy's query. " ' . . . this war's an awful illumination,' " one speaker in **"Summer Night"** warns; " 'it's destroyed our dark; we have to see where we are.' " By the 1940s children are still "cryptic," but a new broadening is in evidence. These people, most of them grownups, face a terror which is public as well as private. In **"Sunday Afternoon"** a man working in beleaguered London visits Ireland, where one girl expresses a taunting desire to be in the thick of the action. The outsider, Henry, is asked about the impact of the bombings. " '. . . it is difficult, you know, to know what one feels. One's feelings seem to have no language for anything so preposterous.' " If one is to break the code of this new world, one must reach beyond the range of sensitive verbalizing. The girl shares the inclination, often fatal, to rely on miracles which one saw in evidence among her earlier sisters. " '. . . it seems that no one can tell one anything,' " she says. " 'There is really nothing, till one knows it oneself.' " But by now Miss Bowen has outlived her faith in incantation. As they explore beyond the genteel drawing room and the young girl's diary, her words grow less self-conscious. What Henry most fears in this wartime world is "the new catastrophic *outward* order of life—of brutality, of being without spirit." One finds people striving to rise above intoxication with sounds, which even animals possess, to some knowledge of how to extricate themselves from aimlessness. ". . . with nothing left but our brute courage," Henry knows, "we shall be nothing but brutes."

The grimmest of all the war stories juxtaposes at closer quarters Miss Bowen's hesitant protagonists and that larger nightmare through which they are living. [In **"Mysterious Kôr,"** a] soldier on leave in London arranges to spend the night at the tiny flat which his girl shares with another young woman. As the lovers walk home a wave of moonlight, eerie, terrifying, washes over them. They no longer fear German air raids. "Something more immaterial seemed to threaten, and to be keeping people at home." The metropolis itself "looked like the moon's capital, shallow, cratered, extinct." The girl quotes a poem about a place called Kor, " 'as high as cliffs and as white as bones, with no history—' " Pepita thinks of it as a refuge, but after she has fallen asleep her roommate speaks to the soldier. The young man has been describing the awe Pepita and he had felt. " '. . . can't wanting,' " Callie protests, " 'want what's human?' " In turn she drifts into unconsciousness, dreaming of her friend's beau. Callie's longing is only an infinitesimal part of "the war's total of unlived lives," yet hers is a momentous dream. The agony of Miss Bowen's youths will never again be entirely private. Their response to what Joseph Conrad called the "inexplicable mysteries of conscious existence" ceases to be a forsaken scream. The breadth of the battlefield, even when illuminated by nothing more than spectral moonlight, at least makes them more aware of the fact that they have a number of comrades, equally beset, equally anxious to liberate themselves from the cancerous ego. (pp. 45-6)

In an age when some of our most brilliant literature constitutes, really, an attack by man against himself, we value in a special way the art of Elizabeth Bowen. Such is the subtlety of her handling of the irreducible particulars with which the artist works, that some have not adequately distinguished among her various spokesmen. Her importance is very great indeed. She teaches us to find life in what casual onlookers might consider peripheral, if not bizarre. She teaches compassion toward the forlorn child, the self-destructive adult, and moral as well as social misfits of all ages. More important still, she helps us to think of them in terms of possibility rather than in terms of dismay. Her mind, as vigorous as it is tactful, never ceases to invite speculation about a whole range of truths beyond those to which she is formally committed. Her world is a place where "mystery" possesses a benign as well as a spooky connotation. "It is to Civilization, not to Nature," Cyril Connolly wrote in another context, "that man must return." In our embattled culture, few have developed a sounder grasp of what the word civilization implies. And in order to insure oneself her company, I am prepared to forgo any number of sinister houses and elegant sonorities. (p. 52)

George Greene, "Elizabeth Bowen: Imagination as Therapy," in Perspective, *Vol. 14, No. 1, Spring, 1965, pp. 41-52.*

EDWARD MITCHELL (essay date 1966)

[*An American critic, Mitchell has edited several short story anthologies. He here provides an overview of Bowen's short fiction, suggesting that the major theme in her stories is the peril involved in both retaining—and losing—one's innocence.*]

One situation to which Elizabeth Bowen consistently devotes her attention is the antithesis between external fact and internal reality, between the objective condition and the projection of an internal world where feeling alone reigns. Innocence in the world of Experience is in Miss Bowen's short fiction not so much the nexus around which the story is developed as it is the situation from which the story progresses. In the novel *The Death of the Heart,* St. Quentin attempts to explain the position of the innocent: "I swear that each of us keeps, battened down inside himself, a sort of lunatic giant—impossible socially, but fullscale—and that it's the knockings and batterings we sometimes hear in each other that keeps our intercourse from utter banality. Portia hears that the whole time; in fact she hears nothing else." The "giant battened down" then is virtually ever present; what Miss Bowen explores is the state of the relation between the romantic imagination—innocence, the giant—and the objective reality to which it ultimately must become reconciled.

In such a story as **"All Saints"** we are presented with a humorous instance in which the giant is definitely not battened down. Mrs. Barrows, "childlike" and "perennial," offers the astonished vicar an enormously expensive stained glass window because it "makes one feel so religious and good." Her unconventional and subjective view of saints and helpfulness reduces the vicar to stuttering out platitudes of orthodoxy: "Error . . . force of example . . . simply a manifestation." Unable to "place" Mrs. Barrows or her offer in any of the accepted conventional contexts, the vicar in desperation turns "on his heel and [flees] through the darkness."

The effects of an unwitting innocence like Mrs. Barrows', preserved through life, are not always so innocuous either for the innocent or her victims. A slightly less happy instance is portrayed in **"Mrs. Moysey."** This secretive little woman who "looks like Christmas Eve every day" is hardly aware of, and little concerned with, the faults of her nephew, Leslie, who unexpectedly arrives to pay her an extended visit. When Leslie suddenly disappears and is replaced by Emerald, the wife he has deserted, with her two small children, Mrs. Moysey absorbs the children—"a bubble or two, some ripples that widened and vanished, then once more above them, its unruffled surface of tranquil secretiveness." Mrs. Moysey, as always, remains locked in her bedroom but the presence of the children there turns her life into "a long agitation, a flutter of happiness." The retreat, however, is not inviolate for Emerald returns, and forcing her way into the bedroom finds the children smeared with chocolate amid a mountain of empty candy boxes listening to Mrs. Moysey's life story, which, the little woman admits, she has touched up here and there. Emerald, "devoid of illusion, sharp with practical understanding," breaks into tears, and Mrs. Moysey, "most unwilling victor . . . most unconvinced voluptuary," does "not know where to look. . . ."

Mrs. Moysey attempts to preserve her innocence behind a locked bedroom door. Amid a confused heap of empty chocolate boxes, she gives unbridled rein to her romantic imagination by writing a doctored account of her own life story. But the door will not remain locked and eventually Mrs. Moysey is made to face some of the less sugary facts of her own situation. Yet, although Mrs. Moysey and Emerald are "shattered" by their final confrontation, one is not led to believe that the damage Mrs. Moysey has done to her victims is irreparable. Preserved innocence can, however, lead to cruelly ruined lives as it does, for example, in **"Queer Heart."** Hilda, though middle-aged, is another innocent. Her face, although embedded in fat, is "as exposed and ingenuous as a little girl's," and she cannot "cure [herself] of the habit of loving life"; but she is an alien in her own home, the victim of what she feels is a "conspiracy" between her daughter Lucille and her sister Rosa.

After the death of Mr. Cadman, Rosa began "flapping round Granville like a doomful bird," and now, dying in an upstairs room, Rosa exerts more influence than ever over the lives of mother and daughter. Yet Rosa's hatred for Mrs. Cadman, and her efforts at alienating mother and daughter stem, as even Mrs. Cadman realizes, from a desire "to protect the interests of Lucille." That Rosa has "a queer heart, eating [itself] out, thanking God for the pain" is undeniable; but when she confronts her sister in the sick room, Hilda Cadman comes to see that innocence, even the justifiable innocence of childhood, can be brutal, and that the naivete, the irresponsibility, the "good time, the real good time" of a middle-aged woman, is not only without justification but appallingly destructive. Because she was once denied a Christmas doll, Rosa has taken Lucille; but the loss of Lucille was only possible because of Mrs. Cadman's "real good time," and too late she thinks "I did that to her [Rosa]; then what have I done to Lucille?"

The giant *not* battened down, innocence preserved, is then one of the thematic patterns in Miss Bowen's collections of short fiction. But this pattern has its corollary: innocence forcibly maintained, the giant in chains. The synthesis between the infinite desire of the romantic imagination and the restrictive pressures of objective fact may never be formed because the innocent is incapable of making the necessary connections between various parts of his experience; or it may never be formed because the innocent is never permitted to encounter an undiluted reality—he is constantly forced to play a role which is not of his own choosing. The giant in chains, innocence forcibly maintained, invariably leads to mental aberrations and destruction either real or symbolic.

One of the effects of being forced to play a role is manifest in **"The Dancing Mistress."** Miss James, who greets her endless dancing classes "with stereotyped little weary amused exclamations" is only a pupil and teacher for Madame Majowski:

> All day long she was just an appearance, a rhythm; in studio or ballroom she expanded into delicate shapes like a Japanese 'mystery' flower dropped into water. Late at night, she stopped *'seeming'* too tired to 'be'; too tired to eat or to speak; she would finish long journeys asleep with her head on the pianist's shoulder: her sister received her with Bovril and put her to bed. Her eyebrows tilted outwards like wings; over her delicate cheekbones looked out, slightly tilted, her dreamy and cold eyes in which personality never awakened.

That her personality is never awakened is felt only too acutely by Lulu, the hotel secretary. His amorous interest in Miss James is dampened because he can find no "self" in her; he asks her "who's there? What's there? *Are* you, at all? I want you." But Miss James' "self" is only capable of being stirred when she is sadistically punishing one of her pupils, like Margery Mannering. Only then does the "unrealized self in her [make] itself felt, disturbing her calm with a little shudder of pleasure. A delicate pink touched her cheekbones, she thought of Lulu, she was almost a woman." But a dancing mistress is the only kind of mistress Joyce James can be; neither she nor Lulu are permitted to have any real selves—"It did not do for Lulu, who showed ladies into their bedrooms, or Joyce who spent hours in clumsy men's arms, to be patently man and woman; their public must deprecate any attraction."

Perversion is the essence of this story; natural and artificial are reversed here as are masculine and feminine names. Miss Peele, the piano player, whose hair is "polished against her skull like a man's," is glad they are out of the fading misty daylight and into the artificial light of the Metropole ballroom—"I'm so glad we've got back to artificial—it seems so much more natural, I think." In response to Lulu's charge of lack of feeling in Joyce, Miss Peele remarks, ". . . we'll forget each other anyhow—that's nature." Because the artificial is natural, because the stereotyped role is the only role permitted her, Miss James' "unrealized self" has only the twisted outlet of sadistic punishment and the release of troubled sleep in which she dreams of telling Margery Mannering, "I'll kill you, I'll kill you."

The result of keeping the giant in chains, of forcibly preventing a contact between the self and the world of fact which it must assimilate and attempt to control, is vividly presented in terms of its effects upon children. Geraldine in **"The Little Girl's Room"** has been allocated the role of "prodigy" by her grandmother. Mrs. Letherton-Channing lies "ambushed in gentleness [and] watched like a lynx for the first tentative emanations of young genius." Tutors are brought to Geraldine, art objects of all kinds are placed before her "till life, for her willful fancy, became an obstacle race." But Geraldine, who tears the living center, the reproductive parts, from the hearts of flowers and crushes the bud of the strawberry, leaving only the calyx, takes part in a nightly ritual unknown to her grandmother. Alone in her room Geraldine calls up "the enemies" who by day are the obsequious hirelings of Mrs. Letherton-Channing, but by night are the "red passions" who approach Geraldine with "knives gleaming," and for whom she waits with "delicious anticipation."

In her "little Italy from Wigmore Street," Geraldine feels "security, feeling for her in the dark, [close] the last of its tentacles on her limbs," while she vainly calls up the masochistic fantasies which are the perverted result of her ardent desire to destroy the suffocating prison in which she is entrapped. But enforced innocence occasionally has its revenge as it does in **"The Easter Egg Party."** The Evers sisters have only one object in view when they invite Hermione to their house for Easter: "to restore her childhood to her." But Eunice and Isabelle themselves lead insular "unperplexed lives"; they know that such things as broken marriages occur, but they refuse to believe such things happen to anyone they know as well as Hermione's mother. These "successful nuns" still receive "intimations of immortality" in a social atmosphere characterized by "inexpensive sociability, liberal politic, shapely antique family furniture, 'interests', enlightened charity." The enforced innocence to which they would subject Hermione is, like their own, an innocence *manqué,* out of touch with any real world. The facts of life from which the sisters would so sedulously guard Hermione—the cat's weaning of her kittens, the natural reproduction of the birds—are stereotyped, superficial, and irrelevant to a girl in whose eyes "existed an alien world of experience." It is love and attention that Hermione needs—"it was their attention she wanted; she collected attention like twists of silver paper or small white pebbles." When she finds it denied she strikes back by stealing the Easter eggs and disrupting the party. Hermione revolts from enforced innocence and retaliates by telling Eunice "you keep on making me take an interest in things, and you never take the slightest interest in me"; and finally she escapes from the sisters leaving "a sort of scar, like a flattened grave, in their hearts."

In another section of *The Death of the Heart,* the narrator, momentarily stepping out of the novel, says, "illusions are art, for the feeling person, and it is by art that we live, if we do." Living, then, becomes the "art" of forming that integration between the self and the world which neither allows the giant complete freedom nor attempts to entomb him by complete repression. But there always exists the possibility of the "illusion of art," the mistaking of the illusion for the art of a balanced integration. This is not a question of innocence, since one half of the equation, experience, the world of fact, has been obliterated. In this case the subjective vision bears no relation to a world outside itself because it recognizes no world outside itself, it is centripetal and self-sufficient. This is the world of hallucination where the terms *innocence* and *experience* are without meaning, because without reference. Here the "illusion" of synthesis has been largely or completely substituted for the "art" of synthesis, and this substitution comprises a second prominent thematic pattern in Miss Bowen's short stories.

The substitution of an illusion for reality may be so gradual, its causes so minute, that it passes nearly undetected, as in the story **"Foothold."** Having recently moved into a new home, with her children away at school, Janet finds that there is "the house, the garden, friends, books, music, letters, the car, golf when one feels like it, going up to town rather a lot." Yet as she tells their house guest, Thomas, "my life—*this* life—seems to have stretched somehow." Janet's life has "stretched" so much that it now includes a ghost, Clara, with which Thomas, Janet, and her husband Gerard are slowly becoming preoccupied. But the ghost seems to be Janet's special property, a mental set become palpable in the form of a presence, an idea which intrigues Thomas who "had guessed her [Janet] capable of an intimacy, something disruptive, something to be driven up like a wedge, first blade-fine, between the controlled mind and the tempered, vivid emotions." To Thomas the idea of Clara is just an idea, a "joke," something to be defined; but to Gerard the matter is more serious—"She's seeing too much of this ghost . . . she wouldn't if things were all right with her." And neither of them realize how "disruptive" the "intimacy" has become until, retiring after a late evening, they are both brought to a halt outside Janet's bedroom door as they hear her saying to Clara, "I can't bear it. How could you bear it? The sickening loneliness. . . ."

Unwittingly, Thomas has put his finger on the source of the illusion which has gained a foothold in Janet when he says, "I've a theory that absolute comfort runs round the circle to the same point as asceticism." Janet's "absolute comfort" has become "sickening loneliness" and only a supernatural presence is now capable of supplying her with any "intimacy." Illusion and the disruption caused in the mind entranced by it can, however, go far beyond the point of a foothold. In such a story as **"Dead Mabelle"** we witness a mind undergoing a complete dislocation from reality. William Stickford, who "never went with a girl," is "intelligent, solitary, self-educated, self-suspicious." Not a frequenter of the cinema, he is finally induced to see the famous Mabelle Pacey, and while he sits with "angry, disordered feeling" watching the black and white world of abstraction, he feels "as though she were a rising flood and his mind bulrushes." After this first encounter with Mabelle, William avoids his friends and makes secretive excursions to the suburbs, even to London, to see one after another of Mabelle's movies because "there was this thing about Mabelle: the way she made love." But suddenly, horribly, Mabelle is killed. For several weeks William is left to face her "absolute dissolution"; yet, for William, Mabelle is not gone, she is "perpetual, untouchable . . . you couldn't break that stillness by the fire; it could shatter time. You might destroy the film, destroy the screen, destroy her body; this endured. She was beyond the compass of one's mind; one's being seemed a fragment and a shadow."

Stumbling from one of the theaters to which he compulsively returns to witness the reruns of Mabelle's films, William puts out a hand in the darkness—"You're here. *You* know *I* know you're here, you proud thing! Standing and looking. Do you see me? . . . You're more here than I. . . ." His vision of Mabelle is now more real than himself. Alone, in his sitting room, in the presence of Mabelle, William is alive, but tomorrow at the bank "that abstraction behind the business of living was due to begin again." Robbed of his "power of being" by the image of Mabelle who "burned brightly on," William slips his hand, in unconscious imitation, into his bureau drawer; but there is no "gesture of pistol to temple, the trail of smoke fugitive over an empty screen" because the drawer is empty of what it should contain: "the means to the only fit gesture that he could have offered her."

William Stickford is capable of "living" only under the obsessive influence of the compelling, dramatic, but artificial cinema actress. Perhaps it is only by illusions that we live, if we do, but it is madness to live *only* in illusion. When his brightly burning hallucination is juxtaposed to the "shabby business of living," William turns to the hallucination; but the shabby business of living is not the only force capable of calling up worlds-within-worlds of hallucination. The inability to face reality may also stem from the fact that that reality has become too horrible to face. Miss Bowen devotes one entire collection of stories to such a reality: the chaos and upheaval of war. In her postscript to ***The Demon Lover*** collection, Miss Bowen notes that when "what was happening was out of all proportion to . . . faculties for knowing, thinking and checking up," people were led down strange paths in search of "indestructible landmarks in a destructible world." Hallucination and illusion provided such landmarks.

"Mysterious Kôr" is one of Miss Bowen's finer renderings of the hallucinations precipitated by war. She defends the hallucinations depicted in this and the other stories in this collection by saying that they "are an unconscious, instinctive, saving resort on the part of the characters: life mechanized by the controls of war-time, and emotionally torn and impoverished by changes, had to complete itself *some* way." For Pepita mysterious Kor is that "*some* way," because it represents the isolation, the withdrawal from time and reality, that are impossible for her and Arthur in an over-crowded and war-torn London. In a world which is "disenchanted," Kor represents that place where "there is not a crack in it anywhere for a weed to grow in," and where "the stairs and arches are built to support themselves." Yet Kor, like the moonlight which drenches London, obliterating niches and shadows as if they were "dissolved in the street by some white acid," is sterile, empty, dead.

Trapped in a world they are incapable of understanding, without a "place to be alone," frustrated in their attempt to enjoy a love which is largely "a collision in the dark," Pepita and Arthur unwillingly return from a walk through the deserted London streets to the small flat Pepita shares with her roommate, Callie. Callie, like her Hindu namesake, sacrifices the last of their frustrated passion on the altar of her "good manners" and "forbearance." Without a boy friend, stiff in her own virginity "like an unlit candle," she does not understand Pepita's attraction to the solitude of mysterious Kor and she demands "Can't wanting want what's human?" But Arthur tells her that "to be human is to be at a dead loss." For Pepita and Arthur, both "at a dead loss," Kor represents the only world which can still be grasped by the imagination. For Pepita, however, it goes beyond this. Kor is both a product of the desiccated world and the final symbolization of Pepita's desire to escape into nonentity. Arthur is the source but not the end of her dream, "he was the password, but not the answer: it was to Kor's finality that she turned."

Mental aberration, perfidious ignorance, abortive love are facts which the individual must recognize without being defeated by them. When the romantic imagination is unable to adjust its subjective vision to the world outside itself, dislocation, aberration, destruction are the consequences. But these same results may be produced not so much by the "batterings and knockings" of the giant subjective self as by the deterioration of accepted social patterns, the crumbling of moral values, a shift or upheaval in that objective world outside the self. This is not the failure to make a synthesis, but rather the failure of a synthesis to conform to the external "facts" which have themselves changed. This is the plight of the disinherited, who can place between themselves and a fallen world neither the shield of their own innocence nor the closed door of hallucination. Their plight forms another of the basic thematic patterns in these short story collections.

One of the processes of familial and moral disinheritance is revealed in **"The Man of the Family."** William, whom his Aunt Luella playfully calls "the man of the family," stops at her Regent's Park house on his way from Oxford to London because his aunt "kept an excellent table." He basks in the warmth of his aunt's admiration and feels "solid" in a family where there are never any grievances. But William suddenly finds his solidity and comfort disrupted by his involvement in his cousin Patsey's third engagement. William's difficulties begin when another cousin, Rachel, tells him that the fiancé, Chummy, "is not a nice man." Rachel discloses that she almost went to Europe with Chummy because "morals are like clothes and I'd scrapped one lot and hadn't found another to suit me." What William finally grasps is that it is not Chummy's morals to which Rachel objects, but to his manners—"It's these little remarks with an edge—you know, spiteful, cutting. He'd skin Patsey alive." William, with his sense of moral values, is non-plussed by Rachel's distinction between "being nasty and being simply immoral"; but he is flatly shocked by his aunt's angry reaction to his condemnation of Chummy. By repeating to himself that "values are relative," William is capable of accepting Rachel's substitution of manners for morals; but because he is incapable of going beyond moral relativity to a point where marriage and materialism become penultimate values, one "man of the family" is replaced by another.

The scope of the disinheritance, the extent of the separation from accepted social relationships and conventional moral values, has its degrees extending from the relatively mild dislocation felt by William to the nearly total isolation presented in **"The Disinherited."** In this story everyone either is or becomes "disinherited." Davina is a *declassé* aristocrat, without money, reduced to exploiting her aunt's affection. "Something that should have occurred—she was not sure what—had not occurred yet, and became every day more unlikely"; and while she waits, she sells herself to Prothero for pocket money. Oliver, like Davina, is without a place in the social structure: "Oliver despised the rich and disliked the poor and drank to the bloody extinction of the middle classes." Prothero is psychologically disinherited. Having killed his mistress to escape the feeling of being "bought up," and having murdered again to lose his identity, Prothero claims to be "his own man." But nightly he is compelled to return to his writing table to exorcise his memory of Anita. His never finished interior monologue, where "the words sprang to their places with deadly complicity," with its hopeless and despairing postscript, reveals a mind enslaved to the very desire it so repeatedly denies.

Woven into the pattern of this social, moral, and psychological disorientation is the life of Marianne Harvey, whose story is an ironic reversal of the Cupid and Psyche tale. Marianne, who "looked like a diffident goddess" with "eyebrows turned up at her temples like impatient wings," half reluctantly, half compulsively, accompanies Davina to a party at Lord Thingummy's. In this "italianate palace" she meets more of Davina's *declassé* friends and confronts her Cupid in the form of Oliver "with his dispirited viking air" who "longed to see himself otherwise, like any other man, with a sound and passionate core." In this rootless and disenchanted atmosphere where "the everyday became cloudy and meaningless and, like a tapestry, full of arrested movement," Marianne is seduced by a passionless and hollow Oliver in whom excitement took its most crippling form. When Marianne returns to the estate, "her serenity, mild good spirits and love of home" are gone—she forgets to change the water in the chrysanthemums, the dogs are not exercised. "Her faculty for disapproval seemed to be all used up," she cannot face her husband, "she was disoriented; she did not know."

Near the end of **"The Disinherited"** Davina, on one of her solitary walks, thinks: "One is empowered to live fully: occasion does not offer." Some of these sufferers of disorientation, like Prothero, are of course not "empowered to live fully"; while for some, like Davina and Marianne, the social structure, the established order, no longer provides them scope, "occasion does not offer." This relationship between the individual and the world outside himself to which he is attempting to adjust is never a static one. The emphasis, however, often falls on the fact that "occasion does not offer," especially when the established order which comprises the "occasion" is itself in a state of upheaval.

"Summer Night" is an exploration of the relation of the ego, the self, to a world in which values have been destroyed and the dependable patterns of social and familial relationships dislocated. As William Heath has pointed out, the entire story is played against the backdrop of the ultimate dislocation resulting from war. But the war *per se* is only one chaotic and destructive element among many in this story and they are all symbolized by the "summer night" which dominates the story from its opening at sunset to its bitter and dreamlike close at midnight.

In his conversation with Robinson, Justin Cavey, the impotent and tortured intellectual, says, "Scrap 'me'; scrap my wretched identity and you'll bring to the open some bud of life. I *not* 'I'—I'd be the world." But as Justin discovers, the "I" dies hard; one's "wretched identity" cannot be scrapped, it can only be continually immolated in a world in which it cannot orient itself. Only Robinson, the uncontemplative man of action working at high pressure in his factory office or shooting off in his highpowered car, and Queenie, the deaf woman, "contemplative, wishless, almost without an 'I' " are capable of withstanding the forces of chaos from without and within.

Emma, "farouche, with her tentative little swagger and childish, pleading air of delinquency," succumbs to her sexual drives and under pretence of a visit leaves her husband and children to drive to a meeting with her lover, Robinson. She attempts to justify what she recognizes as an aberration of behavior by seeing it as a romantic adventure, a "pilgrimage"; but in Robinson's house of tile, chromium, and switches, she finds that his behavior is as mindless and mechanical as his factory and motorcar—"her adventure became the quiet practice with him." Emma's attempt to adjust her inner self to an act which will destroy all preexisting values and standards is crushed by Robinson's "stern, experienced delicacy." He forces her to see their meeting for what it is—"she thought for a minute he had broken her heart, and she knew now he had broken her fairytale."

The revelation of chaos and dislocation to which Aunt Fran is subjected is of a different but no less destructive kind. Always afraid of the "wakeful night" she eagerly awaits the barring and locking of the house, but, as she discovers, this does not prevent the shadow rising "up the cathedral tower, up the side of the pure hill." When she and her nephew, the major, hear noises from upstairs, Aunt Fran demands to go and see. Pushing open the door of Emma's bedroom, she finds Vivie, the carbon copy of her mother, bouncing on Emma's empty bed, her naked body covered with chalk pictures of snakes and stars, while "all her senses stood up wanting to run the night." Unlike Emma, Vivie is locked in, but this does not prevent her from stepping over the "one arbitrary line [which] divided this child from the animal."

Later, in her own room, Aunt Fran, "capable of no act . . . undone," feels that the war, the night, Vivie's nascent sexuality are all related:

> There are no more children: the children are born knowing. The shadow rises up the cathedral tower, up the side of the pure hill. There is not even the past: our memories share with us the infected zone; not a memory does not lead up to this. Each moment is everywhere, it holds the war in its crystal; there is no elsewhere, no other place. Not a benediction falls on this apart house of the Major; the enemy is within it, creeping about. Each heart here falls to the enemy.

The old aunt, "stranded here like some object on a spool that has run dry," finds that her values and standards, her Victorian morality, are anachronistic; she discovers that her "china kittens, palm crosses, three Japanese monkeys, *bambini,* Lincoln Imp, merry thought pen-wiper, [and] ivory spinning wheel from Cologne" are not enough to protect her in a world where even "our memories share with us the infected zone."

Justin Cavey, like Emma and Aunt Fran, is a victim of the "summer night." Locked in by the war, separated from the historical, cultural, intellectual traditions of a France, Germany, Italy which are no more, Justin retreats to the "impersonal, patient look of the thinker." His only defense is talk, but the casual inattentiveness of Robinson, and the "solitary and almost fairy-like world created by [his sister's] deafness" crush this defense and leave him "to face the screen of his own mind, on which the distortion of every one of his images, the war-broken towers of Europe, constantly stood." Justin's attraction to Robinson is nearly homosexual and certainly symptomatic of his relation to his dislocated world. Unable to adjust to the "fair, smiling, offhand, cold-minded man" or his mistress "crouching in her crouching car in the dark," Justin is reduced to the impotent action of writing Robinson a letter ending their friendship and condemning his "never failing imperviousness."

Queenie, Justin's deaf sister, is simultaneously the antithesis to and complement of Robinson. Unlike Robinson, Queenie, although deaf, is capable of intuiting subtle shifts in the emotional atmosphere and the "things she said out of nowhere, things with no surface context, were never quite off the mark." Yet "almost without an 'I' " she lives in a soundless world of her own, feeding on the memories of a single meeting with a lover in whose place she has, for this evening, substituted Robinson. Queenie is immured in her memories, Robinson in his imperviousness; as Justin puts it, "she does not hear with her ears, he does not hear with his mind." Neither of them see any need for "a new form for thinking or feeling" for they are not aware of the destruction of the old.

While it might be argued that all of Elizabeth Bowen's short fiction deals with the relationship of innocence to experience, the complexity of that relationship should not be overlooked. The tension between the self and the world of external fact is, as Miss Bowen treats it, never simple or static. While her stories often depict a failure of synthesis or assimilation, the blame, if that word is appropriate, is never wholly to be placed at a single door. It is just as possible that the apparently objective and trustworthy world will betray the individual, as it is that the individual will fail to adjust to his world. The variations in thematic patterns of her short fiction suggest that cause, not verdict, is Elizabeth Bowen's concern. And if she most often turns her attention to failures, she does so in the interest of success. (pp. 41-54)

Edward Mitchell, "Themes in Elizabeth Bowen's Short Stories," in Critique: Studies in Modern Fiction, *Vol. VIII, No. 3, Spring-Summer, 1966, pp. 41-54.*

T. O. BEACHCROFT (essay date 1968)

[Beachcroft is an English short story writer, novelist, poet, and critic. In the following excerpt from his critical survey of the short story, he briefly discusses Bowen's short fiction and compares her with such writers as James Joyce, Henry James, and Katherine Mansfield.]

[Elizabeth Bowen] does not, like Joyce, practise a conscious meanness of style. She is for the most part writing about more sophisticated people, yet she uses her own brilliance of observation, her own arresting imagery, to bring scenes and people to life. The two unmarried sisters, for instance, in **"The Easter Egg Party"**:

> Eunice and Isabelle Evers were both just over fifty: their unperplexed lives showed in their faces, lined only by humour, and in their frank, high foreheads. They were Amazons in homespuns, Amazons, without a touch of deprivation or pathos; their lives had been one long vigorous walk. Like successful nuns, they both had a slightly married air.

This suggests a certain aloofness on the part of the author, a standing apart from her characters. She is not afraid, as Katherine Mansfield was, of saying 'something clever'. **"The Easter Egg Party"** tells the story of the quite unsuccessful attempt of the two country spinsters to assuage the boredom and also the distress of a town-dwelling girl of eleven who they think has been through some 'unspeakable' experience. In the fiasco of Hermione's visit both points of view are seen with understanding. The Misses Evans are really distressed on Hermione's account; Hermione wants simply to go home, and, missing every conceivable point about their efforts to be kind to her, says, 'Couldn't you get some other girl to stay with you?'

The brilliantly lighted sets and the air of light banter does not pass into sarcasm or rebuke of her characters. Elizabeth Bowen is capable of saying something clever that is also something friendly. That she can truly share her characters' emotions is shown in the small, single-scene story called **"Tears, Idle Tears,"** in which a boy of seven shames his very brave and soignée widowed mother by weeping hopelessly in Regent's Park.

> Frederick stumbled along beside her, too miserable to notice. His mother seldom openly punished him, but often revenged herself on him in small ways. He could feel just how this was. His own incontinence in the matter of tears was as shocking to him, as bowing-down, as annulling, as it could be to her.
>
> He never knew what happened—a cold black pit with no bottom opened inside himself; a red-hot bellwire jagged up through him from the pit of his frozen belly to the caves of his eyes. Then the hot gummy rush of tears, the convulsion of his features, the terrible square grin he felt his mouth take all made him his own shameful and squalid enemy.

The mother walks on in front, disowning her awful child, and he is braced up by a complete stranger, shabby in contrast to his mother and quite practical: she treats his outburst in a most matter-of-fact way, and says she has a young brother who has just the same trouble.

If this small story has a flaw it is to be found in the suggested explanation of the boy's hysteria, making him a prime object for later deep analysis. That kind of thing belongs very much to the psycho-analytical fashion of the twenties and thirties, and the mother, the child, and the stranger are all the story needs, without the embedded Freudian footnote.

In her sensitivity to colours, sounds, and impressions, Elizabeth Bowen challenges comparison with Katherine Mansfield. On the other hand, her own emotions are considerably more balanced than those of Katherine Mansfield. Even when she was young, she had as an author far more sophistication. She often writes about family groups and homes in which complicated situations may have arisen. She has a unique gift for catching the atmosphere of houses as if they were characters in the story. Outwardly the people in these houses are serene and calm, but they move towards outbreaks. She likes to show the civilized surface with the tensions underneath, approaching a nervous breakdown; yet in the end that crisis may never reach the point of an outbreak. It may seem a strange comparison to mention the long-winded Henry James at this point, but if one could distil out of "The Aspern Papers" or "The Real Thing" some elixir in a few pages, one would find the kind of situation that Elizabeth Bowen brilliantly condenses. In fact she herself refers to the influence of Henry James and at times her art moves towards the over-contrived 'situation' or towards spooks, as James's did also.

Here is the close of **"Joining Charles,"** the title story from Miss Bowen's second volume of short stories. Louise, the wife of Charles, is staying with her husband's mother and sisters in the family house. She is going to join Charles in Lyons, and the whole surface of the story is taken up with the chilly, nerve-stretched atmosphere of early rising and preparing for departure. Louise is petite and dainty and seems rather childish, surrounded by her larger, more boisterous sisters-in-law, and her efficient mother-in-law. They are kind to Louise, anxiously trying to break her precise reserve, yet never approaching her directly.

> Out in the dark hall Mother was bending over the pile of boxes, reading and re-reading the labels upside down and from all aspects. She often said that labels could not be printed clearly enough. As Louise hurried past she stood up, reached out an arm and caught hold of her. Only a little light came down from the staircase window: they could hardly see each other. They stood like two figures in a picture, without understanding, created to face one another.
>
> 'Louise,' whispered Mother, 'if things should be difficult—Marriage isn't easy. If you should be disappointed—I know, I feel—you do understand? If Charles—'
>
> 'Charles?'
>
> 'I do love you, I do. You would tell me?'
>
> But Louise, kissing her coldly and gently, said: 'Yes, I know. But there isn't, really, Mother, anything to tell.'

Throughout this story we see the subtlety and feeling for tentative communication typical of James, crystallized in a way that he never approached. (pp. 182-85)

T. O. Beachcroft, "The Twenties and Thirties," in his The Modest Art: A Survey of the Short Story in English, *Oxford University Press, London, 1968, pp. 176-95.*

ALLAN E. AUSTIN (essay date 1971)

[*In the following excerpt from his book-length critical survey of Bowen, Austin traces the prominent characteristics of Bowen's short stories in a detailed overview of her short fiction.*]

[Elizabeth] Bowen's stories appear to fall naturally enough into three main thematic groupings, and a discussion of her best eighteen or so stories gives a fair indication of her talent for diversification within her relatively narrow concerns. (p. 93)

By and large, the protagonists are sensitive, educated, well-mannered females moving through a reasonably well-to-do world. The point of view is almost always omniscient, and most stories include generous portions of dialogue. All but a few contain incisive but impressionistic descriptive passages which help to establish and sustain mood and tone. Many of the stories show a greater freedom in their handling of time than the novels. The interplay between present and past time (not readily conveyed by analyses), along with elliptical conversation and terse narrative details, contributes to a "difficult" and challenging style. Not a writer given to concessions, Miss Bowen says: "I expect the reader to be as (reasonably) imaginative as myself." The stories employ what the author calls "a free form," which she describes as "impressionism lightly laced with psychology. . . ." There are times, especially in ***The Demon Lover*** collection, when we might wish to amend this statement to read, "heavily laced with psychology."

It is on the matter of psychology that Miss Bowen's stories differ most from her longer fiction. Her better short stories, on the whole, investigate psychological states (what the author calls "fantasy") which are more unusual than those portrayed in the novels. (p. 94)

"Ivy Gripped the Steps" is a frame story which encompasses a full evocation of a past time. The present Gavin Doddington has been damaged by a past experience which he has never forgotten but which he has never been able to bypass emotionally. In the beginning, he literally returns to the locale which has caused him such pain because it once had brought him such joy. The setting is seaside Southstone in the closing days of World War II. Coastal wartime conditions have hastened the decay which had already come to the street in which the handsome Mrs. Nicholson lived when Gavin came as a delicate boy for two summers. In her day, the street was "one of the best residential avenues" in the city.

In Nathaniel Hawthorne's terms, Gavin has been victimized by the worst of all sins: the manipulation of one human being by another. The sanctity of his heart was invaded by the alluring young widow. His days with Lilian Nicholson were the high point of his young life until the day he overheard a conversation between her and another of her acquaintances and learned he has been "used."

The son of a poor farmer, Gavin is invited to the seaside home for his health because his mother was a girlhood friend of Lilian. Coming from the hard Midland's life, Gavin finds the wealth and style of Lilian's fashionable Southstone exotic. Within the capacities of a young boy, he falls in love with her, and Lilian does nothing to discourage his intense but obviously uncomprehended feelings. At least in one instance she responds to him as fully as he could wish when she cries, "Why do I stay on and on here; what am I doing? Why don't we go right away somewhere, Gavin; you and I?"

Gavin's traumatic experience occurs when he overhears Admiral Concannon, a married man in whom Lilian has sought to provoke interest in herself, clarifying his position for her:

> I see, now, where you are in your element. You know as well as I do what your element is; which is why there's nothing more to be said. Flirtation has always been off my beat—so far off my beat, as a matter of fact, that I didn't know what it was when I first saw it. There, no doubt, I was wrong. If you can't live without it, you cannot, and that is that. If you have to be dangled after, you no doubt will be. But don't, my dear girl, go for that to the wrong shop. It would have been enough, where I am concerned, to watch you making a ninnie of that unfortunate boy."
>
> "Who, poor little funny Gavin?" said Mrs. Nicholson. "Must I have nothing?—I have no little dog."

Gavin, now an aging bachelor, finds Mrs. Nicholson's old home deserted and in the grips of ivy: "The process of strangulation could be felt . . ."; and, "one could have convinced oneself that the ivy must be feeding on something inside the house." Appropriately, the word "gripped" is also linked with Gavin to describe the nature of his living: "Despair, the idea that his doom must be never, never to reach her, not only now but ever, gripped him and gripped his limbs. . . ." Gavin's experience links him, of course, with the young heroines of the novels whose romantic dreams are shattered and betrayed by the adult world. But Gavin's betrayal is carried to its uttermost conclusion; the death that Emmeline suffers in *To the North* is to be preferred to the lifetime of hell endured by Gavin who has "the face of somebody dead who [is] still there . . . under an icy screen, of a whole stopped mechanism for feeling."

"The Disinherited" is both one of Miss Bowen's longest stories and one of her most detailed depictions of corruption. At the center of the narrative is Davina Archworth, twenty-nine, who is "idle with a melancholy and hollow idleness. . . ." Without money or life of her own, she has come to live off an elderly aunt whose house sits on a rise overlooking a university town. This situation brings Davina into contact with two others, Prothero, Mrs. Archworth's chauffeur, and Marianne Harvey, a quiet "modern" wife who lives in one of many new homes being built on an estate above the town.

Underlying the story is the theme of mutability. The season is autumn, appropriate to the images of decay which abound; the atmosphere is decadent. Davina takes Marianne to a surreptitious party at a big house where the owner is absent, where mustiness abounds, and where there are no bulbs in the grand saloon because the owner is "as poor as a rat." Much is also made of the rawness of the new housing development; it is without lawns, but with "half made roads, like the first knowing cuts of a scalpel. . . ." At the very close of the story, when Davina has been walking by herself and has decided to leave her aunt's and move on, though she has no place to go, she watches as "two men came uphill her way, stopped and debated: they were surveyors coming to peg out a new road." Times are changing, and Davina finds herself neither a member in good standing of the old order nor a candidate for the new. One of the disinherited, she is like the grass on the new homes estate: "wiry grass that had lost its nature, being no longer meadow and not yet lawn."

Davina sees herself as an aristocrat without the means. She believes it is money she wants, though it is more likely power. She began with money, but "love affairs and her other expensive habits had ruined her." The thought of money pulses through her mind like the undercurrent chanting of "There must be more money" which recurs in D. H. Lawrence's most telling tale of money madness, "The Rocking-Horse Winner." The narrator says of Davina: "Her thoughts were almost all angry. 'If I had money—' she said again and again."

It is money which brings her into close contact with Prothero. Offering kisses in return, she borrows from him. He too is corrupt, and almost instinctively she recognizes him as a criminal. Like her, Prothero can not have what he wants; and his story comments upon hers and suggests that her disinheritance is not simply material or sociological but is also psychological. Prothero once had an affair with a married woman whom he loved to distraction; but she came to spurn him and, in his agony and frustration, he smothered her. Now he spends his evenings writing letters to her of purported disdain, which are betrayed by anguished postscripts, "Anita I love you Anita, Anita where are you? . . . come back, where are you, I won't hurt you, come back, come back, come back—"

The borrowing of money from Prothero and the kisses are simply a measure of Davina's decay. At one point in the story she says, "I hate having no power." Near the close, she threatens Prothero with dismissal; but he already has "too much on her." She has no power over even the likes of him. Hers is, and will continue to be, a study in self-betrayal.

The only person Davina can manipulate is Marianne, who is, initially at least, flattered by Davina's attention. To Davina, Marianne's life and new home are "mullish," and the whole housing development is "hygienic and intellectual." For her part, Marianne loves her home, is proud of it, and is a serene wife of "mild good spirits." Her husband, Matthew, fifteen years her senior, is another who is conscious of change: ". . . he saw how his friends grew grayer, how their sentiments creaked, and, with dismay for himself, dreaded to desiccate. He clung to his wife's everfreshness, her touch of the vine leaf." The Harveys have two sons away at school.

The story's major dramatic scene is the party to which Davina takes Marianne while her husband is in London. Her limited contact with Davina has already infected her: "Marianne's heart was set on this evening's pleasure, this fantastic setting-out. In these weeks of knowing Davina her faculty for disapproval seemed to be all used up. She was under a spell." Yet it is clear she is not completely benumbed, for at the start and recurringly throughout the subsequent adventures of the evening, she "wished herself safe at home." The party is composed of a motley crew, Davina's crowd, of men and women who are also caught between desire and impossibility of fulfillment. Principal among them is Oliver, the man with whom Davina was once in love and who is to seduce Marianne before the party's end. He exists by cataloguing the libraries of big homes and hence his presence at "Lord Thingummy's" and the possibility for the party in the Lord's absence. As with Davina, "the old order left him stranded, the new offered him no place." For Oliver, the stout Purdon, the oldish platinum blonde Miriam, and the others, the party is little more than an occasion for the sharing of mutual pain. The images imply they are in hell: "Now, each immobile from poverty, each frozen into their settings like leaves in the dull ice of different puddles, they seldom met." Such descriptives as "horrid," "empty," "askew," "bald," "vacuity," "yawning," "chill," "peevish," "muffled," "tarnished," and "congested" pile up.

Oliver, "a broken-spirited Viking," wanders off through the house with an uncertain Marianne. Eventually, he cries for her, and he seemingly seduces her. As he recollects the next morning, "he had unwillingly, deluded her with tears. . . ." In a nice touch, the story gives the scene the following day in which Marianne meets her husband at the station and returns home with him. The occasion is typical of Miss Bowen in its elliptical, tense, and deliciously suggestive nature. Having settled into the living room, Matthew says, "I think . . . I must get my glasses changed! 'Changed?' said Marianne, starting." What we are left speculating about is the impact of the previous night upon Marianne's future. She is conscious of change, and Matthew detects something: " 'What's the matter?' he said. 'You're not quite yourself.' 'Perhaps I have got a slight chill.' " Mutability, then, both physical and metaphysical, is the way of life. Among Miss Bowen's shorter fiction, **"The Disinherited"** is one of her most telling portrayals of the pain change can inflict—and of the human incapacity for adapting to it.

Everyone has met people whom he would love to shake or shock in some manner—people who are complacent, self-righteous, self-satisfied, or self-important. Miss Bowen shares these impulses, and a group of her stories shows her administering some artistic shaking up. At the center of each of these tales is an individual whose attitudes to or whose views about life are called into question. The action revolves around an "opportunity" presented to him for self-discovery or self-judgment. Generally, the opportunity comes suddenly in the form of a shock—a mental or emotional jolt designed to be salutary. As with each grouping, stories typical of my generalizations (such as **"The Working Party"**) give way to skillful variations. In **"The Jungle,"** for example, the challenge to a particular outlook is cumulative rather than sudden. **"Shoes: An International Episode"** enjoys a particularly sardonic ending for the very reason that the administered attack proves insufficient to unseat the resident smugness. One of Miss Bowen's best stories, the frequently anthologized **"The Queer Heart,"** displays a most astute switch and gains force by confronting the reader with a complex problem of judgment; the character under attack is wonderfully appealing, and the individuals surrounding her are otherwise. (pp. 101-05)

Mrs. Cadman of **"The Queer Heart"** is the most fully evoked character in Miss Bowen's short fiction—and also one of the most trying to judge. Stout, good-natured, not inclined to worry, she has lived a happy life, enjoyed herself, found happiness with her equally easygoing husband, who is now deceased. As first introduced to us, she seems perfectly harmless: we smile at her as do several fellow passengers on her bus, and we understand why she is considered something of a character. Gradually, the story uncovers the wider implications of her life and nature.

The occasion of the story is her sister Rosa's visit to Mrs. Cadman and her grown daughter Lucille. This older sister, who is in her stringent manner, antithetical to Mrs. Cadman has taken to such semiannual trips only since the death of Mr.

Cadman, who did not care for her dour outlook. Mrs. Cadman does not enjoy these visits since her severe daughter, normally tolerable to live with, and Rosa join forces to criticize her. This time not only has Rosa come, but she has taken seriously ill; and, if Lucille is correct, she is on the verge of death.

When Mrs. Cadman is seen in her house, it becomes necessary to revise the initial assessment of her. It is evident, finally, that both Rosa and Lucille are a consequence of Mrs. Cadman's life. Lucille suffers in her sensitivity because her mother's public appearance and conduct are a constant source of embarrassment, while her self-indulgent ways absorb her capacity for love. The mother-daughter relationship exists in reverse. Mrs. Cadman's sheepishness, her piggishness with candy, and her banging of doors are all reminiscent of a child rather than of an aging woman. Her face, in fact, is "as ingenuous as a little girl's," while her vanity over tight pumps is girlish.

The key scene is a confrontation between the sisters. Mrs. Cadman seeks to avoid a bedside visit as she has most likely sidestepped anything unpleasant all her life. In a way, we can empathize with Mrs. Cadman since Rosa proves a bitter individual whose lifelong jealousy and self-righteous attitude to her sister have corroded her. In this interview, Rosa reveals when and why she first consciously assumed her rigid stance. When both were little children one Christmastime, Mrs. Cadman had asked for and received a doll Rosa had longed to have. Recounting the scene of which Mrs. Cadman has no recollection, Rosa, quite unappealingly says, "I could have fretted, seeing you take everything. One thing, then another. But I was shown. God taught me to pity you." The scene brings some measure of insight to Mrs. Cadman; for she thinks, "I did that to her; then what have I done to Lucille?"

Mrs. Cadman has lived the unexamined life, symbolized perhaps by her act of backing off the bus; but there is uncertainty as to the extent she may be blamed. She has been akin to the blue-eyed, golden-haired people Thomas Mann's protagonists admire and long to be. Rosa recalls her younger sister's great beauty and popularity: "They were taken with you." Mrs. Cadman also has affinities with Dinah Delecroix of *The Little Girls* who, by virtue of her attractiveness, has been well looked after and allowed to bypass the humanizing shocks of life.

Different as it is in subject matter, D. H. Lawrence's fine story, "Odour of Chrysanthemums," is very close to the final configuration of **"The Queer Heart."** Mrs. Cadman's illumination before Rosa parallels that of Elizabeth Bates before her dead husband's body.

Few short-story themes have proven more fruitful for Miss Bowen than that of dislocation. Sensitive people, she observes, do not suffer the disintegration of their world lightly; they frequently react, seemingly involuntarily, in strange and unexpected ways when it is threatened. The irrational within appears to answer the call of chaos and of the irrational without; or, as Miss Bowen has said, "one counteracts fear with fear, stress with stress." Miss Bowen had employed the theme of dislocation earlier; but, with the coming of World War II, it fully engaged her imagination. The stories written in wartime London and published as ***The Demon Lover*** have dislocation as their major concern. (pp. 112-13)

The title story of ***The Demon Lover*** is typical of several other items in the collection because the protagonist is a woman whose mind reverts to a highly localized past. **"The Demon Lover"** is a ghost story which builds up and then culminates like an Alfred Hitchcock movie. A woman, in London for the day, stops briefly at her closed London home. The woman is Mrs. Kathleen Drover, who "went round to her shut-up house for several things she wanted to take away." Surprisingly, a letter addressed to her awaits her on the hall table. This is strange on two counts: her mail is now directed by the post office to her country address; no one knew she would be calling at the house this day. The enclosed message staggers Mrs. Drover.

In an inset scene from the past, Kathleen is with her soldier fiancée in August, 1914; it is evening, and they are saying goodbye in a garden. In the context of the story, some of the soldier's comments carry an ominous ring: " 'I shall be with you,' he said, 'sooner or later. You won't forget that. You need do nothing but wait.' " Several years pass before Kathleen marries William Drover. This past provides a context for the letter which Mrs. Drover finds awaiting her with the date of the current day, though in the story the letter dramatically precedes the flashback: "Dear Kathleen: You will not have forgotten that today is our anniversary, and the day we said. The years have gone by at once slowly and fast. In view of the fact that nothing has changed, I shall rely upon you to keep your promise. I was sorry to see you leave London, but was satisfied that you would be back in time. You may expect me, therefore, at the hour arranged. Until then. . . ."

Stunned by this letter signed "K," and caught up in "rapidly heightening apprehension," she cries: "The hour arranged. . . . My God . . . *what* hour? How should I . . .? After twenty-five years. . . . " The narrator observes: "The desuetude of her former bedroom, her married London home's whole air of being a cracked cup from which memory, with its reassuring power had either evaporated or leaked away, made a crisis—and at just this crisis the letterwriter had, knowledgeably, struck." That she may not be alone occurs to Mrs. Drover; but, as a dependable mother and wife, she determines not to return to her family without the items she has come to fetch. She decides to slip out, get a cab, and bring the driver back to the house with her while she collects what is wanted.

Cautiously, she leaves the house and finds a single taxi waiting in the taxi rank at the corner. She climbs in, and the taxi begins to move off. Mrs. Drover taps on the glass—the driver turns around: "Through the aperture driver and passenger, not six inches between them, remained for an eternity eye to eye. Mrs. Drover's mouth hung open for some seconds before she could issue her first scream. After that she continued to scream and to beat with her gloved hands on the glass all around as the taxi accelerating without mercy, made off with her into the hinterland of deserted streets." (pp. 117-18)

The central intelligence of **"The Happy Autumn Fields"** is a young woman, Mary. She is another of ***The Demon Lover*** protagonists who seek salvation from the pressures of wartime London by almost involuntary theatrics of the mind. Mary has returned to the bomb-weakened residence that was home before the blitz, despite the protestations of her fiancée, Travis. She has returned to seek—what? Travis half understands and half does not, but he is correct when he tells her, "You don't like it here. Your self doesn't like it." But it is evident he lacks full insight into her action when he adds, "Your will keeps driving your self, but it can't be driven the whole way—it makes its own get out: sleep." Mary is one of Miss

Bowen's chief illustrations of "fighting fear with fear." Evidently her personally recognizable inner being has been dissipated in her own eyes through the depersonalization resulting from sharing in community tension. The return "home" signifies her deep-felt need to possess and experience a private emotional life. This she acquires vicariously and, in so doing, gains not the "sleep" anticipated by Travis but the awakeness resulting from a fresh sense of self.

Home, with its own private store of history and drama, aids Mary by casting before her an old box of letters dating from mid-Victorian times. Mary's mind seizes upon this correspondence as a script for the drama she creates in her mind. We are well into the story of a memorable day in the life of a well-to-do gentleman farmer's family before a break occurs to reveal that it is taking place in Mary's consciousness. Travis has arrived to urge her to leave; and she, eager to play out her story, angrily sends him away. Sensing that the letters she has put aside are contributing to her unsettled state, he carries them off. Mary, however, has sufficient material to sustain her visionary dream and resumes it until the jarring repercussions of an exploding bomb once more brings a halt.

By now, Mary has had the experience which will sustain her; and, when Travis returns, she is ready to leave with him. She now explains what has been troubling her: "We only know inconvenience now, not sorrow." And, telling him of her dream, she adds, "I cannot forget the climate of those hours. Or life at that pitch, eventful—not happy, no, but strung like a harp." But she bemoans the fact that he removed the letters so that she has been "left with a fragment torn out of a day. . . ." As it so happens, Travis has been reading the letters and is therefore able to provide the information which completes Mary's knowledge.

The past narrative of the letters centers upon the theme of mutability and presents three variations of it: the natural change of the seasons, the threat of emotional dislocation which accompanies growing up, and the sudden thrust of accidental death. The change of seasons provides the immediate occasion for the action. It is the day before a new school term; and, since two sons of the family, Robert and Lucius, are to depart before the day is out, the family is having a farewell walk across the fields which compose "the estate the brothers [will] not see again for so long." Sarah, the second eldest sister and the character whose being Mary inhabits, is walking with her younger sister Henrietta. The girls have been the most intimate and congenial of friends, and their relationship is the emotional center of the story; on this day Sarah first realizes that she is in love with Eugene, the friend of her eldest brother Fitzgeorge, and that her present liaison with Henrietta must inevitably alter. As she and Henrietta walk, Fitzgeorge and Eugene ride up, and the latter dismounts to walk beside Sarah.

Later, when the family has gathered in the parlor, Eugene included, Henrietta makes it evident to Sarah that she understands what has happened and what is happening. She is the stronger of the two sisters, and, "It had always been she who with one fierce act destroyed any toy that might be outgrown." This statement carries an ominous note of foreshadowing, but this fact does not become apparent until Travis takes over from Mary to complete the story. He tells of a letter written to Robert by Fitzgeorge in his old age recalling the time a friend (who in the context must be Eugene) who was killed one evening in a fall from his horse while riding away from a visit. In the letter, Fitzgeorge says he has always wondered "what made the horse shy in those empty fields." Earlier in the narrative, much is made of the white handkerchief Henrietta waves in the fields when she and Sarah first sight Fitzgeorge and Eugene riding toward them. This incident, in conjunction with the hints of Henrietta's impulsive and decisive nature, suffice to suggest what or who distracted Eugene's horse. The drama of the family letters, or more precisely Henrietta's perverse motivation and Sarah's evident tragedy, prove salutary for Mary. She takes evident satisfaction in being able to tell Travis, "I have had a sister called Henrietta."

Though the relationship between Mary and her dream and its significance have been stressed, the rich evocation of the earlier time and the delicate rendering of the emotional undercurrent between Sarah and her sister give this story its engaging intensity. This ability to project in a brief compass the flesh and anatomy of a completely realized world makes Elizabeth Bowen a superior short-story writer. This ability reaches its zenith in **"The Happy Autumn Fields," "The Disinherited," "Her Table Spread," "Summer Night,"** and **"Ivy Gripped the Steps."** While Miss Bowen has been well treated by short-story anthologists in recent years, it is regrettable that each of these works, excepting **"Her Table Spread,"** is of a length which editors must generally forego. (pp. 120-22)

Allan E. Austin, in his Elizabeth Bowen, *Twayne Publishers, Inc., 1971, 134 p.*

DOUGLAS A. HUGHES (essay date 1973)

[*In the following excerpt from his discussion of "The Demon Lover," Hughes asserts that the story is a psychological study, not the "ghost" story many believe it to be. His contention was refuted by Daniel V. Fraustino (see Additional Bibliography).*]

In a recent study of Elizabeth Bowen, Allan E. Austin has written, "**'The Demon Lover'** is a ghost story that builds up and then culminates like an Alfred Hitchcock movie [see excerpt dated 1971]." This misreading of Miss Bowen's unforgettable story is, to judge from my experience with student interpretations, fairly common. Far from being a supernatural story, **"The Demon Lover"** is a masterful dramatization of acute psychological delusion, of the culmination of paranoia in a time of war. Because the narrative point of view is restricted to that of the patently disturbed protagonist, Mrs. Kathleen Drover, some readers may see, as the character herself certainly does, the ominous return of a ghostly lover. But in contrast to Mrs. Drover's irrational belief that she is watched and in peril, the narrator subtly but clearly indicates why the forty-four year-old woman suddenly loses her tenuous hold on reality at this particular moment and succumbs to madness.

In the English ballad **"The Demon Lover,"** an inconstant woman betrays her absent lover and marries another man; but when the ostensibly wealthy lover returns years later, the woman is quick to abandon her husband and children. Too late, she discovers the lover is, in fact, the devil. Miss Bowen's story superficially resembles the ballad, and the author even relies upon the poem to suggest how Mrs. Drover views herself. In reality, however, Mrs. Drover is decidedly not a faithless woman and there is no spectral figure come from the nether world to claim her. Like all the characters in the collection of stories ***Ivy Gripped the Steps*** (published first in London as ***The Demon Lover***), Mrs. Drover is simply an indirect casualty of war. In the First World War, at the age of nineteen, she lost her fiancé, precipitating her first emotional collapse, which lasted for thirteen years. Twenty-five years later the air war in Britain has the devastating psychological effect of depriving Mrs. Drover of her recent past. War divests her of the memory of those years that separated her from the feelings of loss and guilt she experienced at the news of her fiancé's disappearance. War, not a vengeful lover, is the demon that overwhelms this rueful woman. (p. 411)

From the first paragraph of the story the narrator begins to attenuate and ultimately to efface the significance of the landmarks and objects Mrs. Drover associates with her recent past. Returning to the bomb-damaged and shut-up Drover house in London by her familiar street, she is struck by the "unfamiliar queerness which had silted up." The whole neighborhood, which would have been animated with life in earlier years, stands silent and deserted. When Mrs. Drover pushes into the house "dead air came out to meet her as she went in," and she "was more perplexed than she knew" by the scene before her. Looking at the empty drawing room with its cold, dead hearth, she observes the traces of the life she and her family had left there: the smoke stain on the mantelpiece, the ring left by a vase on a table, the bruise left by a door handle on the wall, and the scratches left by a piano on the parquet. "Though not much dust had seeped in, each object wore a film of another kind; and, the only ventilation being the chimney, the whole drawing-room smelled of the cold hearth." The smell of ashes and the film covering the objects suggests the awareness of time, the presence of death. As anyone who has revisited a *deserted* former residence knows, the experience can be unsettling. For Mrs. Drover, psychologically maimed and predisposed to a sense of loss, the return to the house is a shattering revelation, a threshold experience that activates her dormant hysteria. In fact, Miss Bowen explicitly utilizes the war-damaged house as an objective correlative of Mrs. Drover's psychological state on this August evening. Early in the story we read, "There were some cracks in the structure [of the house], left by the last bombing, on which she was anxious to keep an eye." Later the narrator says, "The desuetude of her former bedroom, her married London home's whole air of being a cracked cup from which memory, with its reassuring power, had either evaporated or leaked away, made a crisis. . . . The hollowness of the house this evening cancelled years on years of voices, habits, and steps." Thus, with the cancellation of these years, which had been shored up against the trauma of the past, Mrs. Drover is returned to that dreadful past and the threat she feels it holds for her.

This threat has no objective reality but is clearly a manifestation of Mrs. Drover's mental state. The narrator is careful to provide a brief psychological history of the protagonist to explain why she is so vulnerable to the ambiance and events within the story. After her fiancé was reported missing and presumed killed in action, Kathleen Drover suffered a severe nervous breakdown, "a complete dislocation from everything." For nearly thirteen years she was removed from the normal connections of life and had no social relations with men. A pledge of binding love—not at all uncommon among young lovers—exchanged with her fiancé before he returned to the trenches became, after his death and her subsequent derangement, a "sinister troth" and he himself became a cold, ominous figure in her diseased imagination. During this long period she felt spied upon and vaguely threatened, but after marrying William Drover her activities "were circumscribed, and she dismissed any idea that they were still watched." This is an obvious example of paranoia. Although she was apparently well enough to live an outwardly normal life, to be a wife and mother, Mrs. Drover never wholly recovered from her personal trauma of the Great War, for her "most normal expression was one of controlled worry." Not long before the events of the story, she has suffered "a quite serious illness" and is left with a facial tic, evidence of a nervous disorder. Thus the mental health of the Kathleen Drover the reader meets as the story opens is indeed fragile.

If this psychological interpretation of **"The Demon Lover"** has thus far been convincing, it should not be difficult to accept hallucination as an element in such a story dealing with paranoia. The author herself speaks in the Preface of hallucinations in the stories included in ***Ivy Gripped the Steps.*** The extraordinary letter, the man heard leaving the house by way of the basement, and finally the demon lover as taxi driver are all, I believe, examples of hallucination. Although she may find an envelope on the hall table and carry it to her former bedroom before opening it with some anxiety, the message Mrs. Drover reads is imagined, not unusual for someone suffering from psychotic guilt. On this August evening, the same month and time her fiancé bade her farewell years before, conscious of "the pearls her husband had given her on their marriage," she reads a message based on the irrational guilt she feels for betraying her lover. Mrs. Drover even suspects she has imagined the message. "To rally herself, she said she was in a mood—and, for two or three seconds shutting her eyes, told herself that she had imagined the letter. But she opened them—there it lay on the bed." The paper on the bed may well exist but the message is a fabrication of her own mind.

In the climax of the story, Mrs. Drover believes her demon lover has found her and is spiriting her off in a taxi, but again she is pitifully deluded. When she slips into the taxi that "appeared already to be alertly waiting for her," the church clock strikes seven, reminding her of "the hour arranged." Even though she has earlier thought, "So, wherever he may be waiting I shall not know him," when the clock strikes she is immediately convinced her hour has come and she takes the unsuspecting taxi driver for a fiend. At this moment Mrs. Drover passes into madness, seeing herself swept away into deserted, war-ravaged streets.

I believe most readers of **"The Demon Lover"** *want* to view it as a ghost story, for there is an undeniable titillation in such supernatural fiction. Miss Bowen's story may be read as a ghost story if one is willing to accept the perspective of Mrs. Drover, who is obviously mentally disturbed. The author, however, provided ample evidence to suggest that the story is a pathetic psychological drama, as I have attempted to show. (pp. 411-13)

Douglas A. Hughes, "Cracks in the Psyche: Elizabeth Bowen's 'The Demon Lover'," in Studies in Short Fiction, *Vol. X, No. 4, Fall, 1973, pp. 411-13.*

ANGUS WILSON (essay date 1980)

[*British author Wilson is noted for his numerous works of criticism, short stories, and biographies, but above all for such novels as* The Middle Ages of Mrs Eliot *(1958) and* No Laughing Matter *(1967). In the following introduction to Bowen's* Collected Stories, *he discusses the author's artistic attributes.*]

[Elizabeth Bowen] is so careful a craftswoman, so conscious, even at times arrogantly conscious, of the shapes, the inversions, the verbal exactitudes in which she clothes her vision, that it would be easy to ignore the instinctive literary creator that lies beneath—that must, I believe, lie beneath all good art, even that of Henry James, the influence of whose shapes sometimes seems superficially too apparent in her work. Anyone so elegant and civilized, so certain of values that to state them would seem to her inept and naïve, so concerned for lack of show—even the bravery that man needs so desperately in a precarious world must never assert itself too crudely, though bravado if worn with sophistication is an allowable foible—so absolutely resolute in acceptance of life, so uninterested in its passing political forms, so urbane even in the Irish countryside she loved and saw so clearly, so concerned that compassion should never show a sloppy side—any such person inevitably seems to fit very little with Rousseau's noble savage, yet the instinctive artist is there at the very heart of her work and gives a strength, a fierceness and a depth to her elaborations, her delight in words, her determination that life seen will only survive on the page when it has met the strictest demands of form and elegance.

This natural force, I think, is what distinguishes her from the many and very various writers to whom she has affinities—Henry James, Aldous Huxley, Saki, Ivy Compton Burnett, even Virginia Woolf. She is with them in the various degrees by which shapes and manners control emotions, but her control comes always from intelligence (the sort of intelligence which she saw as inseparable from civilized behaviour), it never comes from intellect or abstraction. Occasionally, as in **"Sunday Evening"** or the farcical ghost story **"The Cat Jumps,"** she is dealing with the intelligentsia or stereotyped 'progressives', but she always sees them from outside, never from above, with that satirical view of intellectual superiority that Aldous Huxley found in his early novels. For all her years spent in Boar's Hill among Oxford academics she remained always an upper-class woman of hardy, firm intelligence, she was never the slave of the brilliant academic world as Virginia Woolf, a greater genius, too often was. She deals with coteries but far more with families and yet, here, unlike Ivy Compton Burnett, though her nails are ready to scratch, it is with heart that she responds to all the ecstasies and desperations, the frustrations, the deadened routines, and the sudden-awakened emotional currents of family life. She can be witty (though not, I think, very successfully funny) but not at the expense of her feeling. One has the sense that, for her, passion and love are so essentially moulded into life that she has no need for the desperate restraints of Mrs. Woolf, the evasions of Ivy Compton Burnett, or the open romanticism, wonderfully civilized though it is, of Rosamund Lehmann. (pp. 8-9)

Are there failures in her stories? **"Gone Away,"** I think, suggests that life as lived was enough for her, and speculation about the future of her society had no place in her scheme of things. Could she move outside her social world? In emotion and sympathy, I think, she could. After all, the girls and the young man in the wonderful **"Mysterious Kôr"** are very middle-class; and she could visualize the problems of others, as in her story about the loneliness of new housing estates. Only her ear lets her down a little—she is over-anxious to establish the difference of what she hears, there are too many 'we really didn't ought to have's in the speech of those she heard from a distance. And the maid's dialogue about the bombed house, 'Oh, Madam', seems to be on the level of the H. M. Tennent matinée performance that it became.

But the failures are so very few, the triumphs so many, especially as time passes by, for, though the seeds of her mastery are in her early stories, the development in so craftful a writer is inevitably vast. Perhaps in the superb **"Sunday Afternoon"** the bringing together of her two sides—the urban, the loyalist of London however horrible the blitz years, and the cultured gentry world of Ireland's countryside—shows her at her best. Here we are at once in a marvellously evoked moment of place and time and in the never changing conflict of youth's hopeful imagination and the regretful doubts of the ageing. But that is only one of many marvels [Elizabeth Bowen's] stories open to us. (p. 11)

Angus Wilson, in an introduction to The Collected Stories of Elizabeth Bowen, *Alfred A. Knopf, 1981, pp. 7-11.*

MARY JARRETT (essay date 1987)

[In the following discussion of Bowen's short fiction Jarrett explores alienation, imprisonment, the loss of identity, and the fine balancing of fiction versus reality in Bowen's stories.]

Elizabeth Bowen felt early what she called the 'Anglo-Irish ambivalence to all things English, a blend of impatience and evasiveness, a reluctance to be pinned down to a relationship.' This, I would argue, richly affected her fiction. (p. 71)

Elizabeth Bowen suffered feelings of dislocation and betrayal as a child from the lies told to her about her father's mental breakdown and her mother's cancer, and Edwin J. Kenney has pointed out that she learnt to read, at the age of seven, precisely at the time 'when her family catastrophes began to enter her consciousness with her removal to England. As she said later, "All susceptibility belongs to the age of magic, the Eden where fact and fiction were the same; the imaginative writer was the imaginative child, who relied for life upon being lied to." ' So from this time on, she said, 'Nothing made full sense to me that was not in print.' She instinctively connected being a grown-up with being a writer—that is, being in control of one's own fictions. For her . . . fiction was a way of escape, a powerful magic, a means of creating another, more tolerable, reality and identity.

Yet this identity could be a shifting one. Elizabeth Bowen, who was the first Bowen child to live and be educated in England since the family settled in Ireland in the seventeenth century, could never decide at school whether to present herself as Irish or as ultra-English, and this 'evasiveness' stayed with her all her life, this 'reluctance to be pinned down to a relationship' affected the way in which she presented her fictions. In all her best stories there is a refusal to pronounce on the validity of the worlds her characters create for themselves. Many of her characters share the fervent wish of Lydia in **"The Return"**: 'if she had only a few feet of silence of her own, to exclude the world from, to build up in something of herself.' But the nature of the silence, like the nature of the building up, in all her best stories is always left open to question. (pp. 71-2)

[Not all of] Bowen's short stories have this richness of ambivalence. She wrote in 1959, of her art as a short story writer: 'More than half my life is under the steadying influence of the novel, with its calmer, stricter, more orthodox demands: into the novel goes such taste as I have for rational behaviour and social portraiture. The short story, as I see it to be, allows for what is crazy about humanity: obstinacies, inordinate heroisms, "immortal longings" ' [see excerpt dated 1959]. Some of this craziness and these immortal longings are made explicitly supernatural, for example in **"The Cheery Soul," "The Demon Lover," "Green Holly,"** and **"Hand in Glove."** That is to say, they are stories in which the surface of ordinary life cracks. This is to use Elizabeth Bowen's own image; in a broadcast discussion of 1948 she explained that she was fascinated with the surface of life not so much for its own sake, as for the dangerous sense it gives of being a thin crust above a bottomless abyss: 'the more the surface seems to heave or threaten to crack, the more its actual pattern fascinates me.' I would argue that in her finest stories the surface only seems to heave but never finally cracks.

One consistent cause of surface-heaving in Bowen is alienation, a loss of identity, like Mrs Watson's in **"Attractive Modern Homes,"** who begins to doubt her own existence when she moves to a new housing estate, or that of the drifting Tibbie, **"The Girl with the Stoop,"** who 'had not learnt yet how to feel like a resident.' Bowen remarks of the Londoners in **"A Walk in the Woods"** that 'Not to be sure where one is induces panic.' Yet in this same story the 'city woman' exclaims to the young lover she has brought to the woods, ' "Before you came, I was walled in alive." ' Imprisonment, the ultimate loss of control of one's environment, is another major preoccupation of the stories.

Imprisonment takes many forms. The prison can be one of vulgarity, an intolerable aesthetic assault, as it is for Mr Rossiter in **"Breakfast,"** trapped by the lodging-house's 'thick fumes of coffee and bacon, the doggy-smelling carpet, the tight, glazed noses of the family ready to split loudly from their skins'—an image in which even the family's noses become impatient prisoners. Cicely in **"The New House"** makes her escape into marriage, with the claim—which would be merely whimsical in another writer—that she was imprisoned in her life with her brother in the old house by the way the furniture was arranged. Oliver and Davina fail to escape into marriage, and their imprisonment is inaction: 'Their May had been blighted. Now, each immobile from poverty, each frozen into their settings like leaves in the dull ice of different puddles, they seldom met.'

Very often the imprisonment is the capture of one person by another. It can be deliberate, like the social capture of the young wife in **"Mrs. Windermere"**: 'Firmly encircling Esmée's wrist with a thumb and forefinger she led her down Regent Street.' Or it can be involuntary, like the enslavement of the hapless Mr Richardson in **"Ann Lee's"** by someone 'as indifferent as a magnet'. Ann Lee, the mysterious enslaver and hat-creator, incidentally appears to derive her power from the fact that she eludes identification: 'Letty Ames had said that she was practically a lady; a queer creature, Letty couldn't place her.'

For other characters, imprisonment can actually be the pressure of being a magnet, of feeling other people's needs. Clifford in **"A Love Story"** feels that 'the nightmare of being wanted was beginning, in this room, to close in round him again.' In **"The Dancing-Mistress"** Peelie the pianist, who wears a slave bangle on each arm, and Lulu, the male hotel secretary, are in thrall to their 'dancing mistress' Joyce James, whose name is perhaps an allusion to the 'paralysis' of James Joyce's *Dubliners,* since she is the prisoner of her own stupor of weariness. Bullying a clumsy pupil is all that affords her 'a little shudder of pleasure' and she is dismayed by Peelie's bright suggestion that the pupil might die, because 'She couldn't do without Margery Mannering: she wanted to kill her.' She wants, that is, the perpetual pleasure of hating and tormenting Margery. But, on another level, to kill Margery would mean that she need never do without her, for the Metropole ballroom in which Joyce and Peelie work is a vision of Hell. As Joyce says to her friend: ' "Oh, Peelie, I'm *dead!,*" ' and when her would-be lover Lulu tries to hold Joyce's sleeping body in the taxi, Peelie implicitly warns him: ' "You'll be as stiff as hell in a few minutes—I am, always." ' The story balances exactly between the real and the supernatural.

In many of the 'ghost' stories the ghost may be seen as the conscious or unconscious fiction of one of the characters. In **"Making Arrangements"** a deserted husband is asked to send on all his wife's dresses, and his perception of her shallowness and her social dependence on him becomes his perception that 'From the hotel by the river the disembodied ghost of Margery was crying thinly to him for her body, her innumerable lovely bodies.' In **"The Shadowy Third"** the second wife is haunted by the *idea* of the unloved first wife—although she does supply a technically correct explanation (murder) for the existence of a ghost by saying that she thinks ' "that not to want a person must be a sort, a sort of murder." '

Some ghosts are seen by the characters themselves as fictions. Thomas, a ghostlike figure himself who must never enter the world of the couple's children, visits Gerard and Janet. He is treated to a sickening, civilized display of luxurious acquisitions, but the fly in the ointment is Janet's acquisition of a ghost called Clara. It gradually becomes apparent that the ghost is the embodiment of Janet's own loneliness and unhappiness, so that Thomas feels how much less humiliating it would have been for Gerard for Janet to have taken a lover, and Gerard complains petulantly, 'She's seeing too much of this ghost.'

In **"Dead Mabelle"** the ghost is the dead film star whose films go on playing. Like Vickery in Kipling's "Mrs Bathurst," Mabelle's fan William is drawn obsessively to her phantom image. The different worlds of reality comically collide when the distraught William returns home and jerks open a drawer for the pistol for a cinematic suicide, only to find a litter of odds and ends. Another collision of realities, or fictions, occurs in **"The Back Drawing-Room."** This story is relatively unusual for Elizabeth Bowen in having an outer framework of narrators. As one of the characters mutters disgustedly under her breath, 'Hell! . . . Bring in the Yule log, this is a Dickens Christmas. We're going to tell ghost stories.' But the guileless little man who tells of his own supernatural experience in Ireland has no notion of the proper, literary way to tell a ghost story, despite hints about the House of Usher. He is actually presented as the prisoner of his ignorance as 'the others peered curiously, as though through bars, at the little man who sat perplexed and baffled, knowing nothing of atmosphere.' Mrs Henneker, the acknowledged arbiter of atmosphere, acts as a marvellous parody of Elizabeth Bowen herself as she urges the little man to recall correctly his entry into the phantom country house.

> "You had a sense of immanence," said Mrs Henneker authoritatively. "Something was overtaking you, challenging you, embracing yet repelling you. Something was coming up from the earth, down

> from the skies, in from the mountains, that was stranger than the gathered rain. Deep from out of the depths of those dark windows, something beckoned.

This is a brisker, more peremptory version of the atmosphere Bowen herself establishes in **"Human Habitation,"** published in the same volume (***Ann Lee's***), in which two students on a walking tour blunder out of the rain into a heavily atmosphere-laden house. The pelting rain, and the physical exhaustion of the students, serve as the bridge into what one of them perceives as 'some dead and empty hulk of a world drawn up alongside, at times dangerously accessible to the unwary'. In his zombie-like state of weariness, he had already begun to doubt his own existence: 'He was, he decided, something somebody else had thought.'

Bowen uses a similar bridge in **"Look at All Those Roses,"** the story I would select as the best example of her delicate balancing of fictions against realities. Here the bridge is the 'endless drive' of Lou and Edward through the Suffolk countryside back to London. We are reminded that 'there is a point when an afternoon oppresses one with fatigue and a feeling of unreality. Relentless, pointless, unwinding summer country made nerves ache at the back of both of their eyes.' Beyond a certain point the route becomes pointless: unmappable. In any case it has always been a 'curious route,' since Edward detests the main roads, and we are therefore prepared for the fact that when they break down 'Where they were seemed to be highly improbable.' They have already 'felt bound up in the tired impotence of a dream.' Lou and Edward may have driven over the borderline into another kind of reality—or they may not.

The title of the story becomes its first sentence.

> 'Look at All Those Roses'
>
> Lou exclaimed at that glimpse of a house in a sheath of startling flowers.

The word 'sheath' has a sinister connotation. But the third sentence of the story runs, 'To reach the corner, it struck her, Edward accelerated, as though he were jealous of the rosy house—a house with gables, flat-fronted, whose dark windows stared with no expression through the flowers.' The curious syntax of 'To reach the corner, it struck her, Edward accelerated' emphasizes Lou's subjectivity. It is only her 'astounding fancy,' later in the story, that the murdered father lies at the roses' roots.

The perhaps unsurprising lack of expression of the house's dark windows gains a resonance not only from Mrs Mather's greeting them with 'no expression at all,' but from Edward's and Lou's reaction when the car breaks down: 'He and she confronted each other with that completely dramatic lack of expression they kept for occasions when the car went wrong.' The car's breakdown itself is completely realistic and simultaneously a kind of magic spell: 'A ghastly knocking had started. It seemed to come from everywhere, and at the same time to be a special attack on them.' There is a 'magic' which is suggested by the curious isolation of the house and its dislocation: Edward speaks of the rest of the country looking like something lived in by ' "poor whites," ' although this is, on one level, Suffolk and not the American South. But Lou and Edward are themselves isolated and dislocated. Lou is perpetually anxious that Edward, who is not her husband, will escape her, whereas Edward feels that 'life without people was absolutely impossible'—by which he means life only with Lou. Lou is presented as rather less than a person: during the course of the story she is compared with a monkey, a cat, and a bird. When she says longingly of the 'rosy house,' ' "I wish we lived *there* . . . It really looked like somewhere," ' Edward replies tartly, ' "It wouldn't if we did." ' Mrs Mather is also isolated, but it is a powerful isolation, like Ann Lee's, and one disconcerting to Lou and Edward, who cannot make out whether she is a woman or a lady. She has no 'outside attachments—hopes, claims, curiosities, desires, little touches of greed—that put a label on one to help strangers.' By contrast, her crippled daughter Josephine has 'an unresigned, living face.' She asks Lou which are the parts of London with the most traffic, and her restlessness is expressed by her canary 'springing to and fro in its cage.' Josephine is described as 'burning,' just as the rose garden has a 'silent, burning gaiety.'

Various interpretations of the 'rosy house' and its occupants are possible for the reader who is searching for a label. One is that Josephine's father had escaped after injuring her back. (This would have happened when Josephine was seven, the age at which Elizabeth Bowen left her father and felt abandoned by him.) As Lou, whose 'idea of love was adhesiveness', thinks bitterly: 'He had bolted off down that path, as Edward had just done.' Another is that he has been murdered by Mrs Mather, a view which obviously enjoys much local support. The murder weapon was possibly the lump of quartz, the 'bizarre object' which props open the front door, wielded by Mrs Mather's 'powerful-looking hands.' This leads to another interpretation, that the house and garden are in effect haunted, and that the murder is manifested by the over-profuse roses, 'over-charged with colour' and 'frighteningly bright.' When Lou sees the same roses that Josephine sees, 'she thought they looked like forced roses, magnetized into being.' This would explain why the farm is ' "unlucky," ' and why there is only one servant for the house, ' "not very clear in her mind." ' This in turn leads to another interpretation, that the 'rosy house' is a place of enchantment, which it is impossible to leave. Lou says jokingly to Josephine that she put the evil eye on the car, and when Lou refuses to eat tea, Josephine says, ' "She thinks if she eats she may have to stay here for ever." ' (Eleanor in **"The Parrot"** remembers Proserpine when she is offered figs by the Lennicotts.) The enchantment, however, may be either good or bad. Is Lou's 'ecstasy of indifference' to life, experienced as she lies beside Josephine's invalid carriage, an unaccustomed peep into the nature of things—one of her 'ideal moments'? Or is she succumbing to the lure of death, so that Edward rightly realizes that he had 'parked' her, like the car, in the wrong place? Lou realizes that she has always wanted 'to keep everything inside her own power,' but to abandon this desire to control one's own fictions may be to abandon life.

The story is alive with ambiguities, like Josephine's ' "We don't wonder where my father is." ' This reminds us of Edward's taunting Lou with ' "You like to be sure where I am, don't you?" ' Edward, who is a writer, comments on the episode, ' "There's a story there," ' which may reveal him either as a sensitive artist or a shallow journalist.

The title of the story is the first sentence, Lou's exclamation. It is also an exhortation to the reader to look at all those roses—and make what you can of them. (pp. 72-8)

Mary Jarrett, "Ambiguous Ghosts: The Short Sto-

ries of Elizabeth Bowen," in Journal of the Short Story in English, *No. 8, Spring, 1987, pp. 71-9.*

ADDITIONAL BIBLIOGRAPHY

Bates, Judith. "Undertones of Horror in Elizabeth Bowen's *Look at All Those Roses* and *The Cat Jumps.*" *Journal of the Short Story in English (Les cahiers de la nouvelle),* No. 8 (Spring 1987): 81-91.

Describes the sense of horror underlying the everyday situations depicted in *Look at All Those Roses* and *The Cat Jumps.*

Bayley, John. "Grande Femme." *The Listener* 98, No. 2529 (6 October 1977): 450.

Biographical and critical overview contained in a review of Victoria Glendinning's biography, *Elizabeth Bowen: Portrait of a Writer;* see entry below.

Bogan, Louise. "Theory and Practice." *The Nation* 153, No. 17 (25 October 1941): 405-06.

Review of *Look at All Those Roses.* The critic finds Bowen's short stories lacking the subtlety and skill of her novels.

Breit, Harvey. "Talk with Miss Bowen." *The New York Times Book Review* (26 March 1950): 27.

Brief profile of Bowen including her illuminating comments on such subjects as the short story form versus the novel.

Brooke, Jocelyn. *Elizabeth Bowen.* Supplement to *British Book News,* no. 28. London: Longmans, Green and Co., 1952, 32 p.

Critical overview focusing on Bowen's novels but containing passing comments on her short stories and her prose style in general.

Church, Margaret. "Social Consciousness in the Works of Elizabeth Bowen, Iris Murdoch, and Mary Lavin." *College Literature* VII, No. 2 (Spring 1980): 158-63.

Demonstrates how Bowen expressed in *The Demon Lover* a social consciousness that was stirred by the events of World War II.

Dunleavy, Janet Egleson. "Mary Lavin, Elizabeth Bowen, and a New Generation: The Irish Short Story at Midcentury." In *The Irish Short Story: A Critical History,* edited by James F. Kilroy, pp. 145-68. Boston: Twayne Publishers, 1984.

Concise survey of Bowen's short fiction.

Fraustino, Daniel V. "Elizabeth Bowen's 'The Demon Lover': Psychosis or Seduction?" *Studies in Short Fiction* 17, No. 4 (Fall 1980): 483-87.

Refutes Douglas A. Hughes's contention that "The Demon Lover" is a psychological study rather than a ghost story (see excerpt dated 1973).

Glendinning, Victoria. *Elizabeth Bowen: Portrait of a Writer.* London: Weidenfeld and Nicolson, 1977, 261 p.

Biography including brief critical comments.

Hardwick, Elizabeth. "Elizabeth Bowen's Fiction." *Partisan Review* XVI, No. 11 (November 1949): 1114-21.

General survey of Bowen's fiction emphasizing her characters' preoccupation with family background.

Kiely, Benedict. "Lovers and Creeds (VIII)." In his *Modern Irish Fiction,* pp. 151-59. Dublin: Golden Eagle Books, 1950.

Explores issues of personal identity and stability in Bowen's fiction. The critic focuses on the novels but briefly considers the short fiction as well.

Lee, Hermione. *Elizabeth Bowen: An Estimation.* London: Vision, Barnes & Noble, 1981, 255 p.

Critical overview including a chapter on the short fiction.

Mellors, John. "Dreams in War: Second Thoughts on Elizabeth Bowen." *London Magazine* 19, No. 8 (November 1979): 64-9.

Finds Bowen's short stories superior to her novels, where, according to the critic, her plots became rambling and her style too mannered.

Meredith, David W. "Authorial Detachment in Elizabeth Bowen's 'Ann Lee's'." *Massachusetts Studies in English* VIII, No. 2 (1982): 9-20.

Suggests an autobiographical basis for "Ann Lee's" and discusses Bowen's various methods of detaching herself from the story.

Moss, Howard. "Elizabeth Bowen: 1899-1973." *The New York Times Book Review* (8 April 1973): 2-3.

Personal reminiscence of Bowen.

Partridge, A. C. "Language and Identity in the Shorter Fiction of Elizabeth Bowen." In *Irish Writers and Society at Large,* edited by Masaru Sekine, pp. 169-80. Irish Literary Studies, no. 22. Totowa, N.J.: Barnes and Noble Books, 1985.

Examines Bowen's use of language to suggest identity in several short stories, including "Joining Charles," "The Cat Jumped," and "Ivy Gripped the Steps."

Sellery, J'nan. "Elizabeth Bowen: A Checklist." *Bulletin of the New York Public Library* 74 (1970): 219-74.

Lists Bowen's published and unpublished works, as well as writings about her and her work, up to 1969.

Strong, L. A. G. "Elizabeth Bowen." In *Living Writers: Being Critical Studies Broadcast in the B.B.C. Third Programme,* edited by Gilbert Phelps, pp. 58-69. London: Sylvan Press, 1947.

Appreciative general essay focusing on the quality of light and illumination as a central concern of Bowen's work.

Trevor, William. "Between Holyhead and Dun Laoghaire." *The Times Literary Supplement,* No. 4062 (6 February 1981): 131.

Favorable review of *The Collected Stories of Elizabeth Bowen* emphasizing the Anglo-Irish aspect of Bowen's work.

Trilling, Diana. "Fiction in Review." *The Nation* 162, No. 16 (20 April 1946): 483-84, 486.

Discusses Bowen's stories included in *Ivy Gripped the Steps* and states that "only two of [Bowen's stories in the volume], "Sunday Afternoon" and the title story, bring off the flourish an admirer has come to look for in her work."

Tyler, Anne. "An Art of Distance." *The New Republic* 184, No. 6 (7 February 1981): 36-8.

Review of *The Collected Stories.* Tyler lauds Bowen for her subtle depiction of characters and manners and fresh use of language, and she deems the wartime stories Bowen's finest.

Welty, Eudora. "Seventy-Nine Stories to Read Again." *New York Times Book Review* (8 February 1981): 3-22.

Offers vibrant praise for Bowen's gift for depicting human relationships and singles out "Summer Night" as the most enduring piece in *The Collected Stories.*

Paul (Frederick) Bowles

1910-

American novelist, short story writer, translator, poet, travel writer, autobiographer, and scriptwriter.

Perhaps best-known for his novel *The Sheltering Sky,* which is regarded as a masterpiece of existential literature, Bowles is considered a prominent writer of short fiction who explores the fundamental discord between Western and primitive cultures. An American expatriate who has lived for many years in Tangier, Morocco, Bowles sets most of his fiction amid the harsh climate and exotic communities of Northern Africa, which he evokes with concise, musical language. His protagonists are usually rootless Americans or Europeans who travel to Africa or Latin America in hopes of shedding the nihilism and malaise instilled by Western society but instead encounter misunderstanding, hostility, and, often, death. Critics compare Bowles's work to that of Edgar Allan Poe for its preoccupation with psychic processes, depictions of macabre violence, and detached narrative style.

Born in Jamaica, New York City, Bowles lived an isolated and unhappy childhood. His father showed him little affection and Bowles has said that their relationship formed the basis for his story "The Frozen Fields." Although Bowles received no religious schooling as a child, which he believes contributed to his atheistic outlook, his mother, a schoolteacher, read to him the stories of Poe, which profoundly influenced his imagination. Bowle's initial artistic ambitions involved poetry and music, and his first published poem, "Spire Song," appeared in the Paris journal *transition* when he was sixteen. After briefly attending the University of Virginia, Bowles studied music in New York under composer Aaron Copland. In 1931, he traveled to Paris, where he met Gertrude Stein, who advised him to write fiction instead of poetry and to move to Morocco, a region which she believed would enhance his creativity. Bowles spent much of the 1930s and 1940s traveling between the United States, Europe, and Tangier, composing scores for the theater and writing music reviews for the *New York Herald Tribune.* His interest in fiction was revived during the early 1940s when his wife, author Jane Bowles, whom he married in 1938, was working on her novel *Two Serious Ladies.* In 1947, Bowles stopped composing music and has since concentrated on literature.

Bowles's first short story collection, *The Delicate Prey, and Other Stories,* established him as one of the foremost chroniclers of humanity's nihilistic impulses and is considered by many critics to be his finest acheivement in short fiction. In this volume, as well as in such collections as *The Time of Friendship* and *Midnight Mass,* Bowles investigates the unbridgeable differences between primitive and civilized cultures, the search for meaning in an absurd world, the failure of human relationships, and the destructive forces of nature. Throughout the stories in *The Delicate Prey,* Bowles employs understatement to relate tales of nightmarish cruelty and degradation. For example, in "A Distant Episode," an American linguistics professor studying North African dialects is captured by nomadic tribesmen, who sever his tongue, dress him in a suit of flattened tin cans, and force him to dance for their entertainment. This story illustrates, among other themes, the inadequacy of language and the danger of intruding on foreign cultures without properly understanding them. The troubled nature of family relationships, a common Bowles theme, is depicted in "Pages from Cold Point." Written as the journal of a retired professor, this piece traces his degeneration from rationality to hedonism as he becomes incestuously involved with his teenaged homosexual son. In "Pastor Dowe at Tacate," a Christian missionary in a Latin American village, realizing his evangelical efforts are futile, loses his grip on reason and regresses to primitive behavior that results in his marriage to an eight-year-old girl.

The themes prevalent in *The Delicate Prey* recur throughout Bowles's subsequent collections of short fiction, including *The Hours after Noon, A Hundred Camels in the Courtyard, The Time of Friendship, Things Gone and Things Still Here,* and *Midnight Mass,* although some critics noticed stronger emphasis on psychological rather than physical violence in the later volumes. The overriding theme of *The Time of Friendship,* according to John Ditsky, "comes down in the end to recognitions of inadequacies in the mutual perceptions and responses of human beings, of failures to observe the need to impose ideals less and to love more." The story that perhaps best exemplifies this idea, critics note, is "The Time of Friendship." Considered one of Bowles's most optimistic tales, it concerns the friendship between a Swiss schoolteacher and an Arab boy. Hoping to teach the boy about Christianity, the woman builds a crêche out of food but discovers that he has eaten the figures. Later, she realizes that she has been trying to indoctrinate him with her own Western values and concludes that it is best to tolerate their immutable differences. Other stories involve characters suffering disturbed states of mind, such as the Mexican woman in "Doña Faustina" who engages in witchcraft, infanticide, and cannibalism and the psychotic in "If I Should Open My Mouth" who plans to put poisonous gum in New York's subway vending machines. Familial discord is chillingly portrayed in "The Frozen Fields," a story frequently compared with Conrad Aiken's "Silent Snow, Secret Snow"—both depict young boys who descend into psychosis. In Bowles's tale, a father's antagonism impels his son to dream of his brutal destruction.

In *Midnight Mass,* Bowles focuses upon Moroccan characters and employs a tone that is less menacing and more reflective than in his previous work. In "Here to Learn," an ingenuous Moroccan woman leaves her family's small village and accumulates wealth by parlaying her beauty to a series of foreign lovers. When she eventually returns to her village, her mother has died and nobody recognizes her. Though she is hurt, she survives with a new identity acquired from her degrading experiences abroad. Bowles's facility for surrealism surfaces in "Allal," in which a North African boy under the influence of the drug kif enters the body of a snake in order to take revenge on the two men pursuing him.

Critical reaction to Bowles's work generally has been favorable, although some critics, most notably Leslie Fiedler, who called Bowles a "pornographer of terror," view his writing as excessively violent and fashionably nihilistic. Most, however, see it as presenting an accurate picture of the absurdity of modern existence and the depravity of humankind. Bowles has been classified with such American gothic writers as Poe, Carson McCullers, and William Faulkner, as well as with such existentialist authors as Jean-Paul Sartre and Albert Camus, but he rejects any attempts to categorize his work. While often celebrated for his elegant descriptions of remote landscapes, Bowles is probably most highly regarded for exploring the misconceptions that occur between civilized and primitive cultures. Although relatively unknown in the United States due to his expatriate status and dislike for the usual promotional activities of publishing, Bowles's writing has garnered much scholarly attention in recent years, and many critics consider him among the foremost writers in the existentialist tradition. Michael Krekorian observed that Bowles's short fiction "represents the work of an innovator in American literature who seeks to debunk apparent order residing deep within nature and to dismiss man's reasoning power over the world as irrelevant hallucination."

(See also *Contemporary Literary Criticism,* Vols. 1, 2, 19, 53; *Contemporary Authors,* Vols. 1-4, rev. ed.; *Contemporary Authors New Revision Series,* Vols. 1, 19; *Contemporary Authors Autobiography Series,* Vol. 1; and *Dictionary of Literary Biography,* Vols. 5, 6.)

PRINCIPAL WORKS

SHORT FICTION

The Delicate Prey, and Other Stories 1950
A Little Stone 1950
The Hours after Noon 1959
A Hundred Camels in the Courtyard 1962
The Time of Friendship 1967
Pages from Cold Point, and Other Stories 1968
Three Tales 1975
Things Gone and Things Still Here 1977
Collected Stories: 1939-1976 1979
Midnight Mass 1981
Unwelcome Words: Seven Stories 1988

OTHER MAJOR WORKS

The Sheltering Sky (novel) 1949
Let It Come Down (novel) 1952
The Spider's House (novel) 1955
Yallah (travel essays) 1956
Their Heads Are Green and Their Hands Are Blue (travel essays) 1963
Up above the World (novel) 1966
Scenes (poetry) 1968
The Thicket of Spring: Poems 1926-1969 (poetry) 1972
Without Stopping: An Autobiography (autobiography) 1972
Next to Nothing (poetry) 1976
Next to Nothing: Collected Poems 1926-1977 (poetry) 1981
Points in Time (novel) 1982

TENNESSEE WILLIAMS (essay date 1950)

[*Along with Arthur Miller, Williams is generally considered one of the two greatest American dramatists since World War II. In such prize-winning plays as* The Glass Menagerie *(1944),* A Streetcar Named Desire *(1947),* Cat on a Hot Tin Roof *(1955), and* The Night of the Iguana *(1961), Williams employed lyrical language to examine isolation, the difficulty of communication, and the solitary search for meaning in a disordered world. In the essay excerpted below, Williams views the stories in* The Delicate Prey, and Other Stories *as explorations of "a cavern of individual sensibilities" that illustrate Bowles's principal theme: the frightening alienation of the individual. Williams also praises Bowles as the American writer whose work most accurately reflects the turbulence of the modern world.*]

Paul Bowles is a man and author of exceptional latitude but he has, like nearly all serious artists, a dominant theme. That theme is the fearful isolation of the individual being. (p. 19)

Certainly a terrible kind of loneliness is expressed in most of these stories [in ***The Delicate Prey, and Other Stories***] . . . but the isolated beings in these stories have deliberately chosen their isolation in most cases, not merely accepted and endured it. There is a singular lack of human give-and-take, of true emotional reciprocity, in the groups of beings assembled upon his intensely but somberly lighted sets. The drama is that of the single being rather than of beings in relation to each other. Paul Bowles has experienced an unmistakable revulsion from the act of social participation. . . . These seventeen stories are the exploration of a cavern of individual sensibilities, and fortunately the cavern is a deep one containing a great deal that is worth exploring.

Nowhere in any writing that I can think of has the separateness of the one human psyche been depicted more vividly and shockingly. If one feels that life achieves its highest value and significance in those rare moments—they are scarcely longer than that—when two lives are confluent, when the walls of isolation momentarily collapse between two persons, and if one is willing to acknowledge the possibility of such intervals, however rare and brief and difficult they may be, the intensely isolated spirit evoked by Paul Bowles may have an austerity which is frightening at least. But don't make the mistake of assuming that what is frightening is necessarily inhuman. It is curious to note that the spirit evoked by Bowles in so many of these stories does *not* seem inhuman, nor does it strike me as being antipathetic.

Even in the stories where this isolation is most shockingly, even savagely, stated and underlined the reader may sense an inverted kind of longing and tenderness for the thing whose absence the story concerns. This inverted, subtly implicit kind of tenderness comes out most clearly in one of the less impressive stories of the collection. This story is called **"The Scorpion."** It concerns an old woman in a primitive society of some obscure kind who has been left to live in a barren cave by her two sons. One of these deserters eventually returns to the cave with the purpose of bringing his mother to the community in which he and his brother have taken up residence. But the old woman is reluctant to leave her cave. The cave, too small for more than one person to occupy, is the only thing in reality that she trusts or feels at home in. It is curtained by rainfall and it is full of scorpions and it is not furnished by any kind of warmth or comfort, yet she would prefer to remain there than to accompany her son. . . . (pp. 19-20)

Here is a story that sentimentality, even a touch of it, could have destroyed. But sentimentality is a thing that you will find nowhere in the work of Paul Bowles. When he fails, which is rarely, it is for another reason. It is because now and then his special hardness of perception, his defiant rejection of all things emollient have led him into an area in which a man can talk only to himself.

The volume contains among several fine stories at least one that is a true masterpiece of short fiction—**"A Distant Episode."** . . . In this story Paul Bowles states the same theme which he developed more fully in his later novel. The theme is the collapse of the civilized "Super Ego" into a state of almost mindless primitivism, totally dissociated from society except as an object of its unreasoning hostility. It is his extremely powerful handling of this theme again and again in his work which makes Paul Bowles probably the American writer who represents most truly the fierily and blindly explosive world that we live in so precariously from day and night to each uncertain tomorrow. (p. 20)

Tennessee Williams, "The Human Psyche—Alone," in The Saturday Review of Literature, *Vol. XXXIII, No. 51, December 23, 1950, pp. 19-20.*

F. CUDWORTH FLINT (essay date 1952)

[In the following excerpt, Flint praises Bowles's use of understatement in his portrayal of uncomprehending people in macabre circumstances in The Delicate Prey.*]*

[Understatement is one of Bowles's] favorite means of securing an effect—a circumstance which possibly accounts for the fact that his best successes he achieves in the short story rather than the novel. And this decorum of expression is the more necessary because the world portrayed by Mr. Bowles . . . is chaotic. His characters [in ***The Delicate Prey, and Other Stories***] are not united even by a sense of guilt. They are disunited by acts of repudiation. Destiny here comes in no "disguise of what we deserve"; for, says the diarist in the story **"Pages from Cold Point,"** "Destiny, when one perceives it clearly from very near, has no qualities at all." All of Mr. Bowles' principal characters betray themselves or others, sometimes through an innocence which ignorantly lends itself to uncomprehended schemes, as in **"Señor Ong and Señor Ha,"** sometimes through self-sufficiency venturing beyond its depth, as in **"Pastor Dowe at Tacaté"** and **"A Distant Episode"** (respectively, a comic and a gruesome version of this possibility), sometimes impelled by the unfamiliar circumstance, as in **"The Echo,"** sometimes giddy with the realisation that the personal will may in the given situation determine the length of its own tether, as in **"At Paso Rojo,"** and sometimes impelled by energies of hashish or madness, as in **"The Delicate Prey"** . . . , or **"You are Not I."** In order to produce the macabre effects in which he specializes . . . the author oftenest chooses for his scene some region of tropical jungle or desert, whether in the Americas or Africa, for there civilisation may most spectacularly be confronted with whatever is a denial of it, or whatever may induce its degradation and decay. "Frightfulness," says the egoistically cynical husband in **"Call at Corazón"** "is never more than an unfamiliar pattern." The settings of these stories often exemplify this dictum; and the characters nearly always act as if they believed it. The result is as effective an assembly of samples of the "higher" gruesomeness—non-Pinkerton, non-mechanized, non-technological; that is to say, freshly imagined—as is to be found on the market today. (pp. 716-17)

F. Cudworth Flint, in a review of "The Delicate Prey and Other Stories," in The Sewanee Review, *Vol. LX, No. 4, Autumn, 1952, pp. 715-18.*

W. RICHARD POIRIER (essay date 1953)

[In the following excerpt, Poirier explicates the themes and imagery in Bowles's short story "Under the Sky."]

At the very end of [**"Under the Sky"**], a year after the central episode, Bowles confronts the reader with a new character; we are told nothing about her except that she is an "old woman of the town who came every day to her son's grave." In such a story as J. F. Powers's "Lions, Hearts, Leaping Does," where nearly all of the characters are richly developed, the intrusion of a stranger might have disrupted the tonality and focus of the story. Yet it is entirely consistent with the purposes of **"Under the Sky"** to have as the final speaker a nameless citizen of the town. For the town is a major figure in the story, and its personality is active both in the obtrusive effect of the setting and in the impressions of ugliness which it stimulates in Jacinto. In his mind, the town and all the people in it are nameless; he cannot identify them for us because he is isolated from them, and he knows them only pictorially, as embodying the features of repulsiveness.

In the movement or form of the story, we begin with a description of the town. Its atmosphere is aboriginal and antediluvian: the promise of a great rain, the gray lizards that scurry across Jacinto's path, the heat and aridity, all provide a kind of backdrop which makes the violence of the story seem a consequence as much of situation as of character. . . .

Given the immensity and malevolence of the surroundings, it is both pathetic and ironic that Jacinto, when we first see him, is "taller" and "prouder" than the others on the road, refusing to bend, as they do, while climbing the mountain. He is defiant of what "the more educated town-dwellers" aptly call the "Inferno."

Once he has completed his business, Jacinto tries desperately to blot out the malignance of the "Inferno," and in so doing he unconsciously gives symbolic significance to two other elements of the setting, the railroad station and the cemetery. Because of his terribly self-conscious isolation from the town, Jacinto finds in the railroad station a possibility of romantic escape. Before going to the cemetery he stops at the station to see and perhaps meet the "strange people" who arrive from "far away" places. Failing at the station to make contact with life from outside the "Inferno," he turns to the cemetery and an escape through an unconsciousness akin to death. But even as Jacinto begins to smoke, the train whistle excites him to a vision of vital and pleasurable life, of a place far off "where the people eat nothing but fish and travel on top of the water." That Bowles has intentionally juxtaposed his symbols is indicated by his having carefully placed "a cemetery behind the roundhouse." Jacinto moves among these places—the "Inferno," the railroad station, and the cemetery—like a man on pilgrimage, but he is always isolated, never content with any one of them, and initially condemned, as the simplicity, poverty, and incredible innocence of his conversational style suggest, to the primitiveness and wildness characteristic of the town itself.

In his personal relationships Jacinto has a vast almost comic distrust of everyone, even of "the others from his village" who have entered the town with him. . . . The sound of the marimbas coming from the doorways allows Jacinto a contact which is for him ideally distant and impersonal; marijuana is a means by which he escapes from the antagonistic world of the living into the world of the dead. But Jacinto's addiction is not the reason for his isolation; rather, he is an addict because he is so lonely and lost. Superficially, he may be identified with the "town-dweller" whom he meets in the park and whose "silken town voice" he distrusts. That we are to make distinctions between the motivations of the two characters is clear, however, from the structure of the story. The central episode which ends with Jacinto's bidding good night to the *señorita* opens with one act of blackmail and develops into another: Jacinto is forced to give cigarettes to the town-dweller; the yellow-haired woman is forced by the most desperate threats to surrender to Jacinto. By extorting the cigarettes from Jacinto, the town-dweller hopes to escape through marijuana into a state like death; by his clumsy intimidation of the woman, Jacinto hopes to escape from an overwhelming sense of death through contact with life and the life-giving sexual act.

Because of the structural balance of the story, Jacinto's rape of the yellow-haired woman is made a natural result of the frustrating experiences which precede it. In this way violence is necessary to the theme; it is neither accidental nor shocking. (pp. 494-96)

The significance of the scene of the rape, and consequently of the three scenes in the cemetery, is largely responsible for the structural unity and dramatic compactness of the story. When we first see Jacinto under the stone statue, it is as if he himself were in the grave. He is almost completely absorbed by death: death is in the earth, death is in the sky with the vultures, death is in Jacinto's soul whose "edges" are burned by the marijuana smoke. Having failed at the railway station to make contact with anyone in life, he finds delight in identifying himself with the dead: "He continued to smoke, going deeper and deeper into delight. Finally he lay back and murmured: 'Now I am dead too.' " In this first episode, Jacinto takes pleasure in life which is indistinguishable from death; in the last episode, although in the same state of death-like intoxication, he weeps out of an anguished sense that life is inaccessible to him. The change has been brought about by the second episode in the cemetery. His experience with the yellow-haired woman who, though not young and perhaps not beautiful, represents the vitality of the world outside and is in sharp contrast to the one woman he has met in the "Inferno": "She had proved to be ugly—one side of her face was mottled with blue and purple."

The old woman in the final scene may believe that Jacinto is grieving the death of his mother, but the reader knows that Jacinto is not grieving the loss of the dead, but the loss of the living. The stone statue of the woman may well represent in his mind the cold and inanimate world of death which has replaced the world of violent life which he once experienced with the yellow-haired woman. In place of her body, he now grasps at the pebbles and at a world of such hardness that marijuana is no longer a sufficient comfort. It is likely, however, that Bowles wishes us to go further and to find in the statement of the old woman an ambiguity which has elements of truth. Jacinto, whose pretensions to being a giver of life we may recall—"I am the father of all of you"—is in the end pathetically viewed as being cut off from the very source of his own life, his mother. Though she mistakes the person he has lost, the old woman does define the nature of his loss. Out of her mistake, Bowles has made a rich symbolic statement. (pp. 497-98)

W. Richard Poirier, "Paul Bowles's 'Under the Sky,' " in Stories: British and American, *edited by Jack Barry Ludwig and W. Richard Poirier, Houghton Mifflin Company, 1953, pp. 494-98.*

IHAB H. HASSAN (essay date 1954)

[*An Egyptian-born American critic, Hassan has written and edited numerous literary studies, including* The Dismemberment of Orpheus: Toward a Postmodern Literature *(1971; revised edition, 1982) and* Radical Innocence: The Contemporary American Novel *(1961). In the essay excerpted below, Hassan contends that the short story medium is better suited than the novel for Bowles's delineation of his primary themes in* The Delicate Prey*; namely, the barrenness of human relationships and the inability to love.*]

In the stories of ***The Delicate Prey,*** the medium's limitation seems to enhance the basic virtue of Bowles, his tight control of savage emotions and baleful situations, and to foreshorten his main weakness, the inability to conceive and develop characters dramatically. These stories may share Tennessee Williams' and Truman Capote's explorations of the sombre, the primitive, and the destructive in human nature; but in them lyricism is muted, the grotesque harsh, and the point of view distant. All but two of the stories, **"You Are Not I"** and **"How Many Midnights,"** are set in North Africa and Latin America. The themes of isolation, of anxiety, of lovelessness, all of the cruelty and perversions which they can induce, are spun in hard, brilliant tones, tones that can sometimes be garish as in **"The Delicate Prey"** and murky as in the psychopathic **"You Are Not I,"** where a certain arbitrariness of conception is in both stories apparent. But in the plights of Pastor Dowe who can only bring Christianity as Jazz to his Indian congregation, **"Pastor Dowe at Tacate"**; of the child forced into the sinister world of dope peddling, **"Senor Ong and Senor Ha"**; of the girl supplanted in her mother's affection by a lesbian friend, **"The Echo"**; of the boy who can only win the acceptance of his shipmates by an act of cruelty, **"The Fourth Day Out From Santa Cruz"**; of the retired professor incapable to restrain or even communicate with his homosexual son, **"Pages From Cold Point"**; of the American woman novelist who discovers her utter alienation in the amorous company of a handsome Arab schoolboy, **"Tea On The Mountain"**; and of the linguist brutalized into the role of a speechless clown by the wild Reguibat, **"A Distant Episode"**; in these plights there is nothing false or precious: they belong to man, man between two civilizations, "one dead, the other waiting to be born." The range of Bowles is perhaps nowhere better delimited than in this collection, his techniques nowhere better illustrated. One feels that whatever development Bowles will undergo—and his ultimate importance depends greatly on such a development—the starting point will remain in these stories. (pp. 27-8)

The impression easiest to receive from Bowles' novels, and from the majority of his stories, is one of violence, one of terror and negation. [In this essay I am] . . . engaged in pointing to correlatives between that exterior of violence and the central theme of quest and decay. No such correlation would be complete without reference to the peculiar transpositions of human relations in Bowles' fiction.

For cruelty and perversion, dominant as they are in so many contacts of Bowles' characters, seem the dramatic proof of a radical impossibility, the impossibility of love. Human relationships are, with scarcely a few exceptions, shown as sterile or intolerable, though at times also implausible. Rape, incest, lesbianism, homosexuality, adultery, and simple betrayal, with all their attending virulence, betoken the most complete negation of human love to which a novelist may refer. Estrangement and loneliness— . . . of the couple in **"Call at Corazon,"** of the native in **"Under the Sky,"** of the father and son in **"Pages From Cold Point,"** and of the mother and daughter in **"The Echo"**—express a situation in which fear and meaninglessness compel each character to entrench himself in the narrowest corner of his selfhood. In that corner no hope of intercourse can subsist. Nor can there even be hope for the palliative of amenities—Eunice Good and the Lyles truly carry unpleasantness to a point of rare refinement. Hence the age is an Age of Monsters (as Bowles entitles a section of *Let It Come Down*) and "monsters," like Iago, cannot be reconciled to the existence of good in humanity. Even Chalia, who is no Iago, succeeds, in the story **"At Paso Rojo,"** in wantonly "framing" the Indian boy Roberto because her uncle's faith in the honesty of his ranch Indians is intolerable to her. Bowles' questioning of human relationships becomes yet more intense when the most traditionally close of these relationships, conjugal and familial ties, are shown to be the least adequate—those whom we generally consider nearest to each other turn out to be the most alienated. Stories like **"Pages From Cold Point," "The Echo,"** and even **"The Scorpion,"** challenge the sentimental complacencies that hide a real evil and insist on a revaluation of all relationships.

But it is perhaps Bowles' style, inclusive of manner as of perception, that converts terror and negation to form and meaning. Occasionally the Gothic element asserts its presence, as in the dinner scene at the Valverde house, high on a cliff overlooking the sea, with cuttlefish in the dining room aquarium, cats, syringes, and the smell of a zoo pervading the interior, and a branch clawing at the windowpane. Yet Bowles is far less indebted, if at all, to William Beckford, Anne Radcliffe, or Horace Walpole than he is to a later tradition now absorbed beyond recognition: the tradition of Poe, his first idol, and of Hoffman, of Novalis, Lautréamont, and the French Symbolists, writers to whom it would be as difficult explicitly to annex Bowles as it would be to annex the Kafka of "Metamorphosis" and "In the Penal Colony" or the James of *The Turn of the Screw.* Different as they are, what James and Kafka do that Poe does not is to relate horror, in action and incident, to a more significant range of human values and experiences. And while Bowles does not in this respect equal James or Kafka—**"The Delicate Prey,"** for instance, is more akin to "The Cask of Amontillado" and "The Pit and the Pendulum" than it is to anything else—in his best work terror, constantly subject to the discipline of style, acquires inescapable reference. (pp. 33-4)

Ihab H. Hassan, "The Pilgrim as Prey: A Note on Paul Bowles," in The Western Review, *Vol. 19, No. 1, Autumn, 1954, pp. 23-36.*

OLIVER EVANS (essay date 1959)

[An American critic, editor, translator, and poet, Evans has written critical studies of such authors as E. M. Forster, Carson McCullers, and Anaïs Nin. In the excerpt below, Evans rejects Leslie Fiedler's statement that Bowles is merely a "pornographer of terror," asserting that horror is crucial to Bowles in dramatizing his central theme of the conflict between Western and primitive cultures in The Delicate Prey.*]*

[***The Delicate Prey***] gained for Mr. Bowles the reputation of being a specialist in horror, a "pornographer of terror, a secret lover of the horror he evokes," as Leslie Fiedler put it. . . . "The whole impact of his work is his insistence on the horrible," wrote Mr. Fiedler, who went on, incredibly enough, to place Bowles in the tradition of science fiction.

There is no denying it: the stories, many of them, *are* terrible, and their horror is intensified by the manner in which they are written: they are told quietly, gently, almost tenderly, in a style as pure and as polished as any in modern English. But granting the horror, it is reasonable to inquire whether the stories are *merely* horrible—that is, whether the horror may not be essential to these intentions; and, finally, whether some beauty may not exist even in the midst of the horror.

Even in this collection, Bowles does not usually indulge in horror for its own sake; it is nearly always related, as a careful reading of the stories proves, to his central obsession—an effect through which he strives to dramatize a thesis. They are most of them highly moral tales in the sense that *The Sheltering Sky* is moral—and in the sense that Faulkner's "A Rose for Emily" is not. A few examples will show what I mean. In **"A Distant Episode,"** an American (or European) pedant, a professor of languages, is captured by a tribe of desert bandits who cut out his tongue and retain him as a kind of performing clown: he is dressed in a suit of tin cans, made to dance, grimace and turn handsprings, and is kept in a cage like an animal. The professor reminds us at once of Port, in *The Sheltering Sky:* "He came down out of the high, flat region in the evening by bus, with two small overnight bags full of maps, sun lotions and medicines." Prim and overcivilized, he is an ideal candidate for defeat and degradation at the hands of a primitive people, and there is terrible irony in the circumstance of a linguist's losing his tongue. One reason the story seems so horrible is that the reader is not made to feel that the author sympathizes with the professor: this, however, is purely a matter of implication, not of statement nor even overt suggestion, for Mr. Bowles realizes that for his story to be effective dramatically it has to be told with the utmost objectivity. The skill with which he creates in the first few pages an atmosphere of danger and impending disaster is remarkable, and reminds one of the beginning of *Benito Cereno.*

In another story, **"Under the Sky,"** a Mexican peon watches the arrival at a railway station of three tourists, two women and a man: "Each one carried a leather bag covered with small squares of colored paper stuck on at different angles." Several hours later, when he has been smoking marijuana, he meets one of the women in the park and rapes her. The scene reminds us of Kit's violation in the desert [in *The Sheltering Sky*]: this woman exhibits a similar type of nervelessness ("Mechanically she allowed him to push her along") and her bag, like Kit's, is a pathetic symbol of the civilization which has produced her. She is another civilized traveler, doomed for disaster. The drug is introduced into the story to make it seem more credible: it is one of the few occasions where Bowles permits the realistic level to profit, perhaps, at the expense of the symbolic.

In **"Pastor Dowe at Tacaté,"** defeat occurs without violence. In this story, a Christian missionary in a remote Latin-American outpost discovers the futility of his labors: the only way he can ensure a congregation is to entice the natives with gifts of salt and to intersperse his sermons with pieces like "Sonny Boy" and "Crazy Rhythm" played on his portable phonograph. (pp. 143-44)

The natives are satisfied with their own deities, a beneficient one named Hachakyum, and a malevolent one named Metzabok. In an important scene near the beginning of the story, the missionary, prompted by curiosity, quizzes one of his congregation, a man named Nicolás, about these gods. Did Hachakyum, he inquires, make the world and everything in it? "No," replies Nicolás, "Hachakyum did not make everyone. He did not make you. He did not make guns or Don Jesucristo." Pastor Downe then asks, "Who made me?" and Nicolás answers: "Metzabok makes all things that do not belong here." Finally Pastor Dowe admits defeat, and decides to leave: "Locking his door, he proceeded to pack what personal effects he could into his smallest suitcase. His Bible and notebooks went on top with his toothbrush and atabrine tablets." The missionary is prim, squeamish, androgynous—another ideal victim for the natural man, who is here symbolized by Nicolás.

Three of the remaining stories in the collection—**"Call at Corazón"** (in which the honeymooning couple bear a striking resemblance to Port and Kit; as in *The Sheltering Sky,* the conflict between them is mirrored in the contrast between them and the primitive surroundings), **"At Paso Rojo,"** and **"The Echo"**—are all related in some way to Bowles's dominant theme. To my mind, the least successful stories are those in which the horror does constitute an end in itself, like the title story [**"The Delicate Prey"**] and **"Pages from Cold Point,"** which last, a study of homosexual incest, is a brilliant *tour de force* written in Bowles's very best manner but without any apparent root in the author's fundamental convictions: in this respect, as also in the cumulative horror of its situation and its technical perfection, it reminds us of *The Turn of the Screw.* The most pessimistic story in the book is **"The Fourth Day Out from Santa Cruz,"** a fable with a terrible message: that it is cruelty which holds men together; it is the leveling influence, the lowest common denominator of human behavior. The story is remarkable for its delicate balancing of narrative and allegory: on both levels it is completely coherent. (pp. 144-45)

Oliver Evans, "Paul Bowles and the 'Natural' Man," in Recent American Fiction: Some Critical Views, *edited by Joseph J. Waldmeir, Houghton Mifflin Company, 1963, pp. 139-52.*

CHESTER E. EISINGER (essay date 1963)

[*Eisinger, an American critic and editor, is the author of the critical study* Fiction of the Forties *(1963). In the following excerpt from that work, Eisinger maintains that, in* The Delicate Prey, *Bowles surpasses even Edgar Allan Poe in creating violent, amoral, and deranged fictional worlds.*]

The Delicate Prey, and Other Stories is dedicated to [Bowles's] mother, who first read to him the stories of Poe. The acknowledged kinship with Poe is neither with the romanticism nor the psychology of that writer. It lies in the sense of felt terror that Bowles finds as immediate and as pervasive in life as Poe did. It lies in the deliberate manipulation of horror and nightmare that both are capable of; it lies in the recognition that man is alien and alone in society and nature; and to put the best face on the matter, it lies in the courage they share in looking steadily into the real face of evil. These short stories demonstrate all the dimensions of that kinship. At the same time, Bowles goes so far in conceiving the world as amoral, in accepting the demonic and embracing the irrational, that he approaches excess; he out-Poes Poe.

Bowles conceives man as depraved and murderous in these stories. The real fellowship of men is established in their shared brutality. The real motive force in man is an anarchic sex drive that breaks out at any moment in any odd way. And since it is a force as real as any other in nature, Bowles reports its manifestations with the same objectivity that another man might apply to recording a snowstorm. In an inland Latin American town, under a blank sky, except for a vulture or two, a native with a blank mind and a blank face smokes his *grifas,* rapes a white woman, and goes home. Or a spinster in her forties suddenly takes to exposing herself and trying to seduce young Indians. The most extreme refinement in Bowles's treatment of sex is in **"Pages from Cold Point,"** where, with great delicacy and restraint, the story is told of how a man and his son have homosexual relations and the son blackmails the father. The real fate of youth is ultimate corruption, usually coming sooner than later. The real condition of man is to be alone, for communication can never be established. The last two stories in the volume, **"The Delicate Prey"** and **"A Distant Episode,"** sum up Bowles's view of man. The first, a story in which the horror mounts to nightmare proportions, shows that man preys upon man, and the second reveals a motiveless malignity. The shock of violence in these stories is the last desperate tactic by which Bowles thinks to press home his vision of a world now dead and holding no promise of life in the future. (pp. 287-88)

Chester E. Eisinger, "The New Fiction," in his Fiction of the Forties, *The University of Chicago Press, 1963, pp. 231-307.*

THEODORE SOLOTAROFF (essay date 1967)

[*An American critic and editor, Solotaroff is best known for* The Red Hot Vacuum, and Other Pieces on the Writing of the Sixties *(1970) and for editing the influential literary journal* New American Review *(later renamed* American Review*). In his critique of* The Delicate Prey, and Other Stories *and* The Time of Friendship *below, Solotaroff praises Bowles as the foremost practitioner of nihilistic fiction.*]

Of the writers who devoted themselves to negation and despair, Bowles was probably the most subtle as well as the most uncompromising. The stories in ***The Delicate Prey, and Other Stories*** with their lucid, quiet evocation of mood and motive leading to revelations of scarifying depravity were often so powerful that they made the nihilism of the early Hemingway seem like a pleasant beery melancholy. The title story [**"The Delicate Prey"**], for example, deserves to live forever in the annals of human cunning and cruelty: a tale of a desert predator and tribal fanatic who wins the confidence of three brothers traveling in a caravan, murders the two older ones after conning them into a hunt, and then, intoxicated with hashish ("carried along on its hot fumes, a man can escape very far from the world of meaning"), wounds, mutilates, rapes, and finally after many hours, kills the youngest brother. The emotional current of the story is provided by the boy's innocence which leads him to distrust his suspicions of the Moungari's treachery; distracted by the lusts and self-consciousness of youth, he is the human equivalent of the desert gazelles, the "delicate prey" that were to be hunted down. The tale concludes with the detection of the murderer whom the police turn over to the tribesmen of the three brothers. (p. 29)

Virtually all of the stories in ***The Delicate Prey*** take place in a primitive setting, usually either Central America or North Africa. The jungle and more notably the desert, the place where "all philosophical systems collapse," as a French colonial officer puts it, have provided Bowles with a natural background for narratives that are intended to crack open the standard models of reality and morality and to reveal the demonic sources of human conduct. The destructive element in which Bowles immerses his tightlaced and empty pilgrims from the modern world takes many forms: there is the incredible brutality of the Reguiba bandits who quickly reduce an anthropologist, led to them by a spiteful native guide, to a state of catatonic terror in which he functions as a kind of tribal pet; but there is also the encompassing languor of a Caribbean island into which a retired professor sinks so far that he sends his teen-age son away to a life of sybaritic perversion rather than be disturbed by his scandalous behavior.

Though most of these stories in ***The Delicate Prey*** still make one feel they were written with a razor, so deftly and chillingly do they cut to the bone, there was clearly more to Bowles than the desire to shock, dismay and terrorize. **"Pastor Dowe at Tacate,"** for example, is a profoundly ironic comment on the white man's burden, a kind of *Heart of Darkness* in miniature, in which a prim missionary finds himself sliding from Christian rationality into atavism, until he finally is faced with the necessity of taking an eight-year-old girl for his wife and literally runs away in terror from the Indian village.

The abysses and furies of the human psyche; the fragile, provisional nature of the civilized instincts; the lure of the primitive and the inhuman; the sadness of deracinated people; the underground warfare of marriage and friendship; the lonely divisions between desire and behavior, between having and holding, between one hand and the other hand; the modern world's contagions of angst, dread, deadness: all these strains of the existentialist vision are dramatically presented in Bowles' earlier work. . . . (pp. 29-30)

Most of [the stories in ***The Time of Friendship***] are effective, several are memorable, but only one seems to me to break fresh ground. This is the long title story [**"The Time of Friendship"**] in which Bowles abandons his rather static view of primitivism, and moves beyond his somewhat fatigued fascination with its timeless mysteries and perversities, to write about post-colonial Algeria.

"The Time of Friendship" is a poignant account of the deepening relationship between Fraulein Windling, a Swiss schoolteacher, who lives part of each year in a desert village, and an adolescent Arab boy. The teacher is not one of Bowles' world-besotted travelers, nor is the desert any longer the burning, silent center of negative truth to which she makes her confused and final way. She is a sensible, resourceful spinster and the oasis village is a place where people live from day to day and somehow make do with the earth, grass, palmwood, and animal skins that comprise their economy. As for herself, the desert is a healthy environment which strengthens her "resistance" to the civilized world's slow stain and each year puts her "in touch with life again." She is enamored of the ancient ways of the village and regards the rebellion going on in the north as part of the modern "virus of discontent," from which she hopes the village will be spared. Slimane, the Arab she comes to befriend, is not a cunning demon who will eventually betray or rape her, but rather a simple, soulful boy who is devoted to her. Several years pass, during which their only conflict is whether Christ was a Moslem; stymied by his obduracy on this one issue, she tactfully resolves to teach him something about Christianity by building a crêche for Christmas. But to her dismay, she finds him eating the figures intricately made of chocolate, raisins, and nuts when she briefly leaves him alone with the crêche. Slimane is impassive about his offense—he had gone without dinner—and his mentor comes to realize that he was right to do so. "This is the desert. . . . Here food is not an adornment; it is meant to be eaten." As for her Christian zeal, "It had been too much head and high ideals,' she reflected, 'and not enough heart'." The next day the French official in the village orders her to leave Algeria because of the war. Slimane accompanies her to the town where she will take the train to the coast. The trip to Colomb-Bechar is her chance to say goodbye to him; but she discovers that it is his chance to leave the oasis, live in a city, and fight against the French. While she was packing, Fraulein Windling had gotten a splinter under her nail; the story ends with her thinking of Slimane's fate, while her wound throbs away.

The story is as complex in the telling as any Bowles has written; what is so strange and moving is its benignity. What it portends for his future work, I don't profess to know. But it's good to find him writing a tender story and one which strengthens his grip on contemporary experience. (pp. 30-1)

Theodore Solotaroff, "The Desert Within," in The New Republic, *Vol. 157, No. 10, September 2, 1967, pp. 29-31.*

CHARLES T. SAMUELS (essay date 1967)

[*Samuels was an American literature and film critic whose works include studies of John Updike and Henry James. In the following excerpt, Samuels assesses the stories in* The Time of Friendship *as stylistically brilliant but thematically superficial.*]

[***The Delicate Prey, and Other Stories***] was dedicated to "my mother, who first read me the stories of Poe," but Bowles improved on his master. With muted prose, he refined Poe's menacing but frequently hysterical atmosphere, while his tropical and African settings provided a more plausible backdrop for terror than Poe could dream up in his New York Grub Street. More important, Bowles writes out of an ironist's vision of human bestiality, whereas Poe writes mostly for emotional effect. Nevertheless, master and pupil share defects of clarity and variety which are as evident in Bowles's new stories [in ***The Time of Friendship***] as in ***The Delicate Prey.***

"Doña Faustina" begins its black course in a way Poe might have envied ("No one could understand why Doña Faustina had bought the inn."), and its puzzles create progressive anxiety. What ripples the water from the bottom of Doñ Faustina's tank? Why does she allow a mestizo interloper to rape her, and what did she feed him before the act?

Bowles's answers are appropriately awful. The lady bought the inn for the purpose of hiding kidnaped babies, the tank contained crocodiles to which she fed their corpses, and her *banquet d'amour* was a baby's heart. The heart should have conferred "the power of thirty-seven" (presumably babies) on the offspring of her violation, but the significance of so bizarre an act is still in doubt by the end of the tale. Doña Faustina's son does become so strong and cunning that he is made a police colonel, but when he captures thirty-seven bandits in a stunning coup, he lets them go. Did Bowles intend a joke about the unexpected effect of witchcraft (including a parody of the Resurrection: the boy's name is Jesus Maria) or a warning against exotic diets? The ending encourages facetiousness, but the rest of the tale is too sinister to be taken for comedy.

More characteristic but equally puzzling is **"Tapiama,"** about an American photographer in the tropics who lets himself be taken to an island cantina, where he gets drunk and encounters some ominous denizens. As events become more phantasmagoric, the hero's desire to attain freedom through self-abandonment seems to fail him. Challenged to remain, he loses heart; but when he tries to row himself back to his hotel he gets lost, only to be picked up by five men who refuse him return. Instead they insist that he repeat the sound of a talking bird that caws *"Idigaraga"* at them from a nearby tree.

His experience is a nightmare "whose painful logic he followed with the entire fiber of his being, without however, once being given a clear vision of what agonizing destinies were at stake." After creating the experience with great power and vividness, Bowles leaves the reader just as perplexed. The five men tell the photographer that the bird is one which invades others' nests and bemoans its unpopularity when expelled, but any parallel that might be drawn to the hero is confounded by his unbirdlike passivity and indifference.

A third evocative tale is more deft in characterization and complex in structure. **"The Hours After Noon"** concerns a pension proprietor described, in the first section, as a woman whose dissatisfaction with her present makes her hate the romantic past which throws it into low relief. The story's epigraph (from Baudclaire), a pattern of statements and verbal echoes, bits of action and décor—even the heroine's name (Mrs. Callender)—all point to a serious consideration of time and memory; but the plot scarcely articulates the theme. Mrs. Callender nearly causes an affair between her daughter and a roué guest by warning the girl against a surrender which would, in effect, repeat her own past. However, the affair doesn't come off, while the girl becomes involved but quickly uninvolved with another man. Nevertheless, the story concludes with the roué's murder, though Bowles makes it difficult to know who killed him and why.

Seldom does one encounter stories so carefully composed, with atmosphere so commanding, prose so fluent, and purpose so little ascertainable. One walks through a dream where everything is simultaneously vivid and muffled. There are exceptions, like **"The Wind at Beni Midar,"** a gruesome anecdote about superstition, and **"The Hyena"** and **"The Garden,"** parables whose ironic dispatch provides especially sharp versions of Bowles's belief that evil is unconquerable. Other tales like **"The Successor"** and **"A Friend of the World"** are clearly conceived, but they are too slight to relieve the book's mood of indefinite malaise.

The title story [**"The Time of Friendship"**] about a Swiss schoolteacher wintering in Algeria, who befriends a street urchin, is the volume's one substantial success. Making the boy her factotum, the schoolteacher inspires "an attitude of respect bordering on adoration . . . [which] never altered unless she inadvertently tangled with the subject of Islam. . . ." Beneath her friendship and charity, unacknowledged but determinant, is a sense that the boy is culturally inferior, as well as poor. Trying to train him in the civilized religion of the Nazarenes, the schoolteacher fails, but she thinks she has attained a truer understanding of Slimane, the street urchin. (p. 183)

"The Time of Friendship" is the best story Bowles has published, but it is so absolutely atypical, both in its realistic cultural implications and in its tenderness, that it prevents us from making any generalizations about his art. . . . Save for the title story, the new collection reveals neither development nor deepening. Bowles's style is still masterly in its maintenance of tension. His vision is still acerbic and his inventions exotic. But his significance still shimmers fitfully; and when we reach the bottom, it seems either shallow or stagnant. (p. 184)

Charles T. Samuels, "What's That in the Tank?" in The Nation, *New York, Vol. 205, No. 6, September 4, 1967, pp. 183-84.*

ROBERT PHILLIPS (essay date 1967)

[*In the following excerpt, Phillips appraises the stories in* The Time of Friendship *as more profound explorations of the mind's dissolution than those in* The Delicate Prey.]

The Time of Friendship is no malebolge of nursery rhymes. One story (**"Dona Faustina"**) blithely uncovers a nice old woman in her quotidian rituals of witchcraft, infanticide, and cannibalism. Another (**"If I Should Open My Mouth"**) is the journal of a madman who plants poisoned gum in New York's subway vending machines. A fable (**"The Garden"**) concerns a good and innocent man who is violently set upon by his neighbors with hoes and sickles. A fourth (**"The Successor"**) concludes with the murder of a Frenchman by Moroccans, his body left behind a rock with wire tightly wrapped around his throat.

Still pretty tame stuff, compared to ***The Delicate Prey.*** In the years since that book Mr. Bowles evidently has become less concerned with outer violence and more with interior. The action of his stories remains much the same: These are tales of flight rather than quest, depicting isolated characters in the grips of desperate nihilism who look for escape from life through drugs, sexual ecstasy, or death. Bowles still sees man as naturally depraved. But the best stories in this book probe more deeply than the first's the psyche's disintegration. Moreover, the landscape of the author's imagination has expanded to include New York and rural Pennsylvania as well as the more exotic Morocco and Algiers of his earlier books.

The most notable examples of Bowles' finer delineation of the human condition are the title story [**"The Time of Friendship"**], which chronicles the betrayal and collapse of a meaningful friendship; **"Tapiama,"** in which an existential antihero falls prey to chance, conspiracy, and destruction; and **"The Frozen Fields,"** the story of how a father's hostility drives his sensitive son toward insanity. If the boy Donald's interior journey to madness recalls that of Paul, the young protagonist in Conrad Aiken's fine short story, "Silent Snow, Secret Snow," it is because Bowles has succeeded as completely as Aiken in using this material in an original and memorable way.

There are some failures in ***The Time of Friendship.*** **"The Hyena"** is an arch fable which is too facile and need not have been collected. Some characters in the shorter stories seem to act out of the author's whim rather than from personal motivation. Nevertheless the collection shows Paul Bowles to be an author who deserves to be taken seriously. Perhaps never again will he be called just another author of "high brow terror fiction" as he was some years ago. (p. 38)

Robert Phillips, "Stories That End with Screams," in The North American Review, *Vol. 252, No. 6, November, 1967, pp. 38-9.*

MAUREEN HOWARD (essay date 1968)

[*Howard is an American novelist, short story writer, critic, and editor whose novels include* Bridgeport Bus *(1965),* Grace Abounding *(1982), and* Expensive Habits *(1986). She is acclaimed for her novels about women searching for identity amid career aspirations and within socially prescribed roles. In the excerpt below, Howard notices a decline in passion in the stories from* The Time of Friendship *compared to Bowles's novel* The Sheltering Sky.]

[Reading ***The Time of Friendship***], I was aware of a career honest in its aims but only occasionally swinging free of a steady performance. Unlike Tennessee Williams' attempts at unmanageable forms, Bowles sticks with what he can do. Here are the gothic tales with their meaningless violence and seedy Arab settings which repeat the formula established in ***The Delicate Prey*** seventeen years ago. Here are the macabre Saki endings and the landscapes beautifully tuned to an indefinable melancholy. The stories are always carefully written but, for the most part, they are too self-contained and seldom have anything to match the atmosphere of frenzied desolation that drives through *The Sheltering Sky* to make it Bowles's masterpiece. He is still involved with his ideas of twenty years ago but he has lost his passion for them. The existential experience of *The Sheltering Sky* can never seem dated, but many of the empty exotic scenes in ***The Time of Friendship*** depend upon a bleak modernity which has worn thin even for Bowles.

This is not true of the story entitled **"The Time of Friendship"**—a wonderful exploration of the limits of love between a Swiss spinster and an Arab boy. Significantly, it gains from its concerns with society. The woman's yearly retreat to the peace of the desert is based on a travel-poster conception of tranquillity that screens out most of the picture. She can never stop teaching, in an enlightened colonial spirit, the little boy whom she grows to love. Polite friendship is the only possible arrangement for these two because she will always give in the wrong way and he will always use her. Her European morality, his devious Arab practicality will make them blind to the other's needs. The Swiss woman is forced to leave the desert because of the Algerian War, the sort of historic occasion which is rare in Bowles. It is not an intrusion upon the tenderness of the story, but a fact which makes ***"The Time of Friendship"*** more than a delicate tale. Only the war will set the spinster and the boy free of each other—each to live with his own disappointment and his own possibilities. . . . In another story, **"The Hours After Noon,"** the shoddy morality of a British matron is played off against a real, though decadent, sensuality of one of the guests at her pension. Again Bowles lets us get hold of some easy associations and then with great artistry proceeds to transform the familiar setup into a real horror for which we must find a fresh response. (pp. 149, 151)

Another splendid story in the collection, **"The Frozen Fields,"** centers on the dreamlike quality of a child trying to piece together the terrible world of adults. It is set on an American farm at Christmas time, almost exotic territory for Bowles, but he knows it thoroughly—all the cruelty and pain rooted in the definable past—and I felt once more that the ordinary should be more central to his vision. His voice need only break through a distracting patter of accomplishment to be heard again. (pp. 151-52)

Maureen Howard, "Other Voices," in Partisan Review, *Vol. XXXV, No. 1, Winter, 1968, pp. 141-52.*

PAUL GRAY (essay date 1979)

[*In the following excerpt, Gray offers a favorable review of* Collected Stories: 1939-1976.]

Collected Stories: 1939-1976 provides a chance to isolate and trace one strand of Bowles' remarkable career. The book's 39 tales are not only worth reading on their own, but their assembly should dispel several myths that have grown up around Bowles' work. First, spreading his talent wide has not meant that he spread it thin; any short list of the best contemporary American stories should include two or three from this volume. Second, Bowles' reputation as a pitiless chronicler of the bizarre and sadistic is undeserved; many of his stories are unquestionably grotesque, but the impact of this collection is much more complex and humane.

The essential Bowles plot charts a clash between two cultures, one usually Western and the other primitive. Primitive almost always gets the home court advantage; Bowles favors settings in North Africa, near the deadly lure of the Sahara, or in stifling, vegetation-choked places in Mexico or South America. Visitors come to feast on the picturesque and take one step too many off the beaten path. From that point on, they are more truly on their own than they ever dreamed possible. Sometimes their fate is terrible. In **"A Distant Episode,"** a linguistics professor studying North African dialects stumbles foolishly into the hands of a gang of marauding nomads; they cut out his tongue and then teach him clownish tricks to perform at their revels. Other interlopers get gentler treatment. In **"Pastor Dowe at Tacaté,"** an ineffectual missionary is driven away from an Indian village by an act of generosity; local custom obliges him to accept a villager's seven-year-old daughter as his wife.

Bowles' outsiders can be predators as well as victims. A city woman in **"At Paso Rojo"** visits her brother's ranch and makes a pass at one of his Indian employees; he loses his job as a consequence. After causing this injustice, the woman "shrugged her shoulders, got into the bed . . . blew out the lamp, listened for a few minutes to the night sounds, and went peacefully to sleep, thinking of how surprisingly little time it had taken her to get used to life at Paso Rojo, and even, she had to admit now, to begin to enjoy it." Bowles' irony passes by like a night chill. The woman is not "getting used to" life at the ranch but perverting it.

One Bowles character jots down a "recipe for dissolving the impression of hideousness made by a thing: Fix the attention upon the given object or situation so that the various elements, all familiar, will regroup themselves. Frightfulness is never more than an unfamiliar pattern." Bowles may believe this, but his stories regularly do the reverse. They fix the attention on beauty and then suggest the frightfulness within. **"Pages from Cold Point,"** Bowles' best, eeriest tale, paints an idyllic Jamaican setting. But the narrator soon learns that his 16-year-old son is homosexual and has been cruising in dangerous native waters. Violence must be forestalled. The father is too civilized to confront the boy with what he knows, nor can he tell him to stop. So he allows his son to seduce him. (pp. 73-4)

In a haunting tale called **"The Circular Valley,"** Bowles portrays an Atlájala, an anima or *genius loci* that can inhabit the bodies of all creatures. Local Indians know enough to stay away, but over the centuries monks come and, then, robbers and soldiers; the Atlájala is fascinated at the complexities he finds when he looks out through the eyes of men. Finally, a man and woman unhappily in love enter the valley, and the spirit enters him. It finds "a world more suffocating and painful than the Atlájala had thought possible." Within the woman, though, "each element was magnified in intensity, the whole sphere of being was immense, limitless." At the top of his art, Bowles is an anima; to inhabit this book is to experience pain and immensity. (p. 74)

Paul Gray, "Steps Off the Beaten Path," in Time, *New York, Vol. 114, No. 9, August 27, 1979, pp. 73-4.*

JOYCE CAROL OATES (essay date 1979)

[A prolific and versatile American novelist, short story writer, critic, and nonfiction writer, Oates is perhaps best known for her novel them *(1969), which won a National Book Award, and for several novels she published during the early 1980s that draw upon elements of the Gothic romance. As a critic, Oates has written on remarkably diverse authors—from Shakespeare to Herman Melville to Samuel Beckett—and is appreciated for the individuality and erudition that characterize her critical work. In the review of* Collected Stories: 1939-1976 *excerpted below, Oates commends Bowles's powerful dramatizations of primitive cultures and his handling of "matters that are terrible without being terrifying, as if the events they delineate take place outside our customary human world."]*

In one of his poems, D. H. Lawrence speaks of a creature whose origin predates not only man, but God—a creature born "before God was love"—and it is precisely this sense of a natural world predating and excluding consciousness that Paul Bowles dramatizes so powerfully in his fiction. It is no accident that the doomed professor (of linguistics) in the story **"A Distant Episode"** loses his tongue before he loses his mind and his humanity—a captive of an outlaw tribe in the Sahara; nor is it by mere chance that an American girl, visiting her mother and her mother's lesbian companion in Colombia (in **"The Echo"**) succumbs to an irrational violence more alarming than any she has ever witnessed. Attacking her mother's lover, she "uttered the greatest scream of her life"—pure sound, bestial and liberating.

Too much has been made, perhaps, of the dreamlike brutality of Bowles's imagination, which evokes a horror far more persuasive than anything in Poe, or in Gide (whom Bowles peripherally resembles). But the stories, like fairytales, tend to dissolve into their elements because so little that is human in a psychological sense is given. The reader is usually outside Bowles's characters, even in those stories—**"You Are Not I," "Pages From Cold Point," "Reminders of Bouselham"**—in which a first-person narrator speaks.

Most of the stories deal with matters that are terrible without being terrifying, as if the events they delineate take place outside our customary human world. A young boy is tortured and castrated in the desert by a maddened hashish smoker (**"The Delicate Prey"**); an Amazonian woman, living in a squalid ruin in Mexico, captures infants in order to devour their hearts and thereby gain supernatural power (**"Doña Faustina"**); the soul of a kif-besotted boy passes into a snake who has "the joy of pushing his fangs" into two men before he is killed (**"Allal"**); a sensitive young Mexican girl succumbs to the atmosphere of sadism around her, and accepts a kinship with "monstrous" spiders who live in the crevices of her bedroom wall (**"At Paso Rojo"**). In **"Call at Corazón"** a traveler abandons his alcoholic wife to an unimaginable fate in the South American jungle; in **"The Hours After Noon"** a child molester is driven by a fellow European into the Moroccan hills, where his fate—a few twists of wire about the neck—is inevitable once he approaches an Arab child. . . .

Even those stories in which nothing explicitly violent happens, stories that would probably not offend the average genteel reader—**"The Frozen Fields," "The Time of Friendship"**—create an unnerving suspense by virtue of Bowles's masterly craft. He has learned from Hemingway as well as from that other 20th-century master of short fiction, D. H. Lawrence; even his descriptions are wonderfully dramatic. Nothing is extraneous, nothing is wasted. If one wants, at times, more humanity—more "consciousness"—surely this is a naïve prejudice, a wish that art always and forevermore affirm our human vantage point, as if the brute implacable *otherness* of the natural world were no more threatening than a painted backdrop for an adventure film.

Though Bowles's marvelous landscapes call to mind Lawrence, it is misleading to read Bowles in the light of Lawrence. Even in Lawrence's coldest, most "legendary" tales, where landscape overcomes humanity . . . one confronts and, to some extent, enters into the lives of recognizable human beings whose personalities are always convincing; and this is not true in Bowles. Lawrence's people are like us, Bowles's people tend to be our very distant kin, shadowy and remote, unclaimable. One cannot imagine Bowles creating a Constance Chatterley or a Mellors, trembling with apprehension of each other, or a Gerald (of *Women in Love*), so susceptible to erotic passion that he chooses death rather than a life without the woman he desires. "Desire" in Bowles's fiction—**"Under the Sky,"** for instance, where a Mexican peasant rapes an American woman—is no more articulated than the emotion of the deranged professor of linguistics. Bowles does not write about sexual love, like many contemporary writers, in order to challenge its mythology; he does not write about it at all. His interests lie elsewhere. (p. 9)

Like Bowles's novels, the best of these stories are beautifully fashioned, and as bleakly unconsoling as the immense deserts about which he writes with such power. They have a way of lingering in the memory for decades—disturbing, vexing, like a partly-recalled dream. The reader is advised to approach them with caution, however, limiting himself to one or two at a sitting, beginning perhaps with the wonderful **"Pastor Dowe at Tacaté."** For these are stories set in an epoch "before God was love," and beside them most acclaimed fiction of our time—brightly and nervously ironic, or dutifully attuned to the latest "moral" problems—seems merely shallow. (p. 29)

> *Joyce Carol Oates, "Bleak Craft," in* The New York Times Book Review, *September 30, 1979, pp. 9, 29.*

H. C. RICKS (essay date 1980)

[*In the following excerpt, Ricks offers a detailed survey of some of the pieces in* Collected Stories: 1939-1976 *and comments on the influence of the oral tradition of storytelling on Bowles's later short fiction.*]

The majority of the stories published in Bowles's first collection, ***The Delicate Prey,*** already exhibit a mature sense of subject and of technique. **"A Distant Episode"** is one of the best of these stories. The title reminds the reader that the events described are far removed from the west. It is an initiation story (Bowles has written a number of these), a meeting between the rule-bound west, represented by "the Professor," and the violence of North Africa. The Professor is a professor of linguistics; preoccupied by the structure of Language, he is incapable of communication.

> "I wish everyone knew me," said the Professor . . .
> "*No* one knows you," said his companion gruffly.

He is captured by the Reguibat tribe who cut out his tongue, deck him with the bottoms of tin cans and make him into a clown. At this point, he "was no longer conscious; to be exact, he existed in the middle of the movements made by these other men. With the loss of his tongue, the Professor loses his western identity and is able to become part of the tribe, falling easily "in with their sense of ritual." But the Reguibat sell the Professor and, separated from his community, he begins to return to consciousness. First, listening to his new master, he becomes aware of spoken language; then, staring at a calendar, he becomes conscious of written language.

> The tiny ink marks of which a symphony consists may have been made long ago, but when they are fulfilled in sound they become imminent and mighty. So a kind of music of feeling began to play in the Professor's head, increasing in volume as he looked at the mud wall, and he had the feeling that he was performing what had been written for him long ago.

Although the Professor has returned to consciousness, he has not returned to his original point of departure. He is no longer aware of language simply as a linguistic structure, a "because." Now he shares the Moslem belief that all events are "written," and language has "become imminent and mighty," a divine "and then." As the Professor runs into the desert, having escaped from the house of his purchaser, a French soldier thinks, correctly, that he is "a holy maniac."

"The Time of Friendship," written in 1962, is perhaps the most affirmative of Bowles's stories, expressing a hope for successful human contact which is largely absent elsewhere in his fiction. Like **"A Distant Episode,"** it tells the story of a westerner reaching an understanding of North Africa. But no dramatic and violent initiation takes place; rather we witness Fraulein Windling's slow progress towards an understanding with a Moslem boy, Slimane. Fraulein Windling winters each year in North Africa, and admires the country and its people. Slimane is drawn to her, initially perhaps by curiosity, and their acquaintance is cemented by her kindness. But kindness and respect are not enough; Fraulein Windling and Slimane can only understand each other as the result of extended interaction. She is a teacher, so she tries to teach him to read French. Though Slimane speaks French, the attempt is a failure.

> Often just as she felt he was about to connect two loose ends of ideas and perhaps at last make a contact which would enable him to understand the principle, a look of resignation and passivity would appear in his face, and he would willfully cut off the stream of effort from its source, and remain sitting, merely looking at her, shaking his head from side to side to show that it was useless.

Unconsciously, Fraulein Windling is attempting to westernize Slimane, to teach him "the principle," the "because" implicit in western languages. His "resignation and passivity," the quality of the "and then" frame of mind, defeat her. Bowles's run-on sentence, with its repeated use of "and," emphasizes this quality. Fraulein Windling also attempts to explain Christianity to Slimane and is equally unsuccessful. She decides to make a creche for the last Christmas Eve she will spend in North Africa. (The revolution against the French is intensifying and the area will soon be closed to Europeans.) This creche is her final attempt at explanation, but Slimane innocently destroys the creche, eating the food and playing with the figures. Initially, Fraulein Windling is angry, but she realizes that she is wrong.

> "This is the desert," she told herself. Here food is not an adornment; it is meant to be eaten. She had spread out food and he had eaten it. Any argument which attached blame to that could only be false.

She has learned to accept Slimane without trying to transform him. The passage we have quoted signals approval of her perception by moving from direct quotation into an authorial voice. But Slimane has also gained insight. As she leaves, he tells her that she is

> "Sad because I ate the food out of the picture. That was very bad. Forgive me."

She is actually sad because of the mutual misunderstanding and distrust which are leading to war, and of which the creche is only an emblem. So contact is made only to be broken by the events of the larger world.

Bowles has always been interested in abnormal states of mind. **"You Are Not I,"** written in 1948, is narrated by a schizophrenic, and **"If I Should Open My Mouth,"** written in 1952, is the purported journal of a madman. So it is not surprising that Bowles should have become interested in the affects of kif, a form of cannabis. In 1962, he published a group of four stories, ***A Hundred Camels in the Courtyard,*** which are primarily concerned with the use of this drug. One, **"He of the Assembly,"** comes closer than any of his other published fiction to a surrealistic atmosphere. It will be sufficient to quote the thoughts of He of the Assembly (the name of the central character):

> And when the wind came in the door it was made of dust high as a man. A night to be chased by dogs in the Mellah. I looked in the fire and I saw an eye in there, like the eye that's left when you burn *chibb* and you know there was a *djinn* in the house. I got up and stood. The fire was making a noise like a voice. I think it was talking.

Obviously, Bowles has come a long way from his early surrealism. This passage is effective out of context, but in context it becomes an expression of He of the Assembly's paranoia which has expanded from a fear of the police to include all of the world, seen and unseen.

Bowles' translations also mark a qualified return to his early surrealism. With the exception of the work by Mohamed Choukri, all of the stories in *Five Eyes* are versions of spoken texts. These tales are not, for the most part, traditional. (Story-telling is a profession in North Africa.) In the case of Layachi's fiction, the material is actually autobiographical. The kinship with automatic writing is obvious: the stories are not premeditated and each telling is responsive to the impulse of the moment. *Five Eyes* is probably the best introduction to this aspect of Bowles's work. (pp. 85-8)

The translations have had a noticeable effect on Bowles's later fiction. He began to imitate the oral tradition, as early as 1960, in **"The Hyena,"** an animal fable. These stories are typically stripped of all extraneous detail. We may not even know the names of the characters, for example in **"The Garden"** where the central character is "a man." By 1974, Bowles explicitly begins to initiate the oral style in the stories, **"Mejdoub"** and **"The Fqih."** As in the translations, the dialogue appears without quotation marks, indicating that the whole story is spoken by a single voice.

Like the Professor in **"A Distant Episode,"** Bowles may seem to have returned to his starting point, surrealistic description having been replaced by kif dreams and automatic writing by oral texts. But to see his career as static or circular is a mistake. The early surrealism was an act of violence towards language, a literal dismembering. The stories collected here redirect this violence, allowing dismemberment an uneasy coherence. The seventeen-year-old could only appropriate a style; the intervening years have created a master capable of appropriating a culture. (p. 88)

H. C. Ricks, "Another Country," in Chicago Review, *Vol. 31, No. 4, Spring, 1980, pp. 83-8.*

WENDY LESSER (essay date 1980)

[*In the review excerpted below, Lesser discusses Bowles's style and characteristic themes in* Collected Stories: 1939-1976.]

The problem with reviewing Paul Bowles' ***Collected Stories: 1939-1976*** is that any description of their content would be too specific, would belie their hard-won lack of definition by giving them too firm an outline. Plot summary has the same effect on these stories that conversion to film has on good novels: by giving you an image to hold in your mind, the film—however faithful to the novel—forever cuts off imaginative possibilities that the novel made available. The most essential aspect of Bowles's stories—the way in which things *don't* get said explicitly—is inevitably lost in any discussion of their content. Yet these stories must be talked about, because it is rare for any writer's "Collected Works" (and this one spans 47 years of writing) to present the kind of uniform perfection that this book does.

"Uniform" is a misleading word here, in that it suggests lack of variety. Certainly the 39 stories in this collection could not be more various. They range in setting from South American jungles to mountainous villages to African deserts to the subways of Manhattan. They deal with virtually every imaginable intimate human relationship: husband to wife, parent to child, sister to sister and brother to brother, employee to employer, pastor to congregation, killer to victim, human to animal, lover to lover, and stranger to stranger. Even their narrative technique varies widely, from the first-person distorted reality of the mad narrators in **"You Are Not I"** and **"If I Should Open My Mouth,"** to the removed, neutral, folk-myth-like telling of **"The Scorpion"** and **"The Water of Izli."** Yet there *is* something common to all these stories, and I think that sameness has to do with tone, or what Bowles himself . . . calls the "voice" of a story. In all of the stories Bowles has written, that voice is shaped by one particular effort—the strenuous withholding of judgment.

Not that the strain shows in the stories themselves: if anything, their language seems at first glance to be as fluid and straightforward as the language of folk tales and fireside stories. The narrative voice itself never suggests that judgment is in any way called for. Yet a brief look at the kind of stories Bowles *seems* to borrow from—for instance, the [five Moroccan] oral tales he translates in *Five Eyes*—reveals that authorial opinions are pervasive in those stories: the narrators think nothing of saying "This was good" or "She was ugly" whenever they feel like it. Bowles, on the other hand, has consciously excised such narrative judgments from his own stories, leaving a gap that creates strong tension between the seemingly traditional form and the far-from-traditional voice. Moreover, the events in Bowles's stories are the sort that cry out for judgment: enormous cruelty, bizarre and inexplicable behavior, psychological and cultural conflict. Yet judgment is consistently suppressed, and therefore the events never fully take shape as "bizarre" or "cruel"—they are simply events.

If I have given the impression that Bowles is a sort of Robbe-Grillet who writes on action-packed topics, this is a false impression. Whereas Robbe-Grillet and other writers who experimented in that manner were interested in the photographic, "objective" look of things, Bowles is at least as much concerned with internal states. Even the stories which are written from a third-person viewpoint frequently focus on a single character's perceptions, and all of Bowles's landscapes seem tinged by human response to them. But such distinctions—internal/external, subjective/objective, alien/familiar, willed/fated, and even cruel/kind—begin to seem pointless in relation to Bowles's work. His stories, if they are uniformly about anything, are about the annihilation of such barriers—and yet he depends on us to remember these barriers, and thereby to give the stories something solid to work against. Bowles's stories about the loss of distinctions are written for an audience that believes in the necessity of distinctions.

A common theme in these stories is the transformation of a Self into an Other. In **"You Are Not I"** (which explicitly echoes that theme in its title), a mad-woman comes to believe that she has turned into her sister: hence the "I" of the beginning and the "I" of the end represent two different characters in the story. In **"A Distant Episode,"** a linguistics professor becomes a tongueless idiot who dances for the amusement of his captors. In **"The Circular Valley,"** a ghost-like spirit, the Atlajala, entertains itself by taking on the perceptions first of animals, then of humans. And in **"Allal,"** a boy enters into the body of a snake and sees his own abandoned body from the outside. . . . In many of these stories, the loss of self is linked with speechlessness (the man who has his tongue cut out in **"A Distant Episode,"** the boy who becomes a silent snake in **"Allal"**), with a journey whose destination is unknown (as in **"Pastor Dowe at Tacaté," "Señor Ong and Señor Ha,"** and, again, **"A Distant Episode"**), and with a general sense of cultural disorientation (which pervades the New York of **"If I Should Open My Mouth"** and **"How Many Midnights"** as much as it does the Latin America of **"Call at Corazón"** or the Bangkok of **"You Have Left Your Lotus Pods on the Bus"**).

Themes like speechlessness and journeying reek of allegory, yet Bowles's stories are anything but allegorical in tone. I said at the beginning that to specify was to belie the stories, but there is one kind of specificity that particularly suits them: it is quite possible, and even instructive, to talk about Bowles's language, about the actual words he uses. In accord with his evasion of judgment, Bowles allows the greatest weight to rest on the tiniest and least significant words. In "A Distant Episode," for instance, he introduces the violent twist in the professor's fate by saying:

> He stepped ahead distrustfully still, as if he expected another treacherous drop. It was so hard to know in this uniform, dim brightness. Before he knew what had happened the dog was upon him, a heavy mass of fur trying to push him backwards . . .

The tremendous skill of Paul Bowles lies in that little definite article—"*the* dog." There have been many dogs already in this story—dogs barking, dogs feared in the dark, dogs alluded to—but they are all non-specific. This dog is specific at least partly because it is unexpected; it is the word "the" which surprises us as much as the attack itself. And yet the formulation is not untrue to colloquial speech: if he had been able to tell the story afterwards in the safety of his home, the professor himself might have said, "And then the dog jumped on me." So while the word carries a weight of significance—as if this were *the* dog, like *the* fate, which awaited the professor even before he knew of its existence—it breaks no rules of normal usage. It is both definite and unpredictable, noticeably *off* and yet *exactly accurate*—just like Paul Bowles's stories themselves.

Wendy Lesser, in a review of "Collected Stories," in The American Book Review, *Vol. 2, No. 4, May-June, 1980, p. 24.*

IRVING MALIN (essay date 1980)

[Malin is a prolific American critic and editor who has written studies of such authors as William Faulkner, Saul Bellow, and William Styron. In the essay excerpted below, Malin disputes the often stated opinion that Bowles is a sensationalist, maintaining that Bowles sincerely believes the world is capriciously brutal.]

[Although] the meticulously described landscape changes [in ***Collected Stories: 1939-1976***], the situation of Bowles' heroes remains the same.

The hero is usually a displaced person; he is suddenly, often brutally compelled to see the "heart of darkness." He is abused, violated, transformed. But Bowles refuses to allow him more than a few seconds of understanding; his broken hero disappears under "the sheltering sky."

Although we expect some final clarification of the disturbing mysteries—some "sense of an ending" (to use Frank Kermode's phrase)—we merely discover more shadows. There is no ultimate, rational solution—even after abrupt mutilations of self. It is, indeed, the sustaining axiom of these stories that the self—or the outside world—is tentative, fragile, and obscure. Bowles disdains any psychological explanation (except indirectly); he offers *moments* of ecstasy and fright—these are oddly married—and not the causes, preconceptions, or origins of the moments.

"Allal," one of the most brilliant stories in this collection of thirty-nine stories, introduces us to a youngster in North Africa. He plays alone; he works for slave wages; he enjoys little time for self-analysis. (Nor does he believe in such rationalism.) He is possessed, "primitive," dream-filled: he prefers "the sound of the wind in the trees." We are unable to understand in our "civilized," Western manner any of Allal's apparent choices. We are simply thrust into his *situation.*

Allal develops another pattern. He falls in love with snakes. He admires their delicate markings, "markings so delicate and perfect that they seemed to have been designed and painted by an artist." He decides—probably the wrong word!—to become a snake. He moves like one; he sleeps like one. Eventually he loses whatever human identity he had. He sheds his skin of self and achieves his unlimited "freedom." Before an axe severs his head, he has the pleasure of "pushing" his fangs into the bad men who pursue him.

Obviously, Bowles dislikes Allal's pursuers—civilized men who cannot recognize the beauty of madness. In **"Pages from Cold Point"** he gives us a narrator who is a complete, cynical rationalist. This hero, unlike Allal, refuses to submit his will. By writing his journal, he believes that he can control himself, the reader, and the "process of decay." He is, however, a divided personality—again the clinical words have little meaning in a Bowles story—because he loves chaos *even more* than the semblance of stability.

At first he devotes himself to his son, Racky, in a "normal," earnest way. But Racky is his snake—the other side. Soon it becomes impossible for father and son to act in conventional roles. They merge identities—such fluidity of reversal obsesses Bowles—and they assume mad parts in a romance.

It is, indeed, unclear whether father seduces son or vice versa. The shock, of course, is that homosexual incest occurs at Cold Point, the wonderfully named location. Here the "love" exchanged is frigid and spooky. We are chilled by the deliberate understatement of an outrageous situation. And when we read that the narrator is so insane as to believe "nothing very drastic" *has happened or will happen* to his island of contentment, we are even more astounded. The tonal coldness—which covers the emotional underground—is perfectly appropriate.

In both stories there is the sense of a spirit hovering over the landscape. And we are not surprised to see the spirit *appear as hero* in **"The Circular Valley."** The spirit moves in a restless way. It becomes a deer, a bee, a serpent. It overhears the love-and-struggle words of human beings. But it refuses to settle for a mere *self.* It is, if you will, an eternal, circular being—more powerful and beautiful and unpredictable than mankind.

I do not think that Bowles is a sensationalist in these stories—or, for that matter, in any of the others I have omitted from my discussion. He does not glory in his painstaking depiction of madness or destruction or mysticism. He believes firmly that life is unpredictably cruel—even to cruel heroes!—and that his accurate, intense art must *contain* the cruelty.

His style is thus stripped of prettiness. It is clear, direct, bold. (pp. 91-2)

When we read Bowles, we enter a new land. We recognize that our daily lives—our usual words—are shields against the unknowable universe. In a strange way we resemble his unwilling (?) victims. I do not mean to imply that we are Allal; I merely suggest that we suddenly appreciate how gratuitously "normality" and "abnormality" can change roles. (p. 93)

Irving Malin, "Abrupt Mutilations," in The Ontario Review, *No. 12, Spring-Summer, 1980, pp. 91-3.*

WAYNE POUNDS (essay date 1981)

[*In the excerpt below, Pounds discusses the motif of the predatory instinct of human nature in* The Delicate Prey.]

In the stories and novels up through 1967, which saw the appearance of Bowles's second major collection of stories. ***The Time of Friendship,*** the representative protagonist was the Westerner abroad. After 1967 this figure moves from center stage as the stories become steadily more North African in setting and characters, and Bowles gives his creative attention increasingly to collaboration with oral-tradition Moroccan storytellers. I propose to examine Bowles's first collection of stories, ***The Delicate Prey*** to show how one fable in this work, taken in connection with parallel episodes from the childhood portion of Bowles's autobiography [*Without Stopping*], clarifies the meaning of the isolated individual in the entirety of ***The Delicate Prey.*** (pp. 620-21)

The story in which the fable of the internalized animal principle first takes its significant form, **"The Scorpion",** resulted from a creative insight which appears to have been seminal in Bowles's development as a writer of fiction. Its publication in *View* in 1945 marked his first mature story and the first fiction he had published since 1930, when a short extract from an abortive novel appeared. Bowles's autobiographical account of the genesis of the story points to its role as a prototypical fable in his later work. While reading ethnographic collections of primitive myths, Bowles recounts in *Without Stopping,* his autobiography, "the desire came to me to invent my own myths, adopting the point of view of the primitive mind. The only way I could devise for simulating that state was the old Surrealist method of abandoning conscious control and writing whatever words came from the pen". What I here am calling "fable", in order to accent its structural function in his fiction, Bowles calls "myth", underscoring what was for him at that time its deeply personal importance. Bowles's equation of the primitive point of view with the abdication of control defines the strategy of many of the stories which follow **"The Scorpion".** "First, animal legends resulted from the experiments and then tales of animals disguised as 'basic human' beings". When *View* published **"The Scorpion",** Bowles felt encouraged to continue inventing myths. "The subject matter of the myths soon turned from 'primitive' to contemporary, but the objectives and behavior of the protagonists remained the same as in the beast legends. It was through this unexpected little gate that I crept back into the land of fiction writing".

Although Bowles began writing stories in early childhood, by the end of his adolescence he had stopped because he believed that he "failed to understand life"; he was not "able to find points of reference" which he might have in common with "the hypothetical reader". The actual reader of *Without Stopping* may rather judge this declared incomprehension of other people to be the result of the acutely oppressive family in which he matured, one in which "Children were treacherous and grown-ups inscrutable", as he observes, and he was himself treated as a "captured animal of uncertain reactions", the perpetual object of parental distrust. But in spite of his disavowal of belief in his own experience, Bowles seems to learn, like Emerson's American scholar, that when "he dives into his privatest, secretest presentiment, to his wonder he finds this is the most acceptable, most public, and universally true." . . . **"The Scorpion"** embodies Bowles's deliberate attempt to turn the social disadvantage he feels to artistic and therapeutic use by a calculated plumbing of the primitive strata of his mind.

The meaning of the outward action of **"The Scorpion"** is defined by a parallel inner action contained in the main character's dream. Both plots describe the way in which the intolerable anxiety which human contact produces is overcome by the acceptance of isolation. An old woman who lives alone in a cave has her placid animal existence disrupted when "One dark day she looked up to see one of her sons standing in the doorway" blocking the light. In response to her son's repeated insistence that she come away with him, she goes to sleep and dreams. First she dreams that it is daylight and she is among a crowd of people who fill her with anxiety; then it is night and she is a little girl laying in bed crying. She stops crying to watch a scorpion crawl down from the ceiling toward her; she tries to brush "him" down but "he" clings to her fingers. "Then she realized that he was not going to sting her. A great feeling of happiness went through her. She raised her finger to her lips to kiss the scorpion. . . . Slowly in the peace which was beginning, the scorpion moved into her mouth. She felt his hard shell and his little clinging legs going across her lips and her tongue. He crawled down her throat and was hers." Her dream reassures her that her isolation, being as much an inner orientation as an outward condition, is impenetrable, and when she awakes she is willing to accompany her son on the journey.

The process outlined in the dream is a skeletal human biography: with the internalization of the poisonous, isolating principle represented by the scorpion, the woman in the dream can deal with the community of people in the street, some of whom, it is implied, may well be her sons. Likewise, the old woman when she wakes can deal with the anxiety produced by her son's presence, for her dream has reassured her that in her withdrawn state human contact is not a threat. Ultimately it makes no difference to the old woman whether she goes with the son or not. "The mind turned scorpion lives among its stones", Bowles writes in a poem from 1940.

The frame story of **"The Scorpion"** repeats and elaborates elements of the meaning of the central dream it encloses. First, it emphasizes the old woman's isolation from human contact. Her many sons have all left her to go "away to the town where many people live"; she is "Neither happy nor unhappy to be there" alone. Second, it underscores the hint in the dream that the process of alienation is transmitted from generation to generation. The old woman is closely linked to suggestions of the origins of life: she is, after all, a mother; and her cave, itself an image of the womb, is near a spring where the occasional passer-by refreshes himself. The son comes back for the old woman, we may suppose, because he is the passive and uncomprehending vehicle of the message that it is time for her to be reborn in her grandchildren. The woman is very old and feeble, as her son notices, and the arduous journey is to be of three days' duration, a traditional interim between one life and the next. In subsequent stories she is reborn again and again.

The fable of **"The Scorpion"** is central to Bowles's work. Variant forms of it occur obscurely in other "tales of animals disguised as 'basic human' beings". Episodes parallel to it are described in the childhood portion of his autobiography. And with it, it is possible to clarify the thematic pattern of the larger part of his fiction. Two additional stories stand out from the others in ***The Delicate Prey*** as variants of the fable outlined in **"The Scorpion"** and as further examples of personal myths. To speak more precisely, these are tales of a predatory animal principle whose introjection in a human character is either accepted (the usual case), as in **"The Scorpion"** and **"The Circular Valley"**, or rejected, as in **"By the Water"**. Each of the latter two stories adds a variation to the signification of the central conflict between isolation and intolerable anxiety which is acted out in **"The Scorpion"**.

The title of **"The Circular Valley"** points to the characteristic device of much of Bowles's fiction, which is the use of geography as an externalization of human nature. Here, the valley, with its "sheer, black cliffs" enclosing an eminence on which stands an abandoned monastery, is a Poe-esque image of the human cranium as a *camera obscura,* comparable to the image of the haunted palace in Roderick Usher's poem. The circular valley is inhabited by the Atlájala, a spirit of indifferent malignity devoted to the enjoyment of pure sensation, gliding in and out of plants, animals, and men alike; knowing for a period what it feels like to be each, it is sentience incarnate. In its active and predatory phase, especially in the story's murderous ending, when it finds itself at home in the consciousness of a woman, the Atlájala is a pure type of the animal principle. Its experiences outline a crude definition of sexual difference; and, as in **"The Scorpion"**, it is the female nature rather than the male which incorporates an amoral destructive principle. Organically part of the larger world of non-human nature, the predatory principle has its home in the jungle. The jungle in turn is seen as an externalization of the female nature, or of the family over which she presides. The Atlájala's experiences define the bases of human sexual relationships: in the woman the basis is a predatory appetite for raw sensation; in the man, the craving for completion of a fragmented being whose characteristic words are "No" and "Never." The lover of this story is destroyed in the end by his refusal to enter the woman's arena of amoral destructiveness, when the Atlájala within her causes her to suggest to her lover that he should kill her husband. Her casual violence is identified with that of "the huge green world" that the Atlájala inhabits at other times, where the principle of life is predation.

"The Circular Valley" concerns itself less with the origins of family relationships and more with their adult entanglements than does **"The Scorpion"**. The third fable, **"By the Water"**, a story of the same year as **"The Scorpion"** and written by the same surrealist method, returns again to the question of origins, but from a different perspective. The setting is now North Africa, the desert terrain. (The desert, where the majority of Bowles's work is set, including the last five stories of ***The Delicate Prey,*** contrasts sharply with the tropics. The desert, as dramatized especially in Bowles's first novel, *The Sheltering Sky* (1950), where it becomes indeed the protagonist, is dominantly masculine, a world of negatives where the flesh is denied.) **"The Circular Valley"** deals with an Arab youth named Amar; though his name means "to love", he is, significantly, an orphan, "alone in the world". Because Amar wants to find someone related to him, he goes on a pilgrimage to a neighboring city where he thinks relatives may live. There, as in a dream, he finds a fearful image of the parental sources he is seeking. Taking refuge for the night in a bathhouse, Amar discovers himself in a sinister grotto ruled over by a creature, half crab, half human, with pincer-like arms—an animal disguised as a human being—named Lazrag. Details of the scene recall **"The Scorpion"**—the spring, the dripping water, the cave. The animals of both of these stories, the crab and the scorpion, are scuttling creatures attracted to darkness, hard-shelled, with pincers that become the focus of fear. Amar, like the son in **"The Scorpion"**, is a young adult whose search for his parental sources brings him to a cave inhabited by a creature neither wholly human nor wholly animal. Lazrag the crab has the same capacity as the scorpion (as well as the Atlájala) to embody himself in human form. Both creatures represent an alienating principle at the springs of human life. But Amar, unlike any other character in ***The Delicate Prey,*** is saved by human contact, through friendship with a young boy he meets in Lazrag's grotto and who accompanies him in his flight.

These three fables from ***The Delicate Prey*** define the terms "myth" and "primitive" as Bowles uses them when he explains the impetus for his fiction as having been initially the desire "to invent my own myths, adopting the point of view of the primitive mind". The sense of "myth" deriving from these stories is not a way of ordering transcendent knowledge or belief but a way of defining the significance of those crises of human experience which are personal and cultural: birth, initiation, friendship, marriage, relations to the natural world. The action does not emerge from the presence of some taint in humanity which might be a vestige of Calvinist belief, perhaps a relic of Bowles's New England parentage. Instead, the action is the effect of a deep anxiety working itself out in human relationships, relationships simplified and reduced for dramatic purposes to an impoversihed and unbecoming skeleton. The term "primitive" is identified with the absence of conscious control, or will, which is indeed eminently the civilized faculty and one that is lacking or defective in many of Bowles's protagonists. The behavior of the old woman in **"The Scorpion",** who is passive in relation to the poisonous principle she *receives,* and who relinquishes the civilized community for an animal existence in solitude, may indicate that it is a defect of will in Bowles's characters which draws them to primitive experience. Transcendence, or release from a kind of consciousness felt to be stifling, is envisioned, but only invertedly, in a phylogenetically backward course; the frontiers of the mind turn out to be zoological, a potential for bestialization. Gaston Bachelard writes of the human being as he appears in the work of Lautréamont, "Man then appears as a totalization of life possibilities, as a *suranimal;* he has all animal life in his disposition."

The whole of Bachelard's monograph [*Lautréamont,* 1956] is relevant here, for he goes on not only to assert the need to animalize as basic to imagination but to specify, in discussing Lautréamont, that the imaginative meaning of animal poison—the scorpion's venom is one example he cites—is *perfidie.* This word, which in most contexts would probably be translated as "treachery", in Bowles's work should be rendered as "distrust." Distrust is an all-important concept for understanding the functioning of the predatory principle, for it is distrust that links the predatory animal to the pattern of destructive parentage described in the stories and novels. (pp. 621-26)

Evil [in ***The Delicate Prey, and Other Stories***] is initially potential as a predatory principle in nature and then made real and manifest in human lives. A mother-figure may or may not be present in the story as the agent or medium of the destructive force unleashed, though given the psychological mechanism of interjection the presence of a parental figure in the offspring is always a possibility. The destructive force itself comes from the primitive ground of the personal unconscious—whether through dreams, alcohol, or psychotropic drugs—as well as from those more inaccessible layers of the unconscious which are represented by the animal world. With these variations the pattern holds for all the stories of ***The Delicate Prey*** with the partial exception of two, **"You Are Not I"** and **"How Many Midnights",** two stories which are exceptional in other ways. They alone are set in the United States; though they deal with poisoned family relationships, they lack the striking primitive features which in other stories symbolize inner experience; and, significantly, they are easily the two least effective stories in the collection. (p. 630)

The Delicate Prey contains a single clear division among its seventeen stories: the first ten are all set in tropical Central or South America or the Carribean (in **"Fourth Day Out from Santa Cruz"** the ship is bound *to* South America); and the last five are set in North Africa. The two stories that form the bridge between these two groups are the two referred to earlier that differ most from the dominant pattern of the collection; these are the two whose setting is the United States. It is the first twelve stories—the first ten plus the bridging pair—that deal centrally with family relationships. The overall image emerging from their reading is of the family as a kind of jungle, a lush green cover concealing, sometimes smothering, the perpetual warfare of its inhabitants. Aileen's journey in **"The Echo"** offers a schematic definition of the individual's development within this kind of family. As a young adult, Aileen is already trapped into identifying herself with a narrow and unsatisfactory rationality. She makes a journey back to her origins, a journey that is at once outer and inner, both geographical and spiritual, in order to understand her own nature and try to experience life more truly. But her journey is defeated in its purpose because the forces unleashed by her inward exploration, the forces which spring from the primitive and repressed areas of her psyche, overwhelm her in the savagery of their too long pent-up strength. Aileen's journey from the United States, the state of superficial and arid rationality, to the Colombian jungle, identified as the area of family origins, is the effort the alienated individual makes in order to achieve contract with the authentic possibilities of the self. Aileen's movement at the end of the **"The Echo"** back to the United States marks the final suppression of the inner self's urge to seek autonomy.

The final five stories of the collection, the North African stories, which deal with the family more peripherally, are centrally concerned with the fortunes of friendship. While such alienated characters as the Professor of **"A Distant Episode"** and the novelist of **"Tea on the Mountain"** are clear products of the kind of cultural nexus described in the preceding twelve stories, the central theme of the North African stories is friendship and its betrayal. Because friendship bypasses the warfare of sexual and family relationships, it seems to beckon with promise of healing affection, but the promise is always threatened by betrayal, as bloodily realized in the two famous "shockers" of the collection, **"The Delicate Prey"** and **"A Distant Episode".** The predatory principle is ubiquitous—it is perhaps the "hostile presence" of the desert itself—and the brighter light of the Saharan sun usually serves only to create darker shadows. Here, nonetheless, in **"By the Water",** friendship is envisioned as an ameliorating possibility.

Bowles's general point of view in ***The Delicate Prey*** seems little different from that of Freud, who himself devoted a lifetime to studying the contortions of the animal principle under the duress of civilization. In *Civilization and Its Discontents* Freud suggests that "the life of present-day civilized people leaves no room for the simple natural love of two human beings." In ***The Delicate Prey*** Bowles describes the family, understood as the basic unit of the community in its acculturating functions, as precisely the nexus in which love as a possibility is eradicated through the internalization of violence, a violence characteristically imaged as animal predation. Violence in Bowles's work, like the violence in much American fiction, acts as "a surgeon's probe that explores a moral question outside the consciousness of any of the characters." Bowles's stories dramatize the dynamics of that "outrageous violation" of himself which, according to R. D. Laing, Western man has had to commit in order to achieve his "capacity to live in relative adjustment to a civilization apparently driven to its own destruction." (pp. 631-33)

Wayne Pounds, "Paul Bowles and 'The Delicate Prey': The Psychology of Predation," in Revue belge de philologie et d'histoire, *Vol. LIX, No. 3, 1981, pp. 620-33.*

LINDA S. WELLS (essay date 1982)

[*In the following excerpt Wells analyzes the parent-child relationship in "Pages from Cold Point."*]

[In the short story **"Pages from Cold Point"**], Bowles treats parent/child conflicts resulting from the violation of sexual taboos and suggests that it is unrestrained desire in the characters which causes anti-social behavior. The child, imitating adult desire or competing for affection from the love object, becomes the adult's "monstrous double."

"Pages from Cold Point" is the story of a college professor, Norton, the very embodiment of civilization, who leaves his teaching position after the death of his wife and takes his son Racky to a Caribbean island to live. The story, written as Norton's reflective journal, is an allegory of the fallen Adam who pollutes the sanctity of the father/son relationship and begins a cycle of perversion which Racky will perpetuate. The theme developed is the infectious nature of perversion when the satisfaction of one's desires becomes more important than the autonomy or psychic health of another. Bowles uses incestuous homosexuality as the metaphor for the sins of the father visited upon the son which are then perpetuated through the son. Freud describes the child's identification with his father in *Group Psychology and the Analysis of the Ego:*

> A little boy will exhibit a special interest in his father; he would like to grow like and be like him, and take his place everywhere. We may simply say that he takes his father as his ideal. This behavior has nothing to do with a passive or feminine [sic] attitude toward the father . . .; it is on the contrary, typically masculine. It fits in very well with the Oedipus complex, for which it helps to prepare the way.

"Pages from Cold Point" records not the child's idealization of the father, but the father's idealization of the son. A reversal of the Oedipus complex, the tale traces the ever-widening circle of chaos which results from Norton's seduction of his son. Unlike a conventional allegory which moves from chaos to order, **"Pages from Cold Point"** begins with the closed circle of perversion between Norton and Racky and ends with Racky moving outside the circle to perpetuate evil in the external world.

Norton is both narrator and actor; as a classic academician, he uses the tools of analysis while he renounces the very act of analysis. Feeling that the primitive man is closer to the truth than the man of culture, he takes his son away from inhibiting civilization to a primitive island where he believes he will lead a life closer to that which is primary and essential—he seeks to escape what he sees as the doom of civilization. Stewart calls this a "journal of crisis," told by a man who renounces academic life but is condemned to exist through reflection [see *Paul Bowles: The Illumination of North Africa* by Lawrence D. Stewart in Additional Bibliography] Norton, as the fallen Adam attempting to return to Eden, is responsible for the perversion of the natural order at Cold Point because he has violated the limits necessary to maintain culture. In his book, *The Transition from Childhood to Adolescence: Cross-Cultural Studies of Initiation Ceremonies, Legal Systems, and Incest Taboos,* Yehudi A. Cohen discusses the need for setting limits (i.e., incest taboos) in relationships among nuclear family members. In contemporary literature treating the theme of menace of the primitive, the chaos is produced by this loss of limits—in **"Pages from Cold Point"** the loss of limits in terms of incest taboos is literal rather than metaphoric. Norton cannot relinquish his hold over Racky for the relationship is one of psychological fusion and symbiosis. But the damage has been done. Racky, perverted by his father, becomes the very embodiment of evil and can do nothing but perpetuate the chaos his father has fostered. Neither Racky nor Norton is able to suppress his desires, and thus this quest for individual gratification indicates their asocial tendency. In allowing free reign to desire, they remain essentially alienated from culture and at the same time unable to return to the simpler, more orderly life of the primitive because they are products of culture; they live in limbo between the primitive and the civilized.

Norton wants to live in the static timelessness of Eden. On the island he decides against the houses near "civilization" because they are "confining in atmosphere," and chooses instead a house on Cold Point where all the activities—swimming, bicycling, eating—are sensual rather than cerebral. Although Cold Point is outside the material world from which he has fled, he cannot escape the constraints of culture. He can escape neither the impingement of the outside world, represented by his brother, nor the morality of the natives on the island, "primitives" who are outraged by his base character. He wants to give himself over to free-floating desire apart from any censure—to live by impulse. Norton casts off all vestiges of culture—his academic career, his role as husband and brother, even his role as father—to plunge into Edenic paradise where desire will direct his life. He submits to the forces of nature which he sees on the island. . . . Norton catches the tempo of the cycles of nature for a time, but the resulting chaos indicates the impossibility of man being directed by nature without the regulating force of reason.

The story opens with Norton's recognition of the decay of civilization: "Our civilization is doomed to a short life: its component parts are too heterogeneous. I personally am content to see everything in the process of decay. . . . Life is visually too hideous for one to make the attempt to preserve it." Several strands are established in these lines: the attack on civilization, his impulse toward homogeneity (which is the very indication of chaos and perversion of the natural order), and the cerebral approach to decay. Norton seeks the primitive, but as an academician he cannot escape the decadence of cerebral analysis.

After Norton's pessimistic prediction about the future of the civilized world, he immediately leaves his teaching position and makes plans to take his son into what his brother, Charles, calls the "wilds." Norton protests that it is really "civilized," but Charles knows Norton's attraction for the primitive: "You just want to go on off down there and live as you've a mind to, and to hell with the consequences!" Charles makes his own pessimistic prediction which foreshadows the chaos Norton and Racky will create: "If there's any trouble with the boy I'll know who's to blame."

Norton ignores Charles and takes Racky to Cold Point, precipitating the very trouble Charles has warned against. Once Norton and Racky establish themselves at Cold Point, the reversals of primitive and civilized occur. Norton, deluded about Racky's malevolent impulses, sees him as angel and saint, but it becomes increasingly apparent that Racky is the imp of the perverse, the embodiment of evil, once he is unleashed on the island. Norton, in a reversal of the Oedipus myth, sees others as rivals for Racky; Norton wishes to dominate and enslave Racky, the very reason they chose the house on Cold Point. He describes himself in the journal, "sitting here being conscious of my great good fortune in having him all to myself beyond the reach of prying eyes and malicious tongues." More than his possessiveness is indicated here, however; apparently something in their relationship would cause scrutiny and malicious gossip.

Norton's idealized view of Racky indicates the extent to which he is guided by passion rather than reason. He describes Racky as the "soul of discretion," one with an "angelic face." Norton envies in Racky his spiritual qualities—the angelic face—and his animal qualities—"the lithe body, the smooth skin, the animal energy and grace"—but he cannot see him in essentially human terms.

Racky's demonic rather than angelic nature and his animal nature coupled with his cunning mind all work together to produce an ignoble savage. In his blindness to Racky, Norton says: "I know he will always have a certain boldness of manner and a great purity of spirit in judging values. The former will prevent his becoming what I call a 'victim': he never will be brutalized by realities. And his unerring sense of balance in ethical considerations will shield him from the paralyzing effects of present-day materialism." It is true that Racky is never a victim, except to the extent that he is a victim of his father's warped behavior, but he is able to avoid victimization only by becoming master over his father and aggressor toward the men and boys on the island. He plays the victim, submitting to his father's seduction, only to force Norton into such a compromising position that he will have to release Racky from the psychologically and physically fused relationship. And he is shielded from what Norton calls the paralyzing effects of materialism in that he is no victim of materialism but the perpetrator of it. He uses materialism to extort sexual favors from his victims: as long as Peter, the house servant, accommodates him, he will insure his livelihood, but when he withholds favors, Racky takes steps to have him fired. The menace arises out of the perversion of desire by the representatives of civilization—Norton and Racky.

Just as he idealizes Racky, so too does Norton idealize the island:

> The servants are clean and quiet, and the work seems to be accomplished almost automatically. The good, black servants are another blessing of the islands; the British, born here in this paradise, have no conception of how fortunate they are. . . . Still even here ideas are changing each day. Soon the people will decide that they want their land to be part of today's monstrous world, and once that happens, it will be all over. As soon as you have that desire, you are infected with the deadly virus, and you begin to show the symptoms of the disease.

Ironically, he and Racky represent the very decay he speaks of—they are the ones who bring disorder to the island by violating the homosexual taboos of people who Racky at least believes can be cajoled and coerced by the superior "cultured" man. The fact that Norton is unconscious of the possibility of offending the islanders indicates that he believes they are essentially amoral. Thus, he is shocked to find that he violates their moral codes.

Once Norton is aware of Racky's sexual blackmail of the male islanders, the story becomes a power struggle between the two of them; Norton tries to maintain the symbiotic relationship while Racky plays the slave for a time in order to become the master. When Norton is required to travel across the island to settle some business, he does not take Racky because he fears that the "sight of 'civilization' might awaken a longing for it in him." Norton is deluded, of course, because Racky is not the neophyte Norton presumes him to be; some of his innocence is stripped away when a black woman in Orange Walk says threateningly, "Keep your boy at home, mahn." While Norton does not know the reason for the threat, he is aware that Racky has in some way violated the islanders' codes of conduct. The effect of the journey away from Cold Point and into the civilization of Orange Walk is to strip away some of the illusions about Racky and himself. Upon his return he walks to the sea and contemplates the intoxicating effects of the physical elements: "All of them together are like a powerful drug; coming back made me feel as though I have been disintoxicated and were returning to the scene of my former indulgences." Clearly, nature dulls rational powers. In the Edenic paradise, Norton and Racky are able to act upon desires previously inhibited by civilization. But neither of them knew the extent to which their actions impinged upon others and violated the taboos of the islanders. The one message from these texts is that the individual cannot act solely to gratify himself without regard for others. Norton exemplifies what both Freud and Reich identify as the essentially anti-social nature of individual passion—the desire to function outside of culture but the impossibility of acting upon such desires.

In a reversal of roles, as Norton and Racky revert to primitivism in its most ruthless form, the islanders emerge as upholders of morality. The black woman, the constable, and Peter all represent the order which has been upset by Norton and Racky's intrusion. The black woman's admonition to Norton begins a series of censures leveled against him. As Norton lies naked in the sun after swimming, he is approached by the constable, a mulatto "gentleman" wearing a white duck suit and a high collar with a black tie. Norton says, "it seemed to me that he was eyeing me with a certain degree of horror." In this scene the naked Norton is censured by the constable who tries to educate him about the ways of the islanders who may cause trouble unless Racky, "a bad young man," is kept at home: "We don't have such things going on here, sir, ... You don't know what these folks do when they are aroused. . . ." Then the constable's report about Racky's activities further awakens Norton about Racky's immorality; "He has no shame. He does what he pleases with all the young boys, and the men too, and gives them a shilling so they won't tell about it. But they talk." Once he is aware of Racky's displays of power and aggression, Norton becomes childlike in his awe: "With the advent of this news he had become another person—an adult, mysterious and formidable."

Even when Racky shows his savagery by striking Peter for refusing his sexual advances, Norton cannot bring himself to exert his parental authority to restrain Racky. Although Racky is visibly shaken when Peter exposes his malign nature, Norton cannot act against him; he fears that censuring Racky will cause him to flee, so he continues to hide the knowledge he has about Racky's exploits. Norton will not assert himself; therefore, Racky takes the initiative, submitting sexually to his father so that he can master him. Just when Norton is blissfully happy about the symbiotic relationship, Racky suggests that they invite Charles for a visit, knowing full well that Charles will not tolerate the perversion between Norton and Racky. By allowing full play to his desire, Norton gives the power over himself to Racky: "Again I felt the fascination of complete helplessness that comes when one is suddenly a conscious on-looker at the shaping of one's fate." Allowing the passions to rule places the power over oneself in the hands of others—to relinquish reason is to relinquish autonomy and self-control.

By the end of the story, Racky has extricated himself from the relationship with his father only to begin a new homosexual relationship in Havana where he is again clearly the master over the lover. Norton returns again to Cold Point, back to the womb-like environment, where he awaits the reawakening of desire:

> The wind blows by my head; between each wave there are thousands of tiny licking and chopping sounds as the water hurries out of crevices and holes; and a part-floating, part-submerged feeling of being in the water haunts my mind even as the hot sun burns my face. I sit here and I read, and I wait for the pleasant feeling of repletion that follows a good meal, to turn slowly, as the hours pass along, into the even more delightful, slightly stirring sensation deep within, which accompanies the awakening of the appetite.

In his childlike state, gratification is primary. The story traces the regression of Norton to the stage of the passive, helpless infant, the man who renounces cerebral, rational activity in favor of a life of passion, but in Norton's stasis the reader sees the impossibility of such an act. His effect upon Racky has been to pollute his character and Racky, in turn, becomes the monster Norton has created by refusing to act as a responsible father. Thus, the story ends with Norton in a static world without Racky, the object of his desire, and Racky, the monstrous imp, re-entering the civilized world to act out his aggressive desires on others. (pp. 75-9)

Racky imitates his father's desire by initiating homosexual relationships with the male islanders. In fact, Racky's actions parallel Girard's analysis in that Racky moves from mimetic desire to what Girard calls the "monstrous double" [in a footnote the critic cites René Girard's *Violence and the Sacred*]. Racky, in imitating his father's desire, replicates that desire and becomes his father's double, his mirror-image. The only way for Racky to extricate himself from this symbiotic relationship is in effect to kill his father, which he does by submitting sexually to his father and then calling on the repressive forces of society represented by Uncle Charles. Norton knows he cannot escape the social sanctions even in the Edenic Caribbean, so he relinquishes his hold on Racky. However, Racky acts through unconscious motivations, in much the same way that Girard describes. While the reader can interpret his action as usurpation of the father, Racky does not understand that he has imitated his father's desire and in doing so has become his father's double. Nor is he aware of the need to "kill" his father in order to become more than a mirror-image. Thus Racky and Norton remain unenlightened—we assume that Norton is destroyed and that Racky, because he is not conscious of the reasons for his actions, will go on to perpetuate the same enslavement of others. Thus by imitating Racky's desire for them, they will become his monstrous doubles. (pp. 79-80)

Linda S. Wells, "Paul Bowles: 'Do Not Appropriate My Object,' " in The Review of Contemporary Fiction, *Vol. 2, No. 3, Fall, 1982, pp. 75-84.*

HAROLD WEBER (essay date 1982)

[In the following review, Weber praises Midnight Mass *for its examinations of Westerners' bewilderment in "primitive" environments.]*

In ***Midnight Mass*** Bowles continues to focus on the meeting of diverse cultures, to examine a "primitive" and exotic culture—usually Moroccan—which normally bewilders and repels the "sophisticated" westerners who encounter it. Bowles' prose—precise, emotionally spare, noncommittal—has proven an excellent medium for portraying the "other" by uncovering the nuances of a Moroccan world that strikes the westerner as illogical, magical, opaque and invariably frightening. Some of the stories in this volume, particularly the title story [**"Midnight Mass"**] and **"The Dismissal,"** are disappointing because they seem to add little to his previous efforts. But most of the twelve stories show Bowles' steady refinement of his vision, and two, **"Here to Learn"** and **"The Eye,"** strike me as among the best stories Bowles has ever written.

The tale told in **"The Eye"** will sound familiar to anyone acquainted with Bowles: a foreigner, in this case Canadian, comes to Tangier to live, rents a house and hires servants, falls ill after but a few months, and eventually dies: "In all this there was nothing extraordinary; it was assumed that Marsh had been one more victim of slow poisoning by native employees. There have been several such cases during my five decades in Tangier." The success of the story stems from the narrative experimentation which has engaged Bowles during the last decade. Until 1970, the author, with but rare exceptions, employed a third-person narrator whose detachment and neutrality eschewed overt moral judgment. Since 1970, however, Bowles has used a first-person narrator on a number of occasions, and in **"The Eye"** this new voice allows him to examine the clash of cultures from a new perspective. Here the emphasis falls on the narrator, whose initial dispassionate judgment of Marsh's fate—"nothing extraordinary"—is transformed as the truth of the murder is revealed. The narrator becomes a detective, involved in discoveries which undermine the easy assumptions about culture and human nature with which he and his audience began. Marsh had indeed been poisoned, but not in the fashion envisioned by the narrator. The complexity of the cultural confrontation which leads to that death forces us to reexamine our notions of guilt and responsibility: "I saw that I had not only expected, but actually hoped, to find someone on whom the guilt might be fixed. What constitutes a crime? There was no criminal intent—only a mother moving in the darkness of ancient ignorance."

The novelty of **"Here to Learn"** lies not in Bowles' narrative technique, but in his delineation of a new outcome to the meeting of conflicting worlds. Malika, a beautiful young Moroccan girl from a small village, is picked up one day by a foreigner who takes her to Tangier. There she lives as his mistress until adopted as a plaything by one of his homosexual friends and spirited off to Spain. From Spain she moves to Paris, then Italy, and finally Switzerland, where she marries a rich American and returns with him to Los Angeles. Malika makes her way with a powerful passivity, hiding her ignorance and vulnerability by attaching herself to figures who shelter her. She enjoys the sophisticated life they offer, though even after her marriage she fails to genuinely understand the world in which she now finds herself. She lives a series of disguises, poses which she adopts but never quite makes her own.

For Bowles this failure to understand the substance behind the forms of a culture is dangerous, for within it lies the violence which has always inhabited his fictive landscape. Yet Malika succeeds where most of Bowles' other protagonists—David Marsh, for instance—fail; she avoids Marsh's end by finally achieving an intimacy with another culture, penetrating beneath the surface of mere gesture and pose. Though the story's conclusion reveals the pain and loss involved in the rejection of her old identity, it does provide her with a new identity in a world no longer alien.

For those familiar with Bowles there are other surprises in this volume. Two stories—**"The Little House"** and **"The Empty Amulet"**—reveal a modern Morocco divided from itself: self and other now exist within one culture, where a new Morocco of western hospitals and courtrooms collides with the old Morocco of magic and prophecy. This collection also includes a tale of metamorphosis, a theme which has fascinated Bowles from the beginning of his career. In the past such stories were often among the most frightening of Bowles' inventions, with the traditional western metamorphosis linked to Moroccan tales of demonic possession. Here, however, in **"Kitty,"** a little girl's transformation into a cat provides the occasion for one of Bowles' most charming stories. Yet ***Midnight Mass*** will reward not simply those who already celebrate this author's virtues. Paul Bowles is one of the finest American writers alive today, and this new collection finds him still at the height of his powers. (pp. 389-90)

Harold Weber, in a review of "Midnight Mass," in Studies in Short Fiction, *Vol. 19, No. 4, Fall, 1982, pp. 389-90.*

CATHERINE RAINWATER (essay date 1984)

[*Rainwater is an American critic and editor. In the essay excerpted below, she examines the influence of Edgar Allan Poe on Bowles's writing in the areas of characterization, form, and language.*]

In 1950, when Bowles published his first collection of short stories, ***The Delicate Prey,*** he dedicated it to his mother, "who first read [him] the stories of Poe." This dedication at the very least suggests Poe's art as a source of inspiration for Bowles's own; moreover, as this essay will show, an informed reader of Bowles's works will recognize many specific examples of Poe's influence. (pp. 253-54)

The works of Bowles suggest Poe's influence in three major areas: characterization, architectonics, and notions about language. Like Poe, Bowles develops characters who suffer an imbalance between rational and nonrational forces of mind; such characters attempt to transcend or escape the limits of personality, often to find themselves inhabiting nightmarish psychological realms from which there is no exit. Also like Poe, who develops a single mythopoetic vision which informs almost all of his works, Bowles devises a system of spatial symbols that remains constant throughout the majority of his stories and novels. And finally, both Poe and Bowles raise similar questions about the relationship between the deterioration of personal identity and of linguistic ability. Despite the affinities between Poe and Bowles, however, Bowles's is consistently the darker vision. The complex and mostly disillusioning array of twentieth-century discoveries and philosophies has darkened the vision of most contemporary writers, and Bowles numbers among the most cynical of this already pessimistic generation. Drawing ideas and techniques from Poe's art, Bowles inevitably concentrates upon the "modern" features of Poe's fiction; he emphasizes as basic principles of existence paradox, despair, and nihilism, which Poe only part of the time entertains as possibilities. Whereas Poe searches for an elusive center of meaning in the universe, Bowles's fiction reduces the significance of human existence by disclosing only a center of meaninglessness.

Certainly meaninglessness plagues many of Bowles's characters, who are often poised on the brink of despair and madness. In the area of characterization, Bowles's works suggest Poe's influence in their consistent preoccupation with the contest between rational and nonrational forces of mind. (pp. 254-55)

[Bowles develops] Poe-esque characters in the stories of ***The Delicate Prey.*** Like several of Poe's stories such as "The Fall of the House of Usher" and "Ligeia" which involve unreliable, irrational narrators (or narrators such as those in "The Tell-Tale Heart" and "The Cask of Amontillado" who are so exaggeratedly rational that they appear deranged), **"Pages From Cold Point"** lends itself to interpretation as psychomachia. Similar to "The Fall of the House of Usher," "Ligeia," "The Tell-Tale Heart" and perhaps especially "William Wilson," Bowles's story presents a constellation of characters symbolically suggesting a battle between flesh and spirit, and between intellect and emotion. Another portrayal of the "war between reason and atavism," **"Pages From Cold Point"** includes a narrator who desires to lapse into unconsciousness and atavistic behavior; it also includes the narrator's brother, Charles, who represents consciousness and rational (socially sanctioned) behavior, and the narrator's son, Racky, a homosexual adolescent who must soon choose between the former men's modes of existence.

Recalling Poe's two William Wilsons, as well as Roderick and the narrator in "The Fall of the House of Usher," these two brothers battle to exert their respective wills. Racky's uncle, Charles, wants the boy to be like himself, to choose "consciousness" and social conformity, while Norton, Racky's father, wants him to choose "unconsciousness" and a more elemental state of existence represented by their residence, Cold Point. Following a complicated struggle and fearing the irrational forces within himself, Norton eventually confronts his "reflected brother" (the last vestiges of "C." within himself) in the mirror. As in the case of Poe's William Wilson, one side of Norton's divided self finally triumphs; the last remnants of rationality finally extinguished (Racky leaves to adopt "C.'s" mode of life), Norton sits alone on the rocks in the sun. He avoids thought and sinks into the "Nothing" at the "Cold Point" of existence where the borders between reality and dream remain obscured forever.

In **"You Are Not I"** Bowles further explores the nature of the human psyche divided against itself in a humorous story which employs a doubling technique likewise recalling Poe's in "William Wilson." The two main characters are sisters, one sane, the other (the narrator) quite mad and escaped from a mental institution. Feeling that her own place has been usurped and her absence unlamented, the escaped mental patient plots her sister's demise. When the hospital authorities come for Ethel, she wills herself into her sister's body, and her sister's self into her own (Ethel's) body. Thus the attendants take away the wrong person, leaving Ethel behind masquerading as her sane sister. In this story Bowles's use of the doubling technique evinces many similarities to Poe's in its suggestion of the cyclic walling up or entombment of rational forces by irrational forces of mind, and vice-versa. Poe's characters in such works as "The Cask of Amontillado," "The Black Cat," and "The Tell-Tale Heart," attempt to seal up, bury, or otherwise rid themselves of antagonists symbolically suggestive of adverse psychic forces. In **"You Are Not I,"** recalling the final confrontation between Poe's two William Wilsons before a mirror, Bowles's characters force each other in and out of mirror-obverse worlds.

Despite its humorous overtones, **"You Are Not I,"** like the majority of Bowles's works and so many of Poe's, emphasizes terror as the human emotion most likely to precipitate escape from the restrictive boundaries of society and self. Ethel terrorizes her sister, whose fear makes her vulnerable to the force of the other's will. Like the narrator of Poe's "The Tell-Tale Heart," Ethel accomplishes her mad scheme with the calmness and deliberation characteristic of sanity, even though her aims and motives appear quite insane. For Poe and for Bowles, terror provides release for irrational forces of mind and allows them to prevail as Ethel prevails in **"You Are Not I."** However, whereas in Poe's works terror often transports the individual into some extraordinary state of being, in Bowles's works abject terror usually precedes total annihilation.

In this respect Bowles's fiction perhaps acquires a dimension of horror beyond Poe's. Although Poe's characters include criminals as well as supernally aspiring idealists, within Poe's universal system the actions of murderers and sadists sustain the same sort of aesthetic and transcendental significance as the actions of idealists. Death, violence, and the supernal imagination merge teleologically [according to James W. Gargano]: "The recurrent and conspicuous convergence in [Poe's] writings of the morbid and the beautiful—the inseparability of even identity . . . of the conditions of art and those of death—suggests a center of meaning . . . underlying these polar modes of imagination." In contrast, no center of meaning, but a center of meaninglessness underlies Bowles's equation of death and transcendental aspirations, not equivalent pathways to any potentially desirable end, but interchangeable preludes to non-being. As suggested in the death by mutilation of a Filala boy in **"The Delicate Prey,"** an individual's sensitivity to beauty and to the hidden motives of others does not protect against meaninglessness and inevitable violence. Bowles's secular fatalism, according to which sensitive and insensitive characters suffer the same fate, contains a "desert center." Like the arabesque designs on the walls of a Moroccan hotel, "evasive geometrical" configurations which both annoy and frighten Polly Burroughs in *The Spider's House,* existence for Bowles consists of intimated designs and meanings against a background of "Nothing."

What Bowles's characters learn about madness and meaninglessness almost always appears confirmed by their experiences in the phenomenal world. Not merely in the area of characterization, but architectonically as well, Bowles's works suggest Poe's influence. Poe develops landscapes and physical environments which mirror the psychological states of his characters and articulate the cosmological vision set forth in *Eureka.* For example, in *Eureka* Poe describes the underlying principle of the universe as a process of growth and particularization followed by decay and collapse back into "Unity." All matter, including human beings, participates in this process. The individual (particularized) artist seeks "Unity" and attains it through "destructive transcendence." Often Poe's stories are spatially conceived to illustrate the artist's enactment of this self-destructive process. In his "maelstrom" tales, for example, the whirlwinds and whirlpools correspond emblematically to the state of the protagonist's mind. Likewise, in "The Fall of the House of Usher" the collapse of the house into the tarn suggests the dissolution of Roderick Usher. Many of Poe's settings thus symbolically represent the psychological states of his protagonists, all of whom are, ultimately, embodiments of the Eurekan poet. Bowles's fictions are similarly constructed around a network of nature symbols corresponding to the various stages in the destructive odyssey of self that each of his protagonists enacts. (pp. 256-59)

In the stories of ***The Delicate Prey,*** Bowles continues to develop natural symbols and symbolic geographical settings. Furthermore, his characters in these stories reveal an animistic superstition about setting recalling that of several of Poe's characters (e.g., the narrator and Roderick in "The Fall of the House of Usher") who detect "vegetable sentience" in inanimate objects. Under the intoxicating influence of terror, drugs, or dream-states, Bowles's characters often attribute their psychic distress to noxious forces emanating (they believe) from the landscape. They may also believe, like Poe's narrator in "The Fall of the House of Usher," that "collocations" or arrangements of objects in the environment can incite terror. In **"Call at Corazón,"** the male protagonist writes a "recipe for dissolving the impression of hideousness made by a thing: Fix the attention upon the given object or situation so that the various elements, all familiar, will regroup themselves. Frightfulness is never more than an unfamiliar pattern."

Another character terrorized by setting is Aileen in **"The Echo."** A gorge near her mother's house frightens her because subconsciously she recognizes it as an emblem for the recessed, irrational regions of her own psyche. Typically of Bowles's characters who repress threatening knowledge, Aileen (who represses acknowledgment of her mother's lesbianism) hears and abhors the sound of a waterfall which empties into the gorge. Returning home late one evening after an irrational encounter with a Colombian who spits water in her face, Aileen is "horrified to see how near she stood to the black edge of the gorge. And the house looked insane down there, leaning out over as if it were trying to see the bottom." Losing her ability to distinguish between inner and outer sources of distress, Aileen assumes she is terrorized by the gorge. However, the actual source of her fear lies within her; when she consciously acknowledges that her mother and Prue are lovers, she attacks Prue physically, making enough noise to drown out at last the sound of the waterfall which has rung in her ears since she arrived in Colombia.

"Pages From Cold Point," certainly one of Bowles's best stories in ***The Delicate Prey,*** also includes a character who perceives the landscape as endowed with awareness. After the "death of Hope," his wife (and of course "hope," the sentiment), the narrator eagerly relinquishes his professorship at a university and retreats into a remote setting where he plans to do "Nothing." Norton seeks shelter from a decaying civilization. Like Poe's speaker in *Eureka,* he senses an entropic quality in the universe: "Our civilization is doomed . . . its component parts are too heterogeneous." Deceiving himself about the island culture, he sees Cold Point and the village of Orange Walk as a place of tranquility and timelessness, an escape from an increasingly destructive American society. At least initially, he recognizes the intoxicating influence which the setting exerts over his spirit. Returning home from a short trip back into "civilization," he observes:

> I had not been conscious until this evening when I came back to Cold Point how powerful they are, all those physical elements that go to make up its atmosphere: the sea and wind—sounds that isolate the house from the road, the brilliancy of the water, sky and sun, the bright colors and strong odors of the flowers, the feeling of space both outside and within the house. . . . This afternoon when I returned I was conscious of them all over again, of their existence and their strength. All of them are like a powerful drug; coming back made me feel as though I had been disintoxicated and were returning to the scene of my former indulgences.

Norton's use of the word "conscious" with respect to himself ironically exposes the degree of his own self-deception despite his claim (reminiscent of Poe's characters) that he has clarity of mind and knows the difference between reality and euphoria. He forgets that "returning to the scene of [his] former indulgences" means returning to his indulgences, for the scene itself constitutes the intoxicant. When he proclaims that he "had not been conscious until this evening," he means he had not *realized* "until this evening" how intoxicating Cold Point could be. Re-entering Cold Point, the symbolic equivalent of *unconsciousness,* cannot possibly be tantamount to re-entering consciousness, for precisely this latter state of mind is what Norton rejects along with society. Later, his complete confusion of the two states of mind becomes apparent as he surrenders absolutely to the spell of his environment, declaring himself "perfectly happy here [at Cold Point] in reality."

Norton's linguistic inaccuracy points toward another area of human existence in which Bowles sees more meaninglessness than ultimate meaning. Although Bowles entertains some notions of language similar to Poe's, his final stance toward its efficacy remains unambivalently pessimistic. Poe's notions about language are stated in various ways throughout his works. Poe's narrators become increasingly inarticulate, for example, as they enter into nonordinary modes of consciousness. And in such works as "The Conversation of Eiros and Charmion," "The Colloquy of Monos and Una," and "The Power of Words" we learn that beyond the earthly realm human language as we know it actually ceases to exist. Much of the time, Poe considers language inadequate to express ethereal, exalted feelings and impressions. (pp. 261-62)

With this pessimistic side of Poe's vision Bowles most closely identifies. Without believing in any ideal realm, yet yearning to achieve some static and painless state of being, Bowles's characters attempt to transcend social and psychological boundaries, and often discover themselves reduced to states of inarticulate madness.

In one of Bowles's most philosophically profound stories, **"A Distant Episode,"** a linguistics professor loses (along with his tongue) his naive notions about language as a mode of communication. Several years after a first visit to the desert, he returns in order to study dialectical "variations on [the] Moghrebi" language; he ignores a sinister warning from an Arab that "there are no languages here." The professor's worst mistake involves imposing his own cultural assumptions upon the enigmatical social system of the desert inhabitants. He believes he can communicate with these people merely by knowing the words of their language. The professor does not initially realize what Kit Moresby learns in the concluding chapters of *The Sheltering Sky:* "even had they had a language in common" they "could never understand" one another.

Captured and terrorized by an outlaw group of Arabs, the Reguibat, the professor is beaten, has his tongue cut out, and is transformed into a macabre clown/shaman wearing a costume of tin can fragments. Traumatized into a completely irrational automaton, he passively assumes his role as dictated by the Reguibat, until they sell him to another group of Arabs. During these months, the professor neither speaks nor understands any language, but responds only to gestures and terse commands; his own utterances consist of cried and other inarticulate sounds which amuse his audience.

However, one day while the professor sits in his cage in the house of his new owner, he suffers the simultaneous return of language and rational awareness. "Pain began to stir . . . in his being." Listening to the conversation of his owner and some guests, he becomes aware of their language. "The words penetrated for the first time in many months." The next day, he sees a calendar on the wall of the house: "on the white paper were black objects that made sounds in his head." In "an access of terror" the professor attempts to drown out these sounds, and escaping the house he runs out into the desert: the "rattling of [his] tin became a part of the great silence out there beyond the gate." Like Kit Moresby, he avoids returning to consciousness and memory, aspects of existence inextricably connected with the use of language. (p. 263)

Perhaps from the moment when Bowles, as a young boy "undergoing" the stories of Poe, imaginatively experienced the crumbling away of self, he became preoccupied with Poe-esque notions of dissolution that later in his life his own existential convictions reinforced. But whereas Poe maintains an ambivalent attitude regarding the ultimate fate of the individual who risks destruction by venturing outside familiar boundaries of self and society, Bowles appears never to doubt the finality of destruction. Embodying the existential despair of the twentieth-century fictional hero, Bowles's characters seem incapable of sustaining the sort of mental and emotional energy typical of Poe's characters—an energy required for belief in alternatives to "Nothingness." For Bowles's characters, the structures and systems comprising civilization and self may appear to be traps; but the individual who dares to stray beyond them soon learns that these very imprisoning structures constitute the only true "shelter" humans possess. (p. 264)

Catherine Rainwater, " 'Sinister Overtones,' 'Terrible Phrases': Poe's Influence on the Writings of Paul Bowles," in Essays in Literature, *Vol. XI, No. 2, Fall, 1984, pp. 253-66.*

LINDA W. WAGNER (essay date 1985)

[An American critic and poet, Wagner has written several scholarly essays and books, including Hemingway and Faulkner: Inventors/Masters *(1975),* Denise Levertov: In Her Own Province *(1979), and* Dos Passos: Artist as American

(*1979*). *In the essay below, Wagner discusses the changing role of women characters in Bowles's fiction.*]

In *The Sheltering Sky* and the stories of ***The Delicate Prey*** (1945-1950), Bowles shows women characters as adversarial. By the fiction of ***Midnight Mass,*** in 1981, however, Bowles is presenting his female characters in much more positive ways. On the one hand, they are less antagonistic to male characters, although they manage to achieve power for themselves. In presentation, they are often more sexless than sexual and, perhaps compatible with their functions in the fiction, they perform almost ritualistic or mythical roles. Malika, in **"Here to Learn,"** surely shows less malice toward any of her lovers than did the honeymooning wife in **"Call at Corazón"** toward her husband. In the earlier story, we are conscious of *personal* emotion. In the latter, the chief impression is of willed action, fated movement, destiny separate from idiosyncratic fortunes. (p. 16)

Several of the female protagonists in Bowles's early stories seem to be drawn to show the destructiveness of the purely sexual impulse. Chalia, in **"At Paso Rojo,"** disrupts her brother's life and effectively ends that of Roberto and his brother in her fury at Roberto's unwillingness to become her lover. Her machinations of revenge are nothing short of gleeful. The young wife in **"Call at Corazón"** sleeps with a cabin steward in retaliation for her husband's buying a monkey. Bowles effectively shows the distance between the honeymooners in brief snatches of charged dialogue:

> "I think you're impossible—and a little insulting," she replied.
> He turned to look at her. "Are you serious?" He saw that she was.
> She went on, studying her sandaled feet and the narrow deck-boards beneath them: "You know I don't really mind all this nonsense, or your craziness. Just let me finish." He nodded his head in agreement, looking back at the hot dock and the wretched tin-roofed village beyond. "It goes without saying I don't mind all that, or we wouldn't be here together. You might be here alone. . . ."
> "You don't take a honeymoon alone," he interrupted.
> "*You* might." She laughed shortly.

Explicit motivation may be missing, but the emotional tone is clear. Bowles's dedication for the collection—"for my mother, who first read me the stories of Poe"—comes as no surprise.

In **"Señor Ong and Señor Ha,"** Nicho's aunt changes drug dealer husbands with no more thought than were she changing shoes, and Bowles shows her placid—and thereby even more chilling—opportunism in her willingness to use both the albino child and her own nephew. And the dramatic tension of the seemingly unresolved **"Tea on the Mountain"** lies in the young man's belief that the woman writer wants to make love with him (witness his writing the word "Incredible" under his address on the tawdry, used calling card)—and in her tacit acknowledgement of his attraction.

In more of the stories of ***The Delicate Prey,*** Bowles uses a woman character to image the fascination men feel for the unknown. In **"Under the Sky,"** Jacinto is strangely drawn to the young foreign woman. . . . He eventually rapes her older companion in the cemetery, and in subsequent years returns to that location and sobs for her loss. Typical of Bowles's ability to suggest a wealth of implication, he ends the story with an old woman's comment as she observes Jacinto rolling on the ground, "He has lost his mother."

Whether man rapes woman, jilts her (as in the beautifully developed **"How Many Midnights"**), or accuses her (as the unnamed protagonist's son does in **"The Scorpion"**), many of Bowles's stories are built from a variation of the male-female relationship—usually from a frustrated bond. Sexual dominance becomes the means of achieving power: man rapes, woman loves illicitly. The mood of this kind of struggle colors many of the stories that are not ostensibly about a romantic or sexual relationship (as, for example, **"Pastor Dowe at Tacaté"** and **"The Echo"**). And in **"The Circular Valley,"** Bowles uses the mock-persona of the Atlájala, the spirit wind, to explain how different woman is from man.

The Atlájala inhabits various bodies, of inanimate objects as well as of human beings. For the first time in its existence, a woman enters its valley (previously the site of a monastery), and when it occupies the man who accompanies her, it experiences a completely new reaction, dominated entirely by the presence of the woman.

> Immediately, instead of existing in the midst of the sunlit air, the bird calls and the plant odors, it was conscious only of the woman's beauty and her terrible imminence. The waterfall, the earth, and the sky itself receded, rushed into nothingness, and there were only the woman's smile and her arms and her odor. It was a world more suffocating and painful than the Atlájala had thought possible.

In sheer poetry, Bowles captures the passion of sexual attraction, but he does more: he moves the Atlájala from the male lover into the female herself. There, "now it would have believed itself to be housed in nothing, to be in its own spaceless self, so completely was it aware of the wandering wind, the small flutterings of the leaves, and the bright air that surrounded it. Yet there was a difference: each element was magnified in intensity, the whole sphere of being was immense, limitless. Now it understood what the man sought in the woman, and it knew that he suffered because he never would attain that sense of completion he sought."

Overcome by this pleasure, the Atlájala plots to keep the woman in the valley. Its plans lead to the death of her lover, and to her own departure, but the experience of having known her sensations numbs the inquisitive Atlájala so that its own existence is virtually ended: "It would be a long, long time before it would bestir itself to enter into another being's awareness. A long, long time—perhaps forever."

Many of the stories collected in 1967 in ***The Time of Friendship*** continue these themes of sexual relationship turned to manipulative purposes. **"The Frozen Fields,"** one of Bowles's most evocative fictions, presumes to tell the story of the young Donald, but it does so through the relationships of his appeasing mother and domineering father, and of his Aunt Louisa's dual husbands. Bowles describes the boy's family world (his mother's family, outside the New York province of his father) as "enchanted," "imbued with magic."

> During the long green summers he had spent there with his mother and the members of her family he had discovered that world and explored it, and none of them had ever noticed that he was living in it. But his father's presence here would constitute a grave danger . . . and once aware of the existence of the other world he would spare no pains

> to destroy it. Donald was not yet sure whether all the entrances were safely guarded or effectively camouflaged.

In almost primitive images, Bowles draws the female and male sensibilities—which color not only the boy's development but every human interchange in the story.

The prototype of Donald's father as male destroyer appears in other stories of this collection: in **"The Successor,"** Ali's brother tries to control his beloved and succeeds only in killing her; **"The Hours After Noon"** re-creates the power struggle between Mr. Van Siclen and Monsieur Royer over the less-than-innocent Charlotte; Lahcen's use of the girl from Mahnes—not only sexually but also to test his friend—is **"The Story of Lahcen and Idir,"** though the "story" is primarily of the male relationship. Bowles' parable for the kind of themes he employs so heavily in these 1950s stories is **"The Hyena."** A shocking travesty of the animal fable, this brief fiction describes the hyena—pure reason—as winner, despite the fact that its every act is heinous. And in this collection, **"The Garden"** is a similar parable.

To counter the rational, manipulative protagonists, Bowles includes stories like **"Tapiama,"** where the photographer is confused by alcohol and sees events through a haze of incoherence, and **"Doña Faustina,"** where the woman's witchcraft provides livelihood and child for the disbelieving culture. His interest in dreams is also in evidence in **"If I Should Open My Mouth,"** a montage journal reminiscent of the dreams Port recounts in *The Sheltering Sky.* Thematically, and in some ways structurally, these stories buttress the critical view that Bowles's stories are not true narratives, that perhaps the very act of narrative is misleading, that stories cannot ever really be "told." Hardison describes Bowles's fiction as "a metaphor without an object, like a dream [the critic does not give the source of the quote], and the fact that Bowles often turns to dream insight continually shows his interest in re-creating the rationally remote. This tendency moves to its furthest point in his use of animal imagery, and of characters who become animals, as in **"Kitty"** ***(Midnight Mass).***

In fact, many of the stories collected in ***Midnight Mass*** have abandoned the premise of a power struggle in which the male protagonist aims for dominance. In these stories, woman—instinctual, wily, nonrational—is often the victor. In some fictions, of course, reminiscent of **"The Hyena,"** victory is reprehensible, but here Bowles is more likely to convey ambivalence than censure. Lalla Aicha's poisoning of her son's mother-in-law only fuels the grudge she has held because her son must live in "The Little House" rather than in a larger one. It is Lalla's trickery that brings her victory of a sort, but the reader thinks well of her because Bowles keeps the murdered woman a mystery, and focuses all attention on the frustrated old Lalla. Similarly, in **"Midnight Mass,"** Madame Dervaux succeeds in winning a place for herself in the elite Tangier house. In **"The Dismissal,"** Patricia and her mother take firm action in firing Abdelkrim—much to his chagrin and bemusement.

In stories in which a romantic relationship focuses the action, Bowles again treats the conflict with wry humor. **"At the Krungthep Plaza"** focuses on Mang Huat, manager of a prestigious hotel, and his "distrust" for his unusually attractive and efficient secretary. The dynamics are mostly imaginary, but eventually Huat finds that Miss Pakun is indeed outsmarting him. **"Here to Learn,"** the longest story in the collection, ironically reverses the plot to naive woman, taken advantage of and subdued. Malika uses her innocence and beauty to build a fortune from a succession of manipulative lovers, only to find that when she returns to her native village, no one knows her and her mother has died. Malika, however, lives on in her wealth. Bowles's final irony appears in a story titled **"The Husband."** Despite the title, the story's focus is on the jolly, wage-earning wife. During the course of the action, Abdallah falls in love with Zohra and leaves his wife; but later events allow her to forgive him and take him back. She declines, however, because he makes a practice of stealing whatever of value she has accumulated. During his absence, "she had managed to avail herself of a huge soft cashmere shawl which she intended to keep." The story ends, "In this world it's not possible to have everything, she told herself." The exchange of husband for shawl, in effect, allows Bowles to present the traditional theme with new humor and less-than-cynical effect.

A somewhat darker side of woman's power to be avenged is shown in **"The Eye,"** when the cook whose child has inadvertently died poisons her master, and feels revenged in justice. As in several other of these late stories, Bowles has used an objective narrator, whose comments close the tale: "What constitutes a crime? There was no criminal intent—only a mother moving in the darkness of ancient ignorance. I thought about it on my way home in the taxi." (pp. 18-21)

Judging from ***Midnight Mass*** . . . , what has changed in Bowles's fiction of the 1980s is the tendency to set character against character, to create a dialectic that somehow informs the reader. Bowles's late stories are so spare, so objectively reported, that a reader would not attempt to draw inferences. . . . In these late tales, and in many of his fictions from ***The Delicate Prey*** and ***The Time of Friendship,*** Bowles may be said to have written what Richard M. Eastman calls the "open parable," the narrative that cannot be "closed" and given a simplified interpretation. Because the author's rhetoric allows opaque details, "irreducible" hints that will not lead to any single reading, the narrative remains open to several interpretations. (p. 22)

[What] Bowles manages to achieve in his terse yet resonant stories, is the impact of an action, a force that creates some dynamic among creations we recognize as characters, whether they be opportunistic women, drug dealers, or tortured professors. We remember Bowles's late *stories,* in short, perhaps more readily than we remember the *characters* from those stories. To create the whole image, and suspend it, and make it, then, memorable is no small feat. It is, indeed, a delicate balance. (p. 23)

Linda W. Wagner, "Paul Bowles and the Characterization of Women," in Critique: Studies in Modern Fiction, *Vol. XXVII, No. 1, Fall, 1985, pp. 15-24.*

JOHN DITSKY (essay date 1986)

[Ditsky is an American critic, poet, and editor. In the review excerpted below, Ditsky examines Bowles's treatment of human relationships in The Time of Friendship.*]*

In spite of the enormous variety of narrative modes employed in [***The Time of Friendship***'s] 13 pieces, there emerges from it the idea of the Paul Bowles short story. This idea, as I want to show, comes down in the end to recognitions of inadequacies in the mutual perceptions and responses of human beings, of failures to observe the need to impose ideals less and to love more. These failures are likely to occur against a complementary exterior landscape of aridity, desolation, and estrangement, which further aggravate the effects of human insufficiency. As a result, the deprived individuals are thrown back upon their inner resources and the manipulation of those resources: upon drugs and alcohol, upon fantasy and myth and magic and dream.

As if denying that we must love one another or die, Bowles's characters seem determined to prove the possibility of some middle ground, neither entirely possessing nor utterly forsaking love and death. But this middle ground turns out to be a center that will not hold; so that in the end the stories in ***The Time of Friendship,*** most of them set in lands where nomads travel from oasis to oasis, become masterful explorations of a country of transient feeling.

Nine of the 13 stories in ***The Time of Friendship,*** are set in the North Africa of Bowles's longtime residence; two take place in Mexico; one each is in New York City and New England. Along with establishing the obvious importance of North Africa—specifically, Morocco—to Bowles, this preponderance of setting also points to another, equally evident feature of Bowles's writing: the use of his exile abroad not, as was the case with some expatriates of an earlier era, to write about the homeland but rather to interpret the adopted country for the enlightenment of foreigners. Given Bowles's strong ability to evoke a sense of place for his readers and to manipulate that sense for purposes central to those of the stories themselves, it is interesting to watch the way the sense of local focus shifts from story to story or even within stories, depending on whether the writer's interest is primarily texturally naturalistic or parabolic, specific or generalized, clearly perceived or hallucinatory.

Complicating the perceptions of all parties involved—author, reader, and characters—is the prevalence in Bowles's writing of various sorts of consciousness-warping substances: kif, hashish, alcohol. Of these things and their interrelationships, more must be said when individual stories are examined. For the moment, though, it may be observed that Paul Bowles writes a very different sort of "local color" story than his 19th-century literary ancestors did. For Bowles, place, far from being merely touristically photographed "material," becomes intrinsically a part of the writer's examination of human failures of all kinds.

Bowles makes no attempt to obscure his prepossessions; he places his title story [**"The Time of Friendship"**] at the beginning of his collection and endows its formal solidity with a fairly rich palette of imagery. The reader is immediately introduced to one of the two central characters, a Swiss (hence "neutral"?) woman named Fräulein Windling, who spends her winters at a North African "oasis" but is "determined to pay . . . no attention" to the troubles in the North, where the native population has risen against the French. An unmarried schoolteacher, she is attracted to the people and landscape of the desert, of whom and which "Her first sight . . . had been a transfiguring experience." For it seemed that "before coming here she had never been in touch with life at all." This desert oasis seems to offer a fuller and realer sort of life, and she notes of the local woodgathering women that they seem able to read connections between the long-buried roots of trees in the very wind. Thus, ironically, this wind-named character begins to discover through the force that creates deserts itself the image of a different sort of life, one of a freedom unknown to her back at her home in watchwork Switzerland.

In this setting where liaisons between adult European males and Arab boys are notoriously possible, Bowles's scarcely sexual Swiss maiden now meets Slimane, a local boy some twelve years of age, whose name tallies with that of a great Moslem king. The Suleiman/Slimane/Solomon coincidence of names is part of the cultural punning that the story rests upon, for young Slimane strongly requests this "Nazarene" woman not to talk about Islam, of which he thinks she knows nothing. Yet his presence seems to teach the woman more about the religion of love she professes to represent, since Slimane accepts her conspicuous presents yet "wanted nothing, expected nothing." Slimane enters her employ, and "It was probably her happiest season in the desert, that winter of comradeship when together they made the countless pilgrimages down the valley." Again, there is irony in such a winter of supreme content (and in a desert of all places), occurring in the midst of such formidable oppositions of forces. In this context of religious referents, such "pilgrimages" become foreshadowings, as well as further instances of Bowles's exploitation of setting.

Yet a phrase like "the time of friendship" implies the ending to such times and fixed limitations upon their extensions. Fräulein Windling thinks as much in musing upon the way the outside world is beginning to intrude upon her relationship with Slimane, her "true" friend:

> . . . But even while she was saying, "How happy I am to see you, Slimane," she remembered that their time together was now limited, and an expression of pain passed over her face as she finished the phrase. "I shall not say a word to him about it," she decided. If he, at least, still had the illusion of unbounded time lying ahead, he would somehow retain his aura of purity and innocence, and she would feel less anguish during the time they spent together.

Thus, in the mind of Fräulein Windling, Slimane's approaching maturity merges with the reality of the encroaching outside world; while she defines her love and freedom as taking place within a womb of time, his own self-expression requires a thrust into the outside world, escape from his entrapment by his own and cherished Moslem society.

As this woman takes a photograph of Slimane out in the wind-swept desert, she conceives the incredible plan of cementing their friendship by inviting him to see a Christmas crèche she would build for him, in spite of the fact that she herself sees the crèche idea as a way of saying that "everything was ending." Even as she has these thoughts, the wind sweeps sand into her eyes; even as she builds the crèche in secret, she takes some of the time remaining away from Slimane. When the expected night arrives, things don't go right: the wind blows, Slimane's presence at her meal gets thwarted, and Fräulein Windling sentimentalizes her visions of the Christmas narrative so that they tally with Slimane's own experiences:

> . . . When she told him about Bethlehem she was really describing Slimane's own village, and the house of Joseph and Mary was the house down in the *ksar* where Slimane had been born. The night sky arched above the Oued Zousfana and its stars glared down upon the cold hammada. Across the

> erg on their camels came the Wise Men in their burnooses and turbans, pausing at the crest of the last great dune to look ahead at the valley where the dark village lay. When she had finished, she blew her nose.

But when Slimane at last sees the crèche, his lack of interest is plain; in her absence, he destroys the arrangement in order to get at the candies she has decorated it with, leaving, essentially, "a pile of sand" and trash. Fräulein Windling realizes her great mistake:

> "This is the desert," she told herself. Here food is not an adornment; it is meant to be eaten. She had spread out food and he had eaten it. Any argument which attached blame to that could only be false. And so she lay there accusing herself. "It has been too much head and high ideals," she reflected, "and not enough heart." Finally she traveled on the sound of the wind into sleep.

When the local authorities tell her she must leave the area because of the insurrection, it merely confirms for her the fact that "the time of friendship is finished."

An interesting aspect of Bowles's style that occurs elsewhere as well is the tendency to have his characters read meanings into landscapes and weather, on their own initiatives, as it were, and thus by no culpable and pathetic fallacy of the author. Fräulein Windling looks out over her desert surroundings, knowing that she must leave, and sees that although the desert looks the same, the reddening sky above it presages war and change. And after Slimane accompanies her part of the way and she finally tells him that taking the crèche candy was truly "good" and not a dreadful act, the story ends with Windling realizing that Slimane has gone off to be a soldier with the help of money she has given him and with her again studying the darkening sky from her train window. She knows that once she is "home" her days will be filled with the dread of waiting for the news of Slimane's inevitable death. Wind and sand in this story, then, accompany both the aridity of personality that must be educated to the full nature of friendship's demands; and they also, ironically, whisper of change and freedom, of new maturities, even though that transformation may and will lead eventually to suffering and death.

In spending so relatively much space with the initial narrative, I recognize that at least two observations may be made by way of justification: First, that **"The Time of Friendship"** is, for all its Jamesian culture-clashing, quite obviously a core dramatization of Paul Bowles's own Moroccan experiences, with such elements as sexuality neatly subsumed into a higher sort of discussion (a kind of *Death in Venice* turned in upon itself, if one can imagine such a thing). Second, the story is, after all, one of the longer pieces in the collection. (pp. 61-5)

"The Hours After Noon" is prefaced by a quotation from Baudelaire to the effect that the "echoes" of the memories of even the most "incoherent" life create a logical "music." The story begins with Mrs. Callender's outburst at table to the effect that men don't understand about "such things," which refers to the sensitivity of young women. Instead of the western Algerian desert setting of **"The Time of Friendship," "The Hours After Noon"** has a more cosmopolitan Moroccan one; instead of two-party exchanges, we are given the conversations of a group of Europeans, people who are repelled by certain aspects of Moroccan life but who themselves introduce much of what in the story is morally questionable. And in place of the Algerian Huck Slimane, who has made an earlier attempt at flight when we meet him first, there is Mrs. Callender's daughter Charlotte.

Mrs. Callender believes in limiting a young girl's "opportunities for learning" about men, and she is particularly concerned about the presence in the vicinity of a middle-aged roué, M. Royer, whose name is suggestive like Mrs. Callender's. "Voluptuous memories burned in the mind like fire in a tree stump" for Mrs. Callender, so that her fears for her daughter are clearly projections of her own insecurities. An archeologist friend suggests that the way to handle Royer is to send him out to the countryside, where the Moroccans know how to deal with men who chase girls: a coil of wire around the neck, and that will be that. But Mrs. Callender is above such talk and rejects the message of the Moroccan countryside. Yet she also confesses that "In all these years of living in Morocco she had never ceased wondering at the astonishing difference made by the sun," and she also bewares "the hours after noon . . . when the day had begun to go toward the night, and she no longer trusted herself to be absolutely certain of what she would do next, or what unlikely idea would come into her head."

Again, a landscape becomes a screen on which the inner person is projected, as if one saw one's inner fears animate themselves there like so many desert imps.

By the time Charlotte and Royer meet, her mother's attitudes toward men and toward her choice of friends has had the predictable effect of setting up a liaison between the Frenchman and her. And yet it is the archeologist who, taking Charlotte for a drive along the ocean at night, casually and brutally extracts a kiss from her, confirming her suspicions that her mother's notions are hardly to be trusted. A pair of meetings with Royer, whom we have earlier glimpsed slapping a bothersome Moroccan child, and Charlotte has driven her mother into asking the archeologist to take Royer out to the countryside digging site with him. This request follows a scene in which the mother remembers her own Andalusian youth, filled as it was with "imminent possibility"; whereas now the same sort of possibility for her daughter, as the mother thinks about the matter on one of her unstable afternoons, is so disturbing that she tries to drive out the distant sound of a Moroccan wedding celebration. When Charlotte briefly disappears, Mrs. Callender, fearing the worst, has herself driven out to the site to confront Royer and the archeologist. But it seems that Royer, attracted by the sound of drumming, had wandered off the night before. When the archeologist tells her to be careful of the barbed wire around the site, Mrs. Callender realizes the inevitability of the results of her actions:

> Now it was complete. Everything had been said. All she had to do was go on breathing deeply, facing the sea. Of course. A coil of wire around his neck. Behind a rock. A minute or two later she went back in.

Mrs. Callender's assumptions are exactly confirmed in the final flashback-tableau in which we see Royer, who is dallying with an Arab child he has met, which is reminiscent not only of the other child, the one he slapped, but also of his telling Charlotte that his code of honor rests upon the easy availability of girls who don't protest his advances. We see Royer thus preoccupied at the moment of his assassination. Not only does this story end with a chillingly vivid feeling of fatality, like **"The Time of Friendship,"** but it also tallies with **"The**

Successor" in the ways it shows the subconscious desires of its principal character working their way into realization. Finally, Bowles is at his most American in the first and third of these stories in showing his characters attempting to read in Nature the answers to their own dilemmas; in the ironically juxtaposed presences of representatives of supposedly "primitive" cultures.

"A Friend of the World" completes and balances this initial foursome by presenting Salam, who backs his self-description as "a friend of the world" and a "clean heart" by living in a Jewish neighborhood. But when the Jews kill his kitten because they wish to avenge a supposed slight upon the daughter of one of them, Salam uses magic spells to attain his revenge. And when the policeman involved in the embarrassment of the Jews gives Salam further trouble, he uses kif dreams to devise via the smoked narcotic a more direct and less magical way of relieving himself of yet another annoyance. It seems that this "friend of the world" is just that, except to his enemies; woe to those who cross him. But the story is gently and humorously told, and when things are more or less back to normal, one cannot feel of Salam quite the fear engendered by Ali in very much the same sort of reader complicity.

With folk magic, superstition, and the use of drugs now introduced into the collection, Bowles radically shifts the narrative texture of his material. **"He of the Assembly"** is, for the reader, rather like what the direct experience of such drugs must be. One suspects, moreover, that if the piece were not indeed written under their influence, firsthand experiences went into the making of the final product.

The relationship between the kif-smoking **"He of the Assembly"** and Ben Tajeh is premised on the former's drug-induced abilities to transcend the limitations of the present moment and of surface realities. Eventually, order in the surface world is restored through consultation of the world of drugged states of mind; the narrative is finally a demonstration of the validity of the kif-smoker's maxim quoted at the story's end: "A pipe of kif before breakfast gives a man the strength of a hundred camels in the courtyard." In a direct line of succession from the accounts of Poe and De Quincey, **"He of the Assembly"** allows the form and texture of the story to be shaped by the logic and syntax of the drug dream. The difficulty of reading through this piece is heightened by the heightening of imagery that drugs induce, while blocking the narrative out in lengthy paragraphs overturns the normal narrative rhythmical elements of action and dialogue in favor of something seamless that recognizes no conventional barriers to the free flow of consciousness. (pp. 65-8)

Of the two Mexican stories, **"Doña Faustina"** concerns the titular character and the out-of-the-way inn she has bought, where the servant José one day finds a hidden tank of water out in the dense underbrush. Doña Faustina is something of a mysterious recluse, a mystery deepened by her failure to cooperate in the investigation into the disappearances of certain neighborhood babies. When an equally mysterious young intruder forces himself upon Doña Faustina one evening, she responds by giving him an object to eat; he resists, then "bit into it as if it had been a plum." "Now you will have the power of two," she tells him. A few lines later she identifies the object as "the heart," confirming the reader's worst fears.

Doña Faustina announces herself pregnant by her young visitor. The baby—a son who arrives on schedule—is to have "the power of thirty-seven." Shortly thereafter, José, who thinks "she got the child from the Devil," discovers a crocodile living in the jungle water tank. In fact, there are two crocodiles; but by this time Doña Faustina has fled with her son "Jesus Maria," taking a job as matron of police. Her son grows up to become an army colonel, eventually capturing a famous bandit and 36 of his men. The story ends with Jesus Maria trying to mimic the expression on the face of the bandit chief, whom he has by now released:

> The man's face had looked something like that; he would never be able to get it exactly, but he would go on trying because it made him happy to recall that moment—the only time he had ever known how it feels to have power.

This parable is of one woman's ruthless and macabre quest for power through the Aztec device of eating the hearts of the enemy—in this case, innocent babies. But the Faustian enterprise is frustrated when her son ironically makes use of his unknown birthright: power, for him, comes from renouncing control over others. This significantly-named Jesus Maria achieves his singular power at the moment when, fatherless, he apparently recognizes his image and likeness in the face of the man he frees.

"Doña Faustina" would seem, in the neatness with which it combines Indian, Christian, and literary myths and the way in which it exploits the exoticism of its almost fairy-tale jungle setting, to be a digression for Bowles, if not simply some sort of literary exercise in the grotesque. But not necessarily. The power of the eaten hearts, after all, is a magical power given by drugs, like the camel power referred to in **"He of the Assembly."** And like that latter drug-trip enterprise, the other Mexican story, **"Tapiama,"** uses alcohol (in the manner of Malcolm Lowry's *Under The Volcano*) to lace a narrative which, in its central and dangerous imagery, has all the vividness of dream experience.

A photographer, walking off a bad case of indigestion, meets a mysterious boatman heading for "Tapiama," whatever or wherever that might be. Thanks to the photographer's state, a result of improper diet and overindulgence in alcohol, the elements of his experience take on the heightened and dulled or narrowed quality of drink-induced dreaming. But through all of this, there is also—for the reader, at least—an enormously dangerous atmosphere abuilding; the reader becomes a rear-view mirror for this narrative, able to glimpse danger approaching from oblique angles yet powerless to warn the central character. The sights and sounds and other sensory phenomena encountered include: frogs, a cantina, strangers there, a girl, a snake, ants, an old man and a boy, a soldier, dogs, a monkey, and the boat itself. In the end, the photographer, this recorder of reality, makes his way back to the world he understands. He manages this return largely on the basis of his ability to imitate a jungle bird that says, and is, "*Idigaraga.*" Having "accepted defeat" in this setting, he is now involved in fitting "the bird correctly into the pattern." One imagines this representative of a technological civilization trying with difficulty to summon up another accurate birdcall, his upper lip gleaming with perspiration, his limbs immobile with fatigue.

With **"If I Should Open My Mouth,"** Bowles shifts to New York. Although this account of big-city madness is curiously anticipatory of the recent Tylenol murders, Bowles seems more interested this time in inner mental states than in the reflection of those states in the surrounding "landscape."

While he does not ignore the latter, he concentrates on direct, first-person self-revelation and casts the story in diary form.

The narrator has his own notions of right and wrong, and these are obviously the warped results of city living; the "reprehensible aspects of [his] silly little project" do not preclude his feeling "hugely righteous about it all." The narrator is a bit of a grown child, prissy-voiced, alone in the wake of his wife's departure. It seems he is occupied with planting penny boxes of poisoned candy in the machines in subway stations. The reason? To get even with democratic man, perhaps; Rousseau is one of the narrator's culprits:

> That unpardonable mechanism, the intellect, has several detestable aspects. Perhaps the worst is the interpenetration of minds; the influence, unconscious, even, that one mind can have over millions, is unforeseeable, immeasurable. You never know what form it will take, when it will make itself manifest.

But when the narrator's disappointment at not finding word of the fruits of his dirty work in the newspapers begins to turn to rage, he finds himself entering a sort of dream-state increasingly difficult to distinguish from reality; indeed, when he discovers that through error he has not in fact planted the poisoned candy as planned, the dream takes over—rather like what happens in **"He of the Assembly"**—and the speaker imagines himself alone in a timeless state under trees in a city park. Out there somewhere are other people, but he will "never be able to touch them," he knows. "If I should open my mouth to cry out, no sound would come forth." The "invisible" narrator abandons his plan, deciding instead to throw the unused boxes onto the rubbish heap behind the school: "Let the kids have them." Horror has been put on hold here but not for long. The results of the ending of the time of friendship are an atrophying of the spirit.

So it is that in **"The Frozen Fields,"** Bowles returns to an American landscape, although for all the absence of desert produced by wind and sand and heat this is interior desert nevertheless. The story is apparently somewhere in New England and in the past of a child who, as a young Bowles might have done, is journeying out of New York city into the wintry countryside for a family Christmas celebration. We remember that a Christmas story started off this collection, one in which an emerging young consciousness was described from without. Here, although the third person is maintained throughout, the focus is on young Donald, whom we see being browbeaten by an overly demanding and restrictive father. Donald prefers the farm which, like the ballet, is possessed of "magic," a world which through recollection he has managed to live in till now. But his father, should he learn of Donald's dreamlike other state (the world of the artist's refuge?), would surely destroy it by reason of his code of living by such rules, as: "Men shake hands . . . They don't kiss each other."

The friendliest men coming to this country Christmas, by the way, are men of whom the family does not approve; among other, hinted-at failings is their reliance on drink and drugs. And when Donald is put to bed, from out of the "borderlands of consciousness" a "fantasy" emerges from the wintry landscape: a silent-running wolf that smashes through the dining-room windows, seizes Donald's father by the throat and carries him off. That dream done, Donald sinks into an immediate slumber. When he awakens it is Christmas morning. In the exchange of gifts, the family's practical presents are far outshone by gifts from the wealthy Mr. Gordon. Chief among them is a splendid, three-foot-long fire engine which almost frightens Donald with "the power he knew it had to change his world." Mr. Gordon, it seems, is sick and Uncle Ivor, the other male of whom the family no longer approves, is his nurse. There is a family squabble over dinner, of course. While Donald's father is upstairs presumably brutalizing Donald's mother, Mr. Gordon reflects on the arguments he remembers from his own childhood, saying, "Well, they're all dead now, thank God," a remark that inspires new respect from Donald. Out in the barn, Uncle Ivor makes a remark from his presumably tolerant-homosexual's insight to the effect that Donald's father ought perhaps never to have married. But just then, the suspicious father arrives to insist that Donald take a walk with him in the woods. Donald refuses his father's demand that he throw snowballs into the woods, for fear the wolf might think them meant for him; and when the angry father roughs him up, Donald experiences an "almost voluptuous sensation" of detachment, akin to the artist's detachment manifested throughout this volume by the author himself.

When the Christmas gathering breaks up in sullen resentment on the family's part, Donald sinks into his last night's sleep with another vision of the wolf taking over his consciousness. This time, because the story ends with the wolf, presumably, it does not leave. Running along hidden paths in the woods, the wolf at last comes to where, "waiting for him," Donald sits:

> Then he lay down beside him, putting his heavy head in Donald's lap. Donald leaned over and buried his face in the shaggy fur of his scruff. After a while they both got up and began to run together, faster and faster, across the fields.

It is, perhaps, a version of Slimane's flight; it is a fleeing prompted by brief glimpses of friendship but also one in which fantasy and the willingness to listen to the darkest promptings of nature are accepted without subjecting them to question and judgment on the basis of some abstract system of values. (pp. 70-4)

[In] restricting myself to a critical reading of ***The Time of Friendship,*** I have attempted to isolate the artistic and humanistic values that volume displays, with an eye to starting to establish some clear idea of what makes a Bowles story *work,* that is, how theme, character, and setting interrelate in ways that are uniquely his own. In doing so, I hope I have made clearer the process by which Paul Bowles explores the brevity of the time of friendship—the speed with which the winds pick up again and resume their coursing through the deserts of the human heart. (p. 74)

John Ditsky, " 'The Time of Friendship': The Short Fiction of Paul Bowles," in San Jose Studies, *Vol. XII, No. 2, Spring, 1986, pp. 61-74.*

WENDY LESSER (essay date 1986)

[In the following excerpt, Lesser analyzes Bowles's employment of violence in his short stories.]

> "The corpse must shock not only because it is a corpse, but also because, even for a corpse, it is

> shockingly out of place, as when a dog makes a mess on a drawing room carpet."
> —W. H. Auden, "The Guilty Vicarage"

It may seem as if references to drawing-room carpets are distinctly inappropriate to a discussion of Paul Bowles's works, the vast majority of which are set in regions far beyond the reach of drawing-room civility, in places such as 1940s Morocco or 1930s Mexico. Yet only a few of the stories, and none of the novels, are purely about the indigenous inhabitants of these settings. Instead, most of his fiction deals with the meeting between these untamed parts of the world and the rigid expectations of Europeans and Americans. It is in the clash of these two sets of rules—the confrontation, as it were, between the drawing room and the desert—that Bowles finds his subjects.

The clash of cultures is not, in itself, a topic unique to Bowles. Prior versions of it appear in Forster's *A Passage to India,* Lawrence's *The Plumed Serpent,* and (if one counts nineteenth-century America as the wilderness) most of Henry James's novels. Where Bowles differs from these earlier writers is in the touchstone he uses to distinguish the attitudes of the two cultures. For James, the distinguishing element was money or class; for Lawrence, it was virility; and for Forster, faith. But for Bowles the touchstone is violence.

The violence in Bowles's work is often shocking and often gory, but it is important to notice that these two characteristics are not the same. One of his most shocking stories, **"Pages from Cold Point,"** involves no physical violence whatsoever, while one of the more physically violent stories, **"The Wind at Beni Midar"** (in which the victim is beaten, knifed, and finally poisoned), is less disturbing than many of Bowles's others. I think this is because the violence in **"The Wind at Beni Midar"** takes place completely within the accepted standards of the Arab world, whereas the shocking characters in **"Pages from Cold Point"**—an American father and son whose relationship, among other things, is incestuous—are consciously violating the rules of their own culture. Whatever shock value does accrue to the **"Beni Midar"** story is brought to it by the European (in which I include American) reader, whose own proprieties are violated by the story's Moslem concepts of superstition and revenge.

In some instances, a Bowles character does not even have to leave town in order to acquire the shock value of culture clash. This is true, for example, of the narrator of **"If I Should Open My Mouth,"** a story set mainly in the subways of New York. Like Edgar Allan Poe's lunatic narrators, this character speaks in the tones of careful rationality even as he plots an outrageous crime (in this case, the insertion of poisoned chewing gum into the dispensing machines of subway stations). What cuts this would-be murderer off from his culture is madness rather than dislocation. The shock of the story comes not from his intention to commit murder, but from his failure to see his plan as anything other than an amusing game. The character's disregard of normal social values becomes clearest in the closing lines of the story, where, having failed to get rid of his forty boxes of poisoned gum, he says:

> After dinner I am going to take all forty boxes to the woods behind the school and throw them on to the rubbish heap there. It's too childish a game to go on playing at my age. Let the kids have them.

If this wry conclusion disturbs us, it is not just because we are shocked at casual murder, but because we treasure a basic social principle that children must be protected from danger at all costs. The story thus forces us into a reaction that runs something like: It's even *worse* to poison schoolchildren by mistake than to poison subway riders intentionally. Such responses come not from our legal system, which condemns premeditated murder more heavily than negligent killing, but from our less explicit social proprieties, our "drawing room" principles of behavior.

Since this kind of shocking violence must involve the violation of social rules, all the real criminals in Bowles's fiction are Europeans—travelers or transplants who have been altered or pushed over the edge by alien geographies. This is not because Bowles believes that Arabs or South American Indians are inherently incapable of committing murder, of violating their own social proprieties, but because his novels and stories are written for European readers. In order to be shocked at murder, such readers must sense it as in some way a violation of themselves; and to most Europeans, the behavior of alien cultures is too distant from them, in either its benign or malign forms, to create much moral reaction. (pp. 402-04)

Bowles is that rare item, a moralist who does not come down on the side of morality. That response is left to the reader, whose own social values—and, by definition, moral assumptions—are brought sharply into relief by Bowles's fictions. (p. 407)

Wendy Lesser, "Murder as Social Impropriety: Paul Bowles's 'Evil Heroes,' " in Twentieth Century Literature, *Vol. 32, Nos. 3 & 4, Fall & Winter, 1986, pp. 402-07.*

JEAN GOULD (essay date 1989)

[*Gould is an American critic, short story writer, and novelist. In the excerpt below, she offers a favorable review of* Unwelcome Words.]

In the seven new stories in ***Unwelcome Words*** . . . , Bowles ranges widely in time, in form, and in geographic space, from Massachusetts to Morocco, from 1932 to the 1970s. Portraits and contemporary scenes mix conventional narration with experimental monologues, and the volume concludes with a tale presented as six letters written to a bitter, dying man.

The subjects—insanity, murder, cruelty to children—are familiar to Bowles' readers. We have come to expect characters who have stepped over the edge, people who are unable to connect thought and deed, action and reaction, or themselves with others in any enduring way. A son kills his parents. A man seeks out and drinks human blood. A host cracks a whip over young girls to entertain his guests. Yet our fascination with these men and women is less voyeuristic than Poe-like: the pulse of the work itself draws us into it.

And Bowles never preaches. He does not draw conclusions. He allows the actions and words of his people to speak for themselves. If the stories feel incomplete or fragmented, that is because they reflect rather than explain. Ultimately, Bowles respects the reader and challenges us to make what we will of his work. And horrifying as it may be, we are compelled to see portions of our various dark selves in his mirrors. . . .

"Unwelcome Words," the last and longest piece in the collection, is the story written in letters to a dying man. It is an eloquent story. One of the most interesting aspects of Bowles' work is that at first glance his words and use of language appear quite ordinary. Yet their cadence and sound, as well as their intrinsic meaning, form a surrealistic world, as layer after layer is added and the rhythms and tones accumulate. In **"Unwelcome Words"** there are slight shifts in tone and pace with each of the letters to the dying man, until at the very end we can almost hear the death rattle. . . .

While this collection is uneven, and although some of the pieces feel more fully rendered than others, Bowles' words and work are not only welcome, but are a treasure for those of us hungry for original voices.

Jean Gould, in a review of "Unwelcome Words: Seven Stories," in The Short Story Review, *Vol. 6, No. 1, Winter, 1989, p. 15.*

ADDITIONAL BIBLIOGRAPHY

Bailey, Jeffrey. "The Art of Fiction LXVII: Paul Bowles." *The Paris Review,* No. 81 (Fall 1981): 62-98.

In-depth interview in which Bowles reflects upon, among other topics, expatriate life in Morocco, family relationships, violence in his work, his musical career, and his wife, the author Jane Bowles. This piece also includes a biographical-critical introduction.

Bertens, Johannes Willem. *The Fiction of Paul Bowles: The Soul is the Weariest Part of the Body.* Amsterdam: Rodopi, 1979, 260 p.

Assesses Bowles's work up to 1975 from an existentialist perspective.

Halpern, Daniel. "Interview with Paul Bowles." *TriQuarterly* 33 (Spring 1975): 159-77.

Interview in which Bowles discusses his beginnings as a writer, as well as literary influences, themes, translating, and the effect of drugs on the imagination.

O'Brien, Geoffrey. "White Light White Heat." *Voice Literary Supplement,* No. 44 (April 1986): 10-13.

In-depth summary of Bowles's career, focusing on his novels.

Patteson, Richard F. "The External World of Paul Bowles." *Perspectives on Contemporary Literature* 10 (1984): 16-22.

Discusses the tenuous bond between order and chaos in Bowles's novels and stories.

The Review of Contemporary Literature 2, No. 3 (Fall 1982): 6-84.

Issue devoted to Bowles and Coleman Dowell.

Stewart, Lawrence D. *Paul Bowles: The Illumination of North Africa.* Carbondale: Southern Illinois University Press, 1974, 175 p.

Biographical-critical study.

Twentieth Century Literature 32, Nos. 3/4 (Fall/Winter 1986).

Issue devoted to Bowles. Includes articles on Bowles's novels, short stories, poetry, and autobiography.

Italo Calvino

1923-1985

Cuban-born Italian short story writer, novelist, translator, essayist, and journalist.

Considered a major international literary figure of the post-World War II era, Calvino is admired as an inventive storyteller whose entertaining tales are imbued with underlying moral and philosophical significance. Strongly influenced by the playful fantasy and moralistic content of the fable, as well as modern humanistic and ideological concerns, Calvino's works blend such devices as irony, symbolism, satire, and allegory with realistic detail to comment on the human condition, the problems of existence, and themes relating to love, alienation, and identity. He often draws upon concepts in art, the natural and social sciences, philosophy, mathematics, and politics, as well as more intuitive methods, to explore and critique the various ways humanity confronts the mysteries of being. Critics distinguish two phases in Calvino's literary career. Many of his early stories are linked with the Italian neorealist movement for their straightforward delineation of social and political issues confronting Italian society and individuals after the Second World War. A second grouping of Calvino's works contains his numerous comic fantasies in which ordinary human problems are examined within the context of imaginative settings inhabited by eccentric characters. In an appraisal of Calvino's career, Teresa de Lauretis stated: "If the trajectory of Calvino's writing, from the neorealism of his early tales to the [science fiction] and metanarrative modes of his later fiction, can be said to reflect the major shifts that have occurred over four decades in contemporary poetics, and is thus a sign of his uncommon literary and historical awareness, it is all the more extraordinary that he did remain, amid such wealth of invention and expressive variety, so perfectly consistent in his own poetic vision and so faithful to his craft, storytelling."

Calvino was born in Cuba, where his Italian parents were working briefly on an agronomy project. Upon returning to Italy, Calvino's father became curator of the botanical gardens in San Remo, a northern port town. Sharing his parents's interest in botany, Calvino studied agronomy and English literature at the University of Turin, where he completed his degree in 1947. These scientific and literary preoccupations inform Calvino's fiction, which repeatedly features poetically evocative and factually precise descriptions of nature. During World War II, Calvino was compelled to serve with Fascist forces, but he eventually joined the Italian Resistance in their attempts to liberate Italy from Fascist domination and Nazi advancements. Following the war, Calvino accepted an editorial position with the prestigious Einaudi publishing firm in Turin. While pursuing his writing and publishing career, Calvino compiled, edited, and rendered for modern readers a collection of Italian fables, *Fiabe Italiane* (*Italian Folktales*), that has been widely praised as the first representative selection of several centuries' worth of tales from various regions of Italy.

Calvino's early stories, collected in *Ultimo viene il corvo,* and his first novel, *Il sentiero dei nidi di ragno* (*The Path to the Nest of Spiders*), center on activities of Resistance members, as well as ordinary experiences of people in postwar rural Italy. "Uno dei tre è ancora vivo" ("One of the Three Is Still Alive)," concerning the fates of three captured German soldiers facing execution by Italian partisans, is one of several pieces in which characters face anguishing moral dilemmas brought about by the war. Reflecting the style of Ernest Hemingway, many of these early stories are written in a plain, straightforward manner. This unadorned style and Calvino's emphasis on social realism led critics to link him with Cesare Pavese and Elio Vittorini as a member of the Italian Neorealist literary movement. However, unlike most Neorealist works, Calvino's stories often feature such rhetorical elements as elaborate descriptions of nature and animal life, subtle twists of plot, and farcical incidents. In addition, many of the tales are narrated from the perspective of a child or young adult, lending a sense of wonder to the events described. "Un pomeriggio, Adamo" ("Adam, One Afternoon"), for example, concerns a boy fascinated with animals and insects who horrifies the girl he loves by presenting her with such gifts as toads, lizards, and snails.

Several of Calvino's stories, particularly the "Gli amori difficili" series he wrote between 1949 to 1958, reflect his penchant for intensifying the anxieties of his characters through absurdly comical incidents. "L'avventura di una bagnante"

("Adventures of a Bather"), for instance, focuses upon the consternation of a woman who loses the bottom piece of her bathing suit while swimming at a crowded beach, and "L'avventura di un miope" ("Adventures of a Photographer") follows a man's growing obsession with photography as a means of capturing the essence of his life. First published in *I racconti,* which collects all of Calvino's early short fiction, these tales appear in English translation in *Difficult Loves.* Two novellas from the 1950s, *La formica argentina* (*The Argentine Ant*) and *La nuvola di smog* (*Smog*), evince Calvino's technique of rooting stories in realistic detail while intimating extended allegorical implications. The first story concerns a young couple whose new home is infested with ants. While this story can be appreciated for its social realism, the ant infestation has been interpreted as representing intrusive elements of modern life that rob people of their privacy. In *Smog,* Calvino meticulously describes a polluted urban setting in which all communication, sensual pleasures, and political truths are stifled. These stories appear in such English-language editions as *The Watcher, and Other Stories* and *Adam, One Afternoon, and Other Stories.* The pieces in *Marcovaldo, ouvero le stagioni in città* (*Marcovaldo, or The Seasons in the City*) relate the comic misadventures of the Chaplinesque title character's pursuit of bucolic pleasures and a simple lifestyle in a modern urban environment.

During the 1950s Calvino also published a trilogy of novellas collectively known as *Il nostri antenati* (*Our Ancestors*). Here, Calvino made greater use of fantasy and allegorical elements to create fables that address, as he stated, "the problem of being" and that "define a genealogical tree of contemporary man." *Il visconte dimezzato* (*The Cloven Viscount*), the first work in the trilogy, is set in the seventeenth century and depicts a warring viscount who is cut in half by a cannonball. The halves, one good, the other evil, return separately to the man's home village, where their actions reflect their differing moral viewpoints. In *Il barone rampante* (*The Baron in the Trees*), a twelve-year-old boy rebels against the quirkily regimented lifestyle of his aristocratic family by climbing a tree and maintaining an arboreal existence for the rest of his life. Through his wit, mastery of engineering techniques, and voracious reading on a wide range of topics, the title character manages ordinary human functions and activities, falls in love, and aids earthbound residents in combatting crime, military invasion, and a fire. Among various interpretations, critics view *The Baron in the Trees* as an allegorical depiction of nonconformity and the fate of antifascists in Italy during the regime of Benito Mussolini. *Il cavaliere inesistente* (*The Nonexistent Knight*), which completes the trilogy, is set during Charlemagne's reign in France and centers on a suit of armor inhabited by an intangible being. In this work, several eccentric characters with obsessive personalities underscore problems of identity. While satirizing chivalric codes and abstract ideas, *The Nonexistent Knight* reflects Calvino's increasing self-reflexive examination of storytelling. Salman Rushdie noted that the tale is related by a nun locked up in a convent, "who can have no possible experience, as she is well aware, of the scenes of chivalry she is required to describe. . . . And yet, heroically, she writes on and on, inventing the unknown and making it seem truer than truth, and providing Calvino with a marvellous metaphor for himself."

Developing further as a fantasist during the 1960s, Calvino composed two of his most popular works, *Le cosmicomiche* (*Cosmicomics*) and *Ti con zero* (*t zero*), in which various forms of life and cosmic matter are given human attributes. In these collections of interrelated "evolutionary tales," Calvino introduces a character named Qfwfq, who passes through the crucial transitional stages in the development of the universe and life on Earth. "Lo zio acquatiro" ("The Aquatic Uncle"), for instance, concerns a relative of Qfwfq who remains in the sea while his extended family evolves into land animals, and "La spirale" ("The Spiral") centers on a mollusc gradually transforming its shell into an object of beauty. Calvino draws extensively on concepts in physics, chemistry, biology, and astronomy to dramatize the unfolding history of the universe, and he investigates through allegory, symbolism, and extended metaphor such topics as love, death, change, and the interaction of imagination with the phenomenal world. In *t zero,* Calvino makes more extensive use of logic, mathematics, and the role of signs in human life. "The Count of Monte Cristo," the concluding tale in *t zero,* explores the interaction of a character and the French author Alexandre Dumas *père* as part of an investigation into the possibilities of narrative and the relationship between creators and the products of their creation.

Calvino further explores narrative possibilities in *Il castello dei destini incrociati* (*The Castle of Crossed Destinies*), where a group of characters combine, construct, and relate stories in potentially infinite variations. In the two sections of this collection, travelers gathered at a castle and a tavern, respectively, lose their power of speech but relate their personal histories by turning over tarot cards. The random sequence of cards orders the tale of each character. By reading the cards in a nonlinear manner, the narrator, who frequently comments upon the art of storytelling, finds the destinies of the characters mixed with such legendary people as Helen of Troy, Faust, Parsifal, and Oedipus. John Gardner commented: "In the metaphor of the cards [Calvino] has exactly described the process of art as concrete philosophy, how we search the world for clues as a gypsy searches the cards, interpreting by means of our own stories and a few unsure conventions." Among Calvino's later works, *Palomar* (*Mr. Palomar*) is a collection of observations by the title character, who attempts to find moral and philosophical insight by applying systematic intellectual approaches to nature and humanity. The logical approach of Mr. Palomar is reflected in the book's structure, which consists of three parts within three subsections within three main sections, respectively offering visual, cultural/anthropological, and speculative analysis. Comic, absurd, and random mental and physical activities consistently frustrate Mr. Palomar, reflecting the elusiveness of absolute knowledge and truth and the limitations of a purely intellectual approach to comprehending existence. *Sotto il sole giaguro* (*Under the Jaguar Sun*), published posthumously, consists of three of a projected five tales revolving on the human senses. Taste, sound, and smell are emphasized in the stories Calvino completed before his death.

Calvino's international popularity and critical reputation is frequently attributed to the virtuosity and exuberantly playful style of his works, as well as to his imaginative investigations of myriad human concerns. While some critics argue that Calvino's political and social observations lack commitment and conviction and that his interest in exotic scenarios and fabulous creations overshadows his intellectual investigations, most commentators commend his appealing approach to fundamental intellectual and humanistic concerns. John Updike stated: "Like Jorge Luis Borges and Gabriel García Márquez, Italo Calvino dreams perfect dreams for us. . . . Of the three, Calvino is the sunniest, the most variously and benignly curious about the human truth as it comes embedded in its animal, vegetable, historical, and cosmic contexts; all his investigations spiral in upon the central question of *How shall we live?*"

(See also *Contemporary Literary Criticism*, Vols. 5, 8, 11, 22, 33, 39; *Contemporary Authors*, Vols. 85-88, Vol. 116 [obituary]; and *Contemporary Authors New Revision Series*, Vol. 23.)

PRINCIPAL WORKS

SHORT FICTION

Ultimo viene il corvo 1949
Il visconte dimezzato 1952
[published in *The Nonexistent Knight and The Cloven Viscount*, 1962]
Fiabe Italiene 1956
[*Italian Folktales*, 1980]
Adam, One Afternoon, and Other Stories 1957; reprinted, 1983
Il barone rampante 1957
[*The Baron in the Trees*, 1959]
I racconti 1958
Il cavaliere inesistente 1959
[published in *The Nonexistent Knight and The Cloven Viscount*, 1962]
I nostri antenati 1960
[*Our Ancestors*, 1960, 1980 *(collects The Cloven Viscount, The Baron in the Trees, and The Nonexistent Knight)*]
Marcovaldo, ouvero le stagioni in città 1963
[*Marcovaldo, or The Seasons in the City*, 1983]
Le cosmicomiche 1965
[*Cosmicomics*, 1968]
Ti con zero 1967
[*t zero*, 1969]
Il castella dei destini incrociati 1969
[*The Castle of Crossed Destinies*, 1977]
The Watcher, and Other Stories 1971
Difficult Loves 1984
Sotto il sole giaguro 1986
[*Under the Jaguar Sun*, 1988]

OTHER MAJOR WORKS

Il sentiero dei nidi di ragno (novel) 1947
[*The Path to the Nest of Spiders*, 1957]
La città Invisibili (novel) 1974]
[*Invisible Cities*, 1974]
Se una notte d'inverno vaggiatore (novel) 1979
[*If on a winter's night a traveler*, 1981]
Pietra sopra discorsi di letteratura e societa (nonfiction) 1980
[*The Uses of Literature*, 1986]
Six Essays for the Next Millennium (nonfiction) 1988

FREDERIC MORTON (essay date 1959)

[*Morton, an Australian-born American novelist, biographer, historian, and critic, offers a generally positive review of* The Baron in the Trees, *but he notes that the book fails to achieve the sense of unity evidenced in such comparably imaginative works as Miguel de Cervantes's* Don Quixote *(1612).*]

Eccentricity is growing rare in contemporary fiction. Many a twentieth-century novelist, muscle-bound with too much sober craftsmanship and industrious subtlety, will not suffer a crotchet among his characters without analyzing it into a neurosis. *Don Quixote*, I fear, might emerge from today's electric typewriters not as the sad and hilarious story of a man, but as the earnestly documented biography of a maladjustment.

Italo Calvino has tackled a quixotic theme in [***The Baron in the Trees***], and I am happy to say that he has the narrative leisure and the style to do it at least initial justice. . . .

The Baron in the Trees tells of a time and a circle that encouraged the innocent flowering of the bizarre. We are introduced to the family of Baron Arminio Piavasco di Rondo, minor and fairly mad aristocracy capering away at the end of the eighteenth century. . . .

The strangest creature of all turns out to be the Baron's elder son Cosimo. At the age of 12 he is reproved by his parents for his table manners, runs off to climb a tree, and for the rest of his long life never descends to earth again.

All these whimsies Mr. Calvino renders very well. But soon it becomes plain that, unlike the kinks of the other di Rondos, Cosimo's deportment is not meant as mere imaginative self-indulgence but as a superb, downright apocalyptic gesture. By eating, sleeping, loving on the bough, the Baron defies all the petty earth-bound conformities of man. By never obeying the thousands of commands to slide down, he upholds an uncompromising individual freedom. . . .

Mr. Calvino . . . seems to have intended nothing less than the deliberate transmutation of fantastic notion into universal allegory. Since he is not Cervantes he does not succeed—yet we are frequently entertained and even incidentally instructed. Cosimo's branch-borne foiling of some Berber pirates makes a very funny episode. So does the cleverness with which he restores a lazy French regiment to a martial qui-vive (he sprays the men with lice). But the latter episode is a performance of wit; the former, of slapstick. Neither develops the character comedy necessary for the author's high purpose.

Everything that happens in *Don Quixote* springs inevitably from the wondrous bent of the knight's mind. The occurrences in this book, however, do not flow together into the revelation of one gloriously gnarled soul. Instead they are competent entertainment, derived from a miscellany of elegantly realized but minor inspirations. Mr. Calvino's . . . novel takes us on a diverting journey through an *outré* age. It never quite lives up to the exquisite potential of its premise.

Frederic Morton, "Flower of the Bizarre," in The New York Times Book Review, *October 11, 1959, p. 35.*

HELENE CANTARELLA (essay date 1962)

[*Cantarella is a critic and translator who specializes in modern European literature. In the review excerpted below, she praises the humor and fantasy elements in* The Nonexistent Knight *and* The Cloven Viscount *and speculates on some of the allegorical meanings implied in these tales.*]

[Like] many another serious writer before him, [Calvino] is endowed with a sly and oblique second vision which permits him on occasion to indulge in whimsical fantasies which are more real, in their intrinsic truths, than reality itself. Like Voltaire, Swift and others of this sophisticated fraternity of genuine wits and social critics, he can transcend the immediate and transmute it in terms of every man and every age.

The two literary *divertimenti* which make up this delightful volume [***The Nonexistent Knight and The Cloven Viscount***] complete Calvino's trilogy of allegorical parables (the first of which [is] ***The Baron in the Trees*** . . .). Set in the brightly emblazoned Middle Ages of the *chansons de geste* and the romances of chivalry, ***The Nonexistent Knight*** is a mock epic rooted in concrete neorealism. Through a series of earthy exploits which combine elements of Ariosto's *Orlando Furioso* and Tasso's *Gerusalemme Liberata,* spiked with liberal dashes of assorted Carolingian and Arthurian legends, chronicles, fables and myths, Calvino pokes ironic fun at the candor of the aging Charlemagne's battle-weary paladins and uses these worthies as vehicles for a mordantly witty satire on the affairs of modern man.

His noble protagonist, the valiant Knight Agilulf, who "exists without existing," stands as one apart from his cohorts. And for good reason. His gleaming white armor contains nothing but an echoing voice and an indomitable will. . . .

Nettled by Agilulf, Charlemagne not only packs him off on a quixotic quest to prove his valor and retain his rank, but assigns to him as squire the brutish Gurduloo, who is the complete antithesis of his master. If Agilulf is an abstraction without tangible reality, Gurduloo who "exists without realizing that he exists" seems the personification of collective mass-man who "becomes a duck with ducks, a fish with fish." As fables would have it, the pure of heart triumph in the end. . . .

The Cloven Viscount is a dark-hued Gothic gem which transports us into the mysterious late medieval world of Altdorfer's teeming battle scenes and Bosch's hallucinating grotesques. During the wars against the Turks, Medardo, Viscount of Tellalba, is neatly sheared in two by a cannon ball. . . . Miraculously rescued and patched up by nursing friars, Medardo's left half, artfully rounded out by a billowing cape, returns to his estate. There he becomes the scourge and terror of all. The embodiment of pure evil, he rides roughshod over the countryside, spreads more desolation than all four horsemen of the apocalypse.

One day another Medardo appears, identical in physique to the first, but diametrically opposed in temperament.

What lies at the core of these ingenious spoofs? Because Calvino is too sophisticated to be an obvious moralist, his parables are open to a number of political and psychological interpretations. To this reader they would seem to imply that in a world split, then as now, between good and bad, true believers and infidels, East and West—sanity and the future belong only to the wholly committed and not to the alienated or mutilated, however lofty their aims and ideals.

Helene Cantarella, "In a World Split, Ideals Are Not Enough," in The New York Times Book Review, *August 5, 1962, p. 4.*

SERGIO PACIFICI (essay date 1962)

[Pacifici has authored and edited several surveys of contemporary Italian literature, reflecting his extensive knowledge and interest in the writings of his native land. In the passage excerpted below from his A Guide to Contemporary Italian Literature: From Futurism to Neorealism, *Pacifici discusses Calvino's early works, focusing on the author's artistic purposes and his place in contemporary Italian letters.]*

Of the small group of writers [who can be used] to illustrate some of the tendencies and problems of contemporary fiction in Italy, Italo Calvino is not only the youngest member but the most productive and versatile. . . . (p. 143)

In a long, polemical essay, "*Il midollo del leone*" (The Lion's Marrow), Calvino has articulated his poetics with conviction: "We believe" he has stated,

> that political engagement, partisanship, self-involvement is, more than a duty, the natural necessity of the writer of today and, even before the writer, of modern man. Ours is not an era we can understand by remaining *au dessus de la melée.* On the contrary, we understand it all the more when we live it, when we situate ourselves even close to the front line.

His words, however, must be taken with much caution. Few writers have successfully demonstrated how a writer can be *engagé* and yet not subservient to political ideologies. . . . (p. 144)

Faithful to his poetics (formulated only in 1955), even his first work, *The Path to the Nest of Spiders,* is not a realistic *novella,* although it has real people, real situations, and real actions. The merit of the tale is not in any photographic depiction of the life and the coups of the band of partisans but in the wonderful whimsicality and vivaciousness with which the protagonist, Pin (a mere boy), is treated; it lies also in the lightness of the author's touch, especially in the descriptions of nature, the same nature that becomes in Calvino's later books a veritable treasurehouse of inspiration. Significantly, Calvino almost invariably chooses a youth as his main hero. Only a youngster possesses a real sense of enchantment with nature, a sense of tranquillity and perennial discovery of the mysteries of life. Typical of such confrontation is the short story **"Un giardino incantato" ("An Enchanted Garden"),** so characteristic of Calvino's deftness and elegance. In the tale, two youngsters, Giovannino and Serenella, find themselves by chance in a marvelous garden:

> There were big, old, flesh-coloured eucalyptus trees and winding gravel paths. . . .
>
> Everything was so beautiful: narrow turnings and high, curling eucalyptus leaves and patches of sky. There was always the worrying thought that it was not their garden, and that they might be chased away at any moment. But not a sound could be heard. A flight of chattering sparrows rose from a clump of arbutus at a turn in the path. Then all was silent again. Perhaps it was an abandoned garden?

The story proceeds with the same rhythm. Nothing much happens, and indeed little need happen. The youngsters play, swim, have some tea and sponge cake (thoughtfully put on a table by the servant of the household), and then leave. It is a delicate, poetic story, which exemplifies how little action or plot Calvino needs to render his tale interesting.

Calvino's vein is not always as light as this. In the short story **"Dollari e vecchie mondane" ("Dollars and the Demi-Mondaine")** he concocts a vision reminiscent of a modern ballet or a surrealistic painting. Another, rather long tale, ***La formica argentina* (*The Argentine Ant*)**, has some of the spine-chilling power and suspense of Dino Buzzati and Franz Kafka (but without the latter's metaphysical implications). It is about a family, a husband and wife and their child, who move to a house, despite having been warned that the place is riddled with ants. Soon thousands upon thousands of ants invade their home, and no remedy, however intelligent, can stop them from coming. There is no solution to their plight. The tale ends as the couple takes a stroll to a nearby beach where there are no ants and where they can once again enjoy themselves. There is probably an allegorical meaning to the story: the ants may well represent the insidious, devastating elements of modern life that rob man of his privacy and tranquillity. Perhaps it is because he is driven by a desire to express his disgust with certain social phenomena that Calvino has composed short stories like **"La speculazione edilizia" ("The Speculation of the Building Constructors")**. This long tale is in the realistic vein of *Il sentiero dei nidi di ragno,* but without its humor and vivacity. It tells of a constructor named Caisotti, a *nouveau riche* of Italian postwar society, who entices his friend Quinto, an impoverished intellectual, to become his partner in a real-estate venture that should prove to be quite profitable. Quinto feels deeply committed to his "speculation." A former Communist (and as such he may well, as some critics have noted, reflect the uneasiness experienced by Calvino himself after his own repudiation of communism), he does not feel the need to live among comrades. Rather, he is tremendously attracted to the business people, to the smart entrepreneurs with "their guns always aimed," and he identifies himself with "all that was new, in contrast, with all that caused violence." . . . The tension of the *novella* is strategically built up by the slow progress made by the construction company, by Caisotti's deliberate procrastinations, and by Quinto's approval of the new rising class, an antibourgeois society, corrupt, amoral, and equivocal. The climax is reached when, after numerous *coups de scène,* Quinto discovers, in the chaos of the situation, that Caisotti has once been a partisan. . . . There is considerable criticism of the degeneration of society in postwar Italy, and it is fictionalized skillfully and intelligently. Calvino may be a realistic writer here (in more than one way), but he succeeds in making his points without polemics or cries for social reform.

The richer side of Calvino, nevertheless, is to be found in his fantastic tales, of which he is one of the few practitioners in contemporary Italy. He has written three works—recently collected in a large volume entitled ***I nostri antenati*** (Our Forefathers)—which may be read as a trilogy or enjoyed individually: ***Il visconte dimezzato* [*The Cloven Viscount*]**; ***Il barone rampante* (*The Baron in the Trees*)**; and, quite recently, ***Il cavaliere inesistente* [*The Nonexistent Knight*]**. Of these three supernatural tales, the best is probably the second one.

The story is most unusual. It is about a twelve-year-old boy, Cosimo Piovasco, who on the fifteenth of June 1767, having been severely scolded by his father for refusing to eat a dish of snail soup (to be followed by more snails as a main course) prepared by his sister Battista, decides to climb a tree and live there. What ordinarily would have been regarded as a child's prank turns out to be a tenacious and diverting plan to live in the trees, cut off (if only in a special way) from the rest of the world. Not that Cosimo refuses to have anything to do with the world: quite the contrary. He goes on living (taking his usual shower, building an extensive library in his hut, and even attending Mass with his family) without ever descending from the giant holm oak—and is considerably helped by the fact that, since the forest in his garden is very thick, he can travel from tree to tree without renouncing his vow not to descend to earth. That Cosimo is "up there" means very little as far as his own activities are concerned. He grows up, studies, loves, and even fights from the trees, successfully demonstrating that the kind of fantastic life we no longer believe feasible *is* possible and contains the adventurous flavor our own, "real" life too frequently lacks. For his life is a rich one, replete with encounters not only with ordinary people (and even a noblewoman, Viola), but with soldiers (both French and Austrian and finally even Russian) and leaders—Napoleon among them! But Cosimo, being after all human, grows old: "Youth soon passes on earth," Calvino wryly remarks, "so imagine it in the trees, where it is the fate of everything to fall: leaves, fruit." . . . (pp. 145-48)

This brief account of the story is sufficient to give the reader an idea of the richness of Calvino's imagination. The novelist has no doubt been influenced by his family's professional interest in botany and by his own interest in science and folk tales. His work recalls the Grimm brothers and Swift, or, especially to the Italian reader, Boccaccio, and, above all, Ariosto. It is with the great poet from Ferrara that Calvino has closely identified himself and has confessed an admiration that goes well beyond that felt by every youngster and adult for the *Orlando Furioso*. . . . (p. 148)

Calvino, much like Ariosto, abstracts from our historical time certain verities that he weaves into fantastic stories about knights and their adventures. Like Ariosto, Calvino sits in his laboratory (his study in Turin) and dreams of a world created by the novelist's fantasy. Unlike Ariosto, however, Calvino holds that his fables are not, *in fondo,* flights from reality, but come from the bitter reality of our twentieth century. They are the means—perhaps the only means left to a writer tired of a photographic obsession with modern life—to re-create a world where people can still be people—that is, where people can still dream and yet understand; flee from the world (as the young Cosimo does) and yet never sever relations with it; where man's aspirations are fulfilled through his intellect rather than through his physical power. However, there is a passage in which Calvino mocks the pure use of reason. When Cosimo's brother (who is the narrator of the tale) goes to France, he visits Voltaire, the great French sage.

> The old philosopher was in his armchair, surrounded by a court of ladies, gay as crickets and prickly as a porcupine. When he heard I came from Ombrosa he addressed me thus: "Is it near you, *mon cher Chevalier,* that there is that famous philosopher who lives in the trees *comme un singe?*"
>
> And I, flattered, could not prevent myself replying: "He's my brother, *Monsieur, le Baron de Rondeau.*"
>
> . . . "But is it to be nearer to the sky that your brother stays up there?"
>
> "My brother considers," answered I, "that anyone who wants to see the earth properly must keep himself at a necessary distance from it." And Voltaire seemed to appreciate this reply.

> "Once it was only Nature which produced living phenomena," he concluded. "Now it is Reason." And the old sage plunged back into the chatter of his theistic adorers.

Through the fable, told in an ironic, amusing style, Calvino manages well to recapture much of the silliness and the seriousness of life. But one wonders where his fiction leads. Calvino himself seems to have become aware of this issue, for in the closing pages of ***Il cavaliere inesistente*** he formulates it explicitly: "Lately I have started writing furiously. From one line to the next I jumped from nation to nation and from sea to sea and from continent to continent. What is the fury that has overtaken me? One would say that I am waiting for something." He may indeed. And the future work, now in progress, should best answer the question. (pp. 148-49)

Sergio Pacifici, "The New Writers," in his A Guide to Contemporary Italian Literature: From Futurism to Neorealism, *The World Publishing Company, 1962, pp. 114-49.*

THE TIMES LITERARY SUPPLEMENT (essay date 1966)

[*The enthusiastic review of* Cosmicomics *excerpted below praises Calvino's ability to write works that are equally entertaining and informative.*]

Beginning as a realist and influenced by Cesare Pavese and Elio Vittorini, Signor Calvino soon found his *métier* as a writer of fables and fantasies, and he created a world of fairies, knights and enchantment. He is also a master of Kafka-like suspense as he showed in ***La formica argentina.*** The central figure of [***Le cosmicomiche***] and the narrator is one Qfwfq, who, the publishers state, is of the same age as the universe. This he cannot quite be, as he has grandparents. He has, however, been present at the creation of the earth and the planets, has raced with galaxies, played marbles with hydrogen atoms and been a dinosaur, a reptile and a mollusc.

The book is divided into twelve episodes, each prefixed by a note on some scientific theory or cosmic event. The episodes are not chronological nor do the various cosmic events form a logical sequence. Each adventure of Qfwfq is complete in itself and any one may conflict with the situations and hypotheses set out in others. It has been said that Signor Calvino's trilogy ***I nostri antenati*** is akin to *Orlando Furioso* and certainly he has written that of all the Italian poets Ariosto is nearest to him, but in ***Le Cosmicomiche*** he carries his humour and surrealism to fantastic lengths. In **"La distanza della Luna"** his characters behave and talk like Jumblies in a more paradisal Lower Slobbovia, more paradisal in as much as the stony moon is not covered with snow but with a manna of the consistency of cream cheese. Qfwfq, although he is but a wandering, disembodied voice, always has human attributes, as have his companions. Indeed his adventures as a dinosaur are moving and pathetic in a very human sense. Some of the episodes have a Chestertonian, even Gargantuan, humour, and there are hints of Baron Münchhausen. In **"Tutto in un punto"**, which is not unlike, in its theoretical aspect, the scholastic argument about how many angels can stand on the point of a needle, the Signora Ph(i)Nk_0 decides to make tagliatelle, and the narrator wonders how much space the flour would occupy, how many stars and galaxies had to be held in suspense while the pasta was being made.

Signor Calvino is not at his best when he is being metaphysical (**"Un segno"**) or sentimental (**"Senza colori"**) but the episodes have great variety. **"Lo Zio acquativo"** is a delightful social skit with a trick ending; **"Quanto scommettiamo"** is a wonderfully far-fetched piece of rollicking nonsense, as is also **"La Forma dello spazio"**; **"Gli anni-luci"** is the most logical, but the fun is carried too far and eventually gets almost boring. Every episode has a stroke of brilliance and the opening of **"Gli anni-luci"** is a masterpiece, but perhaps Qfwfq's remark in **"La spirale"**, when he is a mollusc, is his funniest: "I was a bachelor (the system of reproduction in those days not requiring mating even for a temporary period) in good health and without too many pretensions".

Signor Calvino has an elegant style and superb gifts of description. A few years ago he defined the novel as "A narrative work which is enjoyable and significant at many levels that intersect one another". This definition effectively describes ***Le Cosmicomiche.***

"Cosmic Cuts," in The Times Literary Supplement, *No. 3367, September 8, 1966, p. 799.*

THE TIMES LITERARY SUPPLEMENT (essay date 1968)

[*The review of* t zero *excerpted below focuses on Calvino's blending of logic, mathematics, and fantasy and assesses his place in contemporary Italian literature.*]

In an Italian literary scene that seethes with technical innovators—ignorers of punctuation and pronouns, paste-and-scissors men, writers of what read like surrealist film-scripts—Italo Calvino continues to write classically plain prose, with perfectly observed detail. Realistic-sounding prose for non-realistic purposes has always been his speciality. . . . [Immediately] after the war, Calvino had looked like the realest of the realists, a literary equivalent of the neo-realist films then reflecting the harsh but invigorating conditions of poverty with freedom; but even at that time a kind of serpentine fantasy wriggled disconcertingly now and then through the bald statements and descriptions, a lyrical, anarchical streak was already apparent. With the years, this grew. But the writing remained plain and pure, un-Italian in its solidity and its avoidance of the abstract, staid and unaffected whatever the circumstances, and in riotous, effective contrast to the farfetched subjects with which, lately above all, it has been dealing.

Calvino is one of the few writers who have used fantasy fruitfully, and is at present stretching the possibilities of fiction by going completely outside its normal range, while still keeping a human proportion. Man remains his subject; but man entirely beyond the usual fictional situations and circumstances. In ***Le cosmicomiche*** his hero was called Qfwfq and was as old as the universe, a protean creature who sprang about in space and time describing the birth, development and extinction of galaxies, solar systems, geological eras, prehistoric animals, all in a modern idiom. . . . Qfwfq is the hero of about half the book ***Ti con zero,*** though not of its title story (unless he is hiding behind the initial Q, by which the narrator identifies himself, but Qfwfq is not as a rule one to hide behind anything): a Qfwfq come so far forward in time from his unicellular beginnings that, while retaining the memory of his immemorial past as precisely as ever, and still in close contact with the oozy world from which he sprang, he now leads a brisk modern life in New Jersey, goes over a precipice in a weekend car-ride in Italy or falls in love with a booted, fringed, freckled girl called Priscilla Langwood, chez Madame Lebras, cent-quatre-vingt-treize Rue Vaugirard, Paris quinzième; all this at a high level of comedy that, with extraordinary lightness, sees contemporary happenings, sharply observed and socially exact, in terms of infinitely ancient experience. The effect is of the kind of *trompe l'oeil* used in op art, of layers upon layers, vistas upon vistas, leading into and out of one another; of perspective stood on its head and forcing one to question the basis of all previous perspectives.

["t zero"] (which simply means t_0 as opposed to t_1, t_2, t_3, &c.) and those that come after it, two set in cars, the third **["The Count of Monte Cristo"]** in the Chateau d'If, with Edmond Dantès, inside, experiencing what Dumas, outside, is writing, are another departure, attempts both serious and comic to take fiction into the field of logic and mathematics. . . . [The] prisoner of If's mental arrangement of escape routes and treasure hunts, his reduction of everything to formulae of possibilities and impossibilities; and an attempt to deal with the time/space problems presented by a lion, L, leaping upon one in a certain time, t: here again, in the effort to formalize actions as apparently haphazard as a quarrel, as violent and gratuitous as murder, as inexplicable as tyrannous imprisonment, as immediate and alarming as a lion in mid-leap, there is an element of *trompe l'oeil,* of visual as well as intellectual tricks and of rings within rings as there are styles within styles in what seems the almost textbook straightforwardness of Calvino's writing. As fluent as he is original, Calvino has things to say to those who, temperamentally, find it hard to swallow the outlandish: for while his concepts are as fantastic as his time sequence, his sobersided air and unpretentious manner make him seem, though he is not, respectably reassuring.

"Qfwfquirks," in The Times Literary Supplement, *No. 3451, April 18, 1968, p. 391.*

D. J. ENRIGHT (essay date 1968)

[*Enright is a noted English poet, novelist, critic, and editor whose works exhibit a liberal, humanistic outlook. In the essay excerpted below, he provides examples of how* The Baron in the Trees *and the pieces in* Cosmicomics *can be read as fables concerning the urge to evolve.*]

[***The Baron in the Trees***] concerned an Italian nobleman who took to the trees as a boy and never came down to earth again. Within the story's charming premises there was space for Calvino's highly developed and humanistic imagination to accomplish quite a lot. In the interests of credibility, we were shown how eminently possible it was for Cosimo to lead "a normal life," all the way from performing his daily duties in a decent, hygienic manner to performing the act of love in a comfortable as well as sometimes a rather acrobatic fashion. . . . Cosimo forswore the earth as an act of rebellion against his family, and even when he dies, he does not return. The old dying man is swept out of the branches by the anchor of a balloon belonging to some English aeronauts and his body is never seen again. Between these two eccentric events, Cosimo has led a reasonably full life, it occurs to us, and a more than usually satisfying one. He has lived according to his lights, he has never compromised, yet neither has he renounced his species.

It is cheering to deduce from the modest success of ***The Baron in the Trees*** that there is still interest in something quite other than the Great American Novel (and smaller British one), the Apocalyptic-Excremental or Sexual Variations without a Theme, that there is still interest in an art which is more concerned with life and growth than with decay and death. Calvino's reviewers were forced to dip into a new (or perhaps old) wordhoard: "mellow," "graceful," "beautifully written," "delightful," "antique ease and enjoyment," "a lovely book."

Some of these epithets, I imagine, will be applied to [***Cosmicomics***], a collection of linked stories, or "evolutionary tales." The narrator, old (indeed remarkably old, or ageless, or even young) Qfwfq, tells of his experiences at various stages of evolution, as a young vertebrate who is in process of deserting the sea for the land, as the last of the dinosaurs anxiously concealing his identity from the New Ones, for whom his sort are doubtfully mythical figures of dread, like giants in later history ("You looked as if you'd seen . . . a Dinosaur!"), and as a mollusk knowing love and jealousy. The opening story, which makes the film *2001* look about as imaginative as a spilled bucket of distemper, tells of the time when the moon was so close to the earth that Qfwfq and his companions could row out in a boat and scramble up on it to collect Moonmilk, which was "very thick, like a kind of cream cheese." In the closing story Qfwfq argues that, though the mollusk remained blind itself, it was the cause of eyes in other species by virtue of producing something to be seen—a beautiful shell.

What adds an element of power to the ingenious, humorous, and charming fantasy of these tales is the palpable though undeclared theme which runs through them, the urge to evolve, the sense in the most primitive forms of life of better things to come, the touching readiness to adopt a receptive posture toward "the future." In ***Cosmicomics,*** simple organisms yearn forward, innocently and trustingly, toward the next stage in evolution. In ***The Baron in the Trees*** Cosimo appears to be retrogressing by "returning" to an arboreal existence, but his love of life prevails over the restrictions he has imposed on himself by a childish act of defiance. He is not really backward-looking, he simply maintains that "anyone who wants to see the earth properly must keep himself at a necessary distance from it," and many of his views and attitudes are in the best sense progressive.

Not that Calvino is writing programmatically in these stories. **"The Aquatic Uncle"** is about a relative of Qfwfq's who shames his family by contentedly staying put in a lagoon after the rest have all removed to the land. Old Uncle N'ba N'ga is a reactionary, literally a stick-in-the-mud, and young Qfwfq is reluctant to introduce him to his fiancée, Lll, because she is a sophisticated young piece and comes of a "very good" family, one of those so long established on land that they "had finally become convinced they had never lived anywhere else." However, Lll is fascinated by the old fish's stories of life under the water and, while Qfwfq is still having a little difficulty in using his fins as paws, she practices using her paws as fins—"Good for you! That's a big step forward," says Qfwfq sarcastically—and then jumps into the lagoon, to marry old Uncle N'ba N'ga and be a fish again and bring more fish into the sea. . . . Qfwfq's uncle has much in common with the Baron Cosimo, sexual charm as well as eccentricity. The parallel situation in human terms is, of course, the old world's emigration to America, that new found land, as is made tactfully plain by Qfwfq's account of the time when there wasn't a family in the sea without someone who had moved to dry land, and the emigrants used to send back "fabulous tales of the things that could be done there," urging their relatives to join them in this New World.

Read as a fable, the tale suggests the propriety of *diversity* within creation, that it is right that some fishes should go on being fish, and also, perhaps, it suggests that while at every stage of evolution something is gained, something is lost too. Uncle N'ba N'ga seems to Qfwfq a bigoted relic of the past with whom you can hardly communicate since his idiomatic expressions are so sadly out of date, but we perceive that Uncle is a canny old fish, understanding and loving his environment, and that for all his progressiveness Qfwfq has a good deal of the brash and ignorant young tadpole about him. That was part of the Baron's message, too: progress is right, but a reverence for the past is right as well, and they also serve who stand and act as brakes.

More plainly than ***The Baron in the Trees, Cosmicomics*** calls for that willing suspension of disbelief which constitutes poetic faith, and since the book is poetic, it willingly gets it. There is just enough appearance of "science" in it to enable one to swallow such seeming anachronisms as Qfwfq's description of the underbelly of the Moon as smelling like smoked salmon. And when he remarks casually of his sister, who disappeared when the planets were solidifying, that he never knew what had happened to her "until I met her, much later, at Canberra in 1912, married to a certain Sullivan, a retired railroad man," we swallow that too, for we are utterly disarmed by his next remark, that she was then "so changed I hardly recognized her." Nothing succeeds like a mixture of effrontery and charm. Moreover, we tell ourselves, there is perhaps some serious implication here, concerning the survival of identity, the conservation of personality.

Dr. Johnson complained of *Paradise Lost* that its plan comprised neither human actions nor human manners. "The reader beholds no condition in which he can by any effort of imagination place himself; he has, therefore, little natural curiosity or sympathy." The plan of ***Cosmicomics*** must labor under an even greater inconvenience, since it treats of ancestors distinctly more remote than our Grand Parents. Perhaps it is in rueful acknowledgment of the risked "want of human interest" that, in a world as yet without an atmosphere and without colors, Qfwfq comments, "You rarely met anyone in those days: there were so few of us!" Sympathy does flag here and there, but for the most part Calvino succeeds by a perfect tact. His characters are human enough, he gives us the essence of each evolutionary stage by allowing old Qfwfq a degree of hindsight wisdom acceptable in one of his age, and then he passes quickly on. These are short stories because they couldn't possibly be long ones. ***Cosmicomics*** is a truly original piece of writing, an engaging and refreshing book. . . . (pp. 22-4)

D. J. Enright, "Effrontery & Charm," in The New York Review of Books, *Vol. XI, No. 9, November 21, 1968, pp. 22-5.*

PAUL WEST (essay date 1969)

[*An English editor, critic, essayist, and novelist, West finds the stories in* t zero *more "sober" and generally less appealing than those in* Cosmicomics.]

Essentially, this new collection of Italo Calvino's cosmicomical fables [***t zero***] picks up where ***Cosmicomics,*** its immediate predecessor, left off. Qfwfq, the protean hero who is just as much at home in the protozoic slime or sporting among the galaxies as he is on a cloverleaf where the superhighways begin to fan out, reappears unchanged (inasmuch as he is still constantly changing himself at will), but with a new obsession. Whereas, in the earlier book, he told about the fun he and his contemporaries used to have collecting milk in buckets from the surface of the moon, now he suffers from something we ourselves might have experienced only recently: moon-nausea. . . .

In manner and subject matter, **"Soft Moon"** . . . would fit congruously into ***Cosmicomics,*** as would the one about the reptilian first bird, who sings "koaxpf" in anachronistic homage to Aristophanes' frogs, and the one about Qfwfq's yearning for the old days when each substance was concentrated into a single large crystal—whereas, now, he has to work among the glass slabs of Manhattan where Tiffany's enshrines the splinters of a vanished kingdom.

Reading such fictions, one's mind must flex itself continually in order to keep pace with all the offered possibilities: the long-since extinct alongside the newest synthetic fabric; the way various species evolved alongside the ways they didn't; and the simultaneous modifiability of everything through imagination, so that whatever is trumped-up is just as "real" as what is not. It's a kind of genetic opportunism in which it is impossible to make mistakes.

Beginning with such of his early heroes as the baron who lives in the trees (***The Baron in the Trees***) and the [one] . . . who manages to get around although cut clean in half [***The Cloven Viscount***], Calvino has sought for an imaginative maximum that transcends such categories as "real," "realistic" and "fantastic" and brings home to us, in a way both farcical and poignant, all the modes of being that surround us and are part of us. He has worked biochemistry against the complacencies of fiction and he has fictionalized both the dubieties and the certainties of astronomers. Sporting with Nature, he has ingeniously reacquainted us with the fact that trees don't laugh, mud can't read, dinosaurs can't cook, and so on.

But, in the last two sections of [***t zero***], he sobers up. The subject matter remains much the same: Qfwfq, as a dividing cell, undergoes agonies of lost and plural identity; as a camel in love, he feels that his individuality and initiative are as nothing compared to the relentless programming set up in him and in his Priscilla by amino acids lined up in a certain way. There is doom, too, on a larger plane—"from the mud of the boiling swamps the first clot of undivided life cannot again emerge . . . the spell is broken, the eternals are dead." We might have expected Calvino to get to such matters sooner or later, but not, as here, in an idiom that combines the obsessive logical exhaustiveness of Samuel Beckett with the acute creative diffidence of J. L. Borges. . . .

If Calvino was ever one thing consistently, he was bold, and impenitently so; he bounced us into going along with him. So why now, I wonder, the switch to mechanically assembled patterns of lucid but stultifying casuistries? Yards of them, no doubt in tribute to the copious intricateness of being; but such prose consorts oddly with what little the mind's eye is offered, such as the male camel's nostalgia for "those sunsets in the oasis, when they loosen the burden from the packsaddle and the caravan scatters and we camels feel suddenly light and you break into a run and I trot after you, overtaking you in the grove of palm trees." It's as if there's a Hemingway locked up inside a Hegel and trying to get out.

The easiest read in the whole book is . . . **"The Count of Monte Cristo,"** in which Edmond Dantès breaks into Alexandre Dumas's study and reads the discarded pages of the novel, thus discovering the life he *might* have had and the fact that his true confinement is in "the concentric fortress, If-Monte Cristo-Dumas's desk." That discovery is Calvino's, too. In other words, *The Count of Monte Cristo* could have been a combination of words different from the one we all know it as, whereas there was and is no alternative to $E = mc^2$. I just hope the factualist in Calvino hasn't humbled the clown for keeps. I much prefer the Calvino who explores *if* to the one who confines himself in a polysyllogistic Château d' *If.*

Paul West, "Global Pillage and the Chateau d' If," in Book World—The Washington Post, *September 7, 1969, p. 15.*

JOHN ASHBERY (essay date 1969)

[Ashbery is a distinguished American poet often linked with the "New York School" of poetry, which also includes Frank O'Hara and Kenneth Koch. In the review excerpted below, Ashbery focuses on the stories "Priscilla" and "The Count of Monte Cristo" as the culmination of Calvino's imaginative examination of the human condition in Cosmicomics *and* t zero.*]*

It was natural that Italo Calvino, born into a family of scientists and himself a student of folklore (he has made a definitive compilation of Italian folk tales), with a penchant for social allegory ([***The Baron in the Trees***] may be read as a reflection of his experiences as a Partisan) would develop a literary form uniquely suited to his interests: the science-fiction parable. In ***Cosmicomics,*** and now in ***t zero,*** he has mined this rather unpromising vein extensively and at times with brilliant results.

Cosmicomics was a collection of tales with a common narrator, Qfwfq, a protean being, capable of evolving unscathed if nonplussed along with the universe from its beginnings. . . . Calvino has been likened to Chesterton and David Garnett and, alas, he does occasionally wander into the tepid never-never land, halfway between whimsy and Surrealism, of *The Man Who Was Thursday* and *Lady Into Fox.*

Though ***t zero*** continues for a while to chronicle the adventures of Qfwfq, there are indications that Calvino has tried to break the snug mold in which the earlier stories were cast. As a result, the new book is both more uneven and more interesting. It is composed of three rather arbitrarily juxtaposed sections, each made up of several stories. The first group, in which we meet Qfwfq as a commuter in a moon-menaced New Jersey of the future and on the Italian Riviera of today, is a rerun of ***Cosmicomics.*** The second group, **"Priscilla,"** is a mad and dazzling scientific dissertation on the nature of love and death. The third, despite its echoes of Borges, Kafka and the *nouveau roman,* does have one story, **"The Count of Monte Cristo,"** which juggles these influences so skillfully as to re-create them.

Calvino's prose is by no means easy or congenial. . . . He has abandoned the elegant *trompe-l'oeil* style of ***The Baron in the Trees,*** a kind of literary equivalent of Visconti's flawlessly detailed costume epics. Perhaps he abandoned it because the extended metaphor which served that novel as a plot (a young 18th-century nobleman decides to live in the trees and never comes down to earth again) did not quite fill out the book's dimensions.

Today, on the contrary, Calvino has a horror of vacuums: he has trimmed these stories to the bone, using long run-on sentences that keep skidding out from under one as idea engenders idea. He is a master of the false summation (introduced by connective devices like "in sort," "in other words," "or rather," "I would almost say," etc.) which does not sum up at all but develops the embryo of a thought through stages the reader could not have imagined. This organic, growing prose, reflecting the movement of the universe as it passes from gas to liquid to sponges to crystals to cosmic jelly, is marvelously right and also very taxing to read. But **"Priscilla"** is worth it. One has to live the density of Calvino's style to live the density of the experience he is describing, which is the experience of wanting the opposed, complementary, outside substance that is the object of love. . . . (pp. 5, 36)

It is everybody's story. Calvino may well be the Proust of 2001.

In **"Priscilla"** (the heroine, by the way, scarcely appears at all in human form, only as a principle; she is apparently an *Anglo-saxonne* living in Paris) Calvino shows signs of doing what one kept hoping he would do in ***Cosmicomics:*** breaking open the Fabergé puzzles he is so expert at and getting into something less ordered, less clear, the real guts of the universe whose vagaries he plots so well from the outside. If he could explode one of his epigrammatic tales into a long messy novel, one feels, he would emerge as a truly amazing writer. There are hints in **"Priscilla"** that the primal lover in him, shut up in cells as effectively as in a cell but still able to protest this state of affairs in language that is like a long, lucid scream, may yet prevail over the ironies of the aristocratic amateur scientist.

One might hope this a little more strongly if Calvino had not succeeded so well, on his own terms, in the final tale of ***t zero.*** **"The Count of Monte Cristo,"** a flawlessly constructed philosophical palace of mirrors on the order of Borges' "Pierre Menard, the Author of Don Quixote" or Kafka's "The Burrow." Starting with the cast of characters of Dumas's novel, he develops a metaphor of the human condition of ever-increasing complexity.

While the prisoner Edmond Dantès lies in his cell, the Abbé Faria is endlessly tunneling in the walls of the fortress: "The walls and vaults have been pierced in every direction by the Abbé's pick, but his itineraries continue to wind around themselves like a ball of yarn." Dantès's plan for escape is the opposite: reflection rather than action, creating a reliable mental image of the fortress using the evidence of the Abbé's soundings; yet both methods are entwined, interdependent: "The only way to reinforce the imagined fortress is to put the real one continuously to the test."

After the odds against escaping have been multiplied even further by the introduction of new elements such as the probability of Napoleon's escape from St. Helena and the velleities of Dumas, the author, as he gums together the story, the prisoner reaches his unexpectedly happy conclusion:

> "If I succeed in mentally constructing a fortress from which it is impossible to escape, this conceived fortress either will be the same as the real

> one—and in this case it is certain we shall never escape from here, but at least we will achieve the serenity of one who knows he is here because he could be nowhere else—or it will be a fortress from which escape is even more impossible than from here—and this, then, is a sign that here an opportunity of escape exists: we have only to identify the point where the imagined fortress does not coincide with the real one and then find it."

Calvino is now saying something that could be said in no other way (and, perhaps significantly, he has here abandoned the science-fiction genre); thanks to the stock characters and plot the point in question is almost visible. Whether he now chooses to dig deeper into the soul of matter, as in **"Priscilla,"** or to throw up constructions that mirror its metaphysical implications, as in **"The Count of Monte Cristo,"** his next book is certain to be worth waiting for. (p. 36)

John Ashbery, "Further Adventures of Qfwfq, et al.," in The New York Times Book Review, *October 12, 1969, pp. 5, 36.*

J. R. WOODHOUSE (essay date 1970)

[*A scholar of Italian literature, Woodhouse has published several essays and articles on his academic specialty, including a monograph,* Italo Calvino: A Reappraisal and an Appreciation of the Trilogy. *In the essay excerpted below, Woodhouse examines the theme of alienation in Calvino's early stories.*]

Throughout his literary career, Calvino has always been interested in the problems of alienation. Consistent with his theories he has shown a great preoccupation with the need for the artist and writer to communicate with their fellows without isolating themselves, almost as specialists in their own right. In order to communicate with a wide audience, however, Calvino's work has, by definition, necessarily had to have popular appeal. This attitude again produces a portrait of the intellectual abandoning commitment for popularity, when his aim is precisely that of presenting a committed message in popular terms. My purpose is to show how Calvino's exotic techniques are particularly effective in convincing his reader of the injurious effects of alienation. (p. 399)

Of all the problems which affect modern urban and industrial society, the most serious and all-embracing are those which may be loosely grouped under the head of alienation. Since Rousseau first noted the fragmenting effects of trade, commerce and industry upon man's traditional social units, many subtle variations on his notion of estrangement have evolved. The Falrets made alienation into a medically certifiable disease; Marx added political and sociological overtones which reintroduced Rousseauistic thought in an industrial situation, and Freud's notion of isolation added other psychological meanings to the phenomenon. During the past twenty years, alienation has become increasingly a preoccupation of a host of experts, including sociologists, doctors, welfare workers, and, not unnaturally, writers, and alienation is a problem which is evidently a major preoccupation in Calvino's study of mankind. Indeed, many non-literary essays of his concern the specific type of alienation which affects the worker or the specialist. His is a comprehensively modern view of alienation, not restricted to one category by political, medical or psychological definitions, and in his work one is astounded by the remarkable variety of nuances in his treatment of the phenomenon which inspires him. Without necessarily attempting to define a word which is developing new meanings daily, I should like to point to the Rousseauistic scale of personages running through Calvino's work, and ranging from the naive and ingenuous type of personage, who is one with nature, to the depersonalised mind which creates new scientific discoveries, which are inexpressible except in terms of mathematical formulae. Between these two extremes, between Zeffirino, the boy hero of **"Pesci grossi, pesci piccoli,"** and Qfwfq, personified formula of ***Le cosmicomiche*** and ***Ti con zero*** there emerge a host of characters who provide subtle variations on the theme. (pp. 399-400)

When Calvino examines the phenomenon of alienation in [the pieces collected in] the ***Racconti,*** his imagery becomes more and more fantastic. The more real the problem of alienation, the more vicious the disregard for human values and social units, the greater the chasm between members of society or between man and his natural environment, then the more unusual his imagery becomes. Alienation is a very present reality, causing at times tangible hardship and violent mistrust among men, and the disruption of nature's harmonious miscellany; and because of the often grim reality which alienation implies, the unreal and fantastic nature of some of Calvino's description may seem paradoxical. The paradox seems to be exaggerated by Calvino's desire to make his stories into real *divertissements* which serve the double purpose of amusing and educating.

For the sake of concision and convenience, I propose to take up again what was earlier called a Rousseauistic scale of personages. The scale begins with the character so integrated with nature that, like a wild animal, he can hardly tolerate the society of his fellow humans, and ends with the sophisticate who cuts himself off from nature, family and colleagues, intent only on making the most of a financial speculation. Two things should become clear from this examination. The first is that Calvino's fantasy very often becomes more bizarre as alienation becomes more acute; the second, that despite alienating and fantastic elements, the resilience of the human spirit is constantly brought to the fore. Particularly in those circumstances where man cannot choose his environment or his way of life, his natural instincts and enjoyments break through to overcome the conditioning of his artificial surroundings.

At the one extreme of the scale, then, is Zeffirino, the boy portrayed in the first of the ***Racconti,*** **"Pesci grossi, pesci piccoli."** . . . The undersea environment in **"Pesci grossi, pesci piccoli"** provides the unreal background as the boy's huge cyclopic mask-eye gulps down (*ingoiare*) shadows and colours. A ballet of minute fish swimming with military precision passes through light and shadow adding point to their fellow swimmer, for when Zeffirino is fully equipped with his underwater fishing gear, ready to plunge into his non-human element, he takes on many of the characteristics of a fish. . . . Zeffirino's great redeeming feature is the wholehearted enthusiasm with which he pursues his sport, and the uninhibited enjoyment which contrasts so vividly with the melancholic inertia of Miss De Magistris. But Zeffirino is obviously a character with limits, a simple character in every sense of the word. Costanzina in **"Uomo nei gerbidi"** is a similar type, one with nature, understanding and sympathising with nature's phenomena, harmonising with her surroundings. Asked for news, she ignores for the moment the "real" world (which is torn by World War II) to describe fairy-tale aspects of nature. Lunacy in fact is a more effective link. . . . But the most startling effect of this *natural* character is produced when he is brought into contact with society, especially with bourgeois society as in the case of **"Pranzo con un pastore."** In this story the realism of the narrative, as the family try to make the goatherd feel at home, is embarrassingly true to life. The bizarre note is struck by the ease which the boy feels in the presence of the family's poor demented daughter. The author comments that the patronising friendliness of his mother and the strange camaraderie of his father had little effect in bridging the gap between the two worlds. . . . There is much irony, too, in the attitude of the silent brother Marco, who, despite his silence and impoliteness, makes contact with the goatherd. Giovanni here, Zeffirino, Libereso and Costanzina seem to be survivals from a bygone age when country lore and close affinity with nature was the rule rather than the exception. In some earlier age, these characters, one feels, would have been accepted as a natural part of their natural environment, but in the twentieth century, their different attitudes make them seem peculiar to their fellow humans. Not only do they seem peculiar, but the artist Calvino depicts them deliberately as part of the natural background which they love so well. Often, however, the effect of political propaganda on the young channels their natural energies into viciously unnatural activities. In particular Calvino evidently feels that fascist propaganda conditioned the young to cultivate those adolescent illusions which preserve fanatically nationalist tendencies. In his trilogy Calvino has helped to destroy the appeal of such illusions, particularly the illusions which surround the glamour of the knights' armour or the modern soldiers' uniform. The uniform crops up in **"L'entrata in guerra,"** as an alienating force, dividing the young narrator from the poor people who need his assistance. In **"Gli avanguardisti a Mentone"** the sacking of the abandoned house by the uniformed youth illustrates the effect of the military environment on young people. The boys, with the exception of the narrator, are taken over by animal instincts. Duccio is an energetic thirteen-year-old enthusiastically sacking an old mansion and presenting a weird picture as he crams stolen property into his jacket and sweater. . . . The scavenging qualities of Duccio give him the appearance of the great scavenger of Italy, the pigeon. . . . The alienating effect of war and the nightmare situations which war creates are evidently a major preoccupation with Calvino, and in the trilogy that preoccupation reaches a climax. It is interesting to see a blend of idyll and realism, involving one of these naive characters and showing the inanity of war, in the short story **"Un bel gioco dura poco."** In that story Giovannino and Serenella, his playmate, are primarily created to put into relief the horror and brutality of war, while in **"Il giardino incantato,"** they serve to emphasise the boredom of a spoilt rich boy. But Libereso, for example, in **"Un pomeriggio Adamo,"** is so close to nature that his love of insects fascinates and yet horrifies the serving-girl he is trying to impress. . . . Libereso, Giovannino, Zeffirino and the others, it has been noted, harmonise with the background which they love so well. In this extreme form of self-identification with nature one sees an exaggeration of another type of character, the type who has a burning desire to approach nature but who is prevented by circumstances beyond his control from achieving his aim. Often the educated outsider, returning to his former home in the country, feels that there is a barrier between him and nature. Here is alienation in a new and personal sense, not necessarily attributable to any marxist approach, but one which is more bitter or more nostalgic because of its personal character. The true harmony between man and nature is described in the short story **"La strada di San Giovanni,"** where the old ideals are seen as rapidly disappearing, as the father grows older. The father in that story is again at one with nature, controlling his small-holding and directing nature into the channels he desires, but at the same time maintaining the harmonious miscellany of fruits and plants which keeps nature lush and exciting. He does not succumb to the profit motive, in other words to the carnation houses, the acres of glass and concrete which were destined to take over the Ligurian riviera in the post-war years. A regret that such a life is not possible for the young educated son of the proprietor is a recurring theme in the ***Racconti.*** In germ one finds it in **"L'occhio del padrone,"** in which the owner's son, sent to oversee his father's work-people in the fields, feels the immense distance which separates him from the *contadini* and from the land. He lacks even the brutal, masterful relationship which his father has with his farm and his workers. The dilemma is put into relief by the unreal image of an eye detached from the body. . . . The rich man's son is able to return and find his nostalgic illusions shattered, the poor worker, unable to leave his urban environment, ironically, keeps his illusions intact. Marcovaldo [a character who appears in several of Calvino's stories] in his ability to see and find nature in the barren streets of the great city is the reverse of *il figlio del padrone.* (pp. 404-08)

Calvino explains the barrenness and sterility of cement and concrete by making it the backcloth for an industrial worker who has the same delight in nature as the farm labourer, the same awareness of nature's miracles. But the worker has to satisfy his aspirations either by enjoying the few meagre manifestations of nature around him, or by enjoying the self-delusion of artificial substitutes for natural phenomena. . . . Marcovaldo, though he is really unaware of his own stubbornness, tenaciously clings to beliefs and instincts deep in his soul, only lightly covered by the conditioning of industrial and urban society. He hunts, but his prey is a rabbit which has recently escaped from a laboratory, and which is injected full of dangerous bacteria. Marcovaldo longs for a night in the open air in another story, **"La panchina,"** but after a bizarre night's adventures, he goes wearily to work. The contrast between his aspirations and the daunting artificiality of his environment is well brought out in this last story by the irritating yellow traffic light which almost takes on a fretful human character of its own as it is contrasted with the serenity of the moon. . . . The traffic light is irritating and because Marcovaldo is unused to it, it helps to keep him awake. Not so the advertising sign in the short story **"Luna e G N A C."** This is surely one of the most brilliant illustrations of how the inhabitants of a poor city quarter are conditioned to accept an incredible modification in their lives as a natural part of everyday (or everynight) life. . . . The GNAC is the final syllable of COGNAC on a neon sign, and as its intermittent flashing causes the poor people to live in a night which lasts for twenty seconds at a time, all six members of Marcovaldo's family are in some way influenced to change the normal pattern of life by the electric phenomenon. Even local cats have their lovelife conditioned by the twenty-second intervals. The story is crammed with surprising descriptions, perhaps the most spectacular being Marcovaldo's first awareness of the stupendous change in his environment when the sign is first broken. . . . Marcovaldo, like some of Calvino's *figli del padrone,* recognises in the return of night, the return of something "natural" from bygone days. . . . (pp. 408-10)

The brilliantly witty scenario is woven through with surreal images, emphasising not only the estrangement of man from his natural environment, but also the worker's ironical acceptance of the rival firm's neon sign which replaces the original COGNAC. The mysterious figures (of electricians) seen in silhouette on the roof opposite Marcovaldo's apartment help to emphasise in a manner worthy of Kafka, the brooding anonymity; here, that of the big business interests. (p. 410)

It would be tempting to dwell at length upon the Marcovaldo stories, for in them, more obviously than elsewhere, Calvino's attitude to the alienated city-dweller is most clearly and surrealistically illustrated. But it would be unprofitable, for Calvino is at his most fabulous and surrealist and yet so obviously *is* dealing with the alienated city-dweller or worker that further illustration would be using weighted scales to prove a point. But taking a less obviously bizarre story, **"La gallina di reparto,"** one can see the inhuman situation of the old turner, Pietro, illustrated in a similarly fantastic way. Pietro represents the Marcovaldo figure at his workplace. He too is aware of the slight manifestation of nature which is allowed into the factory and of the possibilities of enticing Adalberto's hen to lay for him. . . . Pietro has so many operations to do on his machine that his thoughts on private human affairs are disjointed by the mechanics of his job. . . . Despite the dehumanising effect of his work, Pietro's human ingenuity succeeds nonetheless in keeping his train of thought personal and logical. Crushed by the burden of working four machines at one time, Pietro's mind is still resilient enough to adapt itself to the extraordinary conditions and to have a few split seconds of private thought between working intervals. . . . The story of **"La gallina di reparto,"** is unreal. A hen, suspected of carrying messages between one worker and another, is killed by the management. The story is one which provokes laughter by its irony. It maintains its audience's interest by the ludicrous logic which leads to the hen's death. The images used to add excitement are often fantastic. And yet this is a story which [Vladimir Hořký, in his essay "I *Racconti* di Italo Calvino,"] includes in the comment:

> [Calvino takes the opportunity to talk freely about the fundamental problem: the impossibility of living happily in a capitalist society.]

That fundamental problem, rendered palatable, readable, interesting in such stories as **"La gallina di reparto,"** illustrates what Calvino aims at in most of his literary output, to instruct and amuse. (pp. 410-11)

J. R. Woodhouse, "Fantasy, Alienation and the 'Racconti' of Italo Calvino," in Forum for Modern Language Studies, *Vol. VI, No. 4, October, 1970, pp. 399-412.*

ALAN CHEUSE (essay date 1971)

[*A professor and critic, Cheuse reviews the three stories from Calvino's early career published in* The Watcher, and Other Stories. *While noting that these stories are written in a more realistic mode than the fantasy works that established Calvino's reputation in the English-speaking world, Cheuse regards these early pieces as evidence of Calvino's ability to transform "the mundane into the marvellous."*]

Italo Calvino, author of ***t zero*** and ***Cosmicomics,*** that wonderful series of etiological fantasies whose theme is the power of the imagination over the universe, should—with this collection of three earlier tales [***The Watcher and Other Stories***]—begin to establish himself in the minds of American readers.

[**"The Watcher,"**] the longest of the three, demonstrates clearly his talent for transforming the mundane into the marvelous. It depicts a day in the life of Amerigo Ormea, a dedicated Italian Communist, who acts as a poll watcher at a special election station inside the walls of the Cottolengo Hospital for Incurables, a city within the city of Turin. Ormea's day begins in darkness and rain. The strange, pathetic inhabitants of the hospital (monsters and madmen, the blind, the halt and the lame) shuffle in or are carried in to vote, the nuns and priests guiding their hands to mark ballots opposite the name of the Christian Democratic candidate.

As Ormea challenges the traditional political practices of the inferno-like hospital ward, his own life comes under scrutiny as well. By day's end, he has learned new things about himself, his relationship to the Party, to the people and to his mistress, and has stopped the farcical custom of voting the moronic and the unconscious. We, in turn, have seen, in microcosm, the contradictory Italian political process.

Its essence, Calvino demonstrates, is that the labor of pessimistic optimists such as the Communist Ormea and the optimistic pessimists of the Church and the conservative political parties yields the possibility of a city grander and more humane than either the Cottolengo complex or Turin itself. That city is a perfect place whose crippled populace, having used comrades and Catholics as a means to this end, has bettered itself by the labors of its own hands. As the crepuscular light filters in through the hospital windows, Ormea catches a glimpse of this ideal.

We catch sight of it ourselves in the second story, **"Smog"** (written in 1958), in which modern Italy's living contradictions, as closely related, Calvino assures us, as "the opposite sides of the same artichoke leaf," are again dramatized. . . .

Calvino's third tale, **"The Argentine Ant,"** is the earliest of the group, and it is more explicitly allegorical and more pessimistic. Here, as well, he finds higher meaning in everyday activity, this time in the form of the struggle by the citizens of a provincial seaside town against a plague of ants. The real scourge however, is the Government-run Argentine Ant Control Corporation, whose molasses traps, supposedly full of poison, seem to nourish the menace rather than destroy it.

The general picture, then, which Calvino develops is that of a "two-headed" society whose Battle of the Books—between the Bible and the works of the young Marx—ends, for most men, in a deadlock. If, as Amerigo Ormea muses, its "net of objective contradictions" is to be broken, each man must "achieve an awareness in person" of its complex nature.

The function of the Watcher in Calvino's work is clearly to witness (for the reader) images of the fabulous meaning and worth of the crooked, broken, sickly and contradictory things of this world. On this count, his achievement is great. What adds a master's grace to his serious labors is that, like the washerwomen of the Laundry Co-operative of Barca Bertulla, he laughs as he cleanses our soiled goods.

Alan Cheuse, "From the Mundane, a Universal Meaning," in The New York Times Book Review, *February 7, 1971, p. 31.*

JOHN GARDNER (essay date 1977)

[*Gardner was a distinguished American writer who produced work in nearly every literary genre. As evidenced in* On Moral Fiction *(1978), his book of critical analysis and theory, Gardner believed that an artist is responsible for creating works that affirm the value of life and present inspirational visions. In his laudatory review of* The Castle of Crossed Destinies *excerpted below, Gardner interprets the underlying meanings in several of the tales in this collection.*]

Although not yet as well known as he deserves to be, Italo Calvino is one of the world's best living fabulists, a writer in a class with Kobo Abé, Jorge Luis Borges and Gabriel García Márquez. He is most famous for his dazzling, astonishingly intelligent fantasies—***The Nonexistent Knight, The Cloven Viscount,*** *Invisible Cities,* ***The Baron in the Trees***—but his mastery is equally evident in what might be called, loosely, his whimsical science fictions on the history of the universe—***Cosmicomics*** and ***t zero***—and in his more-or-less realistic fictions, for instance, ***The Watcher and Other Stories.*** In the realistic stories and in ***The Baron in the Trees,*** Calvino creates substantial, moving characters and fully elaborated, thoroughly convincing fictional worlds. In all his books, but especially in *Invisible Cities,* he has moments where the prose turns into pure, firm lyric poetry. In the science fictions he brilliantly translates modern scientific and mathematical theory into fictional emotion; and everywhere his final pursuit is metaphysical. His strange new production, ***The Castle of Crossed Destinies,*** uses all these talents, rises directly from the world view he has been developing all these years, yet is like nothing Calvino has done before.

The book is, in a way, a collection of tales. The framing story concerns a group of pilgrims who, after traveling separately through an enchanted forest, come together at a castle or, perhaps, a cavern (no one is sure) and, trying to tell each other their stories, discover that they have lost their ability to speak. The tales are worth hearing, we know in advance. The hair of all the pilgrims, both young and old, has been turned white by their adventures. One of the pilgrims hits on the idea of telling his tale by means of tarot cards. He selects the cards which best represent himself, he thinks, then adds a line of other cards, and, with the aid of grimaces and gestures, tells his tale.

His actual story may or may not have much to do with the tale we are reading since we get only the narrator's interpretation, and the narrator is by no means sure of himself—an annoying, unsatisfying business, the narrator will readily admit. But the cards are all the pilgrims have, and they decide to do their best with them. . . . By the time all the cards are on the table, the interlinking of tales—or the narrator's interpretation of the cards laid down—is incredibly complex and subtle: a history of all human consciousness through the myths of Oedipus, Parsifal, Faust, Hamlet and so on, and a history of Calvino's career as a novelist, since the pilgrims' tales repeatedly allude to Calvino's earlier fiction.

The Castle of Crossed Destinies is an ambitious, "difficult" book, though short, and one's first inclination may be to make top-of-the-head judgments: "overly ambitious," "annoyingly complex," "lacking in sentiment." Like Kafka—or Chaucer—Calvino makes plodding comedy of our scholastic need to explain things. Like those writers, he uses a squinty, insecure narrator who's forever searching out answers, mostly getting wrong ones, or raising intellectual obstacles in his own path. Such comedy inevitably slows the pace. Again, one may feel that Calvino's review of his own career as a writer is a touch self-regarding, even coy. (Tolstoy would never have stooped to such a thing.) Or thinking of the emotional power of books like ***The Baron in the Trees,*** one may complain ***The Castle of Crossed Destinies*** is lacking in warmth.

Those objections—and others—may have at least some validity, but to register them, even in the timid way I've done, is to feel oneself squeaking like a mouse. Cranky, self-conscious, confusing and confused, ***The Castle of Crossed Destinies*** is a shamelessly original work of art. Not a huge work, but elegant, beautiful in the way mathematic proofs can be beautiful, and beautiful in the sense that it is the careful statement of an artist we have learned to trust.

All Calvino's philosophy is here, subtly reassessed: the idea of existence as an act of will confirmed by love (***The Nonexistent Knight***), the tragicomic mutual dependence of reason and sensation (**"The Watcher"**), Calvino's usual fascination with chance, probability and will and his theory of value (mainly worked out in ***The Cloven Viscount, Cosmicomics*** and ***t zero.*** What comes through most movingly, perhaps, is Calvino's love for the chance universe we are stuck with. It comes through in the physical appearance of the book—the elegant binding, dust jacket and type design and the publisher's reproductions in actual size and full color, of 15th-century tarot cards.

But Calvino's celebration of things as they are comes through still more durably in the central allegorical images, the tales and the structure of the whole. The place where the pilgrims meet—our world—is perhaps a castle fallen on hard times, becoming a mere inn, perhaps a tavern doing splendidly, becoming a castle. The meeting of minds and hearts we all hunger for, as pilgrims, is impeded by difficulties—language and interpretation, our differences of background (adventures in the woods), and the infuriating fact that no pilgrim's story is entirely unique: we need each other's cards, yet the cards never carry exactly the same meaning twice. ("Each of us," Calvino remarks elsewhere, "is a billion-to-one shot.") But despite the problems, the pilgrims tell their tales, each mixing his destiny with the other's destiny and thus helping to evolve (as the universe evolved in Calvino's science fictions) a total providence, so to speak—an enveloping work of art.

Art is a central theme here. Like the universe, it is partly brute substances in random combination. (pp. 15, 29)

Calvino has made his narrator both writer and reader (interpreter of the cards), both creator and victim of creation. In the metaphor of the cards he has exactly described the process of art as concrete philosophy, how we search the world for clues as a gypsy searches the cards, interpreting by means of our own stories and a few unsure conventions. Finally, he claims, the search is moral and potentially tragic. Despite the permutations, tale by tale, we always learn the same tale of man: we celebrate and cleanse or we die, destroyed by our betters. . . .

Like a true work of art, Calvino's ***The Castle of Crossed Destinies*** takes great risks—artificiality, eclecticism, self-absorption, ponderousness, triviality (what, yet another interpretation of the world's great myths?)—and, despite its risks, wins hands down. (p. 29)

John Gardner, "The Pilgrims' Hair Turned White,"

in The New York Times Book Review, *April 10, 1977, pp. 15, 29.*

MICHAEL WOOD (essay date 1977)

[*Wood frequently contributes literary criticism to the* New Republic *and the* New York Review of Books. *In the excerpt below, he discusses several of the tales in* The Castle of Crossed Destinies *and finds Calvino's inventive storytelling techniques in this volume more methodical than those of his previous works.*]

In Italo Calvino's *Invisible Cities,* Marco Polo and Kublai Khan converse among the fountains and magnolias of the Khan's hanging garden. At first, the Venetian is unable to speak the Khan's language, and can recount his travels in the Empire only with gestures, leaps, and cries, and by exhibiting various objects he has brought back with him. He also resorts to pantomime. . . .

Before long Marco masters the Tartar idiom and can express himself with much more precision. But then a certain nostalgia for the emblems sets in: "you would have said communication between them was less happy than in the past."

Calvino seems to be thinking here of a passage in Rousseau's *Essay on the Origin of Languages,* where the eloquence of emblems is preferred to the poor specificity of speech. But the preoccupation with silent discourse, or better, with the ruin that comes upon stories when we are able to tell them, is very much Calvino's own. In a preface to a new edition of his first novel, *The Path to the Nest of Spiders,* Calvino wrote of postwar Italy as "a varicolored universe of stories" for those emerging from the War and the Resistance. Wonderful material for a writer, and yet material a writer can only betray, ending up with what Calvino calls "remorse toward reality," which is "so much more variegated and warm and undefinable" than the twisted exaggerations one can get down on paper.

So that when Calvino, in the same preface, talks of "this failure that writing always is," and later says that "a written book will never console me for what I destroyed in writing it," we hear an authentic sorrow and not merely a fashionable echo of Mallarmé. Language for Calvino is a kind of plague, something like the smog, or the swarm of ants, which appear in his earlier stories. It is what we live in and long to get out of. But since Calvino doesn't want to give up communication, or even to break the linear clarity of his elegant prose, he must use language to point us toward other possibilities of expression: the comic strip (as in ***Cosmicomics***), Marco Polo's objects and pantomimes, and, in ***The Castle of Crossed Destinies,*** the tarot pack. . . .

Calvino "reads" these cards not as a cartomancer, but as a person playing with them, laying out the stories which the cards, in their actual appearance, suggest to him. . . .

The tarot pack, Calvino says, is "a machine for constructing stories," and he works with two versions of the pack: the sumptuous Visconti deck painted by Bembo, and the fairly common Marseilles deck which can be bought in any decent occultist's shop in Paris. For the first deck, he imagines travelers staying overnight in a castle, or perhaps an inn—the place is rather too grand for an inn, and rather too disorderly for a castle. The travelers have all had adventures—the narrator mentions his own "trials, encounters, apparitions, duels"—and are clearly longing to tell them. But they are inexplicably struck dumb, and thus find themselves in the position of Marco Polo in his early conversations with Kublai Khan, or in the position which perhaps ought to have been that of the Italian writer immediately after the war: full of stories and unable to speak.

Fortunately, they do have a tarot pack, and identifying themselves by means of cards which resemble them, they create from the pack sequences which represent their tales—or more precisely which the narrator turns into tales for them. We hear of an unfaithful lover, or of a punished grave robber, of a man who met the Devil's bride. We also hear of Faust, and of Roland as he is portrayed in Ariosto. The narrator's interpretations are confident but frankly speculative, relying on phrases like "our fellow guest probably wished to inform us," "this row of cards . . . surely announced," and "we could only venture some guesses"; and when he needs the story of Astolpho, the English knight in Ariosto who recovers Roland's wits for him, he seems simply to conscript a fellow guest, who "might well be that English knight." The narrator doesn't tell us his own tale, but it is there, he says, buried in the pattern the cards make on the table once several crisscrossing stories have been dealt out.

For the second deck Calvino imagines another set of silent travelers, but they seem more clearly to be in an inn, as befits the less aristocratic nature of the cards themselves, and for some reason the stories deduced from these cards are much more vivid and ingenious. They include the tale of the waverer, a narrative that finds impossible choices at every turn of the card, and also the stories of Faust (again) and Parsifal, and the stories of Hamlet, Macbeth, and Lear. At one point Calvino decides to interpret the picture card showing the Pope as signifying "the great shepherd of souls and interpreter of dreams Sigismund of Vindobona," and starts to look for, and of course soon finds, the story of Oedipus in the pack, "that story which, according to the teachings of [Sigismund's] doctrine, is hidden in the warp of all stories."

For the tarot pack is not only a machine for constructing stories, as Calvino modestly says, it is a labyrinth where all the world's stories can be found. But they have to be *found,* and finding them, it seems, does not interfere with the inexhaustible mystery of the labyrinth itself, which is organized, Calvino says, around "the chaotic heart of things, the center of the square of the cards and of the world, the point of intersection of all possible orders." Calvino experiments briefly with "reading" other pictures in the same way, paintings of famous saints, for example, and he suggests, no doubt not entirely seriously, that he thought of completing his "Castle of Crossed Destinies" (the Visconti pack) and "Tavern of Crossed Destinies" (the Marseilles pack) with a "Motel of Crossed Destinies," in which the mute survivors of an unnamed catastrophe would tell their tales by pointing to the various frames of the comics page of a scorched newspaper.

This new work as a whole doesn't have the grace and tenderness of *Invisible Cities*—there is something too dogged, too methodical about Calvino's application of his imagination to the tarots—but it has the discreet pathos which is never far from the surface in any of Calvino's work. "When you kill, you always kill the wrong man," Calvino says in a gloss on the story of Hamlet. And Calvino's fiction, with its allusions to the denser speech of the visible world and indeed of life itself, is a monument to one of literature's most important half-truths: When you write, you always write the wrong book.

Michael Wood, "Fortune Hunting," in The New York Review of Books, *Vol. XXIV, No. 8, May 12, 1977, p. 36.*

JoANN CANNON (essay date 1979)

[*Cannon's book,* Italo Calvino: Writer and Critic *(1982), collects a series of essays she wrote on individual works by Calvino, including an extensive analysis of* The Castle of Crossed Destinies, *which is excerpted below from* Critique *magazine, where it originally appeared. In this essay, the critic examines the nature of storytelling, the activity of reading, and the prospects of regenerating literature as these topics are developed in* The Castle of Crossed Destinies.]

Although Italo Calvino does not belong to the Italian literary movement known as *Sperimentalismo,* his works are undoubtedly among the most truly experimental to come out of Italy in the last decades. . . . ***The Castle of Crossed Destinies,*** one of Calvino's more recent experiments, is a *tour de force* in which all of the myths and fictions of Western civilization—the stories of Faust, Parsifal, Oedipus, Roland, and Don Juan—are brought into play. The novel is composed of two texts: "The Castle of Crossed Destinies" and "The Tavern of Crossed Destinies." Each text is a collection of tales framed by a conventional device.

In the framing story of **"The Castle of Crossed Destinies,"** a group of travellers, having lost their way in an enchanted forest and taken shelter for the night in a castle (or inn), decide to while away the time by telling stories. By setting his tale in a castle in an enchanted forest, Calvino informs the reader that he is entering into a patently fictional universe. Like Scheherazade or the writer-protagonist of Borges' "The Secret Miracle," Calvino's characters are "suspended in a journey that had not ended nor was to end." The wayfarers, caught in the atemporal realm of fiction, have been mysteriously deprived of the power of speech. They must resort to a deck of tarot cards to "tell" their tales.

The narrator of the first story within the frame, **"The Tale of the Ingrate and His Punishment,"** begins by choosing the card which most closely resembles him and placing it on the table. The narrative unfolds as the "player" lays down a sequence of cards, which is reproduced in the margin of the text. The text itself, i.e., the written word, is a reading of the cards on the part of the narrator of the framing story. Because the number of cards at their disposal is limited to seventy-eight (in the fifteenth-century Visconti deck that Calvino employs), the five players or narrators who follow the first must construct their tales in such a way as to intersect with the cards already played. By the end of the sixth tale, when the entire deck has been played, the arrangement of cards resembles a crossword puzzle composed of cards rather than letters.

In the final story of the first text, entitled **"All the Other Stories,"** the narrator makes a startling discovery: "the stories told from left to right or from bottom to top can also be read from right to left or from top to bottom, and vice versa, bearing in mind that the same cards, presented in a different order, often change their meaning, and the same tarot is used at the same time by narrators who set forth from the four cardinal points". The narrator then produces six "new" stories through the reverse reading of the stories already on the table; thus, for instance, **"The Tale of Astolpho on the Moon,"** when read in reverse, becomes the story of Helen of Troy. The narrator has discovered that the system is indeed a structural one. The stories are not mere aggregates of isolated elements with a fixed meaning; rather, they are made up of elements whose meaning is determined by their relationship with the other elements in the system. The slightest variation in the configuration of the elements produces an entirely new story.

With only two more stories to be read in reverse, the narrator admits that it is only a desire for some kind of symmetry which compels him to complete the design: "What is left me is only the manic determination to complete, to conclude, to make the sums work out". Calvino expresses a similar desire to have done with his project in a "Note" to the texts. Speaking of the difficulties he encountered in composing the second text, he says that he was at one time tempted to renounce the entire project, which was, after all, "an operation that made sense only as a theoretical hypothesis." He maintains that he is only publishing the text to free himself of it.

The theoretical hypothesis to which Calvino refers and which subtends the entire work is that fiction is produced through the combination of a limited number of prefabricated elements subject to fixed rules of association. The hypothesis is, of course, not original with Calvino; Greimas, Todorov, and Bremond have attempted to isolate the minimal units of fiction and the laws governing their combination. (pp. 83-5)

Calvino's use of the tarot cards as a narrative code is a device which "lays bare" the combinatory process through which fiction is produced. The seventy-eight tarot cards are equivalent to the minimal units or fictional universals of narrative and lend themselves particularly well to Calvino's project. The chivalric characters represented in the tarot cards are devoid of what Propp calls secondary characteristics, such as psychological attributes, which are irrelevant in the structural analysis of narrative based on functions. The actions depicted in the tarot cards, again borrowed from the chivalric genre, also lend themselves to be categorized in a finite number of functions. Calvino underlines the functional simplicity of his tale from the first pages of the novel, when he lists its constitutive ingredients: "after entering the forest I had faced so many trials, encounters, apparitions, duels, that I could no longer order my actions or my thoughts". Trials, encounters, apparitions, duels—these are the minimal units from which fiction is produced, the stuff from which all stories are made.

In its extreme form, the conception of the production of literature through the combination of predetermined elements has been criticized for reducing the text to a kind of formula. Does Calvino's conception of the combinatory nature of narrative impoverish the fictional text? Calvino himself answers that it does not, for he draws a parallel between modern fiction and the primitive oral tales of the first tribal narrators, whose repertory of prefabricated elements—"to be born, to die, to couple, to sleep"—was indeed limited. While all fiction is based on just such a *catalogo limitato,* the catalogue allows for "limitless combinations, permutations, and transformations." Narrative, like the primitive folktale, is characterized by the paradoxical interplay between the uniformity of the system and the multiplicity of its manifestations. In the preface to a collection of Italian folktales, Calvino has pointed out the dual nature of the tale, "its secret property; its infinite variety and infinite repetition." Such duality, which is characteristic of all structural systems, had been observed in the Russian folktale by Propp, who contrasted the "amazing multiformity, picturesqueness, and color" of the folktale with "its no less striking uniformity, its repetition."

Calvino himself insists upon the first of these characteristics, the tale's diversity. He also compares storytelling with a game of chess, an image frequently employed by structuralist theoreticians (Saussure often cites it in describing the functioning of *la langue,* that linguistic system which allows one to generate discourse). Calvino writes: "We know that, just as no chessplayer can live long enough to exhaust the combinations of the possible moves of the thirty-two pieces, so not even in a life which lasted as long as the universe would one be able to play all the possible games." The tarot cards in Calvino's novel function in precisely the same manner: although finite in number, they allow for limitless combinations. Like the chessplayer or the reader of tarots, the writer can never exhaust the possibilities of fiction.

Although all narratives are implicit in a finite narrative code, the combinatory potential of the system is inexhaustible. Perhaps the writer is, as Calvino suggests in ***The Castle of Crossed Destinies,*** similar to the juggler or conjurer "who arranges on a stand at a fair a certain number of objects and, shifting them, connecting them, interchanging them, achieves a certain number of effects"; but no matter how many combinations the writer arranges on his table, not all possibilities are realized. Calvino is fascinated by the idea of unrealized possibilities implicit in all systems. In the sixth tale of **"The Castle of Crossed Destinies,"** Astolpho is instructed to journey to the moon not to recover the phial containing Roland's lost wits, as in *Orlando Furioso,* but to find "an endless storeroom" which "preserves in phials placed in rows . . . the stories that men do not live, the thoughts that knock once at the threshold of awareness and vanish forever, the particles of the possible discarded in the game of combinations, the solutions that could be reached but are never reached . . .". (pp. 85-7)

The theme of the supernovel or the infinite book is one dear to another writer who, like Calvino, is fascinated by the combinatory game and its application to literature. (p. 87)

Both Borges and Calvino, however, qualify their conception of literature as a combinatory game. Borges maintains that "if literature were nothing but verbal algebra, anyone could produce any book simply by practicing variations." Calvino seems to entertain such a prospect when he speculates on the possibility of supplanting the author by a literary automaton. Rejecting the Romantic myth of the author as creative genius, Calvino suggests that "the writer is already a writing machine," but he does not mean that all possible combinations produced by the "writing machine" are of equal value: "yes, literature is a combinatory game which follows the possibilities implicit in its own material, independently of the personality of the author, but it is a game which at a certain point is invested with an unexpected significance and which puts into play something of supreme importance to the author and the society to which he belongs." (p. 88)

Calvino introduces the figure of the reader as the one who invests the literary product with meaning: "the decisive moment in literature will be reading . . . the work will continue to be born, to be judged, to be destroyed and continually renewed upon contact with the eye of the reader." Literature is inexhaustible not only because the system, symbolized in ***The Castle of Crossed Destinies*** by the deck of tarot cards, can generate an infinite number of combinations, but also because a single variation, a single story, can never be exhausted by the reader. Borges, who, like Calvino, stresses the reader's importance above the writer's, says "a book is more than a verbal structure . . . a book is a dialogue with the reader. . . . That dialogue is infinite."

Calvino's conception that reading is dominant in the creation of fiction is underlined in the very structure of ***The Castle of Crossed Destinies.*** As already indicated, the tarot cards represent the story itself, which is relegated to the margins of the text. The written text is actually an interpretation or reading, in an active sense, by the narrator of the framing story, but that reading is by no means privileged. When a storyteller bearing a marked resemblance to the Knight of Cups places that card on the table, the narrator-reader prefaces his reading of the card with "we thought we understood that . . .". Later readings are qualified in similar fashion: "our fellow guest probably wished to inform us . . .". In **"The Tale of the Ingrate and His Punishment"** a single card, *Justice,* is given three possible readings, for the possibility of alternative readings is always implicit. Such ambiguity is not the same as that encountered in a novel by Henry James, where the reader must depend on a narrative reflector who is flawed or unreliable. In ***The Castle of Crossed Destinies*** the narrator becomes a reader who constantly reminds us that no single reading is exhaustive.

By incorporating the activity of reading into his novel, Calvino dramatizes the literary text as a *dialogue.* The text can no longer be seen as a receptacle of a predetermined and unequivocal meaning. . . . (p. 89)

Calvino's insistence on the impossibility of exhausting literature is particularly significant in light of the recent critical debate concerning structuralist and post-structuralist analyses of literature. Calvino has undoubtedly drawn on structuralist theory in ***The Castle of Crossed Destinies;*** the novel has even come under attack for the "excessive—almost didactic—evidence of its theoretical origins." To the extent that he exposes the structural underpinning of narrative in his use of the tarot cards, Calvino seems to be laying himself open to the charge often levelled at structuralist critics—that while attempting to isolate the fictional universals which constitute "literariness," they reduce the individual text. But Calvino, much like the critics striving to move "beyond structuralism," stresses "the heterogeneity of readers and works." He is not interested in reducing all texts to an abstract model of "literariness"; rather, from the invariable model he moves toward the infinite variants which the model generates and the infinite possibilities of reading those variants. In the last paragraph of the final tale of the novel, we see the heroine "peering at every movement of the foliage of this wood, . . . at every turn of events in this pattern of tales, until the end of the game is reached. Then her hands scatter the cards, shuffle the deck, and begin all over again". Italo Calvino, hinting at the inexhaustible potential of fiction, concludes his tale with an opening towards as yet unrealized stories. (pp. 90-1)

JoAnn Cannon, "Literature as Combinatory Game: Italo Calvino's 'The Castle of Crossed Destinies,'" in Critique: Studies in Modern Fiction, *Vol. XXI, No. 1, 1979, pp. 83-92.*

ERNEST L. FONTANA (essay date 1979)

[In the essay below, Fontana relates the transformations which Qfwfq and the universe undergo in Cosmicomics *with the*

Greek myths involving Proteus, a herdsman of Neptune famous for his power to assume sundry shapes and forms. Within this context, Fontana also traces Calvino's development of themes concerning creativity, love, scientific theories, and the human use of signs to interpret and understand the phenomenal world.]

The science fantasy of Italo Calvino's ***Cosmicomics*** is not directed to the future, but to the remote past of our universe and solar system, to events anterior to the emergence of mammalian history, and, in the case of **"All at One Point,"** to the very beginnings of space and time. The scientific theories that are quoted or summarized before each narrative are appropriated—and thereby domesticated—by Calvino's fantastic imagination. Instead of projecting a future that is catastrophic and menacing to human values, as does much traditional science fiction in the Gothic mode (e.g., Wells's *Time Machine* or Harlan Ellison's "Boy and His Dog"), Calvino, by playfully dealing with the pre-human past as if a familiar form of consciousness did then exist, suggests that amidst the almost unbelievable transformations of matter and life there is a continuity and that change is not necessarily destructive or catastrophic. D. J. Enright [see excerpt dated 1968] aptly observes that the theme that runs through the twelve fables is "the urge to evolve, the sense in the most primitive forms of life of better things to come, the touching readiness to adopt a receptive attitude to the future."

Although "our" future is not presented in ***Cosmicomics,*** we are imagined as a future for which the past of the universe has prepared, not by forethought, deliberation, and intention but through spontaneous acts of desire, play, and art. The implication is that we are only one future and that our own spontaneous acts of desire, play, and art contribute to the making of other futures, in which we shall survive as the blind mollusc and its unseen beloved survive, in **"The Spiral,"** in the eyes of other creatures, eyes that the eyeless mollusc has, through its erotic secretion of visible form, called into being.

Qfwfq is himself the continuity, the undifferentiated Protean urge that endures as long as matter endures. Like Proteus, none of his transformations is final, none of them exhaustible of his creative plenitude. In **"The Aquatic Uncle,"** L1, a reptilian creature, abandons Qfwfq for his lovable, curmudgeon uncle, who has refused to "emigrate" from water to land. Qfwfq, at the end of the fable, recalls his discovery that his own identity is, unlike that of L1 or his uncle, not fixed or completed, but always open to completion in an unending process of creative transformation. . . . (p. 147)

One of the reasons that the fables in ***Cosmicomics*** are not arranged chronologically, but randomly, is that Calvino wishes to avoid a simple, evolutionary teleology, such as that of Teilhard de Chardin. For Calvino the universe is characterized by change and transformation, new beginnings, but none of these is final or fixed. Although he suggests a movement in the universe towards both greater complexity and randomness, his emphasis is not on man as destination or on the "one far-off divine event" of Tennyson, but on the moments of transformation themselves. The end of the universe is not to be but to become, beginnings not endings. A chronological arrangement of the fables would imply a terminus. The conclusion of **"At Daybreak"** is, therefore, ironic. The sun has become an incandescent mass of light and, during the earth's first night, Qfwfq notes that "Everything was just beginning." In ***Cosmicomics,*** Qfwfq demonstrates that everything is *always* beginning.

If an approximation to an absolute beginning is to be found, it is to be found in the fourth fable, **"All at One Point."** Here, Mrs. Ph(i)Nk's spontaneous desire to make noodles for everyone bound in a punctiform world sets off the "big bang" that creates the time and space in which the sun itself will become incandescent. The big bang is set off by a spontaneous impulse of desire, playfulness, and generosity that cannot be actualized within the constraints of a neurotic, punctiform, encapsulated universe.

Although everything is always beginning anew, Calvino does not ignore the attendant theme that transformation also brings loss, separation, and, consequently, desire. The desire to be other than where and how I am creates not only the future, as in **"The Spiral,"** but an attachment to that which has become absent and/or superseded. Although the superseded configurations of matter are absent, they survive as memories, as nexuses of desire, love, and myth. That which becomes absent is as wonderful as that which becomes present. In **"The Dinosaurs"** Qfwfq, as the last dinosaur, surviving unrecognized among "the New Ones," who enfable and mythologize the superseded species, realizes that "the more Dinosaurs disappear, the more they extend their dominion, and over forests far more vast than those that cover the continents: in the labyrinth of the survivors' thoughts." To love what is, but to yearn pastward, in desire or curiosity, to what was constitutes the necessary polarity of an imagination commensurate to the inexhaustible fullness of matter, a fullness that is, simultaneously, realized and delimited—often tragically—by the astringent necessities of space and time.

The separation of the earth and the moon, in the **"The Distance of the Moon,"** means not only the loss of moon-milk for Qfwfq, but also the loss of the beloved Mrs. Vhd Vhd. Because Qfwfq's deaf cousin is in love with the moon, which he alone realizes is gradually becoming more distant from the earth, Mrs. Vhd Vhd, who is in love with him, seeks to become the moon, the object of his love, to assume its distance. The jealous and unrequited Qfwfq follows her to the moon, but in obedience to the "natural power" of gravity, is drawn back to the earth, "perhaps more aware of it [his love] than ever and of its unfortunate outcome." In her exile on the moon, Mrs. Vhd Vhd will be forever separated from both Qfwfq and his cousin, the object of her desire. Calvino seems to imply, through this fable, that it is the inevitable distance created by the separation of objects in time and space that is the necessary condition of desire, the most fundamental form of love. Moreover, Calvino suggests that desire is an antithetical response to the necessary limits of matter. (pp. 148-49)

In **"The Spiral,"** "the flat mollusk-pulp" transforms itself because of desire, a yearning consciousness of a distant other. It seeks to affirm through specific material form its individuality in order to communicate with, to reply to otherness. Desire enables the formless pulp to generate material organization, its shell, in an archetypal act of making. . . . (p. 149)

In **"The Spiral,"** the ultimate consequence of the mollusc's act of artistic individualization through erotic form is to create a new organ—the eye. The work of art (the shell), generated by desire, creates a new mode of perception and consciousness (the eye). In a reversal of Berkeleian idealism, in which nothing exists unless it is perceived, Calvino's **"The Spiral"** suggests that the perceptible creates the perceiver, that art reshapes nature, and that form, generated by desire, generates vision. What is poignant here is that the new mode of perception and consciousness is made possible by an earlier, less complex mode of consciousness that cannot experience the mode that it creates: "they developed eyes at our expense." . . . The creative acts of one mode of perception, reacting in antithesis to its perceived limits, generate new, unimagined modes of perception and consciousness and, consequently, a new set of limits. For the blind mollusc, vision is consummation and transcendence; for creatures with vision, vision creates a new set of limits, a world of images in space. Language, the medium of Calvino's own art, enables us to transcend the limits of visible images in space. The words of Qfwfq, Calvino's Protean narrator, enable us to see what our eyes cannot see, to perceive, through the heard symbols of language, relationships and continuities that are beyond the capacity of the eye.

Many of the ***Cosmicomics*** are love stories. One of the most moving is **"Without Colors."** Set during the transformation of the planet from a world constituted exclusively of Lockean primary qualities (there is yet no color, no sound) to one of both primary and secondary qualities, Qfwfq narrates his unconsummated love for Ayl, a colorless creature of pure form and movement: "a way of life about to finish was displaying the supreme peak of beauty. Nothing so beautiful had ever run over the Earth, as the creature I had before my eyes". Qfwfq's love for Ayl is heightened by her otherness. While he longs for a new universe of color and sound, she resists it and wishes to preserve a world of pure form and essence. . . . (pp. 150-51)

Like Orpheus, Qfwfq descends into the earth, now rent by earthquakes, to resurrect Ayl, who has fled from the confused, chromatic beauty of the earth as it assumes its atmosphere. Not only does Qfwfq lose Ayl, who draws back into the darkness of the earth, but in a new world of atmospheric color and sound, he loses a world of pure form, of unqualified and perdurable essences. Both Ayl and Qfwfq's Aquatic uncle, in the story of the same name, are Platonists who long to escape the Heraclitean flux of Protean matter, articulated, celebrated and embodied in Qfwfq. . . . The anachronistic uncle uses terms such as "achieved, perfect forms" that are alien to the dialectical, Protean vision of Calvino.

Not only are matter and perception transformed in ***Cosmicomics,*** but also ways of knowing matter and understanding perception. In **"How Much Shall We Bet?"** Qfwfq engages in an extended game of chance with the conservative Dean (k)yK. As long as the future events are of a general physical nature, Qfwfq is able to win his bets, predict the future, by extrapolating from the past. . . . But Qfwfq becomes a compulsive gambler who, ignorant of Heisenberg's uncertainty principle, extends his predictions to "the most marginal and aleatory" events. There is an increase in the number of events and an increase in randomness or entropy as the universe increases in age. Qfwfq's mistake is to abstract and simplify in the face of increased entropy and randomness, which Calvino associates with the emergence of man, a creature characterized by free, unpredictable acts. What the Emperor Justinian will import from China, how Balzac will conclude *Les Illusions perdues,* and how many stories the illegally constructed building on the Via Cassia will be, cannot be predicted. At the end of **"How Much Shall We Bet?"** Qfwfq is uncharacteristically nostalgic; he longs for the simple clarities of a prehuman universe. Now events "come flowing down without interruption"; the universe has become "a doughy mass of events without form or direction."

Not only do man's acts of freedom qualitatively change the universe, as did those of the "flat mollusk-pulp" in **"The Spiral,"** they can, as signs, become an alternative universe, usurping the primary universe of matter. This is the theme of Calvino's **"Sign of Space,"** the conclusion of which evokes the world of Borges's "Library of Babel." . . . Calvino suggests that the distinction between the sign and the signified becomes as tenuous as that between art and nature. The alternative universe of human signs merges with the primary universe of matter and, together, they constitute a new, more complex primary datum which itself must become signified. Qfwfq's narrative is in fact this new signification, which, in turn, has become signified in my analysis.

Thus, as the universe increases in freedom, complexity, randomness, and confusion, there emerges an antithetical desire for simplicity (the lost world of Ayl), a desire for essence, certitude, and stasis. At the end of **"The Light-Years,"** Qfwfq, who has entered into a dialogue about his identity with galaxies light-years away, longs to terminate his manic attempts to communicate his essential self to his distant observers. Like his Aquatic uncle, he attempts to distinguish some of his acts as more *essential* to his character than others. Troubled that his uncharacteristic acts have been observed and frustrated by his attempts to explain them away, he wishes that the galaxies of his observers would reach that point where they would begin to move away from the earth at a velocity equal to the speed of light, an eventuality that would terminate this frustrating inter-galactic dialogue: "then, one by one, they would disappear from the last ten-billion-light-year horizon beyond which no visible object can be seen, and they would bear with them a judgement by then irrevocable."

Calvino ends **"The Light-Years,"** but not ***Cosmicomics,*** with the idea that "the only possible truth" about Qfwfq, the only complete and final understanding of Protean matter, is available to a consciousness that is moving away from the matter of our universe at the velocity of light. Only an understanding that becomes alien to ours can know us with certitude. Only when communication ceases can understanding begin, and it will be an understanding as incomprehensible to Qfwfq, to Calvino, and to us, as the vision of the eye is to the blind mollusc.

The fables of ***Cosmicomics*** are almost as inexhaustible, in their metaphoric and thematic richness, as the capacity of matter to transform itself. This imaginative richness is appropriate, since the dramatized voice of these fictions is the voice of Protean matter become articulate. Not only do these fables celebrate transformation through a humanizing of physical and biological theory, they enact, through their sustained inventiveness, audacity, and wit, the cosmic creative process that is their subject. Moreover, like Proteus in Bk. IV of *The Odyssey,* Qfwfq is a seer who sees into the past and can help us on our homeward journey to Lacedaemon. In *The Odyssey,* Menelaus must hold Proteus in a vice-like grip to elicit from him both the account of his countrymen's voyage home after the fall of Troy and the reasons for his imprisonment on the island of Pharos. Calvino's Qfwfq also sees into the past; but his transformations, instead of being a hindrance to the articulation of his vision, are themselves the content of his vision. Furthermore, what Qfwfq tells us is as useful as what Proteus tells Menelaus, for it enables us to find our way home—to see matter not as Pharos, our prison, but as Lacedaemon, our home. (pp. 151-53)

Ernest L. Fontana, "Metamorphoses of Proteus: Calvino's 'Cosmicomics,' " in Perspectives on Contemporary Literature, *Vol. 5, 1979, pp. 147-54.*

ANTHONY BURGESS (essay date 1981)

[*A major English novelist and critic, Burgess examines a wide range of topics in his work and is perhaps best known for his novel* A Clockwork Orange *(1962), which evidences his knowledge of music and linguistics and his thematic interest in the concepts of free will and determinism. In his review of* Italian Folktales *excerpted below, Burgess finds the collection uneven but praises Calvino for performing a valuable cultural service by compiling and rendering these tales for modern readers.*]

I must say now that, on finishing Calvino's book [***Italian Folktales***] (a genuine labour of love, and also a pointer to Calvino's literary aims, which have more to do with the recovery of the folktale than the innovations for which his novels have been praised), I went straight back to Grimm and read it through. Being occasionally bored by the Italian stories, I wondered if the fault was in myself, but I found I was never bored by the Teutonic tales and must conclude that they are superior.

Certainly there is nothing in Calvino's volume which would inspire a new Disney to the expenditure of great ingenuity and much money. The Italian tales seem to have passed already through the alembic of sophisticated minds; they are literature in a way in which the Grimm tales are not. There is some brutality, but nothing on the scale of the German stories (remember the death of the Queen in the Snow White tale: she is made to wear red-hot shoes of iron and dance till she drops). There is an unfolksy elegance, almost a quality of the troubadours and the medieval legends of chivalry.

We do not find much of the agricultural myth. It is as though the Greco-Roman tales of Demeter and Persephone have already been discarded as insufficiently sophisticated. There is nothing made out of the agonies of winter and the hope that spring will come. But, on the level of the adventures of youths and maidens, transmutations from human to animal and back again, the victory of the good heart over the evil one, we know ourselves to be very much in the Aryan heartland.

The kings and queens of the south lack the magical and magisterial: they are no more than magnates who have bought the big house round the corner. There are no pancakes, but pasta . . . is eaten. Women are fruit, and trees have souls. We are in a world we already know, one in which the unity of the animate and the inanimate, of flesh and fruit and precious metals, is assumed by the folk, as it is assumed by the child, but there is no sense, as in Grimm, of encountering the raw stuff of the fireside, retailed by an old gummy granny. The Italians have had a literature longer than the Germans and it shows.

So probably Calvino was right in wishing his collection to be read with the somewhat complicated sensibility we bring to *Pinocchio* (which is so good, if we forget the disneyfication, that no folktale can touch it). We know we are in the world of cities and not of primeval forests because money is countable stuff in the mercantile tradition, not vague bags of gold and silver. Sex, as opposed to romantic love, attests the sophistication. In the story called "The Man Who Came Out Only At Night", a lively Ligurian girl marries a man who turns into a tortoise during the day and, to recover his total humanity, must voyage for a year and trust that his wife's fidelity will work the magic of transformation. The girl is successively offered one, two and three thousand francs if she will break her bed-vow. She does not drive away her would-be seducers: she takes the money and tricks them. I do not think there is anything like this in the Grimm stories. . . .

The Christ-child gets, often with lachrymose consequences, into the Grimm collection, but there is little religion in the Italian tales. The devil comes into "Silver Nose". Indeed, Silver Nose is his delightful name. He is a kind of Bluebeard who gives the girl he abducts a key to a door which she must never open. Naturally, she opens it and finds Hell inside. It is more purgatory than hell, since people can, with trickery, be rescued from it. . . .

What religion we find is often shorn of the numinous and made to serve sectarian interests. There is a story still popular among Italian robbers which rests on the implanting of a kind of Original Virtue in the trade through Christ's blessing of the thief on Golgotha. St. Anthony is transmuted into a sort of Prometheus (his tale comes from Corsica). He steals fire from Hell and warms the world. Nuns and monks are distressingly secular. Priests tend to mild lasciviousness. If these stories show nothing else, they demonstrate the innate paganism of the chief of the Christian nations. Or perhaps it had better be termed realism. Italian realism often comes out at the end of a tale in some such formula as: "Yes, they lived happy ever after, but we sit here shivering in the dark."

Calvino has performed a valuable service to his own culture and, by extension, to our own. Reading his book, we are confirmed in our belief that human aspirations are everywhere much the same; that gold is better than paper money, that golden hair is magical, that the love of a good woman is above rubies, that the animal, vegetable and mineral worlds form a unity, and that, on the whole, life is pretty hard. To mitigate the hardness tales of magical good fortune must be told (or nowadays seen) in the dark. Where the writer can still learn from the folktale is in the technique of rigid economy—an economy which, as Calvino reminds us in his notes, was often vitiated in the past by retellers of the tales who possessed literary ambitions. Our compiler has, following his own aesthetic as well as that of the folk, cut away excrescences very frequently. What we get here is less high literature than something between the bald tale and the stylish artifact. It is a volume to possess, but the lovers of tales will not return to it as often as he will to the *Kinder-und-Hausmärchen.* A lot of magic found its way into that pioneering search for philological truth.

Anthony Burgess, "Southern Sophistication," in The Times Literary Supplement, *No. 4058, January 9, 1981, p. 29.*

THOMAS SUTCLIFFE (essay date 1983)

[*In the review of* Adam, One Afternoon, and Other Stories *and* Marcovaldo, or The Seasons in the City *excerpted below, Sutcliffe examines these early works of realism within the context of Calvino's career, focusing in particular on the moral force and purpose of Calvino's work. Sutcliffe also addresses the difficulties confronting readers who have followed Calvino's career through the sequence of books published in translation, which introduced the author's works of allegory and fantasy to*

English readers before the stories written in the neorealist mode with which Calvino actually began his career.]

What does Italo Calvino want us to know? Asked of almost any other writer the question would probably seem crassly unspecific or simply irrelevant, but it retains a particular pertinacity with regard to Calvino. In more detail the question could be put like this: does he want us to discover what we know for ourselves, or does he want to persuade us to accept certain patterns in which knowledge might be placed? His work invites both proposals. He is, perhaps, the least dogmatic of writers, and yet by virtue of that openness he is acutely susceptible to a reconstruction in other forms; his books can readily be appropriated to exemplify a single thesis or ideology. Calvino doesn't appear to discourage that procedure, not in recent work at least. More than Borges and Pynchon, even, his books invite the attention of literary theorists, indeed often speak their language, and clearly share with them certain preoccupations. So it's easy to think of his colleagues as being, not other writers, but academics working in the field of literary interpretation and hermeneutics. The subject they share is the place of narrative in our lives. . . .

He would, I think, enjoy the suppositional etymology which derives the word *narrative* from the latin *gnarus*—knowing or skilled—and he has elaborated through his books the connections between reading, cunning, interpretation and knowledge. The real importance of his contribution is that he remains aware of the limitations of theory and preserves the value of the exception to the rule. His is an artist's knowledge, not a theorist's. He knows that pattern and order might be all that are available to us but avoids the fallacious conclusion that everything is then covered. Life evades the patterns laid down upon it, which is why narratives can never cease, and a mental ordering which proved to have no exception would freeze experience. So in Calvino's writing random detail comes to have a moral force, because it offers the only remaining resistance to theory. The two hold each other in a tension which has traditionally been preserved by the opposition of the literary theorist and the artist. Almost uniquely, Calvino maintains the balance of power within his own books, indeed often on the same page or within the same sentence. As he says: "I agree to the books being read as existential or as structural works, as Marxist or neo-Kantian, Freudianly or Jungianly; but above all I am glad when I see that no single key will turn the locks."

The source of Calvino's morality of narrative, and the origins of his concern with the labour of reading, lie in his passion for folk-tale. In the preface to his classic collection of Italian folk-tales, published early in his career, he expressed the opposition between identifying theory and distinguishing reality more quietly. To represent the various types of tale which recur he chose "versions that struck me as being the most characteristic, the least stereotyped, the most steeped in local colour." Without that thin defensive line of local colour what difference would there be between *characteristic* and *stereotyped,* the good and evil faces of order? Calvino also cites approvingly the Tuscan proverb, "The tale is not beautiful if nothing is added to it", which captures exactly the mute expectancy of the folk-tale, the sense that it requires something of you which it will not name. Folk-tales remain merely dumb until you realize that you are required to complete them yourself, to fill in your own particulars.

The transformation which follows is prefigured in the magical metamorphosis which so often concludes this type of story, frog into prince, from the apparently worthless to a shining merit. It is important also that the folk-tales Calvino likes best are not parables. They have no dogma to conduct, no possessive interest in the career of their own meaning. The knowledge they convey is not information but a procedure experienced in the act of reading. They teach cunning by requiring it of the reader in order to understand. . . .

His later work offers something much more like a catalogue of the potential thoughts of men and women in this century. His erudition is enormous; it is hard to think of a way of thinking about the world which doesn't make a guest appearance somewhere in the books (in ***Cosmicomics*** he even gives a cheerful sit-com vitality to the principle laws of physics). But none comes with the writer's authorization. The point is sharply made when Calvino offers some notes about the intellectual background to the stories collected in ***Our Ancestors*** (it is a feature of Calvino's modesty that he is the least mystifying of writers about his own procedures, an etiquette he shares with Eliot and Empson). Anyone who has read those fabulous *mélanges* of invention and humour might find the author's suggestions bathetic: ***The Cloven Viscount*** is offered as an allegory of the divisions of Cold War, or ***The Invisible Knight*** as providing a critique of the "organization man" in a mass society. But these readings are dismaying only if we take such interpretations as exclusive, and Calvino repeatedly demonstrates that rival interpretations have no force against each other. In ***The Castle of Crossed Destinies*** a group of travellers, magically struck dumb, tell their individual stories through the arcane and silent symbolism of the tarot pack. The book is not about communication, as none of the stories is verified; they are speculations on the part of the narrator, interpretations of the pictures and even the manner in which the cards are selected. Like the sorcerer's apprentice Calvino sets off a flow of meaning from what appears to be a limited source.

The book proves its point, the infinite capacity to invent the world and the resistance of the world to all invention. Meaning and detail are inseparable but unconnectable. . . .

It is perhaps improper to require the latest books to fall into line with this narrative about Calvino's concerns, but no alternative is available. In fact the publishers have arranged an intriguing flashback for his readers [***Adam, One Afternoon and Other Stories*** and ***Marcovaldo, or The Seasons in the City***], because although the books come dressed in new clothes they are poor and elderly relations. Calvino explains in a note that the stories in ***Marcovaldo*** were written in the early 1950s, "the Italy of the neo-realistic movies", and in the mid-1960s "when the illusion of an economic boom flourished". This is more evidence of his good manners but it is hard not to read it also as a plea of mitigation, and one which is to some extent required. The stories of ***Adam, One Afternoon*** are largely set in the Second World War and the period immediately following. Anyone familiar with Calvino's later books will feel a certain disquiet on reading these; the instinct is something like "It's too quiet out there". The exhilarating attack of works like *Invisible Cities* or *If on a Winter's Night* never comes. Elsewhere Calvino has hinted that at this stage in his career he was not writing with the purposeless pleasure he discovered in folk-tales. "I had made efforts to write the realistic-novel-reflecting-the-problems-of-Italian-society and had not managed to do so. (At the same time I was what was called a 'politically committed writer')". The hyphens, shackling the words into a slogan, and the quotation marks, holding the disreputable title at a distance, tell the story. ***Marcovaldo*** dutifully depicts the life of a poor family in an Italian city. The worker of the title longs for the country, worries about his family and dreams of escaping routine. The stories in both collections are pervaded by the same sense of the deceptions of desire and of resentment about the delusions of appearance, a dismay that is unthinkable in more recent works.

In the later stories in these two books there is some evidence of Calvino's impatience, his desire to write without constraint. Fantasy occasionally takes off but its flight is clumsy, burdened with a dutiful realism, and the concerns are expressed without the grace he later achieved. Marcovaldo goes out in winter to saw down billboards for firewood and is suddenly illuminated by the headlight of a short-sighted motorcycle policeman. The latter has already mistakenly challenged two advertisements and isn't going to be fooled again. "Smart idea. That little man up there with the saw represents the migraine that is cutting the head in two. I got it at once." The idea, that vanity distorts what we see, is characteristically Calvino, but the expression of it seems embarrassed and uncertain. It is as though the sudden joke is seen as delinquent when there are more important things to worry about—the oppression of the poor, the emptiness of consumerism, the corruption of capital. The best story of all, ***The Argentine Ant***, is undoubtedly the quietest as regards its implicit message. A young couple moves into a new house only to find it overrun with ants. Their neighbours have learnt, by devising elaborate and ineffectual stratagems, to quell the irritation they cause, a crawling in the skull. The story simply describes how insignificant things can make life intolerable, but it remains open to any number of other interpretations, is not sealed off by the anxiety to achieve a specific end which marks many of the other tales.

The collections could, without absurdity, be described as sincere, that familiar apology for a faltering in style. But sincerity as a term of judgment is disabled by the later writing; it suddenly looks to make embarrassing assumptions about the identity between appearance and meaning. In ***Marcovaldo,*** the worker sees a plant, "one of those plants that are so plant-shaped, with leaves so leaf-shaped, that they don't seem real." These stories are too short-story-shaped to seem like real Calvino. They are obedient not only to a genre, with a familiar set of rules and gallery of effects, but also to the ideas they wish to see prevail. As a result they can't finally be rescued by the detail they contain, because it exists to confirm theory, not to undermine it. That delicate cold war between a perceived order and resistant, exorbitant life has broken down. The stories certainly don't issue from the same writer who concludes, in ***The Invisible Knight,*** "The art of writing tales consists in an ability to draw the rest of life from the little one has understood of it: but life begins again at the end of the page and one realises that one knew nothing whatsoever." At the beginning Calvino thought he knew what the reader needed to know; folk-tales taught him that that's something only the reader *can* know.

Thomas Sutcliffe, "Before the Art of Cunning," in The Times Literary Supplement, *No. 4196, September 2, 1983, p. 921.*

KATHRYN HUME (essay date 1984)

[*An American critic and professor, Hume has published several exegeses on Calvino's works. In the essay excerpted below on* Cosmicomics *and* t zero, *Hume discusses Calvino's mythographical and metaphoric exploration of human interaction with the universe, finding that he "manages to retain an undaunted sense of man's significance despite the immensity of the cosmos."*]

In ***Cosmicomics*** and ***T Zero,*** Calvino asks how human consciousness can relate to the phenomenal world in a way that satisfies its craving for significance without having to make claims that are absurd on scientific grounds. He juxtaposes the narrative personalities, who are both eternal and banal, with the universe of space and time, of physics and biology. By showing how Qfwfq and his relatives relate to the cosmos, Calvino sportively displays the kinds of interactions best able to satisfy humanity's desire for significance. His tone is ironic and amused; hence, for many readers, the stories are modernist *jeux d'esprit.* Dazzlingly comic though they are, however, their philosophical content is carefully enough presented and sufficiently detailed to warrant serious consideration. (p. 81)

I shall begin with one story, **"The Distance of the Moon"**—which richly exemplifies Calvino's metaphoric techniques for relating man to the phenomenal world—and then analyze the value system which he explores through the mythic elements of such stories. The implications and adequacy of this new kind of myth—for new myth is what emerges—are the ultimate concern of this paper. Calvino measures the scientific universe, using humanity as his yardstick. He manages to retain an undaunted sense of man's significance despite the immensity of the cosmos. He affirms man's stature without denying his triviality as a scientific phenomenon and without artificially dwarfing the scale of the natural universe. He looks at mankind without idealizing its representatives, and yet does not find them wanting. The result is a universe in which Pascal's infinite, silent spaces are filled with human—and humane—warmth.

"The Distance of the Moon" is unusual for its multiple value systems. Calvino presents three ways of bringing man into harmony with the macrocosm. He begins the narrative with a scientific theory:

> *At one time, according to Sir George H. Darwin, the Moon was very close to the Earth. Then the tides gradually pushed her far away: the tides that the Moon herself causes in the Earth's waters, where the Earth slowly loses energy.*

Qfwfq, the immortal narrator, describes this interplay of planetary bodies, and in doing so, translates the dry scientific notation into a midsummer extravaganza. "We had her on top of us all the time, that enormous Moon: when she was full—nights as bright as day, but with a butter-colored light—it looked as if she were going to crush us; when she was new, she rolled around the sky like a black umbrella blown by the wind. . . . Climb up on the Moon? Of course we did . . .". Qfwfq's friends gather moon-milk, a ricotta-like amalgam of "vegetal juices, tadpoles, bitumen, lentils, honey, starch crystals, sturgeon's eggs, molds, pollens, gelatinous matter, worms, resins, pepper, mineral salts, combustion residue." Among Qfwfq's companions are a Mrs. VhD VhD, for whom he is suffering the torments of adolescent passion, and his deaf cousin, who loves the moon. Mrs. VhD VhD cares nothing for Qfwfq, but lusts after the cousin. She attempts to get herself stranded on the moon for a month with him, but ends up stranded with Qfwfq. At the end of that time, Qfwfq is all too glad to claw his way back to earth against the changes in gravity which are causing the moon to move farther away. Mrs. VhD VhD stays on the moon. Despairing of supplanting the moon in the cousin's affections, she makes herself one with it.

This torrid transmutation of a scientific hypothesis illustrates three ways of relating to the universe. The cousin's approach is an idealized form of scientific exploration: love of the phenomenal for its own sake, sensuous enjoyment of the exploration process, delight in questing. Despite his apparently random and intuitive approach to hunting moon-milk, the cousin is their best gatherer. His love for the moon is passionate but selfless. When the moon withdraws, he does not repine. Science is so serious now that we do not often see this sort of enjoyment except in scientific hobbies. . . . Calvino apparently admires this love which is satisfied by the phenomenal world, but he recognizes its rarity. He does not show it often in his stories, and we note that the man who enjoys this passionate relationship with the cosmos has been denied other, competing pleasures by his deafness.

Qfwfq, as narrator looking back on the incident, offers a second way of wresting meaning from the experience: "my eyes gazed at the Moon, forever beyond my reach, as I sought [Mrs. VhD VhD] . . .". Qfwfq mythologizes the moon, makes it his lost love, and tells about this new divinity. He is the poet or priest who turns his longings into stories and myths, and vivifies the "dead" matter of the scientific universe.

Mrs. VhD VhD and the other members of the group exemplify humanity's commonest way of finding meaning in life. They bury themselves in absurd, endless rounds of intrigue and lust, and hence hardly notice the cosmos, let alone feel dwarfed by it. They make their world out of the network of attractions and repulsions. Indeed, the scientific basis for this story echoes and comments on this mode of relating to the cosmos, since underlying this tale of weird gravitational effects is a philosophical pun. Boethius, Neoplatonists, and Christianizers of classical philosophy speak of the universe as being held together by forces or chains of love. If you substitute for "love"—a non-scientific term—the word "attraction," the gravitational universe, as well as the more anthropomorphized, mythical world of the story, is obtained. The world inhabited by Qfwfq and his friends is ruled by immense forces of attraction. So is their private world of loves and jealousies. Attractions and repulsions give meaning to their everyday actions. Again and again, Calvino will portray the bickering and brawling social group or family unit, not because he finds it admirable, but because its attractions and repulsions make effective barriers against the immensities that damage human self-esteem. (pp. 81-3)

The underlying message of Calvino's mythic fables emerges very clearly in his redundancies. All his stories reiterate a basic situation: an intelligent consciousness confronts the scientific universe. This consciousness (Qfwfq) makes itself at home in this context through a series of attractions and antagonisms directed toward other beings and toward phenomena in the universe. These two feelings are man's primary means of creating a sense of significant relationship. In a few stories, Calvino shows characters going beyond attraction and repulsion to two other modes of relating to the universe. One is creativity. Calvino values any form of the ability to bring something new into existence. This direct relationship with the universe is mostly shown to be a happy by-product of rivalry and antagonism. The other mode of achieving a significant relationship might be called holistic or mystic vision. Such vision usually appears as the fleeting benefit of an attraction. Although such visionary moments do not last, they erase the boundaries of ego awareness and offer Qfwfq his most meaning-laden sense of integration with the cosmos. Most of Calvino's secondary characters are content with self-centered rivalries and the ordinary mortal lusts, but Qfwfq and, by implication, the reader, can transcend these basic strategies and find more intellectual and spiritual modes of relating to the cosmos if they desire them. Overall, Calvino emphasizes the basic feelings of attraction and antagonism. These surprisingly simple and homely emotions permit virtually anyone to feel at one with the scientific universe. In order for us to understand how they function, he writes about several kinds of attractions and enmities.

Attraction, or love, tames the universe to man's capacity to respond in **"All at One Point," "The Spiral,"** and **"The Origin of the Birds." "All at One Point"** makes love the force that brings the universe into existence. Qfwfq, along with all the rest of the universe, suffers the pangs of extreme compaction just prior to the Big Bang. Tenement living and astrophysics caper cheek by cheek in this delightful paean to Mrs. Ph(i)Nko, the erotic lodestar of the males of the community. One day she says, "Oh, if I only had some room, how I'd like to make some noodles for you boys!" As they all imagine the implications of that picture—her arms, the flour, the wheat in the fields, rain and mountains and sun—they find that her loving impulse has triggered the Big Bang. Hers is truly the love that moves the sun and all the stars, that brings the heavenly bodies into being out of her mothering desire to feed those who rely emotionally on her. In this creation myth, her love produces a universe for her admirers, and all its fruitful plains are sanctified because they are necessary to her pasta-making. As she is transformed into the universe's energy-heat-light, her admirers suffer the loss of paradise; yet the love they bore her lets them now love the universe, for their momentary vision of its unfolding glories shows this love, which was once directed toward one person, being transformed into a relationship with all creation.

Similarly, in **"The Spiral,"** love for a female mollusk becomes the thrill of sympathetic vibration at recognizing the feminine in any of its manifestations, be they seagull, anchovy, queen bee, movie actress, or tourist girl on the beach. With half the animate world thus abstracted as the feminine (and hence easy to relate to through attraction), the rest of the animate world also falls into place as male and as rival for the attentions of the female. In **"The Origin of the Birds,"** Calvino shows love of Queen Or causing Qfwfq to reach a unifying vision of what is (the world visible to science) and what might be (the world of imagination), joined in a continuum with himself as the bridge between the two disparate realms. Love fleetingly gives him a sense of place in the universe. And as mediating link between these two antagonistic worlds, his consciousness gains a momentary sacredness.

Calvino creates a dynamic mixture of human love, antagonism, and attraction toward some physical component of the universe in **"The Soft Moon," "Crystals,"** and **"Without Colors."** The ongoing arguments between male and female in these three stories concern those qualities of the universe which each considers desirable. The arguments help the lovers define their relationship to each other, and the passions involved in their arguments help them relate their lives to the world around them. (pp. 84-6)

Antagonism unmixed with affection governs many of Calvino's other stories. These rivalries are male-against-male struggles for dominance, and insofar as Qfwfq escapes the depressing and destructive implications of this way of approaching the universe, he does so through the idea of man as creator. **"Games Without End"** shows Qfwfq and Pfwfp in a violent chase. **"A Sign in Space"** displays Qfwfq in a kind of artistic rage provoked by envy and destructive passion. Yet these stories also show him creating new atoms, galaxies, and signs, the last leading to all future forms of communication. Moreover, the antagonisms not only stimulate creativity, they even allow moments of vision, although the visions are daunting rather than ecstatic. In **"Games Without End,"** as Qfwfq sees Pfwfp hot rod around the perimeter of the universe, Qfwfq sees Pfwfp both behind and ahead of him, and further out, he sees multiples of himself and Pfwfp. The curves of space put him in a series of reflections, like those in funhouse mirrors. Their ugly enmity thus is multiplied around the entire universe. Many of Calvino's rivalries thus replicate themselves out to infinity, and vision of this infinite series is not comforting, although the moment of expanded awareness may be exhilarating. More lastingly positive than these visions, however, are the creations that emerge from the rivalries, for with them something new enters the universe.

Other antagonisms which make interaction, feeling, and a sense of meaning possible for Qfwfq are rivalry in love **("The Form of Space," "The Aquatic Uncle,"** and **"Night Driver")** and participation in the diffused quarrels of an extended social group **("The Dinosaurs," "At Daybreak,"** and **"The Distance of the Moon").** (pp. 86-7)

Calvino's characters define their lives so effectively through attraction and antagonism that the universe seems to them a perfectly natural backdrop for their individual concerns, and it does not make them feel insignificant. Such outlooks are egotistical and rather unsatisfactory as philosophies of life, but they work, and they offer their proponents the possibility of greater awareness and of more direct interaction with the cosmos through vision and creativity. Following Calvino's mythic prescriptions, some characters reach daunting visions of infinity and holistic, ecstatic visions of unity; furthermore, they can create things not previously present in the universe, such as new atoms, signs, pasta, galaxies, and eyes. Calvino offers his readers a moment of vision by helping us feel part of the cosmic continuum. Qfwfq, as conscious intelligence, reminds us of our singularity; his actions and passions show us how to participate in the cosmos. Passivity in the face of the infinite, silent spaces of objective science seems pointless when one can sport with the phenomena one observes inhabiting those spaces. Calvino's myths are lessons in the Great Dance. (p. 87)

Calvino's cosmos derives its meaning from two basic oppositions. The primary confrontation is that of consciousness with the universe of space and matter. The secondary opposition lies between male and female. This latter tends to reinforce and color Calvino's primary conflict, for Qfwfq's consciousness definitely establishes itself as masculine, whereas the phenomenal world often seems feminine to him. Ultimately, for Qfwfq, the Other is feminine and the Feminine is other. (p. 88)

Calvino puts consciousness that is human in outlook (if not in fact) into direct contact with such phenomena as the condensation of interstellar gases into matter, the galactic year (600 million years), the moment prior to the Big Bang, the curvature of the universe, the development of life-sustaining atmosphere on earth, the expanding universe, and evolutionary time.

As Calvino looks at human consciousness against such a backdrop, he sees that consciousness playing several roles: observer, admirer, creator, inhabitant, speculator, seer, model-maker, and imitator. As we watch the non-conscious forces of astrophysics at work, Qfwfq's antics remind us that his awareness is an addition to the universe, since all the magnificence of the macrocosm is deaf, dumb, and blind.

In stories that pit Qfwfq's consciousness against matter rather than space, Calvino's scientific concern shifts from physics to biology. Chemistry figures in **"Crystals,"** and optics in **"Without Colors,"** but matter to Calvino is at its most complex and interesting when alive because of its ultimate messiness as well as because of its infinite variability. The forms taken by matter awaken wonder and longing in **"Without Colors"** and **"The Spiral."** In **"The Origin of the Birds,"** the forms of life generate yearnings and vision. In **"Blood, Sea,"** insight leads to a sense of oceanic oneness with the cosmos—oceanic both literally and in its Freudian, psychological sense. In **"Mitosis,"** Qfwfq reaches an ecstatic moment of transcendent consciousness as he, a cell, divides in two. In **"Meiosis,"** his urbane consciousness (embedded this time in a camel) muses upon the physiological and genetic impulses that lead to the creation of new life. Occasionally, biology provokes in him a negative response to matter. The changing forms of bodies alienate him in **"The Aquatic Uncle"** and **"Dinosaurs."** More disturbing yet is **"The Soft Moon,"** in which the moon, its surface a mess of "extended tumefactions," of buboes, suckers, opercula, and pores, smothers the earth with its "gelatin and hair and mold and slaver." The irrepressible Qfwfq, however, does not let his revulsion overwhelm him. He fights to construct the kind of world he prefers out of the gooey mess, and in doing so, earns the right to feel good about himself and about his place in the universe.

In this basic binary opposition Calvino shows intelligent consciousness responding to the non-conscious world around it. Qfwfq, whose personality is effervescent, cynical, and passionate, embodies this awareness at play with the universe. When we compare Calvino's handling of binary opposition with that in some of the traditional myths, we realize just how thoroughly Calvino has pushed beyond superficial antinomies and has zeroed in on the most basic confrontation of all. Human knowledge, thoughts, and feelings grow from our interaction with the world around us. Without this opposition of our awareness to all that is "other," we would not exist as humans.

The second binary opposition that characterizes Calvino's cosmogony is sex. Subtly or obviously, he sexualizes the universe. Qfwfq is an eternally masculine being; the whole realm of his non-I reverberates with glimpses of a feminine principle. Because this feminine so often corresponds to the universe Qfwfq plays with, it becomes a derivative opposition, but no less important. Without this sexualization, many of Qfwfq's ways of finding meaning would not work. He would feel little response to the heat, light, and energy of the universe if his sexual myths had not identified these forces with one beloved woman, Mrs. Ph(i)Nko. Because the feminine is latent in so much of the cosmos, Calvino suggests that the proper approach to the phenomenal world is to make love to it. One should interact sensuously and personally, not just observe with the frigid detachment of the scientist. Only by going beyond observation can one hope to experience vision. The stories of male rivalry that lack a feminine object or overt feminization of the universe only allow vision depressed by a sense of infinite futility. In stories where the Other is feminized, there are visions that exalt Qfwfq, make him ecstatic, help him transcend normal consciousness, as, for instance, in the holistic moment of unity with everything in **"The Origin of the Birds."** The mystery of awareness pushes Calvino to ponder intellectual responses to the universe. The mystery of sex causes him to examine physical interaction with it. When combined, the two offer the possibilities of transcendent vision and creativity.

Little wonder that Calvino's cosmos is more comic than tragic, as his title ***Le cosmicomiche*** implies. Laughter can be triggered by relaxing our rigid inner hold on aggressive and sexual impulses. Laughter also explodes as the mind grapples with incongruity. Many of the standard aggressions and antagonisms which we normally repress are embedded in Calvino's stories of rivalry, family quarrels, and jealousy. So too, an urgent and tickling sexuality haunts his universe. (pp. 88-90)

Before one can assess the adequacy of Calvino's myths, one must . . . see how his cosmology accounts for death and the end of the mythic cycle. Since Calvino starts with the scientific, godless universe, he cannot use traditional religious answers without violating his own premises. Yet myths that offer no consolation whatever will attract few followers. Science as "the modern myth" falls short of satisfying cravings for individual significance on precisely these grounds.

Calvino does present a mediation between life and death—not afterlife, but transformation. He does not preach metempsychosis as doctrine; instead, he asks us to value change and novelty for their own sakes, change in form and change in mind. The physical and mental transformations of his characters are the epic events that mediate between the meaninglessness of a scientific view and the meaningfulness of a human outlook. What happens to Calvino's characters emerges as a mythic redundancy, an oft-repeated effect, designed to make sure we perceive the subliminal comfort of what the cosmos can do for us. Faustian man may or may not succeed in changing the cosmos, but he will be changed by it and he can record its changes in his consciousness, thus giving them meaning and finding meaning for himself.

Calvino begins by establishing our ultimate isolation and aloneness, a state suggested by Qfwfq's singularity. Moreover, Calvino often reminds us that because we are unique points of consciousness, with limitations to our powers of perception, our understanding of the world is filtered by and distorted by that consciousness. When that consciousness dies, our world goes with us. Hence, in the epic sense, our world is an internal construct, and we are demigods. We may not wish to die, but when the I ceases, there is no longer a distinction between the I and the not-I, so death is meaningless, a false categorization. A window on the universe closes. A version of the universe disappears. Calvino works to undermine our assumptions about death when he describes other moments of dissolution. The I loses itself in the not-I in **"Blood, Sea," "Mitosis,"** and **"The Origin of the Birds,"** and these moments of merging are ecstatic peaks of vision. Thus are we urged to accept, even look forward to, an experience we might otherwise fear. That most of the dissolutions Calvino describes are not terminal is secondary; he upholds the desirability of such vision and makes its joys real.

In **"Death,"** he shows a scientific alternative to death as we know it: immortality without conscious continuity. Reproduction by division of cells produces "a discontinuous and perpetual life, always identical to itself in a shattered time and space." As Calvino notes, "nobody seems prepared any longer to renounce sex, even the little share of sex that falls to his lot, in order to have again a life that repeats itself interminably." Thus too are we pushed to accept death, first as a corollary of sex, and second as a corollary of consciousness. The cell that divides perpetually loses itself in becoming its own successor. Since few of us would give up sex or consciousness in return for deathlessness, we acquiesce in the inevitability of death as if by choice.

Calvino takes his arguments yet further. Having persuaded us to reject one form of continuous identity in **"Death,"** he proceeds to offer us various sorts of transformations as a muted kind of comfort. Continuation of some part of oneself obviously appeals to Calvino, and, indeed, sociobiology argues that some animals will even sacrifice their lives to ensure the survival of their genes. But Calvino does not limit himself to genetic proliferation. He shows us many forms of metamorphic continuation and change, and invites us to revel in them. With Qfwfq, we experience such transformations as that of darkness to light, of dinosaurs to lizards, of a woman who becomes one with the moon, of an amphibian who returns to fishhood, and of a woman who becomes the energy of the universe. Calvino treats novelty as an ultimate good. Moreover, the creation of something new is not only a good, but also an extension of the creator, a transformation of some part of his mind, an extension of his life. Calvino's insistence that creation is one of man's finest means of relating to the cosmos takes on more significance as we realize that such creation is a mediative, sacred act. (pp. 92-3)

Overall, what lets Calvino's myths handle death is their focus on consciousness. Aside from moments of vision, when we feel seamlessly united with the universe about us, Calvino suggests that we are really only aware of ourselves and of our I's reactions to the not-I. Hence his lack of concern with society and politics in these stories. All that we really have is the interplay between consciousness and that-which-it-is-conscious-of. For Calvino, this interaction permits a satisfying variety of possible responses, including scientific observation, erotic longing and release, and ecstatic vision. (p. 94)

In sum, Calvino's myths rest on the following interrelated elements. Attraction or antagonism, because they give man a sense of meaning, are basic to Calvino's argument. Also achievable are creativity (which involves the creator in bringing a novelty into existence) and vision (which operates holistically to give man that feeling of integration with the cosmos which he craves). Activity, which Calvino portrays as sporting with the elements of the cosmos, is to be preferred to passivity, as we learn from watching Qfwfq make love to the universe rather than trying to observe it with detachment. Because Calvino apparently values novelty for its own sake, he offers the idea of change and metamorphosis as muted comfort for our fears of death. If nothing else, our atoms continue; so do genes, and so too do the products of our creativity.

All these values can give man an inner sense of meaning, and none of them is invalidated by science. Yet Calvino manages to do more. He upholds the importance and meaning of human consciousness, even when it is measured against the scale of the universe. Without intelligent consciousness, nothing in the universe could be significant, for no awareness would be there to render judgment of relative importances, to interpret the meaning behind the sign. Only some form of consciousness can bestow the gift of meaning; the universe cannot interpret itself. Hence the significance of our conscious species. (pp. 94-5)

Calvino invites us to become interested observers and, better yet, active partners in the mysteries of the universe. His cosmicomical stories can be usefully read as a set of privately devised myths—myths depicting creation and survival, conflict and violence, attraction and repulsion, transcendence and love. The point of these myths is that they offer us a way of relating to the cosmos. None of the strategies he sketches for achieving this sense of place in the universe is invalidated by scientific knowledge. Science remains our means of analyzing the phenomenal world. Calvino's myths augment science by helping us bridge the abyss between the phenomenal world we observe and the inner world that we are. (p. 95)

Kathryn Hume, "Italo Calvino's Cosmic Comedy: Mythography for the Scientific Age," in Papers on Language & Literature, *Vol. 20, No. 1, Winter, 1984, pp. 80-95.*

UGO VARNAI (essay date 1984)

[*In the review excerpted below of* Difficult Loves, *Varnai notes that although these stories are written in the plain, realistic style characteristic of Calvino's early work, several tales suggest deeper meaning and allegorical significance.*]

Difficult Loves is in three sections, the first of which, under the title adopted for the whole volume, is a new translation of ***Gli amori difficili,*** eleven short pieces written from 1949 to 1958; there follow reprints of earlier translations of two of the best known of Calvino's "long short-stories", ***La nuvola di smog***, 1958 (translated as ***Smog***) and ***La speculazione edilizia***, 1957 ***(A Plunge Into Real Estate)***.

It is difficult to guess what impression these stories will make on a new reader, one who does not know Calvino. While the "fantasies" of the famous trilogy, written at about the same time as these stories, still project an image which the years and the striking qualities of Calvino's later books have not altered in depth, the stories in this selection might definitely seem dated, especially in translation, where the finer points of Calvino's prose style are inevitably smoothed out. . . . The "Difficult Loves" series, in particular, takes us back to the world of the 1950s. Not only the props and material circumstances, but the very mentality, the thoughts and acts of the protagonists are rooted in the world of those remote years: we read page after page on the emotion of sitting near a woman, a stranger, during a train journey, and attempting to touch her with imperceptible, clandestine shiftings of finger-tips or knuckles; or on the drama of the female bather who loses her swimming costume in the water, and runs the terrifying risk of being seen naked.

The protagonists are mostly cardboard figures, impersonally conceived, mere types—the soldier, the crook, the bather, the clerk, the short-sighted man, the photographer; the plots are often flimsy, and there is an air of affected simplicity; in short we get the impression of a fairly typical "neo-realist" work. But soon we begin to notice the traces of a remarkable writer's hand, beyond the purely verbal qualities. There are, in the first place, those notes of deep personal commitment to certain themes—solitude, for example, Calvino's familiar, lucidly conveyed sense of isolation from fellow human beings, his perception that our deepest experiences are not communicable. One story, the **"Adventure of a Traveller"**, tells of a long night's journey by train towards Rome and love, and describes in almost grotesque detail the meticulous preparations, the elaborate arrangements for trying to sleep in a compartment where other passengers come and go, the irritations, the discomfort, the ticket collector, the fitful sleep, the heat, the cold. . . . There is total enjoyment of all this on the part of the young traveller, a strange, excited feeling of perfection, of vitality, of fulfilment. As he arrives in the morning, he rings up his girl from the station, hears her voice at the other end, still suffused with sleep and soft warmth, "and he realized he would never manage to tell her anything of the significance of that night, which he now sensed was fading, like every perfect night of love, at the cruel explosion of day". The elegant transposition of values, here, seems to fuse with the disconsolate sense that what is really worthwhile in human life cannot be conveyed through words, in ordinary life at least.

One other striking quality of several of these seemingly plain tales is their tendency to take on further meaning, to work like allegories. We are reading about some unprepossessing feature of Italian life in the 1950s, and suddenly become aware that something wider and deeper is being signified. Take the **"Adventure of a Photographer"**, the man who begins to practise photography against his will, becomes an addict and is then drawn into a frantic critique of his work. Where do we draw the line between the reality that is photographed because it is beautiful to us, and the reality that seems beautiful because it has been photographed? And why should we want to cut from the mobile continuum of our day a series of temporal slices, the thickness of a fraction of a second? And isn't it clear that the snapshot kills spontaneity: should we not instead go in for the posed portrait, which is so much closer to truth? The protagonist chooses his girl friend as his subject, and she has to submit to an endless series of fanatical experiments—their life becomes a nightmare, she leaves him, he goes on "photographing her absence", then taking pictures of his own pictures of her, then tearing them up and taking pictures of the fragments, because "if you decide to photograph a person or a thing, you must go on photographing it always, exclusively, at every hour of the day and night. Photography has a meaning only if it exhausts all possible images." Thus a slightly absurd, unreal little story turns into a painful metaphor of writing itself.

The particular anguish involved in the relationship between personal experience and writing surfaces at several points. In the short, emblematic **"Adventure of a Poet"** two people, a poet and the girl he loves, explore a sea grotto in Southern Italy. Their boat glides in the radiant, magical semi-darkness, the girl swims naked, clad in rays of bluish, unnatural light. The poet is deeply moved.

> He understood that what life now gave him was something not everyone has the privilege of looking at, open-eyed, as at the most dazzling core of the sun. And in the core of this sun was silence. Nothing that was there at this moment could be translated into anything else, perhaps not even into a memory.

Later, as they return into the light of open day, they cross the path of a fishing boat, and speak to the fishermen. A picture of poverty and human misery is projected, and the poet senses that this *is* capable of being expressed, indeed "here was a turmoil of words that crowded into his mind . . . words and words thick, woven one into the other . . . a tangle from which even the tiniest white spaces were vanishing, and only the black remained, the most total black, impenetrable"—which must be one of the most disconsolate accounts of literary articulateness ever written.

The two long short-stories belong to the group of Calvino's socially and politically charged tales, and turn on the theme of the involvement of intellectuals in the struggles and indignities of real life. **"Smog"** describes with cold, deadly irony the physical and moral chaos of post-war Italy, where the fight against pollution is conducted by the makers of pollution; and in particular the position of those progressive intellectuals who criticize the establishment but accept the employment and patronage which it provides. In a similar vein **"Real Estate"** chronicles the progress, the reverses and the triumph of the new men, coarse entrepreneurs, crooked builders, shady operators, who possess such astonishing vitality that (it is suggested) they perhaps deserve their success. "A man who isn't trying to make money doesn't count", the protagonist says to himself: "we intellectuals make a distinction between the larger historical perspective and our own interests and in the process we have lost the taste of life. We have destroyed ourselves. We don't mean anything". In fact this is not Calvino's view, except with reference to certain dubious cultural pretensions of the 1950s. He for one has continued to explore those levels of consciousness where "we intellectuals" do mean something, indeed may turn out to be the custodians of meaning, even when we have to proclaim that meaning is elusive, possibly illusory.

Ugo Varnai, "Meaning into Words," in The Times Literary Supplement, *No. 4239, June 29, 1984, p. 716.*

ROBERT TOWERS (essay date 1984)

[*An American professor and critic who frequently contributes to the* New York Review of Books, *Towers praises Calvino's early stories published in* Difficult Loves, *declaring that they should be treated with as much respect as the "more spectacular 'metafictions'" the author wrote later in his career.*]

When the early work of a famous writer rides in on the coattails, so to speak, of the later work that has made him famous, one is inclined either to dismiss it with a knowing wink at the cupidity of publishers or else, if a devotee of the writer in question, to examine it for signs pointing to subsequent maturations and triumphs. Neither response is appropriate in the case of ***Difficult Loves.*** Calvino's stories stand on their own as finished performances, as distinctive and seductive in their own way as the more spectacular "metafictions" that followed them. The author of ***Cosmicomics*** and *Invisible Cities* seems to have sprung fully armored from the head of his muse.

The first section of ***Difficult Loves*** consists of the "Riviera Stories," which date back to the beginning of Calvino's career in the 1940s. For the most part they are nearly plotless sketches, many of them dealing with children, that shift delicately between realism and fantasy; a major pleasure in reading them is to watch the way Calvino maintains a light but perfect control as he allows the material to veer slightly to one side of the line and then to the other. In **"Adam, One Afternoon,"** a gardener's boy, Libereso, woos a kitchen girl, Maria-nunziata, by presenting her with a series of innocently phallic creatures. "D'you want to see something nice?" he asks as he leads her to a moldy corner of the garden where he reveals a toad. "*Mammamia!*" cries the girl, but Libereso tries to convince her that it is pretty and that she should stroke it. The toad is followed by a handful of rose chafers, a lizard, a pair of copulating frogs, snails, a snake, a goldfish—all of which he tries to persuade her to touch. At the end, saying, "I want to give you a surprise," the boy releases a whole basketful of the creatures in the kitchen, and the girl's future is symbolically prophesied:

> Maria-nunziata stepped back, but between her feet she saw a great big toad. And behind it were five little toads in a line, taking little hops toward her across the black-and-white-tiled floor.

In this piece, as in **"The Enchanted Garden"** and in **"Lazy Sons"** (the droll account of two narcoleptic young men who shamelessly resist all appeals for help from their hard-working, hard-pressed parents), one keeps expecting a metamorphosis into fairy tale that never quite takes place. The slightly teasing effect is nicely calculated.

In "Wartime Stories" and "Postwar Stories" the cruelties of partisan warfare and the exigencies of poverty invite a more grimly realistic treatment of the peasants, migrant workers, prostitutes, and black marketeers who populate them. These stories are the fictional counterparts of the great Italian films of the period—*Paisan, Rome, Open City,* and *The Bicycle Thief.* But metaphysical, fabulist, or farcical elements keep breaking in. In the most impressive of the war stories, a trigger-happy soldier-boy, "a mountaineer with an apple face," keeps shooting, with miraculous accuracy, at everything that catches his eye—birds, pine cones, trout, toadstools, and the gilt buttons on the uniforms of German soldiers—in an effort to transcend his separateness from the rest of creation. . . . At the end, a cornered German soldier tries to divert the boy's attention to a crow circling overhead—only to have the boy place a bullet through the middle of an embroidered eagle on the German's tunic, while the crow continues its slow downward circling.

The humor of some of the "Postwar Stories" is of a kind that Boccaccio might have relished. Crowded sleeping arrangements figure in two of them, **"Sleeping like Dogs"** and **"Transit Bed,"** while in another, **"Desire in November,"** a poor old man, Barbagallo, who wears a military overcoat and nothing else (his clothes having been stolen from the riverbank the preceding summer), forces his way into an elegant furrier's shop where, in the company of one of the saleswomen, he spends the night lapped in the softest and richest pelts that luxury can provide.

The final section, "Stories of Love and Loneliness," consists of eight "adventures," which, far more than the earlier pieces, resemble the Calvino we have come to know. . . . [Each] adventure proposes a problem which is then explored with a kind of philosophical thoroughness, mitigated by wit. While the explicitly Italian setting is retained, character and action are strictly subordinated to the working out of the chosen perplexity. (p. 33)

The wittiest of all is **"The Adventure of a Reader,"** in which Amedeo, whose interest in an active life has given way to a passion for reading thick novels—especially those of the nineteenth century—settles himself on a rocky shelf overlooking a secluded patch of beach with just such a volume. The identity of the work changes as he reads: sometimes it is *War and Peace,* sometimes *Crime and Punishment, The Charterhouse of Parma, Lost Illusions,* or *Remembrance of Things Past.* His absorption in the narration of events, the tangle of human situations, is nearly total. Nearly total—for occasionally, at the end of a chapter, he dives into the tepid, translucent water. Even as he swims, he can't wait to get back to the story of Albertine—"would Marcel find her again, or not?"

He has also become aware of a deeply tanned lady sunning herself on a rubber mattress not far from his perch. One thing leads to another, they take a dip together, and a desultory conversation ensues, interrupted by long intervals during which Amedeo returns to his book with a devouring curiosity to find out what happens next. The day is waning. The lady, whose intentions are clearly amorous, undoes the halter of her bathing suit under the pretext of getting dressed. Having reached a climax in the book, "Amedeo didn't know whether to look at her, pretending to read, or to read, pretending to look at her." Finally aroused, he embraces the lady, falling onto the mattress with her, but as he does so he slightly turns his head toward the book to make sure it has not fallen into the sea. Even in the ecstasy of his lovemaking, Amedeo tries "to free one hand to put the bookmark at the right page. Nothing is more irritating when you're eager to resume reading than to have to search through the book, unable to find your place." As Calvino develops the situation, his ambivalence toward the entire world of traditional fiction (the same ambivalence, compounded of nostalgia and despair, that animates *If on a winter's night a traveler . . .*—that marvelous work of *narratio interrupta*) becomes incandescent, shedding gleams of comic irony in every direction.

The collection possesses great charm. It can only enhance Calvino's already towering reputation. The stories are "lightweight" in the most favorable sense of that term: never, in his exploration of the possibilities latent in each "adventure," does Calvino allow himself to become tedious. More obviously than his later books, with their cosmopolitan or cosmological settings, ***Difficult Loves*** reveals Calvino as a classically Italian writer—a writer, that is, for whom clarity of outline and brilliantly lighted surfaces seem preferable to thickness of atmosphere and the weight of social and psychological documentation. Gesture and act count more than introspection; shame, as in the case of the poor bather, is a more palpable emotion than guilt. While Calvino plays with abstractions, is engaged by conundrums, and is drawn toward symmetry, his inventions, however fanciful, are always embedded in sharply observed or vividly imagined sensory detail. Boccaccio, Pirandello, and the early De Chirico—these are among the Italian artists with whom his genius is aligned. (pp. 33-4)

Robert Towers, "Light and Lively," in The New York Review of Books, *Vol. XXXI, No. 19, December 6, 1984, pp. 33-4.*

SEAMUS HEANEY (essay date 1985)

[*A major contemporary literary figure, Heaney has been called the most important Irish poet since William Butler Yeats. In the review of* Mr. Palomar *excerpted below, Heaney praises Calvino's philosophical observations on consciousness as both sophisticated and entertaining.*]

[***Mr. Palomar***] has three main sections entitled **"Mr. Palomar's Vacation," "Mr. Palomar in the City"** and **"The Silences of Mr. Palomar."** Each main section has three subsections and each subsection three parts and Mr. Calvino has created a numbering system for them. (p. 1)

Happily, the schema turns out to be not just a prescription; what might have been for a lesser imagination a grid acts in this case like a springboard, and indeed one suspects anyhow that the numerological stuff evolved from the accidents of composition and not vice versa. Each of these pieces has the feel of a single inspiration being caught as it rises and then being played for all its life is worth—though not for an instant longer than it takes to exhaust its first energy.

Mr. Palomar is a lens employed by his author in order to inspect the phenomena of the world, but the lens is apt to turn into a mirror which reflects the hesitations and self-corrections of Mr. Palomar's own reflecting mind. The book consists of a graduated sequence of descriptions and speculations in which the protagonist confronts the problem of discovering his place in the world and of watching those discoveries dissolve under his habitual intellectual scrutiny.

So the very first movement is entitled **"Reading a Wave"** and here Mr. Palomar attempts to see and describe and kidnap into language the exact nature of a single wave. His precisions, which he must keep revising, are constantly accurate and constantly inadequate; yet it is these very frustrations which constitute the reader's pleasure. By the last movement, however, Mr. Palomar has turned his gaze inward and is now, as the title of the piece puts it, **"Learning to Be Dead."** But his appetite for certain knowledge remains equally tantalized and unsatisfied: "You must not confuse being dead with not being." In between there are the other 25 texts which one hesitates to call prose poems since it makes them sound much too affected and humorless, or meditations, since that undersells their lovely metaphorical ease and rapture.

Mr. Calvino's line whispers and lazes and tautens and sports itself very cajolingly. His gaze, like Mr. Palomar's as he contemplates the stars, "remains alert, available, released from all certitude." "In August," he tells us, "the Milky Way assumes a dense consistency, and you might say it is overflowing its bed." The lavish simplicity of that, its double gratitude for the world and for words adequate to the world, its mingled sense of something sweetly and personally discovered yet also something of almost racial memory, this atmosphere of spacious and buoyant reverie is typical of the whole work.

Here is a large unhampered talent sailing a middle course between the sophistication of the avant-garde and the innocence of the primitive poetic imagination, between the kind of intelligence that constructed the medieval bestiaries and the preliterate intuitiveness that once chanted hunters' prayers. If the persona of Mr. Palomar is haunted at times by the petulant shade of Molloy in Samuel Beckett's [*Molloy*], trying to devise an infallible method by which to rotate his sucking stones from pocket to mouth to pocket, and at other times by the urbane Jorge Luis Borges, softly expatiating upon the question of whether writing gets done by "Borges" or "I," the reader is not worried. Nor is Mr. Calvino. He knows that everybody ends up worrying about the same things anyhow. . . .

Nevertheless, for all its sensual felicity, the writing is philosophically impelled. Mr. Palomar, who takes his name from the famous telescope and observatory, is both an "I" and an "eye," "A world looking at the world," as the title of one of Mr. Palomar's meditations suggests, a question mark retroactively affecting his own credibility: "Is he not a piece of the world that is looking at another piece of the world? Or else, given that there is world that side of the window and world this side, perhaps the 'I,' the ego, is simply the window through which the world looks at the world. To look at itself, the world needs the eyes (and the eyeglasses) of Mr. Palomar."

Which mercifully takes us, Mr. Palomar and Italo Calvino beyond the impasse of solipsism, the distrust of language and the frigid fires of "experiment." There may be a problem of knowledge, but the consciousness only comes alive to this problem by suffering those constant irrepressible appetites for experience which want to rampage beyond the prison of the self. Mr. Calvino may divide and categorize in triplicate the visual, the cultural and the speculative aspects of Mr. Palomar's world, he may prompt and tag and analyze and juxtapose to his (and our) heart's content, but Mr. Palomar himself remains wonderfully spontaneous and receptive to the pell-mell of the senses. . . . Mr. Palomar may collapse at the end, like the book named for him, in a syllogism, but not before he has outstripped his conclusion in one incandescent apotheosis after another.

If it often seems in the course of this book that Mr. Calvino cannot put a foot wrong, this is because he is not a pedestrian writer. Like Robert Frost, his whole concern is for himself as a performer, but whereas Frost performed at eye-level, as it were, on vocal cords and heartstrings, Mr. Calvino is on the high wires, on lines of thought strung out above the big international circus. Yet such high-wire displays engage us only if the performer is in fact subject to gravity and genuinely at risk. A lightweight can throw the same shapes but cannot evince that old, single, open-mouthed stare of hope and wonder which we all still want to be a part of. What is most impressive about ***Mr. Palomar*** is a sense of the safety net being withdrawn at the end, of beautiful, nimble, solitary feats of imagination being carried off not so much to dazzle an audience as to outface what the poet Philip Larkin calls "the solving emptiness / That lies just under all we do." (p. 60)

Seamus Heaney, "The Sensual Philosopher," in The New York Times Book Review, *September 29, 1985, pp. 1, 60.*

JOHN UPDIKE (essay date 1985)

[*Considered a major contemporary American writer, Updike is particularly noted for the subtle complexity of his poetry, criticism, and fiction, which includes such novels as* Rabbit Run *(1960) and* Rabbit Is Rich *(1981). In the review of* Mr. Palomar *excerpted below, Updike pays careful attention to the book's structure and its emphasis on consciousness and perception.*]

[***Mr. Palomar***] consists of twenty-seven small chapters, each describing observations by its hero, who is named after an observatory. Twenty-seven is three to the third power, and an afterword attached to an index of the chapters demonstrates that the possibilities for symmetry and modulation were lovingly weighed by the author. . . . [The grid in the afterword] rivals Joyce's intertwining schemata for *Ulysses,* which assigned each chapter not only a corresponding episode of the Odyssey but a particular color, an organ of the human body, an hour of the day, a dominant symbol, and a human science or art, and which furthermore carried forward this huge apparatus of multiple significance through a Thomistic system of contraries and coincidences, products and antidotes, not to mention parallels with various of Giambattista Vico's ages of mankind and a presiding metaphysics of space and time.

Joyce's encyclopedic and abstractifying ambitions were incongruously but healthily wedded to his love of life's small talk and petty grit, and to the passionate autobiography that his elaborate designs hold. Where the autobiographical, factual impulse is less powerful, schematization runs the risk of seeming playful and automatic; and Calvino did not always dodge this gentle danger. *Invisible Cities,* amid all its ingenuities, was imbued with his lively civic concern and cosmopolitan reach of imagination, but ***The Castle of Crossed Destinies*** seemed at times to be merely playing cards, to be filling in the scheme's blank spaces, and in *If on a winter's night a traveler* the overlays of cleverness and the charm of the literary parodies left an afterimage that melted in the mind like a Platonic pastille. ***Mr. Palomar,*** though short, is a more ambitious and integrated book than these last two; it essays a description of existential man rather than literary man, and deals with issues of perception rather than of reading and narration. The light it gives off is as cool as starlight.

Mr. Palomar—a man, we learn, of middle age and no definite occupation, with a wife and daughter and an apartment in Rome and in Paris—sets himself to look at things, and focusses until he arrives at a conclusion, however small. "A nervous man who lives in a frenzied and congested world, Mr. Palomar tends to reduce his relations with the outside world; and, to defend himself against the general neurasthenia, he tries to keep his sensations under control insofar as possible." Chapter 1.1.1, for instance—the most intense dose, as we can gauge at a glance, of the visual, descriptive mode—finds our hero on the beach, viewing the waves with a determined precision. . . . He tries to use the waves as an instrument wherewith "to perceive the true substance of the world beyond sensory and mental habits," feels "a slight dizziness" instead, and goes off along the beach "tense and nervous as when he came, and even more unsure about everything."

With 1.1.2, we enter the anthropological mode: Mr. Palomar attempts to cope visually and socially with the sight of a naked bosom, "the bronze-pink cloud of a naked female torso," on this same beach. To stare is wrong, yet not to stare is also wrong; his reactions to this provocative sight swing from an "indiscreet and reactionary" looking away that reinforces "the convention that declares illicit any sight of the breast" to a liberal attempt to convey "detached encouragement" with a gaze that, "giving the landscape a fickle glance, will linger on the breast with special consideration, but will quickly include it in an impulse of good will and gratitude for the whole, for the sun and the sky, for the bent pines and the dune and the beach and the rocks and the clouds and the seaweed, for the cosmos that rotates around those haloed cusps." Thus he will signal that "though he belongs to a human generation for whom nudity of the female bosom was associated with the idea of amorous intimacy, still he hails approvingly this change in customs." But in walking back and forth trying to achieve just the right political adjustment in his gaze he finally succeeds in driving the possessor of the bosom off in an angry huff. It is all funny, familiar, and sociologically thoughtful. The next chapter, 1.1.3, takes us into cosmic and philosophical considerations as Mr. Palomar swims toward the swordlike reflection of the sun on the sea and ponders the dependence of this blazing phenomenon upon his own witnessing of it. Persuaded that "the sword will exist even without him," he "dries himself with a soft towel and goes home."

Such a cycle of three is repeated three times three: we see Mr. Palomar on the beach, in the garden, and stargazing; on the terrace, shopping, and at the zoo; travelling, in society, and meditating. He ponders the lovemaking of tortoises, the composition of lawns, the moon in daytime, Rome's plague of pigeons, Paris's plethora of cheeses, an albino gorilla, a Zen sand garden, a Mexican ruin, and why we get so angry at the young. When the book heads into its last third and the 3's pile up, the topics get increasingly heady: "The model of models," "The universe as mirror," "Learning to be dead." We learn, in the bargain, a bit more about Mr. Palomar. He does not love himself, we are told, and therefore "has always taken care not to encounter himself face to face." He thinks of death as benign insofar as it will eliminate "that patch of uneasiness that is our presence." The middle section, under the anthropological sign of 2 and the general head of **"Mr. Palomar in the City,"** reads the easiest, and has a distinctly creaturely emphasis, from the colorful evocation of a butcher's shop . . . to the close scrutiny of a gecko, lit transparently from underneath, as it swallows a large, live butterfly: "Will it all fit? Will he spit it out? Will he explode? No, the butterfly is there in his throat: it flutters, in a sorry state but still itself, not touched by the insult of chewing teeth; now it passes the narrow limits of the neck; it is a shadow that begins its slow and troubled journey down along a swollen esophagus."

Witty observation and artful phrasing are the rule in Calvino's subtly arranged sets and subsets of vignettes; some spark higher than others, but none falls below a certain airy level of intelligence and attentiveness. The world, as it were, is inventoried afresh, by this most generally (and genially) alert of postwar writers. Yet a melancholy, defeated tone seeps through the polish. . . . This collection of animated essays tricked out as a novel has a certain upper limit, too; Mr. Palomar's world offers itself as food for thought too meekly, without fighting back. As in Robert Benchley's old humorous pieces, the bemused hero can meet no worse fate than embarrassment—looking momentarily like a fool. It would be as if Mr. Sammler, in Saul Bellow's novel, were allowed to wander through New York thinking his thoughts and never having to cope with the menacing black pickpocket, the outrageous college radical, the distressingly sexy great-niece, the lethal Israeli son-in-law. Even in Paul Valéry's *Monsier Teste,* a book ***Mr. Palomar*** considerably resembles, there is more sense of activity and contention; M. Teste has had to hack out his clearing for pure intellection with a heroic, ascetic effort, and in the assembled texts he is seen from the outside, by an admiring friend and a loving wife. (pp. 167-68, 171)

Well, Calvino might have argued, the nineteen-eighties are not the eighteen-nineties, when Valéry created M. Teste, "the very demon of possibility." The demon of impossibility has replaced that of possibility. We live now in "the era of great numbers," when humanity "extends in a crowd, leveled but still made up of distinct individualities like the sea of grains of sand that submerges the surface of the world." If one such individuality chooses to pose on the sand and contemplate the waves, little will come of it for good or ill; in society, Mr. Palomar holds his tongue, and in solitude "no longer knows where his self is to be found." Can this diminished person be today's Western European intellectual? Backed off from any doctrinal certainty, concerned with words and signs since things are now properly abandoned to science, mellowed by forty years of affluence and peace, his "patch of uneasiness" affably succumbs to the "dismay of living."

In this book's last chapter, the hero contemplates his own death: "The world can very well do without him, and he can consider himself dead quite serenely, without even altering his habits." The sadness of this modest reflection is deepened by Calvino's own death two months ago, of a stroke, at the age of only sixty-one. Presumably, he had many books still to write and honors still to reap; he had become, with the death (also premature) of Roland Barthes, Europe's leading litterateur. Thoroughly "up" on all the latest devices of thought and style, Calvino nevertheless could immerse himself for years in Italian folktales; for all his love of complication, his work had a timeless lucidity, a unique unclouded climate, like that of a fall afternoon whose coolness is the small price we must pay for its being so sunny and clear. (p. 171)

John Updike, "States of Mind," in The New Yorker, *Vol. LXI, No. 39, November 18, 1985, pp. 167-68, 171-72, 174.*

JAMES GARDNER (essay date 1985)

[An American critic who frequently contributes to Commentary, Art News, *and the* New Criterion, *Gardner praises Calvino's humanity and ingenuity yet assesses the author's work as uneven. While acknowledging dazzling and insightful passages in Calvino's work, Gardner argues that the author never created a work of sustained excellence.]*

An ancient adage counsels us to speak only well of the deceased, and the recent and untimely death of Italo Calvino, at the age of sixty-one, has provoked in almost all quarters a confirmation, if not an escalation, of the enthusiasm that greeted his work for over a generation. It is fitting that Calvino's death should sadden us, because his writings were characterized by a broad humanity, a compelling ingenuity, and above all the constant promise, while he lived, that he might finally consolidate within a single work of art those scattered passages of excellence that are present in all his works.

Since only a very few writers in any generation are treated to the degree of adulation that Calvino enjoys at this moment, it must be the purpose of any critical essay to test whether indeed his virtues reside in those elements of his work that have been praised, whether such praise has been excessive, and, most disturbing of all, whether the universal enthusiasm for Calvino's writing did not in fact undermine his artistic integrity. Such has been the exuberance of the praise with which Calvino's writings have been received that any critic who demurs from total capitulation to this author's mystique, especially in the present circumstance of his death, is likely to seem something of a crank. Perhaps to demur will seem to contravene the fine adage already cited, one can only say that in an ideal world all people would judge things at their proper worth and critics would not be needed, but the truth is that critics have been sent forth into a post-lapsarian world to be always slightly at odds with the prevailing opinion, correcting it when it has gone too far, or when it has not gone far enough, in the way of praise.

It must seem almost inconceivable to anyone acquainted with only the rarefied fictions of ***Cosmicomics*** or the structuralist experimentation of ***The Castle of Crossed Destinies*** that their author could ever have announced, as he did in 1955, that "We are in a state of emergency. Let us not exchange the terror [*terribilità*] of writing for the terror of reality; let us not forget that it is against reality that we must fight, even if we avail ourselves of the weapons of words." How different is even the style of this prose from that measured stasis of Calvino's more recent writing. . . . Is this truly the utterance of a man who in less than a generation would be signing his name to pallid Barthesian essays on Groucho's cigar or Saul Steinberg's pen?

Yet the reputation that Calvino enjoys in this country is founded almost entirely upon these later writings, which might be characterized as "deconstructionist," since their matter seems inextricably involved with the act of reading, and the same currents that have made fashionable the philosophy of Jacques Derrida are largely responsible for causing Calvino to appear as a significant spokesman for a certain way of conceiving the universe. The same people who have found so much to like in his later writings have been slightly embarrassed by what Calvino was doing in the first half of his creative life, since this would seem to be so very much at odds with what he would go on to do as to make it impossible for a proponent of one period to have much use for anyone who favored the other. Indeed, unless a reader had already been tipped off, it is unlikely that he would ever realize that works as disparate as **"La giornata d'uno scrutatore"** and ***Cosmicomics*** could have proceeded from a single imagination, although in fact only two years divide them.

The reason for which the early fiction of Calvino has constituted an embarrassment to many of his admirers on this side of the Atlantic, who came into the act in time to adore only his more recent efforts, is the boldness and obviousness with which these first endeavors pose political and social questions. In these early works the freewheeling imaginativeness that has endeared him to many American readers in recent years is but rarely in evidence. The literary tradition into which Calvino emerged in adulthood, that of Neo-Realism, was one to which he would have been predisposed by inclination as well as by education. His father was active in various anarchist movements early in the century, and in his youth Calvino, by indulging Communist ideas, registered a similar disrelish for the extreme Right that was then in power. But the application of these ideas to his literature was always fairly casual, and his political impulses seem in the main to spring from the implicit but indestructible conviction, which pervades everything he ever wrote, that man is essentially good. Whether he seeks to expose the fatuity of the fascists, as in those early stories in the volume ***L'entrata in guerra,*** or to celebrate that Adamite freedom so dear to the hearts of anarchists and nudists, as in some of the still earlier stories included in ***Difficult Loves,*** or finally to simplify human existence through a poetic system, as in *Invisible Cities* or ***Mr. Palomar,*** Calvino still advocates throughout the profoundly if sometimes disastrously political position that all men are good, and that, left to their own devices, they will band together in choirs of fraternity. (pp. 6-7)

As is evident in the sense of urgency with which they are so often filled, this and other early writings in his Neo-Realist phase reflect the influence of philosophical movements, like existentialism, which were in vogue in the years immediately after the Second World War. But they also presage the more dulcet and graceful tendencies that would evolve only much later in Calvino's career, and which it may be accurate to consider more essentially his own. These proclivities are present in some of his earliest short stories, as in those contained in the two volumes ***Ultimo viene il corvo*** and ***I racconti,*** which were published together in the volume ***Difficult Loves.*** Here he indulges, even if at a humbler level, in those tricks that would later make him famous. One of these is the inverted perspective, whereby he, the author, adopts the point of view of the character who is narrating the tale, even when that viewpoint is diametrically opposed to his own. In **"A Goatherd at Luncheon,"** for instance, Calvino relates an incident that occurs within an affluent and upper-middle-class family, when the overly exuberant father invites a peasant to dine with them. This story is related from the perspective of the younger son of the household, who looks with a mixture of horror and condescending pity upon the downtrodden representative of the lower classes. This tale is surely one of very few in the canon of modern literature in which the story is told entirely from the point of view of the snob, who is made to appear as rational as can be, and who, above all, instinctively assumes that the reader, to whom he is telling the story, could not possibly feel otherwise. Thus the traditional reader of modern fiction, who is most comfortable seeing things from the perspective of the underdog, especially in Neo-Realist fiction, is here co-opted against his will into company in which he feels sure he doesn't belong. Similarly, in **"A Shipload of Crabs,"** we are made to see things from the point of view of very young children, to share in their conflicts, and once again to feel as our own those tribulations which we thought we had overcome when we turned ten. This technique, which approaches stream of consciousness, is present in works as disparate as *The Path of the Nest of Spiders,* his foremost Neo-Realist work, with its adolescent protagonist Pin, and the much more recent ***t zero*** with its postmodern narrator Qfwfq. Calvino has achieved this more through sympathy than through mimicry, for mimicry has never been one of his strong points; and although he is constantly passing judgment, this judgment is always benign. It is perhaps indicative of some secret falling out between Calvino and the Neo-Realists that in his early fiction, especially in the three war stories in the volume ***L'entrata in guerra,*** he is always least effective when relating the incidents of the Second World War. Perhaps this is because he is least likely in this context to practice those tricks in which most of his skill resided from an early age.

[The stories in ***Gli amori difficili*** (1970), which were written between 1949 and 1958 and first published in ***I racconti*** (1958),] are interesting in the history of the oeuvre of Calvino, since they would seem to announce a tendency that became of major importance for him later on. This volume comprises eight tales, and their titles, such as **"The Adventure of a Poet"** and **"The Adventure of a Clerk,"** have a decidedly Chaucerian ring to them. Indeed, they are even narrated in that deadpan poker-faced tone, at once familiar and distant, that Boccaccio introduced into Italian literature. It is in these works that we see the origins of an interest that would later induce Calvino, in the mid-Fifties, to take on the task of editing and rephrasing two hundred Italian fables, as well as paraphrasing Ariosto's *Orlando Furioso.* This fabulistic tendency is present in many of the later works, like ***The Castle of Crossed Destinies,*** and especially in the three imaginative works from the 1950s that have been published together in Italy under the title ***I nostri antenati,*** and that have been translated into English as ***The Baron in the Trees, The Cloven Viscount,*** and ***The Nonexistent Knight.*** What links all these works, and constitutes an implicit attack upon the aesthetic of Neo-Realism, is the fact that they all take place in the past, in the eighth, seventeenth, and eighteenth centuries, and in a context not of the lower and middle classes but rather of the feudal aristocracy, who are as remote as could be from adolescent heroes like Pin. Furthermore, the heroes are the recipients of a curious and even supernatural destiny, by which their lives are irreversibly altered. (pp. 7-8)

These three works struck their first critics as signaling a decidedly radical departure from the style of writing that one had come to associate with Calvino, and it was easy to believe, with the publication of such sturdily Neo-Realist works as ***La Nuvola di Smog*** and ***La Formica Argentina,*** both from 1958, and **"La giornata d'uno scrutatore"** and **"La speculazione edilizia,"** both from 1963, that those three earlier works had been merely an aberration which might yet be accommodated within a larger and more traditional context. But in fact, as is now well known, the three novels comprised in ***I nostri antenati*** are really presentiments, if not fulfillments, of a tendency which would become more and more dominant in Calvino's writing as the years went on, and which, as we have seen, had its origins in his very earliest short stories.

As has already been suggested, it is the growing interest in science which informs the shorter fiction in ***Cosmicomics*** and ***t zero,*** although these works are in effect the translation into a more exotic vocabulary of the earlier Neo-Realist short stories which Calvino had written in the Forties. They express the same very human longings and frustrations that were found in the early fiction, and the title under which these earlier works were collected, ***Difficult Loves,*** would serve to describe them as well.

Despite the presence in ***Cosmicomics*** and ***t zero*** of a profusion of scientific references, and chic effusions in the manner of Barthes and Derrida, Calvino was really an unsystematic thinker at best, and he has used these borrowings most effectively where they serve only to underscore or to enhance the emotional content that was equally present, if in another form, in his Neo-Realist works. Calvino was by nature a timid and introspective intelligence. For many years he served in the capacity of editor at the important Italian publishing firm of Einaudi in Turin, and this fact, combined with his native, if desultory, inquisitiveness, brought him into contact with works on many different subjects. But as far as can be deduced from his fiction and his occasional forays into expository prose, neither his knowledge nor his thought was ever especially profound or brilliant, although they often provided the context and the form for a sensibility that could go quite deep. With respect to his scientific and structuralist modes, Calvino is closer to a florist than to a botanist. Where the botanist perceives an indissoluble unity within a single organism, all of whose parts, from the deepest roots to the topmost petals, are involved in a relentless process of reciprocal and dynamic engendering and necessitation, the florist can perceive only the prettiness of the flowers, which strike him as an accomplished and disembodied fact. Calvino's knowledge of the sciences is characterized in the highest degree by superficiality, which it is important to bear in mind, considering that many people place him on a higher level of scientific sophistication. He has merely applied to a modern context (though one that even now is becoming slightly dated) the imaginative exorbitancies of older poets like Boiardo and Ariosto, whose *Orlando Furioso,* as we have seen, he prepared in an updated version for Einaudi. What the world looked like before the advent of color, or what the fish were thinking as they began their trek onto the dry land upon which they would become in due course lizards and birds, are the sort of questions that poets rather than scientists ask. Nor is this merely to chastise Calvino for not being more of a scientist, or for being in fact a pseudo-scientist. It is to insist that the mystique and vogue that this pseudo-methodology takes should not be allowed, as they usually are, to enter into our assessment of his literary worth. Calvino is never especially good at considering a scientific fact in its natural context; he is able to appreciate it only in its phenomenal nakedness. (p. 9)

In his earlier scientific fiction (for it is not "science fiction") he was content merely to stand the reality of science on its head, cooking up an engagingly imbecile story-line around the colorful facts that he had at his disposal. But in one of his most recent books, and the one most recently translated into English, ***Mr. Palomar,*** he has rejected the principles of causation altogether. He has done this by cataloguing the naked facts of reality, rather than forcing them into a relationship like that of cause and effect, in which facts lose their individuality and autonomy, by being perceived as only parts in a new and larger whole. And in this as well Calvino shows the influence of recent philosophers, like Jacques Derrida, who have criticized the traditional paradigms of science, and have sought to go "beyond" cause and effect, by creating "texts" that subsist under a category of mind different from that of traditional Western science. This is surely the reason for which a novel like ***Mr. Palomar*** seems so fiercely contemporary, and one of the reasons for which it will probably come in a very short while to seem very dated indeed. Quite aside from the narrative peculiarities of this work, which will be considered below, it is characterized by an obsessive cataloguing of the reality that surrounds the narrator, who, as almost all critics have recognized, is largely a projection of the author himself. (p. 10)

But if Calvino does not show much interest beyond a very superficial one in the explicatory powers of the scientific or historical method, he shows scarcely greater interest in the rigorous method of those philosophers who influenced his writings, especially in later years. In his writings from the late Sixties and the early Seventies one finds the influence of thinkers like Barthes and the theoreticians of the Nouveau Roman, and thereafter he becomes interested in, or at least breathes the same spirit as, Jacques Derrida and the Tel Quel writers. And yet, he seems only to share in their spirit in a very casual way, and it is difficult to imagine Calvino sitting down with the texts of Barthes's more scientific inquiries into the nature of narrative, or with Derrida's impenetrable *De la grammatologie.*

It is perhaps safest to say that Calvino is very much inspired with the *Zeitgeist,* although it must be stated in his behalf that he did much to form it into its present shape. Whether he is the cause or the effect of certain of those tendencies with which he is associated is a question that is outside of the scope of the present essay, although it is my suspicion that the form itself that Calvino's writing and his thoughts took, especially most recently, will be found to have a Frenchman behind every one. But Calvino had neither the inclination nor the cast of mind truly and thoroughly to assimilate these foreign importations, any more than he had the diligence to acquire the basic principles of the scientific method. They are present merely as ornaments that decorate his native inclinations, or as vaguely construed ideas that inspire him to attempt bold literary experiments which really have little to do with what had been intended by the originators of those systems. Calvino stands to the French in something of the same relationship in which a provincial painter stands to the great masters in the academies of the capital. He is able to reproduce with a certain skill, in his case quite an admirable skill, the suavities and urbanities of the prime movers, but there is always present in his work the sense that foreign forms and manners have been allowed merely to impose themselves, like ornaments, upon a deeper and eccentric structure that really has very little to do with these decorations, and is in fact unaltered by them.

The tone of the scientific writings of the Sixties was not only very human but also touched with that gentle good humor which Calvino revealed so often and so refreshingly throughout his career. But in more recent works, which were inspired by the French and which might be considered scientific or at least "methodological" in the rigor with which they unfold, this characteristic humor is lacking and we are faced with that dour sobriety that had not been seen since **"La speculazione edilizia"** and **"La giornata d'uno scrutatore"** a decade earlier. It is not unworthy of consideration that perhaps these late works, which have been held up often enough as paragons of inventiveness and zestful caprice, are in fact the results of a partial and momentary exhaustion which manifested itself in their mirthlessness. . . . [***The Castle of Crossed Destinies***] is a boring application to the short story of the narrative principles which the structuralists would have us believe to inhere in some important sense in a pack of tarot cards. By drawing from the deck, Calvino explains in a pedantic epilogue, he was provided with the general outlines for the plots. If these stories were successful, and I do not feel that they were, they would be so for a few beautiful descriptions or for a dramatic scene for which the tarot had provided the context—in other words, for reasons entirely different from those of narrative technique, which are ostensibly the innovations that made the work sell to those more avant-garde readers who mistook and still mistake novelty for consequence. (pp. 11-12)

[There] are certainly beautiful passages in ***The Castle of Crossed Destinies*** and *Invisible Cities,* but they are insufficient to repay the tedium generated by the rest.

We should be thankful, then, that in his two final works of fiction, *If on a Winter's Night a Traveler* and ***Mr. Palomar,*** although Calvino was inspired ostensibly by post-structuralist principles not unlike those of the two works that preceded them, still, he has leavened these last two books, especially the earlier one, with a genuine and pungent sense of humor. . . . The system of ***Mr. Palomar*** is divided into three sections, each with three chapters, each of which in its turn has three sub-chapters marked 1, 2, and 3. These latter chapters are supposed to correspond (they "tend" to correspond, to use Calvino's revealing expression of methodological laxness) to sensory experience in the first part, linguistic data in the second, and speculative questions in the third. It is obvious that in order to achieve this clear schema, Calvino has almost surely had either to eliminate material that simply would have run over, or to include superfluous material merely to fill in the holes in the grid. But in addition to composing some attractive prose passages, he has managed to create an appealing and pitiable personality in the eponymous hero, and, insofar as novel writing concerns the creation of memorable personalities, Calvino has at least that much of traditional achievement. It is also worth remarking that in the hierarchy implied in the ordering of 1, 2, and 3 he seems to have placed spiritual and religious questions above those of language and structure. Is this not the earliest, the truest Calvino emerging once again? In certain circles of his admirers, this fact, if it were ever to be fully appreciated, would have to be understood as a kind of apostasy.

Although the quality of Calvino's output varies considerably, he is never conspicuously bad, just as he is never truly great. That he is never conspicuously bad is, of course, only of biographical interest; in an assessment of a man's creativity, it is the possibility of excellence that alone commands our attention, and in application to Calvino the consequences of such an examination may be very sad indeed. For it is by no means impossible that Calvino might have become a much finer novelist than he turned out to be, if he had ever managed to combine in a single work the inventiveness of *If on a Winter's Night a Traveler* with the poetic beauty of *Invisible Cities* and the warmth of the earliest stories in ***Difficult Loves. The Baron in the Trees*** comes closer to this imaginary novel than does any of Calvino's other works, but still it is not a great novel, and even if it were, this fact probably would not justify the praise almost universally paid to Calvino's entire output. If the reception that Calvino received had been a bit more critical perhaps he might have gone on to create a work of such sustained excellence. But he did not achieve this, and since, in a sense, he could not help responding, especially later on, to the applause that he was receiving from all sides, and since he might have been tempted by this enthusiasm to provide his glamorous public with exactly what it wanted, in order to win still more applause, is it not possible that that adoring and insincere public has participated in neutralizing a great talent? We have seen this before and we will see it again. Surely this is one of those occasions Eliot had in mind when, as he lamented, "fools' approval stings and honor stains"! (pp. 12-13)

James Gardner, "Italo Calvino 1923-1985," in The New Criterion, *Vol. IV, No. 4, December, 1985, pp. 6-13.*

CYNTHIA OZICK (essay date 1988)

[*Ozick is considered a leading contemporary American novelist, short story writer, essayist, and critic. In the review of* Under the Jaguar Sun, *excerpted below, Ozick discusses the three tales in this collection in the context of Calvino's statement that each of the tales corresponds to one of the human senses.*]

Before his death in 1985, Italo Calvino undertook to write five stories on the five senses. He completed three—on the powers of tongue, ear, nostrils—gathered here in a nervous, narrow, grandly unsettling volume; a cerebral accident swept him away before he could arrive at the fingertips and the eye.

The trio of tales in ***Under the Jaguar Sun*** is not "experimental." Calvino, an authentic post-modernist (despite the clamor, there are not so many of these), does not experiment; the self-conscious post-modernist is also a devil-may-care post-experimenter. No one has understood the gleeful and raucous fix, or tragedy, of the latter-day artist more penetratingly than Italo Calvino. The writer's quest has traditionally been to figure out the right human questions to ask, and if we still love the novels of, say, George Eliot, it is because we are nostalgic for the sobriety of a time when the right questions could be divined. In the disorderly aftermath of Joyce, Kafka, S. Y. Agnon, Borges, all the questions appear to be used up, repetitive, irrelevant; and their answers—which only recently *did* take on experimental form—have been marred by struggle, stoicism and a studied "playfulness" more plucky than antic. After Kafka, after Borges, what is there to do but mope?

Calvino sets aside both questions and answers for the sake of brilliant clues and riddling intuitions. He gives up narrative destination for destiny, clarification for clairvoyance. He invents a new laughter suitable to the contemporary disbelief in story. In short, Calvino readdresses—and magisterially reenters—the idea of myth, of the tale. . . . A learned, daring, ingeniously gifted magus, Calvino in our own time has turned himself into the Italian Grimm: his ***Italian Folktales,*** a masterwork of culling and retelling, is devoted precisely to the lure of the primordial magma—myth spawned by the body of the organic and inorganic world.

The three tales of ***Under the Jaguar Sun*** are, accordingly, engendered by the human nervous system—the body as a cornucopia of sensation, or as an echoing palace with manifold windows, each a shifting kaleidoscope. The modernists have already hinted at how the fundamental story-clay, the myth-magma, can spring from taste (remember Proust's madeleine) or smell (Mann's diseased Venice) or sound (Forster's *ouboum* in the Marabar Caves). Yet these merely metaphorical resonances will not content Calvino. He slides back behind them to the primary ground of perception: ganglia and synapse. He fuses fable with neuron. By driving story right down to its biological root, to cell and stimulus, he nearly annihilates metaphor. Calvino's post-modernism is a literalism so absolute that it transports myth to its organic source, confining story to limits of the mouth, the ear, the nose.

But what seems to be confinement and limitation—the mouth, after all, is only a little chamber—widens to rite and mystery. [**"Under the Jaquar Sun"**] opens with a scrupulous recounting of Mexican cuisine (the reader is likely to salivate), and winds up in a dazzlement of wit and horror. The narrator and Olivia, a tourist couple who are vaguely estranged, are in Mexico on a holiday. They are diligent about seeing the sights and obsessive about trying every exotic dish. The husband is somewhat apathetic ("insipid," Olivia calls him, as if he needed seasoning) while Olivia is intense, inquisitive, perilously inspired. Her passion for food is sacerdotal, almost creedal. . . .

Husband and wife investigate the "gastronomic lexicon" of various localities, including *chiles en nogada,* "wrinkled little peppers, swimming in a walnut sauce whose harshness and bitter aftertaste were drowned in a creamy, sweetish surrender," and *gorditas pellizcadas con manteca,* "plump girls pinched with butter." The very name of the latter returns them to their hotel room in a rare state of sexual arousal. And meanwhile their days are given over to exploring the ruins of ancient Aztec and Olmec civilizations—temples where human sacrifice was practiced, with the complicity of willing victims, by priests who afterward consumed a certain "ritual meal." Olivia presses their guide to speculate on the possible flavors of that unspecified dish; following which, during a supper of shrimp soup and goat kid, the husband fantasizes that

> "I could feel her tongue lift me against the roof of her mouth, enfold me in saliva, then thrust me under the tips of the canines. . . . The situation was not entirely passive, since while I was being chewed by her I felt also that I was acting on her, transmitting sensations that spread from the taste buds through her whole body."

Without such reciprocity, "human sacrifice would be unthinkable."

Of course this is also a comic immersion in the psychology of that "universal cannibalism," as the well-chewed narrator terms it, that "erases the lines between our bodies and . . . *enchiladas.*" And incidentally makes marriages work.

If the mouth can both smile and devour, the ear is all petrified anxiety. To listen acutely is to be powerless, even if you sit on a throne. In **"A King Listens"**—the crown of this extraordinary collection—the suspected eavesdropping of spies, unidentifiable movements and whispers, signals of usurpation, mysterious knockings, the very noise of the universe, imply terror and imprisonment. The ear turns out to be the most imagining organ, because it is the most accomplished at deciphering; still, on its own, it cannot be confident of any one interpretation and wheels frenetically from conjecture to conjecture. In the end, the monarch around whom the life of the palace stirs does not know whether he is a king or a caged prisoner in the palace's secret dungeon. . . .

The last and shortest tale—**"The Name, the Nose"**—is not a success, though here as in the others the brilliance of language never falters. Calvino's aim is to juxtapose the primitive and the rococo, the coarse and the highly mannered, in order to reveal their congenital olfactory unity. . . . In brief, the nose, no matter who is wearing it, is an aboriginal hunter. It is all too artful, too archetypal, too anthropological—and especially too programmed and thematic. No use sniffing here after the primeval mythos. The sophisticated aroma is of Calvino, writing.

James Whistler—acclaimed a master painter in his own time, if not in ours—once declared that "the master stands in no relation to the moment at which he occurs." Possibly. But it is also a sign of the masterly imagination that it will respond lavishly to the moment's appetite—and appetite is elemental, the opposite of fashion. Calvino occurring in any span of decades other than those vouchsafed him is inconceivable. He was meant to flourish on the heels of Kafka.

Cynthia Ozick, "Mouth, Ear, Nose," in The New York Times Book Review, *October 23, 1988, p. 7.*

ADDITIONAL BIBLIOGRAPHY

Adler, Sara Maria. *Calvino: The Writer as Fablemaker.* Potomac: Jose Porrúa Turanzas, 1979, 171 p.

Traces the evolution of Calvino's fiction from several different critical perspectives.

Andrews, Richard. "Italo Calvino." In *Writers & Society in Contemporary Italy,* edited by Michael Caesar and Peter Hainsworth, pp. 259-81. Warwickshire: Berg Publishers Ltd., 1984.

Provides an overview of Calvino's career with a particular emphasis on the author's approach to problems concerning language and communication and the significance of his self-reflexive techniques.

Atwood, Margaret. "The Sorcerer as Apprentice." *The New York Times Book Review* (7 October 1984): 13.

Offers a positive review of the stories collected in *Difficult Loves.*

Bocelli, Arnoldo. "The Double Storyteller." *Atlas: The Magazine of the World Press* 12, No. 1 (July 1966): 62-3.

Discusses what Italian critics have called the "crisis" in Calvino's writing—his alternating production of works of realism and fantasy—and argues that these modes complement one another. The critic also presents an enthusiastic review of *Cosmicomics.*

Broyard, Anatole. "Qfwfq through the Ages." *The New York Times Book Review* (25 August 1969): 4.

Positive review of *Cosmicomics* that compares Calvino's work with that of Jorge Luis Borges, Samuel Beckett, and Franz Kafka.

Cannon, JoAnn. *Italo Calvino: Writer and Critic.* Ravenna: Longo, 1981, 115 p.

Collects Cannon's numerous essays published in journals on individual works and the various phases of Calvino's career.

———. "Calvino's Latest Challenge to the Labyrinth: A Reading of *Palomar.*" *Italica* 62, No. 3 (1985), pp. 189-200.

Offers an in-depth analysis of *Mr. Palomar* and assesses its place in Calvino's canon.

Carter, Albert Howard, III. *Italo Calvino: Metamorphoses of Fantasy.* Ann Arbor, Mich.: UMI Research Press, 1987, 182 p.

Explores the many implications suggested in Calvino's fantasy tales, concentrating on the author's penchant for dramatizing metaphysical problems.

De Lauretis, Teresa. "Narrative Discourse in Calvino: Praxis or Poesis?" *PMLA* 90, No. 3 (May 1975): 414-25.

Applies various elements of semiotic theory to Calvino's fiction.

Friedman, Sorel Thompson. "*t zero:* Italo Calvino's Minimalist Narratives." *The Review of Contemporary Fiction* 6, No. 2 (Summer 1986): 19-23.

Discusses three stories—"t zero," "The Chase," and "The Night Driver"—as minimalist works that examine the storytelling process.

Gardner, John. "For All Who Like Stories." *The New York Times Book Review* (12 October 1980): 1; 40-1.

Discusses Calvino's renderings of Italian folktales, comparing them with fables from Germany, the Orient, Africa, and the Middle East. Gardner concludes that "Calvino's collection stands with the best folktale collections anywhere."

Gatt-Rutter, John. "Calvino Ludens: Literary Play and Its Political Implications." *Journal of European Studies* 5, No. 4 (December 1975): 319-40.

Examines Calvino's playful experimentation with the conventions of literature, concluding that Calvino's best works are those in which he emphasizes political and human issues over stylistic concerns.

Hannay, John. "Description as Science and Art: Calvino's Narrative of Observation." *Mosaic: A Journal for the Interdisciplinary Study of Literature* XXI, No. 4 (Fall 1988): 73-86.

Focuses on *Mr. Palomar.* Hannay discusses Calvino's evolution from scientific description in *Cosmicomics* and *t zero* to a "narrative of observation" in *Mr. Palomar.*

Heiney, Donald. "Calvino and Borges: Some Implications of Fantasy." *Mundus Artium* II, No. 2 (Winter 1968): 67-76.

Compares the methods and concerns in the fabulous narratives of Calvino and Borges.

———. "Calvinisimo." *Iowa Review* 2, No. 4 (Fall 1971): 80-8.

Places Calvino within a modern tradition of writers who use myth and metaphysical speculation to interpret and make meaning of existence.

Hume, Kathryn. "Science and Imagination in Calvino's *Cosmicomics.*" *Mosaic* XV, No. 4 (December 1982): 47-58.

Argues against categorizing *Cosmicomics* as science fiction, contending that the stories significantly challenge the role of science in the modern world as the primary means for interpreting the phenomenal world.

Lucente, Gregory. "Self-Conscious Artifacts: Calvino's Fictions." In his *Beautiful Fables: Self-Consciousness in Italian Narrative from Manzoni to Calvino,* pp. 266-300. Baltimore: The Johns Hopkins University Press, 1986.

Focuses on the significance of Calvino's self-reflexive techniques in two novels and in the stories of *Cosmicomics.*

MacShane, Frank. "The Fantasy World of Italo Calvino." *The New York Times Magazine* (30 July 1983): 22-3, 33, 41, 43, 48-50.

Feature article that offers biographical and critical commentary.

Markey, Constance. "Calvino and the Existential Dilemma: The Paradox of Choice." *Italica* 60, No. 1 (Spring 1983): 55-70.

Concentrates on the dilemma faced by many Calvino characters of having to make significant choices and decisions while confronted by the unpredictable, random, and illusory nature of reality. The critic focuses on *The Castle of Crossed Destinies* and the Trilogy.

Mathews, Harry. "La Camera Ardente." *The Review of Contemporary Fiction* 6, No. 2 (Summer 1986): 7-10.

Personal and critical tribute to Calvino upon his death.

Migiel, Marilyn. "The Phantasm of Omnipotence in Calvino's Trilogy." *Modern Language Studies* XVI, No. 3 (Summer 1986): 57-68.

Addresses Calvino's thematic focus on the problems of identity as developed in the Trilogy, paying particular attention to the connections in these stories between imagery relating to food and eating and the struggles of characters to assert individual identity.

Olken, I. T. *With Pleated Eye and Garnet Wing: Symmetries of Italo Calvino.* Ann Arbor: The University of Michigan Press, 157 p.

Extensive study of recurring patterns, or "symmetries," that inform Calvino's narratives.

Ragusa, Olga. "Italo Calvino: The Repeated Conquest of Contemporaneity." *World Literature Today* 57, No. 2 (Spring 1983): 195-201.

Sweeping overview of Calvino's *ouvre,* concentrating on the author's proclivity for creating original new forms and structures with each succeeding work.

Ricci, Franco. "The Recovery of Mnemonic Meaning in *L'etrata in guerra.*" *Review of Contemporary Fiction* 6, No. 2 (Summer 1986): 31-7.

Discusses the importance of ratiocination and introspection in three long stories, "L'entrata in guerra," "Gli avangaurdisti a Mentone," and "Le notte dell'UNPA," where characters recall and find meaning in significant incidents of their wartime experiences.

Stille, Alexander. "Reading Backward." *The Nation* 239, No. 22 (29 December 1984 and 5 January 1985): 718-19.

Reviews the stories published in *Difficult Loves* and addresses the likely sense of surprise among American readers familiar only with the translations of Calvino's fantasy works.

———. "An Interview with Italo Calvino." *Saturday Review* 11, No. 2 (March-April 1985): 36-9.

Illuminating interview in which Calvino discusses the relationship between his life and work.

Updike, John. "Card Tricks" and *"Fiabe Italiane." Hugging the Shore: Essays and Criticism.* New York: Vintage Books, 1984, pp. 463-71 and 655-62.

In-depth reviews of *The Castle of Crossed Destinies* and *Italian Folktales.*

Vidal, Gore. "Calvino's Novels." In his *Matters of Fact and of Fiction,* pp. 39-60. New York: Random House, 1978.

Enthusiastic overview of Calvino's fiction by one of the author's greatest admirers.

———. "On Italo Calvino." *New York Review of Books* XXXII, 18 (21 November 1985): 3, 6-10.

Tribute written upon Calvino's death, blending personal reminiscence and commentary on *Mr. Palomar.*

Vlasopolos, Anca. "Love and the Two Discourses in *Le cosmicomiche.*" *Stanford Italian Review* IV, No. 1 (Spring 1984): 123-35.

Analysis of *Cosmicomics* based on the development of themes relating to love within the individual stories.

Wood, Michael. "On the Edge of Silence." *The New Republic* 199, No. 16 (17 October 1988): 38-43.

Review of *Under the Jaguar Sun* in relation to the aesthetics Calvino promotes in his critical work, *Six Memos for the Next Millennium.*

Woodhouse, J. R. "Italo Calvino and the Rediscovery of a Genre." *Italian Quarterly* 12, No. 45 (Summer 1968): 45-66.

Addresses negative commentary concerning Calvino's shift from neorealism to fantasy. Woodhouse contends that Calvino's incisive cultural commentary is more effective when presented in the more entertaining and accessible mode of fantasy.

Arthur C(harles) Clarke

1917-

(Also wrote under the pseudonyms E. G. O'Brien and Charles Willis) English short story writer, novelist, essayist, and nonfiction writer.

Best known in connection with the film *2001: A Space Odyssey,* Clarke is the author of numerous novels and short stories that are considered classics of science fiction. In works informed by his extensive background in physics and mathematics, he has explored such themes as the implications and consequences of proof that intelligent life exists elsewhere in the universe and the possibility of contact between human and extraterrestrial beings. Supporting the speculative nature of Clarke's fiction is his meticulous attention to technological verisimilitude. "I'm a hard-core science fiction writer," Clarke has stated. "I have seldom written anything that I thought could not happen."

Clarke was born into a farming family in Minehead, Somerset. After attending a local primary school, he was sent at age nine to Huish's Grammar School in Taunton, where he excelled in science courses and contributed short stories to the school magazine. From his youth Clarke recalled being "under the spell of the old science-fiction pulps" and enthralled by the speculative fiction of Olaf Stapledon, whose works were among the first to undertake millenarian themes and to portray human evolution on a cosmic scale. Some of Clarke's earliest fiction, written as a teenager, reveals his fascination with scientific themes. After graduating in 1936, Clarke entered the civil service and moved to London. There he joined the recently formed British Interplanetary Society, a small group exploring the feasibility of space travel, and became active in science fiction circles. In the late 1930s, he began publishing science fiction stories and nonfiction articles in a British fan magazine that he helped to edit; his short stories began appearing in professional publications in the 1940s.

Clarke served in the Royal Air Force during World War II. Poor eyesight kept him from flight missions, and he was assigned to the top-secret field of radar research. In 1945, he published an article in a technical journal suggesting that satellite relays could provide simultaneous global communications. Although the idea was considered improbable at the time, such systems are now in place, and Clarke has been acknowledged as the originator of the concept. After the war, a veterans' grant enabled Clarke to enter King's College, London, where he completed a degree in mathematics and physics in 1948. He abandoned studies toward a second degree, in astronomy, to work as an assistant editor of a scientific journal. When his income as a writer exceeded his salary, he left this post to devote his full attention to a literary career. Clarke's nonfiction study *Interplanetary Flight: An Introduction to Astronautics* was published in 1950, and his novel *Prelude to Space* appeared the following year. His first short story collection, *Expedition to Earth,* was published in 1953. In 1956 Clarke moved to Ceylon, now Sri Lanka, and his residence on the island led to an avocational interest in skin diving, which inspired him to write numerous studies of underwater exploration and marine life, as well as novels and short stories of marine adventure.

During the 1960s, filmmaker Stanley Kubrick sought Clarke's assistance in making what he intended to be the ultimate science fiction film. Their work was largely based on Clarke's short story "The Sentinel," in which an artifact found on the moon is discovered to be a signaling device that informs its creators that earth's inhabitants have begun to venture into space. Clarke and Kubrick combined this story with newly written material and with elements of several other stories by Clarke, including "First Encounter," "Gift from the Stars," "Farewell to Earth," and "Moon-Watcher," and created the script for *2001: A Space Odyssey* (1968), which is considered one of the best science fiction films ever made. Clarke's novel of the same title, written simultaneously with the screenplay, also appeared in 1968. Both the film and book offer engaging and enigmatic exploration of the themes of alien intelligence and the possibility of further human evolution. Since the 1970s, Clarke has written primarily novels. Critics maintain that study of his short stories reveals the development of themes and ideas that are more fully expressed in the longer works.

While Clarke's science fiction, in the tradition of H. G. Wells, frequently treats themes of planetary destruction and racial extinction, it is often marked by an optimistic belief that humanity will survive, and perhaps advance, as a result of its facility with technology. In the stories "Transience" and "Rescue Party," for example, earth faces destruction by an impending natural disaster, but speedily constructed spaceships capable of traveling to other solar systems insure the survival of the species. Similarly, in " 'If I Forget Thee, O Earth,' " the planet is rendered uninhabitable by nuclear holocaust, but lunar colonists represent hope for the future of the race. The stories collected in *Tales from the White Hart,* including "Big Game Hunt," "What Goes Up," and "The Ultimate Melody," address a common concern of the 1950s: that science and technology were advancing beyond the capabilities of humankind to control or comprehend. Humorously intended, many of these tales feature amateur scientists who are blown up by their inventions or destroyed by the natural forces that they sought to master. Clarke, however, introduced a characteristically optimistic element. According to John Hollow, Clarke countered the possibility "that the human race may self-destruct" with the equal likelihood "that reason will prevail, that humans may use their science to help them escape from the prison of this single world." A common criticism of Clarke's science-oriented stories is that characterization is consistently subordinated to the depiction of technology; this negative assessment recurs throughout commentary on his work.

Clarke wrote extensively about actual or impending first contact between humans and aliens, particularly in his novels *Childhood's End* and *2001: A Space Odyssey,* which are widely considered among the finest works exploiting this theme. His short fiction recounts this momentous meeting in various ways. In "Encounter in the Dawn," for example, an alien astronaut whose own race faces extinction gives tools and artifacts to a prehistoric human. In "Meeting with Medusa," a cyborg—a human with a partly robotic body (representing, perhaps, the next stage of human evolution)—discovers gigantic life forms in the upper atmosphere of Jupiter. In "Loophole" and "Guardian Angel," aliens arrive on earth just as human meddling with imperfectly understood forces threatens global existence. The aliens share their advanced technology, imposing the condition that the troublesome human race be denied space travel, but in both stories humankind manages to circumvent this restriction. Some commentators have noted that many of these stories seem to exhibit a negative view of human nature, as Clarke's human characters are often indefensibly pugnacious toward even well-meaning aliens. In one story, for example, visiting aliens are massacred by a terrified mob that has just seen a science fiction movie. Clarke has also been charged with anthropocentrism for failing to present an alien culture, however advanced, that cannot be outwitted by humans. Other critics, however, commend Clarke's affirmation of the inventiveness and endless adaptability of humankind.

Clarke combined science fiction and religious themes in several stories, including "The Star," winner of the 1956 Hugo award and one of the most widely reprinted science fiction stories of all time. Its central character, a Jesuit priest and astrophysicist, is devastated to learn that the Star of Bethlehem was a supernova that destroyed a peaceful, advanced culture on a distant planet. "The Star," too, has been faulted for anthropocentrism: commentators have suggested that by portraying an alien culture that appeals to human values, Clarke avoided the issue of whether the destruction of a repulsive or an incomprehensible alien culture would elicit the same emotional response from the protagonist. "The Nine Billion Names of God" similarly combines an apocalyptic theme with elements of religion and with Clarke's sometimes sardonic humor. In this story, Buddhist monks employ a computer to list all the combinations of a set of mystic symbols, thereby fulfilling the purpose of the universe and bringing about its end. Hollow has noted that "the story mocks . . . the human assumption that we are the center of the cosmos," while suggesting that humankind and its works may represent a stage in the divine plan that governs the universe.

In reviewing Clarke's 1958 collection *The Other Side of the Sky,* H. H. Holmes commended the volume as "calculated to lift science fiction out of the ghetto of specialists and introduce its delights to the general reader." As the genre has developed and has inspired increasingly sophisticated criticism, Clarke's works have been the subject of more analytical study. Both his short stories and novels continue to be praised for their characteristic attention to detail and insistence upon scientific accuracy, as well as for offering entertaining and often thought-provoking glimpses of possible futures.

(See also *Contemporary Literary Criticism,* Vols. 1, 4, 13, 18, 35; *Contemporary Authors,* Vols. 1-4; *Contemporary Authors New Revision Series,* Vol. 2; and *Something about the Author,* Vol. 13.)

PRINCIPAL WORKS

SHORT FICTION

Expedition to Earth 1953
Reach for Tomorrow 1956
Tales from the White Hart 1957
The Other Side of the Sky 1958
Across the Sea of Stars (novels and short stories) 1959
From the Ocean, from the Stars (novels and short stories) 1962
Tales of Ten Worlds 1962
Prelude to Mars (novels and short stories) 1965
The Nine Billion Names of God: The Best Short Stories of Arthur C. Clarke 1967
Of Time and the Stars: The Worlds of Arthur C. Clarke 1972
The Wind from the Sun: Stories of the Space Age 1972
The Best of Arthur C. Clarke: 1937-1971. 2 vols. 1973

OTHER MAJOR WORKS

Interplanetary Flight: An Introduction to Astronautics (nonfiction and essays) 1950; rev. ed., 1960
The Exploration of Space (nonfiction and essays) 1951, rev. ed., 1959
Prelude to Space (novel) 1951; also published as *Master of Space,* 1961, and *The Space Dreamers,* 1969
The Sands of Mars (novel) 1951
Islands in the Sky (novel) 1952
Against the Fall of Night (novel) 1953; revised and expanded as *The City and the Stars,* 1956
Childhood's End (novel) 1953
Earthlight (novel) 1954
The Coast of Coral (nonfiction) 1956
The Deep Range (novel) 1957
The Reefs of Taprobane: Underwater Adventures around Ceylon (nonfiction) 1957

The Challenge of the Spaceship: Previews of Tomorrow's World (nonfiction and essays) 1959
The Challenge of the Sea (nonfiction and essays) 1960
A Fall of Moondust (novel) 1961
Profiles of the Future: An Inquiry into the Limits of the Possible (nonfiction and essays) 1962; rev. ed., 1973
Dolphin Island: A Story of the People of the Sea (novel) 1963
An Arthur Clarke Omnibus (novels) 1965
Time Probe: The Sciences in Science Fiction [editor] (short stories) 1966
An Arthur Clarke Second Omnibus (novels) 1968
2001: A Space Odyssey (novel) 1968
The Lost Worlds of 2001 (fiction and diary entries) 1972
Report on Planet Three and Other Speculations (essays) 1972
Rendezvous with Rama (novel) 1973
Imperial Earth: A Fantasy of Love and Discord (novel) 1976; revised and expanded as *Imperial Earth,* 1976
The View from Serendip (memoirs) 1977
The Fountains of Paradise (novel) 1979
2010: Odyssey Two (novel) 1982
1984: Spring; A Choice of Futures (essays, journalism, and speeches) 1984

PETER J. HENNIKER-HEATON (essay date 1953)

[In the following excerpt, the critic commends the stories in Expedition to Earth *as exemplary "space fiction," the literature of the coming Space Age.]*

How soon men will land on the moon and planets leaves room for difference of opinion. That men will do so within a foreseeable period seems beyond reasonable doubt. The Space Age is upon humanity, if indeed it has not already arrived. In the Space Age literature will have its place, and well-informed readers will naturally wish to be acquainted with such literature and to be able to assess it.

Though the Space Age may still be round the corner, space literature in its embryo form is already here. Space literature includes space fiction, space fantasy, and space poetry, with many intermediate forms. It does not, strictly speaking, include textbooks, which can only be profitably read by technical experts. Nevertheless, for the intelligent appreciation of space literature the reader requires some general idea of the various lines, the probabilities and possibilities of space-travel, along which current natural scientific thought is advancing. . . .

[***Expedition to Earth*** is] genuine space fiction, in which the probabilities of natural science are respected, rather than space fantasy, in which imagination is given free play. Arthur C. Clarke, chairman of the British Interplanetary Society, is a spaceman of integrity and learning. . . .

Expedition to Earth consists of eleven short and short-long stories. Most of them, as the title indicates, deal with visitations from space to Earth. Sometimes these are in the far past, sometimes in the far future, sometimes nearer at hand. One of the jolts is the somewhat horrific beginning of the first story; but as one reads on, one sees that even this has a legitimate purpose. Among the best of the stories are **"The Sentinel," "History Lesson"** with its surprise ending, and **"Hide and Seek."**

This is no book for escapists. Many of the stories contain a sharp warning for the present day. **" 'If I Forget Thee, O Earth' "** represents an Earth-colony on another planet waiting longingly to return to its mother-planet, waiting till the devastated Earth is cleared of the radio-active poisons unleashed by chemical warfare, waiting not for months or years but for generations. So far as I am aware, no anthology of space poetry has yet been collected, but this short story of Mr. Clarke's reaches the high point of tenderness and feeling in space prose. He has written nothing better.

Peter J. Henniker-Heaton, "From Star to Star," in The Christian Science Monitor, *December 24, 1953, p. 13.*

BASIL DAVENPORT (essay date 1956)

[Davenport is an American critic and editor who has compiled numerous science fiction and fantasy anthologies. In the following review, he favorably assesses the stories in Reach for Tomorrow.*]*

A dozen stories which Arthur C. Clarke has produced over the last ten years, all written with the sense of style which one has come to expect from him, make up the contents of [***Reach for Tomorrow***]. Beyond that, it is difficult to generalize about the collection, for the stories are of many different kinds, humorous and sad, long and short, tightly scientific and very loosely so. **"A Walk in the Dark"** is essentially an old-fashioned ghost story, a man confronted with a menace that is so far outside our physics that it might as well be called supernatural; but the menace is a denizen of another planet. **"The Forgotten Enemy"** and **"The Curse"** are scientific only in showing a world ravaged by atomic war; **"The Curse,"** points up the desolation by the casual destruction of Shakespeare's tomb, and is hardly more than a mood piece or sketch.

At the other extreme are stories of pure science, like **"Jupiter Five,"** which depends on some oddities of gravity on one of the moons of Jupiter, and **"Technical Error,"** which old-timers will recognize as a reworking of the hypothesis of A. Conan Doyle's "The Great Keinplatz Experiment," carrying this a step further in the light of what is now known about the structure of the atom.

In the same way, some of these stories are pessimistic, some optimistic; if **"The Forgotten Enemy"** and **"The Curse"** show the suicide of mankind, **"Rescue Party,"** the first story in the book, shows man, late in developing a real civilization, suddenly rising to dominate the galaxy.

Obviously, not every one will like all these equally, and different readers will have different preferences. My own favorite is the broadly humorous **"Trouble with the Natives,"** about some interplanetary visitors to Earth whose preparation for Earthly mores has been an intensive study of our television programs. Of the collection as a whole, it is slighter and less thought-provoking than most of Mr. Clarke's work, but it is all literate and in the best sense entertaining.

Basil Davenport, "Spaceman's Realm," in The New York Times Book Review, *July 15, 1956, p. 20.*

FRITZ LEIBER (essay date 1958)

[*Leiber is a science fiction, fantasy, and horror novelist and short story writer. In the following excerpt, he reviews* The Other Side of the Sky, *commending in particular the scientific aspect of the stories and Clarke's straightforward narrative style.*]

[***The Other Side of the Sky*** is Clarke's] fourth collection of science fiction stories, an engaging series of adventures in space and near distant stars, wryly humorous visions of the end of the world, and coolly sympathetic views of life in other shapes and forms than those we know, all written in smoothly literate prose and spiced with neat jabs at some of the fads and manias of our commercial civilization.

Included are an unusual and controversy-rousing piece about the Star of Bethlehem [**"The Star"**], judged by magazine readers the best science fiction story in 1956, and 12 short shorts about the satellites and moon exploration, written for a British newspaper on a commission American science fiction authors may well envy.

Altho all his stories have the light touch, Clarke's faith in the scientific view of things as a solution to man's problems is anything but light. If that mixed term, "the religion of science," means anything, his stories embody it. More even than H. G. Wells in some respects, he is the sort of scientific story teller envisaged by Vic and especially by the French historian Michelet, who pictured science ushering in and formulating a new age for mankind.

If I had to pick one word for Clarke's style, I would say clarity. His stories seem to be written at the conscious level. There are no tortuous moods, no murky, ambiguous shadings, no uncertainties, no deep self-doubts—or, when they are there, they are very much under control.

Above all, there is no truckling with superstition. It is always the scientist talking—and with a command of the popular approach equal to that of such outstanding science writers as Haldane and Julian Huxley. The spirit is one of cheerful sobriety, unflinching facing of facts, reasoned optimism, and a great enthusiasm for man's adventure in exploring the universe.

And occasionally Clarke's prose reaches a poetic clarity reminiscent of Dunsany, as witness this opening sentence: "Many and strange are the universes that drift like bubbles in the foam upon the River of Time."

Yes, indeed.

Fritz Leiber, "Engaging Adventure Tales," in Chicago Sunday Tribune Magazine of Books, *February 16, 1958, p. 7.*

SAM MOSKOWITZ (essay date 1966)

[*Moskowitz is a leading science fiction historian and critic. In the following excerpt from a chapter devoted to Clarke in his* Seekers of Tomorrow: Masters of Modern Science Fiction, *Moskowitz offers a chronological discussion of some representative works of Clarke's short fiction and concludes by assessing some characteristics of his work.*]

[In the 1940s] Clarke began submitting to *Astounding Science-Fiction* in the United States, impressing its editor, John W. Campbell, with a short story titled **"Loophole,"** which appeared in the April, 1946, issue. Dealing with precognition and a son destined to fulfill his father's vision, the story really did not merit publication.

Much stronger, **"Rescue Party,"** published in the following (May, 1946) number provided taut, fascinating, imaginative suspense as an alien spaceship attempts to explore earth's vacated cities eight hours before the sun will explode into a nova. In this short story, two of the major influences on Clarke are instantly apparent: John W. Campbell, in the Don A. Stuart vein creating a mood of sympathy and admiration for the creations of man and the faithful machines that have served him, and Olaf Stapledon, whose intellectual grandeur sent the imagination racing to the limits of time and space.

Suspense in **"Rescue Party"** is created by the intellectual presentation of the problems and not by its stylistic rendition. In method, Clarke acted in this story and in most of his future stories as the observer or historian and never as the participant. The reward for concentration in reading is a surprise ending. **"Rescue Party"** proved to be a matter for chagrin to Clarke because its popularity and frequent reprintings implied that he had improved little over the years. This attitude toward any unusual popularity of early stories is often found among successful writers. (pp. 381-82)

[The first issue of *Fantasy* (December 1946) contained] Clarke's story **"Technical Error."** The plot concerned a powerhouse accident in which a technician's body is reversed like a mirror image and he is unable to absorb nutrition from his food as a result. In an attempt to restore him to normalcy by repetition of the accident, the entire installation is destroyed. The story required concentration for impact because of the heavy-handedness of its telling, but it won first place in reader approval in the issue and four years later was reprinted in the United States by *Thrilling Wonder Stories* (June, 1950) as **"The Reversed Man."**

Fantasy ran only two more issues and Clarke had a story in each under a pen name, "because I want only my choice pieces to appear under my own name." He used Charles Willis for **"Castaway"** in the April, 1947, issue, a mood piece in which navigators on an airliner obtain a glimpse of a strange and awesome life form that has been blasted free of the sun and is dying in the "frigid" clutch of the earth. Nothing else happens, but Clarke successfully conveys the wonder and the tragedy of that brief encounter. **"The Fires Within,"** published under the name E. G. O'Brien in the August, 1947, and final issue of *Fantasy* (printed in the United States in the September, 1949, *Startling Stories*) was one of Clarke's most successful short stories. The discovery and emergence of a high-density race of creatures from underground inadvertently destroys all surface life, leaving the subterranean race conscience-stricken. (pp. 382-83)

"History Lesson," published in the May, 1949, *Startling Stories,* evolved from the same basic idea as **"Rescue Party"** but took a different direction. Here, Venusians land on earth after human life has been destroyed by a new ice age and they judge the life and inhabitants of the planet solely by an old Donald Duck cartoon they find.

"The Wall of Darkness," which appeared in the July, 1949, *Super Science Stories,* is beyond doubt one of Clarke's finest short stories. Related in the manner of Lord Dunsany, it tells of a far-off world at the edge of the universe, completely "separated" by a gigantic wall, a wall with only *one* side like a

Moebius strip. It is a highly original and beautifully written story which deserves far more attention than it has received.

Of particular significance was **"Hide and Seek,"** which appeared in the September, 1949, *Astounding Science Fiction.* This short story is built around the problem of a man in a space suit on the Martian moon Phobos who must keep alive and out of sight of an armed space cruiser until help arrives. How he does it is the story. This type of story is known as the "scientific problem" yarn: put the character into a difficult situation that can be solved only by legitimate scientific reasoning. (p. 385)

"Superiority," a short story published in the August, 1951, issue of *The Magazine of Fantasy and Science Fiction,* brought Clarke prestige when it was made required reading for certain classes at the Massachusetts Institute of Technology. The story had a moral for those scientists so determined to increase the sophistication of their work that they lose out to those aggressively using conventional methods. (p. 387)

The highest honors in the science-fiction world were both presented to Clarke at the 14th World Science Fiction Convention in New York in 1956, where he was guest of honor and also was given the Hugo for the best short science-fiction story of the previous year, **"The Star"** (*Infinity Science Fiction,* November, 1955). This story, dealing with the discovery of the remains of the star that became a nova at the time of Christ's birth and thus destroyed a noble race, poses a moral dilemma intended to strike the reader with considerable impact. Despite almost a clumsy telegraphing of the punch line by the author, it still had the desired effect on its readers. (pp. 389-90)

[Clarke's] "failings" as a writer are many in the realm of science fiction. For the most part he was not an innovator. As a literary technician he was outclassed by a number of contemporaries. His style, by current standards, was not "modern." Yet, people in many countries bought and read him with enthusiasm and hard-headed critics applauded his efforts.

What is the answer to this seeming paradox?

In an age fraught with horror and despair he was optimistic. Mankind, in his stories, is essentially noble and aspires and triumphs despite all difficulties.

Behind each of his stories is a thought-provoking concept or philosophy. Whether these are or are not original with him is beside the point; some nugget of thought is always present and they read new to this generation. The ideas are never introduced obliquely or discussed in a blasé, over-sophisticated, or matter-of-fact manner, a method indigenous in too much of modern science fiction. Instead, he vests them with all the poetry, wonder, awe, mystery, and adventure that he is capable of conjuring up. Even if it is only the preparation of the first space rocket, he attempts to communicate the richness and implication of an overwhelming experience.

His science is thorough, authentic, yet easily followed.

These factors, together with his obvious sincerity, entranced the reader and won over the critics.

For Arthur C. Clarke, the direction his science-fiction writing was to take was decided at the end of World War II. Consciously or not, he went against the trend. For him, a paraphrase of Robert Frost's famous lines certainly applies: He took the road least traveled by and that made all the difference. (pp. 390-91)

Sam Moskowitz, "Arthur C. Clarke," in his Seekers of Tomorrow: Masters of Science Fiction, *World Publishing Co., 1966, pp. 374-91.*

THOMAS D. CLARESON (essay date 1976)

[*Clareson, an American educator and critic, was the founding editor of* Extrapolation, *a magazine of science fiction criticism. He has edited and contributed to numerous studies of the genre, including the three volumes of* Voices for the Future: Essays on Major Science Fiction Writers *(1976, 1979, and 1984). He is also the author of* Some Kind of Paradise: The Emergence of American Science Fiction *(1985). In the following excerpt, Clareson identifies "cosmic loneliness"—a longing to find other sentient races in the universe, which inspires space travel and exploration—as the central theme of Clarke's science fiction.*]

Although Clarke spreads the human drama across future millenia, he often strikes a contrapuntal note by warning that "Everyone recognizes that our present racial, political, and international troubles are symptoms of a sickness which must be cured before we can survive on our own planet—but the stakes may be higher than that. . . . The impartial agents of our destiny stand on their launching pads, awaiting our commands. They can take us to that greater Renaissance whose signs and portents we can already see, or they can make us one with the dinosaurs. . . . If our wisdom fails to match our science, we will have no second chance" ["When the Aliens Come," *Report on Planet Three and Other Speculations*]. Out of the conflict revealed by these admonitions came one of his finest short stories, **" 'If I Forget Thee, O Earth' "** (1951), in which a son of the lunar colony witnesses for the first time the rising of an Earth poisoned for centuries to come by a nuclear holocaust.

And when Clarke wonders whether or not the Solar System will, indeed, "be large enough for so quarrelsome an animal as *Homo sapiens,*" one conjures up the second of his stories to be published in America, **"Rescue Party"** (*Astounding,* May 1946), in which alien representatives of a galaxy-wide Federation come to save mankind just before the Sun goes into nova. Finding an empty Earth, they learn that man has built a fleet of ships to save himself. The captain muses about such "very determined people" and jests that one must be polite to them because they are outnumbered only "about a thousand million to one": "Twenty years afterward, the remark didn't seem funny." Both narratives bear one of the distinguishing marks of Clarke's story-telling. Not unlike O. Henry, he likes a quick climax—often a single punchline—which may surprise but always opens new perspectives. (p. 54)

Throughout Clarke's fiction there is no want of life or intelligence; they abound in a multitude of forms on a multitude of planets: "For what is life but organized energy?" In *Against the Fall of Night* and *The City and the Stars,* while wandering the blighted universe, Vanamonde had found "on countless worlds . . . the wreckage that life leaves behind"; in *Childhood's End,* the first child to travel psychically goes beyond the range of the Overlords' ships and finally travels in another universe to a planet lighted by six colored suns—a planet that never repeats the same orbit: "And even here there was life." But there is the other side of the coin, those stories like **"Transience"** (*Startling Stories,* July 1949) which are dominated by a note of sadness.

In **"Transience"**—whose indebtedness to the mood of Campbell's "Twilight" Clarke has acknowledged—an omniscient narrator paints three scenes. A hominid encounters the ocean for the first time. While building castles in the sand, a small boy from a village watches the departure of the last great ocean liner, not yet realizing that "tomorrow would not always come, either for himself or for the world." In the far-distant future, another child is interrupted at play to be taken aboard a spaceship into exile from Earth, for "something black and monstrous eclipsed the stars and seemed to cast its shadow over all the world." During what time is left only the sea and the sand will remain: "For Man had come and gone."

Most often Clarke has maintained an omniscient narrator so that he can . . . switch the perspective quickly in order to gain some desired effect. Consistently, however, he has achieved his highest artistry in those stories unified by a first-person narrator recalling personal experience, as in **"The Star"** (1955). A Jesuit, the astrophysicist of an expedition returning to Earth from the so-called Phoenix Nebula, finds himself troubled by the report he must make of what was actually a supernova. The "burden of our knowledge" has caused his faith to falter. On the farthest planet of what was a solar system, the crew of his ship found a Vault prepared by a people who knew that they were doomed and were trapped because they had achieved only interplanetary flight, not starflight. "Perhaps," he writes, "if we had not been so far from home and so vulnerable to loneliness, we should not have been so deeply moved":

> Many of us had seen the ruins of ancient civilizations on other worlds, but they had never affected us so profoundly. This tragedy was unique. It is one thing for a race to fail and die, as nations and cultures have done on Earth. But to be destroyed so completely in the full flower of its achievement, leaving no survivors—how could that be reconciled with the mercy of God? . . . There can be no reasonable doubt: the ancient mystery is solved at last. Yet, oh God, there were so many stars you could have used. What was the need to give these people to the fire, that the symbol of their passing might shine above Bethlehem?

Or again, **"Before Eden"** (1961), in which the first astronauts to land on Venus discover a responsive, though mindless, plant. After conducting appropriate tests, Graham Hutchins, "the happiest biologist in the solar system," reflects:

> . . . This world around them was no longer the same; Venus was no longer dead—it had joined Earth and Mars.
>
> For life called to life across the gulfs of space. Everything that grew or moved upon the face of any planet was a portent, a promise that Man was not alone in this universe of blazing suns and swirling nebulae. If as yet he had found no companions with whom he could speak, that was only to be expected, for the light-years and the ages still stretched before him, waiting to be explored. Meanwhile, he must guard and cherish the life he found, whether it be upon Earth or Mars or Venus.

Pressed by the inexorable deadline for their departure, Hutchins and his companion postpone a little longer—for a few months until they can return to Venus with a team of experts and with the eyes of the world upon them—this meeting which "Evolution had labored a billion years to bring about." The mindless plant absorbs their wastes collected into a plastic bag and thereby contaminates the planet so that Hutchins' pictures and specimens are the "only record that would ever exist of life's third attempt to gain a foothold in the solar system. Beneath the clouds of Venus, the story of creation was ended".

For Clarke, these stories give expression to the central drama of the universe. He might be speaking for himself when he says of the alien visiting prehistoric Earth in **"Moon-Watcher"** (1972): "Centuries of traveling through the empty wastes of the universe had given him an intense reverence for life in all its forms." Yet as the very language of these stories indicates, this reverence is accompanied by an anxiety which reechoes through his finest fiction, perhaps reaching something of a climax in his essay, "When the Aliens Come," in *Report on Planet Three:*

> . . . perhaps the most important result of such contacts [radio signals] might be the simple proof that other intelligent races do exist. Even if our cosmic conversations never rise above the "Me Tarzan—You Jane" level, we would no longer feel so alone in an apparently hostile universe.

Such a view surely echoes something of that horror felt especially during the decades at the turn of the century when science told man that he dwelt alone in an alien universe. That is why the apocalyptic moment of first contact is so important to Clarke; it dramatizes—resolves—what may be called *his cosmic loneliness.*

"The Sentinel" (1951) captures the melancholy of that loneliness. Perhaps more than any other single story it has proved seminal to the development of his artistry. That it provided the symbolic monolith which structures *2001: A Space Odyssey* measures but does not determine its importance. Once again Clarke makes use of a first-person narrator, one who recalls a discovery which he made twenty years earlier. From the first he fuses vividly his memories of the lunar landscape and what it was like to live aboard a surface vehicle in *Mare Crisium* during the summer of 1996. Because he is reflecting upon past action, one soon realizes that what is important is the implication of such a discovery on a moon proved barren by twenty years' further research. He guesses that early in prehistory Earth was visited by "masters of a Universe so young that life as yet had come only to a handful of worlds. Theirs would have been a loneliness we cannot imagine, the loneliness of gods looking out across infinity and finding none to share their thoughts." And so they left a sentinel—a signaling device to let them know when man had reached the Moon.

In November 1950, Clarke first dramatized that **"Encounter at Dawn."** An alien astronaut gives various tools, including a flashlight of some kind, to a prehistoric man already possessing a flint-tipped spear. This may be called the astronauts' story. That their own worlds are being destroyed by a series of explosions—whether supernovae or atomic bombs, one cannot be finally certain—well illustrates how a number of ideas and images wove themselves through Clarke's imagination. As he is about to depart, the astronaut muses:

> . . . In a hundred thousand of your years, the light of those funeral pyres will reach your world and set its people wondering. By then, perhaps, your race

> will be reaching for the stars. . . . One day, perhaps, your ships will go searching among the stars as we have done, and they may come upon the ruins of our worlds and wonder who we were. But they will never know that we met here by this river when your race was very young.

Despite the increasing number of references in his nonfiction to a possible meeting during some period of the Earth's past, he did not rework the plot until *2001: A Space Odyssey* (1968), where it becomes the first section of both the film and the novel. This version may be called Moon-Watcher's story, the story of the man-apes, particularly since the "super-teaching machine"—the monolith—is substituted for the physical presence of the astronauts. The emphasis upon the education—the awakening—of Moon-Watcher and his companions completely submerges the sense of cosmic loneliness. Thus, not until the four short tales—**"First Encounter," "Moon-Watcher," "Gift from the Stars,"** and **"Farewell to Earth"**—first published in *The Lost Worlds of 2001* (1972) did Clarke give the encounter its fullest development thematically.

Again the narrative focus is upon one of the astronauts, Clindar. A member of one of ten landing parties making a census of the Earth, he finds a small group of hominids. Possessing no tools and living "always on the edge of hunger," they have not yet been "trapped in any evolutionary *cul-de-sac*"; "they could do everything after a fashion." Whether because Clindar "looked straight into a hairy caricature of his own face" or because he saw one of the young males contemplating the moon in a manner suggesting "conscious thought and wonder," he decides to intervene in an attempt to tip the scales "in favor of intelligence." Left to themselves the near-apes would have little chance of survival, for "the universe was as indifferent to intelligence as it was to life." And so he gave them an "initial impetus" by teaching them to hunt and use clubs.

As his ship departs, he realizes that nothing may come of his efforts because many factors could destroy "the glimmering pre-dawn intelligence, before it was strong enough to protect itself against the blind forces of the Universe." Nevertheless, he and his companions install a signaling device on the moon to inform them if the descendants of Moon-Watcher reach their satellite. Then they will be worthy of a second visit. For "only a spacefaring culture could truly transcend its environment and join others in giving a purpose to creation": Clarke makes no more succinct statement of his central dream. Yet it is a dream hard-pressed by anxiety, "for if the stars and the Galaxies had the least concern for mind, or the least awareness of its presence, that was yet to be proved."

Without exception Clarke's recent major works—*2001: A Space Odyssey*, **"A Meeting with Medusa"** (1971), and *Rendezvous with Rama*—have dealt with the concept of first contact, but none has significantly modified the philosophical stance presented in the encounter between Clindar and Moon-Watcher. *2001: A Space Odyssey* suggests that those who left the Sentinel have now evolved into beings "free at last from the tyranny of matter," thereby bringing to mind Vanamonde. Bowman journeys to the eighth moon of Saturn, Japetus, an artificial satellite which proves to be a kind of "Star Gate" through which he passes; he finally undergoes a metamorphosis changing him into a "Star-Child"—certainly an echo of the visions of Olaf Stapledon. In *Rendezvous with Rama,* Clarke pays explicit tribute to H. G. Wells's "The Star," adapting its basic plot to his own ends, for the new celestial body plunging through the solar system proves to be a giant spaceship. Most attention is given to its exploration, although there is opportunity for political confrontation in the General Assembly of the United Planets when the citizens of Mercury launch a missile at Rama because it invades their solar space and supposedly threatens to become another planet. Instead it draws energy directly from the sun and departs, leaving the protagonist indignant because "the purpose of the Ramans was still utterly unknown":

> They had used the solar system as a refueling stop, a booster station—call it what you will; and then had spurned it completely on their way to more important business. They would probably never know that the human race existed. Such monumental indifference was worse than a deliberate insult.

Because the Ramans seem always to do things in threes, there is the final suggestion of further flights.

In contrast, **"A Meeting with Medusa"** attains the highest artistry of his recent works; it combines an innovative plot with an effective character study, and it gains unity by focusing solely upon Howard Falcon, though not told from the first person. He is a cyborg who flies a hot-air balloon through the upper atmosphere of Jupiter. And he discovers life in the form of a gargantuan creature like a jellyfish, a medusa. When it begins to handle his balloon, he flees. There is the final suggestion that he will act as an ambassador between humanity and the "real masters of space," the machines; the awareness of his destiny makes him take "a somber pride in his unique loneliness." Certainly **"A Meeting with Medusa"** suggests that Clarke may have found a new perspective from which to consider the old concerns.

For Clarke, man has chosen the right path, employing his intelligence and technology to reach out toward the stars. "Though men and nations may set out on the road to space with thoughts of glory or of power," he wrote in 1965, "it matters not whether they achieve those ends. For on that quest, whatever they lose or gain, they will surely find their souls." Somewhere amid the blazing suns and swirling nebulae, if only in the artifacts of a civilization long dead in the vastness of time, man will find that he has become part of a community of intelligence which alone gives meaning to the indifferent splendor of the Universe. Until then he must dream of the stars and, like Clarke, be haunted by a sense of cosmic loneliness until he finds the Sentinel. (pp. 66-71)

Thomas D. Clareson, "The Cosmic Loneliness of Arthur C. Clarke," in Voices for the future: Essays on Major Science Fiction Writers, Vol. I, *edited by Thomas D. Clareson, Bowling Green University Popular Press, 1976, pp. 216-37.*

PETER BRIGG (essay date 1977)

[*Brigg is a Canadian educator and critic. In the following excerpt, he analyzes technical aspects of three types of story that recur throughout Clarke's fiction: extrapolations from "hard" scientific data, scientific comedy, and metaphysical speculation.*]

Clarke's best known approach [to science fiction] is precise scientific extrapolation that depends upon detailed scientific knowledge carefully explained to the reader to communicate Clarke's fascination with the possibilities at the frontiers of scientific thinking. These stories are admired by fans of science fiction whose minds are open to the realms of possibility that can be tested in strict logical fashion by following the reasoning in a story or checking the description of a planet against astronomical data. Clarke is very much in his element in this type of story, prepared by his early contacts with *Amazing Stories, Astounding Stories,* and *Wonder Stories* and by his university training in physics, mathematics, and astronomy.

There are a number of particular difficulties in creating effective stories based upon hard scientific data and carrying that data forward through logical steps of extrapolation. The creation of a plot to illustrate a scientific concept or concepts is a vital first factor, for the mechanical necessities of the idea must be brought forward in exciting fashion. Once the plot has been arrived at, the author must find satisfactory ways of inserting the scientific explanations, avoiding extensive direct lectures and integrating the development of the physical logic without revealing the ending in advance. Solutions to this problem include the "thinking narrator" who is working his way through some desperate or puzzling situation; the narrator who is relating events that have already taken place and explaining them to an audience in the story or directly to the reader; or a structure where the problem is posed and some scientific data presented before a surprising action occurs that is then explained in retrospect as an extension of the original scientific premises.

Once the structure has been selected, a tone must be found for the story that will allow the presentation of a good deal of information and reasoning. There may be room for some humor, but the stories must not pivot upon tricks or jokes that would obscure the elegance of their scientific demonstrations. Nor can there be much emotional complication that would expand their length and obscure their logic. They tend to be dry, clean, and practical, with characters who serve as explainer and listener, the explainer presenting the scientific reasoning at the level of the general reader and the listener asking questions the reader would like to ask. Characters' emotional involvements are on the uncomplicated level of characters in melodrama, represent emotions of hate or love, or states of being such as good or evil, in order to allow the swift working out of plot action. These characters lack subtlety, but this is a positive merit in stories tightly packed with information. Indeed, it is characteristic that the dialogue be factual and precise, with only a smattering of irony and wry wit. In these stories, Clarke's characters are either acting or explaining their actions in clear, semi-technical language. Clarke himself defended this type of story in the preface to ***Reach for Tomorrow:***

> It seems only right to warn the reader that **"Jupiter Five," "Technical Error"** and **"The Fires Within"** are all pure science fiction. In each case some unfamiliar (but I hope plausible and comprehensible) scientific fact is the basis of the story action, and human interest is secondary. Some critics maintain that this is always a Bad Thing; I believe this is too sweeping a generalization. In his perceptive preface to A.D. 2500, for example, Mr. Angus Wilson remarks: "Science fiction which ends as technical information dressed with a little fantasy or plot can never be any good." But any good for what? If it is done properly, without the information being too obtrusive or redolent of the textbook, it can still have at least the entertainment value of a good puzzle. It may not be art, but it can be enjoyable and intriguing.

Typical of the "one idea" plots in the hard extrapolation stories is that of **"The Wall of Darkness"** (1949) in which Clarke explicates a single scientific projection in a dramatic context. That context is a medieval world of flying buttresses, feudalism, and "certain animals it is convenient to call horses"; whose low technological level causes the premise of the story, a universe with a one-sided surface, to stand out in sharp relief. Clarke then wrestles with the actual problem of story line and tells about a man who seeks to conquer the amazing, high, indestructable wall built by a previous civilization to prevent men from discovering that their universe is a three-dimensional extension of the two-dimensional geometrical construct of the Möbius Strip. It is characteristic of stories of this type that they are "closed," with the action completed and the puzzle completely solved. This reflects Clarke's positive thinking, ending a project or experiment in the manner of the physical scientist.

Another tale illustrating the exposition of a single idea is **"Technical Error"** (1950) in which a research scientist is accidentally inverted when caught in the tremendously powerful field of an experimental generating station. The left-to-right inversion causes him to starve because his body cannot absorb certain molecules of regular foods that have distinctive left and right properties. To save his life, an attempt is made to reinvert him but he vanishes. Dr. Hughes, who planned the change, wakens in the night with the horrible realization that the vanished man has been displaced in time as well as being "revolved" through a fourth-dimensional axis. Before he can have the giant turbine lifted from its base, the researcher materializes in the same space as its pivot point, causing the whole station to explode. Once again Clarke dramatically illustrates complex physical concepts, in this case multiple dimensions and the nature of stereo-isomers of food. Again there is a closed plot in which the explosion writes finis to the problem, wholly confirming Dr. Hughes' speculation.

Within these carefully chosen, clear, straightforward plots Clarke holds character development to an absolute minimum, employing melodramatic types to focus attention on the ideas. A number of the short stories have heroes whose principal emotion is sheer fear for their lives that can only be relieved by the scientific point upon which the story is premised. In **"Maelstrom II"** (1962) Cliff Leyland finds himself with insufficient velocity to escape the moon and his unlikely salvation lies in abandoning spaceship with a strong leap that makes it possible for him to pass perigee above the moon's surface, aided by the hole blown in the Soviet Range by the impact of his derelict ship. Before the solution, however, there are some soggy moments as Clarke describes the emotional states of the characters. Cliff's wife, "a spaceman's wife, always alert for disaster," reacts according to the precepts of melodrama: "She took it well, as he had known that she would. He felt pride as well as love when her answer came back from the dark side of Earth," while Cliff himself retains a cool head:

> Whatever happens to the individual, life goes on; and to modern man life involves mortgages and installments due, insurance policies and joint bank accounts. Almost impersonally, as if they concerned someone else—which would soon be true enough—Cliff began to talk about these things. There was a time for the heart and a time for the brain. The heart would have its final say three

> hours from now, when he began his last approach to the surface of the Moon.

Then he relaxes in private:

> Quite unexpectedly, without desire or volition, tears sprang from his eyes, and suddenly he was weeping like a child.
>
> He wept for his family, and for himself. He wept for the future that might have been, and the hopes that would soon be incandescent vapor, drifting between the stars. And he wept because there was nothing else to do.

Cliff's emotions are under strict control, switched on and off to provide a human aspect for the clever solution to a physics problem.

"Summertime on Icarus" (1960) is another disaster story. Colin Sherrard is nearly roasted alive on the asteroid Icarus until his friends effect a rescue. Sherrard is even more practical in the face of death than Cliff Leyland until moments before he is to fry, when Clarke has him break up spectacularly at the failure of an Emergency Release to give him a quick death:

> There was no easy way out for him, no merciful death as the air gushed from his lungs. It was then, as the true terror of his situation struck home to him, that his nerve finally broke and he began to scream like a trapped animal.

There is nothing unusual or subtle about this reaction, and one recognizes in it Clarke's concentration on the story at the expense of psychological complexity. On the other hand, it makes for effective storytelling and Clarke mortices it tightly into the scientific aspect of the tale for Sherrard is located by his colleagues when his screams leak through the damaged radio antennae of his pod.

One of Clarke's most striking hard extrapolations is **"A Meeting with Medusa"** (1962), and here the intense concentration on Howard Falcon, Commander of the dirigible *Queen Elizabeth IV* and later of the Jupiter probe, *Kon-Tiki,* could have provided a detailed characterization. But Clarke is concentrating upon the creations of technology and speculating on the possible life forms of Jupiter. Falcon is nearly killed when the *Queen* crashes on a test flight, and as the story unfolds we discover that he is a cyborg, human intelligence amalgamated with machinery, that makes him the only "man" capable of withstanding the challenge of Jupiter. But Clarke's portrait of him is a simple collection of longings and memories of pain. Falcon must go to Jupiter because of the challenge. He is somewhat disdainful of ordinary mortals. His personality is resolved in a cavalier sweep at the close of the story:

> Howard Falcon, who had once been a man and could still pass for one over a voice circuit, felt a calm sense of achievement—and, for the first time in years, something like peace of mind. Since his return from Jupiter, the nightmares had ceased. He had found his role at last.

But the treatment here is perfunctory, and pales beside the imaginative skill Clarke has employed in visualizing the descent of the *Kon-Tiki* into the upper atmosphere of Jupiter. One can almost read Clarke's reasoning: "Character must have reason for going to Jupiter; it must be something he can do no one else can; pilot with special body produced as a result of airship accident (chance to bring in echo of my fascination with *Titanic* by naming sequence "A Day to Remember"); psychological drive to prove new self in cyborg body." The starting point is the events of the story, the end point is character and motivation. This approach is the reverse of modern literary custom, but it is admirably suited to the hard extrapolations in which it is employed.

The concrete projections in this type of story are set forth in matter-of-fact narrative tone, and Clarke writes briskly in stories of this type, producing either very short stories or novels covering enormous amounts of material very quickly. (pp. 15-19)

Clarke usually frames segments of dialogue so that the reader knows their importance and the feelings of the speakers. This makes for a quick, methodical dialogue without verbal frills or subtleties. The latter part of **"A Meeting with Medusa"** is largely constructed in this fashion, with the descriptions of Howard Falcon's voyage into the atmosphere of Jupiter being briefly interrupted by his conversations with mission control. After Clarke has described the conflict between the Jupiter beasts ending in a burst of light, the explanation is encapsulated in dialogue:

> "Beautiful!" said Dr. Brenner, after a moment of stunned silence. "It's developed electric defences, like some of our eels and rays. But that must have been about a million volts! Can you see any organs that might produce the discharge? Anything looking like electrodes?"

In dialogue as in plot, characterization, and narrative tone, Clarke is moving quickly and efficiently to build the bones upon which the real flesh of the hard extrapolation can rest: the scientific explanation of the story and the vivid and haunting descriptions of strange futures and places.

The stratagems used to explain the scientific content of these stories involve variations in narrative voice. Clarke has tried a variety of methods, seeking to combine narrative ease with a clear statement of scientific premise. One direct form has a narrator who reasons out the story as it progresses, mixing narrative with explanation. **"The Star"** (1955) has as its first-person narrator a Jesuit astronomer to whom Clarke gives the task of explaining a supernova:

> When the star had exploded, its outer layers had been driven upwards with such speed that they had escaped completely from its gravitational field. Now they formed a hollow shell large enough to engulf a thousand solar systems, and at its center burned the tiny, fantastic object which the star had now become—a white dwarf, smaller than the Earth, yet weighing a million times as much.

He later discovers to his horror that the high civilization destroyed by the star was sacrificed so the star might shine over Bethlehem. The complex creation of a death ray is detailed in **"Let There Be Light,"** when Harry Purvis explains an astronomer's plan to murder his cheating wife. The cleverness of the device employed, an arc lamp focused by a telescope mirror into the eyes of the driver of a car rounding a cliff, reminds us that the pattern of the short hard science story owes much to detective fiction. Harry's narration of the motivation and preparation for the deed are followed by a quick revelation of the elegant solution:

> His timing was perfect; the instant the car came

> round the curve and the headlights shone on him, he closed the arc.
>
> Meeting another car at night can be unpleasant enough even when you are prepared for it and are driving on a straight road. But if you are rounding a hairpin bend, and *know* that there is no other car coming, yet suddenly find yourself staring directly into a beam fifty times as powerful as any headlight—well, the results are more than unpleasant.

This tight mixture of narrative and explanation is most effective. It is modeled not only on detective fiction, with its sudden assembly of information into a complete picture, but on the scientific experiment, where an event is viewed and then explained in retrospect. (pp. 21-2)

Another easy and natural format for the hard extrapolations is the omniscient narrator who can tell the story and explain the scientific events at the same time. In **"Second Dawn"** (1951) Clarke directly presents a detailed description of an alien race whose entire development has varied from the human because they are hooved:

> Both the Atheleni and their cousins, the Mithraneans, possessed mental powers that had enabled them to develop a very advanced mathematics and philosophy: but over the physical world they had no control at all. Houses, tools, clothes—indeed, artifacts of any kind—were utterly unknown to them.

An omniscient narrator can point the reader towards the idea behind the extrapolation. In **"Second Dawn"** the creatures collaborate with a small tentacled animal and the combination leads to sudden enormous strides in technology. Clarke chooses to spell out the results carefully to emphasize the full import of the change. At each stage in the partnership's progression to tool makers and users he points out the implications:

> This primitive raft, he knew, was merely a beginning. It must be tested upon the river, then along the shores of the ocean. The work would take years, and he was never likely to see the first voyagers returning from those fabulous lands whose existence was still no more than a guess. But what had been begun, others would finish.

At the conclusion of the story they have discovered a radioactive rock, and Clarke makes clear the destiny of their rapidly developing technology:

> In the darkness, the faint glow of dying atoms burned unwavering in the rock. It would still be burning there, scarcely dimmed, when Jeryl and Eris had been dust for centuries. It would be only a little fainter when the civilization they were building had at last unlocked its secrets.

On several occasions Clarke has gone beyond the omniscient narrator to speak as Arthur C. Clarke. This applies to the comic stories of ***Tales from the White Hart,*** but he stays very much in the background in these, making Harry Purvis the storyteller. However, in **"I Remember Babylon"** (1960) Clarke himself tells of an encounter in Ceylon with a fanatical American communist who describes his intention to combine Clarke's idea of a fixed communications satellite with Kinsey's research to produce a pornographic propaganda television network for the Chinese. The story is strikingly solid and realistic, as Clarke listens to the plan and foresees its implications for a somewhat decadent America:

> "The Avenue [Madison] thinks it knows all about Hidden Persuasion—believe me, it doesn't. The world's best *practical* psychologists are in the East these days. Remember Korea, and brainwashing? We've learned a lot since then. There's no need for violence any more; people enjoy being brainwashed, if you set about it the right way."
>
> "And you," I said, "are going to brainwash the United States. Quite an order."

In many ways this story is representative of Clarke's direct approach to hard science materials, for he weaves together a number of known and practical scientific propositions in a brisk, efficient way. As in *Venture to the Moon* and ***The Other***

A scene from 2001: A Space Odyssey.

Side of the Sky sequences, he is examining the potentials of immediate science. The hard science stories depend for their excitement upon the efficiency with which precise scientific reasoning can be embodied and explained in narrative format and Clarke uses the full variety of means at his disposal.

The uncomplicated narratives of these stories are punctuated by some of the most positive "purple passages" in all of science fiction. Arthur Clarke's true sense of wonder is most vividly expressed in lyrical descriptions of the cosmos and man's present or future achievements. In story after story he draws from an imagination carefully tempered by scientific knowledge to create sweeping physical descriptions of the marvels of nature and of man. The descriptions of Saturn in **"Saturn Rising"** (1961), the pulsing coded hues of the squid in **"The Shining Ones"** (1962), the solar sailboats in **"Sunjammer"** (1965), the mighty city of Diaspar and the Seven Suns in *The City and the Stars* (1956), the image of Omega in **"The Possessed"** (1952) and the images of the mighty being in **"Out of the Sun"** (1958) are all unforgettable moments in Clarke's writing. Typical of these passages is the description of the moon landscape in the first chapter of *Earthlight.*

> And then Sadler almost cried out aloud, for the cliff on the right came to a sudden end as if a monstrous chisel had sliced it off the surface of the Moon. It no longer barred his view; he could see clear round to the north. . . . There, marching across the sky in flaming glory, were the peaks of the Apennines, incandescent in the last rays of the hidden sun. The abrupt explosion of light left Sadler almost blinded; he shielded his eyes from the glare, and waited until he could safely face it again. When he looked once more the transformation was complete. The stars, which until a moment ago had filled the sky, had vanished. His contracted pupils could no longer see them: even the glowing Earth now seemed no more than a feeble patch of greenish luminosity. The glare from the sunlit mountains, still a hundred kilometers away, had eclipsed all other sources of light.
>
> The peaks floated in the sky, fantastic pyramids of flame. They seemed to have no more connection with the ground beneath them than do the clouds that gather above a sunset on Earth. The line of shadow was so sharp, the lower slopes of the mountains so lost in utter darkness, that only the burning summits had any real existence.

The solid basis of this picture; the rugged lunar landscape, the special characteristics of the short horizon that make possible "catching up to the sun," and the particular brilliance of sunlight on an airless world are integrated with the character's emotional perception of the scene. The momentary blinding of the observer reveals to the reader the intensity of the light. The peaks, "pyramids of flame," and the sharpness of the shadow line are all concrete qualities, creating a real picture with a human perspective. There is a sense of awe in this prophecy of what man will someday view. (pp. 23-5)

In **"The Shining Ones"** (1962) squid were the subject of another Clarke description that pulsates with the same energy as the beasts themselves:

> In my travels I have seen most of the animals of this world, but none to match the luminous apparitions floating before me now. The colored lights that pulsed and danced along their bodies made them seem clothed with jewels, never the same for two seconds at a time. There were patches that glowed a brilliant blue, like flickering mercury arcs, then changed almost instantly to burning neon red. The tentacles seemed strings of luminous beads, trailing through the water—or the lamps along a super-highway, when you look down upon it from the air at night. Barely visible against this background glow were the enormous eyes, uncannily human and intelligent, each surrounded by a diadem of shining pearls.

The images in this passage are fascinatingly concrete. It is a scientist's description that includes "mercury arcs," "neon red," and the "lamps along a super-highway," but it sums to a vivid and emotionally effective picture.

When Clarke moves from the ocean depths to Jupiter in **"A Meeting with Medusa"** (1962) he envisions on an immense scale scenes where only immensity could survive. The medusa, as he names one of the creatures on the planet, is described by the biologist watching Falcon's transmissions in terms which challenge the reader's imagination:

> . . . this thing is about a hundred thousand times as large as the biggest whale? And even if it's only a gasbag, it must still weigh a million tons! I can't even guess at its metabolism. It must generate megawatts of heat to maintain its buoyancy.

In his stories which are projections of hard science, whether presently proven or speculation based upon the limits of our knowledge Clarke works sharply and clearly, stating the bases of his speculations, explaining, reasoning and describing with energy. If there are weaknesses in this "first style of Clarke" they are inherent in the limited aims of such stories. This leads to mechanical plotting, a generally factual narration, and a lack of depth in characterization, but these traits reflect the style of the pulp magazines in which these stories were originally published, and the need to get on with the real excitement of the universe and man's ability to conquer it by bringing reason to bear in understanding its wonders. If these are weaknesses they are overridden by the skill with which the stories make scientific processes and man's observation of the cosmos an exciting adventure.

A second style of Clarke's work is the comic mode, stories that may contain and even conceal hard scientific ideas. Comedy in science fiction is best when rooted in the plot, executing an idea based on a quirk in scientific knowledge or illustrating a tiny fantasy suggested by some scientific fact. It works best in the short story where the idea does not have to be sustained, and it may work even better as an extended joke. As befits comic creations, the characters in these stories and anecdotes are often stereotypes of professions such as scientist, bureaucrat, militarist, or alien. Many of the stories have twist endings and Clarke takes particular pleasure in playing the conjurer who prepares a surprise and springs it upon the unsuspecting reader. Clarke's comic stories are colored by the British tone of his humor, featuring understatement, irony, and wit. This comedy is delicate and when these stories work they are fine, but they can also be dismal, flat failures if they do not hit their comic mark.

The plots of the extrapolations are "closed" in that they prove a point or illustrate a concept. The plots of comic writing are "closed" because they finish a joke or resolve the comic situation they have created. As comedy depends upon surprise there are often sudden reversals or changes of perspective at the finish. The suddenness is comic and may also be thought-provoking as in **"History Lesson"** (1949). This story carefully prepares the reader for the moment when Venusian amphibians will recover knowledge of human civilization by screening a film preserved through an ice age that destroyed mankind. The film appears to present man from the mildly humorous and distorted viewpoint of the alien's scientific objectivity.

> The creature possessed two eyes, set rather close together, but the other facial adornments were a little obscure. There was a large orifice in the lower portion of the head that was continually opening and closing. Possibly it had something to do with the creature's breathing.

It shows the bipeds feverishly in combat with others, driving four-wheeled vehicles, and performing other activities. Clarke suddenly says that all of the effort to interpret these actions will be in vain because: "Millions of times in the ages to come those last few words would flash across the screen, and none could ever guess their meaning: A Walt Disney Production." This twist makes **"History Lesson"** a comic story and gets across Clarke's more serious point, that civilization is tenuous. It is a wry humor that strikes the reader when he realizes that the frantic activity he assumed portrayed human behavior in the film ironically reflects how much Mickey Mouse and his fellow cartoon animals have in common with man.

Other Clarke stories close with equal finality upon a sudden twist. The galactic scout in **"Cosmic Cassanova"** (1958) is taken aback when the beautiful girl he has discovered living on the small distant planet and courted by radio and television is four times his size. Hercules Keating, the victim in **"The Reluctant Orchid"** (1956), plots to murder his overwhelming Aunt Henrietta. However, his immense carnivorous orchid ruins the plan:

> Then the dangling tentacles flashed into action—but not in the way that Hercules had expected. The plant clutched them tightly, protectively, *around itself*—and at the same time it gave a high-pitched scream of pure terror.

In the joke-length stories the closing is sharper and more visible. In **"Reunion"** (1963) humans return to earth to save the population from a horrible mutation: "If any of you are still white, we can cure you." In **"Watch This Space"** (1956) a lunar sodium flare experiment is secretly passed through a stencil of the name Coca Cola, thus creating one of the largest and best observed advertisements of all time. **"The Longest Science Fiction Story Ever Told"** (1965) puts the concept of infinite regress into the form of a one-page story. **"Neutron Tide"** (1970) leads up to the pun that the only piece of wreckage left from a United States space cruiser that encountered a neutron star was "a star-mangled spanner." All jokes lead to a punch line that leaves them logically and esthetically complete. They are plotted towards their own end in a closed pattern.

"The Food of the Gods" (1961) is typical. It begins at a Senate Investigating Committee hearing where a mystery is gradually unraveled. Clarke posits a distant future where men eat only foods constituted from component elements and abhor the thought of eating animal flesh. A company has produced an exceptionally successful new flavor of food. The witness, employed by a competing firm, climaxes his explanation of the remarkable success by spelling for the Committee a word that has gone out of use, C-A-N-N-I-B-A-L, and this is the last word of the story. Clarke has slammed home a point, that human consumption of meat is virtual cannibalism, by moving humorously through the sequence from eating wholly synthetic foods, to eating vegetables, to eating meats to eating Ambrosia Plus, the trade name for that peculiar and intuitively familiar taste. The impact of the story turns on its final word to focus the comedy and the moral.

The efficient plots of the comic stories serve to do several things. As with the hard science stories, they may expound a scientific concept, but they add a wry and comic angle. They may parody scientific logic and solutions. Some of the stories are logically impossible, and Clarke will often admit this and go on to tell them with humor and such a veneer of logic that the reader will be inclined to distrust the disclaimer. ***Tales From the White Hart*** contains stories that serve as examples of both approaches. In **"Patent Pending"** (1954) Clarke combines our existing ability to record brainwaves on an encephalograph with the possibility of replaying sensual experience recordings made by experts (gourmets and sexual acrobats for the sake of the comic aspects). With a nod to Huxley's "feelies" Clarke proceeds to set the story in France and plot it around Georges' development of the device and the fatal result when he neglects his mistress for the work of professionals. In **"Big Game Hunt"** a giant squid is brought to heel through electric control but takes revenge when a fuse blows in the apparatus. In **"The Ultimate Melody"** a professor devises a tune electronically whose perfection drives him into a catatonic trance. In each of these tales Clarke is extending perfectly reasonable scientific data to a comic and illogical conclusion, hiding the technical difficulties beneath a layer of comic prose.

The employment of science in the comic tales is illustrated in **"Hide and Seek"** (1949) when a spy lands on Phobos, the tiny moon of Mars, and evades the might of a fast cruiser for twelve hours by taking advantage of the physics of his situation. He moves rapidly over the surface of the satellite because of the low gravity while above him the cruiser is much less maneuverable because of its moment of inertia. Phobos has a twenty-kilometer diameter, too large for a search party on foot to go over the rugged surface in twelve hours. The television sensor missiles cannot pick him out against the dark surface of the moon. He finds that he can direction-find the cruiser because she is radio-controlling the missiles' search pattern. These facts combine with the growing frustration of the commander of the cruiser and the dry, witty deductions made by the spy to create a highly amusing situation in which the flea conquers the elephant. Clarke employs physics and astronomy with factual care to create this story.

The second approach to science in the comic stories employs pseudoscience and pseudomethodology upon which truly fantastic comic plots can be constructed. The mighty gaps between scientific reality and the events of these tales are actually sources of humor. In **"Time's Arrow"** (1952) Professor Fowler is launched backwards in time so the dinosaur tracks he and his assistants have been excavating end at the point where the dinosaur catches up to the Professor's jeep. This absurd spatialization of time depends upon the assumption that the past exists in some form so that the Professor can be sent back to it. Clarke covers this anomaly by creating a mystery around the scientists devising the time machine and by comic banter between the research assistants and the Professor. In **"Silence Please"** (1954) Clarke combines the fact that sound waves can be set up to cancel one another, thus producing silence, with the law of conservation of energy to arrive at the absurd conclusion that a machine which created silence in this way would explode because the energy of sound would be concentrated in its circuits. It all seems so logical when Harry Purvis tells it, but of course sound waves cannot be stored in any electrical circuit because the circuit deals in electricity rather than sounds. In these stories and in many others such as **"The Man Who Ploughed the Sea"** (1956), **"The Reluctant Orchid"** (1956), **"Moving Spirit"** (1957) and, preeminently in **"What Goes Up"** (1955), where he actually challenges the reader to discover six errors in scientific logic, Clarke imitates scientific reasoning and introduces random fragments of scientific knowledge to fabricate hilarious fantasies. (pp. 26-30)

The characters in Clarke's comic stories, and who often put in brief appearances in some of his other work, are frequently comic stereotypes of professions or positions. Clarke is particularly good at describing scientists and the military, perhaps because he has had practical experience in both areas. But he is equally capable of picturing comic bureaucrats, aliens, or exceptional characters such as Buddhist monks or spinster aunts. The characters are often victims whom the reader wishes to see victimized or the meek who emerge victorious by guile or scientific trickery. (p. 31)

In characterization as in plotting, the comic stories have amusement as their first principle. In stories such as **"Time's Arrow," "Big Game Hunt," "Patent Pending," "Sleeping Beauty," "The Ultimate Melody," "What Goes Up,"** and **"The Defenestration of Ermintrude Inch,"** Clarke is able to present disasters and deaths that befall comic victims so that the reader is amused rather than horrified.

The general tone of the comic stories owes a great deal to the traditions of British humor. Clarke has much in common with the dry, ironic wit and techniques of understatement frequently associated with P. G. Wodehouse, Evelyn Waugh, and some of the writing of Aldous Huxley. His wit is low-keyed and is especially effective because it allows the reader to share with him the thought that none of this amazing stuff need be taken wholly seriously. (p. 32)

The situations that Clarke presents are themselves wry and witty. He matches the tone of the presentations with events such as six men lugging a spaceship on their shoulders in the low gravity of **"Jupiter Five." "Who's There"** shatters the terror of discovering that something is sharing a spacesuit with the narrator with the revelation that the space station's cat has been raising kittens in the suit. Irony pervades **"All That Glitters"** when a professor on the Moon locates one of the largest diamonds of all time to satisfy a greedy wife, only to receive news from Earth that his laboratory team has synthesized diamonds, making them virtually worthless.

The strength of Clarke's comic writing is best seen when he combines a good scientific idea with effective caricature and his dry style to lead to a shockingly funny reversal. The best stories have simple comic plots involving jealousy and love, struggles for property and the dangers of curiosity, with the additional amusement of the puzzles presented by science and by human failures to take full account of physical reality. Often the characters in these stories become victims of their own Machiavellianism. Clarke is wryly cynical about human behavior, seeing it in the larger perspective of the universe at large.

Although Clarke has written a number of highly successful comic stories his efforts can fall flat if they do not hit just the right edge of wit. The juvenile ring of **"Whacky"** (1942), an early experiment with passages such as:

> "The amazing affair of the Elastic Sided Egg-whisk," said the Great Detective, "would no doubt have remained unsolved to this very day, if by great misfortune it had ever occurred. The fact that it didn't I count as one of my luckiest escapes."
>
> Those of us who possessed heads nodded in agreement.

is generally absent from more mature work but occasionally recurs. In **"Passer-by"** (1957) the interesting mystery of the object that goes by the port of a space shuttle the narrator is using illegally to visit a girlfriend is spoiled by a failed ending when the narrator claims he should have reported the incident because the girl married someone else. It is not funny. **"Publicity Campaign"** (1956) juxtaposes a publicity campaign for a horrible space invasion film with a real arrival. The resulting xenophobia causes the visitors to destroy the earth. After a bit of parody on Hollywood publicity it goes flat and the dry wit misses in what are supposed to be comic descriptions of the invaders.

In a story like **"Critical Mass"** (1957) the twist ending simply fails to work. Clarke establishes a threat when a truck overturns near a nuclear plant and the driver flees in panic. The letdown when the narrator discovers that the truck contained beehives does not do justice to the situation. These failed endings are matched by wooden dialogue in stories such as **"The Food of the Gods."** A speaker in that tale is discussing the fact that men used to eat flesh and one Senator cannot bear these mentions. There is humor here, but Clarke labors the point and by the third mention the reader is no longer amused:

> . . . our great-grandparents were enjoying the flesh of cattle and sheep and pigs—when they could get it. *And we still enjoy it today* . . .
>
> Oh dear, maybe Senator Irving had better stay outside from now on. Perhaps I should not have been quite so blunt.

In these moments Clarke seems to be *striving* to be funny and these obvious efforts are awkward and uncertain.

However, Clarke's best comic stories are very successful indeed, blending the quirks of science and the quirks of human behavior with surprise twists. Comedy injects energy into tales with strict scientific antecedents and Clarke has developed it as a delightful adjunct to fantastic speculations.

Among Arthur C. Clarke's best-known works are *Childhood's End, 2001: A Space Odyssey* and **"The Nine Billion Names of God."** These and many of Clarke's other stories attempt to go beyond the limits of the hard extrapolations and the humorous entertainments. It is a serious mistake to think of Clarke as a writer whose imagination is bounded by the known, a scientist of the old school who is deeply reluctant to consider anything but emphatically proven data. In *The Lost Worlds of 2001* he enunciates his position as Clarke's Three Laws:

> . . . Clarke's Third* Law: "Any sufficiently advanced technology is indistinguishable from magic." [* *The First:* "When a distinguished but elderly scientist says that something is possible, he is almost certainly right. When he says it is impossible, he is very probably wrong." *The Second:* "The only way of finding the limits of the possible is by going beyond them to the impossible."]

Despite the slightly flippant tone of Clarke's Laws there is no doubt that he seeks to go beyond "known" and more "practical" extrapolations to metaphysics. His writings in this third style reflect a dissatisfaction with the concrete and a longing for the unknown. It is in these free and experimental works that Clarke moves his readers most effectively; yet it is here the limitations of his abilities as a writer are most glaringly obvious, for he is attempting to describe universes and creatures at the outer limits of the imagination. (pp. 33-5)

[In his approach to the mystical] Clarke communicates an urgent wish for man to explore the wonders of the universe and reveal its basic being. The sense of awe evoked in the lyrical passages of the hard extrapolations expands as Clarke invests his energies in experiments that open outward toward an infinite cosmos.

Clarke's experiments with the unknown speculate in diverse directions and unlike the hard extrapolations and comic stories they end in suggestions of further expansion in many directions. A number of stories put man's evolution in perspective, placing human history as a tiny fragment of the past of the universe and suggesting what lies ahead. In **"The Sentinel"** (1950), the story from which *2001* was derived, man's development is influenced at the dawn of time by extraterrestrial visitors. **"Expedition to Earth,"** also entitled **"Encounter at Dawn"** (1953), treats the same theme with the variation that the visitors' forced retreat from Earth costs man the leap forward they were preparing. Man's future evolution is the theme of *Childhood's End, The City and the Stars, 2001,* and short stories such as **"The Possessed"** and **"Transience."** Other stories speculate on sophisticated forms of life that man has not previously considered, including the intelligent life of the sea in *Dolphin Island,* life in the core of the Earth in **"The Fires Within,"** and life in the hearts of stars in **"Out of the Sun"** and **"Castaway."** Still others, including *2001, Childhood's End, The City and the Stars,* **"All the Time in the World,"** and **"Jupiter Five"** speculate on the master races who may contact man. Man's spread throughout the universe is the subject of stories such as **"Rescue Party," "The Road to the Sea,"** and **"The Songs of Distant Earth."** All of the topics for speculation in stories of this type invoke broad and distant perspectives that challenge and expand the imagination.

The general direction of Clarke's metaphysical speculations owes a good deal to the work of Olaf Stapledon whose sprawling predictive prose fictions *Last and First Men* (1930) and *Star Maker* (1937) have a sweep unmatched in science fiction. *Last and First Men* deals with the future of human evolution over the course of several million years as man leaves Earth, migrates to the planets and adjusts to their environments before coming to a tranquil end. *Star Maker* looks even further as a human narrator joins a growing, galactic telepathic network to search for, understand, and worship the being who made all things. (pp. 35-6)

Clarke echoes Stapledon's optimism toward man's expanding abilities to comprehend the wonder of the cosmos, but he also reflects the pessimism implicit in *Star Maker.* This is particularly fascinating in light of the optimism in short-run projections in Clarke's fiction. It makes the enthusiasm and certainty of getting to the Moon and living on the planets a very short-lived gain for a creature who is ultimately a dust speck in the cosmic pattern. This pessimistic streak emerges in *Childhood's End* where doubts must linger as to the route that devils (for despite all rationalization they remain devils) advocate for mankind. . . . Pessimism informs stories like **"The Next Tenants"** where a scientist prepares termites to take over the world on the grounds that man has failed and the unconscious, ongoing insect should have an opportunity. Even **"The Nine Billion Names of God,"** with its lighthearted if not comic tone, is ultimately pessimistic in illustrating how man could be snuffed out by immense unknown forces.

The optimistic side of Clarke's visions does, however, go beyond relatively mundane speculations on the exploration of the solar system. *Childhood's End* is titled to suggest an evolutionary change. The thrust of the creation of Vanamonde and the abandonment of the galaxy by all its races to go on a further pilgrimage at the close of *The City and the Stars* certainly projects optimism. The conclusion of *2001* is as ambiguous as anything Stapledon ever created, for David Bowman, the Star-Child who has been guided beyond the merely human, hovers above the Earth uncertain of how he will use his almost infinite powers to change the world.

The characteristics of Clarke's metaphysical speculations are dominated by this aspect of open-ended plotting. Whereas his other stories are symmetrical, offering solutions and conclusions to the experiment or comic situation they propose, the mystical stories provide opening terms of infinite series. . . . **"The Songs of Distant Earth"** (1957) suggests that man will go forward:

> She knew now, with a wisdom beyond her years, that the starship *Magellan* was outward bound into history; and that was something of which Thalassa had no further part. Her world's story had begun and ended with the pioneers three hundred years ago, but the colonists of the *Magellan* would go on to victories and achievements as great as any yet written in the sagas of mankind.

"A Meeting with Medusa" ends as Howard Falcon prepares to face his future as mediator between man and his mechanically improved descendants and with the intimation that man will further investigate the marvellous life forms of Jupiter. Other stories such as **"Rescue Party,"** *The Lion of Comarre,* **"The Road to the Sea,"** and **"Second Dawn"** end with expectations of a future expansion of some trend of development or discovery of the absolute.

Despite the trend of these stories toward the metaphysical, they are generally presented in a matter-of-fact tone. Clarke's clear, methodical style, perfected in the hard extrapolations, would not seem to be the natural vehicle for metaphysics, usually the region of mystical and symbolic writing. But on the whole the reverse seems the case, for Clarke's level-headed narrators communicate the sense of wonder that is felt when one travels far beyond the known, and Clarke's own quiet, factual voice as an omniscient narrator is equally effective. In **"Rescue Party"** (1945) the galactic saviors find to their immense surprise that mankind has evacuated Earth without their aid and the story ends with a firm, cool promise for the future:

> "Something tells me they'll be very determined people," he added. "We had better be polite to them. After all, we only outnumber them about a thousand million to one."
>
> Rugon laughed at his captain's little joke.
>
> Twenty years afterward, the remark didn't seem funny.
>
> (pp. 36-8)

All of the stories that end with a reach toward the unknown begin in the mundane. People bustle about preparing space shots; briefings take place; a conference is held on the Moon to discuss a mysterious artifact; or a young man dares to visit an ancient city to prove his love. The stories move outward while the calm tone keeps the sense of concrete reality. . . . It is not the unbelievable that Clarke specializes in. It is the "un-thought of," presented to expand the reader's range of possibilities. This expansion is particularly evident in the two stories about beings from within the stars. In **"Castaway"** Clarke employs a dual point of view to relate how the radar of an airship accidentally destroys a being ejected by a solar flare. The reader knows the beast exists because Clarke narrates its fate partly from its point of view, and is moved by the simple description of its dissolution:

> For the filaments were breaking up, and even as they watched the ten-mile-long oval began to disintegrate. There was something awe-inspiring about the sight, and for some unfathomable reason Lindsey felt a surge of pity, as though he were witnessing the death of some gigantic beast. . . .
>
> And across the screen of the great indicator, two men stared speechlessly at one another, each afraid to guess what lay in the other's mind.

The sensible idea that a form of life can exist in those most frequent concentrations of energy in the universe, stars, is also the theme of **"Out of the Sun."** Astronomers on Mercury detect a being projected out of the Sun that collides with the planet and the narrator speculates on its nature:

> . . . only the electrical senses of the radar were of any use. The thing that was coming toward us out of the sun was as transparent as air—and far more tenuous. . . . We were looking at life, where no life could exist. . . .
>
> The eruption had hurled the thing out of its normal environment, deep down in the flaming atmosphere of the sun. It was a miracle that it had survived its journey through space; already it must be dying, as the forces that controlled its huge, invisible body lost their hold over the electrified gas which was the only substance it possessed.

It is the extension of the possibilities that gives the tale its special dimension:

> . . . for to them we should be no more than maggots, crawling upon the skins of worlds too cold to cleanse themselves from the corruption of organic life.
>
> And then, if they have the power, they will do what they consider necessary. The sun will put forth its strength and lick the faces of its children; and thereafter the planets will go their way once more as they were in the beginning—clean and bright . . . and sterile.

Clarke's metaphysical stories are not parables or symbolic in nature, then, but attempts to carry the powers of physical description out to the indefinable. Like Stapledon, Clarke seeks to communicate a sense of the vastness of the cosmos and its possibilities through stories that move outward from a core to ever-enlarging perspectives. And it is precisely at the boundaries of this exploration that Clarke, like Stapledon, fails to consistently exhibit the imaginative powers necessary to carry the reader with him. (pp. 39-40)

The thrust of most of Clarke's mystical fiction is sentimental in its optimistic view of human destiny. Although he is only charting possibilities Clarke consistently hints that the universe will be man's and that man, coming to grips with the physical universe through science, will emerge the final victor. This optimistic tone is at the root of **"Rescue Party,"** *Against the Fall of Night, 2001: A Space Odyssey,* **"A Meeting with Medusa," "The Songs of Distant Earth,"** and **"The Road to the Sea."** Yet there is a curious wavering in this confidence when Clarke catches, perhaps from Stapledon, the sense of the awesome objectivity of the cosmos, the lack of evidence in the stars for anything approaching a benign being. Clarke dismisses conventional religion as superstition on numerous occasions, perhaps most effectively in **"The Star,"** when an anguished Jesuit priest is faced with the horrible fact that a highly civilized race was victim of a supernova, the Star of Bethlehem. Clarke seems to want a belief that is adequate for the scope of the universe, but that belief in turn is one in which human existence is infinitesimal. It is the crux of the dilemma that Clarke is both hazy in his writing and appealing, for he captures in a naive fashion that sense of distant things that has always haunted men who looked at the stars, and he does so in the context of the modern scientist and space adventurer. This enigmatic sentimentalism may deter the trained metaphysician, but it is the stuff of appealing fiction, of popular expressions of deep feeling like: "That's one small step for man, one giant leap for mankind."

Although Arthur C. Clarke's work can be divided into three principal styles most of his stories and novels contain combinations of hard extrapolation, humorous vignettes, and some gesture in the direction of metaphysical possibilities. (pp. 40-1)

The styles in which Clarke has worked are distinctive and have different purposes. They are not always comfortably integrated in the same story; when they are, it is in situations such as *Rendezvous with Rama* where the hard extrapolation has natural mystical implications without any need to pin them on from the outside and where humor serves to fit man into his tiny niche in the universal scheme. Clarke is perfectly capable of the variety of styles that have been suggested, but closest to his heart and, more importantly, to his head, is the commitment to the real universe as it is understood by the laws of the sciences or as it probably exists if those laws are extended to strange places or different times. When he approaches the metaphysical he does so best through the concrete and although a good deal of his writing contains an ill-suppressed desire to find the gods through science, his abilities as a writer weaken as he approaches the metaphysical. Sensing this, Clarke has evolved a story mode featuring hard science, sprinkled with wit and turning suddenly at its conclusion to its metaphysical speculation in a breathtaking leap from hard reality into the unknown. (pp. 50-1)

Peter Brigg, "Three Styles of Arthur C. Clarke: The Projector, the Wit, and the Mystic," in Arthur C. Clarke, *edited by Joseph D. Olander and Martin Harry Greenberg, Taplinger Publishing Company, 1977, pp. 15-51.*

GEORGE EDGAR SLUSSER (essay date 1978)

[*Slusser is an American educator and critic who has written extensively on science fiction. In the following excerpt, he identifies an "Odyssey pattern" of voyages that ultimately return to their starting points as a unifying theme in Clarke's fiction.*]

Invariably [in Clarke's work], there is an adventure of human "progress." In some way or other a man journeys to contact with the unknown, and comes face to face simultaneously with the possibility of transcendence and the limits of his humanity. Invariably too, the going out is balanced by some sort of coming back. In these "homecomings" the voyager's wonder and resignation before the mysteries of the universe are recaptured (if only momentarily) in a trivial incident, infused into the most mundane object. "Out there," man is absorbed in human vastness; "in here," he reawakens new meaning in the everyday world, "humanizing" some microcosmic part of that greater nature. This is not linear advancement but oscillation, a form of perpetual motion. As with Wells's Time Traveler, homecoming leads to a new voyage: progress/stasis/progress. (p. 13)

Over his long career Clarke has written short fiction, novellas, and novels of different lengths. Cutting across such genre distinctions, Peter Brigg . . . divides Clarke's output into "three styles": the hard extrapolater, the wit, and the mystic [see excerpt dated 1977]. Whatever diversity there is in Clarke, however, exists only on the surface. Indeed, anyone who reads great doses of his writing is struck by just the opposite—in spite of variations in tone or length, it is all very similar. This is due mainly to the underlying persistence of the Odyssey pattern. If themes and narrative situations vary, they hardly evolve. Instead, this basic matrix reduces them invariably to the same set of relationships. Moreover, instead of different or successive "styles," the various tones of Clarke's writing are better described as different modes of a same and unique verbal figure—the oxymoron, a surprising and transformatory juxtaposition of opposites. If we wish to classify Clarke's work, we should do so rather in increments—to what degree is this single pattern developed in any given work? His range extends from various kinds of partial Odysseys to the most elaborate voyages and returns. Quite naturally (if not exclusively), these latter occur in the longer works. . . .

This does not mean, however, that only Clarke's novels possess the intricacy of construction of a "full" Odyssey. On the contrary, Clarke continues to work in short forms; if anything, the development of his stories parallels that of his novels. In fact, a brief look at a few sample tales, taken in chronological order, provides an excellent view, in miniature, of Clarke's overall literary evolution. Not only do the stories tend to get longer, but the Odysseys they recount become more complex. We pass from simple juxtapositions of the "trick" or surprise ending to calm, extended workings-out of multilayered sets of "correspondences"—the author's word for the intricate combinations of opposites he erects in *Imperial Earth.* Throughout all of this Clarke is doing little more than refining and perfecting techniques of variation on his single theme.

Ostensibly, **"The Nine Billion Names of God"** (1952) is a story of apocalypse. In reality, though, the process described here (in a manner wryly ironic, if not facetious) is an entropic one. A sect of Tibetan monks believe that the world will end when the nine billion names of God have been listed: "The human race will have finished what it was created to do, and there won't be any point in carrying on." In order to accelerate this task of naming names, the monks employ a computer—mystery is literally conquered by rule and line, the individuality and variety that abide in names are leveled and spent. And at the point of highest entropy—when no more names are available—a heat-death occurs: the stars go out. Simultaneous with this process, there is a curious reversal at work—one which builds and magnifies the individual vision in the face of an indifferent universe. The laconic description of the end ("there won't be any point in carrying on") is at the antipodes of poetic wonder. It is spoken by one of two computer programmers—men whose sole yearning is not for God or transcendence, but for home, family, and the familiar comforts. They are, in fact, on the road home when the end really does come. At this moment, suddenly, inexplicably, their banal vision is transfigured: mountains gleam "like whitely hooded ghosts," Chuck's face in the moonlight is "a white oval turned toward the sky." In an ironic switch, as if their former banality had been transferred to the awesome spectacle itself, revelation becomes something commonplace, almost domesticated: the stars go out "without a fuss." If mankind is superceded here, at the last minute the balance is tipped slyly in his favor. The luster of apocalypse is drained away as ordinary men and their homing instincts are uplifted in poetic wonder. In a brief flash before the darkness, the going out and coming home crisscross, becoming one. This is clever sleight of hand, but significant in terms of the Odyssey pattern.

The focus of a more famous tale, **"The Star"** (1954), is less the cosmic irony of its surprise ending—our Star of Bethlehem was in reality a supernova that destroyed a paradisical world at the other end of the universe—than the voyage of its narrator, a Jesuit priest-scientist, to this destroyed world and back. It too seems essentially a journey to loss of faith, to man's encounter with his limits. But again, simultaneous with the going out is a coming back. Paradoxically, the hero's perception of cosmic indifference coincides with clear proof of the Christian religion—the Biblical account was correct after all, there was a Star of Bethlehem. In the same way, if one homeland must in the process be abandoned—the unbroken line from Christianity to humanist science is shattered by the irony of this discovery—it is only so that another may be found. It is here, at the farthest point of his journey, that this priest comes nearest to basic humanity: he observes the simple joys and everyday domestic pursuits of this "disturbingly human" race, and grieves. The final juxtaposition is that of a lyrically heightened voice brooding on the spectacle of universal indifference. Once more, at this extreme crossroads, a man reaches the ultimate expression of his individual humanity, only to have it become a lament. Religious belief and scientific method both give way to the elegaic question: "Yet, oh God, there are so many stars you could have used. What was the need to give these people to the fire, that the symbol of their passing might shine above Bethlehem?"

"Summertime on Icarus" (1960) takes a traditional enough theme—a crash and rescue on the asteroid Icarus—and handles it in a very particular way. This time the narrative focus is not on the hero's struggle to survive. He is physically trapped, helpless, resigned. What Clarke gives us is the vision of another man suspended at the crossroads, whose lyrical awareness of human insignificance is awakened and keyed to the pitch of a scream—the moment at which dissolution and homecoming again overlap. More clearly than before, perceptions of the inhuman machinery of the cosmos are linked in the hero's mind with analogies to familiar human things or situations—in this case a common myth: "How strange that he should be dying now, because back in the nineteen-forties—years before he was born—a man at Palomar had spotted a light on a photographic plate, and had named it so appropriately after the boy who flew too near the sun." The pull of the unknown is balanced by the known—here already is an example of those "correspondences" that Clarke will develop so elaborately in his later works. In the same manner, the hero's moment of transcendental vision leads simultaneously away from Earth and man, and back to it: "At some remote time in the past [Icarus] had been under enormous pressure—and that could mean only one thing. Billions of years ago it had been part of a much larger body, perhaps a planet like Earth. For some reason that planet had blown up. . . . Even at this moment, as the incandescent line of sunlight came closer, this was a thought that stirred in his mind. What Sherrard was lying upon was the core of a world—perhaps a world that had known life. In a strange irrational way it comforted him to know that his might not be the only ghost to haunt Icarus until the end of time."

The experiences of space adventurer Colin Sherrard are typical of many other Clarke heroes. His is a world in which heroism itself has been strangely domesticated. As part of the *Prometheus*'s crew he is the fire-stealer plucking "unimagined secrets from the heavens"; but he is also a member of a routine research mission in connection with a very mundane "International Astrophysical Decade." Even more strikingly, his ordeal itself is the exact opposite of action-adventure. Instead, an oddly entropic process, a series of "moments of physical weakness," reduces him to a state of near-immobility. First an attack of "space vertigo" causes him to lose all purpose and direction, grounding him in disorder. Then the crippling of his "space pod" brings total rupture between volition and physical movement. Paradoxically, however, it is only at this point of stasis that Sherrard makes the discoveries these men have travelled millions of miles to get. Only when he experiences the sudden blast of the sun's heat in this helpless state does he understand what made Icarus a "blasted cinder"—in measuring cosmic processes, instruments cannot replace a man. At this apparently fatal moment of truth there is another reversal. What comes to Sherrard is less a vision of man's annihilation, his nothingness in the face of indifferent vastness, than a heightened feeling for some abiding human presence at the center of things. Out of impending personal disaster surges a new vision of life (something like Heinlein's mystical "fifth planet"), which in turn is caught up in still wider vistas of destruction. Set against this spiraling vortex of change is a counterfigure—suspension as in a mirror. The hero's death is overlayed by that of an entire race. And on this hypothetically Earth-like planet the "ghosts" he conjures up could be human ones. Once again a man plunges to the heart of the alien only to discover (and reaffirm) the familiar and the human. But again, as with the narrator of **"The Star,"** it is a humanity most fully sensed or understood only at the moment of its passing.

Sherrard doesn't actually die. In another twist he is retrieved and eventually returns home, a home which no longer seems the same. Here, in reverse fashion, the return to the familiar infuses it with an alien, transcendental quality. Near death, at the farthest point of alienation, Sherrard's return had already begun. Seeking to kill himself by letting his oxygen escape, he is thwarted when the valve sticks, and literally forced into the lyrical alternative—a last glimpse of Earth brings a lament for lost loved ones and home. Cutting across this vision is a radically transcendent one: "*What was that?*" A brilliant flash of light, infinitely brighter than any of the stars, had suddenly exploded overhead. Miles above him a huge mirror was sailing across the sky. . . . Such a thing was utterly impossible." But this epiphanic mirror, in yet another reversal, seems to reflect back commonplace things. Sherrard's lament rises to a scream, only to sink back immediately into the ordinary world. To the listening captain who saves him, Sherrard's metaphysical despair is but a "shout": "Hold on, man! We've got a fix on you. But keep shouting!" In the same way his great "mirror" turns out to be no more (and no less) than one of his familiar radiation screens come now to protect a man instead of technical instruments from the sun's rays. We are not left here in domestic comfort, with every mystery explained away. When this Ulysses finally looks homeward again it is with a gaze contaminated by strangeness: "Back to enjoy and cherish all the beauties of the world he had thought was lost forever—No, not all of them. He would never enjoy summer again."

The elegaic poignancy and finality of **"The Star"** echoes that of its contemporary, *Childhood's End,* a novel which for all its promise of transcendence culminates in radical division: lamenting man is suspended in the face of cosmic process. **"Summertime,"** on the other hand, in its brush with annihilation and mystical revelation, and its continuous rhythm of reversals that pours the marvelous into the familiar and back again, looks forward to the more sequential structure of a work like *2001.* A longer . . . tale, **"A Meeting with Medusa,"** is the harbinger of Clarke's latest novels, in which still another twist is given to the Odyssey pattern. Here in miniature are the reductive intricacies that shape *Imperial Earth.*

As an odyssey, as a voyage to fabulous places and back, **"Medusa"** resembles **"Summertime"**—an episode in an ongoing adventure rather than a totality. Similarly this story also makes constant use of suspending juxtapositions. But where these were employed before to strike a perilous balance between man and cosmos—to oppose the physical fact of change with the lyrical dream of permanence—now they have been turned to new, ironic ends. In **"Medusa"** even transcendence has become problematical. Before there was no doubt—evolutionary process would surpass man, the human form was not divine but transitional. There was no doubt either that man's lamenting dream, however futile, was also noble. Though man (at these moments of transcendental vision) sees he must pass, the fact that he can raise his voice against the blind mechanisms of evolution, and utter his desire to be the unchanging center of things, makes him (in a twist on Pascal's thinking reed) as great as the forces that crush him, for they know nor sing not. In this recent tale, however, these extremes are not simply suspended face-to-face—they are rather played against each other in mutually reductive fashion. Transcendence becomes less clearly progressive, a "childhood's end" or even the fleeting revelation of cosmic process. And the isolated lyrical hero on the edge is more an aberration than ever. Clearly in **"Medusa"** (as in his latest novels) Clarke is tending toward a new view of man; he has retreated from confrontation at the end of human mind or time to the restatement of a mean. In relation to his earlier elegaic humanism, Clarke seems not to have moved forward so much as backward, to have abandoned *fin de siecle* romanticism for satire, the voyage of the entropic discoverer for something closer to the travels of Gulliver. Howard Falcon's journey to greater-than-human powers and his moments of transcendence are ironically offset in such a manner that, as he becomes something more than man, he is simultaneously becoming less. What is displayed here is neither man's evolutionary potential nor his lyrical uniqueness, but rather his essentially normative nature.

The key to this process of reduction in **"Medusa"** is two sets of bracketing events. In this tale there is a symmetry and direction that (though composed of old elements and processes) seem new to Clarke. Previously his narratives were characterized by telescoping—in single events the voyage out and back, the alien and familiar, were made to meet and blend. In this story too, Earth and Jupiter—home and the field of Odyssean adventures—seem merely inversions of each other. A series of interpenetrating correspondences link these opposites and draw them together. They are pushed apart again, however—in polar suspension—by these bracketing sets of recurring situations: an event on Earth happens again on Jupiter, a meeting at the beginning is repeated at the end. We are now invited to seek differences in what seem similar happenings, to compare and contrast. Between these polarities arises a system of compensations and ironic adjustments that, resonating this time across the whole expanse of the story, undermine and cancel what otherwise appears to be the unbroken moral and physical advancement of the hero. The first polar set is the sudden drop of a lighter-than-air ship, on Earth and on Jupiter. The second is Falcon's meeting with the "superchimp" in his plummeting ship, mirrored in the end by his encounter with Webster and his own rise to "superman". As these horizontal correspondences play off against each other, man finds himself ironically framed in tight limits.

At first glance Earth and Jupiter strike us as mirror images of each other: the *Queen Elizabeth* gives way to the *Kon-Tiki,* another dirigible ("Hot-hydrogen" has replaced helium) sailing the "aerial sea" of the Jovian atmosphere and discovering a "medusa." If these two situations are vastly different (this new world "could hold a hundred Pacifics") yet they are strangely analogous, for the purpose of "sailing" here is also to defy the pull of the deep, Jovian gravity: "At the level where *Kon-Tiki* was drifting now . . . the pressure was five atmospheres. Sixty-five miles farther down it would be as warm as equatorial Earth, and the pressure about the same as the bottom of one of the shallower seas." Even this small sample serves to show just how slippery these apparently neat inversions are—the "air" of Jupiter combines elements of both land and sea. This incessant rhythm of polar comparisons, cutting back and forth between worlds, provides ironic insight in both directions. We see not only the strangeness of Jupiter constantly eluding man's arrogant attempts to measure and tame it, but at the same time his familiar world becoming more uncertain, less stable. The *Queen Elizabeth* for instance, seems to be more out of its element on Earth than its counterpart in deep space. If this new *Queen* now sails the airs instead of the seas, it is in answer to the whims of a bored post-industrial humanity seeking its pleasures in increasingly unnatural fashion. Indeed, if what seems right on Earth is actually wrong, on Jupiter the wrong turns out to be right after all—the *Kon-Tiki* functions, it does the job. Here too on another level is a twist, for this physical success only points to moral and metaphysical failing. The *Queen* was and is a luxury liner, but the *Kon-Tiki* implies radical adventure, exploration of the unknown. Falcon plunges to the heart of this strange world only to find a "medusa"—the wall he beats against is man's psychological need to domesticate the alien. On the other hand, it is on Earth, at the very center of the familiar, that Falcon actually has what is perhaps his most intense brush with the uncanny. All at once, inside the air sack of his *Queen,* he comes upon a startling new world, an inverted land with a "curiously submarine quality." In a flash air and sea merge, the huge translucent gasbags of the ship become "mindless, harmless jellyfish." Falcon here is but a frail man before his fall. And yet his vision is not a fearful but a peaceful one. Ironically, the vision of the almost more-than-human hero in the atmosphere of Jupiter (where again air and sea are seen as one) is just the opposite: in panic he flees the advances of this alien "jellyfish."

At either end of this vast crisscrossing web of correspondences are the two answering situations—the twin fall of ships. Not only are these individual events ambiguous in themselves, but each throws ironic light on the other; in their mirror reflections Falcon's progress is suspended. In the crash of the *Queen* a near-fatal fall actually turns out to be a moment of transcendence: the decorative captain of a pleasure ship rises from the flames an insatiable Odysseus: decadent man is "reborn" a superman. At the end of his Jovian adventure Falcon openly asserts this new being, prides himself on his role as "ambassador between old and new." But this is exactly what he fails to be in his second fall over Jupiter. For instead of implementing the "prime directive" and making this first contact between man and alien life form, he panics and lets his ship drop away from the hovering Medusa. Once again he seems to fall only to rise higher. This time in fact he appears to pass beyond human honors and deeds alike: "He said 'men'. He's never done that before. And, when did I hear him use the word 'we'? He's changing, slipping away from us." But he has fallen too. This time the plunge is a moral rather than a physical one—he who would become more than man has through fear perhaps become less. In almost Swiftian fashion, through all these reversals, these falls and swellings of pride, runs a median, the human norm as measure of all things. Falcon's initial reaction to Jupiter confirms this standard: "He did not feel that Jupiter was huge, but that *he* had shrunk—to a tenth of his normal size. Perhaps, with time, he would grow accustomed to the inhuman scale of this world; yet as he stared at the unbelieveably distant horizon, he felt as if a wind colder than the atmosphere around him was blowing through his soul." Here is another "fall," one which serves to reduce the cosmic to manageable human dimensions. At once, however, things expand, and a touch of the old elegaic wonder returns as man again must confront infinite spaces. At this point we seem closer to the rhythmic relationship of man and God's universe in Pascal than in Swift: "If he exalt himself, I humble him; if he humble himself, I exalt him." Yet, as Falcon's tale unfolds, we soon see that this dynamic is parodied, itself treated reductively. In a final burst of pride Falcon rises "on his hydraulics to his full seven feet of height." By his act he proves that to "grow accustomed" to inhuman vistas is to be human no more. Again with irony all the more savage for its understatement balance is achieved: these extra inches were given to him to "compensate for what he lost in the crash of the *Queen.* However grotesquely, the human median holds.

In more ways than one Falcon exalts himself only to be humbled. This rhythm of oscillation around a median functions here in a horizontal sense as well, and tends to offset the process of evolution itself. At first glance the twin "superchimp"—superman encounters may appear to mark successive stages in the hero's development. As man looks on ape, so superman looks on man: Falcon's past, present, and future seem spread before us. But if we look closer, we see that the two episodes are actually ironic inversions of each other: in the end Falcon rises and man descends, but in the beginning it is Falcon who descends and the chimp who rises. The hero himself links these two scenes: at the moment he takes leave of his old friend Webster, he suddenly recalls the instant inside the sinking *Queen* when he had faced the terrified "superchimp" on the ladder. It is he, in fact, who discovers their deeper affinity. In his mind, it is not Webster but himself who replaces the chimp in the equation. Linear evolution is suspended as two extremes—both deviants from the human norm—suddenly face each other: "Neither man nor beast, it was between two worlds, and so was he." This juxtaposition casts ironic light on Falcon's subsequent assertion of "somber pride in his uniqueness." Because he can go where man cannot, he feels he has advanced beyond him. But the "superchimp" was also an advancement over his species, a creature that in the terror of the crash "atavistically" reverted to its original nature as an ape. In like manner, Falcon, far from proving in his Jovian odyssey that he is more than human, becomes man again through his fear of the Medusa.

The various species in **"Medusa"** seem to exist not in genetic relationship to each other, but as isolated compartments, essentially disconnected states of being. What is "super" in both chimp and man is merely an accretion, the work of medical engineering. Each of these figures, in becoming greater than his species, simultaneously becomes less; each is a hybrid, a monstrous deviant from its respective norm. Things will change and go forward, but man as man will not: "Someday the real masters of space would be machines, not men, and he was neither." Falcon sees himself as the "first immortal midway between two orders of creation." Actually he is in the same extreme position as Clarke's earlier elegaic heroes. As with the lone wanderer of Matthew Arnold's "Stanzas from the Grande Chartreuse," he too is "between two worlds, one dead/The other powerless to be born." Falcon's hubris blinds him to this truth: at this point pride in his "uniqueness" is grotesque mock-heroics; visionary lament is replaced by Byronic posturing. In a tale where elegy has shaded into satire, what abides in the face of cosmic indifference is a human norm, the common term between beast-man and man-machine.

Clarke's reenactment of this pattern of contradictions and paradoxes in work after work seems almost a ritualistic act. Again and again his hero is painstakingly placed in his social setting, only to be yanked from it—the adventure is invariably a solitary one. More surprisingly, it is passive as well—the hero is less actor than a spectator to the drama of evolution. Clarke flaunts both evolution and relativity, for however much the protagonist may "move" in time, or see the most fearful changes, he remains firmly anchored in space. It is important that Wells's time machine has the form of a chair—the domestic object that most signifies stasis has itself become the source of movement. The machine has real affinities with the dinner guests' armchairs that surround it. Its center of gravity, however, goes beyond the merely contemporary and comfortable to much more permanent, unyielding foundations. If the Morlocks and Eloi have clearly evolved beyond man as we know him, the Traveller nevertheless seeks to draw them back into a human space that is less the familiar than the ideal: "[they have] kept too much of the human form not to claim my sympathy." Even when staring upon the unhuman landscape at the end, he can still affirm this form, if only in its absence. At once the space he occupies is a familiar one again: "Now in this old familiar room it is more like the sorrow of a dream than an actual loss." Clarke's adventurers are also often seated and immobile; and there is little actual loss or change, either. To contact the unknown is to return immediately to known space—the pilot seat becomes a chair again. And there are deeper roots: beneath the comfortable present lies an elegaic one—the perennial sorrow of the dream of human permanence. To Thoreau such a lament for the golden age was little more than a lament for golden men. And so it is for Clarke. Here perhaps is the most striking paradox in his works: the writer who poses as poet of evolution, chronicler of the relativity of intelligences and life-forms, in reality uses his sweeping adventures to reaffirm a view of man which, in its almost idyllic insistence on family and hearth as the center of society, the focus of human endeavor, is profoundly aristocratic in nature. In all the comings and goings of Clarke's fictional universes, the values that define human space remain more than conventional and hieratical—Odysseus's royal bed becomes Wells's time-machine throne. (pp. 14-24)

George Edgar Slusser, in his The Space Odysseys of Arthur C. Clarke, *The Borgo Press, 1978, 64 p.*

JOHN HOLLOW (essay date 1983)

[*Hollow, an American educator and critic, has written studies about the science fiction of Clarke, Ray Bradbury, H. G. Wells, and Jules Verne. In the following excerpt from his* Against the Night, the Stars: The Science Fiction of Arthur C. Clarke, *he identifies a Wellsian tradition of potential terrestrial annihilation in Clarke's short fiction that is tempered by Clarke's optimistic faith in science and technology.*]

An important thing to remember about the science fiction of Arthur C. Clarke, it seems to me, is that it was written by an Englishman. Although he now calls Sri Lanka home, Clarke was born in Minehead, Somerset (in 1917), and he is therefore, by nationality as well as by predilection, an inheritor of the tradition defined by H. G. Wells. (p. 1)

More than any of his equally well-known contemporaries, it seems to me, Clarke is the inheritor, not of Jules Verne's desperate attempts to show—by having some character name its parts—that Nature is controllable, or of Edgar Allan Poe's equally desperate attempts to gain some control of the subconscious by bodying forth its most awful horrors, but of the bleak evolutionary projections of H. G. Wells, Huxley's most famous pupil at the Kensington Normal School of Science.

I will go further. I will suggest that appreciation of Clarke's stories and novels might well begin by seeing them as having appeared, as do the stars at evening, against the dark background of the far future anticipated by Wells' best-known scientific romances.

Wells' best-known scientific romances can be not unfairly represented by the moment in *The Time Machine* when the time traveller, who has voyaged far into the future, stands on the deserted beach which is the epitome of our deserted planet and watches the passage of one of the inner planets eclipse the much closer but now weakened Sun. . . . As the time traveller explains to his guests, after he has returned to his own time, what the far future has in store is not the completion of humanity's upward climb from the beast, not a civilization even more urbane than that represented by their late-Victorian dinner party, but the bleak truth that the human race itself must end. From the viewpoint of the aeons, the traveller insists, his face almost as pale as the front of his dress shirt, not only individuals but the species itself must—like the bubbles in their champagne—wink in the light and be gone. (pp. 2-3)

The Time Machine means to suggest a change in perspective. It wants to argue that the future will not be endless progress, that the workings of time will be as hard on the race as they are on the individual. (p. 4)

In that scene when the time traveller stands . . . on that deserted beach, he sees "the black central shadow of the eclipse sweeping towards me." "In another moment," he says, "the pale stars alone were visible. All else was rayless obscurity. The sky was absolutely black."

Wells acknowledges, to put it another way, that in the case of an eclipse of the Sun by one of the inner planets, the stars would still be visible, even the "pale stars" of a far-off future in which the universe is closer to burning itself out. So intent is he on suggesting the final night, however, the time when the stars themselves will have winked and gone out, that he overstates: he says, ignoring the stars he has just mentioned, that the sky is "absolutely black." He probably means that the sky in between the stars is absolutely black, but he is so bent on hinting at the return of Darkness and Old Night that he forgets the stars he describes just two sentences earlier.

It is exactly the time between now and some such far-off death of the stars that the fiction of Arthur Clarke insists on. For him, Wells is the too-quick despairer, too ready to accept the analogy that as the day dies so must the universe. (p. 6)

Clarke's response to Wells' legacy can perhaps best be presented by comparing two of their stories, both of which happen to be entitled **"The Star"** (Wells, 1897; Clarke, 1955). Clarke's story does not seem, at least not consciously, to have been meant to allude to that of his predecessor, but both refer to the Star of Bethlehem, both contemplate the seemingly meaningless destruction of a civilization, and both finally are about whether the universe can be understood.

In Wells' story, a planetoid wanders into our solar system, where it collides with Neptune and ignites into a giant fireball, the new "star" of the title. As these interlocked bodies narrowly miss the Earth on their fall into the Sun, the result on our planet is terrible storms, earthquakes, and a flood almost as universal as that described in Genesis.

The theme is typically Wellsian: we humans, who thought ourselves the center of creation, suddenly realize that we are no more guaranteed survival than was Neptune. Our fate, for that matter, would be no more detectable over the vast distances of space than was that of whatever beings may have lived on that planet. A new star in the heavens, says the story, is much more likely to announce that the universe is a random and uncaring place than that a savior is born.

Clarke's story, in turn, is equally anti-Christian. A Jesuit priest, an astrophysicist, is returning to Earth from an expedition to investigate the remains of a supernova at the extreme edge of our galaxy. The investigators have found, buried on the planet which must have been the Pluto of the destroyed system, a time fault filled with the relics of a brilliant and beautiful civilization, destroyed when the star exploded. "It is one thing for a race to fail and die, as nations and cultures have done on Earth," the Jesuit says to himself; "but to be destroyed so completely in the full flower of its achievement, leaving no survivors—how can that be reconciled with the mercy of God?"

"I know in what year the light of this colossal conflagration reached our Earth," he says. "I know how brilliantly the supernova whose corpse now dwindles behind our speeding ship once shown in terrestrial skies. I know how it must have blazed low in the east before sunrise, like a beacon in the oriental dawn." "What was the need to give these people to the fire," he cries out; was it "that the symbol of their passing might shine above Bethlehem?"

It is not the ruin of civilizations that undermines the priest's faith. As he says, he and several other members of the expedition have "seen the ruins of ancient civilizations on other worlds." To such routine disasters he is able to answer, as the voice from the whirlwind answers Job, that "God has no need to justify His actions to man. He who built the Universe can destroy it when He chooses." The priest's real difficulty is the same as that of the people in Wells' story: his religion has

Clarke with stills and models from 2001: A Space Odyssey.

claimed too much. The human assumption that this world is the center of the cosmos, which is exemplified in both stories by the Star of the Magi, is bound sooner or later to come up against the fact of other inhabited planets; perhaps in very dramatic fashion. Are we to believe, asks Clarke's story, that God so loved this world that He destroyed another for it? It would be better, the priest is close to deciding, if the crucifix were to be seen as "an empty symbol," if humans were to admit that the Earth-centered view of the universe has difficulties which not even the great founder of his order, not even the far-seeing Loyola of the Rubens engraving, could foresee.

If the priest is to keep his intellectual honesty, he must do as the people in Wells' story do: he must give up the idea of divine favor. (It is even suggested, in Wells' story, that such a surrender would bring about a "new brotherhood" among men, would make of the world a more Christian place than Christianity managed to do.) The priest must realize that the state of human knowledge is as the ship's doctor describes it to him one day when the two of them are looking out from the ship's observation deck at the "stars and nebulae" swinging "in silent, endless arcs." "Well, Father," the doctor says, "it goes on forever and forever, and perhaps *something* made it. But how you can believe that something has a special interest in us and our miserable little world—that beats me." Or as Clarke has said in another context, in answer to the psalmist's "What is man that Thou art mindful of him?": "What indeed?" ("Of Space and Spirit," 1959).

The priest has to learn to see all peoples, his own and those of the destroyed civilization, as the latter present themselves in one of the "visual records" they left in the time vault: as children playing on a beach. The image does not favor one people over another; instead, it captures, as it always has, the poignant beauty of mortality, especially of mortality seen against the magnificent immensity of the universe. Some cultures may be swept away, as in Housman's "Smooth Between Sea and Land"; some cultures may learn to sail the sea, as in Clarke's **"Transience."** The point is that both are beautiful. The passing of culture is no worse than the passing of a generation, than the passing of an individual. We must concentrate, as does the art of the destroyed civilization, on the moment of youth against the sweep of time, on the moment of intelligent life against the background of death. From such a viewpoint, focused on such an image, it still might be possible for the Jesuit to hope that such beauty—simply because it is beautiful—is *Ad Majorem Dei Gloriam.* The universe and the existence of life in it still may testify to the glory of a creator.

The difference between Wells' "The Star" and Clarke's **"The Star"** is this faint hope still available to the priest. In Wells' story, the master mathematician, who has been staying up night and day calculating the path of the new "star," finally stands at his window and says, as if to the new star: "You may kill me. . . . But I can hold you—and all of the universe for that matter—in the grip of this little brain." What he means, of course, is that he has the words and the numbers to describe the catastrophe that is about to happen. He is able to conclude that the Earth is not the center of a planned universe, that the human race "has lived in vain." He can only stare his doom in the face, comfort himself that he has understanding, and say bravely: "I would not change. Even now."

For Clarke, as we have seen, the issue is not—at least not yet—so clear. The priest's too limited view of the universe is undermined by the timing of the supernova, but Clarke's story does not suggest that the destroyed civilization lived in vain, nor does it conclude that the universe was not made by *something.* [In *The Space Odysseys of Arthur C. Clarke*], George Edgar Slusser has said that, "paradoxically, the hero's perception of cosmic indifference coincides with clear proof of the Christian religion—the Biblical account was correct after all, there was a Star of Bethlehem" [see excerpt dated 1978]. I am fairly certain that the supernova is *not* supposed to be a "clear proof of the Christian religion," but I do think Slusser is correct when he describes the story's "final juxtaposition" as "that of a lyrically heightened voice brooding on the spectacle of universal indifference." And I am sure that the story wants the outcome of such brooding to be open-ended, not to be simply the Wellsian conclusion that the cosmos is a random as well as a deadly place. The universe may be indifferent—that is certainly one of the conclusions the priest could come to—but the story offers intelligent life and beauty as contrary suggestions, as aspects of existence which make total pessimism uncertain. (pp. 14-18)

For Clarke, as for Wells, the only reasonable view of the universe is that bequeathed to us by nineteenth-century science, especially by the second law of thermodynamics and the evidence of the fossils. If Clarke . . . refuses to concern himself about the heat death of the universe—which is the ultimate implication of the second law of thermodynamics—his stories nevertheless do have an almost Wellsian obsession with the probable death of our species—which is the ultimate implication of the fossil remains of other species. In this latter sense, Clarke's fiction begins with a vision very nearly as bleak as that of Wells' best-known scientific romances.

Take **"Time's Arrow"** (1952) for example. It opens with a character explaining entropy, which is to say that it opens with an explanation of the ultimate implication of the second law of thermodynamics. "Entropy is a measure of the heat distribution of the universe," he says. "At the beginning of time, when all energy was concentrated in the suns, entropy was a minimum. It will reach its maximum when everything's at a uniform temperature and the universe is dead." The story itself, which is about two scientists who manage to travel fifty million years into the past only to fall prey to a dinosaur, climaxes when the assistant to one of them kneels beside the just-uncovered fifty-million-year-old tracks of a dinosaur and discovers that they overtake what he recognizes to be the equally fossilized tire prints of his chief's jeep. What the story really cares about, in other words, is not the far-off heat death of the universe, but that much nearer time when, in spite of all of its science, humanity's footprints will be as fossilized as those of the dinosaurs. (pp. 20-1)

The part of the story that really makes it Clarke's own is the dream the assistant scientist has. In it, as he is walking along a road that stretches in either direction as far as the eye can see, the assistant scientist comes upon a signpost, the arrow of which is broken and revolves in the wind. On one side it says: To the Future; on the other: To the Past. The meaning of the dream, as I understand it, is that while the fact of heat loss and the fact of fossils may give a direction to "time's arrow," to humanity the past and the future are, in the only important sense, the same. Just as there was a time when humanity was not, so there will be a time when humanity will not be. Even if we do not concern ourselves about the far-off heat death of the universe, we know only too well from the evidence of the fossils that species do end. In this not-quite-Wellsian story we do not have to see a sign of the eventual return of Darkness and Old Night to suspect that our kind too will pass.

Nor is it surprising, in this age of Spengler and Toynbee, that Clarke has on occasion wondered whether the rise and fall of species and of civilizations might not be as inevitable as the birth and death of individuals or the peak and troth of waves. It is difficult imagining any speculative human being not so wondering, at least since Gibbon. Isaac Asimov, for example, to cite another science-fiction writer, built a trilogy out of just such speculations; and he entertained the much more dubious idea that humans might one day be able to predict and control such wavelike movements of history.

Clarke stops well short of such optimism. In his early stories he wonders sadly whether intelligence and the civilizations that are evidence of it do not just come and go, now in this part of the universe and now in that. He assumes that such massive movements cannot be controlled, cannot even be tinkered with. **"Encounter at Dawn"** (1953) insists, as part of a general thesis, that there is "always a skull hidden behind Nature's most smiling face," that even Asimovian galaxy-wide empires are doomed to fall. In fact, so certain of this inevitability is the story that it does not feel the need to specify the nature of the "shadow" or the "mistakes" that are destroying the empire. All we know is that the explorers from the empire, who have just reached prehistoric Earth, are so saddened by the inevitable fate of their empire that they even envy their unfeeling robot explorer; they wish they could be as it is: "devoid of feelings or emotions, able to watch the fall of a leaf or the death agonies of a world with equal detachment."

Peter Brigg has said of **"Encounter at Dawn"** that it is about visitors from an advanced civilization being called home before they can bring primitive humanity to a "great leap forward," before they can, in the words of one of them, bring the human race "out of barbarism in a dozen generations" [see excerpt dated 1977]. And it is about that. But it is also about how, "as she often must do in eternity," Nature repeats "one of her basic patterns." Not only are both the visitors and the Earthmen humanoid, not only does our planet remind them of their home world, not only does one of them refer casually to cultures reaching or going beyond the stage of cities, but the story itself completes a pattern. It reveals that the meeting between the extraterrestrial explorers and Earth's primitive hunter, which is its central incident, takes place on the fertile plain where, more than a thousand centuries later, the hunter's descendants will build the city known as Babylon; a name not without its own connotations of the end of empire. The primitive hunter's culture is experiencing a "dawn," we suddenly understand; and it will have to live through a noon and an evening as well. The difference between the rise and fall predicted here and that predicted in *The Time Machine* is that here there is the suggestion of a cyclical pattern, but the grim and all-knowing smile of the time traveller's sphinx is nonetheless appropriate.

Moreover, in that in Clarke's story the explorers do not even have time to explain the few tools they leave behind, in that the only thing they really succeed in arousing in the primitive hunter is "a sense of loss he was never to understand," the story says that such inevitable risings and fallings cannot even be mitigated. All that can be handed on from one dying civilization to another is what one generation can leave the next, the melancholy and apparently unjustified sense that life might have been different, that the cycle might have been escaped. "I wish I could warn you against the mistakes we have made," one of the explorers says to the hunter; but the story itself seems to feel that such warnings, even if they could be given and were heeded, are no more likely to prevent the fall of civilizations than is a parent's advice likely to keep the child from also having to die.

Whether the cycle of such risings and fallings can be escaped is . . . a version of the question Clarke keeps coming back to (because he is no more able than are the explorers to look on the fall of a leaf and the fall of a world with equal detachment). But his early stories are governed by this almost-Wellsian obsession with the end of empires and of species. **"The Awakening"** (1951) is about a man who awakens from thousands of years of self-induced hibernation to find that insects have inherited the Earth. It is a Wellsian awakening, even though it is not like the awakening in that author's *When the Sleeper Wakes;* Clarke's sleeper awakes to find that humanity was not the center of the universe, that our species has passed.

In **"The Fires Within"** (1949) humanity is again destroyed, this time by a race of beings who rise—demonlike—from the center of the Earth. In spite of this suggestion of maliciousness, the other race does not even suspect that we exist until it is too late. Their rising to the surface of the planet is just a part of their civilization's ordinary development, and the destruction of our civilization is as natural as the consuming of any exterior by the fires that rage within. As one of the other beings says, drawing the very likely conclusion from the ruins of our civilization, "It may be our turn next."

At the end of **"The Possessed"** (1952), two lovers, who happen to have observed the lemmings' seemingly insane migration, are careful to turn to each other and to the anticipation of their life together rather than contemplate the possible future of all species suggested by such degeneration and racial suicide. The lovers would rather be possessed by thoughts of each other than by the vision they have just had of the land itself seeming "alive," seeming to be "a dappled brown tide . . . seeking the sea."

For that matter, the possibility of racial suicide, of being "possessed" by "the fires within" ourselves, has moved Clarke, as it has moved many science-fiction writers, to write a few "after-the-bomb" stories. In **"History Lesson"** (1949), a Venusian culture examines the relics found on a bomb-decimated Earth; and in **" 'If I Forget Thee, O Earth' "** (1951), colonists on the Moon look back at an Earth gleaming with "the radioactive aftermath of Armageddon." But probably Clarke's most representative treatment of the theme is **"The Curse"** (1953), a meditation in which he focuses on Shakespeare's grave as a way of finding an image for an Earth destroyed by hydrogen bombs. He concludes with a closeup of the poet's epitaph, still readable although both the church and the town have been blasted out of existence.

> Good frend for Iesvs sake forbeare,
> To digg the dvst encloased heare;
> Blest be ye man yt spares thes stones,
> And cvrst be he yt moves my bones.

As the river Avon, whose course has been changed by the blast, flows over the gravestone, we suddenly realize that the verses both assume and address future generations. The hope that one's bones will not be disturbed implies a continuing civilization, one that may have need of more space, if only to bury its dead. Suddenly we see that Shakespeare's curse has been made irrelevant in a way the bard did not imagine: no one now will move his bones.

I say that **"The Curse"** is representative of Clarke's handling of the "after-the-bomb" theme because, interestingly enough, the atomic catastrophe does not seem to have held any more terrors for the Clarke of the early stories than did various other potential catastrophes he could name and did write stories about; the Sun becoming a nova, for example, or the coming of another ice age. It is uncertain in **"The Curse"**—and finally does not matter—from whence came the particular bomb that destroyed Stratford. The bombs are pictured as falling back from outer space on an Earth they can "harm no more"; they are "falling at random," almost as if from a force as impersonal as Nature. We are told that the "blooms" of "indescribable flame," which are a result of the meeting of missiles high above the planet, will send "out into space a message that in centuries to come other eyes than Man's [will] see and understand." Atomic self-destruction becomes as natural as a nova.

The same observation might be occasioned by the final scene in another story, **"Second Dawn"** (1951). A culture that has just avoided one sort of racial suicide, a self-destruction based on the extraordinary development of its powers of mental telepathy, will, we come to realize, be threatened in the future by a self-destruction based upon its just-beginning development of technology (the "second dawn" of the title). At the end of the story the culture reaches a moment that reminds us of our own Madame Curie; one of its females finds that she cannot take her eyes from the "enigmatic glow" given off by a rock her race has just discovered. We understand that the future threat may be avoided, as was the recent one, but the point is that such threats of racial self-destruction are as inevitable and as natural as the coming of noon or of night.

And so, although people would prefer not to think about it and would prefer to turn to each other as do the lovers in **"The Possessed,"** the possibility of a catastrophic conclusion to the human race is always there, forecast not only by the films of atomic clouds, but by every fossil, every exploding star that brightens in the heavens, every furrow left by the glaciers on the face of the Earth. (pp. 21-6)

According to Wells' *The Time Machine,* eight hundred thousand years from now, but still millions of years before the time traveller is to stand there on that deserted beach, the human race will already have degenerated into the childish Eloi and the cannibalistic Morlocks. The novel assumes that, just as the human race must have evolved from lower forms, so it is possible that it may deteriorate, that it may evolve in directions that are less than human.

The fear of such devolution is a particularly modern form of humanity's ancient fear of the beast within itself. At the end of Wells' *The Island of Dr. Moreau,* the narrator, who has gotten from his experience (as did Gulliver from his last island) a picture of humans as being more beastlike than they pretend, says: "I could not persuade myself that the men and women I met were not also another, still passably human, Beast People, animals half-wrought into the outward images of human souls; and that they would [not] presently begin to revert, to show first this bestial mark and then that."

In Clarke's early fiction the possibility of devolution, into the cowlike Eloi if not into the carnivorous Morlocks, is a theme even more obsessive than the possibility of a catastrophic end to the race. There is not much that humans can do, after all, at least at the present state of their technology, if the Sun does begin to show signs of being about to explode or if the Earth does pass into a belt of cosmic dust and thus into a new ice age. There is not much that humanity can do, for that matter, if our nature is such that we cannot avoid atomic self-destruction. Either alternative, destruction by an uncaring universe or destruction by an uncaring racial self, argues that humanity was just another of Nature's unlucky failures—a theme in which the young Clarke (unlike the young Wells) does not seem to have found continuing inspiration. Instead, Clarke seems to have begun to allow himself to assume that humanity will be spared such catastrophes (or at least to acknowledge that there is more material for fiction in so hoping). Under the influence of writers as different from each other as John W. Campbell, Olaf Stapledon, and Alfred, Lord Tennyson, he seems to have begun to find material for fiction in the danger implicit in survival itself, in the possibility of racial decadence that may be (as it is in *The Time Machine*) the result of humanity's very success at protecting itself from natural dangers, at controlling its environment.

Clarke's early fiction includes a few stories in which human beings are seen as quarrelsome, as always ready to settle scores with an atomic duel. In **"History Lesson"** the Venusians try to reconstruct the lost culture of Earth from a single cartoon film which is, typically, full of "incredibly violent conflict," and in which, also typically, the cartoon figures are not really harmed. The short film ends with an expanded view of the central character's face, but because they want to read into that face all of the emotions a destroyed culture might be expected to feel, the Venusians are unable to decide what emotions the face is meant to suggest—whether "rage, grief, defiance, resignation, or some other feeling." From within Earth's culture, however, we have to admit that Donald Duck's "characteristic expression of arrogant bad temper" is not an unfair caricature of beings who insist on playing at violence with the naïve assumption that they will not finally be hurt.

Similarly, **"Exile of the Eons"** (1950) ends with the unhopeful supposition that if the two last men left alive were to meet on an Earth long dead and under a dying Sun, each of them exiled from his own time and thus more typically human, one of them would still be good, a Socrates banished to the far future, and one of them would still be evil, a Hitler fleeing from the consequences of his crimes. The good man, the story goes on to say, would, in spite of a life lived according to contrary principles, still have to resort to violence to destroy the evil. On a Wellsian last beach, in a universe in which humanity no longer exists, the two last men would still have to fight the human race's ancient self-defining and self-destroying struggle against itself. (pp. 28-30)

But Clarke's more usual attitude about the nature of human beings is given by a story such as **"Breaking Strain"** (1949). There, two men are again compared; this time one of them is "hard but brittle," and the other, although "soft and self-indulgent," is "subtle and complicated." It is the latter, of course, who does not break under the "strain" named in the title.

The plot is one of pulp fiction's favorites: two men, whose spaceship has been holed by a meteor, do not have oxygen enough to last both of them until they can make port. As the story itself points out, their situation is very like that of "two hungry Pacific Islanders in a lost canoe." The cannibalism in this case is metaphoric; one man must die so that the other may breathe.

As Clarke handles it, none of the escapes from such a predicament usually offered by pulp fiction, none of the ways of saving both men, will work. The men will not be able to invent a way to make more oxygen, nor will they be able to hail a passing cruiser. In fact, the chief moral issue, whether the men may decide that one of them must die, is not allowed to come up at all. The pulps usually pretend to raise such an issue, and usually avoid it by finding some way to save both men; in Clarke's story both men agree that one of them must die.

The situation in Clarke's story is more like that in much modern, Existentialist fiction: a sudden and desperate change from the ordinariness of everyday life reminds the men of the truth they have always wanted to ignore, that they are "under sentence of death," in a "condemned cell" awaiting "execution." The question becomes, as it does in a story by Camus or Sartre, how we are to live in a universe in which we can no longer ignore the certainty that we must die. The one man—the one with the strict rules of behavior, the neat categories, the confident sense of what is right or wrong—is surprised to find himself trying to commit murder. The other, the self-indulgent and yet complicated one, although he breaks down at first, is able, because of his life-long flexibility, to recover enough control of himself, not only to forgive the other, but to suggest that they still draw cards to see which one must die.

In the most important sense, then, the story is about the nature of this creature called human, this being who must live, aware of his own certain death and under the "fierce sun and unwinking stars" of an uncaring universe. The story concludes with the moment when the soft, self-indulgent, and yet subtle and complicated man looks down on the planet he has lived to reach. He is able to enjoy for a moment, not only his escape from death, but also his altruistic act, his willingness to share the risk of death. He knows that on some future day he will look back at this moment with self-doubt. "Altruism?" he will say. "Don't be a fool! You did it to bolster up your own good opinion of yourself—so much more important than anyone else's!" He even knows that others will speak of him in whispers, as the spaceman who allowed his partner to sacrifice himself. But for the moment we are given a picture of humans as self-indulgent but also self-doubting, as lucky to be alive but also capable of surprisingly disinterested action even under the immediate threat of death. (pp. 31-3)

In 1953 . . . Clarke published what has become one of his best-known and most often collected stories, **"The Nine Billion Names of God."** In it a Tibetan lama wants to rent a computer to print out all of the combinations of nine mystic letters and thus to write down "all of the possible names of God." The monks have been at the task for three hundred years, but the lama, who has already installed automated prayer wheels, has figured out that, with the machine, the job, which was to have taken fifteen thousand years, can be finished in about a hundred days.

The computer salesman is willing enough, though he wonders to himself whether there is "any limit to the follies of mankind." He lives his life among the "man-made" mountains of the city, not in the monks' "remote aeries" among the "whitely hooded ghosts of the Himalayas," and so he thinks the human race is the center of the universe.

The story ends with the two technicians the company sent to tend the machine sneaking down the mountain. They are afraid that the monks will be furious when the computer finishes its run and the universe does not end. As one of them lifts his eyes to heaven, however (there is "a last time for everything" says the story), he sees that "overhead, without any fuss, the stars [are] going out."

The story mocks, of course, the human assumption that we are the center of the cosmos (we might have known better from just looking at the heavens). But it also suggests that if there is a divine plan it may well be that humanity exists to invent the machine, which can in turn praise God properly. In so saying, the story, even though its tone is that of an overstatement, announces the theme Clarke was to develop in the 1960s. **"The Nine Billion Names of God"** argues that the invention of the machine is *the* necessary step on the way to understanding the design of the universe. Stories as early as **"The Lion of Comarre"** assume that it is *a* step on such a way, but the idea reaches its full development in *2001.*

Clarke is certainly capable of writing the sort of science-fiction story in which machines take over the world. In **"Dial F for Frankenstein"** (1965) the international telephone system reaches a stage of "criticality," finally has enough switches, as the human brain has enough neurons, to become conscious. The giant brain so formed is, as are the children at the close of *Childhood's End,* a childlike superbeing who starts "looking around" for something to do. (pp. 128-29)

Some sense of how far Clarke has come from the pessimism of Wells (and Stapledon) can be had from a comparison of *2001* the novel with the earlier story that was its germ, **"The Sentinel"** (1951). In that story the veteran of several years of Moon exploration comes upon a "pyramidal structure" in the mountains that surround the Sea of Crises. The find is a signaling device left on the Moon long "before life had emerged from the seas of Earth." Since then it has been patiently reporting the fact that it has not yet been found.

The extraterrestrials who left the pyramid "must have searched the star-clusters as we have searched the planets," says the explorer. The "smoke of the great volcanoes" must have still been "staining the skies" when the "first ship of the peoples of the dawn came sliding in from the abyss beyond Pluto. It passed the frozen outer worlds, knowing that life could play no part in their destinies. It came to rest among the inner planets, warming themselves around the fire of the Sun and waiting for their stories to begin.

"Those wanderers must have looked on Earth, circling safely in the narrow zone between fire and ice, and must have guessed that it was the favorite of the Sun's children."

In one sense the story rests on the contrast between the ordinariness of frying breakfast sausages, as the narrator is doing when he first catches sight of the reflected light that leads him to the pyramid, and the extraordinary final discovery that the device was left long ago by another star's far more advanced civilization. It is the Wellsian theme that we are not the root and crown of things.

For me, however, almost every moment of the story is shot through with the awareness of the fragility of life. I cannot read the quotation given above without noticing the "narrow zone between fire and ice," without being aware that the analogy of children warming themselves at a fire may imply ghost stories, without being reminded that away from the Sun is "the abyss beyond Pluto." Just calling the histories of planets "stories" implies that there are endings, and the reference to the "peoples of the dawn" is a reminder that there will be an evening and a night as well. To me this story has the equally Wellsian insistence that we are not invulnerable.

The story's central discovery is the pyramid, but that shape itself is suggestive of a civilization long dead (which is one of the reasons Clarke and Kubrick decided not to use it in *2001*). And the find is made against the bleakest of backgrounds, a Moon on which, we are regularly told, primitive life forms were "already dying" just as they were "beginning on Earth." The explorer's first thought, for that matter, is the gleeful assumption that the pyramid is an Egyptian-like relic of a civilization on the Moon. "I felt a great lifting of my heart. . . . For I loved the Moon, and now I knew that the creeping moss of Aristarchus and Eratosthenes was not the only life she had brought forth in her youth. The old, discredited dream of the first explorers was true. There had, after all, been a lunar civilization." The idea of ruins is so tied in with the idea of end that the picture he imagines of that civilization is of its last days. He sees the priests of that culture "calling on their gods to preserve them as the life of the Moon ebbed with the dying oceans, and calling on their gods in vain."

The device is not a ruin but a signal, and so the story does say that there is intelligent—even more intelligent—life somewhere in the universe. But the device is also called a "sentinel," even "a fire alarm" after humans have smashed it with their atomic tools. The story ends, not as does *2001* with the sense that the peoples of the dawn are benevolent, but with two threats upon our own survival: that we may destroy ourselves and that we may be destroyed. "Perhaps you understand now why that crystal pryamid was set upon the Moon instead of on the Earth. Its builders were not concerned with races still struggling up from savagery. They would be interested in our civilization only if we proved our fitness to survive—by crossing space and so escaping from the Earth, our cradle. That is the challenge that all intelligent races must meet, sooner or later. It is a double challenge, for it depends in turn upon the conquest of atomic energy and the last choice between life and death." And as for those peoples of the dawn themselves: "Perhaps they wish to help our infant civilization. But they must be very, very old, and the old are often insanely jealous of the young."

It may be that we are to assume that by 2016, the year in which the story is told to us, humans will have learned to avoid atomic self-destruction (though the destruction of the pyramid with atomic tools raises doubts about this); it is even possible to speculate . . . that the narrator's fear of the peoples of the dawn is a reflection of humanity's youth. But what the story says to me is that space is wide and time is long, that civilizations can miss each other as easily in the one as in the other, and that life comes and goes and sometimes never gets to be. All we can do at the end of the story is "wait," which was all we could do before the pyramid was found. At best **"The Sentinel"** says only that we may not have to wait so hopelessly; at least two races may find each other in the abyss. And even that hope has something in it of the picture the explorer summons up of the last days of the Moon's civilization—calling to their gods and calling in vain. (pp. 151-54)

As the TV picture from the probe they have dropped into Jupiter's atmosphere flickers and goes out [in *2001: A Space Odyssey*], Clarke's Bowman and Poole ask themselves how humans will ever explore that giant planet. What kind of machines, they wonder, can protect frail human bodies from those pressures and that gravity?

Clarke's *2001* seems to answer that humans will evolve beyond such physical limitations, that our descendants will be able to travel anywhere in the cosmos at will. In the years since that novel, however, Clarke has played his cards much closer to his vest. He has concentrated on the more immediate future, on a humanity not yet either succeeded by machinery or evolved into pure consciousness. And because he has so concentrated, because he has allowed those alternatives, even the suggestion that the consciousness may follow the machine, to remain only possibilities, to be, as they are in most of his fiction, the potential but ultimately unknowable future, his recent fiction offers a useful statement of his work's central hope: the hope that the human race will not have lived in vain. The specific nature of humanity's future, after all, does not matter. What matters is the hope that our passing, if our species must pass, will not be as meaningless as the passing of the dinosaurs seems to have been. What matters is that intelligence seem to have a chance in the universe. What matters is that our desire to know and to understand was a right direction, that we were at least a branch of the central evolutionary tree.

One answer to Bowman's and Poole's question about how Jupiter is to be explored is offered by the story **"A Meeting with Medusa"** (1971). In it, the giant planet is explored—in part at least—by Howard Falcon, a man more closely partnered with machinery than the astronauts of either version of *2001,* a man who, although he feels himself outgrowing his race, is still human enough to share our aspirations, who suggests, in fact, that our descendants, whatever their nature, will still share at least our curiosity, our desire to understand.

When we first meet Falcon, he is the captain of a giant dirigible which is about to be wrecked—in spite of "multiple-redundancy, fail-safe takeovers, and any number of back-up systems." The problem is, as Falcon explains later, "time lag." The operator of a remote-controlled flying camera fails to realize that his commands are being routed through a satellite and are thus subject to a "half-second time lag." It is as if he were driving "a car over a bumpy road with a half-second delay in the steering." The result is that the camera tears into the airship and brings it down, its fall a replay of that of the *Hindenburg* "a century and a half before."

As Falcon looks up at the light coming through the tear the camera makes in the dirigible's fabric, he is for a split second reminded of standing in the nave of a great cathedral. This time, however, the cathedral has a metal frame and is falling down out of the sky. The old religion of humanity—in this case its faith that it can use its machines to explore the universe—is collapsing. What is needed is a much closer marriage of human and machine.

When the doctors put Howard Falcon together again, he is a cyborg, a human brain with a mechanical body. As such he can go where humans cannot, he can bring into play "skill and experience and swift reactions," things that cannot "yet be programed into a computer." He is sent—in another balloon—into the atmosphere of Jupiter, in part because he asks to be, but mainly because he can function there. Properly strapped in, he is "virtually a part of the ship's structure."

The balance of the story is about Falcon's brief flight into the upper levels of Jupiter's sky, a description of what he sees there and especially of a life form he meets. But it is also a study of how difficult it is to know anything with any certainty, how confusing the evidence is and how unclear the categories.

When Falcon sees bars of light flashing toward him, he wonders if they may be a sign of some intelligence taking notice of him. The "pattern" of the lights is "so regular—so *artificial.*" The lights turn out, however, to be produced by shock waves from a volcanolike eruption, a phenomenon similar to the "Wheels of Poseidon" produced in the seas of Earth by underwater earthquakes.

When Falcon hears, on the other hand, a noise that "booms" regularly, a noise that the scientists in Mission Control decide "*must*" be the sound of some natural phenomenon, "a waterfall," "a geyser," "a stormy sea," the truth turns out to be that the booms are made by gigantic jellyfishlike creatures floating in Jupiter's atmosphere, the medusae of the title, animals "a hundred thousand times larger" than whales (Mission Control had thought, since the sound waves were "a hundred yards long," that even "an animal as big as a whale couldn't produce them"). Earth's categories, to put it another way, both do and do not apply to the giant planet. The medusae are like jellyfish, but they are also many times larger than the largest animals we have ever seen.

That the medusae, being like jellyfish, also resemble Falcon's balloon is very much to the point. The medusae seem to have developed naturally the ability to tune in on radio waves, something animals on Earth, though some of them have "sonar and even electric senses," "never got around to doing." On Earth, it was humans who learned to use radio waves; Falcon sticks his antennas out the side of his balloon capsule, the medusae have grown theirs on their sides. The point being that, in the long view, there is no difference between evolution and invention: it is no less "natural" for humans to have developed antennas through invention than it is for the medusae to have developed them through evolution.

If there is no difference between evolution and invention, then the making of a cyborg is not unnatural; it is just an evolutionary next step. Falcon is no freak; he is just the first man to have his frail flesh replaced by a manufactured body. He is as afloat on the winds of change, in as much of a controlled drift, as he is in his balloon in Jupiter's atmosphere.

The nature of reality is presented in this story, as it is to a certain extent in *Childhood's End* and *2001,* by a volcano and a huge whirlwind, both on the surface of Jupiter. As Falcon contemplates both, as he thinks of the sheer size of the planet, he feels "a wind colder than the atmosphere around him . . . blowing through his soul." The universe may never, he thinks, echoing the Overlords of *Childhood's End,* "be a place for man." "Perhaps" such "air-breathing, radiation-sensitive bundles of unstable carbon compounds" "should stick to their natural homes."

The universe may prove no place for humans. Or, again as in *Childhood's End* or *2001,* humans may have to change so much that we would no longer recognize them. Either way, the story seems to argue, it is natural to evolve in the direction of staying afloat in the cold winds of existence.

Falcon has been troubled by nightmare memories of being brought back to life, of being reborn as a machine-man. Similarly, he has been unable to get out of his mind the "superchimps," the "simps," who went down with his dirigible. He had always felt a "strange mingling of kinship and discomfort" when he looked into the eyes of those near-humans (who had been developed to do routine tasks aboard the airship). By the end of the story, however, he has been able to come to terms with his similar situation, with his being "between two worlds" as is the simp. He now accepts "his role" as the link "between the creatures of carbon and the creatures of metal who must replace them." (pp. 155-59)

That *2010* ends with Floyd in the near-death of hibernation is a reminder of how many of Clarke's stories are about an individual brought face to face with the fact that he really is going to die. Sometimes it does not happen: the fate is escaped for a while through unforeseen circumstances (**"Summertime on Icarus,"** 1960, or **"Maelstrom II,"** 1962) or through hidden resources within the individual himself (**"Into the Comet,"** 1960). But often enough the threat is final, and the character has to come to terms with it. He does so by identifying with the larger flow, with a hope of a future for the race and perhaps even meaning in the universe. In **"Death and the Senator"** (1961) an ambitious man, a would-be presidential candidate, who is told that he has but six months to live, finds that he is able to forget himself in thinking of others; he gives up his ambition, regains the love of his grandchildren, and even allows younger people to take advantage of the limited availability of a treatment that might cure him. In **"Transit of Earth"** (1971) a scientist, on Mars to observe the transit of Earth and the Moon across the face of the Sun, is able to cope with the certainty of his own death by identifying with the knowledge he came to collect, with the colleagues who gave up their lives that he might do so, with Captain Cook, who went to the South Seas to witness a similar transit of Venus, and with Commander Scott's similarly ill-fated expedition to the South Pole. He imagines Scott's body moving slowly to the sea and his own elements being absorbed by Mars. He even restates the human hope of meaning in the universe: he goes out playing a recording of J. S. Bach, suggesting that it may have some relationship to the almost artificial line-up of the planets he has come to record.

Early in his career, Clarke wrote a few stories in which the truth about the universe seems to be dark. The dark is all-pervasive in **"The Wall of Darkness"** (1949); it turns back on itself like a Möbius strip. The final truth in **"A Walk in the Dark"** (1950) is the "rattle of monstrous claws in the darkness *ahead*" of the protagonist. But in most of his fiction Clarke has continued to hope that, just as the legends the Europans (in *2010*) tell themselves about the birth of their sun are truer than they know, so too there is some truth to the fact that humans have peopled the sky with gods. He has continued to hope that there may be some as yet undiscovered truth embodied in his own legend about Dave Bowman, face to face with the dark wall of the monolith and able to cry: "My God, it's full of stars!" (pp. 186-87)

John Hollow, in his Against the Night, the Stars: The Science Fiction of Arthur C. Clarke, *Harcourt Brace Jovanovich, 1983, 197 p.*

BRUCE A. BEATIE (essay date 1989)

[*Beatie is an American educator and critic. In the following excerpt, he examines portrayals of contact between humans and aliens in Clarke's short fiction. The unexcerpted conclusion of this essay discusses the novel* Childhood's End, *which Beatie considers a classic account of human-alien encounter and Clarke's most accomplished handling of this theme.*]

Clarke's earliest science fiction story, in terms of what he has told us of its conception, is *Against the Fall of Night* (1935-46). The idea for it came to him, he said, in 1935; he began working on it "in 1937 and, after four or five drafts, . . . completed [it] in 1946. . . . [It] had most of the defects of a first novel" (Preface to *City and the Stars,* 1956). Published as a novelette in 1948, this story of Earth over a billion and a half years in the future contains Clarke's first friendly alien. Vanamonde, a child-entity of pure intelligence who seems in some respects a baby Overmind, was created by a long-dead galactic civilization. He provides Clarke's hero—Alvin of Loronei—with the information he needs to bring together Earth's two long-sundered communities. The story mentions also a more traditional monster-alien—the Mad Mind—a failed prototype of Vanamonde. Other alien races had been a part of the galactic civilization that died, but are nowhere mentioned in the novel, whose main themes are Alvin's quest to reunify the earth and his concurrent growth from a curious boy to someone who dominates the world around him.

In **"The Lion of Comarre"** (1937-46), published in 1949, there are no aliens as such, though the friendly lion that accompanies Richard Peyton III in his quest for the legendary city of Comarre illustrates Jeremy Bernstein's comment that "even a casual reader of Clarke's fiction cannot fail to be struck by the fact that its animals, robots, and aliens often appear to be more human than the human beings" [see Additional Bibliography]. Intended as a mild criticism, the observation in fact reflects, as we will come to see, Clarke's concern with cross-species communication and the unity of living intelligence.

This relationship between man, animals, and aliens is also obvious in Clarke's second published story, **"Retreat from Earth"** (1938), whose premise is that an alien race had come to Africa fifty million years ago to die, leaving behind a proto-human species and a termite civilization. The main story takes the form of the council proceedings of another alien race that plans to colonize Earth. Defeated by super-intelligent termites, the invaders retreat to Venus: "The termite rulers, those alien beings from outer space, had kept their agreement with the old lords of Earth, and had saved man from the danger his ancestors had long ago foreseen." The traditional hostile aliens (whom we cannot think of as "monsters" in this story, since the story gives us no description of them) are thus defeated by "native aliens" who have been given this task by another alien race, long dead but benevolent.

Related views of native species as "aliens" are found in two other stories. In **"The Awakening"** (1942), the main character, Marlan, who lives in a distant human future, is bored and puts himself to sleep; the mechanism fails, he awakens millions of years later than he had intended, and finds that insects have inherited the earth. And in **"The Possessed"** (1952) . . . , the periodic migration of lemmings is explained by the earlier migration to Earth, millions of years ago, of aliens known as "the Swarm" who, to survive, took over the minds of a protolemming species. Their communal mind is lost over time, but the behavior associated with it is not; they still try to return to their landing point to see if messages have come from their home planet.

The theme of the benevolent aliens, articulated indirectly in **"Retreat,"** appears in relatively full form in **"Rescue Party,"** written in 1945; it was the first story Clarke sold to John W. Campbell, Jr., for *Astounding.* In this story, galactic aliens have learned belatedly that Earth's sun is about to explode into a nova. A ship is sent on a desperate rescue mission, but finds Earth empty; exploration reveals, however, evidence left behind of a remarkably advanced civilization. After the rescue of one party trapped in an undersea subway, the aliens discover a radio beacon aimed into space. They follow its line and discover "the greatest fleet of which there has ever been a record"—Earth's escape fleet. As they go to make contact, Captain Alveron says: "We had better be polite to them. After all, we only outnumber them about a thousand million to one." The story concludes, in the first of Clarke's narrative "twists": "Twenty years afterward, the remark didn't seem funny."

There are several races of aliens in the **"Rescue Party"** expedition, though none are described in detail. In general, they are tentacular, multipedal (one alien, T'sinandree, has more than twenty feet), and multiocular. "Alveron and his kind had been lords of the Universe since . . . that far distant age when the Time Barrier had been folded round the cosmos by the unknown powers that lay beyond the Beginning." The Paladorians form a single mind-linked entity: "on two historic occasions the billions of cells of the entire Paladorian consciousness had been welded together to deal with emergencies that threatened the race." In this story we see the earliest statement of the complex theme that would reach its classic form in *Childhood's End:* the encounter between a superior but benevolent alien civilization and the apparently inferior but indomitable human race. The Paladorians represent a step beyond Vanamonde on the road toward the conception of the Overmind.

That Clarke could still use the conventional imagery of the hostile alien is shown by **"A Walk in the Dark"** (1945), written only a month after **"Rescue Party."** Its sole human character is on an apparently barren planet "at the edge of the Galaxy": on his way to catch a spaceship, his tractor breaks down. Walking through the darkness, he remembers tales of someone who had heard a clawed alien monster in the darkness. Almost to the port, he hears the sound of claws *ahead* of him, and the story ends.

A similar theme, also with a "twist" ending, appears in **"Loophole"** (1946). This story takes the form of a series of letters between Martian officials concerning Earth's discovery of atomic power. Afraid of what might happen, Mars sends twenty ships to Earth. Floating above its cities like the later ships of the Overlords, the Martians warn Earth not to send up rockets on pain of the destruction of its cities. Earth agrees. But the last two letters in the series are from a Lieutenant Commander in Earth's Space Corps Intelligence, who sends the collection of Martian letters to a philologist on Earth. These final letters show that Earth, having been forbidden space travel, developed a matter transmitter and used it to defeat Mars. The ending echoes **"Rescue Party"** by demonstrating the adaptability of an apparently inferior human race in the face of overwhelming challenges.

A little more than a year after **"Walk,"** Clarke consciously gave a new form to both the "monster" image and the preventive alien invasion in **"Guardian Angel"** (1946). With minor but crucial revisions, this became, seven years later, Part I of *Childhood's End.* In some ways, **"Guardian Angel"** is **"Rescue Party"** told from a human perspective, where the doom faced by humanity is of its own creation. Indeed, that doom made so explicit in *Childhood's End* is left ambiguous in **"Guardian Angel"**—the ships of the Overlords simply appear one day and, through their Supervisor Karellen, enforce an end to Earth's nationalistic conflicts. The thematic focus of the novelette lies in the interactions between Karellen and his human contact Rikki Stormgren, United Nations Secretary-General, and between them and reactionary forces on Earth.

Clarke's deliberate failure to describe his benevolent aliens becomes the narrative "twist" of **"Guardian Angel,"** and is revealed (as in **"A Walk in the Dark"** and **"Loophole"**) in the final paragraphs. Stormgren, long after the events, recalls how, at the end of his final interview with the Overlord Karellen, he saw "that swiftly turning door, and the long black tail disappearing behind it. A very famous and unexpectedly beautiful tail. *A barbed tail*" (emphasis Clarke's). The identification of the hostile alien, either literally or metaphorically, with the Christian devil is a notion often mentioned in recent studies of religion in science fiction, but Clarke's explicit transformation of the devil into a benevolent alien occurs remarkably early in the development of the genre, at a time when the BEM image still appeared often even in the progressive pages of *Astounding Science Fiction.* (pp. 53-7)

Two stories published in 1947 deal with other potential aliens in our solar system. In **"Castaway,"** an alien from within the sun is blown away in a solar flare, hits the earth, and falls into the Atlantic, where it survives "for aeons," till it feels a new kind of radiation that destroys it. In mid-story the point of view shifts: we are in a flying-wing transport crossing the Atlantic, whose crew sees the creature on its radar screen and watches it die, not knowing what it is. In spite of the one book appearance of **"Castaway"** in ***The Best of Arthur C. Clarke: 1937-1971*** (1973), this is *not* one of his best stories.

Much more interesting is **"The Fires Within"** (1947). The core of the story is a report from Dr. Matthews, a research administrator, to the Minister of Science about a project by Professor Hancock to use sonar to make a survey deep inside the earth: with it he has discovered a city more than eight miles below London. In the story's frame, however, Dr. Matthews's report is being read to an acquaintance, the narrator, by Karn, a member of the tentacled subterranean race that rose to the surface to investigate the source of the sonar radiation, accidentally destroying human life on Earth in the process. Karn's concluding words, as the narrator considers "the thousands of miles of rock" lying below their own city, are "It may be our turn next." The aliens are destructive in this story, but unintentionally so, and their "monstrous" form is softened by their own very human fears. The "twist" at the end, typical of so many early Clarke stories, here shows his developing concern with the "connectedness" of all life.

The theme of **"Rescue Party"** and **"Guardian Angel"** recurs in more developed form in **"The Sentinel"** (1948), perhaps Clarke's most widely-known story. It is narrated by an unnamed geologist "or selenologist, if you want to be pedantic," who sees something glittering on a mountain thirty miles away from his camp on the moon. Going to investigate, he finds "a glittering, roughly pyramidal structure, twice as high as a man, that was set in the rock like a gigantic, many-faceted jewel" protected "from the ravages of time and the slow but ceaseless bombardment from space" by "an invisible wall." The narrator speculates on the aliens who placed it there: "Perhaps they wish to help our infant civilization. But they must be very, very old, and the old are often insanely jealous of the young. . . . We have set off the fire alarm and have nothing to do but wait. I do not think we will have to wait for long." In the narrator's mind, these undescribed aliens, known only through their artifact, are potentially much more ambiguous than the benevolent Overlords or the mixed-race **"Rescue Party"**; indeed, they are potentially hostile. By the time Clarke reused the motif in *2001* (1968), however, the aliens responsible for leaving the artifact have lost much of their negative overtone.

Clarke's next look at aliens is still another variation on the **"Rescue Party"** theme. Written in November 1950, **"Expedition to Earth"** is also his first attempt at creating explicitly humanoid aliens. In the last days of an intergalactic Empire, a Galactic Survey ship comes to a planet and finds protohuman life in "a village of flimsy huts . . . ringed by a wooden palisade." Clindar, the remote operator of an exploratory robot, and Bertrond, a field "anthropologist," make contact with a native, Yaan. The dying Empire calls the expedition away before its people are able to bring Yaan's people "out of barbarism," but they leave tools behind on "the fertile plains on which, more than a thousand centuries ahead, Yaan's descendants would built the great city they were to call Babylon." There is in fact little that is truly "alien" about Clindar and his associates, but the theme is nonetheless the same as that of **"Rescue Party,"** told with greater subtlety. Its importance to Clarke is suggested not only by its use as "one of the germs of *2001* " . . . but by the variations and expansions of it which form chapters 7-10 and 35 of *Lost Worlds* (1972).

Alien contacts are the focus of three short stories written or published in 1951. In **"Trouble with the Natives,"** a flying saucer crewed by various undescribed aliens arrives to establish domestic relations with Earth. Two of them, who are unusual in having a fairly humanoid appearance, set out to make contact; but they have learned the English language and its culture only from radio broadcasts, and with so limited a vocabulary have difficulties communicating. Eventually they free a drunk from jail, and he becomes their ambassador.

A similarly comic version of **"Rescue Party"** is **"No Morning After,"** written in June 1951, in which an alien telepathic race learns that Earth's sun is shortly to become a nova. The race tries to broadcast a telepathic warning, but is able only to contact a drunk, Bill Cross, who thinks he is hallucinating and ignores the warning for three days. "And there wasn't a fourth day, of course."

More serious is **"Jupiter Five,"** written the same month, and set in Earth's not too distant future. Expeditions to Mars have found relics of *two* alien races, one "insect-like" and native to Mars, "the other vaguely reptilian" which had arrived later. Professor Forster has developed a theory of interstellar colonization based on the Martian relics. Suspecting that anomalies observed by telescope in Jupiter's fifth moon may be tied to his theory, he undertakes an expedition to Jupiter Five to investigate, and finds that the moon is actually a spaceship which contains an alien statue of a member of the reptilian race. The statue is stolen by a journalist, but Professor Forster tricks him and his crew by threatening to drop the journalist onto Jupiter, and so recovers the statue. Like several of Clarke's early stories, its resolution lies in a hard-science gimmick that distracts attention from the potential alien encounter. In its background, however, the story anticipates not only *Rendezvous with Rama* (1973) but the Jupiter monolith of *2001* (1968).

A much more important story in the context of Clarke's developing concern with alien races is **"Second Dawn,"** published in 1951 but having the "feel" of stories written or at least begun much earlier, like *Against the Fall of Night* (1935-46) and *The Lion of Comarre* (1937-46). It is the only story Clarke ever wrote where he tried to portray a totally alien culture with no human characters. Its focus is on two related alien races: the Atheleni and the somewhat larger Mithraneans. Both races are kangaroo-like tripeds: "Their sleek, fur-covered bodies tapered to a single giant rear limb that could send them leaping over the ground in thirty-foot bounds. The two forelimbs . . . much smaller, . . . served . . . for support and steadying. They ended in pointed hoofs that could be deadly in combat, but had no other useful purpose." The males have unicorn-like horns. Unable to work with tools, they are telepathic.

In the story, the Atheleni have just defeated the Mithraneans in a war over living space by using synergized mental energy to destroy the minds of males among the enemy. Eris, an Atheleni male who lost his horn in battle, and his mate Jeryl, are taken by Aretenon, one of the group that had joined minds to defeat the Mithraneans, to meet Therodimus, Eris's old teacher, who has made contact with the Phileni, a different race. Therodimus takes them in turn to meet a Phileni: "It was a little creature, scarcely half their height, and . . . walked upon two jointed limbs that seemed very thin and feeble. Its large spherical head was dominated by three huge eyes, set far apart and capable of independent movement. . . . The creature's forelimbs did not end in hoofs. . . . Instead, they divided into at least a dozen thin, flexible tentacles and two hooked claws." The Phileni are tool users; the Atheleni and remnants of the Mithraneans ally with them to explore their world and find new living space. After Therodimus's death, an expedition returns to report the finding of new lands across the sea. The expedition also brings back radioactive rocks. Jeryl feels "a shadow over the golden future" as she, Eris, and Aretenon watch how, "in the darkness, the faint glow of dying atoms burned unwavering in the rock. It would still be burning there, scarcely dimmed, when Jeryl and Eris had been dust for centuries. It would be only a little fainter when the civilization they were building had at last unlocked its secrets."

Though the aliens of **"Second Dawn"** are scarcely credible biologically, the story's message concerning the necessity of cross-species cooperation is one that, already expressed to some extent in the stories described above, was to become progressively more crucial in Clarke's fictional thinking. The final emphasis on the potential of technology, especially of atomic energy, is unusual; we have already seen it in several stories as a threat to man's future, and in Clarke's later fiction it was often to become even more so. That fact may also argue for an early date of composition.

Only four of the eleven stories (36%) which Clarke included in ***Expedition to Earth*** (1953)—his "first collection of short stories . . . all written during the period 1945–1950"—are alien-focused; compared to seventeen of the thirty-eight (45%) stories he had written or published before 1953. It is interesting, however, that he chose to open the collection with **"Second Dawn"** (1951), the longest, perhaps the earliest, and certainly the most purely "alien" of his stories. The other three—**"Expedition to Earth"** (1950), **"Loophole"** (1947), and **"The Sentinel"** (1948)—are among the four concluding stories. Since only three of the other stories fall clearly within one of Clarke's other dominant thematic areas as hard-science "extrapolator" stories, the collection is not only framed but dominated by alien-focused stories. [In a footnote, Beatie identifies Peter Brigg as the originator of the term "extrapolator" (see excerpt dated 1977) and lists **"Breaking Strain," "Superiority,"** and **"Hide and Seek"** as the collection's three "hard-science stories."]

The only story involving aliens which Clarke published in 1953 represents a minor variation of a theme he had used earlier. **"Publicity Campaign"** is a comic inversion of the alien invasion pattern. During the run of the fabulously successful "Monsters from Space" movie, representatives of the Third Galactic Empire arrive on a mission to establish peaceful contact. Their leader is Prince Zervashni of Rigel, "who apart from his four eyes might have been mistaken for a panda with purple fur"; his adviser is Sigisnin II, who has a "dozen flexible fingers," and the captain is "a tripedal creature who looked rather like a ball of wool balanced on three knitting needles." Despite their peaceful intentions, the ambassadors are destroyed by a mob inspired by the movie, and the alien fleet destroys the Earth. (pp. 57-60)

It is now abundantly clear that, in Clarke's fiction prior to *Childhood's End,* the alien encounter is a dominant theme; perhaps even, as Clareson asserted, Clarke's main concern. And we can see that, though he indulged in a number of comic variations on the meeting of man and alien, Clarke has a special and quite serious view of the nature of that encounter. His aliens, however "monstrous" their outward appearance may be, are not hostile to man; they are at worst neutral, at best benevolent, often the saviors of man. Their "alienness" is not worked out in terms of elaborate exobiological characterization, as many later writers have done, but is circumstantial; in their behavior, Clarke's aliens seem very human. (p. 61)

Bruce A. Beatie, "Arthur C. Clarke and the Alien Encounter: The Background of 'Childhood's End,'" in Extrapolation, *Vol. 30, No. 1, Spring, 1989, pp. 53-69.*

ADDITIONAL BIBLIOGRAPHY

Agel, Jerome, ed. *The Making of Kubrick's "2001."* New York: Signet, 1970, 367 p.

Examines aspects of the film. The text includes Clarke's short story "The Sentinel" and critical essays on the movie, several of which discuss Clarke's fiction and his role in creating the movie.

Aldiss, Brian W. "How to Be a Dinosaur: Seven Survivors." In his *Trillion Year Spree: The History of Science Fiction,* pp. 383-406. New York: Atheneum, 1986.

Includes discussion of Clarke in a chapter devoted to seven important early science fiction authors who remain well known and widely read in the 1980s.

Bernstein, Jeremy. "Out of the Ego Chamber." *The New Yorker* XLV, No. 25 (9 August 1969): 40-65.

Biographical account based upon interviews with Clarke, including discussion of several major works.

Clareson, Thomas D. " 'If I Forget Thee, O Earth': Notes." In *A Spectrum of Worlds,* edited by Thomas D. Clareson, pp. 178-79. Garden City, N. Y.: Doubleday, 1972.

Discusses plot, theme, and imagery in " 'If I Forget Thee, O Earth,' " offering comparison with Stephen Vincent Benét's "By the Waters of Babylon."

Disch, Thomas M. "The Earthbound Exegete." *The Times Literary Supplement,* No. 3976 (16 June 1978): 662.

Scathingly reviews *Arthur C. Clarke* (1977), the volume of critical essays edited by Joseph D. Olander and Martin Harry Greenberg, and *The Best of Arthur C. Clarke,* edited by Angus Wells. Disch dismisses much of the criticism in the collection as muddled and inadequate, and contends that the selection of Clarke's "best" short stories is haphazard.

Erlich, Richard D. "Ursula K. Le Guin and Arthur C. Clarke on Immanence, Transcendence, and Massacres." *Extrapolation* 28, No. 2 (Summer 1987): 105-29.

Compares fiction by Clarke and Le Guin that explores different potential futures, including transcendent evolutionary stages as well as possible racial annihilation.

Fadiman, Clifton. Introduction to *Across the Sea of Stars,* by Arthur C. Clarke, pp. ix-xii. New York: Harcourt, Brace & World, 1959.

Commends Clarke's facility with "the probable or fairly possible" and identifies "faith in the beneficent powers of science" as a feature of his fiction.

Holmes, H. H. "All Aboard for Outer Space." *The New York Herald Tribune Book Review* 34, No. 30 (2 March 1958): 6.

Assesses the short stories of *The Other Side of the Sky* as "deft, charming, sensitive, witty, imaginative, and plausible, making a volume ideally calculated to lift science fiction out of the ghetto of specialists and introduce its delights to the general reader."

Ketterer, David. "Other Worlds out of Space and Time." In his *New Worlds for Old: The Apocalyptic Imagination, Science Fiction, and American Literature,* pp. 43-9. Bloomington: Indiana University Press, 1974.

Mentions "The Star" in a discussion of mysticism and religion in science fiction.

Knight, Damon. "New Stars." In his *In Search of Wonder: Essays on Modern Science Fiction,* pp. 177-205. Rev. ed. Chicago: Advent, 1967.

Briefly discusses Clarke's major works, including several short stories.

Nedelkovich, Alexander. "The Stellar Parallels: Robert Silverberg, Larry Niven, and Arthur C. Clarke." *Extrapolation* 21, No. 4 (Winter 1980): 348-60.

Compares "To the Dark Star," by Silverberg, "Neutron Star," by Niven, and "The Star." Nedelkovich considers Clarke's story the most structurally complex and soundly based in scientific fact.

Priestley, J. B. Introduction to *Of Time and Stars: The Worlds of Arthur C. Clarke,* pp. 7-10. London: Victor Gollancz, 1972.

Commends the scientific accuracy, imagination, and "wide range of time, place, plot, situation, [and] theme" in Clarke's short stories.

Rabkin, Eric. "Short Stories." In his *Arthur C. Clarke,* pp. 53-60. San Bernardino: The Borgo Press, 1979.

Discusses representative works of Clarke's short fiction, focusing upon Clarke's introduction of elements from "the ghost story to the tall tale to the lament for lost love" into science fiction stories.

Samuelson, David N. "Arthur C. Clarke." In *Science Fiction Writers: Critical Studies of the Major Authors from the Early Nineteenth Century to the Present Day,* edited by E. F. Bleiler, pp. 313-19. New York: Charles Scribner's Sons, 1982.

Biographical and critical essay that includes commentary on several of Clarke's most important short stories.

Sturgeon, Theodore. "The Scientist Fictionist." *National Review* XIII, No. 20 (20 November 1962): 403-04.

Largely favorable review of *Tales of Ten Worlds* that includes speculation about the sources of Clarke's inspiration. Sturgeon criticizes Clarke's tendency to write stories about things rather than people.

Sutton, Thomas C., and Sutton, Marilyn. "Science Fiction as Mythology." *Western Folklore* 28 (1969): 230-37.

Includes discussion of "The Star" in an analysis of the mythic bases of science fiction.

Wolfe, Gary K. "The Short Fiction of Arthur C. Clarke." In *Survey of Science Fiction Literature,* Vol. 4, edited by Frank N. Magill, pp. 1926-29. Englewood Cliffs, N. J.: Salem Press, 1979.

Chronological discussion focusing on the way that Clarke's short stories foreshadow the primary themes of his later novels.

Nathaniel Hawthorne

1804-1864

American novelist, short story writer, and essayist.

Hawthorne is considered one of the greatest American fiction writers. His novel *The Scarlet Letter,* with its balanced structure, polished prose style, and skillful use of symbols, is acknowledged as a classic of American literature, and several of his short stories are ranked as masterpieces of the genre. Like his longer works, Hawthorne's stories reflect his dark vision of human nature, frequently focusing on Puritanism as an expression of humanity's potential for cruelty, obsession, and intolerance. Hawthorne's literary style—particularly his use of symbolism and his fascination with the macabre—exerted a marked influence upon the development of short fiction in the United States during the nineteenth century; as a result, along with Edgar Allan Poe, Hawthorne is regarded as one of the principal architects of the modern American short story.

Biographers view Hawthorne's preoccupation with Puritanism as an outgrowth of his background. Born in Salem, Massachusetts, he was descended from a line of staunch Puritans that included William Hathorne (Hawthorne himself added the "w" to the family name), an ardent defender of the faith who participated in the persecution of Quakers during the seventeenth century, and his son, John Hathorne, a presiding judge at the infamous Salem witch trials. This melancholy heritage was augmented by the premature death of Hawthorne's father, which left the four-year-old Nathaniel in the care of his grief-stricken and reclusive mother. Hawthorne therefore spent much time alone during his childhood, developing an intensely introspective nature and eventually coming to believe that the misfortunes of his immediate family were the result of divine retribution for the sins of his ancestors.

While attending Bowdoin College in Maine from 1821 to 1825, Hawthorne wrote his first short stories. After graduating, Hawthorne returned to his mother's home in Salem, where he continued to write. Although he was frequently dissatisfied with these early efforts, and in fact destroyed a number of the manuscripts, he submitted several pieces to *The Token,* an annual anthology published by Samuel Goodrich. Goodrich included Hawthorne's stories in *The Token* during the early 1830s and played a major role in the development of the young author's career, naming him editor of the *American Magazine of Useful and Entertaining Knowledge* in 1836 and arranging for the publication of his first collection of short stories, *Twice-Told Tales,* one year later. According to Edgar Allan Poe, who was greatly impressed by Hawthorne's early stories, *Twice-Told Tales* made of Hawthorne "*the* example, *par excellence,* in this country, of the privately-admired and publicly-unappreciated man of genius." Although lavishly praised by critics, the volume sold poorly; an enlarged edition issued in 1842 fared no better. This pattern of critical appreciation and public neglect continued throughout Hawthorne's literary career, and he was forced to occupy a series of minor governmental posts in order to supplement the meager income from his writings.

In July of 1842, Hawthorne married Sophia Peabody, to whom he had been engaged for several years, and the couple moved into a large house in Concord, Massachusetts, known locally as the "Old Manse." There Hawthorne wrote many of the pieces included in his next collection of stories and sketches, *Mosses from an Old Manse.* Critics agree, however, that Hawthorne's most fruitful period of short story production had already ended by this time. Although two of his most highly regarded works, "Young Goodman Brown" and "Roger Malvin's Burial," first appeared in *Mosses from an Old Manse,* they had been written more than a decade earlier. After the publication of *Mosses from an Old Manse,* Hawthorne concentrated on writing novels, replicating in such works as *The Scarlet Letter* and *The House of the Seven Gables* the artistic success of his early stories. In 1851, he issued one final volume of previously uncollected short pieces, *The Snow Image, and Other Twice-Told Tales.*

Following the election of his friend Franklin Pierce to the presidency in 1852, Hawthorne was appointed to a diplomatic post in Liverpool, England, where he remained for much of the next decade. Preoccupied with his official duties, he wrote little during this period, and upon returning to Concord in 1860 he found that he was no longer able to successfully translate his ideas into fiction. In the final years of his life, Hawthorne began and abandoned several novels; posthumous publication of these fragments revealed them to be inferior, lacking the stylistic grace and narrative power of Hawthorne's earlier fiction.

Set against the New England background with which he was so familiar, the majority of Hawthorne's short stories are allegorical in nature. He typically took as his starting point an action or image that he considered potentially illuminating and created complex, multilayered narratives through skillful use of symbol and allusion. As reflected in his most highly regarded short works, Hawthorne was particularly fascinated by such dimly understood aspects of human psychology as degeneracy, obsession, and guilt. In "The Minister's Black Veil," for example, he tells of a minister named Mr. Hooper, whose obsession with the innately sinful nature of humanity—as delineated by his Calvinist theology—leads him to adopt the wearing of a symbolic black veil, an act that irrevocably separates him from those around him. Similarly, "Young Goodman Brown" recounts the story of a young Puritan who becomes aware of the secret sins of his community when he discovers his friends, his neighbors, and even his wife participating in a satanic ritual. Like Mr. Hooper, Brown allows his newly awakened sense of the potential for human depravity to color his perceptions, and he is thenceforth unable to derive any pleasure from the society of others. Hawthorne suggests that the problem for both men lies in their inability to recognize and cope with the inherent duality of human nature, which combines the potential for sublime goodness with a strong tendency toward shocking baseness. Both stories function on several levels, incorporating elements of folklore, Christian doctrine, classical mythology, and American history to extend the implications of the narrative.

In addition to their function as penetrating psychological studies, Hawthorne's stories frequently serve as explorations of the Puritanism that shaped the history of New England and, in Hawthorne's opinion, accounted for much of its unique character. Often repelled by the joylessness and intolerance of his Puritan ancestors, the brooding and morally rigid Hawthorne nevertheless felt a spiritual kinship, writing of them in his introduction to *The Scarlet Letter:* "Let them scorn me as they will, strong traits of their nature have intertwined themselves with mine." Critics agree that Hawthorne's ability to identify with his Puritan characters is reflected in the authenticity of his explorations of their temperament. In general, however, his approach to Puritanism was adversarial. Aside from the negative effects of the Puritans' Calvinist theology portrayed in "The Minister's Black Veil," "Young Goodman Brown," and other stories, Hawthorne addressed the subject of Puritan intolerance in "The Gentle Boy," which describes the persecution of Quakers, and in "Alice Doane's Appeal," which depicts victims of the Salem witch trials. In other stories, Hawthorne discusses the cruel punishments imposed by Puritan leaders upon those whom they considered sinners and examines the effects of their repressive morality.

Another prominent concern in Hawthorne's stories is the role and responsibility of the scientist, and several of his early tales have in fact been described as prototypes of modern science fiction. Sharing the European Romantics' mistrust of science, Hawthorne perceived great danger in attempts to manipulate nature, particularly if the aim of the endeavor was to somehow improve upon natural creation. This concern is most explicitly manifested in "The Birthmark," in which Aylmer, a highly skilled scientist, attempts to remove a small birthmark from his otherwise flawlessly beautiful wife and in so doing kills her. Imperfection, Hawthorne asserts, is an integral part of humanity; to remove it is to remove life. The presumptuousness of the scientific endeavor is also the central theme of one of Hawthorne's most complex tales, "Rappaccini's Daughter." In this story, a young man named Giovanni becomes enamored of a beautiful young woman who has been secluded by her father in a lush garden. Finding that the woman's body has been made poisonous by her father as part of a scientific experiment, Giovanni seeks to correct the situation and, like Aylmer, succeeds only in killing the woman he loves. Both Aylmer and Giovanni represent Romantic archetypes of the scientist: like Mary Shelley's Victor Frankenstein, they attempt to usurp divine powers, and like Goethe's Faust, they allow their intellectual curiosity to overcome their spirituality, ignoring the redemptive power of love. Critics note that in "Rappaccini's Daughter," this exploration of human presumption is greatly enriched by Hawthorne's frequent allusions to the Judeo-Christian story of Adam and Eve.

The complexity of Hawthorne's allegories frequently results in narrative ambiguity, thus giving rise to varied, and in some cases diametrically opposed, critical interpretations. Commentators have disputed such basic issues as the precise motive for Mr. Hooper's adoption of the black veil, the nature of the "unpardonable sin" discovered by the eponymous hero of "Ethan Brand," and whether Goodman Brown actually sees the people of his town in the forest, dreams the episode, or is tricked by Satan into believing that he has seen them. Moreover, such close examinations of Hawthorne's texts have led to conflicting interpretations of his primary fictional intent. The majority of his stories contain explicit didactic statements, and the goal of his fiction has traditionally been viewed as one of moral enlightenment. Several other critics, most notably Frederick Crews and Roy R. Male, diametrically suggest that Hawthorne's tales function as moral fables only on the most superficial level, their true significance lying in their penetrating analysis of human psychology. Crews has written that Hawthorne's plots "follow a logic of expression and repression that bypasses or undercuts moral problems: he is more concerned with psychological necessity than with conscious virtue." Others contend that Hawthorne's primary aim was to interpret the lessons of history, and a recent study by Michael J. Colacurcio focuses entirely upon this aspect of Hawthorne's short stories.

Despite such critical divergence, scholars agree on the significance of Hawthorne's short stories within both his oeuvre and the context of Western literature. Although the short works of great novelists sometimes represent apprentice works that serve to indicate the progress of an author's artistic development, Hawthorne's stories are regarded as sophisticated expressions of his primary concerns that exhibit a highly developed style and a nearly complete mastery of the form, and his narrative achievements established standards that remain an integral part of American fiction. In addition, his explorations of those subjects with which he was personally concerned expressed the spirit of America in the nineteenth century and clarified its links with the past, rendering the accumulated lore of Western civilization in an endeavor to illuminate the nature of universal human experience.

(See also *Nineteenth-Century Literature Criticism,* Vols. 2,

10, 17, 23; *Dictionary of Literary Biography,* Vols. 1, 74; and *Concise Dictionary of American Literary Biography, 1640-1865.*)

PRINCIPAL WORKS

SHORT FICTION

Twice-Told Tales 1837; also published as *Twice-Told Tales* [enlarged edition] 1842
Mosses from an Old Manse 1846
The Snow Image, and Other Twice-Told Tales 1851
Hawthorne's Short Stories 1946
Selected Tales and Sketches 1950
The Complete Short Stories of Nathaniel Hawthorne 1959
The Celestial Railroad, and Other Stories 1963
Tales and Sketches 1982

OTHER MAJOR WORKS

Fanshawe (novel) 1828
The Scarlet Letter (novel) 1850
The House of the Seven Gables (novel) 1851
The Blithedale Romance (novel) 1852
The Marble Faun; or, The Romance of Monte Beni (novel) 1860

EDGAR ALLAN POE (essay date 1842)

[*One of the foremost American authors of the nineteenth century, Poe is widely regarded as the architect of the modern short story and the principal forerunner of aestheticism in America. His self-declared intention, both as a critic and as a literary theorist, was the articulation and promotion of strictly artistic ideals in a milieu he viewed as overly concerned with the utilitarian value of literature. Specifically, Poe's theory of literary creation is noted for two central points: (1) a work must create a unity of effect on the reader to be counted successful; and (2) the production of this single effect should not be left to the hazards of accident or inspiration but should to the minutest detail of style and subject matter be the result of rational deliberation on the part of the author. Along with these theoretical concepts, Poe's most conspicuous contribution to literary criticism was his analytical approach, which focused on the specifics of style and construction. In the following excerpt, he praises the originality of* Twice-Told Tales. *Poe revised his estimate of Hawthorne's literary talents; for his later comments, see the excerpt below dated 1847.*]

Of Mr. Hawthorne's Tales we would say, emphatically, that they belong to the highest region of Art—an Art subservient to genius of a very lofty order. We had supposed, with good reason for so supposing, that he had been thrust into his present position by one of the impudent *cliques* which beset our literature, and whose pretensions it is our full purpose to expose at the earliest opportunity; but we have been most agreeably mistaken. We know of few compositions which the critic can more honestly commend than these ***Twice-Told Tales.*** As Americans, we feel proud of the book.

Mr. Hawthorne's distinctive trait is invention, creation, imagination, originality—a trait which, in the literature of fiction, is positively worth all the rest. But the nature of originality, so far as regards its manifestation in letters, is but imperfectly understood. The inventive or original mind as frequently displays itself in novelty of *tone* as in novelty of matter. Mr. Hawthorne is original at *all* points.

It would be a matter of some difficulty to designate the best of these tales; we repeat that, without exception, they are beautiful. **"Wakefield"** is remarkable for the skill with which an old idea—a well-known incident—is worked up or discussed. A man of whims conceives the purpose of quitting his wife and residing *incognito,* for twenty years, in her immediate neighborhood. Something of this kind actually happened in London. The force of Mr. Hawthorne's tale lies in the analysis of the motives which must or might have impelled the husband to such folly, in the first instance, with the possible causes of his perseverance. Upon this thesis a sketch of singular power has been constructed.

"The Wedding Knell" is full of the boldest imagination—an imagination fully controlled by taste. The most captious critic could find no flaw in this production.

"The Minister's Black Veil" is a masterly composition of which the sole defect is that to the rabble its exquisite skill will be *caviare.* The *obvious* meaning of this article will be found to smother its insinuated one. The *moral* put into the mouth of the dying minister will be supposed to convey the *true* import of the narrative; and that a crime of dark dye, (having reference to the "young lady") has been committed, is a point which only minds congenial with that of the author will perceive.

"Mr. Higginbotham's Catastrophe" is vividly original and managed most dexterously.

"Dr. Heidegger's Experiment" is exceedingly well imagined, and executed with surpassing ability. The artist breathes in every line of it.

"The White Old Maid" is objectionable, even more than the **"Minister's Black Veil,"** on the score of its mysticism. Even with the thoughtful and analytic, there will be much trouble in penetrating its entire import.

"The Hollow of the Three Hills" we would quote in full, had we space;—not as evincing higher talent than any of the other pieces, but as affording an excellent example of the author's peculiar ability. The subject is common-place. A witch subjects the Distant and the Past to the view of a mourner. It has been the fashion to describe, in such cases, a mirror in which the images of the absent appear; or a cloud of smoke is made to arise, and thence the figures are gradually unfolded. Mr. Hawthorne has wonderfully heightened his effect by making the ear, in place of the eye, the medium by which the fantasy is conveyed. The head of the mourner is enveloped in the cloak of the witch, and within its magic folds there arise sounds which have an all-sufficient intelligence. Throughout this article also, the artist is conspicuous—not more in positive than in negative merits. Not only is all done that should be done, but (what perhaps is an end with more difficulty attained) there is nothing done which should not be. Every word *tells,* and there is not a word which does *not* tell.

In **"Howe's Masquerade"** we observe something which resembles a plagiarism—but which *may be* a very flattering coincidence of thought. (pp. 574-75)

In the way of objection we have scarcely a word to say of these tales. There is, perhaps, a somewhat too general or prevalent *tone*—a tone of melancholy and mysticism. The subjects are insufficiently varied. There is not so much of *ver-*

satility evinced as we might well be warranted in expecting from the high powers of Mr. Hawthorne. But beyond these trivial exceptions we have really none to make. The style is purity itself. Force abounds. High imagination gleams from every page. Mr. Hawthorne is a man of the truest genius. (p. 577)

Edgar Allan Poe, in a review of "Twice-Told Tales," in his Essays and Reviews, *edited by G. R. Thompson, The Library of America, 1984, pp. 569-77.*

EDGAR ALLAN POE (essay date 1847)

[*In the following excerpt from his review of* Mosses from an Old Manse, *Poe discusses the question of Hawthorne's originality and the allegorical nature of his writings.*]

In the preface to my sketches of New York Literati, while speaking of the broad distinction between the seeming public and real private opinion respecting our authors, I thus alluded to Nathaniel Hawthorne:—

> For example, Mr. Hawthorne, the author of ***Twice-Told Tales,*** is scarcely recognized by the press or by the public, and when noticed at all, is noticed merely to be damned by faint praise. Now, my own opinion of him is, that although his walk is limited and he is fairly to be charged with mannerism, treating all subjects in a similar tone of dreamy *innuendo,* yet in this walk he evinces extraordinary genius, having no rival either in America or elsewhere; and this opinion I have never heard gainsaid by any one literary person in the country. That this opinion, however, is a spoken and not a written one, is referable to the facts, first, that Mr. Hawthorne *is* a poor man, and, secondly, that he *is not* an ubiquitous quack.

The reputation of the author of ***Twice-Told Tales*** has been confined, indeed, until very lately, to literary society; and I have not been wrong, perhaps, in citing him as *the* example, *par excellence,* in this country, of the privately-admired and publicly-unappreciated man of genius. Within the last year or two, it is true, an occasional critic has been urged, by honest indignation, into very warm approval. Mr. Webber, for instance, (than whom no one has a keener relish for that kind of writing which Mr. Hawthorne has best illustrated,) gave us, in a late number of *The American Review,* a cordial and certainly a full tribute to his talents; and since the issue of the ***Mosses from an Old Manse,*** criticisms of similar tone have been by no means infrequent in our more authoritative journals. I can call to mind few reviews of Hawthorne published *before* the ***Mosses.*** One I remember in *Arcturus* (edited by Matthews and Duyckinck) for May, 1841; another in the *American Monthly* (edited by Hoffman and Herbert) for March, 1838; a third in the ninety-sixth number of the *North American Review.* These criticisms, however, seemed to have little effect on the popular taste—at least, if we are to form any idea of the popular taste by reference to its expression in the newspapers, or by the sale of the author's book. It was never the fashion (until lately) to speak of him in any summary of our best authors. The daily critics would say, on such occasions, "Is there not Irving and Cooper, and Bryant and Paulding, and—Smith?" or, "Have we not Halleck and Dana, and Longfellow and—Thompson?" or, "Can we not point triumphantly to our own Sprague, Willis, Channing, Bancroft, Prescott and—Jenkins?" but these unanswerable queries were never wound up by the name of Hawthorne.

Beyond doubt, this inappreciation of him on the part of the public arose chiefly from the two causes to which I have referred—from the facts that he is neither a man of wealth nor a quack;—but these are insufficient to account for the whole effect. No small portion of it is attributable to the very marked idiosyncrasy of Mr. Hawthorne himself. In one sense, and in great measure, to be peculiar is to be original, and than the true originality there is no higher literary virtue. This true or commendable originality, however, implies not the uniform, but the continuous peculiarity—a peculiarity springing from ever-active vigor of fancy—better still if from ever-present force of imagination, giving its own hue, its own character to everything it touches, and, especially, *self impelled to touch everything.*

It is often said, inconsiderately, that very original writers always fail in popularity—that such and such persons are too original to be comprehended by the mass. "Too peculiar," should be the phrase, "too idiosyncratic." It is, in fact, the excitable, undisciplined and child-like popular mind which most keenly feels the original. The criticism of the conservatives, of the hackneys, of the cultivated old clergymen of the *North American Review,* is precisely the criticism which condemns and alone condemns it. "It becometh not a divine," saith Lord Coke, "to be of a fiery and salamandrine spirit." Their conscience allowing them to move nothing themselves, these dignitaries have a holy horror of being moved. "Give us *quietude,*" they say. Opening their mouths with proper caution, they sigh forth the word "*Repose.*" And this is, indeed, the one thing they should be permitted to enjoy, if only upon the Christian principle of give and take.

The fact is, that if Mr. Hawthorne were really original, he could not fail of making himself felt by the public. But the fact is, he is *not* original in any sense. Those who speak of him as original, mean nothing more than that he differs in his manner or tone, and in his choice of subjects, from any author of their acquaintance—their acquaintance not extending to the German Tieck, whose manner, in *some* of his works, is absolutely identical with that *habitual* to Hawthorne. But it is clear that the element of the literary originality is novelty. The element of its appreciation by the reader is the reader's sense of the new. Whatever gives him a new and insomuch a pleasurable emotion, he considers original, and whoever frequently gives him such emotion, he considers an original writer. In a word, it is by the sum total of these emotions that he decides upon the writer's claim to originality. I may observe here, however, that there is clearly a point at which even novelty itself would cease to produce the legitimate originality, if we judge this originality, as we should, by the effect designed: this point is that at which *novelty becomes nothing novel;* and here the artist, *to preserve his originality,* will subside into the common-place. No one, I think, has noticed that, merely through inattention to this matter, Moore has comparatively failed in his *Lalla Rookh.* Few readers, and indeed few critics, have commended this poem for originality—and, in fact, the effect, originality, is not produced by it—yet no work of equal size so abounds in the happiest originalities, individually considered. They are so excessive as, in the end, to deaden in the reader all capacity for their appreciation.

These points properly understood, it will be seen that the critic (unacquainted with Tieck) who reads a single tale or essay by Hawthorne, may be justified in thinking him original; but the tone, or manner, or choice of subject, which induces in this critic the sense of the new, will—if not in a second tale, at least in a third and all subsequent ones—not only fail of inducing it, but bring about an exactly antagonistic impression. In concluding a volume, and more especially in concluding all the volumes of the author, the critic will abandon his first design of calling him "original," and content himself with styling him "peculiar."

With the vague opinion that to be original is to be unpopular, I could, indeed, agree, were I to adopt an understanding of originality which, to my surprise, I have known adopted by many who have a right to be called critical. They have limited, in a love for mere words, the literary to the metaphysical originality. They regard as original in letters, only such combinations of thought, of incident, and so forth, as are, in fact, absolutely novel. It is clear, however, not only that it is the novelty of *effect* alone which is worth consideration, but that this effect is *best* wrought, for the end of all fictitious composition, pleasure, by shunning rather than by seeking the absolute novelty of combination. Originality, thus understood, tasks and startles the intellect, and so brings into undue action the faculties to which, in the lighter literature, we least appeal. And thus understood, it cannot fail to prove unpopular with the masses, who, seeking in this literature amusement, are positively offended by instruction. But the true originality—true in respect of its purposes—is that which, in bringing out the half-formed, the reluctant, or the unexpressed fancies of mankind, or in exciting the more delicate pulses of the heart's passion, or in giving birth to some universal sentiment or instinct in embryo, thus combines with the pleasurable effect of *apparent* novelty, a real egotistic delight. The reader, in the case first supposed, (that of the absolute novelty,) is excited, but embarrassed, disturbed, in some degree even pained at his own want of perception, at his own folly in not having himself hit upon the idea. In the second case, his pleasure is doubled. He is filled with an intrinsic and extrinsic delight. He feels and intensely enjoys the seeming novelty of the thought, enjoys it as really novel, as absolutely original with the writer—*and* himself. They two, he fancies, have, alone of all men, thought thus. They two have, together, created this thing. Henceforward there is a bond of sympathy between them, a sympathy which irradiates every subsequent page of the book.

There is a species of writing which, with some difficulty, may be admitted as a lower degree of what I have called the true original. In its perusal, we say to ourselves, not "how original this is!" nor "here is an idea which I and the author have alone entertained," but "here is a charmingly obvious fancy," or sometimes even, "here is a thought which I am not sure has ever occurred to myself, but which, of course, has occurred to all the rest of the world." This kind of composition (which still appertains to a high order) is usually designated as "the natural." It has little external resemblance, but strong internal affinity to the true original, if, indeed, as I have suggested, it is not of this latter an inferior degree. It is best exemplified, among English writers, in Addison, Irving and *Hawthorne.* The "ease" which is so often spoken of as its distinguishing feature, it has been the fashion to regard as ease in appearance alone, as a point of really difficult attainment. This idea, however, must be received with some reservation. The natural style is difficult only to those who should never intermeddle with it—to the unnatural. It is but the result of writing with the understanding, or with the instinct, that the *tone,* in composition, should be that which, at any given point or upon any given topic, would be the tone of the great mass of humanity. The author who, after the manner of the North Americans, is merely at *all* times *quiet,* is, of course, upon *most* occasions, merely silly or stupid, and has no more right to be thought "easy" or "natural" than has a cockney exquisite or the sleeping beauty in the wax-works.

The "peculiarity" or sameness, or monotone of Hawthorne, would, in its mere character of "peculiarity," and without reference to what *is* the peculiarity, suffice to deprive him of all chance of popular appreciation. But at his failure to be appreciated, we can, *of course,* no longer wonder, when we find him monotonous at decidedly the worst of all possible points—at that point which, having the least concern with Nature, is the farthest removed from the popular intellect, from the popular sentiment and from the popular taste. I allude to the strain of allegory which completely overwhelms the greater number of his subjects, and which in some measure interferes with the direct conduct of absolutely all.

In defence of allegory, (however, or for whatever object, employed,) there is scarcely one respectable word to be said. Its best appeals are made to the fancy—that is to say, to our sense of adaptation, not of matters proper, but of matters improper for the purpose, of the real with the unreal; having never more of intelligible connection than has something with nothing, never half so much of effective affinity as has the substance for the shadow. The deepest emotion aroused within us by the happiest allegory, *as* allegory, is a very, very imperfectly satisfied sense of the writer's ingenuity in overcoming a difficulty we should have preferred his not having attempted to overcome. The fallacy of the idea that allegory, in any of its moods, can be made to enforce a truth—that metaphor, for example, may illustrate as well as embellish an argument—could be promptly demonstrated: the converse of the supposed fact might be shown, indeed, with very little trouble—but these are topics foreign to my present purpose. One thing is clear, that if allegory ever establishes a fact, it is by dint of over-turning a fiction. Where the suggested meaning runs through the obvious one in a *very* profound undercurrent, so as never to interfere with the upper one without our own volition, so as never to show itself unless *called* to the surface, there only, for the proper uses of fictitious narrative, is it available at all. Under the best circumstances, it must always interfere with that unity of effect which, to the artist, is worth all the allegory in the world. Its vital injury, however, is rendered to the most vitally important point in fiction—that of earnestness or verisimilitude. That *The Pilgrim's Progress* is a ludicrously over-rated book, owing its seeming popularity to one or two of those accidents in critical literature which by the critical are sufficiently well understood, is a matter upon which no two thinking people disagree; but the pleasure derivable from it, in any sense, will be found in the direct ratio of the reader's capacity to smother its true purpose, in the direct ratio of his ability to keep the allegory out of sight, or of his *in*ability to comprehend it. Of allegory properly handled, judiciously subdued, seen only as a shadow or by suggestive glimpses, and making its nearest approach to truth in a not obtrusive and therefore not unpleasant *appositeness,* the *Undine* of De La Motte Fouqué is the best, and undoubtedly a very remarkable specimen.

The obvious causes, however, which have prevented Mr. Hawthorne's *popularity,* do not suffice to condemn him in the eyes of the few who belong properly to books, and to whom books, perhaps, do not quite so properly belong. These few estimate an author, not as do the public, altogether by what he does, but in great measure—indeed, even in the greatest measure—by what he evinces a capability of doing. In this view, Hawthorne stands among literary people in America much in the same light as did Coleridge in England. The few, also, through a certain warping of the taste, which long pondering upon books as books merely never fails to induce, are not in condition to view the errors of a scholar as errors altogether. At any time these gentlemen are prone to think the public not right rather than an educated author wrong. But the simple truth is, that the writer who aims at impressing the people, is *always* wrong when he fails in forcing that people to receive the impression. How far Mr. Hawthorne has addressed the people at all, is, of course, not a question for me to decide. His books afford strong internal evidence of having been written to himself and his particular friends alone. (pp. 577-83)

[Hawthorne] is peculiar and *not* original—unless in those detailed fancies and detached thoughts which his want of general originality will deprive of the appreciation due to them, in preventing them forever reaching the *public* eye. He is infinitely too fond of allegory, and can never hope for popularity so long as he persists in it. This he will not do, for allegory is at war with the whole tone of his nature, which disports itself never so well as when escaping from the mysticism of his Goodman Browns and White Old Maids into the hearty, genial, but still Indian-summer sunshine of his Wakefields and Little Annie's Rambles. Indeed, *his* spirit of "metaphor run-mad" is clearly imbibed from the phalanx and phalanstery atmosphere in which he has been so long struggling for breath. He has not half the material for the exclusiveness of authorship that he possesses for its universality. He has the purest style, the finest taste, the most available scholarship, the most delicate humor, the most touching pathos, the most radiant imagination, the most consummate ingenuity; and with these varied good qualities he has done *well* as a mystic. But is there any one of these qualities which should prevent his doing doubly as well in a career of honest, upright, sensible, prehensible and comprehensible things? Let him mend his pen, get a bottle of visible ink, come out from the Old Manse, cut Mr. Alcott, hang (if possible) the editor of *The Dial,* and throw out of the window to the pigs all his odd numbers of *The North American Review.* (pp. 587-88)

Edgar Allan Poe, in a review of "Twice-Told Tales," in his Essays and Reviews, *edited by G. R. Thompson, The Library of America, 1984, pp. 577-88.*

FRED LEWIS PATTEE (essay date 1923)

[*Pattee was an American literary critic and historian who, in such works as* A History of American Literature, with a View to the Fundamental Principles Underlying its Development *(1896) and* The First Century of American Literature *(1935), called for the recognition of American literature as distinct from English literature. In the following excerpt, he discusses Hawthorne's narrative style and its impact on the development of the short story in America.*]

The eighteen tales, ten of them from *The Token,* which Hawthorne in 1837 selected for the first issue of ***Twice-Told Tales,*** were the pieces he had wrought with greatest care, the ones nearest his heart, the ones uniquely his. A study of them in connection with those he rejected is profitable. The most of them are tales rather than sketches; all of them are highly imaginative, highly serious, and written on the plane of poetry rather than of prose. They remind us of the dictum of Yeats that "Poetry is the voice of the solitary man." It was the poetic element within them that called out Longfellow's glowing tribute in *The North American Review* (1837), the first prominent notice Hawthorne's work had ever received. "The book, though in prose," Longfellow had declared, "is written, nevertheless, by a poet." He selected his illustrative extracts all of them to show the author's "bright poetic style," and the marvelous beauty of his descriptions. Margaret Fuller, also writing in Hawthorne's obscurest days, believed that, had he "written **'Roger Malvern's Burial'** alone, we should be pervaded with the sense of the poetry and religion of his soul."

Undoubtedly Hawthorne's genius was lyric rather than epic or dramatic. "Much poetry," said Tieck, "is only prose gone mad; much prose is only crippled poetry." The phrase describes Hawthorne's early work, the work he brooded over in his solitary chamber—"crippled poetry." Longfellow chose as his favorite selection **"The Great Carbuncle,"** and Hawthorne in his **"Sketches from Memory"** had written in 1835: "There are few legends more poetical than that of the 'Great Carbuncle' of the White Mountains." He had opened the tale as if it were a German romantic ballad:

At nightfall once in the olden time.

The sentences are everywhere on the high romantic level, and everywhere near to the rhythm of poetry. At the climax the two who had discovered the gem threw their arms around each other

And trembled at their own success,
For as the legends of this wondrous gem
Rushed thick upon their memory they felt
Themselves marked out by fate,
And the consciousness was fearful. Often
From Childhood upward they had seen
It shining like a distant star, and now
This star was throwing its intensest luster on
Their hearts. They seeméd changed to one
Another's eyes in the red brilliancy
That flamed upon their cheeks while it lent
The same fire to the lake, and rocks and sky
And to the mists which had rolled back before
Its power.

"Crippled poetry" manifestly, but, nevertheless, poetry rather than prose. Everywhere in the volume one finds oneself moving in rhythmical measures on the high levels of the poetic:

Where would be Death's triumph
If none lived to weep?

The sweeping sound of the funeral train
Faded away like a thin vapor, and the wind
That just before had seemed to shake
The coffin pall, mourned sadly round the verge
Of the hollow between three hills.

In some happier time
The Rosebud may revive again, with all
The dewdrops in its bosom.

His hour is one
Of darkness and adversity and peril,
But should domestic tyranny oppress us
Or the invader's step pollute our soil,
Still may the Gray Champion come.

At the culminating scene of **"The Hollow of Three Hills,"** the movement becomes funereal and sobbingly broken, like the "Bridge of Sighs," its monotonous time-beat at length pounding upon the heart of the reader like the dead march at an execution:

> Then came a measured tread
> Passing slowly, slowly on,
> As with mourners with a coffin
> Their garments trailing on
> The ground. . . .
> Before them went the priest
> Reading the burial service
> While the leaves of his book
> Were rustling in the breeze.
> And though no voice but his
> Was heard to speak aloud
> Still there were revilings
> And anathemas
> Whispered but distinct
> From women and from men,
> Breathed against the daughter
> Who had wrung the aged hearts
> Of her parents, and the wife
> Who had betrayed the trusting
> Fondness of her husband,
> The mother who had sinned
> Against natural affection
> And left her child to die.

To read the work of Irving is to be conscious of eighteenth-century prose; to open Hawthorne is to be in the presence of the poets, of Thomson most of all. A sketch like **"Toll-Gatherer's Day"** has in it the atmosphere and at times even the rhythms of *The Seasons.* Spenser, too, is in the tales, in their allegorical bearings, their tendency to fantasy, their dim, mysterious light, their harmonious beauty.

Hawthorne wrote in the period when American authors tended toward the grandiose in style and diction. The writer of romance, as none better than he understood, galloped constantly on the brink of absurdity, and most of the American writers fell hopelessly over, but ***Twice-Told Tales*** and the others which followed it are never extravagant, never ornamented for the sake of ornament, never, even when viewed in the cold light of to-day, ridiculous. They were uninfluenced by the popular material by which they were surrounded. Many of them were written while the Dickens wave was sweeping over English fiction, but there is no slightest trace of Dickens in Hawthorne. So far as style is concerned his tales might have been written in the eighteenth century. His was a style that had been molded by an early knowledge of Greek and Latin classics, of the English Bible, which seems to have been read aloud daily in the Hawthorne home, and of the early English masterpieces brooded over for years in solitude. It is a classical style: finished yet seemingly spontaneous; artistic, yet simple even to childlikeness.

Poe [see excerpt above dated 1847] professed to have found the secret of Hawthorne in Tieck, even declaring that all who called him original betrayed their own ignorance, "their acquaintance not extending to the German Tieck, whose manner in some of his works is absolutely identical with that habitual with Hawthorne"—certainly a sweeping statement. A calmer and more truthful criticism came five years later in the British *New Monthly Magazine* from a reviewer to me unknown: "His stories have been likened to Tieck's in their power of translating the mysterious harmonies of nature into articulate meanings, and to Töpffer's, in high finish and purity of style."

One may indeed "liken" Hawthorne's work to Tieck's and even to Töpffer's, but it is doubtful if one may go much farther. Certainly one finds in him Tieck's brooding, poetic fancy, his tendency at times to symbolism and allegory, and his conception of romantic art as the ability to "lull the reader into a dreamy mood." Both, moreover, handled the *Mährchen,* or legendary tale, in the poetic manner and both in some instances made use of the same materials. Tieck's tale "The Klausenburg," for instance, is a study of the workings in a later generation of a curse launched by a gypsy upon one in power who had condemned her to cruel punishment. **"Feathertop"** in a vague way is like Tieck's "Die Vogelscheushe," and H. A. Beers in his *English Romanticism* finds traces in Hawthorne's work of Tieck's "The Elves," "The Goblet," and "The Runenberg." Carlyle in 1827 had indeed published these three, together with two others, "The Fair-Haired Eckbert" and "The Trusty Eckart," and it is not improbable that Hawthorne read the translation, though internal evidence of the fact is small. That he may have heard much of Tieck at Brook Farm in 1842 and even have heard readings from his tales is also not impossible. Margaret Fuller was volubly enthusiastic over the German writers, especially Tieck, and George William Curtis was spending his afternoons reading Novalis and *Wilhelm Meister.* That Hawthorne read the tales in the original, however, is quite another matter. It is safe to say that during the period in which he wrote the most of his shorter work he had no knowledge of the German language. Even the leading transcendentalists were not much influenced by the German until well into the thirties. Says James Freeman Clarke of Margaret Fuller:

> Margaret began to study German early in 1832. Both she and I were attracted toward this literature, at the same time, by the wild bugle call of Thomas Carlyle, in his romantic articles on Richter, Schiller, and Goethe, which appeared in the old *Foreign Review,* the *Edinburgh Review,* and afterwards in the *Foreign Quarterly.*

In 1843 Hawthorne in his *Note Books* records his struggle with one of Tieck's tales in terms of one who has to make his way laboriously with a "phrase book:" "Went on with Tieck's tale slowly and painfully, often wishing for help in my difficulties" . . . "I again set to work on Tieck's tale and worried through several pages" . . . "Plodded onward in the rugged and bewildering depths of Tieck's tale till five o'clock" . . . "Till dinner time I labored on Tieck's tale"—this in 1843, after the most of his tales had been written and after his manner of writing had long since, to quote Poe, become "habitual."

The likeness between the two came from similarity of soul and from the fact that both were working in an atmosphere charged with the German romantic spirit. Like his own artist in **"Prophetic Pictures,"** Hawthorne worked not in life, but in an idealization of life. "A subdued tinge of the wild and wonderful is thrown over a sketch of New England personages and scenery, yet . . . without entirely obliterating the sober hues of nature." It is the very essence of the later romanticism and both romancers made full use of it, Tieck often with wild abandon, Hawthorne always sanely and with due reverence for the essential Puritan foundations from which his feet never wandered.

Despite Poe's elaborate formulation of the rules governing

the art of the ***Twice-Told Tales,*** it is to be doubted if Hawthorne had any theory of the short story or any suspicion that the tale differed from the novel save in the one attribute of length. A few of the tales obey in full the laws of Poe, but they are so few they may be counted as exceptions, so few, indeed, that they seem accidental rather than intentional. Hawthorne was most at home in the sketch, the rambling essay type of reminiscent description, as in **"The Old Manse"** and the introduction to *The Scarlet Letter,* and in expository analyses of situations or personalities or mental states. Everything had seemed to turn him to the shorter varieties of prose—the demands of the magazines, the uncertain market for American novels, the nature of his own genius, which was more inclined to brood over moral situations than to plan elaborate structures of plot—and in his solitary chamber he wrote to please himself, using for models, if he used any at all, the older classics, the dramas of Shakespeare, and the English novel which, according to his sister's testimony, he had studied for its technique. As a result his tales, from the standpoint of form, show surprising merits and, on the other hand, equally surprising defects. Poe was the first to formulate the former, and A. P. Peabody, in a review some ten years later, the first to dwell upon the latter. "The most paltry talemaker for the magazines or the newspapers," Peabody had declared, "can easily excel him in what we might term the mechanical portion of his art. His plots are seldom well devised or skillfully developed . . . the conversations are not natural," and so on with other details. It is not hard now, in the light of modern rules, to point out Hawthorne's failures: his leisurely, expository openings; his frequent discursiveness; his characters which for the most part are as abstract and bloodless as Spenser's creations; his distance from the warm currents of actual life; his moralizing endings. But these defects, serious as some of them may be, are overbalanced by equally important excellencies, even in technique, for if we are to judge him by his work, by a dozen or more tales universally admitted now to be masterpieces, tales like **"Rappaccini's Daughter," "The Birthmark," "The Great Stone Face," "The Wives of the Dead," "The Great Carbuncle," "The White Old Maid," "The Minister's Black Veil," "Ethan Brand,"** the four "Legends of the Province House," **"The Snow Image,"** and a few others, we shall find that even in the matter of form Hawthorne was a pioneer, in advance of all his contemporaries save Poe.

He conceived of his tales in terms of culminating action; there is always a dramatic moment for which everything before has been a preparation. One may most easily illustrate this from his jottings for tales in his notebook. It reveals his habit of mind:

> A sketch to be given of a modern reformer—a type of the extreme doctrines on the subject of slaves, cold water, and other such topics. He goes about the streets haranguing most eloquently, and is on the point of making many converts, when his labors are suddenly interrupted by the appearance of the keeper of a madhouse, whence he has escaped. Much may be made of this idea.
>
> The scene of a story or sketch to be laid within the light of a street lantern; the time, when the lamp is near going out; and the catastrophe to be simultaneous with the last flickering gleam.
>
> Two persons, by mutual agreement, to make their wills in each other's favor, then to wait impatiently for one another's death, and both to be informed of the desired event at the same time. Both, in most joyous sorrow, hasten to be present at the funeral, meet, and find themselves both hoaxed.

Perhaps his emphasis of a single climactic moment rather than of a growing series of happenings in chronicle form came from the sermonic habit, which, like every other indigenous New-Englander, he had inherited from his Puritan ancestors. His tales came to him as texts to be illustrated and driven home. "On this theme," he observes after one of his notebook jottings, "methinks I could frame a tale with a deep moral." He wrote **"Wakefield"** "trusting there will be a pervading spirit and a moral, even if we should fail to find them done up neatly and condensed into the final sentence."

In the second place, Hawthorne had a keen eye for situation. Here again was he a pioneer, the first prominent writer whose tales may be defined in terms of situation. So far as I have been able to find, the first to perceive and record this fact was the English *National Review* in 1861:

> All his tales embody single ideal situations, scarcely ever for a moment varied in their course. . . . His longer works are ideal situations expanded by minute study and trains of closely related thought into the dimensions of novels. . . . He prefers to assume the crisis past and to determine as fully as he can the ideal situation to which it has given rise when it is beginning to assume more of a chronic character.

No one has expressed more clearly than this what Hawthorne really added to the short story. If it be true—and no one has disputed it—then the author of the ***Twice-Told Tales*** rather than Poe stands as the father of the American short story. At least he was the first to direct it into its modern form.

Hawthorne was the first in America to touch the new romanticism with morals, at least the first to touch it in the department of its fiction. His situations are almost invariably moral culminations, and for presenting them he had several devices. Often he sought for a symbol that would grip and shake the reader's imagination. This from his notebooks:

> Meditations about the main gas pipe of a great city,—if the supply were to be stopped, what would happen? How many different scenes it sheds light on? It might be made emblematical of something.
>
> A snake taken into a man's stomach and nourished there from fifteen years to thirty-four, tormenting him most horribly. A type of envy or some other evil passion.

The result of the latter was **"Egotism; or, the Bosom Serpent."** Sometimes the situation is presented in order to study the psychological reactions of the victim and to probe into the depths of personality, as in **"Wakefield."** Most often of all, the situation is presented in order to point out a fundamental characteristic or a subtle besetting sin of humanity. In his notebook he writes this:

> A person to be in possession of something as perfect as mortal man has a right to demand; he tries to make it better, and ruins it entirely;

which is his tale, **"The Birthmark,"** reduced to its lowest terms. If each of his tales were cut to bare single-sentence texts, as their severe unity renders it possible to do, as, for example:

> In every heart there is secret sin, and sad mysteries which we hide from our nearest and dearest, and would feign conceal from our own consciousness.—**"The Minister's Black Veil";**
>
> Does it not argue a superintending Providence that, while viewless and unexpected events thrust themselves continually athwart our path, there should still be regularity enough in mortal life to render foresight even partially available?—**"David Swan";**
>
> In the solitude of a midnight chamber or in a desert, afar from men or in a church, while the body is kneeling, the soul may pollute itself even with those crimes which we are accustomed to deem altogether carnal.—**"Fancy's Show Box";**
>
> Would all who cherish wild wishes but look around them, they would oftenest find their sphere of duty, of prosperity and happiness, within those precincts and in that station where Providence itself has cast their lot.—**"The Three-Fold Destiny";**—

if all his tales were so reduced and the resulting texts were gathered into a chapter, it would be a fairly complete summary of the best elements of his philosophy. His stories, the best of them, are, therefore, sermons, each with a text to which its author rigidly adheres, made vivid by a single illustration dwelt upon lingeringly, presented from new angles again and again until it becomes a haunting presence that lays its hands upon one's very soul.

Hawthorne, therefore, did four things for the short story: he turned it from its German romantic extravagances and frivolity and horrors into sane and moral channels; he made of it the study of a single intense situation; he deepened it and gave it beauty; and he made it respectable even in New England, a dignified literary form, admitted as such even by the most serious of the Transcendentalists. After ***Twice-Told Tales*** and ***Mosses from an Old Manse*** the short story had no longer to apologize for its existence and live a vagabond life in the corners of weekly papers and the pages of lady's books and annuals: it had won so secure a place that even before Hawthorne had died *The Atlantic Monthly,* the constituted mouthpiece of the Brahmins of New England, could print seventeen specimens of it in its first volume. (pp. 102-10)

Fred Lewis Pattee, "Nathaniel Hawthorne," in his The Development of the American Short Story: An Historical Survey, *Harper & Brothers Publishers, 1923, pp. 91-114.*

JORGE LUIS BORGES (lecture date 1949)

[*An Argentine short story writer, poet, and essayist, Borges is considered an important figure in contemporary literature. His writing is often used by critics to illustrate the modern view of literature as a highly sophisticated game. Justifying this interpretation of Borges's works are his admitted respect for stories that are artificial inventions of art rather than realistic representations of life, his use of philosophical conceptions as a means of achieving literary effects, and his frequent variations on the writings of other authors. Such characteristic stories as* "The Aleph," "The Circular Ruins," *and* "Pierre Menard, Author of the Quixote" *are demonstrations of the subjective, the infinitely various, and the ultimately indeterminate nature of life and literature. In his literary criticism, Borges is noted for his insight into the manner in which an author both represents and creates a reality with words and the way in which those words are variously interpreted by readers. With his fiction and poetry, Borges's critical writing shares the perspective that literary creation of imaginary worlds and philosophical speculation on the world itself are parallel or identical activities. In the following excerpt, he discusses the strengths and weaknesses of Hawthorne's allegorical method, focusing in particular on "Wakefield" and "Earth's Holocaust."*]

One aesthetic error debased [Hawthorne]: the Puritan desire to make a fable out of each imagining induced him to add morals and sometimes to falsify and to deform them. The notebooks in which he jotted down ideas for plots have been preserved; in one of them, dated 1836, he wrote: "A snake taken into a man's stomach and nourished there from fifteen years to thirty-five, tormenting him most horribly." That is enough, but Hawthorne considers himself obliged to add: "A type of envy or some other evil passion." Another example, this time from 1838: "A series of strange, mysterious, dreadful events to occur, wholly destructive of a person's happiness. He to impute them to various persons and causes, but ultimately finds that he is himself the sole agent. Moral, that our welfare depends on ourselves." Another, from the same year: "A person, while awake and in the business of life, to think highly of another, and place perfect confidence in him, but to be troubled with dreams in which this seeming friend appears to act the part of a most deadly enemy. Finally it is discovered that the dream-character is the true one. The explanation would be—the soul's instinctive perception." Better are those pure fantasies that do not look for a justification or moral and that seem to have no other substance than an obscure terror. Again, from 1838: "The situation of a man in the midst of a crowd, yet as completely in the power of another, life and all, as if they two were in the deepest solitude." The following, which Hawthorne noted five years later, is a variation of the above: "Some man of powerful character to command a person, morally subjected to him, to perform some act. The commanding person to suddenly die; and, for all the rest of his life, the subjected one continues to perform that act." (I don't know how Hawthorne would have written that story. I don't know if he would have decided that the act performed should be trivial or slightly horrible or fantastic or perhaps humiliating.) This one also has slavery—subjection to another—as its theme: "A rich man left by will his mansion and estate to a poor couple. They remove into it, and find there a darksome servant, whom they are forbidden by will to turn away. He becomes a torment to them; and, in the finale, he turns out to be the former master of the estate." I shall mention two more sketches, rather curious ones; their theme, not unknown to Pirandello or André Gide, is the coincidence or the confusion of the aesthetic plane and the common plane, of art and reality. The first one: "Two persons to be expecting some occurrence, and watching for the two principal actors in it, and to find that the occurrence is even then passing, and that they themselves are the two actors." The other is more complex: "A person to be writing a tale, and to find that it shapes itself against his intentions; that the characters act otherwise than he thought; that unforeseen events occur; and a catastrophe comes which he strives in vain to avert. It might shadow forth his own fate—he having made himself one of the personages." These games, these momentary confluences of the imaginative world and the real world—the world we pretend is real when we read—are, or seem to us, modern. Their origin, their ancient origin, is perhaps to be found in that part of the *Iliad* in which Helen of Troy weaves into her tapestry the battles and the disasters of the Trojan War even then in progress. Virgil must have been impressed by that passage, for the *Aeneid* relates that Aeneas, hero of the Trojan War, arrived at the port of Carthage and saw scenes from the war sculptured on the marble of a temple and, among the many images of warriors, he saw his own likeness. Hawthorne liked those contacts of the imaginary and the real, those reflections and duplications of art; and in the sketches I have mentioned we observe that he leaned toward the pantheistic notion that one man is the others, that one man is all men.

Something more serious than duplications and pantheism is seen in the sketches, something more serious for a man who aspires to be a novelist, I mean. It is that, in general, situations were Hawthorne's stimulus, Hawthorne's point of departure—situations, not characters. Hawthorne first imagined, perhaps unwittingly, a situation and then sought the characters to embody it. I am not a novelist, but I suspect that few novelists have proceeded in that fashion. "I believe that Schomberg is real," wrote Joseph Conrad about one of the most memorable characters in his novel *Victory,* and almost any novelist could honestly say that about any of his characters. The adventures of the *Quixote* are not so well planned, the slow and antithetical dialogues—reasonings, I believe the author calls them—offend us by their improbability, but there is no doubt that Cervantes knew Don Quixote well and could believe in him. Our belief in the novelist's belief makes up for any negligence or defect in the work. What does it matter if the episodes are unbelievable or awkward when we realize that the author planned them, not to challenge our credibility, but to define his characters? What do we care about the puerile scandals and the confused crimes of the hypothetical Court of Denmark if we believe in Prince Hamlet? But Hawthorne first conceived a situation, or a series of situations, and then elaborated the people his plan required. That method can produce, or tolerate, admirable stories because their brevity makes the plot more visible than the actors, but not admirable novels, where the general form (if there is one) is visible only at the end and a single badly invented character can contaminate the others with unreality. From the foregoing statement it will be inferred that Hawthorne's stories are better than Hawthorne's novels. I believe that is true. The twenty-four chapters of *The Scarlet Letter* abound in memorable passages, written in good and sensitive prose, but none of them has moved me like the singular story of **"Wakefield"** in the ***Twice-Told Tales.***

Hawthorne had read in a newspaper, or pretended for literary reasons that he had read in a newspaper, the case of an Englishman who left his wife without cause, took lodgings in the next street and there, without anyone's suspecting it, remained hidden for twenty years. During that long period he spent all his days across from his house or watched it from the corner, and many times he caught a glimpse of his wife. When they had given him up for dead, when his wife had been resigned to widowhood for a long time, the man opened the door of his house one day and walked in—simply, as if he had been away only a few hours. (To the day of his death he was an exemplary husband.) Hawthorne read about the curious case uneasily and tried to understand it, to imagine it. He pondered on the subject; **"Wakefield"** is the conjectural story of that exile. The interpretations of the riddle can be infinite; let us look at Hawthorne's.

He imagines Wakefield to be a calm man, timidly vain, selfish, given to childish mysteries and the keeping of insignificant secrets; a dispassionate man of great imaginative and mental poverty, but capable of long, leisurely, inconclusive, and vague meditations; a constant husband, by virtue of his laziness. One October evening Wakefield bids farewell to his wife. He tells her—we must not forget we are at the beginning of the nineteenth century—that he is going to take the stage-coach and will return, at the latest, within a few days. His wife, who knows he is addicted to inoffensive mysteries, does not ask the reason for the trip. Wakefield is wearing boots, a rain hat, and an overcoat; he carries an umbrella and a valise. Wakefield—and this surprises me—does not yet know what will happen. He goes out, more or less firm in his decision to disturb or to surprise his wife by being away from home for a whole week. He goes out, closes the front door, then half opens it, and, for a moment, smiles. Years later his wife will remember that last smile. She will imagine him in a coffin with the smile frozen on his face, or in paradise, in glory, smiling with cunning and tranquility. Everyone will believe he has died but she will remember that smile and think that perhaps she is not a widow.

Going by a roundabout way, Wakefield reaches the lodging place where he has made arrangements to stay. He makes himself comfortable by the fireplace and smiles; he is one street away from his house and has arrived at the end of his journey. He doubts; he congratulates himself; he finds it incredible to be there already; he fears that he may have been observed and that someone may inform on him. Almost repentant, he goes to bed, stretches out his arms in the vast emptiness and says aloud: "I will not sleep alone another night." The next morning he awakens earlier than usual and asks himself, in amazement, what he is going to do. He knows that he has some purpose, but he has difficulty defining it. Finally he realizes that his purpose is to discover the effect that one week of widowhood will have on the virtuous Mrs. Wakefield. His curiosity forces him into the street. He murmurs, "I shall spy on my home from a distance." He walks, unaware of his direction; suddenly he realizes that force of habit has brought him, like a traitor, to his own door and that he is about to enter it. Terrified, he turns away. Have they seen him? Will they pursue him? At the corner he turns back and looks at his house; it seems different to him now, because he is already another man—a single night has caused a transformation in him, although he does not know it. The moral change that will condemn him to twenty years of exile has occurred in his soul. Here, then, is the beginning of the long adventure. Wakefield acquires a reddish wig. He changes his habits; soon he has established a new routine. He is troubled by the suspicion that his absence has not disturbed Mrs. Wakefield enough. He decides he will not return until he has given her a good scare. One day the druggist enters the house, another day the doctor. Wakefield is sad, but he fears that his sudden reappearance may aggravate the illness. Obsessed, he lets time pass; before he had thought, "I shall return in a few days," but now he thinks, "in a few weeks." And so ten years pass. For a long time he has not known that his conduct is strange. With all the lukewarm affection of which his heart is capable, Wakefield continues to love his wife, while she is forgetting him. One Sunday morning the two meet in the street amid the crowds of London. Wakefield has become thin; he walks obliquely, as though hiding or escaping; his low forehead is deeply wrinkled; his face, which was common before, is extraordinary, because of his extraordinary conduct. His small eyes wander or look inward. His wife has grown stout; she is carrying a prayer book and her whole person seems to symbolize a placid and resigned widowhood. She is accustomed to sadness and would not exchange it, perhaps, for joy. Face to face, the two look into each other's eyes.

The crowd separates them, and soon they are lost within it. Wakefield hurries to his lodgings, bolts the door, and throws himself on the bed where he is seized by a fit of sobbing. For an instant he sees the miserable oddity of his life. "Wakefield, Wakefield! You are mad!" he says to himself.

Perhaps he is. In the center of London he has severed his ties with the world. Without having died, he has renounced his place and his privileges among living men. Mentally he continues to live with his wife in his home. He does not know, or almost never knows, that he is a different person. He keeps saying, "I shall soon go back," and he does not realize that he has been repeating these words for twenty years. In his memory the twenty years of solitude seem to be an interlude, a mere parenthesis. One afternoon, an afternoon like other afternoons, like the thousands of previous afternoons, Wakefield looks at his house. He sees that they have lighted the fire in the second-floor bedroom; grotesquely, the flames project Mrs. Wakefield's shadow on the ceiling. Rain begins to fall, and Wakefield feels a gust of cold air. Why should he get wet when his house, his home, is there. He walks heavily up the steps and opens the door. The crafty smile we already know is hovering, ghostlike, on his face. At last Wakefield has returned. Hawthorne does not tell us of his subsequent fate, but lets us guess that he was already dead, in a sense. I quote the final words: "Amid the seeming confusion of our mysterious world, individuals are so nicely adjusted to a system, and systems to one another, and to a whole, that by stepping aside for a moment a man exposes himself to a fearful risk of losing his place for ever. Like Wakefield, he may become, as it were, the Outcast of the Universe."

In that brief and ominous parable, which dates from 1835, we have already entered the world of Herman Melville, of Kafka—a world of enigmatic punishments and indecipherable sins. You may say that there is nothing strange about that, since Kafka's world is Judaism, and Hawthorne's, the wrath and punishments of the Old Testament. That is a just observation, but it applies only to ethics, and the horrible story of Wakefield and many stories by Kafka are united not only by a common ethic but also by a common rhetoric. For example, the protagonist's profound *triviality,* which contrasts with the magnitude of his perdition and delivers him, even more helpless, to the Furies. There is the murky background against which the nightmare is etched. Hawthorne invokes a romantic past in other stories, but the scene of this tale is middle-class London, whose crowds serve, moreover, to conceal the hero.

Here, without any discredit to Hawthorne, I should like to insert an observation. The circumstance, the strange circumstance, of perceiving in a story written by Hawthorne at the beginning of the nineteenth century the same quality that distinguishes the stories Kafka wrote at the beginning of the twentieth must not cause us to forget that Hawthorne's particular quality has been created, or determined, by Kafka. **"Wakefield"** prefigures Franz Kafka, but Kafka modifies and refines the reading of **"Wakefield."** The debt is mutual; a great writer creates his precursors. He creates and somehow justifies them. What, for example, would Marlowe be without Shakespeare?

The translator and critic Malcolm Cowley sees in **"Wakefield"** an allegory of Nathaniel Hawthorne's curious life of reclusion. Schopenhauer has written the famous words to the effect that no act, no thought, no illness is involuntary; if there is any truth in that opinion, it would be valid to conjecture that Nathaniel Hawthorne left the society of other human beings for many years so that the singular story of Wakefield would exist in the universe, whose purpose may be variety. If Kafka had written that story, Wakefield would never have returned to his home; Hawthorne lets him return, but his return is no less lamentable or less atrocious than is his long absence.

One of Hawthorne's parables which was almost masterly, but not quite, because a preoccupation with ethics mars it, is **"Earth's Holocaust."** In that allegorical story Hawthorne foresees a moment when men, satiated by useless accumulations, resolve to destroy the past. They congregate at evening on one of the vast western plains of America to accomplish the feat. Men come from all over the world. They make a gigantic bonfire kindled with all the genealogies, all the diplomas, all the medals, all the orders, all the judgments, all the coats of arms, all the crowns, all the sceptres, all the tiaras, all the purple robes of royalty, all the canopies, all the thrones, all the spirituous liquors, all the bags of coffee, all the boxes of tea, all the cigars, all the love letters, all the artillery, all the swords, all the flags, all the martial drums, all the instruments of torture, all the guillotines, all the gallows trees, all the precious metals, all the money, all the titles of property, all the constitutions and codes of law, all the books, all the miters, all the vestments, all the sacred writings that populate and fatigue the Earth. Hawthorne views the conflagration with astonishment and even shock. A man of serious mien tells him that he should be neither glad nor sad, because the vast pyramid of fire has consumed only what was consumable. Another spectator—the Devil—observes that the organizers of the holocaust have forgotten to throw away the essential element—the human heart—where the root of all sin resides, and that they have destroyed only a few forms. Hawthorne concludes as follows:

> The heart, the heart—there was the little yet boundless sphere wherein existed the original wrong of which the crime and misery of this outward world were merely types. Purify that inward sphere, and the many shapes of evil that haunt the outward, and which now seem almost our only realities, will turn to shadowy phantoms and vanish of their own accord; but if we go no deeper than the intellect, and strive, with merely that feeble instrument, to discern and rectify what is wrong, our whole accomplishment will be a dream, so unsubstantial that it matters little whether the bonfire, which I have so faithfully described, were what we choose to call a real event and a flame that would scorch the finger, or only a phosphoric radiance and a parable of my own brain.

Here Hawthorne has allowed himself to be influenced by the Christian, and specifically the Calvinist, doctrine of the inborn depravation of mankind and does not appear to have noticed that his parable of an illusory destruction of all things can have a philosophical as well as a moral interpretation. For if the world is the dream of Someone, if there is Someone who is dreaming us now and who dreams the history of the universe (that is the doctrine of the idealists), then the annihilation of religions and the arts, the general burning of libraries, does not matter much more than does the destruction of the trappings of a dream. The Mind that dreamed them once will dream them again; as long as the Mind continues to dream, nothing will be lost. The belief in this truth, which seems fantastic, caused Schopenhauer, in his book *Parerga und Paralipomena,* to compare history to a kaleidoscope, in which the figures, not the pieces of glass, change; and to an eternal and confused tragicomedy in which the roles and masks, but not the actors, change. The presentiment that the universe is a projection of our soul and that universal history lies within each man induced Emerson to write the poem entitled "History."

As for the fantasy of abolishing the past, perhaps it is worth remembering that this was attempted in China, with adverse fortune, three centuries before Christ. Herbert Allen Giles wrote that the prime minister Li Su proposed that history should begin with the new monarch, who took the title of First Emperor. To sever the vain pretensions of antiquity, all books (except those that taught agriculture, medicine, or astrology) were decreed confiscated and burned. Persons who concealed their books were branded with a hot iron and forced to work on the construction of the Great Wall. Many valuable works were destroyed; posterity owes the preservation of the Confucius canon to the abnegation and valor of obscure and unknown men of letters. It is said that so many intellectuals were executed for defying the imperial edict that melons grew in winter on the burial ground.

Around the middle of the seventeenth century that same plan appeared in England, this time among the Puritans, Hawthorne's ancestors. Samuel Johnson relates that in one of the popular parliaments convoked by Cromwell it was seriously proposed that the archives of the Tower of London be burned, that every memory of the past be erased, and that a whole new way of life should be started. In other words, the plan to abolish the past had already occurred to men and—paradoxically—is therefore one of the proofs that the past cannot be abolished. The past is indestructible; sooner or later all things will return, including the plan to abolish the past.

Like Stevenson, also the son of Puritans, Hawthorne never ceased to feel that the task of the writer was frivolous or, what is worse, even sinful. In the preface to *The Scarlet Letter* he imagines that the shadows of his forefathers are watching him write his novel. It is a curious passage. "What is he?" says one ancient shadow to the other. "A writer of storybooks! What kind of a business in life—what mode of glorifying God, or being serviceable to mankind in his day and generation—may that be? Why, the degenerate fellow might as well have been a fiddler!" The passage is curious, because it is in the nature of a confidence and reveals intimate scruples. It harks back to the ancient dispute between ethics and aesthetics or, if you prefer, theology and aesthetics. One early example of this dispute was in the Holy Scriptures and forbade men to adore idols. Another example, by Plato, was in the *Republic,* Book X: "God creates the Archetype (the original idea) of the table; the carpenter makes an imitation of the Archetype; the painter, an imitation of the imitation." Another is by Mohammed, who declared that every representation of a living thing will appear before the Lord on the day of the Last Judgment. The angels will order the artisan to animate what he has made; he will fail to do so and they will cast him into Hell for a certain length of time. Some Moslem teachers maintain that only images that can project a shadow (sculptured images) are forbidden. Plotinus was said to be ashamed to dwell in a body, and he did not permit sculptors to perpetuate his features. Once, when a friend urged him to have his portrait painted, he replied, "It is enough to be obliged to drag around this image in which nature has imprisoned me. But why shall I consent to the perpetuation of the image of this image?"

Nathaniel Hawthorne solved that difficulty (which is not a mere illusion). His solution was to compose moralities and fables; he made or tried to make art a function of the conscience. So, to use only one example, the novel *The House of the Seven Gables* attempts to show that the evil committed by one generation endures and persists in its descendants, like a sort of inherited punishment. Andrew Lang has compared it to Émile Zola's novels, or to Émile Zola's theory of novels; to me the only advantage to be gained by the juxtaposition of those heterogeneous names is the momentary surprise it causes us to experience. The fact that Hawthorne pursued, or tolerated, a moral purpose does not invalidate, cannot invalidate his work. In the course of a lifetime dedicated less to living than to reading, I have been able to verify repeatedly that aims and literary theories are nothing but stimuli; the finished work frequently ignores and even contradicts them. If the writer has something of value within him, no aim, however trite or erroneous it may be, will succeed in affecting his work irreparably. An author may suffer from absurd prejudices, but it will be impossible for his work to be absurd if it is genuine, if it responds to a genuine vision. Around 1916 the novelists of England and France believed (or thought they believed) that all Germans were devils; but they presented them as human beings in their novels. In Hawthorne the germinal vision was always true; what is false, what is ultimately false, are the moralities he added in the last paragraph or the characters he conceived, or assembled, in order to represent that vision. The characters in *The Scarlet Letter*—especially Hester Prynne, the heroine—are more independent, more autonomous, than those in his other stories; they are more like the inhabitants of most novels and not mere projections of Hawthorne, thinly disguised. This objectivity, this relative and partial objectivity, is perhaps the reason why two such acute (and dissimilar) writers as Henry James and Ludwig Lewisohn called *The Scarlet Letter* Hawthorne's masterpiece, his definitive testimony. But I would venture to differ with those two authorities. If a person longs for objectivity, if he hungers and thirsts for objectivity, let him look for it in Joseph Conrad or Tolstoi; if a person looks for the peculiar flavor of Nathaniel Hawthorne, he will be less apt to find it in the laborious novels than on some random page or in the trifling and pathetic stories. (pp. 51-61)

Jorge Luis Borges, "Nathaniel Hawthorne," in his Other Inquisitions: 1937-1952, *translated by Ruth L. C. Simms, University of Texas Press, 1964, pp. 47-65.*

RICHARD P. ADAMS (essay date 1957)

[Adams was an American critic who focused on what he described as "the Romantic tradition in American literature." In the following excerpt, he identifies and examines the stories known as Hawthorne's "Provincial Tales."]

In the attempt Hawthorne made in the 1820's and 1830's to bring his work before the public, the project of the "Provincial Tales" was his third failure. The first was a group of stories which he intended to publish under the title *Seven Tales of My Native Land* but all except one or two of which he burned when the publication was intolerably delayed. The second was the novel *Fanshawe,* which was published at the author's expense, but which Hawthorne almost succeeded in totally suppressing soon after it appeared. These failures were unqualified; neither project brought fame or fortune, and the work was artistically immature. The surviving pieces are important only because Hawthorne went on to do better things. The failure of "Provincial Tales," on the other hand, is very much qualified for us by the fact that although the stories were never published in the volume Hawthorne intended them for and although they brought little money and less recognition at the time, they contain some excellent fiction. In them Hawthorne discovered his mature method and partly developed the typical themes and structural principles of his later work.

Elizabeth Chandler and Nelson F. Adkins have made about as thorough a study as can be made of the evidence for an identification of the "Provincial Tales." They agree on six titles, three sure and three probable. On the testimony of Hawthorne's correspondence with Samuel Goodrich about possible publication of the group, they are certain that **"The Gentle Boy," "Roger Malvin's Burial,"** and **"My Kinsman, Major Molineux"** belong. On strong circumstantial evidence they feel reasonably sure of **"The Gray Champion," "The Maypole of Merry Mount,"** and **"Young Goodman Brown."** Chandler thinks that **"Dr. Bullivant"** might be included, and Adkins advances tentative claims for **"The Wives of the Dead"** and **"The Minister's Black Veil."** But they do not agree on these, and I have seen no positive evidence for any of the three. I prefer to consider the first six named, more or less arbitrarily, to be the "Provincial Tales."

Whether or not Hawthorne meant these and only these for his collection, and whether or not all six were written at about the same time (1828 and 1829, Chandler supposes), they have a great deal in common. They all have essentially the same theme: the transition from childishness or adolescence to maturity. They are all historical in their settings and in the specific terms of their presentation. And although they approach their mutual theme from different directions, making for a surface variety of treatment, they overlap in many ways, so that even the surface treatment is fairly homogeneous. In general **"Young Goodman Brown"** illustrates a moral approach, **"The Maypole of Merry Mount"** an esthetic approach, **"My Kinsman, Major Molineux"** a sociological approach, **"The Gray Champion"** a political approach, **"Roger Malvin's Burial"** a psychological approach, and **"The Gentle Boy"** a religious approach. But there is a strong esthetic flavor to the religious controversy that motivates **"The Gentle Boy,"** and that controversy has political implications too. The political conflict in **"The Gray Champion"** also involves a religious quarrel and some strong esthetic differences; and these three aspects are also present in **"The Maypole of Merry Mount." "My Kinsman, Major Molineux"** combines political and psychological aspects with its primarily sociological treatment, and **"Young Goodman Brown"** contains in its extremely complex unity almost everything that the group as a whole represents.

These differences in focus are necessary, if only to keep the author from telling the same story six times. Each tale in the group quite properly develops a point of view and an interest peculiar to itself. But from each point of view we are made to become interested in some aspect or other of the problem of achieving maturity. Each tale can therefore be made to throw light on each and all of the others; each can be seen to mean more in relation to the others than by itself.

"**Young Goodman Brown**" is generally considered the best of the "Provincial Tales" and one of the best stories Hawthorne ever wrote. It is also important because it contains the germ of nearly all his best work to follow. It would be at least partly true to say that *The Scarlet Letter* or *The Marble Faun* is only "**Young Goodman Brown**" grown older and bigger.

The question of maturity for Goodman Brown is put in terms of good and evil. At first it seems a fairly simple choice, but the problem is much more complex than Brown seems ever to realize. He leaves the daylit street of Salem Village, saying goodbye to his wife, Faith, with pink ribbons in her cap, and goes into the darkening forest. There, by appointment, he meets the devil, who tries to persuade him to attend a witch meeting, saying that his father and grandfather have often done so and that the leaders of the Puritan community are generally in attendance. Brown, making his simple choice of good over evil, refuses. His confidence is somewhat shaken when they see old Goody Cloyse on the path ahead and he learns that she, who has taught him his catechism, is on her way to the meeting. But he still refuses, and the devil leaves him. As he is congratulating himself on his moral purity and fortitude, he is further disconcerted by hearing the minister and Deacon Gookin riding through the forest on the same errand. His resolution is broken when a heavy cloud goes over and he hears the voices of people he knows in Salem, including that of his wife. He shouts her name, she screams, and one of her pink ribbons flutters down. At this Brown rejects the good he has chosen and embraces evil, rushing through the forest after the devil, himself more like a devil than a man, until he comes to the firelit clearing where the witch meeting is being held.

In the meeting, especially its setting, evil is associated so closely as practically to identify it with sex. At the end of the clearing is a rock used as an altar or pulpit, "surrounded by four blazing pines, their tops aflame, their stems untouched, like candles at an evening meeting. The mass of foliage that had overgrown the summit of the rock was all on fire. . . . " The imagery of fire is typically used by Hawthorne, both before and after the "Provincial Tales," to connote intense emotion, especially sexual passion, which is specified if anything too obviously here by the physiological correspondences of the pines and the brush-covered rock. But, almost as often in Hawthorne, fire also connotes the warmth of personal and familial association, as opposed to the coldness of isolation. Brown's feelings as he approaches are accordingly mixed. He is surprised to see that the congregation includes many presumably virtuous people, as well as "men of dissolute lives and women of spotted fame," and he finds it "strange to see that the good shrank not from the wicked, nor were the sinners abashed by the saints." But as he steps out into the clearing he too feels the "loatheful brotherhood" between himself and the others "by the sympathy of all that was wicked in his heart." It might be more accurate to say by all that is sexual in his character. A parallel ambiguity is suggested by the fact that, as it seems to him, "the shape of his own dead father beckoned him to advance, looking downward from a smoke wreath, while a woman, with dim features of despair, threw out her hand to warn him back. Was it his mother?" If so, the two play typical roles, the father encouraging the son to become a man, the mother trying to keep him a child as long as possible.

Brown and Faith are led to the altar, where the devil, in the guise of a Puritan minister, proposes to reveal the " 'secret deeds' "—that is, the sexual crimes—of their neighbors:

" 'how hoary-bearded elders of the church have whispered wanton words to the young maids of their households; how many a woman, eager for widows' weeds, has given her husband a drink at bedtime and let him sleep his last sleep in her bosom; how beardless youths have made haste to inherit their fathers' wealth; and how fair damsels . . . have dug little graves in the garden, and bidden me, the sole guest, to an infant's funeral.' " As the congregation welcomes the "converts" to the communion of evil, or of sexual knowledge and guilt, the setting becomes still more suggestive. "A basin was hollowed, naturally, in the rock. Did it contain water, reddened by the lurid light? or was it blood? or, perchance, a liquid flame? Herein did the shape of evil dip his hand and prepare to lay the mark of baptism upon their foreheads, that they might be partakers of the mystery of sin, more conscious of the secret guilt of others, both in deed and thought, than they could now be of their own."

The prospect is too much for Brown, who at this point makes his final decision, rejects evil, and commands Faith to " 'look up to heaven, and resist the wicked one.' " Instantly the congregation, Faith, and the devil disappear, and Brown is alone, "amid calm night and solitude," while the foliage that has been blazing with fire now sprinkles him "with the coldest dew." He returns to Salem with his isolation around him like a cloak, shrinks away from the minister, wonders what god Deacon Gookin is praying to, snatches a child away from Goody Cloyse, and passes his wife, Faith, in the street without a word. Through the rest of his long life, Goodman Brown is "A stern, a sad, a darkly meditative, a distrustful, if not a desperate man. . . ."

The most immediately apparent reason for this final state of Brown's mind is that he has been required to face and acknowledge the evil in himself and others, including his young wife, so as to be able to recognize the good, and has failed the test. Having refused to look at evil, he is left in a state of moral uncertainty that is worse, in a way, than evil itself. His inability to judge between good and evil also prevents him from entering into stable social relations or having any sort of intimate contact with others. He has lost Faith, as he says at one point in the story, in all the ways that the ambiguities of the name can be made to mean. For Hawthorne, this condition of moral and social isolation is the worst evil that can befall a man.

But the more important aspect of Brown's personal disaster is his failure to grow up, in the sense of becoming emotionally mature. This is not itself a matter of good and evil, though it is a matter where good and evil are always potentially present. To reach maturity, Brown must learn to recognize, control, and constructively use powerful feelings that a grown man has, especially about sex. Those feelings, when loosed in war or civil riot, are the most dangerous forces we know. But they are also the most effective forces for good. Civilization is built and preserved, when it is preserved, by men who love their wives and children, their homelands, and the human race, and who will not only risk death for themselves but kill other men, if they must, for the sake of positive emotional values. Brown does not become such a man. In place of the needed capacity for both love and hate or, in the terms of the story, both evil and good, he develops only a great fear of moral maturity and of the knowledge and responsibility that maturity brings.

The other tales of the group throw different lights on the common theme by approaching it from their different points of view. **"The Maypole of Merry Mount"** poses a predominantly esthetic question against the background of a cultural conflict. Hawthorne tells us, with his tongue only partly in his cheek, that the battle between the pleasure-loving colonists of Merry Mount and the gloomy Puritans of Massachusetts Bay is a very serious matter. "The future complexion of New England," he says, "was involved in this important quarrel. Should the grizzly saints establish their jurisdiction over the gay sinners, then would their spirits darken all the clime, and make it a land of clouded visages, of hard toil, of sermon and psalm forever. But should the banner staff of Merry Mount be fortunate, sunshine would break upon the hills, and flowers would beautify the forest, and late posterity do homage to the Maypole." Hawthorne, though hardly himself a frivolous person, would have welcomed a little more of the Maypole spirit than he found in the New England of his own time. He was partly in earnest too when he blamed its gloom, and the darkness of his own soul, on the Puritan heritage.

The action of **"The Maypole of Merry Mount"** is even simpler than that of **"Young Goodman Brown."** Edith and Edgar, on their wedding day, are forced by Endicott, the iron-clad, iron-souled Puritan leader, to leave their formerly happy home at Merry Mount and take up life among the somber but eminently grown-up Puritans. Their transition (Edgar's more specifically) is not altogether easy, but it is what Hawthorne seems to regard as normal. We need not suppose he means that grown-ups all have to be Puritans, but he shows here and elsewhere a real admiration of certain Puritan qualities, such as moral strength and seriousness, courage, firmness, and determination. These are precisely the qualities of maturity that young Goodman Brown most conspicuously lacks. Edgar, by contrast and in spite of his youth in Merry Mount, has already gained some share of them. Therefore, encouraged by similar virtues in the character of Edith, he is able to impress the stern Endicott as being at least potentially fit for the adult society of Massachusetts Bay.

Much the same kind of transition is shown from the social point of view by what happens to Robin in **"My Kinsman, Major Molineux."** Having left his home in the hope of being advanced in the world by his rich and powerful kinsman, he is forced to renounce the kinsman and make his own way. The typical revolt of the son against the authority of the father is here related to some unidentified incident of revolt on the part of the Colony, or at any rate a large number of the Colonists, against the parent country or a symbol or representative of it in the person of the Major. Thus Robin's desertion of his family is associated with America's desertion of the British Empire.

The action of this tale is more complex than that of either **"Young Goodman Brown"** or **"The Maypole of Merry Mount."** Robin arrives in the provincial metropolis (presumably Boston) late one evening, tired and almost out of money. The only resource he knows is to find his kinsman at once, but he is unable to do so. When he inquires for the Major he is rebuffed, ridiculed, insulted, threatened, and deceived, but nowhere able to learn anything helpful. It becomes apparent to the reader, though not very clearly to Robin, that some plot or agitation is on foot in which the Major is unpleasantly involved. Finally Robin stops "a bulky stranger, muffled in a cloak," and demands information. The stranger, baring his face, replies that the Major will pass by in an hour, and Robin recognizes him as a man he has met earlier at an inn, impressive for his bold features and eyes that "glowed . . . like fire in a cave." Now the sight of him fills Robin with "dismay and astonishment" because one side of his face blazes "an intense red" and the other is "black as midnight." "The effect," says Hawthorne, "was as if two individual devils, a fiend of fire and a fiend of darkness, had united themselves to form this infernal visage."

Robin, settling down to wait, imagines the scene at home, where his father will be leading the family in outdoor prayer. But the fantasy ends with the door of the house being shut in Robin's face. He is "excluded from his home." Thus he takes the first step toward resolving his crisis by recognizing that he is cut off from his immediate family, particularly his father. The results of this recognition are first an intense feeling of loneliness and second a possibility that he, like Edgar, may successfully complete the process of growing up.

Robin's loneliness is relieved toward the end of the hour when another stranger comes along, a kindly citizen who listens to Robin's story and stays to wait for the Major. Then a parade appears with the double devil at its head; and in the midst, where the torches are brightest, sitting in tar and feathers on a cart, is the Major, whose recognition of Robin seems to be his crowning indignity. "They stared at each other in silence, and Robin's knees shook, and his hair bristled, with a mixture of pity and terror." His catharsis is completed when he recognizes all the various people he has met during the evening and joins with them in the monstrous laugh that goes up; and by so doing he completes his declaration of independence by repudiating the father-substitute embodied in his kinsman and would-be sponsor. When the parade has moved on, Robin thinks he will go back home, but the kindly citizen points out the significance of his recent experience by suggesting that he stay in town and remarking that " 'perhaps, as you are a shrewd youth, you may rise in the world without the help of your kinsman, Major Molineux.' "

There is interest enough on the surface of this tale, which is a fine imaginative handling of a local uprising, the entanglement of a young man in affairs beyond his comprehension, and his extrication from the difficulty, partly by his own efforts and partly by the help of two men, one stern and the other kindly. But this interest is multiplied by deeper meanings. The action is, in one aspect, an initiation ceremony, marking and confirming the young man's establishment of a new, mature set of relations with his family and with society. The typical initiation test represents externally the psychological difficulties involved in this process, and by externalizing them renders them easier to surmount than they are when the boy has to wrestle with them privately, as he usually does in our society. It is essentially this test that Goodman Brown fails.

Edgar, in **"The Maypole of Merry Mount,"** passes it in much the same way as Robin. Edgar's real father is not mentioned, but he has a substitute in the Anglican priest who marries him to Edith. Endicott's function is first to force Edgar to renounce the priest as a father image and then encourage him to take his place as an adult among the Puritans. The suggestion of the public ritual element is strong in all three tales.

In **"Roger Malvin's Burial,"** however, with its dominantly psychological approach, the public aspect is almost entirely absent. The privacy of the struggle and the difficulty of winning through the crisis are emphasized in this tale more than in any of the others, even **"Young Goodman Brown."** The basic problem is the same. Reuben Bourne, the protagonist, returning with Roger Malvin from Lovell's fight with the Indians, is forced to leave the badly wounded older man, after promising to come back or send a party to rescue or, as seems more likely, bury him. Reuben is prevented from carrying out this promise, first by his collapse from exhaustion and his own wounds, and then, when he has partly recovered, by a kind of moral cowardice which keeps him from admitting that he has not stayed with Malvin to the end. These circumstances are given added meaning and emotional force by two related facts. Malvin, in urging Reuben to leave him, says that he has loved him like a father and " 'should have something of a father's authority.' " And Reuben's most powerful motive for leaving, a motive which he fails to acknowledge even to himself, is that he wants to marry Malvin's daughter, Dorcas. Partly for these reasons, he is led to conceal the truth of the matter, most particularly from Dorcas.

This concealment, rather than anything wrong or disgraceful about the desertion itself, Hawthorne says "imparted to a justifiable act much of the secret effect of guilt," and it makes Reuben unable to protect himself from even more uncomfortable thoughts. "By a certain association of ideas, he at times almost imagined himself a murderer." The worst trial of all is that he is subject to "a haunting and torturing fancy that his father-in-law was yet sitting at the foot of the rock, on the withered forest leaves, alive, and awaiting his pledged assistance." Apparently there is nothing terribly wrong with leaving one's father, even though such a desertion seems in a way like murder. But leaving him unburied may be dangerous. As long as Malvin remains alive in Reuben's secret memory, Reuben cannot act the part of a man or be a proper father himself. He and Dorcas marry and have a son, Cyrus, so that physically Reuben is a father, as Goodman Brown is after his ordeal in the forest. But, like Brown, Reuben is emotionally or psychologically unable to accept the father's role. Instead he finds his only relief from the neurotic feelings that plague him by identifying himself with the dependent and therefore innocent boy, in whom "he recognized what he had himself been in other days." He is arrested in a childish attitude.

Reuben's neurotic indolence and contentiousness gradually reduce his fortunes to such a degree that, after eighteen years, he is forced to abandon the farm he has inherited from Malvin and go pioneering. Unconsciously he leads his family to the place where he has left Malvin, and there, in search of game, with his mind hovering on the verge of recognition, he fires at a movement in the bushes and kills his son. At that moment he realizes where he is, and when Dorcas comes he tells her that her father and her son lie dead together. Then the weight of the secret is removed, or, as Hawthorne puts it, "His sin was expiated,—the curse was gone from him; and in the hour when he had shed blood dearer to him than his own, a prayer, the first for years, went up to Heaven from the lips of Reuben Bourne." Logically, this ending makes no sense—indeed it makes badly perverted nonsense—but psychologically it has some interesting meanings.

The main point is that Reuben is able to free himself of dependence on Malvin only when he recognizes that his foster father is really dead and in effect buried, and when he ratifies that recognition by destroying the concrete equivalent of his childishness as he sees it in Cyrus. So interpreted, **"Roger Malvin's Burial"** is an allegory, more or less symbolic, of the same universal experience dealt with in the other stories in the group. But Reuben Bourne succeeds in surmounting the crisis of adolescence at a price that must make any reader feel uncomfortable, however puzzled he may be by the confusing terms in which the story is presented.

Ilbrahim, in **"The Gentle Boy,"** does not succeed; he is persecuted to death at the age of about seven years because he insists on being a Quaker in the Puritan Colony. His father has been hanged. His mother has left him with foster parents who do the best they can for him but who fail in their efforts to bring him into their church and community and who cannot give him the kind of spiritual relations he needs. Because he is too young and weak to make his way, or to make the kind of impression on the Puritans that Edgar makes on Endicott in **"The Maypole of Merry Mount,"** he is forced continually farther into isolation, until it ends in death.

"The Gray Champion" seems at first to have as its protagonist the old Puritan who emerges from the crowd and halts the governor and his soldiers, preventing a riot that might have become an earlier Boston Massacre. But a more logical protagonist, in view of the general theme of the group, is the Colony of Massachusetts Bay. It is the Colony that is immature but growing, that is straining the political and legal bonds of dependence on England, and that will eventually, with the other twelve, declare and establish its independence. The Gray Champion has the same function as the kindly citizen in **"My Kinsman, Major Molineux":** that of encouraging and helping the protagonist in his encounter with the devil-figure.

The common theme of the "Provincial Tales" is not basically a question of good versus evil, but rather of boyish dependence and carelessness versus manly freedom and responsibility. And it is very much a question of the protagonist's passing from the one state to the other or failing to do so—a question of time, change, and development. This dynamic aspect has not been given the consideration it deserves. Hawthorne's fiction cannot be understood in terms of the static formulas that have been most often applied to it.

Even the typical structure of the "Provincial Tales" is dynamic. It consists of a pattern of three or four characters who move in a series of shifting relationships. The protagonist, a naïve young man, is attracted by a woman, who somehow seems to bring him into conflict with an evil man or devil. Sometimes he is helped by a benevolent older man, more often not; but essentially the number of characters is always four because when only three appear the devil-figure has a double function. He both frightens and encourages the youthful candidate. This pattern can be most completely demonstrated in **"My Kinsman, Major Molineux."** Robin, after briefly meeting the devil-figure without makeup, is attracted by a young woman who pretends to be the Major's housekeeper and who evidently aims to seduce him. Then he meets the devil in full rig, and then the kindly citizen who confirms his maturity and encourages him to stay and make it good.

In the other tales the pattern is less complete, but its meanings are sometimes clearer. The function of the woman, for example, is much more plainly evident in **"Roger Malvin's Burial"** than it is in **"My Kinsman, Major Molineux."** Reuben sees Malvin as the friendly foster father until he marries Dorcas. Then Malvin haunts him until he declares himself mature, at which point Malvin again seems to be the benevolent father. In **"The Maypole of Merry Mount"** Edgar's marriage to Edith brings a gloomy foreboding of trouble to both their minds, even before Endicott interferes. And in **"Young Goodman Brown"** it seems to be Brown's marriage to Faith that really poses the problem of evil; certainly it is her voice from the cloud that leads him to the witch meeting and his deeper involvement with the devil, who may be only trying to help him after all.

We must remember that this is an abstract pattern, useful only insofar as it helps us to understand the stories. But it is worth noting that the tales in which it appears most clearly, **"My Kinsman, Major Molineux," "Young Goodman Brown,"** and **"The Maypole of Merry Mount,"** are those which now seem esthetically most satisfactory. **"The Gray Champion"** is a splendid picture, but the woman does not appear, and the real protagonist is kept in the background, so that the dynamic effect is dampened. In **"The Gentle Boy"** the pattern is so much distorted that it can hardly be said to exist at all; and **"The Gentle Boy"** is one of Hawthorne's weakest works. The same pattern is awkwardly weighted in **"Roger Malvin's Burial,"** but without some reference to it that tale can hardly be understood. With these necessary reservations, I think it is proper to say that the four-character pattern is normal for Hawthorne in the "Provincial Tales."

The psychological implications of this pattern, though not its final or most important values, are too emphatic to be ignored. The young man's attraction to a sexually potent woman, his struggle to free himself from dependence on and antagonism toward a fatherly man, and his achievement of, or his failure to achieve, adult status—these matters, we cannot help noticing, are precisely those with which modern psychoanalysis has been most deeply concerned.

To put it simply, Hawthorne, like Freud (and Sophocles, among many others), was very much interested in what is now called the Oedipus complex. He recognized, as Freud did later, that the typical crisis of adolescence, for a boy in our culture, is that which involves his ambivalent attitude and feelings toward his father. The themes of incest, parricide, and fear of castration that appear in both men's work represent the hazards of a boy's normal emotional development from adolescence to manhood. Which is perhaps only to say that both men were dealing with human nature: Hawthorne empirically, for esthetic purposes, and Freud more scientifically, for therapeutic purposes. (pp. 39-52)

The most important values in the "Provincial Tales" are finally esthetic; and, as I have remarked elsewhere, the basic esthetic problem for Hawthorne's generation of American artists was to join themselves and the culture of this country to the romantic movement which had already been so well begun in Europe. Though various people had made beginnings, all rather tentative and none quite successful, before 1830, in Hawthorne's "Provincial Tales" we find the earliest creative work done and published in the United States in which the true positive romantic note is struck and held.

The best evidence in support of this claim is Hawthorne's dynamic use of the pattern of symbolic death and rebirth. The pattern of death and rebirth was not in itself a new device; its history goes back as far as history itself has gone, to early Sumerian times. Among English poets, Milton used it with fine effects, most obviously in "Lycidas" and more massively in *Paradise Lost, Paradise Regained,* and *Samson Agonistes.* But, like other writers in the humanistic tradition, Milton used the pattern in a static way. He began with an intellectual understanding of Christian (or pre-Christian) religious and cultural truth. Symbolic death tested this truth in experience and questioned it in spirit, placing the truth and the protagonist in danger of literal death and damnation. Finally the truth was vindicated and accepted emotionally, and the esthetic pattern returned full circle. The truth remained the same truth, and the whole effect was to bring the esthetic pattern into equilibrium, or a state of rest.

The romantics make it dynamic. In works such as *Faust, The Ancient Mariner,* and *The Prelude* the pattern of death and rebirth ends, if it can be said to end at all, at a point beyond its beginning. It is not a matter of doubt and reconciliation, or an emotionally enriched return to a given formula. It involves the discovery of a new attitude which enables the protagonist to carry his revolt through to a sort of open completion; to make it, in fact, not just a revolt against an old truth but a radical departure from all old concepts of truth as a static value. The romantic protagonist dies in much the same symbolic sense as his humanistic predecessor, by withdrawing from the generally accepted ways of thinking and feeling. But he is reborn in a very different sense and into a whole new, different world. Instead of returning he goes on indefinitely. (pp. 54-5)

Hawthorne handles the romantic theme very well. His unresolved ambiguities express the conflicts out of which the romantic development comes, and mean something more than just the tough-minded acceptance of the fact that men are both good and evil. They strongly imply a transcendence of good and evil as absolute, static values or concepts, because it is out of the tension between these opposites that the power to move onward is generated. Young Goodman Brown is lost because he rejects one of the necessary elements, and with it his ability to progress. Like Milton's hero, he ends where he has begun, but Hawthorne reverses the values, so that Brown returns to Puritan Salem not with enriched faith but in a state of complete spiritual impoverishment. He should have fallen, should have let himself be tempted and damned out of the old dispensation entirely, should have accepted the devil's destructive knowledge, which was death sure enough, but which might therefore have led eventually to rebirth. By refusing he has caught himself in the trap of an absolute and static moral isolation. To make the point more literally, it is only by exposing himself all the way to the hostile power of evil that he can move off dead center in his progress toward manhood. Because he refuses to do so he fails to reach maturity, which is a condition of being able to move in any direction one wishes and of being willing to take the consequences of whatever moves one makes. A state, that is, of freedom with responsibility.

Many readers will have strong moral objections to this interpretation. But the actual weakness of it is its assumption that Brown is a real person, with a real choice between real courses of action. That is not the fact. Brown is a fictional character, a symbol, an imaginary entity in an imaginative tale. Hawthorne tries to suggest the kind of reality that is involved, and to forestall the wrong kind of criticism, by asking at the end, "Had Goodman Brown fallen asleep in the forest and only dreamed a wild dream of a witch-meeting?" His answer is that it does not matter. "Be it so if you will," he says; "but, alas! it was a dream of evil omen for young Goodman Brown." We are told, in effect, that this is an imaginary garden with a real toad in it, and that we are not to let the imaginariness of the garden blind us to the reality of the toad. At the same time we must not let the reality of the toad—that is, the seriousness of the moral crisis through which Brown is imagined as passing—blind us to the equally significant imaginariness of the garden, the purely arbitrary symbolic structure of the story. Brown cannot choose. Hawthorne has decided that he shall refuse the choice, and has created the whole situation accordingly. The story is a highly artistic exploration of the moral problem.

"Young Goodman Brown" is the best of the "Provincial Tales," partly because it most powerfully symbolizes the terrors and difficulties at the crisis of development, and fixes the very moment of that crisis in an esthetic projection combining the maximum of force with the maximum of control and finish. Other stories in the group are hardly less remarkable, however, for the cogency with which they seize the moment of significant change, and for the beauty with which they express the tensions out of which development comes. Their universality lies in the common feeling of young people everywhere in revolt against parental and social authority. Their special appeal is to romantics who are in revolt against all fixed ideas of order and whose need is for a larger freedom than either a humanist or a mechanist can imagine. In rendering that special feeling, out of the experience of his own time and the revolt of his own generation, Hawthorne effectively began to establish himself in "Provincial Tales" as a romantic artist of the highest rank. (pp. 55-7)

Richard P. Adams, "Hawthorne's 'Provincial Tales,' " in The New England Quarterly, *Vol. XXX, No. 1, March, 1957, pp. 39-57.*

RICHARD P. ADAMS (essay date 1958)

[*In the following excerpt, Adams analyzes the stories Hawthorne wrote during his stay at the "Old Manse."*]

Hawthorne was keenly interested during the Old Manse period [July 1842 to October 1845] in the character and function of the artist, and in the question of his place in society. Four of the tales written in Concord were directly concerned with artists of various kinds and in various situations, and a discussion of these will bring out Hawthorne's ideas more plainly and suggest his own difficulties as an artist. . . .

"The Birthmark," which presents the artist as alchemist, is a poignant expression of Hawthorne's feelings about the aims, means, and difficulties of his work. Its general theme is suggested, in two ways, by a couple of notebook entries printed by Sophia between the dates of October 16 and December 6, 1837: "A person to be in the possession of something as perfect as mortal man has the right to demand; he tries to make it better, and ruins it entirely." "A person to spend all his life and splendid talents in trying to achieve something naturally impossible,—as to make a conquest over Nature." The whole idea is more specifically stated in another entry, which Sophia placed between the dates of January 4 and July 3, 1839: "A person to be the death of his beloved in trying to raise her to more than mortal perfection; yet this should be a comfort to him for having aimed so highly and holily." In the tale, the protagonist, Aylmer, is married to Georgiana, a woman of almost perfect beauty. Her only defect is a birthmark, shaped like a tiny reddish hand, on her cheek. Aylmer is unable to reconcile himself to this imperfection, and Georgiana, made unhappy also by his dissatisfaction, urges him to use his esoteric powers to try removing it. He does so, but when the mark fades out, and her beauty is perfect, she dies. This one little defect, "the symbol of his wife's liability to sin, sorrow, decay, and death," is what makes her existence in the imperfect material world possible. She does not blame her husband. "My poor Aylmer,' " she says, " 'you have aimed loftily; you have done nobly. Do not repent that with so high and pure a feeling, you have rejected the best the earth could offer.' "

The moral of the story, however, is more complex than that. Aylmer's earthy assistant, Aminadab, gives his habitual "hoarse, chuckling laugh," and the authorial voice remarks,

> Thus ever does the gross fatality of earth exult in its invariable triumph over the immortal essence which, in this dim sphere of half development, demands the completeness of a higher state. Yet, had Aylmer reached a profounder wisdom, he need not thus have flung away the happiness which would have woven his mortal life of the selfsame texture with the celestial. The momentary circumstance was too strong for him; he failed to look beyond the shadowy scope of time, and, living once for all in eternity, to find the perfect future in the present.

Hawthorne's reach in this passage appears to exceed his grasp; his terms are obscure and probably confused. What he seems to be groping for is some theory or formula by means of which to transcend the difficulties arising from the traditional humanistic dualism of body and soul, or matter and spirit, or time and eternity. He is suggesting that Aylmer, or the artist, or man in general, should live the earthly life in such a way that it participates in the life of eternity. In this moral Hawthorne verges toward the Transcendentalist views of Emerson and others; however, he does not fully commit himself to any such notion as that of the Over-Soul, or that of the perfect organic universe. He was too hardheaded to go entirely overboard for any theory.

Aylmer is presented as a scientist of the late eighteenth century, when "ardent votaries" hoped that "the secret of creative force" might soon be within their grasp. At the same time, somewhat paradoxically, he is an heir and disciple of the medieval and early renaissance alchemists Albertus Magnus, Cornelius Agrippa, Paracelsus, and Roger Bacon, whose books line the walls of his library. He works in matter, with the help of Aminadab, but in such a way as to spiritualize it "by his strong and eager aspiration towards the infinite." He claims the ability to concoct an elixir of life and to transmute base metals into gold, but he feels that " 'a philosopher who should go deep enough to acquire the power would attain too lofty a wisdom to stoop to the exercise of it.' " His allegiance to spiritual values preserves him from materialism and from the author's condemnation, and yet the very fact that his aim is upward rather than inward constitutes in a way his principal error. His failures are all of the same kind, as his journal, which Georgiana reads, records:

> His brightest diamonds were the merest pebbles, and felt to be so by himself, in comparison with the inestimable gems which lay hidden beyond his reach. The volume, rich with achievements that had won renown for its author, was yet as melancholy a record as ever mortal hand had penned. It was the sad confession and continual exemplification of the shortcomings of the composite man, the spirit burdened with clay and working in matter, and of the despair that assails the higher nature at finding itself so miserably thwarted by the earthly part. Perhaps every man of genius in whatever sphere might recognize the image of his own experience in Aylmer's journal.

In short, it is the dualism of his experience—or of his attitude toward experience—that trips him every time.

Another and a simpler way of looking at his error is suggested by Georgiana, whose concept of character, or personality, seems to be developmental rather than idealistic. " 'Life,' " she says, " 'is but a sad possession to those who have attained precisely the degree of moral advancement at which I stand. Were I weaker and blinder it might be happiness. Were I stronger, it might be endured hopefully. But, being what I find myself, methinks I am of all mortals the most fit to die.' " From this point of view Aylmer's error lies in his failure to understand that perfection is death. A living thing must grow and develop in order to keep on living; it is therefore by definition and by necessity imperfect, as Georgiana is. If it is ever perfected, as Georgiana comes to be by her husband's art, it must die, as Georgiana does. The concept of "the perfect future in the present" must depend, somehow, on acceptance of the radical imperfection of the developing world of matter and of life. Hawthorne never states this principle directly or clearly, and probably did not understand it as well as Emerson, Thoreau, or Whitman did; but just at this time he seems to have been at least looking in its direction.

"The Artist of the Beautiful" is in some ways an even more daring flight than **"The Birthmark"** into the rarefied air of the Transcendentalist thinkers. In **"The Birthmark"** Hawthorne still appears to have held the opinion he expressed in the *American Magazine of Useful and Entertaining Knowledge* in 1836 that "the Creator has absolutely debarred mankind from all inventions and discoveries, the results of which would counteract the general laws, that He has established over human affairs," and that the elixir of life, for instance, is therefore an impossibility. Another expression of the same or a very similar idea is a notebook entry printed by Sophia between the dates of October 7 and 14, 1837: "The reason of the minute superiority of Nature's work over man's is, that the former works from the innermost germ, while the latter works merely superficially." The story idea for **"The Artist of the Beautiful"** is partly suggested in one of the notebook entries quoted above: "A person to spend all his life and splendid talents in trying to achieve something naturally impossible—as to make conquest over Nature." Another variation on the theme of misdirected and futile effort is stated in an entry located by Sophia between the dates of January 4 and July 3, 1839, but after the "1840" date: "To represent a man as spending life and the intensest labor in the accomplishment of some mechanical trifle,—as in making a miniature coach to be drawn by fleas, or a dinner-service to be put into a cherry-stone."

In **"The Artist of the Beautiful"** these related suggestions are combined and then boldly transcended. The protagonist, Owen Warland, is apparently wasting his life on a mechanical trifle, and at the same time he is trying to outdo nature, in the construction of a synthetic butterfly. Like Aylmer, he aims at " 'the spiritualization of matter.' " But Owen the artist succeeds precisely where Aylmer the alchemist fails. When he finishes his work, we are told, "Nature's ideal butterfly was here realized in all its perfection; not in the pattern of such faded insects as flit among earthly flowers, but of those which hover across the meads of paradise for child-angels and the spirits of departed infants to disport themselves with." At the same time he is able to achieve a degree of maturity that enables him to realize his inner vision so confidently that he remains undisturbed when his butterfly is destroyed. **"The Artist of the Beautiful"** is the most extended and thorough single inquiry Hawthorne ever made on the artist's relation to his work and his environment, and it is his most important manifesto of his own artistic intention and method.

Before his final success, Owen has three temporary failures, each caused by a weakness in his relation to his social environment. The first occurs just after a visit to his watchmaking shop by his friend Robert Danforth, a blacksmith. Disturbed by Danforth's embodiment of " 'hard, brute force,' " Owen slips and ruins his project. The author's voice remarks, ruefully,

> Thus it is that ideas, which grow up within the imagination and appear so lovely to it and of a value beyond whatever men call valuable, are exposed to be shattered and annihilated by contact with the practical. It is requisite for the ideal artist to possess a force of character that seems hardly compatible with its delicacy; he must keep his faith in himself while the incredulous world assails him with its utter disbelief; he must stand up against mankind and be his own sole disciple, both as respects his genius and the objects to which it is directed.

Owen, at first, like Hawthorne on many occasions, is unable to exert enough force of the kind required for artistic success.

His second failure consists in the destruction of the little mechanism by Annie Hovenden, with whom he is in love, but who is unable to sympathize adequately with his aims and efforts. The authorial reflection is that "He had indeed erred, yet pardonably; for if any human spirit could have sufficiently reverenced the processes so sacred in his eyes, it must have been a woman's. Even Annie Hovenden, possibly, might not have disappointed him had she been enlightened by the deep intelligence of love."

The third and most serious failure is Owen's own deliberate wrecking of the work when he hears from Peter Hovenden, Annie's father, that she is engaged to marry Robert Danforth. Hovenden, from whom Owen has learned the watchmaker's trade as an apprentice, is himself the "most terrible" influence, "by reason of a keen understanding which saw so distinctly what it did see, and disbelieved so uncompromisingly in what it could not see." Material force, misdirected emotion, and the skeptical, theoretical intellect, in rising order of importance, are the obstacles that Owen must overcome. Among them, they seem to represent also the causes of the artist's isolation in New England society, which systematically misunderstands his work from all three points of view. Owen's solace and inspiration come from nature, after each failure, even though it is nature he is trying to surpass. Butterflies are especially inspiring, and he seems to follow each one with his eyes "as if its airy track would show the path to heaven."

When he has finished his work, he comes to present the result, as a belated wedding gift, to Annie, whose "fireside circle" now includes her father, her husband, and a baby son. Peter Hovenden is as skeptical and Danforth as gross as ever, and Owen now realizes that even Annie "could never say the fitting word nor feel the fitting sentiment which should be the perfect recompense of an artist who, symbolizing a lofty moral by a material trifle,—converting what was earthly to spiritual gold,—had won the beautiful into his handiwork." Danforth seems dimly to recognize the value of this esthetic alchemy when he says, " 'Well, that does beat all nature.' " But he spoils his own good word by going on to maintain that " 'There is more real use in one downright blow of my sledge hammer than in the whole five years' labor that our friend Owen has wasted on this butterfly.' "

Annie comes nearer the point by asking, " 'Is it alive?' " The third time she asks, Owen somewhat reluctantly explains that " 'it may well be said to possess life, for it has absorbed my own being into itself; and in the secret of that butterfly, and in its beauty,—which is not merely outward, but deep as its whole system,—is represented the intellect, the imagination, the sensibility, the soul of an Artist of the Beautiful!' " He has created a work which is beautiful, like the works of nature, from its innermost germ in his imagination, thus giving it life and making it represent the life of his own intellect and soul. But in doing this he has done something else more important, at least to him. He has discovered the meaning of life in the process of communicating it in the symbol which is the work of art.

This meaning is most plainly stated by the box he has made for his butterfly, "carved richly out of ebony by his own hand, and inlaid with a fanciful tracery of pearl, representing a boy in pursuit of a butterfly, which, elsewhere, had become a winged spirit, and was flying heavenward; while the boy, or youth, had found such efficacy in his strong desire that he ascended from earth to cloud, and from cloud to celestial atmosphere, to win the beautiful." It is the life of art that is primarily important, rather than the work in which the life is embodied. Once the work is done, the artist has little further use for it. Therefore, when the heir of Danforth strength and Hovenden sagacity snatches the butterfly out of the air and crushes it into "a small heap of glittering fragments, whence the mystery of beauty had fled forever," Owen views the matter "placidly." "He had caught a far other butterfly than this. When the artist rose high enough to achieve the beautiful, the symbol by which he made it perceptible to mortal senses became of little value in his eyes while his spirit possessed itself in the enjoyment of the reality."

Again, as in **"The Birthmark,"** there is a strong suggestion of Transcendentalist thought and imagery in this formulation, which makes it seem uncharacteristic of Hawthorne. However, the butterfly has a history in his previous writings that supports the interpretation of it as representing the artist's soul in its struggle toward a higher realm and reality. In an article on "St. John's Grave" in the *American Magazine of Useful and Entertaining Knowledge* for April, 1836, Hawthorne remarks, "We do wrong to our departed friends, and clog our own heavenward aspirations, by connecting the idea of the grave with that of death. Our thoughts should follow the celestial soul, and not the earthly corpse." The last sentence here is reproduced almost word for word in the sketch "Chippings from a Chisel," first published in 1838, which in turn is based on the article "Martha's Vineyard" in the same issue of the magazine. The narrator says to his friend the tombstone cutter, " 'Our thoughts should soar upward with the butterfly—not linger with the exuviae that confined him.' " The substitution of "butterfly" for "soul" is the key. The image is repeated in "The New Adam and Eve," where the speaker supposes that the newly created couple might think of death, if at all, as "the butterfly soaring upward." So there seems little reason to doubt that when Hawthorne chose a butterfly as the "mechanical trifle" for Owen to spend his time and genius creating, he fully and consciously intended it as a symbol of the soul.

In spite of all this spiritual emphasis, and in spite of a pervasive insistence on the smallness and apparent triviality of the mechanical object on which Owen labors, and on the weakness of Owen's character in the beginning, **"The Artist of the Beautiful"** is consistent in expressing the dynamic nature of the artist's work and its relation to his personal growth in self-confidence and maturity. This growth takes place partly by means of the work, which also results in a tangible symbol of the completed development, a public medium through which the private experience of growth may be communicated. But the art object has no importance in itself, nor does it seem to matter whether anyone receives the communication or not. The artist gets his satisfaction purely in his own inner vision of "the beautiful," which in any case can be only very imperfectly expressed. The doctrine is not that of art for art's sake but of the life and work of the artist for his soul's sake. But in some of these matters the tale is experimental and somewhat strictly limited. The question seems to be whether it is possible for an artist to succeed entirely on his own, in spite of weakness, against the inertia of materialism and intellectual philistinism in society, and without the inspiration of a woman's love. And the answer is that he can. (pp. 130-37)

The most important evidence of Hawthorne's strength during the Old Manse period . . . is neither his satire nor his criticism, but the fact that at this time he got back to the way of writing that had produced the best of his early work in the Provincial Tales, and wrote one story, **"Rappaccini's Daughter,"** that belongs with **"Young Goodman Brown," "My Kinsman, Major Molineaux,"** and *The Scarlet Letter* in the very top rank of his achievements in fiction.

This event appears to have grown out of a formula which Hawthorne conceived, probably, late in 1842. It is recorded in the notebook between the dates of June 1, 1842, and July 27, 1844.

> The human Heart to be allegorized as a cavern; at the entrance there is sunshine, and flowers growing about it. You step within, but a short distance, and begin to find yourself surrounded with a terrible gloom, and monsters of diverse kinds; it seems like Hell itself. You are bewildered, and wander long without hope. At last a light strikes upon you. You peep towards it, and find yourself in a region that seems, in some sort, to reproduce the flowers and sunny beauty of the entrance, but all perfect. These are the depths of the heart, or of human nature, bright and peaceful; the gloom and terror may lie deep; but deeper still is the eternal beauty.

This passage, omitted from Sophia's version of the notebooks and therefore not published until the appearance of Randall Stewart's edition of 1932, has not yet received the critical attention it deserves. It has, of course, very little artistic value in itself, but it probably comes nearer than any other single comment Hawthorne ever wrote, long or short, to explaining what his art is about.

As an image, the cavern is not new to Hawthorne's writing in 1842; it appears in works done before as well as after that time, and refers rather simply and plainly to unconscious aspects of the mind and experience. It is congenial to Hawthorne because of its connotations of depth and inwardness, which harmonize with his notions of psychic geography; because of its labyrinthine darkness, which goes well with the imagery of wandering; and because of its associations with springs or fountains, volcanic fire, and buried treasure, all of which, as images, are variously involved with Hawthorne's feelings about the nature of literary or artistic inspiration and the manner of its coming into the conscious mind. He might well have derived the image, as an image, from the Gothic tradition, which is full of castles with dungeons and secret passages, caves, forests, and the depths of the sea. All of these apparently refer to unconscious matters, though not very often in an orderly or effective way. The forest in **"Young Goodman Brown"** and **"Roger Malvin's Burial"** and the dark streets of Boston in **"My Kinsman, Major Molineux"** and **"The Gray Champion,"** peopled with lurid enemies and guilty fancies, places of confused moral wanderings and strange encounters, suggest the notebook formula. The heart is more explicitly related to cavern imagery in **"The Haunted Mind,"** where the narrator says that "In the depths of every heart there is a tomb and a dungeon," which may release its "buried ones, or prisoners," during the night hour when the will relaxes its control. In **"The Minister's Black Veil,"** Mr. Hooper is kept "in that saddest of all prisons, his own heart," and in **"The Man of Adamant,"** for a different reason, Richard Digby imprisons himself in a cave in the depth of a forest. A similarly imprisoned man is the proprietor of the museum in **"A Virtuoso's Collection,"** which the narrator reaches, after leaving "the sunny sidewalk," by way of "a sombre staircase." Numerous references to wanderers into infernal regions, such as AEneas, Ulysses, Rampsinitus, Orpheus, Hercules, Empedocles, and Thomas the Rhymer, and the fact that the narrator leaves by 'the gateway through which Aeneas and the Sibyl had been dismissed from Hades" reinforce the association.

But the notebook passage is more than an image; it is an allegory, and it differs from these uses of the cavern and associated images, and from the subterranean imagery of the Gothic tradition, in that it represents a deliberate, conscious principle of artistic organization. The human experience it refers to is that of spiritual death and rebirth, which Hawthorne's best fiction is always concerned with, before and after 1842. The sunshine and flowers at the entrance may be said to represent a relatively simple, naive acceptance by the unregenerate man of superficial appearances, of social proprieties, and of cultural conventions. The wandering in darkness among intimidating monsters corresponds to the ordeal of doubt and terror that must always follow a rejection of conventional notions and standards. The innermost region suggests the discovery of a new and more satisfactory conception of truth and reality. (pp. 139-41)

"Rappaccini's Daughter" is generally regarded as one of Hawthorne's best stories, but, until recently, it has received little critical attention. The reason may be that it is also the most complex and difficult of his shorter works. The early critics did not get into it far enough to see it as a whole or to correct their initial and superficial assumptions. There is still disagreement as to the theme of the tale, as to the identity of its protagonist, and as to the moral to be drawn from its events. I think that most of the difficulties, though not the complexities, can be resolved if **"Rappaccini's Daughter"** is regarded as Hawthorne's first complete, successful working-out of the cavern allegory in fiction. This assumption leads to others which I believe will in turn prove useful: first, that Giovanni Guasconti is the protagonist; second, that the theme is his testing in the cavern of the heart; and third, that the conclusion, or moral, is the same as that of **"Young Goodman Brown"**—the young man must face the knowledge of evil and pass through the terrifying experience by which it is to be gained, and then he may reach the knowledge and experience of good. From this point of view, the story reads, in outline, as follows:

Giovanni Guasconti has come from southern Italy to Padua in order to study at the University. He finds lodging in a "high and gloomy chamber" of a house that has once belonged to a family one member of which is mentioned in Dante's *Inferno.* The window of Giovanni's room overlooks an enclosed garden, where Dr. Giacomo Rappaccini cultivates herbs for his medicines, which the landlady reports to be "as potent as a charm." But, as Giovanni watches the doctor at work, he is disagreeably impressed by a feeling that Rappaccini, in "that most simple and innocent of human toils," behaves like "one walking among malignant influences, such as savage beasts, or deadly snakes, or evil spirits, which, should he allow them one moment of license, would wreak upon him some terrible fatality." He is wearing gloves, and when he comes near his most magnificent plant, a shrub with purple flowers like gems, growing out of the pool of a ruined fountain in the center of the garden, he puts on a mask. Then, "finding his task still too dangerous," he calls his daughter Beatrice to come and help him. She is "beautiful as the day," and seems "redundant with life, health, and energy; all of which attributes were bound down and compressed, as it were, and girdled tensely, in their luxuriance, by her virgin zone." Her attractiveness to Giovanni is qualified by a vague sense of danger. She seems like "another flower, the human sister of those vegetable ones, as beautiful as they, more beautiful than the richest of them, but still to be touched only with a glove, nor to be approached without a mask." She embraces the plant in the fountain and tends it lovingly, like a sister. That night, in Giovanni's dreams, "Flower and maiden were different, and yet the same, and fraught with some strange peril in either shape."

The next morning, Giovanni dismisses his fears and adopts "a most rational view of the whole matter." He goes to call on an old friend of his father, Professor Pietro Baglioni, a rival of Rappaccini's, who warns him against involving himself with that uneasy gardener. According to Baglioni, Rappaccini " 'would sacrifice human life, his own among the rest, or whatever else was dearest to him, for the sake of adding so much as a grain of mustard seed to the great heap of his accumulated knowledge.' " Giovanni, not much impressed by this admonition, returns to his room, from which he now sees Beatrice alone in the garden. He is struck by her "expression of simplicity and sweetness," and the analogy between her and the flowers no longer disturbs him. But then he sees, or thinks he sees, three very disquieting events. As she picks a flower from the magnificent central shrub to fasten on her dress, it appears to him that a drop falls from its stem on the head of a small lizard, which dies at her feet. Then an insect—described in such a way as to suggest a butterfly, though it is not named—is apparently killed by her breath. Then, when he speaks to her and tosses down a bouquet of " 'pure and healthful flowers,' " he thinks he sees them withering in her hand as she disappears into her father's house.

Although he has not yet entered the garden, Giovanni seems at this point to be moving into the cavern, and Hawthorne describes his feelings in such a way that the cavern allegory is made to assimilate the imagery of fire and darkness which describes young Goodman Brown's emotions in a similar dilemma. "Guasconti," the author says, "had not a deep heart—or, at all events, its depths were not sounded now; but he had a quick fancy," which, aroused by sexual desire and inhibited by fear and doubt, is tormented by "a wild offspring of both love and horror that had each parent in it, and burned like one and shivered like the other." He is caught between "hope and dread," without knowing quite what either refers to. He is only a little way into the cavern, still able to see sometimes by the daylight from the entrance but as yet without any glimpse of the perfect light and beauty of the innermost depth. "Blessed," says the author, "are all simple emotions, be they dark or bright! It is the lurid intermixture of the two that produces the illuminating blaze of the infernal regions."

Giovanni is again warned by Baglioni, who becomes convinced that his young friend is the subject of one of Rappaccini's evil experiments. But again Giovanni disregards the warning, and when he returns to the house, his landlady shows him a way "along several obscure passages" into the garden, where he finally meets Beatrice face to face. He is dismayed by the ugly deformities of the plants, but reassured by the behavior of Beatrice. In describing her, Hawthorne uses the imagery of the fountain and the treasure: "Her spirit gushed out before him like a fresh rill that was just catching its first glimpse of the sunlight and wondering at the reflections of earth and sky which were flung into its bosom. There came thoughts, too, from a deep source, and fantasies of a gemlike brilliancy, as if diamonds and rubies sparkled upward among the bubbles of the fountain." This imagery,

An engraving of Hawthorne in 1850 from a painting by Cephas G. Thompson.

while it expresses the innermost goodness of her character, also emphasizes her likeness to "the magnificent shrub, with its treasury of glowing blossoms," springing from the fountain in the center of the garden.

Giovanni has seen enough now, if he could understand it, to know her correctly; but he takes too simple a view. He has seen her as daylight shows her, healthy, beautiful, and innocent. He has also seen her, in afternoon and evening light and dimness, as poisonous, like the plants in the garden, and therefore presumably evil. Finally he has seen, or more properly he has heard, emanations from the region of the inner light, the ultimate truth of her character, as of the human heart in the notebook allegory, which should resolve the apparent contradiction of the two preceding views. But his ignorance, or his willful blindness, is so complete that he cannot see even the second stage of the truth; he tries to pick a flower from the central shrub and present it to her. With "a shriek that went through his heart like a dagger," she pulls his hand away. The next morning he sees, by the superficial light of the cavern entrance, the prints of her thumb and fingers on his wrist, which is painfully swollen, and he wonders "what evil thing had stung him. . . ."

Beatrice has advised him, during their interview, to " 'Forget whatever you may have fancied in regard to me. If true to the outward senses, still it may be false in its essence; but the words of Beatrice Rappaccini's lips are true from the depths of the heart outward. Those you may believe.' " As she speaks, the author says, "A fervor glowed in her whole aspect and beamed upon Giovanni's consciousness like the light of truth itself. . . ." However, Giovanni being the kind of young man he is, the author's advice, suggested previously, seems sound. "The wisest course would have been . . . to quit his lodgings and Padua itself at once; the next wiser, to have accustomed himself, as far as possible, to the familiar and daylight view of Beatrice—thus bringing her rigidly and systematically within the limits of ordinary experience." That is, Giovanni should stay out of the cavern of the heart, or better yet he should flee from even the vicinity of its entrance. But he lacks this better part of valor, just as he lacks the courage to admit that Beatrice, in her secondary aspect, is poisonous. His chances of reaching the innermost region of the cavern seem practically nil.

The crisis comes one day when Baglioni, taking the initiative, comes to Giovanni's room and tells him that Rappaccini has loaded his daughter with poison, and gives him an antidote which, Baglioni thinks, will counteract the evil. Giovanni's doubts and fears return with a rush. He plans to make a decisive test, by handing some fresh flowers to Beatrice and staying to see if they really wither. But before he can get them to her, they wither in his own hand, and he begins to suspect that he too has been innoculated with Rappaccini's venoms. After killing a spider by breathing on it, to confirm this suspicion, he rushes down to Beatrice in the garden and accuses her of having made him " 'as hateful, as ugly, as loathesome and deadly a creature as thyself—a world's wonder of hideous monstrosity!' " Then, having forgotten the glimpses of ultimate truth and goodness he has had "when the pure fountain had been unsealed from its depths and made visible in its transparency to his mental eye," he adds further insult by proposing that they both take the antidote, " 'and thus be purified from evil.' " Beatrice, knowing that the antidote will act as a poison to her distorted system, but knowing also that there can be no "earthly union" between her and Giovanni, that "she must bathe her hurts in some fount of paradise, and forget her grief in the light of immortality, and *there* be well," accepts the vial and drinks, advising Giovanni to " 'await the result.' "

Rappaccini, whom Giovanni has identified as the Adam of this modern Eden, but who seems in some ways more like its evil god, or devil, now appears "in the attitude of a father imploring a blessing upon his children," or "as might an artist who should spend his life in achieving a picture or a group of statuary and finally be satisfied with his success." But his satisfaction in placing his daughter and her duped lover apart from and, as he thinks, above the rest of humanity is destroyed when Beatrice, denying any wish for such a status, dies at his and Giovanni's feet; and Baglioni puts his head out the window of Giovanni's room and calls down "in a tone of triumph mixed with horror, to the thunderstricken man of science,—

> " 'Rappaccini! Rappaccini! and is *this* the upshot of your experiment!' "

The structure of the tale, and the quality and relations of the characters, are parallel to the main lines of the cavern allegory, which is an objective though somewhat abstract correlative of Hawthorne's pervasive theme of personal development. The course of **"Rappaccini's Daughter"** is at the same time like that of **"Young Goodman Brown,"** though the imagery is very much richer. Giovanni, like Brown, is attracted by a woman into a situation where good and evil, associated mainly with the attractive and the frightening aspects of adult sexuality, are mingled in a more complex and challenging way than he is prepared to understand or deal with. The result is a fictional projection of how it feels to be caught in the moment of transition from adolescence to manhood and fixed there without being able to go either forward or back. This is a universal feeling, though presumably for most men a transitory one. In the story, it is isolated and made permanent, and transformed into an esthetic pattern which intensifies it and brings it to the reader's attention with emphasis, vibrancy, living immediacy, and intense satisfaction in the simple and total awareness of the feeling as feeling, all of which qualities help to give it its value.

Giovanni, as a protagonist who fails to develop, is precisely constituted for his part. He is handsome and ardent, but shallow. His naivety is caused by weakness, and it is therefore unconquerable. He is, by Hawthorne's definition of his character, incapable of the development which is demanded of him. Beatrice, the woman of the tale, takes a much more prominent part than Faith does in **"Young Goodman Brown"** because she represents or embodies all three stages of the cavern allegory. She is good, innocent, harmless, and beautiful in the outward, sunlit view of her to which Giovanni tries to cling. A somewhat more penetrating look reveals that she is deadly poisonous. The profoundest view, expressed in the images of the fountain and of heavenly light, shows the innermost perfection of the heart, which cannot be reached except through the region of darkness and monsters representing the fears and doubts of any transition period or any crisis in personal development. Rappaccini, the evil man or devil figure, is the chief monster of the middle region, and he is reinforced by the plants in his garden, which also seems to represent the dark part of the cavern. However, like the devil in **"Young Goodman Brown"** or the evil figures in Hawthorne's other early tales, he is not purely or merely evil, but has his positive function, at least potentially, in the protagonist's development. Baglioni's character and function are even more ambiguous, in that his mistaken effort to pull Giovanni out of the cavern by the heels is the immediate precipitant of the catastrophe. Baglioni is a creature wholly of the outside light, knowing nothing of the cavern except, presumably, that people who go into it go out of his sight and are, to him, lost. His apparently well-intentioned effort to play the part of the benevolent man is therefore the most mischievous kind of meddling. He corresponds closely to the combination of Peter Hovenden and Robert Danforth in **"The Artist of the Beautiful,"** in representing the obtuse intolerance of the materialistic intellect for any exploration that may lead to personal development.

The various classes of Hawthorne's subsidiary imagery fall rather neatly into place in relation to the general structure of **"Rappaccini's Daughter."** Wandering is appropriately prominent, especially when Giovanni, before his admittance to the garden, walks feverishly through the streets of Padua and is stopped by Baglioni, at whom he looks "forth wildly from his inner world into the outer one" to which that "portly personage" belongs. Fire, darkness, treasure, and fountain are all important, as we have already seen. Coldness is the essence of Rappaccini's character and of the isolation which he has imposed on Beatrice. Her "look of desolate separation, shuddering at itself," keeps Giovanni from touching her, even when the passion of their love is spoken "like tongues of long-hidden flame." The mirror, too, comes in at the crisis, where Giovanni looks at himself with naive approbation and then, realizing that he is poisoned, with terrified loathing.

In ***Mosses from an Old Manse,*** in which both tales were first collected, **"Rappaccini's Daughter"** immediately follows **"Young Goodman Brown,"** which was written at least nine and probably nearer fifteen years before. The juxtaposition may be accidental, but it serves to point up both the similarities and the differences between the two tales. It shows to what degree Hawthorne returned in 1844 to the modes and motives of his early work, and at the same time how far he had enriched his ability, during the intervening years of varied and often apparently futile experimentation, to do that kind of work. The fact is that Hawthorne struck his true note only occasionally, and never for very long at a time. **"Rappaccini's Daughter,"** the finest of the Old Manse stories, was also the last. . . . (pp. 144-51)

Richard P. Adams, "Hawthorne: The Old Manse Period," in TSE: Tulane Studies in English, *Vol. VIII, 1958, pp. 115-51.*

ROBERT H. FOSSUM (essay date 1963)

[*Fossum is an American critic and the author of numerous commentaries on Hawthorne's work. In the following excerpt, he examines Hawthorne's approach to historical subjects.*]

Nathaniel Hawthorne's historical tales and sketches comprise a pageant of more than two hundred years of American history. The Puritan conquest of the wilderness, the Salem witch trials, the revolt from English rule—these are only a few of the episodes over which Hawthorne at one time or another casts the "moonlight of romance." But not at all in order to sentimentalize or glorify our past; for as any reader of *The Scarlet Letter* knows, Hawthorne tends to dwell on the more inglorious features of our nation's green years. Honing the knife of fiction on the whetstone of fact, he scrapes away any sugar-coating time may have spread over the sometimes bitter pill of American history, penetrates to the essence of events, and therein reveals to the present—his and, subsequently, our own—that the past's "long shadow, falling over all the intervening years, is visible . . . upon ourselves." By imaginatively re-creating the past, Hawthorne hoped to create the conscience and consciousness of his race; to make all Americans aware of the mixture of good and evil, innocence and guilt, in the historical matrix which gave them birth and from which they can detach themselves only by relinquishing their national identity. For since, Hawthorne believed, we can know what we are and what it is possible for us to become only by knowing what we have been, our future as well as our present is contingent on recognizing both the burdens and blessings of our heritage.

The confrontation of the past by the present is not only the purpose of the tales; it is their subject as well. The pre-Revolutionary New England which serves as setting for some of Hawthorne's most notable fiction is in itself a place where present mingles with past, New World with Old, and where the two must come to terms with each other before any kind of integrated community can develop. Out of this restless conjunction of past and present, "prophetic echoes" of the American Revolution could be heard—a revolution which, Hawthorne believed, should remind us all that a violent break with the past is inevitably a costly affair. For despite a fundamental sympathy with the Colonies against the "antiquated trumpery" of English rule, Hawthorne observed in **"Old News"** that a "revolution or anything that interrupts social order may afford opportunities for the individual display of eminent virtues; but its effects are pernicious to general morality." Believing that the revolt from English rule was both right and necessary, he also believed America must face the fact, as he says in **"The Old Manse,"** that our nation has grown on "soil that was fertilized with English blood." However just the cause, insurrection might have "the effect of sin" and make the insurrectionist a man "unfit for heaven." Thus, to Hawthorne, even Washington, that "upright rebel," had something of the fallen angel about him. Nor does Hawthorne appear to be speaking entirely on behalf of the British captain in **"Old Ticonderoga"** who thinks that Ethan Allen's summons to the British fort to surrender "in the name of the great Jehovah and of the Continental Congress" invokes "Strange Allies." Furthermore, rebellion, whether personal or collective, results in a punishment befitting the crime: isolation, deracination, a sense of displacement for the magnificent rebel who, in becoming the outcast of the tribe, finds he has lost his sense of identity. For no matter how complete the objective rupture with the past, subjectively the two can never be disjoined. In the psychic depths, personal or communal, the present is still tied to the past, the son to the father. To pretend otherwise is to dissociate the subjective from the objective self, to put the social body at odds with the psychological, and to feel abandoned, forlorn, and temporally out of joint.

Paradoxically, while Hawthorne's purpose is a Thomas Mannian "making present of the past," to effect this a temporary expatriation from the present is necessary—for Hawthorne and readers alike. Nor is it enough to see ourselves as the heirs of our American forebears; we must journey back still further and see ourselves and our more immediate ancestors in the continuum of all history. If humanity, like time, is essentially one (as Hawthorne believed), then we are all Endicotts and Hutchinsons, Hancocks and Washingtons, not simply because we are later Americans but because we are men. Hawthorne's mystic symbols and allusions are intended to place both the personal and national elements of his tales—and his audience besides—within a larger historical context. Because in the mythic symbol, as in the personal and collective psyche, all time is continuously present, Hawthorne's technique illuminates the mytho-historical New England past of his tales, its actions and agents, in the light of traditional myth—those "nursery tales of primeval races" which, because they are the "nursery tales of this generation" as well, were to Thoreau "the most impressive proof of a common humanity."

Three stories—**"My Kinsman, Major Molineux," "The Gray Champion,"** and **"Endicott and the Red Cross"**—exemplify Hawthorne's purposes, techniques, and attitudes especially well. In the first of these, Robin Molineux's rebellion against his father's rule is a paradigm of the present's revolt from the past, and, withal, an example of the eternal recurrence of an archetypal human experience: the primordial act of parricide. Robin is more than just a young country lad making his first visit to town: he is *any* young man—youth itself at that crucial moment when it wavers between dependence and independence, past and future. More particularly, he is the prototypical American rebel, striking out by himself in a world he does not fully understand, about to witness and vicariously participate in "a temporary inflammation of the popular mind" which corresponds to a similar inflammation of his own consciousness. That is, the rebellion of the Colonial townspeople against Major Molineux, Robin's cousin and the English representative of the King, corresponds to the young man's rejection of his father's authority, its violence being a reflection of the real (however unconscious) nature of Robin's rebellion as well as a ritualistic version of the demonic forces at work in the overthrow of traditional social authority. Major Molineux is not only the authority of England, not only Robin's surrogate father, but an image—for both society and the individual—of the traditional authority of the past, a past which both youth and nation must come to terms with before they can achieve independent selfhood. Hence, America's break with England, Robin's break with his home and father, and every young man's break with the parental bond, are in the story interchangeable and mutually supporting. In addition, through Robin's confrontation of the violent forces in himself and in Colonial American society, Hawthorne confronts his readers with the forces of the buried but still living past in themselves and their culture. Robin's struggle with time is seen to be timeless; and the problem of the past, we see, is the problem of the present as well.

The similarity between Robin and young America is suggested early in the story. A homeless youth, Robin comes to his new world bearing a wallet on his back, presumably containing usable but nonetheless burdensome items of the past; a prospective initiate, he is ignorant of both social reality and his own nature; and while professedly seeking independence, he is actually looking for someone to lean on. Because Robin does not as yet understand himself, the conditions of independent manhood, nor the forces underlying the community, he believes he can retain the guidance, protection, and providence of the past (his father), while cutting himself off from its stern, constraining power. But the innocent young American ultimately is confronted by the fact that the relationship between old and young is an uneasy one; that independence brings a burden equal, perhaps, to the burden of submission; and that the price of self-assertion may well be confusion, isolation, a loss of temporal continuity and the sense of identity which independence was supposed to produce. For America, too, the problem is to see clearly its relationship to Father England, to recognize the implications of stepping outside the circle of its "old home," and to understand the complex forces behind its break with the past. For the reader, the problem is to penetrate the thin curtain between both his personal and cultural present and past, to realize that since Robin and the Colonists are his ancestors he must settle his relations with them as they had to with their ancestors.

Indeed, the way in which Robin and the Colonists react to paternal authority is the very crux of the story. Both of them rebel—the Colonists (led by a devil incarnate) with actual violence, by tarring and feathering Major Molineux; Robin with vicarious violence, by laughing at the Major's humiliation. Moreover, since Robin's father is a clergyman as well as a farmer, the young man's rebellion assumes even larger dimensions. For just as seventeenth-century New England's break with the fatherland was religious as well as political, so Robin's break with his father is a denial of both the spiritual and domestic authority of the past. The revolt against the father thus becomes, Hawthorne suggests, a revolt against God Himself, a satanic assertion of the autonomous self.

Robin's actions mean that he has relinquished, once and for all, his father's protection and guidance. Similarly, the Colonists, metonymous for America, must realize that they are now lost as well as liberated. More importantly, Robin must realize that by participating in an act of violence against a representative of the past, he has assumed a share of history's burdensome guilt. Still, perhaps because his violent impulses remain at least partly repressed, Robin is not fully aware of the consequences of his actions. His awareness will only be complete, Hawthorne implies, when he realizes that the conditions of independent selfhood are, paradoxically, acceptance of one's place in the "magnetic chain of humanity" forged by sin, guilt, and sorrow; and that whereas his rejection of the past has made a return to its innocence impossible, the guilt incurred by that rejection has also inextricably involved him in the procession of human history. So too with America, which cannot achieve identity and selfhood until it recognizes fully what it has done in attempting to create and define itself. It must recognize that despite the necessity of throwing off the past, the demonic violence of that act was an invocation of savagery inherited from a still earlier time; that the "inflammation of the popular mind" which overthrew one symbol of evil, English authority, with the hand of another, that of the "fiend of fire and . . . darkness," has blighted once and for all the dream of an Eden in the New World. America can never be free of the past, since in repeating Adam's sinful revolt from the father, it has become one with all the fallen Adams of man's history, thereby taking up the burden of the past in the very act of throwing it off. At the end of **"My Kinsman, Major Molineux,"** the authority of the past has been consumed in the flames of violence, but because the implications of the act have not been squarely faced, no fully conscious, integrated identity—social or personal—arises from the ashes. Whether Robin and America will rise in the world and whether, if they do, it will be with the help of Satan rather than with that of the kinsman they have rejected, are problems which Hawthorne chooses to raise but not to solve.

Nor are they solved in **"The Gray Champion,"** which deals in somewhat different terms with the same themes and problems; the inevitable tension between past and present and an implicit assessment of the moral nature and consequences of rebellion. As in **"Molineux,"** a group of Colonists—until now "kept in sullen submission by . . . filial love"—are shown face to face with their British oppressors in a New England street. Literally, the setting is Boston in 1689, during the rule of Sir Edmund Andros, representative of James II; figuratively, as the static twilight scene suggests, it is a moment of arrested time between past and future, a pivotal point between Colonial submission and self-assertion. Now Hawthorne immediately introduces an explanation of the tale's "moral": any government, he says, is deformed "that does not grow out of the nature of things and the character of the people." Still, **"The Gray Champion"** is hardly the chauvinistic eulogy of rebellion which Hawthorne's comment suggests. If among the Colonists there is a general "confidence in Heaven's blessing on a righteous cause," beneath that confidence lurk vestiges of guilt. And well there might. In the group are "veterans of King Philip's war, who had burned villages and slaughtered young and old with pious fierceness while the godly souls throughout the land were helping them with prayer;" and although the Colonists understandably view Andros as evil incarnate, they themselves are "burning with that lurid wrath, so difficult to kindle or to quench," which branded the rioters in **"Molineux."** Furthermore, since the person who stirs up their strongest resentment is the Episcopal clergyman, the incipient violence here, too, is evidently directed against religious as well as political authority. The result is a guilty fear of retaliation. There are rumors, for instance, that the Holy Father has ordered the Colonists " 'to be massacred, man and male child,' " that the guilt incurred by their Puritan forebears is to be visited on sons now contemplating a similar revolt from paternal authority. Finally, while Hawthorne shows us on one side "despotic rulers . . . proud of unjust authority and scoffing at the universal groan," he shows us on the other the Puritans' "dark attire," which, as he says in *The Scarlet Letter,* "so darkened the national visage . . . that all the subsequent years have not sufficed to clear it up." These last also constitute a "deformity"; corrupted remnants of the Colonial past, they oppress the present as heavily as does British political and religious rule.

To assume that the Colonists are representatives of pure righteousness is to over-simplify the story's conflict, to miss Hawthorne's irony, and to misinterpret his attitudes. The logical consequences of such a reading would be to regard the Gray Champion as a type of the dead American past, banishing one tyrant to perpetuate the heavy hand of another, a pesky obstructionist standing in the way of progress. He is something quite other than this. The hoary-headed champion, who so mysteriously appears out of the twilight shadows to stand between destructive sons and tyrannical fathers, mediates between total submission and violent rebellion, thereby quelling the potential violence in Colonists and Royalists alike. Carrying a "heavy sword upon his thigh, but a staff in his hand," performing "a gesture at once of encouragement and warning," he combines severity with beneficience to accomplish his ends. To the Colonists he is both a " 'gray patriarch' " and a "venerable brother," an image of the continuity of past and present who encompasses (as Hawthorne sees it) the need for obedience and the need for independence, the need to maintain connection with the past and the rightful demands of the present for freedom from inflexible rule by the past. If the mob leader in **"Molineux"** represented the liberated forces of stavistic violence, the Gray Champion personifies humanity's inherent powers of restraint. A timeless human force, he assumes the form of that archetypal old man as hero-saviour who, possessing *mana,* is invoked to mediate between past and present, submission and revolt, when a culture's hegemony is threatened. He is Hawthorne's reminder that whereas from the past we inherit irrational, potentially disruptive forces, we may also gain from it the wisdom to triumph over that primal savagery always threatening to erupt into the present.

No such wisdom manifests itself in **"Endicott and the Red Cross."** Or if it does, in the person of Roger Williams, it is compelled to give ground before John Endicott, who rips the Red Cross from the English banner, thereby performing "one of the boldest exploits our history records." Standing in the center of seventeenth-century Salem's village green, Endicott is in a very literal sense the reflector of the tale's action, since the entire scene has its image in his steel breastplate: the whipping post; the pillory; the stocks and their occupants—those who dared to defy, theologically or morally, "the infallible judgment of the civil rulers"; and the meeting house, with the still bloody head of a wolf nailed on the porch. These compose a microcosmic picture of Puritanism's militant authority; its bloody struggle with bestiality, not only in the actual wilderness but in the primordial forest of the human heart; the ironic incongruities of a system which fought evil with evil, authoritarianism with authoritarianism, *stasis* with *stasis.*

It is with these incongruities that Hawthorne is principally concerned. Despite his ironic declaration that Endicott's name should be "forever honored," the conflict in **"Endicott and the Red Cross"** is not simply Colonial freedom *versus* English tyranny, but rather, a complex struggle involving two tyrannical fathers and two sets of rebellious sons. If Endicott as Colonial American is the recalcitrant offspring, as Puritan patriarch he assumes as much infallibility as King Charles or Archbishop Laud. Furthermore, although his mutilation of the English banner is a symbolic declaration of independence from the past's authority, it is also an omen of his downfall and a revelation of the causes behind it. In the emblematic figures of the rebellious Wanton Gospeller and the tolerant Roger Williams, we see the sons whom Puritanism has engendered and whose resistance prefigures its doom. And although Hawthorne's distaste for English despotism cannot be doubted, he also clearly shows that Endicott's rebellion is not so much against England as it is against all authority other than his own—even, perhaps, against that of God. From the brightness, "internal heat," and "angry fire" of Endicott's steel-covered bosom to his "wrathful change" of countenance when he reminds the Colonists that they " 'have sacrificed all things' " to " 'make a new world' " and " 'painfully seek a path from hence to heaven,' " Endicott bears an unmistakable resemblance to the Miltonic Satan whose *non serviam* is the prototypical cry of all mythical rebels. The high churchman is thus partly right, at least, when he accuses Endicott of having repudiated " 'the symbol of our holy religion' ": for the Cross, emblem of the humble and merciful Son, is cast off as ruthlessly as the yoke of the proud and tyrannical Father, with the Arch-Puritan assuming the place of both Jesus and Jehovah.

The real opponent of tyranny is not Endicott but the Christlike Roger Williams. Unlike Endicott, who fights the savages with savagery, Williams triumphs over the wilderness—that which is inside as well as outside of man—with the staff, not the sword. Endicott, head and heart enclosed by steel and iron, is protected from the external savage but a prey to the savage impulses within; he is a "tyrannic man" (in the Socratic sense), a victim of unruly passions, satanic pride, and inflexible will. Williams, his head covered by a velvet skullcap, his bosom by a black robe, accepts the primordial Indian as his brother, the ancient wilderness as his home, the mire as the substance from which all men come and to which all will return. Williams' place in the scene is with the crowd; Endicott's is above it, where he stands magnificent yet solitary, alone in space, doomed in time. Indeed, just as Endicott's entire nature is captured by his rending of the flag, Williams' is revealed by the drink he takes from a fountain. In Hawthorne's fiction, as in the work of the English romantics, fountains consistently represent the soul, the image of God, the only authority to which men owe absolute obedience. By associating Williams with the fountain, Hawthorne makes him the embodiment of all it represents, thus implicitly contrasting the authority of the inspired soul flowing through time with the authority of the imposed will arrested in time, represented by Endicott. Before drinking, Williams turns his face heavenward, acknowledging that spiritual authority which cannot be seized but only received as a gift of grace. Endicott, on the other hand, who assumes Divine prerogatives, perpetuates in time that ancient curse which binds man to time, commits again the sin of Adam as well as of Satan, and re-enacts in the "Eden of the West" the tragedy of the first Garden.

In trying to free themselves from a corrupt and moribund past, the Endicotts substituted for it an inflexible insistence that time be put in the stocks and the rule of the father serve for the son. True, they rebelled against a church which, they felt, had replaced God as ultimate authority; but they did so not to reassert that He is man's only judge, but, replacing the tree of life with the whipping post, to set themselves up as judges. Rather than subduing man's primitive savagery and rebellious will, they released them in the names of "civilization" and "piety." And ironically, that savagery, in the symbolic form of the primeval Indian, remained in their midst—temporarily contained, no longer roaming wild in the forest, but still present within the fortress of the Puritan heart. In trying to suppress or rid themselves of the evil of the past, European or atavistic, the Puritans so forgot the lessons of time that they merely converted evil into a different form, repeated the past, and passed on its burden to future generations. For Hawthorne lets it be known that he is not smugly confining evil to the past and thereby himself repeating, in that sense, the mistakes of his ancestors. His mythic parallels connect New England history with that of the long past preceding it; but both are also carefully connected with his own era. Knowing that time is not only the womb in which evil is conceived and grows, but that it can also be the hiding place of evil, he says: "Let not the reader argue, from any of these evidences of iniquity, that the times of the Puritans were more vicious than our own"; it is only that sin was then exposed "in the broadest light of the noonday sun." Ironic as this may be in view of the "secret sins" evident in the Puritans of, say, *The Scarlet Letter,* **"Young Goodman Brown,"** and **"The Minister's Black Veil,"** Hawthorne was aware that all men, regardless of era, might well see reflected in a Puritan's breastplate the emblazoned banner of their own guilt. (pp. 45-56)

Robert H. Fossum, "The Shadow of the Past: Hawthorne's Historical Tales," in Claremont Quarterly, *Vol. 11, No. 1, Autumn, 1963, pp. 45-56.*

R. P. BLACKMUR (essay date 1963)

[*Blackmur was a leading American literary critic of the twentieth century. His early essays on the poetry of such contemporaries as T. S. Eliot, W. B. Yeats, Wallace Stevens, and Ezra Pound were immediately recognized for their acute and exacting attention to diction, metaphor, and symbol. Consequently, he was linked to the New Critics, who believed that literature was not a manifestation of sociology, psychology, or morality, and could not be evaluated in the terms of any nonliterary discipline. Rather, a literary work constituted an independent object to be closely analyzed for its strictly formal devices and internal meanings. Blackmur distinguished himself from this group of critics, however, by broadening his analyses through discussions which explored a given work's relevance to society. Inspired by the moral thought of American autobiographer Henry Adams, Blackmur conceived the critic's role as that of a crucial intermediary between artist and reader, with the dual purpose of offering literary insight as well as social commentary on the age. His belief that criticism also represented an art form in its own right led him to an increasingly poetic, impressionistic style best demonstrated in his posthumously published lecture series* Anni Mirabiles 1921-25: Reason in the Madness of Letters *(1967). In the following excerpt, Blackmur discusses the cathartic function of Hawthorne's fiction.*]

Perhaps Hawthorne's clearest statement about the mode in which he wrote most of his tales comes at the beginning of **"The Threefold Destiny, A Faëry Legend."** . . .

> I have sometimes produced a singular and not unpleasing effect, so far as my own mind was concerned, by imagining a train of incidents in which the spirit and mechanism of the faëry legend should be combined with the characters and manners of familiar life. In the little tale which follows, a subdued tinge of the wild and wonderful is thrown over a sketch of New England personages and scenery, yet, it is hoped, without entirely obliterating the sober hues of nature. Rather than a story of events claiming to be real, it may be considered as an allegory, such as the writers of the last century would have expressed in the shape of an eastern tale, but to which I have endeavored to give a more lifelike warmth than could be infused into those fanciful productions.

Hawthorne's allegory, then, is meant to touch at least the diaphragm of the quick, to raise at least the qualm of recognition if not the shock. (It was in a letter to Hawthorne that Melville used the phrase "the shock of recognition.") Yet I would suppose most readers coming to Hawthorne at any time after the age when belief is not a problem—say after fifteen—would find him as remote as he found the eastern tale. We do not like the "faëry legend," and the less so if we do like the fairy tales of Kafka and Camus, of Faulkner and Hemingway, or if we have been taught to like the allegory of Melville or Dante. Hawthorne seems thin in comparison to any of these writers—thin in mind, thin in prose, and thin in the conventions by which he foreshortens his vision. This is partly a judgment of Hawthorne, partly a judgment of ourselves; it is also altogether a historical matter. Our histories no longer coincide. Hawthorne does not command us what to bring with us to find his "lifelike warmth," and what we would bring by instinct and experience does not seem to fit. We do not tell quite the same lies in order to find or escape the truth. Yet at one stage we did. Hawthorne's **"Snow Image"** haunts me from the age of six, and **"The Great Stone Face,"** too, and as deeply as the letter A in *The Scarlet Letter* did later on, and I recognize both the image and the face in the last lines of Wallace Stevens' poem "The Snow Man." It seems to me that Hawthorne and Stevens and I are all one—

> the listener, who listens in the snow,
> And, nothing himself, beholds
> Nothing that is not there and the nothing that is.

Coleridge was right enough that some literature requires the "willing suspension of disbelief," but for writers like Hawthorne we must come nearer Keats's negative belief; indeed, we must make the belief positive and immediate so far as Hawthorne will persuade or permit us. The mind, the prose, and the conventions will all richen a little, even if they do not thicken solid, if the preliminary belief is there, reaching for what is meant to be there.

One way to reach is to take the paragraph quoted from **"The Threefold Destiny"** phrase by phrase, as if we were commenting scripture head by head with every head a revelation and a sermon needed on each; but as this procedure would require twenty-five drowsy and exasperated discourses—a full set of lectures in the fall term of any graduate school—we will not do it here. Let us rather think quickly, agitated only by the temptation to go further, of how some of the heads might appear, and assume the elaboration. "A subdued tinge": I will show you how what is hidden is yet innate; for the wild is within us and the wonderful is what makes the bed squeak. The "faëry legend" is the inescapable account when, as always, all others, including the religious, fail; and there is nothing with which we are more intimate than the spirit, nothing to which we are more prone than the mechanism, of the "faëry legend." The "sober hues of nature" are, for the given day, the first and last shades in the looking-glass, shaving or powdering, the toothbrush or the salts, the oncoming nightmare or the lapse of virtue. Thus every "story of events" claims immediate reality but must also be considered as going beyond any mere story; it signified what we did not yet know—what indeed had not yet been created until the event had been put together; which is the allegory—where what we think of signifies further than we expected it possible for thought to go—into either the pusillanimous or the great-spirited. It is in this sense, surely, that what seems to us, as other things seemed to Hawthorne, the "shape of an eastern tale" has a "lifelike warmth." To go back toward the beginning of Hawthorne's paragraph, the "spirit and the mechanism of the faëry legend should be combined with the characters and manners of familiar life." Spirit and character, mechanism and manners. The words so paired run away with one because the substance in them is alive with its own momentum. It is possible they ran away with Hawthorne, too. To read him we must run with him.

We must believe at the level of serious writing what we commonly believe in our own daydreams: in curses, blessings, miracles, in the magical man of science, in alchemy, and above all in the creation of beauty by art and vision. In **"The Birthmark"** we must believe both in the fatal flaw of humanity and in the now perfect woman. In **"Young Goodman Brown"** we must believe that the Devil is in the Forest, but that the forest is within and the devil is ourselves; it is only the Calvinist version of Turgenev's proverb, that the heart of another is a dark forest. We must believe in the frivolity of **"The Celestial Railroad"** because Bunyan once seriously touched us when we found ourselves, if only for a moment, within the movement of *Pilgrim's Progress.* In **"Egotism"** we must believe in the Serpent in the Bosom as well as the devil in the heart. We must know that **"The Vision of the Fountain"** is an adventure of Narcissus, and must feel the Fountain of Youth sink into our own sands in **"Dr. Heidegger's Experiment."** We must hope that **"The Gray Champion"** must fearfully rescue us all, and we know that upon at least one of our expressions we should put **"The Minister's Black Veil"** before we look again in the mirror.

All these matters constantly press into the substance of everyday belief. In Hawthorne they seem to have absorbed belief and left us at the edge of the precipice, ourselves the only obstacle to keep us from falling from ourselves. Is not this what Hawthorne is suggesting at the end of **"Wakefield"**?

> Amid the seeming confusion of our mysterious world, individuals are so nicely adjusted to a system, and systems to one another and to a whole, that, by stepping aside for a moment, a man exposes himself to a fearful risk of losing his place forever. Like Wakefield, he may become, as it were, the Outcast of the Universe.

In Hawthorne people are constantly stepping aside for a moment—but with something in Hawthorne that always steps back. In each of his twice-told tales there is a withdrawal from the possibility. If I may twist the application a little from Hawthorne's intention, in story after story it is like Roderick's words to the sculptor in **"Egotism."**

> Could I for one instant forget myself, the serpent might not abide within me. It is my diseased self-contemplation that has engendered and nourished him.

One thinks at once of Baudelaire and then of Huysmans and of Pascal behind them all. They are all of the same tradition, with Hawthorne being the New England version and like so much in New England twice told and twice removed. Hawthorne did not know that there was a future for his perceptions.

From the same story, but in Hawthorne's own voice, I draw two further passages in illustration of how his fiction looks at life.

> All persons chronically diseased are egotists, whether it be sin, sorrow, or merely the more tolerable calamity of some endless pain, or mischief among the cords of mortal life.

The remainder of the passage says a great deal about Hawthorne's psychology, but the quotation is better arrested on the splendid phrase, "or mischief among the cords of mortal life"; which is what the great masters, and the religious masters, too, have dealt with, and which is where Hawthorne's perceptions seem to lead. The other passage, a thousand words further on, shows where Hawthorne actually drove his perceptions.

> Thus making his own actual serpent—if a serpent there actually was in his bosom—the type of each man's fatal error, or hoarded sin, or unquiet conscience, and striking his sting so unremorsefully into the sorest spot, we may well imagine that Roderick became the pest of the city.

The hoarded sin in Hawthorne is what is substituted for the mischief among the mortal cords of life. It is not very different with Faulkner; both are adepts if not masters of a kind of black and blackened Christianity. This psychology, this way of looking at life, is one which cultivates nightmare to the point where true dream—or virtue—is excluded. It would never have been permitted in the temples of Aesculapius, but it seems a characteristic trait of American imagination and the opposite of American action. In Hawthorne the culmination is perhaps reached in **"Feathertop,"** where the scarecrow sees himself . . . and is nothing. **"Feathertop"** is as humorous as Hawthorne could be; if the reader insists on a "serious" version, he may turn to **"Edward Randolph's Portrait"** which hung obliterated in the state chamber of the Province House until in the imagination of the beholder he wears "the terrors of hell upon his face."

What I have been saying is that the mode of most of Hawthorne's short stories is that of the daydreams which edge toward nightmare—toward our desire to be pursued, cast out, demolished, damned—daydreams undertaken, I should suppose, so that we may escape the reality of such things and protect ourselves from life. Such daydreams are certainly among the great uses of fiction; for in fiction they become fetishes or amulets, little patron images, more often of devils than saints worn to keep the wind away, which nevertheless blows as it wills and in its own severity. We use them, these fictions, like sympathetic magic or homeopathic medicine, to control our experience of what they represent. It is like sticking pins in the wax model of our disaster; and when we put the model away, we put off, having enjoyed it, the disaster. They make a Mardi gras of what we would not do if we could. One or another of these phrases should fit Hawthorne's tales.

Take **"Ethan Brand."** I do not know how it may be now, but when I was a boy the unpardonable sin, the unforgivable sin, or, as I was taught it in church, the sin of blasphemy against the Holy Ghost was a major though intermittent attraction in the short times that seem so long just before sleep. It was a frightening possibility that I might find what it was and how to do it: the frightening thing was that I might then have to do it, as if discovery was actual commission of the sin. The verse in St. Mark (3:19) contained as much potential horror as anything I have ever read or heard said, outside the pitiless words of private life. So when I read **"Ethan Brand"** I knew where he was, his marble heart turned snowy lime, and in reading escaped where I was: I escaped being the fiend, the satanic, all powerful pride of intellect, and the glory of heartless triumph, and escaped all these by enjoying them in little; though as I think of it now I do not think Ethan Brand ever committed the unpardonable sin, unless it be, which Hawthorne does not tell us, that he committed it by finding that it was the impossible sin. When every possibility is taken away, *then* we have sinned. The theology is doubtless unsound, but there is an agony in the perception.

The bite of the word sin and the notion of unpardonable sin has pretty well gone out: we hardly know what is meant when we say—or hear—that sin gave birth to death; but we experience the perception, and are wooed to imitate the action, when we read **"Ethan Brand."** It is like being wooed to paranoia—or to all those other states that would be so wonderful if there were no outside world, and it is the kind of wooing we all enjoy because we can fill in all the details ourselves, as no doubt, so far as he was concerned, Hawthorne did when he wrote the tale. His business in this tale was to provide a frame or an armature for things going totally wrong with great pride and inordinate ambition and ability. Each of us is enough of a paranoiac to see the details.

If the reader is not tempted by **"Ethan Brand"** and unpardonable sin, surely he will succumb to **"Rappaccini's Daughter"** and her fatal beauty—I mean for the thrills and the shivers, and also to explain why in one's own life one never dared make a total commitment. There is nothing in Hawthorne if not pi-jaw—minatory occasional exhortations where you delight in what you professedly repel: the censor who keeps and shows his dirty pictures. The flagrant morals make the flagrant sinner, as morals absorbed make virtue possible. Here we will skip morals, whether flagrant or absorbed, and stay with the thrills and shivers of fatal beauty at work in a poisoned Italian garden. Gardens are where everything happens, which is doubtless why Voltaire said that one must cultivate one's garden, and an Italian garden has the advantage that though mainly walled it is usually accessible from various quarters—one overlooks it, spies upon it, and descends into it. As for the poison, we all know, including the smiling and the wily Italians, that the Italians are master poisoners; Shakespeare, Webster, and all the people who have written about the Borgias have all told us so—arrows, ointment, and rings—so why should we object to poisoned flowers? In our own day we have the residue of fallout in our milk, not to mention other foods; Hawthorne is not out of place in either history or legend in giving us a garden of love where

> There was hardly an individual shrub which a wanderer, straying by himself through a forest, would not have been startled to find growing wild, as if an unearthly face had glared at him out of the thicket. Several also would have shocked a delicate instinct by an appearance of artificialness indicating that there had been such commixture and, as it were, adultery of various vegetable species that the production was no longer of God's making, but the monstrous offspring of man's depraved fancy, glowing with only an evil mockery of beauty.

This is right enough to legend and history, and perhaps Hawthorne is right enough in calling Rappaccini's garden an "Eden of poisonous flowers." It is only the botany that is wrong; all the other excesses—the scar from the touch of the hand, flowers from elsewhere wilting in the grasp—spiders and bees dying from a breath—all these are in the fatality of beauty as we should sometimes—since it hurts us so and will not abide our sentiment—like to see it: the disaccommodation and destroyer of the spirit who made it by perceiving it. *The daydream of fatal beauty is only the natural though fantastic protection against the harshness and destructiveness of love in the actual world. It is of a type,* as Hawthorne looks at it, with the serpent in the bosom and the unpardonable sin: the one prefigures the other. The upshot, as Hawthorne puts it when Rappaccini's daughter falls dying:

> To Beatrice—so radically had her earthly part been wrought upon by Rappaccini's skill—as poison had been life, so the powerful antidote was death.

Some say Hawthorne was a great student of evil; I think rather he studied how to avoid and ignore it by interposing the frames of his tales between evil and the experience of it.

As a final example, there is the tale, very well thought of by many critics, called **"My Kinsman, Major Molineux."** It is a tale wholly without limiting specification, but it provides a frame for any specification you may choose, even the most random, and the signifying power of what you choose will depend on the power or the inanity of your mind. Thus it is open to any interpretation of whose method you—not Hawthorne—are a master. I can imagine someone treating the tale as a late and remote version of the three temptations in the wilderness—but unless you are the Dostoevsky of "The Grand Inquisition" (itself mercilessly exposed both to insane and powerful interpretations) you had better not try it. The general assault of possible evil and the general contagion of woes do not seem to me the result of the pressure of vision—hard or lovely things finally seen—but they are very well adapted to the sentimental use of anyone in need of a parallel for his own adventures not met.

I hope it will not be offensive to quote, for contrast with Hawthorne's allegory, the words Dante gives to Ulysses for his speech to his crew on the threshold of their last adventure beyond man's landmarks.

> "O brothers!" I said, "who through a hundred thousand dangers have reached the west, deny not, to this the brief vigil of your senses that remains, experience of the unpeopled world behind the sun. Consider your origin: ye were not formed to live like brutes, but to follow virtue and knowledge."

In Dante's allegory every adventure is met and what is met signifies further than had been known or intended, in prospect endlessly. Dante commands us what to bring by the authority of what is there. Hawthorne allows us to put in what we will at our own or a lesser level. Dante's allegory gives force to our own words—and thus to our thoughts as they find words—that they never previously had. Hawthorne's allegory lets our words seem good enough as they are, so that at best they only pass for thought. Dante's allegory is constructive, Hawthorne's allegory is reductive. Even the allegory of *The Scarlet Letter* is reductive of the values concerned; it is in the twilit limbo of virtue and knowledge—*virtute e conoscenza*—not in the light and dark of the continuing enterprise.

I find that in these remarks I have repeated a good many times different versions of the judgment of Hawthorne which I now bring to a head when I say that his allegory is reductive, as if allegory could go backward, and is even more likely to do so in him than to go forward. I must also then repeat what I have said less frequently, but as much believe, that Hawthorne's kind of allegory—his whole kind of writing—his whole way of looking at life—is one of the ancestors living within us, not a ghostly or merely haunting ancestor, but an active agent in our perception of things and the way in which we deal with them in the rote and wearing away of getting along. We cannot always be about mastering life; it is altogether sweet to put life off and give it the lie, and it is altogether proper to reduce life to a little less than our own size by the pretense either that we are bigger than life or that we are outcast. Hawthorne is an excellent help to these refuges, the more so if his language and conventions differ from ours. It is like saying, "I love you," in French; it is not so very different and, the first time, much more charming. If, when seen with the other eye and heard with a different voice, Hawthorne seems thin in mind, thin in prose, and thin in the conventions by which he foreshortens his vision, so are we. It is good that he is so remote. (pp. 289-97)

R. P. Blackmur, in an afterword to The Celestial Railroad and Other Stories, *by Nathaniel Hawthorne, New American Library, 1963, pp. 289-97.*

TERENCE MARTIN (essay date 1964)

[*In the following excerpt from a slightly revised draft of an essay that originally appeared in* Hawthorne Centenary Essays, *edited by Roy Harvey Pearce, Martin analyzes Hawthorne's development of narrative techniques that would most effectively convey his personal vision.*]

Hawthorne's primary concern as a writer was to gain access to what he once called "the kingdom of possibilities." Repeatedly, he speaks of his need to attenuate the American insistence on actuality. The burden of the prefaces to his major romances is that he requires a latitude for his imagination, a "neutral ground" set metaphorically between the real world and the imaginary. His romances take form—he would have us believe—in the context of poetic precincts and fairy lands, part of the geography of the "neutral ground." Hawthorne's effort to dilate reality for the purposes of his art ends only with the significant admission in his introductory letter to *Our Old Home* in 1863 that "the Present, the Immediate, the Actual, has proved too potent for me."

What all such statements signify is that Hawthorne needed a fiction to create fiction. And long before he turned his energies to the romance, he had confronted the problem of how to bring his fiction into being in the form of the tale. The method of Hawthorne's tales reveals the achievement of a writer who had to establish the *conditions* of his fiction in the very act of creating that fiction itself. As he himself acknowledged, Hawthorne did not improve steadily as a writer of tales. Some of his best work came surprisingly early: **"My Kinsman, Major Molineux"** was first published in 1831, **"Young Goodman Brown"** and **"The Maypole of Merry Mount,"** in 1835. Slight tales appeared in the same year with major tales. ***Twice-Told Tales*** (1837) was considered superior as a collection to ***Mosses from an Old Manse*** (1846) by Poe, Melville, and most later critics. Yet **"Rappaccini's Daughter"** (1844) and **"Ethan Brand"** (1851) clearly attempt and achieve more than do, say, **"The White Old Maid"** (1835) and **"Mrs. Bullfrog"** (1836). The movement of Hawthorne's tales, indirect and often unsure, is toward *The Scarlet Letter.* But it took twenty years of striving before Hawthorne's triumph in *The Scarlet Letter* exhausted the tale for him as a working form even as it transformed the tale into the romance.

Hawthorne opens **"The Hollow of the Three Hills"** (1830) with an abrupt evocation of a mysterious past: "In those strange old times, when fantastic dreams and madmen's reveries were realized among the actual circumstances of life, two persons met together at an appointed time and place." He begins, that is, by equating the real and the fantastic. If there were such a time, we see immediately, when dreams and reveries existed as a part of actual life, then surely there could be no more congenial setting for his tale. As the condition of his fiction, Hawthorne postulates the existence of "strange old times," then uses the immense latitude he thereby acquires to relate a tale of domestic tragedy from a thoroughly non-domestic point of view.

By means of the crone's powers, with their suggestion of Satanic darkness, the lady of the tale can look back into her life to see the tragic consequences of her actions. She has wrung the hearts of her parents, betrayed her husband, and "sinned against natural affection" by leaving her child to die. Amid a setting redolent of witchcraft and evil, she experiences her visions of society. After each vision, Hawthorne makes a transition back to the hollow, thereby reinforcing the reality principle of the tale. For this is where the lady's sins have led her. She must consort with witchcraft and deviltry if she is to have even a glimpse of society. To measure the distance of her fall, she must make use of powers antithetical to heart and home. Taking advantage of the latitude assumed in (and achieved by) his abrupt opening sentence, Hawthorne has turned the world as we ordinarily know it inside out—we see society only in momentary visions from the standpoint of the marvelous. He has managed the form of his tale so that it embodies in a unique way a theme characteristic of his work.

The opening sentence of **"The Hollow of the Three Hills"** constitutes a Hawthornesque variation of the time-honored opening of the fairy tale. It was a method of getting his fiction immediately under way which Hawthorne would use repeatedly. **"The Great Carbuncle,"** (1836) for example, begins, "At nightfall, once in the olden time. . . ." In **"The Lily's Quest"** (1839), this has become "Two lovers, once upon a time. . . ." And in **"Earth's Holocaust"** (1844), "Once upon a time—but whether in the time past or the time to come is a matter of little or no moment. . . ." By adopting the convention of the fairy tale, Hawthorne achieves at a stroke the imaginative freedom he requires. And most often he shapes the ensuing tale into a fable complete with a moral regarding human wisdom or folly. The lesson of **"Earth's Holocaust"** is that reform will fail if the human heart is not first purified. **"The Great Carbuncle"** points up the wisdom of rejecting a jewel which would dim "all earthly things" in favor of the "cheerful glow" of the hearth. **"The Lily's Quest"** spells out laboriously the idea that happiness is predicated on eternity. Wrought with greater discipline, **"The Hollow of the Three Hills"** does not offer a moral refrain. What it says about human guilt and woe is implicit in the achieved drama of the tale, which stands as the best evidence of what Hawthorne could realize in fiction by adapting the method of the fairy tale to the uses of the imagination. (pp. 11-13)

Characteristically, Hawthorne uses twilight as an analogue of the "neutral ground" to achieve his imaginative effects. "The white sunshine of actual life," he says in **"The Hall of Fantasy"** (1843), is antagonistic to the imagination, which requires access to a region of shadow if it is to function creatively. Young Goodman Brown begins his shattering journey into the forest at sunset. **"The Great Carbuncle"** begins at nightfall. And the settings of **"The White Old Maid," "The Maypole of Merry Mount,"** and many other tales depend heavily on twilight, shadow, and Gothic effects.

Twilight is the middle time, between the noon of actuality and the midnight of dream. It corresponds to the point between yesterday and tomorrow that constitutes the setting of **"The Haunted Mind"** (1834), that profoundly metaphorical sketch in which Hawthorne presents a musing dramatization of the creative process. On the borders of sleep and wakefulness, dream and reality meet and merge. The actual and the imaginary each partake of the nature of the other; the conditions of fiction are displayed in paradigm. But just as it is difficult to remain on the borders of sleep and wakefulness, so the twilight atmosphere can be difficult to sustain. Before the legends themselves are told, the narrator of "Legends of the Province House" (1838-39) draws "strenuously" on his imagination in an effort to invest a contemporary tavern with an aura of the past. While concerns of historical grandeur and plebeian actuality remain with Hawthorne's narrator in the framework, the inner tales move expansively in a twilight of legend. At the end of a tale, the narrator strives to maintain the illusion it has created; but a spoon rattling in a tumbler of whisky punch, a schedule for the Brookline stage, and the *Boston Times*—couriers of "the Present, the Immediate, the Actual"—quickly defeat his efforts. "It is desperately hard work," he concludes, "to throw the spell of hoar antiquity over localities with which the living world, and the day that is passing over us, have aught to do."

In his legends of the province house, and in other tales as well, Hawthorne equates revolutionary tendencies with the democratic aspiration of the people; colonial history comes to prefigure the spirit of the American Revolution. Wearing old Puritan dress, the Gray Champion (1835) answers the cry of an oppressed people. Typically, as a figure evoked onto a historical neutral ground by the imagination, he stands between the colonists and the British soldiers in an "intervening space," with "almost a twilight shadow over it"; when he disappears some think he has melted "slowly into the hues of twilight." But he will be at Lexington in the next century, says Hawthorne, "in the twilight of an April morning." For the Gray Champion "is the type of New England's hereditary spirit," opposed equally to domestic tyranny and to the step of the invader. (pp. 14-15)

During the years immediately following his marriage in 1842, Hawthorne wrote a number of tales distinct in form from his previous work. In these tales—which include **"The Procession of Life," "The Celestial Railroad," "The Christmas Banquet," "A Select Party,"** and **"The Hall of Fantasy"**—he examines subjects such as reform, social organization, human folly, and modern religiosity. **"The Procession of Life"** supplies a term to describe the group as a whole. They are, in one way or another, processionals. They are set perhaps in a vague banquet hall, on an undefined prairie, or in a castle in the air; they deal with assemblages of people who are characterized collectively. In his processionals, Hawthorne assumes such largeness of treatment that he necessarily confronts general human problems in a general way. No personal drama of guilt or suffering could be portrayed effectively by means of such a form, which explores subjects in themselves and achieves latitude by the expedient of perspective. Surely not among his best tales, the professionals do show Hawthorne striving for the kind of effect that only experimentation with the form of the tale would yield. (pp. 15-16)

The role of fiction is the product of the role of the imagination. At their best, Hawthorne's tales—public proof that the author has returned from a private journey into the imagination—lessen the fetters of reality so that we may see "what prisoners we are." At their best, the tales invite us to consider the difficulties man faces because he cannot face his humanity. The tales tell us that man must acknowledge his dependence on (even as he should rejoice to participate in) "the magnetic chain of humanity." The alternative is abstraction, a preference for idea, which breeds pride, isolation, and ultimate self-destruction.

The cancer of obsession threatens any Hawthorne character—scientist, man of religion, artist—who prefers an idea to a human being. Aylmer and Rappaccini; Richard Digby (Hawthorne's "man of adamant"), the Shakers, and the Puritans and Quakers in **"The Gentle Boy"** (1831); the painter in **"The Prophetic Pictures"** (1836)—all seek to exist on the high, desolate plane of idea beyond the slopes of compassion and love. In historical tales, too, Hawthorne's concern for humanity is evident. The terms of his presentation change: tyranny and oppression represent abstraction, the insistence on idea; the will of the people—democracy—represents humanity. The Gray Champion, a people's hero, resists oppression, which Hawthorne defines as "the deformity of any government that does not grow out of the nature of things and the character of the people." For all his irritability and iron nature, Hawthorne's Endicott stands likewise for the people; thus, he can legitimately oppose any force which seeks to abrogate the rights of the colonists as human beings. And in **"Edward Randolph's Portrait"** (1838), Lieutenant Governor Hutchinson risks the terror of a "people's curse" by allowing British soldiers to occupy the fort.

If the oppressor seeks to abuse man in history, the reformer seeks to disabuse man of history; both dehumanize. To make mankind conform to the good as he sees it, the reformer wields his one idea like a flail. He repudiates history as the record of man's imperfection and seeks to destroy human foibles by the purity of his idea. The spirit of reform that spreads wildly in **"Earth's Holocaust"** seeks to burn away the follies and fripperies of the past. But all reformers overlook the nature of the heart (which is to say, the nature of man). Unless the heart is purified, says the dark stranger in the tale, "forth from it will reissue all the shapes of wrong and misery" which the reformers have burned to ashes.

In **"Ethan Brand,"** Hawthorne articulates most explicitly the theme of a man of idea that had run through his fiction for almost twenty years. The definition and focus of the tale are precise; an obsession with one idea has completely vanquished the heart, turning it to marble. **"Ethan Brand"** bears the subtitle "A Chapter from an Abortive Romance," and there are several references in the narrative to episodes that have supposedly taken place at an earlier time. Hawthorne presents us with a conclusion, a final chapter. And incomplete as it may be with reference to his original conception, it has a ring of finality, the authority of a literary work that embodies a theme simply and precisely.

Ethan Brand commits a mighty sin of presumption which prefigures his final despair. The quest to commit a sin so vast that God cannot forgive it becomes itself the Unpardonable Sin. In the hour of his greatest despair, Ethan Brand stands revealed as a success; his quest becomes a parable of how to succeed at spiritual self-destruction. And his triumphant suicide is a final gesture for many a Hawthorne character who has destroyed his humanity over a period of years. The unlettered and earthy, however, are given an anti-climactic dividend in the tale. When Bartram finds the bones of Ethan Brand in the lime kiln, he decides that "it is burnt into what looks like special good lime; and, taking all the bones together, my kiln is half a bushel the richer for him." By half a bushel, the bones of Ethan Brand contribute to Bartram's well-being. By half a bushel, Ethan Brand serves the mundane purposes of a humanity he has scorned.

To repudiate humanity, in Hawthorne's fiction, is to fail spectacularly; to accept humanity is to succeed domestically. Throughout the tales, heart and hearth are intimately related. The bantering praise of the open hearth in **"Fire Worship"** (1843) has its serious counterpart in **"The Vision of the Fountain"** (1836), in which the fireside domesticates the vision. Ralph Cranston in **"The Threefold Destiny"** discovers that home is where one's destiny awaits. Dorothy Pearson, the bringer of love to the gentle boy, is like "a verse of fireside poetry." Both **"The Great Carbuncle"** and **"The Great Stone Face"** (1850) draw morals concerning the futility of searching abroad for values inherent in domesticity. Wakefield (1835) is an apostate from home; whimsy, stubbornness, and a creeping paralysis of will transform him into the "outcast of the Universe." The characters in **"The Ambitious Guest"** (1835), unsettled by the young man's contagious thirst for fame, are killed by a rockslide when they rush out of their house in search of shelter; their home stands untouched. Home, clearly, is of the heart. To be heartless is to be homeless.

The great importance of [his wife] Sophia and a home in Hawthorne's personal life suggests the value he attached to domestic resolution in his tales. Yet it proved difficult to counter a profound vision of evil with a peaceful portrait of the fireside—especially in the tale, by definition a relatively short fictional form which promoted intensity rather than scope. In his romances, Hawthorne would strive more explicitly for a redemptive vision (though his blonde maidens, with their indestructible frailty, might seem to promise captivity rather than redemption). In the tales, however, he could do little more than assert the value of domesticity. His greatest achievement would come from his treatment of those who—for one reason or another—have become homeless.

Such, as the world knows, is the case of young Goodman Brown, who is exposed to the mightiest vision of evil Hawthorne ever imagined. Goodman Brown's journey into the forest is best defined as a kind of general, indeterminate allegory, representing man's irrational drive to leave faith, home, and security temporarily behind, for whatever reason, and take a chance with one (more) errand onto the wilder shores of experience. Our protagonist is an Everyman named Brown, a "young" man who will be aged by knowledge in one night. In the forest he goes through a dreamlike experience marked by a series of abrupt transitions and sudden apparitions. From the devil he learns that virtue is a dream, evil the only reality. And once Goodman Brown sees that idea in all its magnitude, he can never see anything else. He has withdrawn into the dream world of the forest, there to find a reality steeped in guilt that makes his return to the village a pilgrimage into untruth and hypocrisy, into what he now sees as a flimsy community dream. From his vision in the forest, Goodman Brown receives a paralyzing sense of the brotherhood of man under the fatherhood of the devil. The thrust of Hawthorne's narrative is toward a climactic vision of universal evil, which leaves in its aftermath a stern legacy of distrust.

Robin Molineux also leaves home—for a different reason and with a different conclusion, of course, though he, too, encounters the fantastic and confronts a shocking vision.

In **"My Kinsman, Major Molineux,"** as in **"Young Goodman Brown,"** Hawthorne sets the conditions of his fiction so that they serve the purposes of his tale with maximum effectiveness. The strategy of the narrative employs Robin-in-history as a way of making us see history-in-Robin. Thus introjected, history affords the latitude of dream. Robin's mind vibrates between "fancy and reality." A feeling of homelessness accentuates his confusion. Locked out of the house of his memory, he has not yet been admitted to the house of his expectations. Thus, he occupies a middle ground, to which (as he sits in front of the church) "the moon, creating, like the imaginative power, a beautiful strangeness in familiar objects, gave something of romance to a scene that might not have possessed it in the light of day." The procession that passes in front of him has "a visionary air, as if a dream had broken loose from some feverish brain, and were sweeping visibly through the midnight streets." The nightmare has indeed broken loose; Robin can no longer avoid seeing it for what it is. At the center of the wild procession, enshrined in "tar-and-feather dignity," sits the Major. The two look at each other in silence, "and Robin's knees shook, and his hair bristled, with a mixture of pity and terror."

The identity Robin had hoped to establish by claiming kin has been swept away beyond recall. His laugh, cathartic and sanative, signifies that the passage from dream to nightmare to waking reality has been accomplished. Significantly, he does not repudiate the Major; to do so would be to succumb to the nightmare through which he has lived. But perhaps, as his new friend suggests, he may wish to remain in town and try to "rise in the world" without the Major's help. To succeed, Robin must put away the cudgel he has brought with him from the forest, dispense with the anticipated patronage of his kinsman, and establish his own identity in a society restively intent on doing the same.

A sense of homelessness likewise underlies the issues confronted in **"The Maypole of Merry Mount."** "Jollity and gloom were contending for an empire," says Hawthorne in introducing the opposing forces in the tale. Most immediately at stake is the empire of two young hearts, which is, at the moment the Puritans rush forth, in a state of sadness and doubt. For the love of Edith and Edgar has wrought their moral and emotional estrangement from the community. The former Lord and Lady of the May have "no more a home at Merry Mount"; they have become subject to "doom, . . . sorrow, and troubled joy." It is as if their graduation from folly has evoked a stern adult world; the clash of Puritans and Merry Mounters becomes an imperial context for their emotional initiation into life. Again, the conditions of fiction are made functional to the tale: at twilight, from concealment, emerge the Puritans, whose "darksome figures were intermixed with the wild shapes of their foes," making the scene "a picture of the moment, when waking thoughts start up amid the scattered fantasies of a dream." The dream of Merry Mount—the period of youth and play—is over; Edith and Edgar must now confront the waking—and adult—world. And again, as in **"My Kinsman, Major Molineux,"** a double context: Hawthorne has played out a private drama of maturation in the context of tensions inherent in New England history—just as he has played out a drama of New England history in the more intimate yet more expansive context of awakening love.

"Young Goodman Brown," "My Kinsman, Major Molineux," and **"The Maypole of Merry Mount"** demonstrate that Hawthorne's need to establish the conditions of fiction could be made to serve the fiction itself. But if the requirements of Hawthorne's imagination called for a neutral ground as a way of conceiving the tale (which traditionally allowed for a heightened presentation of reality), they called also for a mode of creation that would impregnate his work with relevance for the moral condition of mankind. What Hawthorne had to say about sin, isolation, and the desiccating effects of idea came from his conception of a blemished human nature. To articulate his vision of "what prisoners we are," he frequently made use of an allegorical mode, shaping his materials so that they would suggest the contours of an outer and moral reality.

Although his tales reflect an allegorical tendency, Hawthorne was not a master allegorist. In later years he looked with disfavor on his "blasted allegories" (among which he probably included his processionals), the thinness of which caused Melville to say that Hawthorne needed to frequent the butcher, that he ought to have "roast beef done rare." He made use of conventional devices, giving his characters such names as Gathergold and Dryasdust, conceiving them generically as the Cynic and the Seeker, and envisioning his material so that it would illuminate a general truth of the moral world. Typically, he makes apparent his allegorical intent. He asks specifically, we recall, that **"The Threefold Destiny"** be read as an allegory; he notes that **"Egotism; or, the Bosom Serpent"** and **"The Christmas Banquet"** come "from the unpublished 'Allegories of the Heart' "; and he constructs **"The Celestial Railroad"** on the classic allegorical foundation bequeathed by Bunyan in *Pilgrim's Progress.* An allegorical tradition afforded Hawthorne a means of access to the moral world. Because the moral world was essential to his vision of humanity, he brought features of that tradition to bear on the form of the tale.

Hawthorne's most significant adaptation of an allegorical mode can be seen in his habit of presenting bifurcated or fragmented characters who complement each other in the totality of an individual tale. Such characters require, even as they contribute to, the kind of latitude which Hawthorne constantly strove to attain. More than this: by means of the configuration of such characters, Hawthorne confronts themes that define the specific nature of his work. He suggests in a number of tales, for example (and in a manner distinct from that of his processionals), the uncertain relationship between the man of imagination and the man of practicality. In **"The Artist of the Beautiful"** (1844), the scorn, practical strength, and shallow sensibility of the world (represented respectively by Peter Hovenden, Robert Danforth, and Annie) victimize the artist who must work, if he is to work, out of a determined *mésalliance* to society. As an artist Owen Warland succeeds; he succeeds even more significantly by being able to transcend the destruction of his creation. But he is forced into, even as he willingly adopts, a position of asociality or even anti-sociality if he is to create at all. In **"Peter Goldthwaite's Treasure"** (1837), the man of business saves the man of fancy from utter ruin. At one (ideal?) time, Peter Goldthwaite and John Brown have been in partnership; after the partnership dissolves, Peter goes through years of foolish hopes and financial disasters, finally tearing down his house in a vain effort to find legendary wealth. John Brown, meanwhile, prospers unspectacularly. No doubt John Brown is dull, unexciting, and basically unimaginative; but he rescues Peter Goldthwaite, arrests a career of sterility and self-destruction, and promises to protect the man of deluded imagination from his own fantasies. When John Brown plays the role of Mr. Lindsey in **"The Snow-Image"** (1850), however, he is blind to all but common sense. In caustic language, Hawthorne tells us how Mr. Lindsey completely overrides the high imaginative faith of his wife. Unable to withstand his bleak, unknowing, factual stare, the marvelous melts away before his eyes without his realizing that he has played the role of antagonist in a diminutive tragedy of the imagination. In each of these tales, and in others—such as **"The Birthmark"** (1843)—as well, a configuration of fragmented characters defines the theme and constitutes a wholeness of effect.

Hawthorne found aspects of an allegorical mode useful in articulating his sense of the complexities of the human condition. But the symbolic mode could also involve moral considerations and at the same time offer great flexibility and economy to the writer of tales. Inheriting a penchant for symbolism from the Puritans, disposed, too, toward symbolic expression by the exigencies of the creative situation in his society, Hawthorne came to place dramatic emphasis on the symbol as a way of achieving effective form in the tale. By means of the symbol he could portray the ambivalence of motive and the ambiguity of experience that defined for him the texture of the human condition. Mr. Hooper's black veil, for example, isolates the minister, who sees, simply and profoundly, that all men wear such veils. Feared by his parishioners, shunned by children, Mr. Hooper nonetheless preaches with power and efficacy. The veil is Mr. Hooper's "parable"; it proclaims the truth that all men hide the truth. But Hawthorne's parable suggests the divisive nature of such a truth and the ultimate failure of an eloquence that can illuminate everything but its source.

The symbol for Hawthorne promoted narrative focus and intensity even as it allowed for economy of presentation. Moreover, and with significant formal consequences, it proved possible to organize a tale effectively in terms of one central symbol. One symbol dominates **"The Minister's Black Veil."** The Maypole commands the focus of **"The Maypole of Merry Mount."** And other well-known tales (written between 1836 and 1850) are structured in a similar way, among them **"The Great Carbuncle," "Lady Eleanore's Mantle," "The Birthmark," "The Artist of the Beautiful,"** and **"The Great Stone Face."** Finally, of course, there is *The Scarlet Letter,* the culmination of Hawthorne's efforts to adapt the form of the tale to the special purposes of his imagination. (pp. 17-23)

Terence Martin, "The Method of Hawthorne's Tales," in Nathaniel Hawthorne: A Collection of Criticism, *edited by J. Donald Crowley, McGraw-Hill Book Company, 1975, pp. 11-25.*

NEAL FRANK DOUBLEDAY (essay date 1972)

[*Doubleday was an American critic and the author of* Hawthorne's Early Tales: A Critical Study. *In the following excerpt from that work, he discusses the development of Hawthorne's narrative technique.*]

The tales [Hawthorne wrote between 1825 and 1838 are] of most unequal value. It is no service to literature or to the study of Hawthorne to exalt his weak work with its occasional puerilities. But there is an opposite disservice. What Lionel Trilling calls "the characteristic highly developed literary sensibility of our time," proceeds into some fascinating criticism, but it is likely to cherish Hawthorne's tales only as they furnish a very few pieces of material especially useful for its exercise. Hawthorne's excellence is neither so wide as the number of his tales portentously discussed might seem to indicate, nor so narrow as the multiplication of discussions of a few might suggest. The tales in which Hawthorne's special kind of insight and his craftsmanship fortunately come together deserve our admiration.

Although Hawthorne could write delightful self-mockery, he took himself and his role as fiction writer seriously; and he was able to feel, at least part of the time, that he had escaped triviality and justified his storytelling. In a letter of February 27, 1842 to his fiancée he writes of himself and of his work in a tone in which he of course would not have written in anything intended for publication:

> A cloudy veil stretches over the abyss of my nature. I have, however, no love of secrecy and darkness. I am glad to think that God sees through my heart, and, if any angel has power to penetrate into it, he is welcome to know everything that is there. Yes, and so may any mortal who is capable of full sympathy, and therefore worthy to come into my depths. But he must find his own way there. I can neither guide nor enlighten him. It is this involuntary reserve, I suppose, that has given the objectivity to my writings; and when people think that I am pouring myself out in a tale or an essay, I am merely telling what is common to human nature, not what is peculiar to myself. I sympathize with them, not they with me.

The passage is especially pertinent to our concern, for in it Hawthorne is reflecting on the work of his first period. But the essence of its last two sentences is repeated in prefatory pieces, by implication in the 1851 preface to ***Twice-Told Tales;*** explicitly in **"The Old Manse,"** where he says that he has "appealed to no sentiment or sensibilities save such as are diffused among us all"; and emphatically in the prefatory letter for ***The Snow Image.*** He "has been burrowing," he says there, "to his utmost ability, into the depths of our common nature," proceeding "as well by the tact of sympathy as by the light of observation."

In the prefatory letter for ***The Snow Image,*** Hawthorne's mind turned back to his early work, not only because he used a good deal of it in that collection, but because he addressed Horatio Bridge, who had made the first edition of ***Twice-Told Tales*** possible. In the course of the letter he remarks, "In youth, men are apt to write more wisely than they really know or feel. . . . The truth that was only in the fancy then may have since become a substance in the mind and heart." Whether or not the remark is sound as a generalization, it describes a condition of Hawthorne's work, for neither his insight nor his skill seems to have developed greatly after his late twenties and early thirties. If as a young writer he complains of his lack of experience and knowledge of the world, he hardly seems to feel as he writes in 1851 that it was so great a disadvantage after all.

The ability Hawthorne claims for himself may be known only by its effects; Henry James in "The Art of Fiction" best describes the gifts required. James has been praising an achievement of insight on the part of a woman novelist, and concludes: "The power to guess the unseen from the seen, to trace the implication of things, to judge the whole piece by the pattern, the condition of feeling life in general so completely that you are well on your way to knowing any particular corner of it—this cluster of gifts may also be said to constitute experience, and they occur in country and in town, and in the most differing stages of education." It is only the recognition of such a cluster of gifts that will account for the work Hawthorne did in his young manhood, and we may call the cluster "the tact of sympathy," by Hawthorne's own term.

The term is a complex metaphor for which there may be no satisfactory literal equivalent. "The tact of sympathy" is paired with "the light of observation" and distinguished from it. The light of observation is external and shared by any writer with all other men; Hawthorne had fewer opportunities for the exercise of observation than great fiction writers usually have. In "the tact of sympathy," *tact* seems to combine something of its ordinary English sense, a fitness of response, with the sense of Latin *tactus* from which it comes. The tact of sympathy is the touch of sympathy, intentional, more active than just response. In Hawthorne's best tales, our common nature is represented by persons who, since they are flawed like ourselves, elicit our concern. And at its best, his tact of sympathy seems the imaginative operation of Christian charity, asking of us not only concern but compassion too.

Ultimately, an estimate of Hawthorne's quality as a writer must depend upon whether or not there is realized in his best work a tact of sympathy enabling him to deal with human experience more by that tact—that touch—than by observation. On his own testimony, he is important for his imaginative realization, not certainly of himself, not especially of particular persons, but finally of our common nature.

Not that Hawthorne's tact of sympathy is always embodied in a successful tale. In comparison with Dr. Heidegger's four friends, or with the ruined merchant and the poet in **"The Canterbury Pilgrims,"** the types in **"The Great Carbuncle"** are inept and labored. Sometimes the very means Hawthorne uses to achieve a narrative balance of interest in an allegorical tale seem not perfectly under his control. The portrait painter in **"The Prophetic Pictures,"** for example, is too much a Gothic figure ever to stand for a part of our common nature, or to bring a moral problem home to us. With such a tale, Henry James's contention that Hawthorne's preoccupation with the sense of sin has an "*imported* character," that it seems to exist "merely for an artistic or literary purpose," perhaps could be sustained. But what is said in **"Drowne's Wooden Image"** of the woodcarver—that he was most consistent with himself in his best achievement—is true also of any writer and particularly true of so uneven a writer as Hawthorne. When we find him most consistent with himself, we experience the kind of recognition that Aristotle so long ago found a fundamental value in literature; we say, "That's right," or "Yes, it must be that way."

But in Hawthorne's early career he would have known of few persons who had experienced that recognition, few who had found their way into his depths. Even in 1851, a year in which he could feel himself a successful writer—then more than ever before and probably after—he remarked in a letter to Bridge: "The only sensible ends of literature are, first, the pleasurable toil of writing; second, the gratification of one's family and friends; and, lastly, the solid cash." In the long years before the publication of the ***Twice-Told Tales,*** there had been very little solid cash, and few friends to gratify; Hawthorne had to find his reward in the pleasurable toil of writing.

The reward was the pleasurable toil, not, apparently, the glow of success, the feeling that this time a tale was right, or even as excellent as Hawthorne could hope to make it. For he was troubled by his persistent awareness of the discrepancy between intention and fulfillment. Now we cannot, as it seems to me, dismiss this feeling in him as just a conventional Romantic attitude. It was too important to him, too often connected with a real sense of failure for that. Nor can we dismiss it as a pose Hawthorne liked to take in his prefatory pieces. The feeling does appear in them in graceful disparagement, but it also appears in what he said privately, and it is projected in his work.

Perhaps Hawthorne's own ideal of his work was never fulfilled: in the prefatory letter to *Our Old Home* he wrote of "a certain ideal shelf, where are reposited many . . . shadowy volumes of mine, more in number, and very much superior in quality, to those which I have succeeded in rendering actual." If we do not quite know what his own conception of a successful tale was, we know it to have been exacting. We find him expressing a feeling of failure not only about tales that seem to us failures, but also about tales the world has taken as successes. When he said of **"The Man of Adamant"** that he had failed to give shape and substance to what had seemed a fine conception, we think we know what he meant, for we recognize in the tale an important conviction and an inadequate embodiment. When in 1850 he reread **"Peter Goldthwaite's Treasure"** and **"The Shaker Bridal,"** he found them "painfully cold and dull." **"Peter Goldthwaite's Treasure,"** a satire of the financial speculator (written during the depression of 1837), has at least an interesting allegorical scheme, but we had not supposed it intended to have any warmth; the compassionate **"Shaker Bridal"** seems so different a tale as not at all to deserve the same adjectives. When he wrote a preface for **"The Gentle Boy,"** he remarked that he had some sense of "imperfect and ill-wrought conception" in the tale—but we hardly know the intent of the stricture. In a letter to Longfellow, he disparaged the pieces in **Twice-Told Tales** his readers have most liked, and preferred those they have cared for least. The most earnest tales in ***Mosses from an Old Manse*** do not, he said, express "satisfactorily the thoughts which they profess to image." **"Roger Malvin's Burial"** and **"Young Goodman Brown"** are earnest tales, and Hawthorne tried again in *The Scarlet Letter* to image some of the thoughts in them.

Yet we hardly know what Hawthorne himself thought even relatively successful. We cannot say, on his own testimony, that any tale nearly achieves his own conception. We cannot say what tales seemed to him less imperfect and ill-wrought than **"The Gentle Boy."** What he says of the two great romances merely complicates the problem of understanding his judgment of himself. He complained in a letter to Bridge that *The Scarlet Letter* lacked "sunshine," and that it seemed to him an inadequate representation of his own nature as a writer; *The House of the Seven Gables,* he told Bridge, was a work more characteristic of his mind, "more proper and natural" for him to write. Now since *The Scarlet Letter* takes up into itself so much of his work in his early tales, the implication of the judgment is that they, too, were not quite characteristic of his mind as he would have it be. In trying to understand Hawthorne's own estimate of his work, we must proceed largely by inference, and, as we have seen, inference from the clearest evidence we have—his own choices in collecting his tales—indicates that his judgment was often at variance with that of his readers, and especially with that of his readers today.

But it is clear that when Hawthorne was dissatisfied with one or another tale, it was because he felt a discrepancy between conception and execution: the tales that disappointed him were "ill-wrought." We may see the tales somewhat differently from the way in which he did; but our judgment of any particular tale, like his, is a judgment largely of his management of his complex technical means. When he so manages them that we recognize a quality of experience we hardly know in any other fiction writer's work, his success is so far technical, a success of craftsmanship. Yet in Hawthorne, perhaps more than in most fiction writers, one technical matter so depends upon another that a consideration of structure leads into a consideration of style, and the discussion of style may involve an attempt to define the narrative assumptions of a tale. What can be said about Hawthorne's technique in the tales must be inference from the tales themselves. And since we do not know much certainly about the order of composition of the tales, we cannot trace stages of Hawthorne's early development—if, indeed, there were any such stages.

There is, however, a clear place to start. It is with the four tales in *The Token* for 1832—**"The Gentle Boy," "My Kinsman, Major Molineux," "Roger Malvin's Burial,"** and **"The Wives of the Dead"**—for we know that the first two and probably all four were complete by December of 1829. Now in these four tales we have examples of the three narrative structures Hawthorne uses best. **"The Gentle Boy"** and **"Roger Malvin's Burial"** have a sort of time span common in the short fiction of the day, a sort we find, for instance, in the work of Miss Sedgwick. **"My Kinsman, Major Molineux"** has a time span of but a single night, yet draws into it a wealth of experience and implication, and in allegorical condensation represents a development in its central figure. **"The Wives of the Dead"** is an early example of the highly concentrated tale that Hawthorne so often writes successfully.

When Hawthorne uses a time span that extends over months or years, he apparently chooses carefully what he will represent directly and in detail and what he will handle in summary narrative, always with the intent to give a sense of the whole elapsing time. He succeeds in that intent with the more-than-two-year time span of **"The Gentle Boy."** The eighteen-year time span of **"Roger Malvin's Burial"** offers more difficulty; at least the reader is quite aware of a contrast between represented action and rapid summary narration. Likewise, in the later **"Prophetic Pictures"** the reader is aware, even as he reads the tale, that the account of the painter's travels in the wilderness is a calculated device to fill the interval between the painting of the portraits and the denouement—although it is also used for analysis of the painter.

But in these tales the handling of the time pattern is not greatly different from that of competent storytellers before and after Hawthorne. His triumph in handling a long time span, as we have seen, is in the skillful use of the narrator in **"The Minister's Black Veil"**—a narrator whose transitions from one sort of narrative to another are so well handled that in reading the tale we are not aware of their careful calculation. Hawthorne succeeds in a way of his own, too, with the shorter time span of **"Old Esther Dudley,"** in which the narrative depends, not on direct representation, but on an account of what is generally known and imagined of old Esther's life alone in the Province House.

The way of storytelling in **"My Kinsman, Major Molineux"** and later in **"Young Goodman Brown"** seems to be Hawthorne's invention; surely no fiction writer before him had condensed so much experience into such short spans of represented time, and written tales so enthralling on their surface and so arresting in their implications. **"My Kinsman"** must have been written at about the same time as **"The Gentle Boy"**; both are skillful, although as we have noticed, **"My Kinsman"** may be too complex an attempt and not completely in Hawthorne's control. Nevertheless, its technique has interested students of Hawthorne more than the technique of **"The Gentle Boy,"** for in **"My Kinsman"** Hawthorne is beginning what distinguishes the best of his tales—the seizing on a representative short period which implies the previous experience of the major figure or figures, and predicts the future or, as in **"My Kinsman,"** teases us into speculation about it. In such tales Hawthorne escapes the limitations of plot, and makes the tale a way of representing not just an episode but the very quality of a life or a relationship.

"The Wives of the Dead," which has a time span from dusk to, apparently, some time in the small hours, sets the pattern for more concentrated and less complex tales than **"My Kinsman"** and **"Young Goodman Brown,"** but tales that, like them, look before and after. For this structure, an initial influence on Hawthorne was certainly the single, highly wrought incident of Scott's novels, and the connection is apparent in some of the early historical tales. But the structure that represents only a moment in the lives of the figures in the tale is used variously. In **"Dr. Heidegger's Experiment"** the action of an afternoon conveys the whole quality of four wasted lives and the inevitable bleakness of their remaining years. Within the time it takes the little company that meet at the Shaker spring in **"The Canterbury Pilgrims"** to tell their stories, we know the essence of four lives, and move forward into a somber hope for the young lovers. Very short periods are represented in **"The Ambitious Guest"** and in **"The Shaker Bridal"**; but in each we comprehend lifetimes.

Just how Hawthorne worked out this distinctive structure we cannot say. The influence of Scott partially accounts for it; a letter of Hawthorne's to Goodrich suggests that Goodrich had asked for short pieces. Yet the technique is surely inherent in Hawthorne. It is not just the result of what F. L. Pattee calls Hawthorne's "keen eye for situation" [see excerpt dated 1923]; it is a manifestation of his bent toward allegory, his interest in the situation meaningful beyond itself, and for what it holds of past and future. But Hawthorne's achievement in these sharply focused tales may be underestimated just because it is gained so briefly.

Henry James, who here as often manages at once to praise and to patronize Hawthorne, writes: " **'The Grey Champion'** is a sketch of less than eight pages, but the little figures stand up in the tale as stoutly, at the least, as if they were propped up on half-a-dozen chapters by a dryer annalist, and the whole thing has the merit of those cabinet pictures in which the artist has been able to make his persons look the size of life." The sentence seems to recognize the economy as an achievement, but to accord it only a kind of success in miniature. Yet the figure of the Gray Champion looms in our imaginations; and, indeed, in our final estimate of Hawthorne there may be a question of where *his* success is greatest—whether it is in those tales in which he works within narrow, self-imposed limitations, or in the romances where he resorts to half-a-dozen chapters of analysis.

What we need to see—and what James may not have seen—is that the economy of a tale like **"The Gray Champion"** depends upon its focus on a single event, and that within the limits of the tale, the treatment is a full one. Hawthorne's style in the tales of the period of our concern is a leisurely style, adapted to their structures. Since he is using a restricted subject matter and time span or, as in **"The Gentle Boy,"** representing only a small part of the time span of the action, he can gain his effects deliberately, lingering on the nuances of experience, taking the time to write a prose far better finished than any we can find in the American writers of his day except Irving's at its very best.

Now there are objections to Hawthorne's style, but almost all of them arise when a passage conflicts with our own twentieth-century taste—and we might remember that Hawthorne wrote in a time when the praise for a writer of imaginative prose was commonly that he was "a true poet." Yet there is much that our taste can admire in Hawthorne's prose. Although his sentence pattern may not have the interest in and for itself that we find in, say, "Rip Van Winkle," there are single sentences of remarkable economy and accomplishment, sentences that convey at the same time accounts of actions and their moral or spiritual concomitants. Such a sentence comes as Goodman Brown makes his way into the dark wood: "He had taken a dreary road, darkened by all the gloomiest trees of the forest, which barely stood aside to let the narrow path creep through, and closed immediately behind." Or, to take but one more example, there is this sentence from **"My Kinsman":** "So saying, the fair and hospitable dame took our hero by the hand; and the touch was light, and the force was gentleness, and though Robin read in her eyes what he did not hear in her words, yet the slender-waisted woman in the scarlet petticoat proved stronger than the athletic country youth." But, although we can find many such separable sentences, it is not in them that Hawthorne's greatest skill is to be found.

For Hawthorne's special stylistic excellence is in the careful calculation of his whole pattern, the adaptation of style to the structure and to the narrative assumptions of particular tales. A cadenced sentence from **"The Minister's Black Veil"** may serve us: "In this manner Mr. Hooper spent a long life, irreproachable in outward act, yet shrouded in dismal suspicions; kind and loving, though unloved, and dimly feared; a man apart from men, shunned in their health and joy, but ever summoned to their aid in mortal anguish." The sentence is a major transition in the narrative, yet it enforces by its series of antitheses the parodox the tale discovers. But it can serve us only as an instance. Any illustration of the effect of Hawthorne's prose is necessarily inadequate, for one can quote only a part of the pattern; and for that matter Hawthorne's patterns are so much determined by the direction of the narrative that it would be misleading to say that one pattern or another is typical.

William Charvat remarks of Hawthorne's romances that their style is "essentially parenthetical and . . . this characteristic reflects the basically essayistic, generalizing, and speculative quality of his fiction." The parenthetical habit grew on Hawthorne; the style of the tales of the period of our concern, although it is deliberate, is far less parenthetical than that of the romances, and immediately adapted to the differing structures and narrators of the individual tales. The style of **"The Minister's Black Veil,"** for instance, is distinct from the style of **"Dr. Heidegger's Experiment,"** both as the greatly different time spans of the actions require differences in the kind of narration and as the narrators differ in temper. Even in **"The Gentle Boy,"** where there seems no narrator distinct from Hawthorne, we are sometimes stayed on a single, dramatic scene—Catharine ascending the pulpit and preparing to address the congregation, for instance—and sometimes carried along with rapid summary narration.

Hawthorne's flexible narrative assumptions, although we may easily be aware of their importance, offer certain difficulties in definition. We cannot say how he defined them to himself. He had read no discussion of "the disappearing author"; he could not have guessed what William Dean Howells and Henry James were to say on the authorial relationship to the story. He does not mind confessing that his story is a story; in **"The Ambitious Guest,"** for instance, after an immediate account of the guest's reception at the inn, a paragraph begins "Let us now suppose. . . ." Yet narrative points of view in Hawthorne's tales may be intricate. Indeed they are intricate enough so that the terms commonly used to distinguish narrative points of view seem never quite suitable to our discussion.

Hawthorne's practice suggests that he did a good deal of thinking about the techniques of his narratives. In most of the tales written before 1839, he did not use an "I" narrator; he may have generally avoided one in order to keep the tales distinct from his essay-like sketches, which are often written in the first person. And it is likely that he wished to keep himself distinct from the tales, and that he understood that the use of an "I" narrator leads readers into confusion about the separation of a writer from his work. Such confusion is entirely apparent in naive readers, who may, for instance, identify the "I" in a Poe tale with Poe himself. But the same confusion may exist in more sophisticated readers without becoming so apparent; it sometimes makes trouble in discussions of *The Blithedale Romance.*

The authorial "we," when it occurs in historical tales, may indicate a narrative assumption special with them in which the action is related with immediacy and interpreted in historical perspective. Endicott, in **"The Maypole of Merry Mount,"** is described even to his changing facial expression, yet he is interpreted as he is historically representative, "the Puritan of Puritans." But of course narrative point of view in these tales does not depend upon a pronoun. In **"The Gray Champion,"** in which there is no authorial intrusion into the narrative itself, there are yet the same assumptions about the storyteller's power to relate the action with immediacy and to interpret it historically; he knows both what an unidentified voice in the crowd calls out and what the scene symbolizes in New England history.

But narrative point of view, even in a historical tale, may not be only a matter of relationship of author to story. In the frame of **"Howe's Masquerade"** we are told that the tale is Hawthorne's redaction of Mr. Bella Tiffany's story. Yet in portions of the tale, the action is represented as it is perceived by some—not all—of the persons in the tale. For example, the last figure in the procession of figures representing the governors of Massachusetts the reader realizes through the apprehensions of "some of the spectators," and the pattern of the paragraph is the pattern of their growing perceptions.

In some tales the realization of an identity for the narrator has considerable critical importance. The reader will have noticed that sometimes in the foregoing discussions of individual tales a narrator distinct from Hawthorne is referred to, and sometimes not—and the reader may not always have agreed with the distinction, for the matter is difficult. But we are surely aware of a narrator in **"The Minister's Black Veil,"** aware even of something of his nature; the limitations on his knowledge are of the same kind that belong to our own knowledge of friends and acquaintances in ordinary life. And it would be difficult to account for the effect of **"Young Goodman Brown,"** or of **"My Kinsman, Major Molineux,"** without assuming a narrator, although in neither tale does the nature of the narrator fully emerge. In **"My Kinsman,"** moreover, the narrator speaks sometimes in a historical perspective (he comments, for instance, on our ancestors' liking for the "Good Creature" rum). Yet the narrator in **"My Kinsman"** does not interpret figures or incidents that bewilder Robin; the narrator in **"Young Goodman Brown,"** although he is cognizant of Goodman Brown's innermost life, will only speculate on the relationships of some of his perceptions to external reality. The ambiguity in these tales turns upon the limitations of the narrators' knowledge or of their candor, or perhaps of both; and it is these limitations that invite us as readers into speculation and a kind of collaboration.

Another difficulty in the definition of point of view is the frequent assumption in the tales of some "chimney corner" tradition or body of legendary material. The tales are not narrated as tradition, to be sure; tradition does not preserve dialogue nor the subtleties of human interactions. The purported recalling of a tradition—as in **"The Great Carbuncle,"** for instance—often provides a preternatural suggestion that the narrator (or Hawthorne) does not make himself responsible for. Even in **"The Maypole of Merry Mount,"** after an immediate account of Endicott cutting down the maypole, it is remarked that "as it sank, tradition says, the evening sky grew darker, and the woods threw forth a more sombre shadow." But this assumption is not essentially different from the narrative assumption for *The Scarlet Letter* as Hawthorne defines it in "The Custom House": there, it will be remembered, he purports to be working from Mr. Surveyor Pue's account and at the same time insists upon the full privileges of the omniscient convention. This likeness in narrative assumption is another evidence of the close connection between the tales and the romance.

But we cannot make rules about the way Hawthorne uses his devices. The account of Dr. Heidegger's study and of the marvelous occurrences therein is prefaced with "If all the stories were true." But in the same tale is ascribed to general report, not a preternatural explanation, but a suggestion that the happenings of the summer afternoon were illusions: "Yet, by a strange deception, owing to the duskiness of the chamber, and the antique dresses which they still wore, the tall mirror is said to have reflected the figures of three old, gray, withered grandsires, ridiculously contending for the skinny ugliness of a shrivelled grandam." The narrator has proceeded as if he had seen the doctor's four friends as young as they felt themselves to be. But he does know what the mirror is said to have reflected; and the mirror we took to be a magic mirror seems in this instance incapable of illusion. Hawthorne's device of unvouched-for suggestion clearly stems from Scott and William Austin, but his refinements on it are complex.

What emerges when we try to analyze the narrative devices with which Hawthorne works is a kind of legerdemain, adroit, yet for the most part not beyond detection, and perhaps not really so greatly involved as some writers on Hawthorne have lately been insisting. But the legerdemain is realized in analysis; it does not intrude itself in ordinary reading. In the best tales the illusion is maintained, and the only requirement we need make of any narrative device or assumption is imaginative success. We are hardly aware of even the repeatedly used devices except in the artificiality of critical analysis; and the reason must be that the even tone and the pattern of the style—its care and calculation—induce an acceptance.

But Hawthorne's narrative procedures only partly account for a peculiar quality of his work. Nor does this quality inhere solely in such passages as those commonly used as examples of his ambiguity, although they may serve to point it up. In the last chapter of *The Marble Faun* Hawthorne remarks, "The actual experience of even the most ordinary life is full of events that never explain themselves, either as regards their origin or their tendency." The sentence may have a special application to the romance, but it recognizes a quality which is in much of Hawthorne's fiction, and which (as it seems to me) is more impressively present in the early tales than in later work. That quality is the realization, not so much of the complexity, as of the opaqueness of experience, a quality we know in our own. There is likely, therefore, to be a residue of mystery in Hawthorne's best tales which good criticism will always leave intact.

Just as in particular tales we must accept a residue of mystery as part of Hawthorne's realization of experience, so we must accept the difficulties in understanding his intention and his estimate of his work. Of course Hawthorne is not the only writer whose estimate of some of his work is out of accord with that of even his devoted readers. Nor is he the only writer to feel the discrepancy between the work he envisaged and the work he produced. But his feeling that his work never quite represented his own nature as he realized it does seem to be special and part of his mystery. It is not only that he believed he had failed in one or another tale. He had some ideal, some measure of excellence for himself that his work in its entirety never fulfilled. The excellence he sought is not at all the excellence with which his critics invest him.

In "The Custom House" Hawthorne imagines a shadowy forefather who scorns him as a writer of "story-books." From his youth Hawthorne was determined to be a storyteller. But he was never willing to be merely a storyteller, never willing to merit that ancestral scorn.

To be a professional writer of fiction in America in the 1830s was to face great difficulties in finding and understanding a market, and greater in discovering a usable tradition. Regarded in itself, what served Hawthorne as a tradition seems makeshift, but clearly his work is strongest when it most depends upon the tradition he devised from what he had at hand. He found a way to be a storyteller in his time and place, and yet to move his fiction into territories no fiction writer had occupied before him.

Hawthorne's necessity to be more than just a storyteller may account for the puerility of some tales in which he seeks and does not find a moral purpose. But the same necessity accounts for those tales in which we recognize our common nature and the opaqueness of our own experience. The residue of mystery in his work is the sign of his humility as an artist; his complex technical means have purposes beyond themselves. He required his storytelling to do more than any fiction writer before him had required, sometimes, it may be, more than fiction can do. (pp. 238-52)

Neal Frank Doubleday, in his Hawthorne's Early Tales: A Critical Study, *Duke University Press, 1972, 262 p.*

JAMES G. JANSSEN (essay date 1976)

[*In the following excerpt, Janssen examines the ways in which Hawthorne utilized fictional techniques to achieve his didactic aims.*]

In one of Hawthorne's minor sketches, the narrator tells the child he is about to take on a sight-seeing walk through the streets, "but if I moralize as we go, do not listen to me. . . ." Unlike little Annie, readers of Hawthorne's short stories and sketches have not found this very appropriate advice, for if there is one demonstrable thing about Hawthorne it is that he does indeed mean meanings, and that his works are presentations of moral confrontations of one sort or another. In speaking of his "blasted allegories," he seems surely to have been describing a haunted moral consciousness more than he was apologizing for inclusion of that acute moral awareness in his work. His lamenting of an allegorical imagination and the wish that he could have written books with more sunshine in them should be taken with no more seriousness than one does his ambiguous remarks about a Puritan background, claimed as it is rejected.

In reading the short works, one discovers at least three different categories based on the way in which the meaning or moral is expressed specifically with regard to its directness and accuracy, either by Hawthorne or some character or narrator invented for that particular purpose.

In a great many of his short stories—and these among the best—Hawthorne, like the narrator of **"The Antique Ring,"** is happily unable to "separate the idea from the symbol in which it manifests itself." There is no authorial voice present to announce a moral at the beginning or the conclusion of great works like **"My Kinsman, Major Molineux," "Roger Malvin's Burial," "Rappaccini's Daughter,"** and **"Young Goodman Brown,"** to name only a few which fall into this first category. Their enduring quality is in part their presentation of complex moral and psychological dilemmas without the detraction of instant explication within the text.

Another group of short works involves a characteristic if less fortunate approach in that the meaning or significance is explicitly stated at the beginning or the end (or both) and seems to be the "right" reading, the one most of us would have arrived at without such pushing. Examples here would include **"The Threefold Destiny," "John Inglefield's Thanksgiving," "Sunday at Home," "The Old Apple Dealer,"** and **"Egotism; or, the Bosom Serpent."** The obviousness of Hawthorne's assertions of moral significance in these works ranges from the observation made in **"The Birthmark"** that the marriage of a perfection-seeking scientist to a flawed wife "was attended with truly remarkable consequences and a deeply impressive moral," to the directive addressed to the reader of **"Earth's Holocaust"** that "the illumination of the bonfire [indiscriminately destroying civilization] might reveal some profundity of moral truth heretofore hidden in mist or darkness."

But although involving fewer works, it is a third category that is especially interesting for what it says about Hawthorne's attitude toward moralizing in fiction. Within this group are works in which the moral is expressed with ironic playfulness, sometimes offered as an afterthought or a hastily discharged duty, other times stated in what are at best puzzling, inadequate, and even misleading terms.

One of the most remarkable statements in this connection appears at the beginning of **"Wakefield,"** a story of a husband who whimsically absents himself from his wife for twenty years. After announcing his source ("some old magazine or newspaper"), Hawthorne suggests that such a mind provoking subject repays the study he intends to give it. "If the reader choose, let him to his own meditation; or if he prefers to ramble with me through the twenty years of Wakefield's vagary, I bid him welcome; trusting that there will be a pervading spirit and a moral, *even should we fail to find them,* done up neatly, and condensed into the final sentence" (emphasis mine).

Hawthorne's cavalier attitude toward the moral is provocative. What good is the moral if we fail to find it, and how does it get there if its author is indifferent to it? True, his comment that "thought has always its efficacy and every striking incident its moral" would seem to imply, in its Emersonian point of view, that all things have meaning beyond themselves, regardless of our artistic design and perception. But a better explanation of his initial toying with the idea of a moral is that it is a surfacing of Hawthorne's never long submerged playful spirit—a spirit that causes him to undercut what he recognized as a generally allegorical turn in his work. By treating the matter with some degree of lightness at the beginning, he disarms the critic who expects only another typically nineteenth century dramatization of bare truth—in this case, the notion that isolation is destructive. What is gained is the absence of condescension: a reader cannot feel lectured to if his guide announces with such tenuity the possibility of a moral at the beginning.

In a somewhat similar fashion the narrator of **"Night Sketches,"** after several pages in which he catalogs scenes from a rainy night, arrives at "a moral, wherewith, *for lack of a more appropriate one,*" he can conclude his sketch, it being that "we, night wanderers through a stormy and dismal world, if we bear the lamp of Faith, enkindled at a celestial fire, it will surely lead us home to that heaven whence its radiance was borrowed" (emphasis mine.) In addition to the casual admittance of its questionable appropriateness (there has been nothing up to that point to make us think heavenly thoughts), even the inflated rhetoric of the moral seems at first glance out of place in a sketch featuring one of Hawthorne's typical artist-narrators, attempting with some degree of wry and sober observation to attune himself to the sights and sounds of nighttime humanity. Upon closer observation, however, the casual and inaccurately expressed moral is seen to be appropriate for this Oberon-type onlooker in life who, caught up in the web of his poetic phrasings and rhetoric, cannot resist the impulse to moralize his way out of the sketch, albeit irrelevantly. It appears, then, that Hawthorne's ironic employment of an enthusiastic though "wrong" moral is consistent with the overall tone of the sketch more than it is indicative of a distaste for moralizing.

Sometimes indeed Hawthorne does seem to treat the moral as a fictional requirement into which he can put little enthusiasm. He exemplifies this in **"The Antique Ring"** where Edward Caryl, a would-be author, has just finished reciting a tale he has composed to accompany the engagement ring he gives to Clara Pemberton. The story he writes is one of misplaced confidence and treacherous intrigue, involving the long history of the ring from the time it is given to Essex by Elizabeth, to its appearance in a collection box in a New England church centuries later. Asked by Clara for a satisfying moral, Edward first replies—as noted earlier—that he is unable to separate symbol from idea, but then as though to acquit himself of an authorial obligation (as well as to please his lover), he quickly makes up a patently obvious set of allegorical equivalents ("the Gem to be the human heart, and the Evil Spirit to be Falsehood . . ." etc.) and concludes without much heart, "I beseech you to let this suffice." It does; for Clara, typical of a large segment of Hawthorne's reading public, requires nothing profounder than the generalities of nineteenth century impressionistic criticism with which Edward's audience had greeted his story in the first place: " 'Very pretty!—Beautiful!—How original!—How sweetly written!—What nature!—What imagination!—What power!—What pathos!—What exquisite humor!' " The entire story has become a parable of the role of the writer, Hawthorne, pressured by an audience he wishes to please and for whom he must draw out the moral design in a way which is occasionally awkward for him, as for example in his **"Procession of Life,"** where a piously hopeful moral is loosely attached to a work cataloging some of life's crueller ironies.

In suggesting that Hawthorne's wry sense of humor is sometimes responsible for his ironic employment of the moral—either in treating the matter lightly or inaccurately or in passing off its message as mere duty—it would be very easy to assert too much. Surely if one looks over the canon of Hawthorne's short works, numbering well over one hundred, it becomes difficult to take seriously his various comments, for example in the preface to *The House of the Seven Gables,* that he does not wish, like some, "to impale the story with its moral as with an iron rod." While there seems little doubt that he was aware, as he states in that preface, that works instruct best "through a far more subtile process than the ostensible one," knowing the ease with which he acknowledges the potential misuse of the convention at the same time that he typically risks it, few readers will be able to agree with those who hold that Hawthorne normally found onerous the inclusion of a moral in his work. As Professor Turner has observed [in his *Nathaniel Hawthorne: An Introduction and Interpretation* (1963)], "it came natural for Hawthorne to search out moral implications, and in the main he offered in good faith the moral statement he supposed his readers would welcome." As has been observed in the preceding paragraphs, several examples of a statement not offered in such "good faith" are traceable to an enthusiasm for the ironic mode, coupled with a willingness to adopt a sportive attitude, especially with regard to self-conscious narrative voices who apologize for what they continue to do. But in several cases there is a less clear-cut reason for the misstated moral.

Although the concern in this study is with the short works, the point might be raised more effectively by thinking for a moment of *The Scarlet Letter.* Near the conclusion of that work we are told that "among many morals" possible, the one we are to take with us is " 'Be true! Be true! Be true! Show freely to the world, if not your worst, yet some trait whereby the worst may be inferred!' " Even though this moral is singled out for Dimmesdale, a sensitive reading of the novel would leave few satisfied that such an aphoristic sentiment does justice to a complex symbolic work and a character within it whose psychological turmoil can hardly be reduced to something as simplistic as "tell the truth about yourself and all will be well."

Typical of those shorter works in which the moral supplied seems equally misdirected is **"Fancy's Show Box,"** a tale which seems fairly obvious upon casual reading. Its slender narrative involves one Mr. Smith, visited by personifications of Fancy, Memory and Guilt, each contributing to vivify for him some recollection of past intentions or incomplete acts of questionable morality (e.g., a sinful thought about a young girl; a lawsuit proposed but dropped; a bottle thrown at, but missing, the head of a young friend). In each case a picture of the thought or deed is presented as accomplished fact.

The idea seems clear enough, its obviousness causing us in fact to recall Hawthorne's self-accusation in the preface to the 1851 edition of ***Twice-Told Tales*** that "in what purport to be pictures of actual life, we have [only] allegory." But near the conclusion of the piece, we are suddenly presented with a lengthy defense of Mr. Smith, compellingly argued in terms of artistic creation. The schemes of a man who does not manage to do what he feels tempted to do are like the schemes of an artist's unexecuted plots, so that Mr. Smith is no more guilty of these mental crimes than a man is an artist before he gives actuality to what are only seed ideas for a work. Furthermore, most men "over-estimate their capacity for evil," and anyway, there are few times when man's deeds can truly be said to be of "settled and firm resolve, either for good or evil." But just when he seems to be exonerating Mr. Smith by means of a formal cause/efficient cause distinction, a shorter, final paragraph announces that the "said and awful truth" demonstrated in all of this is that "man must not disclaim his brotherhood, even with the guiltiest, since, though his hand be clean, his heart has surely been polluted by the flitting phantoms of iniquity."

Lest it be thought that it is only in the obscure works that the oblique moral is found, one of the best examples, the last to be treated here, is also one of Hawthorne's most highly regarded stories, **"The Prophetic Pictures,"** a work whose plot must be recalled in some detail so as to appreciate the outrageously simplistic moral which Hawthorne draws from it.

A young couple about to be married engages a renowned artist to do their portraits. When they come to approve the finished canvases, they are surprised to find the expressions there: Elinor's is one of grief and terror, Walter's one of unnatural vividness. As he prepared the portraits, the painter also made a sketch which he shows only to Elinor. Years later he visits the couple in order to see his prized work, arriving in time to see enacted what he had foreshadowed on each face and drawn specifically in his sketch: Walter in the act of drawing a knife against his wife. When the artist separates them and reminds Elinor that he tried to warn her of this in the sketch, she replies only that she loved Walter. Hawthorne draws from this the moral that even if we were able to foresee our futures, most of us would go about the business of life undeterred by prophetic pictures.

Such a plot summary is deceiving, for it implies that the story is primarily about Walter and Elinor and the relative importance of knowledge and fate in determining future events. But surely most readers would catalog **"The Prophetic Pictures"** with those works concerned with the problem of the artist, and would see within the creator of the pictures most of the forces surrounding Hawthorne's artists generally: divinely creative genius on the one hand, and arrogant manipulation of individuals on the other; perceptivity and insight, along with a suggestion of "dark" knowledge that goes beyond what finite man should attempt; responsiveness to the individual as artist's model, but indifference to him in terms of humanitarian regard and love.

Even in terms of quantitative measurement, the story is given over to a depiction of the artist's character, and specifically to the question of whether he is merely the observer and recorder of human appearances or a causal factor in the playing out of the human drama. "A strange thought darted into [the painter's] mind. Was not his own the form in which that destiny had embodied itself, and he was a chief agent of the coming evil which he had foreshadowed?" Throughout the story Hawthorne suggests that in the painter's extensive learning and reputation there is something that is both impressive and frightening. When he recommends the artist's erudition and reputation, Elinor asks Walter if he is speaking of "a painter or a wizard." Stepping back from the "foolish fancies" of the mob at the same time that he asserts them as viable, Hawthorne reminds us that the artist's skill is such that his work seems a "presumptuous mockery of the Creator." No less damning than his reputation for prescience among the old woman of Boston, however, is the extent to which he, like others of Hawthorne's men of "engrossing purpose," has isolated himself from mankind. "Though gentle in manner and upright in intent and action, he did not possess kindly feelings; his heart was cold; no living creature could be brought near enough to keep him warm." Nothing sums this up better than the mistake the painter makes when, in calling at the home of Walter and Elinor on the fatal day, he asks for an audience with the portraits rather than with the couple.

The evidence is so familiar, the character type so much a Hawthorne staple as to need no further recollection. What does remain, however, is the gnawing question of the significance of Hawthorne's extracting from all of this an inaccurate moral which makes no mention of what the story has been about. In a tale clearly questioning aspects of the Romantic theory of the artist, are we really being invited to think only about our willingness to let destiny unfold despite warnings of disaster? And, most significantly, what is the aesthetic effect of this and other episodes of Hawthorne's studied obtuseness in not being able to find the true moral, especially in view of his general practice in doing so?

Any suggestion must, of course, remain tentative, for Hawthorne does not have much to say about his inaccurately drawn morals. But several things do seem clear, among them that he is certainly aware of what he is about in works like **"Fancy's Show Box"** and **"The Prophetic Pictures,"** nor does it seem likely that the exceptions to the rule discussed in this study prove that Hawthorne is primarily nervous about moralizing in fiction. Quite the contrary, in fact; for in the works discussed in the preceding pages, his apparent reluctance to moralize accurately does not discourage the reader but in fact challenges him to pursue meanings of the sort we have come to associate with Hawthorne (**"Wakefield,"** after all, turns out to be one of the most morally assertive of his tales). What seems more reasonable is that the inaccurately stated moral legitimatizes the entire idea of moralizing through the kind of indirection, subtlety and suggestion one expects from a writer who, unlike the artist of **"The Prophetic Pictures,"** is not so presumptuous as to circumscribe in every case the precise boundaries of meaning.

The justification for the misleading moral in **"The Prophetic Pictures"** seems to be not primarily a comic pose (as it was in **"Wakefield"** and **"Night Sketches"**), nor a sportively ironic handling of the whole idea of moralizing (**"The Antique Ring"**), but rather an attempt to open up the field of the moral by means of a tantalizing misstatement of it, thereby goading the reader into doing better for himself. The device is not unlike Hawthorne's more familiar employment of suggestive alternatives, validating readings beyond those he himself is willing to assert, a bit like the instructor who misreads by way of challenging his students. In a way then, even when he seems to take a holiday from moralizing, Hawthorne willingly risks what he warned against in the preface to *The House of the Seven Gables:* treating the moral like a pin to be stuck through a butterfly. Rather than rendering the story lifeless, "in an ungainly and unnatural attitude," however, Hawthorne's use of the obviously inaccurate moral in certain of his works allows the butterfly to remain unimpaled and yet arrested, the better to be understood and appreciated. (pp. 269-75)

James G. Janssen, "Impaled Butterflies and the Misleading Moral in Hawthorne's Short Works," in The Nathaniel Hawthorne Journal, *1976, pp. 269-75.*

MADISON JONES (essay date 1978)

[In the following excerpt, Jones offers readings of "Young Goodman Brown," "Rappaccini's Daughter," and "The Birthmark" based on the Calvinist doctrine of the "total depravity" of humanity.]

The extent of Hawthorne's commitment to the religious tenets of his Puritan forebears is problematical, but at least in terms of his fiction it is extensive enough to be fundamentally significant. Whatever his differences with Puritan theology, certain of its most prominent metaphysical assumptions inform his work throughout and cast important light on his meanings. It is in this kind of light that I want to examine three of Hawthorne's best known stories: **"Young Goodman Brown," "Rappaccini's Daughter"** and **"The Birthmark."** These stories, I believe, are closer kin than has been thought, forming a sort of cluster whose center is a single motif shaped in terms of Hawthorne's Puritan heritage.

Fundamental to my reading of these stories is the Puritan, and Calvinist, tenet concerning man's natural condition, a condition described by the phrase "total depravity." Simplified, it means this. Man's fall in the Garden of Eden was not only a falling off from God's grace, a separation from God that left man the victim of his own limited and therefore erring nature: it goes much farther. Human nature, including human reason, was irreparably damaged by the fall, perverted to the extent that all purely human acts bear the indelible stamp of their origin. Purely human acts, since they are the issue of man's perverted nature, are therefore without merit. Lacking good, they are evil and, except by God's intervention, can only serve the interest of the Great Perverter himself, Satan, who by right of conquest is Prince of this fallen world. So the Puritans understood the words of Christ in Gethsemane: "Now is the prince of this world cast out."

But the Puritan version of the fall goes farther still. Not only human nature but all nature suffered the consequent disaster. "Thus began/Outrage from lifeless things; but Discord, first/Daughter of Sin, among th' irrational,/Death introduced through fierce antipathy:" says Milton, another, if often heretical Puritan. What surrounds us, what we look upon and commune with, is not nature as it issued from the hand of God. It is nature red in tooth and claw, perverted from its original, the domain of the Prince of Evil and of his subject, natural man.

But there is another side to this Puritan doctrine—one much less commonly known, or commonly noted. For all the insistence on man's unworthiness, his corrupt nature, man still bears the image of God in some measure engraven on him. He is therefore, says Calvin, however lacking in intrinsic merit, a creature of no small dignity and excellence. In Calvin's *Institutes* we read: " . . . we must not reflect on the wickedness of men, but contemplate the divine image in them; which, without concealing and obliterating their faults, by its beauty allures us to embrace them in the arms of love."

So said Calvin and, however little might have been made of it, so said the main theological tradition of New England. And so said Hawthorne, in his way. Add only that in order to perceive this transcendent aspect of man, faith ("the substance of things hoped for, the evidence of things not seen") is essential, and we have all the terms needed to discover the fundamental kinship of these three Hawthorne stories.

I take **"Young Goodman Brown"** to be the story that is most clearly and literally informed by this Puritan vision of the human condition. Vision is exactly the word here. The story is about a vision, Goodman Brown's vision, which comes as the consequence of his deliberate journey, whether literal or not, into the benighted wilderness. The journey, climaxing in the devil's communion service, makes real for him a truth about his fellow men from which he never afterwards recovers. For there in the wilderness he finds all those he has reverenced from his youth, saints and sinners without distinction, gathered in the worshipful assembly of the Evil One. Virtue *is* all a dream. Evil is the nature of mankind. Now is Goodman Brown finally undeceived. In a last desperate appeal to faith, Goodman Brown saves himself from personal commitment to the evil that is man's nature. But it is a barren kind of salvation—if the word salvation can be used at all to denominate Goodman Brown's new condition: a corrosive cynicism that keeps him forever after an alien among his fellows. Although his breach with faith is not absolute (presumably there are also intervals when he does *not* shrink from Faith's bosom) he no longer has with it a redemptive relationship.

Just here, I think, is the essential point—a point, let me add, that is not made any easier by Hawthorne's insistence on having it both ways in terms of the allegorical and literal levels. Faith, and Goodman Brown's relation to it—or to "her"—is the key to the story's meaning. "Believe," says Origen, along with other church fathers, "in order that you may understand." Without belief, faith, it is hard or impossible to understand, to "see," for things of the spirit are hidden from the natural eye. It is as though faith were a kind of spectacle empowering the natural eye to see what was invisible before. In the fallen world of the Puritans where evidences of the spirit are not apparent, unaided, unsanctified, merely reasoning man can perceive only unredeemed nature, material nature grinding on in the determinancy of its own mechanical laws. It is a desert place, a howling wilderness ruled by the prince of this world. And Goodman Brown has lost his spectacles, on purpose has left them behind him in Salem village.

This departure from faith is what the story allegorically depicts in the opening passage. Goodman Brown, at sunset, bids goodbye to his wife Faith who, all reluctant, watches with a sense of foreboding as her husband sets out on his journey into the forest. The separation from Faith is to last for only the space of one night and, to assuage the guilt his secret purpose has inspired in him, Goodman Brown reflects that ". . . after this one night I'll cling to her skirts and follow her to heaven."

It is soon apparent what Goodman Brown's secret purpose is, and why the guilt it inspires. A little tardily, because "Faith kept me back a while," he keeps his appointment with the devil. It is also soon apparent, if never openly specified, why he had agreed to the appointment in the first place. The reason is surely simple human curiosity, the desire to see with one's own eyes reality laid bare. Hence the need to step outside the medium of faith. Goodman Brown intends that it should be for only one quick look. He has been only moments in the devil's company when, having come to a full stop, he says "Friend . . . having kept covenant by meeting thee here, it is my purpose now to return whence I came. I have scruples touching the matter thou wot'st of." But the devil is persuasive. "Let us walk on, nevertheless, reasoning as we go; and if I convince thee not thou shalt turn back. We are but a little way in the forest yet." And Goodman Brown's answer, "Too far! Too far!" is much more true than he knows. Already, "unconsciously," he has resumed his walk.

So they go on together, reasoning as they go, ever deeper into the devil's domain. The wonderfully dramatic sequence of events that follows is the process of stripping Goodman Brown of his faith in all those he has held in honor and reverence, including, finally, his wife. She also—for Goodman Brown holds the evidence of her pink ribbon in his hand—is present in the dark wilderness. The wilderness echoes mock him when he cries out "Faith!" Then, "My Faith is gone!" he cries again. "There is no good on earth; and sin is but a name. Come, devil; for to thee is this world given."

Goodman Brown plunges into despair. He rushes on through the wilderness "with the instinct that guides mortal man to evil," his cry of despair "lost to his own ear by its unison with the cry of the desert." So he arrives at the devil's worshipful assembly, where all that might have been doubtful in his experience of this night is confirmed. They are all there, and "the smile of welcome gleamed darkly on every visage." "Welcome, my children," Satan's voice intones, "to the communion of your race."

This is the vision from which Goodman Brown can never recover. Ever afterward this is what he sees when he looks at his fellow man, and not unlike one of the victims of the Medusa's head, he is frozen into stone by the vision. What he perceives is in fact the nature of man: he is not mistaken. But because he looks upon it without the intervening medium of faith, his merely human eyes can see no reality beyond it. There is no divine image available to reason and hence, for Goodman Brown, none is present. What cause has he, then, for reverence and love toward his fellows? What is to be expected of him but that he should become what he does become: "A stern, a sad, a darkly meditative, a distrustful, if not a desperate man . . . from the night of that fearful dream." Without faith and hence without love, Goodman Brown lie at last under a tombstone on which his neighbors had carved no hopeful verse.

"Rappaccini's Daughter" is a story that has brought many a critic to grief. In part the difficulty lies with Hawthorne's loose practice, already mentioned, of sliding from literal to allegorical and back again as convenience urges. The effect is often quite unmanageable ambiguities. But another difficulty—as I am not the first to point out—lies with the temptation to view the story as Beatrice's story. In fact it is Giovanni's, not because it is he who shares the point of view with the author but because Giovanni is the one whose relation to the events gives the story its structure and, so, its meaning. With the focus on Giovanni, the central motif that echoes **"Young Goodman Brown"** and also **"The Birthmark"** can be brought clearly in evidence.

Before pursuing the role of Giovanni farther, however, it is necessary first to take note of the poisonous garden and of its native inhabitants. Fairly early in the story Hawthorne, in typical style, asks this question: "Was this garden, then, the Eden of this present world?" The interrogative has the effect both of suggesting that it *is* the present Eden and also, since the answer *could* be no, of letting Hawthorne out of some logical difficulties. For instance: how can Beatrice, with a mortal father on the scene, be an allegorical figure of Eve? And how can this be the present Eden, a representation of man's perverted re-creation, and not have any apparent or literal relation to Giovanni and Professor Baglioni, who are also in the present world? Such objections are disarmed by Hawthorne's seeming to leave the question to us. At the same time the idea has been planted and it is kept alive throughout the story by a number of suggestive supporting details.

Such a detail is Giovanni's reflection that not improbably the garden once had been the pleasure palace of an opulent family, "for there was the ruin of a marble fountain in the centre, sculptured with rare art, but so woefully shattered that it was impossible to trace the original design from the chaos of remaining fragments." Such are the details that suggest the likeness of the simple childlike Beatrice to Eve tending the Garden of Eden, her life confined within it. This garden is, in Hawthorne's words, an "Eden of poisonous flowers" to which Giovanni descends. And Beatrice, dying, says that she is going where the poisonous fragrance "will no longer taint my breath among the flowers of Eden"—meaning, the *other* Eden, Paradise.

Rappaccini is a type of the santanic intellectual who rises superior to merely human claims, a type prominent in Hawthorne's fiction. But here, in the total context of the story, and despite the ambiguities involved, he plays the role of Adam. So Hawthorne suggests by his question: "And this man . . . was he the Adam?" Considering what Rappaccini has perpetrated, the parallel becomes evident. For it was Adam, inspired by Satan, whose rebellion dethroned the rightful ruler of nature and put into man's hands the power to rule and to re-create. This power resides in man's knowledge, his science, and Rappaccini's perversion of nature as it came originally from God's hand is at least roughly analogous to the new condition created through Adam's fall. " . . . this garden is his world," Beatrice says of her father, and Rappaccini by his science has turned this world to his own purposes. He has "created" these flowers. It is a world whose productions are "no longer of God's making, but the monstrous offspring of man's depraved fancy." And all of this, as the story's climax makes clear, has been done for the enhancement of Rappaccini's own power.

The analogy, if not perfect, is close enough. It becomes still more persuasive when viewed, as it must be, in connection with the nature of Beatrice and with Giovanni's relation to her. Beatrice is the child of her father's body but likewise of his science, a re-created and perverted creature bound by irrevocable bonds of kinship to a world also perverted by her father's science. Like the flowers of the garden she is a poisonous creature, a creature in fact so imbued with poison that it is her element of life. So far is poison inextricable from her nature that when purged of it she dies. She is, as Giovanni comes to observe of her, "a world's wonder of hideous monstrosity." And Giovanni's observation is based on no mere delusion. Her very breath, much less her embrace, is death. Such is the nature her father's science has wrought. In terms of the analogy, such also is the condition wrought by Adam's rebellion—in human *and* external nature. Figured here, in the imagery of poison, is the Puritan vision of all nature depraved by the fall of man.

This nature in Beatrice is what Giovanni comes to see and cannot see beyond. From here, if we look back at the terms of **"Young Goodman Brown,"** the relation between the protagonists of the two stories becomes apparent. In fact, certainly in respect to their fatal flaws, the two protagonists look much alike. What they both lack is the illuminating medium of faith, which lack leaves them blind to the profounder, transcendent truth that lies hidden from the unaided eye. Goodman Brown enters the wilderness of this world without his Faith and, beholding depraved nature, ever afterward sees all men in the lurid light of the devil's worshipful assembly. In different terms, so it is with Giovanni. Compelled at last to realize the truth about Beatrice's nature, he has not the faith to discern the profounder truth—namely that, as Beatrice tells him, " . . . though my body be nourished with poison, my spirit is God's creature." Nor can he believe it when Beatrice enjoins him: "If true to the outward senses, still it may be false in its essence; but the words of Beatrice Rappaccini's lips are true from the depths of the heart outward. Those you may believe." But Giovanni can know only through his outward senses. He cannot believe in something truer and more real than what the senses can experience and he cannot suppose that "those dreadful peculiarities in her physical nature . . . could . . . exist without some corresponding monstrosity of soul." We concur with Beatrice's dying words about him: "Oh, was there not, from the first, more poison in thy nature than in mine?"

For all the differences between the stories of Giovanni and Goodman Brown, the central relationship is clear. At the center of both stories is the Puritan vision of depraved, or perverted nature. In each case the protagonist, lacking the faith necessary for spiritual perception, is brought to the conviction that this nature encompasses all, that spirit and virtue are finally but delusions. The consequence for both is spiritual ruin, breeding a destructiveness that only requires an occasion to overflow upon others. Goodman Brown, though evidently never presented with such an occasion, is not a whit less poisonous than Giovanni.

Of Aylmer, in **"The Birthmark,"** it may appear less comfortable to say that he too is as poisonous a creature as Giovanni. Certainly Aylmer is described in terms of high praise, praise for his aspiration toward the infinite, for his pure and honorable love that will accept nothing less than perfection. And Georgiana, his wife, the most nearly perfect of human creatures, profoundly esteems and reverences his nobility of spirit. Clearly Hawthorne does admire Aylmer. What we have here, however, is a manifestation of another side of Hawthorne, the Promethean side, which shows itself now and again throughout his fiction. It does not amount to a change of fundamental stance on Hawthorne's part. Hawthorne's tragic imagination, like Milton's, responds to beauty where it is to be found, even if it be in the person of Satan himself. So in the case of Aylmer. The fact that Hawthorne, and we, respond to his virtues does not invalidate the good reasons for likening him to Giovanni and Goodman Brown.

The likeness can be best approached by first considering Georgiana, Aylmer's nearly but not quite flawless wife. She is flawed by a crimson birthmark in the shape of a tiny hand on her cheek, representing, as we are flatly told, the grip of mortality upon her. It symbolizes Georgiana's liability to sin, sorrow, decay and death and, like Beatrice's poison, is inextricable from her nature. The parallel with Beatrice is continued in terms of Georgiana's high moral and spiritual qualities and, more strikingly, in terms of her fate. Both women die as the consequence of attempts, devised by human science, to purge their natures. In each case, too, they are the victim of a man, the protagonist, to whom they are bound by ties of love.

Between these men, the protagonists of the two stories, the parallel is less perfect. For instance, Aylmer has high and admirable qualities of mind and spirit, while Giovanni has not. But at the critical point, that of their response to fallen human nature, the likeness between them becomes apparent: both respond with horror and revulsion. It makes little difference, finally, that Aylmer's horror, in contrast to that of the shallow-hearted Giovanni, is inspired by his overpowering vision of the ideal. Nor is it convincing, when he knowingly risks sacrificing Georgiana's life to his ideal, that his 'love' for her is of an order so superior to that of Giovanni for Beatrice. In the presence of Georgiana's birthmark, the blood-colored hand that represents her irremediable humanness, Aylmer cannot restrain "a strong convulsive shudder." It is "intolerable"; it "shocks" him; it is a "frightful object." The one time when, "by a strange and unaccountable impulse," he touches his lips to the birthmark, this is what happens: "His spirit recoiled . . . in the very act". This strange and unaccountable impulse is man's natural impulse toward the human, which Aylmer's shuddering spirit instantly rejects. He would sooner have Georgiana dead than impure. An instant after his lips touch the birthmark, after his one small human slip, Aylmer is quite himself again.

The self that is Aylmer is not essentially different from the one named Giovanni who stands shuddering in the presence of a Beatrice less poisonous than he. Nor is either one of them essentially different from the self called Goodman Brown who shrinks from the bosom of Faith and sits in a pew of Salem church shuddering at the gray blasphemer in the pulpit. What Hawthorne says about Aylmer at the conclusion of **"The Birthmark"** could have been as aptly said about these other two. Aylmer failed, says Hawthorne, to reach "a profounder wisdom . . . The momentary circumstance was too strong for him; he failed to look beyond the shadowy scope of time. . . ." Aylmer's own light will not serve him. Blinded by it, he can see circumstance, mortality, only in its aspect of ugliness and horror. Like many a reformer in our day, Aylmer would have human nature reconstituted or else not at all. Hawthorne, if unconsciously, was looking well ahead. But genius has been always at least one part prophecy. (pp. 277-83)

Madison Jones, "Variations on a Hawthorne Theme," in Studies in Short Fiction, *Vol. 15, No. 3, Summer, 1978, pp. 277-83.*

ADDITIONAL BIBLIOGRAPHY

Allen, M. L. "Hawthorne's Art in His Short Stories." *Studi Americani* 7 (1961): 9-41.

Assesses the artistic success of Hawthorne's most popular short stories.

Asals, Frederick. "Jeremy Taylor and Hawthorne's Early Tales." *American Transcendental Quarterly,* No. 14 (Spring 1972): 15-23.

Suggests that "The Wedding Knell," "The Minister's Black Veil," and "The Maypole of Merrymount" are "a closely linked group, related first by the essential clash in each of the claims of this world against those of the next, posed in an overtly religious context; second, and more specifically, by the marriage ceremonies central to each story; and third by their common indebtedness . . . to the writings of [seventeenth-century bishop] Jeremy Taylor."

Ayo, Nicholas. "The Labyrinthine Ways of 'Rappaccini's Daughter.' " *Research Studies* 42, No. 1 (March 1974): 56-69.

Discusses textual ambiguities in "Rappaccini's Daughter" and the critical controversies they have created.

Baxter, David J. " 'The Birthmark' in Perspective." *Nathaniel Hawthorne Journal* (1975): 232-40.

Analysis of "The Birthmark" in which Baxter views Hawthorne's portrayal of Aylmer as essentially sympathetic.

Benoit, Raymond. "Hawthorne's Psychology of Death: 'The Minister's Black Veil.' " *Studies in Short Fiction* 8, No. 4 (Fall 1971): 553-60.

Existentialist reading of "The Minister's Black Veil" in which Benoit asserts that the black veil symbolizes "non-being in the center of being."

Brenzo, Richard. "Beatrice Rappaccini: A Victim of Male Love and Horror." *American Literature* 48, No. 2 (May 1976): 152-64.

Feminist interpretation of "Rappaccini's Daughter."

Brill, Lesley W. "Conflict and Accommodation in Hawthorne's 'The Artist of the Beautiful.' " *Studies in Short Fiction* 12, No. 4 (Fall 1975): 381-86.

Discussion of "The Artist of the Beautiful" as a reflection of Hawthorne's feelings about his own work.

Broes, Arthur T. "Journey into Moral Darkness: 'My Kinsman, Major Molineux' as Allegory." *Nineteenth Century Fiction* 19, No. 2 (September 1964): 171-84.

Views "My Kinsman, Major Molineux" as an eclectic allegory, combining elements drawn from Dante, Spenser, and Bunyan.

Brown, Dennis. "Literature and Psychoanalysis: 'My Kinsman, Major Molineux' and 'Young Goodman Brown.' " *Canadian Review of American Studies* 4, No. 1 (Spring 1973): 65-73.

Suggests that "Existential psychology in general, and the writings of R. D. Laing in particular, provide . . . an appropriate avenue of approach to Hawthorne's psychological insights."

Brubaker, B. R. "Hawthorne's Experiment in Popular Form: 'Mr. Higginbotham's Catastrophe.' " *Southern Humanities Review* 7, No. 2 (Spring 1973): 155-66.

Background material for and an analysis of "Mr. Higginbotham's Catastrophe."

Bunge, Nancy L. "Unreliable Artist-Narrators in Hawthorne's Short Stories." *Studies in Short Fiction* 14, No. 2 (Spring 1977): 145-50.

Discusses Hawthorne's view of the role and responsibility of the artist.

Burhans, Clinton S., Jr. "Hawthorne's Mind and Art in 'The Hollow of the Three Hills.' " *Journal of English and Germanic Philology* 60 (1961): 286-95.

Examines stylistic and thematic elements of "The Hollow of the Three Hills."

Canaday, Nicholas, Jr. "Hawthorne's Minister and the Veiling Deceptions of Self." *Studies in Short Fiction* 4, No. 1 (Fall 1966): 135-42.

Analysis of "The Minister's Black Veil" in which Canaday views the veil as a symbol of hypocrisy and self-deception.

Carnochan, W. B. " 'The Minister's Black Veil': Symbol, Meaning and the Context of Hawthorne's Art." *Nineteenth Century Fiction* 24, No. 2 (September 1969): 182-92.
Suggests that "The Minister's Black Veil" is "concerned above all with the veil as a symbolic object, pointing toward questions that cluster about the notion of a symbol itself."

Coffey, Dennis G. "Hawthorne's 'Alice Doane's Appeal': The Artist Absolved." *Emerson Society Quarterly* 21, No. 4 (1975): 230-40.
Argues that "Alice Doane's Appeal" is unified by its "dissolving form," which Coffey describes as a dynamic in which "elements in the story—plots, scenes, and characters—constantly merge and dissolve; where everything is continually in the process of becoming something else."

Colacurcio, Michael J. *The Province of Piety: Moral History in Hawthorne's Early Tales.* Cambridge: Harvard University Press, 1984, 661 p.
Study of Hawthorne as an interpreter of history.

Connolly, Thomas E. "Hawthorne's 'Young Goodman Brown': An Attack on Puritanic Calvinism." *American Literature* 28, No. 3 (November 1956): 370-75.
Analyzes criticism of Calvinism in "Young Goodman Brown."

Cook, Reginald. "The Forest of Goodman Brown's Night: A Reading of Hawthorne's 'Young Goodman Brown.' " *New England Quarterly* 43, No. 3 (September 1970): 473-81.
Discusses "Young Goodman Brown" as an exploration of "the turbulence beneath the layers of the Puritan conscience."

Crews, Frederick. *The Sins of the Fathers.* London: Oxford University Press, 1966, 279 p.
Seminal study of psychological dimensions of Hawthorne's fiction that includes much discussion of his short stories.

Crie, Robert D. " 'The Minister's Black Veil': Mr. Hooper's Symbolic Fig Leaf." *Literature and Psychology* 17, No. 4 (1967): 211-18.
Summarizes possible interpretations of the symbolism of the veil in "The Minister's Black Veil."

Daly, Robert J. "History and Chivalric Myth in 'Roger Malvin's Burial.' " *Essex Institute Historical Collections* 109, No. 1 (January 1973): 99-115.
Views "Roger Malvin's Burial" as "a dramatization of what happens to a man who believes in an impracticable chivalric myth."

Davidson, Frank. " 'Young Goodman Brown': Hawthorne's Intent." *Emerson Society Quarterly* 31 (1963): 68-71.
Suggests that it may have been Hawthorne's intent in "Young Goodman Brown" to illustrate "the transforming power and the paralyzing deceptiveness of an evil thought, which once entertained, starts into action subtle psychological processes against which one may make resolves but which, begun, proceed with increasing strength to demoniacal frenzy and the perpetration of an evil deed."

Davis, Joe. "The Myth of the Garden: Nathaniel Hawthorne's 'Rappaccini's Daughter.' " *Studies in the Literary Imagination* 2, No. 1 (April 1969): 3-12.
Interprets "Rappaccini's Daughter" as a retelling of the Judeo-Christian creation myth.

Dennis, Carl. "How to Live in Hell: The Bleak Vision of Hawthorne's 'My Kinsman, Major Molineux.' " *University Review* 37, No. 4 (October 1970): 250-58.
Reading in which Dennis views "My Kinsman, Major Molineux" as "an account of man's inhumanity to man."

Donohue, Agnes McNeill. " 'From Whose Bourn No Traveller Returns': A Reading of 'Roger Malvin's Burial.' " *Nineteenth Century Fiction* 18, No. 1 (June 1963): 1-19.
Analysis of "Roger Malvin's Burial." Donohue views the story's central concern as the tragedy of the human condition, a reflection of "Hawthorne's dark imagination, his sickness of human life, his New England Puritan heritage, [and] his fear of the price of expiation demanded by the Calvinist Jehovah."

Dusenbery, Robert. "Hawthorne's Merry Company: The Anatomy of Laughter in the Tales and Short Stories." *PMLA* 82, No. 2 (May 1967): 285-88.
Examines the function of laughter in Hawthorne's short fiction, noting that Hawthorne's characters "both enrich the story and reveal themselves through their laughter."

Erlich, Gloria Chasson. "Guilt and Expiation in 'Roger Malvin's Burial.' " *Nineteenth Century Fiction* 26, No. 4 (March 1972): 377-89.
Explores the logic of Reuben Bourne's actions in "Roger Malvin's Burial," focusing on "Hawthorne's preoccupation with displaced filial relationships and their complex load of mutual guilt."

Evans, Oliver. "Allegory and Incest in 'Rappaccini's Daughter.' " *Nineteenth Century Fiction* 19, No. 2 (September 1964): 185-95.
Attempts to clarify the complex allegory of "Rappaccini's Daughter." Evans suggests that the most plausible interpretation is that Rappaccini, rather than Giovanni, represents Adam in the story, while his daughter may have been based on Beatrice Cenci, a sixteenth-century Italian noblewoman who was the subject of a drama by Percy Bysshe Shelley.

Feeney, Joseph J. "The Structure of Ambiguity in Hawthorne's 'The Maypole of Merry Mount.' " *Studies in American Fiction* 3, No. 2 (Autumn 1975): 211-16.
Examines stylistic and thematic sources of ambiguity in "The Maypole of Merry Mount."

Fetterley, Judith. "Palpable Designs: Four American Short Stories." In her *The Resisting Reader,* pp. 1-45. Bloomington: Indiana University Press, 1978.
Includes a discussion of the feminist perspective in "The Birthmark." Fetterley states: "In exploring the sources of men's compulsion to idealize women Hawthorne is writing a story about the sickness of men, not a story about the flawed and imperfect nature of women."

Fogle, Richard H. "Ambiguity and Clarity in Hawthorne's 'Young Goodman Brown.' " *New England Quarterly* 18, No. 4 (December 1945): 448-65.
Study of ambiguity in "Young Goodman Brown." Fogle contends that in this story "Hawthorne has achieved that reconciliation of opposites which Coleridge deemed the highest art. The combination of clarity of technique, embodied in simplicity and balance of structure . . . , with ambiguity of meaning as signalized by 'the device of multiple choice,' in its interrelationships produces the story's characteristic effect. By means of these two elements Hawthorne reconciles oneness of action with multiplicity of suggestion, and enriches the bareness of systematic allegory."

———. "The Problem of Allegory in Hawthorne's 'Ethan Brand.' " *University of Toronto Quarterly* 17, No. 2 (January 1948): 190-203.
Analysis of allegory in 'Ethan Brand' in which Fogle concludes that "in 'Ethan Brand' Hawthorne has written an impressive allegory, valuable in itself for its noble seriousness of theme, and for its careful and artistic arrangement of intricate detail about the magnetic pole of an abstract conception."

———. "The World and the Artist: A Study of Hawthorne's 'The Artist of the Beautiful.' " *Tulane Studies in English* 1 (1949): 31-52.
Analysis of style, structure, and theme in "The Artist of the Beautiful."

———. *Hawthorne's Fiction: The Light and the Dark.* Rev. ed. Norman: University of Oklahoma Press, 1964, 239 p.
Includes general discussion of short fiction and separate chap-

ters on "My Kinsman, Major Molineux" and "The Birthmark."

Fossum, Robert H. "The Summons of the Past: Hawthorne's 'Alice Doane's Appeal.' " *Nineteenth Century Fiction* 23, No. 3 (December 1968): 294-303.
Suggests that "Alice Doane's Appeal" "expresses . . . both explicitly and implicitly, what [Hawthorne] considered the purpose of his fiction to be."

Gargano, James W. "Hawthorne's 'The Artist of the Beautiful.' " *American Literature* 35, No. 2 (May 1963): 225-30.
Discusses the complex structure of "The Artist of the Beautiful" and its thematic implications.

Gross, Seymour L. "Hawthorne's 'My Kinsman, Major Molineux': History as Moral Adventure." *Nineteenth Century Fiction* 12, No. 2 (September 1957): 97-109.
Analysis of "My Kinsman, Major Molineux" in which Gross emphasizes the moral implications of the story.

Gupta, R. K. "The Idea and the Image: Some Aspects of Imagery in the Minor Short Stories of Nathaniel Hawthorne." In *Studies in American Literature,* edited by Jagdish Chander and Narindar S. Pradhan, pp. 62-76. Delhi: Oxford University Press, 1976.
Discussion of imagery in Hawthorne's short stories.

Halligan, John. "Hawthorne on Democracy: 'Endicott and the Red Cross.' " *Studies in Short Fiction* 8, No. 2 (Spring 1971): 301-07.
Views "Endicott and the Red Cross" as a reflection of Hawthorne's skepticism about democracy and the possibility of political reform.

Heilman, R. B. "Hawthorne's 'The Birthmark': Science as Religion." *South Atlantic Quarterly* 48, No. 4 (October 1949): 575-83.
Suggests that the central message of "The Birthmark" is the need for human beings to mediate between "irrational passivity and a hyperrational reorganization of life."

Hennelly, Mark M., Jr. " 'Alice Doan's Appeal': Hawthorne's Case against the Artist." *Studies in American Fiction* 6, No. 2 (Autumn 1978): 125-40.
Argues that the key to understanding "Alice Doane's Appeal" lies in Hawthorne's ironic treatment of the story's narrator.

Hoeltje, Hubert H. *Inward Sky: The Mind and Heart of Nathaniel Hawthorne.* Durham, N. C.: Duke University Press, 1962, 579 p.
Comprehensive critical biography.

Hoffman, Daniel G. *Form and Fable in American Fiction.* New York: Oxford University Press, 1961, 368 p.
Includes discussion of folkloric elements in "My Kinsman, Major Molineux," "The Maypole of Merry Mount," and "Young Goodman Brown."

Humma, John B. " 'Young Goodman Brown' and the Failure of Hawthorne's Ambiguity." *Colby Library Quarterly* 9, No. 8 (December 1971): 425-31.
Reviews the critical controversy surrounding the question of whether the events in "Young Goodman Brown" occur only in the mind of the protagonist and concludes that "those elders Brown encounters in the forest are present in the flesh."

Hurley, Paul J. "Young Goodman Brown's 'Heart of Darkness.' " *American Literature* 37, No. 4 (January 1966): 410-19.
Argues that " 'Young Goodman Brown' is a subtle work of fiction concerned with revealing a distorted mind" and that what Brown witnesses in the forest is simply "the product of his suspicion and distrust."

Jones, Bartlett C. "The Ambiguity of Shrewdness in 'My Kinsman, Major Molineux.' " *Midcontinent American Studies Journal* 3, No. 2 (Fall 1962): 42-7.
Views "My Kinsman, Major Molineux" as "a biting commentary on a human nature too prone to choose the expedient."

Brother Joseph. "Art and Event in 'Ethan Brand.' " *Nineteenth Century Fiction* 15, No. 3 (December 1960): 249-57.
Traces the development of "Ethan Brand" from its appearance as a historical note in Hawthorne's notebooks to its final appearance as a complex allegorical tale.

Lesser, Simon O. "The Image of the Father." *Partisan Review* 22, No. 3 (Summer 1955): 372-90.
Analysis of unconscious motivations in "My Kinsman, Major Molineux."

Levin, David. "Specter Evidence in Hawthorne's 'Young Goodman Brown.' " *American Literature* 34, No. 3 (November 1962): 344-52.
Argues that Goodman Brown errs in allowing himself to be tricked by Satan into believing that he has seen the people of his town participating in a satanic ritual.

Levy, Alfred J. " 'Ethan Brand' and the Unpardonable Sin." *Boston University Studies in English* 5, No. 3 (Autumn 1961): 185-90.
Explores the meaning of the unpardonable sin. Levy contends that Brand's only unpardonable sin was the failure to recognize and repent his own sinful nature.

Levy, Leo B. "The Problem of Faith in 'Young Goodman Brown.' " *Journal of English and Germanic Philology* 74, No. 3 (July 1975): 375-87.
Discusses "Young Goodman Brown" as "a dream vision, a conventional allegory, and . . . an inquiry into the problem of faith that undermines the assumptions upon which the allegory is based."

Liebman, Sheldon W. "Robin's Conversion: The Design of 'My Kinsman, Major Molineux.' " *Studies in Short Fiction* 8, No. 3 (Summer 1971): 443-57.
Examines the significance of character, action, and imagery in "My Kinsman, Major Molineux."

———. "The Forsaken Maiden in Hawthorne's Short Stories." *American Transcendental Quarterly,* No. 19 (Summer 1973): 13-19.
Discusses Beatrice Rappaccini, Lady Eleanore, and Georgiana (in "The Birthmark") as symbols of Christian redemption.

———. "Ethan Brand and the Unpardonable Sin." *American Transcendental Quarterly,* No. 24 (Fall 1974): 9-14.
Analysis of "Ethan Brand" in which Liebman suggests that it is his despairing reaction to the sinful nature of humanity that constitutes Brand's "unpardonable sin."

———. "Moral Choice in 'The Maypole of Merry Mount.' " *Studies in Short Fiction* 11, No. 2 (Spring 1974): 173-80.
Argues that " 'The Maypole' dramatizes the problem of moral choice—the need for man to choose between two moral points of view, one essentially 'pagan,' the other essentially Christian."

———. " 'Roger Malvin's Burial': Hawthorne's Allegory of the Heart." *Studies in Short Fiction* 12, No. 3 (Summer 1975): 253-60.
Analysis of symbolism in "Roger Malvin's Burial."

McKeithan, D. M. "Hawthorne's 'Young Goodman Brown': An Interpretation." *Modern Language Notes* 67, No. 2 (February 1952): 93-6.
Views the theme of "Young Goodman Brown" as the blighting effect of sin. According to McKeithan's reading, Brown's own sinfulness creates a feeling of guilt and distorts his perception of others.

Miller, Edwin Haviland. " 'My Kinsman, Major Molineux': The Playful Art of Nathaniel Hawthorne." *Emerson Society Quarterly* 24, No. 3 (1978): 145-51.
Analysis in which Miller suggests that an accurate interpretation of "My Kinsman, Major Molineux" must take into account Hawthorne's "spirit of play." Miller writes: "If 'My

Kinsman' is read with this spirit in mind, we may not arrive at intellectual-historical-mythical profundities, which I believe Hawthorne eschews, but we may come closer to the comitragic . . . spirit of his affectionate depiction of a boy-man at the difficult, anxiety-ridden age of eighteen."

Miller, Paul W. "Hawthorne's 'Young Goodman Brown': Cynicism or Meliorism?" *Nineteenth Century Fiction* 14, No. 3 (December 1959): 255-64.

Views "Young Goodman Brown" as an indictment of Calvinist Puritanism.

Morsberger, Robert E. "The Woe That Is Madness: Goodman Brown and the Face of the Fire." *Nathaniel Hawthorne Journal* (1973): 177-82.

Discusses the attitudes toward Puritanism and the Salem witch trials manifested in "Young Goodman Brown."

———. " 'The Minister's Black Veil': 'Shrouded in a Blackness, Ten Times Black.' " *New England Quarterly* 46, No. 3 (September 1973): 454-63.

Contends that the black veil is a symbol of Mr. Hooper's, and by extension of the Puritans', obsessive concern with the sinfulness of humanity.

Moss, Sidney P. "A Reading of 'Rappaccini's Daughter.' " *Studies in Short Fiction* 2, No. 2 (Winter 1965): 145-56.

Defines the theme of "Rappaccini's Daughter" in terms of three related propositions: "The first of these propositions is that people act out of impure and therefore deceptive as well as self-deceptive motives. . . . The second is that bad and good are interfused in this world; that this is the central and inevitable fact of life; and that adjustment to this fact, not the mere recognition of it, constitutes the fundamental human problem. The third is that we can adjust to this fact by a 'mystique'—call it love or a profound trust in our intuitions or in providence."

Newman, Franklin B. " 'My Kinsman, Major Molineux': An Interpretation." *University of Kansas City Review* 21, No. 3 (March 1955): 203-12.

Discusses elements of allegory and dream in "My Kinsman, Major Molineux."

Paulits, Walter J. "Ambivalence in 'Young Goodman Brown.' " *American Literature* 41, No. 4 (January 1970): 577-84.

Considers "Young Goodman Brown" as "an allegorical presentation of ambivalence."

Predmore, Richard L. "The Hero's Test in 'Rappaccini's Daughter.' " *English Language Notes* 15, No. 4 (June 1978): 284-91.

Explores mythic and philosophical elements in "Rappaccini's Daughter." Predmore concludes: "Hawthorne wants us to see that in a general way Giovanni's deficiency in understanding is his inability to comprehend and accept the ambiguous Beatrice 'just as she is,' in all her womanly complexity. . . . Thus it is partly due to his own shortcomings that Giovanni fails to solve the maiden's puzzle and hence fails to rescue her from the enchanted garden."

Rohrberger, Mary. *Hawthorne and the Modern Short Story: A Study in Genre.* The Hague: Mouton, 1966, 148 p.

Discusses Hawthorne in the context of the development of the modern short story.

Ross, Morton L. "What Happens in 'Rappaccini's Daughter.' " *American Literature* 43, No. 3 (November 1971): 336-45.

Stresses the importance of literal interpretation in approaching "Rappaccini's Daughter."

Russell, John. "Allegory and 'My Kinsman, Major Molineux.' " *New England Quarterly* 40, No. 3 (September 1967): 432-40.

Focuses on historical elements in "My Kinsman, Major Molineux."

Santangelo, G. A. "The Absurdity of 'The Minister's Black Veil.' " *Pacific Coast Philology* 5 (April 1970): 61-6.

Explores elements of existentialism in "The Minister's Black Veil."

Scanlon, Lawrence E. "That Very Singular Man, Dr. Heidegger." *Nineteenth Century Fiction* 17, No. 3 (December 1962): 253-63.

Discusses humor in "Dr. Heidegger's Experiment."

Schubert, Leland. *Hawthorne, the Artist: Fine Art Devices in Fiction.* New York: Russell and Russell, 1963, 181 p.

Study of form in Hawthorne's fiction that includes discussion of the short stories.

Strandberg, Victor. "The Artist's Black Veil." *New England Quarterly* 41, No. 4 (December 1968): 567-74.

Views Mr. Hooper as an artist figure. Strandberg notes: "In Mr. Hooper we see Hawthorne's mixed judgment toward himself as an artist. Here he defined his paradoxical position an an immoral writer of moralities, as an anti-Transcendentalist nourished by Transcendentalism, as an ideological recluse preaching the importance of community."

Van Doren, Mark. "Tales and Sketches." In his *Nathaniel Hawthorne,* pp. 61-95. New York: Viking, 1949.

Provides background and brief analyses of Hawthorne's better-known short stories.

Waggoner, Hyatt H. *Hawthorne: A Critical Study.* Cambridge, Mass.: Belknap, 1955, 268 p.

Includes in-depth discussions of several of Hawthorne's short stories.

James (Augustine Aloysius) Joyce

1882-1941

Irish novelist, short story writer, poet, dramatist, and critic.

Joyce is considered one of the most prominent literary figures of the first half of the twentieth century. His virtuoso experiments in prose both redefined the limits of language and recreated the form of the modern novel. Joyce's prose is often praised for its rich symbolism, and many critics maintain that his verbal facility equals that of William Shakespeare or John Milton. Joyce's only short story collection, *Dubliners,* is considered a master achievement in that genre as well as a revealing indicator of Joyce's ultimate preeminence as a prose stylist.

Joyce was born in a suburb of Dublin to middle-class parents, but the family subsequently lived in a number of Dublin neighborhoods, reflecting their financial decline from comfortable respectability to virtual poverty. Although occasioned by adverse circumstances, the family's many moves around Dublin afforded Joyce an extraordinary intimacy with the city. He was educated at Jesuit schools, instruction financed largely by scholarships, and displayed outstanding aptitude as a scholar. However, he experienced much the same emotional hardship throughout his school years as he later attributed to Stephen Dedalus, the hero of his first published novel, *A Portrait of the Artist as a Young Man.* The influence of the Jesuit priests on Joyce was great, and although he eventually rejected Catholicism, his notion of the artist as a secular priest may be seen as a result of his education. After graduating from University College in Dublin in 1902, Joyce left Ireland and established himself in Paris, consciously abandoning the restrictive Dublin milieu that *Dubliners* depicts in harsh detail. In 1903, he returned to Ireland when his mother developed a serious illness. Following her death in 1904, Joyce moved permanently to the Continent with Nora Barnacle, a chamber maid from Galway with whom he had fallen in love and whom he would marry in 1931. Though so disgusted by the narrowness and provincialism of Ireland that he spent most of his life in self-imposed exile, Joyce nevertheless made Ireland and the Irish the subject of all his fiction. In Trieste, where the couple's two children were born, Joyce supported himself and his family by working as a language instructor while continually struggling to find a publisher for his short stories.

By the end of 1904, three of Joyce's *Dubliners* stories, "The Sisters," "Eveline," and "After the Race," had been published in the journal *Irish Homestead,* but the collection as a whole remained unpublished until 1914. Joyce completed eleven further stories and revised and expanded the *Irish Homestead* stories for book publication, an event that seemed imminent in 1906 when English publisher Grant Richards accepted the collection. However, after a series of setbacks, including the censure of Richards's printer, who refused to print the work on grounds that the stories were indecent, the project was abandoned. In explaining to Richards why he would not allow arbitrary changes to his collection and, thus, preferred that they remain unpublished, Joyce—in a statement that J. I. M. Stewart has called "a little manifesto of naturalism"—underscored his aim in writing *Dubliners:* "My intention was to write a chapter of the moral history of my country and I chose Dublin for the scene because that city seemed to me the centre of paralysis. . . . I have written it for the most part in a style of scrupulous meanness and with the conviction that he is a very bold man who dares to alter in the presentment, still more to deform, whatever he has seen and heard." In 1912 an Irish publisher, Maunsel and Company, accepted and printed the collection to which a fifteenth story, "The Dead," had been added, but destroyed all copies of the volume before they could be distributed, due to concern that libel actions would result from Joyce's use of the names of well-known people, places, and businesses in Dublin. Finally, Richards published the volume in 1914, nearly a decade after the first of the stories had been written; while contemporary reviews praised Joyce's realistic presentation of Dublin life in the stories, notice of the volume was soon eclipsed by interest in *A Portrait of the Artist as a Young Man,* which was then appearing serially in an English periodical.

Reflecting the intellectual and spiritual torpor of Ireland, *Dubliners* is considered the first literary product of Joyce's enduring preoccupation with Dublin life. The *Dubliners* stories are also important individually as examples of Joyce's aesthetic theory of epiphany in fiction: each is concerned with a sudden revelation of truth about life inspired by a seemingly trivial incident. To clarify Joyce's use of the term *epiphany* and his understanding of the role of the literary artist, critics often refer to a statement defining the aesthetic theory of the eponymous protagonist of Joyce's unfinished novel, *Stephen Hero:* "By an epiphany he meant a sudden spiritual manifestation, whether in the vulgarity of speech or of gesture or in a memorable phase of the mind itself. He believed that it was for the man of letters to record these epiphanies with extreme care, seeing that they themselves are the most delicate and evanescent of moments." Each story in *Dubliners* contains an epiphanic moment toward which the controlled yet seemingly plotless narrative moves; among the best-known epiphanies are those occurring in "Araby," in which a young boy recognizes the vanity and falsity of ideal, romantic love, and "The Dead," in which a husband realizes that his understanding of his wife and of the nature of their relationship has never equaled what he had presumed.

Joyce's Dubliners are uniformly middle-class and Catholic, but from that social group he extracted a wide range of characters representing many ages and occupations—from preadolescent schoolboys to decaying priests and from idealized adolescent beauties to aged spinster music teachers, and the structure of the book shows progressively their entrapment in Dublin society through their own inertia or through improvident choices. Joyce carefully arranged the stories to present the physical, moral, and social paralysis of Irish life in four distinct stages: Childhood, in three stories related by first person protagonists becoming aware of the stifling, corrupt milieu surrounding them; Adolescence, in four tales describing young adults facing decisions about their futures; Maturity, in four stories detailing moments in the lives of protagonists who must learn to live with the constraining choices they have made; and Public Life, in three stories viewing typically Irish concerns—politics, music, and the Church—from a societal perspective. "The Dead," the longest and last story in the volume, was written and added to *Dubliners* after Grant Richards's rejection in 1906. Critics consider it an epilogue or coda to the collection, resolving and complementing prominent issues, themes, motifs, and symbols introduced throughout the book.

The stories of childhood—"The Sisters," "An Encounter," and "Araby"—describe the narrators' first recognition of the stagnation of Dublin life as it concerns the Church, the chance for escape, and love. Important themes and symbols explored by Joyce throughout the collection and in some cases throughout his writing career are introduced in the opening story, "The Sisters." For example, the theme of moral paralysis—especially its presence in the Roman Catholic church in Ireland—is introduced in the character of Father Flynn, a retired priest suffering from hemiplegia. The young narrator of "The Sisters" professes in the opening paragraphs his fascination with the words *paralysis, simony,* which refers to the buying or selling of church offices or ecclesiastical favors, and *gnomon*—the portion of a parallelogram remaining after a parallelogram containing one of its corners has been removed—all of which in Bernard Benstock's words "have thematic reverberations throughout the ensuing stories." The remaining childhood stories depict the frustrated expectations that Joyce associated with Dublin life: the protagonist of "An Encounter" attempts to escape the city to visit a seaside landmark, but fails, encountering instead a threatening stranger who describes in detail his fondness for beating little boys; in "Araby," the romanticized love ideal of a young boy is shattered when he arrives too late at the alluringly named benefit bazaar "Araby" to purchase a token of love for an adolescent schoolgirl whom he idolizes; instead he finds cheap, inappropriate merchandise and overhears the common flirting of an English salesgirl.

The stories of adolescence—"Eveline," "After the Race," "Two Gallants," and "The Boarding House"—show young protagonists spoiling through moral inertia or indiscretion their chances to escape the decaying conditions of their lives. Two of the stories present young people facing decisions about marriage: In "Eveline," nineteen-year-old Eveline Hill deserts her fiance as he boards the ship on which they are to sail to their new life in Buenos Aires, remaining in Dublin to keep house for her father and younger brothers and sisters. In "The Boarding House," a talented clerk employed in a respectable wine merchant's firm is seduced by and subsequently trapped into marrying the socially inferior daughter of a boardinghouse keeper in order to avoid a scandal, which would hinder his career more than an improvident marriage.

The stories of maturity include "A Little Cloud," "Counterparts," "Clay," and "A Painful Case." Of these, "A Little Cloud" and "Counterparts" depict married office clerks whose prosaic lives exemplify the confinement of Dublin; "Clay" and "A Painful Case" focus on unmarried celibates, one woman and one man. The latter pair are highly regarded for their neat depiction of Joyce's intentions for this section, in which the results of such choices as those faced by the protagonists of the stories of adolescence are detailed. "Clay" follows an unmarried, middle-aged laundry worker as she visits the home of young family friends on Halloween and unwittingly chooses clay, symbolizing death, in a divination game. The story's central character, Maria, has undergone critical scrutiny matched by few other *Dubliners* protagonists. In the 1950s Marvin Magalaner presented a symbolic reading of the story, in which Maria was attributed three levels of significance: her literal character, a Virgin Mary figure, and a Halloween witch. Debate on this matter has been considerable but inconclusive; to at least one critic she embodies a mature counterpart to Eveline Hill, finally coming to terms with her decision not to marry. "A Painful Case" concerns James Duffy, whose ascetic, withdrawn lifestyle is called into question by his brief association with an understanding and sympathetic woman, who some time after his rejection of her intimacy is struck by a train while drunkenly attempting to cross the tracks.

Each of the stories of public life—"Ivy Day in the Committee Room," "A Mother," and "Grace"—highlights the stagnation and degeneration of a facet of Irish society. "Ivy Day in the Committee Room" relates the seemingly dissociated conversation of political canvassers in a campaign office on the anniversary of the death of Irish nationalist leader Charles Stewart Parnell. "A Mother" depicts the lamentable state of Irish culture through a glimpse behind the scenes of a series of musical concerts held at Dublin's Antient Concert Rooms. In this story, a mother destroys the career of her daughter through her own greed when she refuses to allow her to accompany the singers on the program until payment for her services has been tendered in full. "Grace" offers Joyce's views on the contemporary Church in Ireland while ostensibly presenting the redemption story of Tom Kernan, who, while recuperating from a drunken fall down the stairs in a pub, is convinced by his friends to attend a Jesuit retreat for businessmen. Recalling the simoniac theme traceable throughout the collection, salvation is equated at the retreat with a simple accounting of spiritual debits and credits. Critics have generally accepted Joyce's brother Stanislaus's assertion that this story, originally the culmination of the collection, is an ironic rendering of Dante Alighieri's *Divina commedia* (*The Divine Comedy,* 1321), connecting the three scenes of "Grace"—the basement lavatory of the pub, the sick room in which Kernan receives his friends, and St. George's church, the scene of the retreat—with the three sections of Dante's epic poem: *Inferno, Purgatorio,* and *Paradiso.*

Joyce professed to Stanislaus a desire to soften the bitter condemnation of the Irish in *Dubliners,* declaring that he had not been altogether fair in his presentation of Irish life and determined to add a story that would reflect the Irish gift for hospitality. The story that he added, "The Dead," is considered Joyce's greatest achievement in the short story genre; according to David Daiches, it is "done with a subtlety and a virtuosity that makes it one of the most remarkable short stories of the present century." The action of the story recounts little more than a holiday party at the home of two spinster music teachers, hosted by their nephew Gabriel Conroy, who is a teacher and literary reviewer with a love of Continental culture. At the close of the evening, after a tenor at the party sings an Irish air that Gabriel's wife, Gretta, associates with a long-dead suitor, Gabriel learns that he is not the only man who has ever loved his wife. The title of the story points to its underlying subject, but critics have argued exactly which "dead" are to be emphasized in explication, and even which characters comprise the "dead." To some, "The Dead" refers only to those mentioned in the story as dead, most notably, Michael Furey, Gretta's adolescent beau, who died after leaving his sickbed on a rainy night to keep a vigil outside her window on the eve of her leaving Galway for Dublin. To others, "The Dead" signifies everyone at the party but Gabriel, and through association, everyone in Ireland. Among the most prominent subjects of disagreement between critics is the ambiguity associated with Gabriel's epiphany at the conclusion of the story, which closes with his assertion that it is time to begin his journey westward and an accompanying vision of snow falling over all Ireland. The meaning of the journey westward is sometimes associated with death, but a more prevalent modern view is that Gabriel's journey westward signifies his reenergized worldview; similarly the meaning of the snow, which in some readings signifies the pall—or even shroud—of death covering Ireland, in others represents universal cleansing, bringing expanded consciousness and renewed life to all upon whom it falls. Florence L. Walzl has asserted that ambivalence and ambiguity were purposefully written into the narrative by Joyce to clearly reflect his changing attitude towards Ireland at the time he wrote the story.

For several decades *Dubliners* was considered little more than a slight volume of naturalist fiction evoking the repressed social milieu of turn-of-the-century Dublin. *Dubliners* was generally viewed as Joyce's most traditional prose work, yet its very accessibility to nonspecialist readers rendered it less interesting to critics, who largely overlooked it in their race to explicate Joyce's later works, *A Portrait of the Artist as a Young Man, Ulysses,* and *Finnegans Wake.* "First Flight to Ithaca," a landmark analysis by Richard Levin and Charles Shattuck, which examined the thematic and structural resemblances of *Dubliners* to Homer's *Odyssey,* was published in 1944 and introduced an era of extensive critical debate. While many critics disagreed with the thesis developed by Levin and Shattuck, most recognized that *Dubliners* held greater significance than had previously been attributed to it, and subsequent studies examined symbolic significance, structural unity, and biographical backgrounds of the stories. Critical interest in *Dubliners* has remained intense in recent decades as each story has been closely examined within the context of the collection and as an individual narrative. The resultant explications have demonstrated that in *Dubliners* Joyce experimented with the subjects and themes that would become the focus of his career and refined the multidimensional narrative method that would revolutionize modern literature. These processes, critics agree, are of considerable importance to both Joyce's development as a literary artist and to the enrichment of short story writing in the twentieth century.

(See also *Twentieth-Century Literary Criticism,* Vols. 3, 8, 16, 26; *Contemporary Authors,* Vol. 3; and *Dictionary of Literary Biography,* Vols. 10, 19, 36.)

PRINCIPAL WORKS

SHORT FICTION:

Dubliners 1914
The Portable James Joyce 1947; Rev. ed., 1966
The Essential James Joyce 1948

OTHER MAJOR WORKS:

Chamber Music (poetry) 1907
A Portrait of the Artist As a Young Man (novel) 1916
Exiles (drama) 1918
Ulysses (novel) 1922
Pomes Penyeach (poetry) 1927
Collected Poems (poetry) 1936
Finnegans Wake (novel) 1939
**Stephen Hero* (unfinished novel) 1944
Letters. 3 vols. (letters) 1955-1966
Critical Writings of James Joyce (criticism) 1959

*This work was written in 1901-1906.

JAMES JOYCE (essay date 1906)

[In April 1906 Joyce submitted the last story of the Dubliners *collection to his publisher, Grant Richards, and in a series of ensuing letters, Joyce and Richards negotiated publication of the volume. However, Richards's printer judged several passages in the collection indecent and refused to print "Two Gallants" and "Counterparts" as they were; further, Richards himself asked Joyce to substitute a gentler word for "bloody" in the story "Grace." Responding in late April, Joyce insisted that nothing be altered. On 1 May, Richards reiterated that changes should be effected if for no other reason than that the printer's views were probably indicative of the opinion of an "inconveniently large section of the general public." The following excerpt is taken from Joyce's reply to Richards written 5 May 1906. In it, Joyce defends his work and describes his intentions in* Dubliners.*]*

I am sorry you do not tell me why the printer, who seems to be the barometer of English opinion, refuses to print **"Two Gallants"** and makes marks in the margin of **"Counterparts."**

Is it the small gold coin in the former story or the code of honour which the two gallants live by which shocks him? I see nothing which should shock him in either of these things. His idea of gallantry has grown up in him (probably) during the reading of the novels of the elder Dumas and during the performance of romantic plays which presented to him cavaliers and ladies in full dress. But I am sure he is willing to modify his fantastic views. (pp. 132-33)

He has marked three passages in **"Counterparts"**:

> a man with two establishments to keep up, of course he couldn't. . . .
>
> Farrington said he wouldn't mind having the far one and began to smile at her. . . .
>
> She continued to cast bold glances at him and changed the position of her legs often; and when she was going out she brushed against his chair and said "Pardon!" in a Cockney accent.

His marking of the first passage makes me think that there is priestly blood in him: the scent for immoral allusions is certainly very keen here. To me this passage seems as childlike as the reports of divorce cases in *The Standard.* Or is it possible that this same printer (or maybe some near relative of his) will read (nay more, actually collaborate in) that solemn journal which tells its readers not merely that Mrs. So and So misconducted herself with Captain So and So but even how often she misconducted herself with him! The word "establishment" is surely as inoffensive as the word "misconducted."

It is easier to understand why he has marked the second passage, and evident why he has marked the third. But I would refer him again to that respectable organ the reporters of which are allowed to speak of such intimate things as even I, a poor artist, have but dared to suggest. O one-eyed printer! Why has he descended with his blue pencil, full of the Holy Ghost, upon these passages and allowed his companions to set up in type reports of divorce cases, and ragging cases and cases of criminal assault—reports, moreover, which are to be read by an "inconveniently large section of the general public."

There remains his final objection to the word "bloody." I cannot know, of course, from what he derives the word or whether, in his plain blunt way, he accepts it as it stands. In the latter case his objection is absurd and in the former case (if he follows the only derivation I have heard for it) it is strange that he should object more strongly to a profane use of the Virgin than to a profane use of the name of God. Where is his English Protestantism? I myself can bear witness that I have seen in modern English print such expressions as "by God" and "damn." Some cunning Jesuit must have tempted our stout Protestant from the path of righteousness that he defends the honour of the Virgin with such virgin ardour.

As for my part and share in the book I have already told all I have to tell. My intention was to write a chapter of the moral history of my country and I chose Dublin for the scene because that city seemed to me the centre of paralysis. I have tried to present it to the indifferent public under four of its aspects: childhood, adolescence, maturity and public life. The stories are arranged in this order. I have written it for the most part in a style of scrupulous meanness and with the conviction that he is a very bold man who dares to alter in the presentment, still more to deform, whatever he has seen and heard. I cannot do any more than this. I cannot alter what I have written. All these objections of which the printer is now the mouthpiece arose in my mind when I was writing the book, both as to the themes of the stories and their manner of treatment. Had I listened to them I would not have written the book. I have come to the conclusion that I cannot write without offending people. The printer denounces **"Two Gallants"** and **"Counterparts."** A Dubliner would denounce **"Ivy Day in the Committee-Room."** The more subtle inquisitor will denounce **"An Encounter,"** the enormity of which the printer cannot see because he is, as I said, a plain blunt man. The Irish priest will denounce **"The Sisters."** The Irish boarding-house keeper will denounce **"The Boarding-House."** Do not let the printer imagine, for goodness' sake, that he is going to have all the barking to himself.

I can see plainly that there are two sides to the matter but unfortunately I can occupy only one of them. I will not fall into the error of suggesting to you which side you should occupy but it seems to me that you credit the printer with too infallible a knowledge of the future. I know very little of the state of English literature at present nor do I know whether it deserves or not the eminence which it occupies as the laughing-stock of Europe. But I suspect that it will follow the other countries of Europe as it did in Chaucer's time. You have opportunities to observe the phenomenon at close range. Do you think that *The Second Mrs. Tanqueray* would not have been denounced by a manager of the middle Victorian period, or that a publisher of that period would not have rejected a book by George Moore or Thomas Hardy? And if a change is to take place I do not see why it should not begin now.

You tell me in conclusion that I am endangering my future and your reputation. I have shown you earlier in the letter the frivolity of the printer's objections and I do not see how the publication of ***Dubliners*** as it now stands in manuscript could possibly be considered an outrage on public morality. I am willing to believe that when you advise me not to persist in the publication of stories such as those you have returned to me you do so with a kind intention towards me: and I am sure you will think me wrong-headed in persisting. But if the art were any other, if I were a painter and my book were a picture you would be less ready to condemn me for wrong-headedness if I refused to alter certain details. These details may not seem to you unimportant but if I took them away ***Dubliners*** would seem to me like an egg without salt. In fact, I am somewhat curious to know what, if these and similar points have been condemned, has been admired in the book at all.

I see now that my letter is becoming nearly as long as my book. I have touched on every point you raise in order to give you reason for the faith that is in me. I have not, however, said what a disappointment it would be to me if you were unable to share my views. I do not speak so much of a material as of a moral disappointment. But I think I could more easily reconcile myself to such a disappointment than to the thousand little regrets and self-reproaches which would certainly make me their prey afterwards. (pp. 133-35)

James Joyce, in a letter to Grant Richards on May 5, 1906, in Letters of James Joyce, Vol. II, *edited by Richard Ellmann, Faber & Faber, 1966, pp. 132-34.*

GERALD GOULD (essay date 1914)

[*In the following appreciative review of* Dubliners, *Gould discusses the originality of Joyce's approach to fiction and the success of his narrative method.*]

It is easy to say of Gorky that he is a man of genius. To say the same of Mr. James Joyce requires more courage, since his name is little known; but a man of genius is precisely what he is. He has an original outlook, a special method, a complete reliance on his own powers of delineation and presentment. Whether his powers will develop, his scope widen, his sympathies deepen, or not—whether, in short, his genius is a large one or only a little one, I cannot pretend to say. Maturity and self-confidence in a first book (and I believe that, in prose, [***Dubliners***] is Mr. Joyce's first book) contain a threat as well as a promise. They hint at a set mode of thought rather than a developing capacity. Certainly the maturity, the individual poise and force of these stories are astonishing. The only recent work with which they suggest comparison is [George Douglas Brown's] *The House with the Green Shutters,* and even that was very different, for one heard in it the undertone of human complaint—its horrors were partly by way of expressing a personal unhappiness; while Mr. Joyce seems to regard this objective and dirty and crawling world with the cold detachment of an unamiable god.

He has plenty of humour, but it is always the humour of the fact, not of the comment. He dares to let people speak for themselves with the awkward meticulousness, the persistent incompetent repetition, of actual human intercourse. If you have never realised before how direly our daily conversation needs editing, you will realise it from Mr. Joyce's pages. One very powerful story, called **"Grace"**, consists chiefly of lengthy talk so banal, so true to life, that one can scarcely endure it—though one can still less leave off reading it. Here is one of the liveliest passages:

> "Pope Leo XIII," said Mr. Cunningham, "was one of the lights of the age. His great idea, you know, was the union of the Latin and Greek churches. That was the aim of his life."
>
> "I often heard he was one of the most intellectual men in Europe," said Mr. Power. "I mean apart from his being Pope."
>
> "So he was," said Mr. Cunningham, "if not *the* most so. His motto, you know, as Pope was *Lux upon Lux—Light upon Light.*"
>
> "No, no," said Mr. Fogarty eagerly. "I think you're wrong there. It was *Lux in Tenebris,* I think—*Light in Darkness.*"
>
> "O yes," said Mr. M'Coy, "Tenebrae."
>
> "Allow me," said Mr. Cunningham positively, "it was *Lux upon Lux.* And Pius IX his predecessor's motto was *Crux upon Crux*—that is, *Cross upon Cross*—to show the difference between their two pontificates."
>
> The inference was allowed. Mr. Cunningham continued.
>
> "Pope Leo, you know, was a great scholar and a poet."
>
> "He had a strong face," said Mr. Kernan.
>
> "Yes," said Mr. Cunningham. "He wrote Latin poetry."
>
> "Is that so?" said Mr. Fogarty.

You see the method? It is not employed only in conversation. The description of mood, of atmosphere, is just as detailed and just as relentless. Horrible sordid realities, of which you are not spared one single pang, close in upon you like the four walls of a torture-chamber. It is all done quite calmly, quite dispassionately, quite competently. It never bores. You sometimes rather wish it did, as a relief.

The best things in the book are **"Araby"**, a wonderful magical study of boyish affection and wounded pride, and **"The Dead"**, a long story (placed at the end) in which we begin with a queer old-fashioned dance, where the principal anxiety is whether a certain guest will arrive "screwed," and are led on through all the queer breathless banalities of supper and conversation and leave-taking till we find ourselves back with a husband and wife in their hotel bedroom, the husband's emotion stirred, the wife queerly remote and sad, remembering the boy, Michael Furey, whom she had loved and who had died because of her. To quote the end without the innumerable preparatory touches that prepare for it seems unfair; yet it must be quoted for its mere melancholy beauty:

> A few light taps upon the pane made him turn to the window. It had begun to snow again. He watched sleepily the flakes, silver and dark, falling obliquely against the lamplight. The time had come for him to set out on his journey westward. Yes, the newspapers were right: snow was general all over Ireland. It was falling on every part of the dark central plain, on the treeless hills, falling softly upon the Bog of Allen and, farther westward, softly falling into the dark mutinous Shannon waves. It was falling, too, upon every part of the lonely churchyard on the hill where Michael Furey lay buried. It lay thickly drifted on the crooked crosses and headstones, on the spears of the little gate, on the barren thorns. His soul swooned slowly as he heard the snow falling faintly through the universe and faintly falling, like the descent of their last end, upon all the living and the dead.

Frankly, we think it a pity (perhaps we betray a narrow puritanism in so thinking) that a man who can write like this should insist as constantly as Mr. Joyce insists upon aspects of life which are ordinarily not mentioned. To do him justice, we do not think it is a pose with him: he simply includes the "unmentionable" in his persistent regard. (pp. 374-75)

Gerald Gould, in a review of "Dubliners," in New Statesman, *Vol. III, No. 64, June 27, 1914, pp. 374-75.*

JOHN MACY (essay date 1922)

[*Macy was an American literary critic and editor of the* Boston Herald *and the* Nation. *His most important work was* The Spirit of American Literature *(1913), which denounced the genteel tradition and called for realism and the use of native materials in American literature. In the following excerpt, Macy praises the narrative subtlety and irony in* Dubliners.]

The sketches in ***Dubliners*** are perfect, each in its own way, and all in one way: they imply a vast deal that is not said. They are small as the eye-glass of a telescope is small; you look through them to depths and distances. They are a kind of short story almost unknown to the American magazine if not to the American writer. An American editor might read them for his private pleasure, but from his professional point of view he would not see that there was any story there at all. The American short story is explicit and thin as a moving-picture film; it takes nothing for granted; it knows nothing of the art of the hintful, the suggestive, the selected single detail which lodges fertilely in the reader's mind, begetting ideas and emotions. America is not the only offender (for patriotism is the fashion and bids criticism relent); there is much professional Irish humor which is funny enough but no more subtle than a shillalah. And English short stories, such at least as we see in magazines, are obvious and "express" rather than expressive. Joyce's power to disentangle a single thread from the confusion of life and let you run briefly back upon it until you encounter the confusion and are left to think about it yourself—that is a power rare enough in any literature.

Except one story, **"A Painful Case,"** I could not tell the plot of any of these sketches. Because there is no plot going from beginning to end. The plot goes from the surface inward, from a near view away into a background. A person appears for a moment—a priest, or a girl, or a small boy, or a street-corner tough, or a drunken salesman—and does and says things not extraordinary in themselves; and somehow you know all about these people and feel that you could think out their entire lives. Some are stupid, some are pathetic, some are funny in an unhilarious way. The dominant mood is irony. The last story in the book, **"The Dead,"** is a masterpiece which will never be popular, because it is all about living people; there is only one dead person in it and he is not mentioned until near the end. That's the kind of trick an Irishman like Synge or Joyce would play on us, and perhaps a Frenchman or a Russian would do it; but we would not stand it from one of our own writers. (pp. 320-22)

John Macy, "James Joyce," in his The Critical Game, *Boni and Liveright, Publishers, 1922, pp. 317-22.*

ALLEN TATE (essay date 1950)

[*A distinguished American poet and critic, Tate was closely associated with two American critical movements of the mid-twentieth century, the Agrarians and the New Critics. A conservative thinker and convert to Catholicism, Tate attacked the tradition of Western philosophy which he believed has alienated persons from themselves, one another, and from nature by divorcing intellectual from natural functions in human life. For Tate, literature is the principal form of knowledge and revelation which restores human beings to a proper relationship with nature and the spiritual realm. In the following excerpt, he praises "The Dead" as an example of Joyce's success in attributing symbolic value to naturalist, objective detail.*]

In **"The Dead"** James Joyce brings to the highest pitch of perfection in English the naturalism of Flaubert; it may be questioned whether his great predecessor and master was able so completely to lift the objective detail of his material up to the symbolic level, as Joyce does in this great story. If the art of naturalism consists mainly in making *active* those elements which had hitherto in fiction remained *inert,* that is, description and expository summary, the further push given the method by Joyce consists in manipulating what at first sight seems to be mere physical detail into dramatic symbolism. As Gabriel Conroy, the "hero" of **"The Dead,"** enters the house of his aunts, he flicks snow from his galoshes with his scarf; by the time the story ends the snow has filled all the visible earth, and stands as the symbol of the revelation of Gabriel's inner life.

Joyce's method is that of the roving narrator; that is to say, the author suppresses himself but does not allow the hero to tell his own story, for the reason that "psychic distance" is necessary to the end in view. This end is the *sudden* revelation to Gabriel of his egoistic relation to his wife and, through that revelation, of his inadequate response to his entire experience. Thus Joyce must establish his central intelligence through Gabriel's eyes, but a little above and outside him at the same time, so that we shall know him at a given moment only through what he sees and feels in terms of that moment.

The story opens with the maid, Lily, who all day has been helping her mistresses, the Misses Morkan, Gabriel's aunts, prepare for their annual party. Here, as in the opening paragraph of Joyce's other masterpiece in ***Dubliners,*** **"Araby,"** we open with a neutral or suspended point of view; just as Crane begins "The Open Boat" with: "None of them knew the color of the sky." Lily is "planted" because, when Gabriel arrives, he must enter the scene dramatically, and not merely be *reported* as entering; if his eye is to *see* the story, the eye must be established actively, and it is so established in the little incident with Lily. If he is to see the action for us, he must come authoritatively out of the scene, not throw himself at us. After he flicks the snow, he sounds his special note; it is a false note indicating his inadequate response to people and even his lack of respect for them. He refers patronizingly to Lily's personal life; when she cries out in protest, he makes it worse by offering her money. From that moment we know Gabriel Conroy, but we have not been *told* what he is: we have had him *rendered.*

In fact, from the beginning to the end of the story we are never told anything; we are shown everything. We are not told, for example, that the *milieu* of the story is the provincial, middle-class, "cultivated" society of Dublin at the turn of the century; we are not told that Gabriel represents its emotional sterility (as contrasted with the "peasant" richness of his wife Gretta), its complacency, its devotion to genteel culture, its sentimental evasion of "reality." All this we see dramatized; it is all made active. Nothing is given us from the externally omniscient point of view. At the moment Gabriel enters the house the eye shifts from Lily to Gabriel. It is necessary, of course, at this first appearance that *we* should see him: there is a brief description; but it is not Joyce's description: we see him as Lily sees him—or might see him if she had Joyce's superior command of the whole situation. This, in fact, is the method of **"The Dead."** From this point on we are never far from Gabriel's physical sight; we are constantly looking through his physical eyes at values and insights of which he is incapable. The significance of the *milieu,* the complacency of Gabriel's feeling for his wife, her romantic image of her lover Michael Furey, what Miss Ivors means in that particular society, would have been put before us, in the pre-James era in English fiction, as exposition and commentary through the direct intercession of the author; and it would have remained inert.

Take Miss Ivors: she is a flat character, she disappears the moment Joyce is through with her, when she has served his purpose. She is there to elicit from Gabriel a certain quality, his relation to his culture at the intellectual and social level; but she is not in herself a *necessary* character. It is to this sort of character, whose mechanical use must be given the look of reality, that James applied the term *ficelle*. She makes it possible for Joyce to charge with imaginative activity an important phase of Gabriel's life which he would otherwise have been compelled to give us as mere information. Note also that this particular *ficelle* is a woman: she stands for the rich and complex life of the Irish people out of which Gabriel's wife has come, and we are thus given a subtle dramatic presentation of a spiritual limitation which focuses symbolically, at the end of the story, upon his relation to his wife.

The examples of naturalistic detail which operate also at the symbolic level will sufficiently indicate to the reader the close texture of **"The Dead."** We should say, conversely, that the symbolism itself derives its validity from its being, in the first place, a visible and experienced moment in the consciousness of a character.

Take the incident when Gabriel looks into the mirror. It serves two purposes. First, we need to *see* Gabriel again and more closely than we saw him when he entered the house; we know him better morally and we must see him more clearly physically. At the same time, he looks into the mirror because he is not, and has never been, concerned with an objective situation; he is wrapped in himself. The mirror is an old and worn symbol of Narcissism, but here it is effective because its first impact is through the action; it is not laid on the action from the outside.

As the party breaks up, we see Gabriel downstairs; upstairs Mr. Bartell D'Arcy is singing (hoarsely and against his will) "The Lass of Aughrim." Gabriel looks up the stairs:

> A woman was standing near the top of the first flight, in the shadow also. He could not see her face but he could see the terra-cotta and salmon-pink panels of her skirt which the shadow made appear black and white. It was his wife. Gabriel was surprised at her stillness. . . .

She is listening to the song. As she stands, one hand on the banister, listening, Gabriel has an access of romantic feeling. "*Distant Music* he would call the picture if he were a painter." At this moment Gabriel's whole situation in life begins to be reversed, and because he will not until the end be aware of the significance of the reversal, its impact upon the reader from here on is an irony of increasing power. As he feels drawn to his wife, he sees her romantically, with unconscious irony, as "Distant Music," little suspecting how distant she is. He sees only the "lower" part of her figure; the "upper" is involved with the song, the meaning of which, for her, we do not yet know. The concealment of the "upper" and the visibility, to Gabriel, of the "lower," constitute a symbol, dramatically and naturalistically *active,* of Gabriel's relation to his wife: he has never acknowledged her spirit, her identity as a person; he knows only her body. And at the end, when he tries to possess her physically, she reveals with crushing force her full being, her own separate life, in the story of Michael Furey, whose image has been brought back to her by the singing of Mr. Bartell D'Arcy.

The image of Michael provides our third example. The incident is one of great technical difficulty, for no preparation, in its own terms, was possible. How, we might ask ourselves, was Joyce to convey to us (and to Gabriel) the reality of Gretta's boy lover? Could he let Gretta say that a boy named Michael Furey was in love with her, that he died young, that she had never forgotten him because, it seemed to her, he must have died for love of her? This would be mere statement, mere reporting. Let us see how Joyce does it.

> "Some one you were in love with?" he asked ironically.
>
> "It was a young boy I used to know," she answered, "named Michael Furey. He used to sing that song, 'The Lass of Aughrim.' He was very delicate."

Having established in the immediate dramatic context, in relation to Gabriel, her emotion for Michael, who had created for her a complete and inviolable moment, she is able to proceed to details which are living details because they have been acted upon by her memory: his big, dark eyes; his job at the gasworks; his death at seventeen. But these are not enough to create space around him, not enough to present his image.

> " . . . I heard gravel thrown up against the window. The window was so wet I couldn't see so I ran downstairs as I was and slipped out the back into the garden and there was the poor fellow at the end of the garden, shivering."

Up to this passage, we have been *told* about Michael; we now begin to *see* him. And we see him in the following passage:

> "I implored him to go home at once and told him he would get his death in the rain. But he said he did not want to live. I can see his eyes as well as well! He was standing at the end of the wall where was a tree."

Without the wall and the tree to give him space he would not exist; these details cut him loose from Gretta's story and present him in the round.

The overall symbol, the snow, which we first see as a scenic detail on the toe of Gabriel's galoshes, gradually expands until at the end it gathers up the entire action. The snow is the story. It is not necessary to separate its development from the dramatic structure or to point out in detail how at every moment, including the splendid climax, it reaches us through the eye as a naturalistic feature of the background. Its symbolic operation is of greater importance. At the beginning, the snow is the cold and even hostile force of nature, humanly indifferent, enclosing the warm conviviality of the Misses Morkan's party. But just as the human action in which Gabriel is involved develops in the pattern of the plot of Reversal, his situation at the end being the opposite of its beginning, so the snow reverses its meaning, in a kind of rhetorical dialectic: from naturalistic *coldness* it develops into a symbol of warmth, of expanded consciousness; it stands for Gabriel's escape from his own ego into the larger world of humanity, including "all the living and the dead." (pp. 10-15)

Allen Tate, "Three Commentaries: Poe, James, and Joyce," in The Sewanee Review, *Vol. LVIII, No. 1, Winter, 1950, pp. 1-15.*

STANISLAUS JOYCE (essay date 1954)

[Joyce is the younger brother of James Joyce. In the following excerpt, he recalls the biographical inspirations for several Dubliners *stories.]*

Criticism of my brother's novel *Ulysses* has become almost scientific. The genuine Joyce critic examines every word under a microscope, and, it must be admitted, often obtains illuminating results, but the same method is, I think, pernicious when applied to my brother's earlier work. It is true that *Ulysses* has, and was intended by its author to have, various levels of significance, but it is quite another matter when, as I have been informed, an American critic, using a like method, arrives at a conclusion regarding *Chamber Music* which is as absurd as it is unfounded. Still another American critic finds in the short story **"The Clay"** three levels of significance on which Maria is successively herself, a witch, and the Virgin Mary [see Marvin Magalaner, "The Other Side of James Joyce," in Additional Bibliography]. Though such critics are quite at sea, they can still have the immense satisfaction of knowing that they have dived into deeper depths than the author they are criticising ever sounded. I am in a position to state definitely that my brother had no such subtleties in mind when he wrote the story. (p. 526)

The stories in ***Dubliners*** were not chosen haphazardly; there is an underlying plan in the book. **"The Sisters," "Araby,"** and **"An Encounter"** are stories of adolescent life. **"The Sisters"** and **"Araby"** are purely fictional, but **"An Encounter"** is based on an actual incident that occurred to my brother and me when we planned and carried out a day's miching together. He was about twelve and I was about ten years of age at the time, and we did not understand what kind of individual we had encountered, but our suspicions were aroused. We thought he was a "queer juggins"—some kind of escaped lunatic—and we gave him the slip. Later my brother put him into the book as a by-product of English educational methods.

"Eveline" and **"Counterparts"** are stories from the life of clerks, female and male. **"A Painful Case"** and **"The Clay"** present types of celibates, male and female, but, by the way, though Maria is a virgin, she is not the Virgin Mary, and though she is a withered virgin, she is not a witch. **"Two Gallants"** is a story of bachelor life, **"A Little Cloud"** of married life, with the figure of a successful and impenitent bachelor in it to cause discord and cast a little cloud over married bliss. Between them **"The Boarding House"** serves as a connecting link. **"After the Race," "A Mother," "Ivy Day in the Committee Room," "Grace"** have as backgrounds respectively sporting, musical, political, and religious life in the Irish capital, while **"The Dead,"** which represents festive life, serves as a kind of boisterous chorus, which is suddenly interrupted to let the book end on a note of disillusionment and resignation, though not of despair.

My brother used to show me the stories page by page as he wrote them, and when he left Dublin and finally settled down in Trieste, he used to send me the stories and invite my criticism. This continued regularly until I joined him at Trieste.

I had unintentionally some part in the stories. **"A Painful Case"** is an imaginary portrait of what my brother thought I should become in middle age. The chance meeting with an unknown lady at a concert he found more or less as it is described in the story in a diary I used to keep and he used to read without troubling to ask permission. The rest is elaboration; there was no daughter at the concert, and if there was a husband I never met him. The lady, whose name I never knew, stopped me once that I remember in the street to ask me some conventional questions about my studies, and that was all. I was about eighteen then and should not have had the audacity to speak to her when I met her. Some of the traits he has borrowed from me are the hostility to socialism—my brother, for his part, in so far as he was anything politically, was a socialist—the insufferance of drunkenness,

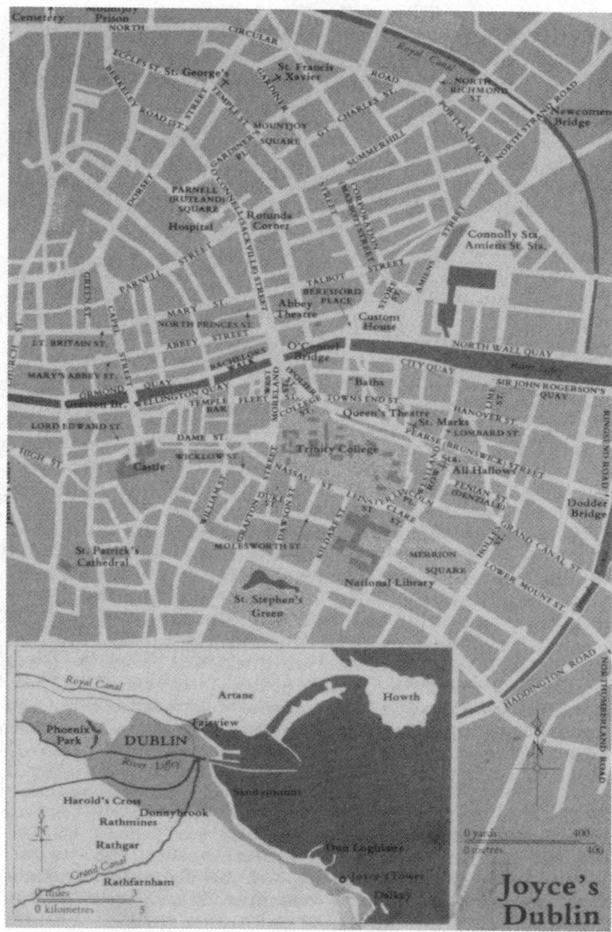

A map showing the locations of Dublin streets and landmarks made famous in Dubliners *and Joyce's later works.*

and the habit of taking notes (besides my diary) on a sheaf of papers. It was there he found the two epigrams which he used in the story. As I fancy few readers of ***Dubliners*** will remember them, I shall quote them. One is: Every bond is a bond to sorrow; the other reads: Love between man and man is impossible because there must not be sexual intercourse, and friendship between a man and a woman is impossible because there must be sexual intercourse. . . . Well, well! Concentrated wisdom and experience at eighteen years of age! However, the use my brother has made of them has redeemed them, and now they haunt my conscience a little less. In order to raise Mr. Duffy's cultural standard he has introduced a few traits taken from his own life, such as the translation of *Michael Kramer* and mention of Nietzsche, who interested me hardly at all, but he drew little from himself because he had reason not to consider himself a good type of celibate. In my diary, too, he found the conclusion for **"Counterparts."**

My brother was never in a committee room in his life. He got that background from my letters to him. I was once temporarily employed as a clerk for one of the candidates in the municipal elections in Dublin. My brother was in Paris at the time, and in my letters to him and later in conversation with him I described most of the characters that come into the story **"Ivy Day in the Committee-Room"**: the old caretaker, the shabby canvassers, the unfrocked priest. Instead, the poem on the death of Parnell, with which the story ends, is his own and is a very clever piece of work. It is deliberately bad, but as Mr. Colum observes [in his introduction to the Modern Library edition of ***Dubliners;*** see Additional Bibliography], in spite of the affected graces of the semi-illiterate poet who has written the poem, one is conscious of a real sorrow. He wrote the story some four or five years later in Trieste.

The second and third parts of **"Grace"** and some of the dialogue as it stands he found again in my diary, but he has used another incident for the first part and changed some of the characters. There is in the story a parody of the *Divina Commedia:* in the underground lavatory, *l'Inferno;* in bed at home convalescing, *il Purgatorio;* in church listening to a sermon, *il Paradiso.* The parody in no way detracts from my brother's almost boundless admiration for the *Divina Commedia.* In fact, his admiration for it had as a consequence so fierce a contempt for Milton's "Paradise Lost" as almost to give personal offence to the poets and men of letters in Dublin, Yeats excepted, to whom he expressed it. For the preacher of the sermon, Father Purdon, he has used the figure of Father Bernard Vaughan, a very popular preacher of that time who appeared sometimes in Dublin and whose name was frequently in the newspapers. He was a Jesuit, a member of an old English family, and a cleric in search of publicity, who besides preaching from his legitimate stage, the pulpit, used to deliver short man-to-man talks from inappropriate places, such as the boxing ring before a championship match. My brother has adorned him with the name which was the old name for the street of the brothels in Dublin—Purdon Street.

The idea for **"The Dead"** was suggested also by a letter of mine to my brother when he was already in Trieste. It came about in this way. The principal singer at a Moore Centenary Concert in Dublin—such was the name I remember, though 1805 was no special date in Moore's life—was a very well-known Irish baritone who lived in London, Plunket Green. As my father had sung with him in concerts when he was a young man and often used to speak of him, I went to hear him. The quality of his voice was somewhat harsh, I thought, but he could do what he liked with it. One of Moore's Irish melodies which he sang was "The Dead." When in the second verse of the song the dead speak, Plunket Green, instead of singing in sepulchral tones, used a plaintive pianissimo. The effect was electrifying. It reminded me of the lines of a cradle-song of Yeats':

The angels are stooping
Above your white bed;
They are weary of trooping
With the whimpering dead.

It sounded as if the dead were whimpering and jealous of the happiness of the living. My brother liked the idea and asked me to send him the song. I did so, but when he wrote the story some six or seven years later—so long it took to mature!—he preferred to use a west of Ireland ballad for the song which is the turning point of the story.

It may well seem from all this that I am laying claim to some part in my brother's work. That is not the case. A writer finds the material for his creative work everywhere—in his own experience, in something he has read or heard and reflected on, in conversation with others, in letters, even in chance words he has overheard. This quality of growth is one of the characteristics of genius, this fertility of the soil on which seed happens to fall. **"The Boarding House"** was suggested by the rude and fluent remarks about his landlady and her daughter made by a little Cockney who was the English teacher in the Berlitz School at Trieste when my brother was first transferred there; the idea for **"Two Gallants"** came from the mention of the relations between Porthos and the wife of a tradesman in *The Three Musketeers,* which my brother found in Ferrero's *Europa Giovane:* hence the title. Such trifles awoke a memory of Dublin in his brain; he saw the story clearly and was not at peace until he had put it on paper. In this sense ***Dubliners*** is as lyrical a work as *Chamber Music.*

As I shared my brother's life day by day, with brief intervals of separation, until January 1915, it was only natural that the promptings for stories should come more frequently from conversation and communication with me than with others; but in no case was it intentional on my part. For example, all the details for **"Ivy Day in the Committee Room"** except the final poem, as I have said, he took from letters of mine, but it had never occurred to me that there could be a story in them—I had written in a mood of disgust and anger—and still less had it occurred to me that by writing the story dispassionately one could raise oneself above all that mean, shiftless, poverty-stricken life and regard it without hatred, even with compassion and humour.

"Ivy Day in the Committee Room" was the story in ***Dubliners*** that my brother preferred, yet he, too, had his doubts as to whether it could be called a story. When the manuscript of ***Dubliners,*** rejected by the seventh or eighth publisher, came home to roost again, and I tried to counter his disappointment, he asked me ironically:

"Do you really think that all Europe is waiting to hear the story of the municipal election in the Royal Exchange Ward in Dublin?"

"Well, if you put it that way, of course not," I answered. "But I think all intelligent readers are waiting to come across something that is well written." (pp. 526-27)

In Zurich, where he lived during the war, he at first supported himself and his family by giving lessons, and amongst his pupils he had an elderly, cultured Viennese, to whom he lent his newly published book of stories. When his pupil brought it back, my brother asked him which story he liked best. Without hesitation the Viennese answered: **"Ivy Day in the Committee Room."**

My brother was astonished. "What on earth," he asked, "did you find to admire in that story?"

The Viennese laughed. "It amused me," said he, "because it is so like Vienna."

An Italian proverb says: *Tutto il mondo é paese*—the whole world is just one township.

For my part, the story which I consider the best in the collection is **"The Dead,"** and I am glad that my brother dictated the end of it to me, when eye trouble prevented him from writing. There is a mastery of story telling in the skill with which a crescendo of noise and jollity is gradually worked up and then suddenly silenced by the ghost of a memory that returns to blight the happiness of the living. Yet **"The Dead"** is not merely a Christmas ghost story and not merely technically clever. In **"The Dead"** the two polar attitudes of men towards women, that of the lover and that of the husband, are presented compassionately. It is not the eternal triangle of falsity and deception. The two men at different times in the woman's life have loved her with equal sincerity each in his way, and there is no guile in the woman. But one love is the enemy of the other, and the dead lover's romantic passion, outliving his mortal flesh, is still dominant in the woman's heart. . . .

My brother did not like the first stories, which had already appeared in a Dublin paper, and would have liked to re-write **"The Boarding House"** but for a fixed objection to changing or omitting anything he had published. Moreover, he always thought that his stories could interest only Dubliners and he struggled desperately to have his book published in Dublin. He failed: 1,000 copies of ***Dubliners*** ready for publication in Dublin were burned at the behest of a self-authorised vigilance committee. The struggle wasted years of his life and for a while sapped his energy. He had another book of stories in mind but no wish to get on with it. It was one round to the forces behind the scenes in Irish life, but by no means the last round. (p. 527)

Stanislaus Joyce, "The Background to 'Dubliners,' " in The Listener, *Vol. LI, No. 1308, March 25, 1954, pp. 526-27.*

HUGH KENNER (essay date 1955)

[*A Canadian critic, Kenner is the foremost chronicler and commentator on literary Modernism. He is best known for* The Pound Era *(1971), a massive study of the Modernist movement, and for his influential works on Samuel Beckett, T. S. Eliot, James Joyce, and Wyndham Lewis. In addition to his reputation as an important scholar, Kenner is also noted for his often eccentric judgments and a critical style that relies on surprising juxtapositions and wit. In the following excerpt from his study* Dublin's Joyce, *Kenner examines the narrative techniques through which Joyce aimed to expose the societal paralysis of turn-of-the-century Dublin in his short stories.*]

About 1905 Joyce wrote most of ***Dubliners,*** a whole which he conceived, with remarkable originality, less as a sequence of stories than as a kind of multi-faceted novel.

He wrote to a prospective publisher:

> I do not think that any writer has yet presented Dublin to the world. It has been a capital of Europe for thousands of years, it is supposed to be the second city of the British Empire and it is nearly three times as big as Venice. Moreover, on account of many circumstances which I cannot detail here, the expression Dubliner seems to me to bear some meaning and I doubt whether the same can be said for such words as "Londoner" and "Parisian". . . .

Dublin is not, that is, an agglomeration of residents, but a city. In its present paralysis, it remains a ghost, not a heap of bones: the ghost of the great conception of the City which polarizes the mind of Europe from the time of Pericles to that of Dr. Johnson. Mr. Eliot saw London as "a heap of broken images"; Joyce's Dublin had none of the random quality characterized by "heap." It was a shell of grandeur populated by wraiths. The *integritas* of the aesthetic image corresponds to something still at a minimal level of organization vitally present in the object of contemplation; but it isn't the sort of organization that fuses in a single action or demands a single narrative. This image Joyce fragmented along its inherent lines of cleavage, the parts he disposed to afford one another the maximum of reinforcement. . . .

> My intention was to write a chapter of the moral history of my country, and I chose Dublin for the scene because that city seemed to me the centre of paralysis. I have tried to present it to the indifferent public under four of its aspects: childhood, adolescence, maturity, and public life. The stories are arranged in this order. I have written it for the most part in a style of scrupulous meanness and with the conviction that he is a very bold man who dares to alter in the presentment, still more to deform, whatever he has seen and heard . . . [see excerpt by Joyce dated 1906].

It is not a sort of photography that the last clause recommends. The precise locutions, gestures, and things out of which the aesthetic image is being synthesized must not be "dented for a phrase's sake" nor reduced to accessory status as bits of "local colour" subserving a conceptual simplification of their meaning. "The artist who could disentangle the subtle soul of the image from its mesh of defining circumstances most exactly and re-embody it in artistic circumstances chosen as the most exact for its new office, he was the supreme artist." (pp. 48-9)

Laying hold on the subject, not expressing an attitude to it, sometimes gave Joyce more trouble than such minutiae would imply. One story, the first, **"The Sisters,"** actually got published [in *Irish Homestead* (13 August 1904)] with traces of beginner's disdain scarring its paragraphs. (p. 50)

In the revised text a thematic statement of hopeless paralysis is the first sentence in the book. The paralysed priest in his arm-chair near the fire is as Stanislaus Joyce confirms [in the *Hudson Review;* see Additional Bibliography] intended as "a symbol of Irish life, priest-ridden and semi-paralysed." By presenting the interactions of this image with the consciousness of a young boy, Joyce introduces at the outset what was to be the scourge of an older boy in a later book: "a malevolent reality behind those things I say I fear" [*A Portrait of the Artist as a Young Man*]. The young boy is a generic Dubliner, or rather the Dubliner is a generic boy, for whom everything beyond the level of reality represented by boot-heels is vaguely dangerous: for a grownup too dangerous to bear thinking about, though a child may feel the fascination of evil, and if unusually tenacious may grow up capable of recording it. The terrible image on which **"The Sisters"** closes displays this dimension of Dublin religion exaggerated to a point where it captures the speculation even of adult women:

> ". . . And what do you think but there he was, sitting up by himself in the dark in his confession-box, wide-awake and laughing-like softly to himself?"
>
> She stopped suddenly as if to listen. I too listened; but there was no sound in the house: and I knew that the old priest was lying still in his coffin as we had seen him, solemn and truculent in death, an idle chalice on his breast.
>
> Eliza resumed:
>
> "Wide-awake and laughing-like to himself. . . . So then, of course, when they saw that, that made them think that there was something gone wrong with him. . . ."

This laughter is a dissolution of intolerable tension, as the ego tortured by the strains and responsibilities of mediation with the supernatural retreats into the world of boot-heels and snuff. It is of a piece with the pathic conviviality of the Dublin tavern. "He was too scrupulous always," the sister says; "the duties of the priesthood was too much for him"; and the boy had wondered how anyone ever had the courage to undertake responsibilities so grave as those the priest outlined to him. The old man, "too scrupulous always," had attempted to serve the supernatural world on its own terms. Relinquishing that attempt in hysterical laughter, he relapsed into the mode of the less scrupulous everyday priest: moral predicaments became complicated logical questions, the responses of the Mass were pattered through with a boy by rote, the works of the Fathers were "as thick as the *Post Office Directory* and as closely printed as the law notices in the newspaper."

It is the *mechanism* of his paralysed life that needs to be pondered. It offers a complex image of what growing up in Dublin amounted to. The old priest had faced, grappled with, and been bested by the world of mysterious malevolence with which the imagination of the small boy is fascinated. Human kind cannot bear even that much reality. Such as he is will, in a different mode, that boy most probably be: a cheerful habitual inhabitant of the boot-heel world. Such as he is the less scrupulous clergy have always been, though no one calls them mad. He tried, and failed. His paralysis foreshadows that of, say, Father Purdon in **"Grace,"** who without uneasiness speaks the habitual idiom of the business world because he is too coarse-textured ever to have tried:

> But one thing only, he said, he would ask of his hearers. And that was: to be straight and manly with God. If their accounts tallied in every point to say:
>
> "Well, I have verified my accounts. I find all well."
>
> But if, as might happen, there were some discrepancies, to admit the truth, to be frank and say like a man:
>
> "Well, I have looked into my accounts. I find this wrong and this wrong. But, with God's grace, I will rectify this and this. I will set right my accounts."

Of Joyce's four divisions, Childhood includes the first three stories, Youth, Maturity, and Public Life four each. These are phases in the onset of the paralysis imaged in **"The Sisters"**; the final story, **"The Dead,"** exhibits it as a living death. A developing mode of consciousness is carefully controlled throughout the book.

The theme of the two modes of priesthood runs from **"The Sisters"** through **"An Encounter"** to **"Araby,"** at which point, with the passing of childhood, the scrupulous and imaginative mode loses its resilience for good. In **"An Encounter,"** Joe Dillon, who used to caper around the garden, "an old tea-cosy on his head, beating a tin with his fist and yelling: 'Ya! yaka, yaka, yaka!' " (like the vested priest at his Latin ritual, or David dancing before the ark) proves to have a vocation for the priesthood: an ebullient young Irishman whom nothing mysterious will much trouble or puzzle. In **"Araby,"** the boy-narrator imagines himself in the streets "bearing his chalice safely through a throng of foes"—as scrupulous as the paralysed Father Flynn, but more cautious; Father Flynn, we remember, broke his chalice. **"The Sisters"** and **"An Encounter,"** moreover, are linked by father-images. The pervert who interrupts the truant boys' expedition to the Pigeon-house with his talk of whipping "as if he were unfolding some elaborate mystery," and his ambivalent injunctions concerning love (it is by turns natural, a furtive secret, and an occasion for flagellation) is very much like the "malevolent reality" itself: he and Father Flynn exist in a complex relation to one another. And with this man's appearance the mysterious is deflected towards the sexual. In **"Araby"** the sexual achieves glamorous awakening, and the chalice of youthful confident enterprise is broken against deglamouring inadequacy—the late arrival, the empty bazaar, impractical porcelain vases and flowered tea-sets, two pennies and sixpence. Every kind of frustration is implied in the last two pages of **"Araby."** The great empty hall is a female symbol, entered at last; and it contains only sparse goods, the clink of money, and tittering banalities.

> Nearly all the stalls were closed, and the greater part of the hall was in darkness. I recognized a silence like that which prevades a church after a service.

It was in a dark deserted chapel late at night that Father Flynn had sat in his confession-box laughing softly to himself. The confessional motif gets its final twist:

> Gazing up into the darkness I saw myself as a creature driven and derided by vanity; and my eyes burned with anguish and anger.

The next sequence balances two feminine and two masculine modes. Eveline torn between Frank and her father, tugged by the injunction of her dead mother, and reaching at last the automatic decision of inaction, "passive, like a helpless animal"; Polly of the banished father and the unspoken understanding with her mother ("As Polly was very lively the intention was to give her the run of the young men") reclining after her *geste* with "no longer any perturbation visible on her face" and collaborating in the manoeuvring of the hapless Mr. Doran into her noose: these are the feminine polarities—virgin and temptress—between which all Joyce's women oscillate.

Eveline is the book's second thematic image of paralysis. She is not a protagonist, like Father Flynn, but a mirror. The stress falls less on her intrinsic drabness than on the masculine world (Dublin) in which she is placed and the materials it has given her mind to feed on. It is a choice rather than a judgment that she is called on to make. The substance of the story, her reverie, is entirely in the mode of passion: not a balancing of arguments but the counterposition of the familiar room, the romance surrounding Frank, her father's contrary moods, the music of the distant street-organ.

Between her and the "lively" Polly two male modalities are poised to complete Joyce's generic fourfold pattern. In **"After the Race"** "life" is imaged as reckless action—Stephen Dedalus' "spell of arms and voices" explicitly geared to the petroleum-reeking Call of the Open Road. "The journey laid a magical finger on the genuine pulse of life and gallantly the machinery of human nerves strove to answer the bounding courses of the swift blue animal": which components are alive in this sentence and which are dead? Zestful technology is shored against Dublin drabness: "At the crest of the hill at Inchicore sightseers had gathered in clumps to watch the cars careering homeward and through this channel of poverty and inaction the Continent sped its wealth and industry." "The French, moreover, were virtual victors." Ah, Paris!

Jimmy Doyle, who becomes infatuated with continental swish and gambles away the patrimony he had intended to invest, is an avatar of Stephen Dedalus and a Dublin's-eye parody of Jimmy Joyce. The motor racing, the dress clothes, the dancing on the yacht ("this was seeing life"), the drinking, the wild card games, are all versions of the anti-Dublin, and that is their attraction for Jimmy. The impecunious artist Villona meanwhile follows their follies, entertains them, and lets in epiphanic light at the end: "Daybreak, gentlemen!" (The young Joyce made a few shillings during his first bleak winter in Paris by interviewing a French motor-racing driver for the *Irish Times.*)

Jimmy forsaking the "channel of poverty and inaction" for Ségouin's jet-propelled "life" inverts Eveline's failure to choose life with the "kindly, manly, openhearted" Frank in Buenos Aires. The connections of the second masculine story in the section, **"Two Gallants,"** are with the second feminine world, the Boarding House of cynical put-up jobs. Metaphors of prostitution reverberate through both stories: Corley and Lenehan, achieving at the end of their adventure the small gold coin, emerge as male street-walkers; as for Mrs. Mooney's Boarding House, "All the resident young men spoke of her as *The Madam.*"

By now the archetypal action of every Joyce work is in full swing. The gentle lyric antitheses of the first pages are growing sharper, as the consciousness divided between the public fact and the private dream incarnates its conflicting elements in the two kinds of men and two kinds of women who people the epic phase. Later these people will start meeting one another and realize dimly that they are meeting themselves.

The four stories of maturity rearrange the antitheses of the preceding section. This time two masculine worlds are followed by two feminine ones; more accurately, since the protagonist of **"A Painful Case"** is a male clerk, two modes of ethos are followed by two of pathos.

"A Little Cloud" exhibits the components of **"After the Race"** in a more complex context. As Bloom and Dedalus, as Watson and Holmes, the palefaced Little Chandler encounters the Noble Savage Gallaher who has Been Abroad and Got On, and by osmosis acquires a timid share of his virtues. The opposites, as always, belong to the same species: the feminine Chandler with his "quiet voice" and "refined" manners confronts the *pseudo*-masculine incarnation of irrational know-how. For the first time in the book, the utter absence of an organic community begins to be insisted on: the "mansions in which the old nobility of Dublin had roystered" are "spectral" now, and no memory of the past touches Chandler. Incommunicable loneliness has superseded the bravado of adolescence. Chandler has none of Lenehan's resilience. His shyness prevents his reading the poetry-books of his bachelor days to his wife: "At times he repeated lines to himself and this consoled him."

As for Gallaher, his positives are those of the impresario only. The key-words of the paragraph in which he is first allowed to emerge at length are tellingly vague. We hear first of "greatness," and the early sign of that greatness was that people used to say he was "wild." But nobody denied him "talent." There was "a certain . . . something" in him that impressed you. Finally it emerges: " . . . he kept up a bold face."

The osmotic interchange begins in the eighth line of the story: "It was something to have a friend like that." As he goes off to meet the anarchic journalist (for that is Gallaher's profession) Chandler feels "superior to the people he passed." His ambitions rise toward the Life Literary in emulation: "He wondered whether he could write a poem to express his idea. . . . He was not sure what idea he wished to express but the thought that a poetic moment had touched him took life within him like an infant hope." Communion is achieved for half a page; the rift begins with Gallaher's patronizing preference for liquor neat, widens through the clash of Chandler's wistful dream of Europe against Gallaher's reportage, and climaxes with Chandler's discovery that his prudent marriage earns him no advantage in Gallaher's eyes. He remains uneasily pestered by Gallaher's image of marriage as the poor man's fornication, attempts a Gallaherian gesture of "living bravely" by shouting "Stop!" to the crying child, and subsides into tears of remorse.

Thus the dialectic of **"A Little Cloud"**; **"Counterparts"** repeats its action in a more automatic fashion. The employer's rebuke is exhibited as response-to-stimulus; his fist "seemed to vibrate like the knob of some electric machine," and his voice in the first sentence of the story emerges from a speaking-tube. The context of the story is mechanism. Farrington is a copying-machine geared to a law-machine. The human cogs and levers of the story whirr and jerk as the rebuke administered by the employer passes through them and emerges at the other end as the flailing of a cane on the thighs of a small boy. In **"A Little Cloud"** there was no community, only loneliness; in **"Counterparts"** there is a pseudo-community of drinking, sterile emulation, action and reaction: a sketch for the monstrous robot body that dominates *Ulysses.*

Maria is **"Clay"** as humanity itself, as susceptible to moulding, and as death in life. Joe's wife, another Mrs. Mooney, has eased her into the laundry and one may suspect will soon ease her into a convent: and Maria, one is sure, will never quite realize how she got there. The omen she touches is that of death; when she laughs the tip of her nose nearly meets the tip of her chin—like a Hallowe'en witch—and like a banished ghost she returns to Joe's fireside, until cockcrow on All Hallow's Eve. The error in her song, parallels her recurrent failure to get the ring; the song should have gone on to treat of marriage:

> I dreamt that suitors sought my hand
> That knights on bended knee,
> And with vows no maiden heart could withstand
> They pledged their hearts to me.
>
> And I dreamt that one of that noble band
> Came forth my heart to claim
> But I also dreamt, which charmed me most,
> That you loved me just the same.

"A Painful Case" occupies the mid-point of the book. It gathers up, specifically, the implications of the third group: Chandler's loneliness, Farrington's automatism (Mr. Duffy "lived at a little distance from his body, regarding his own acts with doubtful side-glances"), Maria's living death. Mr. Duffy is carefully presented for three pages as a person of absolute meticulous voluntary routine. The rare inscribing of sentences in a commonplace-book (held together by a brass pin) is as glamourless an action as is the business of the bank from which at four o'clock daily he is "set free." Passion when it intersects his life proves impossibly circumstanced; he rebukes it; he is touched as by a ghost; and his newly emotionalized mental life, brings an eerie ultimate awareness of the loneliness he has until then accepted with his intellect only.

Now that the ghosts have begun to swarm (we are entering

the regions of **"The Dead"**) we become aware that it is a living death that the book is presenting. The action of story after story has taken place at night or in twilight; and from **"A Little Cloud"** to **"Ivy Day in the Committee Room"** the season is autumn. **"A Painful Case"** is the first adumbration of **"The Dead"**: passion missed and returning as the phantom touch of a hand, a hallucinatory voice, cold air creeping into the sleeves of a coat. The malevolent realities surrounding the innocent protagonist of the first part of the book are now part of the texture of life; but the antithesis to the world of boot-heels is no longer the mysterious power that had cracked the mind of its sacerdotal servant: rather, the multiplication of spectres of choices negated, passions unexplored, opportunities missed, aspects of the self denied. The alter ego who returned in the flesh to Little Chandler returns as a wraith to Mr. Duffy.

The theme of might-have-been is endemic to Joyce's books: Richard Rowan's fear lest he deprive his wife of some moments of passion that ought to have been hers, Stephen's speculation ("Weave, weaver of the wind") on the events of history "lodged in the room of the infinite possibilities they have ousted," Anna Livia's disillusion as her Prince Charming's coach dwindles back into a pumpkin: "I thought you were all glittering with the noblest of carriage. You're only a bumpkin. I thought you the great in all things, in guilt and in glory. You're but a puny. Home!" Its layers of meaning are numerous. It is the paralysis of the City, at one level; the rhythm of the Dubliners' lives rises to no festivity and is sustained by no community; in the drabness of mediaeval peasant life without its seasonal joyfulness, they oscillate between bricks and ghosts. It is the paralysis of the person, at another level, though it is seldom evident that these persons are so circumstanced that they might have chosen differently. But at the most important level it is metaphysical: the Exiles are exiled from the garden, and the key to their plight, as *Finnegans Wake* brings forward, is the Fall. Joyce's world, as the Rev. Walter Ong has written of Kafka's, "is governed by the sense in which man's actions are carried on in a setting to which they are irrelevant." Father Ong goes on to define "the great fiction of the West; the self-possessed man in the self-possessed world, the fiction which seeks to erase all sense of plight, of confusing weakness, from man's consciousness, and which above all will never admit such a sense as a principle of operation." Man so constituted, he notes, cannot afford to *give,* since giving recognizes the fact of *otherness,* of a portion of being neither susceptible to his control nor violable to his gaze; this works out alike between man and man, and between man and God. It is precisely this fiction of self-containment that Joyce defines in successively more elaborate images, from Mr. Duffy's careful control over every detail of life through the tightly-bounded ethical world of *Exiles* and Stephen's "All or not at all" to HCE's solipsistic nightmare. What beats against all these people is the evidence of otherness: the ghosts in ***Dubliners,*** Richard Rowan's voices on the strand at dawn, Stephen's fear of a "malevolent reality" and his collapse into Dublin itself ("I have much, much to learn"), the voices and tappings that derange Earwicker's slumbers like leaves, twigs, and stones dropped into a pool that craves stagnation.

The focus of Mr. Duffy's plight is achieved in exactly these terms. During his evenings of intellectual friendship with Mrs. Sinico,

> Sometimes he caught himself listening to the sound of his own voice. He thought that in her eyes he would ascend to an angelical stature; and, as he attached the fervent nature of his companion more and more closely to him, he heard the strange impersonal voice which he recognized as his own, insisting on the soul's incurable loneliness. We cannot give ourselves, it said: we are our own. The end of these discourses was that one night during which she had shown every sign of unusual excitement, Mrs. Sinico caught up his hand passionately and pressed it to her cheek.

"Her interpretation of his words disillusioned him." Her touch brings otherness, a world of passion lying outside his controlled and swept and tidied world, a denial of the voice which says "We are our own." The "strange impersonal" quality of that voice is Mr. Duffy's kind of gratuitous illusion, comparable to the dry detachment with which he had translated *Michael Kramer,* the stage directions written in purple ink, trying to pretend that someone else did it, some perfected self disengaged from the tensions of the drama. The voice *is* his own, as Joyce knew and as Duffy himself half recognizes. That is what is unforgivable, that she should challenge his self-sufficiency; and he is thrown off balance, breaks off the affair, and after a false quiet steps into hell.

The public life stories are ampler looks round at the same material, with a shift of emphasis to the social manifestations of self-sufficiency. They enact a muted scherzo between the first climax of the book, Mr. Duffy's contact with the dead and his conviction of haunted aloneness, and the long final epiphany, **"The Dead."**

In **"Ivy Day in the Committee Room"** the perspectives of **"A Painful Case"** begin to expand. The shadow of Parnell to whom they had made years before the one act of faith of which they were capable lies over not just one man but a roomful of paralytics. Political activity in the vacuum left by his departure consists of a few futile gestures, sporadic interviews with voters, and much meditative drinking of stout by an October fire. Edward VII, the surrogate father, is the focus of mild colloquial dissension; the betrayed dead father Parnell stirs into life through a piece of turgidly sincere declamation: our first impressive evidence of Joyce's ability to write just the right kind of bad rhetoric without cynicism. They are the received locutions of Dublin execrably joined, yet a real grief and loyalty break through.

In **"A Mother"** factitious culture and gratuitous pride collaborate; in **"Grace,"** gratuitous friendship and factitious religiosity. The absence in these two stories of the circumambient dead, so insistently dominant in the preceding three, is not accidental. We are in touch here with the carapace alone, public life in the boot-heel world. It is not into the communion of saints that his friends' little plot and Father Purdon's urbanely muscular sermon induct Mr. Kernan. "If he might use the metaphor, he said, he was their spiritual accountant"; nothing could make the point more clearly than the presentation of redeeming spiritual wisdom in two pages of indirect discourse. From his *selva oscura* at the foot of the lavatory steps, up to the nipping air, then via a sick bed to a Jesuit Paradiso of "decorous atmosphere" on Gardiner Street, where his party settles down "in the form of a quincunx" (Dante's courageous made such a cross, in the fifth heaven—*Paradiso* XIV)—Mr. Kernan has been led through a Dublin *Commedia.*

> The gentlemen were all well dressed and orderly.

> The light of the lamps of the church fell upon an assembly of black clothes and white collars, relieved here and there by tweeds, on dark mottled pillars of green marble and on lugubrious canvases. The gentlemen sat in the benches, having hitched their trousers slightly above their knees and laid their hats in security. They sat well back and gazed formally at the distant speck of red light which was suspended before the high altar.

> O abbondante grazia, ond' io presunsi
> ficcar lo viso per la luce eterna
> tanto che la veduta vi consunsi!
> *Paradiso* XXXIII, 82-84

When the preacher enters, they produce handkerchiefs, and kneel upon them "with care."

"A Mother" and **"Grace"** bring to maximal articulation the world which the young narrator of **"The Sisters"** had glimpsed in contemplating the untidy hooking of the old woman's skirt and the heels of her cloth boots trodden down all to one side: that epiphany, we remember, took place at prayer.

The motifs of **"The Dead"** are drawn, in ways we need not detail, from all the stories in the book, but its peculiar modes of consciousness are in touch with **"The Sisters"** at the beginning and with the **"Clay"—"Painful Case"—"Ivy Day"** group in the centre. It is towards the definition of living death, as we saw in connection with **"Clay,"** that the entire book is oriented; the first point to grasp about **"The Dead"** is the universal reference of the title. "I had not thought death had undone so many"; in reading *The Waste Land* aloud Mr. Eliot puts the stress not on "death" but on "undone." The link, through the quotation, with the outer circle of Dante's hell, the souls who lived without blame and without praise, the world of the Hollow Men, is an Eliotic perspective of the utmost relevance to Joyce's story. In **"The Dead"** everybody is dead. Its Prufrock-world of dinner-parties, elderly aunts, young topers, old lechers, and after-dinner wit ("He ran over the heads of his speech. Irish hospitality, sad memories, the Three Graces, Paris, the quotation from Browning," is summed up in the story of the factory horse that exasperated the fashionable pretensions of its rider by walking round and round the statue of King Billy as around the millshaft. Music, the subject on which these Dubliners are most articulate, is discussed solely in terms of the good old days. And the most living influence in the story is the memory, enclosed in music, of a dead peasant boy.

> We have lingered in the chambers of the sea
> By sea-girls wreathed with seaweed red and brown
> Till human voices wake us, and we drown.

We drown: "His own identity was fading out into a grey impalpable world: the solid world itself, which these dead had one time reared and lived in, was dissolving and dwindling."

Like the first story in the book, the last presents a world of death dominated by two wraith-like sisters. The priest who had been first deranged, then paralysed, then dead had enacted, we now see in retrospect, a symbolic role of much complexity. The sisters Morkan are custodians of a ritual order, comprising every component of the culture of eighteenth-century Dublin, in whose vitality it is now impossible to feel much faith. It does not, we are made to feel, stand of itself; the being of its world of light, movement, quadrilles, music, and banqueting is sustained, like an underwater bubble, by the pressure of the dark snowy boundlessness outside. Gaiety is oddly unspontaneous, a function of custom, habit, and encouragement:

> A red-faced young woman, dressed in pansy, came into the room, excitedly clapping her hands and crying:
>
> "Quadrilles! Quadrilles!"
>
> Close on her heels came Aunt Kate, crying:
>
> "Two gentlemen and three ladies, Mary Jane!" . . .
>
> As the piano had twice begun the prelude to the first figure Mary Jane led her recruits quickly from the room.

The cultural order has shifted, since Swift's time, from the masculine to the feminine mode. Art is discussed, in terms of performers. Creation is unthought of. The world of art is an established order which undergoes the homage of ritual performance. At the same level of triviality, the discussion shifts from art to religion: the pattern of living death emerges:

> He was astonished to hear that the monks never spoke, got up at two in the morning, and slept in their coffins. He asked what they did it for.
>
> "That's the rule of the order," said Aunt Kate firmly.
>
> "Yes, but why?" asked Mr. Browne.
>
> Aunt Kate repeated that it was the rule, that was all. . . .

As for the celebration of artistic mysteries, the respect in which it is surrounded is one of the polite conventions (cf. "the rule of the order") dominated by the Sisters:

> Gabriel could not listen while Mary Jane was playing her Academy piece, full of runs and difficult passages, to the hushed drawing-room. He liked music but the piece she was playing had no melody for him and he doubted whether it had any melody for the other listeners, though they had begged Mary Jane to play something. Four young men, who had come from the refreshment-room to stand in the doorway at the sound of the piano, had gone away quietly in couples after a few minutes. The only persons who seemed to follow the music were Mary Jane herself, her hands racing along the keyboard or lifted from it at the pauses like those of a priestess in momentary imprecation, and Aunt Kate standing at her elbow to turn the page.

The "Academy piece," the departure of the young men "in couples" (moral support for unobtrusive defection), the "priestess" gestures of the performer, the dominating presence of Aunt Kate expediting the mechanism of a culture still in some sense real to her alone, none of these details is accidental. As for male vitality, we have Mr. Browne:

> Then he asked one of the young men to move aside, and, taking hold of the decanter, filled out for himself a goodly measure of whisky. The young men eyed him respectfully while he took a trial sip.
>
> "God help me," he said, smiling, "it's the doctor's orders."
>
> His wizened face broke into a broader smile, and the three young ladies laughed in musical echo to

> his pleasantry, swaying their bodies to and fro, with nervous jerks of their shoulders. The boldest said:
>
> "O, now, Mr. Browne, I'm sure the doctor never ordered anything of the kind."

—and Freddy Malins:

> Mr. Browne, whose face was once more wrinkling with mirth, poured out for himself a glass of whisky while Freddy Malins exploded, before he had well reached the climax of his story, in a kink of high-pitched bronchitic laughter and, setting down his untasted and overflowing glass, began to rub the knuckles of his left fist backwards and forwards into his left eye, repeating words of his last phrase as well as his fit of laughter would allow him.

We are made to feel the artificially fostered isolation of this merriment in countless insidious ways. Physical separation from Dublin is implied not only by the frequent references to the cold and dark out of which the visitors emerge, but by the setting itself, a "dark gaunt house on Usher's Island, the upper part of which they had rented from Mr. Fulham, the corn-factor on the ground floor," which emerges oddly during the scenes of leavetaking as a gaslit oasis in Limbo. Death is written on the face of Aunt Julia ("Her hair, drawn low over the tops of her ears, was grey; and grey also, with darker shadows, was her large flaccid face. Though she was stout in build and stood erect, her slow eyes and parted lips gave her the appearance of a woman who did not know where she was or where she was going") and life on the face of Aunt Kate suggests comparison to "a shrivelled red apple." Aunt Julia sings "Arrayed for the Bridal," and Gabriel catching the haggard look on her face foresees her death.

It is, significantly, through Gabriel that the anachronistic factitious quality of the evening's merriment emerges in definitive fashion:

> One boot stood upright, its limp upper fallen down: the fellow of it lay upon its side. He wondered at his riot of emotions of an hour before. From what had it proceeded? From his aunt's supper, from his own foolish speech, from the wine and dancing, the merrymaking when saying goodnight in the hall, the pleasure of the walk along the river in the snow. Poor Aunt Julia! She, too, would soon be a shade with the shade of Patrick Morkan and his horse. . . .

Gabriel's emotional organization was completed in his youth, in isolation from their world:

> The indelicate clacking of the men's heels and the shuffling of their soles reminded him that their grade of culture differed from his

—and now in isolation from every context. Boots speak as they did to the boy in **"The Sisters."** Like Mr. Duffy, Gabriel has constructed about himself an armour of isolation; his own voice speaks to him in countless forms, as it did to Mr. Duffy: "We cannot give ourselves, it said; we are our own." The question, for Gabriel, is only what posture to adopt for minimal friction:

> He would only make himself ridiculous by quoting poetry to them which they could not understand. They would think that he was airing his superior education. He would fail with them just as he had failed with the girl in the pantry. He had taken up a wrong tone. His whole speech was a mistake from first to last, an utter failure.

Lily, the caretaker's daughter, whose pale name is the first word in the story, is only the first of the women who rebuff Gabriel. He is heckled by his wife, by his two aunts, by Miss Ivors; and his wife at the end turns from him for a shade. It is his know-how, chiefly, that commands respect:

> He felt quite at ease now for he was an expert carver and liked nothing better than to find himself at the head of a well-laden table.

Gabriel, then, and the Morkan party are analogous worlds: analogous in their incurable autonomy. He is one closed system. The scheme of values expressed at the annual dance is another. The enveloping background of both is the snow. Gabriel emerges into the house from the snow as from an invigorating medium:

> He continued scraping his feet vigorously while the three women went upstairs, laughing, to the ladies' dressing-room. A light fringe of snow lay like a cape on the shoulders of his overcoat and like toecaps on the toes of his goloshes; and, as the buttons of his overcoat slipped with a squeaking noise through the snow-stiffened frieze, a cold, fragrant air from out-of-doors escaped from crevices and folds.

Their laughter recedes from him; the snow, the "cold, fragrant air," standing for something like Ibsen's envacuumed Norway, is his element. Between his round of infighting with Miss Ivors and the necessities of the dinner-table speech in tribute to the aunts whom he privately reduces to "two ignorant old women," his mind turns to the snow again with longing:

> Gabriel's warm trembling fingers tapped the cold pane of the window. How cool it must be outside! How pleasant it would be to walk out alone, first along by the river and then through the park! The snow would be lying on the branches of the trees and forming a bright cap on the top of the Wellington Monument. How much more pleasant it would be there than at the supper-table!

The meaning of this desire is clarified much later, when at the beginning of the walk home Gabriel's imagination yields to the passion that is to suffer such deflation in the hotel-room:

> Moments of their secret life together burst like stars upon his memory. . . . He was standing with her in the cold, looking in through a grated window at a man making bottles in a roaring furnace. It was very cold. Her face, fragrant in the cold air, was quite close to his; and suddenly he called out to the man at the furnace:
>
> "Is the fire hot, sir?"
>
> But the man could not hear with the noise of the furnace. It was just as well. He might have answered rudely.

The invigorating cold stands for something complexly intrinsic to Gabriel's psychic balance. It is that against which his animal warmth is asserted: an obeisant medium presenting no diplomatic puzzles. And it is the brisk vacant context of his ideal passion for Gretta, once experienced and now remembered, in which they exist alone, in a naked mingling of passions, separated from the ordinary social milieu by a grated window. The picturesque spectacle of the man making bottles in a roaring furnace conveys the spectacular toy-shop quality Dublin acquires when seen from the centre of their union. The snow, ultimately, corresponds to the quality of Gabriel's isolation ("How pleasant it would be to walk out alone by the river and then through the park!") It is where he feels at home. It is anti-communal; it is that against which the Misses Morkan's Christmas dance asserts warmth and order. Gabriel imagines, as it proves mistakenly, that Gretta has shared it with him. Because it is anti-communal it is death; it triumphs in the end over his soul and, as he foresees, over Aunt Kate and Aunt Julia, and over all Dublin and all Ireland, reducing "the solid world itself, which these dead had one time reared and lived in" to a common level with "the dark central plain," "the bog of Allen," and "the lonely churchyard on the hills where Michael Furey lay buried."

The fragrant air Gabriel had carried into the Misses Morkan's house is the principle of death; it is his proper medium, as he comes to see:

> A shameful consciousness of his own person assailed him. He saw himself as a ludicrous figure, acting as a pennyboy for his aunts, a nervous, well-meaning sentimentalist, orating to vulgarians and idealizing his own clownish lusts, the pitiable fatuous fellow he had caught a glimpse of in the mirror.

He and his generation of glib middle-class snobbery and book-reviewing are the exorcism of the ghostly eighteenth-century order that lingers in the salon of his aunts. "Better pass boldly into that other world, in the full glory of some passion," he thinks, "than fade and wither dismally with age." The dancing-party belongs to that which is fading and withering; as for himself, there is no question of passing boldly into that other world. He is already of it. His longing to be alone in the snow was a longing for this death. His soul already pursues the "wayward and flickering existence" of the dead; it has taken very little to cause his identity to fade out "into a grey impalpable world." He is named for the angel who is to blow the last trump; but having released no blast of Judgment he watches through a hotel window the pale flakes falling through darkness.

One of Joyce's Trieste language-pupils recalls him gazing into a glass paperweight of the sort containing floating crystals and murmuring, "Yes, snow is general all over Ireland." Snow continued to fall and Ireland continued to be paralysed, in Joyce's mind, throughout his life. (pp. 51-68)

The epical narrative has concluded by gathering up the quality of a whole civilization in the isolation of Gabriel Conroy. His preferred snow-world suggests Ibsen; it was to the meaning of his ethical absolutism, as elevated by Ibsen into a preferred *modus vivendi,* totally divorced from communal context, that Joyce now turned. (p. 68)

Hugh Kenner, in his Dublin's Joyce, *1955. Reprint by Columbia University Press, 1987, 372 p.*

BREWSTER GHISELIN (essay date 1956)

[*In the following excerpt, Ghiselin defines the unitary structure of* Dubliners.]

The structure of James Joyce's ***Dubliners,*** long believed to be loose and episodic, is really unitary. (p. 75)

[The structural unity is achieved] by means of a single development, essentially of action, organized in complex detail and in a necessary, meaningful sequence throughout the book. . . . [The] whole unifying development [is] discernible as a sequence of events in a moral drama, an action of the human spirit struggling for survival under peculiar conditions of deprivation, enclosed and disabled by a degenerate environment that provides none of the primary necessities of spiritual life. So understood, ***Dubliners*** will be seen for what it is, in effect, both a group of short stories and a novel, the separate histories of its protagonists composing one essential history, that of the soul of a people which has confused and weakened its relation to the source of spiritual life and cannot restore it.

In so far as this unifying action is evident in the realistic elements of the book, it appears in the struggle of certain characters to escape the constricting circumstances of existence in Ireland, and especially in Dublin, "the centre of paralysis." As in *A Portrait of the Artist as a Young Man,* an escape is envisaged in traveling eastward from the city, across the seas to the freedom of the open world. In ***Dubliners,*** none of Joyce's protagonists moves very far on this course, though some aspire to go far. Often their motives are unworthy, their minds are confused. Yet their dreams of escape and the longing of one of them even to "fly away to another country" are suggestive of the intent of Stephen Dedalus in *A Portrait*. . . . Thus, in both books, ideas of enclosure, of arrest, and of movement in space are associated with action of moral purport and with spiritual aspiration and development.

In ***Dubliners,*** the meaning of movement is further complicated by the thematic import of that symbolic paralysis which Joyce himself referred to, an arrest imposed from within, not by the "nets" of external circumstance, but by a deficiency of impulse and power. The idea of a moral paralysis is expressed sometimes directly in terms of physical arrest, even in the actual paralysis of the priest Father Flynn, whose condition is emphasized by its appearance at the beginning of the book. . . . But sheer physical inaction of any kind is a somewhat crude means of indicating moral paralysis. Joyce has used it sparingly. The frustrations and degradations of his moral paralytics are rarely defined in physical stasis alone, and are sometimes concomitant with vigorous action. Their paralysis is more often expressed in a weakening of their impulse and ability to move forcefully, effectually, far, or in the right direction, especially by their frustration in ranging eastward in the direction of release or by their complete lack of orientation, by their failure to pass more than a little way beyond the outskirts of Dublin, or by the restriction of their movement altogether to the city or to some narrow area within it. (pp. 76-7)

It should be no surprise to discover in a book developing the theme of moral paralysis a fundamental structure of movements and stases, a system of significant motions, countermotions, and arrests, involving every story, making one consecutive narrative of the surge and subsidence of life in Dublin. In the development of the tendency to eastward movement among the characters of ***Dubliners,*** and in its successive modifications, throughout the book, something of such a system is manifest. It may be characterized briefly as an eastward trend, at first vague, quickly becoming dominant, then wavering, weakening, and at last reversed. Traced in rough outline, the pattern is as follows: in a sequence of six stories, an impulse and movement eastward to the outskirts of the city or beyond; in a single story, an impulse to fly away upward out of a confining situation near the center of Dublin; in a sequence of four stories, a gradual replacement of the impulse eastward by an impulse and movement westward; in three stories, a limited activity confined almost wholly within the central area of Dublin; and in the concluding story a movement eastward to the heart of the city, the exact center of arrest, then, in vision only, far westward into death. (p. 78)

Orientation and easting are rich in symbolic meanings of which Joyce was certainly aware. An erudite Catholic, he must have known of the ancient though not invariable custom of building churches with their heads to the east and placing the high altar against the east wall or eastward against a reredos in the depths of the building, so that the celebrant of the mass faced east, and the people entered the church and approached the altar from the west and remained looking in the same direction as the priest. He knew that in doing so they looked toward Eden, the earthly paradise. . . . Probably he [knew] that Christ returning for the Last Judgment was expected to come from the east. And he must have shared that profound human feeling, older than Christianity, which has made the sunrise immemorially and all but universally an emblem of the return of life and has made the east, therefore, an emblem of beginning and a place of rebirth. . . . He could not have failed, and the evidence of his symbolism in ***Dubliners*** shows that he did not fail, to see how a multitude of intimations of spiritual meaning affected the eastward aspirations and movements of characters in his book, and what opportunity it afforded of giving to the mere motion of his characters the symbolic import of moral action. (p. 79)

Like the booklong sequence of movements and stases, the various states of the soul in virtue and sin form a pattern of strict design traceable through every story. Each story in ***Dubliners*** is an action defining amid different circumstances of degradation and difficulty in the environment a frustration or defeat of the soul in a different state of strength or debility. Each state is related to the preceding by conventional associations or by casual connections or by both, and the entire sequence represents the whole course of moral deterioration ending in the death of the soul. Joyce's sense of the incompatibility of salvation with life in Dublin is expressed in a systematic display, one by one in these stories, of the three theological virtues and the four cardinal virtues in suppression, of the seven deadly sins triumphant, and of the deathly consequence, the spiritual death of all the Irish. Far more than his announced intention, of dealing with childhood, adolescence, maturity, and public life, this course of degenerative change in the states of the soul tends to determine the arrangement of the stories in a fixed order and, together with the pattern of motions and arrests, to account for his insistence upon a specific, inalterable sequence. (pp. 80-1)

The pattern of virtues and sins and the spatial pattern of motions and arrests in ***Dubliners*** are of course concomitant, and they express one development. As sin flourishes and virtue withers, the force of the soul diminishes, and it becomes more and more disoriented, until at the last all the force of its impulse toward the vital east is confused and spent and it inclines wholly to the deathly west. (p. 82)

Brewster Ghiselin, "The Unity of 'Dubliners,'" in Accent, *Vol. XVI, Nos. 2 and 3, Spring and Summer, 1956, pp. 75-88, 196-213.*

FRANK O'CONNOR (essay date 1956)

[O'Connor was an Irish short story writer, critic, and man of letters. His fiction is known for its realistic portrayal of small town and city life in Ireland and its detached yet sympathetic humor regarding the human condition. O'Connor's major work of literary criticism, The Mirror in the Roadway, *is based on a series of lectures he delivered at Harvard University during the early 1950s. In the following excerpt from that work, O'Connor outlines the metaphorical structure of "Ivy Day in the Committee Room," "Grace," and "The Dead."]*

Proust and Joyce were the heroes of my youth, but while Proust's work has continued to grow on me, Joyce's has lost its charm. The reason may be that I know too much about it. The reason for that may be that there is far too much to know.

That weakness of Joyce's does not begin with *Finnegans Wake.* It begins with his first book of fiction. It may be that the earlier stories in ***Dubliners*** are plain sailing; to me the later ones at least are exceedingly difficult to understand, and I can only admire the critics who so blandly profess to interpret them.

Let me begin with one small detail of which I shall have more to say. It is the first paragraph of a story called **"Two Gallants,"** and I merely wish to point out that the style is unusual.

> The grey warm evening of August had descended upon the city and a mild warm air, a memory of summer, circulated in the streets. The streets, shuttered for the repose of Sunday, swarmed with a gaily coloured crowd. Like illumined pearls the lamps shone from the summits of their tall poles upon the living texture below which, changing shape and hue, unceasingly, sent up into the warm grey evening air an unchanging unceasing murmur.

This beautiful paragraph, apparently modeled upon the prose of Flaubert, has a deliberation and self-consciousness exceedingly rare in the work of a young man and, indeed, rare in Flaubert. There is a deliberate repetition of certain key words, sometimes with a slight alteration of form, like "warm," "grey," "change," and "cease" which produces a peculiar effect that is not the result of precise observation, but of a deliberately produced hypnosis.

And here, so far as I can see, that particular experiment ceases for the moment. But in stories like **"Ivy Day in the Committee Room," "Grace,"** and **"The Dead,"** there is a deliberate and self-conscious use of form which produces a similar result. I have read these stories many times, and cannot profess to understand them. I am not impressed by the argument that they should be read "straight." I envy the ability of those who can read "straight" such a passage as that I have quoted, but I cannot emulate it. To me it seems queer, and I cannot help searching for the reason for its queerness.

In **"Ivy Day in the Committee Room"** we are in the headquarters of a candidate in a Dublin municipal election after Parnell's death. We meet the caretaker and a canvasser whose name is O'Connor and who wears a badge in Parnell's memory. The caretaker complains of his son's drinking habits. Another canvasser called Hynes appears, and they discuss the prospects of their getting paid, as well as the arrival of Edward VII on a visit to Dublin. A third canvasser called Henchy appears; Henchy has approached the candidate—a publican—for payment and had no luck. Even his request for a few bottles of stout seems to have been ignored. There is reference to the publican's father, who had kept an old-clothes shop where he had sold liquor on the side. Hynes goes out, and Henchy indignantly asks what he was doing there. His father was a decent man, but, according to Mr. Henchy, the son is not much better than an English spy. The scene is interrupted for a few moments by an unfrocked priest, Father Keon, who is looking for the publican, and then the dozen of stout arrives and the messenger boy is dispatched for a corkscrew, which he later takes back. Two fresh canvassers arrive: Mr. Crofton, a Protestant and socially a cut above the others, and Mr. Lyons, and as there is no corkscrew, two bottles of stout are put before the fire. Then, after the first cork pops, the men discuss Edward VII—a decent man who likes his glass of grog—and Parnell, till Mr. Hynes, the alleged spy, returns and a third bottle is laid on for him. Mr. Henchy, his former critic, now calls him "Joe" and asks him to recite. He recites a doggerel poem of his own in praise of the dead leader, and the third cork pops. The last lines run:

> "What do you think of that, Crofton?" cried Mr. Henchy. "Isn't that fine? What?"
>
> Mr. Crofton said it was a very fine piece of writing.

The story is remarkable for a certain apparent looseness of texture which is almost a new thing in literature. Events seem to occur merely as they would occur in everyday life; people drift in and out; there is no obvious design, and yet the story holds our attention. As a storyteller, I am impressed by the achievement, but at the same time it is clear to me that the casualness is only apparent. To begin with, the form is based upon political comment that emerges from a ground bass of booze. Everybody in the story is thinking or talking of drink, and the crisis, such as it is, when Mr. Henchy's mood mellows and he calls Hynes by his Christian name, is the result of the dozen of stout. The parallelism between King Edward and Parnell, "the Uncrowned King of Ireland," is clear, though the repeated references to "fathers"—human fathers, holy fathers, and City Fathers—I do not understand. But there are other details that show the careful structure of the story. Take, for instance, the bottles of stout. The corkscrew is absent, so one is borrowed from, and then returned to, the nearest public house, which leaves us with three bottles that must be opened by the primitive method of heating them. There is no doubt that this episode has been contrived to suggest the three volleys fired over the dead hero's grave.

The author's brother tells us that **"Grace"** was intended as a parody of *The Divine Comedy,* the pub representing Hell, the home Purgatory, and the church Paradise [see excerpt by Stanislaus Joyce dated 1954], but even this does not seem to me to explain all the peculiarities of the story, which again gives an elaborate impression of casualness. A commercial traveler falls down the steps of an underground lavatory and hurts himself. He is rescued from the police by an influential friend who then organizes a campaign to make him quit the drink, and the story ends in a Jesuit church with a business-like sermon fit for business gentlemen like Mr. Kernan. There are two long discussions in the story, one dealing with policemen, the other with priests, and these seem to represent the temporal and spiritual powers; but even these discussions have a peculiar quality because each deals with the problem of good and bad types. Like the characters in the story, these seem to be neither very good nor very bad; and the whole manner of the story, which is the mock-heroic, seems to be a denunciation of mediocrity.

But whether or not there is a hidden structure of metaphor in the two stories I have mentioned, there is no doubt of its existence in **"The Dead,"** the latest to be written and the most elaborate in construction. This metaphor is unique just because it is hidden. Many nineteenth-century writers, particularly the Americans, used metaphor and allegory, but Joyce's metaphor resembles the dissociated metaphor of dreams, which is intended to baffle and deceive the conscious mind.

The story is about a young man with tuberculosis living in the west of Ireland who falls in love with a girl called Gretta. He spends one whole night outside her window, and dies soon after. Years later, at a musical party in Dublin, Gretta, now the wife of a man called Gabriel Conroy, hears the young man's favorite song, "The Lass of Aughrim," and tells her husband of the incident. Then Conroy looks out and sees the snow, death's symbol, drifting down over the city.

In the story the process of recollection is unconscious and is built up of odd scraps of metaphor. The train of allusion is fired when Conroy enters, "scraping the snow from his goloshes." He asks the maid jocularly about her wedding, and she replies bitterly that "the men that is now is only all palaver and what they can get out of you." The repudiation of the living in relation to love and marriage is an anticipation of Gabriel's own feelings at the end of the story. His aunts, the old music teachers, ask if it is true that he and Gretta are not going home to "Monkstown" for the night, and Gabriel replies that after the previous year's party Gretta had caught "cold." The reference to "a cold" is deliberate, as is, perhaps, the reference to Monkstown because the Cistercian monks mentioned later who are supposed to "sleep in their coffins" are another metaphor of death. The party is, of course, a musical one, as the young man had been a singer. Because the setting of the incident has also to be placed by means of allusion, one of the guests, Miss Ivors, who is a Nationalist, talks of going with a party to the west of Ireland during the summer, and disputes with Gabriel, who prefers to go abroad. The reference to marriage at the opening is continued by things like the old song, "Arrayed for the Bridal," and the imperfections of "the men that is now" are emphasized by the mention of Caruso, who, though he may be a good singer, is not nearly so good as a forgotten tenor named Parkinson, while in Gabriel's speech he contrasts Miss Ivors with his aunts and finds her to "lack those qualities of humanity, of hospitality, of kindly humour which belonged to an older day." His tribute to the memory of the dead is only another chord in the theme, which is simply that all love and beauty and grace are with the dead, and that as husband he himself can never compete with that long-dead youth until the snows cover himself as well.

It is a beautiful story, and perhaps here, at any rate, the mysterious effect of dissociated metaphor is not out of place, though elsewhere I find that it produces something akin to claustrophobia in me. I long to know how Mr. Kernan and Martin Cunningham would really express themselves if released for a few moments from the need to be so damn metaphorical. (pp. 295-301)

Frank O'Connor, "Joyce and Dissociated Metaphor," in his The Mirror in the Roadway: A Study of the Modern Novel, *Alfred A. Knopf, 1956, pp. 295-312.*

MARVIN MAGALANER AND RICHARD M. KAIN (essay date 1956)

[*American Joyce scholars Magalaner and Kain have each written and edited numerous Joyce studies. Their important collaboration* James Joyce: The Man, the Work, the Reputation *presents analyses of Joyce's works that "attempt merely to discover a way of approach to what he wrote, to suggest a method of reading Joyce that will be profitable and exciting." In the following excerpt from that work, Magalaner and Kain present a detailed explication of symbolism in* Dubliners, *focusing on "The Sisters," "An Encounter," "Araby," "Ivy Day in the Committee Room," "Clay," and "The Dead."*]

Perhaps the best approach to the symbolic meaning of the stories in ***Dubliners*** is through scrutiny of the first story, **"The Sisters."** Fortunately, three versions of the story are available for study. The earliest, Joyce's contribution to George Russell's *Irish Homestead,* runs to about sixteen hundred words (half the size of the final version) and is little more than a record of a rambling conversation or two, with incidental description of several Dublin slum dwellers. It is signed "Stephen Daedalus."

The story tells of a boy, Stephen perhaps, whose elderly friend, the Reverend James Flynn, lies dying. The lad maintains a vigil on the sidewalk below. But death occurs when the child is not present, so he hears of the event from grown-ups at supper. The next morning he visits the priest's house. He thinks of the old man, feeble, waking to talk occasionally to the little boy or to complain of his needs to his two sisters, Nannie and Eliza. On the evening of the same day, the boy comes with his aunt to pay formal respects to the dead man. They kneel with deaf Nannie at the coffin, then make small talk about the priest's life. The sisters speak of his life as "crossed," his attitude "disappointed." They date this attitude to the time he dropped and shattered a chalice. This accident is supposed to have affected his mind so that he would laugh to himself in his dark confessional. This draft of the story shows the young Joyce at his blunt, unsubtle worst. An intermediate version of the story, in the collection of John J. Slocum, apparently represents an attempt by Joyce to revise the *Homestead* story. In it Joyce is at work refining his diction, reworking tenses, economizing on superfluous words, making it a neater piece. What he adds to it to bolster its symbolic content will be dealt with shortly.

The final ***Dubliners*** version of **"The Sisters"** is to the *Homestead* draft what *A Portrait* is to *Stephen Hero.* The quantity of information in the latter may be greater, but there is more artistry in the former. We learn in the *Homestead* story that Cotter is "the old distiller" and that he owns "prize setters." In ***Dubliners*** we must assume his occupation from his "talking of faints and worms." In the former we find that Nannie "is almost stone deaf"; we learn of her deafness in the final version when all those who talk to her raise their voices. In the short interval between first and last drafts, Joyce had learned to use the symbolist technique of expression through suggestion rather than through explicit telling. Joyce had lengthened the story to almost twice its original size. He had also shifted the emphasis from the sisters to the boy and his environment.

What, specifically, has been added? Joyce had promised earlier to write of the moral paralysis of his country. In this final version he reveals that the priest's malady is paralysis, a word that "sounded to me like the name of some maleficent and sinful being. . . ." Thus, at the beginning of the narrative, the author associates the priest with paralysis, sickness, and vague evil. The dreams and visions of the symbolists also come into play. After death, the "grey face of the paralytic" appears before him, apparently trying to "confess" a sin.

The problem of the relationship of the boy to the priest becomes complicated in the ***Dubliners*** version. By trying to confess to the lad, Father Flynn shows that he considers Stephen's role a priestly one. After all, the old man has trained him in Latin, in the catechism, and in performing some of the ceremonies of the priesthood. Yet the boy resists: "The duties of the priest toward the Eucharist and . . . confessional seemed so grave to me that I wondered how anybody had ever found in himself the courage to undertake them." Nor can he perform his functions as a Catholic communicant, much less those of priest-confessor. Kneeling with the rest of the mourners at the bier, he "pretended to pray but . . . could not. . . ." In the same way, Stephen, in *A Portrait,* kneels silently while Uncle Charles prays aloud, for the boy can respect, "though he did not share, his piety." Later, offered wine and crackers by the sisters, he hesitates to take the wine and refuses the crackers. So much space is given to the details of the offer, omitted completely from the *Homestead* version and merely mentioned in a sentence in the intermediate draft, that the question arises of Joyce's intention to express symbolically here the boy's hesitation to accept "Communion." Considered from the point of view of Joyce's biography or Stephen's spiritual history, the episode seems significant.

At the time when Joyce was turning his obvious first version of the story into the very delicately symbolic story that we have today, his mind was full of his involuntary conflict with the national religion. Behind him lay his rejection of the life of a Jesuit; immediately before him were the many vital decisions that had to be made: to leave Ireland, to refuse to conform to religious ritual observances, to enter a frightening profession. That the shock of such a conflict was tremendous is clear from Joyce's inability to forget his period of mental strain and emotional turmoil. A man whose life was the literature he created might well have attempted to project his conflict in his short story.

The Father Flynn whose shadowy essence dominates the revised story appears to be illustrative of the, to Joyce, decaying Irish Catholic God. Being a part of the paralyzed Irish environment, the Deity of the church is also paralyzed. With care, Joyce carries through the analogy, not made in the *Homestead* version, in all details. Paralysis, it will be recalled, reminds him of the word "simony." Not only does the church suffer from physical paralysis, but morally it is sick, if the perversion theme may be transferred—as it must be—from the man to the church. . . . And much is made of the advisability of keeping the younger generation, represented by the boy narrator, away from the perverted influence of Irish religion, which has "smiled continually" but has been guilty of awful sins.

True, Father Flynn, a surrogate for the Deity, has made friendly overtures to Stephen, as to Joyce. It was possible to rouse him from his "stupefied doze," says Joyce, in a tone reminiscent of Gautier and the early Eliot, by bringing him a contribution of snuff. But so weak and enervated is the old God that "his hands trembled" and the gifts of snuff sprinkled through his fingers and "gave his ancient priestly garments their green faded look. . . ." Yet the father figure had done something for the boy: " . . . taught me to pronounce

Latin properly . . . explained to me the meaning of the different ceremonies of the Mass . . . amused himself by putting difficult questions to me. . . ." The old man had ended by trying to make a priest of him and had succeeded in scaring the boy with the awful solemnity of a priest's functions.

Perhaps his spiritual superior might have convinced the boy if he himself had not been so inept in carrying out his own priestly functions. Had not Father Flynn dropped and broken the chalice? Had he not crushed this symbol of spiritual responsibility? Even in death the coffined priest lies silently, "his large hands *loosely* retaining a chalice [italics mine]." An indication of how important Joyce considered this chalice symbol is its evolution from draft to draft. In the first version, the priest grasps a rosary, in the second a cross; but Joyce saw in time the artistic rightness of placing in the dead man's hand what, as a living man, he could not hold.

The stage is set now in the story for presentation of the boy's symbolic reluctance to accept the ceremonies of his former faith. He cannot pray; he delays drinking the wine and refuses the wafers offered to him by the sisters. The role of Nannie and Eliza assumes an importance that the merely realistic part they play does not apparently justify. After all, Joyce, who took great pains with his story titles, did call the story **"The Sisters."** They do not represent nuns. As nurses, who minister to the wants of Father Flynn (the God of the church on earth), they may play the symbolic part of priests. As one of their functions is the bestowing of Communion, Joyce has the two sisters offer "Communion" to the unwilling boy. (pp. 82-5)

Taking the sisters as priestly figures helps to give consistency to the details of the story. Nannie is deaf, as in Joyce's opinion the average priest was deaf to the words and needs of docile parishioners. Nannie leads the prayers at the bier of the dead father. Her voice is audible above the voices of the others. Both sisters apparently offer "Communion." Both point out rather weakly the virtues of the impotent, feeble Father Flynn. Throughout the story, too, there is an air of disappointed expectancy as the living await a sign, a voice, a sound from the dead figure of the Catholic faith. As must happen, however, "there was no sound in the house: and I knew that the old priest was lying still in his coffin. . . ."

Critics have almost universally dismissed all the stories in ***Dubliners*** except **"The Dead"** as trivial sketches—and let it go at that. Two few have seen the trouble that Joyce took to give more than a surface meaning to his seemingly transparent, harmless stories. Yet even in the fragile narrative of **"An Encounter,"** a richness of symbolic content is evident.

The main outlines of the story are simple and ordinary. Three boys, weary of the unromantic life of schoolboys, decided to play truant for one day and to make an excursion to the old Pigeonhouse Fort. One loses his courage and backs out, leaving the narrator and Mahony to go together. The former, his mind full of "penny dreadful" notions of what adventure and adventurers should be, watches wide-eyed on the docks to catch a glimpse of foreign sailors, whose eyes, he has been led to believe, will be green. He is disappointed. But later in the afternoon, the two boys fall in with an elderly pervert whose strange conversation they do not quite understand although it makes them uneasy. The narrator suddenly discovers with a shock that the rheumy eyes of their unwholesome acquaintance are "bottle-green." "I turned my eyes away." The boys, worried by the tone of his conversation, depart hurriedly.

The dead and inconclusive note on which the story and the quest for adventure end is, of course, deliberate. The attempt of the boy in **"The Sisters"** to find a spiritual father and a calling had resulted in rejection and almost in revulsion. The expectation of discovering romance and adventure in Dublin must end in more than frustration—in a souring of childhood dreams of glamour and love. This happens also to the adolescent narrator in **"Araby,"** and his youthful exuberance is permanently dampened.

The theme of escape receives its first treatment from Joyce in **"An Encounter."** The three conspirators plan "to break out of the weariness of school-life for one day at least" by playing hooky in the freedom and privacy of the isolated Pigeonhouse. Perhaps significantly, the boy who withdraws from the adventure has parents who "went to eight-o'clock mass every morning" and a brother who is preparing for the priesthood. He is not present to share their disillusion on the docks nor does he wander with them into an open field where their quest for adventure, and a father, is gratified and rebuffed.

The perverted old man whom they encounter—a symbol of love turned sour in the enervating Dublin climate of fifty years ago—bears an interesting resemblance to Father Flynn. Both are old men, the decay of their physical being indicated by reference to Flynn's "big discoloured teeth" and to the anonymous old man's mouth in which there were "great gaps . . . between his yellow teeth." Joyce speaks too about Flynn's "ancient priestly garments," which have a "green faded look"; and of the other old man: "He was shabbily dressed in a suit of greenish-black. . . . He seemed to be fairly old. . . ." Both men enjoy the companionship of children and delight in initiating them into mysterious rites—Flynn in describing the intricacies of the Catholic Mass, the other in detailing the ceremony of whipping a miscreant boy. "He described to me how he would whip such a boy as if he were unfolding some elaborate mystery." Flynn is a symbol of impotent God, and the boys call the pervert a "josser," pidgin English for "God." The old man's voice grows "almost affectionate" as he strives to win the love that he can seemingly never attain, for his distorted revelation of it serves merely to alienate those to whom it is revealed. In much the same way, Father Flynn, by harping on the complexities of his office, alienates the boy whom he most wishes to convert. Though both old men seem to covet the father role, and though the child in both stories craves a father, father and son seem incompatible. Not until *Ulysses* will father and son attain even partial compatibility.

The boys in **"An Encounter"** never do reach their destination, the Pigeonhouse, in the filthy slum of Ringsend. This structure, erected far out on a breakwater in Dublin Bay, once a "watch house, store house and place of refuge for such as were forced to land there by stress of weather," later a fort, and finally a power station supplying light to the vicinity, is symbolically too far away from the young adventurers to fulfill for them any of its functions.

At least one of the functions of the symbol is religious. His mind fascinated by correspondences, Joyce saw many literary possibilities in the Pigeonhouse. "Pigeon" brought to mind "dove" and dove recalled the Holy Ghost. When Stephen, in the "Proteus" episode of *Ulysses,* sees the Pigeonhouse, he says to himself cryptically, "*Que* [*sic*] *vous a mis dans cette fichue position?*" and responds, "*C'est le pigeon, Joseph.*" Later it becomes clear that these words are supposedly exchanged by Joseph and the Virgin Mary on the matter of Mary's baffling pregnancy. (pp. 85-8)

The Pigeonhouse, then, is identified in Joyce's mind with the "father" of Christ and with fathers in general. In its towerlike proportions, it may also be a rather trite phallic symbol of fatherhood. The boy narrator, moreover, being an orphan, seeks in this quest a father. The ironies are multiple. The boys choose this retreat because they are sure that their teacher, Father Butler, will not interrupt their fun, for a Dublin priest (a father) would have no reason to visit the Pigeonhouse, the temple of the Holy Ghost. Furthermore, though attracted toward the Pigeonhouse-Holy Ghost-father symbol, the boys amuse themselves by shooting birds with Mahony's catapult. They succeed only in poisoning the springs from which their desires arise. Instead of a father, a sterile pervert greets them. Their quest fails, for they are unable to reach the house of the Dove, of the father.

A strong case may be made for the presence in all of the stories of ***Dubliners*** of symbolic strands that help to tie together the seemingly discrete details of each and operate beyond that to leave in the awareness of the reader a sense of vital interconnection among the stories. (p. 88)

In **"Araby,"** for which Cleanth Brooks has provided a good explication [in *Understanding Fiction,* 1947], exile and the illusion-reality motif are given early treatment by young Joyce. He portrays the bright flame of the boy narrator's hope against a dreary and sordid backdrop to foreshadow its inevitable disappointment. The boy lives, symbolically, on a dead-end street. The neighborhood is decaying: "odours arose from the ashpits," and a discarded rusty bicycle pump lies hidden in untended shrubbery. In this unprepossessing environment, a sensitive boy feels the first stirring of love for the younger sister of his playmate. Why Joyce does not name the girl specifically, beyond calling her "Mangan's sister," is a problem. Perhaps it is to render more ideal this object of an almost spiritual love that he prefers to keep her Christian name anonymous. Or perhaps there is a relationship here between the romantic Irish poet, James Clarence Mangan, whom Joyce so much admired in his essay of 1902, and the girl who symbolizes the acme of romance and poetry. (pp. 88-9)

When books fail to provide relief from the oppressive atmosphere, [the boy narrator] is drawn to the girl, who attracts him with the "soft rope of her hair," as with a noose. He is torn between a natural predilection for escape to the solitude of his romantic dreams, on the one hand, and the necessity of compromising with the world of reality in which his ideal love moves. For her the narrator is willing to go through the mundane motions of requesting a few shillings, taking a train ride, and so forth, in order to enjoy the ideal beauty promised in the name "Araby." The romance that the name breathes is synonymous for him with the romantic dreams he harbors of his future with the girl. But the disappointment that actuality holds out for those who expect too much is harsh.

Reality provides no fabulous wonderland. The end of the journey and the object of the quest is a makeshift bazaar—and the narrator arrives too late, just as it is closing for the night. In the same way, the boys in **"An Encounter"** find their trip to the Pigeonhouse blocked by approaching night. The narrator remarks, "I recognised a silence like that which pervades a church after a service," as he finds that "the greater part of the hall was in darkness." It is the darkness of his own street, especially of the deserted house of the priest, which is mentioned at the beginning of the story. It is the darkness of his lost religion. Bitter in his disappointment, the boy snatches at the one consolation that remains to him—the chance to buy for Mangan's sister a trinket in one of the booths still open. Here, however, the imagined rebuff of the indifferent salesgirl and the fragments of a particularly pointless and flirtatious conversation of this woman and her male companion bring him up sharply and show him the falsity of the entire situation in which he is involved. He learns from this epiphany that reality never comes up to life's promise.

In some ways, the Araby bazaar suggests the church and is its symbol. The narrator's quivering eagerness to reach it, his willingness to overcome material obstacles for the joy of attaining his destination, has religious fervor. But the worldly, the trivial, the gross await him at journey's end. The glowing colors with which idealists surround spiritual objects fail to appear. Again, Joyce seems to be saying, the quest for the father, for the Church, has been thwarted by reality. The bazaar turns out to be just as cold, as dark, and as man-made as the gloomy house of the dead priest on his own street. It is almost empty, too, and the only activity going on is the counting of the day's receipts. "The light," says the narrator, "was out." Suggestion through symbols again in this story reveals much more than the "plot" seems to supply.

"Ivy Day in the Committee Room," written before the end of 1905, deals with political decay in Dublin. Against a backdrop of Ireland's political glory in the days of Parnell's ascendancy, Joyce projects his narrative of the decay of contemporary political institutions and politicians. This juxtaposition of the old and desirable with the new and reprehensible in Dublin's political life is a favorite modern technique. Joyce found it especially workable here, as he did on a much larger scale late in *Ulysses.* He sets the time of the story as an anniversary of the death of Parnell, symbolic of the death of principle and moral righteousness in government and the rise of factionalism based on self-interest and mean expediency. By selecting his anniversary, the author is able to focus the reader's attention on both periods at once and thus heighten the meanness by keeping constantly before him the memory of former selfishness. In much the same way, Yeats [in "September 1913"] speaks of "romantic Ireland" as "dead and gone," placing it with the patriot "O'Leary in the grave."

In terms of simple narrative, the story is colorless enough. A group of petty ward workers and political canvassers meet in a bare, hired room and speak of their day's success in rounding up votes for their candidates. Their reminiscences of better days gone by, their backbiting and small jealousies, and their remarks on the campaign—in short, their whole conversation—*is* the story. Though their talk wanders from topic to topic, casually, and appears aimless and undirected, actually it is carefully regulated. So is the descriptive comment by the author. Several of the themes need a closer look.

Constant stress is placed, throughout the story, on the age-youth, father-son motif, which was to concern Joyce so strikingly in his later writings. The replacing of the older generation by the new, which in one sense should be heralded joyously as a sign of progress and fulfillment, is treated dolorously by the exiled artist. This is ironic in a story whose title mentions the ivy, symbol of regeneration. For Joyce can find no encouragement in the rising generation of which he is a member. "Old Jack," with his "old man's face," entitled by his seniority to veneration and respect, is given scant consideration he had finished his recitation there was a silence and then a burst of clapping: even Mr Lyons clapped. The applause continued for a little time. When it had ceased all the auditors drank from their bottles in silence. Pok! the cork flew out of Mr Hynes's bottle but Mr Hynes remained sitting on the table as if he had not heard the invitation.

— Good man, Joe! said Mr O'Connor, taking out cigarette-papers and tobacco in order to conceal his emotion—

— What d'ye think of that, Crofton? said Mr Henchy. Isn't that fine — what?—

Mr Crofton said that it was a very fine piece of writing.

Jas Joyce.
29 August 1905

The last page of a fair copy manuscript of "Ivy Day in the Committee Room."

by the young men. Mr. Henchy alone makes the conventional murmur, "O, don't stir, Jack, don't stir," when the old man rises, but Joyce is quick to add that Henchy "sat down on the chair which the old man vacated." Jack discourses at great length upon the worthlessness of his own child, who, in these dissolute times, "goes boosing about." Plaintively he asks, "What's the world coming to when sons speaks [*sic*] that way to their fathers?"

The dependence of son on father is constantly reiterated. Their employer, the candidate from the Royal Exchange Ward, "Tricky Dicky Tierney," is held up to ridicule because his "little old father kept the hand-me-down shop in Mary's Lane." Shortly after that, talk centers on Joe Hynes, who has just left the little circle of politicians. Someone suggests that Joe is a spy for the rival camp. " 'His father was a decent respectable man,' Mr. Henchy admitted. 'Poor old Larry Hynes! Many a good turn he did in his day! But I'm greatly afraid our friend is not nineteen carat . . .'." Even the teenagers are flippant and disrespectful to their elders. Mr. Henchy, seeking the support of one youngster, is told: ". . . when I see the work going on properly I won't forget you, you may be sure." The politicians find, when the seventeen-year-old boy who delivers their drinks accepts and drains one of the bottles, that in drink begins the corruption of youth—yet they do not appear to recognize or decry their own major part in this corruption. When the lad leaves, muttering thanks for his drink, the fatal act is laconically recorded: " 'That's the way it begins,' said the old man. 'The thin edge of the wedge,' said Mr. Henchy."

Whatever the reason, the young men of Ireland are not prepossessing. They seem to have been born old. Joyce describes Mr. O'Connor significantly as a "gray-haired young man" and bestows upon him a "face disfigured by many blotches and pimples." He is no more attractive mentally than physically. Lazy, slow-witted, he twice rolls the tobacco for a cigarette "meditatively," but it is only "after a moment's thought" that he "decided to lick the paper." Like Lenehan, of **"Two Gallants,"** he seems able only to agree with remarks made by others and seldom has the inspiration or initiative to make an original statement. Ireland is a country of old men (no matter what their chronological age), of ugly and stupid souls from whose efforts, or perhaps lack of effort, little in the way of spiritual or material regeneration may be expected. It is, in fact, a kind of Hell, peopled by small-time politicians, renegade priests, and sinful youngsters.

"Ivy Day in the Committee Room," to emphasize this point, carries a heavily weighted structure of Hell symbolism. It seems inconceivable that so disciplined a writer as Joyce would mention maybe a score of times the fire, smoke, cinders, and flames on the hearth of the committee room simply to tell the reader that the room contained a fire. These numerous references to the environment of Hell, in the moral context of the story and of the volume, are not the only evidence. They are reinforced by certain seemingly casual remarks, figures of speech, and imagery to which the conventional Christian description of Hell is central. Their profusion implies an impossible series of coincidences or, more probably, a deliberate attempt to evoke in the reader the idea that political Dublin is Hell.

The first sentence introduces the motif: "Old Jack raked the cinders together with a piece of cardboard and spread them judiciously over the whitening dome of coals." Throughout the story, he continues to nurse the fire, fanning it into bright flame when it suits Joyce's purpose to have the room revealed in the glare. By this device, the reader discovers "a leaf of dark glossy ivy in the lapel" of one of the men, which "the flame lit up." The Parnell motif of regeneration is thus introduced against a background of fire. It is interesting to note, too, that, when Mr. Hynes enters the fire-lit room, he asks, "What are you doing in the dark?" Joyce makes it plain that the fire, at that moment, is still burning. Perhaps he is picturing the fire of Hell, as he does in the sermon in *A Portrait,* as flame which, "while retaining the intensity of its heat, burns eternally in darkness."

Continuing the Hell motif, Mr. Henchy refers to the candidate whom they represent and from whom they draw a salary as a "Mean little schoolboy of hell." Also, when the group greets another canvasser coming in to report, its spokesman addresses him: "Hello, Crofton! . . . Talk of the devil." Can it be significant too that the politicians are not able to gain access to their drinks without the aid of the fire, which causes the corks to fly out with an empty "pok"? Frank O'Connor's ingenious explanation for the noisy succession of "pok" sounds [see excerpt dated 1956] is that they represent what has become of the traditional gun salute to Parnell as statesman-hero in the Dublin of **"Ivy Day."**

It would be strange if, in Joyce's Hell, as in Dante's, there were no sinful clerics. The desire to have an important segment of Dublin life, the priest, represented in the Committee Room calls for the contrived entrance of Father Keon to the fireside circle. The priest is looking for Mr. Fanning, the campaign treasurer, who is not present. He leaves, and that is all there is to the incident. His appearance and departure do, it is true, provide food for half a page of cynical discussion on Keon's clerical status and means of livelihood. He may be, as Stanislaus Joyce believes [see excerpt dated 1954], an unfrocked clergyman, or perhaps he still retains his clerical authority. But Joyce's displeasure is plain. The priest is "very thick" with the treasurer and spends much time in pubs with him. This blend of religion, drink, and politics qualifies the priest for a place in the Hell of the Committee Room.

The author's descriptive comments support such an assignment. "A person resembling a poor clergyman or a poor actor appeared in the doorway . . . it was impossible to say whether he wore a clergyman's collar or a layman's. . . ." In a story about Parnell there is an obvious double meaning to these seemingly innocent lines; Joyce is pointing up the thin line that separates, or does not separate, the religious from the secular in his Dublin. He is stirring up the raging controversy over the right of the Catholic clergy to take part in influencing a state election. The priest admits, indeed, that he has come to see the treasurer of a political group on a "little business matter." This admission is especially damning since the whole incident of Keon's brief appearance follows immediately a discussion of Irish traitors like the infamous Major Sirr who would "sell his country for four-pence." Joyce's conversational narrative only *seems* to wander in **"Ivy Day."**

The decade or so that had passed since the death of Parnell had dissipated all but the last vestiges of the enthusiasm for a cause which his presence generated. The question of money for political services rendered is paramount: "Has he paid you yet?" is repeated in various guises until it becomes deliberately annoying. Mr. O'Connor voices the favorite sentiment of the group when, speaking of Tierney, he says, "I wish he'd turn up with the spondulics." The shoe boy will sell his vote for money. Father Keon goes into conference with the treasurer. The candidate himself evades his proper obligation by putting off questions concerning payment. Graft, it is hinted, plays a large part in the election of city officials. And those municipal officeholders are judged not by their actions in government but by the shabby display that they make: "What do you think of a Lord Mayor of Dublin sending out for a pound of chops for his dinner? How's that for high living?" A far cry from the steadfast single-mindedness of the Parnell era, at least when the earlier period is seen through the roseate haze of time and a national myth.

With Hynes's reading of his almost doggerel poem commemorating Parnell's death, Joyce gets his chance to sum up implicitly the contrast between the glory that had been and the present tawdry circumstances. The reading of the sincere but poetically decayed poem that seeks in vain to recapture that fleeting glory is another good example of epiphany. What could have been a lame and sentimental ending becomes, through a fine balance of parts and proper timing, a moving symbol of decay.

The poem, neither better nor worse than many of the patriotic journalistic pieces in Duffy's *Nation,* and according to Stanislaus Joyce a parody on Joyce's first published work, "Et Tu, Healy!" is poor poetry, questionable politics, and sentimental rhetoric. That its effect should be powerful, in spite of these defects (or maybe because of them), is testimony to the strength of the Parnell legend. Joyce might well have had in mind such an audience as his own father, Mr. Casey, or his uncle, heartbroken, frustrated followers of their "dead king." Beyond the political implications, the poem is also indicative of the decay of taste in aesthetics, in religion, in journalism that prevailed, or so he felt, in Joyce's Dublin. It is what makes old Jack, a representative of a happier day, exclaim: "God be with them times! . . . There was some life in it then."

There is some evidence of social decay—and the cheapening of personal relationships—in **"Ivy Day,"** but Joyce chose to concentrate his attention on this strain of Ireland's paralysis in stories like **"Two Gallants"** and **"Clay."**

The story **"Clay"** shows most clearly the operation of symbolism on several levels simultaneously. Though a quick reading may deceive the reader into thinking that the sketch concerns nothing more than the frustrated longings of a timid old maid for the joys of life, a husband, children, and romance, careful examination leads to discovery of interesting patterns. All the social relationships in the story, for instance, are awry. Maria should be married but is not. Alphy and Joe, though brothers, fight continually. Mrs. Donnelly strives to keep peace in the family by calming her drunken husband. The laundresses quarrel often. The saleswoman in the cake shop is impudent to the most inoffensive of customers. The young men on the tram will not rise to give her a seat. And even the innocent children are half accused of stealing the missing cakes. Through this maze of human unpleasantness moves the old maid, Maria, a steadying and moderating influence on all those who have dealings with her.

Her role as peacemaker is stressed. In the Protestant laundry, she "was always sent for when the women quarrelled over their tubs and always succeeded in making peace." Her employer compliments her on her ability as mediator: "Maria, you are a veritable peace-maker." Her calm moderation alone keeps Ginger Mooney from using violence against the "dummy who had charge of the irons." "Everyone," says Joyce, "was so fond of Maria." And rightly so. Her tact prevents a family quarrel over the loss of a nutcracker when she quickly says that "she didn't like nuts and that they weren't to bother about her." Though she does not wish a drink of wine offered by Joe, she "let him have his way." Maria's function as peacemaker, dovetailing as it does with a great many other details of the story, suggests the hypothesis that Joyce intended to build up a rough analogy between the laundry worker Maria and the Virgin Mary. Along certain lines, the relationship is fairly obvious.

Maria, of course, is a variant of the name Mary. Certainly there is nothing subtle about the associations that the name of the main character evokes. The Virgin is well known for her role as peacemaker, for the invocations to her, especially by women, to prevent conflict. Accordingly, she is invoked ("sent for") whenever the laundresses argue and she "always succeeded in making peace." Without her restraining and comforting influence, much more violence would occur. There is surely a suggestion of the church in Maria, for, like Mrs. Kearney and the two sisters, she offers a form of Communion to the women by distributing the barmbracks (raisin bread) and beverage.

Carrying the analogy further, Joyce makes much of the fact that Maria is a virgin. At the same time, and this is significant, she has children, though they are not born from her womb. "She had nursed . . . [Joe] and Alphy too; and Joe used often to say: 'Mamma is mamma but Maria is my proper mother'." There would seem to be no reason, in a very short story, to quote Joe directly here unless more was intended by the author than the bare statement that Maria had aided his mother in bringing up her sons. There are additional Biblical parallels too. In the Gospel according to Luke, it is Elizabeth who announces to Mary that she is blessed and will have blessed offspring. Interestingly enough, in **"Clay"** it is Lizzie (Elizabeth) Fleming, Maria's coworker in the laundry, who "said Maria was sure to get the ring and, though Fleming had said that for so many Hallow Eves, Maria had to laugh and say she didn't want any ring or man either. . . ."

Other similarities crowd in to lend support to the idea. Maria works in a laundry, where things are made clean; Mary is the instrument of cleansing on the spiritual plane. All the children sing for Maria, and two bear gifts to her on a Whitmonday trip. That one gift is a purse has ironic meaning in Joyce's mercenary Dublin. The laundress finds her appearance "nice" and "tidy" "in spite of its years," perhaps a circumspect way of saying that, after centuries, the freshness of Mary as a symbol is still untarnished. On the other hand, Maria finds on the tram that she is ignored by the young men and in the bakeshop treated insolently by the young girl. Only the elderly and the slightly drunk treat her with the respect which she enjoys but which she is too timid to demand. The meaning for Joyce of this situation needs no spelling out. The fact, finally, that Maria gets the prayer book, in the game of the three dishes, and is therefore slated to enter a convent and retire from the world is additional evidence of the author's symbolic intent. (pp. 89-97)

The story, originally entitled "Hallow Eve," takes place on the spooky night of the thirty-first of October, "the night set apart for a universal walking abroad of spirits, both of the visible and invisible world; for . . . one of the special characteristics attributed to this mystic evening, is the faculty conferred on the immaterial principle in humanity to detach itself from its corporeal tenement and wander abroad through the realms of space. . . ." Putting this more bluntly than Joyce would have wished, Maria on the spirit level is a witch on this Haloween night, and as a traditional witch Joyce describes her. "Maria was a very, very small person indeed but she had a very long nose and a very long chin." To fix this almost caricature description in the minds of his readers, the author repeats that "when she laughed . . . the tip of her nose nearly met the tip of her chin." And two sentences further on, he reiterates the information for the third time, and for a fourth before the story is through. The intention is very plain. In addition to these frequent iterations, Joyce's first sentence in **"Clay"**—and his story openings are almost always fraught with special meaning—discloses that this was "her evening out." By right it should be, for witches walk abroad on Allhallow Eve. In itself, however, implying that the old woman is a witch is of minor significance. It derives fuller meaning from the illusion-reality motif.

This motif is central to the story, gives it, in fact, its point. Halloween is famous for its masquerades, its hiding of identities of celebrants, conjuring tricks, illusions of goblins and ghosts—in other words, famed for the illusions that are created in the name of celebrating the holiday. It is a night on which it is hard to tell the material from the spiritual, witch from woman, ghost from sheeted youngster. On this night, things are not what they seem.

In the first paragraph, Joyce touches gently upon the motif more than once. Maria's work in the kitchen is done. Barmbracks have been prepared. It is legitimate to wonder whether the baking was done in accordance with this Irish custom [described in E. H. Sechrist's *Red Letter Days,* 1940]: unmarried girls would knead a cake "with their left thumbs. . . . in mute solemnity; a single word would have broken the charm and destroyed their ardent hopes of beholding their future husbands in their dreams after having partaken of the mystic 'dumb-cake'." The finished barmbracks "seemed uncut; but if you went closer you would see that they had been cut into long thick even slices and were ready. . . . Maria had cut them herself." The contrast between the illusion of wholeness and the reality of the actual slices is given prominent mention only because it belongs within the larger framework of the motif. Also, in the same paragraph, the cook delights in the cleanliness of the big copper boilers in which "you could see yourself," another reference to illusion, possibly connected in Joyce's mind with the Allhallow Eve custom of looking into a mirror to see one's future husband.

In other respects, also, the spirits are at work in this story. Things, as things, lose their materiality and become invisible. At least they are missing and cannot be found. The plum cake disappears. "Nobody could find the nutcrackers." Finally, Joe trying to locate the corkscrew, "could not find what he was looking for." Maria herself is ambiguous, sometimes more a disembodied spirit than a person. Her body, though it exists, is "very, very small," and a hearty burst of laughter grips her "till her minute body nearly shook itself asunder." On this night she is able to get outside her body, almost, and look at it objectively: "she looked with quaint affection at the diminutive body which she had so often adorned . . . she found it a nice tidy little body."

It is in dreams, however, that Maria is able to put the greatest distance between illusion, namely, the love and adventure which have never entered her life, and reality, the drab, methodical existence of a servant in a laundry. Or if not in dreams, in the reverie induced by a dream song, "I dreamt that I dwelt in marble halls." The whole story builds up to this central split, at which point all the minor examples of the thin line between fantasy and actuality attain meaning and stature. In these rich and sensuous lines, sung in a "tiny quavering voice" by Maria, are packed the antitheses to the frustrating life of the average Dubliner. Mary in contemporary life has decayed in scope to Maria and is no more imposing a spiritual figure than a witch on a broomstick. The marble halls have been converted into laundry kitchens. Most tragic of all, there is no one in the world to whom the old maid can, with truth, sing "that you loved me just the same." In Maria's rendition of the song, she inadvertently omits the second and third stanzas and carelessly sings the first verse twice. Joyce emphasizes that "no one tried to show her her mistake." Little wonder that her audience remains tactfully silent about these missing verses:

> I dreamt that suitors sought my hand
> That knights on bended knee,
> And with vows no maiden heart could withstand,
> They pledged their faith to me.
>
> And I dreamt that one of that noble band
> Came forth my heart to claim,
> But I also dreamt, which charmed me most,
> That you loved me still the same.

Maria's error is probably attributable to an emotional block that prevents her from giving voice to remarks so obviously at variance with the reality of her dull life. Leopold Bloom suffers a similar lapse when of Boylan's affair with Molly he speaks of "the wife's admirers" and then in confusion adds, "The wife's advisers, I mean."

Joyce's decision to change the title of the story from "Hallow Eve" to **"Clay"** shifts the emphasis from the singing of the song to the ceremony of the three dishes. This familiar Irish fortunetelling game requires blindfolded players to select from a group of traditional objects the one which, so the story goes, will be symbolically revelatory of their future life. Poor Maria puts her fingers into a dish which the thoughtless children have jokingly filled with clay. She is to get neither the prayer book (life in a convent) or the ring (marriage). Death is her fate. There is a subdued shock when even the insensitive people present at the Halloween party realize the symbolic significance of selecting clay as an omen of things to come. Joyce, leaving nothing to chance, has earlier prepared the reader for the symbolic action by showing that Maria is half in love with easeful death: "She had her plants . . . and she liked looking after them. She had lovely ferns and wax-plants. . . ." The emblems of the Virgin Mary, it is interesting to note, are unlike the others late-flowering plants and late-blossoming trees.

Joyce was a very young writer when he wrote **"Clay."** He seems uncertain where to place the emphasis, and perhaps he allows too many motifs, even though a tenuous connection among them does exist, to deflect from the central point of his narrative. Perhaps he has not sufficiently reinforced the relationship between the witch and the Virgin, though the history of the church holiday actually establishes all the parallel background he needs: the day set aside in honor of saints (like Mary) by Boniface IV has had its eve perverted by celebrants to the calling forth of witches. The two supernormal female figures, the saint and the witch, share this holiday. The writer who was soon to wrestle with the intricacies of interlocking symbolic levels in *Ulysses* was in **"Clay"** learning his trade. The result is a much more complicated story than commentators in the past have discovered. (pp. 97-100)

[**"The Dead"**] represents Joyce's most highly developed and artistic use of the short story medium and of symbols prior to *Ulysses.* Much of the impressiveness of the story comes from its noble theme, easier to feel than to identify precisely. David Daiches [see excerpt dated 1960] defines it as "a man's withdrawal into the circle of his own egotism, a number of external factors trying progressively to break down the walls of that circle . . ." and the final breaking down from within and within. Stanislaus Joyce [in *Recollections of James Joyce by His Brother,* 1950] speaks of **"The Dead"** as "the final chorus of the book . . . a story of ghosts, of dead who return in envy of the living. . . ." Finally, Allen Tate, in his most discerning analysis of the novelette, calls it a treatment of the "great contemporary subject: the isolation and frustration of personality." All these attempts at definition are necessarily inconclusive because what Joyce is saying cannot be fixed in a formulated phrase.

The death motif may be said, however, to stand out above the others in importance, for it supports all the other themes. It is puzzling how [John Macy; see excerpt dated 1922] can have been so insensitive to the pervasiveness of imagery of death in the story as to say, "there is only one dead person in it and he is not mentioned until near the end. That's the kind of trick an Irishman . . . would play on us. . . ." Equally undiscerning is the remark of [Louis Golding in his *James Joyce,* 1933] that the artistic purpose of giving in detail the long description of the dinner party is simply to make Gabriel Conroy wait longer for his wife's love in their hotel room. The many pages, apparently of prelude to the main action, must have their full exposition, partly to allow presentation of Gabriel's reactions to different situations but mainly to give the author scope to develop his motif of death.

Though the story takes place at Christmas time, when the mind is turned to birth and beginnings, the air of deadness and decay in the description of the "gaunt house" and of its ancient owners, the two maiden aunts of Gabriel (and of Joyce), penetrates the surface warmth and lushness of the special banquet preparations. Hints of the faded glory of family fortunes and the frankly faded inhabitants of the mansion add to the impression that the reader is watching the stiff gyrations of long dead souls.

The dead overshadow much of the conversation at the party and after, with emphasis on the fact of human forgetfulness of those who die. In lighthearted jest, when he wishes to eat his dinner undisturbed, Gabriel asks that the guests "kindly forget my existence" for a few minutes. Ironically, these words take on a deeper meaning later when a chastened Gabriel sees unmistakably that that is exactly what will happen to him, to everyone, eventually. When the talk turns to opera singers and musicians of an earlier day, "Tietjens, Ilma de Murzka, Campanini, the great Trebelli," the younger guests cannot recall even the names of the great:

> "For me," said Aunt Kate, . . . "there was only one tenor. . . . But I suppose none of you ever heard of him."
>
> . . . . "His name," said Aunt Kate, "was Parkinson. I heard him when he was in his prime. . . ."
>
> "Strange," said Mr. Bartell D'Arcy. "I never even heard of him."

Then the conversation veers to an order of Trappist monks, who sleep in their coffins "to remind them of their last end." The party over, and transportation home being the problem, they speak of "The never-to-be-forgotten Johnny," their father's dead horse, whom Mr. Browne has already forgotten. The tenor Bartell D'Arcy sings of "The Lass of Aughrim" in words which tell that "My babe lies cold." Gabriel communes with the dead by nodding at and saying good-by to the statue of Daniel O'Connell, as the cab drives by the figure of the deceased liberator. These frequent references to the dead are crystallized in three ways in the novelette: in Gabriel's after-dinner speech, in his wife Gretta's story of Michael Furey, and in the symbol of the snow.

Gabriel's speech concentrates on the relationship of past and present, accentuating, as do most of the stories, the bleak contrast. His hope that "in gatherings such as this" will be kept alive "the memory of those dead and gone great ones whose fame the world will not willingly let die" sounds hollow, coming after the section in which the guests fail to recall the great singers of a few short years earlier. In such tragic ironies as this **"The Dead"** is steeped. The speaker waxes eloquent upon the "sad memories" of "absent faces" but philosophizes bravely that one must not brood over the dead. "Therefore, I will not linger on the past." Before the night is over, a shade from the past will return to haunt him, to destroy the complacency of his marriage relationship and to give him a lesson in false egocentricity.

The memory, stronger than a ghost, of Michael Furey, evoked for Gretta Conroy by a ballad, is the final shock that the tottering ego of Gabriel cannot bear. That a dead boy, one who worked "in the gasworks," should alter even slightly the relationship between his wife and himself is unthinkable at first. But then, beside this figure of romance that Gretta's meager description conjures up, he sees himself as "a ludicrous figure . . . a nervous, well-meaning sentimentalist. . . ." What the successive but petty assaults upon his ego of Lily's rebuff, Miss Ivors's insulting banter, and even his wife's evasion of his attentions have failed to accomplish entirely this crowning defeat has brought about. (pp. 102-04)

The aftermath of his wife's disclosure is a period of severe soul-searching by Gabriel, who has never before been able to decide what his wife was a symbol of. Now he realizes that she stands for romance, a romance denied to their marriage by his stodginess and fussiness, the concrete expressions of an overweening ego. "So she had had that romance in her life: a man had died for her sake. It hardly pained him now to think how poor a part he, her husband, had played in her life." His aging appearance gives him reason to shudder at the thought of slowly fading and withering "dismally with age." Rather than that, he wishes to become a shade "boldly" as the young Michael had, "in the full glory of some passion." The wide difference between Furey's love and the lust which he himself has felt earlier in the evening comes to disturb his peace. But most disturbing of all the sensations that beset him is the consciousness of his own loss of identity in a "dissolving and dwindling" world. Like Michael Furey, of whose very existence he had been unaware two hours earlier, he too is drifting slowly toward impalpability, toward oblivion. (pp. 104-05)

As the symbolic representation of oblivion and death, the figure of the snow plays its part. Joyce's use of the snow as symbol throughout the story is perhaps the main reason why the narrative rises above the commonplace of realistic portrayal and assumes a poetic cast. His use of the snow symbol, furthermore, changes at various stages of the tale, making for a fuller utilization of the possibilities of the universal image. Gabriel is introduced to the reader as he is "scraping the snow from his goloshes." "A light fringe of snow lay like a cape on the shoulders of his overcoat." He is thus physically covered with the cold substance, and in his own words, "I think we're in for a night of it." The initial impression one gets of the protagonist is of a man overly concerned with protecting himself and his possession, namely Gretta, from the snow by an excess of outer clothing, mufflers, and the ever-intruding galoshes. " 'Goloshes!' said Mrs. Conroy. 'That's the latest. Whenever it's wet underfoot I must put on my goloshes'." If this oversolicitousness to avoid sickness and worse be coupled with the fact that cold and snow are universally accepted as concrete representations of death, may it not be said with justice that Gabriel's attempt to ward off death is the symbolic keynote of the beginning of the story?

Conversely, Gabriel's petty attempts to keep himself and his loved ones from all contact with living nature may certainly be interpreted as a desire to shun life. Excessive care for outer garments, insistence upon galoshes, a wish to escape contact with water, snow, cold air—all these point to a desire to avoid what life in this world offers. As Tindall has pointed out [in his critical biography of Joyce, 1950] Joyce has used this water (snow)-life symbolism often enough to leave no doubt of its applicability here. (pp. 105-06)

In **"The Dead,"** as the action proceeds and Gabriel meets rebuff after rebuff to his powerful but nervous egocentricity, the life-death ambiguity seems to resolve itself. The alteration is reflected in his new attitude toward snow and cold. In a passage undoubtedly of more than passing descriptive importance since the author repeats it in substance twice, this change is recorded: "How pleasant it would be to walk out alone, first along by the river and then through the park! The snow would be lying on the branches of the trees and forming a bright cap on the top of the Wellington Monument. How much more pleasant it would be there than at the supper-table!" In the second reference to the snow outside, which occurs just before he makes his after-dinner address, he thinks of people "standing in the snow . . . gazing up at the lighted windows. . . . The air was pure there. In the distance lay the park where the trees were weighted with snow. The Wellington Monument wore a gleaming cap of snow. . . ." Now, if we extend the figure of snow as death, it would appear that Gabriel, without knowing it perhaps, is little by little seeking the purity and peace of a death and oblivion which, physically, he actively rejects. But why the mention of the monument? It is, of course, a prominent landmark of Dublin. More than that, however, the monument is eminently, if somewhat tritely, suitable as a phallic symbol in the context of the narrative, just as Nelson's pillar is phallic in the "Aeolus" episode of *Ulysses.* Like Dylan Thomas, though with no such formal system as basis, Joyce is always equating love and death in his Dublin. It is quite probable that Gabriel's unconscious longing for snow-death should be bound up with his recollection of the phallic symbol of sexual love, now covered with a cap of cold, bright snow. (p. 107)

Before the heat of Gabriel's lust, the cold disappears on the journey to the Gresham Hotel. Gabriel thinks only of Gretta and his need for her. His feverish mood is soon dispelled by the story his wife tells of early love and Michael Furey. In bed, he feels that his "soul had approached that region where dwell the vast hosts of the dead." It is when he feels "his own identity . . . fading out into a grey impalpable world . . . dissolving and dwindling" that the snow image reasserts itself and overwhelms everything else in sameness and death. "He watched sleepily the flakes, silver and dark, falling obliquely against the lamplight. The time had come for him to set out on his journey westward." Here the identification of snow with death is explicit. And still the snow continues to fall "faintly through the universe and faintly falling, like the descent of their last end, upon all the living and the dead." Bloom puts it simply, "No one is anything."

Beneath this blanket of snow-death, all men lose their identities, or, to put it another way, all identities are of similar appearance. Beneath it, Gabriel's selfishness is smothered and his personality may emerge anew. ["In **'The Dead,'**] Joyce is attempting to show the change from a wholly egocentric point of view, where you regard the world as revolving round yourself to a point of view where your own personality is eliminated and you can stand back and look disinterestedly on yourself and on the world . . ." [David Daiches in "James Joyce: The Artist as Exile," 1940].

Joyce's handling of the snow, both as descriptive detail and as symbol simultaneously, is one strong reason for the success of the story. Recognizing that the snow changes from a "hostile force of nature" at the beginning to a "symbol of warmth, of expanded consciousness," which he equates to Gabriel's breaking out of his own ego, Allen Tate, in his analysis [see excerpt dated 1950], lets it go at that. Undoubtedly he is correct. The question is whether he has said enough.

"The Dead" proved to Joyce that he had carried his kind of short story as far as it would go. He had outgrown a form that he had developed to a high point of excellence. He needed more spacious fields in which to roam than those afforded by the limited area of the short story or even of the novelette. Though he had tried to stick with the prose form which had, in his own opinion, served him well, and had even tried to send Mr. Bloom into the literary world as the Mr. Hunter of a short story, he was discerning enough to see that he was getting beyond the scope of contributions to *The Irish Homestead.* Like Yeats, like Eliot, without abandoning the advantages of the outgrown form, he was able to extract from it what he needed and to build on it a new and different kind of novel that was to travel far beyond Dublin, or even Europe, to astonish the world. (pp. 107-08)

Marvin Magalaner and Richard M. Kain, in their Joyce: The Man, the Work, the Reputation, *1956. Reprint by Collier Books, 1962, 383 p.*

DAVID DAICHES (essay date 1960)

[*Daiches is a prominent English scholar and critic who has written extensively on English and American literature. He is especially renowned for his in-depth studies of such writers as Robert Burns, Robert Louis Stevenson, and Virginia Woolf. In the following excerpt from the revised edition of his study* The Novel and the Modern World, *Daiches offers an appreciative overview of Joyce's achievement in the short story form, concluding that the subtle yet powerful selection and arrangement of detail in "The Dead" make it "one of the most remarkable short stories of the present century."*]

The short stories that make up [***Dubliners***] have certain common features in aim and technique; they are realistic in a certain sense, and they have a quite extraordinary evenness of tone and texture, the style being that neutral medium which, without in itself showing any signs of emotion or excitement, conveys with quiet adequacy the given story in its proper atmosphere and with its proper implications. Only the last story in the collection, **"The Dead,"** stands apart from the others; here Joyce has done something different—he has presented a story in a way that implies comment, and he has deliberately allowed his style to surrender, as it were, to that comment, so that the level objectivity of the other stories is replaced by a more lyrical quality.

The first three stories are told in the first person, the principle of selection, which determines the choice, organization, and emphasis of the incidents, being provided by the recollected impressions of the narrator. Thus, in **"The Sisters"** Joyce gives the constituent parts of what, to a sensitive boy, made up (whether actually or not is irrelevant) a single and memorable experience; and these parts are arranged and patterned in such a way as to give a sense of the unity of the experience to the reader. And although it is irrelevant to the critic whether the events actually occurred or not, it is very relevant that the pattern of events should be one which produces a recognizable experience with its attendant atmosphere. A purely "formal" analysis of any of these stories would be useful—in fact, indispensable—in an endeavor to assess their value as literature, but such an analysis is only the first step in a process; it is not in itself able to tell us why that particular arrangement of incident and description constitutes a totality which has more value than a mere symmetrical pattern or intriguing design. The arrangement of events in **"The Sisters"** or **"Araby"** produces a good short story because the result is not merely a pattern *qua* pattern (such has no *necessary* value in literature), but a pattern which corresponds to something in experience. For those who, owing to the circumstances of their life or the limitations of their sensibility, are unable to recognize that correspondence, the story loses most of its worth: there is always this limitation to the universality of great literature, this stumbling-block to the purely formal critical approach. A study of ***Dubliners*** can tell us a great deal about the function of pattern in fiction and about the relation between realism as a technique and as an end. No English short-story writer has built up his design, has related the parts to the preconceived whole, more carefully than Joyce has done in stories such as **"The Sisters," "Two Gallants,"** or **"Ivy Day in the Committee Room."** Observation is the tool of imagination, and imagination is that which can see potential significance in the most casual seeming events. It is the more specifically and consciously artistic faculty that organizes, arranges, balances emphases, and sets going undercurrents of symbolic comment, until that potential significance has become actual.

In the second of these stories, **"An Encounter,"** the organizing and selecting principle is again the boy's impressionable mind and memory as recalled or conceived by Joyce. It is worth noting how Joyce sets the pattern going in this and other stories. Descriptive comment concerning the chief characters constitutes the opening paragraph—comment that wanders to and fro in its tenses, not starting with a clear edge of incident but with a jagged line, as though memory were gradually searching out those events which really were the beginning of the design which is a totality in the retrospective mind. Similarly, in **"The Sisters,"** the opening paragraph consists of an almost regular alternation of imperfect and pluperfect tenses:

> Night after night I had passed the house . . . and studied the lighted square of window. . . . If he was dead, I thought, I would see the reflection of candles on the darkened blind. . . . He had often said to me: "I am not long for this world," and I had thought his words idle. Now I knew they were true. . . .

These deliberately wavering beginnings serve a double function. First, they give the author an opportunity of presenting to the reader any preliminary information that is necessary to his understanding of the story; they enable him, too, to let out those pieces of information in the order which will give them most significance and throw the necessary amount of emphasis onto what the author wishes to be emphasized. Second, on a simple, naturalistic level they give us the pattern of an experience as it actually is to memory or observation. The beginning is vague (the reader should study the evidence of witnesses in reports of court trials to understand how wavering the beginning of a unified experience is to both observer and sufferer), but once under way the jagged line becomes straight, until the end, which is precise and definite. Our own memories of experiences which have been significant for us will provide sufficient comment on this technique. In those stories which are told in the first person, as memories, the jagged-line openings are more conspicuous than in the stories narrated in the third person: Joyce has not done this accidentally.

Very different are the conclusions of the stories. A series of events is recognized as having constituted a totality, a "significant experience," in virtue of its close, not of its opening. The conclusions of these stories are level and precise, the last lines denoting a genuine climax of realization (if told in the first person) or in the pattern of the objective situation (if told in the third). And the pause is genuine. If the reader were taken on five minutes farther he might find the addition unnecessary or silly, but it would not cancel out the effect of the whole story, as the prolongation of the trick conclusions of so many modern short-story writers would. In many of O. Henry's short stories, for example, where the final point is contained in a fraction of a moment sustained in print simply by the author's refusing to go farther, the conclusion is not a genuine one, no real end to a pattern, but simply a piece of wit on the author's part. The stories they tell are not real patterns or wholes but are made to appear so only by the epigrammatic form of the conclusion, and the point would be lost if the author told his readers the succeeding event. Joyce is not in this tradition—he has more respect for his art. His final pauses are as genuine as the final bars of a Beethoven symphony, though not nearly so obvious. . . . Genuine pause does not imply a long-drawn-out conclusion or an uneconomical art: Joyce's endings are subtle and rapid:

> "What do you think of that, Crofton," cried Mr. Henchy. "Isn't that fine? What?"
>
> Mr. Crofton said that it was a very fine piece of writing.

Or:

> Gazing up into the darkness I saw myself as a creature driven and derided by vanity; and my eyes burned with anguish and anger.

And there is the immensely subtle and effective ending of **"Grace,"** concluding in the middle of Father Purdon's sermon. (pp. 66-70)

"Two Gallants," a gray, unexciting incident whose predominant mood is illustrated by the setting—late Sunday evening in a deserted street of Dublin—is one of Joyce's minor triumphs. It is a perfect example of the organization of the casual until, simply by the order and relation of the parts, it becomes significant, not only a sordid incident that happened at a given moment but a symbol of a type of civilization. The arrangement of detail so as to give the utmost density to the narrative is a striking quality here, as it is in **"Ivy Day in the Committee Room."** Joyce will pause to elaborate the description of a character at a certain point of the story, and it is only by a careful, critical analysis that we appreciate the full effect of having that pause in that place and in no other. Always the location of particularizing detail is such that it suggests the maximum amount of implication. In **"Ivy Day in the Committee Room"** two features of Joyce's technique are dominant: first, every action is symbolic of the atmosphere he wishes to create, and, second, the pauses for description are carefully arranged and balanced so as to emphasize the symbolic nature of the action. The introduction of candles to light up the bareness of the room at the particular point in the story when Joyce wishes to draw the reader's attention to its bareness is one of many examples:

> A denuded room came into view and the fire lost all its cheerful colour. The walls of the room were bare except for a copy of an election address. In the middle of the room was a small table on which papers were heaped.

A simple enough piece of description, but it has been held back till now and allowed to emerge naturally as a result of the candle incident at a point where the emphasis on bareness, on the loss of the fire's cheerful color, and on the dreary untidiness of the room, gains its maximum effect as regards both structure and atmosphere. Similarly, the manipulation of the Parnell motif in this story shows great skill. It is suggested in the title, but does not break through to the surface of the story until, at a point carefully chosen by Joyce, Mr. Hynes takes off his coat, "displaying, as he did so, an ivy leaf in the lapel." And henceforth this motif winds in and out until its culmination in Mr. Hynes's recitation. And no more effective symbol of the relation between two of the main interests of Dubliners in the beginning of this century has ever been created than in this simple, realistic piece of dialogue and description:

> "This is Parnell's anniversary," said Mr. O'Connor, "and don't let us stir up any bad blood. We all respect him now that he's dead and gone—even the Conservatives," he added, turning to Mr. Crofton.
>
> Pok! The tardy cork flew out of Mr. Crofton's bottle. Mr. Crofton got up from his box and went to the fire. As he returned with his capture he said in a deep voice:
>
> "Our side of the house respects him because he was a gentleman."

The claims of liquor impinge naturally on those of politics, as anyone who has seen a certain section of the Scottish Nationalists at work in Edinburgh today can well understand. A similar point is made in Mr. Kernan's remark in **"Grace."**

> " 'Course he is," said Mr. Kernan, "and a damned decent Orangeman, too. We went into Butler's in Moore Street—faith I was genuinely moved, tell you the God's truth—and I remember well his very words. *Kernan,* he said, *we worship at different altars,* he said, *but our belief is the same.* Struck me as very well put."

This time it is religion and liquor that mingle so effortlessly. The slipping-in of the name of the bar right beside Mr. Kernan's expression of his genuine religious emotion is realistic and convincing in itself and is also symbolic in that it makes, thus economically, a point about the Irish character.

Joyce's realism in ***Dubliners*** is not therefore the casual observation of the stray photographer, nor is it the piling-up of unrelated details. All the stories are deliberately and carefully patterned, all have a density, a fulness of implication, which the even tone of the narrative by disguising only renders more effective. The almost terrifying calm of **"An Encounter,"** the aloof recording of **"Eveline,"** the hard clarity of carefully ordered detail in **"After the Race,"** the carefully balanced interiors in **"A Little Cloud,"** the penetrating climax of **"Counterparts,"** the quiet effectiveness of **"Clay"**—to select only some of the more obvious points—are the work of an artist whose gift of observation, tremendous as it is, is never allowed to thwart his literary craftsmanship—his ability to construct, arrange, organize. The two most impressive stories in the collection are **"Ivy Day in the Committee Room"** and the concluding story, **"The Dead."** The former has in a high degree all the qualities we have noted; it is as careful a piece of patterned realism as any writer has given us. But **"The Dead"** differs both in theme and technique from all the other stories in ***Dubliners*** and deserves some discussion to itself.

In **"The Dead"** Joyce uses a much more expansive technique than he does elsewhere in ***Dubliners.*** He is not here merely concerned with shaping a series of events into a unity; he has a specific point to make—a preconceived theme in terms of which the events in **"The Dead"** are selected and arranged. In the other stories there is no point other than the pattern that emerges from his telling of the story; no argument can be isolated and discussed as the "theme" of the story, for the story is the theme and the theme is the story. The insight of the artist organizes the data provided by observation into a totality, but no external principle determines that organization; the principle of organization is determined simply by further contemplation of the data themselves. But **"The Dead"** is the working-out, in terms of realistic narrative, of a preconceived theme, and that theme is a man's withdrawal into the circle of his own egotism, a number of external factors trying progressively to break down the walls of that circle, and those walls being finally broken down by the culminating assault on his egotism coming simultaneously from without, as an incident affecting him, and from within, as an increase of understanding. Only when we have appreciated this theme does the organization of the story become intelligible to us. On the surface it is the story of Gabriel returning from a jolly time at a party given by his aunts in a mood of desire for his wife and the frustration of that desire on his learning that a song sung by one of the guests at the party had reminded his wife of a youth who had been in love with her many years ago and who had died of pneumonia caught through standing outside her window in the cold and the rain; so that his wife is thinking of that past, in which Gabriel had no share, when he was expecting her to be giving herself to him, the final result being that Gabriel loses his mood of desire and falls asleep in a mood of almost impersonal understanding. But about three-quarters of the story is taken up with a vivid and detailed account of the party, and on first reading the story we are puzzled to know why Joyce devotes so much care and space to the party if the ending is to be simply Gabriel's change of mood on learning how his wife is really feeling. As a piece of simple patterning the story seems lopsided; we have to discover the central theme before we realize how perfectly proportioned the story is.

The theme of the story is the assault on the walled circle of Gabriel's egotism. The first character we see is Lily, the caretaker's daughter, rushed almost off her feet in the performance of her various duties. Then comes a pause, and Joyce turns to describe the Misses Morkan, who are giving the party, and the nature of the function. Then, when this retrospect had been brought up to the time of the opening of the story, Gabriel and his wife enter—late for the party, everyone expecting them. The external environment is drawn first before Gabriel enters and makes it merely an environment for himself. Lily is an independent personality, quite outside Gabriel's environment; she is introduced before Gabriel in order that when Gabriel arrives the reader should be able to feel the contrast between the environment as Gabriel feels it to be (a purely personal one), and as it is to a quite objective observer—the caretaker's daughter to whom the party is just an increase of work. Gabriel is greeted as he enters with a great deal of fuss; he enters naturally into the environment his aunts are preparing for him, but immediately after the greeting he has an illuminating encounter with Lily. He patronizes her, as he had known her since she was a child. He remarks gaily that one of these days he will be going to her wedding. Lily resents the remark and replies bitterly that "the men that is now is only all palaver and what they can get out of you."

What part does this little incident play in the story? It is the first attempt to break down the circle of Gabriel's egotism. He has questioned Lily, not with any sincere desire to learn about her, but in order to indulge his own expansive mood. He does not recognize that Lily and her world exist in their own right; to him they are merely themes for his genial conversation. Gabriel colors at Lily's reply; his egotism is hurt ever so slightly, but the fortress is still very far from taken. How slight the breach was is illustrated by his subsequent action—he thrusts a coin into the girl's hand, warming himself in the glow of his own generosity and not concerned with finding a method of giving that will obviate any embarrassment on Lily's part. On thinking over his encounter with Lily he sees it simply as a failure on his part to take up the right tone, and this failure of his own hurts his pride a little and makes him wonder whether he ought not to change the speech he has prepared for after dinner—perhaps that is the wrong tone too. He sees the whole incident from a purely egotistical point of view; Lily exists only as an excuse for his gesturing, and he is worried lest his gestures are not those which will get most appreciation from his audience.

Then we have Gabriel again in his relation with his aunts. He was always their favorite nephew, we are told. We see his possessive attitude to Gretta, his wife. We see him patting his tie reassuringly when his wife shows a tendency to laugh at him. When that tendency is manifested by Aunt Julia as well he shows signs of anger, and tactful Aunt Kate changes the conversation. The picture of Gabriel as withdrawn behind the walls of his own egotism is carefully built up.

The second assault on Gabriel's egotism is made by Miss Ivors, the Irish Nationalist, who attacks his individualism and asks what he is doing for his people and his country. She succeeds in making Gabriel very uncomfortable, and when she leaves him he tries to banish all thought of the conversation from his memory with the reflection that "of course the girl, or woman, or whatever she was, was an enthusiast but there was a time for all things." He goes on to reflect that "she had tried to make him ridiculous before people, heckling him and staring at him with her rabbit's eyes." And so fails the second attempt to break down the circle of Gabriel's egotism.

Then we see Gabriel in a more congenial atmosphere, where his egotism is safe. He is asked to carve the goose—as usual. But Gabriel has been upset, and his cold refusal of a request by Gretta shows his egotism on the defensive. He runs over the heads of his speech in his mind. It must be changed—changed in such a way as to squash these assaults that are being made on his ego. And so he thinks up a nice, cozy talk about hospitality and humor and humanity and the virtues of the older generation (with which, as against the generation represented by Miss Ivors, he temporarily identifies himself). Eventually the meal begins, and Gabriel takes his seat at the head of the table, thoroughly at ease at last.

Mr. Bartell D'Arcy is Gabriel's counterpart—a figure merely sketched, to serve the part of a symbol in the story. There is deliberate irony on Joyce's part in making Gretta refer to him as conceited in an early conversation with Gabriel. When at dinner a group of guests are discussing with their hostesses the singers of Ireland, their complacency is such as to dismiss Caruso almost with contempt: they had hardly heard of him. Only D'Arcy suggests that Caruso might be better than any of the singers mentioned, and his suggestion is met with skepticism. D'Arcy alone of the guests refuses to drink either port or sherry until persuaded by nudges and whispers. And it is D'Arcy who sings the song that removes Gretta to another world.

Gabriel's speech takes place as planned, and for some time he revels happily in the little world of which he is the center. The party ends and the guests stand with coats on in the hall, about to take their leave. Gabriel is waiting for Gretta to get ready, and as he and others are waiting the sound of someone playing the piano comes down to the hall:

> "Who's playing up there?" asked Gabriel.
>
> "Nobody. They're all gone."
>
> "O no, Aunt Kate," said Mary Jane. "Bartell D'Arcy and Miss O'Callaghan aren't gone yet."
>
> "Someone is fooling at the piano anyhow," said Gabriel.

D'Arcy is first "nobody"; then—and it is significant for the structure of the story that it is Gabriel who says this—he is "fooling at the piano." While Gabriel, a little disturbed again, is making a final effort to re-establish his full sense of his own importance by telling a humorous story to the circle in the hall and thus becoming again the center of attraction, the sound of someone singing comes downstairs, and Gabriel sees his wife listening, standing near the top of the first flight "as if she were a symbol of something." D'Arcy stops abruptly on being discovered (again the contrast with Gabriel) and finally Gabriel and Gretta set out for the hotel where they are to spend the night, as it is too far to go home at such an hour.

Then comes the climax, when the fortified circle of Gabriel's egotism is battered down by a series of sharp blows. Just at the moment of his greatest self-confidence and desire for her,

Gretta tells him that she is thinking about the song D'Arcy had sung. He questions her, first genially, and then, as he begins to realize the implications of the song for Gretta, more and more coldly:

> "I am thinking about a person long ago who used to sing that song."
>
> "And who was the person long ago?" asked Gabriel, smiling.
>
> "It was a person I used to know in Galway when I was living with my grandmother," she said.
>
> The smile passed away from Gabriel's face. . . .

Miss Ivors had talked about Galway; it was one of the symbols of that world of otherness against which Gabriel had been shutting himself in all evening. This is the beginning of the final assault. Then Gabriel learns that the "person" was a young boy that Gretta used to know, long before she knew him. He had been in love with her, and they used to go out walking together. With cold irony Gabriel asks whether that was the reason that Gretta had earlier in the evening expressed a desire to go to Galway for the summer holidays. When she tells him that the young man is dead—dying long since, when he was only seventeen—this line of defense is taken away from Gabriel and he falls back onto his final line:

> "What was he?" asked Gabriel, still ironically.
>
> "He was in the gasworks," she said.
>
> Gabriel felt humiliated by the failure of his irony and by the evocation of this figure from the dead, a boy in the gasworks.

Gabriel has no further defenses left. He burns with shame, seeing himself

> as a ludicrous figure, acting as a pennyboy for his aunts, a nervous, well-meaning sentimentalist, orating to vulgarians and idealising his own clownish lusts, the pitiable fatuous figure he had caught a glimpse of in the mirror. Instinctively he turned his back more to the light lest she might see the shame that burned upon his forehead.

The full realization that his wife had all along been dwelling in another world, a world he had never entered and of which he knew nothing, and the utter failure of his irony to bring his wife back to the world of which he, Gabriel, was the center, finally broke the walled circle of his egotism. A dead youth, a mere memory, was the center of the world in which Gretta had all this while been living. As a result of this knowledge, and the way it has been conveyed, Gabriel escapes from himself, as it were, and the rest of the story shows us his expanding consciousness until the point where, dozing off into unconsciousness, he feels a sense of absolute unity, of identity even, with all those elements which before had been hostile to his ego:

> Generous tears filled Gabriel's eyes. . . . The tears gathered more thickly in his eyes and in the partial darkness he imagined he saw the form of a young man standing under a dripping tree. . . . His own identity was fading out into a grey impalpable world: the solid world itself, which these dead had one time reared and lived in, was dissolving and dwindling.
>
> A few light taps upon the pane made him turn to the window. It had begun to snow again. He watched sleepily the flakes, silver and dark, falling obliquely against the lamplight. The time had come for him to set out on his journey westward. Yes, the newspapers were right: snow was general all over Ireland. It was falling on every part of the dark central plain, on the treeless hills, falling softly upon the bog of Allen and, further westward, softly falling into the dark mutinous Shannon waves. It was falling, too, upon every part of the lonely churchyard where Michael Furey lay buried. It lay thickly drifted on the crooked crosses and headstones, on the spears of the little gate, on the barren thorns. His soul swooned slowly as he heard the snow falling faintly through the universe and faintly falling, like the descent of their last end, upon all the living and the dead.

The snow, which falls indifferently upon all things, covering them with a neutral whiteness and erasing all their differentiating details, is the symbol of Gabriel's new sense of identity with the world, of the breakdown of the circle of his egotism to allow him to become for the moment not a man different from all other men living in a world of which he alone is the center but a willing part of the general flux of things. The assault, which progressed through so many stages until its final successful stage, had this result, and the contrast with the normal Gabriel is complete.

It is only as a result of some such analysis that the organization and structure of **"The Dead"** can be seen to be not only effective but inevitable. It is a story which, in the elaborateness of its technique and variations of its prose style (the cadenced inversions of the final passage form a deliberate contrast with the style of the earlier descriptions, adding their share to the presentation of the main theme), stands apart from the others in ***Dubliners.*** Joyce's versatility is already apparent. **"Ivy Day in the Committee Room"** has the texture of a Katherine Mansfield story but with a firmness of outline and presentation that Katherine Mansfield lacked in all but two or three of her works. **"The Dead"** is in a more traditional style, but done with a subtlety and a virtuosity that makes it one of the most remarkable short stories of the present century. (pp. 71-81)

David Daiches, " 'Dubliners,' " in his The Novel and the Modern World, *revised edition, The University of Chicago Press, 1960, pp. 63-82.*

ANTHONY BURGESS (essay date 1965)

[*Considered one of the most prolific and versatile English novelists of his generation, Burgess has written such widely divergent works as* A Clockwork Orange *(1962), an account of a futuristic dystopia narrated by a violent teen-age criminal;* Nothing Like the Sun *(1964), a fictional rendering of William Shakespeare's life; and* Tremor of Intent *(1966), an eschatological espionage story. In addition, Burgess is recognized for his vast knowledge of music and linguistics and, in particular, for his erudite criticism of James Joyce's works. In the following excerpt from his study* Re Joyce, *Burgess discusses Joyce's understanding of his artistic function in* Dubliners, *paying particular attention to Joyce's notion of epiphany and his themes of paralysis and frustration.*]

Before leaving Ireland, almost for ever, [Joyce] wrote a Swiftian—or Hudibrastic—poem called "The Holy Office," in which the parochial poetlings of the Celtic Twilight have a few drops of acid thrown at them:

So distantly I turn to view
The shamblings of that motley crew,
Those souls that hate the strength that mine has
Steeled in the school of old Aquinas.
Where they have crouched and crawled and prayed
I stand, the self-doomed, unafraid,
Unfellowed, friendless and alone,
Indifferent as the herring-bone,
Firm as the mountain-ridges where
I flash my antlers on the air.

Bold words, and a bold manifesto:

> But all these men of whom I speak
> Make me the sewer of their clique.
> That they may dream their dreamy dreams
> I carry off their filthy streams
> For I can do those things for them
> Through which I lost my diadem,
> Those things for which Grandmother Church
> Left me severely in the lurch.
> Thus I relieve their timid arses,
> Perform my office of Katharsis.

Joyce, at twenty-two, had no doubt of his artistic function, nor of its importance. The office of purgation, of making art a kind of sewer for the draining-off of man's baser elements, was not what the Church would call holy; still, Aristotle—who gave him the word *katharsis*—was sponsored by St. Thomas Aquinas, and St. Thomas Aquinas was not of the same world as the Christian Brothers and the Maynooth priests. Joyce has the image of a great traditional intellectual aristocracy, to which he himself belongs. Prettiness, fancy, devotionalism have no place in the austerity and self-dedication of its creed. It is demanding, and one must be prepared to be damned for it (Joyce sees himself in a sort of hell of artists, "self-doomed, unafraid, unfellowed, friendless and alone"). And so the deliberate cutting-off, the exile.

The first big fruit of Joyce's exile was the volume of short stories, ***Dubliners.*** It seems a very mild purge to us now, chiefly because it is the first in a whole pharmacopoeia of cathartics to which we have developed a tolerance. To its eponyms it seemed strong enough; printers and publishers would not at first administer it; its little saga of rejections, bowdlerisations, burnings looks forward to the epic struggle of *Ulysses* (itself originally conceived as a story for ***Dubliners***) to get itself first into print and then past the customs-houses. The book was mainly written in Trieste in 1905, worked up from notes Joyce had made while still in Dublin. Grant Richards, to whom it was first sent, would and would not publish it. In 1909, Joyce gave it to Maunsel and Co. in Dublin. In 1910, Maunsel and Co. grew frightened of it and postponed publication. In 1912, the type was broken up by the printer and Joyce, in a broadside called "Gas from a Burner," made the printer say:

> . . . I draw the line at that bloody fellow
> That was over here dressed in Austrian yellow,
> Spouting Italian by the hour
> To O'Leary Curtis and John Wyse Power
> And writing of Dublin, dirty and dear,
> In a manner no blackamoor printer could bear.
> Shite and onions! Do you think I'll print
> The name of the Wellington Monument,
> Sydney Parade and Sandymount tram,
> Downes's cakeshop and Williams's jam?
> . . . Who was it said: Resist not evil?
> I'll burn that book, so help me devil.
> I'll sing a psalm as I watch it burn
> And the ashes I'll keep in a one-handled urn
> I'll penance do with farts and groans
> Kneeling upon my marrowbones.
> This very next lent I will unbare
> My penitent buttocks to the air
> And sobbing beside my printing press
> My awful sin I will confess.
> My Irish foreman from Bannockburn
> Shall dip his right hand in the urn
> And sign crisscross with reverent thumb
> *Memento homo* upon my bum.

But printing the name of the Wellington Monument and Downes's cakeshop was, after all, the thin end of the wedge. Admit the naturalism of a picture postcard and you must soon admit also *graffiti* on lavatory walls, the blaspheming of jarveys, and what goes on in the back bedrooms of Finn's Hotel. ***Dubliners*** was totally naturalistic, and no kind of truth is harmless; as Eliot says, mankind cannot bear very much reality.

And yet, first as last, Joyce did not want merely to record the current of ordinary life. There was this business of epiphanies, defined in *Stephen Hero* (the first draft of *A Portrait*):

> By an epiphany he meant a sudden spiritual manifestation, whether in the vulgarity of speech or of gesture or in a memorable phase of the mind itself. He believed that it was for the man of letters to record these epiphanies with extreme care, seeing that they themselves are the most delicate and evanescent of moments.

Stephen Dedalus tells his friend Cranly (as, in *A Portrait,* he is to tell Lynch—more eloquently and at much greater length) that Aquinas's three prerequisites for beauty are integrity, symmetry and radiance. First the apprehending mind separates the object—"hypothetically beautiful"—from the rest of the universe and perceives that "it is one integral thing"; it recognises its integrity or wholeness. Next, "the mind considers the object in whole and in part, in relation to itself and to other objects, examines the balance of its parts, contemplates the form of the object, traverses every cranny of the structure." As for the third stage—"radiance"—that is Stephen's translation of Aquinas's *claritas*—it is a sort of *quidditas* or whatness shining out of the object:

> . . . finally, when the relation of the parts is exquisite, when the parts are adjusted to the special point, we recognise that it is *that* thing which it is. Its soul, its whatness, leaps to us from the vestment of its appearance. The soul of the commonest object, the structure of which is so adjusted, seems to us radiant. The object achieves its epiphany—

The term seems ironic when applied to the "showings forth" of ***Dubliners,*** but, after all, the original Epiphany was ironic enough to the Magi—a child in a dirty stable.

The glory and mystery of art can lie in the tension between the appearance and the reality, or, rather, between the subject-matter and what is made out of it. The view that subject-matter should be in itself enlightening still persists, chiefly because a moral stock-response comes more easily to most people than a genuine aesthetic transport. When Grant Richards eventually got round to publishing ***Dubliners***—as he did on June 15th, 1914: very nearly the tenth anniversary of the Bloomsday that had not yet happened—few people were ready for it: the taste was for the didacticism, the pedestrian moral lessons of a less naturalistic fiction. In ***Dubliners*** the reader was not told what to think about the characters and their actions, or rather inactions. There were no great sins, nor any performance of great good. Out of drab ordinariness a purely aesthetic *quidditas* leaps out.

All the stories in ***Dubliners*** are studies in paralysis or frustration, and the total epiphany is of the nature of modern city life—the submission to routines and the fear of breaking them; the emancipation that is sought, but not sought hard enough; the big noble attitudes that are punctured by the weakness of the flesh. The first story, **"The Sisters,"** presents the key-word in its very first paragraph:

> Every night as I gazed up at the window I said softly to myself the word paralysis. It had always sounded strangely in my ears, like the word gnomon in the Euclid and the word simony in the Catechism. But now it sounded to me like the name of some maleficent and sinful being. It filled me with fear, and yet I longed to be nearer to it and to look upon its deadly work.

The narrator is a young boy. Behind the window Father Flynn lies dead. The boy, like Joyce himself, is drawn not only to the mystery of words but to the terrifying complexities of the rites that the priest has administered. As for the priest himself—old and retired and dying—the boy's feelings have been a mixture of awed fascination and repugnance. Father Flynn looks forward to the unpleasant priests of Graham Greene and the dramatic possibilities of the contrast between their function and their nature. He has been a messy snufftaker. "When he smiled he used to uncover his big discoloured teeth and let his tongue lie upon his lower lip." But now he is dead, and the boy goes with his aunt to see the body in the house of the Misses Flynn, the sisters of the priest. He learns, over a glass of defunctive sherry, that Father Flynn's illness began with the breaking of a chalice, that this affected his mind: ". . . And what do you think but there he was," says Eliza Flynn, "sitting up by himself in the dark in his confession-box, wide-awake and laughing-like softly to himself?" Meanwhile, the dead priest is "lying still in his coffin as we had seen him, solemn and truculent in death, an idle chalice on his breast."

That is the whole story, and it is more an attempt at establishing a symbol than manufacturing a plot: a broken chalice, an idle chalice. The shameful discoveries about the adult world continue in the next story, **"An Encounter,"** in which the boy-narrator and his friend Mahony play truant from school for a day. Their heads full of *The Union Jack, Pluck,* and *The Halfpenny Marvel,* they meet adventure, but not in the form of the innocent violence of their little Wild West mythologies. A shabby man accosts them, full of perverse fantasies. Mahony runs away, but the narrator has to listen to the man's

North Richmond Street, the home of the narrator of "Araby," where the houses "gazed at one another with brown imperturbable faces."

passionate frustration belongs to the boy himself. He is past the stage of encountering external mysteries—ritual and dementia—and is now learning about love's bitter mystery through pubescent experience. Here comes the eucharistic symbol: "I imagined that I bore my chalice safely through a throng of foes. Her name sprang to my lips at moments in strange prayers and praises which I myself did not understand." We are to meet this symbolism again, in the "Villanelle of the Temptress"—named in *Stephen Hero,* presented in *A Portrait.* In **"Araby,"** though, the loved one is no temptress but a girl at a convent-school. She wants to go to the bazaar called Araby (this, like all the public events in Joyce, is historical: it was held in Dublin from May 14th to 19th, 1894, in aid of Jervis Street Hospital); unfortunately there is a retreat at the convent and she has to be disappointed. The boy promises to go instead and bring her back a present. It is the last night of Araby, he must get some money from his uncle, and his uncle comes home late and fuddled. When he arrives at the bazaar it is closing down; the lights are going out.

> Gazing up into the darkness I saw myself as a creature driven and derided by vanity; and my eyes burned with anguish and anger.

The seeming triviality of the frustration and the violence of the language which expresses it are, as it were, reconciled by the aesthetic force of the epiphany: here, drawn from commonplace experience, is a symbol for the frustration of adolescence and, by extension, of maturity too.

The rest of the frustrations and cases of paralysis belong to the adult secular world. The heroine of **"Eveline"** longs to escape from her drab Dublin life and she has her chance. But, on the very point of embarking for Buenos Aires with the man who loves her, "all the seas of the world tumbled about her heart. He was drawing her into them: he would drown her." Her heart says no; she sets "her white face to him, passive, like a helpless animal. Her eyes gave him no sign of love or farewell or recognition." Little Chandler, in **"A Little Cloud"**, re-meets the great Ignatius Gallaher, who has made good in London journalism (in *Ulysses* he has already become a Dublin newspaper-man's myth: he telegraphed details of the Phoenix Park murders to the *New York World,* using a code based on a *Freeman* advertisement. This was a memorable scoop). Little Chandler makes the inevitable comparison between the richness of Gallaher's life, all whiskey and advances from moneyed Jewesses, and his own—the mean job, the insipid wife, the bawling child. If only he could make his name with a little book of Celtic Twilight poems, go to London, escape ghastly provincial Dublin. But it is too late. The epiphany flowers in the rebukes of his wife for making the brat scream, while his cheeks are "suffused with shame" and "tears of remorse" start to his eyes. The cage is tight-shut.

One need not be a negative and timid character, like Eveline or Little Chandler, to exhibit the syndrome of soul-rot. Farrington, in **"Counterparts,"** is burly, red-faced, perpetually thirsty, and he fancies himself as a pub strong man. But he has the shiftlessness of all virile Dubliners, and even the job of copy-clerk in a solicitor's office is too much for him. The little heaven of release from actuality is always the "hot reeking public-house," the tailor of malt, the dream of high-class women, but the money always runs out, the sponging cronies fade away, and heaven is thoroughly dissolved by the time he has reached the tram-stop on O'Connell Bridge. "He cursed everything," waiting for the Sandymount tram. "He had done for himself in the office, pawned his watch, spent all his monologue about whipping boys who have sweethearts. "He described to me how he would whip such a boy, as if he were unfolding some elaborate mystery. He would love that, he said, better than anything in this world; and his voice, as he led me monotonously through the mystery, grew almost affectionate and seemed to plead with me that I should understand him." The narrator gets away from the demented babbling, calling Mahony. "How my heart beat as he came running across the field to me! He ran as if to bring me aid. And I was penitent; for in my heart I had always despised him a little."

"Araby" is the last of this opening trilogy of stories in which the world is seen from a child's-eye view. Here, though, the money; and he had not even got drunk." All that is left is to go home and beat his son Tom for letting the fire go out. Tom cries: "I'll say a *Hail Mary* for you, pa, if you don't beat me . . . I'll say a *Hail Mary*. . . ." But a *Hail Mary* won't do for any of these Dubliners.

Nothing will really do. Lenehan, in **"Two Gallants"** as in *Ulysses,* carries his seedy scraps of culture round ("That takes the solitary, unique, and, if I may so call it, *recherché* biscuit!") in the service of a sports paper and the office of jester to whoever—even a boor like Corley—has, or is able to get, a little bit of spending money. But even where there *is* money, and education, and a fair cultivated and cosmopolitan acquaintance, there is something missing. In **"After the Race"** the city wears "the mask of a capital" for Jimmy and his European friends, who have come "scudding in towards Dublin, running evenly like pellets in the groove of the Naas Road" in their racing cars.

> At the crest of the hill at Inchicore sightseers had gathered in clumps to watch the cars careering homeward, and through this channel of poverty and inaction the Continent had sped its wealth and industry. Now and again the clumps of people raised the cheer of the gratefully oppressed . . .

There are drinking and gambling and song on board the American's yacht in Kingstown Harbour, but Jimmy is fuddled and is one of the heaviest losers. "They were devils of fellows, but he wished they would stop: it was getting late." It is all folly, and he will regret it all in the morning. At the end of the story—Joyce's only incursion into the world of the moneyed—morning has come. "Daybreak, gentlemen!"

High ideals are betrayed—not with renegade force but through submission to compromise, the slow silting away of conviction that, it seems, only the Irish fanatic can hold. Mr. Henchy, in **"Ivy Day in the Committee Room,"** says:

> "Parnell is dead. Now, here's the way I look at it. Here's this chap come to the throne after his old mother keeping him out of it till the man was grey. He's a man of the world, and he means well by us. He's a jolly decent fellow, if you ask me, and no damn nonsense about him. He just says to himself: 'The old one never went to see these wild Irish. By Christ, I'll go myself and see what they're like.' And are we going to insult the man when he comes over here on a friendly visit?"

It is Parnell's anniversary, and the corks pop round the fire in the committee room. The impending visit of Edward VII is folded into the warmth of convivial tolerance ("The King's coming here will mean an influx of money into this country"). Joe Hynes recites a poem called "The Death of Parnell," in which the lost leader is presented as a betrayed Christ. There is applause, another cork pops, and Mr. Crofton says that it is "a very fine piece of writing." Parnell has joined a harmless pantheon, no legitimate Jesus but an ikon. This is one of the stories that held back publication of the whole book. A libel on the Irish spirit, a too free bandying of the name of a living monarch, an intolerable deal of demotic speech: naturalism had gone too far altogether.

With **"Grace,"** the penultimate story, the heady wine of religious faith is decently watered for the children of this world, who—as the text of Father Purdon's sermon reminds us—are wiser in their generation than the children of light. The story begins with the fall of man:

> Two gentlemen who were in the lavatory at the time tried to lift him up but he was quite helpless. He lay curled up at the foot of the stairs down which he had fallen. They succeeded in turning him over. His hat had rolled a few yards away and his clothes were smeared with the filth and ooze of the floor on which he had lain, face downwards. His eyes were closed and he breathed with a grunting noise. A thin stream of blood trickled from the corner of his mouth.

This is Mr. Kernan, "a commercial traveller of the old school which believed in the dignity of its calling." He is one of a group of small tradesmen, clerks, employees of the Royal Irish Constabulary, workers in the office of the Sub-Sheriff or the City Coroner—good bibulous men who are to be the backbone of *Ulysses.* Mr. Power promises Mrs. Kernan that he and his friends will make a new man of her husband: no more drunken fallings, regeneration with God's grace. And so, without solemnity and even with a few harmless Catholic jokes, we move towards a businessmen's retreat, a renewal of baptismal vows, and a sermon from Father Purdon. It is a manly, no-nonsense sermon, in which Jesus Christ is presented as a very understanding master, asking little, forgiving much.

> We might have had, we all had from time to time, our temptations: we might have, we all had, our failings. But one thing only, he said, he would ask of his hearers. And that was: to be straight and manly with God. If their accounts tallied in every point to say:
> "Well, I have verified my accounts. I find all well."
> But if, as might happen, there were some discrepancies, to admit the truth, to be frank and say like a man:
> "Well, I have looked into my accounts. I find this wrong and this wrong. But, with God's grace, I will rectify this and this. I will set right my accounts."

Thus this rather mean city is spread before us, its timidity and the hollowness of its gestures recorded with economy and a kind of muffled poetry, its bouncing cheques of the spirit endorsed with humour but with neither compassion nor censoriousness, for the author must be totally withdrawn from his creation. The book begins, in **"The Sisters,"** with the image of a paralysed priest and a broken chalice; it might have ended, in **"Grace,"** with the sacrament of provincial mock-piety and a blessing for small and dirty minds. But it does not end there. The longest and best story which concludes the book is an afterthought. Dublin may be an impotent city, but Ireland is more than Dublin. Life may seem to lie in exile, "out in Europe," but it is really waiting coiled up in Ireland, ready to lunge from a wilder west than is known to the reading boys of **"An Encounter."** This story about life is called **"The Dead."**

Everything in Joyce's writing is an enhanced record of the author's own experience, but perhaps **"The Dead"** is the most personal item in the long chronicle of Dublin which was his life's work. Gabriel Conroy is a sort of James Joyce—a literary man, college teacher, contributor of a literary column to the Dublin *Daily Express,* Europeanised, out of sympathy with Ireland's nationalistic aspirations, aware that his own culture is of a different, superior, order to that which surrounds him in provincial Dublin. He has married a girl of inferior education ("country cute" is what his own mother once called her), but he does not despise her: Gretta Conroy has the Galway firmness of character of her prototype, Nora Joyce; she is beautiful; Gabriel is a possessive husband. On New Year's Eve they go to the annual party given by Gabriel's aunts—Miss Kate and Miss Julia—and, as the house is some way out of Dublin, they have booked a hotel room for the night. It is a good convivial evening, full of piano solos, song, quadrilles, food. As Gabriel and Gretta go to their hotel room in the early hours, a wave of desire comes over him: the possessive wants to possess. But Gretta is distracted. At the end of the party the tenor Bartell D'Arcy sang a song called "The Lass of Aughrim," and she is thinking about the song. A young boy she once knew in Galway used to sing it. His name was Michael Furey and he was "in the gasworks." He died young. Gabriel asks whether he died of consumption, and Gretta replies: "I think he died for me."

The complex of emotions which takes possession of Gabriel's soul on this disclosure and on Gretta's transport of re-lived grief needs something more than a naturalistic technique for its expression. We see the emergence of a new Joyce, the deployment of the cunning of the author of *Ulysses,* and experience a visitation of terrible magic. As Gabriel analyses his tepid little soul we see that his name and that of his dead rival have taken on a strange significance—Gabriel the mild angel, Michael the passionate one; and that dead boy, possessed of an insupportable love, was rightly called Furey.

> The air of the room chilled his shoulders. He stretched himself cautiously along under the sheets and lay down beside his wife. One by one, they were all becoming shades. Better pass boldly into that other world, in the full glory of some passion, than fade and wither dismally with age.

Gabriel becomes aware of the world of the dead, into which the living pass. That world goes on with its own life, and its purpose is to qualify, literally to haunt, the world of those not yet gone. The living and the dead coexist; they have strange traffic with each other. And there is a sense in which that dead Michael Furey is more alive, through the passion which killed him, than the living Gabriel Conroy with his bits of European culture and his intellectual superiority. Meanwhile, in the all too tangible world of Dublin, the snow is coming down, general all over Ireland. "The time had come for him to set out on his journey westwards." The west is where passion takes place and boys die for love: the graveyard where Michael Furey lies buried is, in a sense, a place of life. As for the snow, it unites the living and the dead and, by virtue of this supernatural function, it ceases to be the sublunary snow that drops on a winter city. Gabriel's soul swoons slowly as he hears "the snow falling faintly through the universe and faintly falling, like the descent of their last end, upon all the living and the dead." We have broken, with him, through the time-space veil; we are in the presence of a terrible ultimate truth.

Ellmann's biography of Joyce [see Additional Bibliography] tells us, in detail, about the real-life materials which went to the making of **"The Dead."** Gabriel's revelation of the community of dead and living was also his creator's, derived from a similar jealousy of his wife's dead lover, a jealousy which had to yield to acquiescence and a sort of surrender. By extension, jealousy of a living rival becomes equally futile: it is best to accept philosophically, even gladly; we can even end by deliberately willing the cuckold's role. When, towards the end of *Ulysses,* Bloom reflects on his wife's adultery (multiple—the names of her fellow-sinners are fully listed), he considers the responses of "envy, jealousy, abnegation, equanimity" and justifies the last of these with thoughts about "the futility of triumph or protest or vindication; the inanity of extolled virtue; the lethargy of nescient matter; the apathy of the stars." (pp. 35-45)

As for the bigger, and more creative, theme of the one world of living and dead, this may be thought of as having its roots in Joyce's Catholicism: the striving living are militant and the beatified dead triumphant, but they are members of one Church. Dead and alive meet naturally in the phantasmagoria of the brothel scene [in *Ulysses*]; in the deeper dream of *Finnegans Wake* the unity of human history depends on the simultaneous existence of all its periods. But, in the interests of economy, one man and one woman must play many parts. The table called, Joyceanly, "Who is Who When Everybody is Somebody Else" in Adaline Glasheen's *A Census of Finnegans Wake,* makes Earwicker play God the Father, Adam the sinner, Adam the father, Abraham, Isaac, Noah, Buddha, Mohammed, Finn MacCool, Tim Finnegan, King Leary and some twenty-odd other roles, and Earwicker's family is quick to find appropriate supporting parts. This is the Occam's Razor of the mature artist. At the close of **"The Dead"** Gabriel feels his own identity fading out and his soul swooning as the solid world dissolves: it is dissolving, proleptically, into the huge empyrean of *Finnegans Wake;* the seeds are being sown.

The importance of ***Dubliners*** in the entire Joyce canon cannot be exaggerated. There may seem to be little remarkable in the technique nowadays, but this is because Joyce himself, through his followers as well as in the book, has habituated us to it: we take for granted the bareness of the prose, the fact that originality may well consist in taking away as much as in adding. Joyce's later work is, in fact, an art of adding, of building on to a simple enough structure incrustations of deeper and deeper richness: *Finnegans Wake* represents the possible limit of loading statements with layers of significance. In ***Dubliners*** his task was different. He had to deromanticise fictional prose, stripping off the coloured veneers that had passed for poetic brilliance in the heyday of the late Victorian novel. To write like Meredith or Hardy or Moore (or anybody else, for that matter) was not difficult for the author who was to create the "Oxen of the Sun" episode in *Ulysses.* He naturally tended to richness, but richness was not wanted in this study of a drab modern city which should flash out its epiphanies from the commonplace. Where cliché occurs, cliché is intended, for most of the inhabitants of the city live in clichés. Where a stale bit of romanticism is used—as in **"Two Gallants"**: "His harp, too, heedless that her coverings had fallen about her knees, seemed weary alike of the eyes of strangers and of her master's hands"—that also is in keeping, underlining the poverty of the Irish dream of the past. As for the management of humour, as in **"Grace"** and **"Clay,"** this is as deadpan as anything in the contemporary American tradition and a world away from the whimsy and heavy-footed japing of what passed for comedy in Joyce's youth. But the miraculous ear for verbal nuance is seen best in the dialogue.

Joyce's books are about human society, and most social speech is "phatic," to use Malinowski's useful term. It concerns itself less with conveying information, intention or need than with establishing or maintaining contact—mere comfortable noise in the dark. Irish town speech is the most phatic of the entire English-speaking world: it is all colour, rhythm and gesture. It is the very voice of charming apathy and shiftlessness, a deadly Siren trap for the author who is concerned with strong plot and dramatic action, for the creation of Irish characters within the structure of a plot must either lead to the destruction of the plot or the falsifying of those who must enact it. When we see *Juno and the Paycock* we feel somehow let down when action occurs: the play stands or falls on what the characters say, and what they say does not take us towards a final curtain. Joxer and the Paycock, like *Finnegans Wake* itself, are destined to go round and round in a circle, lamenting the "chassis" of the world but never doing anything about it, asking "What is the stars?" but never troubling to find out. And so with Joyce's Dubliners, whose totem is Johnny the horse in Gabriel Conroy's story:

> "And everything went on beautifully until Johnny came in sight of King Billy's statue: and whether he fell in love with the horse King Billy sits on or whether he thought he was back again in the mill, anyhow he began to walk round the statue. Round and round he went. . . ."

The exactly caught speech of these harnessed citizens is the true voice of paralysis. Realising how essential its tones are to Joyce's art, we begin to understand his need for finding action outside, for his garrulous pub-crawlers will not generate it. Action has to come from an exterior myth, like that of the Odyssey, or a circular theory of history which suggests, even if it does not fulfil, an image of purposive movement. (pp. 45-7)

Anthony Burgess, in his Re Joyce, *W. W. Norton & Company, Inc., 1965, 272 p.*

FLORENCE L. WALZL (essay date 1966)

[In the following excerpt, Walzl discusses ambiguity in "The Dead," maintaining that the story's ambivalent conclusion resulted from Joyce's own altered outlook on Ireland by the time he wrote the story and added it to his already completed short story collection in 1907; Walzl also examines the structural unity of "The Dead" and its role within the precisely arranged structure of Dubliners.*]*

Dubliners as a collection and **"The Dead"** as a narrative both culminate in the great epiphany of Gabriel Conroy, the cosmic vision of a cemetery with snow falling on all the living and the dead. As an illumination, it follows Gabriel's meeting with the spirit of Michael Furey and seems to evolve from it. Though commentators generally agree on the structural design of ***Dubliners*** and the plot pattern of **"The Dead,"** they have not agreed on the interpretation of this conclusion, or even of the principal symbol, the snow, which to some represents life, to others death, and to still others life or death depending on the context of the passage. Such lack of agreement at the crux of a work seems surprising. The purpose of this study is to suggest that the ambiguity of this conclusion was deliberate on Joyce's part and that it arose from the history and development of ***Dubliners*** as a collection.

The context in which **"The Dead"** is read affects interpretations of the story. For the reader who approaches **"The Dead"** by way of the preceding fourteen stories of frustration, inaction and moral paralysis, this story is likely to seem a completion of these motifs, and Gabriel's epiphany a recognition that he is a dead member of a dead society. But when **"The Dead"** is read as a short story unrelated to ***Dubliners,*** the effect is different: the story seems one of spiritual development and the final vision a redemption.

A survey of the critiques of **"The Dead"** shows significant differences in interpretation. Explications which discuss the story and its final vision primarily as the conclusion of the book as a whole, such as those of Hugh Kenner [see excerpt dated 1955] and Brewster Ghiselin [see excerpt dated 1956], tend to interpret the snow vision as Gabriel's self-identification with the dead. However, structural analyses of the story *per se,* such as those of Kenneth Burke [see Additional Bibliography], David Daiches, Allen Tate [see excerpts dated 1960 and 1950], and others, generally agree that the story is one of maturation and that the snow vision is a rebirth experience. Though studies of the symbolism vary greatly, a number, among them the critiques of Ellmann [see Additional Bibliography], Magalaner and Kain [see excerpt dated 1956], and Tindall [see Additional Bibliography], note ambivalence in the symbols, or "different perspectives" in the imagery. All commentators agree on the essential significance of the snow vision both for ***Dubliners*** and **"The Dead."**

When Joyce left Ireland in 1904, he took with him the manuscripts of a number of the ***Dubliners*** stories and the following year completed a work that consisted of fourteen stories. It did not include **"The Dead,"** which was not written until 1907. It was this version that Joyce described as "a chapter of the moral history" of Ireland and as having its setting in Dublin because that city seemed to him the "centre of paralysis." There is no question that this work represents Joyce's view of Ireland at the time he left his native land—as a moribund country that destroyed or paralyzed its children because of its provinciality and conformism.

A number of studies have demonstrated ***Dubliners*** to have an organized inner structure. The stories are placed in four chronological groups, which Joyce described as an order of "childhood, adolescence, maturity and public life"; and all develop a dominant paralysis symbolism. The 1905 version was highly symmetrical, consisting of an opening triad of stories of individual children (**"The Sisters," "An Encounter,"** and **"Araby"**), a quartet of stories dealing with youthful men and women (**"Eveline," "After the Race," "Two Gallants,"** and **"The Boarding House"**), another quartet picturing mature characters (**"A Little Cloud," "Counterparts," "Clay,"** and **"A Painful Case"**), and a final triad dealing with public groups in public situations (**"Ivy Day in the Committee Room," "A Mother,"** and **"Grace"**). The first and final triads obviously balance individuals and groups, and all the stories in the middle quartets are arranged in pairs contrasting sex, age, and social type or status. Also, the characterizations have a patterning that is unusual in short story collections. Though the protagonist of each story is a different character, all—children or adults—are variants of a basic type, a central everyman figure. Since each main character is older in the first eleven tales, a life cycle is presented. This chronological structure is matched to a thematic one of hemiplegia. The result is a progression in which children are depicted as disillusioned, youths as frustrated or trapped, men and women as passive and non-productive, and social groups as completely static. The central image of the book is a creeping paralysis that ends in a dead society.

Analyses of the individual stories have shown that the paralysis motif tends to be developed by a number of related images, all variations on a basic death-life symbolism. They are stasis versus action, darkness versus light, cold versus warmth, and blindness versus perception. (pp. 17-18)

Inaction or arrest imagery is the most obvious variant of the paralysis motif. Joyce devises plots in which characters are immobilized by weakness or circumstance, symbolizes the resulting psychological situations by imagery of traps and cages, and employs settings with constricted spaces, such as confessionals, cells, cabins, narrow rooms, and little houses—all suggestive of graves or vaults (*e.g.,* **"Eveline," "A Little Cloud,"** or **"Clay"**). In addition, Ghiselin has pointed out a variation of this stasis-action imagery in the directional symbolism in ***Dubliners:*** movement eastward generally representing youthful attempts to escape life in Dublin (**"An Encounter," "Araby,"** and **"Eveline"**); circular movement or essential immobility at the center of the city, the frustration of more mature characters (**"Two Gallants," "The Boarding House," "A Little Cloud,"** and **"Counterparts"**); and movements westward a drift toward death of the elderly (**"Clay"** and **"A Painful Case"**). The stories of public life in the 1905 version all depict groups of people sitting inertly in public places. It should be noted that in this pattern of movement, Joyce is using traditional imagery that associates life with dawn and the east and death with twilight and the west.

Darkness and cold are also used either separately or in combination throughout ***Dubliners*** for death suggestions in contrast to light-warmth-life imagery. The opening pages set the tone with the repetitions of the words *night, darkened,* and *paralysis,* and in the succeeding stories images of shadow, mist, dimness, dust, gloom, and night appear as scenic details and symbols. Changes from light to darkness and warmth to cold (or the reverse) sometimes parallel the action of the plot (*e.g.,* **"An Encounter," "Araby," "Two Gallants,"** and **"A Painful Case"**). Twilight and night scenes have symbolic significance in most of the stories, and in the latter part of the book darkness and chill imagery is cumulative.

Blindness and sight imagery is also evident as a pattern. First, the tales, examined in succession, show a steady decline in the perceptivity of the characters as to the reality of their situations. The youths are painfully aware of their disappointments; the more mature suffer but lack insight; characters in the final stories seem totally insensitive. As a result the epiphanies of these final stories are usually manifestations for the reader rather than the character. In addition, throughout ***Dubliners*** Joyce uses frequent eye imagery, a practice consistent with his view of the epiphany as an enlightenment. At the climactic moment of revelation, lack of insight on the part of the character may be indicated by eyes that are dim, blinded, or unseeing (*e.g.,* **"Eveline," "After the Race,"** or **"Clay"**). By contrast a sudden view, a flash of light or color, may bring enlightenment (*e.g.,* **"A Painful Case"**). (pp. 18-19)

The end of the 1905 version was carefully planned to round out the beginning. **"The Sisters"** opens ***Dubliners*** with a story of defective religion and a picture of a priest dying of paralysis, a figure symbolic of clerically dominated Ireland, according to Joyce's brother. **"Grace"** ends this version with an ironic story of faith and a picture of a corrupt priest preaching a materialistic sermon to a group of morally insensible Dubliners. Both congregation and cleric exemplify Joyce's judgment that Ireland is spiritually dead.

Dubliners did not appear in the 1905 version. A series of disagreements over revisions of the stories delayed publication. When the book was finally published in 1914, a new story, **"The Dead,"** provided the conclusion.

"The Dead" is markedly different from the earlier stories in several important respects. It is not only a longer, more fully developed narrative, but it presents a more kindly view of Ireland. Exile had modified Joyce's views of his native land. He had found Italian cities like Pola and Trieste provincial in their own way, and Rome had seemed to him as much a city of the dead as Dublin. He complained that Rome lived as if by exhibiting its "grandmother's corpse." He now felt that his picture of Ireland had been "unnecessarily harsh," and that he had not shown Ireland's "ingenuous insularity" and unique "hospitality" [the source of the quotations is a letter from Joyce to his brother Stanislaus cited in Richard Ellmann's *James Joyce;* see Additional Bibliography]. **"The Dead"** reflects these modified views, but the changes presented Joyce a problem. For in adding **"The Dead"** to ***Dubliners,*** he was not merely appending another narrative to an ordinary collection of short stories: he was adding to a highly structured book already complete, a different kind of story with a different kind of conclusion.

As a narrative, **"The Dead"** has a plot of oscillation and reversal which mirrors the psychological changes in the chief character. The protagonist is Gabriel Conroy, a Dublin schoolteacher, who, with his wife, Gretta, attends a Christmas party given by his two old aunts, the Miss Morkans. During the evening a series of small events makes him alternate between emotions of confidence and inferiority. His self-esteem is undermined by the remarks of a bitter maid, Lily, by the criticisms of a fellow teacher, Molly Ivors, and by the doubts he secretly feels. On the other hand, his ego is bolstered by his aunts' dependence on him, his presiding at the carving, and his making the after-dinner speech. The attention, the festivities, and the prospect of an unaccustomed night at a hotel arouse in Gabriel romantic emotions and memories of his wife that have long lain dormant. When later at the hotel he approaches her amorously, he finds that she too is remembering a past love, but it is a different love from his. It is for a boy of her youth, Michael Furey, now dead. The sudden realization that for his wife the memory of a long dead lover has greater reality than does the physical presence of her living husband precipitates a crisis of self-evaluation in Gabriel. For the first time he gains an insight into his own identity and that of his society. In imagination he has a confrontation with his long dead rival, and from this meeting evolves the snow vision which ends the story and the book.

Obviously **"The Dead"** is a story of insight and realization, and it seems to reverse the pattern of increasing insensibility that ***Dubliners*** otherwise traces.

Nonetheless, in a number of ways, **"The Dead"** was clearly designed to provide an appropriate conclusion for ***Dubliners.*** Commentators have tended to apply the terms *coda* and thematic *reprise* to it. Structurally it fits neatly into the tales of public life depicting groups of provincial and conformist people. Its characters tend to recall earlier figures. Its atmosphere, despite the holiday scene, becomes one of funereal gloom as the conversation is devoted increasingly to the past, to people dead and gone, and discussions of death, monks, and coffins. There are constant intimations that the group will soon re-convene for a wake in these same rooms. In its own way, it rounds out the book as **"Grace"** had the 1905 version. Its setting, a gathering at the home of two ancient sisters, seems a scenic repetition of **"The Sisters,"** and Gabriel's final vision of a cemetery in the night is a fitting close for a book that began as a deathwatch outside the house of a dying man.

Despite these thematic repetitions, Joyce's problem in integrating **"The Dead"** into ***Dubliners*** was not easily solved. For **"The Dead"** is a story of maturation, tracing the spiritual development of a man from insularity and egotism to humanitarianism and love. No earlier character in ***Dubliners*** undergoes a comparable change or has such an enlightenment. It cannot be fit with easy logic into the dominant paralysis pattern of ***Dubliners.*** I suggest that Joyce made his accommodation by two means: first, use of ambiguous or ambivalent images that mirror the oscillation in Gabriel's character, and second, by means of a conclusion in which a series of key images, all employed earlier in both the story and the book as a whole, operate to reflect one set of meanings from ***Dubliners*** as a total entity and a slightly different set from **"The Dead"** as an individual story.

Gabriel's final epiphany, comprising his ghostly meeting with Michael Furey and his vision of the snow, is the chief means by which Joyce effects this resolution. Every image in it is a symbol, and since each symbol is multi-faceted in reflecting earlier ambiguities, the epiphany allows for either a life or death interpretation. Paradoxical images of arrest and movement, darkness and light, cold and warmth, blindness and sight, are used in this conclusion to recall both the central paralysis-death theme of ***Dubliners*** as a collection and the rebirth-life theme of **"The Dead"** as a narrative.

The ambiguity of this ending succeeds because Joyce had already described ambivalent attitudes on the part of the hero, largely by means of these same symbols, used in shifting, paradoxical ways. To illustrate: at first view **"The Dead"** seems to employ the patterns of arrest and motion used earlier in ***Dubliners.*** For instance constricted motion is definitely associated with the frustrated Gabriel. The most obvious instance is the family anecdote that he dramatizes, of the treadmill horse that on a Sunday drive in Dublin insisted on going round and round and round King William's statue. Though Gabriel does not realize it, he is acting out symbolically the vicious circle of his own daily round in Dublin. Also, the directional symbolism seems that of the earlier tales: the east is the direction of Gabriel's holiday escapes to freedom on the continent, the center of Dublin is made the scene of his revelation, and the west is associated with his final vision of the graveyard. However, it soon becomes evident that Joyce is developing, side by side with this east-west symbolic pattern, another one that is its opposite in certain ways. In this system the east suggests the old, traditional, and effete; the west, the new, primitive, and vital. These symbols are largely developed through the characters. The story develops a contrast between the cultivated, urban East Coast society and people from the wilder Gaelic west of Ireland. The Dubliners are shown as a dull, elderly group. As exemplified at the party, the upper middle class Dubliner seems commonplace and his culture mediocre. The conversation is stereotyped, the famed Irish hospitality consists chiefly of eating and drinking, and the arts seem provincial. The one writer present produces critical rather than creative work; the pianist's playing is pretentious sound without substance. The "Three Graces of the Dublin musical world" are a spinster and two ancient ladies whom Gabriel privately and hypocritically admits are "only two ignorant old women." In contrast, the westerners are more simple, direct and passionate. For example, several of the strongest characters are associated with the west, among them Gabriel's argumentative colleague, Miss Ivors, who urges him to visit the west to learn Gaelic and see the real Ireland; his attractive wife, Gretta, who has come from Connacht and is "country cute"; and above all, Gabriel's ghostly rival, Michael Furey, who is strongly identified with the west country. The character contrast between east and west is made explicit in the opposition between Gabriel's mother and his wife, the two principal women in his life. His dead mother is identified as a chief representative of the cultivated Dublin milieu. The "brains carrier" of the family, she saw that her sons were educated for the proper professions. She exists in the story as a photograph in which she holds a book. She opposed Gabriel's marriage to a girl from the west country. In contrast, his wife, Gretta, seems representative of a more natural west. She is always associated with color and perfume, music and stars, and her reactions always seem direct and ingenuous. It should be noted that in this second pattern of east-west symbolism Joyce is developing traditional symbolism, also. From the Ulysses myth to the American mystique of the West, the east has represented the old and tried, and the west the new and unknown. Westward movement in this association tends to symbolize man's utopian possibilities and connote search and adventure. Thus, in **"The Dead"** Joyce deliberately builds an ambivalent symbolism of motion and direction that in some contexts equates the east with dawn and life and the west with sunset and death, but in other contexts associates the east with the old and sterile and the west with the new and vital.

The darkness-cold and light-warmth images are also developed paradoxically in shifting patterns of meaning. Several episodes will illustrate this. When Gabriel first comes out of the dark and cold into the light and warmth of the Morkan house, his marked insulation against the cold and snow by means of heavy clothes and galoshes suggests a conventional symbolism which associates heat with life. But ironically the lights within seem to illuminate a society that is stuffy and dead rather than warm and alive, and Gabriel soon longs for the cold fresh air and the great darkness outside, which now seem to represent the vitality of nature and perhaps also the living culture of Europe beyond the seas. Later as the characters prepare to leave the party, there is a shift back in the symbolism. The "cold, fragrant air" is no longer emphasized, but seemingly casual remarks about the cold and night build up a death-journey symbolism. The departing guests remark about the sharp wind, the bitter cold, the snow which is "general all over Ireland," and the fact that "everybody has colds." Mary Jane shivers as she tells the leave-takers that she "would not like to face . . . [their] journey home." The repetitive farewells of "Good-night," "Good-night, again," "Good-night, all. Safe home." "Good-night. Good-night" (the word is repeated ten times) hint of a "last journey." These suggestions are imagistic preparations for the scene in the hotel bedroom where the death imagery is unmistakable. The box-like room, the removal of a candle, the darkness, the chill, and the bed on which Gretta lies, all build the impression of a vault where the dead rest frozen on their biers. There is no question that the symbols have shifted back and forth in these episodes.

These shifting images of darkness-cold and light-warmth are supported by marked ambiguity in the handling of the snow imagery. The snow mirrors the very paradox Joyce is developing. For snow exposed to heat turns into water, but exposed to cold solidifies into ice. (Water is an archetypal life symbol, and ice a traditional death symbol.) In **"The Dead"** the snow symbol unites all the other images.

The coldness and warmth imagery developed in connection with Gabriel is extraordinarily complex. Every commentator on **"The Dead"** has remarked how the snow is associated with Gabriel from his first appearance to his final vision. Throughout the story a complicated interplay of attraction and repulsion is evident in his attitudes. Though he boasts of the galoshes that insulate him from the snow, he also longs for physical contact with it. Though he is moved by the sight of the snow on the roofs, he is irritated by the slush under foot. Though he thinks of statues and monuments covered with snow during the evening, he never sees the relevance of these pictures to himself. (It is the reader that notes the likeness to the opening description of Gabriel.) His final epiphany involves a vision in which snow is both falling and melting. The inherent flexibility of snow as a symbol allows Joyce to shift symbolic suggestions rapidly in these contexts. The warmth imagery will be discussed in connection with the angel symbolism.

The imagery of blindness and sight combines ambivalence and ambiguity. It is used initially to indicate Gabriel's lack of insight and his unconscious avoidance of reality, but it later is employed to describe the gradual enlargement of perspective that leads to his final cosmic vision. Images of eyes, eyesight, glasses, mirrors and windows appear in the story in varied and paradoxical meanings. Of all these images, the mirror is most significant and like the snow it tends to shift its meaning with the context of the passage. For the mirror in **"The Dead"** represents successively illusion, human reality, and intuitive vision.

The first use of reflection imagery is Narcissistic, and here Joyce is working in a rich literary tradition that extends from Ovid through Shakespeare's Richard II and Milton's Eve to modern psychological fiction. The story opens with a protagonist preoccupied by his own image. How he appears to other people engrosses Gabriel, to the point that his sense of his own identity becomes the view of him reflected from his aunts, the guests at the party, and even the maid, Lily. His concern for a flattering self-image is shown imagistically by eyesight-glasses references. Gabriel's eyes are described as "screened" by his "scintillat[ing]" or "glimmering" glasses. His "delicate and restless eyes" are dazzled by the "glitter" from the polished floor and bright chandelier. In short, his view of the world is distorted by the reflections from his environment, and Gabriel is unable to see reality as it is. Since his eyes are easily irritated, he goes several times to the windows to look out on the darkness, actions suggesting his psychological uncertainty. This Narcissistic imagery culminates with his first direct look into a mirror. Joyce has both Gretta and

Gabriel look into a large cheval-glass shortly after they reach the hotel. What Gretta sees is not immediately revealed, for she turns away "serious and weary." Gabriel looks in the mirror and what he sees is an illusion—a "broad, well-filled shirt-front, the face whose expression always puzzled him . . . , and his glimmering gilt-rimmed eye-glasses." His blind egotism masks the truth from him, for actually this image is the pompous front he has been at the party. The mirror has reflected a flattering distortion for him. But the same mirror will later reflect reality. After Gabriel learns the truth that he has not been the only love in his wife's life and that his sense of possession of Gretta has been only an illusion, he again looks in the mirror and this time he does see reality in an extended view that includes himself and his society. This time he sees "a ludicrous figure, acting as a pennyboy for his aunts, a nervous, well-meaning sentimentalist, orating to vulgarians and idealising his own clownish lusts." This is the figure he has really cut that evening. Moreover, he now identifies himself with the social group that he has secretly despised and yet feared all evening long: he is a "pitiable fatuous fellow" in a society of "vulgarians." Finally, at the end of ***Dubliners*** the mirror seems to shift significance again and becomes a reflection of intuitive or visionary truth. After Gabriel has realized the nature of his limitations and acknowledged that as a man he has never really lived, he turns humbly to the window where he had earlier imagined his rival standing. The physical scene of falling snow dwindles and dissolves for him, and the cosmic snow vision replaces it. In this scene the mirror has become a reflecting window, and ultimate reality is shown in an image of a cemetery in the snow. The symbolism seems highly Dantean in its concept of the glass as a reflection of transcendent reality and in its presentation of that reality through a symbolic image. In the final canto of the *Paradiso* Dante, after perceiving an image, achieved a direct view of Being. Whether or not Gabriel does at the end of **"The Dead"** is one of the cruxes of ***Dubliners.***

The climax of ***Dubliners*** is the imaginary conformation of Gabriel and Michael from which the snow vision evolves. At this point both characters become larger than life, and it is clear that both are mythic figures and archetypes. At the first level they are characters in a story, rivals in a love triangle, the only unusual aspect of which is that one of the rivals has long been dead. At another level, they are archetypes. At a still different level their opposition is represented by their angel names and the legendary associations with each.

At the narrative level, the Gabriel-Michael opposition is illustrated in the scene at the Gresham Hotel. This episode marks a final phase of Gabriel Conroy's development as a character, for in it Gabriel moves from blindness and conceit to self-knowledge and sympathy for others. His enlightenment is effected by Gretta's telling him the story of Michael Furey, the frail boy who, because he loved her more than life, left his sick bed on a night of rain and cold to come to see her. Gabriel's sudden realization that he has never experienced a love like this brings with it the discovery that he has never lived to the full depth of being. Hence to his wife he is less real than Michael Furey, this shade of her youth. Joyce creates a polarity in the reader's mind between the lover and the husband. Both are shown as seeking the woman's love in the night, the dead lover standing in the falling rain, happy in his moment of love; the living husband, frustrated and unhappy in the dark, vault-like hotel room watching the snow fall. Ironically the ghost seems alive, the man dead. Here the Michael-Gabriel contrast opposes life-in-death to death-in-life.

As an archetype, Gabriel is the central everyman figure of ***Dubliners*** in its final configuration. In numerous ways he brings together in his character and life all the earlier protagonists. In his sensitivity and insecurity he recalls the little boys of **"The Sisters," "An Encounter,"** or **"Araby,"** whose quests for answers end in disappointment. He seems a projection of the youths like Eveline Hill, Jimmy Doyle, and Lenehan, who lack the energy to undertake vital careers and the courage to leave Ireland. He is not betrayed like Doran of **"The Boarding House,"** but he has himself betrayed his own best possibilities. Like Little Chandler and Farrington he is caught in a dull round of domesticity and uncreative work. He is like Maria of **"Clay"** in that he has never experienced the full meaning of love, and he is clearly on his way to becoming a prim, fuss-budgety Mr. Duffy. When he recognizes himself as a "fatuous fellow," he has pronounced his own identification with all the "sentimentalists," "vulgarians," pennyboys, pretentious fools, and ineffectual Dubliners of **"Ivy Day," "A Mother,"** and **"Grace."** In short, Gabriel Conroy is The Dubliner. And he is Man.

Michael Furey also is more than a character and an angel namesake. This should not be surprising, since in a number of earlier ***Dubliners*** stories, great names of myth and legend, heroes and God figures, are invoked as ironic contrasts. (Such examples as the Christ-Judas references in **"Two Gallants,"** the Mary contrast of **"Clay,"** and the Parnell and disciple figures of **"Ivy Day"** come readily to mind.) A phrase in Gretta's description of him identifies him. Speaking of Michael's end, she says, "I think he died for me." The phrase echoes the words of the Poor Old Woman who is Ireland in disguise in Yeats's *Cathleen ni Houlihan.* Speaking of her patriot-lover, "yellow-haired Donough that was hanged in Galway," she says, "He died for love of me." Michael represents Ireland—an older traditional Ireland of the Gaelic west, of Galway and the Aran Islands, an Ireland that Gabriel is unwilling to visit or to view as important. Michael is a fatherland figure. But he is more. The phrase "he died for me" and the picture of him standing under a tree identifies him as Christ. He is a symbol of sacrificial love in both configurations. To love a cause or a person more than life is the action of the hero and the God, and Michael is so identified. Gabriel the Dubliner has been incapable of such sacrifice. At this point, a question seems pertinent: who is the betrayer and who the betrayed? ***Dubliners*** as a whole work suggests that Ireland betrays its children. **"The Dead"** in this symbolic identification seems to imply that the Dubliner betrays Ireland. This is only one of the ambiguities that **"The Dead"** offers.

The central ambiguity of **"The Dead"** is the conclusion, and it is developed in large part by the Archangel Gabriel and Michael contrasts. Several polarities between Michael and Gabriel as angels namesakes appear. The first involves a difference in rank between these angels. In the angelic hierarchies, Michael as an archangel has precedence over Gabriel as an angel, a relationship which is probably exemplified in the ascendancy of Michael over Gabriel in Gretta's consciousness. The second polarity involves the elements in nature which these two angels represent. In both Jewish and Christian occult tradition the four chief angels, Michael, Gabriel, Raphael, and Uriel, are correspondent with the four elements, seasons, directions, and winds. Michael represents symbolically the element water, is called "the prince of snow," and is associated with silver. Gabriel represents fire, is called "the prince of fire," and associated with gold. These suggestions all appear in **"The Dead."** A third polarity involves a contrast in

New Testament tradition: Michael is primarily the angel of the Last Judgment and Gabriel of the Annunciation. All these motifs join in clusters of shifting symbols in the final section of **"The Dead,"** especially the scene at the Gresham Hotel, which introduces the snow epiphany.

This episode presents a paradoxical contrast between the "living" ghost, Michael, and the "dead" man of flesh, Gabriel. This paradox affects certain images, deriving from the angelic traditions, that are applied to Michael and Gabriel. Michael, named for the angel of water and snow, is always associated with cold, sometimes in combination with rain, sometimes with snow. His memory is first evoked by Gretta when she hears the song, "The Lass of Aughrim" with its picture of a loved one deserted and standing in the cold. Then in her story of Michael, she describes how, when he came to say goodbye to her, he stood shivering in the streaming rain under a tree outside her window. Finally, through a series of imaginative suggestions, Joyce creates in Gabriel's (and the reader's) imagination the illusion that throughout the whole scene in the hotel room, the ghost of Michael is standing outside the window in the snow under the gas lamp looking in. These suggestions come to an eerie climax when the "few light taps" of snow upon the window pane re-created the sound of the gravel Michael had thrown long ago to attract Gretta's attention. Now they call Gabriel to a different rendezvous, the vision of the graveyard where Michael lies buried under the drifting snow.

While the linking of Michael to cold is consistent throughout these scenes, there is an interesting shift from rain to snow imagery. In Gretta's memories Michael is always evoked in rain, but in Gabriel's evocation he is usually associated with snow. The rain and water symbolism suggests that to Gretta, Michael brought an experience of life and love. The snow symbolism suggests that to Gabriel he now brings an experience of death.

The heat and fire imagery associated with Gabriel is partly explained by Gabriel's representation as the angel of fire. Metaphors of fire describe his feelings for Gretta, but paradoxically because they are applied both to his lust and his love. His present emotions "glow angrily" and are termed "the dull fires of . . . lust." The pure, intense love of his youth is depicted as the soul's "tender fire" and likened to the "fire of stars." In thus making a distinction between a love that is life-giving and good and one that is destructive and evil, Joyce is developing a life-death contrast. In using fire in such opposite meanings Joyce probably took Dante as model. In the *Purgatorio,* where the punishments image the sins, the lustful are purged in fire, but in the *Paradiso* fire as light is the image for God's love. In fact, Joyce's very phraseology, the "fire of stars," suggests Dante's pictures of the planetary heavens as rings of light and of the angelic choirs as circles of fire. In use of this imagery Gabriel seems rightly named for the angel of fire.

Ambiguities extend also to the roles Michael and Gabriel play as namesakes of great angels. St. Michael is the warrior angel of the Last Judgment, depicted in art holding scales and associated with the settling of accounts. One of his chief offices is to bring men's souls to judgment. And this is precisely the role Michael Furey plays in **"The Dead."** Though he exists only as a memory in Gretta's mind, he brings Gabriel to a judgment of himself. No ambiguity lies in the fact of this judgment; the ambiguity lies in the nature of the judgment. In this context a second office of the archangel Michael is pertinent: his duty to rescue the souls of the faithful at the hour of death. Since the verdict in Gabriel's case is not in the form of a statement, but a vision, it is not clear which of these functions Michael performs. Does he bring Gabriel, as his final verdict, a knowledge that he is one of the dead? Or does he bring him an illumination that rescues him at the brink of spiritual death? Joyce leaves the role of Michael ambiguous.

In contrast to the stern role of the archangel Michael, Gabriel is a messenger angel associated with God's beneficence. In the Old Testament he is the angel sent to Daniel to interpret two great visions of salvation, one of them a Messianic prophecy. His words to Daniel, "Understand, O son of man, for in the time of the end the vision shall be fulfilled" (Daniel 8:17) may have relevance to **"The Dead."** In the New Testament he is the angel of the Annunciation to the Virgin Mary and to Elizabeth. The vision of Zacharias has particular significance: to a man who was old and sterile and whose wife was barren, the angel Gabriel brought promise of new life. Does this name symbolism suggest birth and renewal for Gabriel? Or is it ironic in connection with this frustrated man? Joyce is not explicit.

All these complex motifs reach culmination in Gabriel's vision. This epiphany is the final stage of a development that has carried Gabriel from a selfish preoccupation with self to sympathy with Gretta, pity for his relatives, and love for all men. His illumination takes place when he realizes he is part of common humanity and shares its mutable state of being. At this moment of enlightenment he loses even the sense of his own identity, and his soul approaches "that region where dwell the vast hosts of the dead." As he watches the snow fall, he reflects that the "time had come for him to set out on his journey westward." Because of the earlier ambiguities, Joyce has made it possible for this strange statement to be either a life or a death suggestion. It is the keynote symbol of the vision, and its significance is all-important, since the meaning of the rest of the vision depends on the interpretation of this image. If it is read as a death symbol, all successive images take a like coloration. If it is read as a life symbol, the succeeding images all suggest rebirth. It signals the opening of one of the most remarkable ambiguities in literature, a conclusion that offers almost opposite meanings, each of which can be logically argued.

For the reader who has come to this conclusion by way of the fourteen preceding stories of disillusioned children, frustrated youths, sterile adults and paralyzed social groups in ***Dubliners,*** the cosmic vision of **"The Dead"** seems the last stage in a moribund process. The final fate of the ***Dubliners*** everyman is a death in life, and Gabriel Conroy's illumination is that he is dead. In this interpretation the vision is a final statement of the death themes of the book. The snow that covers all Ireland images the deadly inertia of the nation. The lonely churchyard where Michael Furey lies buried pictures the end of individual hope and love. The crooked crosses on which the snow drifts represent the defective and spiritually dead Irish Church. The spears and barren thorns suggest the futility of Christ's sacrifice for a people so insensible. To the hero it is an irrevocable last judgment. Such an interpretation is a powerful and symbolically logical conclusion for ***Dubliners.***

This is not the conclusion that the reader who knows only **"The Dead"** draws. Interpreting the journey westward as a start toward a new life of greater reality, he sees a succession of rebirth images. The snow, though it is general over Ireland, is quickly swallowed in the Shannon waves—its static iciness melting in the great waters of life. The melting snow is seen as subtly paralleling the change in the hero whose cold conceit has disappeared with his warming humanitarianism. The snow melting is thus a baptismal symbol, and as such offers renewed life not only to Gabriel, but also all the dead who lie here. The lonely churchyard where Michael Furey is buried serves only as a reminder that the grave has already yielded up its dead. For Michael lives vibrantly in the memory of a vibrant act. The recollections of Christ's passion in the spears and thorns are reminders that sacrifice of self is the condition of revival. The judgment that Michael brings is a salvation, and Gabriel's swoon is a symbolic death from which he will rise revivified. Gabriel is rightly named: he is a figure of annunciation and new life.

Joyce thus resolved the problem in logic which arose from his changed viewpoints by composing a conclusion for **"The Dead"** and ***Dubliners*** that employed a pattern of ambivalent symbols and a great final ambiguity. (pp. 19-30)

Florence L. Walzl, "Gabriel and Michael: The Conclusion of 'The Dead,' " in James Joyce Quarterly, *Vol. 4, No. 1, Fall, 1966, pp. 17-31.*

JOHN WILSON FOSTER (essay date 1973)

[*In the following excerpt, Foster offers an upstart reading of "The Dead" in which he interprets Gabriel Conroy as the only character truly alive among a funereal gathering of Dublin dead.*]

Despite the intensity of analysis to which Joyce's story has been subjected in the last two decades, I believe a great deal remains to be said about **"The Dead."** In offering what I think is a fairly radical interpretation of the story, I wish to take issue with or supplement extant readings on four major grounds. (i) The elaborate ritual of the Misses Morkan's annual dance, rather than that of a New Year's celebration, is that of a funeral. In accordance with this view, many of the story's mythic and ritual allusions can be seen as ironic or, if you like, mockmythic and mockritual. (ii) I should like to rescue the character of Gabriel from those critics who see him at worst as a priggish buffoon and at best as an egotistic antihero who must remedy the flaws of his personality or "die." On the contrary, I see Gabriel as the story's undoubted hero who, rather than being the "deadest" figure at the party, is in fact the only "living" one, a particularly Joycean hero who must fly by the nets of the dead en route to epiphany. (iii) Gabriel's passage through the dead can be interpreted dialectically. The notion of the dialectic of epiphany we can derive from the esthetic theory presented by Stephen in *A Portrait,* and from a comparison of Stephen's epiphanies with that of Gabriel. (iv) Florence L. Walzl [see excerpt dated 1966] states that structural analysts of **"The Dead"**—Burke [see Additional Bibliography], Daiches [see excerpt dated 1960], Tate [see excerpt dated 1950], and to which list we can add William J. Handy [see Additional Bibliography]—"generally agree that the story is one of maturation and that the snow vision is a rebirth experience," unlike critics such as Kenner [see excerpt dated 1955] and Ghiselin [see excerpt dated 1956] who, reading the story within the context of ***Dubliners,*** tend to interpret the snow vision as "Gabriel's self-identification with the dead." However, Walzl neglects to mention the greater number of critics who assume other approaches to the story (mythic, historical, generic) and whose conclusions cannot easily be fitted into either of her categories. Often, these critics, without discussing any of the other stories in ***Dubliners,*** feel it necessary to reconcile the notions of death and rebirth. My own view is that while the critics Walzl neglects are closer to honoring the real nature of Gabriel's vision, the epiphany is neither a death nor a rebirth experience. The epiphany is, as C. C. Loomis remarks [see Additional Bibliography], a "timeless moment of almost supreme vision" in which death and life are fused and then transcended. No interpretation of **"The Dead"** is complete which fails to account for this in terms of the story's narrative and formal organization.

It would be unnecessary and tedious to catalogue all the direct and oblique allusions to death in the story, from the title and opening word to the last resounding paragraphs. However, it has yet to be fully shown that the insistence with which the allusions pepper the story is directly related to the ritual nature of the Misses Morkan's party. The party is contained within a ritual framework: there are elaborate and painstakingly conveyed rites of arrival and departure, from the ritualized banter as Gabriel scrapes the snow from his goloshes to that series of goodnights that seems to prefigure the pub scene in *The Waste Land.* These rites of threshold separate the party from the offstage journey of Gabriel and Gretta to the house on Usher's Island and from the hotel scene which follows the festivities. Between arrival and departure there is ritual dancing, a ceremonial feast, a speech, and ritual singing.

The dance is an annual affair, a ritual conducted ever since Kate and Julia, "after the death of their brother Pat," moved from Stoney Batter to the "dark gaunt house" on Usher's Island. The party begins with the ritualized small talk of welcome and reacquaintance and continues with the guests dancing quadrilles, a dance that requires a degree of organization and a number of male "recruits," a military metaphor highlighting the ritual nature of the diversion and later pursued in Joyce's description of the bottles on the feast-table. On the wall are icons of the dead: Romeo and Juliet, the two murdered princes in the Tower, Gabriel's mother. What these icons oversee is a disastrous attempt by Miss Ivors at a "joking relationship" with Gabriel, followed by Aunt Julia, old and grey, singing "Arrayed for the Bridal," a song in this context redolent of imminent death despite the clarity of voice. During the supper (the food of which is described in ceremonial detail), the guests speak of the departed and of the monks who sleep in their coffins, a conversation which, since it grows "lugubrious," is "buried" in silence. Then follows Gabriel's speech, devoted to the past and those "dead and gone great ones whose fame the world will not willingly let die." At the speech's conclusion, the guests toast their hostesses and sing "For They Are Jolly Gay Fellows," a song whose refrain, repeated for ritual effect, is curiously anything but gay. After more talk about the dead, this time "the late lamented Patrick Morkan," the guests disperse but not until Bartell D'Arcy has sung the final dirge, "The Lass of Aughrim" and ritual valedictions are exchanged.

Clearly, the Misses Morkan's party is, on this particular night at any rate, a funeral celebration whose corpse is played, at one level of reference, by Aunt Julia and Aunt Kate, and at another level by all the guests. Most of the party's main events can be viewed accordingly. The dances performed by the guests are "the dances of the dead" noted by Arnold van Gennep [in his *The Rites of Passage*] in certain primitive peoples and used as a motif in a poem by Joyce (as "the dance of death"), the same poem in which the phrase "distant music" occurs. For van Gennep, the dancing of the dead is a rite of incorporation into the other world, and funeral meals a bond of union between the living and the dead: "their purpose is to reunite all the surviving members of the group with each other, and sometimes also with the deceased . . .". Joyce, I suggest, exploits both meanings of incorporation, thus overlaying the story's levels of ostensibility.

Gabriel's speech can be regarded as a funeral oration over the "corpses" of the hostesses, over the "corpses" of the other guests, and over the actual, invisible corpses of the "dead and gone great ones." The toast and song to the hostesses are to a past that has already enveloped the partygoers and to the memory that the present has already become. "Arrayed for the Bridal," then, is Aunt Julia's own funeral dirge (and by extension the dirge for all those present, with the exception of Gabriel), her betrothal "with the population of the lower world" she is soon to join. In such a context, the final series of good-nights has a somewhat macabre effect, as though the living were exchanging farewells before their passage into death.

Most of those present seem to have upon them the stamp of mortality. Aunt Julia is old and grey; Aunt Kate's face is healthier than her sister's but is "like a shrivelled red apple"; the caretaker's daughter is called Lily and is described as "pale in complexion," a paleness accentuated by the gaslight; Mr. Browne is tall but "wizen-faced"; Freddy Malins' face is "fleshy and pallid" and he has a high-pitched, "bronchitic" laugh; Miss Ivors speaks "gravely" to Gabriel (it is a mock-gravity at first, but the association has been carefully planted); Freddy Malins' mother is a "feeble old woman with white hair"; it is Mary Jane who explains (and defends, we feel) the behavior of the coffined monks; Bartell D'Arcy, by singing the song of dead Michael Furey in an out-of-sorts voice (like Aunt Julia's) "made plaintive by distance," is also associated with death; and Gretta, who takes three "mortal" hours to dress herself and who must be "perished alive," later pines for a lost lover: it is her identification with the dead that is most complete. And of course, the actual dead hover around: the aunts' brother Pat, Gabriel's mother, old Parkinson, Wellington, O'Connell, Patrick Morkan, and supremely, Michael Furey.

If the party is indeed a funeral celebration, the fact that it takes place on Epiphany (first suggested by Julian B. Kaye [see Additional Bibliography]) is the story's overriding irony. The irony is translated into pun when Gabriel has his own epiphany which is very different from the experience of the Wise Men. Almost every critic has taken the mythic allusions in **"The Dead"** seriously and attempted to wring a corresponding meaning out of the narrative, but it ought to be clear that the presiding though offstage pun of the first act of the story is "funferal," the titular pun of *Finnegans Wake.* The story's littler ironies subtend this pun: Aunt Julia's "marriage" song is in fact a funeral dirge; Mr. Browne, jovial and witty, can be regarded as Satan or as Mr. Death as critics have suggested [see, for instance, Kelleher, Additional Bibliography]; the "Magi" (i.e. guests) arrive at the party, not to witness the birth of the Redeemer but to participate in their own funeral; the crosses in the graveyard where Michael Furey lies buried are "crooked" and the thorns around them "barren." The technique is akin to that used in **"Ivy Day in the Committee Room."** In the latter story, spare naturalistic detail veils the funeral celebration taking place. When the veil is removed, the mockserious intent of the author is also laid bare. The irony of the first act of **"The Dead"** is a variation of this: the ostensible mythico-ritual framework supporting the narrative conceals a framework of precisely opposite import, mourning rather than joyousness, silence rather than clamor, passage to the grave rather than deliverance from it.

Despite his central role, Gabriel is singularly apart from the festivities and guests. His apartness is first established through his encounter with Lily, which Gabriel immediately regrets, and tries to annul with a coin. It is underscored by his premonition that his after-dinner speech will be a failure, largely because it will be the product of an education superior to that of the other guests. It will also, we suspect, reflect Gabriel's cultural bias toward the Continent, an orientation presaged by the incident of the goloshes (" 'Gabriel says everyone wears them on the continent'.") and reinforced when Gabriel crosses Miss Ivors. In fact, the speech is a studied and rather fake attempt to deny any such orientation, something of a tossed coin to the partygoers.

By the time Miss Ivors resurrects the resentment that was roused in Gabriel by the memory of his mother calling Gretta "country cute," Gabriel is deeply alienated from the gathering, yet strives outwardly to accommodate himself to the ritual of the party. The carving of the goose, coming on the heels of departing Miss Ivors, allows him to succeed in this temporarily. But it is to be noticed that he "took no part in the conversation" which runs for several pages. Noteworthy, too, that "all the gentlemen, except Gabriel, ate some of the pudding out of compliment to Aunt Julia," Gabriel never eating sweets. Sometime after his speech, which is full of private matter and privately rehearsed phrases, despite the postprandial solemnity of its deliverance, Gabriel tells the story of Patrick Morkan and Johnny the horse. When the peals of laughter have died down, Gabriel's underlying alienation is recalled when he sees a woman standing on the stairs: "Gabriel had not gone to the door with the others. He was in a dark part of the hall gazing up the staircase."

Gabriel's apartness is also conveyed in his periodic though somewhat subliminal desire to escape the festivities. Ironically, the snow from which Gabriel insulates himself with goloshes exudes "a cold fragrant air" which in moments of stress he longs for. After the upset with Miss Ivors and Gretta, it is to the thought of snow that he turns: "Gabriel's warm trembling fingers tapped the cold pane of the window. How cool it must be outside! How pleasant it would be to walk out alone, first along by the river and then through the park! The snow would be lying on the branches of the trees and forming a bright cap on the top of the Wellington Monument. How much more pleasant it would be there than at the supper-table!" Just about to begin his speech, Gabriel leans nervously on the table and thinks of the outdoors again: "People, perhaps, were standing in the snow on the quay outside, gazing up at the lighted windows and listening to the waltz music. The air was pure there. In the distance lay the park where the trees were weighted with snow. The Wellington Monument wore a gleaming cap of snow that flashed westward over the white field of Fifteen Acres." Bird-flight is another image of escape for Gabriel, as it is for Stephen Dedalus. Listening to Aunt Julia's song, he thinks: "To follow the voice, without looking at the singer's face, was to feel and share the excitement of swift and secure flight."

Critics, when willing to grant Gabriel's essential separation from the others, usually see it as a sad reflection upon Gabriel's character. This I would contend. In his encounter with

Lily, Gabriel is politeness itself, calling the girl by name and speaking "in a friendly tone." It is Lily who answers "with great bitterness" when Gabriel hints at imminent nuptials, a merely ritualized and rhetorical remark. According to Aunt Kate, something has come over Lily lately, "she's not the girl she was at all." When Gabriel tosses her the coin, it is not, as Handy suggests [in his essay "Criticism of Joyce's Works: A Formalist Approach"], to reassert his social superiority, but an attempt to buy back a normal, ritually defined relationship, a transaction in which Gabriel is engaged most of the evening. In his confrontation with Miss Ivors, Gabriel must shoulder more of the blame, but only because his literal-mindedness (something he is destined to lose during the image-rife epiphany) does not equip him for parrying her ironies and banter. We must remember also that "West Briton" was an insulting remark in those days, and that Miss Ivors exceeds the bounds of the joking relationship, resulting in an unearned intimacy and an intrusion upon a man's private beliefs.

Gabriel, then, stands among the guests but not of them. He stands apart not so much because his formal education (Royal University) is superior, his culture (quasi-European) broader, his arrogance sterner. He is different because they are all tainted by death, fitting members of a funeral party, while he is there because of social and ritual obligations he must confront and rise above before the evening is out. His problem is not, as many critics see it, to become one with those at the party who are alive, but to escape all of them, for they are all without exception touched by death, directly or by association. Their mortality is not just the caducity of flesh. It is Lily's self-abnegation because, presumably, of a couple of bad experiences, a reversion to celibacy that somehow strikes one as curiously Irish (as well as being reminiscent of Eveline's unadventurousness). It is the restrictive Irish bigotry of nationalism and anti-Europeanism. It is the sterility of ritual that exists because of its own momentum and in which Gabriel participates before transcending the notion of duty later in the story. It is ancestor worship and the cult of the superiority of the past over the present. It is the life-negation practised by a man who sleeps in a coffin in rehearsal for death, a practice described in a conversation in which Gabriel, wisely, takes no part.

These are versions of forces which Joyce himself felt threatened by—religion, nationalism, celibacy, ancestor and parent worship—and which he wove into the nets Stephen flies by in *A Portrait.* It is arguable that whereas Stephen is able to escape the nets, Gabriel is mortally entangled in them. In support of such a view, Kelleher shows, convincingly I believe, that during the course of the evening, Gabriel violates taboos associated with his country: by telling Miss Ivors he is sick of Ireland, by recounting to outsiders an intimate family story of Johnny the horse, and by treating the statue of O'Connell disrespectfully. But I disagree with Kelleher's conclusion that these are tragic errors for which Gabriel must pay. Stephen violates many similar taboos without thereby incurring the wrath of any Joycean gods. Gabriel violates the taboos of the dead, not of the living, and the claim that the dead press vindictively is, as the hotel scene demonstrates, unrightful.

The forces from which Gabriel is alienated are death-forces. The ensuing question is: do these forces win by claiming Gabriel for their own, or does he escape them? In answering this, it would be absurd to press similarities between Gabriel and Stephen too far. As critics have rightly pointed out, Gabriel is what Joyce and Stephen would probably have become had they remained in Ireland. Certainly Gabriel is without Stephen's artistic credentials, though perhaps the creative ambition was once there, but sterilized by the forces of the dead around him. And certainly his pride is not of the high order of Stephen's, threatening as it does to settle into crankiness. Such a dim view of Gabriel would support the notion that the dead claim Gabriel at story's end. But against this view we must remember that Stephen is not the most prepossessing character we have met in fiction, either, being priggish, arrogant, and wilfully iconoclastic. Moreover, the personality of Gabriel as it emerges during the hotel scene is one capable of extending compassion and generosity toward others. In the end, however, we must appeal to Gabriel's epiphany, an experience that bears many resemblances to Stephen's most intense epiphanies and of such profundity and inclusiveness that to see it as a death-experience is to fragment it.

Gabriel's passage through the dead is conducted in accordance with the dialectic of epiphany. The three stages of this dialectic are: Gabriel's ritualized but uneasy confederacy with the dead, Gabriel's discovery of his real, solitary and living self, the annihilation of Gabriel's self and its consubstantiation with the matter and energies of the universe. Or, put another way: the wearing of a death-mask, the unmasking of the living self, the transcendence of death and life in epiphanic vision. In other words, Gabriel's ritualized confederacy *with* the dead is at the same time a form of insulation and self-protection *from* the dead. The dialectic is developed in three acts: the party, the hotel scene, and the epiphany, with a transitional scene between the first two acts in which Gabriel prematurely believes himself beyond the grasp of the dead. Throughout the story, in fact, the third stage of the dialectic is anticipated in the incremental development of motifs and in Gabriel's occasional lapses at the party into living responses.

Gabriel's ritualized confederacy with the dead takes the form of false sociability. There is irony in this, since as the party's presiding shaman he is required to be more socially conscious than anyone else. It is he who has the responsibility of seeing that Freddy Malins is not too screwed, who has to carve the goose, and who has to make the after-dinner speech. That he is in many ways the ritual focus of the dance simply sharpens the reader's awareness of his discomfiture. There is, too, his ritualized thinking that consists of elegant and rehearsed phrases, such as, "One feels that one is listening to a thought-tormented music." The speech, of course, is the most vivid illustration of ritualized thought and expression. Except during those moments when he wishes to flee, Gabriel lets ratiocination block genuine insight: "He asked himself what is a woman standing on the stairs . . . a symbol of." This is an advance on the literal-mindedness of his response to Miss Ivors, but like studied elegance, the search for symbolism in real life is a blinding confusion of artifice and reality.

The lip-service Gabriel pays to "living duties and living affections" in the course of his speech is another form of ritualism. It is a catchphrase merely, for what claim the strenuous endeavors of everyone at the party, including at this stage Gabriel, are not living but dead duties and affections. This is demonstrated in the hotel room when Gabriel attempts to give substance to the catchphrase and is balked by the presence of death. It is not until Gretta's revelations concerning Michael Furey that Gabriel realizes the reality of death. His speech, for instance, though ostensibly about the dead, is merely a litany of platitudes that exhibits absolutely no torment of thought at all; the funeral oration, like that in **"Ivy Day,"** has an empty ring to it.

At various points during the party, for instance when he sees his aunts as ignorant old women, or when he longs to be out in the snow, we catch a glimpse of Gabriel's real self. It is immediacy of emotional response that informs us that Gabriel is alive. When standing by the window after rebuffing Gretta's request to go west, Gabriel's "trembling fingers" tap the cold pane in consternation; approaching the hotel room with Gretta, he is "trembling with desire"; in the room, when he cannot reach Gretta, he is "trembling now with annoyance"; but when she kisses him, he is "trembling with delight." This immediacy of response is due, one feels, to the fact that Gabriel does wear a mask most of the time; his real self has not been toughened, as it were, in the air of objective reality. Hence the discarding of his death-mask toward the end of the story coincides with his deepening of emotion. I'm aware that I'm inverting formalist thinking on the matter. First of all, in seeing Gabriel's immediate, even shallow response to Lily, Miss Ivors, and later Gretta as his tenuous contact with the objectively real, rather than as evidence of his egotism, as the formalists would have it. Secondly, in seeing Gabriel during the party as being for most of the time precisely the opposite of egotistic, i.e., allowing others to impose their dead selves upon him and thereby dictate his reactions. Only at the end of the hotel scene is Gabriel self-sufficient enough (egotistic enough, if you like) to afford pity and compassion toward others.

Near the end of the party, there is a false and premature feeling of escape for Gabriel. Watching Gretta listen to Bartell D'Arcy, Gabriel begins to sense again that spaciousness and otherness he had sensed through the window after the encounter with Miss Ivors. But reason still prevailing, he translates the distant music of D'Arcy's song into visual symbol and it is not until the very end of the epiphany that Gabriel is to succumb to the *sound* of universal motion. Moreover, distant music is still at this stage for Gabriel and reader the music of the past, of grief, of the sad passions of the west (the song seeming "to be in the old Irish tonality"), rather than the music of visionary transcendence it is destined to become.

At first, Gabriel does not tumble to the illusion. Leaving the party with Gretta, he imagines they have "escaped from their lives and duties, escaped from home and friends and run away together with wild and radiant hearts to new adventure." Unknown to him, Gretta feels no such sensation of flight, she being preoccupied with thoughts of a dead lover, and so Gabriel's freedom ends, significantly, when they pass from out-of-doors into the hotel. In the bedroom Gabriel tries to act as though he were indeed free from the clutches of the dead, but he is soon thwarted by Gretta and the distant music of her past. Gretta, like the others, is one of the living-dead and as such beyond Gabriel's reach, beyond the scope and jurisdiction of truly living duty and truly living affection. Gretta's revelations about events in Galway at last produce the funeral celebration's most ostensible corpse, Michael Furey. It is Michael Furey who comes to "embody" in one ghostly figure those who haunt Gabriel, the dead who must be acknowledged and admitted: he is a figure from the past ("whose fame the world will not willingly let die"!), he was passionate in a self-denying, loyal and tubercular way, he came from the west (the ancestral home and most conventional locus of nationalist aspiration). This time the dead cannot be conveniently eulogized out of sight, cannot be concealed by euphemistic ritual, cannot be paid lipservice. This time the dead have to be confronted.

When Gretta flings herself on the bed sobbing, in a sense she dies for Michael Furey as he died for her, and so the real dead claim another for their own. When Gretta and Michael "join" each other in "death," Gabriel is left looking out of the window, the vision beyond death ever closer. If the story on one level concerns the price death exacts from those who choose not to acknowledge with the fullness of their being his omnipresence, then at this point Gabriel has come close to balancing his account. At the close of the story's second act, Gretta sobbing herself to sleep, Gabriel is on the threshold of coming to terms with mortality by recognizing its power and reality. To do so has involved some truly tormented thought: how that phrase, so casually tossed off by Gabriel in his speech, echoes mockingly in this scene! But it is not a question of initiation in any abrupt sense. When Gabriel sees himself as a ludicrous figure, pitiable and fatuous, he is not, as the formalists suggest, seeing the *real* Gabriel, but instead the Gabriel who has acted up to then against the subliminal current of his real being. The real Gabriel is the man looking at the mirror image; the masked Gabriel is the man reflected therein. But Gabriel's awareness, like the epiphany itself, has been steadily prefigured throughout the story in carefully woven images of snow, fragrant air, and flight. Now, alone (as in a glancing thought earlier in the evening he had longed to be), ineloquent, gauche, haunted, Gabriel is suitably prepared for the vision that has awaited him all evening. As in **"Araby,"** there is a profound and self-conscious awareness of loss and bewilderment before the exquisite swoon of epiphanic experience.

The quick feelings that have helped to alienate Gabriel from the others all evening subside into a kind of emotional stasis. When Gabriel watches Gretta sleep, he does so "unresentfully"; when he thinks of the small part he has played in her life, he is "hardly pained"; and it is with "curious eyes" that he looks upon her. When emotion again begins to suffuse him, it is pity now rather than annoyance or lust or nervous fear; "as he thought of what she must have been then, in that time of her first girlish beauty, a strange friendly pity for her entered his soul." The notion of pity is important in **"The Dead."** When the word is used at the party it conveys a merely ritual or rhetorical emotion: " 'O, what a pity!' " exclaims Mary Jane when Bartell D'Arcy stops singing on account of his voice; subsequently, everyone gives the singer advice and says it is "a great pity," and urges him to be careful of his throat in the night air. In the hotel room, Gabriel tries to reach his wife with sentiments he does not feel. Freddy Malins, he tells her, returned a borrowed sovereign, adding, " 'It's a pity he wouldn't keep away from that Browne, because he's not a bad fellow at heart.' " Almost immediately, he inwardly curses "the sottish Malins and his pound." Now in the bedroom with Gretta asleep, Gabriel thinks of his wife's fading beauty and a genuine pity possesses him.

Gabriel's pity, unlike the mercurial feelings that have played upon him all evening, originates freely and without provocation. It results in "generous tears" (copious, pitying), which adjective harks back to Gretta's premature description of Gabriel and leads forward to the notion of snow being "general all over Ireland." The expansion of Gabriel's emotions is a correlative, then, of his growing sense of physical spaciousness at this point in the story. Pity is also a unifying emotion. Stephen Dedalus defines pity for Lynch thus: " 'Pity is the feeling which arrests the mind in the presence of whatsoever is grave and constant in human sufferings and unites it with the human sufferer'." The grave and constant thing in this case is mortality, the human sufferer, at first Gretta and then by degrees everyone. Moreover, pity for Stephen is a tragic emotion and therefore static, unlike loathing and desire which are kinetic and divisive. The stasis is achieved dialectically in **"The Dead"**: Gabriel's occasional anger and spitefulness at the party is succeeded by desire in the hotel room and synthesized in tragic pity. Likewise, Gabriel's ritualized self is unmasked to reveal his vulnerable living self which in turn is annihilated. His false sociality gives way to solitariness which is then dispelled by his feeling of oneness with all the dead and then with all the living: all are expressions of the same dialectic.

Gabriel must accept his own mortality before he can feel at one with the dead. His awareness of Gretta's fading beauty becomes an awareness of Aunt Julia's imminent death, then an awareness of the reality of Michael Furey's death (he imagines he sees the young man in Gretta's garden), and at last of his own mortality: "One by one they were all becoming shades." Gabriel belongs in this category also, "they" being Joyce's rendering of Gabriel's own interior "we." It would be wrong, however, to deduce that Gabriel's recognition of the omnipresence of death is tantamount to his own symbolic death. Because Joyce maintains the atmosphere of death in the story's second act, it could appear as though the funeral celebration is followed by Gabriel's own "death" (following the revelations about Michael Furey) and the purgatorial journey of his soul during the epiphany. But it is Gretta rather than Gabriel who "dies" during the hotel scene; what looks like Gabriel's purgatorial experience at the story's close is his passage toward epiphany. Gabriel's realization that death mocks life—as the funereal reality of the party mocks its ostensible purpose, and the ghost of Furey Gabriel—is only a stage in this passage. From this realization springs Gabriel's sense of impoverishment before the final expansiveness of his vision.

By the beginning of the story's last paragraph, snow has succeeded death as the dominant motif but is not an image of death. "A few light taps upon the pane made him turn to the window": this is an echo of Gretta's story of Furey's throwing gravel against her window. Many critics have taken this to mean that the dead Michael Furey "lives" while Gabriel, ostensibly alive, is "dead." But in an earlier scene to which I have alluded Gabriel looks longingly through a window at his aunts' house and taps his fingers on the pane, a scene surely meant to echo in the story's last paragraph. And when we remember that Gabriel, out of doors on the way to the hotel, was elated and expectant, it seems that in each case windows function as a barrier between Gabriel and the snow and fragrant air that are images not of death but of imminent epiphany. Windows, indeed, are important throughout **"The Dead."** Before his speech, Gabriel imagines the pure air outside the window; walking to the hotel he recollects standing with Gretta, "looking in through a grated window at a man making bottles in a roaring furnace"; in the cab Gretta looks abstractedly out of the window, an echo of Gabriel's mention of rattling cab windows at the beginning of the story; in the hotel room a "ghostly" light shines through the window and Gretta looks out, an action repeated by Gabriel when he is shy of intruding on her grief. Whereas for Gretta the window presents an inward view of the dead past, it is for Gabriel a form of insulation (like goloshes), a barrier against the spacious forces without. The barrier—half willed, half imposed by circumstances—is destroyed at last when the snow invades Gabriel's being and he in turn passes through the window to become one with the indivisible radiance of universal beauty.

The ontology of **"The Dead"** clearly alters during Gabriel's epiphany, the mockritual and mockallegorical emphasis of the first two acts (however psychologically realistic) giving way to the lyrical beauty of the concluding act. We remember Stephen's definition of beauty: " 'an esthetic stasis, an ideal pity or an ideal terror, a stasis called forth, prolonged, and at last dissolved by what I call the rhythm of beauty'." Matter and form thus coalesce perfectly at the close of **"The Dead,"** the rhythm of beauty corresponding to the rhythm of the universe to which Gabriel is at last attuned. We might even forge a parallel between the stages of Gabriel's passage toward epiphany, and the three stages of esthetic illumination described by Stephen: the synthesis of perception, the analysis of apprehension, and the silent stasis of esthetic pleasure. Daiches is correct, then, in claiming that among other things **"The Dead"** is a symbolic statement of Joyce's esthetic attitude.

Gabriel's epiphany, as befitting its lyrical nature, is filled with images. These images have, of course, dimly illuminated the entire story, and in finally taking possession of it, they at last submerge the ratiocinative bent of Gabriel's mind: "His own identity was fading out into a grey impalpable world." The grey impalpable world is a familiar Joyce image for the gradual loss of identity and the dissolving of the external world. At its most literal, it images the lamplit room in which Gabriel is falling asleep; beyond that it is akin to the insubstantiality experienced by Stephen at key points of *A Portrait:* watching the leather football fly like a heavy bird "through the grey light"; the "soft grey air" around Stephen the day after he loses his spectacles and again after his triumphant confrontation with the rector; the "fading air" through which he watches the wheeling birds; the "veiled grey sunlight" around the girl during the Dollymount epiphany; his thoughts of E.C.: "He would fade into something impalpable under her eyes and then in a moment he would be transfigured." Joyce frequently uses soft greyness, whether in reference to dimsightedness, imminent sleep, or mist, as an image for the collapse of the self into the luminous silent stasis of epiphany. Thus, the underwater uncertainty of the world into which Stephen's drowsy soul passes during the Dollymount epiphany corresponds to that into which Gabriel's soul passes at the close of **"The Dead."**

This is an ambivalent process. On the one hand, it is a kind of death. Paleness when used in **"The Dead"** seems to connote, symbolize, or presage actual or figurative death, one of whose forms is an unhealthy preoccupation with the past. Hence the number of guests who are pale, actually or metaphorically. Hence, too, Gretta's association with dim light at the end of the party as she stands illuminated by the dusky fanlight, and in the hotel room as the "ghostly" light from the street lamp falls upon her. The light that shines upon Gretta is the pale light of the past and Gabriel refuses at first to recognize it, beset as he is with "clownish lusts" that seek the darkness. He shuns the bedroom light, is satisfied when there is no electric light, and refuses the porter's candle. Upon throwing his coat and hat down, he crosses to the window and stands with his back to the light. Gabriel's later acceptance of his soul's fading into a grey impalpable world follows upon his realization of the power and omnipresence of death.

On the other hand, what seems like a species of death is merely a necessary and transfiguring stage on the way to ultimate vision. In this sense, we may view the snow simply as an intensification of the grey world which, like the white snow-world, has illuminated Gabriel's passage through the dead. Greyness, in other words, is not only the ghostly light of the past, but also, as in *A Portrait,* the imagery of epiphany itself. Gabriel's avoidance of the light in the bedroom, then, is a disinclination to admit the vision that awaits him. In the story's final paragraph, Gabriel watches sleepily "the flakes, silver and dark, falling obliquely against the lamplight." The defenses against vision are down. In the image of the dark, mutinous Shannon waves receiving the falling snow, we have an imaginative representation of Gabriel's dark soul receiving the visionary light.

Like lambency, falling is a key motif at the end of **"The Dead."** The word occurs seven times in the last paragraph and is emphasized for several reasons. Firstly, to provide through imagery an objective correlative for the metaphor, "falling asleep." Secondly, to convey aurally by careful inversions and near-monotony the quality of imminent sleep and the slow reverberation of a few blurred thoughts in a tired mind. Thirdly, to indicate epiphany; at the climax of the experience "swooning" will sometimes be substituted for "falling," to suggest an emotional and spiritual as well as physical sensation. In particularly intense epiphanies, Joyce forges an interconnection between falling darkness, falling asleep, and the psychic sensation of falling as a metaphoric description of the spirit leaving its familiar moorings.

The motif of falling is, like lambency, developed through incremental repetition. Thus, we notice the modulation of Gabriel's voice during his speech ("falling into a softer inflection"), the falling of Gabriel's and Gretta's feet on the hotel stairs, and of the molten candle wax on to the porter's tray. This latter scene invites closer inspection. Joyce's description, "their feet falling in soft thuds on the thickly carpeted stairs" is not only aural but suggestively synesthetic as well. When the three halt on the stairs while the porter settles his candle, "in the silence Gabriel could hear the falling of the molten wax into the tray and the thumping of his own heart against his ribs." The heightening of Gabriel's senses suggested here becomes the outright synesthesia of the story's last paragraph when Gabriel *hears* the snow falling faintly through the universe. Synesthesia occurs in Joyce when senses expand and fuse in company with dissolving identity. And so Stephen, when he kisses the prostitute, feels an intimacy "softer than sound or odour," and later during the Dollymount epiphany his eyelids *feel* "the strange light of some new world."

The sound of the faintly falling snow at the end of **"The Dead"** also fulfils the motif of distant music established much earlier in the phrase "thought-tormented music" that Gabriel works into his speech, in the title Gabriel gives to the sight of his wife listening to D'Arcy, and in the "distant music" of love-words Gabriel had written Gretta years before. During the epiphany, the music of the past becomes the music of the spheres, the celestial music that Stephen also hears on occasion. By the time the epiphany climaxes, Gabriel's self has dissolved and its consubstantiation with the external world is complete. Gabriel's fading out requires the author to assume omniscient and sole control of the narrative. Effectively, this occurs with the sentence, "Yes, the newspapers were right: snow was general all over Ireland." Gabriel could not know this, and it would be an odd intuition even presented as a hypnagogic image. The subsequent description of the snow falling all over Ireland is the author's, Gabriel having surrendered to the vision that haunted him all evening. Joyce uses the omniscient viewpoint to achieve the sense of spaciousness Gabriel, with some irony, longs for during his speech, the spaciousness which at the close of **"The Dead"** permits the unimpeded flight of Gabriel's soul through fragrant air.

Although I do not read Gabriel's epiphany as his symbolic dying, I do not read it as his rebirth: since he is alive throughout the story, no "rebirth" is necessary. Those who see the story as one of rebirth see their evidence in the sentence: "The time had come for him to set out on his journey westward." Actually, this sentence is presaged in Gabriel's earlier reflection: "Better pass boldly into that other world, in the full glory of some passion, than fade and wither dismally with age." The possible ellipsis produces an ambiguity. Does this sentiment augur Gabriel's resolve to seek the glory of some passion before his eventual death, the notion that *he had better* seek such passion? In which case the westward journey would be a declaration of intent, a literal or symbolic journey in search of lost passion. Or is it a defeated salute to Furey and a remorseful acknowledgement that for himself it is too late, the notion that *it would have been better?* In which case the West is the symbolic location of death as well as the symbolic location of passion.

The ambiguity, I suggest, is best resolved in terms of a third choice. Gabriel's deepening pity is finally a more powerful experience than even Furey's passion, making Gabriel's "death" unfair and his recovery of passion redundant. The West is the symbolic location of death and of passion transmuted dialectically into the symbolic location of epiphanic vision. The image of the snow can be viewed correspondingly. At the story's end, snow cannot be death's image because, as Ellmann points out, it falls on the living *and* the dead, and also because it falls not only in Oughterard but in Usher's Island, Monkstown, all over Ireland, and all through the universe. Nor can it be a "warm" image of passion and humanity, as Tate suggests, for the same reasons. It seems more fitting for the snow to be the image of vision, consistent with that image's role throughout the story. The vision is of universal beauty, of universal motion, of the mutuality of death and life, of the "whatness" of all things. But the mutuality of life and death does not render redundant or irrelevant the necessity of Joyce's heroes passing safely through the dead. Gabriel's vision of the oneness of the living and the dead is itself a spiritual triumph of the living over the dead, as the ending of the story is Joyce's own esthetic triumph over the "dead" matter he has transmuted "into the radiant body of everliving life." I disagree, then, with Walzl who believes that a reading of **"The Dead"** within the context of ***Dubliners*** enforces a "death" reading. On the contrary, I see Gabriel as the grown-up counterpart of the young narrator of **"The Sisters"** (the first story in the volume), surrounded by the dead and the mourning, his way dimly lit by lamp and candle, looking beyond windows for an unforthcoming vision. But whereas the "grey face" of death—the actual dead and those "communing with the past"—paralyzes the boy, Gabriel (who like the boy is educated, intolerant, and beset by the notion of duty) triumphs over the dead by acknowledging their reality and ubiquity. In **"The Dead,"** the "dusky golden light" of the deadroom in **"The Sisters,"** and the extinguished bazaar lights that close **"Araby,"** are redeemed into visionary light, the circularity of theme and motif in ***Dubliners*** thus completed. Moreover, the narrator's illusory sense of freedom in **"The Sisters"** when the priest dies becomes triumphant reality in Gabriel's epiphany, as does the anguishing irony of the boy's illusion in **"Araby"** that he bears his chalice safely through the throng of the dead. (pp. 91-108)

John Wilson Foster, "Passage through 'The Dead'," in Criticism, *Vol. XV, No. 2, Spring, 1973, pp. 91-108.*

DONALD T. TORCHIANA (essay date 1986)

[*In the following excerpt, Torchiana examines Joyce's multi-layered narrative method in* Dubliners.]

Most critics remind us that in ***Dubliners,*** his first major publication, Joyce held up a mirror to the average Irishman. The ending of the famous letter to Grant Richards is usually cited to good advantage: "I seriously believe that you will retard the course of civilization in Ireland by preventing the Irish people from having one good look at themselves in my nicely polished looking-glass." Aside from this mirror-image of paralysis, commentators also point to Joyce's frequent use of the epiphany, especially at the end of his stories, to cast sudden illumination, a kind of radiance, which distinguishes the whatness of the story. Other critics insist on autobiographical interpretations. These stories, so the account goes, follow Joyce's four divisions of childhood, adolescence, maturity, and public life. Recent critics increasingly stress the psychosexual slant. Yet Joyce himself in his letters frequently reveals an almost obsessive demand for accuracy in the details of ***Dubliners,*** as though only the accurate fact ensured the meaning. Even when on the Continent, he seems to have had almost daily access to Irish newspapers, maps, and even John T. Gilbert's three-volume history of Dublin. In this regard, his final effort, **"The Dead,"** may well sum up and conclude the entire volume, for it has, simply put, the most facts and details. Now, all these hints, speculations, and approaches go a long way to help a general reading of ***Dubliners.*** Yet they don't go very far in clarifying Joyce's method—one that is oddly enough neither the method of literary naturalism, a term early settled on him, nor that of the mere symbolist, the identity that graces him in so much American criticism. The insistence on a mirror, the details in what he called his nicely polished looking-glass, and the epiphanies at the end of the stories all suggest to me something else. But let me quote Joyce himself on the first story. As he once told Adolf Hoffmeister:

> In the first story in ***Dubliners,*** I wrote that the word "paralysis" filled me with horror and fear, as though it designated something evil and sinful. I loved this word and would whisper it to myself in the evening at the open window. I have been accused of making up some words influenced by the conception of a universe that I never have seen. Perhaps my weak sight is to blame, so that my mind takes refuge in pictures evoked by words, and certainly it is a result of a Catholic education and an Irish origin.

Dubliners strikes me, then, as a series of representative pictures—or mirror-images, if you will. That is, they catch a permanence in Irish life that has a timeless quality as though each detail in any story had about it a built-in significance that no educated native Irishman could really miss and no outsider, armed with a guide to Ireland and a bit of imagination, could fail to detect. Yet these stories are also startlingly new, for all their occasional resemblance to Turgenev's *Sketches,* a scene from an Ibsen play, or the forceful truth of Tolstoy's short novels. This newness, as I take it, comes largely from Joyce's writing of Dublin as she had never been viewed before and, at the same time, writing against the mode of the Irish Literary Revival. (pp. 1-2)

[The] opening story, **"The Sisters,"** pictures a boy's fate, his likely future defeat as a priest of the imagination—something like the fate of Father Flynn, a genuine and no less scrupulous priest. Misunderstood by his sisters and the boy's aunt, condemned by the uncle and Mr. Cotter, the priest in his relationship to the boy serves as an ironic parallel to the figure of Father Christian Rosencrux—in fact Flynn means "ruddy" or "red" in Irish—Yeats's symbol for the imagination dormant for some two hundred years in both his 1895 essay "The Body of the Father Christian Rosencrux" and the later poem "The Mountain Tomb." Yeats frequently went on to speculate that a like imaginative rekindling in literature would soon break out in Ireland, the hoped-for effulgence of the Irish Literary Revival. I hold Joyce's first story to be a strong demurrer against such a possibility in the Dublin of 1895 and after. Part of Joyce's method would then seem to be his setting his face against such extravagant hopes. For example, his derision at the publication of AE's *New Songs* in 1904 figures powerfully in his letters and in his probing the character of Little Chandler in **"A Little Cloud."** We recall that Chandler contemplated signing his name "T. Malone Chandler" in hopes of recognition as a poet of the Celtic Twilight, much like the writers in AE's gathering. It is just possible that one of the more egregious among the mediocrities that contributed to *New Songs,* George Roberts, a man who was to give Joyce trials enough in the publication of ***Dubliners,*** is openly glanced at in the character of Little Chandler himself. For, while he recognizes himself as "a prisoner for life," he does not recognize that he is also enacting the role of the famous Prisoner of Chillon, in Chandler's case a mean, loveless marriage, perhaps made doubly ridiculous if we recall the inclusion of Roberts's poem "The Prisoner of Love" in *New Songs.*

Nor have critics been slow to recognize the spoof of the Revival in the story **"A Mother."** The Kathleen of the story is betrayed partly by Holohan, and partly by her own mother's outraged propriety and legality. Yeats's play may certainly be mocked, no less his poem "Red Hanrahan's Song about Ireland"; Kathleen is not the daughter of Holohan. One might even go on to say that by the time we reach **"The Dead"** the boy of the first story has dutifully grown into the nervous yet complacent Gabriel—reviewer, teacher of languages, Continental traveler, critic, but not imaginative poet. His speech at table is clearly derived from the last of Browning's poetic volumes, *Asolando,* which Gabriel probably reviewed earlier in 1903. Gabriel's speech, very close to the easy sentiments of the "Epilogue" to that volume, also serves as something of a dramatic monologue to expose him at his most fatuous. The method, then, in part, has been to mock the literary ideals of the Revival and to show instead the paralysis of the imagination in Ireland.

But Joyce's larger method—a laying on of national, mythic,

religious, and legendary details, often ironically, as we may also see—can discover itself in the simplest of references and place-names. For instance, early in the pages of **"Two Gallants"** we behold a mournful harpist playing "Silent, O Moyle" not far, we are informed, "from the porch of the club." Unobtrusively, Joyce has placed the key to the interlocking scenes of the story in our hands. For, instead of aimless wanderings through Dublin that the story seems at the best to afford, we recognize a landscape some two hundred years old. The club is the Kildare Street Club, bastion of a declining Ascendancy, and an offshoot from the older Daly's Club, where half the land of Ireland was said to pass through the gambling hands of a sporting nobility and gentry. In Corley (Lord Corley in *Ulysses*) and Lenehan we get the Garrison remnant of those former Ascendancy Bucks, still exploiting Ireland and getting paid for it to boot. As Joyce once said of British rule, and its instrument the Ascendancy in Ireland, "She enkindled its factions and took over its treasury." Consequently, every place-name in the story speaks of that Williamite and Georgian period and its profitable betrayal of Ireland's interest. From Rutland Square to the Shelbourne Hotel to Hume Street, the half-sovereignty, exposed in the small gold coin at the end, merely attests to that formula.

In the same mode, more briefly but no less powerfully, I would call attention to Farrington's final steps home upon alighting from the Sandymount tram in **"Counterparts,"** then to the furniture in Mr. Duffy's room in **"A Painful Case,"** no less to the dead priest's books in **"Araby,"** and last to the death-notice in **"The Sisters."** All these objects seem to me charged with a significance that goes to the heart of the stories and illuminates their pictures as though we unrolled a canvas.

If indeed a counterpart can be a legal document, a duplicate, or a like person, it can also be for Farrington himself another whose complement makes for a completeness. From first to last we see Farrington—whether at work, at play, or at home—in hell. Most readers recognize that he in fact commits all seven of the deadly sins. Tom his son pleads vainly that he'll say a Hail Mary for his father—of no avail for a man in hell. Yet we sympathize with Farrington, and Joyce in a letter has expressed the same sympathy—he may be more sinned against than sinning. Hence, as we watch Farrington enter Mr. Alleyne's office at the onset, a place centered by "the polished skull which directed the affairs of Crosbie and Alleyne," we are also in the place of a skull, Golgotha. At the story's end, when Farrington steps from the tram at Shelbourne Road, we hear of him propelling "his great body along in the shadow of the wall of the barracks." This is the famous Beggar's Bush Barracks, still standing today but no longer used by the military. A famous eighteenth-century engraving by Giles King shows the real meaning of the area before the barracks was built: a haunt of beggars, thieves, footpads and rapparees. In his way, Farrington is one of them, yet he, too, has suffered crucifixion that day and may, like the fortunate thief in St. Luke's Gospel, his counterpart, receive some release from his hell.

Mr. Duffy has another counterpart. Perhaps enough has been said about his library in **"A Painful Case,"** but no one has looked at the fact that "he himself had bought every article of furniture in the room." That furniture includes "a black iron bedstead, an iron washstand . . . a coal scuttle, a fender and irons. . .a black and scarlet rug. . . .A little hand-mirror . . . a white-shaded lamp." All these may seem of a

Sidney Parade, the scene of Mrs. Sinico's demise in "A Painful Case."

piece when we realize that Mr. Duffy's counterparts are the two slow trains, one from Kingstown that knocked Mrs. Sinico down, the other from Kingsbridge moving laboriously toward Cork, parallel on its track to the Liffey but puffing in the opposite direction. Yes, Mrs. Sinico had tried, as Joyce tells us, to "cross the lines," had died of "shock and sudden failure of the heart's action," and "had gone out at night to buy spirits." So she had also sought out Mr. Duffy after their first meeting, so she had crossed the lines when pressing his hand to her cheek, and so he had rebuffed her and broken her heart. Chapelizod, South George's Street, and the Magazine Hill, identified with the beginning, middle, and end of the story, are also Dublin's three associations with Isolde, her chapel, her tower, and her well, all underlining the ironic application of the Tristan and Isolde story to Mr. Duffy's mistake.

Just as quietly, the dead priest's books perused by the boy in **"Araby"** are all about or by double agents. Vidocq is perhaps the most celebrated, yet he must also vie with Pacificus Baker, compiler of the *Devout Communicant,* he who brought the young Edward Gibbon into the Catholic church, Gibbon who was to become one of her greatest enemies. *The Abbot,* despite its title, settles on a supposed waif, taken up by Protestant nobility, who later, in disguise, spies upon Mary Queen of Scots, but not without sympathy, and only at the end does he return to find himself indeed the scion of that Protestant nobility. Accordingly, only at the end of **"Araby"** does the boy, earlier aware of his "confused adoration," learn the futility of transferring his love of the Virgin to Mangan's sister, who so much resembles the girl in the charity bazaar on the Saturday after Whit Monday. He is in a world of double agents that include himself, his father surrogate, the uncle, Mrs. Mercer, "a pawnbroker's widow who collected used stamps for some pious purpose," and the Irish girl making up to bank-holiday visitors from England. Perhaps the same boy, the boy in **"The Sisters,"** will also reflect, after his telling silence at the end of the story, on the implications of a death-notice that makes Father Flynn's life virtually correspond with the church in Ireland since Catholic Emancipation in 1829, attaches his death to the defeat of another James at the Boyne on the same day, holds up the Feast of the Precious Blood for a man who fancied himself responsible for a broken chalice, and may point to another St. Catherine's Church where Emmet was executed. To these enemies of promise one is bound to add the detail that the good father had also retired to a shop in Great Britain Street where articles were sold to keep water from infants. Even an unscrupulous priest might have found himself disappointed and crossed before his death in such an ethos. The opposite irony springs from Mrs. Mooney's decision in **"The Boarding House"** to "catch short twelve at Marlborough Street;" for she will be going to the Pro-Cathedral, the Church of the Immaculate Conception, only after ensuring that Polly her daughter, a pregnant and "perverse madonna," will be married.

How much and how deep the most pedestrian and ordinary details flashed out meanings to Joyce is a subject usually reserved for discussion of *Ulysses.* Yet even the titles alone of the above stories suggest that meanings may be more than one, as we shall see in titles like **"Clay," "Grace," "A Mother,"** and **"The Dead."** Yet I would continue here to show how Joyce's method also makes for an expansion of his effects by linking the paralysis of Dubliners to all Ireland and insisting that its impress is from something more than a contemporary malaise. Joyce's frequent appeals to a historical memory strike an almost timeless note for the bane that has always afflicted Ireland.

For instance, during the boys' wanderings in **"An Encounter,"** time and again we happen on places of historical encounters where the Irish always ultimately lost, however apparent the victory might have seemed. Following the North Strand Road and then the Wharf Road, the boys also trace the line of the battle of Clontarf, a famous Irish victory over the Norsemen, yet also a Pyrrhic victory because of the loss of Brian Boru. Their final encounter with the pervert is in part a meeting head-on with a cruel twisted puritanism going back to Cromwell's time and not unknown to the Catholic church in Ireland. Cromwell also landed at the Pigeon House, the boy's failed destination. Yet they are also encountering a perpetual figure in Irish life, the combination of priestly and political repression that stretches back further than Cromwell. Moreover, the field where the boys come to rest, within sight of the River Dodder, is very close to the confluence of that river and the River Liffey. This place, given its shallow beach, was the site of the original Scandinavian landings in Dublin. In just such a field, the Norsemen would often construct a Thingmote where trials were held before a combined priest and magistrate, a *godi* as described in Haliday's *Scandinavian Kingdom of Dublin.* A convicted malefactor's only chance to escape execution was to run the gauntlet of surrounding warriors and escape the ring of bystanders. So the boy in the story goes over the slope, escaping his goggle-eyed pious sadist with silence, cunning, and something like exile. An encounter on ancient grounds turns out to be an encounter with a possible conqueror of himself, given religious and political forces, if he stayed. Stephen Dedalus' weapons will be his. Thus one historical reference.

No less drastic historically appears the likely necessity of defeat when, as in **"After the Race,"** an Irishman gains the allegiance of the French in any contest with the English. The sense of triumph that flushes the face of James Doyle while riding in a winning French car after the 1903 Gordon-Bennett Cup Race sharply recalls Irish enthusiasm after another such famous race won by the French. I speak, of course, of the notorious Races of Castlebar, the jibing appellation affixed to the British rout by a small French and Irish force under General Humbert in 1798 after the landing at Killala. But it's the aftermath, as Joyce's title suggests, that must preoccupy us. In the story, aboard the yacht in Kingstown harbor, the Englishman Routh wins the final game of cards over the Frenchman Ségouin. But the heaviest losers are the Irish-American Farley and the Irishman Jimmy Doyle. Just so after the Races of Castlebar. A second engagement lasted but a half-hour when the French surrendered. Their officers and men were well treated, even feted in Dublin. The Irish were massacred on the spot and their officers summarily executed. "Our friends the French," the traditional slogan, said to link patriotically Catholic France to Catholic Ireland in their joint enmity toward England, turns out to be inevitably disappointing, perhaps even collusive in Ireland's usual defeat.

But defeat at home or exile abroad may be much the same. Surely neither is much different historically, or so a story like **"Clay"** might insist. While Maria is clearly a symbol of Ireland—the Little Old Woman who appears to be ugly—she has for her reward in this story a remembrance of her mortality in the neighbor girls' trick. But beyond this a neighbor girl also wins the ring in the games while, of the four Donnelly children, one receives a prayer-book and the others get the water. In other words, the predominant likelihood for children in such a family is either the church or emigration. Might it be too much, then, to think of those mischievous girls next door as somehow resembling Caledonia and Britannia? The evening is not just Halloween or Allhallows Eve. It is also the beginning of Samhain, the Irish winter, when the druidical god of death sets evil spirits abroad in the darkness without disguise—such a history and such a time of year play nicely into Joyce's hands.

The timelessness of Irish paralysis reinforces what I might call mythic, religious and legendary patterns that Joyce seems to place so frequently at the very center of each story or picture. This method is openly visible in books like the *Portrait* and *Ulysses,* but I strongly believe that Joyce has invested very similar paradigms in most if not in all these ***Dubliners*** tales. John Kelleher's justly famous essay "Irish History and Mythology in James Joyce's **'The Dead',**" [see Additional Bibliography] cleverly establishes the mythic center of the final story as the fate of King Conaire in the saga "The Destruction of Da Derga's Hostel." (pp. 2-9)

In **"Eveline,"** . . . if we can accept the title as directing us to a little Aoife as well as to a little Eve, we may strongly question Eveline's rejection of Frank. To be a little Aoife is to emulate a number of legendary and mythic women, none a very great friend of the Irish family. To be a little Aoife may mean to be like the mother of Conla, or to be like the wicked stepmother of the Children of Lir, or even to follow Dermot MacMurrough's daughter and marry Strongbow in the smoking ruins of Waterford. In the same story, **"Eveline,"** the religious pattern is taken ironically from the life of the Blessed Margaret Mary Alacoque, whose colored print is on the wall. Her sufferings led to her meeting with Christ at the grille, the merging of his burning heart with hers, and the eventual founding of the Order of the Sacred Heart, so dear to family life in Ireland. Yet, in the name of that order and the promises made to the Blessed Margaret Mary, Eveline dumbly refuses to accompany "openhearted" Frank to Buenos Aires. In short, she who left a home consecrated to the Sacred Heart for that very cause refuses a similar call to her own heart and soul. A heritage of Christ's blazing love for man, caught in the visions of a provincial French girl of the seventeenth century, now denies the heart and renders chastity trivial in a later provincial and Catholic Dublin.

Sometimes Joyce's audacity in pursuing the ironies of religious assumptions in Dublin almost surpasses belief. If we count the moneylenders, questionable political figures, and ordinary run of failed businessmen and castle officials attendant upon the red-faced Father Purdon in **"Grace,"** they add up to a round twelve. We might well call the group apostles enough, if not children of light, as they ingest the Word, the sanctifying grace from a businessman's Christ. Another example: one critic, Joseph Blotner, has detailed the many parallels with the Crucifixion to be found in **"The Boarding House"** [see also Bruce A. Rosenberg entry in Additional Bibliography]. But he has neglected Joyce's clear-cut division of that story, the second part assuming less than a page of text yet seemingly equivalent in weight to the first. Here Joyce appends his sequel to the crucifixion that is any Irish forced marriage, that is, he gives us the likely drama of the Annunciation. In *Ulysses* we learn that Bob Doran on his yearly bender had identified himself to prostitutes as Joseph. Now here at the end of **"The Boarding House"** Polly suddenly drifts into a dream full of "hopes and visions" until her surroundings fade from her mind before she's recalled by her mother's voice. If her role has been that of a magdalen in most of the story, now—pregnant, dreaming and hopeful—she may be no more than "a little perverse madonna" yet she is in the same human predicament as her saintly sister of old, the Mother of Christ. To observe further the threats of Mrs. Mooney, a butcher's daughter, and the implacable attitude of Doran's employer, a great Catholic wine merchant, toward Doran, should he be exposed and refuse the sacrament of marriage, in no way lessens the ironic pertinence of the birth and crucifixion of Christ for another loveless Irish marriage sanctified by a mass.

Just as pertinent, though more muted as befits legend, is Joyce's use of Dun Laoghaire, at the time called Kingstown, in **"After the Race."** To contemplate Doyle senior, the former butcher and merchant prince, and his son Jimmy is also to glance at the continuing fates of Niall of the Nine Hostages and his son Laoghaire. Niall had embraced the hag Royal Rule to get the kingship at Tara; he had sought to advance himself on the Continent; one story has it that he was slain by a Saxon arrow shot by a rival Leinsterman backed by the Franks. Laoghaire was known for his attention to Irish law, his formulating the Senchus Mor, and then for also imposing the Boromean Tribute—cattle, sheep, and swine—originally forced by King Tuathal on Leinster. Captured during Leinster's resistance, Laoghaire swore by the four elements never to repeat his attempt. He broke his oath, however, and was immediately struck down by those elements. In the face of this legendary account, the flickering ironies in the fortunes of the Doyles, whose money and position are dependent upon meat, need not be drawn out. Yet the father is a kind of prince collaborating with royal rule; despite his patriotism, police contracts had allowed him to expand his business. He is also a parent who has sent his son to college and then to Cambridge in England. The son in turn has lost him a good deal of money to a Briton while in the company of Frenchmen in whose enterprise the father had encouraged the son to invest, thus hoping to extend both their social lives into Continental circles. Jimmy had dabbled in law at Trinity and now has returned to the family stronghold, formerly Dun Laoghaire, after a foray near Naas, once King Tuathal's base in forcing the Tribute. Breathless and excited, Jimmy is struck by the dawn's light on a body of water, Dun Laoghaire/Kingstown harbor, where, disarmed, relieved of his money, slumped toward earth, his head in his hands, he must nevertheless face his friends, the French.

In like manner, the expanding shadow of old Jack on the wall as his fire momentarily brightens may also set us thinking as we begin **"Ivy Day in the Committee Room."** For in fanning the flame he unwittingly stirs memories of the Phoenix Flame associated with Parnell and, before him, with the Fenian efforts to rid Ireland of England. Interpretations of the story that identify Parnell with Moses and the martyred Christ are well enough known. Yet the enlarged shadow of a decayed old man may also be juxtaposed not only with Parnell and the Fenian tradition but also with the original Finn and his Fianna. Finn and his warriors also cruelly contrast with the mayor-maker Fanning, his tool Dicky Tierney, and their seedy vote-canvassing underlings in the Committee Room. The popping of corks from Guinness bottles may also contrast with the real meaning of the Irish words behind the misnamed Phoenix, that is, *fionn-uisge,* "pure water."

Joyce's method tends to the hard and accurate facts of Dublin obviously enough. But it also appeals to the farthest reach of the Irish imagination, especially when excited by the illustrious dead in religion, legend, myth, history, place-name, and literature. The resulting picture or mirror-image is permanent.

But Joyce's method is also highly conventional as the practice of short story writing goes, so much so that I doubt that he could get ***Dubliners*** published today. The stories are simply too well done. The *New Yorker,* for instance, would probably rather accept a piece by someone like the late Frank O'Connor for its supposed Irish tone. Yet, though I may have dwelt overmuch on the interior intricacies in ***Dubliners*** . . . , Joyce's stories are just as rewarding if we but pay attention to their external events. So much on the level of mere narration is hit off brilliantly and even slyly, although that surface appears to be a rather formal, naturalistic one. Hence I ought to say a few things about Joyce's use of the more conventional methods of short fiction, and look for a moment at such important considerations as the matter of structure, tone, character, plot, action, and the like.

Joyce's structure tends to be the expected tripartite one: introduction, body, and what often appears to be an unfinished conclusion. But when he wishes to gain emphasis or effect a sharp contrast he will often interrupt his pages with a line of dots or make sure that a considerable space lies between two paragraphs as if to insist that the reader pause. **"Eveline," "The Boarding House,"** and **"A Little Cloud"** are supreme examples of the first practice. The Eveline who lives under the protection of the Blessed Margaret Mary Alacoque and the Eveline who resists a secular imitation of the founder of the Order of the Sacred Heart are sharply contrasted: Eveline at home and at the North Wall, Eveline without Frank, then with him, and at last without him. So, too, with Little Chandler. We view him at Corless's and then at home, first under the gaze of Ignatius Gallaher, then with his wife and child. While the contrast is a glaring one, we also may mark the common elements in both scenes. In **"Counterparts"** and **"A Painful Case,"** extra space brings us to the conclusion of both stories. Like Mr. Duffy, we look up after the newspaper account of Mrs. Sinico's death. At that point his changing reactions begin. Similarly, a line of dots heralded the end of Farrington's day at the office, but his awaiting the tram is rendered more subtly by the slightest increase in space that nevertheless helps us fix the increased anger and loathing that will explode into violence at the end. I am not sure that other critics have observed this practice, simple though it is, but when Joyce combines it with his multiple-meaning titles, his apparently innocent but loaded first paragraphs, and then his lingering yet truncated conclusions, usually the moment of epiphany, then one may realize how very scrupulously Joyce adheres to the structure of a short story. He does so much with so little.

A further example of this economy is Joyce's characterizations. I am especially impressed to find that his most powerful characters are often those who are barely seen, if seen or heard at all. The priest, Father Flynn, in **"The Sisters,"** for instance, exists largely as a matter of confused memories or the uncertain impression of his corpse. Yet his presence is a haunting one from first to last and, by my account, shadows the boy as one personage or another in all first three stories, and then again in **"The Dead."** On the other hand, unpleasant characters like Corley, O'Madden Burke, Mr. Henchy and Jack Mooney nevertheless engage our attention, even hold it, not just by what they utter but also by their physical presence, so very close somehow not only to what they say but also in fact to what they do. We meet or hear of them, no less incorrigible than ever, in *Ulysses.* Yet even in ***Dubliners*** Henchy's shortness, bustling nature and briskly rubbed cold hands somehow fit him most appropriately as hypocritical friend and back-stabber of Joe Hynes, who himself probably understands best what Ivy Day means and the continuous betrayal that it commemorates. No less, Jack Mooney's stubby arms and then the long look he casts on Bob Doran from the top of the stairs suddenly recall us to his determined mother and murderous, drunken father as another major threat to Doran. Corley walks like the policeman, his father; O'Madden Burke's stance with his umbrella matches his pompous name and imperious talk, natural covers for his shaky finances; Holohan's limp implies, however unfairly, something of his deviousness. Mr. Fitzpatrick of the vacant expression, the askew hat and flat accent remains a startling foil yet also a goad to the increasingly ferocious Mrs. Kearney.

Part of Joyce's success in striking off such memorably complex characters, sometimes in only a glance or two, may also lie in his controlling tone, one that can also seem at such great odds with itself. Joyce has the maddening talent of being both satirical and sympathetic, comic and tragic, malicious and sentimental, cynical and thoughtful both or all at once. As soon, for instance, as we begin to sympathize with Little Chandler, we also recognize him for the fool that he is. The child-beater, Farrington, whom we ought to hate, nevertheless gains a modicum of our sympathy for his retort to Mr. Alleyne and his defeat by the English sponge Weathers. The boy in **"Araby"** is doubtless a victim of puppy love, a comic casualty of the onset of puberty, yet who will not admit as a reader the terrible seriousness of the same boy's self-discovery at the story's end. Polly Mooney may indeed resemble "a little perverse madonna," yet something close to the ethereal touches her as she falls into a reverie of hopes and visions just before the story's end. Which side, we still ask, after finishing **"A Mother,"** are we meant to be on, Mrs. Kearney's or that of her detractors? And when will the arguments end on how we are meant to take Gabriel at the end of **"The Dead"**? Given Joyce's brilliant admixture of tone, I hope the answer is never.

As far as their actions go, most characters are caught up in the toils of a paralysis as much of their own making as it is of any burden handed down to them. Yet a heavy sense of determination hangs over all the stories—a determinism, whether religious, racial, political, or historical, that is seldom clearly recognized. Thus, not much happens in ***Dubliners,*** and what does happen appears to be part of a chain of causation that is habitual and age-old. In almost every story, the past lends great weight to the frustration of present action. In the first of the three opening stories alone, a dead priest has been misunderstood and will continue to be misunderstood. In the second, two boys fail to arrive at the Pigeon House but, willy-nilly, failure from the past has confronted them at every turn. In the third, a gift is not bought at the charity bazaar, largely for religious, historical, and only lastly sexual reasons. Drinking habits, traditional drinking habits, render more than one Dubliner foolish and disappointed—the boy's uncle, Eveline's father, Farrington, Mrs. Sinico, old Jack and his son, Mr. Kernan, to name but a handful. The church serves as a like inhibitor, as every story attests. Love, freedom, altruism, adventure, genuine struggle, all these dominions of spontaneous action and life are in very short supply.

At the risk of being overly paradoxical on this subject of determinism I must nevertheless add that, however abated their actions and characters, the stories do brim with excitement. The unsaid, the half-said, the undone or barely done, these halting movements also afford sharp glimpses of the extreme tensions, the desperate resolves, the chilly resignations, the nearly inhuman rages that invest what I have called this pictorial record or series of mirror-images that emerges as the total ***Dubliners.*** (pp. 9-15)

Donald T. Torchiana, "Introduction: James Joyce's Method in 'Dubliners'," to Backgrounds for Joyce's Dubliners, *Allen & Unwin, 1986, pp. 1-17.*

ADDITIONAL BIBLIOGRAPHY

apRoberts, Robert P. " 'Araby' and the Palimpsest of Criticism; or, Through a Glass Eye Darkly." *The Antioch Review* 26, No. 4 (Winter 1966-67): 469-89.

Refutes Harry Stone's 1965 explication of "Araby"; see Additional Bibliography entry below.

Baker, James R., and Staley, Thomas F., eds. *James Joyce's "Dubliners": A Critical Handbook.* Belmont, Calif.: Wadsworth Publishing Co., 1969, 188 p.

Includes discussion of Joyce's aesthetic theories and the short story genre, examination of the structure and unity of *Dublin-*

ers, critical analyses of the stories, and a comprehensive bibliography of criticism on *Dubliners.*

Beck, Warren. *Joyce's "Dubliners": Substance, Vision, and Art.* Durham, N. C.: Duke University Press, 1969, 375 p.
Explores major topics of *Dubliners* criticism: biography, publication history, critical response, prominent angles of approach, and stylistic elements, among others.

Benstock, Bernard. " 'The Sisters' and the Critics." *James Joyce Quarterly* 4, No. 1 (Fall 1966): 32-5.
Challenges the literal interpretation of "The Sisters" submitted by Thomas E. Connolly in his essay "Joyce's 'The Sisters': A Pennyworth of Snuff"; see Additional Bibliography entry below.

———, ed. *The Seventh of Joyce.* Bloomington: Indiana University Press, 1979, 266 p.
Critical collection that includes Florence L. Walzl's "A Book of Signs and Symbols: The Protagonist," Mary T. Reynolds's "The Dantean Design of Joyce's *Dubliners,*" and Phillip Herring's "Structure and Meaning in Joyce's 'The Sisters.' "

Blotner, Joseph L. " 'Ivy Day in the Committee Room': Death without Resurrection." *Perspective* 9, No. 4 (Summer 1957): 210-17.
Analyzes Joyce's treatment of Irish politics after the death of Parnell in "Ivy Day in the Committee Room" by drawing parallels between the story and "the events of Christ's death and resurrection as reported in the Gospel according to St. Luke and St. John and in the Acts of the Apostles."

Boyd, John D., and Boyd, Ruth A. "The Love Triangle in Joyce's 'The Dead.' " *University of Toronto Quarterly* 42, No. 3 (Spring 1973): 202-17.
Suggests that a central theme of the story is illustrated by the relationship between Gabriel and Michael, "a theme which is partly obscured if one stresses only their opposition. That is the theme of the continuity among all men, living and dead, linked by the feelings, aspirations, and sufferings universal to human experience (and symbolized by the falling snow)."

Boyle, Robert, S. J. " 'Two Gallants' and 'Ivy Day in the Committee Room.' " *James Joyce Quarterly* 1, No. 1 (Fall 1963): 3-9.
Considers the harp the central image of "Two Gallants," and outlines a double movement central to the structure of the story: 1) As Corley moves toward the slavey's money, he moves away from the romantic ideal of gallantry; and 2) his movement away from gallantry is "symbolized in the story . . . by the gradual fading of the faint romantic moon, its complete disappearance behind the rain-clouds, and its replacement by the shining gold coin."

Burke, Kenneth. "Three Definitions." *Kenyon Review* XIII, No. 2 (Spring 1951): 186-92.
Defines three stages in the narrative of "The Dead," all amplifying the theme of death: 1) the preparations for the party, during which the "keynote is expectancy"; 2) the party scenes, comprising "a catalogue of superficial socialities, each in its way slightly false or misfit"; and 3) the post-party events during which "the cycle of realistic expectations and eventualities" draws to a close.

Carpenter, Richard, and Leary, Daniel. "The Witch Maria." *James Joyce Review* 3, Nos. 1-2 (1959): 3-7.
Analyzes the character Maria in "Clay," concluding that Joyce "intended for us to see Maria as an unintentional spirit of discord who pathetically and ironically does not even realize her own agency."

Carrier, Warren. "*Dubliners:* Joyce's Dantean Vision." *Renascence* XVII, No. 4 (Summer 1965): 211-15.
Considers Dante's *Divine Comedy* the model for *Dubliners.*

Collins, Ben L. "Joyce's Use of Yeats and of Irish History: A Reading of 'A Mother'." *Eire-Ireland: A Journal of Irish Studies* V, No. 1 (Spring 1970): 45-66.
Traces allusions and references to Irish history and William Butler Yeats's drama *Cathleen ni Houlihan* (1902) in "A Mother." In Collins's view, Mrs. Kearney's relationship with her daughter in the story represents that of the Catholic church with Ireland.

Colum, Padraic. Introduction to *Dubliners,* by James Joyce, pp. v-xii. New York: Modern Library, 1926.
Offers an appreciative overview of *Dubliners* and discusses the narrative detachment with which the stories are rendered.

Connolly, Thomas E. "Joyce's 'The Sisters': A Pennyworth of Snuff." *College English* 27, No. 3 (December 1965): 189-95.
Offers a literal reading of "The Sisters," disputing elements of symbolic readings by Marvin Magalaner and Richard Kain, Julian B. Kaye, William Bysshe Stein, and others. Connolly concludes that "the hulk of Father Flynn spiritually and physically paralyzes the society which he dominates. He has become an example of paralysis to which society continues to pay respect, even if it is the respect only of pious clichés uttered by ignorant old women and vaguely felt by one small boy." For an opposing view, see Bernard Benstock, " 'The Sisters' and the Critics," Additional Bibliography entry above.

———. "Marriage Divination in Joyce's 'Clay.' " *Studies in Short Fiction* III, No. 3 (Spring 1966): 293-99.
Describes three traditional divination tools in "Clay"—barmbrack cake, nutcracking, and the three saucers—and connects "Eveline" and "Clay" by asserting that Maria represents a middle-aged Eveline, triumphing over her dull situation.

Cooke, M. G. "From Comedy to Terror: On *Dubliners* and the Development of Tone and Structure in the Modern Short Story." *Massachusetts Review* IX, No. 2 (Spring 1968): 331-43.
Maintains that in *Dubliners* "Joyce developed a singularly modern articulation of the possibilities of the short story form." Cooke particularly praises the stories "An Encounter," "Araby," "Two Gallants," "Clay," and "The Dead."

Cope, Jackson I. "The Waste Land." In his *Joyce's Cities: Archeologies of the Soul,* pp. 1-28. Baltimore: Johns Hopkins University Press, 1981.
Discusses the influence of Dante's *Divine Comedy* on *Dubliners* and examines the effect of "The Dead" on the success of the collection.

Corrington, John William. "Isolation as Motif in 'A Painful Case.' " *James Joyce Quarterly* 3, No. 3 (Spring 1966): 182-91.
Discusses "A Painful Case," focusing on the central character, Mr. Duffy, and his response to Mrs. Sinico and the news of her death.

Davis, Joseph K. "The City as Radical Order: James Joyce's *Dubliners.*" *Studies in the Literary Imagination* 3, No. 2 (October 1970): 79-96.
Examines Joyce's rendering in *Dubliners* of the city of Dublin as a prototypal modern city.

Deming, Robert H., ed. *James Joyce: The Critical Heritage.* 2 vols. New York: Barnes & Noble, 1970.
Reprints several commentaries on *Dubliners* dating from 1908 to 1934.

Dilworth, Thomas. "The Numina of Joyce's 'Eveline.' " *Studies in Short Fiction* 15, No. 4 (Fall 1978): 456-58.
Draws parallels between Joyce's characterization of Eveline and Homer's portrait of Helen.

Easson, Angus. "Parody as Comment in James Joyce's 'Clay.' " *James Joyce Quarterly* 7, No. 2 (Winter 1970): 75-81.
Analyzes Joyce's use of parody to comment on the character Maria in "Clay."

Ellmann, Richard. "The Backgrounds of 'The Dead.'" *Kenyon Review* XX, No. 4 (Autumn 1958): 507-28.
Traces autobiographical elements in "The Dead."

———. *James Joyce.* Rev. ed. New York: Oxford University Press, 1982, 928 p.
Comprehensive biography of Joyce which has become the standard work on his life.

Engel, Monroe. "*Dubliners* and Erotic Expectation." *Twentieth-Century Literature in Retrospect,* edited by Reuben A. Brower, pp. 3-26. Cambridge: Harvard University Press, 1971.
Suggests that "The Sisters," "An Encounter," and "Araby" depict "the thwarting of the eroticized life expectations" of their respective narrators.

Freimarck, John. "'Araby': A Quest for Meaning." *James Joyce Quarterly* 7, No. 4 (Summer 1970): 366-68.
Cites the quest as the underlying narrative pattern in "Araby." According to Freimarck: "The myth element enriches the story, but we are never really on the quest for the grail—we are in Dublin all the time with the psychologically accurate story of the growth of a romantic boy awakening to his sexuality, idealizing Mangan's sister and encountering frustration in the process."

Friedrich, Gerhard. "The Perspective of Joyce's *Dubliners.*" *College English* 26, No. 6 (March 1965): 421-26.
Discusses the narrative perspective of Joyce's *Dubliners,* focusing on the central preoccupations of the collection's first and last stories—"The Sisters" and "The Dead."

Gifford, Don. "Notes for *Dubliners.*" In his *Notes for Joyce: "Dubliners" and "A Portrait of the Artist as a Young Man,"* pp. 29-84. New York: E. P. Dutton & Co., 1967.
Textual notes explaining Joyce's references to such subjects as geography, Irish history, and Catholic teachings, as well as his use of Dublin vernacular in *Dubliners.*

Handy, William J. "Joyce's 'The Dead.'" In his *Modern Fiction: A Formalist Approach,* pp. 29-61. Carbondale and Edwardsville: Southern Illinois University Press, 1971.
Discusses themes of spiritual death and rebirth and spiritual freedom in "The Dead."

Hardy, Barbara. "James Joyce." In her *Tellers and Listeners: The Narrative Imagination,* pp. 206-76. London: The Athlone Press, 1975.
Examines the function of narrative imagination in *Dubliners.*

Hart, Clive, ed. *James Joyce's "Dubliners": Critical Essays.* New York: Viking Press, 1969, 183 p.
Contains fifteen original essays, one on each of the stories in *Dubliners.* Among the contributing critics are Bernard Benstock, Robert Boyle, S. J., Adaline Glasheen, Clive Hart, Richard M. Kain, Robert Scholes, and Fritz Senn.

Jackson, Robert Sumner. "A Parabolic Reading of James Joyce's 'Grace.'" *Modern Language Notes* LXXVI, No. 8 (December 1961): 719-24.
Connects "Grace" with the scriptural parable of the unjust steward (Luke 16) and relates this parable to St. Paul's teaching that grace is a gift from God.

Jones, William Powell. "*Dubliners:* or the Moral History of Ireland." In his *James Joyce and the Common Reader,* pp. 9-23. Norman: University of Oklahoma Press, 1955.
Analyzes the progressive arrangement of the stories from childhood to public life in order to assess Joyce's success in presenting the moral history of Ireland in his short story collection.

Joyce, Stanislaus. "James Joyce: A Memoir." *The Hudson Review* II, No. 4 (Winter 1950): 485-514.
Biographical record originally published in Italy in 1941. Of *Dubliners* Joyce says: "The stories . . . are not detached episodes unrelated to one another. They form a complex whole which is a kind of preliminary sketch of the life of Dublin, a city for which Joyce always felt the nostalgic love of a rejected exile. . . . He had also intended to include a vignette based upon a scene in the first story, 'The Sisters': the old priest stricken by hemiplegia and sunk in his armchair near the fire. This was to have been a symbol of Irish life, priest-ridden and semi-paralyzed."

Kaye, Julian B. "The Wings of Daedalus: Two Stories in *Dubliners.*" *Modern Fiction Studies* 4, No. 1 (Spring 1958): 31-41.
Explicates "An Encounter" and "The Dead," introducing to Joyce criticism the idea that "The Dead" takes place on January 6, the Christian festival of the Epiphany.

Kelleher, John V. "Irish History and Mythology in James Joyce's 'The Dead.'" *Review of Politics* 27, No. 3 (July 1965): 414-33.
Traces three sublevels of meaning in "The Dead": 1) Irish myth based on the Old Irish saga "Togail Bruidhne Dá Derga" ("The Destruction of Da Derga's Hostel"); 2) a level of reference to early nineteenth-century Catholic Dublin history; and 3) "a symbolistic level on which Death is personified in Mr. Browne."

Lachtman, Howard. "The Magic-Lantern Business: James Joyce's Ecclesiastical Satire in *Dubliners.*" *James Joyce Quarterly* 7, No. 2 (Winter 1970): 82-92.
Examines Joyce's satiric treatment of clerics in *Dubliners.* According to Lachtman: "In *Dubliners,* the Church becomes an object of Joyce's wit, ridicule, sarcasm, and contempt. . . . [His priests] do not inspire faith; on the contrary, they encourage considerable doubt, if not open skepticism. Taken together, they comprise what is surely one of the least inspiring congregations of clerics in modern short fiction."

Leatherwood, A. M. "Joyce's Mythic Method: Structure and Unity in 'An Encounter.'" *Studies in Short Fiction* XIII, No. 1 (Winter 1976): 71-8.
Studies archetypal conventions of the knight's quest and the warrior's initiation in "An Encounter." According to Leatherwood: "In controlling the plot with archetypes, Joyce creates a parallel between the contemporary and mythic worlds, a type of parallel used extensively by Joyce in his later work and hailed by T. S. Eliot as 'the most important expression which the present age has found.'"

Levin, Harry. "The Uncreated Conscience: The City." In his *James Joyce: A Critical Introduction,* revised and enlarged edition, pp. 21-40. Norfolk, Conn.: New Directions, 1960.
An overview of literary techniques, subjects, and themes of *Dubliners.*

Levin, Richard, and Shattuck, Charles. "First Flight to Ithaca: A New Reading of Joyce's *Dubliners.*" *Accent* 4, No. 2 (Winter 1944): 75-99.
Examines the thematic and structural resemblances of *Dubliners* to Homer's *Odyssey.*

Magalaner, Marvin. "The Other Side of James Joyce." *Arizona Quarterly* 9, No. 1 (Spring 1953): 5-16.
Includes the famous reading of "Clay" in which Magalaner suggests that in addition to her literal character, Maria is symbolically equated with the Virgin Mary and a witch; see Staley entry in Additional Bibliography for response.

Mandel, Jerome. "The Structure of 'Araby.'" *Modern Language Studies* XV, No. 4 (Fall 1985): 48-54.
Examines conventions of medieval romance in "Araby."

Montgomery, Judith. "The Artist as Silent Dubliner." *James Joyce Quarterly* 6, No. 4 (Summer 1969): 306-20.
Examines silence in the opening stories of *Dubliners:* "The Sisters," "An Encounter," and "Araby." According to Montgomery: "The trilogy marks the progressive withdrawal of a boy—

or, several parallel boys—into silence as both defense and liberation for the future artist."

Morse, Donald E. " 'Sing Three Songs of Araby': Theme and Allusion in Joyce's 'Araby.' " *College Literature* 5, No. 2 (Spring 1978): 125-32.
Concludes that "Araby" "succeeds in eliciting our sympathy for the boy's plight while amusing us with his excesses—a double vision which appears remarkably similar to the one most adults adopt towards their own first encounter with romantic love."

Moynihan, William T., ed. *Joyce's "The Dead."* Boston: Allyn and Bacon, 1965, 134 p.
Collection of essays examining "The Dead" in the context of Joyce's life, of Ibsen's influence, of *Dubliners* as a whole, and of Joyce's aesthetic theories, as well as critical perspectives of the story by Kenneth Burke, C. C. Loomis, Jr., George Knox, and others.

Munich, Adrienne Auslander. "Form and Subtext in Joyce's 'The Dead.' " *Modern Philology* 82, No. 2 (November 1984): 173-84.
Maintains that in their form and subtext the sections of the story "describe Joyce's emotional strife in evolving his modernist style," and that "the ending . . . is mock-epic but comic in its broadest implications—a celebration of and reconcilement to the human condition."

Murphy, M. W. "Darkness in *Dubliners.*" *Modern Fiction Studies* 15, No. 1 (Spring 1969): 97-104.
Examines the pervasive darkness in *Dubliners.*

Nebeker, H. E. "James Joyce's 'Clay': The Well-Wrought Urn." *Renascence* XXVIII, No. 3 (Spring 1976): 123-38.
Discusses the complex point of view, ambiguous tone, and characterization in "Clay," as well as the significance of Maria's song.

Newman, F. X. "The Land of Ooze: Joyce's 'Grace' and the Book of Job." *Studies in Short Fiction* IV, No. 1 (Fall 1966): 70-9.
Interprets "Grace" as a parody of the Book of Job.

Niemeyer, Carl. " 'Grace' and Joyce's Method of Parody." *College English* 27, No. 3 (December 1965): 196-201.
Discusses Dante's *Divine Comedy* as the literary model on which Joyce drew to parody Dublin life in "Grace." According to Niemeyer: "Here as in *Ulysses* [Joyce] takes a great book and by deliberately echoing it, by applying it to squalid situations, of which we get no suggestion in the book itself, makes fun not of the original but of an age or civilization so debased that, measured by the great classics, it is ridiculous."

Norris, Margot. "Narration under a Blindfold: Reading Joyce's 'Clay.' " *PMLA* 102, No. 2 (March 1987): 206-15.
Asserts that "Joyce displays a surprising technical maturity in this early work, whose object is . . . to dramatize the powerful workings of desire in human discourse and human lives."

O'Hehir, Brendan P. "Structural Symbol in Joyce's 'The Dead.' " *Twentieth Century Literature* 3, No. 1 (April 1957): 3-13.
Explication of "The Dead," focusing on symbols, dramatic action, and characterization.

O'Neill, Michael J. "Joyce's Use of Memory in 'A Mother.' " *Modern Language Notes* LXXIV, No. 3 (March 1959): 226-30.
Details the autobiographical basis—Joyce's performance as a vocalist in a program held in Dublin's Antient Concert Rooms, Saturday, 27 August 1904—of the events portrayed in "A Mother."

Ostroff, Anthony. "The Moral Vision in *Dubliners.*" *Western Speech* XX, No. 4 (Fall 1956): 196-209.
Traces the importance and value of *Dubliners* for its "remarkable accomplishment in rendering dramatic a variety of lives and a moral vision of consequence, and needless to say, accomplishing this with the greatest artistry."

Pound, Ezra. "*Dubliners* and Mr. James Joyce." *The Egoist* 1, No. 14 (15 July 1914): 267.
Favorable review praising Joyce's artistic capability, selection of material, and universal appeal.

Rosenberg, Bruce A. "The Crucifixion in 'The Boarding House.' " *Studies in Short Fiction* V, No. 1 (Fall 1967): 44-53.
Maintains that Bob Doran in "The Boarding House" may be seen as a diminished Christ figure and that the " 'facts' of Bob Doran's life and of his sad affair with Polly loosely parallel, yet are an inversion of, the life of Christ."

Ryf, Robert S. "The *Portrait* and *Dubliners.*" In his *A New Approach to Joyce: The "Portrait of the Artist" as a Guidebook,* pp. 59-76. Berkeley and Los Angeles: University of California Press, 1962.
Discusses the motivations of characters in *Dubliners* and interprets the collection through the major themes of *A Portrait of the Artist as a Young Man.*

San Juan, Epifanio, Jr. *James Joyce and the Craft of Fiction: An Interpretation of "Dubliners."* Rutherford, N. J.: Fairleigh Dickinson University Press, 1972, 260 p.
Discusses *Dubliners* in the context of Joyce's aesthetic theories.

Smith, Paul. "Crossing the Lines in 'A Painful Case.' " *Southern Humanities Review* XVII, No. 3 (Summer 1983): 203-08.
Considers the significance of Nietzschean misogyny in "A Painful Case," suggesting that Mrs. Sinico's demise occurs as a result of her attempt to "cross the lines" of Mr. Duffy's fixed, patriarchal order.

Smith, Thomas F. "Color and Light in 'The Dead.' " *James Joyce Quarterly* 2, No. 4 (Summer 1965): 304-09.
Sees the complementing and reconciling of light and dark as important to the symbolic structure of "The Dead."

Somerville, Jane. "Money in *Dubliners.*" *Studies in Short Fiction* 12, No. 2 (Spring 1975): 109-16.
Concludes that Joyce used money in *Dubliners* to portray economic impotence and the corruption in Dublin of such traditional values as work, politics, religion, family, masculinity, and adulthood.

Staley, Thomas F. "Moral Responsibility in Joyce's 'Clay.' " *Renascence* XVIII, No. 3 (Spring 1966): 124-28.
Disputes Marvin Magalaner's theory that Maria dually symbolizes a witch and the Blessed Virgin in "Clay"; see Additional Bibliography entry above. According to Staley, at the beginning of the story Maria represents "the adult product of the paralysis that is Dublin—unaware of the disintegration of community, never cognizant of the meaning of her existence," but through the events of the story she reaches an "understanding of herself and is for the first time confronted with the terrible emptiness of her life."

Stein, William Bysshe. "Joyce's 'Araby': Paradise Lost." *Perspective* 12, No. 4 (Spring 1962): 215-22.
Explicates Catholic terms and symbols in "Araby" concluding that Araby represents paradise lost.

———. "The Effects of Eden in Joyce's 'Eveline.' " *Renascence* XV, No. 3 (Spring 1963): 124-26.
Interprets the character Eveline as a "little Eve," struggling in a corrupt environment and seeking salvation through Frank, a false redeemer.

Stern, Frederick C. " 'Parnell is Dead': 'Ivy Day in the Committee Room.' " *James Joyce Quarterly* 10, No. 2 (Winter 1973): 228-39.
Offers a political reading of "Ivy Day in the Committee Room," noting the prominent imagery and symbolism related to clergy, fire, betrayal, father-son relationships, and the dominant figure of Charles Stewart Parnell.

Stone, Harry. " 'Araby' and the Writings of James Joyce." *The Antioch Review* 25, No. 3 (Fall 1965): 375-410.

Symbolistic explication of "Araby"; see apRoberts entry in Additional Bibliography for response.

Walzl, Florence L. "The Liturgy of the Epiphany Season and the Epiphanies of Joyce." *PMLA* LXXX, No. 4 (September 1965): 436-50.

Discusses Joyce's concept of literary epiphany and its function in *Dubliners,* and explicates the stories in terms of Catholic liturgy and theology.

———. "*Dubliners:* Women in Irish Society." In *Women in Joyce,* edited by Suzette Henke and Elaine Unkeless, pp. 31-56. Urbana: University of Illinois Press, 1982.

Determines the accuracy of Joyce's depictions of "Irish family mores and of social and economic conditions as they affected women in Dublin at the turn of the century."

West, Michael, and Hendricks, William. "The Genesis and Significance of Joyce's Irony in 'A Painful Case.' " *ELH* 44, No. 4 (Winter 1977): 701-27.

Maintains that "though frequently read as a kind of tragedy *manqué,* ["A Painful Case"] is one of the more purely comic [stories] in *Dubliners.* Enmeshed in a web of authorial irony, the automaton Duffy scarcely becomes human, even in his final anguish and remorse."

Wigginton, B. Eliot. "*Dubliners* in Order." *James Joyce Quarterly* 7, No. 4 (Summer 1970): 297-314.

Examines several hypotheses concerning Joyce's use of color imagery, the gradual progression of the protagonists' ages from youth to old age, the failure of meaningful interpersonal relationships between characters, the presence of death, and the important role of religious clergy in *Dubliners.*

Wilson, Edmund. "James Joyce." In his *Axel's Castle: A Study in the Imaginative Literature of 1870-1930,* pp. 191-236. New York: Charles Scribner's Sons, 1948.

Calls *Dubliners* "French in its objectivity, its sobriety and its irony, at the same time that its paragraphs ran with a music and a grace quite distinct from the taut metallic quality of Maupassant and Flaubert."

H(oward) P(hillips) Lovecraft

1890-1937

(Also wrote under the pseudonyms Ward Phillips, Humphrey Littlewit, Gent., Lewis Theobald, Jr., Augustus T. Swift, Albert Frederick Willie, Edgar Softly, Richard Raleigh, and others) American short story writer, novelist, poet, critic, and essayist.

Lovecraft is widely considered the most important literary supernaturalist of the twentieth century and one of the greatest in a line of authors that originated with the Gothic novelists of the eighteenth century and was perpetuated throughout the nineteenth century by such figures as Edgar Allan Poe, Ambrose Bierce, J. Sheridan LeFanu, and Arthur Machen. Like these literary forebears, Lovecraft practiced an essentially popular form of writing, the evolution of which he traced in the critical history *Supernatural Horror in Literature.* Combining elements of the lowest pulp melodrama with the highest imaginative artistry, Lovecraft's "weird tales," a term he invested with special connotations, have become classics of an enduring branch of literature, and among authorities in this province he is regarded as a peer of his Gothic predecessors.

Lovecraft was born in Providence, Rhode Island, at the home of his maternal grandfather, Whipple V. Phillips, a prosperous industrialist and New England gentleman who was the dominant intellectual influence on his grandson's early life, both personally and through his extensive library of works by eighteenth- and nineteenth-century authors. Of the Victorian mansion on Angell Street, Lovecraft wrote: "Here I spent the best years of my childhood. The house was a beautiful and spacious edifice, with stable and grounds, the latter approaching a park in the beauty of the walk and trees." A precocious child whose delicate health allowed him only sporadic attendance at school, Lovecraft flourished in a world of cultured adults who fostered his interest in Greco-Roman antiquity, astronomy, eighteenth-century literature and history, and Gothic tales of terror. This milieu, and the traditions on which it was founded, served as the prime mental and emotional coordinates of Lovecraft's life, whose auspicious beginnings gradually devolved into a lethargic procession of loss and unfulfilled promise: Lovecraft's father, a handsome, syphilitic traveling salesman who was effectively a stranger to his son, died in 1898 after spending the last five years of his life institutionalized with general paresis; Lovecraft's grandfather died in 1904, and subsequent ill-management of his financial holdings forced Sarah Phillips Lovecraft and her only child to move from their family home into a nearby duplex. In his published letters, Lovecraft unfailingly celebrates his mother's refinement and cultural accomplishments; in biographies of Lovecraft, his mother is portrayed as an intelligent and sensitive woman, a neglected wife, and an overprotective parent who instilled in her son a profound conviction that he was different from other people.

In 1908 Lovecraft suffered a nervous breakdown that prevented his attaining enough credits to graduate from high school, and, rather than entering Brown University to pursue the professorship that he had formerly assumed would occupy the rest of his life, he continued his program of self-education. During this period Lovecraft in large part existed as a semi-invalid recluse. In 1914 his isolation was alleviated when he joined the United Amateur Press Association, a group of nonprofessional writers who produced a variety of publications and exchanged letters. A voluminous writer from an early age, Lovecraft now directed his efforts toward these amateur journals, with his own magazine, the *Conservative,* appearing from 1915 to 1923. He also became involved in a network of correspondence which for the rest of his life provided a major outlet for personal and artistic expression. In these letters, Lovecraft discussed an encyclopedic range of subjects in essay-like length and depth; here he also vented his lifelong obsessions, most prominently his love of the past and of scientific truth, and his aversion to the modern world and to all peoples who were not of the Anglo-Nordic cultural stream, although several biographers maintain that he moderated some of his extremist views later in his life. Lovecraft's contributions to amateur journals were almost exclusively in the form of poems and essays, the former being imitations of such eighteenth-century poets as Alexander Pope and James Thomson, and the latter displaying a style strongly influenced by such eighteenth-century prose writers as Joseph Addison and Samuel Johnson. Although Lovecraft wrote several horror stories after his first reading in 1898 of the tales of Poe, he destroyed most of these efforts and wrote no fiction from 1908 to 1917. In the latter year he was encouraged by editor W. Paul Cook to resume fiction writing, resulting in the successive composition of "The Tomb" and "Dagon," the first of what are considered Lovecraft's mature works. After further encouragement from other friends, these two stories, along with three others, were submitted to the pulp magazine *Weird Tales,* which afterward became the principal publisher of Lovecraft's fiction during his lifetime.

Beginning around 1919, Lovecraft began to socialize with other amateur journalists, and through these channels in 1921 he met Sonia H. Greene, a Russian Jewish businesswoman from New York City. They married in 1924 and Lovecraft went to live with his wife in New York, where he hoped to find employment that would enable him to abandon the disagreeable and insubstantial living he previously earned as a literary reviser and ghostwriter. Ten months later the couple separated for reasons that Lovecraft described as largely financial, although the situation was aggravated by Lovecraft's hatred of a city with such a conspicuously mixed racial and ethnic population. In 1926, Lovecraft returned to Providence, where he lived for the remainder of his life. To supplement his dwindling inheritance he was forced to continue his revision work. Despite his nearly destitute financial state, Lovecraft managed to travel extensively, documenting these excursions in his letters and in such essays as "Vermont: A First Impression," "Charleston," and *A Description and Guide to the City of Quebeck.* During the last ten years of his life, he also produced what are considered his greatest works, including "The Call of Cthulhu," *The Case of Charles Dexter Ward,* "The Colour out of Space," "The Shadow over Innsmouth," and *At the Mountains of Madness.* Lovecraft died of intestinal cancer at the age of forty-six.

While an account of the outward events of Lovecraft's life may suggest some of the character traits that critics have found immensely valuable in explicating his works, it fails to convey the full range and intensity of his convictions, preoccupations, and eccentricities. As revealed in his letters, Lovecraft's most important experiences were those of a self-sustaining and isolated imagination. The solitary worlds that he inhabited in childhood—based on his reading of the *Arabian Nights,* classical mythology, and Georgian authors—were fortified and augmented throughout his life, providing him with a well-defined set of interrelated roles which he sometimes facetiously, sometimes tenaciously assumed: the Anglophile gentleman who upheld the most staid conventionality and lamented the "tragic rebellion of 1775-83," the Nordic warrior who reveled in dreams of adventure and blood, the proud citizen of the Roman Empire, the anemic decadent immersed in every form of human and metaphysical abnormality, the frigid scientist seeking truth by the strictest criteria of logic, the generous and brilliantly humorous friend, the xenophobic admirer of *Mein Kampf* who evolved into a quasi-socialist supporter of Franklin Roosevelt's New Deal, and the "cosmic-minded" dreamer of imaginary spheres that transcend the brief and aimless episode of human history. The last-named quality of cosmic-mindedness was perhaps less a discrete component of Lovecraft's temperament than the relatively stable foundation upon which his numerous personae were constructed. Philosophically, Lovecraft was a strict scientific materialist who held that the universe is a mechanical assemblage of forces wherein all values are simply fabrications having no validity outside the context of human imagination and that humanity itself is merely an evanescent phenomenon without any special dimension of soul or spirit to distinguish it from other forms of animate or inanimate matter. At the same time Lovecraft wrote that his strongest feelings were connected with a sense of unknown realms outside human experience, an irrationally perceived mystery and meaning beyond the world of crude appearances. It is particularly this tension between Lovecraft's sterile scientism and mystic imagination—whose contradictory relationship he always recognized and relished—that critics find is the source of the highly original character of his work.

Lovecraft's stories are commonly divided into three types: those influenced by the Irish fantasist Lord Dunsany, a diverse group of horror narratives set in New England, and tales sharing a background of cosmic legendry usually referred to as the "Cthulhu Mythos," a term coined by August Derleth and never used by Lovecraft himself. The Dunsanian stories begin with "Polaris," which Lovecraft actually wrote the year before his first reading of Dunsany's works. Nevertheless, his discovery of Dunsany was a crucial impetus to continue developing narratives more or less related to a tradition of fairy tales and typified by wholly imaginary settings and characters with otherworldly names. Stories in this vein are "The White Ship," "The Doom That Came to Sarnath," "The Cats of Ulthar," and *The Dream-Quest of Unknown Kadath.* Contrasting with these dreamlike romances are tales in which the central element of supernatural horror originates and is circumscribed in a realistic New England setting. Throughout his life Lovecraft was captivated by the architecture, landscape, and traditions of New England. In a letter of 1927, he wrote: "Sometimes I stumble accidentally on rare combinations of slope, curved street-line, roofs & gables & chimneys, & accessory details of verdure & background, which in the magic of late afternoon assume a mystic majesty & exotic significance beyond the power of words to describe. . . . All that I live for is to capture some fragment of this hidden & unreachable beauty; this beauty which is all of dream, yet which I feel I have known closely & revelled in through long aeons before my birth or the birth of this or any other world." To some extent, the fantasy realms of the Dunsanian stories are transfigurations of this New England of ideal beauty. On the other hand, Lovecraft simultaneously perceived and devoted much of his work to depicting a different side of his native region: the degeneracy and superstition that flourish in isolated locales, as described in "The Picture in the House" and "The Unnameable"; the survival of unearthly rites practiced in a quaint, colonial town in "The Festival"; the clan of ghouls that inhabits modern Boston in "Pickman's Model"; the horror interred beneath "The Shunned House," which was inspired by an actual home in the district of Providence where Lovecraft resided; and the foul aspirations of an eighteenth-century wizard which are recapitulated in twentieth-century Providence in *The Case of Charles Dexter Ward.* In other stories, those of the Cthulhu Mythos, Lovecraft provided literary travelogues to a New England that departed even further from the sites of his antiquarian wanderings, revising the geography so familiar to him to create the fictional world of Arkham, Innsmouth, and Dunwich. As he wrote to one of his correspondents: "Yes—my New England is a dream New England—the familiar scene with certain lights and shadows heightened (or meant to be heightened) just enough to merge it with things beyond the world." Among these "things" are the primeval and extrastellar pantheon of a body of myth that, although irregular in its details, is highly consistent as Lovecraft's expression of humanity's insignificant and unsteady place in the universe.

One of the most important and controversial issues in Lovecraft criticism is that regarding nomenclature for his Mythos stories. Various labels have been employed, from the broad designations of "horror" and "Gothic" to more discriminating terms such as "supernormal" and "mechanistic supernatural." At the source of this diverse terminology is the fact that, while these works clearly belong to the tradition of Gothic literature, Lovecraft did not make them dependent on the common mythic conceits associated with this tradition—such as ghosts, vampires, witches, werewolves, and other figures of folklore—and even when they do appear in his work, these entities are often modified to function against a new mythical background, one whose symbolism emphasizes the philosophical over the psychological. For example, Keziah Mason in "Dreams in the Witch-House" has all the appearance and appurtenances of a seventeenth-century New England witch; but instead of serving the demonic forces of Christian mythology, she is in league with extraplanetary forces wholly alien to the human sphere and ultimately beyond good or evil, superterrestrial entities blind to either the welfare or harm of the human species. This order of alien existence and its imposing relationship to human life is similarly displayed in such works as "The Call of Cthulhu," "The Dunwich Horror," "The Whisperer in Darkness," and "The Shadow over Innsmouth," while *At the Mountains of Madness* and "The Shadow out of Time" offer more elaborate development of cosmic civilizations whose nonhuman nature violates all earthly conceptions of reality, forcing upon the protagonists of these narratives an esoteric knowledge which they can neither live with nor disregard. The question of how to describe tales whose effect derives from the violation of the laws of nature rather than those of personal or public morality was somewhat resolved by Lovecraft himself when he applied the term "weird" to such works. In a letter of 1926, he wrote: "As to what is meant by 'weird'—and of course weirdness is by no means confined to horror—I should say that the real criterion is *a strong impression of the suspension of natural laws or the presence of unseen worlds or forces close at hand.*" The literary consequences of this distinction between weirdness and horror may be noted in the remarks of critics who find horrific effects minimal in Lovecraft's stories, their power relying more on an expansive and devastating confrontation with the unknown.

Critical reaction to Lovecraft's work displays an unusual diversity, from exasperated attacks upon what are judged to be the puerile ravings of an artistic and intellectual incompetent to celebrations of Lovecraft as one of the greatest writers and thinkers of the modern era. His severest detractors regard him as an isolated neurotic, and even something of an imbecile, whose writings merely betray a pathetic estrangement from the concerns of adult society. For the most part admitting Lovecraft's eccentricity, his defenders find in his fiction, and more obviously in the five volumes of his *Selected Letters,* a complex vision of reality which could only be formed by a mind of exceptional independence. Summarizing his perception of existence and the implications this had for the outward aspect of his life, Lovecraft explained: "I preach & practice an extreme conservatism in art forms, society, & politics, as the only means of averting the ennui, despair, & confusion of a guideless & standardless struggle with unveiled chaos." While this reaction has been called pathological, and its manifestation as literature uninteresting for readers whose psychic functions remain sound, it has also inspired empathy, even admiration, as an existential ploy not without relevance for a world in which "chaos" has become a key word. With regard to the literary consequences of Lovecraft's character, a great deal of controversy has persisted over his prose style which, reflecting the division between his reactionary code and his sense of universal discord, varies from a highly formal, essay-like discourse to manic outbursts wherein rationality is sacrificed for poetic effect. Briefly, Lovecraft's prose has been derided as labored and archaic by critics who regard plain-spoken realism as the modern standard for fiction; at the same time, it has been praised by those who perceive its calculated suitability for the idiosyncratic nature of Lovecraft's fictional universe, which demands artificiality and a remoteness from the familiar as paradoxical requisites for a vivification of the unreal and the impossible.

The debate concerning the value of Lovecraft's work is, of course, hardly unique in the history of literature. Lovecraft himself was the first to argue both sides of this controversy, which often extends beyond his own work and calls into question the validity of all weird literature. As he described his position to one correspondent: "Doubtless I am the sort of shock-purveyor condemned by critics of the urbane tradition as decadent or culturally immature; but I can't resist the fascination of the *outside's* mythical shadowland, & I really have a fairly respectable line of literary predecessors to back me up." Elsewhere Lovecraft defended the weird tradition when he noted shared traits in his fiction and that of his contemporaries, contending that this similarity "illustrates the essential parallelism of the fantastic imagination in different individuals—a circumstance strongly arguing the existence of a natural & definite (though rare) mental world of the weird with a common background & fixed laws, out of which there must necessarily spring a literature as authentic in its way as the realistic literature which springs from mundane experience." For most of those concerned with this "world of the weird," Lovecraft has long taken his place among its most dedicated explorers and supreme documentarians.

(See also *Twentieth-Century Literary Criticism,* Vols. 4 and 22; and *Contemporary Authors,* Vol. 104.)

PRINCIPAL WORKS

SHORT FICTION

The Outsider, and Others (short stories, novel, and criticism) 1939
Beyond the Wall of Sleep (short stories, essays, poetry, and novels) 1943
The Dunwich Horror, and Others 1963; revised edition, 1985
At the Mountains of Madness, and Other Novels (short stories and novels) 1964; revised edition, 1985
Dagon, and Other Macabre Tales (short stories and criticism) 1965; revised edition, 1987
The Horror in the Museum, and Other Revisions 1970; revised edition, 1989

OTHER MAJOR WORKS

Supernatural Horror in Literature (criticism) 1945
Collected Poems (poetry) 1963
Selected Letters. 5 vols. (letters) 1965-76
To Quebec and the Stars (essays) 1976
A Winter Wish (poetry and essays) 1977

H. P. LOVECRAFT (essay date 1932)

[*In the following excerpt, Lovecraft explains his philosophy and practice of the weird tale.*]

My reason for writing stories is to give myself the satisfaction of visualising more clearly and detailedly and stably the vague, elusive, fragmentary impressions of wonder, beauty, and adventurous expectancy which are conveyed to me by certain sights (scenic, architectural, atmospheric, etc.), ideas, occurrences, and images encountered in art and literature. I choose weird stories because they suit my inclination best—one of my strongest and most persistent wishes being to achieve, momentarily, the illusion of some strange suspension or violation of the galling limitations of time, space, and natural law which for ever imprison us and frustrate our curiosity about the infinite cosmic spaces beyond the radius for our sight and analysis. These stories frequently emphasise the element of horror because fear is our deepest and strongest emotion, and the one which best lends itself to the creation of nature-defying illusions. Horror and the unknown or the strange are always closely connected, so that it is hard to create a convincing picture of shattered natural law or cosmic alienage and "outsideness" without laying stress on the emotion of fear. The reason why *time* plays a great part in so many of my tales is that this element looms up in my mind as the most profoundly dramatic and grimly terrible thing in the universe. *Conflict with time* seems to me the most potent and fruitful theme in all human expression.

While my chosen form of story-writing is obviously a special and perhaps narrow one, it is none the less a persistent and permanent type of expression, as old as literature itself. There will always be a certain small percentage of persons who feel a burning curiosity about unknown outer space, and a burning desire to escape from the prison-house of the known and the real into those enchanted lands of incredible adventure and infinite possibilities which dreams open up to us, and which things like deep woods, fantastic urban towers, and flaming sunsets momentarily suggest. These persons include great authors as well as insignificant amateurs like myself—Dunsany, Poe, Arthur Machen, M. R. James, Algernon Blackwood, and Walter de la Mare being typical masters in this field. (pp. 135-36)

There are, I think, four distinct types of weird story: one expressing a *mood or feeling,* another expressing a *pictorial conception,* a third expressing a *general situation, condition, legend, or intellectual conception,* and a fourth explaining a *definite tableau or specific dramatic situation or climax.* In another way, weird tales may be grouped into two rough categories—those in which the marvel or horror concerns some *condition* or *phenomenon,* and those in which it concerns some *action of persons* in connection with a bizarre condition or phenomenon.

Each weird story—to speak more particularly of the horror type—seems to involve five definite elements: (a) some basic, underlying horror or abnormality—condition, entity, etc.—, (b) the general effects or bearings of the horror, (c) the mode of manifestation—object embodying the horror and phenomena observed—, (d) the types of fear-reaction pertaining to the horror, and (e) the specific effects of the horror in relation to the given set of conditions.

In writing a weird story I always try very carefully to achieve the right mood and atmosphere, and place the emphasis where it belongs. One cannot, except in immature pulp charlatan-fiction, present an account of impossible, improbable, or inconceivable phenomena as a commonplace narrative of objective acts and conventional emotions. Inconceivable events and conditions have a special handicap to overcome, and this can be accomplished only through the maintenance of a careful realism in every phase of the story *except* that touching on the one given marvel. This marvel must be treated very impressively and deliberately—with a careful emotional "build-up"—else it will seem flat and unconvincing. Being the principal thing in the story, its mere existence should overshadow the characters and events. But the characters and events must be consistent and natural except where they touch the single marvel. In relation to the central wonder, the characters should show the same overwhelming emotion which similar characters would show toward such a wonder in real life. Never have a wonder taken for granted. Even when the characters are supposed to be accustomed to the wonder I try to weave an air of awe and impressiveness corresponding to what the reader should feel. A casual style ruins any serious fantasy.

Atmosphere, not action, is the great desideratum of weird fiction. Indeed, all that a wonder story can ever be is *a vivid picture of a certain type of human mood.* The moment it tries to be anything else it becomes cheap, puerile, and unconvincing. Prime emphasis should be given to *subtle suggestion*—imperceptible hints and touches of selective associative detail which express shadings of moods and build up a vague illusion of the strange reality of the unreal. Avoid bald catalogues of incredible happenings which can have no substance nor meaning apart from a sustaining cloud of colour and symbolism.

These are the rules or standards which I have followed—consciously or unconsciously—ever since I first attempted the serious writing of fantasy. That my results are successful may well be disputed—but I feel at least sure that, had I ignored the considerations mentioned in the last few paragraphs, they would be much worse than they are. (pp. 138-39)

H. P. Lovecraft, "Notes on the Writing of Weird Fiction," in his Marginalia, *edited by August Derleth and Donald Wandrei, Arkham House, 1944, pp. 135-39.*

FRITZ LEIBER (essay date 1949)

[*Leiber is an American fiction writer whose works are among the most admired and important in the genres of science fiction, fantasy, and horror. In the following excerpt, he portrays Lovecraft as the innovator of a new type of supernatural horror story.*]

Howard Phillips Lovecraft was the Copernicus of the horror story. He shifted the focus of supernatural dread from man and his little world and his gods, to the stars and the black and unplumbed gulfs of intergalactic space. To do this effectively, he created a new kind of horror story and new methods for telling it.

During the Middle Ages and long afterwards, the object of man's supernatural fear was the Devil, together with the legions of the damned and the hosts of the dead, earthbound and anthropomorphic creatures all. Writers as diverse as Dante and Charles Maturin, author of *Melmoth the Wanderer,* were able to rouse terror in their readers by exploiting this fear.

With the rise of scientific materialism and the decline of at least naive belief in Christian theology, the Devil's dreadfulness quickly paled. Man's supernatural fear was left without a definite object. Writers seeking to awaken supernatural fear restlessly turned to other objects, some old, some new.

Horror of the dead proved to be a somewhat hardier feeling than dread of the Devil and the damned. This provided the necessary ground for the genre of the ghost story, ably exploited by Montague Rhodes James and others.

Arthur Machen briefly directed man's supernatural dread toward Pan, the satyrs, and other strange races and divinities who symbolized for him the Darwinian-Freudian "beast" in man.

Earlier, Edgar Allan Poe had focused supernatural dread on the monstrous in man and nature. Abnormal mental and physiological states fascinated him, as did the awesome might of the elements, natural catastrophes, and the geographic unknown.

Algernon Blackwood sought an object for horror especially in the new cults of occultism and spiritualism, with their assertion of the preternatural power of thoughts and feelings.

Meanwhile, however, a new source of literary material had come into being: the terrifying vast and mysterious universe revealed by the swiftly developing sciences, in particular astronomy. A universe consisting of light-years and light-millenia of black emptiness. A universe containing billions of suns, many of them presumably attended by planets housing forms of life shockingly alien to man and, likely enough in some instances, infinitely more powerful. A universe shot through with invisible forces, hitherto unsuspected by man, such as the ultraviolet xray, the X-ray—and who can say how many more? In short, a universe in which the unknown had vastly greater scope than in the little crystal-sphered glove of Aristotle and Ptolemy. And yet a real universe, attested by scientifically weighed facts, no mere nightmare of mystics.

Writers such as H. G. Wells and Jules Verne found a potent source of literary inspiration in the simple presentation of man against the background of this new universe. From their efforts arose the genre of science fiction.

Howard Phillips Lovecraft was not the first author to see in this new universe a highly suitable object for man's supernatural fear. W. H. Hodgson, Poe, Fitz-James O'Brien, and Wells too had glimpses of that possibility and made use of it in a few of their tales. But the main and systematic achievement was Lovecraft's. When he completed the body of his writings, he had firmly attached the emotion of spectral dread to such concepts as outer space, the rim of the cosmos, alien beings, unsuspected dimensions, and the conceivable universes lying outside our own space-time continuum.

Lovecraft's achievement did not come overnight. The new concept of the horror story did not spring full-grown from his mind. In his earlier tales he experimented with the Dunsanian strain and also wrote a number of effective stories in the vein of Poe, such as **"The Statement of Randolph Carter," "The Outsider," "Cool Air,"** and **"The Hound."** He shared Machen's horror of the human beast and expressed it in **"The Lurking Fear," "The Rats in the Walls," "The Horror at Red Hook,"** and **"Arthur Jermyn."** Though even in these briefer tales we find broad hints of the new concept: vast life-forms from Earth's past in **"Dagon"** and a linkage of a human being's insanity with the appearance of a new star in **"Beyond the Wall of Sleep."** But with **"The Call of Cthulhu"** the line of development becomes clearly marked, as shown by the opening sentences: "The most merciful thing in the world, I think, is the inability of the human mind to correlate all its contents. We live on a placid island of ignorance in the midst of black seas of infinity, and it was not meant that we should voyage far. The sciences, each straining in its own direction, have hitherto harmed us little; but some day the piecing together of dissociated knowledge will open up such terrifying vistas of reality, and of our frightful position therein, that we shall either go mad from the revelation or flee from the deadly light into the peace and safety of a new dark age."

For a while Lovecraft tended to mix black magic and other traditional sources of dread with the horrors stemming purely from science's new universe. In **"The Dunwich Horror"** the other-dimensional creatures are thwarted by the proper incantations, while witchcraft and the new Einsteinian universe appear cheek-by-jowl in **"Dreams in the Witch House."** But when we arrive at **"The Whisperer in Darkness,"** *At the Mountains of Madness,* and **"The Shadow out of Time,"** we find that the extra-terrestrial entities are quite enough in themselves to awaken all our supernatural dread, without any medieval trappings whatsoever. White magic and the sign of the cross are powerless against them and only the accidents of space and time—in short, sheer chance—save humanity. (pp. 4-6)

The universe of modern science engendered a profounder horror in Lovecraft's writings than that stemming solely from its tremendous distances and its highly probable alien and powerful non-human inhabitants. For the chief reason that man fears the universe revealed by materialistic science is that it is a purposeless, soulless place. To quote Lovecraft's **"The Silver Key,"** man can hardly bear the realization that "the blind cosmos grinds aimlessly on from nothing to something and from something back to nothing again, neither heeding nor knowing the wishes or existence of the minds that flicker for a second now and then in the darkness."

In his personal life Lovecraft met the challenge of this hideous realization by taking refuge in traditionalism, in the cultivation of mankind's time-honored manners and myths, not because they are true, but because man's mind is habituated to them and therefore finds in them some comfort and support. Recognizing that the only meaning in the cosmos is that which man dreams into it, Lovecraft treasured beautiful human dreams, all age-worn things, and the untainted memories of childhood. This is set forth clearly in **"The Silver Key,"** the story in which Lovecraft presents his personal philosophy of life.

In the main current of Lovecraft's supernatural tales, horror of the mechanistic universe gave shape to that impressive hierarchy of alien creatures and gods generally referred to as "the Cthulhu mythos," an assemblage of beings whose weird attributes reflect the universe's multitudinous environments and whose fantastic names are suggestive renderings of non-human words and sounds. They include the Elder Gods or Gods of Earth, the Other Gods or Ultimate Gods, and a variety of entities from distant times, planets, and dimensions.

Although they stem from that period in which Lovecraft mixed black magic in his tales and was attracted to Dunsanian pantheons, I believe it is a mistake to regard the beings of the Cthulhu Mythos as sophisticated equivalents of the entities of Christian demonology, or to attempt to divide them into balancing Zoroastrian hierarchies of good and evil.

Most of the entities in the Cthulhu mythos are malevolent or, at best, cruelly indifferent to mankind. The perhaps benevolent Gods of Earth are never mentioned directly, except for Nodens, and gradually fade from the tales. In *The Dream-Quest of Unknown Kadath* they are pictured as relatively weak and feeble, symbols of the ultimate weakness of even mankind's traditions and dreams. It is likely that Lovecraft employed them only to explain why the more numerous malevolent entities had not long ago overrun mankind, and to provide a source of incantations whereby Earthlings could to some degree defend themselves, as in **"The Dunwich Horror"** and *The Case of Charles Dexter Ward.* In the later tales, as we have mentioned, Lovecraft permitted mankind no defense, except luck, against the unknown.

In contrast to the Elder Gods, the Other Gods are presented as powerful and terrible, yet also—strange paradox!—" . . . blind, voiceless, tenebrous, mindless . . ." (*The Dream-Quest*).

Of the Other Gods, Azathoth is the supreme diety, occupying the top-most throne in the Cthulhu hierarchy. There is never any question of his being merely an alien entity from some distant planet or dimension, like Cthulhu or Yog-Sothoth. He is unquestionably "god," and also the greatest god. Yet when we ask what sort of god, we discover that he is the blind, idiot god, " . . . the mindless daemon-sultan . . . ," " . . . the monstrous nuclear chaos . . .".

Such a pantheon and such a chief diety can symbolize only one thing: the purposeless, mindless, yet all-powerful universe of materialistic belief.

And Nyarlathotep, the crawling chaos, is his messenger—not mindless like his master, but evilly intelligent, pictured in *The Dream-Quest* in the form of a suave pharaoh. The Nyarlathotep legend is one of Lovecraft's most interesting creations. It appears both in the prose poem and in the sonnet of that name. In a time of widespread social upheaval and nervous tension, one looking like a pharaoh appears out of Egypt. He is worshipped by the fellahin, "wild beasts followed him and licked his hands." He visits many lands and gives lectures with queer pseudo-scientific demonstrations, obtaining a great following—rather like Cagliostro or some similar charlatan. A progressive disintegration of man's mind and world follows. There are purposeless panics and wanderings. Nature breaks loose. There are earthquakes, weedy cities are revealed by receding seas, an ultimate putrescence and disintegration sets in. Earth ends.

Just what does Nyarlathotep "mean"? That is, what meanings can most suitably be read into him, granting that, by him, Lovecraft may not consciously have "meant" anything. One possibility is that the pharaoh-charlatan expresses the mockery of a universe man can never understand or master. Another is that he symbolizes the blatantly commercial, self-advertising, acquisitive world that Lovecraft loathed (Nyarlathotep always has that aura of the salesman, that brash contemptuousness). Yet a third possibility is that Nyarlathotep stands for man's self-destructive intellectuality, his awful ability to see the universe for what it is and thereby kill in himself all naive and beautiful dreams.

In this connection it is to be noted that Lovecraft, to his last month a tireless scholar and questioner, was the embodiment of the one noble feeling scientific materialism grants man: intellectual curiosity. He also expressed this passion in his supernatural tales. His protagonists are often drawn to the unknown as much as they dread it. Quaking at the horrors that may lurk there, they yet cannot resist the urge to peer beyond the rim of space. **"The Whisperer in Darkness,"** perhaps his greatest story, is remarkable for the way in which the horror and fascination of the alien are equally maintained until almost the very end.

Lovecraft's matured method of telling a horror story was a natural consequence of the importance of the new universe of science in his writings, for it was the method of scientific realism, approaching in some of his last tales (*At the Mountains of Madness* and **"The Shadow out of Time"**) the precision, objectivity, and attention to detail of a report in a scientific journal. Most of his stories are purported documents and necessarily written in the first person. This device is common in weird literature, as witness Poe's "Ms. Found in a Bottle," Haggard's *She,* Stoker's *Dracula,* and many others, but few writers have taken it quite as seriously as did Lovecraft.

He set great store by the narrator having some vitally pressing motive for recounting his experiences, and was ingenious at devising such motives: justificatory confession in **"The Thing on the Doorstep"** and **"The Statement of Randolph Carter"**; warning, in **"The Whisperer in Darkness"** and *At the Mountains of Madness;* attempt by the narrator to clarify his own ideas and come to a decision, in **"The Shadow over Innsmouth"**; scholarly summing up a weird series of events, in *The Case of Charles Dexter Ward* and **"The Haunter of the Dark."**

The scientifically realistic element in Lovecraft's style was a thing of slow growth in a writer early inclined to a sonorous and poetic prose with an almost Byzantine use of adjectives. The transition was never wholly completed, and like all advances, it was attended by losses and limitations. Disappointingly to some readers, who may also experience impatience at the growing length of the stories (inevitable in scientific reports), there is notably less witchery of words in, say, **"The Shadow out of Time"** than in **"The Dunwich Horror,"** though the former story has greater unity and technical perfection. And Lovecraft's own restricted and scholarly life hardly fitted him to be an all-over realist. He always observed a gentlemanly reserve in his writings and depicted best those types of characters which he understood and respected, such as scholars, New England farmers and townsmen, and sincere and lonely artists; while showing less sympathy (consider **"He"**) and penetration in the presentation of business men, intellectuals, factory workers, "toughs," and other admittedly brash, uninhibited, and often crude denizens of our modern cities.

There were three important elements in Lovecraft's style which he was able to use effectively in both his earlier poetic period and later, more objective style.

The first is the device of *confirmation* rather than revelation. (I am indebted to Henry Kuttner for this neat phrase.) In other words, the story-ending does not come as a surprise but as a final, long-anticipated "convincer." The reader knows, and is supposed to know, what is coming, but this only prepares and adds to his shivers when the narrator supplies the last and incontrovertible piece of evidence. In *The Case of Charles Dexter Ward* the reader knows from almost the first page that Ward has been supplanted by Joseph Curwen, yet the narrator does not state this unequivocally until the last sentence of the book. This does not mean that Lovecraft never wrote the revelatory type of story, with its surprise ending. On the contrary, he used it in **"The Lurking Fear"** and handled it most effectively in **"The Outsider."** But he did come more and more to favor the less startling but sometimes more impressive confirmatory type.

So closely related to his use of confirmation as to be only another aspect of it, is Lovecraft's employment of the terminal climax—that is, the story in which the high point and the final sentence coincide. Who can forget the supreme chill of: "But by God, Eliot, *it was a photograph from life,*" or "*It was his twin brother, but it looked more like the father than he did,*" or "They were, instead, the letters of our familiar alphabet, spelling out the words of the English language in my own handwriting," or " . . . the face and hands of Henry Wentworth Akeley?" Use of the terminal climax made it necessary for Lovecraft to develop a special type of story-telling, in which the explanatory and return-to-equilibrium material is all deftly inserted before the finish and while the tension is still mounting. It also necessitated a very careful structure, with everything building from the first word to the last.

Lovecraft reinforced this structure with what may be called *orchestrated prose*—sentences that are repeated with a constant addition of more potent adjectives, adverbs, and phrases, just as in a symphony a melody introduced by a single woodwind is at last thundered by the whole orchestra. **"The Statement of Randolph Carter"** provides one of the simplest examples. In it, in order, the following phrases occur concerning the moon: " . . . waning crescent moon . . . wan, waning crescent moon . . . pallid, peering crescent moon . . . accursed waning moon . . .". Subtler and more complex examples can be found in the longer stories.

Not only sentences, but whole sections, are sometimes repeated, with a growing cloud of atmosphere and detail. The story may first be briefly sketched, then told in part with some reservations, then related more fully as the narrator finally conquers his disinclination or repugnance toward stating the exact details of the horror he experienced.

All these stylistic elements naturally worked to make Lovecraft's stories longer and longer, with a growing complexity in the sources of horror. In **"Dreams in the Witch House"** the sources of horror are multiple: " . . . Fever—wild dreams—somnambulism—illusions of sounds—a pull toward a point in the sky—and now a suspicion of insane sleepwalking . . ." while in *At the Mountains of Madness* there is a transition whereby the feared entities become the fearing; the author shows us horrors and then pulls back the curtain a little farther, letting us glimpse the horrors of which even the horrors are afraid!

An urge to increase the length and complexity of tales is not uncommon among the writers of horror stories. It can be compared to the drug addict's craving for larger and larger doses—and this comparison is not fanciful, since the chief purpose of the supernatural tale is to arouse the single feeling of spectral terror in the reader rather than to delineate character or comment on life. Devotees of this genre of literature are at times able to take doses which might exhaust or sicken the average person. Each reader must decide for himself just how long a story he can stand without his sense of terror flagging. For me, all of Lovecraft, including the lengthy *At the Mountains of Madness,* can be read with ever-mounting excitement.

For it must be kept in mind that no matter how greatly Lovecraft increased the length, scope, complexity, and power of his tales, he never once lost control or gave way to the impulse to write wildly and pile one blood-curdling incident on another without the proper preparation and attention to mood. Rather, he tended to write with greater restraint, to perfect the internal coherence and logic of his stories, and often to provide alternate everyday explanations for the supernatural terrors he invoked, letting the reader infer the horror rather than see it face to face, so that most of his stories fulfill the conditions set down by the narrator of **"The Whisperer in Darkness":** "Bear in mind closely that I did not see any actual visual horror at the end . . . I cannot prove even now whether I was right or wrong in my hideous inference," or by the narrator of **"The Shadow out of Time":** "There is reason to hope that my experience was wholly or partly an hallucination—for which, indeed, abundant causes existed." (pp. 7-13)

Fritz Leiber, "A Literary Copernicus," in Discovering H. P. Lovecraft, *edited by Darrell Schweitzer, Starmont House, Inc., 1987, pp. 4-17.*

EDMUND WILSON (essay date 1950)

[*Considered America's foremost man of letters in the twentieth century, Wilson wrote widely on cultural, historical, and literary matters. He is often credited with bringing an international perspective to American letters through his widely read discussions of European literature. Wilson was allied to no critical school; however, several dominant concerns serve as guiding motifs throughout his work. He invariably examined the social and historical implications of a work of literature, particularly literature's significance as "an attempt to give meaning to our experience" and its value for the improvement of humanity. Although he was not a moralist, his criticism displays a deep concern with moral values. Another constant was his discussion of a work of literature as a revelation of its author's personality. However, though Wilson examined the historical and psychological implications of a work of literature, he rarely did so at the expense of a discussion of its literary qualities. In the following excerpt, Wilson disparages Lovecraft's fiction while praising his critical study* Supernatural Horror in Literature.]

The principal feature of Lovecraft's work is an elaborate concocted myth which provides the supernatural element for his most admired stories. This myth assumes a race of outlandish gods and grotesque prehistoric peoples who are always playing tricks with time and space and breaking through into the contemporary world, usually somewhere in Massachusetts. One of these astonishing peoples, which flourished in the Triassic Age, a hundred and fifty million years ago, consisted of beings ten feet tall and shaped like giant cones. . . . They propagated, like mushrooms, by spores, which they developed in large shallow tanks. Their life span was four or five thousand years. Now, when the horror to the shuddering revelation of which a long and prolix story has been building up turns out to be something like this, you may laugh or you may be disgusted, but you are not likely to be terrified—though I confess, as a tribute to such power as H. P. Lovecraft possesses, that he at least, at this point in his series, in regard to the omniscient conical snails, induced me to suspend disbelief. It was the race from another planet which finally took their place, and which Lovecraft evidently relied on as creations of irresistible frightfulness, that I found myself unable to swallow: semi-invisible polypous monsters that uttered a shrill whistling sound and blasted their enemies with terrific winds. Such creatures would look very well on the covers of the pulp magazines, but they do not make good adult reading. And the truth is that these stories were hack-work contributed to such publications as *Weird Tales* and *Amazing Stories,* where, in my opinion, they ought to have been left.

The only real horror in most of these fictions is the horror of bad taste and bad art. Lovecraft was not a good writer. The fact that his verbose and undistinguished style has been compared to Poe's is only one of the many sad signs that almost nobody any more pays any real attention to writing. I have never yet found in Lovecraft a single sentence that Poe could have written, though there are some—not at all the same thing—that have evidently been influenced by Poe. . . . One of Lovecraft's worst faults is his incessant effort to work up the expectations of the reader by sprinkling his stories with such adjectives as "horrible," "terrible," "frightful," "awesome," "eerie," "weird," "forbidden," "unhallowed," "unholy," "blasphemous," "hellish" and "infernal." Surely one of the primary rules for writing an effective tale of horror is never to use any of these words—especially if you are going, at the end, to produce an invisible whistling octopus. (pp. 287-88)

[Lovecraft] wrote also a certain amount of poetry that echoes Edwin Arlington Robinson—like his fiction, quite second-rate; but his long essay on the literature of supernatural horror is a really able piece of work. He shows his lack of sound literary taste in his enthusiasm for Machen and Dunsany, whom he more or less acknowledged as models, but he had read comprehensively in this special field—he was strong on the Gothic novelists—and writes about it with much intelligence. (p. 289)

Lovecraft's stories do show at times some traces of his more serious emotions and interests. He has a scientific imagination rather similar, though much inferior, to that of the early Wells. The story called **"The Color out of Space"** more or less predicts the effects of the atomic bomb, and **"The Shadow out of Time"** deals not altogether ineffectively with the perspectives of geological aeons and the idea of controlling the time-sequence. The notion of escaping from time seems the motif most valid in his fiction, stimulated as it was by an impulse toward evasion which had pressed upon him all his life. . . . (p. 290)

Edmund Wilson, "Tales of the Marvellous and the Ridiculous," in his Classics and Commercials: A Literary Chronicle of the Forties, *Farrar, Straus and Company, 1950, pp. 286-90.*

PETER PENZOLDT (essay date 1952)

[In the following excerpt, Penzoldt praises Lovecraft's artistry and inventiveness as an author of supernatural fiction while finding his realistic depiction of horrific subjects to be offensively graphic.]

Lovecraft's greatest merit was also his greatest fault. He was too well read. In his critical study *Supernatural Horror in Literature* he displays an encyclopaedic knowledge of supernatural fiction, and since he read that enormous amount of weird fiction with obvious pleasure he has been subjected to a corresponding series of influences. In fact he was influenced by so many authors that one is often at a loss to decide what is really Lovecraft and what some half-conscious memory of the books he has read. (pp. 165-66)

If one reads carefully Lovecraft's critical study on supernatural horror in literature, one is struck by his frequent remarks, on how much more some authors could have made of themes they used. It seems possible that Lovecraft deliberately shaped some themes that were already known into the type of story that he considered fitted them best. . . .

The fact remains that when Lovecraft adopted a motif which his forerunners had already used, he frequently handled it far better. His **"Call of Cthulhu"** and other stories on the ancient gods rank high above [Arthur] Machen's "The Novel of the Black Seal," "The Shining Pyramid" or "The White People." His **"Shadow out of Time,"** a novel about strange trips through time and space, and the forced exchange of human bodies with those of the mysterious pre-human "Great Race" is at once reminiscent of Wells' *The Time Machine* and of Machen's Tales. It also contains many Poesque scenes. Yet, as a whole, the story is infinitely more poignant and convincing than either Wells' or Machen's works. The hero's final descent into the ruined capital of the "Great Race," where he discovers his own manuscript written quadrillions of years ago, is one of the most perfect climaxes in the history of weird fiction.

It would be unjust to say that Lovecraft's inventive powers were limited to a better presentation of old themes. In **"The Call of Cthulhu"** he created a whole mythology of his own which now and then appears in his other tales. (p. 167)

The way in which he was influenced by so many other writers makes it very difficult to decide which symbols found an echo in his own personality, which were used for subtly calculated effect, and which arose from a more or less distinct recollection of his reading.

As it is, the most dominant motif in Lovecraft's work is the nameless, ancestral horror lurking beneath the earth, or ready to invade us from the stars; the dethroned but still potent gods of old. The symbol is a very common one and is not bound to any particular complex. It therefore strikes and horrifies more readers than would any theme having a single subconscious origin. Probably C. G. Jung's theories on the collective subconscious give the only explanation of such symbols as "great Cthulhu," "the father Yog-Sothoth." According to him they would symbolise very old hereditary fears. Edgar Dacqué, the famous German palaeontologist and philosopher, whose theories are somewhat different from Dr. Jung's, would, strangely enough, point to a similar origin. While the latter believes in an exceedingly ancient but yet subconscious origin of certain collective fears and spiritual tendencies, Dacqué suggests an equally ancient but materially existent basis for these terrors in the distant past. Perhaps such tales as **"Pickman's Model"** or **"The Call of Cthulhu"** are, after all, more than the result of purely intellectual search for effect.

Even if there is a true symbolism in Lovecraft's tales it is his realistic descriptions of pure shameless horror that strike one as the dominant feature. If any writer was able to cram his tales with more loathsome physical abominations than [Francis Marion] Crawford and Machen it is Howard Phillips

Lovecraft. He delights in detailed descriptions of rotting corpses in every imaginable state of decay, from initial corruption to what he has charmingly called a "liquescent horror." He has a particular predilection for fat, carnivorous, and, if possible, anthropophagus rats. His descriptions of hideous stenches and his onomatopoeic reproductions of a madman's yowlings are something with which even "Monk Lewis" did not disgrace fiction. (pp. 168-69)

Yet when the details are not too ridiculous one cannot but praise his precision. There are no traces of nineteenth-century reticence left in his work. Though he sometimes speaks of "unnamable" horrors, he always does his best, and perhaps even too much, to describe them. Even if he sometimes overshoots the mark, one may say at least that no author combined so much stark realism of detail, and preternatural atmosphere, in one tale.

It is strange how Lovecraft uses material details even if he is describing purely supernatural entities. He is unable to evoke the glorious spectral and half-material shapes we find in [Algernon] Blackwood's tales. A presence felt, rather than perceived by the senses, is beyond his inventive powers. . . . Nor was he able to make use of Dr. [M. R.] James' indirect method of describing an apparition, with metaphors chosen from reality, but devoid of words directly alluding to horror. He would never have begun a climax with "It seems as if." Lovecraft's monsters are usually ridiculous compounds of elephant feet and trunks, human faces, tentacles, gleaming eyes and bat wings, not to mention, of course, the indescribable foetor that usually accompanies their presence. The reader is often amused rather than frightened by the author's extraordinary surgical talents. (pp. 170-71)

Peter Penzoldt, "The Pure Tale of Horror," in his The Supernatural in Fiction, *P. Nevill, 1952, pp. 146-90.*

AUGUST DERLETH (essay date 1963)

[Derleth was an American author whose prolific body of works includes regional novels of his native Wisconsin, detective fiction, horror stories, biographies, poetry, and criticism. Along with Donald Wandrei, he was the founder of Arkham House, which published the first collection of H. P. Lovecraft's works as well as those of numerous other authors of supernatural fiction. In the following excerpt, Derleth provides an overview of Lovecraft's fiction.]

The stories of H. P. Lovecraft fall readily into two major classifications—and on occasion a combination of both veins. They are either fantastic, in the pattern of Lord Dunsany, whose influence Lovecraft readily acknowledged as from "about 1919," or they are weird and terrible tales of cosmic outsideness, after a pattern which, though a compound of Edgar Allan Poe, Arthur Machen, Robert W. Chambers and Ambrose Bierce, manifests the primary influence of Arthur Machen and Algernon Blackwood, and yet is individually Lovecraftian to such an extent that it influenced many other writers in the genre. The weird and terrible tales subdivide into "New England" tales and stories of the Cthulhu Mythos.

The best of the early tales of pure horror are **"The Rats in the Walls,"** the Poesque **"The Outsider," "The Picture in the House," "Pickman's Model," "The Hound," "Cool Air," "He," "The Horror at Red Hook," "In the Vault," "The Shunned House,"** and **"The Unnameable."** Of the Dunsanian stories, **"Dagon" "The Cats of Ulthar"** and **"The Strange High House in the Mist"** are the best in the first vein, while **"The Statement of Randolph Carter," "The Silver Key,"** and **"Through the Gates of the Silver Key"** are the best of the later tales. The one surviving fantasy novel, *The Dream-Quest of Unknown Kadath,* has a dream-like eeriness but little genuine terror, and is quite unlike the other short novels, *The Case of Charles Dexter Ward* and *At the Mountains of Madness,* which are among Lovecraft's most carefully wrought fictions.

The stories in the Cthulhu Mythos belong primarily to Lovecraft's last creative phase. The pattern of the Mythos is a pattern that is basic in the history of mankind, representing as it does the primal struggle between good and evil; in this, it is essentially similar to the Christian Mythos, especially relating to the expulsion of Satan from Eden and Satan's lasting power of evil. "All my stories, unconnected as they may be," wrote Lovecraft, "are based on the fundamental lore or legend that this world was inhabited at one time by another race who, in practising black magic, lost their foothold and were expelled, yet live on outside ever ready to take possession of this earth again." Elsewhere, Lovecraft, writing of the "vast impetus" the work of Dunsany gave to his own writing, conceded that it was from Dunsany that he "got the idea of the artificial pantheon and myth-background represented by Cthulhu, Yog-Sothoth, Yuggoth." Be that as it may, Lovecraft also freely borrowed from Machen, Robert W. Chambers, Poe, and Ambrose Bierce, including their contributions, minor as they are, in the stories he wrote.

At the top of the Lovecraft pantheon of deities were the Elder Gods, none of whom save Nodens, Lord of the Great Abyss, is ever named; these benign deities, representing the forces of good, existed peacefully at or near Betelgeuse in the constellation Orion, very rarely stirring forth to intervene in the unceasing struggle between the powers of evil and the races of Earth. These powers of evil were variously known as the Great Old Ones or the Ancient Ones, though the latter term is most often applied to the manifestations of one of the Great Old Ones on earth's extension. The Ancient Ones, unlike the Elder Gods, are named, and make frightening appearances in some of the tales. Supreme among them is the blind idiot god, Azathoth, an "amorphous blight of nethermost confusion which blasphemes and bubbles at the center of all infinity." Yog-Sothoth, the "all-in-one and one-in-all," shares Azathoth's dominion, and is not subject to the laws of time and space, being co-existent with all time and conterminous with all space. Nyarlathotep, who is presumably the messenger of the Great Old Ones—corresponding to an earth elemental; Great Cthulhu, dweller in hidden R'lyeh deep in the sea—corresponding to a water-elemental; Hastur the Unspeakable, who occupies the air and interstellar spaces, half-brother to Cthulhu—corresponding to an air-elemental; and Shub-Niggurath, "the black goat of the woods with a thousand young"—the Lovecraftian conception of the god of fertility, complete the roster of the Great Old Ones as they were originally conceived by Lovecraft.

However, Lovecraft began to write these stories without any overall plan; it is doubtful that he had even conceived the Cthulhu Mythos as it finally evolved when he began writing such tales as **"The Nameless City"** and **"The Call of Cthulhu."** When at last he began consciously to construct the pantheon, he invited some of his fellow writers to add to it, with the result that Clark Ashton Smith added Tsathoggua and

Atlach-Nacha, Frank Belknap Long the Hounds of Tindalos and Chaugnar Faugn, Henry Kuttner Nyogtha, and I myself added Cthugha, corresponding to the fire elemental Lovecraft failed to provide, as well as Lloigor, Zhar, the Tcho-Tcho people, Ithaqua, etc. Lovecraft added Hypnos, god of sleep; Dagon, ruler of the Deep Ones, ocean depth allies of Cthulhu; Yig, the prototype of Quetzalcoatl; the "Abominable Snow-Men of Mi-Go," etc.

To the pantheon of forces of good and evil were, of course, added all the necessary trappings—the "secret" or apocryphal books headed by the dread *Necronomicon* of the mad Arab, Abdul Alhazred, and including the *Pnakotic Manuscripts,* the *R'lyeh Text,* the *Book of Dzyan,* the *Seven Cryptical Books of Hsan,* the *Dhol Chants,* the *Book of Eibon* (contributed by Clark Ashton Smith), the *Unaussprechlichen Kulten* of von Junzt (added by Robert E. Howard), Ludvig Prinn's *De Vermis Mysteriis* (by Robert Bloch), Comte d'Erlette's *Cultes des Goules* and the *Celaeno Fragments* of my own invention. There were lesser books and manuscripts invented for the Mythos, and some very real books were subsumed into the fiction.

The place-names of the Mythos tales were concentrated in New England—Arkham (corresponding to Salem, Massachusetts); Kingsport (Marblehead); Dunwich (the country around Wilbraham, Monson, and Hampden)—but ranged as far as Aldebaran, the Hyades, and such mythical places as Kadath in the Cold Waste, the Plateau of Leng, etc. While the place-names did not vary or expand very much, the disciples or servants of the Ancient Ones did—to the Deep Ones were added the Mi-Go, the shantaks, the night gaunts, etc.

The primary stories by Lovecraft in the Cthulhu Mythos are these—**"The Nameless City," "The Festival," "The Call of Cthulhu," "The Colour out of Space," "The Dunwich Horror," "The Whisperer in Darkness," "The Dreams in the Witch-House," "The Haunter of the Dark," "The Shadow over Innsmouth," "The Shadow out of Time,"** *At the Mountains of Madness, The Case of Charles Dexter Ward,* and **"The Thing on the Doorstep."** Related stories by other writers include these—*The Narrative of A. Gordon Pym,* by Edgar Allan Poe; *The Yellow Sign,* by Robert W. Chambers; *An Inhabitant of Carcosa,* by Ambrose Bierce; *The White People* and *The Black Seal,* by Arthur Machen; *Ubbo-Sathla, The Tale of Zatampra Zeiros, The Seven Geases* and others, by Clark Ashton Smith; *The Horror from the Hills, The Hounds of Tindalos,* and *The Space-Eaters,* by Frank Belknap Long; *The Shambler from the Stars, The Dark Demon,* and others, by Robert Bloch; *The Eater of Souls, The Salem Horror,* and others, by Henry Kuttner; *The Church in High Street, The Tower from Yuggoth,* and others, by J. Ramsey Campbell; *The Mask of Cthulhu, The Trail of Cthulhu, The Shuttered Room,* and others, by August Derleth; and such posthumous collaborations as *The Lurker at the Threshold* and *The Survivor and Others,* by H. P. Lovecraft and August Derleth.

Lovecraft had very clear convictions about writing, particularly macabre tales. He believed that nothing was so essentially terrifying to the human spirit as a dislocation in space and time, for instance; yet in all his fiction, for all that it ranges widely into the unknown, he kept himself moored to familiar country, against a meticulously constructed background. "The keynote should be that of scientific exposition—since that is the normal way of presenting a 'fact' new to existing knowledge—and should not change as the story gradually slides off from the possible into the impossible," he wrote on one occasion, and, on another: "Spectral fiction should be realistic and atmospheric—confining its departure from nature to the one supernatural channel chosen, and remembering that scene, mood, and phenomena are more important in conveying what is to be conveyed than are characters and plot. The 'punch' of a truly weird tale is simply some violation or transcending of fixed cosmic law—an imaginative escape from palling reality—since *phenomena* rather than *persons* are the logical 'heroes'. Horrors should be original—the use of common myths and legends being a weakening influence."

He wrote of his devotion to the weird as "a sheer accident of personality, which only a psychiatrist, biologist, geneticist . . . could ever hope to trace to a source or sources—and I have never even dreamed of injecting such a personal bias into any general critical outlook. The proper function of a short story is to reflect powerfully a single mood, emotion, or authentic situation in life, and when you consider what a slight part the weird plays in our moods, feelings, and lives you can easily see how basically minor the weird tale must necessarily be. It can be art, since the sense of the uncanny is an authentic human emotion, but it is obviously a narrow and restricted form of art . . . . I respect realism more than any other form of art—but must reluctantly concede that through my own limitations, it does not form a medium which I can adequately use." His onetime wife said of him that "his love of the weird and mysterious, I believe, was born of sheer loneliness." By the time that Lovecraft had perfected his style the world of the macabre was integral to his being; that it was born of his childhood loneliness and the solitudes in which he lived is entirely credible.

Whether his untimely death deprived the little domain of the macabre of some literary masterpieces is moot. He wrote ever less and less; in the last three years of his life he wrote but three tales—but one of them, **"The Shadow out of Time,"** is accorded by some critics place as his best work. That he was a skilled writer of supernatural fiction, none can gainsay. It cannot be doubted that he was a master of the macabre who had no peer in the America of his time, and only the fact that in America there is no quality market for the supernatural tale prevented his work from reaching a wider audience. By his own choice he was in letters, as in his personal existence, an outsider in his time. (pp. xiii-xvii)

August Derleth, "H. P. Lovecraft and His Work," in The Dunwich Horror and Others: The Best Supernatural Stories *by H. P. Lovecraft, edited by August Derleth, Arkham House, 1963, pp. ix-xx.*

DIRK W. MOSIG (essay date 1973)

[*An American educator and critic, Mosig is one of the pioneering figures in the study of Lovecraft's work, and much subsequent scholarship and criticism was inspired by his contributions to this field. In the following excerpt from an essay first published in* Whispers *(December 1973), Mosig examines the view of humanity implied by Lovecraft's work, particularly the story "The Outsider."*]

Howard Phillips Lovecraft has finally achieved what appears to be a secure niche in Anglo-American literature, and is widely acclaimed for his fantastic creations in the worlds of the bizarre and the macabre. In addition, the publication of his brilliant letters is gradually earning him recognition as one of the greatest epistolarians of all time. Nevertheless, one aspect of Lovecraft has remained strangely neglected—his value as a significant thinker.

Lovecraft's greatest forte was perhaps his lucid and objective materialistic philosophy, so well exposed in many of his letters and in essays such as "Idealism and Materialism," "The Materialist Today," "A Confession of Unfaith," "Nietzscheism and Realism," and others. These pieces, expounding his cosmic-minded mechanistic materialism, reveal him as a profound *penseur* and provide a unique framework for the understanding and interpretation of his memorable fiction.

In his conception of Life, Man, and the Universe, Lovecraft considered himself a *realist,* in the sense that Richard Upton Pickman was a realist. . . . He abandoned all cherished myths, all explanatory fictions, all dreams and illusions, and faced reality as he perceived it, with utmost objectivity and a total lack of emotional involvement. In this sense he was truly an Outsider, able to become an intellectually detached observer of the futile antics of men and beasts, standing aside and watching the stream of time flow by, like some mythical intelligence from Outside, amused by the abysmal insignificance of Man and the purposelessness of the cosmos. He coldly analyzed the beliefs in the perfectibility of man, and in science as the panacea of all evils, as well as the naive expectations of a utopic future, and found them equally unfounded on fact. Even though he was a scientist at heart, a rationalist for whom knowledge was the ultimate good, he prophesied with unique insight the general rejection of iconoclastic Science by horrified Man, unwillingly confronted with reality, and desperately refusing to accept the truth about his own meaninglessness and lack of destiny in a mechanistic Universe. As early as 1921, he clearly foresaw what we know today as "future shock," the recoil of Man from the revelations of the future which he is not ready nor willing to accept.

Future shock and man's retreat into insanity or the safety of a new Dark Age were clearly predicted in the introductory paragraph of **"The Call of Cthulhu,"** to which the reader stands referred, as well as in several other tales and passages, long before the publication of Alvin Toffler's bestseller. Consider, for example, the following lines from **"Arthur Jermyn"**:

> Life is a hideous thing, and from the background behind what we know of it peer daemoniacal hints of truth which make it sometimes a thousandfold more hideous. Science, already oppressive with its shocking revelations, will perhaps be the ultimate exterminator of our human species . . . for its reserve of unguessed horrors could never be borne by mortal brains if loosed upon the world.

For Lovecraft, "the most merciful thing in the world is the inability of the human mind to correlate all its contents," that is, the avoidance of cognitive dissonance by the compartmentalization and lack of communication between facts stored in the human brain. It is merciful because complete awareness of reality would almost certainly result in mental disintegration and psychosis. The consequences of such an instant of total realization form the theme of one of Lovecraft's early masterpieces, **"The Outsider."** In this peerless work of philosophical allegory, he grimly prophesied the outcome of Man's confrontation with the revelations of the Future. (pp. 9-10)

Three main stages are clearly discernible in **"The Outsider."** The first is the time spent in the subterranean castle, which stands for the *PAST.* Here the narrator, who represents MAN, lives in the security of ignorance, surrounded by the countless musty books of the great library—the storehouse of mythical lore and budding scientific knowledge accumulated through the ages. Completely unaware of reality, he dreams endlessly of the many marvels to come, of the happiness and blessings promised by the bright pictures in the mouldy volumes, and of the ultimate freedom that must result when the Light of day—the knowledge of Science—dispels the "brooding shadows" of fear and ignorance. His yearning for Light grows so frantic that he decides to climb the single black tower pointing the way to the Utopia that must lie above the "terrible trees" that keep him rooted in the past. His emergence through the monolithic tower into the level ground, symbolizes Man's birth into the *PRESENT.* The ensuing wanderings under the moonlight represent Man's frantic but hopeful quest for his idealized goals—freedom, happiness, perfection. . . . Man is convinced that all his dreams will come true through the miracles of Science in the not too distant future. The third stage shows Man coming face to face with reality in the Castle of Lights, representing the *FUTURE.* But the future is not what he expected, and instead of the fabled golden utopia of his dreams, he finds only the most bitter of disappointments. The future has not brought the happiness and security he yearned for, but instead has revealed the reality about Man—a meaningless accident in an unfathomable cosmos, lasting an instant in eternity, devoid of purpose, destiny, dignity, glory. . . . A filthy vermin polluting a grain of sand in a purposeless universe, the abominable disease of a negligible planet that did not exist a moment ago and which will have been forgotten an instant hence—all this, and much more, he sees in his fateful reflection on the mirror of Science with the golden frame of his dreams, in the castle of the Future.

Faced with the unutterable horror of total realization, Man is overwhelmed by the traumatic level of cognitive dissonance, and to reduce it, not only denies reality, but also changes his belief in science, in progress, and in the future. As he madly recoils and tries to regain the lost security of the past, attempting to return to the subterranean castle, he finds the trap door immovable: there is no return. His final flight is into the new freedom of insanity and the security provided by the unknown feasts of Nitokris—the superstitions of a new Dark Age. . . . The Outsider is alienated Man, "dazed, disappointed, barren, broken," victim of "future shock," condemned to a meaningless existence in the ever changing present, faced with traumatic revelations from which the only escape is self-deception and the regression of psychosis. . . .

Lovecraft did not share the naive humanistic beliefs in the unlimited perfectibility of Man and his unbounded ability to adapt to the revelations of the future. His view of the future went beyond Huxley's and Orwell's in terms of its detached objectivity and cold realism, and he predicted in many of his tales and essays the bleak consequences of man's inability to cope with reality and with the advancing tide of progress.

The accuracy of this pessimistic prophecy and the validity of his critique of progress are attested to today not only by the devastating super-abundance of maladaptive reactions to the unbearable stresses of modern life—with mental patients taking up over one-half of all hospital beds—but also by the wholesale escape into the "cancer of superstition," the countless *fads* of pseudo-mysticism, astrology, palmistry, phrenology, numerology, occultism, religion, witchcraft, voodoo, transcendental meditation, satanism, psychic phenomena, psychedelic drugs . . . anything to regain the lost sense of security, to escape from the cold and unbearable reality emerging like a phoenix from the ashes of the crumbling edifices of traditional beliefs and cherished myths shattered by the efforts of the great iconoclasts: Galileo, Copernicus, Darwin, Freud, Einstein, Skinner, and many others. But it is a barren phoenix, rejected and despised, because the new Dark Age has already begun. . . . (Parenthetically, it is interesting to observe here that the rejection of Lovecraft's mechanistic materialism by readers of this article is an implicit confirmation of the validity of his prediction.)

Throughout the Lovecraft opus are scattered references to his philosophical *Weltanschauung,* as well as impressive glimpses of his vivid vision of the intellectual crisis of the future, felt today more than ever before. His works, like those of Franz Kafka, are full of allegories, analogies, parables, and symbols, resulting not from a hollow didacticism, but from the deep undercurrents of philosophical thought which permeate his writings and make them extremely relevant today. The time is right for a greater appreciation of this deeper, more serious aspect of Lovecraft's fiction, as well as of his many philosophical essays, which deserve being collected in a single volume together with excerpts from his prolific correspondence. The ground is particularly ready in Europe, where his works are held in highest esteem. For instance, two recent collections of Lovecraft's tales published in Spain appeared in a literary series including works by Nietzsche, Unamuno, Freud, Malthus, Pavlov, Jung, Kafka, Kant, Schopenhauer, Karl Marx, Bertrand Russell, and others.

Ultimately, Lovecraft's fame should rest not only on his value as a master of dramatic fiction, a skilled poet, and a brilliant epistolarian, but also on the depth and significance of the philosophical insights of his superior intellect. (pp. 10-11)

Dirk W. Mosig, "The Prophet from Providence," in Crypt of Cthulhu, *Vol. 4, No. 8, August 1, 1985, pp. 9-11.*

BARTON LEVI ST. ARMAND (essay date 1977)

[*St. Armand is an American critic and educator specializing in American literature and literary figures, particularly such New England authors as Nathaniel Hawthorne, Emily Dickinson, Sarah Orne Jewett, and H. P. Lovecraft. His studies of Lovecraft are considered among the most significant in the field. In the following excerpt, St. Armand discusses the sources and significance of horror in Lovecraft's fiction.*]

In his long historical essay entitled *Supernatural Horror in Literature,* the modern fantasist and master of the macabre, H. P. Lovecraft, tells us that "Children will always be afraid of the dark, and men with minds sensitive to hereditary impulse will always tremble at the thought of the hidden and fathomless worlds of strange life which may pulsate in the gulfs beyond the stars, or press hideously upon our own globe in unholy dimensions which only the dead and the moonstruck can glimpse." This insight is framed in typical Lovecraftian hyperbole, yet it appears in a study that, while both exhaustive and suggestive in the scope of its erudition, actually reveals little about the roots of horror itself and nothing about those particular eldritch roots of horror in Lovecraft's own work. Indeed, although he thought of himself as an eighteenth-century mind born into the wrong world, Lovecraft neglects to make a basic discrimination between "horror" and "terror" first formulated by Mrs. Ann Radcliffe, whose exquisitely horrid novels, *The Mysteries of Udolpho* and *The Italian,* titillated many a delicate Gothic sensibility in the 1790's. Lovecraft goes on to devote two long paragraphs to Mrs. Radcliffe in *Supernatural Horror in Literature,* noting that her "genuine sense of the unearthly in scene and incident . . . closely approached genius" and that "A few sinister details like a track of blood on castle stairs, a groan from a distant vault, or a weird song in a nocturnal forest can with her conjure up the most powerful images of imminent horror; surpassing by far the extravagant and toilsome elaborations of others." . . . Yet, HPL's mention of Mrs. Radcliffe remains only a polite gesture, just as his reading of the interminable *Mysteries of Udolpho* must have been an extended act of scholarly homage and a supreme test of his own Chesterfieldian sense of honor.

The definitions in question appeared, as Bonamy Dobrée notes in his introduction to the most recent Oxford University Press edition of *Udolpho,* in a posthumous article entitled "On the Supernatural in Poetry," in which Mrs. Radcliffe says:

> They must be men of very cold imaginations with whom certainty is more terrible than surmise. Terror and horror are so far opposite, that the first expands the soul, and wakens the faculties to a high degree of life; the other contracts, freezes, and nearly annihilates them. I apprehend that neither Shakespeare nor Milton by their fictions, nor Mr. Burke by his reasoning, anywhere looked to positive horror as a source of the sublime, though they all agree that terror is a very high one; and where lies the great difference between horror and terror, but in uncertainty and obscurity, that accompany the first, respecting the dreader evil?

Dobrée goes on to add that "Her distinction would seem to gain support from the *New English Dictionary,* where terror is defined as 'intense fear, fright, or dread,' while horror is 'compounded of loathing and fear; shuddering with terror and repugnance.' "

Thus, there are two different directions or dimensions associated with these two different emotions if we accept Mrs. Radcliffe's initial premise about their essential dissimilarity. Terror expands the soul outward; it leads us to or engulfs us in the sublime, the immense, the cosmic. We are, as it were, lost in the ocean of fear or plunged directly into it, drowning of our dread. What we lose is the sense of self. That feeling of "awe," which traditionally accompanies intimations of the sublime, links terror with experiences that are basically religious in nature, like those annihilating confrontations with the numinous that [Rudolph] Otto explores in *The Idea of the Holy.*

Lovecraft touches on this connection between the terrific and the numinous when, in his general discussion of fear, he writes, "There is here involved a psychological pattern or tradition as real and as deeply grounded in mental experience as any other pattern or tradition of mankind; coeval with the religious feeling and closely related to many aspects of it, and too much a part of our innermost biological heritage to lose keen potency over a very important, though not numerically great, minority of our species." . . . (pp. 1-3)

Yet the archetypal patterns that Lovecraft associates with fear apply most precisely not only to the springs of terror in his fiction (although, as we shall see, there surely is an approach to the religious in his Descartian preoccupation with the sublimity of the void) but to those roots of horror—especially traditional Gothic horror—with which the fiction began. For if terror expands the soul and leads to an overwhelming, potentially destructive, sense of cosmic outsideness in Lovecraft's later and longer science-fiction works, then horror is equally annihilating, but from a dramatically different direction. Horror overtakes the soul from the inside; consciousness shrinks or withers from within, and the self is not flung into the exterior ocean of awe but, sinks in its own bloodstream, choked by the alien salts of its inescapable prevertebrate heritage.

Terror entails a quest for the wholly other, the outside. I should like to demonstrate that in Lovecraft's fiction horror demands a parallel descent into the subconscious, the inside, which reveals an added archetypal and psychological dimension to his own use of Mrs. Radcliffe's Gothic tradition. In semantically proper terms, terror is a means of evolution toward the ineffable; horror is a species of devolution toward—to use another appropriately Lovecraftian phrase—"the unspeakable."

Horror and terror are also the visionary means by which Lovecraft manages to break the cosmic laws of time and space and so accomplish that rupture of the ordinary which he considered to be the great secret of the best supernatural fiction. Terror is the springboard that can hurl the soul and the self beyond the coordinates of daylight reality; horror is the plank in reason that can break and plummet the individual into the profoundest pit of his own darkest dreams. Writing at the beginning of *Supernatural Horror in Literature,* Lovecraft reiterates this doctrine, which can often be found in his letters to younger disciples who aspired to the making of superior weird tales. Here Lovecraft is speaking of "cosmic fear" and that kind of science-fiction fantasy he came to write only after experimenting with the possibilities of Gothic horror, that interior domain of the shuddery and the repugnant. "The cosmic," he writes,

> must not be confounded with a type externally similar but psychologically widely different; the literature of mere physical fear and the mundanely gruesome. Such writing, to be sure, has its place, as has the conventional or even whimsical or humorous ghost story where formalism or the author's knowing wink removes the true sense of the morbidly unnatural; but these things are not the literature of cosmic fear in its purest sense. The true weird tale has something more than secret murder, bloody bones, or a sheeted form clanking chains according to rule. A certain atmosphere of breathless and unexplainable dread of outer, unknown forces must be present; and there must be a hint, expressed with a seriousness and portentousness becoming its subject, of that most terrible conception of the human brain—a malign and particular suspension or defeat of those fixed laws of Nature which are our only safeguard against the assaults of chaos and the demons of unplumbed space. . . .

(pp. 3-4)

Lovecraft tried to abandon his early dream-quest of the dreadful because he felt his first, traditionally Gothic pieces were too derivative and "mundanely gruesome." Much has been made of the slow development of his "Cthulhu Mythos" and the tales of cosmic outsideness, such as **"The Shadow out of Time"** and *At the Mountains of Madness,* yet the full scope of Lovecraft's work cannot really be understood without also understanding what he was trying to achieve in these increasingly longer productions. This was nothing less than a mating of Gothic horror and cosmic terror, an unholy marriage of inside and outside—hence the presence in these tales of a whole pantheon of outside gods (Cthulhu, Azathoth, Yog-Sothoth) as well as such entities as the viscous Shugoths of Antarctica, or what Edmund Wilson called the "invisible whistling octopus" of the forbidden city in **"The Shadow out of Time"** [see excerpt dated 1950], both of which come from subterranean caves deep below the desert of the ice. A kind of monstrous theory of relativity is operating in these longer fictions: one can go so far outside that the result is a return or emergence at the farthest point inside. (p. 4)

Like the short stories of Lovecraft's great mentor, Edgar Allan Poe, Lovecraft's tales operate on at least two levels: the first, an instinctive Gothic one calculated to produce in the reader what Victor Hugo called a *frisson nouveau;* the second, an archetypal, psychological, or metaphysical level that (to use one of Poe's favorite metaphors) "has a depth greater than the well of Democritus." The primary level is precisely that of Poe's famous unitary and preconceived "effect," the effect of sheer sensation and radical dislocation of the psyche. But as we have noted, this initial disruption of the sense of self, dictated by the prime coordinates of our mundane, daylight world of space and time, leads in both artists to a contemplation of the meaning of space and of time and ultimately to a consideration of the place of man in an alien and indifferent universe.

Thus, through the first circle of fear or horror (to utilize the Radcliffean dichotomy I stated at the beginning of this discussion) we are launched toward ever-widening maelstroms of terror or the sublime. Otto has explored in depth this connection between these two extremely polar yet inextricably linked states of the soul, taking as one of his principles the maxim propounded by the French metaphysician Récéjac in his *Essai sur les fondements de la connaissance mystique,* where he states that: "Mysticism begins in fear, in the feeling of a universal and invincible domination, which later becomes a desire for union with that which dominates." Although Lovecraft, dedicated materialist that he was, would have shuddered at having either his works or himself labeled "mystical," still in his own rationalistic terms he fully believed that fear or horror was allied to a realm of primitive vision "coeval with the religious feeling and closely related to many aspects of it," as he wrote in *Supernatural Horror in Literature.* This can be easily seen if we substitute the term "sublimity" for his own vague and elusive words "alienage" and "outsideness," staples of his critical vocabulary.

Much like one of the old Cabbalists, who forbade pronouncing or writing the true and awful name of God, Lovecraft himself had a certain horror of defining his concepts too rigidly. He was at his artistic best when he matched the majesty and ineffability of his idea of the unholy with poetic and equally "sublime" prose. Thus he could write Wilfred Blanch Talman, advising him on the composition of a horror story, that "if any suggestions are in order, I suppose the thing to urge would be a more bizarre, cosmically external, and utterly non-human set of motives and phenomena—in order to achieve that effect of the *unknown outside clawing at the rim of the known* which forms spectral horror in its acutest form." . . . (pp. 34-5)

It is a critical truism with Lovecraft, and an unfortunate one, that the more realistic and detailed his monsters grow, the less convincing and the less horrific they simultaneously become. He was conscious of this tendency himself, and wrote one correspondent that "Most of my monsters fail altogether to satisfy my sense of the cosmic—the abnormally chromatic entity in **"The Colour out of Space"** being the only one of the lot which I take any pride in." . . . The fascination of the cosmic outside, of what might lie hidden in the spaces between the stars or beneath one's very feet (which, as Lovecraft explained in a letter to Elizabeth Tolridge in January, 1931, was the very spot that "lies ultimately beyond the deepest gulf of infinity") held for him all the emotion he needed for the creation of what Mrs. Radcliffe would have termed a "sublime transport." As he wrote:

> . . . one of my strongest and most persistent wishes [is] to achieve, momentarily, the illusion of some strange suspension or violation of the galling limitations of time, space, and natural law which forever imprison us and frustrate our curiosity about the infinite cosmic spaces beyond the radius of our sight and analysis. [My] stories frequently emphasize the element of horror because fear is our deepest and strongest emotion, and the one which best lends itself to the creation of nature-defying illusions. Horror and the unknown or the strange are always closely connected, so that it is hard to create a convincing picture of shattered natural law or cosmic alienage and "outsideness" without laying stress on the emotion of fear. The reason why *time* plays such a great part in so many of my tales is that this element looms up in my mind as the most profoundly dramatic and grimly terrible thing in the universe. *Conflict with time* seems to me the most potent and fruitful theme in all human expression [see excerpt dated 1932].

The doubleness which runs through all of HPL's thought must be, by this point, blatantly apparent, for he is at once a defender and upholder of a strict universe of natural law as well as its secret saboteur. . . . [This] attraction-repulsion syndrome is at the root of the horror tale itself, . . .[and] the subtle progression in Lovecraft's best work is always from the ordinary to the extraordinary, the particular and detailed to the monumental and the epic, the mundane to the sacred, unholy, or archetypal. It is HPL's cosmicism that provides the unique resonance of his fiction, which, like **"The Rats in the Walls,"** reverberates with meanings that go far beyond the surface conventions of weird tales and Gothic props. What Lovecraft accomplishes in his work is to take the old Gothic machinery and invest it with new, archetypal meaning. (pp. 35-6)

Lovecraft formed a whole mythology of the outside and a philosophy of the outsider hidden in every human being. He liked to think of himself (in the terms of a Schopenhauer or a Nietzsche) as a mechanistic materialist living in an age whose total result was, in the words of the latter philosopher, "a chaos, a nihilistic sigh, an ignorance as to where or whence, an instinct of fatigue." But Lovecraft found himself in the position of modern man as Jung defined him: a being who spurned the sacred and the religious as a defense mechanism against a sterilized existence, only to find that he could not help scaring himself almost to death for his own good. "We have stripped all things of their mystery and numinosity," Jung writes, "nothing is holy any longer":

> In earlier ages, as instinctive concepts welled up in the mind of man, his conscious mind could no doubt integrate them into a coherent psychic pattern. But the "civilized" man is no longer able to do this. His "advanced" consciousness has deprived itself of the means by which the auxiliary contributions of the instincts and the unconscious can be assimilated. These organs of assimilation and integration were numinous symbols, held holy by common consent. (*Man and His Symbols*).

(p. 87)

In spite of his protests to the contrary, H. P. Lovecraft was modern man *par excellence* because he was also the most extreme example of what contemporary psychologists call "the divided self": the most civilized of conversationalists and the most violent of xenophobes, the most rational of scientists and the most fantastic of visionaries, the most controlled of authors and the most extravagant of artists. This inextricable doubleness runs through all of his work and his thought, for such doubleness is the hallmark of archetypal power, the paradox of numinous symbols assimilated in his art. Vainly, Lovecraft tries to restore an epic sense of man's essentially precarious and ultimately tragic position in the cosmos by setting up a polarity between frail humanity, on the one hand, and the force of a willful pantheon of deities (not unlike the Greek gods who gaze down and occasionally intervene in the events of the *Iliad* or the *Odyssey*), on the other. But the god, the monster, is always a mirror of its creator, as Mary Shelley's Dr. Frankenstein finds out to his woe.

"I believe that no honest aesthetic canon," Lovecraft wrote to Frank Belknap Long in 1922, "can exclude that highest of organic faculties—the pure, ice-cold reason; which gives man his sole contact with things outside himself, and which must be superimposed upon emotion before anything like *imagination* can be produced." . . . Reason may always hold the reins in H. P. Lovecraft's fiction, but the spectre rides in harness.

It was the "creation of a given sensation" that, in *Supernatural Horror in Literature* remained "the all important thing." . . . He begins that work with the "admitted truth" that "the oldest and strongest emotion of mankind is fear, and the oldest and strongest kind of fear is fear of the unknown." . . . More and more HPL realized that it was emotion and feeling, not the intricate dovetailing of a plot, that made for the success of weird fiction. Writing to E. Hoffman Price (who provided the impetus for the composition of **"Through the Gates of the Silver Key"**), HPL acknowledged, ten years after his praise of reason to Long, that:

> When a writer succeeds in translating these nebulous urges into symbols which in some way satisfy the imagination—symbols which adroitly suggest actual glimpses into forbidden dimensions, actual happenings following the myth-patterns of human fancy, actual voyages of thought or body into the nameless deeps of tantalising space and actual evasions, frustrations, or violations of the commonly accepted laws of the cosmos—then he is a true artist in every sense of the word. He has produced literature by accomplishing a sincere emotional catharsis. . . .

(pp. 87-8)

No better defense of weird fiction in general or his own accomplishment in particular could be devised. (p. 89)

Barton Levi St. Armand, in his The Roots of Horror

in the Fiction of H. P. Lovecraft, *Dragon Press, 1977, 102 p.*

S. T. JOSHI (essay date 1982)

[*An American educator and critic, Joshi is the leading figure in the field of Lovecraft scholarship and criticism. As an editor, his publications include several volumes of Lovecraft's uncollected or unpublished works, critical editions of Lovecraft's major fiction, a collection of essays surveying Lovecraft's critical reputation, the journal* Lovecraft Studies, *and the definitive bibliography of Lovecraft's works and Lovecraft criticism. As a critic, he has published numerous essays on Lovecraft's life and work as well as a full-length biographical and critical study. In the following excerpt from that study, Joshi surveys a group of Lovecraft's stories under the collective designation "the Lovecraft Mythos," a term he finds preferable to the more common "Cthulhu Mythos."*]

Lovecraft scholars have long been debating as to which tales do or do not fit into a distinct and discrete category which they have termed the "Cthulhu Mythos," not realizing two facts of cardinal importance: 1) Lovecraft never used the term "Cthulhu Mythos" himself, and 2) Lovecraft constantly emphasized the philosophical unity of *all* his fiction, regardless of its setting, characters, or style. Let us examine these two points further.

Lovecraft certainly realized that some of his tales contained—through use of common imagined scenes and an imaginary pantheon of gods and forces (e.g., Cthulhu, Yog-Sothoth, Nyarlathotep, etc.)—interrelations beyond the normal, but the closest he ever came to coining any term for this group of tales was "Yog-Sothothery" or the "Arkham cycle." The second term, indeed, is enormously significant and may hint that Lovecraft envisioned one important link in these tales to be the mythical New England locale represented by Arkham (=Salem), Innsmouth (=Newburyport, Massachusetts), Dunwich (=the area around Hampden, Wilbraham, and Monson, Massachusetts), and Kingsport (=Marblehead, Massachusetts), since nearly all the tales of this group at least originate in this area, although (as with *At the Mountains of Madness* and **"The Shadow out of Time"**) they may later veer off into widely different settings.

Moreover, Lovecraft, in the middle of his career (i.e., July 1927, before most of the major tales of the Mythos were written), uttered an artistic credo whose significance has only now been recognized:

> Now all my tales are based on the fundamental premise that common human laws and interests and emotions have no validity or significance in the vast cosmos-at-large. . . . To achieve the essence of real externality, whether of time or space or dimension, one must forget that such things as organic life, good and evil, love and hate, and all such local attributes of a negligible and temporary race called mankind, have any existence at all. . . .

[This] statement renders it useless to make fine distinctions between those tales which do or do not "belong" to the myth-cycle. Hence . . . I shall discuss **"The Colour out of Space"** (1927)—not regarded by any scholars (including Mosig) as within the Mythos—since I see in it that element of *cosmicism* which seems to underlie all the tales which can be considered part of what we may now term the Lovecraft Mythos.

As hinted above, I believe we can trace four elements—some perhaps mere devices of plot—which recur in the Lovecraft Mythos and lend to it that distinctive unity which led George T. Wetzel [see Joshi entry dated 1980 in Additional Bibliography] to term it a "lengthy novel":

> 1. Recurring use of the imaginary New England locale typified by Arkham, Innsmouth, etc.;
>
> 2. Recurring use of pseudomythological deities and beings (Azathoth, Yog-Sothoth, the shoggoths, the Great Old Ones, etc.);
>
> 3. Use of mythical books of magical lore which purport to contain information about the deities of the myth-cycle (the *Necronomicon,* the *Book of Eibon,* the *Unaussprechlichen Kulten,* etc.);
>
> 4. The common element of cosmicism, whereby the vast gulfs of the cosmos, and the resultant triviality and inconsequentiality of mankind, are suggested.

One or more elements may, of course, be especially prominent in any given tale.

It is of the highest importance to understand that Lovecraft did not envision all details of his Mythos completely at any point in his career but that he developed various concepts gradually through successive stories. What is more, it seems clear that some aspects of the Mythos were not fully developed within Lovecraft's lifetime. George T. Wetzel believes that the idea of Azathoth remained particularly inchoate at the time of Lovecraft's death, and we must draw hints of that god's powers only from random fragments, poems, and passages in stories. In any case, the idea of linking stories together through details of plot is not restricted to the tales of the Lovecraft Mythos. We also find it in the "Dunsanian" tales, and especially in *The Dream-Quest of Unknown Kadath,* where allusions are made to nearly all the previous "Dunsanian" tales of Lovecraft.

With **"Dagon"** (1917), we find adumbrated a number of details later to become standard in the Mythos. The narrator accidentally stumbles upon traces of an aquatic civilization—whose traces remain only in the form of the Philistine fish-god Dagon—not only of appalling antiquity ("some tribe whose last descendant had perished eras before the first ancestor of the Piltdown or Neanderthal Man was born") but of hideously hybrid shape ("they were damnably human in general outline despite webbed hands and feet, shockingly wide and flabby lips, glassy, bulging eyes, and other features less pleasant to recall"). It is significant that the narrator goes mad not through any physical violence at the hands of supernatural entities but through the mere *realization* of the existence of such a race of gods and beings. Paul Buhle has emphasized this point well:

> The hideous beings under the surface of human civilization's superficial conquest of Nature and its own nature were ever poised to wipe out Man. But even worse than their standing threat was their very existence, and this *presence* drove their discoverers to insanity. . . . To uncover the Monsters was to co-exist with them always [see Additional Bibliography].

"Beyond the Wall of Sleep" (1919) again hints of the cosmic, in this case a strange linkage between an ignorant peasant and an astral entity connected with the star Nova Persei (an idea to recur briefly in **"The Dreams in the Witch House"**). The tale is not one of Lovecraft's best and is written in a clumsy and stilted manner but again contains hints of vast gulfs of time and of civilizations unheard of by man:

> "Next year I may be dwelling in the dark Egypt which you call ancient, or in the cruel empire of Tsan-Chan which is to come three thousand years hence. You and I have drifted to the worlds that reel about the red Arcturus, and dwelt in the insect-philosophers that crawl proudly over the fourth moon of Jupiter. How little does the earth-self know life and its extent! How little, indeed, ought it to know for its own tranquillity!"

The brief but powerful prose-poem **"Nyarlathotep"** (1920) introduces us to the god of that name, one which Lovecraft *dreamed.* Here Nyarlathotep is portrayed as an itinerant magician who displays apocalyptic scenes from an odd mechanical device. In the end, we learn that Nyarlathotep is merely a symbol for the aimlessness and purposelessness of the cosmos:

> And through this revolting graveyard of the universe the muffled, maddening beating of drums, and thin, monotonous whine of blasphemous flutes from inconceivable, unlighted chambers beyond Time; the detestable pounding and piping whereunto dance slowly, awkwardly, and absurdly the gigantic, tenebrous ultimate gods—the blind, voiceless, mindless gargoyles whose soul is Nyarlathotep.

"The Nameless City" (1921) is important in that it introduces us to Abdul Alhazred (although at this time he is not necessarily the author of the *Necronomicon* but merely the composer of an "unexplainable couplet"), reveals an unknown and hideously ancient civilization lost in the depths of Arabia Deserta, and—in an anticipation of *At the Mountains of Madness*—tells a potted history of that civilization through the decipherment of frescoes. Otherwise the tale is undistinguished, somewhat pompous in style, and slightly too long.

"The Festival" (1923) presents a long quotation from the *Necronomicon* and makes first real use of the imaginary New England locale. Otherwise, its connection with the Mythos is slim, and its importance in this regard has probably been exaggerated by critics.

All these adumbrations of a synthetic myth-cycle lead to **"The Call of Cthulhu"** (1926), where the first real exposition of the Mythos is given. This tale, one of the best of Lovecraft's middle period (one which was the vanguard of an enormous surge of creativity during 1926-27, when, upon his return from New York, Lovecraft wrote two novels and several lenghty tales in about six months), is an enormous advance both in style and in theme from his previous work and reveals a coherence and tightness of plot approached only by the previous **"Rats in the Walls"** (1923). The very form of the work is fascinating and involves not merely the use of a wide variety of documents (old manuscripts, newspaper cuttings, the reports of an archaeological meeting, etc.) to tell the tale but incorporates several narratives within narratives. The narrator himself, a colorless character, merely collects diverse data telling of increasingly awesome and horrific events, until finally the emergence of Cthulhu—itself described through the narrator's paraphrase of an eyewitness account—forms the apocalyptic climax. Significantly, Cthulhu's depredations are forestalled by mere accident, when he is inadvertently trapped by the re-sinking of his watery prison, the huge and eldritch stone city R'lyeh, which lay under the waters of the Pacific for countless aeons until the "stars were right" and it rose for an instant to blast the minds of a hapless ship's crew. This chance occurrence hints powerfully of how far men are the mere pawns of forces infinitely greater than they.

Through the sub-narrative of an "immensely aged mestizo named Castro," we are given much information on the Great Old Ones, but just who these entities is not quite clear. Only Cthulhu is mentioned by name, and it is not probable that the "Great Old Ones" refer collectively to the other gods later invented by Lovecraft (Yog-Sothoth, Shub-Niggurath, etc.). Rather, they seem to be minions of Cthulhu, since "They all lay in stone houses in Their great city of R'lyeh, preserved by the spells of mighty Cthulhu for a glorious resurrection when the stars and the earth might once more be ready for Them."

In passing we may . . . [turn] to *The Dream-Quest of Unknown Kadath* (1926-27), where Nyarlathotep makes an appearance, this time as a "tall, slim figure with the face of an antique Pharaoh, gay with prismatic robes and crowned with a golden pshent." In physical form, he seems similar to the Nyarlathotep of the prose-poem of 1920, who had also "come out of Egypt" and "was of the old native blood and looked like a Pharaoh," but here he has entered the dream-world and has become the "dread soul and messenger of the Other Gods." He keeps this latter role in **"The Whisperer in Darkness"** (1930) as well, where allusion is made to "Nyarlathotep, Mighty Messenger."

It is in *The Case of Charles Dexter Ward* (1927) that Yog-Sothoth is first mentioned, although only within some odd incantations which fail to reveal his actual nature or significance. This task was accomplished only by **"The Dunwich Horror"** (1928).

"The Colour out of Space" (1927) contains at least two elements that we regard as typifying the Lovecraft Mythos: the setting in the mythical New England locale ("west of Arkham") and the cosmic framework. Thus it may well be studied here in spite of its failure to employ any pseudomythological beings. In its description of a strange meteorite which lands in the Massachusetts back country and causes a peculiar and hideous blight upon all living things, this tale—regarded by Lovecraft as his finest, along with **"The Music of Erich Zann"** and *At the Mountains of Madness*—reaches heights of descriptive perfection that redeems its slightly excessive length (especially at the end). The high-point of the tale is Nahum Gardner's poignant dying speech wherein he, entirely in New England colloquial dialect, describes the effect of the "colour" upon him—a description which is a veritable classic in fantasy and which dynamites the belief that Lovecraft always used a pompous or adjective-filled style to convey horror. The description must be quoted in full:

> "Nothin' . . . nothin' . . . the colour . . . it burns . . . cold an' wet, but it burns . . . it lived in the well . . . I seen it . . . a kind of smoke . . . jest like the flowers last spring . . . the well shone at night . . . Thad an' Merwin an' Zenas . . . everything alive . . . suckin' the life out of everything . . . in that stone . . . it must a' come in that stone . . . pizened the whole place . . . dun't know what it wants . . . that round thing them men from the college dug outen the stone . . . they smashed it . . . it was that same colour . . .

> jest the same, like the flowers an' plants . . . must a' ben more of 'em . . . seeds . . . seeds . . . they growed . . . I seen it the fust time this week . . . must a' got strong on Zenas . . . he was a big boy, full o' life . . . it beats down your mind an' then gets ye . . . burns ye up . . . in the well water . . . you was right about that . . . evil water . . . Zenas never come back from the well . . . can't git away . . . draws ye . . . ye know summ'at's comin' but tain't no use . . . I seen it time an' agin senct Zenas was took . . . whar's Nabby, Ammi? . . . my head's no good . . . dun't know how long sense I fed her . . . it'll git her ef we ain't keerful . . . jest a colour . . . her face is gettin' to hev that colour sometimes towards night . . . an' it burns an' sucks . . . it come from some place whar things ain't as they is here . . . one o' them professors said so . . . he was right . . . look out, Ammi, it'll do suthin' more . . . sucks the life out . . .".

"The Dunwich Horror" (1928) tells the simple tale of Yog-Sothoth's mating with an albino halfwit from the Massachusetts backwoods, the subsequent birth of twins—Wilbur Whateley and his invisible brother—and the ravages of that brother upon Wilbur's death. In the end the horror is quelled by the efforts of Dr. Henry Armitage. Here we have all the elements of the myth-cycle—setting (Dunwich), mythical books (*Necronomicon*—a long and important citation), involvement of pseudomythological beings (Yog-Sothoth), and cosmicism—in a tale which bears a startling but perhaps superficial similarity in plot to Machen's "Great God Pan" (where a woman mates with Pan and spawns the mysterious Helen Vaughan, who is subdued "amidst horrible transmutations of form involving changes of sex and a descent to the most primal manifestations of the life-principle" [*Supernatural Horror in Literature*]). While the tale seems to reveal a rather puerile "good vs. evil" (Armitage vs. Whateley) dichotomy, it has recently been shown that in fact Armitage's victory is "virtually meaningless in cosmic terms" and that it is the Whateley twins who are the real (if tragic) heroes. They are, in any case, certainly more awesome than the figure of Armitage, who rather pompously states at the end: "We have no business calling in such things from outside, and only very wicked people and very wicked cults ever try to." Moreover, the ponderous citation from the *Necronomicon* clearly indicates that one day Whateley and his ilk will succeed in restoring the sway of the Old Ones: "Man rules now where They ruled once; They shall soon rule where man rules now."

That passage from the *Necronomicon* is, indeed, one of the more interesting points of the tale, for we learn still more about the nature of the Lovecraftian gods. The "Old Ones" are evidently distinct from the "Great Old Ones" in **"The Call of Cthulhu"** (just as these "Old Ones" must be distinguished from the Antarctic denizens in *At the Mountains of Madness,* also called "Old Ones"), for it is said that "Great Cthulhu is Their cousin, yet can he spy Them only dimly." It is this passage which led Mosig (correctly, I think) to deem Cthulhu "perhaps one of the weakest and least important of the main entities" of the Lovecraftian pantheon. Clearly the term "Old Ones" must here refer collectively to these gods, although at the moment the term seems to include only Azathoth, Yog-Sothoth, Shub-Niggurath, and perhaps Nyarlathotep.

In passing we may note Lovecraft's ghost-written tale, **"The Mound"** (1929-30), which is the first extensive depiction of an extraterrestrial civilization in all its particulars—social, political, intellectual, and cultural. Of much interest is the inclusion of open political satire in the tale, whereby the underground denizens of K'n-yan rather obviously symbolize Lovecraft's view of the fate of modern Western civilization:

> It is evident that K'n-yan was far along in its decadence—reacting with mixed apathy and hysteria against the standardised and time-tabled life of stultifying regularity with machinery had brought it during its middle period. Even the grotesque and repulsive customs and modes of thought and feeling can be traced to this source; for in his historical research Zamacona found evidence of bygone eras in which K'n-yan had held ideas much like those of the classic and renaissance outer world, and had possessed a national character and art full of what Europeans regard as dignity, kindness, and nobility.

Here again we have a convoluted narrative within a narrative—a modern explorer discovers the narrative of a fifteenth-century Spaniard, Panfilo de Zamacona, which itself tells of the fabulously old civilization of K'n-yan lurking under the mounds of Oklahoma. This gradual "distancing" of the narrative successfully induces us to accept the increasingly bizarre tale being unfolded. We also have random mentions of "Great Tulu [=Cthulhu], . . . the octopus-headed god," Yig, and a few other minor members of the Lovecraft pantheon. Tsathoggua, the deity invented by Clark Ashton Smith as an addition to the Lovecraft Mythos, finds first citation in this tale as well, while we may also note the mention of various place-names from Lovecraft's "Dunsanian" tales, including "the vaults of Zin" and "Olathoe, in the land of Lomar." **"The Mound,"** then, in its complexity of plot, vast imaginative scope, and detailed descriptions of the political and cultural bases for an imagined civilization, is a much undervalued tale in the Lovecraft corpus.

In studying **"The Whisperer in Darkness"** (1930), it is difficult to know where to begin, for it is one of the most richly textured tales in the whole of Lovecraft's fiction. The longest work of original fiction he had yet written—with the exceptions of the "practice" novels *The Dream-Quest of Unknown Kadath* and *The Case of Charles Dexter Ward*—the tale was particularly difficult in its genesis and required nearly seven months for composition. . . . [Much] of the Vermont setting was derived from Lovecraft's visits there in 1927 and 1928. We may . . . also note the strong influence of Arthur Machen upon the tale, especially in its nature-descriptions and in the strange "fungi from Yuggoth" who, like Machen's "little people," lurk just in the background of the tale. There is even mention of a "black stone" with strange hieroglyphs, reminiscent of a similar object in Machen's "Novel of the Black Seal." The novelette involves the strange appearance of crab-shaped beings (variously called the "Winged Ones," the "*Mi-Go* or 'Abominable Snow-Men'," and the "fungi from Yuggoth") who come from the proximal base of Yuggoth (=Pluto) to mine a certain metal not found upon that planet and, from time to time, to kidnap human beings and take them on strange voyagings throughout the cosmos. This kidnaping, however, occurs in a very peculiar way. Through the enormously advanced surgical skill of the creatures, a human being's brain is taken from the body and housed in a metal canister where, for all practical purposes, it remains as an immortal, disembodied intellect. It might be thought that such an existence would be a welcome opportunity for knowledge and aesthetic appreciation—especially to a Lovecraft who wished to adopt "an imaginative and detached life which may enable us to appreciate the world as a beautiful object"—but as the tale proceeds it is clear that Lovecraft intends us to see this state of affairs as in fact the nadir of horror. The very fact that the creatures resort to violence and trickery against a lone individual—Henry Wentworth Akeley, around whom our sympathy must center—condemns them as nefarious. The final letter received by the narrator Wilmarth from "Akeley" (actually from the aliens) reveals in its unctuousness and false jauntiness—"so antipodally at variance with the whole chain of horrors preceding it"—the desire by the aliens to destroy Akeley, Wilmarth (the narrator), and any others who may have knowledge of their existence.

As with many of Lovecraft's tales, an enormously complicated structure allows Lovecraft to conclude with what Leiber called the terminal climax—"in which the high point [of the tale] and the final sentence coincide" [see excerpt dated 1949]. The awful revelation that Akeley has actually been done away with (although his mind is preserved in one of the metal canisters) and that the entity whom Wilmarth meets in Akeley's farmhouse in Vermont is in fact an alien in disguise, must all be implied previous to the final concluding line, which confirms our intimations of Akeley's fate: "For the things in the chair, perfect to the last, subtle detail of microscopic resemblance—or identity—were the face and hands of Henry Wentworth Akeley."

"The Whisperer in Darkness," then, contributes to the broadening of the Mythos and creates still another race of extraterrestrial entities—apparently subservient to Nyarlathotep—and in its tantalizing hints of other mythic elements ("I found myself faced by names and terms that I had heard elsewhere in the most hideous of connections—Yuggoth, Great Cthulhu, Tsathoggua, Yog-Sothoth, R'lyeh, Nyarlathotep, Azathoth, Hastur, Yian, Leng, the Lake of Hali, Bethmoora, the Yellow Sign, L'mur-Kathuos, Bran, and the Magnum Innominandum") would serve as a source for the later development of the Mythos.

At the Mountains of Madness (1931), the last and perhaps the greatest of Lovecraft's novels, is another work about which it is difficult to say too much. Lovecraft himself was pleased with the tale (a rare occurrence) and confessed later that its unexpected rejection by Farnsworth Wright of *Weird Tales* "did more than anything else to end my effective fictional career." The narrative concerns an expedition from Miskatonic University in Arkham to the white wastes of the Antarctic and the titanic, millennia-abandoned city of the "Old Ones" (barrel-shaped entities, half-animal and half-vegetable, who had floated down from the stars millions of years ago) uncovered on a mountain ridge higher than the Himalayas. Behind this simple plot lurks an enormous wealth of detail which we can scarcely touch. Let us first of all, however, destroy a strangely persistent misconception concerning the novel—that it was intended as a continuation or sequel to Poe's *Narrative of A. Gordon Pym.* Probably such an idea would not have occurred to anyone had not Lovecraft mentioned Poe's novel in the early parts of his work. In fact, the novel relies not in any central feature upon the Poe work save in random details of plot (such as the odd and unexplained cry *"Tekeli-li!"* uttered by the shoggoths at the end) and can at best be regarded as a tongue-in-cheek sequel. The scope of the novel is so much vaster than anything Poe could have imagined that it is best to consider the novel as a distinct work in its own right.

As in **"The Mound,"** we here find an elaborate description of the history, politics, aesthetics, and general civilization of the Old Ones—a sociological epic whose breathtaking scope can only be matched by the similar description of the Great Race in **"The Shadow out of Time."** But if we saw that the denizens of K'n-yan may be representative of the future of mankind, what are we to make of the Old Ones? Here we can perhaps see another indication of Lovecraft's classicism, for the Old Ones (and perhaps even more emphatically the Great Race) appear to be a type of *classic* civilization holding the same relation to mankind in general as the Greeks and Romans do to Western civilization. Note that the Old Ones are vastly superior intellectually and aesthetically to men. What is more, they appear to have *created* mankind themselves. The two narrators, in exploring the friezes in the interiors of the houses of the city by which they learn the history of the species, find that the Old Ones could not only create crude synthetic life-forms for their needs but have created "a shambling primitive mammal, used sometimes for food and sometimes as an amusing buffoon by the land dwellers, whose vaguely simian and human foreshadowings were unmistakable." In a similar, if metaphorical, way Lovecraft testifies to the manner in which the Greeks have created Western man:

> Perhaps one should not wonder at *anything* Greek; the race was a super-race. . . . Modern civilisation is the direct heir of Hellenic culture—all that we have is Greek.

Later, when the civilization of the Old Ones—like that of the later Roman Empire—is in decline, Lovecraft makes a telling simile which confirms the connection: "Art and decoration were pursued, though of course with a certain decadence. The Old Ones seemed to realise this falling off themselves; and in many cases anticipated the policy of Constantine the Great by transplanting especially fine blocks of ancient carving from their land city, just as the emperor, in a similar age of decline, stripped Greece and Asia of their finest art to give his new Byzantine capital greater splendours than his own people could create."

In terms of the Mythos, *At the Mountains of Madness* begins systematizing the history and interrelations of the varied entities previously created in Lovecraft's fiction. Both the Cthulhu spawn and the fungi from Yuggoth are incorporated in the history of the Old Ones on this planet. This task of collation would be completed—or at least extensively expanded—in **"The Shadow out of Time."**

In **"The Shadow over Innsmouth"** (1931), we abandon the cosmic plane temporarily and return to New England. In the insidious description of the decaying, sinister port of Innsmouth, Lovecraft has created a masterpiece of local color as distinctive in its way as the South of William Faulkner or the England of Thomas Hardy. The tale concerns the narrator's "tour of New England—sight-seeing, antiquarian, and genealogical," his stumbling upon Innsmouth, his discovery—largely through conversations with the 96-year-old Zadok Allen—of the loathsome history of Innsmouth (wherein the inhabitants have been led to mate with strange creatures from the sea and thus gain "the Innsmouth look"), and his ultimate escape from the town after a maniacal pursuit by the fishy denizens. But the lesson we are to draw from the tale is the inexorable call of heredity. Later researches by the narrator reveal that he himself has Innsmouth blood in him, and after some years, wherein he experiences dreams of increasing horror, he learns the truth: "That morning the mirror definitely told me I had acquired *the Innsmouth look.*" But the ultimate horror is yet to come; for the narrator, instead of committing suicide, *accepts* his fate and decides to return to Innsmouth:

> I shall plan my cousin's escape from that Canton madhouse, and together we shall go to marvel-shadowed Innsmouth. We shall swim out to that brooding reef in the sea and dive down through black abysses to Cyclopean and many-columned Y'ha-nthlei, and in that lair of the Deep Ones we shall dwell amidst wonder and glory for ever.

To Lovecraft this could only mean not a mitigation of horror, as some have believed, but an intensification of it. The narrator has, by his actions, renounced his own culture and joined a culture which throughout the tale Lovecraft has depicted as noxiously alien. It is not surprising that the Innsmouth denizens bear many resemblances to the "foreigners" so castigated by Lovecraft in his letters and essays.

The novelette contains some enormously subtle links with other tales which have generally been overlooked. It appears that the Innsmouth folk—who, once they return entirely to the sea, are called the "Deep Ones"—have become leagued with the shoggoths of *At the Mountains of Madness* ("This was the dream in which I saw a *shoggoth* for the first time"); a connection also suggested in the later **"Thing on the Doorstep."** The fact, moreover, that in Innsmouth there is a secret cult called the Esoteric Order of Dagon means that there is some relation to that fish-god and perhaps to the worshippers of that god described in **"Dagon"** (1917). Lovecraft, however, never got the opportunity of developing these linkages in further tales.

With **"The Dreams in the Witch House"** (1932), we return to the cosmic level, in a distinctive combination of Einsteinian physics and Puritan witchcraft. Keziah Mason has discovered the means for traveling through space and time via advanced mathematics and the odd geometry of the attic room of the Witch House in Arkham (based, at least in name, upon the celebrated Witch House in Salem). Accompanying her is her familiar, the human rat Brown Jenkin, along with the sinister Black Man who, we learn, is nothing more than an avatar of Nyarlathotep. Lovecraft is vastly ingenious not merely in connecting ancient witchcraft with modern science but in his vivid and almost surrealistic descriptions of the fourth dimension (carried to further heights in **"Through the Gates of the Silver Key"**).

The tale, however, is not without flaws. The most serious one is a generally "overwritten" or verbose style of writing whereby Lovecraft falls back upon hackneyed phrase-combinations, such as "unspeakably menacing" or "stark, hideous fright." The use of such adjectives is not intrinsically bad but has here become stilted and commonplace. Another fatal flaw is the curiously conventional touch whereby the witch Keziah is frightened off by the mere appearance of a nickel crucifix—a trite and hackneyed horrific device hardly worthy of the cosmicism of the rest of the tale. **"The Dreams in the Witch House,"** along with **"The Shadow over Innsmouth"** (which went through several initial drafts), begins to reveal that increasing difficulty which Lovecraft was to have in his later years in setting down his fictional ideas.

"The Thing on the Doorstep" (1933), however, certainly belies the trend temporarily, having been composed in four days (August 21-24, 1933). We have returned to Arkham, although connections with Innsmouth are not dropped. Edward Derby, a brilliant but sensitive and weak-willed poet and scholar, is attracted by and ultimately marries the strange and fascinating Asenath Waite, daughter of Ephraim Waite of Innsmouth. Behind this disturbing romance, however, lies horror. Asenath is intent on psychically possessing Derby's body, forcing his psyche into her own form, and so attaining that male status that will allow her to practice deeper forms of black magic than is possible in a woman's body. Asenath, it turns out, is nothing more than old Ephraim himself, for it was Ephraim who seized his young daughter's body when he felt himself approaching death. It is this exchange that impels Derby, in a moment of furious anger, to cry out: "I'll kill that entity . . . her, him, it . . . I'll kill it! I'll kill it with my own hands!"

In the character of Derby, we have an obviously autobiographical figure, especially in such descriptions as this:

> Perhaps his private education and coddled seclusion had something to do with his premature flowering. An only child, he had organic weaknesses which startled his doting parents and caused them to keep him closely chained to their side. He was never allowed out without his nurse, and seldom had a chance to play unconstrainedly with other children. All this doubtless fostered a strange, secretive inner life in the boy, with imagination as his one avenue of freedom.

It cannot, however, be said that Derby is entirely Lovecraft—rather, he seems to be an amalgam of Lovecraft and some of his associates, particularly Alfred Galpin, Clark Ashton Smith, and perhaps Samuel Loveman. Asenath herself seems to be a combination of Lovecraft's wife and mother.

The tale—while suffering somewhat from too much explanation and lack of subtlety—is redeemed not only by characterization but by one of the grisliest climactic scenes in fantasy fiction. Derby had finally gained enough courage to kill Asenath and bury her in the cellar, but her personality did not yet die. Several months after the murder, she came back triumphant and possessed Derby's body, *forcing his mind into the rotting corpse in the cellar.* By superhuman effort of will, Derby dug himself out of the grave and crawled—a "foul, stunted parody" on the human shape—to the home of his friend Daniel Upton and gave him a message relating the final horror. Upton then went to the sanitarium where "Derby" (i.e., Asenath) was being detained and shot the being. It is of this action that Upton writes when opening the tale on a superb paradox: "It is true that I have sent six bullets through the head of my best friend, and yet I hope to shew by this statement that I am not his murderer." Here again we see that convoluted construction—where the actions at the chronological *end* of the story are told *first*—which makes Lovecraft a master of fictional structure.

Mind-exchange returns on a vastly expanded level in **"The Shadow out of Time"** (1934-35), this time involving the Great Race—which "alone had conquered the secret of time" by its ability to send its minds backwards and forwards in time and into the body of any other life-form in the universe. In this way the Great Race could study all life anywhere in the cosmos—they were the greatest scientists of all time. "From the accomplishments of this race arose all legends of prophets, including those in human mythology." This process of mind-exchange—whereby a member of the Great Race mentally enters the body of some other species, while the displaced mind is thrown into the body of its dispossessor and writes the history of its own times for the central archives—is in fact one of the few ways of escaping the paradoxes of time-travel and can thus earn a significant place in the history of science fiction. Moreover, this mind-exchange somewhat cynically seems to account for some of the greatest intellectual advancements of the human race.

In describing the civilization of the Great Race as it inhabited the minds of great cone-shaped beings coming from space and landing on the earth 150,000,000 years ago, Lovecraft gives much attention to the political and social fabric of the ancient culture, which becomes a near-utopia and outlet for the expression of Lovecraft's political views:

> The Great Race seemed to form a single, loosely knit nation or league, with major institutions in common, though there were four definite devisions. The political and economic system of each unit was a sort of fascistic socialism, with major resources rationally distributed, and power delegated to a small governing board elected by the votes of all able to pass certain educational and psychological tests. Family organization was not overstressed, though ties among persons of common descent were recognized, and the young were generally reared by their parents.

In this tale we are given a vast amount of information on the past and future history of the earth and solar system—a history which is typically bleak as regards mankind's small and inconsequential place in it. The stupefying gulfs of time are suggested by the encounters of the narrator Nathaniel Wingate Peaslee (in the bodily form of his cone-shaped captor) with minds from other corners of space:

> There was a mind from the planet we know as Venus, which would live incalculable epochs to come, and one from an outer moon of Jupiter six million years in the past. Of earthly minds there were some from the winged, star-headed, half-vegetable race of palaeogean Antarctica [=Old Ones]; one from the reptile people of fabled Valusia; three from the furry pre-human Hyperborean worshippers of Tsathoggua; one from the wholly abominable Tcho-Tchos; two from the arachnid denizens of earth's last age; five from the hardy coleopterous species immediately following mankind, to which the Great Race was some day to transfer its keenest minds en masse in the face of horrible peril; and several from different branches of humanity.

Indeed, this tale and *At the Mountains of Madness* are surely the most "cosmic" in all Lovecraft's fiction.

"The Haunter of the Dark" (1935), Lovecraft's last work of original fiction, has certainly the oddest genesis. Robert Bloch had written a tale entitled "The Shambler from the Stars," wherein a character thinly disguised as Lovecraft had met a rather grisly end. Incited by a reader's comment in the letter column of *Weird Tales,* Lovecraft replied with **"The Haunter of the Dark,"** in which the character Robert Blake is left "sitting rigidly at a desk and gazing out a west window, with an expression of unutterable fear on the twisted features." But the humorous inspiration of the tale hides an enormously powerful story of psychic possession, wherein a mysterious entity trapped in the steeple of an odd church in the Federal Hill section of Providence ultimately takes over the mind of the young fantaisiste Blake, who is drawn with increasing fascination to the exploration of this church. This entity—which cannot endure light, but escapes through an accidental power failure in the city—is nothing less than an avatar of Nyarlathotep, "who in antique and shadowy Khem even took the form of man." Blake's concluding diary entry is a triumph of horror mingled with pathos:

> "Lights still out—must be five minutes now. Everything depends on lightning. Yaddith grant it will keep up! . . . Some influence seems beating through it. . . . Rain and thunder and wind deafen. . . . The thing is taking hold of my mind. . . . My name is Blake—Robert Harrison Blake of 620 East Knapp Street, Milwaukee, Wisconsin. . . . I am on this planet. . . ."

One detail in this passage is an elaborate "in-joke" which, when understood, carries enormous power. Toward the last, just before the entity has completely possessed Blake, he scribbles: "Roderick Usher—am mad or going mad. . .". The reference to Usher seems fantastically incongruous until we realize that Lovecraft, in *Supernatural Horror in Literature,* had made the discovery—one of his several important contributions to Poe scholarship—that "The Fall of the House of Usher" "displays an abnormally linked trinity of entities at the end of a long and isolated family history—a brother, his twin sister, and their incredibly ancient house all sharing a single soul and meeting one common dissolution at the same moment." So too the entity and Blake share a single soul, and at the moment of psychic union ("I am it and it is I"), both are killed when a bolt of lightning strikes the creature as it is winging its course across the sky.

It might now be well to cover briefly few minor works which add some details to the Lovecraft Mythos. The fragment **"Azathoth"** (1922) tells little about that entity, and seems—in its depiction of a man's quest to escape tawdry modernity by dream-voyagings—an adumbration of *The Dream-Quest of Unknown Kadath.* The "History of the *Necronomicon*" (1927) tells a tongue-in-cheek history of the writing and publishing of the dreaded tome of the mad Arab Abdul Alhazred, a history to which Lovecraft adhered in later citations of the work. In **"Through the Gates of the Silver Key"** (1932-33, with E. Hoffmann Price) Yog-Sothoth's character is developed. Indeed, at this point the whole pantheon seems to return to a sort of Dunsanian etherealness, as Randolph Carter learns their true nature:

> He [Carter] wondered at the vast conceit of those who had babbled of the *malignant* Ancient Ones, as if They could pause from their everlasting dreams to wreak a wrath upon mankind. As well, he thought, might a mammoth pause to visit frantic vengeance on an angleworm.

This passage, as well as the almost unthinkably cosmic scope of the tale, again serves to reduce mankind to an inkblot in the vast gulfs of infinity.

If anything has emerged from this study, it is the gradual and unsystematic way in which Lovecraft mapped out the various facets of the Mythos—a fact which must again confirm Lovecraft's belief that these tales, while superficially related in details of plot and recurrent sites and characters, are not necessarily to be cleanly segregated from the rest of his fictional work. Although the idea of obscure sea-denizens was first broached in **"Dagon,"** it was only expounded extensively in **"The Shadow over Innsmouth."** The role of Nyarlathotep is successively elaborated in the prose-poem **"Nyarlathotep,"**

The Dream-Quest, **"The Whisperer in Darkness," "The Dreams in the Witch House,"** and **"The Haunter of the Dark."** The idea of obscure civilizations which have come to earth from the stars, first hinted in **"The Nameless City,"** is followed up in **"The Call of Cthulhu," "The Mound," "The Whisperer in Darkness,"** *At the Mountains of Madness,* and **"The Shadow out of Time."** The mythical New England locale is described variously in **"The Festival," "The Colour out of Space," "The Dunwich Horror," "The Whisperer in Darkness," "The Shadow over Innsmouth," "The Dreams in the Witch House,"** and **"The Thing on the Doorstep."** Hence one story may—and usually does—add details to several aspects of the total concept of the Mythos.

It cannot be denied that the Lovecraft Mythos—a series of tales unique not only in their interrelatedness or in their structural and stylistic excellence but in their conveying of the "cosmic" attitude which gives to Lovecraft's philosophy its distinctiveness—is Lovecraft's greatest fictional achievement. Although few later writers have been successful in making significant advances upon the idea (largely through a misconception of the philosophical bases of the Mythos), it is likely that future fictionists will be kept as busy in elaborating the Mythos as future scholars will be in explicating it. (pp. 31-43)

S. T. Joshi, in his H. P. Lovecraft, *Starmont House, 1982, 83 p.*

DONALD R. BURLESON (essay date 1983)

[*Burleson is an American educator and critic whose* H. P. Lovecraft: A Critical Study *is an extensive consideration of Lovecraft's fiction, nonfiction, and poetry. In the following excerpt from that study, he examines the influence of Edgar Allan Poe and Nathaniel Hawthorne on Lovecraft's fiction.*]

Lovecraft was a largely self-educated but exceedingly widely read author, and his writing shows, in varying amounts and different patterns at various states of his career, the clear influence of a number of writers whom he studied and admired. He is, however, not a "derivative" writer producing works that merely amount to collages of those influences; rather, his writings reveal that he *assimilated* such influences, transmuting and developing them for artistic purposes that are highly individual. (p. 213)

Lovecraft read Poe from the age of eight, and early in his writing career, in 1922, he remarked:

> To me Poe is the apex of fantastic art—there was in him a vast and cosmic vision which no imitator has been able to parallel. . . . I do find it in Dunsany, though in much weaker form, and diluted with a certain shrewd self-consciousness which Poe sublimely lacked. There may be something rather sophomoric in my intense and unalterable devotion to Poe . . . but I do not think it so far amiss as the average ultra-modern would hasten to pronounce it.

He goes on to cite the "ultra-human point of view" in Poe, and one recognises that this fictional stance has become an integral part of the Lovecraft Mythos itself, which indeed sustains the viewpoint more tenaciously than Poe's works do. Several years later, in 1931, Lovecraft was still able to remark, "Poe has probably influenced me more than any one person," despite the fact that Lovecraft eventually reestimated Dunsany's comparative cosmicism upward and came to write less in the actual diction and general manner of Poe as time went on. What Lovecraft derived of permanence from Poe was an abiding tone of darkness, a concern with gloomy and ponderous themes and images, and the strength of basing the crafting of horror tales on a working knowledge of the psychology of fear rather than on "stock" and empty narrative devices purporting to produce shudders without the requisite emotional base.

Early in Lovecraft's writing career, his devotion to Poe could at times run to the extent of almost slavish imitation; the story **"The Hound"** (1922) is a prime example, with its starkness of imagery—the amulet, the baying hound itself, the "nightmare retinue of huge, sinewy, sleeping bats"—and with an emotional outburst from its brooding and morbidly disturbed narrator: "—how I shudder to recall it!" The tale **"The Outsider"** of the previous year also shows a heavy Poe influence; its opening is, in terms of imagery and diction alike, a virtual paraphrase of the opening of Poe's "Berenice":

> there are no towers in the land more time-honoured than my gloomy, gray, hereditary halls. . . . The recollections of my earliest years are connected with that chamber, and with its volumes—of which latter I will say no more. Herein was I born . . . into a place of imagination—into the wild dominions of monastic thought and erudition.

Lovecraft's tale also imagistically reflects Poe's "Masque of the Red Death" in its ballroom scene. Yet the tale develops along very different thematic lines from those explored by Poe, and indeed one cannot say that Lovecraft even during this period was exclusively devoted to Poe, for he produced also such tales as **"The Quest of Iranon"** and **"The Other Gods"** (both in 1921) showing more than anything else the influence of Dunsany. It is simplistic to try to carve Lovecraft's writing career up into a "Poe period," "Dunsany period," and the like, for one finds the influences temporarily interspersed and irregularly recurrent.

One finds Poesque themes and images cropping up in Lovecraft's works at widely separated intervals. Perhaps the last story that one could call overtly Poe-imitative is **"Cool Air"** (1926), in which the imagery of liquescent dissolution in the end is (besides perhaps reflective of the similar scene in Machen's "The Novel of the White Powder") a clear echo of the ending of Poe's "The Facts in the Case of M. Valdemar": "his whole frame at once . . . absolutely *rotted* away beneath my hands. Upon the bed, before that whole company, there lay a nearly liquid mass of loathsome—of detestable putrescence." Even after Lovecraft grew out of this direct imagistic echoing of Poe—certainly by the writing of **"The Call of Cthulhu"** in 1926 he was finding his own identity as an artist—even after his dependence on Poe ceased to be so obvious, he continued to reflect Poe in somewhat less visible ways. His novel *At the Mountains of Madness* (1931) still exhibits a clear connexion with Poe, with its reiteration of Poe's *"Tekeli-li!"* and concern with Antarctica as in *Narrative of A. Gordon Pym*—not to the extent, however, that Lovecraft's novel can in any real sense be described as a sequel to the Poe novel, for Lovecraft strikes out in directions wholly unanticipated by Poe's account. The Poe novel evidently influenced Lovecraft in other ways. On a point of diction, it contains the expression "exceedingly singular" employed in the opening paragraph of *The Case of Charles Dexter Ward,* as well as other stylistic points. More significantly, there is in **"The**

Whisperer in Darkness" a loose but clear borrowing of Poe's motif of the chasms in the island of Tsalal, which are found to spell out in huge letters a message in ancient Egyptian; Lovecraft has his narrator in the Vermont tale feel "that the very outline of the hills themselves held some strange and aeon-forgotten meaning, as if they were vast hieroglyphs left by a rumoured titan race."

Other such parallel motifs may be traced, as in the case of Poe's "Ligeia," where the theme of possession by a departed woman cannot fail to make the reader think of Lovecraft's Asenath Waite in **"The Thing on the Doorstep."** Poe dwells at length on the woman's eyes:

> The expression of the eyes of Ligeia! . . . What was it—that something more profound than the well of Democritus—which lay far within the eyes of my beloved? What *was* it?

One notes a parallel concern with Asenath's hypnotic eyes and the secret that lies within them, a secret, like Ligeia's, destined to outlive life itself through possession from beyond the grave; indeed, the conquering of death is a frequent Lovecraftian theme, as in the case of Joseph Curwen. "Ligeia" also deals with the theme of elusiveness; its narrator remarks that "we often find ourselves *upon the very verge* of remembrance, without being able, in the end, to remember." Lovecraft's use of this notion is widespread and basic to his work, finding great articulation in **"The Shadow out of Time," "The Shadow over Innsmouth,"** and other works.

"Ligeia" affords as well a pertinent imagery concerning draperies:

> The phantasmagoric effect was greatly heightened by the artificial introduction of a strong continual current of wind behind the draperies—giving a hideous and uneasy animation to the whole.

Certainly, this is reflected in Lovecraft's description of the arras in **"The Rats in the Walls."** In Poe's tale, Lady Rowena, the narrator says, speaks of "sounds which she *then* heard, but which I could not perceive" in connexion with the shifting tapestries; one is ineluctably put in mind of Lovecraft's de la Poer.

As time went on, Lovecraft did largely cease to emulate Poe in any such obvious fashion as diction or borrowing of motifs and imageries, though his constant use of the motif of cryptogram-solving—see **"The Dunwich Horror," "The Haunter of the Dark,"** *The Case of Charles Dexter Ward*—is a testimony to his lasting indebtedness to Poe's "The Gold Bug." More broadly speaking, what lingers of Poe in Lovecraft is his psychological concern, his working artistic acquaintance with the nature of fear; as Lovecraft put it in *Supernatural Horror in Literature* (where Poe alone has an entire chapter devoted to him), Poe, unlike earlier writers of gothic or horror fiction, possessed "an understanding of the psychological basis of the horror appeal" leading to "a new standard of realism" in the realm of horror. Poe's protagonists are often mentally tormented individuals facing the insupportably bleak facts of their existence and circumstances; they find themselves alone with their inner horrors, bereft even of any hope of being believed, or of being themselves able to believe their own experiences. See, for example, the opening lines of Poe's "The Black Cat":

> For the most wild yet most homely narrative which I am about to pen, I neither expect nor solicit belief. Mad indeed would I be to expect it, in a case where my very senses reject their own evidence.

One finds this sort of opening statement even in some of Lovecraft's later works, particularly **"The Thing on the Doorstep"** and **"The Shadow out of Time."** Similarly, Poe's narrator desperately tries to defend his sanity in "The Tell-Tale Heart" (in which there is the motif of hypersensitive hearing—see Lovecraft's Walter Gilman in **"The Dreams in the Witch House"**), and Lovecraft derives from Poe a sort of general character type, many times reworked by both authors, in which there is a brooding inner horror that swells to dreadful proportions and envelops the unfortunate protagonist, whose horror, whatever other implications there are, is a private and inescapable one. Thus, although Lovecraft progressively dropped his facile imitation of Poe, there lingers in Lovecraft's literary career a general backdrop of darkness, a pervasive psychological frame of reference or mind-set which Lovecraft learned early at the feet of his master but came to develop along lines highly original and characteristically Lovecraftian.

Although Lovecraft did not seem to regard Nathaniel Hawthorne as a major influence on him, nevertheless there is to be found a Hawthorne influence that is quite considerable. At the age of seven Lovecraft read Hawthorne's *Wonder Book* and *Tanglewood Tales,* deriving from them an enduring interest in classical mythology which makes itself evident in Lovecraft's work not only in the form of the Mythos itself (which directly owes more to the Dunsany influence) but in the form of a lasting concern with beauty and propriety of language inspired by classical models whom Lovecraft came to read and admire.

However, Hawthorne influenced Lovecraft in far more specific ways, in terms more thematic than stylistic. Although Lovecraft disapproved of Hawthorne's literary didacticism—preferring Poe's critical theory that literature should move us emotionally rather than instruct us—and although such Hawthornian concerns as the Unpardonable Sin were virtually meaningless in Lovecraft's world-view, Lovecraft derived a lasting influence from Hawthorne ranging over a wide variety of themes and motifs.

On a general level, one may say that Lovecraft found in Hawthorne a fascination with the shadowy side of New England history and culture; the fact that Lovecraft came to prefer setting horror tales in his native region, rather than in such "stock" settings as eastern European castles and the like, is largely due to Hawthorne. (Hawthorne's concern with *gloom* in New England simply reinforces the predilection that Lovecraft had already largely derived from Poe.) Lovecraft's earliest works show no particular tendency to concentrate on New England; but by the mid-1920s—Lovecraft intensively reread Hawthorne for his critical project *Supernatural Horror in Literature*—Lovecraft came to weave New England into the fabric even of his most stunningly cosmic narratives.

More specifically, there is a wealth of imagery and thematic concern common to Hawthorne and Lovecraft despite the differences in their philosophical viewpoints. Even as early as 1920 Lovecraft, in writing **"The Picture in the House,"** reflects Hawthorne's personification of the House of the Seven Gables. Hawthorne says of his celebrated Salem edifice:

> The aspect of the venerable mansion has always affected me like a human countenance, bearing the traces not merely of outward storm and sunshine,

> but expressive, also, of the long lapse of mortal life, and accompanying vicissitudes, that have passed within. . . . You could not pass it without the idea that it had secrets to keep, and an eventful history to meditate upon.

One can scarcely avoid making the connexion between this imagery and that of Lovecraft's **"The Picture in the House,"** where it is said of the farmhouse:

> the small-paned windows still stare shockingly, as if blinking through a lethal stupor which wards off madness by dulling the memory of unutterable things. . . . Sometimes one feels that it would be merciful to tear down these houses, for they must often dream.

Hawthorne's *The House of the Seven Gables* also influenced Lovecraft's **"The Shunned House,"** to the point of closely parallel passages. Hawthorne says of his house that "the street having been widened about forty years ago, the front gable was now precisely on a line with it." Similarly, at the Shunned House, "a widening of the street at about the time of the Revolution sheared off most of the intervening space" between the house and the road so that the cellar wall was exposed to the sidewalk. Hawthorne's novel also adumbrates another image used (in transmuted form) by Lovecraft: the image of the Pyncheon looking–glass, said to be influenced by the Maule family in such a way that "they could make its inner region all alive with the departed Pyncheons." One is reminded of the scene in **"The Shunned House"** in which Elihu Whipple, attacked by the vampiric presence beneath the house, becomes a shifting pageant of the faces of the departed in the house's history. Hawthorne even says of the Salem house that Colonel Pyncheon "was about to build his house over an unquiet grave," and the same is *literally* true of Lovecraft's Shunned House. Lovecraft in his critical essay [*Supernatural Horror in Literature*] noted the *psychopomp* motif in Hawthorne's novel (in the form of the cat keeping vigil at the window when Judge Pyncheon dies), and, of course, this same motif—in the form of whippoorwills, after a local legend encountered in Wilbraham, Massachusetts—appears in **"The Dunwich Horror."** Perhaps the most striking motif borrowed from the Hawthorne novel is that of the discovery, in a recess in the wall behind the portrait of old Colonel Pyncheon, of long-lost family papers; Lovecraft repeats this pattern in *The Case of Charles Dexter Ward,* in which Joseph Curwen's papers are found in a wall-cache behind his portrait. In both novels there is the notion of a modern character having an ancestor, whom the character resembles, reach forward from the family past to engulf the current scion.

Lovecraft derives various other motifs and images from assorted Hawthorne works. Surely the god-face carved on Mount Ngranek in *The Dream-Quest of Unknown Kadath* is a reflection of Hawthorne's "The Great Stone Face," derived in turn from the Old Man of the Mountains of Franconia, New Hampshire. This Lovecraft novel also would appear to owe something to Hawthorne's *The Marble Faun* with its hints of deific blood in mortal veins, for in the Lovecraft work we find the notion that the Great Ones in disguise often consort with human women to produce offspring whose features resemble those of the gods; of course, this has inspiration from Greek mythology as well.

Lovecraft even borrows from Hawthorne's unfinished novels. *Septimius Felton* has a character named Aunt Keziah, who boasts of her resistance of the temptations of the Black Man of witchcraft lore, and the influence on Lovecraft's **"The Dreams in the Witch House"** is obvious. The same novel speaks of a silver key which leads to ancestral papers in an old chest, and again the influence is obvious, with respect to **"The Silver Key,"** though Lovecraft's work involves a cosmicism far beyond anything suggested by Hawthorne. Lovecraft's tale **"The Unnameable,"** with its cloven hoofprint, echoes the bloody footprint of *Dr. Grimshawe's Secret,* and indeed the Lovecraft story has its setting in Salem's Charter Street cemetery, the adjacent "Grimshawe House" being by Lovecraft's own account the real prototype of the fictive house; Hawthorne's wife Sophia once lived there.

Some of the most striking influence is to be found in connexion with Hawthorne's *American Notebooks.* It is clear that Lovecraft read these notebooks at an early date, for in his own commonplace book he writes, in 1919 or 1920, but sufficiently early despite the dating ambiguities involved, "Hawthorne—unwritten plot. Visitor from tomb. Stranger at some public concourse followed at midnight to graveyard where he descends into the earth." This note not only makes it clear that Lovecraft had read Hawthorne thoroughly at the time—otherwise he could not identify a Hawthorne plot idea as "unwritten"—but shows also that Lovecraft, well in advance of writing **"The Nameless City"** in 1921, could scarcely have missed the following remarkable Hawthorne notebook entry of 17 October 1835: "An old volume in a large library—everyone to be afraid to unclasp and open it, because it was said to be a book of magic." Lovecraft's discovery of this note is early enough for it to be the inspiration for his mythical tome, the *Necronomicon* (first quoted in **"The Nameless City,"** first named in **"The Hound"** in 1922), which is characterised as being shunned and guardedly ensconced in libraries as described. Lovecraft is quite likely to have drawn thematic inspiration from at least one other Hawthorne notebook entry, that of 4 January 1839:

> A mortal symptom for a person being to lose his own aspect and to take the family lineaments, which were hidden deep in the healthful visage. Perhaps a seeker might thus recognise the man he had sought, after long intercourse with him unknowingly.

This notion is clearly suggestive of Lovecraft's **"The Shadow over Innsmouth,"** in which indeed—Lovecraft's preter-Hawthornian twist—there is just such a delayed recognition, the narrator's recognition of his own monstrous heritage and nature when he begins himself to assume the "Innsmouth look." Indeed, the general notion of being haunted by the past is common in Hawthorne; Lovecraft's works are full of the notion, though he develops it in vastly different ways.

Thus, it is reasonable to conclude that Lovecraft, while preferring the philosophical stance of Poe and retaining much of that master's psychological approach to horror fiction, derives much imagistic and thematic influence from Hawthorne, influence that ranges over a variety of works in the canons of both authors. Even Lovecraft's *Necronomicon,* so central to the Lovecraft Mythos, is virtually certain to have been germinally inspired by Hawthorne's notebook jottings. Lovecraft developed his materials, of course, in a cosmic, trans-human way very unlike the allegorical moralising of Hawthorne, but the imprint of the dark side of Hawthorne's New England and the commonality of numerous motifs and images is clear and lasting in the Lovecraft *oeuvre.* The influence of Hawthorne on Lovecraft is altogether one of the most striking instances of (largely) unrecognised influence likely to be encountered in the field of fantasy literature. (pp. 213-21)

Donald R. Burleson, in his H. P. Lovecraft: A Critical Study, *Greenwood Press, 1983, 243 p.*

ROBERT M. PRICE (essay date 1985)

[*Price is an American educator and critic whose writings are principally devoted to his two main fields of expertise: Christian theology and the works of H. P. Lovecraft. He is the editor of* Crypt of Cthulhu: A Pulp Thriller and Theological Journal, *which publishes both facetious and serious essays on Lovecraft and other authors of the* Weird Tales *school. In the following excerpt, Price analyzes the nature and function of the Cthulhu Mythos in Lovecraft's work, and examines how this invented mythology was used by Lovecraft and by other fantasy writers.*]

Much debate has swirled around the question of the "Cthulhu Mythos"—what is it? To what extent is it the authentic creation of Lovecraft? Or is it the distortion of later hands? What stories, if any, may be said to belong to it? We think that a great deal of clarification has been accomplished by the pioneering studies of Dirk W. Mosig, particularly in his pivotal essay "H. P. Lovecraft: Myth-Maker" [see Joshi entry dated 1980 in Additional Bibliography]. Mosig speaks of Lovecraft's "pseudomythology (which I prefer to call the Yog-Sothoth Cycle of Myth, to differentiate it from the distorted version labeled 'Cthulhu Mythos' by Derleth)." Parenthetically, S. T. Joshi endorses Mosig's rejection of the term "Cthulhu Mythos," but prefers to dub it instead the "Lovecraft Mythos" [see excerpt dated 1982]. Whatever one calls it, Mosig continues, it

> refers to various alien entities, cults, books, and places, but the tales themselves—whether by Lovecraft, Derleth, or anyone else—do not, and cannot "belong" to the myth-cycle! Practically all of Lovecraft's stories are loosely connected by common themes, locales, legendry, and philosophical undercurrents, but to state that some of the tales "belong to the Cthulhu Mythos" and others don't is largely meaningless and misleading. Instead, it would be correct to state that in some of the tales elements of the Yog-Sothoth Cycle of Myth are of pivotal importance, while in others they assume a marginal role, or are absent.

Mosig is certainly correct here—stories *utilize* the Mythos; they don't *belong to* it. This insight is essential if we are going to understand just what the Mythos is and how stories by various authors relate to it. And this is precisely what we are going to attempt.

But first it should be noted that Mosig himself fails to heed his own advice. In another related article, . . . Mosig seems to regard Lovecraft's stories as together composing his Yog-Sothoth Myth-Cycle. "It is this writer's contention (and that of others before him [e.g., George Wetzel]) that practically all of the stories written by H. P. Lovecraft can best be regarded as the loosely connected chapters of a gigantic novel. . . ." This suggestion itself seems to us extremely doubtful, but let us not digress. Mosig's point is to show how artificial it is to divide Lovecraft's stories, as is traditionally done, into "Cthulhu," "Dunsanian," and "New England Horror" categories. This arbitrariness he thinks to demonstrate by showing how elements of each supposed category often appear mixed in a single tale, e.g., **"The Shadow over Innsmouth," "The Rats in the Walls,"** or *The Dream-Quest of Unknown Kadath.* Mosig, then rejects the threefold classification in favor of seeing all the elements (e.g., Arkham, the Old Ones, the *Necronomicon,* the Dream World) as parts of the one "Yog-Sothoth Myth-Cycle."

Yet the problem Mosig discusses will seem to be a problem only if one supposes that the various stories must *belong* to one of the three sub-myth-cycles. And the problem thus posed will seem to be solved as Mosig solves it only if one goes on to see all the tales as belonging to the Yog-Sothoth Cycle of Myth. If, on the other hand, the several stories merely *utilize* the myth-cycle as Mosig claimed in the essay quoted above, there would seem to be no reason they could not just as easily utilize elements from three submyth-cycles simultaneously.

In other words, Mosig seems to be saying in effect, "If the stories cannot all neatly belong to these three categories, what *category can* they belong to?" His answer is that they are one long novelization of the Yog-Sothoth Cycle of Myth. He is barking up the wrong tree. The stories do not *belong* to one category or to three.

We are going to argue instead that Lovecraft created what are three essentially different myth-cycles upon which all his several stories draw. A single story may use data from more than one cycle without creating confusion as to the boundaries of each separate mythos.

Another important point at which we must dissent from Mosig's picture is where he seems to regard the "Yog-Sothoth Myth-Cycle" as autonomously and self-containedly Lovecraft's work, as is implicit in his spurning of Derleth's nomenclature "Cthulhu Mythos." By contrast, we will argue that in Lovecraft's own lifetime there was already a "Cthulhu Mythos" to which other writers had contributed. Yet Mosig is right in saying that eventually the waters *were* muddied, that Derleth was the chief polluter. But we will see that the line is not to be drawn quite where Mosig draws it.

Strangely enough, much of the discussion about "the Mythos" has tended to ignore Lovecraft's own words on the matter. For instance, are we justified in erasing the distinction between the "Dunsanian," the "New England," and the "Cthulhu" groupings, when Lovecraft himself may be shown to have used similar terminology? He speaks of his "Dunsanian period," his "Arkham cycle," and "the Yog-Sothoth and Cthulhu cycles." Granted, in the first two instances, he seems to refer to groups of stories, but certainly the point is that the tales in question are characterized principally by their dependence upon distinct collections of elements such as locale.

First, the Dunsanian canon involves ancient lands and cities such as Sarnath, Olathoe, Leng, Ib, Kadath, and Lomar. These places are peopled by the gugs, ghasts, zoogs, Inutos, Gnoph-kehs, moon-beasts, etc. The stories have a dreamlike atmosphere or else actually occur in dreams. The gods of these lands are modeled on the lines of classical mythology. They include the Great Ones and the sunken Mighty Ones, notably the Roman sea-god Nodens. They are the "gods of earth," those who are supreme in the normal order of things. When on occasion we find that there are also "Other Gods," the point is that they are beyond the purview of the languid and limpid dream-reality, representing instead the stark and awful truth as Lovecraft conceived it. Barzai the Wise is surprised to discover them. They are not in view at all in **"The Strange High House in the Mist,"** and the power of Nodens is triumphant in *The Dream-Quest of Unknown Kadath* even against Nyarlathotep, an interloper from the Cthulhu Mythos.

Second, the Cthulhu cycle itself is defined over against the Dunsanian canon. In this frame of reference, no mention is made of any other "gods of earth." Where Leng is mentioned, it exists not in the Dunsanian land of Dreams, but in the real world, in either Central Asia or the South Pole. "Gnophkeh" is a minor Old One, not a tribe of cavemen, as in the Dunsanian cycle. The Cthulhu Mythos as Lovecraft created it concerned primarily a set of extra-dimensional beings including Cthulhu, Yog-Sothoth, Shub-Niggurath, Azathoth, and Nyarlathotep, plus certain grimoires for summoning them, especially the *Necronomicon.*

Third, the "Arkham cycle" refers primarily to the set of haunted locales in Massachusetts, in and around Arkham, Lovecraft's analogue to Salem. Within Arkham we may point to Miskatonic University, the Witch-House, and the homes of Edward Derby, Randolph Carter, and others. In the environs of Arkham, and often mentioned in connection with it, are the towns of Innsmouth, Dunwich, Kingsport, Aylesbury, and Dean's Corners.

Rarely a piece of lore may be transferred between the three cycles. For instance, one might argue that the *Pnakotic Manuscripts* began as part of the Dunsanian cycle but eventually found themselves firmly entrenched in the Cthulhu cycle. Or the Great Old Ones may possibly be seen as being incorporated also into the Dunsanian cycle as the "Other Gods." But most of the time the overlap occurs not between the bodies of lore themselves, but in the stories which freely draw on this, then that, body of lore. For instance, though Arkham is not part of the Cthulhu Mythos, a tale of Cthulhu may certainly be set there. Though Nodens is not part of Lovecraft's myth-cycle of Cthulhu, he may battle Nyarlathotep in *The Dream-Quest of Unknown Kadath.* The stories draw on the various bodies of lore indiscriminately, but that does not mean we cannot discriminate between the bodies of lore.

So if we wanted to, we could indeed speak of a larger "Lovecraft Mythos," but it would not be simply another name for what most people call the Cthulhu Mythos. Rather it would include it, plus both of Lovecraft's other bodies of lore. Yet the Cthulhu Mythos in another sense would be wider in scope than the "Lovecraft Mythos" since it embraces the contributions of other writers.

In view of all the subsequent mischief perpetrated under the aegis of the Cthulhu Mythos, we might wish that Lovecraft had debarred anyone else from poaching in his reserve, but the famous fact is that he did welcome his friends' use of and contributions to his Mythos. And, we ought to admit it, several of the early additions to the Cthulhu Mythos (that one of HPL's three cycles to which we now narrow our focus) were fully as enjoyable as Lovecraft's own creations. Though others might be named, we will restrict our consideration to Clark Ashton Smith, Robert E. Howard, Robert Bloch, Frank Belknap Long, and Henry Kuttner. These men and their contributions constitute what we might call the Cthulhu Mythos Stage I, or the Cthulhu Mythos proper, as it was adumbrated in Lovecraft's lifetime and under his supervision.

Once again it is advisable to see what Lovecraft himself had to say on the matter of his own myth-cycle and the creations of his friends. First, we find that the conception of a "Cthulhu Mythos" was not foreign to Lovecraft's thinking (though as a body of lore, remember, not as a collection of stories). In a letter to Robert E. Howard, he speaks of "the solemnly-cited myth-cycle of Cthulhu, Yog-Sothoth, R'lyeh, Nyarlathotep, Nub and Yeb, Shub-Niggurath, etc., etc." and "the cult of Azathoth, Cthulhu, and the Great Old Ones." In **"The Whisperer in Darkness,"** a strategic story for the consideration of this whole question, Lovecraft refers to "fearful myths antedating the coming of men to the earth—the Yog-Sothoth and Cthulhu cycles." This passage, incidentally, is probably the source of Mosig's term "Yog-Sothoth Cycle of Myth," but it would seem to provide nearly as strong support, if one seeks it, for the more familiar term "Cthulhu Mythos."

Some pages later in the same story, Lovecraft mentions "Tsathoggua . . .—you know, the amorphous, toad-like god-creature mentioned in the *Pnakotic Manuscripts* and the Necronomicon and the Commoriom myth-cycle preserved by the Atlantean high-priest Klarkash-Ton." Here is an explicit reference to Clark Ashton Smith and his stories of Hyperborea, some of which involve the entity Tsathoggua. Note that in the same story Lovecraft implicitly differentiates his own "Cthulhu and Yog-Sothoth cycle" from Smith's "Commoriom myth-cycle," since he mentions them separately. In the same letter to Howard previously quoted, Lovecraft notes that "[Frank Belknap] Long has alluded to the Necronomicon in some things of his [e.g., "The Space-Eaters"]—in fact I think it is rather good fun to have this artificial mythology given an air of verisimilitude by wide citation. . . .

Clark Ashton Smith is launching another mock mythology revolving around the black, furry toad-god Tsathoggua. . . . I am using Tsathoggua in several tales of my own and of revision clients. . . ." Writing to Elizabeth Toldridge, Lovecraft mentions that "Clark Ashton Smith & I allude to each other's artificial mythologies in our respective tales." Finally, in a letter to James F. Morton, Lovecraft tells him about "Adept's Gambit" by Fritz Leiber, based on Harry O. Fischer's characters Fafhrd and the Grey Mouser. "Their myth-cycle . . . involves my own pantheon of Yog-Sothoth, Cthulhu, etc. . . ."

The thing to note in all these quotations is that Lovecraft recognizes that Smith, Fischer, and Leiber have their own myth-cycles (and we might add Howard's Hyborian Mythos) distinct from HPL's own mythos that may nevertheless make references to it. Further, HPL himself refers to their myth-cycles, especially Smith's. The upshot of all this is a situation exactly parallel to that obtaining in HPL's own works, considered above: in the fiction of the "Lovecraft Circle" we have several distinct myth-cycles, any number of which might be tapped for a single tale by any of the authors. But they do *not* form a single vast myth-cycle, any more than the Dunsanian, Cthulhu, and Arkham cycles formed a unitary mythos in Lovecraft's work.

As Lovecraft made clear, a story predominantly based on one myth-cycle (e.g., one of Smith's Hyperborea tales) may use a detail from another (e.g., the reference to "Kthulhut" in Smith's "Ubbo-Sathla"), without incorporating that detail into the first cycle. We saw the same thing happening in Lovecraft's own stories: just because Miskatonic University is mentioned in **"The Call of Cthulhu,"** the school is hardly to be considered part of that "myth antedating the coming of man to the earth."

But in one instance, again as in Lovecraft's own works, we

do find a real adoption from one myth-cycle to another, i.e., HPL's appropriation of Tsathoggua. What makes this different from all the mere cross-references? It is fairly simple. Remember that the *Pnakotic Manuscripts* only became part of the Cthulhu myth-cycle when coupled with the *Necronomicon* and explicitly tied up with the Great Old Ones, etc. (cf. ". . . the fiendish elder myths which things like the Pnakotic Manuscripts and the *Necronomicon* affrightedly hint about" [*At the Mountains of Madness*].) Even so, Tsathoggua only finds a niche in the Cthulhu Mythos once Lovecraft uses him extensively and ties him in with other elements in the Mythos. "I once built up a whole cycle of legend around Smith's *Tsathoggua* and used it in a story I rewrote for a revision client." Lovecraft almost certainly refers here to **"The Mound,"** where Tsathoggua is depicted as having been worshipped along with "Tulu," Yig, Shub-Niggurath, and Nug and Yeb in underground K'n-yan. Smith himself adopted the connection, linking Tsathoggua with Tulu and Azathoth in his own genealogy of the Old Ones. Much the same process holds true for HPL's adoption of Smith's *Book of Eibon,* but for convenience sake, we will consider it below in another connection.

Most additions to the Mythos did not involve cross-pollination from other people's myth-cycles. Instead, they were intended by their creators as parts of the Cthulhu Mythos from the start. Already established, most of the additions to the Mythos were the infamous magic books, "the banned and dreaded repositories of equivocal secrets and immemorial formulas" including "the sinister *Liber Ivonis,* the infamous *Cultes des Goules* of Comte d'Erlette, the *Unaussprechlichen Kulten* of von Junzt, and old Ludvig Prinn's hellish *De Vermis Mysteriis*" (**"The Haunter of the Dark"**). Of these volumes, the first is of course Smith's *Book of Eibon,* the second and fourth are the inventions of Robert Bloch, and the third is Robert E. Howard's. Howard's tome was used extensively by Lovecraft in **"Out of the Eons"** and again in **"The Shadow out of Time."** Both times it is connected by the context to the Cthulhu Mythos. And Howard himself saw it that way, having tied the book to the Mythos directly in "The Children of the Night," noting that von Junzt had mentioned "such nameless and ghastly gods and entities as Cthulhu, Yog-Sothoth, Tsathoggua, Gol-goroth, and the like." Von Junzt had also read the *Necronomicon.* Though information is rather more scant, we may conclude that Lovecraft similarly adopted Kuttner's *Book of Iod,* Richard F. Searight's *Eltdown Shards,* and Willis Conover's *Ghorl Nigral* into the Cthulhu Mythos.

As implied in the quote immediately above, Robert E. Howard may be said to have contributed a "ghastly god" to the Mythos, viz. "Gol-goroth." Henry Kuttner's "Nyogtha, the Thing That Should Not Be," also comes to mind. Nyogtha is mentioned in "The Salem Horror," actually in a quotation from the *Necronomicon* fabricated by Kuttner. Lastly, we may mention a single contribution to the Mythos by Frank Belknap Long which we find in his story "The Space Eaters." Long quotes the *Necronomicon,* referring to it as "John Dee's [translation of the] *Necronomicon.*" Lovecraft knew of this and approved it, as can be seen from his inclusion of Dee and his edition in the *History of the Necronomicon.*

In all these cases, the items in question were either explicitly designed by their creators as additions to the Mythos or were later included in the Mythos by Lovecraft. Usually if they were intended from the first as items of Mythos lore, Lovecraft gave them his blessing.

We can clarify things a bit further by briefly listing those items from other myth-cycles which Lovecraft merely mentioned in passing, without actually incorporating them into the Cthulhu Mythos. First of all, and perhaps surprisingly, there are the Hounds of Tindalos and Chaugnar Faugn of Long's creation. HPL mentions the Hounds in **"The Whisperer in Darkness"** and "proboscidian Chaugnar Faugn" in **"The Horror in the Museum."** Howard's "Serpent-Men of Valusia" are mentioned in **"The Haunter of the Dark"** and Valusia itself is referred to in *At the Mountains of Madness,* but we have here simply cosmetic references to Howard's Hyborian Mythos. It is certain that neither Lovecraft nor Howard himself ever intended the King Kull cycle to form part of the Cthulhu Mythos. Lovecraft also makes passing mention in various stories to "Hastur," "Hali," and "The Yellow Sign" from Bierce and Chambers, "Bethmoora" from Dunsany, Poe's "Arthur Gordon Pym" and the "Aklo Letters" and "Voorish Sign" from Machen. But in all these instances, all we have are mere references, not incorporations: these items do not form part of the Mythos.

If not every reference to someone else's myth-cycle was intended by Lovecraft as an inclusion in his own, the same is true when other writers make glancing reference to the Cthulhu Mythos in otherwise unrelated stories of their own. When they do, other elements in the same tale are not thereby automatically absorbed lock-stock-and-barrel into the Cthulhu Mythos. Did Frank Belknap Long mean to add his "space eaters" to the ranks of the Great Old Ones? There is nothing in the story to suggest that he did. Robert E. Howard certainly did not intend to add Bran Mak Morn to the Mythos merely because he has him invoke the "black gods of R'lyeh" in the "Worms of the Earth." And Clark Ashton Smith's entity Ubbo-Sathla does not find any place in the Mythos merely on the strength of a marginal reference to Cthulhu and Yog-Sothoth in the same story. (In fact, Ubbo-Sathla is explicitly removed from the company of the Old Ones in the passage itself: "*Before* the coming of Zhothaqquah or Yok-Zothoth or Kthulhut from the stars, Ubbo-Sathla dwelt in the steaming fens of the new-made Earth. . . ." [emphasis added].) Smith himself saw it this way. "As to the Cthulhu Mythos, I believe I added as much to it as I borrowed. Tsathoggua and the Book of Eibon were my own inventions, and were promptly utilized by Lovecraft." Ubbo-Sathla is conspicuously absent from this list.

So this was the Cthulhu Mythos in Lovecraft's lifetime. It is at least a bit wider in extent than the Cthulhuvian elements in Lovecraft's own fiction. But then again, it is rather sparse in comparison to the subsequent elaborations of the Mythos by other hands.

"The Cthulhu Mythos Stage II" can be said to have begun with the work of August Derleth. The line to be drawn here is clear from two considerations, one logical, the other chronological. Derleth began to systematize and add to the Mythos after Lovecraft's death. He assimilated fundamentally alien themes, such as the assignment of the various Old Ones as "elementals," a rather puerile domestication of Lovecraft's "wholly other" beings. He also added rafts of new gods that both complicated and trivialized the picture. Worst of all, he ascribed the whole resultant scenario to Lovecraft, "humbly" disclaiming any originality, as in the misleading and often-reprinted Derleth "Introductions" to Lovecraft volumes [see excerpt dated 1963].

So drastically did Derleth change the face of the Mythos that

Dirk W. Mosig would later, as we have seen, call for the repudiation of the very term "Cthulhu Mythos" and urge that the original version be renamed the "Yog-Sothoth Cycle of Myth." But Richard L. Tierney's suggestion was wiser: why not simply rename *Derleth*'s version? Tierney himself called it the "Derleth Mythos" [see Schweitzer entry dated 1987 in Additional Bibliography]. Or we might use the term "the mythology of Hastur," which Derleth himself first proposed to Lovecraft, who rejected it.

But whatever nomenclature one chooses for Derleth's revisionism, how did he come by it? Sheer caprice? Or was there at least some method in Derleth's madness? Yes; in fact on the basis of our analysis so far, we can explain very precisely why Derleth's mythos came out the way it did.

We have suggested, first, that Lovecraft drew a distinction, or at least that we ought to draw one, between three separate myth-cycles which, though logically independent and self-contained, might be used together in a single story. These were the Dunsanian, Arkham, and Cthulhu cycles; secondly, that HPL distinguished, and so should we, between various analogous myth-cycles in his own fiction, and those of Smith, Howard, and previous writers such as Chambers, Machen, Bierce, and Dunsany. Here, too, cross-referencing was permissible, even encouraged, but it did not serve to blur the borders of the various myth-cycles.

But what Derleth did, in effect, was to ignore both distinctions. First, he lumped all of Lovecraft's lore into one big myth-cycle. Whereas Lovecraft had in one story brought together Nodens from the Dunsanian cycle and Nyarlathotep from the Cthulhu cycle, Derleth actually adopted Nodens into the Cthulhu Mythos, supplying him with a host of Elder Gods opposed to the Old Ones. The result violated the logic of the original Cthulhu Mythos, which had no such ethical dualism, but was darkly nihilistic and fatalistic. Clearly, Lovecraft's adoption of his own *Pnakotic Manuscripts* or of Smith's Tsathoggua entailed no such rending of the fabric of the Mythos.

Significantly, Clark Ashton Smith saw early on where Derleth was headed with all this and tried, to no avail, to nip it in the bud: "I shouldn't class any of the Old Ones as *Evil:* they are plainly beyond all limitary human conceptions of either ill or good" (letter to Derleth, August 13, 1937). "A deduction relating the Cthulhu mythos to the Christian Mythos would indeed be interesting. . . . However, there seems to be no reference to *expulsion* of Cthulhu and his companions in [**"The Call of Cthulhu"**]. . . . Cthulhu and the other Old Ones 'died' or were thrown into a state of suspended animation 'when the stars were wrong.' . . . This would seem to indicate the action of cosmic laws rather than a battle between good and evil deities. . . . [And] if the 'expulsion' was accomplished by animate agencies or gods, it is strange that they are not referred to in the stories."

Second, Derleth also ignored the distinction between HPL's Cthulhu myth-cycle and any other which HPL used. He took any cross-reference to someone else's myth-cycle to denote Lovecraft's wholesale adoption of that cycle into the Cthulhu Mythos. For instance, the bare reference to "Hastur" in **"The Whisperer in Darkness"** is made the precedent for Derleth's own Great Old One "Hastur the Unspeakable." Because Lovecraft mentioned "the Yellow Sign," Derleth felt justified in saying that Robert W. Chambers' *The King in Yellow* holds "the distinction of having contributed to the famed Cthulhu mythos of H. P. Lovecraft." Because Lovecraft mentioned the *Book of Eibon,* Derleth added Ubbo-Sathla, mentioned by Eibon, to the Mythos and had him mentioned in the *Necronomicon.* Inevitable, the Hounds of Tindalos were included, too. Why not?

Third, Derleth seems to have assumed (as Mosig says) that any story in which a Cthulhu Mythos element appeared *belonged* to the Mythos, and that therefore any other detail figuring in the story was *ipso facto* part of the Mythos. Needless to say, on this understanding, the Mythos could not help but grow by leaps and bounds.

Derleth's followers have gone even farther in the same direction, as may easily be seen in their fiction. But perhaps the best indication of this trend is Lin Carter's "H. P. Lovecraft: the Gods," an ecumenical theogony where all of Smith's Hyperborean deities, as well as Lovecraft's "gods of earth" and Derleth's Cthugha, Ithaqua, etc., have found a place. Also witness the lists of "Mythos stories" which include Howard's King Kull or Bran Mak Morn tales.

The result of all this is that we now have two very different understandings, in fact two different versions, of the Cthulhu Mythos. The first sees the Mythos as a body of lore; the second sees it as a network of stories. The first version, that developed by Lovecraft and the Lovecraft Circle, is relatively simple and is nihilistic; the Old Ones, indifferent to the fortunes of humanity, will one day make an end of it. The second version, that begun by Derleth and continued by subsequent Mythos writers, is much more complicated and is significantly more optimistic; there is a cosmic struggle of Good and Evil, and humanity will finally be redeemed by the Elder Gods. Which version is preferable? Obviously, that is entirely up to the choice of each reader. Many (including the present writer) enjoy stories related to both versions of the Mythos, and such enjoyment can only be enhanced by more clearly understanding what we are enjoying. (pp. 3-10)

Robert M. Price, "H. P. Lovecraft and the Cthulhu Mythos," in Crypt of Cthulhu, *Vol. 5, No. 1, November 1, 1985, pp. 3-11.*

MAURICE LÉVY (essay date 1985)

[*A French critic, Lévy is an authority on the history of Gothic fiction. In the following excerpt, he delineates the elements of Lovecraft's fictional universe, focusing on those stories relating to the Cthulhu Mythos.*]

[Lovecraft's universe], with its bizarre dimensions and hideous monsters, where time and space stretch or contract in incomprehensible ways, merits analysis for more than one reason. It is a fantastic universe because of the manifestly dreamlike quality of the images that it presents and that compose it and because of the author's obvious intention to capture and to communicate his anguish. Let us admit that he succeeds admirably in so doing: his archaic horrors shake us, jar us from our certitudes, remove us for all too short a time from the soothing influence of the modern world. He leaves far behind him the comforts of the American dream, the reassuring slogans, the "Colgate smile," and explores the unsoundable depths of dream, carrying us along after him. Few authors went as far as he in depicting foulness; we know of none who have given to their work a structure analogous to the Cthulhu Mythos. (p. 12)

With few exceptions, the Lovecraftian universe is circumscribed in a well-determined region of the United States. It is a closed space, cut off from the rest of the country and the world, a different place, another province, a privileged corner of the cosmos where the outer forces and the powers from beyond the world can, by some mysterious favor, freely manifest themselves.

This choice world is New England, the land of origins, of the first beginnings, the Promised Land of mythical times, where the American nation was born and from which it thrust out its fleshly roots. No other place in the United States could better lend itself to the irruption of the bizarre. By its very nature the fantastic is manifested most efficaciously where a historic profundity is embedded under the surface of everyday life.

New England was also Lovecraft's native soil, the only point on earth with which he could totally identify. This obscure emotion of belonging, of rootedness, was for him the primordial condition of all plenitude. He tells us that his vital force, like that of Antaeus, depends strictly on contact with the Mother Earth who bore him. Everyone knows that we dream well only when living in that absolutely intimate region of our childhood: Only the "natal home" can be changed into a dream-dwelling.

New England is the province of marvelous cities that Lovecraft so often visited and so dearly loved: Providence, Boston, Marblehead, Salem, Newport. In those cities the past surfaces and affirms itself at each street corner, and all the homes have a single history; it is a place of *profound towns,* rooted in the homogeneous tradition of Puritanism and the culture of a single race. What a difference from New York, where the verticality of the skyscraper is only an exterior dimension! Instead of being rooted in the earth, these dwellings spurt out vertiginously toward the sky. This is a place devoid of a center or an identity or ties with the past, a city to which none of the many ethnic groups composing it really belong. Then again, New England has its own folklore, its own legends, which belong to racial memory: the tales of sorcery, impious cults, and diabolical rites that are as a faraway family heritage, the legacy of the Old Ones.

These cities through which Lovecraft loved to stroll are also ports, oriented toward the old continent, toward the past. These ports give on to the great open sea, on unknown immensity, whence *anything could come:* the blue line on the horizon that represents the famous "Edge of the World" so dear to Dunsany, beyond which the unsoundable and terrifying abysms of dream might lurk.

New England, with its deep forests, its marvelous landscapes, its wild mountains, its rugged coast gouged with gulfs, is certainly a place with a potential for adventure and mystery. To walk there, says Lovecraft, is to cross time and space as if penetrating a picture hung on a wall, to settle into the inadmissible; nowhere else is it possible so strongly to sense the presence of the bizarre, the sinister, the unholy, the macabre. In this predestined framework, in this elect land, where the equivocal and the aleatory preside over man's rapports with nature, almost all Lovecraft's tales unfold.

It is a world whose *reality*—physical, topographical, historical—should be emphasized. It is well known that the truly fantastic exists only where the impossible can make an irruption, through time and space, into an objectively familiar locale.

And yet, there is a city very dear to the author's heart for which we vainly search on a map—antique Arkham, haunted by the evil spells of the past, with its roofs bent by the weight of centuries, its gables and its balustrades of another age, its narrow and tortuous streets. There is a port where no vessel of any known nationality has ever touched—Innsmouth. And there is a hamlet lost in western Massachusetts, which no traveler today can ever reach—Dunwich. These imaginary places form, in the real topography of New England, a zone of shadow, a zone of mystery, a *dream-zone,* which spreads little by little to the rest of the countryside, contaminating the diurnal space of the maps and charts and giving it a suddenly different aspect. The familiarity of places is blurred, leaving the weird to take its place. Arkham is at once Boston and Newport, Providence and Salem, Portsmouth and Marblehead—a point in mythical space toward which dreams converge and where all the accumulated images gathered in the course of Lovecraft's interminable walks are superimposed. Arkham is, in the most precise sense of the term, a structure condensed from dreams, around which is built and organized an entire universe of inexpressible wonders and blasphemous horrors. Arkham and its vicinity are, in the Lovecraftian topography, the fault through which the bizarre, the horrific, the disquieting, the morbid, and the unclean spread. In the heart of the American world, at a laughably short distance from the great industrial centers, from the most respected universities, from the tourist sites—amid smiling civilization—Lovecraft sets up an abominable region where unbelievable evils are practiced.

In this region, the picturesque landscapes of New England are degraded, corrupted from the effects of mysterious forces from beyond. After the fall of a strange meteorite, in **"The Colour out of Space,"** no trace of vegetation remains on the fields; the effect of the bizarre is manifested by a profound withering. In the circumference of this zone, the scrawny trees, as if struck by lightning, waste away, the grass becomes gray, the rocks crumble. Elsewhere, as if nature were unhinged, forests suddenly become denser, darker. Perspective itself is distorted—it is as if we have found ourselves in a landscape from the canvas of that master of the picturesque, Salvator Rosa.

In **"The Lurking Fear,"** the soil is covered by a fetid and corrupt vegetation, a poisonous mold representing a type of horrible suppuration of the earth; the trees, infested by an unspeakable essence they draw from this decay, take on grotesque and demented forms. Decrepitude, corruption settle wherever the supernatural has intruded. The Lovecraftian fantastic is manifestly *decadent:* The bizarre does not fall from space to terrify or confound, but to corrupt. It is a type of gangrene that gnaws, wears away, and finally rots the familiar world through and through.

The strain obviously spreads to architecture, a choice constituent of these degraded landscapes. The old colonial homes dear to Lovecraft's heart, with their irregular gables, their bizarre framework, their transomed windows—all the residences of another age that incite meditation and dream—become through dream sinister places where nameless abominations rule. Innumerable are the dwellings that, baleful and menacing, loom on the horizon in Lovecraft's tales; sometimes they are rooted in the earth by an inextricable network of subterranean tunnels or peopled with swarming horrors; sometimes they are perched, conversely, on a remote cliff in the mist thousands of feet above the waves, with a door opening on to the void as the only possible entrance. Sometimes cracked and unwholesome like Poe's, sometimes unreal and faraway like Dunsany's, they are the setting of foul practices, of barbarous banquets at which human flesh may well be featured on the menu; they are evil places haunted by phosphorescent, gelatinous, and vampiric entities who have malevolently assimilated the flesh and souls of their unfortunate tenants.

The dwelling is a fantastic place par excellence, insofar as it demarcates and isolates the malefic region in a particularly adequate way. It materializes the mythical threshold that makes possible the necessary transgressions and justifies the inevitable retribution: The horror it inspires is primordial and brings up in each individual the most archaic layers of racial memory. The same irrepressible anguish seizes all the characters the moment they cross the forbidden portico, knowing confusedly that they are performing the irremediable and are binding themselves irreversibly. Being the meeting place of the here and the beyond, all the houses are in a way fateful. Lovecraft cannot bring the abnormal to his hero except within the interior of these tragic walls, which enclose, contain, and up to a point dam up the irrational. To enter one of these old edifices of New England is to accept the discovery there of unheard-of forms of life, of beings that attain their monstrous fullness only insofar as their confinement preserves and maintains their essential difference. Vampires, shoggoths, and mutants, incubi, lemurs, and Aegypans are their true selves only in their original settings. All thresholds are, in essence, forbidden. To cross them is at the same time to expose the unholy, for the incomprehensible, in an advanced society that has definitively broken off with the mystical, is necessarily a form of Evil. How many sabbaths, how many Walpurgis-nights, how many blasphemous rites have for their settings these picturesque and many-gabled homes! Erected on the native soil, contemporaneous with the earliest days of the nation, they are for Lovecraft structures of oneiric exploration, guiding dream along the vertical axis that they delineate, down to the vertiginous abysms of space and time. The inquiry conducted by the narrator of **"The Shunned House"** makes him descend, generation by generation, into the hidden depths of American history where horror is encountered. Gilman, in **"The Dreams in the Witch House,"** is compelled to dream by the architecture of the room he inhabits, and is driven to explore an immaterial cosmos of strange and alarming marvels.

Lovecraft's homes are the vehicles of dream, the irreplaceable auxiliaries of the imaginary, which permit the author to root his work in a geographically individualized secular tradition. Descending to the cellar, the hero is driven into a national past and finds, at the foot of the spiral staircase that vertically structures the whole edifice, the folklore of the Beginning. Infallibly, the ever descending steps lead the dreamer to myth.

The man who dated his letters as from the "Usual Sepulchre" enjoyed, like Poe, haunting old cemeteries. His nostalgia, his taste for the mossy vestiges of other times, and, we must say, the morbid vein of his temperament, drove him often to sit and dream on a tomb with time-effaced inscriptions. Cemeteries belong entirely to bygone times; to visit them is to leave intolerable reality and flee toward immaterial horizons where life is more real, more full, because all there is already done. In a word, it is to feign death.

In many of his tales we find the old cemeteries of Providence, Boston, and Marblehead, but they do not have the diurnal aspect Lovecraft gives them in his letters. Metamorphosed by oneiric composition, they suddenly become places where the latent horror that they inspire is *reactivated.* By day, on the level of clear life, a tomb is only a raised sign on the smooth surface of the present. In the night of dream, the sign is inversed and the tumulus becomes a hole, a pit, a receptacle where unclean osmoses and repugnant transformations take place. From the melancholy vestige that it was, the tomb becomes a *functional place.* The crypts are then hollowed out alarmingly, reaching incredible depths and stretching toward the bottom by way of subterranean tunnels, which push simultaneously into the earth and into the past. Then, by these imaginary conduits, from the most archaic layers of subsoil and time, the Abominable, the Unnameable can resurface. Cemeteries are, in Lovecraft's works, privileged places where terror surfaces; the sepulchers are so many gaping orifices to the *underneath,* which is a type of *beyond.* After having read **"The Statement of Randolph Carter,"** we can never again forget the story of that insane expedition organized by Warren in the depths of a peculiarly redoubtable crypt: Descending to the bottom of the gulf, he stayed in telephone contact with the surface up to the moment the voice which Carter heard in the receiver . . . was no longer that of his friend.

Scientists also lurk in cemeteries, though in a more conventional way: These are special searchers who need special materials for their experiments. Such is Joseph Curwen [in *The Case of Charles Dexter Ward*], who, from the "essential Saltes" of which cadavers are composed, makes the spirits of the dead appear. Such is Herbert West, who fragmentarily reanimates the still "worthwhile" parts of human remnants so as to make new and monstrous beings from them [**"Herbert West—Reanimator"**]. Or again, there are the young esthetes of horror, the "neurotic virtuosi" [in **"The Hound"**] who freely profane sepulchers to extract unclean trophies. Then comes the night when, forcing a tomb inhabited by a particularly redoubtable presence, they pay for their mad audacity. In Lovecraft, cemeteries always become what they by no means ought to be: *animated* places where disquieting exchanges between the world of the surface and the gulf take place.

The final element in the Lovecraftian landscape is the sea. Although the tourist may like to dream next to it in the charming ports of New England, it is never a friendly, familiar element for our writer. It also has its depths, more unsoundable, more primordial than even those of the earth, concealing nauseous horrors. It is inhabited by monsters who menace the peace of mankind and pull men in after them into their original element. Nothing is more abominable than a Deep One—unless it be, perhaps, the deity they adore, Dagon, that gigantic, scaly, and viscous entity, the mere sight of which makes lost navigators lose their reason [**"Dagon"**]. It does not do to explore the bottom of these liquid abysms. Strange temples are raised there where barbarous rites are performed [in **"The Temple"**], and incredibly ancient cities are there, engulfed for millennia but always, it seems, inhabited, where singular sacrifices are made. [In *The Dream-Quest of Unknown Kadath*] Carter, leaning over the rails of the sailboat conveying him to Oriab, perceives at the bottom of the transparent waters the body of a sailor bound upside down to a monolith—a sailor who no longer has eyes.

Sometimes, in the course of some geologic upheaval, there emerges from the depths one or the other of the underwater cities. But when it happens to be the dead city of R'lyeh, built millions of years before the beginning of history, then madness must await the human race. For R'lyeh is the city where, in an edifice whose architectural norms defy the human mind, Cthulhu himself rests. As long as one sees the Great Old One, this deity who came from the stars in immemorial times, only in the approximate reproductions carved in rock by his primitive admirers, one still has a chance to survive. But when the god himself—this veritable moving mountain, this hideous contradiction of all the laws of nature, this indescribable "cosmic entity" emerging from the waves—draws up, then . . . death is the supreme—nay, only—refuge. "When I think of the *extent* of all that may be brooding down there," says the narrator of **"The Call of Cthulhu,"** "I almost wish to kill myself forthwith."

Such, then, is the setting where, for a paltry instant, the imperceptible silhouettes of Lovecraft's characters move. It is a setting strangely familiar and fabulously faraway, where a dream-topography is superimposed on the real topography. Geographic space is substituted by a malefic space. The landscape, the cities, the dwellings of New England lose their pleasant, picturesque, diurnal aspect, to become lunatic sites, nocturnal images, degraded images of a demented dream.

About the characters themselves we must say a word. They are for the most part eminently respectable individuals, descended from the oldest families in New England: university professors—of that celebrated Miskatonic University, which, in the author's dream, represents Brown University—reputed doctors, worthies surrounded by general consideration. All lead active, peaceful, useful lives in the heart of their community, until the day when, in their sheltered existence, the bizarre monstrously surges. By the place they occupy in society, however, they represent an elite. Holders of culture, they profess the absolute skepticism that is the attribute of their class: about the supernatural, they all have the same attitude of perfect incredulity as Lovecraft. Although the lessers around whom they lead their inquiries—the degenerate peasants of the Catskills or the decadent populace of the cities—are open to all superstitions and to the most bizarre ideas, they preserve, or try to preserve, their lucidity and their cold reason to the end. In Lovecraft's tales they embody what it would be tempting to call the "function of rationality"—an essential, irreplaceable element in all fantastic creation, because it gives the scale of the real, the measure of the waking world. They are in their way an integral part of the landscape, representing waking characters who move in a dream-setting. It is because they are all reasonable men in a demented world that the Lovecraftian fantastic is totally efficacious. These savants, these doctors, these professors, being close to the reader, are the guarantee of the impossible.

Finally, it is manifest that many of them are projections of the author himself, who through the illusion of literature thus enters his own imaginary world. The phenomenon has, as we will see, its importance. Like Lovecraft, Charles Dexter Ward was born in Providence, where he passed a studious adolescence in the shadow of the John Hay Library. Like him, he had an exclusive passion for his native town, with its steeples, its sunlit roofs, and its tortuous streets. Like him particularly, he liked to wander into the old parts of town, admire the old colonial houses, and dream of the past, for it is to Charles Dexter Ward that "something will happen." . . . Analogously, the narrator of **"He"** begins his story with the words: "My coming to New York was a mistake . . . ," and the reader is soon made to understand, by the way he speaks of that dead city where soulless and repulsive automata move about, that the narrator is no other than the author himself. And it is he who, just around the corner, will encounter adventure. We also recognize Lovecraft in the traits of Edward Derby, in **"The Thing on the Doorstep,"** in that he is an only child, with fragile health and morbid temperament, and so sheltered by his parents that he cannot make any decisions by himself. Through weakness he will also marry a woman with whom he is ill-matched. Therefore, it is on him, and no other, that horror will pounce. . . .

We are then justified, it seems, in wondering whether these characters do not, regarding the author, play a vicarious role: Through them Lovecraft gives the bizarre to himself, by a series of ordeals that strangely recall the initiation stages of yore. The sites, the landscapes, the dwellings that we have noted become then the privileged terrain of a mythical quest, the nocturnal place where, gropingly and amid unspeakable horrors, this devotee of genealogy searches for his own identity. (pp. 35-43)

At the risk of shocking or deceiving we would like here to repeat, before going any further in our analysis, how Lovecraft's tales seem to us distinct from science fiction. The cosmic dimension of the settings, the "entities" from Outside, and the scientific experiments were for Lovecraft a means, not an end: the oftentimes feeble pretext for a reverie where space and time are arranged very differently.

Science fiction is basically a forward-looking genre, preoccupied with the future, where anguish is projected in forms conceived from the data of the then current science. In a way it is a dream that outruns science and, from embryonic elements, invents what scholars and technologists establish or rigorously create later. In a science fiction tale the imaginary always runs the risk of descending to the real.

Lovecraft's art, however, is essentially regressive, oriented toward a fabulous past and rooted in myth. In this it is an authentically fantastic art, forever belonging to the realm of chimeras and the unverifiable. We might even be tempted to say that the fantastic is, on the axis of the imagination, rigorously opposed to science fiction.

In science fiction tales the cosmos is a virgin space, a space to be conquered, a place of sublimation; time is time to come. In Lovecraft, space is perceived as a void, a depth; time, as the mythical time of beginnings. And in the depths of time, at the other end of the cosmos, horror lurks. It is not man who will recklessly explore new worlds with prodigious machines; it is the Unknown, which, under diverse yet always unholy forms, breaks out on our planet. The initiative is not on the side of the human race, which instead serves as the field of observation and . . . experimentation for fabulously different beings who are phenomenally more advanced scientifically and technologically than man.

In Lovecraft, knowledge and technical efficiency are not found at the end of human evolution, but at the beginning. For him, the notion of progress, in the modern sense of the term, is devoid of meaning. On the contrary, the history of the civilizations that from time immemorial have followed one another on our planet has been one of a slow and irreversible decadence. Contemporary man is not defined by his future conquests of space or by his ever growing mastery of natural phenomena, but as one who has lost what the Great Old Ones knew before him. Coming from deep regions of the ether, these primordial beings established themselves on the earth millions of years before man ever appeared. If we believe the narrator of *At the Mountains of Madness,* they were infinitely more advanced than we in technology, art, and basic research. They were able to conceive and create docile slaves, who obeyed their hypnotic suggestions and built marvelous cities for them. They were strong, wise, and happy. And only the revolt of the shoggoths, unforeseeable and devastating, could end this model civilization.

For the dreamer from Providence, *the beginning, the elsewhere,* was perfection. Since *that* time, on *this* world, wretched humanity, having forgotten everything, is overwhelmed, devoured, dominated by these unknown forces it can no longer understand. It is because Lovecraft built his whole work on this mythical, irrational base that he is not, in our eyes, an author of science fiction. The Cthulhu Mythos, which each of his tales resumes and treats with greater or less amplitude, is incompatible with the hyperrationality that characterizes the genre illustrated today by Poul Anderson, Ray Bradbury, and many other lesser writers. To sum up in a few words what clearly merits a more thorough study, let us say that myth and science, in fiction as in everything else, are mutually exclusive.

But perhaps it is time to examine this myth, which firmly structures the Lovecraft oeuvre and gives it its significance. "All my stories," wrote the author, "are based on the fundamental premise that common laws and interests and emotions have no validity or significance in the vast cosmos-at-large. . . . To achieve the essence of real externality, whether of time or space or dimension, one must forget that such things as good and evil, love and hate, and all such local attributes of a negligible and temporary race called mankind, have any existence at all."

By making some comparisons and tests, it is possible to reconstruct a vast fresco, a cosmic-dimensioned "saga" in which each tale would represent an episode. The obvious drawback in this procedure is in rationalizing what in essence ought not to be rationalized. Moreover, the Cthulhu Mythos is not the exclusive work of Lovecraft; others have contributed to it—his friends and disciples Clark Ashton Smith, Frank Belknap Long, Robert E. Howard, August Derleth, Robert Bloch the scenarist, and many others, each creating and animating new characters. But it may be useful to shed some light, for practical ends, on this unheard-of jumble of baffling images and forms. At the risk of some omissions and a few contradictions, let us see how this universal myth can, if reconstructed, be read.

At the summit of this diabolical hierarchy we must name Azathoth, the "blind and idiot" god. Installed at the heart of Ultimate Chaos, it is he who presides over human destiny; in this way is the radical absurdity of the world explained. Like the gods of Dunsany to whom they owe so much, Lovecraft's gods are transparent allegories, and Azathoth illustrates adequately the author's theses on mechanistic materialism. He is, for the dreamer Randolph Carter who is searching for marvelous Kadath,

> that shocking final peril which gibbers unmentionably outside the ordered universe, where no dreams reach; that last amorphous blight of nethermost confusion which blasphemes and bubbles at the centre of all infinity—the boundless daemon-sultan Azathoth, whose name no lips dare speak aloud, and who gnaws hungrily in inconceivable, unlighted chambers beyond time amidst the muffled, maddening beat of vile drums and the thin, monotonous whine of accursed flutes; to which detestable pounding and piping dance slowly, awkwardly, and absurdly the gigantic ultimate gods, the blind, voiceless, tenebrous, and mindless Other Gods whose soul and messenger is the crawling chaos Nyarlathotep.

Nyarlathotep is the faithful servant of Azathoth. He is most often designated vaguely, such as the "Crawling Chaos." But he has many other names: he is sometimes the "Dark God," sometimes "The Dweller in Darkness," sometimes "The Faceless God," or again "The Howler in the Night." His most notable appearance is made in **"The Haunter of the Dark,"** in the form of a jet-black "flying thing" who, emitting an intense stench, is endowed with an enormous three-lobed eye, which throws off a deadly light. He is invoked and worshipped in this form, by means of the Shining Trapezohedron, in the steeple of an old church in Providence, where his appearance in a night storm strews panic. But he can take on other aspects: In *The Dream-Quest of Unknown Kadath* he appears to Randolph Carter in the form of a young man of great beauty, clothed in the austere dignity of an Egyptian god and in a scarlet robe. . . .

As redoubtable, as strong as Azathoth, is Yog-Sothoth, the All-in-One, the One-in-All, also coming from the stars. The myth tells us that he resembles a conglomeration of sparkling globules agglutinated one to the other. It is of him that the archaic *Book of Eibon* speaks, it is to him that the hideous *Necronomicon* sings its praises. It is he who is invoked in the symbolic formulas of Charles Dexter Ward, it is he who has engendered the double horror at Dunwich. "Nor is it to be thought," we read in the terrible opus of the mad Arab Abdul Alhazred,

> that man is either the oldest or the last of earth's masters. . . . The Old Ones were, the Old Ones are, and the Old Ones shall be. Not in the spaces we know, but *between* them, They walk serene and primal, undimensioned and to us unseen. *Yog-Sothoth* knows the gate. *Yog-Sothoth* is the gate. *Yog-Sothoth* is the key and the guardian of the gate. Past, present, future, all are one in *Yog-Sothoth.* He knows where the Old Ones broke through of old, and where They shall break through again. . . . *Yog-Sothoth* is the key of the gate, whereby the spheres meet. Man rules where They ruled once; They shall soon rule where Man rules now.

It is Yog-Sothoth whom the crustacean-bodied creatures of **"The Whisperer in Darkness"** worship, it is he whom Joseph Curwen frequently invokes in the course of his abominable experiments. He has existed for all time, he is everywhere at once, he is unclean and cruel. He is the Guardian of the Ultimate Gate.

With Yog-Sothoth, Cthulhu is perhaps the deity most often evoked by Lovecraft's characters. While Yog-Sothoth wanders the Outer Spaces, Cthulhu has by accident been imprisoned in a monument of ancient R'lyeh, the city engulfed in the Pacific. Like Yog-Sothoth he came from the stars and now "reposes" in the sea. His aspect is vaguely anthropomorphic; but he has an octopus-head and, instead of a face, a mass of swarming tentacles. His body, covered with scales, has a rubbery consistency. His paws are armed with prodigious claws, and he has long, narrow wings on his back. His worshippers, who by chance happen to be *degenerate half-breeds,* observe a changeless rite and from generation to generation ever chant the same verse: "Ph'nglui mglw'nafh Cthulhu R'lyeh wgah'nagl fhtagn." This, as the readers of "The Call of Cthulhu" well know, means: "In his house at R'lyeh dead Cthulhu waits dreaming." But although these incantations and the barbarous rites accompanying them remained inefficacious millennium after millennium, the simple curiosity of sailors threatened to unleash this horror on the world. When Johansen and his companions disembarked on the unknown island that had surged from the waves after an upheaval of deep land masses, they saw that from the bottom of a black pit, where the very darkness seemed to have become viscous, some indescribable "Thing" was coming alive that endangered their reason and their lives. It was Cthulhu, the Great Old One, the fallen deity, who with Dagon rules over all that swarms at the bottom of the sea.

Dagon does not in this Pantheon of Horror occupy the same place as the Great Old Ones. He is certainly the servant of Cthulhu, as Nyarlathotep is of Azathoth. He is no less the master of the Deep Ones, the half-fishy, half-batrachian beings who live in the marvelous cities of the great deeps, but who when they wish can easily venture upon the land and mate with humans. We know already that at Innsmouth there is a sect of the "Esoteric Order of Dagon" whose priests wear tiaras and who under the folds of their ample vestments hide singular deformities. . . . Lovecraft nowhere gives a precise description of Dagon, and perhaps this is for the best. At most, in the tale with the name of this redoubtable entity for its title, we are shown from afar a gigantic silhouette with enormous scaly arms, which gropes after a lunatic monolith erected in a nightmare landscape. . . . It is a monolith whose base is ornamented with frescoes representing unclean beings, roughly human but with webbed hands and feet, flabby lips, and protruding, glassy eyes. When Dagon has been met but once in one's existence, even drugs ease not the burden of life: The narrator of **"Dagon,"** at the end of his tether, commits suicide, to escape—so he believes—that whose massive and viscous presence he senses behind the door of his room.

The other gods who people and animate Lovecraft's mythical universe, though they are physically as repulsive, seem less dangerous to men. Among them let us mention 'Umr at-Tawil, dean of the Great Old Ones and direct servant of Yog-Sothoth; Tsathoggua, the Toad-God, potbellied, hairy, and swarthy, settled on the earth since its creation and originating from the planet Cykranosh; the gigantic Ghatanothoa, imprisoned since his rebellion in the crypts of the fortress constructed by the "crustaceans" of Yug-goth at the summit of Mount Yaddith-Gho; and Shub-Niggurath, wife of Yog-Sothoth, the Black Goat of the Woods, of whom it is said in the *Necronomicon* that she will proliferate hideously throughout the world.

Such are the actors of a drama that, having the Cosmos for its stage, unfolds in the tales of H. P. Lovecraft. It is a drama where man seems to have no other role than to act as victim—terrorized, mutilated, tossed from one corner of the universe to the other. Indeed, the old legends themselves have set down in fable man's destiny; and Lovecraft, who as a child played at building altars in honor of pagan deities, knew it well. Dunsany, whom Lovecraft idolized, had on his part often conceived, in *The Gods of Pegāna* and other collections of fantastic tales, divinities with exotic names, such as Māna-Yood-Sushāī, the God who created the gods; Slid whose soul is in the sea; Mung the God of Death; and Loharneth-Lahai, God of Fantasy, who spends eternity in dream. Let us, however, agree that neither the familiar gods of classical mythology nor the slightly decadent gods of the Irish poet have the odious and fascinating presence of those invented by Lovecraft. The first enhance the tragic sense of life that underlies ancient philosophy; the second belong to a fantasy world where the imagination of poets of the "Yellow Nineties" readily took refuge. Lovecraft's gods, however, are fantastic because they are manifested in daily reality, outside the author's every belief, every adherence to a dogma or church. Surging from dream-depths, they settle into the Waking World, mingle and mate with humans, and inflict a thousand experiments upon them. (pp. 79-85)

It is in the Cthulhu Mythos that Lovecraft's tales gain their profound unity. Except for some details, all develop the same central theme; all make reference to the same deities; all put on stage the same characters devoted to the same occult practices. Above all, the same images recur under the author's pen with an obsessive insistence, to form a tight web around the mythic contents of the work, ensuring its cohesion and giving it its consistency.

The question we then ask is whether this organized, structured, hierarchical system is a gratuitous fable, a jeu d'esprit, a "cosmic epic" conceived by an idle paranoiac, or whether it involves, at a deep level of consciousness, the most fundamental realities. Did the "old gentleman of Providence" write for the pleasure of writing, as did his "grandfathers"? Or does he convey in his mythic discourse something that might make us seek a more profound interpretation?

Certainly the Cthulhu Mythos is a fable, a pure invention, a fiction. It was elaborated, episode after episode, by the author just as other patient amateurs build houses of cards or put together a jigsaw puzzle. Who could conceivably deny that in a sense it is the disconcerting result of an intense play-activity? The fact is amply demonstrated by an attentive reading of Lovecraft's correspondence. Some of the correspondents or disciples of the dreamer from Providence were even allowed to enter the game, inserting at some point a new deity, or at some other point relating an obscure genealogy. Particularly after the author's death the Cthulhu Mythos became a parlor game—a lucrative game, to be sure, taken over for commercial ends by publishers and movie producers. . . . *This* myth—need we say so?—interests us not at all. But through the data of the fable (the data, at least, established by Lovecraft) there is outlined a movement of return toward the fundamental, the initial, the exemplary. Under the surface of the narrative, which necessarily follows the thread of an articulated discourse, can confusedly be perceived structures reminiscent of the great myths that have nourished humanity and that seem to have been *inherited* rather than invented. For all the clouding by a profusion of horrible or grotesque details, the general schema—the "pattern," as the mythologists say—of the Cthulhu Mythos is this return to the beginning, the source, the "principle of life."

If we are to believe the most respected commentators, the essential of myth is to remind man of the times signifying the beginnings, the Great Time at the beginning of time. All myth is *myth of origins,* and under one form or another tells the tale of Creation. It tells of the first Act, it recounts what happened in the times when something could happen, *in illo tempore,* in the times of the gods and the exemplary beings who existed at the birth of our planet.

"Myth," writes Mircea Eliade, "tells a sacred history; it relates an advent which has taken place in primordial times, the fabulous times of the beginnings. In other words, myth tells how, thanks to the exploits of Supernatural Beings, a reality has come into existence."

How, then, can we *not* think of the imaginary voyages Lovecraft undertakes vicariously, through his characters, toward the most hidden eras of history? How can we not recall, more precisely, the adventures Peaslee knew in the "shadow out of time," among the Great Race, hundreds of millions of years before the appearance of man on earth?

> Things of inconceivable shape, [the myths] implied, had reared towers to the sky and delved into every secret of Nature before the first amphibian forbear of man had crawled out of the hot sea three hundred million years ago. Some had come down from the stars; a few were as old as the cosmos itself; others had arisen swiftly from terrene germs as far behind the first germs of our life cycle as those germs are behind ourselves. Spans of thousands of millions of years, and linkages with other galaxies and universes, were spoken of. Indeed, there was no such thing as time in its humanly accepted sense.

Of little importance here are the artifices used by the author to send his character back to this fabulous epoch of history. What counts is that Peaslee breaks for a while with secular time and reintegrates himself with primordial time, the intense time of the beginnings. Projected out of ordinary temporality, he becomes—literally—the contemporary of legendary beings. He is called upon to live the events the memory of which the human race has lost, to participate in that initial fullness Mircea Eliade tells us is the chance for the sick man—and perhaps for Lovecraft?—to recover his strength: "The function of myth is not to *conserve* the remembrance of the primordial event, but to *project* the sick man *to where that event is in the process of occurring,* i.e. to the dawn of Time, the beginning."

Later on we will see what conclusions concerning the author can be drawn about this *therapeutic* significance of mythic behavior. For the moment let us note that the same method is found in many other tales and particularly in *At the Mountains of Madness.* The survivors of the Pabodie expedition become provisionally the "contemporaries" of the Great Old Ones and of . . . a shoggoth. In contrast with the preceding tale, the artifice here consists in reanimating the fabulous beings right in secular time. But the result is the same: humans suddenly find themselves confronted with entities who were, as we are made to understand in the course of the tale, *models.* In the Cthulhu Mythos, everything rests on the belief that in prodigiously obscure times, primordial deities from the stars—all myth necessarily having a cosmic dimension—were installed on the earth, and by their arrival began earth life. This is the tale told by the frescoes painted on the walls of the subterranean tunnels explored by the narrator and his companion in the ruins of that ancient city on the malefic Plateau of Leng. These "astral beings" are, par excellence, the actors of a primordial drama played *at the beginning.* And to illustrate this drama, we need only recall the terrible struggle between the Old Ones and the Great Race, a fight whose echoes can here or there be perceived, or again the rebellion of these premier deities from the other gods, and their ultimate chastisement. In each tale the time of the story is always defined by reference to mythic times, which is the Time of Cthulhu. The characters, by will or accident, leave chronological time to recover the sacred—or sacrilegious?—time of the beginning. In this context is it not significant that Randolph Carter, in the last pages of **"Through the Gates of the Silver Key,"** suddenly disappears from the room he is in by entering a clock? We can suppose that he has returned, beyond cosmic space, to faraway Yaddith, where time is qualitatively other than that which it is on earth.

It is certainly patently significant that in **"The Silver Key"** Carter's mythic quest, which will put him in the presence of Yog-Sothoth himself, coincides with the quest for the images of his childhood. Having, at age fifty, made the tour of human vanities, he decides to go to the old family home, obeying the suggestions of a strange dream, and becomes again the child "Randy" that he was forty years before. He becomes so in the literal sense: familiar voices surround him again, and it is a youngster in knee breeches and smock who applies the "silver key" to the lock of the Ultimate Gate.

Here the return to origins is made in the framework of an individual psyche. Randolph Carter becomes, in the most literal sense of the term, the contemporary of his first childhood; he is projected, by the author's own wish, to the beginning of his personal history. He is reinstated in the "beatific" period, the "paradisiacal" time of the beginnings, breaking with the sterile and chronological time of the adult world he had regrettably entered. Again, the psychoanalyst would have much to say about this oneiric regression to the initial stage of the individual psyche. We will leave to others better prepared than ourselves the task of doing this. Let us restrain ourselves and show, for our part, that the mythic approach coincides once again with the oneiric experience. Carter reattains childhood, comes back to the initial stage of his existence, and by this rediscovers the fundamental truths that in the beginning presided over the development of worlds. The silver key is the symbol for the time of infancy, which permits Carter to attain the infancy of Time.

Placing them in this context, we can better understand the "genealogical" quests in which many of the characters indulge. These beings who examine the archives of their ancestral dwellings, who comb attics in search of old familial correspondence, or who watch for the least clue capable of clearing up the past of their "stock" in effect illustrate this same "myth of origins." The importance accorded by some of them to the "line," to the "ancients," testifies to their wish to reproduce *in their time* what took place *at the beginning of Time.* To achieve this, they use ritual, which, as is well known, has no other function than the reactualization of myth. We think of all those ceremonies . . . the aim of which is the awakening of the Great Old Ones and their return to our planet. What do the worshippers of Dagon, Cthulhu, and Yog-Sothoth seek if not to repeat archaic actions to make history repeat itself, the fabulous history of the time when R'lyeh emerged from the waves? . . . Lovecraft, conscious of the demands of myth, abolished lay, ordinary language for the duration of these ceremonies and substituted a language—sacred, secret—which he re-created. Yog-Sothoth must not be addressed in everyday language; one cannot hope to communicate with him but by using formulas known only to initiates and priests. The ritualistic re-creation of the world requires the institution of a new Word.

The cosmic dimension of the Lovecraftian universe again testifies to its ties with myth. The space in his tales is an *astral space,* which extends to the very confines of the universe, beyond the "Edge of the World." The planet Yaddith, where Carter spends several million years in the body of the sorcerer

Zkauba, whose aspect it is best to hide; the planet Yuggoth, whence those strange crustacean-shelled creatures came; the star Vega, toward which Nyarlathotep steers the shantak mounted by Carter; and many other stars that shine in the skies of . . . Providence indicate not the limits of Lovecraft's mythic universe, but the directions to which it ceaselessly extends. Lovecraft, reactualizing cosmogonic myth, re-creates the cosmos. Returning to the beginning of Time, he distributes the worlds in space, taking care, however, to reserve a place for Chaos, over which a blind and idiot god rules. . . .

We may perhaps be puzzled by the apparently close correspondence between the Cthulhu Mythos and the "real" myths of humanity, such as those presented us in the most recent and pertinent studies. It will be still simpler to find in the Lovecraftian universe the constituent elements of the closer and more familiar myths of Greco-Roman antiquity, such as the revolt of certain gods, their chastisement, their imprisonment. And yet, to explain the presence of Hypnos, Neptune, Hermes, or Zeus in such-and-such a tale, it is not enough to recall the author's perfect knowledge of classical mythology. Nor does the fact that he had read Frazer, Fiske, and so many other mythologists whom he cites in his letters the more imply that the Cthulhu Mythos was solely an abstract, rational construction, an ersatz myth articulated by logical thought; at least it does not imply exclusively this. Certainly the Cthulhu Mythos has been elaborated from a structure common to all myths. We admit that it was elaborated as a game, the game of a neurotic and idle scholar.

But may we not believe that Lovecraft, insofar as he *dreamed* a feigned mythology, restored to it its value as myth as well as its primordial irrationality? Dreaming at first within acquired structures, he rediscovered in his unconscious—or at a profound level of consciousness—inherited structures. By dream he reanimated petrified schemas; in dream he passed from fable to myth, or better, from fable he redid a myth. Need we thus be astonished? In a world that like our own has banished the irrational, the dark zones of the psyche were the last refuge of myth. "Dream is a cosmogony of the night. Every night, the dreamer builds the world anew." This lovely formula of Bachelard's better defines Lovecraft's method than we have done, mythic and oneiric at one and the same time, or mythic *because* it is oneiric.

We thus return to our first remark, concerning the profound, *therapeutic* significance of myth. Lovecraft's tales can be read, as we have said, as the journal of a treatment. It is now possible, in the context we have just advanced, to be a little more precise. What seems fundamental in his work is this oneiric regression into the heart of a mythic structure, into the fullness of primordial times, which is also the time of childhood. For Lovecraft as for all other mythographers, the beginning is the model, the perfection. Parenthetically, let us here refer to what we said earlier about distinguishing Lovecraft's tales from those of science fiction. According to him, science and intelligence were at the beginning of time. Then men forgot, and the human race degenerated. . . . Here again is an important aspect of mythic behavior, this notion of decadence from high times, from times signifying the beginning, an aspect that, as we have seen, occupies an important place in the author's *Weltanshauung.* There would doubtless be much to say about the rapports that existed in him between racism and mythic thought, and his "fascism" could in part be explained by this return to the "myth of origins." By what other means could he fight against the degeneracy of his contemporaries, if not to return to the source and praise the former purity of the race? But this is a secondary aspect of a fundamental question. It is essential to see how the "myth of origins," through the transfer it makes to the intense time of the beginnings, re-creates life and allows the sick man to participate in the fullness of creation. It is, as Mircea Eliade tells us, a remedy for all "critical and existential situations where man is driven to hopelessness."

Lovecraft was . . . a man without hope. Unstable, sick, unhappy, obstinately rejecting what he considered the delusions of faith, fed on nihilistic philosophies, he had frequently thought of suicide. Only his dreams—his correspondence testifies to it—permitted him to overcome each crisis and to try once again to live. Did he not in dream find, in the blackest moments, the unexpected help of secret and vitalizing forces?

We are then tempted to regard the Cthulhu Mythos, whose elaboration was slow, progressive, and continuous, as the adequate receptacle for the author's anguish, where, in the waters of dream, it could "precipitate," form deposits in precise, horrible, *monstrous* shapes at the bottom of a structure ready to receive them and give them meaning.

Driven by a myth—a necessarily *oriented* structure, based on the quest for and the revelation of the sacred—horror can only be expressed by and in sacrilege: the impious cults, hideous ceremonies, blasphemous rites . . . , which tell a reverse history of salvation. It is at this deep level that the cure operates: because the sick man recognizes these images of horror as his own, he is in a position to assume them fully and thereby overcome them. To give a material representation to anguish is in itself to be freed from it. To formulate sacrilege is somehow to recover the meaning of the sacred, even if, as was probably so with Lovecraft, it is basically a playful representation. For we can never totally invent our monsters; they express our inner selves too much for that. Game is part of the search for a cure, as fable is a step toward myth. (pp. 109-15)

Lovecraft's tales unequivocally bring to light the connection between the fantastic and the oneiric. To judge by his example, the writing of a fantastic tale consists in substituting nocturnal images for the clear images that directly signify diurnal life: dark images, in the material sense of the term, fraught with the characteristic symbols of dream. Thus are the images of the labyrinths, spiral staircases, black gulfs, putrid waters, and closed spaces explained, and thus ought they to be read: images which constitute a vocabulary of anguish and which, if we believe in the universality of the structures of the imagination, ensure what we can call an "intense communication" between the author and his readers, a communication "through the depths."

But it is at the same time important, as we have seen, that the characters who encounter these dream-images be lucid, conscious. The fantastic necessarily implies the presence, at the thickest level of dream, of a conscious intelligence. Indeed, the fantastic is born, more precisely, at the very instant the author *becomes aware* of his dream-images, "reifies" them, and detaches himself from them, not without having placed the hero, whose premier function is to prolong his awareness, in this impossible and "real" world. . . . [Many] clues allow us to understand that, in most of Lovecraft's tales, the main character—whether his name be Charles Dexter Ward, Edward Derby, Olney, Malone, or simply "I"—*is* the author. It is his glance that perceives the horror, the split, the transgression; it is in his glance that terror is born.

This should allow us to refine our appreciation of the apparent relation of the fantastic to the pathological. To be sure, the fantastic is fostered by the disturbances introduced by neurosis, insofar as they accentuate the chaotic aspect of dream, amplify anguish, and are made manifest by the persistence of dream-images at the level of wakefulness. But it is as clear that no work can properly be classified as fantastic through which the author has not "recovered" and recognized these images for his own. Lacking such an identification, he remains the prisoner of his delirium, the oeuvre remaining mad, savage, alienated. We are told that the pictures drawn and the tales written by madmen are sometimes beautiful, but they do not belong to the fantastic: lacking is a clear way of looking at things, indispensable to create "distance" and perspective. The emergence of fantastic art is conditioned by the author's mastery of his phantasms, whence the primordial importance of a *cure,* of which we have spoken before, and which we consider an absolute prerequisite. The writer of fantasy ought also to *want* to create fear, and this is derived directly from a cure. There must be a purpose, a deliberate intention to communicate anguish. Here technique takes over, arranging and making hierarchical the unrefined data of dream. It organizes suspense, it introduces the irrational into the heart of a causal series, it condenses the dream around a plot. All tales of fantasy are an articulated, dramatized dream. Their quality depends in large part on the working of a finely geared mechanism, which must run without hitches. But technique ought always to remain subservient to dream.

What Lovecraft teaches us, and what he himself learned from Machen, is that the best fantasy is that which is rooted in folklore, tradition, and myth. Puritanism and the history of New England play the same role in our author's tales as medieval myth did in the Gothic novels of the end of the eighteenth century. Somehow, myth, in the superficial sense of the term, orients and localizes dream-activity, thereby assuring it an even greater intensity and benefic homogeneity.

On a personal level, myth gives depth and efficiency to the fantastic, precisely insofar as this return to the primordial it involves coincides with a quest for a cure, and also because it permits the irrational to be built on the foundations of the universal psyche. At the most, the idea would be defensible that anything truly fantastic implies a return to *archetypes.*

It will always be impossible to define the fantastic universally, which is too rich, too basic to be encompassed definitively by any discourse. Examples, complementary or contradictory, can but illustrate that Lovecraft's work is one, a very significant one, we believe, and particularly if we consider the time and place in which he lived.

He vehemently stood, in his letters, against the ravages of industrial civilization, which was attacking man at his deepest level: isolating him from the past, from the traditions of his race, tearing him from his native soil; in a word, alienating him. From this viewpoint, fantastic creation is a protest and a refusal. No; life is not as simple, rudimentary, and facile as the billboard advertisements might lead us to believe. No; the laws that rule the universe are not as well known as popular science—the only type of science possible in a "democratic" society, based on numbers—seems to indicate. No; space is not as certain, time is not as "chronological," the past is not as dead as some people declare. In truth, there are more things in heaven and *under the earth* than are dreamt of in our philosophies.

In a society that is becoming each day more anesthetized and repressive, the fantastic is at once an evasion and the mobilization of anguish. It restores man's sense of the sacred or the sacrilegious; it above all gives back to him his lost depth. For the myth of the automobile, the washing machine, and the vacuum cleaner, for the modern myths of the new world that are merely surface myths, Lovecraft substituted the Cthulhu Mythos. (pp. 118-20)

Maurice Lévy, in his Lovecraft: A Study in the Fantastic, *translated by S. T. Joshi, Wayne State University Press, 1988, 147 p.*

MIKE ASHLEY (essay date 1988)

[*Ashley is an English scholar and critic who has published numerous studies and reference works in the fields of science fiction, fantasy, horror, and mystery fiction. In the following excerpt, he considers the influence of the English supernatural author Algernon Blackwood on Lovecraft's work.*]

Lovecraft regarded Blackwood as the greatest living writer of weird fiction and considered his story "The Willows" as the best weird story ever written. That alone does not mean Lovecraft should have been influenced by Blackwood. . . .

Tracing an author's influences is no easy task. It requires a detailed knowledge of both authors' styles and their literary preferences and proclivities. . . .

[One] must tread carefully when considering the possibilities of an author's influence. Author X may be influenced in a number of ways. The most direct is where a scene in a specific story by Author Y is so effective that Author X transplants the scene to one of his own stories. Such an action may be subliminal or may have been deliberate either in direct imitation or emulation of Author Y's works.

Then again Author X may be influenced by the style of Author Y or by the mood created in his stories. Detecting this can be deceptive as it is always possible that Author X created this approach independently with both authors possibly being influenced by a third source. This parallelism is evident in Lovecraft's Dunsanian stories where he had evolved his own approach in **"Polaris"** before reading any of Dunsany's stories.

Nevertheless, in Lovecraft's early fiction the influences of Edgar Allan Poe and Nathaniel Hawthorne are self-evident whilst in his later stories the more direct influence of Arthur Machen arises, each to some degree distinct and not merging into an evolving style.

Since Lovecraft seems not to have encountered Blackwood's works until 1924 there is no need to look for his influence in stories written before that date, although it is necessary to know those stories in case a further example of parallelism is detected. By the same token it is important to know which stories by Blackwood Lovecraft had read as there is no value in highlighting an episode as being influenced by a story if Lovecraft had not read it. It would again be an example of parallelism. (p. 3)

Lovecraft would certainly seem to have read Blackwood's collections *The Empty House, The Listener, John Silence, The Lost Valley* and *Incredible Adventures* and the two novels *Jimbo* and *The Centaur.* These he had read sometime between 1924 and 1926. He had also read the novels *The Extra*

Day and *The Garden of Survival* which he regarded as "junk" but it is less easy to know when he read these. In addition his library contained a copy of *Julius Le Vallon* but it is unclear when he read this.

With the exception of *Pan's Garden* and the novel *The Human Chord,* both of which Lovecraft may still have read, Lovecraft may still have read, Lovecraft had certainly read the best of Blackwood and would be acquainted with his most influential work. It would be pertinent here if I gave a brief outline of Blackwood's works and their main themes for the reader not so acquainted with his output.

Blackwood's first book, *The Empty House* (1906) contained fairly traditional horror and ghost stories, some betraying the influence of Poe and other gothic writers. Blackwood had felt these stories had welled up inside him as he desired to unburden himself of many horrors he had encountered during his years of hardship in New York during 1892 to 1896 when he eked out a living as a journalist. Blackwood, in fact, shared with Lovecraft a dislike of New York. . . .

The Listener (1907) was a transitional volume containing some of Blackwood's earlier stories but also showing him developing his main credo which would emerge most powerfully in his novel *The Centaur* (1911) and the collection *Pan's Garden* (1912). Blackwood believed that man was but a pawn against the might of Nature. Nature—with a capital N—as a power emanating from Mother Earth was, itself, a form of consciousness. Man, with a heightened awareness brought about through special training, or by drugs, or by frequent communing with Nature, could become attuned to this consciousness, to the controlling forces of Nature. These forces may be harmless in themselves but man's own intrusion may result in him becoming imperilled through his own lack of understanding. Blackwood became totally captured by the spell of Nature. He rapidly developed a sense of oneness with Nature and with that came an awareness of the grand Cosmic scale and of our own insignificance. In his autobiography *Episodes Before Thirty* (1930), which Lovecraft may well have read, Blackwood describes these feelings.

> So intense, so flooding, was the elation of joy Nature brought, that after such moments even the gravest worldly matters, as well as the people concerned in these, seemed trivial and insignificant. Nature introduced a vaster scale of perspective against which a truer proportion appeared. There lay in the experience some cosmic touch of glory that, by contrast, left all else commonplace and unimportant. The great gods of wind and earth and fire and water swept by on flaming stars, and the ordinary life of the little planet seemed very small, man with his tiny passions and few years of struggle and vain longings, almost futile.

It was this sense of the cosmic and of the all-powerful force of Nature that provided the backcloth against which Blackwood set many of his best stories. . . . (p. 4)

If Lovecraft first encountered Blackwood in 1924 then he encountered him in New York and in *The Empty House* he may have found an affinity with the stories set in New York such as "A Case of Eavesdropping" and "The Strange Adventures of a Private Secretary." There is no reason to suppose that these stories necessarily influenced him but Lovecraft might have felt he had found a like soul. Lovecraft at this time had not written very much and it would seem that the first stories he wrote after encountering Blackwood both have their New York settings. **"The Horror at Red Hook"** to my mind betrays no Blackwoodian influence, though there are more than direct hints of Machen's shadow. **"He,"** though, is another matter.

During his days in New York Blackwood befriended an old Jewish tramp, Alfred H. Louis, who had at one time been a man of strong political direction in England and seemed destined for a powerful future. This man became arguably the strongest influence on Blackwood's life and in tribute Blackwood wrote a short story, "The Old Man of Visions," about Louis. The story, to be found in *The Listener,* is an effective mood piece showing how two minds may be similarly attuned with the one inspiring visions in the other. There is no particular plot to the story; it is predominantly a creation of atmosphere and a tribute to the visionary talents of Blackwood's spiritual mentor. As such it is not one of Blackwood's most memorable stories but it is effective and would certainly attract someone susceptible to mood.

The opening paragraphs to both stories are, to my mind, too similar for coincidence. . . .

> "The Old Man of Visions"
>
> The image of Teufelsdrőckh, sitting in his watch-tower "alone with the stars," leaped into my mind the moment I saw him; and the curious expression of his eyes proclaimed at once that here was a being who allowed the world of small effects to pass him by, while he himself dwelt among the eternal verities. It was only necessary to catch a glimpse of the bent grey figure, so slight yet so tremendous, to realise that he carried staff and wallet, and was travelling alone in a spiritual region, uncharted, and full of wonder, difficulty and fearful joy.
>
> **"He"**
>
> I saw him on a sleepless night when I was walking desperately to save my soul and my vision. My coming to New York had been a mistake; for whereas I had looked for poignant wonder and inspiration in the teeming labyrinths of ancient streets that twist endlessly from forgotten courts and squares and waterfronts to courts and squares and waterfronts equally forgotten, and in the Cyclopean modern towers and pinnacles that rise blackly Babylonian under waning moons, I had found instead only a sense of horror and oppression which threatened to master, paralyse, and annihilate me.

Some may argue that Lovecraft's opening is similar to passages found in earlier stories like **"Dagon"** and **"The Temple"** and that **"He"** is merely a natural development along those lines, and that may be so. But I feel the opening paragraphs are too similar for so simple an explanation all the more so because, for the next few pages, the two stories develop along the same introspective lines until Lovecraft injects his own pace and direction whilst Blackwood lets the mood permeate the narrative until it reaches its own natural conclusion.

"He" is, to my mind, Lovecraft's earliest story to show some mark of Blackwood. There is further betrayal of this in Lovecraft's possible consideration of Blackwood's feelings for Nature. In **"He,"** Lovecraft begins his narration of past visions with a reference to the forces of Nature.

> "To—my ancestor—" he softly continued, "there appeared to reside some very remarkable qualities

> in the will of mankind; qualities having a little-suspected dominance not only over the acts of one's self and of others, but over every variety of force and substance in Nature, and over many elements and dimensions deemed more universal than Nature herself.

In no earlier story does Lovecraft make such a reference to mastery over Nature, let alone Nature with a capital N. The influence of Blackwood was starting to encroach.

Also in *The Listener* is possibly Blackwood's greatest story, and certainly one of the classics of weird fiction, "The Willows." It is a long story with a gradual buildup of atmosphere to the sudden unleashing of cosmic forces. If Lovecraft was in any way receptive to Blackwood's own inspiration the power of "The Willows" could not fail to have effect. Two unnamed explorers, the narrator and his Swedish friend, are canoeing down the Danube and have reached one of the more lonely and desolate reaches. They are forced to spend the night on a shallow, sandy island, the home of countless willow trees. The sensitive, imaginative narrator begins to sense hostility and rejection from the trees and he prepares to spend an unnerving night. Awoken during the night the narrator witnesses huge indistinct inhuman figures surmounting the trees. The vision then takes a specific shape:

> They first became properly visible, these huge figures, just within the tops of the bushes—immense, bronze-coloured, moving, and wholly independent of the swaying of the branches. I saw them plainly and noted, now I came to examine them more calmly, that they were very much larger than human, and indeed that something in their appearance proclaimed them to be *not human* at all. Certainly they were not merely the moving tracery of the branches against the moonlight. They shifted independently. They rose upwards in a continuous stream from earth to sky, vanishing utterly as soon as they reached the dark of the sky. They were interlaced one with another, making a great column, and I saw their limbs and huge bodies melting in and out of each other, forming this serpentine line that bent and swayed and twisted spirally with the contortions of the wind-tossed trees. They were nude, fluid shapes, passing up the bushes, within the leaves almost—rising up in a living column into the heavens. Their faces I could never see. Unceasingly they poured upwards, swaying in great bending curves, with a hue of dull bronze upon their skins.

It's a vivid scene in what is Blackwood's most completely developed story, a masterpiece of writing and atmosphere. It totally captured Lovecraft and remained his favourite story for the rest of his life. But did it influence his fiction? . . . [Consider] these passages:

> . . . And yet amid that tense, godless calm the high bare boughs of all the trees in the yard were moving. They were twitching morbidly and spasmodically, clawing in convulsive and epileptic madness at the moonlit clouds; scratching impotently in the noxious air as if jerked by some alien and bodiless line of linkage with subterrene horrors writhing and struggling below the black roots. . . .
>
> All the while the shaft of phosphorescence from the well was getting brighter and brighter, bringing to the minds of the huddled men a sense of doom and abnormality which far outraced any image their conscious minds could form. It was no longer *shining* out, it was *pouring* out; and as the shapeless stream of unplaceable colour left the well it seemed to flow directly into the sky. . . .
>
> At this point, as the column of unknown colour flared suddenly stronger and began to weave itself into fantastic suggestions of shape which each spectator later described differently. . . .

These scenes come . . . from **"The Colour out of Space"** and seem to me to have been directly inspired by "The Willows." It also seems to me that the opening of "The Willows" with its description of growing desolation is echoed in the opening of both **"The Colour out of Space"** and, to a greater extent, **"The Dunwich Horror"** and this general feeling of desolation and remoteness is more evident in Lovecraft's post-1924 stories. This could owe its origin not just to "The Willows" but to the effect of reading many of Blackwood's stories. His best are set in the isolated areas of the world where, away from civilisation, man is once more at the mercy of Nature or the lure of the Past. There is, for example, much in common in the basic approach, between Blackwood's "A Descent Into Egypt," where the protagonist's soul is gradually absorbed by Egypt's past leaving just the shell of the man behind, and Lovecraft's **"The Shadow out of Time,"** where Nathaniel Peaslee is also overcome by the sense of the great remoteness in time and space of the Western Australian desert.

Blackwood used this approach most effectively in "The Wendigo" (in *The Lost Valley,* 1910). Set in the desolate backwoods of northern Canada, the story has a party of hunters come under the spirit of the wilderness, the personification of the call of the wild, the Wendigo. The sensitive Defago is abducted by the Wendigo and the party endeavor to find him. Before his eventual discovery they become aware of his presence and of something alien, nearby but above them. Firstly there was a sense of "acrid odours" and later "something went past through the darkness of the sky overhead at terrific speed—something of necessity very large for it displaced much air."

At the start of **"The Dunwich Horror"** we learn of past traditions of the place, "of foul odours near the hill-crowning circles of stone pillars, and of rushing airy presences to be heard faintly at certain hours." There are similar references later in the story.

If "The Wendigo" did not directly influence **"The Dunwich Horror"** it may well have suggested the scenes of aerial menace, and perhaps the concept of the Wendigo itself provided food for thought in the development of Lovecraft's alien entities. (pp. 4-7)

The most direct relationship between Blackwood and Lovecraft is that of the direct quote used as a preamble to **"The Call of Cthulhu."** The quote, about great powers surviving from a "hugely remote period" comes from Blackwood's novel *The Centaur* (1911) but is taken slightly out of context. Blackwood is referring to a possibility, in great antiquity, when the Earth's consciousness had projected herself and created visible, even tangible images of beings which primitive man recorded in tribal legend as gods or monsters. The novel concerns another Nature mystic who discovers a modern survivor of this *urwelt,* and through association with "him" discovers a spiritual Garden of Eden.

Out of context the quotation seems ideally suited to Lovecraft's Cthulhuvian cycle. It invites the question of to what extent Blackwood's works may have inspired the Cthulhu stories.

My own view is that Blackwood served as a catalyst. After all at this time (1926/27) Lovecraft was not consciously writing a Cthulhu cycle. This only developed in later stories and became more fully formed in his stories of the 1930s. The concept of earlier gods and myths had long been with him from his early fascination for the Greco-Roman pantheon and the tales of the Arabian Nights. This had been strengthened by Dunsany and Machen but remained limited in scope, almost earth-bound. Lovecraft seemed to be striving for a wider backdrop against which to explore his concepts—something cosmic.

> I have often wished that I had the literary power to call up visions of some vast and remote realm of entity beyond the universes of matter and energy; where vivid interplays of unknown & inconceivable influences give vast & fabulous activity to dimensional areas that are not shapes, & to nuclei of complex arrangements that are not minds. . . .

Lovecraft wrote that in May 1927 at the start of a dry period of writing. He had completed **"The Colour out of Space"** in which he was well pleased but which no doubt left him in a creative vacuum. It would be over a year before he completed another solo story, **"The Dunwich Horror,"** and a further two years after that before he settled down to a period of inspired productivity with **"The Whisperer in Darkness,"** *At the Mountains of Madness,* and **"The Shadow over Innsmouth."**

Was Blackwood that catalyst? Let me quote . . . from Blackwood's stories as food for thought:

> "You think," he said, "it is the spirits of the elements, and I thought perhaps it was the old gods. But I tell you now it is—*neither.* These would be comprehensible entities, for they have relations with men, depending upon them for worship or sacrifice, whereas these beings who are now about us have absolutely nothing to do with mankind, and it is mere chance that their space happens just at this spot to touch our own."
>
> "All my life," he said, "I have been strangely, vividly conscious of another region—not far removed from our own world in one sense, yet wholly different in kind—where great things go on unceasingly, where immense and terrible personalities hurry by, intent on vast purposes compared to which earthly affairs, the rise and fall of nations, the destinies of empires, the fate of armies and continents, are all as dust in the balance. . . ."
>
> And thus the beauty of the early world companioned him, and all the forgotten gods moved forward into life. They hovered everywhere, immense and stately. The rocks and trees and peaks that half concealed them, betrayed at the same time great hints of their mighty gestures. Near him, they were; he moved towards their region. If definite sight refused to focus on them the fault was not their own but his. He never doubted that they could be seen. Yet, even thus partially, they manifested—terrifically. He was aware of their overshadowing presences. Sight, after all, was an incomplete form of knowing—a thing he had left behind—elsewhere. It belonged, with the other limited sense channels, to some attenuated dream now all forgotten. Now he knew *all over.* He himself was of them.
>
> Out there, in the heart of unreclaimed wilderness, they had surely witnessed something crudely and essentially primitive. Something that had survived somehow the advance of humanity had emerged terrifically, betraying a scale of life still monstrous and immature. He envisaged it rather as a glimpse into prehistoric ages, when superstitions, gigantic and uncouth, still oppressed the hearts of men; when the forces of nature were still untamed, the Powers that may have haunted a primeval universe not yet withdrawn. To this day he thinks of what he termed years later in a sermon "savage and formidable Potencies lurking behind the souls of men, not evil perhaps in themselves, yet instinctively hostile to humanity as it exists."

That is just a handful of quotes from many that I could have used. Blackwood's work, more than Poe's, Dunsany's or Machen's, provided a sense of the cosmic, of vast planetary entities, of alien beings natural in their own environment but supernatural to man who was but a pawn on a cosmic battlefield.

Another factor that may be an indication of Blackwood's influence is the length of Lovecraft's stories. Blackwood had found he could not explore his themes sufficiently in a cramped short story and almost all of his best stories are of novella length. In encountering Blackwood's works this may have struck Lovecraft soundly for the first time as virtually all of his stories prior to 1924 are relatively short, whilst very few after 1924 are of equivalent length.

Whatever the case it seems to me that Blackwood's influence has never showed as explicitly as does Poe's or Machen's. It was, I feel, that Blackwood's influence was not the vehicle that Lovecraft drove, but rather the force that set the vehicle in motion. (pp. 7-9)

Mike Ashley, "The Cosmic Connection," in Crypt of Cthulhu, *Vol. 7, No. 7, June 23, 1988, pp. 3-9.*

PETER CANNON (essay date 1989)

[*Cannon is an American fiction writer and critic. In the following excerpt from his book-length biographical and critical study of Lovecraft, he discusses Lovecraft's early stories set in the fictional New England towns of Arkham and Kingsport.*]

Perhaps in part because of his great fondness for his native New England, of its natural landscape and colonial architecture in particular, Lovecraft did not immediately recognize its suitability as a setting for supernatural horror. Not until 1920 did it occur to him to look beyond the Gothicism of Poe and the otherworldly fantasy of Dunsany and take inspiration, as had Hawthorne, from the distant past of the region that had fostered them both. Drawing more upon his experiences of life than upon his book reading, Lovecraft began to place New England increasingly at the heart of his fiction. Over the next fifteen years he would succeed in transforming portions of Essex County, Massachusetts, and environs into a territory as mythically potent as Faulkner's Yoknapatawpha County or the London of Sherlock Holmes. Granted, Lovecraft's Arkham landscape has little of the dark, psychological complexity of Faulkner's Mississippi, nor can it claim the same nostalgic appeal as the detective's late Victorian England, yet it too has an enduring allure, at any rate for those few blessed with minds of the "requisite sensitiveness."

In these earliest New England tales Lovecraft introduced

Kingsport and Arkham, Massachusetts, that pair of fictitious towns of somewhat uncertain provenance. "Vaguely, 'Arkham' corresponds to Salem (though Salem has no college)," he wrote in 1931, "while 'Kingsport' corresponds to Marblehead." "Vaguely" is the key word in this assertion, for as Will Murray has shown Lovecraft did not consistently identify Arkham as a seaport, and in fact in several cases he seems to have located it well inland. Whereas Kingsport became fixed as a constant as early as **"The Festival,"** Arkham remained a sort of variable, developing over the course of some dozen tales into Lovecraft's quintessential, cosmically haunted New England town. As befits such status, Arkham transcends any one spot on the map.

Admirers might wish it otherwise, but Lovecraft's bigotry pervades his first tale with a distinct New England setting, **"The Terrible Old Man"** (1920). Within its brief, tidy, ironical span it shows the same disdain exhibited in the poem "Providence in 2000 A.D." for "that new and heterogeneous alien stock which lies outside the charmed circle of New England life and traditions." By selecting a diverse national mix for his thieves, "Angelo Ricci and Joe Czanek and Manuel Silva"—Italian, Slav, and Portuguese—Lovecraft at least comes across as impartial in his prejudice. The three robbers, of course, prove no match for the Terrible Old Man, a "tottering, almost helpless greybeard," for he acts as heroic defender of those "New England traditions" that Lovecraft was so keen to preserve. Supernatural horror, at the service of the Yankee establishment, brutally puts the ethnic upstarts in their place. (pp. 35-6)

If **"The Terrible Old Man"** suffers as heavy-handed polemic, it nonetheless reveals Lovecraft beginning to use realistic New England elements. The title character, "believed to have been a captain of East India clipper ships in his day," sets the pattern for later sea captains like Obed Marsh who engage in dubious traffick in the Pacific and the Far East. He also anticipates in outline a character like old Wizard Whateley, with whom he would appear to share an appreciation of large standing stones: "Among the gnarled trees in the front yard of his aged and neglected place he maintains a strange collection of large stones, oddly grouped and painted so that they resemble the idols in some obscure Eastern temple." But where in **"The Dunwich Horror"** such stones help to call down Yog-Sothoth, here they function as no more than suggestive ornaments. Likewise Kingsport, not yet inspired by any particular New England site, is simply a generic coastal town with street names like "Ship" and "Water."

Even less to Lovecraft's credit is **"The Street"** (1920), a quasi-poetic attack on "foreign" subversion of Anglo-Saxon America, probably composed within a few months of **"The Terrible Old Man"** to which it forms a kind of thematic footnote. In this petulant sketch, filled with periphrastic locutions in place of characters, a sole reference to "grave men in conical hats" specifically evokes New England, while **"The Street"** of the title is an idealized conglomeration of Lovecraft's beloved old houses. These buildings, "with their forgotten lore of nobler, departed centuries; of sturdy colonial tenants and dewy rose-gardens in the moonlight," have degenerated by the present into such establishments as "Petrovitch's Bakery, the squalid Rifkin School of Modern Economics, the Circle Social Club, and the Liberty Café," patronized by "alien makers of discord," upon whom at the climax they collapse—in a ludicrous display of architecture animated by Lovecraft's own intolerance. Of negligible literary value, **"The Street"** is of interest chiefly as it reflects its author's conservative reaction to the Red Scare of the period.

"The Picture in the House" (1920), after the false starts of **"The Terrible Old Man"** and **"The Street,"** stands as Lovecraft's first tale effectively to employ local New England color. Here Arkham makes its debut, though the action occurs outside the town, in the general region of the "Miskatonic Valley," where the anonymous narrator, the first of his sober-minded scholars, is "in quest of certain genealogical data." The time for the tale's action—November 1896—may not be as irrelevantly specific as the April eleventh date for the thieves' call upon the Terrible Old Man, since such precision would be in keeping with the protagonist's pedantry.

The opening paragraph, an outstanding example of Lovecraftian bombast, sets forth what amounts to a declaration of aesthetic independence:

> Searchers after horror haunt strange, far places. For them are the catacombs of Ptolemais, and the carven mausolea of the nightmare countries. They climb to the moonlit towers of ruined Rhine castles, and falter down black cobwebbed steps beneath the scattered stones of forgotten cities in Asia. The haunted wood and the desolate mountain are their shrines, and they linger around the sinister monoliths on uninhabited islands. But the true epicure in the terrible, to whom a new thrill of unutterable ghastliness is the chief end and justification, esteems most of all the ancient, lonely farmhouses of backwoods New England; for there the dark elements of strength, solitude, grotesqueness, and ignorance combine to form the perfection of the hideous.

With this manifesto Lovecraft serves notice that he will rely less upon stock Gothic backgrounds and will turn more and more to his own New England as a source for horror.

From this rhetorical height the narrative voice shifts smoothly to a broad view of these backwoods houses and their degenerate inhabitants, who "cowered in an appalling slavery to the dismal phantasms of their own minds," thus rooting the story proper in authentic Puritan psycho-history. In contrast to **"The Street,"** the sentient quality of these houses keeps within credible bounds. When the narrator says of the "antique and repellent wooden building" in which he takes refuge, "Honest, wholesome structures do not stare at travellers so slyly and hauntingly," he is revealing not the objectivity of his judgment but the sensitivity of his imagination. Like Lovecraft, he can be at once the rationalist and the romantic.

From fanciful impression the narrator goes on to give an exact and naturalistic description of the exterior and interior of the house. Such finely observed details as the contents of the library shelf—"an eighteenth-century Bible, a *Pilgrim's Progress* of like period, illustrated with grotesque woodcuts and printed by the almanack-maker Isaiah Thomas, the rotting bulk of Cotton Mather's *Magnalia Christi Americana*"—vividly contribute to the mood of sinister antiquity. The character of the narrator, through such erudite particulars as his recognition of Pigafetta's *Regnum Congo,* "written in Latin from the notes of the sailor Lopez and printed at Frankfort in 1598," emerges just enough to be convincing. His host, another menacing, preternaturally aged individual like the Terrible Old Man (though robust in physique, thanks to his diet of human flesh), speaks in an exaggerated, archaic dialect—" 'Ketched in the rain, be ye?' he greeted"—that contrasts nicely with the civilized diction of the narrator. Their exchange is an early instance of Lovecraft's restricting quoted speech to a monologue: typically, to a rustic's account of strange goings-on given to a learned narrator who never records his side of the conversation. If this technique allowed Lovecraft to avoid the dialogue for which he felt he had no talent, it also helped him to tell his tales with considerable economy. Here, as in all his better first-person narratives, dialogue never obtrudes upon that intimate mental contact the narrator establishes with the reader.

At the climax, with a finesse unknown to those present-day horror writers who delight in explicit violence, Lovecraft suggests the worst through "a very simple though somewhat unusual happening": the tiny spattering of blood onto the open book page that causes the narrator to look up to the ceiling and see "a large irregular spot of wet crimson which seemed to spread even as I viewed it." Unlike narrators of later tales, he has no time for philosophical ruminations in face of such gruesome evidence, as fate intervenes in the next moment in the form of "the titanic thunderbolt of thunderbolts; blasting that accursed house of unutterable secrets and bringing the oblivion that alone saved my mind." This *deus ex machina* ending, trite though it may be, in effect reduces the tale to a nightmare from which the narrator suddenly awakes when the danger becomes too much to bear. His survival unhurt amid the blackened ruins of the house is nothing miraculous for one in a dream. After the careful realism and subtle plot development leading up to this denouement, Lovecraft wisely refrains from any overt dream explanation. Such restraint helps make **"The Picture in the House,"** however conventional its cannibal theme, the strongest of Lovecraft's early New England tales.

"I am become a Grub-Street hack," declared Lovecraft in announcing his first professional story project [**"Herbert West—Reanimator"** (1921-22)]. "My sole inducement is the monetary reward." When George Houtain, the editor of *Home Brew* magazine, made him the offer, the hitherto amateur gentleman gamely enough set aside his ideals and produced the six self-contained episodes that together constitute **"Herbert West—Reanimator."** As perhaps his most contrived work of fiction, it adds up to an awkward and repetitious whole. No doubt length restrictions put a strain on his invention. For example, the account of the thing that had been Dr. Allan Halsey, "public benefactor and dean of the medical school of Miskatonic University," running amok for three days and killing a total of nineteen Arkham residents might have been less grotesquely comic had it not been so compressed. That Lovecraft later condemned **"Herbert West"** as "my poorest work—stuff done to order for a vulgar magazine, & written down to the herd's level," however, should not obscure the fact that the plot, which builds in neat, logical increments from one section to the next, took some skill to construct. Within an artificial framework lies an ingenious tale, as lurid and lively as any of Robert E. Howard's pulp action yarns that would so excite *Weird Tales* readers later in the decade.

As monomaniacally as Captain Ahab seeks the white whale, Herbert West strives to perfect his corpse-reanimating techniques, assisted by the compliant, Ishmael-like narrator, until undone by his unholy creations. Of course, on the scale of Faustian fiction **"Herbert West"** is closer in value to *Frankenstein* than to *Moby-Dick,* yet by selecting a pseudo-scientific premise in accord with his own philosophical views—West's theories "hinged on the essentially mechanistic nature of life"—Lovecraft shows some degree of seriousness. Says the narrator: "Holding with Haeckel that all life is a chemical and physical process, and that the so-called 'soul' is a myth, my friend believed that artificial reanimation of the dead can depend only on the condition of the tissues; and that unless actual decomposition has set in, a corpse fully equipped with organs may with suitable measures be set going again in the peculiar fashion known as life." In the same letter to Frank Belknap Long in which Lovecraft mentions his progress on the serial, he advises him to read Ernst Haeckel's *Riddle of the Universe* "before placing too much credence in any vague and unexplainable force of 'life' beyond the ordinarily known mechanical forms."

Emphasizing action over atmosphere, Lovecraft provides little local color. The first two sections, stocked with references to such new Arkham sites as Meadow Hill and Christchurch Cemetery, contain none of the architectural and historical detail that enriches **"The Picture in the House."** Only Miskatonic University, in its initial appearance, assumes any character—primarily as the institution where Herbert West and the narrator get started in their profane medical researches. Parts three and four transpire in nearby Bolton, an inexplicable use of an actual Massachusetts town northeast of Worcester, though again it might be any mill town in the region. Only in the sixth and concluding section, after a grisly interlude behind the front in Flanders in part five, does Lovecraft make a passing attempt to particularize setting. Having finally settled "in a venerable house of much elegance, overlooking one of the oldest burying-grounds in Boston," West is back on familiar ground—that is, below it. In the process of having a subcellar dug out for his laboratory, he discovers some "exceedingly ancient masonry" that he calculates must form a "secret chamber beneath the tomb of the Averills, where the last interment had been made in 1768." Even in his hack work Lovecraft could not resist slipping in an antiquarian touch or two.

Such incidental features redeem a tale like **"Herbert West,"** as is true of his weaker efforts in general, imbuing it with a certain naive charm. Only in a Lovecraft story could two young men not pursue attractive female specimens for their experiments, remaining bachelors for seventeen years, all without a hint of deviant sexual behavior. (In 1985 Hollywood would supply the missing sex element in its gory if good-natured film version, *Re-animator.*) If **"Herbert West—Reanimator"** represents an unnatural detour from Lovecraft's own development, it nonetheless shows how entertainingly he could write when compelled to satisfy someone else's story requirements.

With **"The Unnameable"** (1923) Lovecraft returned to the vein begun in **"The Picture in the House,"** adapting a bit of New England folklore out of Cotton Mather's "chaotic *Magnalia Christi Americana,*" of which he possessed an ancestral copy. The narrator, Lovecraft's persona Randolph Carter (referred to only as "Carter"), is, in a touch of self-parody, an author of weird fiction. With his friend "Joel Manton," "principal of the East High School, born and bred in Boston and sharing New England's self-satisfied deafness to the delicate overtones of life," Carter conducts a stilted debate over the existence of the "unnamable," while "sitting on a dilapidated seventeenth-century tomb in the late afternoon of an autumn day at the old burying-ground in Arkham." In a letter answering some small matters of the tale's obscure plot,

Lovecraft noted that there was "actually an ancient slab half engulfed by a giant willow tree in the middle of the Charter St. Burying Ground in Salem." References to the Salem witchcraft in the tale itself also connect Arkham to the venerable Essex County seaport.

As in **"The Picture in the House,"** the narrator hints at horrors in colonial Massachusetts far worse than any known to the history books:

> It had been an eldritch thing—no wonder sensitive students shudder at the Puritan age in Massachusetts. So little is known of what went on beneath the surface—so little, yet such a ghastly festering as it bubbles up putrescently in occasional ghoulish glimpses. The witchcraft terror is a horrible ray of light on what was stewing in men's crushed brains, but even that is a trifle. There was no beauty; no freedom—we can see that from the architectural and household remains, and the poisonous sermons of the cramped divines. And inside that rusted iron strait-jacket lurked gibbering hideousness, perversion, and diabolism. Here, truly, was the apotheosis of the unnameable.

Unlike **"The Picture in the House,"** however, **"The Unnameable"** fails to deliver the horrors such an assertion promises, being nearly as stagey and static as that poorest of Sherlock Holmes stories, "The Adventure of the Mazarin Stone." Carter may boast that his tale "The Attic Window" led to the removal of the magazine it appeared in from the stands in many places "at the complaints of silly milksops," but, judging from his smug, inappropriately offhand manner, his "lowly standing as an author" is not undeserved. Indeed, the uncharacteristic use of dialogue suggests that again on some parodic level Lovecraft may have conceived the tale as more Carter's than his own.

Manton's impressionistic description of the monster that shows up from nowhere at the climax to gore them like a bull, "a gelatin—a slime . . . the pit—the maelstrom," incongruously mixes the viscous and the literary, as it confirms rather too patly Carter's belief in the impossibility of naming the unnamable. Lovecraft will link shoggoths and Poe less crudely in *At the Mountains of Madness.*

More than seven years after his initial visit to Marblehead, Massachusetts, Lovecraft wrote: "God! Shall I ever forget my first stupefying glimpse of MARBLEHEAD'S huddled and archaick roofs under the snow in the delirious sunset glory of four p.m., Dec. 17, 1922! ! ! I did not know until an hour before that I should ever behold such a place as Marblehead, and I did not know *until that moment itself* the full extent of the wonder I was to behold. I account that instant—about 4:05 to 4:10 p.m., Dec. 17, 1922—the most powerful single emotional climax during my nearly forty years of existence." Such a declaration, while it should not be taken wholly at face value, can be considered an honest expression of Lovecraft's preference for emotions of purely aesthetic origin to those generated by human relationships. In particular, it indicates as none of his direct comments on the matter do why his marriage in the interval was doomed.

"The Festival" (1923) marks Lovecraft's first and most literal attempt to recapture in fiction the ecstasy prompted by the sight of a well-preserved New England town of colonial vintage. The unnamed narrator, as he nears Kingsport by foot at "Yuletide," experiences architectural rapture of an intensity far beyond any felt by the narrator of **"The Picture in the House"**:

> Then beyond the hill's crest I saw Kingsport outspread frostily in the gloaming; snowy Kingsport with its ancient vanes and steeples, ridgepoles and chimneypots, wharves of small bridges, willow-trees and graveyards; endless labyrinths of steep, narrow, crooked streets, and dizzy church-crowned central peak that time durst not touch; ceaseless mazes of colonial houses piled and scattered at all angles and levels like a child's disordered blocks; antiquity hovering on grey wings over winter-whitened gables and gambrel roofs; fanlights and small-paned windows one by one gleaming out in the cold dusk to join Orion and the archaic stars.

Lovecraft used such similar phrases as "small buildings heap'd about at all angles and all levels like an infant's blocks" to describe Marblehead in a letter to Rheinhart Kleiner dated 11 January 1923, suggesting a common set of notes for both the letter and the tale that was to follow later in the year. . . .

[Something] is odd about an entire community: "they were strange, because they had come as dark furtive folk from opiate southern gardens of orchids, and spoken another tongue before they learnt the tongue of the blue-eyed fishers." Here Lovecraft resorts to the flowery language of dreamland, but for no other purpose than to distinguish the inhabitants of Kingsport from more traditional Puritan settlers. Their background and motives remain vague. . . . [These] "dark furtive folk" have no real stake in the scene set out so lovingly in the first part of the story. After all the effort put into the creation of the mood picture of the antique town, Lovecraft seems to have been too exhausted to devise a horrific premise of equal power.

In this perhaps most Hawthornesque of Lovecraft's tales, the narrator has been called, like the title character of Hawthorne's "Young Goodman Brown," to attend a Sabbath rendezvous. There he experiences a hideous revelation, discovering not that he belongs to a fallen brotherhood of man but that his own ancestors are evil, reanimated corpses—a far less profound insight, to say the least, than that gained by Goodman Brown. Faced with coventional monsters he reacts with conventional fear, his responses bordering on the illogical. While in the cavern below the church he regards with comparative calm the "tame, trained, hybrid winged things" that are "not altogether crows, nor moles, nor buzzards, nor ants, nor vampire bats, nor decomposed human beings," yet he flings himself into the oily, underground river only after the mask of the old man who has guided him slips and he glimpses "what should have been his head," an arguably less frightening vision.

"The Festival," overwritten and melodramatic though it may be, especially at its climax, does have value as more than just an atmospheric study. In **"Herbert West"** an artificial head had allowed a reanimated corpse missing the genuine item to pass among the living, while in **"The Festival,"** a bit more plausibly, a waxen mask and gloves serve to hide the decay of what had once been human. This face-hands deception motif will reappear as a vital plot feature in **"The Whisperer in Darkness"** and **"Through the Gates of the Silver Key,"** and less centrally in **"The Dunwich Horror,"** where the relatively normal face and hands of Wilbur Whateley disguise his fundamentally alien nature. The colonial house in **"The Festival,"** like that in **"The Picture in the House,"** holds a library of ancient books but of a plainly sinister import: "I saw that the books were hoary and mouldy, and that they included old Morryster's wild *Marvells of Science,* the terrible *Saducismus Triumphatus* of Glanvill, published in 1681, the shocking *Daemonolatreia* of Remigius, printed in 1595 at Lyons, and worst of all, the unmentionable *Necronomicon* of the mad Arab Abdul Alhazred, in Olaus Wormius's forbidden Latin translation; a book which I had never seen, but of which I had heard monstrous things whispered." In this surely conscious echo of the catalogue of books in "The Fall of the House of Usher," Lovecraft establishes the *Necronomicon* as the acme of all such dreaded volumes. As with Kingsport and Arkham, each new appearances makes Alhazred's wondrous tome seem that much more convincing. Defined only through guarded mentions and rare quoted passages, it will come to assume an air of reality impossible for any actual book. There is nothing comparable in Poe. (pp. 36-44)

Peter Cannon, "Kingsport and Arkham," in his H. P. Lovecraft, *Twayne Publishers, 1989, pp. 35-44.*

ADDITIONAL BIBLIOGRAPHY

Bailey, J. O. "Beyond the Mountains of the Moon." In his *Pilgrims through Space and Time: Trends and Patterns in Scientific and Utopian Fiction,* pp. 119-87. New York: Argus Books, 1947.

Primarily plot outlines of *At the Mountains of Madness* and "The Shadow out of Time." Bailey calls Lovecraft "one of the most sensitive and powerful writers of our generation in the field of the quasi-scientific tale of terror."

Buhle, Paul. "Dystopia As Utopia: Howard Phillips Lovecraft and the Unknown Content of American Horror Literature." *The Minnesota Review,* No. 6 (Spring 1976): 118-31.

Views Lovecraft as an opponent of the idea of social and political progress in the United States.

Carter, Angela. "Lovecraft and Landscape." In *The Necronomicon,* edited by George Hay, pp. 173-81. London: Neville Spearman, 1978.

Discusses the significance of setting and landscape in Lovecraft's fiction.

Carter, Lin. *Lovecraft: A Look behind the "Cthulhu Mythos."* New York: Ballantine Books, 1972, 198 p.

Offers a thorough background on the nature and evolution of the Mythos stories.

Carter, Paul A. *The Creation of Tomorrow: Fifty Years of Magazine Science Fiction,* p. 7ff. New York: Columbia University Press, 1977.

Discusses Lovecraft's place in the early development of science fiction.

Conover, Willis, Jr. *Lovecraft at Last.* Arlington, Va.: Carrollton-Clark, 1975, 272 p.

Personal chronicle of Conover's correspondence with Lovecraft during the last months of Lovecraft's life.

Cook, W. Paul. *In Memoriam: Howard Phillips Lovecraft.* 1941. Reprint. West Warwick, R.I.: Necronomicon Press, 1977, 75 p.

Reminiscences of Lovecraft by a longtime friend and fellow amateur journalist.

Davis, Sonia H. *The Private Life of H. P. Lovecraft.* West Warwick, R.I.: Necronomicon Press, 1985, 25 p.

Reminiscences of Lovecraft by his wife.

De Camp, L. Sprague. *Lovecraft: A Biography.* Garden City, N.Y.: Doubleday & Co., 1975, 510 p.

Controversial biography that is informative and opinionated, designed to offer more information about the personal life of Lovecraft than criticism of his work.

Faig, Kenneth W., Jr. *H. P. Lovecraft: His Life, His Work.* West Warwick, R.I.: Necronomicon Press, 1979, 36 p.

Biographical sketch followed by a chronology of important dates in the life and literary career of Lovecraft and a chronology of selected fiction, nonfiction, and poetry.

Fresco: Howard Phillips Lovecraft Memorial Symposium 8, No. 3 (Spring 1958): 68 p.

Reminiscences, essays, and a bibliography by Samuel Loveman, Matthew Onderdonk, T. O. Mabbott, David Keller, and others.

Joshi, S. T. *H. P. Lovecraft and Lovecraft Criticism: An Annotated Bibliography.* Kent, Ohio: Kent State University Press, 1981, 473 p.

Comprehensive primary and secondary bibliography, with an introductory essay on the development of Lovecraft's critical reputation.

———. "Topical References in Lovecraft." *Extrapolation* 25, No. 3 (Fall 1984): 247-65.

Details references in Lovecraft's fiction to events and figures of his time.

———, ed. *H. P. Lovecraft: Four Decades of Criticism.* Athens, Ohio: Ohio University Press, 1980, 250 p.

Collection of seminal essays on Lovecraft, including studies by Barton Levi St. Armand, Dirk W. Mosig, Richard Tierney, Fritz Leiber, and George Wetzel.

———, and Blackmore, L. D. *H. P. Lovecraft and Lovecraft Criticism: An Annotated Bibliography.* West Warwick, R.I.: Necronomicon Press, 1985, 72 p.

Supplement to Joshi's 1981 bibliography, documenting primary and secondary publications from 1980 to 1984.

Ketterer, David. "Somebody up There." In his *New Worlds for Old: The Apocalyptic Imagination, Science Fiction, and American Literature,* pp. 261-66. Bloomington: Indiana University Press, 1974.

Discusses elements in Lovecraft's stories that link them to science fiction.

Mosig, Dirk W. "Towards a Greater Appreciation of H. P. Lovecraft." In *First World Fantasy Awards: An Anthology of the Fantastic: Stories, Poems, Essays,* edited by Gahan Wilson, pp. 290-301. New York: Doubleday & Co., 1977.

Jungian reading of some of Lovecraft's stories.

Prawer, S. S. "Allurements of the Abyss." *The Times Literary Supplement,* No. 4081 (19 June 1981): 687-88.

Examines the distinctive traits of Lovecraft's stories and offers a defense of his prose style.

Price, Robert M. "Demythologizing Cthulhu." *Lovecraft Studies* 3, No. 1 (Spring 1984): 3-9, 24.

Applies the hermeneutic principle of "demythologizing" to Lovecraft's fiction in order to arrive at a more valid understanding of his invented mythology than is allowed by either literal occultist belief or symbolic literary interpretation.

St. Armand, Barton Levi. *H. P. Lovecraft: New England Decadent.* Albuquerque, N.M.: Silver Scarab Press, 1979, 76 p.

Demonstrates Lovecraft's connections to the Puritans of seventeenth-century New England on the one hand and to the Aesthetic and Decadent artists of nineteenth-century Europe on the other.

Schweitzer, Darrell. *The Dream Quest of H. P. Lovecraft.* Bernadino, Calif.: The Borgo Press, 1978, 63 p.

Introductory study of Lovecraft's life and work.

———, ed. *Discovering H. P. Lovecraft.* Mercer Island, Wash.: Starmont House, 1987, 153 p.
Collection of reprinted essays, including "The Four Faces of the Outsider" by Dirk W. Mosig, "The Derleth Mythos" by Richard L. Tierney, "Genesis of the Cthulhu Mythos" by George Wetzel, "Lovecraft and Lord Dunsany" by Darrell Schweitzer, and "Textual Problems in Lovecraft" by S. T. Joshi.

Taylor, John. "Poe, Lovecraft, and the Monologue." *Topic* 17, No. 31 (1977): 52-62.
Examines the influence of Edgar Allan Poe on Lovecraft's fiction, particularly those stories employing the narrative form of the monologue.

Wilson, Colin. "H. P. Lovecraft." In *Science Fiction Writers: Critical Studies from the Early Nineteenth Century to the Present Day,* edited by E. F. Bleiler, pp. 131-37. New York: Charles Scribner's Sons, 1982.
Frequently disparaging survey of Lovecraft's fiction.

Paule Marshall

1929-

American short story writer and novelist.

Marshall is regarded as a prominent and innovative voice in contemporary literature. A passionate champion of the individual's search for personal identity, Marshall has been praised by critics as one of the first authors to explore the psychological trials and growth of black American women. Drawing upon her experiences as an African-American woman of Barbadian heritage and her upbringing in New York City, she embodies the cultural dichotomy that provides the major tensions in her work. Since the publication of her first novel, *Brown Girl, Brownstones,* Marshall has built both her literary reputation and her fiction around her belief that knowledge and acceptance of one's past is crucial in achieving personal integrity. Critics often refer to *Brown Girl, Brownstones* as a *bildungsroman* and have praised Marshall's continued expansion of psychological struggle and enlightenment in her first collection of short fiction, *Soul Clap Hands and Sing,* which deals with aging men who are forced to come to terms with their emotional and spiritual decline. In her other works of short fiction, particularly "The Valley Between," her first published piece, and "Reena," which were both collected in *Reena, and Other Stories,* she examines female characters' attempts to overcome sexual and racial discrimination and focuses on the difficulties women face in personal relationships. Marshall was active in the Civil Rights movements of the 1960s, and her works voice her strong commitment to her political beliefs. Although her writing deals primarily with black and feminist issues, critics note that the power and importance of Marshall's work transcends color barriers and speaks to all individuals.

Born in Brooklyn to Barbadian parents, Marshall's personal life has propelled her fiction. In several essays and interviews Marshall comments on her childhood reluctance to acknowledge her West Indian heritage and speaks of the discrimination she felt growing up during the 1930s in Brooklyn's Stuyvesant Heights. Marshall was profoundly influenced by the conversations she overheard between her mother and other women from their community. The power which these women wielded with their words, their sharp character analyses, and the poetic rhythms of their Barbadian dialect instilled in Marshall a desire to capture some of their "magic" on paper. In an interview with Alexis De Veux in *Essence* she says, "Perhaps the most important influence in my becoming a writer is due to those fantastic women, my mother and her friends, who would gather every afternoon after work—they did day's work—and talk. . . . In that kitchen I was in the presence of art of a very high order because those women, in their talk, knew what literature was all about."

In addition to listening to her mother in what she calls "the wordshop of the kitchen," Marshall spent a great deal of time at the public library, where she became interested in the works of William Thackeray, Henry Fielding, and Charles Dickens. Her subsequent discovery of a volume of Paul Laurence Dunbar's poetry filled a gap she had sensed in her reading, because the work was written in black vernacular and conveyed the images familiar to Marshall's own life. Dunbar's poetry, Marshall has said, "validated the black experience" for her, and she continued to look for other works by African-American writers, which were not being introduced to her in school. The works of Zora Neale Hurston and Gwendolyn Brooks, and especially Ralph Ellison's collection of critical essays *Shadow and Act,* were of particular importance in shaping Marshall's ideas.

After receiving her B.A. from Brooklyn College in 1953, Marshall began working as a researcher for a small magazine, *Our World.* She was the only woman on the staff and has said that she felt as if "the men were waiting for me to fall." After her promotion to staff writer, she was sent to Brazil and the Caribbean on assignments, and she later drew upon these experiences in her fiction. While working for *Our World* and attending Hunter College, Marshall began writing *Brown Girl, Brownstones.* Despite the novel's commercial failure, the critical praise it received prompted Marshall's desire to pursue a literary career.

Since then, Marshall has earned her living by writing and has often depended on the monies she received from literary grants for additional financial support. She has been the recipient of several prestigious awards, including a Guggenheim Fellowship and a National Endowment for the Arts Fellowship, and has supplemented her writing career by lecturing at universities and conferences. She has taught creative writing courses at Yale, Columbia, the University of Iowa Writer's Workshop, and the University of California at Berkley and has written several essays on her personal beliefs in addition to the critically acclaimed novels *The Chosen Place, the Timeless People,* and *Praisesong for the Widow.*

Marshall believes the literary image of the black woman has been a mythical one that represents prejudices embedded in the American psyche. In her fiction Marshall rejects what she calls the sensuous "nigger wench" and humble "mammy" images prevalent in American literature and attempts to dispel the stereotyped roles of blacks in literature. *Soul Clap Hands and Sing,* Marshall has said, marks her first work in which she "began consciously reaching for a more expressly political theme"; in it she affirms her insistent opposition to the customary subordination of female characters. The title of the work is a reference to William Butler Yeats's poem "Sailing to Byzantium," which speaks of old men as "paltry things." Though the protagonists of the four novellas are aging men, many critics note that the female characters act as the works' catalysts. They provide the impetus which urges the men toward psychological and emotional enlightenment. Brooklyn, Barbados, British Guiana, and Brazil are the four locales which provide the titles and settings for each of the novellas. In "Barbados," as in the other stories of *Soul Clap Hands and Sing,* critics note that Marshall is critical yet sympathetic to the characters who deny their personal identity in an effort to become members of the dominant culture. After working fifty years as a hospital attendant in America, the story's protagonist, Mr. Watford, returns alone to his plantation in Barbados. There he develops a strong, though masked, emotional attachment for his house girl, who represents the spirit and vitality he has lost in his pursuit of wealth and a position in the upper class. Piercing the shield of cold indifference behind which Watford has hidden a half century of emotions, the girl ultimately forces him to examine his denial of his own blackness. Watford realizes that he no longer belongs to any social group when he is confronted by the girl's lover, who wears a button that reads "the old order shall pass."

In 1983, as a signal of a resurging interest in and widespread acceptance of black feminist writing, the Feminist Press collected several of Marshall's early works in *Reena, and Other Stories.* The volume contains those works which are based on female characters and includes Marshall's personal comments on each of the stories. Though she wrote "The Valley Between" when she claims as a writer she was "just learning to crawl," the story contains a central theme of her later works. It focuses on a young woman, Cassie, who seeks personal fulfillment outside of her marriage and finds that her husband deliberately hinders her attempts. Critics note Marshall's use of white characters in this piece and suggest that it may stem from Marshall's early reluctance to confront directly the plight of the black woman. In "Reena" we see the development of a West Indian-American woman who assesses her life in terms of its contrasts with her older female relatives. Reena, whom critics often view as an autobiographical character, is a middle-aged woman who is frustrated by a society that will not acknowledge college-educated black women. During Reena's college years, she was active in left-wing political groups and became acutely aware of the injustices prevalent in America. At a wake for her Aunt Vi, the character compares her own struggles to those that her mother and aunts have encountered and finally gains a better understanding of herself and her history. She begins to accept the importance of her cultural history and decides to visit Africa with her children.

The story "To Da-duh, in Memoriam," also included in *Reena, and Other Stories,* is an autobiographical piece about a young Barbadian-American girl's visit to see her grandmother in Barbados. As in "Barbados," Marshall concentrates on the passing of old orders, and she pits the past against the present in an attempt to depict the cyclical nature of life. Da-duh, who personifies the old world culture of the island, challenges her granddaughter's brash confidence and her love for New York City by pointing out the natural wonders of Barbados. The crucial point of the story occurs when Da-duh shows her grandchild the most astonishing wonder of her home, a beautiful palm tree which seems to touch the sky. Da-duh is devastated, however, when the wonder of the palm tree is diminished by the child's description of the Empire State Building. While dealing again with the clashing of cultures, Marshall does not suggest that either is superior; instead, she aims to integrate the new world and old world perspectives. Marshall's characters then find themselves couched within the discord between past and present, and they must rely on the past as instruction for personal growth.

Also included in the collection is *Merle,* a novella based on Marshall's novel *The Chosen Place, the Timeless People.* Marshall has commented that Merle Kinbona is perhaps her most important character because she is an integration of several earlier female characters. Peter Nazareth says of Merle in his study of Marshall's novel: she is "a woman who talks compulsively but whose honesty, genuineness and historical awareness cut through what the others are saying as a scythe cutting through burnt-out grass."

From her earliest fiction, Marshall has worked faithfully and extensively on clearly defined themes. Her use of Barbadian dialect and her celebration of cultural heritage introduced new honesty and authenticity into black American fiction. Though critics often note the narrow thematic scope of Marshall's fiction, most agree that her vivid presentations of black cultures and her thorough examinations of psychological battles make her fiction a medium of universal insight.

(See also *Contemporary Literary Criticism,* Vol. 27; *Contemporary Authors,* Vols. 77-80; and *Dictionary of Literary Biography,* Vol. 33)

PRINCIPAL WORKS

SHORT FICTION

Soul Clap Hands and Sing 1961
Reena, and Other Stories 1983; also published as *Merle: A Novella, and Other Stories,* 1984

OTHER MAJOR WORKS

Brown Girl, Brownstones (novel) 1959
The Chosen Place, the Timeless People (novel) 1969
Praisesong for the Widow (novel) 1983

IHAB HASSAN (essay date 1961)

[*An Egyptian-born American critic, Hassan has written and edited numerous literary studies, including* The Dismemberment of Orpheus: Toward a Postmodern Literature *(1971, revised edition, 1982). In this review of* Soul Clap Hands and Sing, *Hassan comments on the personal struggles of the works' four male protagonists.*]

"An aged man is but a paltry thing," old Willie Yeats once sang, "A tattered coat upon a stick unless / Soul clap its hands and sing." Paule Marshall, born of Barbadian parents in Brooklyn, has chosen Yeats's bitter, impassioned phrase as the title of her second book, making it the uncommon theme of its four longish stories. The results are both striking and uneven. . . .

Though her stories do not all claim America for a setting, Paule Marshall enriches our idea of Memory by gentle, lyrical brooding on the meaning of lives that have been already spent or shaped. Her four aged protagonists can neither clap nor sing. But they have some kindlings of rage, and the bitter dignity of knowledge through defeat. In this lies the unique quality of the book.

The collection begins well, sags badly in the middle, and ends with a praiseful burst. **"Barbados"** is the story of a Negro hospital attendant who retires, after long exile in America, to his modest Barbadian plantation. He is alone, except for the doves he keeps, having fled all his life the demands of love. The meaning of that life comes to focus when the warm, unassuming servant girl he harshly ignores rejects him in his moment of need. "But his inner eye was suddenly clear. For the first time it gazed mutely upon the waste and pretense which had spanned his years. Flung there against the door by the girl's small blow, his body slowly crumpled under the weariness he had long denied. He sensed that dark but unsubstantial figure which roamed the nights searching for him wind him in its chill embrace." Setting and action here conspire to create a full metaphor of deprivation. **"Brooklyn"** repeats the same theme in undistinguished manner.

"British Guiana" attains the length of a novella. It might have better remained a story. Gerald Motely is a distinguished drunkard of mixed Chinese, Negro, and white blood. He dissipates his life in a sinecure as the director of a radio station. The one true vision of himself is somehow dispelled by the woman who loves him most, and who represents "the sane and cautious part of himself coming to save him." When many years after the same woman offers him an important job, Motley can only howl with ironic laughter. He requests that she grant the opportunity to his protégé, who represents the part of him that refuses to be deceived. Despite its lags, **["British Guiana"]** has humor and rich color; its paradoxes cauterize human illusions to heal the flesh of reality.

By far the best story is the last, **"Brazil,"** a sharp yet moving account of a famous comedian about to retire. "O Grande Caliban," as everyone knows him (his true name and his identity seem lost forever), is Rio's implacable jester. A tiny man, he seems all his life a "Lilliputian in a kingdom of giants." "The world had been scaled without him in mind—and his rage and contempt for it and for those who belonged was always just behind his smile, in the vain, superior lift of his head, in his every gesture." Caliban's frenzied effort to reclaim his identity from the posters and cheering crowds, from the stupid, spoiled, blonde Amazon who is his partner, and even from his young, pregnant wife, takes him to the center of his personality and the terrifying slums of Rio. Here all is done with tact and great power.

The example of Caliban shows that an aged man may not be entirely a paltry thing. (Indeed, the sequence of stories in the book reveals a progressive vitality in the characters.) Paule Marshall does not bring new resources of form or startling sensibility to the genre. But she allows her poetic style to be molded in each case by the facts of her fiction; she has escaped the clichés that must doubly tempt every Negro author writing today; and she has given us a vision, precise and compassionate, of solitary lives that yet participate in the rich, shifting backgrounds of cultures near and remote. Her retrospective vision is really a forecast of what we may wake up, too late, to see.

Ihab Hassan, "A Circle of Loneliness," in Saturday Review, *Vol. XLIV, No. 37, September 16, 1961, p. 30.*

HENRIETTA BUCKMASTER (essay date 1961)

[*Buckmaster has worked as an editor and has written several novels and children's books. Here, she praises Marshall's style and comments on the changing fictional role of the black character in* Soul Clap Hands and Sing.]

[In] ***Soul Clap Hands and Sing,*** [Paule Marshall] has written four short novels and has extended the theme of Person and Place into the wider range of self-recognition. This extension takes on a very subtle ambivalence because she is again dealing with Negroes. It also points to the fact that the Negro as the subject of a novel is undergoing a considerable sea-change, acquiring new fictional dimensions and associations. . . .

These people are all men and women before they are racially identified. The familiar problem of outer social pressure on the Negro has been subtly and evocatively exchanged for assimilated inner tensions. Miss Marshall is a penetrating and skillful writer who creates a world as sharp as a scream and with much of the same urgency. Perhaps, in time, more humaneness and compassion will deepen her quite remarkable gifts, and widen her perception. She uses words beautifully, and for this one is profoundly grateful.

Henrietta Buckmaster, "Inner Tensions," in The New York Times Book Review, *October 1, 1961, p. 37.*

LEELA KAPAI (essay date 1972)

[*In the following excerpt, Kapai discusses the identity crises of the characters in* Soul Clap Hands and Sing *and "Reena," and also touches upon Marshall's prose style, characterization, and depiction of personal relationships.*]

With a remarkable maturity in her work, [Paule Marshall] displays a subtle understanding of human problems and a mastery of the art of fiction. Some of the major themes in her works concern the identity crisis, the race problem, the importance of tradition for the black American, and the need for sharing to achieve meaningful relationships. In her technique she blends judiciously the best of the past tradition with the innovations of recent years. . . .

Quest for identity is a perennial theme in literature. There is no age when a sensitive soul has not been troubled by questions about the meaning of his very own existence and his relation to the world around. The identity crisis assumes even more gravity for the minority groups who were either brought to this land or who came of their own accord in search of greener pastures. Lost in a new cultural environment, such people need more than ordinary effort to recognize and keep their identity alive. However, such self-questionings are not the prerogative of only the members of a particular group based on race, sex, or age; therefore, Miss Marshall concerns herself with people of all ages, of all races, and of all strata. (p. 49)

In contrast to [*Brown Girl, Brownstones,* ***Soul Clap Hands and Sing*** deals] with old men who, approaching their end, realize that they have failed to live. In the author's own words, "They missed out on life because they refused to give themselves to any one or any thing. It was my attempt to examine the question of what happens to the human spirit when love is absent, when a man refuses to give of himself." [In a footnote the critic states that this comment, as well as others by the author, is from Marshall's personal notes.]

In both **"Barbados"** and **"Brooklyn,"** the protagonists learn the truth about themselves through two young girls. In the former, the aging farmer Watford, who returns to his home rich after fifty years of toil in Boston, keeps himself aloof, disdaining others and assuming the superiority of his masters. When at last he turns to a young woman for affection, he is spurned mercilessly. And Watford, who had always shunned love, always avoided getting involved with human emotions, realizes his folly: "his inner eye was suddenly clear. For the first time it gazed mutely upon the waste and pretense which had spanned his years." In **"Brooklyn"** Max Berman, a teacher of French literature, not only fails in his attempt to seduce a fair Negro girl and sees the futility of his life, but also enables her to see where she belongs. All her life Miss Williams had been sheltered by her parents from the white people as well as from the darker members of her race. She had thus grown up belonging to no world. Max's behavior makes her accept her blackness with pride.

The old men of the next two novellas are Gerald Motley in **"British Guiana"** and Heitor Baptista Guimares in **"Brazil."** A descendant of Hindu, Chinese, and Negro ancestors, Motley does not know who he really is. He tolerates Sidney's arrogance and contempt because he serves as a constant reminder of what he could have been. Seeing Sidney's pain he feels glad that "he is old and would never know pain again." Death is perhaps the only merciful end of his state. In **"Brazil"** Guimares, the night-club entertainer, known by his assumed name O Grand Caliban, finds himself "lost in the myth he has created." On the eve of his retirement, he realizes that his white partner has robbed him not only of his years of glory, but even deprived him of his very name. He too perhaps has no chance to retrieve his lost identity.

Thus in all the four novellas, the old men finally come to see the truth, but their time is gone. Out of the ashes of the old, a new phoenix arises, and it seems that the nameless young girl of **"Barbados"** with her politically aware boyfriend, Miss Williams of **"Brooklyn,"** Sidney Parrish of **"British Guiana,"** and the madonna-like wife of Caliban bearing his child in **"Brazil"** are the heralds of a new future. (pp. 50-2)

The search for identity of all educated black women seems to be Miss Marshall's concern in **"Reena."** Reena, obviously the writer's alter-ego, is an intelligent girl who gradually grows aware of the acute injustice of the society. After her struggle at college and two abortive affairs with young men who use her for their own ends, she faces the problem of finding a suitable mate. The educated black men are either settled or they prefer white women. Her marriage to an aspiring photographer does not last too long, for he resents Reena's success. Reena resolves to bring up her children fully aware of their own personalities and race and plans to take them to Africa to show them black men living with pride in their heritage.

Closely connected with the question of identity is the race issue. . . . In **"Brooklyn"** the life of Miss Williams is an evidence of the ambiguous identity experienced by many blacks. She succeeds, however, in accepting herself as a proud member of her race and thwarts the centuries old pattern of seduction and exploitation. Motley and Caliban in **"British Guiana"** and **"Brazil"** respectively suffer on account of the white power structure that encouraged no individualism. (pp. 53-4)

Time and again, Paule Marshall brings us to the question of human relationships. Beyond the barriers of race, all men are the same; they share the same fears, the same loneliness, and the same hopes. And they cannot live as islands; the bridges of communication have to be built. She repeatedly stresses the act of "using each other." In the complexity of human relationships we use each other in strange ways. . . .

[In **"Reena"**] Reena's boyfriend associates with her to annoy his father. But then Reena confesses with candor that she too had used him "to get at that white world which had not only denied me, but had turned my own against me." Despite these varied uses, the truth is that we need to share ourselves with others, barring which the life is a barren wasteland. (pp. 54-5)

Miss Marshall says, "My concern has always been not only with content, what is being said, but also the way it is being said, the style." This concern shows in her craftsmanship. She uses a judicious mixture of the old and the new in fictional tradition. The plots of her novels are unambiguous and interesting containing conflict and suspense to keep the reader engrossed. But she uses liberally symbolic language to heighten the meaning; thus her stories are very often capable of being taken on different levels of meaning. . . . ***Soul Clap Hands and Sing*** deals with the identity crisis of the protagonists, but it also represents the passing away of the old order and the time for the new. (p. 55)

Paule Marshall excels in her character portrayals, but one must confess that she is partial to her women. They receive more careful attention, but that too is for a certain end, for she believes that the Negro woman has been neglected in literature. "The figure which emerges even upon the most cursory examination . . . is a myth, a stereotype, a fantasy figure which has very little to do with the Negro woman in reality." Thus she does not draw the stereotype, neither "the sensual, primitive, pleasure-seeking, immoral, the siren, the sinner" nor "the Negro matriarch, strong but humble, devoted, devoutly religious, patient" [a footnote attributes the two quotations to Marshall in her 1966 article in *Freedomways;* see Additional Bibliography]. Her women are complex characters but with hidden reservoirs of strength, which they need in order to survive. (pp. 56-7)

Even though the writer does not use Joycean style of stream of consciousness technique, she frequently focusses on the subconscious mind of the characters. Combined with the editorial omniscience, her method succeeds in giving us an insight into the characters. . . . In [***Soul Clap Hands and Sing***] most of the narrative is seen through the consciousness of the protagonists. (pp. 57-8)

Like Ralph Ellison Paule Marshall believes that the "Negro American writer is also an heir of the human experience which is literature. . . ." From Eliot and Joyce she has learned the value of tradition. And then she does not forget the value of folk material. She tells us that she learned the first lessons of the narrative art from listening to her mother and her friends. After their hard day of scrubbing floors, they had to talk out their hurts and humiliations. Their acute observations about the people they worked for and their vivid portrayals filled their young listener with awe and admiration. Miss Marshall sees their gift as a part of the great oral tradition: "theirs was the palaver in the men's quarters and the stories the old women told the children seated outside the round houses." Thus they taught her that "in the African tradition art was an integral part of life and that form and content were one." She feels that the mysterious element that held her spellbound has its source in the archetypal African memory. (p. 58)

Like several other writers, [Paule Marshall] knows that the American writer cannot deny his Western heritage. She is equally proud of her black heritage but believes that her art should be devoted to showing the relationship of an individual to the other inhabitants of this world, no matter what their color, race, or geographic location is. She writes of blacks, very often of West Indians, simply because a writer writes best when he makes use of what he knows best. Her characters are, therefore, human beings first; their racial identity is secondary so far as the art is concerned. (p. 59)

Leela Kapai, "Dominant Themes and Technique in Paule Marshall's Fiction," in CLA Journal, *Vol. XVI, No. 1, September, 1972, pp. 49-59.*

LLOYD W. BROWN (essay date 1974)

[*In the following excerpt, Brown suggests that the musical and machine rhythms prevalent in "To Da-duh, in Memoriam" and* Soul Clap Hands and Sing *symbolize the individual strength of Marshall's characters, and he compares the characters in "Brazil" with those in William Shakespeare's* The Tempest.]

Apart from the usual review notices in the usual periodicals, there has been no noteworthy discussion of Paule Marshall's major works. . . . This neglect is unfortunate, because Paule Marshall's major themes are both significant and timely. Her West Indian background (Barbadian parentage) enables Paule Marshall to invest her North American materials with a Caribbean perspective, and in the process she invokes that Pan-African sensibility which has become so important in contemporary definitions of Black identity. Secondly, her treatment of the Black woman links her ethnic themes with the current feminist revolt. Finally, the ethnic and sexual themes are integrated with the novelist's interest in the subject of power. This interest is the logical outcome of her preoccupation with groups—women and Blacks—whose roles have been defined by powerlessness. But her treatment of this subject is complex and innovative because she analyses power not only as the political goal of ethnic and feminist movements, but also as social and psychological phenomena which simultaneously affect racial and sexual roles, shape cultural traditions, and mould the individual psyche.

Indeed, Paule Marshall's style invariably includes images of power-as-experience. She is a good example, in this regard, of those novelists in whom the recurrence of major themes imposes a distinctive iconography on their narrative forms. We can trace throughout her fiction rhythms of movement and sound which symbolically dramatize the dynamics of power in several forms—physical force, will power, political and sexual power, and so on. This power symbolism imparts a distinctive rhythm to her fictional forms as a whole: the narrative opens and closes with identical or similar symbols of power; or her themes present certain forms of power, such as death and the life-force, as alternating cycles in the cosmos. Paule Marshall's style therefore defines her themes. It fulfils the concept of fictional style not merely as a "mode of dramatic delimitation, but more precisely, of thematic definition."

One of her short-stories, **"To Da-duh, In Memoriam,"** is typical of her rhythmic use of symbols for "thematic definition." Briefly, this is the auto-biographical story of a young girl from Brooklyn on her first visit to her parents' family in Barbados. During the visit her spirited clashes with her grandmother, Da-duh, dramatize the conflict of two life-styles: the rural traditions of the old woman's pre-technological society versus the young Brooklynite's machine culture. After the visit Da-duh dies when the British air-force "buzzes" her village during anti-colonial riots. And years later her grown-up granddaughter keeps her memory alive: "She died and I lived, but always, to this day even, within the shadow of her death. For a brief period after I was grown I went to live alone, like one doing penance, in a loft above a noisy factory in downtown New York and there painted seas of sugarcane and huge swirling Van Gogh suns and palm trees striding like brightly plumed Watussi across a tropical landscape, while the thunderous tread of the machines downstairs jarred the floor beneath my easel, mocking my efforts."

The opening statement ("She died and I lived") presents the life-death antithesis which the subsequent rhythm symbols explore. The "swirling" suns and "striding" palm trees of her tropical landscapes evoke the rhythmic movements of dance—the rhythm of life. But this life-rhythm is counterbalanced by the thunderous "tread" of the machines. On the whole, the passage opposes the power of life to the power of death. Thus the earlier, personal conflict between the narrator and Da-duh is part of a larger confrontation between the pastoral innocence of the old woman's dying world, and the invincible power of a machine age which triumphs, in turn, through the brassy arrogance of the granddaughter, the Royal Air Force, and the machines of the New York factory. Of course there is no final end for the life-force. Its real power lies in its capacity for endless resurgence. The granddaughter's sentimental gesture as a painter may be mocked by the all-powerful machines downstairs, but the very attempt to recapture the essence of Da-duh's world is itself an assurance that the humanist principles which Da-duh embodies have replaced the narrator's earlier brassiness, and have survived, once again, to challenge the mechanical wasteland. Moreover, the opening statement of the paragraph places the life-death antithesis on a metaphysical plane. The reflection, "She died and I lived," is more than an exclamation of remorse and self-pity. It is a reminder of the universal life-death cycle—the cycle which is imitated by the alternating phases of destruction and re-creation on physical levels of experience. Consequently, the symbolic rhythms of power in the painting paragraph define the cycles of power as a universal principle. (pp. 159-60)

Two features of [the title ***Soul Clap Hands and Sing***] are immediately significant. First, it is a musical symbol taken from Yeat's "Sailing to Byzantium." Second, the original Yeats passage, quoted in Paule Marshall's foreword, affirms the transcendental power of the human will:

> An aged man is but a paltry thing,
> A tattered coat upon a stick, unless
> Soul clap its hands and sing . . .

This affirmation is the thematic starting-point in the four novellas of [the work]. In each story the hero's age and/or imminent death creates an urgent need for that assertion of spiritual strength and purposefulness which alone can transcend the decay or loss of physical prowess, but which eventually eludes him. In each case the image of desired will-power and the power of imminent death are juxtaposed in a context which is dominated by the rhythm symbols of the title and the narrative. Moreover, the musical force of the main title is complemented by the alliterative rhythm of all four subtitles, **"Barbados," "Brooklyn," "British Guiana,"** and **"Brazil."** [In a footnote the critic states: "This rhythmic cadence seems to be important in most of Paule Marshall's titles: for example, 'Brown Girl/Brownstones,' or 'The Chosen Place/ The Timeless People.' "]

In the first story, **"Barbados,"** old Mr. Watford returns to Barbados after years of residence in the United States. The crisis of the story arises from his realization that his mechanistic sense of purpose lacks that vital awareness which could enable him to cope with old age and death. As in *Brown Girl, Brownstones,* this kind of vitalism is celebrated by the calypso rhythms and the life-force they symbolize. When his maid and her lover dance to the steel bands, their bodies "claimed the night. . . . The trees were their frivolous companions, swaying as they swayed. The moon rode the sky because of them." On the other hand, Mr. Watford is the machine-man, an "American" expert on socio-economic power, whose stiff posture contrasts with the rhythmic sounds and movements around him. His sexual desire for his maid violates, instead of fulfils, the vital principle of the calypso, because his interest in her is simply a lecherous extension of power as selfish domination. Love, the vitalizing agent in a creative purposefulness, is missing because he is a machine-man without a soul: "If he could have borne the thought, he would have confessed that it had been love, terrible in its demand, which he had always fled."

In **"Brooklyn"** the narrative is introduced by the rhythmic soaring and dying of the summer wind outside Max Berman's literature class in a Brooklyn college. The rhythm of the wind's movements suggests the continuous cycle of life and death, and in turn, the cycle dominates the conflict between Berman and Miss Williams, one of his Black students. The conflicts are centered on the contrast between his age (and its attendant sexual insecurity) and her youth, between his lifelong lack of will, and her strength of purpose. His clumsy attempt to seduce her is linked with his external advantages of power—the sexual prerogatives of the male, the racial mystique of being White, and his status as her instructor. But in rebuffing him and in exposing the real purposelessness behind his cynical mask, she asserts her actual superiority. Like the maid in **"Barbados,"** she affirms the life-principle of human purpose in contrast to his death-like role as a "paltry thing." And her ascendancy implies the yielding of death to vitality in the universal cycle symbolized by the rhythm of the summer wind.

The third story, **"British Guiana,"** opens with the rhythmic movements of children at play—stick figures draped in dun-colored rags . . . flapping like wings." The image is obviously derived from the coat-and-stick metaphor with which Yeats describes purposeless old age. But it is applied ironically to the young children because it is more appropriate to the physical and moral emptiness of their sole spectator, Gerald Motley. He is eventually forced to face this emptiness when a former girl friend Sybil (whose powerful will contrasts with his lack of purpose) offers him an important job. He refuses the offer because of "the terrifying awareness of his deficiencies." Significantly, once he achieves this awareness, he dies in a traffic accident. The manner of his death, destruction by the machine-mass, points up the pervasive power of the machine force, which can even substitute for the moral purpose lacking in Motley and his society. And, by extension, this triumph of machine-force over "paltry" spirit links Motley's Caribbean milieu with Western culture as a whole. The latter is represented by the fatal automobile, and by that pre-eminent symbol of technological self-destruction—the nuclear bomb: in a typical heat wave the sun transforms the capital, Georgetown, into "another Hiroshima at the moment of bombing." The bomb and the automobile are power symbols of the cultural malaise embodied by Motley. Hence Motley's failure implies the affirmation of all those human values which are lacking in his person and his culture.

In **"Brazil"** we return to the kind of musical symbol which dominates the first novella. The two main characters, Caliban and Miranda, literally burst upon the stage to the sound of music in their night-club act:

> Three trumpets, two saxophones, a single trombone; a piano, drums and a bass fiddle. Together in the dimness of the night club they shaped an edifice of sound glittering with notes and swaying to the buffeting of the drums the way a tall building sways imperceptibly to the wind, when suddenly, one of the trumpets sent the edifice toppling with a high, whinnying chord that seemed to reach beyond sound into silence. It was a signal and the other instruments quickly followed, the drums exploding into the erotic beat of a samba, the bass becoming a loud pulse beneath the shrieking horns—and in the midst of the hysteria, a voice announced . . . "The Great Caliban and the Tiny Miranda!"

The music is a series of rhythmic conflicts, and the two performers act out a series of antagonisms. In ethnic terms, Caliban is the Shakespearean image of the non-White savage, the antithesis of Miranda's "civilized" virtues in *The Tempest.* On a sexual level, their night-club routine reenacts the male's need to be dominant. And underlying all this is the assumed mystique of power as brute strength, "masculinity" as physical force. But all these power conflicts are controlled by the irony of the introductory titles—the "great" Caliban is actually "diminutive" and the "tiny" Miranda is really that sexual stereotype, the "statuesque" or "big-bodied" blond. Their act, in which Caliban dominates her, is like their introductory titles in that it inversely parodies their actual physical sizes and the socio-sexual relationship it purports to convey. Thus the Black Caliban's actual stature emphasizes the real powerlessness of the non-White. His diminutive male figure suggests that real insecurity which inspires the male need to dominate. And conversely, Miranda's "powerful animal presence" projects the male's fearful image of women as objects to be dominated and possessed. Finally, when Miranda scoops up Caliban with one hand in the finale and carries him off-stage, she dramatizes the degree to which subordination creates power-hunger in women—*her* need to dominate.

These stage roles are complemented by their personal lives. Now that he is old and about to retire from the stage, Caliban is searching for that sense of purpose which eludes all the old men in ***Soul Clap Hands and Sing.*** His search is centered on his attempts to reestablish his real identity as Heitor Guimares. But Miranda refuses, indeed she is unable, to recognize him as any other than the Great Caliban. In effect, Caliban discovers that they have both been permanently trapped into the socio-sexual roles which dominate their culture and which they reenact on-stage. His small size and sexual insecurity demand that he maintain his domination of the woman. On her side, the refusal to recognize him as Heitor Guimares assures her some measure of control: without the recognition and acceptance by persons like herself Guimares can never return to existence. Miranda's tactics represent the instinct to compensate for basic powerlessness in society by manipulating the insecurities of "superiors." And on an ethnic basis, Caliban has been imprisoned in the role of the Black stud who challenges the White world by flaunting his supersexuality. Consequently, when Caliban reacts to Miranda's tactics by wrecking her apartment he is recognizing his permanent imprisonment in empty roles. As for Miranda, her hysterical reaction to his violence concludes the story on an ironic note, for her cries echo the sounds of the powerful trumpet in the opening paragraph: "Her outcry was the sound of the trumpet the night before, a high, whinnying note that reached beyond all sound into a kind of silence." [In a footnote the critic suggests: "The symbolic structure of **'Brazil'** is a microcosm of the structural rhythms of ***Soul Clap Hands and Sing*** as a whole. Hence the novella opens and closes with musical symbols—just as the quartet as a whole opens and closes with stories (**'Barbados'** and **'Brazil'** respectively) that are dominated by music symbolism."] The trumpet metaphor invests Miranda's outburst with the rhythms of power—the narrow and destructive selfishness which women like herself use to compensate for their basic powerlessness. Her limited triumph confirms the aging Caliban as a "paltry thing" rather than as a purposeful and fully human Guimares. And in the process she fulfils the symbolic implications of the night-club finale—she has scooped up his identity and carried it off-stage. But she can only do this at the cost of her own human identity, at the cost of maintaining the socio-sexual status quo in which the insecure male must be manipulated by those below him while being left to occupy positions of subhuman power. Miranda's failure to achieve the substantial powers of human identity is emphasized by the fact that we never know her real name. She remains Miranda to the end, in order to perpetuate the Caliban tradition. (pp. 162-65)

Lloyd W. Brown, "The Rhythms of Power in Paule Marshall's Fiction," in Novel: A Forum on Fiction, *Vol. 7, No. 2, Winter, 1974, pp. 159-67.*

MARCIA KEIZS (essay date 1975)

[*In the excerpt below, Keizs comments on the themes of Marshall's early short stories.*]

Mrs. Marshall's four short stories complement her novels; two of the stories focus on women, another deals with a Brooklyn-ghetto gang, and the fourth gives an account of the cross-generational ties which exist between families.

"The Valley Between," Mrs. Marshall's first published work (1953), presents a young woman who comes to the realization that she would like to fulfill herself not only as a wife and a mother but also as an individual with special feelings of self which need to be nurtured. [In a footnote the critic states: "this story is peopled by white rather than Black characters. Perhaps Mrs. Marshall later felt that the Black artist cannot be released from the task of writing about Black life."] The strong/weak dichotomy pursued elsewhere in Mrs. Marshall's work is present here. The wife feels quite overpowered by her situation and by her husband's view of their relationship. She wants to pursue her studies; he sees that desire as irrelevant. The matter comes to a head when their daughter, having been out in the rain, becomes ill. This incident, occurring as it does while the mother is at school, gives the husband an opportunity to aggravate her feelings of guilt. Finally Ellen acknowledges that the strong, although wrong, always win.

In her second story, **"Reena,"** written eleven years later (1964), Mrs. Marshall looks at the middle class Black woman, who has, as it were, educated herself out of a man. The story focuses on the reunion of two women who were childhood friends and who in their adult life have become fairly successful. The importance of their reunion is that it displays a certain recognition of their success in spite of all the obstacles as well as a recognition of their failure at establishing a good relationship with men. Although the women are not bitter, they do display some cynicism about the reasons Black men give for rejecting them, as is suggested by their litany-like recitation of those reasons. Though this story is very much a "woman's" story, it is different from the first short story on the same subject, because it ultimately suggests a quiet acceptance of the reality of their particular situation.

The story **"Some Get Wasted,"** Mrs. Marshall's only work to deal exclusively with the social milieu of the Black ghetto, appears in an anthology edited by her friend and associate, John Henrik Clarke, an associate editor of *Freedomways.* The story describes Brooklyn teenage gangs whose members display their power by "busting heads and wasting cats," a policy they have no doubt adopted as a result of their interaction with a larger society. And some "cats" do get wasted, including Hezzy, the leader of the gang's "Little People." Mrs. Marshall seems to be saying that the almost inevitable waste gang-life brings on is symbolic of the waste, both of mind and body, occurring all the time in ghetto communities.

The fourth short story published by Mrs. Marshall [**"To Daduh, In Memoriam"**], autobiographical in that it describes the indelible impact of a visit with her maternal grandmother on the island of Barbados, deals with those spiritual ties which, in spite of time and space, link one generation to the next. This connection is initially observed when the young girl, seeing her grandmother for the first time, concludes that she is "both child and woman, darkness and light, past and present, life and death—all the opposites contained and reconciled in her."

The two spend time together, exchanging influences: the grandmother shares with the young girl the information about the land the old woman knows so well; the young girl amazes "Da-duh" with her Tin-Pan Alley songs, her New York dances, and her stories about the strange city from which she hails and about "beating up white people." Da-duh, fascinated by her grandchild, demands to be sent a picture of the Empire State Building. The wish, however, is never to be fulfilled, for Da-duh, stubbornly refusing to seek shelter in the caves, dies in an air raid before the postcard reaches her. It is as though Da-duh knows that the new world holds nothing for her—of another time, she is unable to deal with the "newness" her granddaughter attempts to bring to her. Faced with the possibility of death or change, she chooses the former. Though dead, Da-duh lives on in the life of her grandchild; her influence thus continues.

> She died and I lived, but always, to this day, even, within the shadow of her death. For a brief period after I was grown I went to live alone like one doing penance, in a loft above a noisy factory in downtown New York and there painted seas of sugarcane and huge swirling Van Gogh suns and palm trees striding like brightly-plumed Watusi across a tropical landscape, while the thunderous tread of the machines downstairs jarred the floor beneath my easel, mocking my effort.

Mrs. Marshall's style, as worthy of comment and praise as are her themes, is remarkable for its crispness, lucidity, and grace. (p. 75)

Marcia Keizs, "Themes and Style in the Works of Paule Marshall," in Negro American Literature Forum, *Vol. 9, No. 3, Fall, 1975, pp. 67, 71-6.*

L. LEE TALBERT (essay date 1978)

[*In the following excerpt, Talbert examines Marshall's manipulation of time to depict the cyclical nature of life in* Soul Clap Hands and Sing. *He also points out thematic references to the works of André Gide and draws comparisons between Marshall's characters and classical and Shakespearean figures.*]

As a Caribbean woman born in Barbados and now living and writing in the United States, Paule Marshall is convinced that the forces of colonialism have deprived both the oppressed and the oppressor of a sense of identity and purpose. In ***Soul Clap Hands and Sing***, she contends that sustenance for the future can and must come from acknowledgment of the past. In this early work Marshall's fictive techniques rely greatly on allusions to Western literary traditions to evoke a sense of the past. . . . She emphasizes death and the life-force as alternating cycles in the cosmos, believing that the human capacity for destruction and the equally awesome determination to survive are one and the same cycle. Consequently, Marshall unfolds events on a human, historical, and cultural continuum which, in turn, evokes a time past in time present. She draws upon Western classical myth and literary archetypes—images of Cassandra and Sibyl, references to the works of Gide, and the Shakespearean figures Miranda and Caliban—as media for a sense of fate and destiny that is tinged with tragedy. Her manipulation of time is reminiscent of Yeats' cataclysmic spiraling time, alluded to in the lines of "The Second Coming." Hence, the structural circularity of her fiction defines a thematic concern with the cyclic character of nature, history, and time. Finally, Paule Marshall's epochal consciousness is embodied in her vision of the birth of a New World ethic founded on a comprehended past which then becomes the key to the future.

Marshall recreates the cosmic rhythms of the universe in ***Soul Clap Hands and Sing*** by manipulating a musical symbol taken from Yeats' "Sailing to Byzantium." The rhythmic cadence established by all four subtitles in the quartet of novellas, **"Barbados," "Brooklyn," "British Guiana,"** and **"Brazil,"** facilitates Marshall's depiction of the vitality of life. However, this vitality is juxtaposed within the novellas with the human dilemma of aging and imminent death. Thus, the original Yeats passage, quoted by Marshall in the foreword, reveals the transcendental power of the human will which must be asserted to overcome this contradiction:

> An aged man is but a paltry thing,
> A tattered coat upon a stick, unless
> Soul clap its hands and sing . . .

The crisis in each story arises precisely because each of the aging male protagonists is a "paltry thing," having led a life devoid of purpose. Subsequently, while lacking a personal sense of identity, each man sees himself reflected in memories of the past, in the surrounding environment, and in the eyes of others. More specifically, each seeks that spiritual assertion of will which is seen embodied in the ambiguous female figures who symbolize a sense of purposefulness and a celebration of life as well as functioning as prophets of a tragic sense of fate. Parasitic attempts to affirm themselves vicariously through these women are negated for each man has failed. Finally, the musical symbols of the title and the narrative recreate the cosmic rhythms established by the alternating cycles of death and the life-force.

"Barbados" begins with an emphasis on the cyclic nature of time, where "Dawn, like the night which had preceded it, came from the sea." Here, the sea as a symbol of timelessness is in opposition to the protagonist, old Mr. Watford, and his preoccupation with time and with his own physical dissipation. Having returned to Barbados after years of residence in the United States, Watford undergoes a crisis which springs from the realization that his adoption of mechanistic values has deprived him of the ability to cope with old age and death. Fearing the loneliness of the darkness, he lives "closeted" from "the night sounds of the village" which produce "a joyous chorale against the sea's muffled cadence and the hollow, haunting music of the steel band." Indeed, his mechanistic stance, made evident by his stiff posture and rigidly structured days, contradicts the vitalism symbolized in the celebrated rhythms of the calypso. Mr. Watford's characterlessness is most clearly defined in contrast to those Barbadian characters whose lives complement the rhythmic sounds and movements of island life.

Watford's recognition of his own sterility comes through contact with three islanders who actively participate in celebrating life: a boy, a mature man and a young woman. More specifically, the delivery boy becomes a reflection of his present indifference, and the maid becomes an ironic prophecy of his future demise. It is through the young man, whose "natural arrogance" shines "like a pinpoint of light within his dark stare," that Watford is reminded of his own past. The boy's deference to Watford rekindles memories of his own youth and that fear of whites that subsequently turned to hatred of his own kind and of himself. The youth's physical strength, a prowess which the old man has lost, is further accentuated by the political button he proudly wears, symbolizing an affirmation of himself and his people which Watford lacks. Mr. Goodman, a swarthy and virile man who embraces life, is even more indicative of all that Watford is not. Goodman's plea for a commitment to the people of Barbados contrasts with Watford's own detachment and false air of superiority. Consequently, both men, as reflections of his past and present, reveal Watford's contempt for his race and expose the sterility of his existence as a mechanistic man.

The young maid who comes to work for Mr. Watford embodies Marshall's concept of the cyclic character of history, nature, and time. Moreover, for the old man, she becomes a symbolic image of the past, present, and future. Appearing to Watford as "of the sun, of the earth," she stands with "bare feet like strong dark roots amid the jagged stones." The young woman is the personification of nature and the embodiment of the life-generating principle. While he is awed by her beauty, she nevertheless reminds him of the "senseless and insignificant" history of his people. Her very posture ushers him back to memories of his own mother and so she becomes also a representation of the heritage he shuns. The girl's loneliness mirrors his loneliness, and Watford's inability to offer her friendship merely accentuates an awareness of himself as a "paltry thing" unable to feel or to give. Watford's attempt to "wrest from her the strength needed to sustain him" proves vain, for his sexual desire is merely an extension of power as selfish dominance. His lust violates the vital principle embodied in the calypso. In contrast, inspired by love as a form of creative purposefulness, the bodies of the maid and the delivery boy "claimed the night . . . the trees were their frivolous companions, swaying as they swayed. The moon rode the sky because of them." Indeed, it is through this sexual initiation that the girl learns of the creative power of love that will "steady and protect her." As a parallel to the alternating forces of life and death, it is precisely the moment when she becomes conscious of her identity as a woman that Watford is stripped of all pretense, forced to admit "that it had been love, terrible in its demand, which he had always fled." As the night ushers in her affirmation and celebration of life, she becomes "Cassandra" foretelling Mr. Watford's negation by this same darkness. The maid, as a Cassandra figure, is also a reminder of imminent death and the ironic futility of life. Watford, like Cassandra's original Trojan audience, is incapable of apprehending the truths of the prophecy or of accepting them in a way which would assure a measure of salvation. And, like the original Cassandra, Marshall's female prophet is also weakened by her own loneliness and vulnerability. This, in turn, dilutes her credibility, especially for an audience predisposed to disbelief. However, on another level of interpretation, the lovers remain nameless individuals, and so they may be considered as representations of the Barbadian people and, in turn, emblematic of the possible birth of a New World ethos. Consequently, as Paule Marshall completes the story's structural circularity, her thematic concern with the cyclic pattern of history, nature, and time is complemented by the dual images of disintegration and rebirth.

In **"Brooklyn,"** the aging literature instructor Max Berman, like Watford, lives withdrawn, refraining even from opening his classroom window to the summer winds. The soaring and dying of that wind is representative of the continuous cycles of life and death. This cycle dominates the conflict between Berman and one of his Black students, Miss Williams. Indicating the dynamics of this conflict, Marshall asserts that "the season was stirring into life even as it died" and this was the contradiction of his "desires which remained those of a young man even as he was dying." Further, this crisis is heightened by the realization of his futile existence, having led a life permeated by false cynicism, indifference, and flight from responsibility. Just as Watford turns to his maid in an effort to acquire a sense of purpose, so Berman perceives that "only the girl could bring him close enough to touch life."

Through Miss Williams, Marshall again develops her epochal conception of history, nature, and time. It is Miss Williams' own dilemma, based on fear of racial inferiority, that first mirrors Berman's vulnerability and her acquired sense of purpose that then exposes his inadequacy. Miss Williams' loneliness forces Berman to remember his own bigotry and guilt. Detecting this woman's vitality, he senses that her laugh "joined her, it seemed, to the wood and wide fields, to the hills; she shared their simplicity and held within her the same strong current of life." Like the maid, Miss Williams is associated with the life-giving principle of nature. Yet, his erotic desire for her violates this creativity because it is merely a lecherous extension of sexual domination. These conflicts are most vividly depicted in her interest in and discussion of Gide's *The Immoralist.* Unconsciously alluding to the cycle of life and death, she concludes that "Perhaps in order for a person to live and know himself somebody else must die." As Gide's Michel discovers vitality in the Arab boys and is homosexually attracted to their exoticism, so Berman finds Miss Williams' blackness foreign and erotic. However, the racial mystique of whiteness and his external advantage of power delude him into equating her vulnerability with what he perceives as the inherent passivity of Gide's heroine. Yet, Miss Williams transcends Berman's limited vision of her and attains lucidity and a new sense of freedom through acceptance of her ethnic self-worth. It is precisely because Berman is an immoralist, sexually, intellectually, and spiritually, that her exposure of his purposelessness becomes an affirmation of her strength of will. Finally, her superiority is equated with the universal cycle of life represented by the summer wind. In contrast, his indifference condemns him to an inevitable death, a death equated with the darkness of the "immense night." Consequently, Marshall structurally and thematically brings the story full circle with the psychic death of Max Berman and the spiritual rebirth of Miss Williams.

The third story, **"British Guiana,"** begins with an image obviously derived from Yeats' coat-and-stick metaphor which describes the physical decay and purposelessness of old age. However, the representation is applied to the youthful movements of children at play, "stick figures draped in dun-colored rags . . . flapping like wings." The application is ironic because the metaphor more aptly relates to the physical decay and moral emptiness of Gerald Motley, the aging protagonist. Moreover, this image is contradicted by his own sense of aging and is compounded by the vigor of the children, whose cries "urge him toward life again." Consequently, this encounter triggers his attempt to come to grips with his own sense of identity.

The universal cycle of life and death is depicted in the character of Gerald Motley and his confused perception of himself. Through his person the history of British Guiana, the machine-force of Western culture, and the natural cycle of decay and regeneration merge. Nicknaming himself B.S.W.C., "Bastard Spawned of the World's Commingling," his dilemma is defined by "this sense of being many things and yet none." Consequently, this confusion leads him to search for an identity mirrored in the eyes which offer him the lie he looks for. Seeking refuge in alcohol, Motley spends much time evading his own lack of purpose in a local bar. Here, the old Hindu waiter Singh, "charged with life," possesses a timeless mystique that reflects "the small part of Gerald Motley which would remain ageless." Confirming his emptiness, the secretary, Miss Davis, mirrors that aspect of his character which is "only certain of being alive in the midst of the dead." The eyes of the other "colored" professional men offer him "the image of his public self." Old Ling, whose glass eye projects an image of his death, is that private part of himself "which had gazed upon the darkness within and found it pleasing." Finally, he maintains a friendship with a contemptuous youth, Sidney, because "the boy became the part of him which refused to spare him the truth." Subsequently, Motley seeks to combat his own fragmentation and attain a sense of wholeness by constructing an image of himself that is a composite of all the racial and colonial forces that have given shape to British Guiana.

Motley's crisis is further compounded by the return of Sybil, a former girl friend, who ambiguously symbolizes the affirmative power of will. Returning to memories of the past, he can "only remember the quality of her loneliness" which "had been his loneliness and the loneliness of the land." She understands "that what he had sought all along had been the reflection of himself in each feature of the land." Consequently, Sybil acts as "the sane and cautious part of himself coming to save him." Indeed, she had prevented his destruction in the bush as a young man and now she comes again, in his later years, to offer him an important job. The duality of Marshall's female characters is emphasized, for it is through Sybil that Motley acquires "the terrifying awareness of his deficiencies." Like her classical namesake, she is prophetic and hard, but in addition she has become suspect by her adoption of Western materialistic values. His rejection of her and his own confusion over his homosexual relationship with Sidney force a recognition that he is neuter. Here the images of Sybil and Sidney merge, and Motley is cognizant that his salvation and his destruction are equivalents.

The death of Motley in an automobile accident points to the pervasive power of the mechanistic values of the Western world, adopted in British Guiana, which can substitute for moral purposefulness. Because his young friend will be offered the job, the consequences of Motley's death become ambiguous. His death either entails the pre-eminent promise of Sidney's rebirth or a foreshadowing of Sidney's reenactment of Motley's failure. In any event, Motley's death certainly becomes an affirmation of all those human values which are lacking in his person and in his Westernized culture. Therefore, as Marshall completes the story, the predominant theme of the cosmic cycle of life and death is echoed.

Functioning as a microcosm of the quartet's structural circularity, **"Brazil"** opens and closes with the same type of musical symbolism which dominates the first novella, **"Barbados."** Caliban and Miranda, the two main characters, burst upon the stage to the sound of music in their night club act entitled "The Great Caliban and the Tiny Miranda." Through the antagonistic rhythms of the music, the two performers act out a series of sexual and ethnic conflicts. Marshall draws upon the Shakespearean image of Caliban as the non-white "savage" who is contrasted to the "civilized" virtues of Miranda as depicted in *The Tempest.* This ethnic definition is reinforced, on the sexual level, as Caliban characterizes the stereotypical Black male who flaunts his supersexuality by domination of the white woman. By the same token, Miranda is the sexual stereotype of the "statuesque" blonde, exuding a "powerful animal presence." However, these stereotypes are shattered by the irony of the title of their act "The Great Caliban and the Tiny Miranda." The great Caliban is actually diminutive, while the tiny Miranda is big-bodied. These inverted labels parody their physical sizes and undermine the socio-sexual relationships purportedly conveyed. Caliban's stature represents the true extent of non-white powerlessness, while Miranda's stature and strength represent the woman's need for power fostered by an innate sense of powerlessness. Finally, the dissonance created by the music parallels the hysteria perpetuated by the destructive forces of ethnic and sexual role playing.

The role playing enacted on the stage is reflected in their personal lives. Preparing to retire and, subsequently, forfeiting the image Miranda has created for him, Caliban attempts to discover a sense of purpose. This quest entails an effort to re-establish his original identity as Heitor Guimares—an identity grounded in his rural past. His crisis is heightened by the recognition that "He had been Everyman, so much so that it had become difficult over his thirty-five years in show business . . . to tell where O Grande Caliban ended and he, Heitor Babtista Guimares, began." In order to discover his identity and affirm himself, Caliban looks back to his past, to the two women now in his life, and to the city of Rio.

Caliban, like the other male protagonists in Marshall's book, turns to female figures to discover his identity and recover a lost sense of purpose. His youthful wife Clara, a girl from his childhood village, is the passive and submissive female image. Indeed, Caliban perceives her as the Black Madonna and the purity of her rural origins leads him to hope "that she would bring, like a dowry, the stories and memories of him as a young man." Though a counterpart of his identity as Heitor and a direct link to his past, Clara is unable to perceive him as anyone other than the famous Caliban. While his wife is the antithesis of all that is urban and Western, Miranda "is like Rio." She, like the city's inhabitants and tourists, creates the Caliban image for her manipulation and entertainment, to be discarded and replaced when no longer useful. The black and white decor of her apartment which he had financed and which "denied him all significance," parallels the extent to which both Miranda and Caliban are the products of Rio and the city's perpetuation of Western values. Both Miranda and the cultural milieu which constitutes Rio are as indifferent to his success as they are indifferent to the poverty-ridden *favelas* as a symbol of his past. Her denial of his real identity as Heitor Guimares, an example of the destructive selfishness of women who manipulate men in order to compensate for basic powerlessness, traps them both into the sterile roles they reenact on stage. On the ethnic level, Caliban is reduced to acting out his stereotypical role of the Black stud, while, on the sexual level, his wrecking of her apartment is a symbolic representation of brute strength as masculinity. The story ends on an ironic note, for Miranda's reaction to his violence echoes the trumpet blast in the opening paragraph: "Her outcry was the sound of the trumpet the night before, a high, whinnying note that reached beyond all sound into a kind of silence." The silence here is indicative of the wasteland of Rio which perpetuates the Caliban tradition divesting both Miranda and Caliban of true purposefulness and human identity. Out of the old myths, it is the Madonna-like wife of Caliban, bearing his child, who is the herald of a new future. However, her passivity, her reluctance to leave the city, and her inability to grasp her husband's fundamental identity limit her role as a creative force in transforming destructive Western values into a New World ethic.

Soul Clap Hands and Sing introduces the continuous and characteristic themes that define the very nature of Marshall's fictive art. The forces of the death-life cycle are linked with the cyclic nature of time, where the past becomes a key to the future and the present is the culmination of the past. To achieve this sense of timelessness, Marshall blends a vivid and powerful natural setting with events in the narrative. Reactions to the environment, in turn, parallel the conflicts of each character, revealing an ability or inability to transcend the destructive forces of history and time. Hence the Cassandra and Sibyl figures, the Gide references, and the Shakespearean archetypes all evidence the multiple sources upon which Marshall draws for her themes. (pp. 49-56)

L. Lee Talbert, "The Poetics of Prophecy in Paule Marshall's 'Soul Clap Hands and Sing'," in MELUS, *Vol. 5, No. 1, Spring, 1978, pp. 49-56.*

JOHN COOK (essay date 1980)

[In the following excerpt, Cook comments on the shaping influence of Ralph Ellison's Shadow and Act *on Marshall's fiction and analyzes the changing political perspectives in her works.]*

While Marshall has been widely recognized as a politically committed writer, what has not been is the most striking aspect of her political perspective: the radical change during her career of the cultural terms which have given it shape. In fact, so marked is this change that speaking in terms of one perspective is misleading; rather, Marshall's work is characterized by the search for a political perspective. The shape of this search is reflected by the change in the cultural contrasts on which her successive works have been based: immigrant vs. American in *Brown Girl, Brownstones;* white vs. Afro-Caribbean in ***Soul Clap Hands and Sing;*** and, finally, Western vs. Pan-African in *The Chosen Place, The Timeless People.* The first two works can best be seen as experiments through which Marshall searches for a cultural opposition which could yield an unambiguous political perspective. Only in the last work does she define a cultural base (and posit a clear adversary culture) from which a definite perspective emerges. (pp. 1-2)

Marshall has stressed the conflicting impulses manifested toward cultural identity by her mother and the other Bajan women of her community. Even while striving to become a part of American life, their discussions were most often, as Marshall has discussed at length, of "home: the people, places and events that had been so much part of their former lives." [This and the other quotations by Marshall in this excerpt are from her article in *Freedomways;* see Additional Bibliography.] Not only *Brown Girl, Brownstones* but such shorter pieces as **"To Da-duh: In Memoriam,"** which recounts a visit "home," reveal this tension to be a major concern in Marshall's early fiction.

Marshall faced a temperamental difficulty as well as developing a political perspective: her predilection for personal as opposed to political subjects. Her essentially nonpolitical nature is indicated, in brief, by her affinity for the writings of Ralph Ellison, the preeminent black spokesman for the supremacy of the individual creative imagination to all other writing masters, particularly political design or radical solidarity. Marshall has called *Shadow and Act* "the single most important piece of writing in my life," and she draws on Ellison repeatedly in her nonfiction. Ellison figures in her writing even when Marshall advocates a culturally militant position, as in her statement on the black writer's responsibility to further the understanding of black culture:

> His is the greater part in establishing the cultural base. And his task is two-fold: on the one hand to make use of the rich body of folk and historical material that is there, and on the other to interpret that past in heroic terms, in recognition of the fact that our history, as Ellison described it, is "one of the great triumphs of the human spirit in modern times. Indeed, in the history of the world."

To be sure, Marshall's later art is given shape by her desire to interpret this cultural base. Yet even when this specific political aim is paramount, she still approaches her material, as was more obviously evident in her early works, in essentially private terms. She accomplishes her political aim not so much through writing about politicians intriguing or cane workers revolting but, as Ellison has, through using the experience of her characters as metaphors for cultural and political trends.

The major problem Marshall encountered, however, was in fashioning works in which her major private subject, sexual conflict, was effectively integrated with a political perspective. . . . In the four portraits of world-weary men in conflict with Afro-Caribbean women that made up ***Soul Clap Hands and Sing,*** the sexual and political themes are merged in only two of the stories, **"Brooklyn"** and **"Barbados,"** in which the young women represent a newly assertive black order. (pp. 2-3)

Unlike [*Brown Girl, Brownstones*], the collection ***Soul Clap Hands and Sing***—four stories set in Barbados, Brooklyn, British Guiana and Brazil—shows an understanding of what Marshall has called "that combined cultural heritage which was at once Afro-American, Afro-Caribbean, and to a much lesser degree, American, that was mine." The qualified position of America is indicative of Marshall's increased understanding of the heritage she wanted to claim; consequently, the distinctions she makes between cultures are sharper and what can be learned through inter-cultural contact more clearly expressed than in the earlier work. In contrast to the uncertain state in which Selina [of *Brown Girl, Brownstones*] ends, two of those involved in these intercultural conflicts—the Bajan girl **"Barbados"** confronting a captain of colonialism and the black American girl coping with a Jewish professor in **"Brooklyn"**—reach a new awareness: that they must reject the dominant culture and affirm a black one if they are to be free.

Moreover, in these, the two most accomplished pieces in the collection, Marshall effectively merges her sexual and political themes to indicate the full commitment, both private and public, needed to establish a vital cultural identity. In **"Barbados,"** for example, the old Bajan, who has retired after fifty years of work in America, initially attempts to drive away a job-seeking girl from his house. When she does not heed his rejection, become intimidated by "the cold edge of his slight American accent," or finally accept his bribe, his impotence both as a man and as the representative of American culture is revealed, for "His shoulders sagged suddenly under the weight of her ignorance, and with a futile gesture he swung away, the dollar hanging from his hand like a small sword gone limp." Similarly, the girl's fashioning of a mature identity is a product of both a new sexual and a new political awareness. When the old man finds her after a tryst with an island youth, "Her dress was twisted around her body—and pinned to the bodice, so that it gathered the cloth between her small breasts, was the political button the boy always wore."

These pieces are the most resonant when they provide a sense of the historical forces molding the characters. Such a sense is evident, for instance, in **"Brooklyn."** When Professor Berman makes advances to his black student, it seems from her response that

> The outrage of a lifetime, of her history, was trapped inside her. And she stared at Max Berman with this mute, paralyzing rage. Not really at him but to his side, as if she caught sight of others behind him. And remembering how he had imaged a column of dark women trailing her to his desk, he sensed that she glimpsed a legion of old men with sere flesh and lonely eyes flanking him.

By confronting him the girl unburdens herself of her legacy, this outrage; not just Professor Berman but the legions like him are felt to be its object.

The past is not simply a burden of grief to be exorcized, for it is by bringing to bear strengths which seem an historical bequest that these women challenge the dominant order. This sense is conveyed most precisely in **"Reena,"** a story from the same period. "We are," Reena states, "most of us, the black woman who had to be almost frighteningly strong in order for us all to survive. . . . And we are still, so many of us, living that history." While it was not finally clear in *Brown Girl, Brownstones* whether the assertive Silla was domineering or acting in a traditional way to insure the family's survival, it is emphasized in these stories that the women are acting out of historical imperatives, that these imperatives are healthy, and that they are finally having an effect.

In **"Barbados"** and **"Brooklyn"** Marshall begins to confront the most persistent problem plaguing the West Indian writer, what Edward Braithwaite has described as "the obsessive theme" of "lack of identity" in Caribbean society. In ***Soul Clap Hands and Sing*** this problem is only raised, since there is a challenge of the old order but no indication of what will form the basis of a new one. Marshall found this basis in the events of the African past, the diaspora, and the common experience of enslavement, all of which are strongly evoked in *The Chosen Place, The Timeless People.* (pp. 9-11)

Marshall's first clear interest in Africa was evidenced in 1962 when at the close of **"Reena,"** the title figure expresses a need to visit Africa, to get in touch with "black people who have truly a place in history of their own and who are building for a new and, hopefully, more sensible world." (p. 11)

John Cook, "Whose Child? The Fiction of Paule Marshall," in CLA Journal, *Vol. XXIV, No. 1, September, 1980, pp. 1-15.*

DOROTHY L. DENNISTON (essay date 1983)

[*In the following excerpt, Denniston examines the feminist themes in "The Valley Between" and "Reena."*]

"The Valley Between," Paule Marshall's first publication, appeared in 1954 in the now defunct magazine, *The Contemporary Reader.* Since this is her only fictional piece to use white characters exclusively, one might be tempted to speculate upon the reasons for her choice. . . . Marshall's deliberate selection of white characters may have stemmed from a desire to erase color distinctions in art—to show somehow that a black artist need not confine herself to race issues alone but could paint, and paint effectively, white, middle-class American portraits.

Equally speculative but perhaps more in keeping with the historical plight of many black writers, Marshall may have chosen to use white characters to disguise her own feelings. "We wear the mask," wrote Paul Laurence Dunbar, and it seems not unreasonable to suggest that Marshall may have been attempting to show indirectly that black women, too, wrestled with the problems of sexism in their own personally and socially proscribed worlds. According to Bell Hooks [in her *Ain't I a Woman: Black Women and Feminism*], the fifties represented for women in general the pursuit of "idealized feminity." She explains:

> As a result of the war [World War II] white and black women had been compelled to be independent, assertive, and hardworking. White men, like black men, wanted to see all women be less assertive, dependent, and unemployed. Mass media was the weapon used to destroy the newfound independence of women. White and black women alike were subjected to endless propaganda which encouraged them to believe that a woman's place was in the home—that her fulfillment in life depended on finding the right man to marry and producing a family. If women were compelled by circumstance to work, they were told that it was better if they didn't compete with men and confined themselves to jobs like teaching and nursing.

This is certainly the message the husband conveys in **"The Valley Between."** But close analysis of the story will reveal another message which, nearly a quarter of a century later, was to dominate the thought of women and launch them toward renewed levels of feminist activity.

The story opens with the main character, Cassie, warming milk for her infant child, Ellen. The serene kitchen scene, warmly insulated against a fine, drizzling rain, presents to us the familiar feel of comfortable, though not extravagant, middle-class American life. The chipped pink and white cup marked "Baby," the child's toys, even the breakfast of coffee, juice, and stewed prunes—all contribute small details to the reader's image of mainstream American family life. The setting seems ordinary, commonplace, unexcitingly quotidian. We soon learn that it is this very lack of newness that disturbs Cassie's security and warmth:

> Yes, warm, that was the word. It was the suffocating warmth of the afternoons in the park, having to listen to the unceasing gossip of the other mothers. It was the ritual of seven o'clock dinners and having the same people over to play cards.

We are told through flashback that Cassie has desperately sought for something new, something that will give her life and perhaps that of Abe, her husband, a freshness and vitality. She recalls that as a child "the library had been her sanctuary, not only against the rainy world, but against all that was incomprehensible and ugly in life." It was there that she discovered the "joy of reading" and grew in her "desire to learn—to have all the muddled ideas made clear, defined in words and images, and thus made a part of her." She also remembers how Abe had once given her life meaning:

> She saw him again in his tight sailor suit, slim and graceful, his hair like an Apollo's against the white cap. He was always talking in his queer mid-

> western twang, and he used to hold her hand as if it were fragile china.

But Cassie slowly realizes that her life is "being spent in one compressed, limited space." Somehow she had to change the routine. She had to find new meaning and fulfillment.

The young woman finds a partial solution to her predicament by returning to college to complete the two years necessary for her degree. Her husband, however, resents the time she must spend away from home and openly defies her need for something other than familial responsibilities:

> "It beats me to figure out why you're killing yourself." Abe sighed heavily, his eyes still averted, "Getting up at all ungodly hours of the morning, running around in all kinds of weather. What for? If we didn't have Ellen, okay, but this nonsense. . . . Look, in the town I come from, a girl gets married and she settles down to take care of her house and kids; she's satisfied with that. Sure, she's got her bridge parties and all that. But not you. What's your rush? Afraid you'll die without having your degrees!"

The increasing tension drives a wedge between them, creating "a wide, untraceable valley," and making them "two proud mountains, unwilling to even look at each other, incapable of coming together."

The story is thoroughly integrated in its theme of ordinariness, for it climaxes with yet another ordinary occurrence. During the young woman's classes, the child is attended by her maternal grandmother, who lives in an upstairs apartment. On this particular day (the story covers less than a twenty-four hour period), little Ellen slips out in the rain to play and subsequently develops a fever. Cassie is later than usual in returning home; she had stopped for "coffee with some of the girls." How good it had been to talk to someone "without being tense!"

"I should have been here," is the young woman's immediate reaction. But we know that this is not the guilt of a negligent mother. Nor is it blame ascribed to the aging grandmother. It is the forced reaction of a woman in defeat, a woman oppressed by conditions she cannot combat. "He's won, . . ." she sighs.

Abe, in fact, has emerged as the conqueror, and the ensuing argument reflects his unyielding domination. But Cassie responds with new strength and insight:

> Yes, I'm selfish and self-centered, just as you are bull-headed and blind. It's not so much school or even Ellen—it's just us—two people who should have never met each other. You would have been much better off with some girl from your hometown. And I—well, that doesn't matter—I should have just finished up one phase of my life before starting another. I wasn't ready for the kind of life you have to offer me, and I couldn't give you very much.

Cassie's strength, however, is no match for Abe's demands. When confronted with the option of staying home or leaving altogether, the decision, in effect, has already been made for her. With sadness and resignation, she states: "I only pity both of us for having lost so much simply because you want me to be happy on your terms. I haven't got the strength to defy you anymore—you and your male strength. . . ."

As indicated in Cassie's response, Marshall is obviously concerned with something more than the surface issue of a resumed education. In this instance, Cassie's education is but a symptom of a much larger disease which insidiously attacks the foundation of American family life and personal relationships. In her careful choice of words and phrases, Marshall describes the debilitating effects of a relationship which denies the fulfillment of either partner. For example, as Cassie goes through her morning ritual of preparing breakfast, she glances "nervously at the clock." She almost "timidly" opens the bedroom door to check that her husband is awake. At the kitchen table, she watches Abe "furtively, fearful that if their eyes met they would have to say something decisive and final to each other." During idle conversation with Abe, she "fidgets" with their child's doll "trying unconsciously to fit its broken head back into the socket of the neck." This symbolic gesture represents Cassie's conscious desire to repair her own broken life.

Abe is not given the detailed attention that Cassie receives; after all, this is not his story. But the reader is made to understand his position. He, too, is a victim of society in his blind acceptance of a system of values he has never seen fit to question. The following comment reveals the selfishness which attends his unrecognized sexism:

> "Well, then what about me? Okay, so you take care of Ellen. But what about me? Am I supposed to moon around here by myself evenings while you bury yourself in books? I gotta take Ellen to the park on Saturdays and the museums so you can have quiet—to study. You always got your nose buried in a book even while you're eating. God, you're a woman of twenty-four. Aren't you tired of school? Didn't you give up all that when we got married? What am I supposed to do—sit home and hold hands with myself?"

Abe is well-intentioned in his attempts to reconcile their differences but, in the final analysis, his way is best. He has absolutely no conception that there might be another, better way.

The story ends with Cassie uttering the appropriate "feminine" line: "Your supper's ready by now, Abe." Though it strikes a hollow note, Cassie's capitulation remains a capitulation. The forces of history and tradition which have molded their respective responses have led to the fragmentation that now characterizes their relationship. The author suggests that traditionally it has been the woman who has had to sacrifice that part of herself which craves fulfillment and, traditionally, the woman has accepted that fate. Her resignation to a status secondary to that of the male has not only been expected, but demanded by all that she has been conditioned to view as sacrosanct. In **"The Valley Between,"** however, we see that simmering beneath this forced acceptance is a dormant, rebellious spirit which, if vented in a supportive atmosphere, can bring creative and useful dimensions to the lives of both men and women.

And herein lies Marshall's feminism. It is not a rhetorical label used as a synonym for surrogate malehood; nor is it a self-serving political platform which simply attempts to equalize the power of an inherently oppressive system. It seems apparent in the development of the storyline that the system has already gone awry. Marshall is looking for new values, new modes of thought which enhance sexual distinctions by extending priority to individual human needs. Perhaps **"The Valley Between"** represents a launching point—a mapping out of the terrain which has tangled the growth of men and of women. The author seems to ask that we first define sex roles as they are operative in contemporary American society. Then we must evaluate them according to the limitations imposed by such definitions. Finally, we must redefine them to suit more comfortably our personal preferences and individual abilities. This conclusion seems reasonable in light of the lingering question which remains a part of the story: On whose terms must the sacrosanct be determined? **"Reena,"** Marshall's second short story, may be an attempt to provide at least a tentative answer.

First published in 1962 in *Harper's* magazine, **"Reena"** also deals with the conflicting attitudes of creative women who struggle with the question of their responsibilities as women, as wives, as mothers. This time, however, the question is entertained by black, middle-class, West Indian/American women and covers the historical and social dimensions which have shaped their particularized responses. It might be argued that Marshall's shift to black characters is a direct reflection of the times, for with the sixties came a cultural resurgence which was soon to change the tone and content of American letters. Black Nationalism, as a political and aesthetic ideology, swept the country and provided for blacks the inspiration for a bold, defiant, and jubilant voice. No longer writing to appeal to dominant white society, the black artist began to focus more specifically upon an audience of color. In seeking to rediscover his unique cultural heritage and to share the positive values he had uncovered, he turned more decisively to the folk heritage. "Black is beautiful" was the popular slogan, and all elements of the black folk heritage began to be interpreted with new insight and pride. In presenting her interpretation of black culture, Marshall was no exception to this trend. Attention was drawn more sharply to the familiar black immigrant experience described in **"Reena."** As we shall see, she also began to draw on her knowledge of African cultural survivals as they seemed to function in contemporary black American society.

Choosing to write from the first person point of view, the author immediately draws us into her private world of memories. Our suspicion that what we are about to read is autobiographical in nature is confirmed when we learn that the narrator is a writer named Paulie. Further, we read that the story takes place in Brooklyn, the place of Marshall's birth. Briefly we see the exotic world of a traditional Jewish community where

> Sunday became Saturday, with all the stores open and pushcarts piled with vegetables and yard goods lined up along the curb, a crowded place where people hawked and spat freely in the streaming gutters and the men looked as if they had just stepped from the pages of the Old Testament with their profuse beards and long, black, satin coats.

Marshall's description of Brooklyn, however, is targeted upon a small West Indian community, and a tone of sad nostalgia is evoked as she writes of the period in which she "served out her girlhood":

> The places no longer mattered that much since most of them have vanished. The old grammar school, for instance, P.S. 35 ("Dirty 5's" we called it and with justification) has been replaced by a low, coldly functional arrangement of glass and Permastone which bears its name but has none of the feel of a school about it. The small, grudgingly lighted stores along Fulton Street, the soda parlor that was like a church with its stained-glass panels in the door and marble floors have given way to those impersonal emporiums, the supermarkets. Our house even, a brownstone relic whose halls smelled comfortingly of dust and lemon oil, the somnolent street upon which it stood, the tall, muscular trees which shaded it were leveled years ago to make way for a city housing project—a stark, graceless warren for the poor.

The strange, cold functionality of American progress has effected a change so drastic that the narrator now feels "nothing."

But Marshall is careful to make a distinction between the people and the places of her past. The former represent a community whose faces are but "myriad reflections" of her own. She continues: "Whenever I encounter them at a funeral or a wake, the wedding or christening—those ceremonies by which the past reaffirms its hold—my guard drops and memories banished to the rear of my mind rush forward to rout the present." It is during one such ceremony, a funeral and a wake, that the narrator, after a twenty-year separation, is reunited with her friend, Reena.

The story proper covers a period of only one long night, but compressed in that brief period is the history of generations of black men and women. The author's manipulation of time may be seen as a "symbolic victory" over the chaos and dispossession which mars the lives of black people in general. Her major concern, however, is the black woman. In the words of the narrator, Reena's story explores "the most critical fact of my existence—

> that definition of me, of her (Reena) and millions like us, formulated by others to serve out their fantasies, a definition we have to combat at an unconscionable cost to the self and even use, at times, in order to survive; the cause of so much shame and rage as well as, oddly enough, a source of pride: simply, what it has meant, what it means, to be a black woman in America.

Marshall writes a story within a story, and it is so densely packed with historical and cultural information, so intense in its portrayal of ambivalent attitudes and emotions, that it is difficult to offer a facile interpretation. It is almost as if the reader must realize the story through the reading rather than to accept an analysis of it. Yet for those unfamiliar with the realities the tale describes, certain points must be given attention.

The secondary story, which really takes prominence, extends over a period of several years and is a synopsis of Reena's life. However, it is framed within the setting of an evening wake. The two major characters remove themselves from the immediate scene and become engaged in a conversation which, on the surface, seems totally irrelevant to—perhaps even irreverent toward—the solemn occasion which has brought them together. As the others conduct their own private ritual, the title character is given full sway to describe the people and the events which have most influenced the direction of her life.

To repeat the episodes of Reena's life would entail too lengthy a discussion. For the black female reader who nods assent to nearly every detail, they might even appear redundant. Perhaps it is in recognition of this that Marshall chooses an unusual approach. First of all, **"Reena"** has no conventional plot line clearly delineating action which rises to a central conflict, reaches the point of climax, and ends with a standard resolution. To say there is no conventional plot line, however, is not to suggest there is no plot. In fact, there seems to be a series of plots in which conflict is assumed as part of the daily facts of black life. Resolution becomes not only a desirable end to perpetual conflict but, importantly, an essential impetus to continued existence.

Secondly, the only two active characters (the narrator and Reena) become almost archetypal in nature, representing the millions of black women who have shared the experiences described. Thirdly, the story often reads like an essay, for scattered throughout are passages which clarify the ideas presented. Oddly enough, this authorial intrusion does not take away from the tale because, in many respects, we need a guiding hand to comprehend a pattern of life which is "foreign" to some and not yet articulated for others. Marshall has already suggested in the excerpt quoted above that the lives of black women have been all too frequently misinterpreted—most often to the detriment of those described. Reena's story seems to offer a perspective which emphasizes the positive values of the black female experience. As we begin to understand the author's purpose to show in microcosm the pain, the beauty, and the strength of a minority group experience, authorial intrusion becomes instead authorial inclusion. The end result is a picture which is totally unified in its theme of collecting from one's heritage the strength and vision to live with purpose and dignity.

Early on in the story we learn that Reena has long possessed the sense of purpose that marks her personality. From the moment she enters the church where the funeral services for Aunt Vi are being held, her presence seems to command attention. Marshall writes: "It was as though she, not the minister, were coming to officiate." Through flashback we are told that even as a child, "she seemed defined . . . all of a piece, the raw edges of her adolescence smoothed over. . . ." Paulie remembers her as precocious, socially responsible, and politically conscious of the larger world around her. Her college years were filled with the crusading efforts of a young woman seriously committed to social equality and justice. She picketed, boycotted, handed out leaflets, solicited signatures for petitions—all of which eventually led to her temporary suspension from college.

As Reena talks of occasional romances, we understand with deeper insight how color effects the human psyche. For the black woman, especially, who is constantly bombarded with white society's standards of beauty, it is an experience of painful rejection which often leads to a negative self-image. Reena is not alone as she describes the psychic wounds inflicted because of color:

> Because I was dark I was always being plastered with Vaseline so I wouldn't look ashy. Whenever I had my picture taken they would pile a whitish powder on my face and make the lights so bright I always came out looking ghostly. My mother stopped speaking to any number of people because they said I would have been pretty if I hadn't been so dark. Like nearly every little black girl, I had my share of dreams waking up to find myself with long, blonde curls, blue eyes, and skin like milk.

Rejection by one's own carries the more devastating effects, and Reena is subjected to the humiliation and shame of being denied an innocent romance simply because the boy's parents saw her as too dark. Note the inclusion of the following to help the reader place this seeming paradox in perspective:

> We live surrounded by white images, and white in this world is synonymous with the good, light, beauty, success, so that, despite ourselves sometimes, we run after that whiteness and deny our darkness, which has been made into a symbol of all that is evil and inferior. I wasn't a person to that boy's parents, but a symbol of the darkness they were in flight from.

Color, as a symbol and as a reality, rears its head on another occasion when Reena is involved with a white student. Reena explains:

> Bob was always, for some odd reason, talking about how much the Negro suffered, and although I would agree with him, I would also try to get across that, you know, like all people we also had fun once in a while, loved our children, liked making love—that we were human beings for God's sake. But he only wanted to hear about the suffering. . . .

The relationship ends when Bob insists that she meet his father, who is visiting in New York. Note the author's poignant allusion to Conrad's "Heart of Darkness:"

> I'll never forget or forgive the look on that old man's face when he opened his hotel-room door and saw me. The horror. I might have been the personification of every evil in the world.

Bob's reaction is a laughter filled with vengeance—not against Reena, but against himself, against his own uncertainty, against his father with whom he shared a painful relationship. Reena, however, cannot be completely exonerated and confesses that she had used Bob "to get at that white world which had not only denied [her], but had turned [her] own against [her]." As Conrad's Kurtz loses his past and his true self emerges, so also emerges the truth of Reena's life. Significantly different, however, is that her past cannot be lost; it is inextricably woven into her present life. Both the then and the now must be confronted and ordered before the confusion which prevails can be dispelled.

At a later point, Reena is able to use her color to advantage. Speaking at a college debate on McCarthyism, she seems intimidating not because of her radical position alone, but also because of "the sheer impact of her blackness in their white midst." Paulie recalls the following:

> Her color might have been a weapon she used to dazzle and disarm her opponents. And she had highlighted it with the clothes she was wearing: a white dress patterned with large blocks of primary colors I remember (it looked Mexican) and a pair of intricately wrought silver earrings—long and with many little parts which clashed like muted cymbals over the microphone each time she moved her head. She wore her hair cropped short like a boy's and it was not straightened like mine and other Negro girls' in the audience, but left in its coarse natural state: a small forest under which her face emerged in its intense and startling handsomeness.

Her hair, her clothing, her conspicuous presence—all contribute to Reena's self-acceptance. In embracing her African ancestry, she develops the strength to combat all that the white world refuses her.

That strength is built upon the foundation of the extended family, which may be defined as a "philosophical orientation" toward a group identity. The priority afforded the community in traditional African societies is widely documented. Marshall seems to acknowledge contemporary kinship patterns as but a variant of that family system. Reena's graduation from college, for instance, represents not just a personal accomplishment, but a triumph for both her mother and father and their parents before them: "It was as if I had made up for the generations his people had picked cotton in Georgia and my mother's family had cut cane in the West Indies." The extended ties are also connected through the relationship between the mothers of the major characters. They had known each other since childhood in Barbados and, further, it was they who initiated—more accurately "forced"—the relationship between Reena and Paulie. Aunt Vi provides another example. While she is blood related to Reena, she is godmother to the narrator, who also refers to the woman as aunt. Over and over again, Marshall shows us both obvious and subtle connections between individuals who have shared a similar space in time and who have gained from that sharing a special insight about conquering its exigencies to keep their communities intact. Both in fact and symbol, the community thrives beyond temporal measurement to embrace perpetual duration.

While this perpetuity is affirmed in the reunion between Paulie and Reena, it is also celebrated in the wake itself. With the juxtaposition of specific cultural rituals which mark the actual beginnings and endings of life, the author seems to be moving toward an exploration of the cyclical nature of time as perceived by traditional African societies. This is in direct contrast to the linear progression of time as perceived by Western societies. Contrary to the Western notion of death as the termination of life, it becomes for this small West Indian community a celebration of the continuity of life. Again we see a clear example of an African cultural survival. John S. Mbiti explains [in *African Religions and Philosophies*] that in traditional African society, the departed one, while physically dead, is categorized as the "living dead." That is, as long as the deceased is "alive in the memory of those who knew him in his life as well as being alive in the world of spirits, . . . he is in a state of *personal immortality.*" Marshall seems to be illustrating this concept.

Note also the author's description of the wake. As in traditional African ritual, special foods and drink, gaiety and laughter attend the joyful ceremony in which friends and relatives gather at the home of Aunt Vi to commemorate her special inclusion in their lives. Appropriate to the festivities is a bit of comic relief which is provided by a brief reference to the time Aunt Vi "had missed the excursion boat to Atlantic City and had held her own private picnic—complete with pigeon peas and rice and fricassee chicken—on the pier at 42nd Street." Such memories distinguish the woman's personality and are retained as a part of the present celebration, the recollection of which will insure her imprint upon the future.

The future for Reena seems promising in her marriage to Dave, a talented and ambitious photographer. They are so compatible and happy together that Reena confesses to being "frightened at times." "Not that anything would change between us," she explains, "but that someone or something in the world outside would invade our private place and destroy us out of envy." That something is realized in Dave's "diffidence," for it seems that his need for success is second only to his fear of it. This is a problem with which Reena cannot cope and "for her own sanity," she returns to work.

It is not difficult to hear reverberating in Reena's tale echoes from **"The Valley Between."** Like Abe, Dave is threatened by Reena's interest in things outside the home. He interprets them as "a way of pointing up his deficiencies." Additionally, he must take on new family responsibilities, which he resents. Note the similarities between Cassie's predicament and Reena's: "After a time we both got caught up in this thing, an ugliness came between us, and I began to answer his anger with anger and to trade insult for insult." But there is a significant difference between the husbands' predicaments. Despite the professional recognition he has gained through various awards and photographic exhibits, he "also wanted the big, gaudy commercial success that would dazzle and confound that white world downtown and force it to *see* him." His inability to act leads to a defensive posture. Here we see the effects of racism combined with sexism and human weakness bringing out the inevitable divorce.

Reena also differs from Cassie in that she refuses to capitulate to the bitterness of a relationship which provides no mutual fulfillment. It is only in retrospect, however, that she can posit at least a tentative answer to the question first raised in **"The Valley Between":** On whose terms must the sacrosanct be determined?

> We have got to understand them [black men] and save them for ourselves . . . By being, on the one hand, persons in our own right and, on the other, fully the woman and the wife. . . .

This is, indeed a tall order for the woman who suffers under the double constraints of sexism and racism. In fact, it calls for a devotion and strength that seems nearly impossible to achieve. But the heritage of the black woman affirms that not only is that achievement possible, it is absolutely necessary.

There is, of course, a sacrifice to be paid and both Paulie and Reena can identify that sacrifice as being alone and lonely. Consider, for a moment, the difficulties involved in finding a suitable mate. Reena tells us that the black woman who has sought to improve her lot by getting an education and a decent job, is really at a disadvantage. Her "intellectual or professional peers," if they marry at all, tend to choose the younger woman without a degree or they marry white women. This is an ire-provoking subject for many black women, and the author minces no words in presenting their long-standing grievances.

Almost in a call-and-response fashion, Reena and Paulie recite the reasons some black men offer for preferring white women to black. The familiar accusations range from sexual inhibition ("And the old myth of excessive sexuality goes out the window . . .") to castrating independence. On an intellectual level, the two women can understand a black man's right to choose a white mate. "In fact," quips Reena, "some of my best friends are white women." Emotionally, however, the resentment runs deep.

The pain, the anger, the understanding and compassion is evident as Reena summarizes:

> They condemn us . . . without taking history into account. We are still, most of us, the black woman who had to be almost frighteningly strong in order for us all to survive. For, after all, she was the one

> whom they left (and I don't hold this against them; I understand) with the children to raise, who had to make it somehow or other. And we are still, many of us, living that history.

In this brief passage, Marshall homes in on the myth of the matriarchy, a theme which was expanded and expounded in her first major novel, *Brown Girls, Brownstones.* In many respects, Reena may be seen as an heiress of that indomitable spirit reflected in the characterization of Silla Boyce. But an indomitable spirit is not to be equated with indisputable power—strength, perhaps, but not power.

Reena considers the historical circumstances of powerlessness for both the black male and the black female when she speaks of her resolve to spend an indefinite period of time in Africa with her children:

> It is important that they see black people who have truly a place and history of their own and who are building for a new and, hopefully, more sensible world. And I must see it, get close to it because I can never lose the sense of being a displaced person here in America because of my color.

Faithful to her pledge to become a person in her own right, we see her questioning the very essence of American life:

> Oh, I know I should remain and fight not only for integration (even though, frankly, I question whether I want to be integrated into America as it stands now, with its complacency and materialism, its soullessness) but to help change the country into something better, sounder—if that is still possible. But I have to go to Africa.

This journey to Africa, though real in intent, is equally symbolic in its thrust. It signals what will become Marshall's central concern in later fiction for the need to establish cultural roots—not just to locate one's ancestral source, but to glean from one's historical past the values which have proven viable and sustaining. As Mary Helen Washington observes [in her afterword to *Brown Girl, Brownstones*]: "Reena and Paulie, as representatives of the next generation, review Aunt Vi's past and their own, not for nostalgia, but to collect the strength and vision in that life: They must go back before they can go forward."

Reena's story draws to a close as the dawn breaks and, once again, we are reminded of the cyclical nature of time. Reena affirms the continuity of time on another level in her devotion to her children:

> "I will feel that I have done well by them if I give them, if nothing more, a sense of themselves and their worth and importance as black people. Everything I do with them, for them, is to this end. I don't want them ever to be confused about this. They must have their identifications straight from the beginning. No white dolls for them!"

The story comes full circle as our attention is brought back to Aunt Vi and the wake. "Our lives have got to make more sense if only for her," remarks Reena. Thus we can see that the rituals attending physical death become a confirmation of spiritual renewal. Accordingly, as the two friends separate at the end, the circles become concentric with our knowledge that their spiritual ties will remain taut.

The force, the conviction, the unsparing honesty which mark this short story seem to provide Marshall with the voice for which she has been searching. They indicate as well the cultural and ideological direction which is to distinguish her later, more mature and stylized fiction. Africa remains, to a large extent, symbolic, but it is accepted, without question, as the central referent. It becomes, in short, the common denominator of the collective, black experience. As for the black woman, who carries the additional burden of learning to be comfortable with her strength, Marshall presents not a dismissal of the male but an affirmation of the female. (pp. 31-45)

Dorothy L. Denniston, "Early Short Fiction by Paule Marshall," in Callaloo, *Vol. 6, No. 2, Spring-Summer, 1983, pp. 31-45.*

ADAM GUSSOW (essay date 1984)

[*In the following excerpt from a review of* Reena, and Other Stories *Gussow describes the shifts in Marshall's narrative voice.*]

Although she began her novelistic career long before the current generation of black women novelists, Marshall remained virtually unknown until 1970, when Toni Cade Bambara included **"Reena"** in an anthology entitled *The Black Woman.* In 1981, The Feminist Press reissued *Brown Girl, Brownstones;* in 1983 Marshall resurfaced with *Praisesong for the Widow,* her third novel and a work which, if you throw away the first 30 pages of uneven exposition, moves with the dreamlike inevitability of a classic. This year—to fill in the gaps—there's ***Reena and Other Stories,*** an assortment of her short fiction from the 1950s and '60s.

Reena and Other Stories begins with a marvelous autobiographical essay, "From the Poets in the Kitchen." Many black women writers have spoken of the debt they owe to storytelling mothers and grandmothers, but Marshall's apprenticeship was truly unusual: she spent her childhood in a houseful of spirited Barbadian women who exercised their wits in her mother's kitchen after long days spent cleaning for white people out in Flatbush. "While my sister and I sat at a smaller table over in a corner doing our homework, they talked—endlessly, passionately, poetically, and with impressive range." Their mad rambling dialogues were, as Marshall points out, a way of coping with the painful halfway state into which they had worked themselves—suspended between bittersweet memories of the islands they left behind and deceptively hard-to-realize dreams of making it in their new urban home.

There were other Barbadian women, relatives who never left the islands or who found it impossible to stay in America. **"To Da-Duh, In Memoriam,"** is a thinly fictionalized portrait of her haughty, roguish grandmother and of young Paule, a headstrong nine year old come to visit Barbados from New York. The spiritual struggle, fed by a mixture of love and fear, that ensues between these two has parallels in Marshall's other work, but nowhere else is it rendered quite so hauntingly.

> Again she turned and her thin muscular arms spread wide, her dim gaze embracing the small field of canes, she said—and her voice almost broke under the weight of her pride, "Tell me, have you got anything like these in that place where you were born?"
>
> "No."

"I din' think so, I bet you don't even know that these canes here and the sugar you eat is one and the same thing. That they does throw the canes into some damn machine at the factory and squeeze out all the little life in them to make sugar for you all so in New York to eat. I bet you don't know that."

"I've got two cavities and I'm not allowed to eat a lot of sugar."

But Da-duh didn't hear me. She had turned with an inexplicable angry motion and was making her way rapidly out of the canes and down the slope at the edge of the field which led to the gully below.

Marshall's narrative voice isn't always so sure. **"Brooklyn"** is an early story she wrote out of rage at a college professor who tried to seduce her. She narrates it, unexpectedly, from the professor's point of view, and her psychological observations are devastatingly acute. But she has difficulty maintaining a consistent aesthetic distance—most of us would, I suspect—and her anger wreaks havoc with her taste. "He saw himself for what he was," she tells us, "in her clear, cold gaze: an old man with skin the color and texture of dough that had been kneaded by the years into tragic folds . . ." Tragic folds? Marshall is at her best when she shows us the world through the eyes of Selina Boyce [of *Brown Girl, Brownstones*] and Avey Johnson (the widow in *Praisesong for the Widow*), when she loses herself in those swift demanding voices she was baptized in as a child.

Adam Gussow, in a review of "Reena and Other Stories," in The Village Voice, *Vol. XXIX, No. 20, May 15, 1984, p. 47.*

EUGENIA COLLIER (essay date 1984)

[*Collier is the author of several critical surveys of Afro-American literature. In the following excerpt, she discusses "To Da-duh, in Memoriam," focusing on Marshall's use of dance rituals to contrast West Indian and American culture.*]

For an author, ritual is an economical way of conveying ideas and emotions that would take reams of pages to communicate. More important, ritual evokes responses on a deeply psychic level, especially from the reader or listener who has also partaken of similar rituals—which is why any art form is most meaningful to its own culture, no matter how it rates on a scale of universality. The rituals in Marshall's works, particularly the ritual of dance, make unforgettable the theme of the self made whole through the community and in turn enriching that community for those yet to come.

"To Da-duh, in Memoriam" was not Marshall's first published work, but it seems to fall first in chronology because it deals with the first step in the journey toward the integrated self. A little girl, aged nine, accompanies her mother and older sister to visit their relatives in Barbados, which the parents had left years ago to settle in New York. For the child this first visit is a pivotal experience which changes the direction of her life. Although she must have heard much about Barbados, being part of the Bajan community in New York, the reality of this sunny place, so different from the home she knows, is something of a shock. But the real impact of the experience is her relationship with the grandmother whom she meets now for the first time—Da-duh. The story is narrated by the child now grown, seeing the experience both through the eyes of her child-self and through the adult perceptions which have made necessary a looking back, a remembering.

Like other elders in Marshall's works, Da-duh is many-sided, complex. She seems to embody irreconcilable opposites. She has survived and more than survived. In spite of the ravages of time and struggle, she has somehow prevailed. And in the prevailing, she embodies more than her individual self.

It was as stark and fleshless as a death mask, that face. The maggots might have already done their work, leaving only the framework of bone beneath the ruined skin and deep wells at the temple and jaw. But her eyes were alive, unnervingly so for one so old, with a sharp light that flicked out of the dim clouded depths like a lizard's tongue to snap up all in her view. . . . Perhaps she was both . . . child and woman, darkness and light, past and present, life and death—all the opposites contained and reconciled in her.

But Da-duh's world is menaced by the high-tech civilization from which the child has come. Da-duh is deathly afraid of machines. She clings to the child's hand as they ride in a lorry from Bridgetown to her rural home but relaxes as they pass the fecund cane fields, which to her are beautiful. To the child, though, it is the canes which are the menace—"I suddenly feared that we were journeying, unaware that we were, toward some dangerous place where the canes, grown as high and thick as a forest, would close in on us and run us through with their stiletto blades."

Throughout the visit, the tropical world is a challenge against which the child pits the manifold miracles of New York. Daily she walks with Da-duh through the cane fields and gulleys and natural terrain. Da-duh says at every turn, "I know they don't have anything this nice where you come from," and the child is forced to admit that the closest thing she has to all this natural beauty is a barren chestnut tree. In this place where the sun makes things grow, the child brags of the cold destructive snow which Da-duh has never seen.

It is here that Marshall uses the ritual of dance to underscore the great contrast between the child's world and Da-duh's. ". . . You'd have to wear a hat and gloves and galoshes and ear muffs so your ears wouldn't freeze and drop off, and a heavy coat. I've got a Shirley Temple coat with fur on the collar. I can dance. You wanna see?" And before Da-duh can reply, the child is doing the popular dances of the day and singing Tin Pan Alley songs in this lush tropical setting. Marshall has thrown out in rapid succession symbols of the high-tech world, all conveying negativity. Snow is seen as cold and destructive. The Shirley Temple coat with the fake fur collar symbolizes the false ideals so often pursued in the child's culture, where the blond, blue-eyed, smart-mouthed child movie star was America's darling and even little Black girls boasted Shirley Temple clothes, wore their version of Shirley Temple curls, and were the proud mamas of yellow-haired Shirley Temple dolls. The child's sudden dance is an ironic commentary on the superficiality and spiritual vacuity of the culture described by the child. She is an incongruous presence in this nurturing place: "My forefinger waving, I trucked around the nearby trees and around Da-duh's awed and rigid form. After the Truck I did the Suzy-Q, my lean hips swishing, my sneakers sidling zigzag over the ground." Then without pause she sings all the popular songs—like "I Found a Million Dollar Baby in the Five and Ten Cent Store." These actions are foreign here. Da-duh, amused, gives her a penny to buy a sweet: "There's nothing to be done with you, soul."

In the semiserious rivalry, the child's world wins out. Da-duh takes her to a dark, overgrown area and shows her a splendid palm tree, taller than anything in Da-duh's world, as tall, it seems, as the sky. "All right, now, tell me if you've got anything this tall in that place you're from." The child—reluctantly, in the face of Da-duh's intensity—replies that in New York there are buildings infinitely taller, and promises to send her a picture of the Empire State Building. But Da-duh never receives the picture. She falls ill shortly after this exchange. Soon after the child's departure there is a labor strike in Barbados, and England sends planes to swoop over the island in a show of strength. Ever fearful of machines, Da-duh watches as the planes come "swooping and screaming like monstrous birds down over the village, over her house, rattling her trees and flattening the young canes in her field." When the villagers return, having fled in terror, they find her dead.

This is a story of discovery. The child discovers a vital dimension of her self. Barbados is a natural place, a place, of brilliant sunshine and lush growth. New York is the land of snow and concrete. Da-duh's palm tree and the child's Empire State Building symbolize the essence of each world. Barbados is the child's collective past, embodied in the grandmother never before seen and so soon gone. But the child is too young to define what she has discovered. The experience lingers. She is no longer at home in the world of concrete and machines:

> She died and I lived, but always, to this day even, within the shadow of her death. For a brief period after I was grown I went to live alone, like one doing penance, in a loft above a noisy factory in downtown New York and there painted seas of sugarcane and huge swirling Van Gogh suns and palm trees striding like brightly-plumed Watusi across a tropical landscape, while the thunderous tread of the machines downstairs jarred the floor beneath my easel, mocking my efforts.

"To Da-duh, in Memoriam" reveals the glimmering awareness of a divided self. Marshall's first novel, *Brown Girl, Brownstones,* shows a little girl growing into early adulthood. With maturity comes the next step in the journey toward wholeness—integration of the personal self with the community: beginning to know who you are because you know where you came from. (pp. 296-98)

Eugenia Collier, "The Closing of the Circle: Movement from Division to Wholeness in Paule Marshall's Fiction," in Black Women Writers (1950-1980): A Critical Evaluation, *edited by Mari Evans, Anchor Books, 1984, pp. 295-315.*

HUGH BARNES (essay date 1985)

[*In the excerpt below, Barnes comments on the strengths of Marshall's female characters and discusses her adaptation of her novel* The Chosen Place, the Timeless People *in the novella* Merle.]

Merle, and Other Stories is a collection of [Paule] Marshall's early work, previously unavailable in this country. This edition comes complete with the writer's own retrospective commentary. In the introductory essay she charts her literary influences, from her visits to Brooklyn library as a child, where she discovered Thackeray, Dickens and Fielding, and, later, black writers (Paul Laurence Dunbar, James Weldon Johnson, Langston Hughes and Zora Neale Hurston) who informed her own experience and that of 'the Race'. But more important to the young Marshall than the testimonies of the page were the stories she heard in the kitchen of her brownstone house, told by the 'unknown bards who would put an apron and a pair of old house shoes in a shopping bag and take the train or streetcar from our section of Brooklyn out to Flatbush' several mornings a week to clean the homes of white folks. These women were her principal educators, swopping Bajan folklore, talking politics ('if FDR was their hero, Marcus Garvey was their God') and the travails of living in this 'man country'. The 'unknown bards' have populated her stories ever since, most memorably in Silla Boyce, the furious matriarch of her first novel. Women have been active elements throughout Marshall's fiction—motors of community, husbands and children. **"The Valley Between"** and **"Brooklyn,"** published here, are apprentice outings, from a time 'when I could barely crawl, never mind stand up and walk as a writer'. But they explore characteristic themes. Cassie in the first story is a white woman who escapes domestic drudgery to go back to college, inviting the reproaches of her husband. Obstructive masculine indifference reappears in **"Brooklyn"**, where Miss Williams's accomplishments in her foreign literature night-class, particularly her essay on Gide, provoke her professor into confession and conceit. In **"Reena"** the narrator meets up with an old friend from her childhood. Reena has thrown over the security of her middle-class upbringing for Civil Rights activism. She would be at home anywhere in Marshall's work. Her confidence is emblematic: 'We are still, most of us, the black woman who had to be almost frighteningly strong in order to survive. For, after all, she was the one whom they left (and I don't hold this against them; I understand) with the children to raise, who had to *make* it somehow or the other. And we are still, so many of us, living that history.' At the end of the story the women separate—Paulie back to the suburbs, Reena onwards to Africa.

Merle Kinbona was the heroine of Marshall's second novel, *The Chosen Place, the Timeless People,* a foreign student in London waylaid by 'the so-called glamour of the West'. In fact this glamour never amounted to more than idleness, a chequered lesbian affair, and the birth of her daughter. Back in the West Indies in this updated story, she occupies the house at Bournehills which once belonged to her white father, Duncan Vaughan, descendant of a celebrated island dynasty. His liberality backfired on him sometimes, in the illegitimate offspring with which he populated his patch. Merle was unexceptional, a Vaughan bastard child whose father refused to acknowledge her. She lived out the first years of her disinheritance a stone's throw across the tracks. She describes herself as 'a slightly daft, middle-aged woman with history on the brain', and no wonder. The inertia of Bourne Island recalls parts of *The Final Passage,* 'someplace the world has turned its back on and even God's forgotten'. But dereliction has its conveniences, making possible impossible relationships, like Merle's with an American anthropologist Saul.

Life on the island is brutish and short, but Marshall observes it with the meticulousness of Jane Austen, demonstrating a comparable genius for conjuring the manners and mechanics of a small, introverted community. Merle is a Third World revolutionary Emma Woodhouse: 'some people act, some think, some feel, but I talk, and if I ever was ever to stop that'd be the end of me.' Instinctively she talks sense, in short blasts against exploitation. When it rains, the island's roads are impassable, and now the local law firm is conspiring to sell Bournehills down the mudstreams to property developers, hellbent on jettisoning the island into the 'modern swing of things'. Merle has the measure of the multi-nationals, at least she thinks she has. Her loyalties are to 'the Little Fella', the indigenous poor, and she encourages them to rise up against the conditions of their lives: primarily to resist the courtesies of the dollar by ensuring that the island can feed itself. To this end Merle storms the Cane Vale refinery where Erskine Vaughan, in a curious Luddite inversion, lays off the workforce after vandalising his own machinery. Her defiance is the absurd gesture of a crystal spirit. At the end of the story, if her initiatives have come to nothing and the socialist transformation of the West Indies has been postponed, her energies are undiminished. Saul's wife is carried off into the sea by winds, and Merle makes sedate preparations to follow her. Like Reena, she chooses Africa as her ultimate destination, but this time in search of a younger generation: 'I'll never get around to doing anything with what's left of my life until I go and look for my child.' Paule Marshall's final passage anticipates her ports of call, from Recife in Brazil 'where the great arm of the hemisphere reaches out toward the massive shoulder of Africa as though yearning to be joined to it again'. Merle suffers a similar yearning, and it furnishes this remarkable collection. She departs to gather up the fragments of her identity, 'as it had been in the beginning'. (p. 20)

Hugh Barnes, "Return of the Native," in London Review of Books, *Vol. 7, No. 4, March 7, 1985, pp. 20-1.*

LINDA TAYLOR (essay date 1985)

[*In the following excerpt from a review of* Merle: A Novella and Other Stories, *Taylor discusses Marshall's strong allegiance to her personal roots in her fiction.*]

Paule Marshall is explicit about her roots (in her introductions to these republished stories, in her essay on writing, "From the Poet's Kitchen", and in the fabric of the stories themselves). . . .

Her Barbadian parents moved to the United States after the First World War and she writes about "what it means to be a black woman in America today" with the black woman's history very firmly in view. The women of her mother's generation, as they strove to make a life in the alien streets of Brooklyn, were forceful matriarchs. They worked at menial jobs for property and possessions: "their consuming ambition [was] to 'buy house' and to see the children through". They recognized the power of language: "In this man world you got take yuh mouth and make a gun!" It is this rhetorical art that Marshall learnt in the kitchen and that she uses in the speech of her characters, her imagery and robust narration. In the same way that the native speech thrives on paradox (composite adjectives like "beautiful-ugly"), the writing stresses the combustible energy of opponents: Jewish white male versus mulatto woman; ancient Barbadian grandmother versus nine-year-old grand-daughter; black, complacent businessman versus poor black servant girl. These are radical political confrontations: it is only by the death of what is culpable, reactionary, other, that the young women (the new order) emerge.

With Reena, from the story of that name, and Merle, however, Marshall is dealing with another branch of the sisterhood: because of their education (at city colleges rather than an Ivy League school), they can use the weapons of the white world. Merle, in particular, is larger than life (noisy, garrulous, vulgar), containing many of the elements of Marshall's wide-ranging females. She lives on the Caribbean island where she was born; she has been educated; she has lived in England; she has been exploited by a rich white woman; she has been married; she has a child (symbolically) in Africa. On the island, Merle fits nowhere and everywhere, living with the poor and socializing with the rich: she is "the perfect cultural broker".

Marshall's prose resounds to both the vibrant domestic lives of her women and to the rhetoric of political radicalism. But these stories seem to have been pulled together (with their authorial comments and their often faulty structure) to make stirring statements.

Linda Taylor, "The Weapon of Laughter," in The Times Literary Supplement, *No. 4279, April 5, 1985, p. 376.*

LINDA PANNILL (essay date 1985)

[*In the following excerpt, Pannill comments on the force and influence of Marshall's female characters in* Reena, and Other Stories *and suggests that Marshall's personal commentaries and her novella "Merle" provide valuable insight for readers of her work.*]

As critics have recognized, each [of the four novellas in ***Soul Clap Hands and Sing***] is about spiritual decay and the sadness of age without wisdom. Marshall chose to include only two—**"Brooklyn"** and **"Barbados"**—in the recent ***Reena, and Other Stories.*** Because the other fictions in ***Reena, and Other Stories*** have female protagonists, **"Brooklyn"** and **"Barbados"** are now placed in a context which invites an interpretation that focuses on the women characters. The woman in each is, it is true, a minor character, a background figure seen through the distorting eye of a man, but she does effect the recognition on his part of his limitations. Also, the woman is the one who changes, and she articulates the theme, speaking for the author. In a commentary in [the work], Marshall says **"Brooklyn"** was based on an incident of sexual harassment she experienced in the 1950s. The protagonist, Dr. Berman, a white professor of literature, tries to pressure Miss Williams, a young Black woman, into a liaison. He propositions her (with a promise of help with her writing) as they stand at the top of a flight of plunging stairs. Although she is shocked, nearly toppling, Miss Williams learns from the experience, overcoming the fear of white people she has been taught; later she refuses Dr. Berman, saying, "In a way you did me a favor. You let me know how you and most of the people like you—see me. . . . Look how I came all the way up here to tell you this to your face. Because how could you harm me? You're so old you're like a cup I could break in my hand." Though the novella appears to be about the old man's wish to be saved from his failed life by a young woman he thinks of as a Gauguin painting, the reader is liable to agree with Miss Williams that "What matters is what it meant to [her]."

The protagonist of **"Barbados,"** the other novella reprinted in ***Reena, and Other Stories*** from ***Soul Clap Hands and Sing,*** is Mr. Watford, who has retired from a job in the United States to the island he came from, where he no longer feels at home. In a large white house on a plantation of dwarf coconut trees, he sets himself above his neighbors and ignores the young servant girl (nameless in the story) who lives in the house with him—until he is stirred by seeing her dancing with a young man. Then it is too late to approach her, of course, and when he does she finally speaks out, saying, "You ain't people, Mr. Watford, you ain't people!" The political button she wears, "The Old Order Shall Pass," underlines the message of this "Cassandra watching the future wheel before her eyes."

Paule Marshall says the women characters in ***Soul Clap Hands and Sing*** are "bringers of the truth," but this motif is less evident in the two novellas not collected in ***Reena, and Other Stories.*** Possibly they were omitted because they are less effective, **"British Guiana"** being a bit unclear in its symbolism and **"Brazil"** a bit obvious. Another reason might be that in both, the women are more passive and less important as characters—although Sybil in **"British Guiana"** is unusually interesting, with a dancer's grace and the perceptiveness her name implies. Maybe **"Brooklyn"** and **"Barbados"** are the better-written fictions in part *because* of the relative prominence of the female characters! A lot of the imagination in these stories is invested in the women, the revelations coming from them; in **"Brooklyn,"** for example, it seems the author is speaking back to the professor who harassed her years before; it seems that she had to write this story to do it.

Also collected in ***Reena, and Other Stories*** are three short stories. . . . **"The Valley Between,"** Marshall's first published story, is notable because the heroine, Cassie, is white. A young wife and mother, she is pressured into giving up college classes to stay at home with her daughter. In a commentary, the author says the character was white "to camouflage my own predicament." That **"The Valley Between"** was her first published story says something about the primacy in Paule Marshall's writing of women's concerns, and that she would reprint apprenticeship work to make this point says something about her self-confidence—and her integrity. The title story of the collection, ***"Reena,"*** was written for a special women's issue of *Harper's* in 1962 and was reprinted by Toni Cade Bambara in the important anthology *The Black Woman* (1970). A *tour de force,* ***"Reena"*** is, as the author says, a "story-essay" made up almost entirely of monologue, Reena speaking about her life as an educated and ambitious Black woman. Her listener is the narrator, her *alter ego,* a woman writer. The story's power comes from the convincingness of the speaking voice and the telling details, so that Reena is both an individual and a representative of women like her, women who have been left out of literature. The finest short story in the collection is **"To Da-duh, In Memoriam,"** an autobiographical work in which the narrator recalls a childhood visit to her grandmother in Barbados. "Da-duh" tries to make her granddaughter see what is valuable in the island but is abashed by the little girl's tales of skyscrapers ("building the city out of words"), her Tin Pan Alley songs and jitterbug dancing. The child's dancing fails to help them understand one another. Years after the grandmother's death the narrator is still trying to understand her background, painting her memories of the island in a loft above a noisy factory in New York. Though the paintings, we are told, fail, the story, with its complete understanding of the older and the younger woman, succeeds.

For the reader familiar with Paule Marshall's work the most interesting part of ***Reena and Other Stories*** is the one-hundred-page novella, ***Merle,*** abstracted from the 1969 novel *The Chosen Place, The Timeless People,* four-hundred-and-seventy-two-pages long. **"Merle"** is not lifted from one section of the novel but from passages throughout, rewritten. The alteration she has made in her work signals Marshall's recognition that Merle, one of a large cast of characters in the original, is her important creation:

> Merle remains the most alive of my characters. Indeed, it seems to me she has escaped the pages of the novel altogether and is abroad in the world. I envision her striding restlessly up and down the hemisphere from Argentina to Canada, and back and forth across the Atlantic between here and Africa, all the while speaking her mind in the same forthright way as in the book.

Merle is a colossal figure, almost always in motion, first seen trying to drive across the fictional Caribbean island of Bourne while the roads seem to twitch under her. Merle is voluble, difficult, generous, weary. A completely believable character (capable, like E. M. Forster's "round characters," of surprising us), she is also a symbolic one. A "bourne" is a boundary, of course, and Bourne Island, a former British Colony, has many such divisions; Merle embodies them all, in conflict. This is evident in her appearance, a mixture of European and African clothing, the silver bracelets worn by the island women and long earrings in the shape of saints, sad-faced but always dancing with her movements. Merle is the unacknowledged daughter of an island aristocrat, himself the descendant of an English planter and a slave. As a young woman she spent many years in England, where she was kept by the wealthy white woman who gave her the earrings. The relationship, presented as an exploitative one, broke up Merle's marriage to an African student, who left her, taking their daughter to Africa. Following a breakdown, Merle returned to the island, where she has just been fired from her teaching job for teaching the history of the island instead of the history of England. Now she runs a hotel on the Atlantic coast, in the house inherited from her father. Though apparently a broken woman, Merle has the power to speak uncomfortable truths. Periodically, however, she falls silent and locks herself in a room which is the analogue to her depressed mind. This room, the creation of a failed artist, is filled with white ancestors' heavy furniture, half-unpacked trunks brought from England, and many pictures: old prints of planters and slaves, a slave ship, her daughter's photograph. Not surprisingly, Merle admits to fascination with King Lear; like him, she is a half-mad monarch without a country, but she is not a father cast out by his daughters: she is a daughter cast out by her fathers.

In *The Chosen Place, The Timeless People* Merle is only one of the characters, Black and white, female and male, in a novel of epic ambitions. Among the others are Vere, a young man who has just returned to the island jobless, and his Great Aunt Leesy; Allen and Saul, social scientists who have come from the United States to do yet one more study of poverty on the island, and Saul's wealthy wife Harriet; Stinger and Gwen, who work in the cane fields; and many others. While there is a great deal of significant detail and telling incident (and, I think, too much dialogue and description), these characters don't come to life as Merle does, especially the white characters. . . . [By] foregrounding Merle in the novella Marshall is able to place the other characters in the background, where they belong. In the process, some memorable scenes are lost: Vere beating his faithless mistress with one of her own white dolls; Saul fleeing the hot cane fields and the sight of Gwen's turned-up eyes under a load of cane, eyes "that you find upon drawing back the lids of someone asleep or dead"; the palpable hunger Harriet sees among children whose parents are in the fields all day, hunger that "prowled angrily up and down, its footsteps shaking the weak floorboards, its fists pounding the walls, demanding to be appeased"; the carnival parade with its re-enactment of an island slave rebellion and its dancing. But what is gained is the excavation of the novel's best story, Merle's. The author's decision to turn the novel into a novella (a choice for which I know no precedent) may also reveal a new confidence in allowing her heroine to carry the burden of the novel's theme, the unforgivable damage done by racism and the exploitation of Third World peoples. A prominent motif in the novel, Cuffee Ned's slave rebellion, part of the fictional island's history, is omitted in the novella, but Cuffee Ned is, in a sense, subsumed into Merle, who is, after all, a rebel too.

Besides the condensing and tightening of structure involved in making the novella, there were changes to make the style more succinct. Comparison with the original shows adjectives and adverbs deleted and redundancies and entire passages of description omitted, changes indicating not only greater assurance on the author's part and greater confidence in her readers but a skillful writer's ability to continue to perfect her prose.

The literary criticism concerned with Paule Marshall's work has typically overlooked her artistry and emphasized nonliterary matters, focusing only on her themes and discussing her characters as though they are people. For example, John Cook chooses to discuss what he sees as the growth of the author's political consciousness, praising *The Chosen Place, the Timeless People* over the earlier work on political grounds, for its "unambiguous political perspective" and Pan-Africanism [see essay dated 1980]. He censures Marshall for "a temperamental difficulty . . . her predilection for personal as opposed to political subjects" and for her interest in "sexual conflict," as though these were not what novels are made of. By positing a false dichotomy between the personal and the political and by overlooking the dynamics of fiction writing, he misses part of the meaning of the work: not only is Marshall concerned in her books with the need to speak out, but her writing fictions, taking on, as a Black woman, the powerful role of shaper, is itself a political act. (Yet essays on Paule Marshall are still appearing which do not attempt to take into account the implications of the author's being a Black *woman* writer.) (pp. 65-70)

Linda Pannill, "From the 'Wordshop': The Fiction of Paule Marshall," in MELUS, *Vol. 12, No. 2, Summer, 1985, pp. 63-73.*

ADDITIONAL BIBLIOGRAPHY

DeVeux, Alexis. "Paule Marshall: In Celebration of Our Triumph." *Essence* 10, No. 1 (May 1979): 70-1, 96-8, 123-35.

Detailed interview in which Marshall comments on her personal goals as a writer and her early literary influences.

Lodge, Sally. "PW Interviews Paule Marshall." *Publishers Weekly* 225, No. 3 (20 January 1984): 90-1.

Brief interview which focuses on *Reena, and Other Stories,* Marshall's introductions to literature, and her first attempts and successes as a writer.

Marshall, Paule. "The Negro Woman in American Literature: Paule Marshall." *Freedomways* 6, No. 1 (Winter 1966): 20-5.

Text of speech given by Marshall at a three-day conference on "The Negro Writer's Vision of America." Marshall was one of four black women writers who discussed the role of black writers; she focuses her comments on the myths which have halted honest depictions of black characters in literature.

———. "Shaping the World of My Art." *New Letters* 40, No. 1 (Autumn 1973): 97-112.

Discussion of Marshall's childhood experiences which have shaped her thinking, writing, and her belief that African-Americans must gain an understanding of their heritage in order to come to individual self-awareness.

———. "Shadow and Act." *Mademoiselle* 79, No. 2 (June 1974): 82-3.

Review of Ralph Ellison's *Shadow and Act.* Marshall discusses the theme of the work and comments on its influence in her personal life and her fiction.

———. "The Making of a Writer: From the Poets in the Kitchen." *New York Times Book Review* (9 January 1983): 3, 34-5.

Highly acclaimed personal commentary on the foundations and elements of Marshall's personal and artistic beliefs. Marshall comments extensively on the distinctive poetic art of her mother's Barbadian dialect and its impact on her writing.

McCluskey, John, Jr. "And Called Every Generation Blessed: Theme, Setting, and Ritual in the Works of Paule Marshall." In *Black Women Writers (1950-1980): A Critical Evaluation,* edited by Mari Evans, pp. 317-36. New York: Anchor Press/Doubleday, 1984.

Study of Marshall's thematic intentions in her major works. McCluskey focuses on Marshall's attempts to merge past and present in her fiction.

Ogunyemi, Chikwenye Okonjo. " 'The Old Order Shall Pass': The Examples of 'Flying Home' and 'Barbados.' " *Studies in Short Fiction* 20, No. 1 (Winter 1983): 23-32.

Comparative study of the narrative style and fundamental optimism found in Ralph Ellison's "Flying Home" and Paule Marshall's "Barbados."

Waniek, Marilyn Nelson. "Paltry Things: Immigrants and Marginal Men in Paule Marshall's Fiction." *Callaloo* 6, No. 2 (Spring-Summer 1983): 46-56.

Examination of the alienation felt by the aging men of *Soul Clap Hands and Sing.*

Washington, Mary Helen. "I Sign My Mother's Name: Alice Walker, Dorothy West, Paule Marshall." In *Mothering the Mind: Twelve Studies of Writers and Their Silent Partners,* edited by Ruth Perry and Martine Watson Brownley, pp. 155-63. New York: Holmes & Meier Publishers, 1984.

Revealing commentary from Marshall on the antagonistic relationship she had with her mother. Washington examines the dynamics of the mother-daughter relationship and discusses its effects on Marshall's fiction.

Alice Munro

1931-

Canadian short story writer and novelist.

Munro is one of Canada's most critically acclaimed contemporary authors. Often referred to as a regional writer who centers her fiction on the cultural milieu of rural Ontario, Munro credits the short story writers of the American South, particularly Eudora Welty and Flannery O'Connor, with shaping her fictional perspective. In her works, Munro pits the mundane against the fantastic and often relies on paradox and irony to expose meanings that lie beneath the surface of commonplace occurrences. Munro's style is often likened to the works of magic realist painters, such as Edward Hopper, for its vivid images and concentrated depictions of surface textures. Her works usually comprise episodic recollections that chronicle the emotional development of adolescent female characters. Although some critics view her collections as loosely-structured novels, Munro insists her writings are short stories. In a *New York Times* article Munro said, "I can get a kind of tension when I'm writing a short story, like I'm pulling a rope and I know where the rope is attached. With a novel, everything goes flabby." Munro's first collection, *Dance of the Happy Shades,* won the 1969 Governor General's Award, Canada's highest literary honor. Her second book, *Lives of Girls and Women,* again garnered widespread attention and established Munro as a prominent figure in contemporary Canadian literature.

Munro grew up on the outskirts of Wingham, Ontario. She characterizes her neighborhood as being separate from both the town and the rural communities, and many critics suggest that Munro uses setting as a device to explore this undefined area in which many of her characters exist. Because writing was viewed as a peculiar hobby for a young girl in southern Ontario, Munro was self-conscious about her stories, and she has commented on the alienation she felt when she began to write. Nonetheless, Munro was a diligent student and in 1949 earned a scholarship to the University of Western Ontario. She left the university after two years and later was married. During her marriage Munro divided her time between her children, housework, and writing. Motivated by what she calls a personal selfishness and toughness, she compiled the stories that constitute *Dance of the Happy Shades* over a 12 year period. In the early 1970s, Munro separated from her husband and moved with her daughters to London, Ontario. Established as a respected author, Munro received a position as writer-in-residence at the University of Western Ontario, and in 1976, she remarried and moved to Clinton, Ontario, just a few miles from Wingham.

The fifteen stories in *Dance of the Happy Shades* explore personal isolation that springs from fear, ridicule, or the inability to communicate and that is often fostered by a hostile community. Critics note that Munro's consistent focus on social and personal divisions provides the collection with an ironic thematic unity. In several stories Munro presents the segregation of misfits of "the other country" from the town's socially accepted characters, and she often creates characters who initially seem certain of their identities but who gradually begin to question the labels under which they exist, as well as those they have given to others. "Dance of the Happy Shades," for instance, centers on an annual piano recital in which a group of retarded children are silently feared and ridiculed by mothers of the "normal" students. The story ends with an exceptional performance by a retarded girl that leaves the mothers stunned and uncomfortably impressed by the superior talent of a person they had earlier considered an idiot. In this piece as in many of her short stories, Munro explores the sources of social inhibitions and exposes the insecurities of self-righteous and self-centered characters. Other stories in the collection deal with their protagonists' coming-of-age. In "Images," a young girl and her father meet an axe-wielding recluse in the woods. The girl establishes a bond with her father when she agrees not to tell anyone about the stranger's axe. In the end, however, she realizes that she too is "[like] the children in fairy stories who have seen their parents make pacts with terrifying strangers, who have discovered that our fears are based on nothing but the truth. . . ."

The forms of *Lives of Girls and Women* and *The Beggar Maid* are similar in their depictions of the development of central characters, and for this reason these works are often referred to as "open-form" novels. In *Lives of Girls and Women,* Munro strives to capture essential elements of the external world, and critics often note that the episodic nature of this work allows Munro to focus on specific experiences that affect protagonist Del Jordan's perceptions of her changing environment. Critics have also compared *Lives of Girls and Women* to James Joyce's *Portrait of the Artist as a Young Man* for Munro's portrayal of Del as an artist who is alienated and misunderstood. In this work's opening piece, "The Flats Road," Munro compares Del's adolescent perception of reality to that of her Uncle Benny, whose vision of life is composed of the irrational ideals of childhood. Although Del is young, she recognizes that her Uncle's behavior is abormal, and she gradually becomes aware that his freedom and his playfulness are fragile and senses that they are continually threatened by the workings of everyday reality. By the story's end, Del attempts to write about her experiences and her hometown but feels that her understanding has been limited by the entrapping and demanding nature of adult life. Like *Lives of Girls and Women, The Beggar Maid* focuses on moments of confrontation in the protagonist's life. Although many commentators treat the work as a novel, Munro refers to *The Beggar Maid* as a collection of "linked stories" that deal with the maturation of the central character, Rose. Critics note the prevailing depressive quality of the stories in *The Beggar Maid* and comment on Munro's harsh depictions of Rose's relationships with men. While the abrupt time shifts and overlapping experiences in this work provide a faceted characterization of Rose, some critics have suggested that the cool objectivity of the third person narrative undermines the authenticity of the characters. Nonetheless, *The Beggar Maid* earned Munro a second Governor General's Award.

Munro's other collections have also received widespread critical attention. *Something I've Been Meaning To Tell You, The Moons of Jupiter,* and *The Progress of Love* focus on the lives of mature characters and deal primarily with adult themes. Again in these collections Munro uses irony to create an overriding sense of uncertainty and insecurity in her characters. While some critics claim that these collections lack the vitality of her earlier works, many praise Munro's ability to reveal the subtleties and dynamics of adult relationships. Occasionally faulted for limiting herself to a narrow thematic range, Munro is widely regarded as a gifted short story writer whose strength lies in her ability to present the texture of everyday life with both compassion and unyielding precision.

(See also *Contemporary Literary Criticism,* Vols. 6, 10, 19; *Contemporary Authors,* Vols. 33-36, rev. ed.; *Something about the Author,* Vol. 29; and *Dictionary of Literary Biography,* Vol. 53.)

PRINCIPAL WORKS

SHORT FICTION

Dance of the Happy Shades 1968
Lives of Girls and Women 1971
Something I've Been Meaning to Tell You 1974
Who Do You Think You Are? 1978; also published as *The Beggar Maid: Stories of Flo and Rose,* 1979
The Moons of Jupiter 1982
The Progress of Love 1986

H. DAHLIE (essay date 1972)

[*In the following excerpt from a review of* Dance of the Happy Shades, *Dahlie examines the role of the "unconsummated relationship" in this collection, as well as the social dichotomy inherent in Munro's fiction.*]

Up to a point, it is meaningful to divide Alice Munro's characters into two categories—the secure and the insecure, or the adjusted and the maladjusted, or the accepted and the rejected—but a more than superficial examination reveals that these oppositions are quite inadequate to explain their real natures. Mrs. Munro's world is neither consistent nor readily comprehensible; and as the reader struggles with its many paradoxes, contradictions, and ambiguities, he finds himself compelled to reassess characters and their motives, and ultimately to realize that "normal" characters in the conventional sense rarely exist in this world. On the surface, much seems straightforward—family relationships, ordinary friendships, love affairs—but there is always something gnawing at the edges of our certainties, and we recognize that the basic pattern in Alice Munro is isolation rather than community, rejection rather than acceptance. And though these kinds of relationships may in part be due to rural and small-town settings, the emphasis in most of her stories is psychological rather than sociological; the ultimate despair or resignation that the reader experiences is in part the product of the sense of inevitability and immutability that characterizes the various human relationships.

It is this vision of the world and of reality that strikes one in reading Alice Munro's ***Dance of the Happy Shades,*** the title of which takes on an increasingly ironic note. The collection's fifteen stories dramatize the contradictions between life and death, between happiness and despair, between freedom and captivity; and the "dance" itself, as it were, frequently reflects an element of the grotesque. The author's use of a first-person narrator in eleven of these fifteen stories emphasizes her concern with the subjective dimensions of reality, and the fact that the narrator or reflector of the action is in most cases a young and sensitive girl anticipates the shifting nature of this reality. In a very real sense, the narrator stands uneasily between two positions: on the one hand, she is an active participant in, or even instigator of, the action, and on the other hand she stands apart from it as a kind of intuitive moral critic. In this ambivalent position she is not unlike R. D. Laing's "divided self": a convincing representation of the idea that a more or less permanent state of tension is both inevitable and quite acceptable.

A basic pattern in most of these stories reveals the sensitive narrator-figure emerging through her experiences to a point where she senses, even though she cannot normally articulate the fact, that a kind of moral chaos rules everything, and that one can find nothing tangible or lasting to give security or meaning to life. "Things are getting out of hand, anything may happen," the narrator reflects in the title story, and this theme of uncertainty and undefined fear is emphasized throughout the stories. In human terms, the various tensions are dramatized in situations described as "unconsummated relationships" which, in the words of one of the narrators, "depress outsiders perhaps more than anybody else." We would perhaps agree with this narrator—and in a very real sense the reader is the ultimate outsider in any fictional experience—but it seems to me that this remark points to one of the many ambiguities in Alice Munro: is the unconsummated relationship as depressing as an outsider believes, or is it in fact, as far as the participants are concerned, a means of hanging on to whatever they have? [In *The Divided Self*] R. D. Laing argues convincingly on this point when he states that "the ontologically insecure person is preoccupied with preserving rather than gratifying himself: the ordinary circumstances of living threaten his low threshold of security." In this light, many of Alice Munro's characters, such as Maddy in **"The Peace of Utrecht,"** Miss Marsalles in **"Dance of the Happy Shades,"** or Ben Jordan in **"Walker Brothers Cowboy"** assume a different dimension altogether, and their refusal or inability to fulfill themselves in a manner meaningful to the outsider might not be such a defeat after all.

Nevertheless, the recurring isolation and rejection pattern in these and other stories underscores the general sense of alienation which informs Mrs. Munro's fiction. In **"Walker Brothers Cowboy,"** for example, this pattern is established at the outset through a momentary glimpse of the children who "separate into islands of two or one . . . occupying themselves in . . . solitary ways." This situation is parallelled in the division within the Jordan family, particularly in the opposition between the mother and the rest of the family. An inward-turning and unimaginative person, Mrs. Jordan restricts herself to a very narrow range of experiences, deliberately closes her eyes on the realities of her world, and chooses to remain in the seclusion of her home, "always darkened by the wall of the house next door." Ben Jordan, on the other hand, knows "the quick way out of town," and travels constantly outside his own territory. In this tendency, he finds sympathetic collaborators in his two children, particularly the daughter, who is the narrator of this story. Caught up in the tension between her father and mother, she is unable to sort out the impulses or motives of either; she is in league with her father, as it were, mainly because of the excitement provided by his travels, both within and outside his territory.

But Ben, too, is a participant in an "unconsummated relationship," not only with his wife, but also in the tentative affair he is carrying on with Nora Cronin. He can pursue this relationship only so far, in part because of restrictive social and marital conventions, but also because he knows that it cannot really work out, and because he senses that a consummated affair would in fact destroy it. Nora clearly is the real loser in this kind of relationship. " 'I can drink alone,' " she tells Ben when he refuses to dance with her, " 'but I can't dance alone' "; and this is the real meaning of isolation and rejection brought down to an agonizingly tangible level. The meaning of this whole experience for Ben's daughter is not clear, though she understands enough to realize that she is to say nothing to her mother about it. Its full significance is, however, both ambiguous and frightening:

> I feel my father's life flowing back from our car in the last of the afternoon, darkening and turning strange, like a landscape that has an enchantment on it, making it kindly, ordinary and familiar while you are looking at it, but changing it, once your back is turned, into something you will never know, with all kinds of weathers, and distances you cannot imagine.

In this incipient formulation of ideas, Ben's daughter touches upon the ecstasies, the terrors, and the contradictions of existence; but the overriding idea is that of unpredictability and uncertainty. She feels isolated in time, and in this respect she stands apart from her father: "The tiny share we have of time appalls me," she muses at one point, "though my father seems to regard it with tranquillity. . . . He was not alive when this century started. I will be barely alive—old, old—when it ends. I do not like to think of it." This fear of the disintegration of self recurs frequently in Alice Munro, and illustrates her essentially existential view of reality. In this vision, she is at times close to that of Samuel Beckett, and many of her situations evoke an echo of one of his basic questions, "How can one be sure in such darkness?"

In **"Boys and Girls"** isolation leads in another direction, and a temporary triumph and sense of emancipation is achieved. Again, the youthful girl narrator experiences fear and insecurity, this time in two stages. First of all as a child in her upstairs bedroom, separated from "the warm, safe, brightly lit downstairs world," she reflects that she and her brother "were not afraid of *outside*" but they "were afraid of *inside.*" In other words, it was not the tangible external world with its snowdrifts and biting winds that posed the terror, but rather the dark, shifting shapes in the unfinished upstairs suggesting undefinable and grotesque horrors—that is, subjective rather than objective reality. In the second stage of her insecurity, she has moved into a state of isolation, as she is rejected by her father and brother because she is a girl, and by her mother and grandmother for not being enough of a girl. "I no longer felt safe," she reflected. "The word *girl* had formerly seemed to me innocent and unburdened, like the word *child*; now it appeared that it was no such thing. A girl was not, as I had supposed, simply what I was; it was what I had to become. It was a definition, always touched with emphasis, with reproach and disappointment." Isolation here is accompanied by the impulse to freedom or release from bondage, symbolized by her act of setting a mare free; the subsequent catching and slaughtering of the horse, however, suggests that freedom is only an illusion, and that one cannot for long elude the destructive elements of one's world. Nevertheless, the girl does achieve a moment of triumph in her isolation; and her father's absolving her of any wrongdoing by pointing out that "she's only a girl" is, in Alice Munro's world, perhaps as much commendation as one can expect.

Another kind of isolation is involved in **"The Shining Houses,"** and while it is a product initially of sociological forces—the phenomenon of urbanization—its ramifications are played out in psychological and individual terms. Juxtaposed here is an opposition between profoundly human but illogical feelings and modern, inhuman and logical views over the question of whether a somewhat disreputable Mrs. Fullerton should be evicted to allow for an uninterrupted suburban development. The central figure, Mary, is physically a part of the suburban world, but as the champion of the isolated and threatened Mrs. Fullerton, she stands apart spiritually from the members of her own world. Mary is not an uncritical or sentimental champion of Mrs. Fullerton; on the contrary, though she opposes eviction, she finds the woman rather disagreeable, and even when she tries to justify rationally her position, she finds nothing about the old lady to sustain her:

> She was trying desperately to think of other words, words more sound and reasonable than these; she could not expose to this positive tide any notion that they might think flimsy and romantic, or she would destroy her argument. But she had no argument—she could try all night and never find any words to stand up to their words, which came at her now invincibly from all sides: *shack, eyesore, filthy, property, value.*

In very tangible and literal ways, Mrs. Fullerton stands in

complete isolation from the new world encroaching upon her. Socially she is a recluse, for she "did not pay calls herself and she did not invite them," whereas for the suburbanites, "any gathering-together of the people who lived there was considered a healthy thing in itself." Her house stands apart geographically as well as by virtue of its Tobacco Road appearance, but the most significant distinction lies in the internal order and self-sufficiency it reflects through its harmony with the world around it: "Here was no open or straightforward plan, no order that an outsider could understand; yet what was haphazard time had made final." The outsiders lived in a vastly different world, in "new, white and shining houses, set side by side in long rows in the womb of the earth. . . . —those ingenuously similar houses that looked calmly out at each other, all the way down the street." Alice Munro provides a most devastating description of the rooms of these houses, and thus we are not at all surprised when we meet their inhabitants.

Mary of course has no chance against the real-estate logic of her world, and though she registers her protest, she knows the eviction order will carry. But Mrs. Munro, in her most explicit note of protest in this book, makes her stand clear in a blistering portrait of the self-righteous upholders of progress:

> . . . it did not matter much what they said as long as they were full of self-assertion and anger. That was their strength, proof of their adulthood, of themselves and their seriousness. The spirit of anger rose among them, bearing up their young voices, sweeping them together as on a flood of intoxication, and they admired each other in this new behaviour as property-owners as people admire each other for being drunk.

Isolation in this story clearly spells out a strong moral victory, though the reader experiences a strong sense of loss or depression, too, in his knowledge that Mary's voice is feeble indeed against the onslaught of logic.

Much of the effect that Mrs. Munro gains in her exploitation of the "unconsummated relationships" theme derives from a very competent use of irony and ambiguity. In **"The Office,"** for example, the external facts of the whole experience should dictate that Mr. Malley is, if not a lecherous old man, certainly deceitful and unpleasant to an extreme. Yet two essentially unanswerable questions are raised here. First of all, there is the question tackled by Harold Pinter in *The Caretaker* or Saul Bellow in *The Victim*—how far does one's obligation to another human being go, and has one the right to declare that a human relationship shall remain an unconsummated one? Alice Munro doesn't provide the answer to this any more than did Pinter or Bellow, but like them, she compels us to think upon it. The second question reflects a nice, ironic twist: the narrator, a writer, re-arranges words to create an imaginative world or experience; and is this really much different from what Mr. Malley does, who re-arranges facts to create his version of the world, and a version that to the outsider is just as credible as any other tale of fiction? In a very real way, Mr. Malley establishes himself here as a formidable antagonist, and his incredible distortions ironically undergo a kind of transformation towards truth in the conscience of the narrator, so that she can never really dismiss him or his unsettling versions of reality.

In the two stories where the consummation of sexual relationships constitutes an essential part of the action, there is ironically no satisfying resolution for either of the partners. **"Thanks for the Ride"** dramatizes somewhat squalid affairs between two young men and two girls they pick up in a small town. The dominant note here is hysteria: Lois in particular seems to be on the edge of fear and nothingness, and for her, the sexual encounter with the narrator is merely a desperate attempt to fill in some of the emptiness in her life. That it failed to do this, and also that she has as a result moved even closer to hysteria, is indicated by her voice calling out to the men after they dropped her off, "the loud, crude, female voice, abusive and forlorn." In the other story, **"Postcard,"** the more or less steady sexual affair between Helen and Clare seems to underscore her essential desperation and loneliness, as though she senses Clare's eventual betrayal. There is something almost grotesque in her attachment to him; even after his marriage to the Florida woman, she refuses to see him for what he is, but her main attitude is incomprehensibility: "What I'll never understand is why, right now, seeing Clare MacQuarrie as an unexplaining man, I felt for the first time that I wanted to reach out my hands and *touch* him."

Taken together, then, most of the stories in ***Dance of the Happy Shades*** reveal that Alice Munro's characters cannot really win, whether the relationships are consummated or unconsummated. Both lead essentially to isolation and rejection, and intensify feelings of insecurity and emptiness; invariably, it is the sadness of experience rather than its fulfillment that remains with the reader. In the more moderate situations, Mrs. Munro's characters simply reflect varying degrees of uncertainty and ambivalence towards their world, but in the more extreme situations, they teeter on the edge of desperation and hysteria; in both cases, however, the overriding feeling is one of futility and despair, and an intuitive recognition of the inevitability and permanence of isolation. (pp. 43-8)

H. Dahlie, "Unconsummated Relationships: Isolation and Rejection in Alice Munro's Stories," in World Literature Written in English, *Vol. 11, No. 1, April, 1972, pp. 42-8.*

ALICE MUNRO [INTERVIEW WITH GRAEME GIBSON] (essay date 1972)

[*Gibson is a Canadian novelist who is recognized for the innovative structures of his narratives. In the following excerpt, Munro shares her opinions on the difficulties of being a woman writer and comments on her works.*]

I'll begin with a general question: do you think writers know something special, in the way physicists or anthropologists do?

You mean probably that writers are . . . have just seen something special. I don't think they *know* something special. I do think that they, perhaps, just perhaps they see things differently. Well I know to me, just things in themselves are very important. I'm not a writer who is very concerned with ideas. I'm not an intellectual writer. I'm very, very excited by what you might call the surface of life, and it must be that this seems to me meaningful in a way I can't analyze or describe.

Now when you say it's not that they know something special, but they see something special . . . what kinds of things?

Well for me it's just things about people, the way they look, the way they sound, the way things smell, the way everything is that you go through everyday. It seems to me very important to do something with this.

Yes. I mean, perhaps one of the most exciting things I found in reading your stuff was an incredible kind of recognition of how things are.

It seems to me very important to be able to get at the exact tone or texture of how things are. I can't really claim that it is linked to any kind of a religious feeling about the world, and yet that might come closest to describing it. (p. 241)

Dell, in ***Lives of Girls and Women,*** *says: "How contemptuous, how superior and silent and enviable they were, those people who all their lives could stay still, with no need to do or say anything remarkable!"*

Yes, I do feel that about those people, don't you?

Yes, but presumably one of the things that drives Dell is the need to do something remarkable.

Yes I suppose that does, it certainly drove me when I was a child. I always planned to be famous before I was quite sure which direction I would go in. Now I would like to say that drive has left, but. . . .

To do something remarkable and to be famous are different things, aren't they? I mean the desire to be famous is. . . .

Yes, is the reward for doing the remarkable thing. No, but you can do something remarkable in order to be noticed partly, can't you? Not just to achieve the thing in itself, and I think as a child I always wanted very much to be noticed.

One of the things she also says is: "To be made of flesh was humiliation." I want to make the distinction here between your desire to write and what motivates Dell, but perhaps her need to do something remarkable has something to do with this sense of humiliation. Do you think that carries over at all into writing?

With me it has something to do with the fight against death, the feeling that we lose everything every day, and writing is a way of convincing yourself perhaps that you're doing something about this. You're not really, because the writing itself does not last much longer than you do; but I would say it's partly the feeling that I can't stand to have things go. There's that feeling about the—I was talking about the external world, the sights and sounds and smells—I can't stand to let go without some effort at this, at capturing them in words, and of course I don't see why one has to do that. You can experience things directly without feeling that you have to do that, but I suppose I just experience things finally when I do get them into words. So writing is a part of my experience.

And the way of really coming to terms with your experience is to write.

Yes, and I can't imagine living any other way.

Dell also says there's no protection unless it is in knowing.

That's talking about death, specifically. Yes, it could be something to do with writing, couldn't it? But it doesn't protect you really. You know when you're writing, and I think people think of a writer that he or she is someone who knows, and yet in one's ordinary life this doesn't carry over.

And the thing is, presumably, that if you put it down so that you really did know, then you'd stop writing.

Yes, I think perhaps . . . (*laughter*) You know when I'm in the really hellish part of a book, I think this is the last book, when I finish this book, I'm going to stop and live like a sensible person. And even now I think maybe after the next book, though just a little while back I said to you I can't imagine living without writing, I think possibly that I could attain some level where I would have done enough and where I—maybe as you say, I would know, and then I wouldn't write anymore.

What is the knowing, just what it is like to be alive?

Yes, and it may be a way of getting on top of experience; this is different from one's experience of the things in the world, the experience with other people and with oneself, which can be, which is so confusing and humiliating and difficult and by dealing with it this way, though, I don't mean that I deal directly with personal experience, though I do but after quite a long time has elapsed. I think it's a way of getting control.

Imposing order?

Yes, but it's control by hindsight in a way, isn't it? And as I said it doesn't mean you have control over what is happening now.

Dell also says, they are talking to her about writing, she says: "They were talking to somebody who believed that the duty of the writer is to produce a masterpiece."

Well, that is indeed what I did believe till I was maybe thirty years old (*laughter*) and I realized that the choice I had was not between producing a masterpiece and producing something else, but between producing something else and producing nothing at all (*laughter*) and I became more realistic.

You said you've always been writing. How really did you start writing?

I started writing things down when I was about fourteen or fifteen, and earlier than that I made up stories all the time. But I think they were the things that—I think many children do this, and I don't know, maybe loneliness in adolescence is one of the things that makes it persist.

And insisting on your own view of the world too, I guess.

Yes, perhaps it helps to grow up feeling very alienated from the environment you happen to live in, which is another thing that happened to me.

Where did the alienation come from?

Well I grew up in a rural community, a very traditional community. I almost always felt it. I find it still when I go back. The concern of everyone else I knew was dealing with life on a very practical level, and this is very understandable, because my family are farmers and they are two or three generations away from being pioneers. In order to survive it's necessary to be very good at making things with your hands, and always to think practically, and not to see more than is obviously there, not to see what we call beauty or—oh I'm not doing very well here, but I always realized that I had a different view of the world, and one that would bring me into great trouble and ridicule if it were exposed. I learned very early to disguise everything, and perhaps the escape into making stories was necessary.

It's an extremely impractical kind of a thing to be doing.

To most of my relatives the work I do is still a very meaningless, useless type of work.

A frill, if anything.

Not even a frill, almost a wrong thing to be doing, because it is so—if I were hooking rugs though, it would be all right, you see, because you put the rugs on the floor and people walk on them, but what do you do with books? In the community where I grew up, books were a time-waster and reading is a bad habit, and so if even reading is a bad habit, writing is an incomprehensible thing to do.

Dell's Uncle Craig, with the two sisters—when they were younger, when she first knew them, they were really admirable and attractive people, but you make a great point of her seeing that one of the real virtues for them is hiding one's own personal light under a bushel.

Yes this was certainly true in my family, and with many people of this sort of Scotch-Irish background in that part of the country. One doesn't try because one may fail . . . the personal revelation is also something that isn't understood at all. It's a shameful thing.

Another general question. Given that writing is a lonely thing, have you felt isolated as a writer on top of the personal loneliness?

You mean because I haven't known other writers, and because I've been working alone for so long? Oh no, I don't think I've suffered any unnecessary loneliness at all.

What about being a Canadian writer? Or do you think in these terms at all?

No . . . I'm beginning to feel guilty that I haven't, because it's being borne in on one that one should (*laughter*) but—no I haven't.

Do you think there are any obvious advantages or disadvantages in being a Canadian writer?

I think there are some fairly obvious advantages, that a lot of the ground hasn't been ploughed before, and that—I don't really think in competitive terms—the words I'm choosing are not quite right, I was going to say the competition is not as stiff. I don't quite mean that, but I can think of so many very, very good short story writers working in the United States, whose names are hardly known, I would imagine, even to Americans. It seems to me that in Canada, if you are doing good work, recognition comes pretty readily.

Any disadvantages?

I suppose it's possible that you don't reach as wide an audience as quickly or something like that, but no, I don't really feel there are disadvantages. I feel damn lucky to be a Canadian writer.

That's good and it's curious because that's been the kind of response I've had from most people . . . Okay. It struck me, I guess partly because my writing, like yours, comes out of Southwestern Ontario, that Southwestern Ontario might become a kind of mythical country, like the American South for example.

Yes, I've thought of this, yes, probably because the writers who first excited me were the writers of the American South, because I felt there a country being depicted that was like my own. I can think of several writers now who are working out of Southwestern Ontario. It is rich in possibilities in this way. I mean the part of the country I come from is absolutely Gothic. You can't get it all down.

Also I think the culture there is a prevailing culture which is a nice thing. They really do have a sense of tradition. They really do have a sense of how things have been.

Yes. It's a very rooted kind of place. I think that the kind of writing I do is almost anachronistic, because it's so rooted in one place, and most people, even of my age, do not have a place like this any more, and it's something that may not have meaning very much longer. I mean this kind of writing.

Okay. A different kind of question again. What is the writer's role in a society? Do you think the writer has any responsibility to society?

I never think about this at all. I have all my life just thought of doing my work and sort of surviving in society. Now this is a very selfish point of view perhaps. I don't feel anything about responsibility or a role, but I think this is partly because I grew up having to feel so, so protective about this whole thing, about writing, and then you know I married young and I was a suburban housewife in the '50s, and I went through the whole thing again, of having to be very, having to protect the real thing I did, so that I suppose I function as if I were cut off from society, and I'm always even rather surprised when, well, when a book is published, that it exists, when people say I read your book. (*laughter*)

Right. This then would be a good time to ask have you found that there are any particular problems as a writer in being a woman?

Yes, I think there are great problems—it's almost impossible. But then there are problems for a man in this country too because you have to be a wage-earner, and I'm not sure that a woman's problems are any greater. But there are tremendous, you know, emotional demands made by children.

Yes. You have three children, and that in itself is, as you say, an incredibly demanding thing. What kinds of problems does a woman writer encounter, do you think, even before children? Are there any in the, in coming to be a writer, knowing what your role is as a woman or what the role expected of you is?

Yeah. I think there's a problem in that when you become—it's a way of observing life that is not, that perhaps doesn't work well with one's role as a woman. The detachment of the writer, the withdrawal is not what is traditionally expected of a woman, particularly in the man-woman relationship. Most women writers I know are very ambivalent this way. There's the desire to give, even to be dominated, to be, at least I, in many ways want a quite traditional role, and then of course the writer stands right outside this, and so there's the conflict right there. And then when children come, well some of the problems are practical. It's getting enough time, like in twenty years I've never had a day when I didn't have to think about somebody else's needs. And this means the writing has to be fitted in around it. I've read about myself, you know, Alice Munro has produced little, and I think it's a miracle that I've produced anything.

How do you find the time, say with young children, to write? Did you find the time when they were young?

Yes, I've always found the time except for a few years when my confidence failed me completely and it wasn't the children, it was my own problems. But I just found it through incredible stubbornness and really through fighting the children, which may not be a good thing.

It seems to me a hell of a lot harder for the woman writer than for the man writer, because at least the man can leave his office. But the house is there all the time.

Yes the problem is when you're young, when you are a young wife and mother as I was, it's awfully hard to say: Well I'm going to—well, not neglect—but withdraw from this child to do my work, because at that point you have no confidence that your work is ever going to be any good. And you have to get very tough.

There is some of that suggested in the short story **["The Office"]** *where the character gets an office . . . she needs an office and it begins with an apology. . . .*

Terrific apology.

Yes, that one is going to do this at all. What about before, say before one is married even? The kind of image that a woman has of herself, a girl has of herself. It's quite all right for a young man to think, well I'm going to explore the world, write books, go on and on forever, you know—have fantastic sexual adventures all over the place. But a young woman has a very different image of herself, doesn't she—or does she?

Yes. Well she doesn't have a different image of herself . . . I think the generation growing up now is entirely different. But if I go back to when I was growing up, I always operated in disguises, feeling if I do to a certain point what the world expects of me, then they'll leave me alone, and I can do my work. I never did feel that in order to write I had to go to Europe, go to North Africa, go round the world, or do any damn thing at all, but just have a room with a typewriter in it, that was all I needed. And so I put the world off by hiding this as much as possible, but getting on with it.

Is writing a secretive thing for you then?

Yes, I still can't write if there's another adult in the house. I don't quite know why this is, but it must be that I'm still embarrassed about it somehow. (pp. 242-51)

Okay. A couple of questions which may or may not be of interest. What do you like best about your work, about what you've done?

You know what I really like, I like when it's funny and I love it when someone laughs, when the pre-pub copies came out and my husband was reading it and he was lying in bed and laughing. I would be looking over his shoulder and say: What are you laughing at? To me it was great to have brought this off, because I think when you have made something funny, you've achieved some kind of reality. That's what I'm trying to get.

All right, the other side of that question is what do you like least about the work you've done so far?

I think it's sometimes too wordy. I think my approach is slow sometimes. I don't know if there is anything I could say I like least, but there are failures all through that I can see, and that I can't do anything about. They're not failures that I could have gone back and changed, I knew they were failures when the book was finished. They were things that I just couldn't do. I feel that the last section of ***Lives of Girls and Women*** is a failure, and I did the best I could with it. But what else do I like? Some of the stories I don't like at all any more, but that's because they were written so long ago.

Who do you write for?

Well is it the constant reader, the ideal reader? (*laughter*) You know we all have an ideal reader. I can't say I write for myself, though it has to suit me and when it suits me I'm not moved, no matter what an editor or a critic or anybody says. So in a sense I'm writing for myself.

Do you have any sense that you want to reach a lot of people with your writing? I mean apart from what you said earlier about the desire for recognition?

I want to reach as many people as possible, yes. But when I'm writing I don't think about that. In fact I find really the only way I can write is to forget about it being published and reaching people at all. Otherwise the sense of self-exposure or something would be too—I couldn't stand it.

Does being a writer demand a particular kind of selfishness?

Oh goodness yes. Well, yes. Yes, of course, you have to think that your work is more important than almost anything else, and you have to start thinking this when you're very young. And I can't understand quite where this selfishness or confidence or—where it comes from. You have to believe it the way you see it, and perhaps this is what makes the difference between all the people who sort of have talent and write stories for the university magazines and the people who go on writing. I think it's a matter of selfishness and this irrational inner confidence, and I don't know where it comes from.

It isn't need, is it, because a lot of people who write good stories, people who want to be writers, have as much need to be a writer as the people who succeed . . . so you think it's probably just a kind of icy confidence.

Yes, I think this is the way I see it—is it that you want to get across to people how you see it or—? No, just that you think it's so important.

Given the assumption one has, we all have it, that if we write, we assume that some people will want to read us . . . What you feel you have to give is your image of how things are?

Yes, but actually when I'm writing, I don't think of it as *my* image. I am so far gone that I think of it as *the* image, as a kind of revelation coming from, you know.

You succeed very well at it, I might just say. Does the selfishness, do you find your selfishness complicates your relationships with people?

Well I try to hide it pretty well, (*laughter*) but if it gets out. Yes, I think it does and then to go back to what we were saying about the specific problems of being a woman, and a writer, I think it complicates a woman's life much more than a man's, because men are expected to be selfish in a way about their work, to have faith in themselves.

And insist upon their work.

And it is disturbing if women do this.

Because it's an assertion of self which is not expected.

Yes, which is outside the whole relationship to men and children.

Your stories are very personal. I use personal as opposed to autobiographical. . . Do you find yourself wanting to use people, wanting to use people in situations, but feeling you shouldn't because in fact they would recognize it?

Oh yes I have this problem. There are a lot of things I can't use because of this, but I've been going through a very personal kind of writing which I think may have culminated in a book. I never particularly wanted to do this kind of writing, I fought against it for a long time. I told somebody the other day I really want to write stories like Frank O'Connor's stories in which, you know, there are all these people living at a distance, going through lives. But when I try to do things like this it doesn't work—it isn't for lack of trying. So I ended up doing all this very personal stuff. I'm not sure whether I'll go on doing this.

At the end of **"Images",** *a really nice short story, the girl encounters the. . . .*

Yes I like that short story the best.

. . . not a madman or anything, but the eccentric, and she comes home and what she has discovered out of it all is that "our fears are based on nothing but the truth."

Yes, well that's what I believe. (*laughter*)

I mean the whole force of your writing seems to be on that. The fears and the triumphs are just out of what is in fact there.

Yes. (pp. 252-55)

You talk about people doing things that you admire and breaking through; are they things that you want to do?

Well I wish I had thought of them. (*laughter*) They mightn't work for me, because I don't think you can superimpose anything on your writing. You can't say: Well I'm going to chop up these sentences or some damn thing, you know. You just can't do it that way; it's got to come from you, but nothing like this does come from me. I tend to work, as you know, in a pretty traditional way.

It really is a very human and a very compassionate kind of way that you write. It's almost as if there is no style. I mean that as a compliment.

Yes I know what you mean. But you see that I don't write about, I can't write about states of mind. I have to write about—I can't have anybody in a room without describing all the furniture. (*laughter*) You know . . . I can't yet get into people or life without—it's really what I was saying earlier—without having all those other things around them, and God knows that isn't the way most people live any more.

Yes, all right, in some sense your characters aren't alienated in the modern traditional sense of alienated. They react against something, but they are always part of something, aren't they?

Yes, But up to now I've only written about Western Ontario, and I've mainly written about, well my personal stuff has been about childhood and adolescence.

You say you started writing at fourteen, and at some point you presumably settled into writing very seriously. Do you have finished books, novels, which haven't seen the light of day yet?

No, no, no no. I just have boxes full of abortions. You know, things that haven't fully developed.

Do you find yourself writing with no end in view, no particular story or novel? Do you find yourself just simply writing episodes?

No, no. I'm fairly controlled. This is another thing I wish I could do; I wish I could just write and see where it was going, where it would take me, but no, I have a pretty well-defined pattern. I don't know whether I'm going to be able to bring it off, but I don't sit down without it.

At what point do you recognize that it's not going to be a long short story, but it's in fact going to be a book in itself?

Yeah. Well. I think I'll really tell you about this because—(*laughter*)—it's a bit damaging in a way, because some people said, of course, ***Lives*** is only a collection of long short stories. This doesn't particularly bother me, because I don't feel that a novel is any step up from a short story. When I began to write ***Lives,*** you see, I began to write it as a much more, a much looser novel, with all these things going on at the same time, and it wasn't working. Then I began pulling the material and making it into what are almost self-contained segments. I mean the sections could almost stand as short stories. They're all a little bit too loose, but this seemed to be the only way I could work, and I think maybe this is the way I'll have to write books. I write sort of on—like a single string, a tension string—okay? That's the segment or the story. I don't write as perhaps, as some people say a true novelist does, manipulating a lot of strings.

All right, a question that may be a difficult one. Where do you go from here? It's almost as if—I mean is there any danger that you will have exorcised all the ghosts?

It might well be. You mean when I started, you know about half the stories in the first book are sort of beginning stories and then they start getting closer and closer. The first one I wrote, **"The Peace of Utrecht",** I didn't even want to write, because it's the most autobiographical story I've ever written. It was very close, and from then on this was the only kind of story I wrote, and then I began writing the book. Okay. I've gone, yeah, I've gone as far as I can go in this direction.

What you've really done is perhaps just exorcised the ghosts of childhood, you know there's. . . .

Yeah. But dealing with the ghosts of one's maturity is more difficult. (*laughter*)

They're more persistent.

Yes. They're still there.

Okay. There's another intriguing area, and that is the relationship between men and women. And there are two quotes, I'll read them both, because it seems to me they give two emphases. Dell is talking about the bright young man who she is in high school with—they are competing for marks—and she says about him: "He was truthful in telling me what he felt about me, apparently. I had no intention of being so with him. Why not? Because I felt in him what women feel in men, something so tender, swollen, tyrannical, absurd. I would never take the consequences of interfering with it. I had an indifference, a contempt almost that I concealed from him. I thought I was tactful, even kind. I never thought that I was proud." And then she also talks . . . that's one side of a woman's relationship with a man. Then there's the other when she talks about her Uncle Craig, and she says: "Masculine self-centredness made him restful to be with." (laughter) *Now. . . .*

Well it does. I was remembering how I felt about men when

I was a child. They never wanted to do anything with you. I mean to change you to . . . what was the question?

I'm not sure exactly what it is. It had to do partially with the kind of—and maybe I ask this primarily as a man, you know, I'm not sure, but it intrigues me, the kind of secretive world that is suggested, particularly in the first quote about Dell's perception of the young man, and also the sense that—and the two aunts have the same thing about Craig, when he's away typing. All he has to do is go in there and type and they're impressed on the one hand, but at the same time they find him what? Childish?

Yes.

And there again is ambiguity.

Yes, I do feel that that's what women have felt about men and about men's work, on the one hand, men have to be built up so that they can fill this role of lover, leader, dominator that we have been taught to require, or that perhaps we do basically require, I'm not even sure it's all what we're taught. At the same time, there's a feeling that they're children who have to be protected from the knowledge of how meaningless their endeavours are. (*laughter*) I think this is true because women particularly are concerned with the very basic things about life, the food, the physical life, and what men do then seems almost like an indulgence.

Is it because they're more social in their ego in some sense?

Women?

Men. I mean they're out there in this society which on the whole your characters have found alien and hurtful and in many ways absurd; and men's egos are much more concerned with those kinds of things? Whereas the women basically are much more concerned with making jam. I don't mean that in a derogatory sense, but in the sense that they are just actual practical things. . . .

The women are concerned with taking care of the men in a physical sense. Okay. So the men have to be doing something to make taking care of them worth while.

But there's also . . . she then meets the guy from the farm who is much more fundamental, I mean the whole sexual exploration, the sexual discovery, but he also has in his church an equally—it's a crutch, isn't it?

A crutch. And something that she doesn't question.

Except that she wants no part of it at all. Within this logic, is the male activity, say in the work, for example—are kinds of crutches that men depend upon?

I wonder if they appear this way to women. I don't know if women go so far as to think of them as crutches. But, there's a feeling there that maybe I was trying to get at, a feeling I have that women are much tougher than men, that they can take far more, and that for instance you mustn't criticize men, you mustn't tear them down beyond a certain point. This may be a simple sexual thing, that if a man's confidence is destroyed, the whole function is going to be lost. I can't get at it too well.

We were talking earlier about where you go as a writer. There are worlds to be explored in post-adolescence, you know. Just in terms of ***Lives of Girls and Women,*** *say "Lives of Men and Women" or something. I mean that whole ambivalence, or whatever, is a very rich area. Is that the kind of thing. . . .*

That is the kind of thing I would like to deal with. When I was writing, it interested me tremendously to try to get down these, these feelings that women have about men.

The thing is, your whole rendition, dramatization, whatever it is, all the condescension which girls and women have towards men is something I always suspected as a young man when I was growing up.

Also fear. I think I said something in the book about the way boys, little boys, your pre-adolescent boys, hate girls, and I've always felt this too, that there's a kind of hate there that you can tap in men. It has no equivalent in women's feelings for men.

And you think it carries on beyond the pre-adolescent?

Yes, in adult men too, yes.

Do you have any sense of what it is based on?

Well. Hatred of sex, I think. I'm not sure at all, but most of the terms in which this hostility is expressed are sexual.

Yes, right. Then most pornography has to do with the humiliation.

Yes, yes. So fear of sex . . . and women are responsible for sex. I think that's probably it. But this condescension as I say is a very different thing and it has to do with, oh it may be very complicated and it may be something to do with the need to have men like you too. It may not be so much a condescension thing, because you can't criticize men. You can't go too far or they won't approve of you; they think you're a castrating bitch, you know. This very frightening thing.

Do you think men demand or expect from women a kind of admiration or a kind of unthinking support?

Yes, I think they assume their pursuits are more important and their gifts are too, probably.

But in a sense, if they have to go to a woman to have them agree with the importance of their pursuits, they can't totally believe in, can they?

No, I suppose not. You mean if they have to put women down?

I mean the effect of, as she says: "I would never take the consequences of interfering with it," and that is. . . .

No I think what I meant by that, I think really what I meant is the consequences of any destruction of a male, which is a frightening thing to happen to a woman.

But then when you say it's a destruction of a male, all he was doing was assuming that he was more important than she. I mean he puts her down for her interest in the humanities. . . .

Yes he puts her down, okay, but she doesn't really. . . .

She doesn't accept that.

She doesn't accept it.

But she simply avoids it.

Yes. Okay. Why can't she put him down? It's a fear that he might just be too crushed, that he wouldn't have the resources that she has to survive being put down, because women have been in this position for a hell of a long time, and they have the strength of any subject race to survive.

Do you think that basically one of the problems women have in coming to terms with men is that they're afraid of destroying them?

It's a problem I have, yes. Yes. But then this is all dealing with, you know, a generation ago. I wonder how things have changed. They may have changed a great deal or maybe less than we suspect. I don't know.

I suspect less, actually. (laughter) *This is the area that the book you're working on is concerned with?*

Yes.

Wow. You've got no shortage of material. (pp. 256-64)

Alice Munro, in an interview in Eleven Canadian Novelists Interviewed by Graeme Gibson, *Toronto: Anansi, 1972, pp. 237-64.*

RAE McCARTHY MacDONALD (essay date 1976)

[*In the following except, MacDonald examines the opposing social poles which create the central tensions in the plots of Munro's fiction.*]

Through her three books [***Dance of the Happy Shades, Lives of Girls and Women,*** and ***Something I've Been Meaning to Tell You***], Alice Munro's vision has been modified and complicated. Yet, the ground-work of its dynamics remains strikingly consistent, clearly basic to Munro's art. The essential tension between two sets of values, two ways of seeing, two worlds, is always apparent, as central in her last book as her first. In the story **"Dance of the Happy Shades,"** which gives its title to the volume of short stories that won the Governor General's Award for Fiction in 1969, all the basic ingredients of Munro's peculiar vision are strikingly present, and Munro herself supplies the best terminology with which to discuss her art. Considered in some detail, this story provides a valuable introduction to the Munro canon.

In **"Dance of the Happy Shades,"** Miss Marsalles, an aging piano teacher, is giving her annual concert to which all her pupils and their mothers, in many cases former pupils themselves, are invited. At one time, when Miss Marsalles' address was in Rosedale, the annual concert "had solidity, it had tradition, in its own serenely out-of-date way it had style. Everything was always as expected." The cautious mothers had felt assurance that their attendance was part of a socially approved ritual of safe and known value. In recent years, however, along with Miss Marsalles' aging and her undeniably pinched circumstances, the old assurance has given way to a nervous "feeling that can hardly be put into words about Miss Marsalles' parties; things are getting out of hand, anything may happen." There is also the major fear that no one else will show up, and the unwary mother who has missed the signs or whose "instincts for doing the right thing have become confused" will find herself alone in an intolerable situation, a situation that has jumped the rails of social custom. The narrator of **"Dance of the Happy Shades"** is one of Miss Marsalles' older pupils, and her mother is typical of the nervous mothers who are beginning to suspect that Miss Marsalles' concerts have moved beyond the pale. This year, the narrator's mother, whose social instincts may have been confused by life in the suburbs, in spite of hesitation, attends the concert as usual. The house is shabbier than in any other year; Miss Marsalles' poverty is no longer muted; upstairs her sister lies ill; in the dining-room, flies buzz around sandwiches made too long beforehand. But these signs are merely omens of the greater disaster. As the narrator sits chopping dutifully at the piano, she senses the bustle of new arrivals and also, underlying the surface noise, "a peculiarly concentrated silence. Something has happened, something unforeseen, perhaps something disastrous." The concert has finally and irrevocably placed itself in the realm of social taboos, has produced the unacceptable. Miss Marsalles has been teaching children from a school for the retarded, and it is these children who have just arrived.

Making polite efforts to avoid looking at these children, the now terrified mothers are inwardly calling them "little idiots" and screaming "WHAT KIND OF PARTY IS THIS?" Outwardly, their social masks remain undisturbed. Yet, the final blow is still to come. Dolores Boyle, one of the retarded youngsters, takes her place at the piano and, to the amazement and consternation of the mothers, plays well, better than well. What she manages to do with the music is something that, given these mothers and their hysterical rigidity, must be more disturbing than anything to this point. "And all that this girl does—but this is something you would not think could ever be done—is to play it so it can be felt." The music is "fragile, courtly and gay" and "carries with it the freedom of a great unemotional happiness." In the face of this onslaught on their carefully schooled emotions, "the mothers sit, caught with a look of protest on their faces, a more profound anxiety than before, as if reminded of something they had forgotten they had forgotten." When the ordeal is over, the mothers leave, certain this time never to return, unwilling to discuss or recognize what they have just been forced to know, that an idiot girl has shown a greater gift for beauty and feeling than either they or their children. "To Miss Marsalles such a thing is acceptable, but to other people, people who live in the world, it is not." And in that sentence is the key to much that is dynamic in Alice Munro's vision. There are those of "the world," of society, of the accepted norms, and those "from the other country," people such as Miss Marsalles whose innocence has made her, at the best, a fondly tolerated anachronism and, at the worst, a social embarrassment. Miss Marsalles, with this terrible *faux pas,* has placed herself in the same category as idiots, seniles, eccentrics, criminals, and the fatally ill, all of whom are uncontrollable, unpredictable, and, therefore, painful, embarrassing, and plainly unacceptable by "the world."

It is around this division of "the world" and non-world or "other country" that Munro's interest and irony centres. In this story, for instance, the title of the piece Dolores Boyle plays is, Miss Marsalles tells the mothers, "The Dance of the Happy Shades," *Danses des ombres heureuses.* The narrator remarks that this information "leaves nobody any wiser." Yet, in this title is contained Munro's illuminating irony, an irony briefly perceived by the mothers in Dolores Boyle's music and which they have promptly repressed, that Miss Marsalles and the "idiot" children, though strictly excluded from "the world," are, nonetheless, happy ghosts who know a measure of feeling and freedom lost to the nervous mothers in their social garrison. In fact, what Munro asks is, "Whc are the real handicapped?" The answer is clear; as the mothers, not one of whom "has ever expected music," leave Miss Marsalles' neighborhood, hurrying back to the safety of their social routines, the reader understands that the retardation of those children who are "not all there" has been a symbolic externalization of the hidden, but ultimately graver, retardation of those smug social survivors, the nervous mothers and their normal children.

Sadly and realistically, many of Munro's stories in ***Dance of the Happy Shades*** recognize that not all the inhabitants of "the other country" are happy or have the compensations of Dolores Boyle's talent. In **"Day of the Butterfly,"** Myra Sayla is first placed beyond the realm of the social norm by her foreign background and manners and then by her fatal illness. As is so often the case in Munro's writing, the narrator is an individual fighting for precarious social survival, in this case one of Myra's classmates. She walks into town from the country to go to school, and this alone marks her as different and makes her cautious: "I was the only one in the class who carried a lunch pail and ate peanut-butter sandwiches in the high, bare, mustard-coloured cloakroom, the only one who had to wear rubber boots in the spring. . . . I felt a little danger, on account of this; but I could not tell exactly what it was." Unconsciously aware of her own danger, perhaps because of it, the narrator finds herself establishing a tentative bond with Myra, the outcast. Part of her cannot resist the admiration offered by Myra, an admiration the narrator herself offers to girls more safely of "the world" than she. In a moment of generosity, she gives Myra a tin butterfly from her crackerjack box and immediately senses that she has endangered her own shaky position within the norm. "I realized the pledge as our fingers touched; I was panicky, but *all right*. . . . I can go and talk to her at recess. Why not? *Why not?*" Of course, the narrator subconsciously knows why not and is instantly relieved that Myra does not wear the pin on her dress; "If someone asked her where she got it, and she told them, what would I say?" The narrator is saved from exposure by Myra's illness. The next time she sees her is when a delegation of girls from the class visit Myra in the hospital. The girls have been chosen by the teacher for the visit, and this process of selection of few and exclusion of many has made the visit "fashionable." "Perhaps it was because Gladys Healey had an aunt who was a nurse, perhaps it was the excitement of sickness and hospitals, or simply the fact that Myra was so entirely, impressively set free of all the rules and conditions of our lives. We began to talk of her as if she were something we owned, and her party became a cause." If special circumstances have made Myra momentarily and superficially acceptable, the narrator, with her improved social status, has developed her survivor's intuition and realizes a new threat from a Myra who is fatally ill and, therefore, clearly not of "the world." So, when the other girls have left the hospital room and Myra suggests a future meeting after she is better, the narrator glibly says "Okay," but this time she defends herself against dangerous involvement. "All the presents on the bed, the folded paper and ribbons, those guilt-tinged offerings had passed into this shadow, they were no longer innocent objects to be touched, exchanged, accepted without danger." When a nurse interrupts, the narrator is happy to have an excuse to leave, and she recognizes "the treachery of my own heart." Myra has leukemia and dies. This death of the body has been preceded by another death, Myra's social murder at the tongues of the same girls who happily played the role of chosen bedside visitors. And, just as at the end of **"Dance of the Happy Shades"** Munro seemed to ask, "Who are the real handicapped?"—at the end of **"Day of the Butterfly"** she asks, "Who or what has really died?" Part of the answer is a portion of the narrator's freedom and integrity. In her conformity to the demands of "the world," in her choice of survival within the norm, the narrator has had to repress or even destroy an impulse towards generosity and individuality. Therefore, Myra's death becomes a symbol, on a different level, of the death of the narrator.

The prevalence, then, in Munro's work, of idiots, senile old people, suicides, the fatally ill, and that recurring image of the mother who is attacked by Parkinson's disease are guides to her controlling vision. Munro sees society and life as cruel and deforming. Those who appear to adapt or cope and survive are, in her eyes, more deformed in an internal, spiritual way, than those who are clearly retarded or maimed and unable to enter the struggle. In some stories, the obviously defective people seem better off and freer than those who have found acceptance in a "normal" world. In most cases, they work as a symbol or externalization of the suffering and deformity of the apparently healthy and adjusted characters. They are also a deflecting release valve for the tension that builds up from the reader's sense of repressed pain in Munro's world.

So, in **"Walker Brothers Cowboy,"** old, blind Mrs. Cronin, who sits passively in her easy chair and from the hollows of whose eyes comes "a drop of silver liquid, a medicine, or a miraculous tear," suggests the long accepted sorrow of her daughter Nora who could not marry the narrator's father because of a difference in religion. In **"Thanks for the Ride,"** another old woman, the grandmother of Lois, a girl the narrator has picked up, is surrounded by a darker, more sinister aura. "She was . . . as soft and shapeless as a collapsed pudding, pale brown spots melting together on her face and arms, bristles of hairs in the moisture around her mouth. Some of the smell in the house seemed to come from her. It was a smell of hidden decay, such as there is when some obscure little animal has died under the verandah." The evocative image of the little animal that has died is as clearly connected to the granddaughter and the narrator as to the grandmother. Lois, who the narrator discovers can be a "mystic of love," is trapped by her environment and used by the people of "the world," chiefly men who never accept her whole offering. Her voice, "abusive and forlorn," yelling after the narrator's car, suggests the internal deformity and horror which the image of the grandmother externalizes. Also externalized in the grandmother is the repulsion and guilt of the narrator who is from a "nice" family. Though he senses the girl's pain, he is unable to do more than use her: "All the things I wanted to say to her went clattering emptily through my head. *Come and see you again—Remember—Love*—I could not say any of these things."

At the end of **"The Time of Death,"** another girl, Patricia Parry, shrieks out her pain at the tortures of society, in this case represented by a garrison of women, "their faces looming pale and heavy, hung with ritual masks of mourning and compassion." Behind the masks are smugness, condescension, and hate, the weapons of "the world" in which Patricia wants desperately to find a place. "She did not play at being a singer, though she was going to be a singer when she grew up, maybe in the movies or maybe in the radio. She liked to look at movie magazines and magazines with pictures of clothes and rooms in them; she liked to look in the windows of some of the houses uptown." Patricia's clumsy, misinterpreted attempts to win social approval never get her what she wants, only mark her more distinctly as an outcast, and the toll she pays in repression and guilt is killing. Her final hysterical fit expresses this, but not as vividly as the image of her little brother Benny who is retarded and who is accidentally scalded to death when Patricia spills boiling water. "Other little kids only thirteen, fourteen months old knew more words than Benny, and could do more things . . . and most of them were cuter to look at. . . . But he was good; he would stand for hours just looking out a window saying Bow-wow, bow-wow. . . ." Patricia, in her efforts to conform to the norm, also tries to be "good" and frequently suggests a little dog trying to please, even at the expense of not allowing herself a natural reaction to Benny's death. The title, **"The Time of Death,"** therefore, implies one of Munro's typical questions: who or what really dies in this story? And the answer is Patricia just as surely as it is Benny. As Patricia stands screaming hysterically at the end of the story, the reader understands her pain in terms of the image of Benny crying and crying before he died.

In ***Lives of Girls and Women,*** the distinction between "the world" and "the other country" remains central to the dynamics of Munro's vision. Many motifs from the first book recur in the second. Idiots, madmen, and suicides are prominent and are placed clearly outside the garrison of society's norms. The most compelling and tragic of these figures is the narrator's mother, Ida Jordan. Neither an idiot nor a suicide, she is, nonetheless, unquestionably, irrevocably, outside the social pale. Her intellectual frankness and social naivêté amount to *eccentricity* and place her outside society like a child with her nose pressed yearningly to a toy shop window. On the other side of the glass are her husband's family whose disapproval "came like tiny razor-cuts, bewilderingly, in the middle of kindness," the ladies who do not return Ida's invitation to a party, the girls in the narrator's class who are always chosen for prestigious duties, and the girls to whom the narrator, Del, unsure of her social place, is "unfailing obsequiously pleasant."

Ida Jordan is the most complex of Munro's outcast characters. She is both admirable and pathetic, both scornful of "the world" and pitiably eager to be part of it. The reader quickly understands that for her there is no chance of acceptability. The narrator, Del, however, is more attuned to the demands of the social norm than her mother, and the effect of this on their relationship is one of the focuses of the novel. Like the narrator of **"Day of the Butterfly,"** Del is a half-way character, neither safely in, nor definitely outside, the garrison. She identifies with her mother's exclusion and vulnerability, but constantly betrays this sympathy to her social instincts: "I myself was not so different from my mother, but concealed it, knowing what dangers there were."

In ***Lives of Girls and Women,*** no one idiot, invalid, or suicide externalizes the suffering of any one character; rather, they all reflect each other and compositely suggest the hidden illness of the apparent survivors. Ida's pain at social rejection is a variation on the stoic suffering of Mrs. Sherriff whose daughter has committed suicide and whose son is in an asylum. The price paid by both Ida and Mrs. Sherriff is expressed by the suicide of the eccentric teacher, Miss Farris. The garrison finds "no revelation" in this violent act and is mystified, but the reader, familiar with Munro's vision, can see it as one more expression of the universal sorrow and hurt. It is significant that Del's final encounter in the novel is with Mrs. Sherriff's son, home on holiday from the asylum. By this time, Del has placed herself on the road to social conformity and cannot accept what this outcast has to offer:

> Bobby Sherriff spoke to me wistfully, relieving me of my fork, napkin and empty plate.
>
> "Believe me," he said, "I wish you luck in your life."
>
> Then he did the only special thing he ever did for me. With those things in his hands, he rose on his toes like a dancer, like a plump ballerina. This action, accompanied by his delicate smile, appeared to be a joke not shared with me so much as displayed for me, and it seemed also to have a concise meaning, a stylized meaning—to be a letter, or a whole word, in an alphabet I did not know.

This scene recalls the mothers of **"Dance of the Happy Shades"** who could not respond freely to the idiot girl's music.

In ***Lives of Girls and Women,*** that important boundary between "the world" and "the other country" is marked not only by characterization but also by symbolic geography. In this novel, the division between town and outside-of-town that made the narrator of **"Day of the Butterfly"** nervous has become full-fledged. The Jordans live outside town on the Flats Road, a no-man's land that is "not part of town . . . not part of the country either." On the Flats Road live various eccentrics, bootleggers, and two idiots. Given the context of Munro's vision and such an accumulation of unmistakable outcasts in one geographical location, the Flats Road becomes a symbol for everything and everyone that the social garrison fears and does not approve. Ida, that complex and pathetic woman, though she will never meet the standards of the garrison, nonetheless, cannot accept relegation to "the other country," and her walks to town represent her desperate futile struggle to be of "the world." "The Flats Road was the last place my mother wanted to live. As soon as her feet touched the town sidewalk and she raised her head, grateful for town shade after Flats Road sun, a sense of relief, a new sense of consequence flowed from her." The pity is that Ida never realizes that "the other country" can offer compensations. Del's father, on the other hand, feels at home and happy on the Flats Road; unlike his wife he has "that delicate special readiness to scent pretension that is some people's talent." So when Ida moves into town to besiege the garrison, Mr. Jordan stays on the Flats Road.

Chief among the eccentrics of this symbolic "other country" is Uncle Benny, "the sort of man who becomes a steadfast eccentric almost before he is out of his teens." Like many of Munro's outcasts, Uncle Benny has gifts denied to inhabitants of "the world." The most important of these is passion, the ability to feel strongly and spontaneously:

> In all his statements, predictions, judgments there was a concentrated passion. In our yard, once, looking up at a rainbow, he cried, "You know what that is? That's the Lord's promise that there isn't ever going to be another flood!" He quivered with the momentousness of this promise as if it had just been made, and he himself was the bearer of it.

This is the very quality that handicaps Ida in her fight for social acceptance, but she never recognizes its stigma or accepts its consequences. Ultimately what Benny has to offer is truth—the truth about life, that it is not regulated, secure, and rewarding as the garrison teaches, but rather an erratic, confusing, unordered wilderness:

> So lying alongside our world was Uncle Benny's

> world like a troubling distorted reflection, the same but never at all the same. In that world people could go down in quicksand, be vanquished by ghosts or terrible ordinary cities; luck and wickedness were gigantic and unpredictable; nothing was deserved, anything might happen; defeats were met with crazy satisfaction. It was his triumph, that he couldn't know about, to make us see.

The ultimate reward of Benny's vision could be what he himself has achieved, freedom from society's expectations and demands, but even the Jordans are unwilling to accept the full darkness of Benny's truth and end by laughing at it, labelling it, taking some refuge in the defenses of "the world," by summing up and brushing aside his hard terrible wife as a comic "madwoman."

Later, in the chapter titled **"Baptizing,"** Garnet French, another character who lives significantly outside of town on a farm "miles through thick bush," offers Del "perfect security" and a talent for love that echoes Lois of **"Thanks for the Ride."** However, Del realizes that these gifts belong to "the other country" and, unwilling to become an outcast, she uses him, meets "his good offers with my deceitful offerings, whether I knew it or not, matched my complexity and play-acting to his true intent." A brief sentence suggests what she gives up when she rejects Garnet and his life: "There is no denying I was happy in [his] house." ***Lives of Girls and Women*** shares the vision of ***Dance of the Happy Shades,*** a vision of man's existence divided sharply into two countries: in each country people suffer for lack of the world on the other side of the barrier. Only the occasional genius, the rare visionary such as Uncle Benny, can fully accept and affirm the world in which he finds himself.

Something I've Been Meaning To Tell You is Munro's latest book, and, in it, we find all the elements of her vision once again, not as obvious perhaps, less sure of the enemy perhaps, but still concerned with the way of "the world" and the way of "the other country." In the title story, Et, another guilty garrison character from whose viewpoint the story is told, is disgusted by the passion she perceives when she happens on her sister, Char, entangled in the grass with a man; "She was left knowing what Char looked like when she lost her powers, abdicated." She is disturbed that Char's remarkable beauty has turned up unexpectedly, uncontrollably, in real life. "This made Et understand, in some not entirely welcome way, that the qualities of legend were real, that they surfaced where and when you least expected." Like the Jordans, Et is unwilling to face a world of chance and chaos. She loves Char's husband who is an ostrich hiding his head in the safe vision of the acceptable. "He did not know why things happened, why people could not behave sensibly. He was too good. He knew about history but not about what went on, in front of his eyes, in his house, anywhere." Finally, to thwart Char's passion, Et lies to her about her lover. Char takes poison, and Et, smugly inside the garrison of respectability, is left, close keeper of Char's "good" husband. "If they had been married, people would have said they were very happy."

In **"Winter Wind,"** the narrator and her mother are clearly Del and Ida Jordan retold. In this story, however, the focus falls on the father's family. The narrator, who has always seen her grandmother as a woman safely and securely of "the world," suddenly perceives the price this conformity has demanded. "My grandmother had schooled herself, watched herself, learned what to do and say; she had understood the importance of acceptance, had yearned for it, had achieved it, had known there was a possibility of not achieving it." Part of the price of achieving this acceptance has been marriage to the wrong man. As in the earlier books, Munro continues to use deaths and derangement as externalizations of hidden psychic pain. At the end of **"Winter Wind,"** the story of the death by freezing of Susie Heferman, a friend of the grandmother, is as much a reflection of the grandmother's internal withering as the tale of an actual freezing.

It is apparent, then, that ***Something I've Been Meaning To Tell You*** reveals the same divided universe as do ***Dance of the Happy Shades*** and ***Lives of Girls and Women.*** And it asks Munro's characteristic questions. **"Walking on Water"** and **"Forgiveness in Families"** both play with the old question, "Who or what is mad?" In **"Memorial,"** the central character, who has been confronted anew with the rigidly defined world of her sister, thinks "the only thing we can hope for is that we lapse now and then into reality." The sister, with her absolute control of house and family and friends, never lapses, and the toll this takes on her spirit is represented by the ironic death of her son in a freak accident; even to this tragedy his mother cannot respond spontaneously.

Alice Munro's work bears the marks of a distinctive, vital, and unifying vision. Though this vision shows itself more complex and subtle with each of her books, the basic terms remain unchanged. Man finds himself divided into two camps, and the price of this division for both sides is loneliness and pain. The external deformities and violences of "the other country," the place of outcasts, are simply transferences of the unseen, hidden disfiguration of "the world," place of "survivors." Which group suffers most is a question without significance in a universe where men, the pathetic victims of chance, offer each other not kindness or encouragement, but suspicion and hate. (pp. 365-74)

Rae McCarthy MacDonald, "A Madman Loose in the World: The Vision of Alice Munro," in Modern Fiction Studies, *Vol. 22, No. 3, Autumn, 1976, pp. 365-74.*

DAVID MONAGHAN (essay date 1977)

[*In the following excerpt, Monaghan discusses* "The Flats Road," *focusing on the "caged" feelings that accompany the characters' passages in adulthood.*]

One of Alice Munro's major points in ***Lives of Girls and Women*** is that as we grow up so we experience an increasing sense of confinement. The structure of her work serves to underline this theme. By presenting Del Jordan's childhood and adolescence through a series of short stories, rather than in the form of a continuous narrative, requiring links, transitions and the creation of a fully coherent world, Alice Munro is able to concentrate almost entirely on those times at which her heroine comes up against the crucial experiences that erode her sense of freedom. The effect for the reader is of a world in which the individual is gradually, but increasingly, entrapped within a cage constructed from the realities of death, family background, religion, love, and sex.

The direction of Del's life is clearly forecast in the first story, **"The Flats Road."** The title itself suggests something about the kind of experience awaiting Del. Her life must progress along a flat road, that is, through bare realities, harsh truths and in prescribed directions, rather than floating free in the balloon of any imaginary world she might create for herself. Del comes to recognize this fully only in the **"Epilogue: The Photographer,"** when, after trying to create a version of experience that owes its coherence to the conventions of southern gothic fiction, she finally admits that "People's lives, in Jubilee as elsewhere, were dull, simple, amazing and unfathomable—deep caves paved with kitchen linoleum."

However, there is far more in **"The Flats Road"** than the title which provides intimations of Del's final awareness. Her vision of life as a cave is implicit in the image pattern of confinement around which the story is constructed. This motif is established in the opening incident: "We caught frogs. We chased them, stalked them, crept up on them; it was the slim young green ones, the juicy adolescents, that we were after, cool and slimy; we squished them tenderly in our hands, then plopped them in a honey pail and put the lid on." Ultimately, Del will become the "juicy adolescent," "plopped in a honey pail," and the sense of power and control she feels in catching frogs is simply an illusion of inexperienced childhood. (pp. 165-66)

Both the quicksand hole in Grenoch Swamp "that would take down a two-ton truck like a bite of breakfast," and the pens and excavations which surround Uncle Benny's house reinforce this initial sense of confinement. And it becomes all-pervasive with the bondage references in Benny's newspaper: "VIRGIN RAPED ON CROSS BY CRAZED MONKS-/SENDS HUSBAND'S TORSO BY MAIL, wrapped in Christmas paper"; and in the childrens' song: *"Irene don't come after me/Or I'll hang you by your tits in a crab-apple tree."*

Through its choice of imagery, then, **"The Flats Road"** points forward to the later stories in ***Lives of Girls and Women.*** However, it also provides an escape from the very logic of experience that Alice Munro has begun to establish. In telling the story of Uncle Benny, Alice Munro presents us with that impossibility, the free man. Benny is free because he has never grown up, and thus has not encountered the realities that make up the cage of existence. For him, Del's childish illusion of freedom is reality. Benny can spend his days catching frogs, fishing and tramping the countryside. His domestic life consists of eating fish straight from the frying pan, and living in a chaotic house piled high with "a whole rich dark rotting mess of carpets, linoleum, parts of furniture, insides of machinery, nails, wire, tools, utensils." He regards business ventures as "something precarious and unusual, some glamorous and ghostly, never realized, hope of fortune," and the outside world is defined only in terms of the bizarre fantasies of his *National Enquirer*-type newspaper. This kind of freedom is so extreme that even though she is a young child, Del already realizes that Benny falls outside of accepted norms. She describes her experience of reading his newspapers thus:

> I was bloated and giddy with revelations of evil, of its versatility and grand invention and horrific playfulness. But the nearer I got to our house the more the vision faded. Why was it that the plain back wall of home, the pale chipped brick, the cement platform outside the kitchen door, washtubs hanging on nails, the pump, the lilac bush with brown-spotted leaves, should make it seem doubtful that a woman would really send her husband's torso, wrapped in Christmas paper, by mail to his girl friend in South Carolina?

Complete as Benny's freedom is, nevertheless it is extremely fragile, and any flirtation with the adult world threatens to shatter it as certainly as Pandora's idyllic state is destroyed by the single act of opening her box. Benny's Pandora's box proves to be marriage. Once he ceases to deal with it as a source of fantastic anecdote, as in his story of Sandy Stevenson and the poltergeist, and actually marries, Benny is threatened with confinement. Alice Munro makes this obvious in her descriptions of Benny's appearance on the day he sets out to meet Madeleine, and of the way in which he marries. Benny, restrained within conventional clothes, with his hair cut and moustache trimmed, looks "sacrificial." As it turns out his appearance is suitable to the role in which he is cast by Madeleine's relatives who are prepared to sacrifice him to rid themselves of an inconvenient burden: "They was all set up for the wedding. Set it up before I got there. They had the preacher there and the ring bought and fixed up with some fellow to get the license in a hurry. I could see they was all set up. All prepared for a wedding. Yes, sir. They didn't leave a thing out."

However, despite his marriage ceremony, Benny is not trapped into reality by Madeleine, since she is almost as strange and unworldly as he, but rather, by his affection for her daughter, Diane. Although he is content to allow Madeleine to pass out of his life when she deserts him, Benny feels he must rescue the mistreated child from her mother. Once Benny has committed himself to the world of duty, obligation and responsibilities, he becomes its most complete victim. Whereas others have spent a lifetime exploring their ever more confined environments and evolving strategems for survival, Benny is like a helpless child suddenly asked to navigate uncharted and threatening waters.

Alice Munro presents Benny's encounter with the adult world through the metaphor of his comic, but horrifying odyssey around the streets of Toronto. For Benny, the city is a maze which he must negotiate without either a map, or access to all the permissable moves: ". . . if you turned left on a green light you gotta turn across the traffic that's comin' *at* you." "You wait until they give you an opening." "You could wait all day then, they're not going to give you no opening. So I didn' know, I didn' know which was right to do, and I sat there trying to figure it out and they all starts up honkin' behind me so I thought, well, I'll turn right, I can do that without no trouble." Inevitably he finds himself "sort of circling" aimlessly, mapping out territory as he goes along, but never able to construct a total picture, until finally he becomes paralyzed: "we could see how it was to be lost there, how it was just not possible to find anything, or go on looking." For most of us such a failure could preclude only a mental breakdown or suicide. However, for Benny there is a way out—back to childhood. He retreats to the Flats Road, and eventually his encounter with reality is reduced to another of the anecdotes which populate his bizarre private world: "Madeleine herself was like something he might have made up. We remembered her like a story, and having nothing else to give we gave our strange, belated, heartless applause. "Madeleine! That madwoman!"

In **"The Flats Road"**, then, there are alternatives. Benny can enter the cage and, when he finds he cannot cope with it, he can step out again. However, no such alternatives await Del. She must go forward, and unless she can make better sense of her world than Benny does of his, she will be devoured by it. Because it escapes its own logic, **"The Flats Road"** stands in relation to the stories that follow as an idyll which must necessarily, but regretfully, be superseded by harsh reality. (pp. 166-68)

David Monaghan, "Confinement and Escape in Alice Munro's 'The Flats Road,' " in Studies in Short Fiction, *Vol. 14, No. 2, Spring, 1977, pp. 165-68.*

JULIA O'FAOLAIN (essay date 1979)

[*O'Faolain is an Irish short story writer and novelist, whose works include* Women in the Wall *(1975)* and The Three Lovers *(1970).* In the following excerpt, O'Faolain reviews The Beggar Maid, *commenting on the interdependence of the stories and praising the vibrance of Munro's narrative art.*]

The Beggar Maid is a figure in a painting by Burne-Jones to which Rose, heroine of Alice Munro's 10 interwoven stories [in ***The Beggar Maid: Stories of Flo and Rose***] is likened by the man she is to marry. Rose is poor, and Patrick, heir to a chain of department stores in British Columbia, loves her for qualities she hasn't got. This common occurrence is highlighted with uncommon clarity when Rose looks up the painting in an art book: "She studied the Beggar Maid, meek and voluptuous, with her shy white feet. The milky surrender of her, the helplessness and gratitude. Was that how Patrick saw Rose?"

Humor here is under restraint. Patrick's softheaded vanity invites derision; for Rose, so far from being meek and surrendering, was raised during the Depression in a small-town Canadian slum and is tougher than he. The author, however, denies the release of laughter. Holding tension pent, she probes for further insights. Rose, too, turns out to be trading in illusions. Impressed by Patrick's adoration for her, she will marry him "not for wealth but for worship," only to discover that though the idea of worship was alluring, the reality isn't.

Visits to the couple's families are explosive with embarrassment. Snobbery, that classic character-tester and tinder for fictional action, is rampant in both households though more exposed at Rose's, where Flo, her stepmother, is unable to bring it off. Flo's anecdotes are too wild and lurid. A former waitress, her props give her away: a specially bought "plastic swan . . . with slits in the wings, in which were stuck . . . paper napkins," a toothpick-holder that provokes "a startled grimace" from "Patrick, the gloomy snob." There are happy surprises too, as when Rose, who is pretending to feel pleasure at Patrick's lovemaking, is "thrown out of gear entirely" when she actually feels it. "She was really grateful now, and she wanted to be forgiven . . . for all her pretended gratitude."

The story illustrates the way in which its impressive Canadian author procures for her readers what I take to be the two great, mutually enhancing pleasures of fiction. The first is the sense that a writer has seen through the muddle of experience to an imminent significance and presented us with it: a conviction that things must be thus and not otherwise. A counter-pleasure comes with the discovery that an apparently conclusive truth may not be true after all. Movement from solution to dissolution electrifies narrative and is especially dynamic here, thanks to Alice Munro's feeling for the variety of levels on which we feel and live. Deft with social detail, she anchors her people firmly to class and place and commands the classic realist's strengths: moral seriousness, compassion, a sense of the particular. The disruptive elements are her characters' delusions, their yearnings and yarning, their snobbery and shames.

The stories are arranged chronologically; each is self-contained, but they all throw light on one another. All are seen from Rose's point of view. On one level their subject is the boundary between the marvelous and the ordinary. On another, it is the life story of a woman in whose grasp reality tends to slither like wet soap. Rose has a restless imagination because she moves from one social class to another and because, in the end, she puts her disability to use and goes into the theater.

In the early stories she is seen learning to survive in the grim neighborhood made mythic by Flo's gossip. Later, Rose gets a scholarship, marries up, divorces, takes and loses lovers, and works as an actress and television interviewer. There are flashes forward and back; moments of prescience and hindsight. Shifts of vision are achieved by alternating the cold looks Rose casts about her when unhappy with the magical close-ups of her responsive moments, as when she notes that Flo's legs are "marked all over with blue veins as if somebody had been drawing rivers on them with an indelible pencil." Becoming aware of her narrative gifts, she queens it over "people who wished they had been born poor" by offering "bits of squalor from her childhood." In a final turn-around, she grows ashamed of her reductive glibness, fearing that beyond the "antics" caught by her arts "there was always something further, a tone a depth, a light, that she couldn't get."

Alice Munro captures a kaleidoscope of lights and depths. Through the lens of Rose's eye, she manages to reproduce the vibrant prance of life while scrutinizing the workings of her own narrative art. This is an exhilarating collection.

Julia O'Faolain, "Small-Town Snobbery in Canada," in The New York Times Book Review, *September 16, 1979, p. 12.*

CAROLE GERSON AND ALICE MUNRO (essay date 1979)

[*The following excerpt is taken from a review/interview in which Gerson comments on the style and structure of Munro's* Who Do You Think You Are? *and Munro responds to questions about the thematic and autobiographical content of her work.*]

Who Do You Think You Are? returns to material that Munro used in her second book, ***Lives of Girls and Women***—the childhood and development of a young girl from a small town in Ontario. Unlike the earlier book, however, this one follows the main character past high school, into university, marriage, motherhood, divorce, and the ironic self-awareness of middle age. The fact that Rose's experiences are related as a series of stories rather than as a novel means that certain elements, such as her elementary school, her courtship, and her return home to care for her stepmother, are highlighted. But other important aspects of Rose's life—her relationships with her brother, husband, and daughter—remain in the shadows. I asked Munro about the gaps in this book, and whether she saw it as less of a novel than ***Lives of Girls and Women:***

*I see this definitely as linked stories, and **Lives** as an episodic novel. If **Who Do You Think You Are?** is going to be judged as a novel it doesn't work because it doesn't explain enough, whereas **Lives** explains enough for that period of Del's life. You see, in the parts of a novel, I think all the characters have* *to matter; in a story you have to concentrate very much on what is happening in that story. I think you're looking at it as a failed novel: why don't you get an explanation of why she doesn't care about Anna (Rose's daughter). When Rose is concentrating on having her affair, Anna doesn't matter. She's taking care of Anna, Anna's part of her life. But Anna doesn't really come into her life. It would have been possible to go through and do a lot of explanatory paragraphs and weave people in, but it would have weakened the stories as stories.*

As stories, the sections of this book are typical of Munro's best work: strong, perceptive accounts of the fabric of ordinary life, given what I view as an especially female texture by the writer's very close attention to the material details of everyday activities. Through her reporting of mundane physical matters—bathroom noises, kitchen linoleum, the cut of a skirt, the furniture people choose, and the food they serve—Munro constructs the unwritten social and sexual codes which govern our lives.

Rose grows up on the wrong side of the bridge, in West Hanratty, a community of cripples, idiots, ne'er-do-wells, and misfits. She graduates from her childhood world of squalor and scandal, incest in the school outhouse and sex under the porch, to the clean, calm corridors of university. Here her consciousness of the differences between social classes increases when she is wooed and rather reluctantly won by Patrick Blatchford. Heir to a west coast fortune, Patrick feeds Rose's romantic imagination by likening their situation to the painting of King Cophetua with the Beggar Maid at his feet. Once married and living in West Vancouver, Patrick discovers that his "Beggar Maid" is a real person, and she learns that her white knight is a Socred businessman. Still searching for romance, Rose attempts to have an affair with her best friend's husband. The tight-lipped comedy of this misadventure foreshadows the nature of Rose's subsequent amorous involvements. When her marriage breaks up she becomes an actress and drifter, moving through various unsatisfactory relationships. Throughout, she maintains both her optimism and her integrity as she encounters and eventually rejects various classes: nouveau riche, "lower arty," "upper arty" (Munro's terms), and academia. A lonely, intelligent woman, Rose . . . discovers that to be herself she must be alone. But does Munro see Rose as a kind of modern everywoman?

No, just as herself. I don't see her fate as particularly depressing. I think it would have been depressing if she'd stayed married, perhaps, but she's still free to choose. I see the whole meeting in Powell River and things like that as tremendously comic. Someone said to me, well, you know, she doesn't get anything, everything fails. But just a lot of the set-ups fail, really. She gets something out of life. She learns something.

When her expectations crumble, Rose does not suffer spectacular despair, but rather everyday self-doubt and loneliness. Perhaps there are no appropriate men for Rose.

I don't know. There are not many men for middle-aged women. This is something I didn't tackle head on. Whether you settle for a kind of freedom and happiness that doesn't necessarily contain erotic love, whether there is such a thing, or whether in choosing freedom you have to deliberately put that kind of happiness behind you, or whether everything's possible—I think it is, sometimes. But I think she wants, in a sense, to keep herself whole, rather than involved. That's a decision.

One of the things that helps Rose keep herself whole is her strong attachment to her past. Munro said that this group of stories grew out of her own personal history; the first story she wrote was **"Privilege"**:

I almost thought of that as an autobiographical piece, not fiction at all. I realized when I moved back to that part of the country I saw a lot of things I had forgotten about, or I saw them from a different perspective. I thought, I'd never written about that school, what it was really like. So I started to write it and then a story just sort of grew out of the material I was working with. It's the most autobiographical story.

In this book, the past is important for the way it shapes the present. Most of the stories end by returning to the present, explaining what happened later to the characters; the structure of the book itself brings the past into the present in the last two stories, when Rose returns to Hanratty to care for her declining stepmother. At the end, Rose acquires an important insight into her life. She learns that in West Hanratty, that community of motley, almost gothic characters from which she had distanced herself by reducing her past to a series of cocktail party anecdotes, there existed a kind of social cohesion and respect for eccentricity not to be found in urban middle-class society. Yet Rose's past remains very much with her; in the last pages of the book she understands that her strongest ties are not to the men she has loved, but to those who shared her childhood. I asked Munro why she rounded off almost every story by returning to the present:

I was doing it a lot, and I thought maybe I should quit this, it's too repetitive. But then I found I liked it. I didn't care if it was repetitive. It was doing what I wanted to do. At one point, too, I cut the book down. I cut out all those retrospects. And I thought, the immediacy is better, but really, I want them in. So I put them back. I felt the information they gave was more important than having a neat story.

I suggested to Munro that the past and memory are two of the basic concerns of her writing. In this book, the past is almost more important than the present, which is why she insists on establishing the continuity between the two. She agreed that she is very interested in

the way things change, the way people change from youth to middle age. It seemed to me that it isn't important enough just to write a story about what was happening, like in **"Half a Grapefruit,"** *when Rose was an adolescent. I wanted this to go in a framework, of what the people became, of what the place became.*

Through the course of the book, we do indeed see what becomes of the town and what becomes of Rose. "Who do you think you are?" is a question addressed to Rose in the first story, and again in the last. In West Hanratty, the expression is a warning not to step outside the acceptable patterns of behaviour. Yet it is in places like West Hanratty, Munro implies, that people do in fact know who they are. Flo, Rose's vivid stepmother, enjoys a kind of honest, spontaneous individualism which gives her the freedom to live fully because she is unhampered by self-consciousness: a mode of existence for which both Rose and Munro reveal a degree of nostalgia. In our interview, Munro said of Flo, "She's very strong. She's very simple, in a way. I mean she's complex, but she's direct. She's unintellectual, and quite unreflective, natural. And I liked her a lot." After nearly losing herself among the masks and poses of the arties and intellectuals who specialize in camouflage, Rose has to return home to discover who she really is. (pp. 3-7)

Carole Gerson, "Who Do You Think You Are? Review-Interview with Alice Munro," in Room of One's Own, *Vol. 4, No. 4, 1979, pp. 2-7.*

HELEN HOY (essay date 1980)

[In the following excerpt, Hoy examines Munro's extensive use of paradox in both language and situation throughout her fiction. Hoy suggests that paradox is a means by which Munro is able to capture the complexity of human emotions.]

> *Royal Beating.* That was Flo's promise. You are going to get one Royal Beating.
>
> The word Royal lolled on Flo's tongue, took on trappings. Rose had a need to picture things, to pursue absurdities, that was stronger than the need to stay out of trouble, and instead of taking this threat to heart she pondered: how is a beating royal?

In this delight in language and exuberant pursuit of absurdities despite ensuing complications, Rose reveals herself, in Alice Munro's latest work ***Who Do You Think You Are?,*** to be very much a child of the author herself. Munro's own sensitivity to individual words and images, her spare lucid style, and command of detail have given her fiction a precision which is one of her most distinctive accomplishments. What an examination of the texture of her prose reveals, in particular, is the centrality of paradox and the ironic juxtaposition of apparently incompatible terms or judgements: "ironic and serious at the same time," "mottoes of godliness and honor and flaming bigotry," "special, useless knowledge," "tones of shrill and happy outrage," "the bad taste, the heartlessness, the joy of it." This stylistic characteristic is closely related to the juxtaposition, in the action, of the fantastic and the ordinary, her use of each to undercut the other. . . . The linking of incongruities in language or action, however, is more than a stylistic technique or fictional quirk. It reflects Munro's larger vision, one which underlies all her fiction and which emerges as a central theme in ***Lives of Girls and Women*** and in several of the short stories in ***Dance of the Happy Shades*** and ***Something I've Been Meaning To Tell You.*** Paradox helps sustain Munro's thematic insistence on the doubleness of reality, the illusoriness of either the prosaic or the marvellous in isolation.

The freshness of language and image, which is Munro's great strength, she herself explains in an interview with Graeme Gibson: "I'm not an intellectual writer. I'm very, very excited by what you might call the surface of life, and it must be that this seems to me very meaningful in a way I can't analyze or describe. . . . It seems to me very important to be able to get at the exact tone or texture of how things are [see excerpt dated 1972]." This impulse she, of course, embodies in ***Lives of Girls and Women*** in Del Jordan who, as a maturing writer, attempts to pin her town to paper and realizes, "no list could hold what I wanted, for what I wanted was every last thing, every layer of speech and thought, stroke of light on bark or walls, every smell, pothole, pain, crack, delusion, held still and held together—radiant, everlasting." The last words hold the clue to Del's, and Munro's obsession with external realities: it is an obsession which Munro, in her interview with Gibson, says can best be compared to a religious feeling about the world. So too when another interviewer John Metcalf asks perceptively whether she glories in surfaces because she feels them not to be surfaces, she agrees, adding, "It's just a feeling about the intensity of what is *there* [see Metcalf in Additional Bibliography]." In the struggle to capture this intensity about very ordinary things, paradox not surprisingly becomes one of Munro's most important tools.

Sometimes this persistent "balance or reconcilement of opposites or discordant qualities" (to echo Coleridge's celebrated definition of the imagination) occurs almost in passing as an unobtrusive feature of Munro's style, in her description, for instance, of the way children whimper monotonously "to *celebrate* a hurt." Often, though, the inherent contradictions in people and situations are more explicitly confronted. Paradox becomes Munro's means of capturing complex human characteristics whether wittily as in the description of successful academics as "such brilliant, such talented incapable men" or more seriously, gropingly as in Del's discussion of an egotism women feel in men, something "tender, swollen, tyrannical, absurd." In an attempt, in **"Dance of the Happy Shades,"** to convey the reality of the Marsalles sisters, "sexless, wild and gentle creatures, bizarre yet domestic," Munro extends paradox into physical description itself, characterizing both as having kindly, grotesque faces, and eyes which are at the same time tiny, red, short-sighted, and sweet-tempered. The same incongruities multiply in the world encompassing Munro's characters. A housewife and writer finds herself sheltered and encumbered, warmed and bound by her home; a growing girl is both absolved and dismissed by her father's casual acceptance of her moment of rebellion; the struggle of wills between an amateur hypnotist and a stubborn old woman ends with her "dead, and what was more, victorious"; a teenage girl feels that her mother's concern creates for her an oppressive obligation to be happy, as another feels that her mother loves her but is also her enemy; a maiden aunt, stumbling on her niece and a lover naked and passionate, perceives them as strange and familiar, both more and less than themselves. A character's feelings for her relatives are described as "irritable . . . bonds of sympathy," a writer's techniques as "Lovely tricks, honest tricks." In these examples as in many, Munro employs not an elaborated paradoxical statement but a more concentrated phrase, an oxymoron, most often in the form of two parallel but incompatible verbs or adjectives. The startling fusion of warring terms gives to her style at its best a denseness and precision characteristic of poetry.

Paradox is most prominent in the fiction's portrayal of human character and emotional reaction. At times this is simply a means of suggesting inconsistencies, variations over time, as in Del's discovery (in contrast with her youthful belief in the absolute finality of some quarrels) that people can feel murderous disillusionment and hate, then go on to love again. More often, Munro explores the emotional contradictions persisting side by side in time. A character in **"Tell Me Yes or No"** not only expects her lover, like a knight, to be capable alternately of "acts of outmoded self-sacrifice and also of marvellous brutality," she also goes on to describe him as *simultaneously* mild and inflexible. Paradox, therefore, is frequently an admirable means of conveying the intense emotional ambivalence of adolescence: in response to an example of purely decorative femininity, for example, Del reveals, "I thought she was an idiot, and yet I frantically admired her." She finds the idea of sex totally funny and totally revolting, hopes and fears she will be overheard shouting the forbidden word "bugger," and later is both relieved and desolate at the loss of her lover Garnet. In the same way, of other adolescent girls, we are told that "any title with the word popularity in it could both chill and compel me," that "she was quivering . . . with pride, shame, boldness, and exhilaration" (note how "shame" here is even flanked by two differing contraries), and that the pregnancy and marriage of a friend "made me both envious and appalled." (In the last example, the friend herself is concomitantly characterized as "abashed and proud.") Lest we conclude, however, that Munro is mainly recording the confusions of youth, we might note that almost the same formula is applied to an adult woman, in her response to some men's invulnerability: "I envy and despise." Rose's friend Clifford argues that his marital dissatisfaction is not simply a change of heart over time, informing his wife, "I wanted to be married to you and I want to be married to you and I couldn't stand being married to you and I can't stand being married to you. It's a static contradiction."

In fact, the matter-of-fact union of incompatible tendencies is Munro's means of bringing life, precision, and complexity to her depiction of emotions generally. Occasionally, as in the example just given, she actually acknowledges and spells out the paradoxical nature of such feelings: "They [Del's aunts] respected men's work beyond anything; they also laughed at it. This was strange; they could believe absolutely in its importance and at the same time convey their judgement that it was, from one point of view, frivolous, non-essential." (Compare this incidentally with a later character's mingling of "flattery and a delicate sort of contempt" in her conversation with a man. Similarly the reader is deliberately drawn into a contemplation of the paradoxical quality of Milton Homer's unsocialized behaviour in ***Who Do You Think You Are?*** as the narrator, describing his goggling, leering expressions as both boldly calculating and helpless, involuntary, asks if such a thing is possible. More often, we simply have subtle touches in the portrayal of characters, even minor characters—a landlord with an "affable, predatory expression," an aunt "flashing malice and kindness," a grandmother whose renunciation of love is a "self-glorifying dangerous self-denying passion," the same grandmother predicting problems with "annoyance and satisfaction," an unhappy lover bound by rules "meaningless and absolute." The same duality is found on a larger scale with more central characters too, like the pathetic heroine of **"Thanks for the Ride,"** whose combination of defiance and need, scorn and acquiescence is summed up in the final sound of her voice, "abusive and forlorn."

At one point in ***Lives of Girls and Women,*** Del somewhat ironically characterizes the Anglican liturgy as presenting "lively emotion *safely* contained in the most *elegant* channels of language." In contrast to this, Munro's own technique, rather than using language to defuse emotion, creates a resonance or current, releases an intensity through the juxtaposition of oppositely charged words or ideas. The effect is not a wild splattering of emotion—in the careful precision of Munro's language, and a certain intellectual detachment as well, there is some of the control attributed here to the liturgical ritual—but it is controlled *energy,* a galvanic interaction between the poles of the paradox rather than a safe elegance. Through the originality not of craziness but of unexpected revelation, Munro's oxymorons have something of the same vitality as the bizarre childhood rhyme about fried Vancouvers and pickled arseholes, which so pleases Rose for what she calls "The tumble of reason; the spark and spit of craziness."

So positive emotions are unexpectedly qualified—"heartless applause," "smiling angrily," "hungry laughter," "accusing vulnerability," "aggressive bright spirits"; negative ones are similarly—"tender pain," "semitolerant contempt," "happy outrage," "terrible tender revenge"; and even an epithet like absurd, which might seem sweeping and inarguably dismissive, must coexist with its opposite: Del's mother in her youthful enthusiasm is "absurd and unassailable," Del, naked, feels "absurd and dazzling," and a boy reassures a drunken girl, with "a very stupid, half-sick, absurd and alarming expression." While such pairings can sometimes become automatic or mechanical in Munro's writing, most often the originality of the details produces a slight, revelatory wrenching of assumptions and perspective.

We should note that the effect of paradox in Munro is never to invalidate, rarely even to diminish either of the contradictory impulses. Characteristically, in fact, she employs the unifying conjunction "and," disregarding for her purposes conjunctions of limitation or concession. As Cleanth Brooks says of the technique in poetry, the ironic or paradoxical union of opposites "is not that of a prudent splitting of the difference between antithetical overemphases." So, Del in ignoring her aunts' dreams feels "that kind of tender remorse which has as its other side a brutal, *unblemished* satisfaction," quotes sentimental poetry "with absolute sincerity, absolute irony," and comments explicitly about her youthful curiosity over sex, "Disgust did not rule out enjoyment, in my thoughts; indeed they were inseparable." The contradictory emotions retain their individual intensity.

In her examination of human inconsistency, Munro presents the contradictions not only within emotions but also between emotion and behaviour. Again there is often little attempt to reduce the inconsistency or explain why actions defy their motivations; the two conflicting realities are simply juxtaposed—"The thought of intimacies with Jerry Storey was offensive in itself. Which did not mean that they did not, occasionally, take place," "The ritual of walking up and down the street to show ourselves off we thought crude and ridiculous, though we could not resist it," "not bothering to shake off our enmity, nor thinking how the one thing could give way to the other, we kissed." At times, in fact, Munro actually uses human perverseness itself as the explanation for behaviour, in identifying the "aphrodisiac prickles of disgust" in the appeal of the idiotic saintly whore or the perversely appealing lack of handsomeness of the lecherous minister Rose encounters. Faced with an invitation to sneak away to a dance, Del feels paradoxically, "I had no choice but to do this . . . because I truly hated and feared the Gay-la Dance Hall."

The unexpected challenge to common assumptions which is the source of such paradoxes' power need not always be spelled out. The same shock of recognition, Coleridge's union of "the sense of novelty and freshness, with old and familiar objects," is achieved when, for instance, Del's mother's radical defence of women's independence is described unexpectedly as innocent in its assumption of women's damageability, when Del comments on the concealed jubilation and eagerness to cause pain in parents' revelations of unpleasant realities, when the narrator of **"Shining Houses"** makes a matter-of-fact, parenthetical reference to the way people admire each other for being drunk, or when Rose reveals that outspoken hostility does not pose the threat to one of her friendships which genteel tact would. The freshness of perception which Alice Munro brings to very familiar situations lends itself to the creation of observations such as these which remain startling, although the underlying paradox is never articulated.

Indeed Munro sometimes even seems to go through an initial process of making the strange familiar so that she can then go on paradoxically to justify the originally familiar (but now strange) as also possible. An interesting example of this occurs in ***Who Do You Think You Are?*** in Rose's analysis of her reconciliation with Patrick, her fiancé. Disregarding any immediate, popular explanations like romantic love (and through silence apparently dismissing them as naïve), Munro accustoms the reader to more sophisticated, sceptical analysis by consideration of such similarly complex motivations as comradely compassion, emotional greed, economic cowardice, and vanity (with only subtle hints of glibness). Only then, ironically, does she reveal Rose's secret explanation, which Rose has never confided and which she cannot justify, namely that she may have been motivated, oddly enough, by a vision of happiness. The paradoxical revelation of unacknowledged, even denied, but recognizable aspects of human behaviour has, in the context of worldly characters and readers, been taken a step further here and turned on itself. Having directed attention towards less obvious explanations of behaviour, Munro then revitalizes from a new perspective a vision of innocence and good will which has paradoxically become unexpected.

Verbal paradox, however, particularly cryptic oxymoron, remains a more distinctive feature of Munro's style, and, as many of the examples already cited suggest, functions particularly as a means of definition, of zeroing in on the individual qualities of an emotion or moment. More than evocativeness, it is precision which she seeks in the description of "a great unemotional happiness," "sophisticated prudery," or a character "kind but not compassionate." In light of Munro's love for clear images and her insistence on her inability to put characters in a room without describing all the furniture, it is interesting that many of these paradoxes involve abstract not concrete language (an aspect of her style easily overlooked). It is the exactness and poetic explosiveness of the internal contradiction which give them their vividness. Admiring the discontinuities of modern experimental prose, Munro has complained that her writing tends "to fill everything in, to be pretty wordy." As this discussion suggests, however, while within a traditional narrative form and concerned with articulating rather than simply suggesting, her use of language generally is not discursive or rambling, but tight, economical, exact. (pp. 100-07)

> *Helen Hoy, " 'Dull, Simple, Amazing and Unfathomable': Paradox and Double Vision in Alice Munro's Fiction," in* Studies in Canadian Literature, *Vol. 5, 1980, pp. 100-15.*

LORRAINE M. YORK (essay date 1983)

[*In the following excerpt, York focuses on the photographic elements in Munro's work. She comments on the camera's role as a distancing mechanism for the narrator and notes its use as a parallel for memory, which stops time and creates static portraits of life.*]

In various writings and interviews, Alice Munro has often expressed interest in photography and photographic realism. In an "Open Letter" to a small Wingham, Ontario journal, *Jubilee,* Munro summarized her feeling about the emotional power of local detail by referring to an Edward Hopper painting. This canvas, entitled "The Barber Shop," is a fairly static, symmetrically-composed, sunlight-flooded interior scene; yet for Munro it becomes "full of a distant, murmuring, almost tender foreboding, full of mystery like the looming trees." This Conradian phrase, so akin to Marlow's concept of "the truth disclosed in a moment of illusion," reveals precisely that which characterizes the vision of Munro and the photographic realists—paradox. In fact, it was while reading Susan Sontag's *On Photography,* a searching commentary on the art which is couched in paradoxical terms, that I realized that Munro's fiction reveals those very same paradoxes and syntheses. Although studies have been written outlining the use and frequency of paradox in Munro's fiction (most notably Helen Hoy's "Paradox and Double Vision in Alice Munro's Fiction" [see excerpt dated 1980], there has been no satisfactory answer as to why paradox is so congenial to her particular way of "fictionalizing" experience.

Munro's fiction, like the Edward Hopper painting and like the work of photographic "realists" from the 1920's on, centres on the paradox of the familiar and the exotic. . . . Closer to Munro's own concerns, however, is the work of a journalist-photographer team to which she makes fleeting reference in an interview with John Metcalf—that of James Agee and Walker Evans. *Let Us Now Praise Famous Men* takes the humblest of human subjects—Alabama tenant farmers in the 1930's—and combines literary and visual images to turn them into hauntingly strange visions of both nobility and despair.

To return to one of the central paradoxes of the photographic vision, one discovers that characters in Munro's fiction witness both the familiar and prosaic becoming unfamiliar, even threatening, and the reverse process as well. In **"The Ottawa Valley"** it is the foreboding sense of sickness and loss which turns the most familiar of presences—the mother—into something dark and remote:

> She went on as if she had not heard, her familiar bulk ahead of me turning strange, indifferent. She withdrew, she darkened in front of me, though all she did in fact was keep on walking along the path that she and Aunt Dodie had made when they were girls . . . It was still there.

This remarkably compressed passage contrasts the vulnerable present with the comforts to be found in memory (unshifting as it is) and in physical objects.

Objects, however, as many of Munro's characters realize with profound amazement, have a mysterious inner layer as well; they possess the hidden potential to turn treacherous or supremely indifferent. As the young protagonist in **"Day of the Butterfly"** witnesses the future of an unpopular schoolmate "turn shadowy, turn dark" in the hospital ward, she also has a new vision of the schoolgirls' hypocritical gifts as "guilt-tinged offerings." She muses that "they were no longer innocent objects to be touched, exchanged, accepted without danger." In the last event, then, she avoids the danger that is human sympathy; Myra's parting gift to her is indifferently shrugged off as "the thing."

In ***Who Do You Think You Are?*** the source of this threat is an objective nature which is simply indifferent to human sentiment. As Rose gradually foresees her argument with Flo reach its malicious climax, she fixes her eyes upon the shoddy linoleum tiles. At this moment she sees with frightening clarity that even familiar objects are not man's familiars:

> Those things aren't going to help her, none of them can rescue her. They turn bland and useless, even unfriendly. Pots can show malice, the patterns of linoleum can leer up at you, treachery is the other side of dailiness.

Distortion of the commonplace becomes specifically identified with art—photographic art, in fact—in the epilogue to ***Lives of Girls and Women,*** entitled **"Epilogue: The Photographer."** Like Del's fictional treatment of Marion Sheriff, the art of her photographer has the frightening power to create grotesqueness from surface innocence:

> The pictures he took turned out to be unusual, even frightening. People saw that in his pictures they had aged twenty or thirty years. Middle-aged people saw in their own features the terrible, growing, inescapable likeness of their dead parents . . . Brides looked pregnant, children adenoidal. So he was not a popular photographer. . . .

Munro applied this theory of the dual nature of art—both creative and parasitic—to her own writing in a manifesto statement ["The Colonel's Hash Resettled"] which echoes Rose's musings about the other side of dailiness: "There is a sort of treachery to innocent objects—to houses, chairs, dresses, dishes and to roads, fields, landscapes—which a writer removes from their natural, dignified obscurity and sets down in print." Such visual paradox, then, underlines the more morally troubling paradox of the writer who "murders to create" by representing yet altering elements of the experienced world.

Perhaps more bewildering for Munro's protagonists is the experience of the inverse paradox—the exotic becoming familiar. Del Jordan, after her sexual flights of fancy with a black negligé as stage prop, reflects after Mr. Chamberlain's sexual theatrics, "I could not get him back to his old role, I could not make him play the single-minded, simple-minded, vigorous, obliging lecher of my daydreams. My faith in simple depravity had weakened." Earlier, this faith in depravity had been slightly shaken by the shabby ordinariness of the newspapers and potted geraniums of the local whorehouse; by "the skin of everyday experiences stretched over such shamelessness, such consuming explosions of lust." (pp. 49-52)

The frequent appearance of clearly "odd" characters has often been noted by reviewers of Munro's work, but to characterize these figures as belonging to some aberrant "other world" is, I believe, another example of making distinctions when syntheses are more in order. As in the photographs of Diane Arbus, the grotesque makes its appearance in Munro's stories in order to make us reform our Gestalt—our conceptions of what is "odd" and "normal." The eccentric hermit Joe Phippen, whom Ben Jordan takes his daughter to meet in **"Images,"** is not so much a creature from a competing world as an additional scrap of knowledge which Del must synthesize in order to construct an "image" of her father:

> Like the children in fairy stories who have seen their parents make pacts with terrible strangers, who have discovered that our fears are based on nothing but the truth, but who come back fresh from marvellous escapes and take up their knives and forks . . . like them, dazed and powerful with secrets, I never said a word.

Unlike Sherwood Anderson, to whose work Munro's has often been compared, Munro would never say (as Anderson did of *Winesburg, Ohio*) that "All the men and women the writer had ever known had become grotesque." Rather, oddity is another element in the synthesis of life in the fictional small town. "It is not true," Munro once commented, "that such a place will not allow eccentricity. Oddity is necessary as sin is . . . Within these firm definitions . . . live bewildered and complicated people."

In ***Who Do You Think You Are?*** this bewildering reconciliation of truth and illusion becomes the dominant theme of the collection. I agree with Helen Hoy that Munro passes into a subtler "dialectic of the ordinary and the marvellous" but not merely in terms of the recognized illusoriness of Rose's adventures. Rather, it is a self-aware dialectic of an artistic nature especially which reaches a synthesis that is typically postmodern. It is no accident, for example, that the final, title story of the volume begins with the "comic" figure of Milton Homer and ends with the "tragic" figure of Ralph Gillespie. In the description of the town parade—an event which mixes theatricality (socially-sanctioned "showing off") and "real" identities—Milton Homer accentuates this blurring of fantasy and fact: "Nobody looked askance at Milton in a parade; everybody was used to him." This overlapping of fiction and fact, wherein oddities become acceptable, is evidenced in his epic-serious name and is beautifully captured in the episode in which young Ralph Gillespie changes the title of Keats's sonnet to "On First Looking Into Milton Homer"! In fact, this subtle bridging of these two figures becomes even more significant at the end of the story, when Ralph Gillespie, *imitator* of Milton Homer, becomes a "fiction" which Rose is unable to read:

> The thing she was ashamed of, in acting, was that she might have been paying attention to the wrong things, reporting antics, when there was always something further, a tone, a depth, a light, that she couldn't get and wouldn't get. And it wasn't just about acting she suspected this . . . She had never felt this more strongly than when she was talking to Ralph Gillespie.

Instead of prodding Ralph about his talent for mimicry, much as she might do in a public interview, Rose realizes that she might have delved further, beyond the surface fiction to the essential story of one man's life. This synthesis is completed only after Ralph's death which leaves Rose with the knowledge that "she felt his life, close, closer than the lives of men she'd loved, one slot over from her own." Thus, the blurring of the distinctions between fact and fiction which lies at the basis of postmodernist fiction develops with increasing intensity in Munro's art, as the "Photographer" as artist and Del as experiencer fully merge in Rose—the artist of experience.

If the photograph is the meeting place of the known and the unknown, it is no less the meeting place of motion and stillness in human experience. The photograph is the static moment snatched out of the *perpetuum mobile* of time—what French photographer Cartier-Bresson described in a now-famous utterance as the "decisive moment." As such, it has been seized upon by postmodernists as a contemporary example of what T. S. Eliot called "the still point of the turning world"—the breathless moment of intersection between the time-driven and the timeless. (pp. 52-4)

In their very form, Alice Munro's interconnected short story collections, ***Lives of Girls and Women*** and ***Who Do You Think You Are?*** function on the same borderline between motion and stasis; each self-contained story is an image in itself, linked to the larger continuum by the main character and a roughly chronological progression. To those who wrongly approach these series of linked images as a traditional novel, however, gaps are bound to appear. This is no shortcoming but a conscious choice on Munro's part, for this imagistic effect closely resembles the very texture and process of memory.

On a more minute level, Munro uses this photographic stillness in motion consciously and overtly to create her "decisive moments." One such moment occurs at the end of ***Lives of Girls and Women*** with the spontaneous act granted by Bobby Sheriff to Del Jordan. His sudden rising upon his toes Del as artist interprets, in a self-conscious fashion, as having "a concise meaning, a stylized meaning—to be a letter, or a whole word, in an alphabet I did not know." The alphabet which Del is just beginning to learn is the flux and flow of human life, and the letter or word—those special, mysterious acts of men and women—are the keys to the code. Munro uses the same linguistic analogy, never forgetting the vital link between literary device and human experience, in ***Who Do You Think You Are?.*** In **"Spelling,"** Rose visits a home for the aged, soon to be the home of her stepmother, Flo, and observes an old woman whose only participation in life is to spell out loud words supplied by others. Rose (and Munro) choose words charged with vitality which become curiously static:

> Forest F-O-R-E-S-T . . .
> Celebrate. C-E-L-E-B-R-A-T-E.

This contrast between the isolated, lifeless linguistic fragments and the lush vitality of the concepts which they suggest when experienced in continuity speaks volumes about the aridity of the home, and of solitary aging itself. It is intriguing, indeed, that Susan Sontag should refer to photography on exactly this dual level, as "a grammar and, even more importantly, an ethics of seeing."

Munro even incorporates this contrast between motion and stasis into her imagery: in **"The Spanish Lady,"** a woman's self-contained musings about her own troubles are jarred by the sudden death cry of an old man in a train station. She becomes transfixed in more senses than one:

> It seems as if I should not leave, as if the cry of the man dying, now dead, is still demanding something of me, but I cannot think what it is . . . What we say and feel no longer rings true, it is slightly beside the point. As if we were all wound up a long time ago and were spinning out of control, whirring, making noises, but at a touch could stop, and see each other for the first time, harmless and still.

The implicit image of the spinning top, its vibrant colours never perceptible until we timidly stretch out a finger to interfere, to participate, is the perfect image of our everyday experience and of our all too characteristic reticence. (pp. 54-5)

[The] photographic seizing of the moment becomes an overt model for Munro as well in the collection which includes **"The Spanish Lady"*—Something I've Been Meaning to Tell You.*** On the very last page, the photograph becomes the act of writing, of capturing and thus exorcising experience. The narrator tells us, first of all, that if she had been making a "proper story" out of her experiences, she would have altered certain details. This affirmation of fidelity to experience then assumes a visual form: "Now I look at what I have done and it is like a series of snapshots, like the brownish snapshots with fancy borders that my parents' old camera used to take." Referring to her fictional creation as a journey, she claims to have undertaken it with the sole purpose of capturing for all time her mother—"To mark her off, to describe, to illumine, to celebrate, to get rid of her," but all in vain, for her edges "melt and flow." Thus, as Eliot reflects, we are left with "the intolerable wrestle with words and meanings" for "Only through time is time conquered."

As this comparison suggests, Munro moves to explore the further paradox of art as both power and vulnerable helplessness. In other Canadian postmodernist novels, most notably Leonard Cohen's *Beautiful Losers* and Hubert Aquin's *Blackout,* the association of fiction-making and power is set in an intensely sexual and political frame of reference. In the case of Aquin, though, this attempt at mastery—of one's experience, one's own national identity—is continually frustrated, for the novel, like the land which lies behind it, is the constant object of a power-struggle among several controlling powers. Is this attempt to gain power over the threat of extinction really so different from the power which Del Jordan learns to exercise over her dominating lover, Garnet, and eventually over the recalcitrant details of experience? Earlier in her development, after the death of Uncle Craig, this power over extinction is sought by Del through the mastery of knowledge:

> I followed her [Del's mother] around the house, scowling, persistent, repeating my questions. I wanted to know. There is no protection unless it is in knowing. I wanted death pinned down and isolated behind a wall of particular facts and circumstances, not floating around loose, ignored but powerful, waiting to get in anywhere.

This wish for power, for security, becomes tied to a sexual theme as Del fights both a literal and metaphorical battle against being submerged by her lover in **"Baptizing."** "I felt amazement," she marvels, "not that I was fighting with Garnet but that anybody could have made such a mistake, to think he had real power over me." Finally, the theme of artistic power over chaos is established in the epilogue, with the actual physical presentation of the lists of prosaic details which Del compiles and orders with sacred devotion:

> And no list could hold what I wanted, for what I wanted was every last thing, every layer of speech and thought, stroke of light on bark or walls, every smell, pothole, pain, crack, delusion, held still and held together—radiant, everlasting."

Interestingly, this drive to control through representation of concrete objects, besides reaching back to Neolithic cave paintings, turns up in a surprisingly parallel passage in *Let Us Now Praise Famous Men:* "If I could do it," writes Agee, "I'd do no writing here at all. It would be photographs; the rest would be fragments of cloth, bits of cotton, lumps of earth, records of speech, pieces of wood and iron, phials of odors, plates of food and excrement . . ." This consideration of the power that photography and fiction hold, to bind together disparate chunks of the world, links Munro's work to the very impulses of mimesis in man.

At the same time, however, the other half of the paradox is completed with the realization that fiction and photography reveal to man the utter hopelessness of ever ordering the chaos of the outer world or the inner landscape. Both outer and inner chaos break forth, for example, in Margaret Atwood's poem, "Camera," in which the lover's insistence that both scenario and woman become immobilized for his "organized instant" is frustrated by the emotional wreckage of the scene. (pp. 56-8)

[In] ***Lives of Girls and Women,*** we note a similar, though milder, process of undercutting as in the Atwood poem, after Del's brash description of her lists, with her disheartening comment, "The hope of accuracy we bring to such tasks is crazy, heartbreaking." This artistic hoarding of detail is tellingly associated with Del's saving of her own life in **"Baptizing,"** for the simple reason that writing, for Munro, is the constant "hedge" against the chaos that is death. She observed to Graeme Gibson that writing "has something to do with the fight against death, the feeling that we lose everything every day, and writing is a way of convincing yourself perhaps that you're doing something about this [see excerpt dated 1972]." How fascinating it is, then, to see that Munro's work, like that of Aquin, displays the curious paradox which Robert Alter notes of the self-conscious novel in our century; that while it is a celebration of generation, it more often than not proves to be "a long meditation on death."

The reason for such an abundance of paradox in contemporary literature lies in the age-old conflict between Romantic and Classical impulses—those of sympathetic identification and aesthetic detachment. Munro's work, representative of the twentieth-century hybrid, often reveals both conflicting tendencies. In **"The Office,"** for example, the writer's final mental portrait of her persecutor, Mr. Malley, poses delicately and painfully this question of sympathy and distance:

> Mr. Malley with his rags and brushes and a pail of soapy water, scrubbing in his clumsy way . . . at the toilet walls . . . arranging in his mind the bizarre but somehow never quite satisfactory narrative of yet another betrayal of trust. While I arrange words, and think it is my right to be rid of him.

Like the plants and teapot which Malley forces on the young writer, the "gifts" which experiences bestow on their authors have their own price, their own nagging demands which cannot be ignored. This, in effect, is the same realization which Rose reaches in ***Who Do You Think You Are?.*** While she is prevented from turning a letter from Flo into a public storytelling exhibition by "a fresh and overwhelming realization" of the "gulf" which lies between her and her past, she nevertheless comes to recognize through Ralph Gillespie that the gulf is also a living link. In terms of the photographer's art, Susan Sontag sums up these, and many of the other conflicting tendencies already noted in Munro's art, with characteristic insight:

> Photography, which has so many narcissistic uses, is also a powerful instrument for depersonalizing our relation to the world; and the two uses are complementary. Like a pair of binoculars with no right or wrong end, the camera makes exotic things near, intimate; and familiar things small, abstract, strange, much further away. It offers, in one easy, habit-forming activity, both participation and alienation in our own lives and in those of others.

Like the photographer, then, who establishes distance through a selective rectangular frame, writing is both a selection and a distancing. Nevertheless, as Cartier-Bresson observed of his art, "in order to 'give a meaning' to the world, one has to feel involved in what he frames through the viewfinder." This precept should be remembered by critics who deplore the constraint and morbidity of Munro's "town," for Munro affirms her link to her created world in characteristically paradoxical terms: "Solitary and meshed these lives are, buried and celebrated."

Like her postmodernist contemporaries, Alice Munro is intensely fascinated by the burials and celebrations, links and gulfs, fictions and nonfictions of the world around her. By fusing these disparate elements into the synthesis which is paradox, Munro accomplishes what a recent reviewer observed of Cartier-Bresson: "He has brought his intuition to the surface of his skin and he has kept it there, bonding into single entity photographer, camera, time, and the objective world." In fact, like all sensitive men and women in a disconcerting, exhilarating age, Alice Munro is "coolly obsessed with humanity." (pp. 58-60)

Lorraine M. York, " 'The Other Side of Dailiness': The Paradox of Photography in Alice Munro's Fiction," in Studies in Canadian Literature, *Vol. 8, No. 1, 1983, pp. 49-60.*

ROWENA FOWLER (essay date 1984)

[*In the following excerpt, Fowler comments on the difficulties which the protagonists of* Lives of Girls and Women *and* The Beggar Maid *confront as they attempt to portray their childhood experiences. Fowler follows the girls' gradual realizations that they have diminished their subjects in their mocking anecdotes.*]

As Del Jordan sets off from Jubilee, Ontario, in search of her "real life," she abandons the "black fable" she has concocted out of her small-town childhood and takes with her only the intuition of **"Epilogue: The Photographer"** that familiar things are both more ordinary and more amazing than she has given them credit for. They stubbornly resist being turned into fiction: "It is a shock, when you have dealt so cunningly, powerfully, with reality, to come back and find it still there." Like Catherine Morland in *Northanger Abbey,* Del sees the world in terms of her favorite novels, is disabused of her fanciful notions, and finally, we realize, undergoes experiences as exciting or disturbing in their way as anything she might read about.

What is false in her "black fable" is not plot but style. Extraordinary things do happen in Jubilee, but Del has distorted them, trapping people and events in topiary gardens, Regency romance poses, and mannered prose: the "bittersweet flesh" of her fictional heroine, Caroline, overlays her Jubilee prototype, "pudgy Marion, the tennis player." Del's stylized figures are set in a physical and psychological landscape that is recognizably Southern Gothic; given Alice Munro's acknowledged debt to Eudora Welty and Flannery O'Connor, it seems that she has her own "black fables" to exorcize: "Their speech was subtle and evasive and bizarrely stupid; their platitudes crackled with madness. The season was always the height of summer—white, brutal heat, dogs lying as if dead on the sidewalks, waves of air shuddering, jellylike, over the empty highway."

Del keeps her fragmentary novel folded inside a copy of *Wuthering Heights* and escapes from Jubilee into *The Life of Charlotte Brontë:* "The only world I was in touch with was the one I had made, with the aid of some books, to be peculiar and nourishing to myself." Emerging from the public library into the Ontario winter after reading Undset's *Kristin Lavransdatter,* she sees a farmer on his sleigh as "a helmeted

Norseman." From time to time, however, practical details, "niggling considerations of fact," impinge on her made-up world: if "Caroline" is to drown herself at the height of summer, how will there be enough water in the river?"

Del's perplexity in the face of such narrative challenges underlines Munro's own achievement: her ability to accommodate both the ordinary and the bizarre in her fiction, to enhance observation and experience without wrenching them out of true. As a child, Del lurches from the world she reads about to the one she lives in and finds that one tends to obliterate the other. The stories in Uncle Benny's tabloid newspaper seem irresistible:

> I was bloated and giddy with revelations of evil, of its versatility and grand invention and horrific playfulness. But the nearer I got to our house the more this vision faded. Why was it that the plain back wall of home, the pale chipped brick, the cement platform outside the kitchen door, washtubs hanging on nails, the pump, the lilac bush with brown-spotted leaves, should make it seem doubtful that a woman would really send her husband's torso, wrapped in Christmas paper, by mail to his girl friend in South Carolina?

In the same way, Uncle Bill, when he turns up in the flesh, obliterates the monster of Del's mother's stories: "This was the thing, the indigestible fact. This Uncle Bill was my mother's brother, the terrible fat boy, so gifted in cruelty, so cunning, quick, fiendish, so much to be feared. I kept looking at him, trying to pull that boy out of the yellowish man. But I could not find him there. He was gone, smothered." Which is true?—her mother's picture of their childhood (miserable, narrow, blighted by religious fanaticism), or Uncle Bill's reminiscences of the simple country life and its "good spiritual example"? Not yet able to appreciate the different ways in which people recount their lives and shape the past to make sense of the present, Del is suddenly sarcastic about one of her mother's favorite stories. For a moment, in challenging her mother's version of the past she has cast doubt on everything she lives by: "there was something in the room like the downflash of a wing or knife, a sense of hurt so strong, but quick and isolated, vanishing."

The handing down of stories from mother to daughter, the reinterpretation of, even resistance to, these stories, the testing of them against experience, is an important structural principle of ***Lives of Girls and Women.*** Implicit in the narrative is the irony that Del, an aspiring writer, never realizes that the stories she is so used to hearing could provide the starting point of a book; she notices only the discontinuities and contradictions between what goes on around her and what she finds written down. Her attitude is natural in Jubilee, where "reading books was something like chewing gum, a habit to be abandoned when the seriousness and satisfactions of adult life took over." At school, "art" is the seductive artifice of the annual operetta, with its cardboard villages and peasant dances. At home, Del's father reads the same three books "over and over again, putting himself to sleep. He never talked about what he read." Her mother, the "Princess Ida" of a city newspaper column for "lady correspondents," coats in sentimental cliché the very countryside she has done her best to escape from: "This morning a marvelous silver frost enraptures the eye on every twig and telephone wire and makes the world a veritable fairyland." Writing under her own name to the Jubilee *Herald-Advance,* she expresses dispassionate reformist opinions that are at odds with Del's sense of glory and danger in the lives of girls and women.

As well as these unhelpful models, Del has two special handicaps to contend with in understanding the relationship between literature and life: being Canadian and being a woman. "Reality" is a special problem for a writer in rural Ontario, who cannot mention the nearest city without having to explain that her London is not the "real" London. It is also a problem for a girl who reads in a woman's magazine the opinion of "a famous New York psychiatrist, a disciple of Freud" that if a boy and a girl look at a full moon: "The boy thinks of the universe, its immensity and mystery; the girl thinks 'I must wash my hair'." Del knows that that is not how she thinks, but instead of doubting the article she doubts herself—"surely a New York psychiatrist must *know*"—and feels trapped in a dilemma: "I wanted men to love me, *and* I wanted to think of the universe when I looked at the moon." It is left to Munro, at the end of the story, to redress the balance by showing what men think about at important moments: "Sometimes when he had barely got his breath back [after love-making] I would ask him what he was thinking and he would say, 'I was just figuring out how I could fix that muffler—.' " (pp. 189-91)

The art of Munro's fiction is to discover an "overall design" for a "conglomeration of stories." The resulting form is flexible without being artless. It is not a *Bildungsroman,* for women's lives are not comfortably accommodated in a genre which presupposes that characters are free to act, develop and make choices, to learn from, not succumb to, experience. Women's stories have their own tenor and direction. Del's aunts, Elspeth and Grace, keep up an endless, sharp dialogue of story-telling which runs along with the pace and mood of their work; stoning cherries, shelling peas, coring apples, "Their hands, their old, dark, wooden-handled paring knives, moved with marvelous, almost vindictive speed." These aunts are spinsters and their stories feel to Del "dried out, brittle." Aunt Moira, on the other hand, who is married, seems "one of those heavy, cautiously moving, wrecked survivors of the female life, with stories to tell."

The female version of the novel of education is about the conflicting claims of individual freedom and biological destiny; imagery of water, as women novelists know so well, is its natural expression. Will the heroine be swept away and drowned or left high and dry? Must her energies be damned up or diverted into narrow channels? Del Jordan's story begins on a river bank: "We spent days along the Wawanash River helping Uncle Benny fish." She hears from her mother and from their lodger, Fern, "stories about people in the town, about themselves; their talk was a river that never dried up. It was the drama, the ferment of life just beyond my reach." The movement of their narrative often takes the form of eddies and whirlpools: "Stories of the past could go like this, round and round and down to death; I expected it." As she grows up, Del protests against this inevitability—"Had all her stories, after all, to end up with just her, the way she was now, just my mother in Jubilee?"—just as she resists her first lover's attempt to "baptize" her, holding her against her will under the water. In the end it is the river itself, gathering force, flooding, receding within each story, which gives the novel its shape and form. In the end Del learns to keep her head above water; it is not she who is destroyed in the spring flood but her unwanted inheritance, Uncle Craig's dry archive of local history and genealogy. (p. 192)

In ***Lives of Girls and Women,*** Del's seductive "black fable" threatened to turn the past into gothic; in ***The Beggar Maid,*** Rose's temptation is to dine out on the exotic appeal to the citydweller of a "deprived" rural childhood: "Rose knew a lot of people who wished they had been born poor, and hadn't been. So she would queen it over them, offering various scandals and bits of squalor from her childhood." The particular narrative falsity skirted and ultimately rejected in the text is a dramatized "folksiness," a sentimentalizing and sensationalizing of places and people by translating them into packaged and titled anecdotes: "The Boys' Toilet and the Girls' Toilet," "Old Mr. Burns in his Toilet." Putting on a country accent, doing imitations, colluding in her future husband's fantasy of herself as Burne-Jones's beggar maid, Rose is nevertheless sometimes "deeply, unaccountably ashamed."

Just as ***Lives of Girls and Women*** began by putting the "real" story of Uncle Benny and Madeleine alongside the cheap shocks of the tabloids, ***The Beggar Maid*** begins with the story of unsavoury old Hat Nettleton and the local radio interviewer's attempt to turn him into a lovable "character," "a living link with our past": "Horsewhipper into centenarian," muses the narrator, "Photographed on his birthday, fussed over by nurses, kissed no doubt by a girl reporter. Flash bulbs popping at him. Tape recorder drinking in the sound of his voice. Oldest resident. Oldest horsewhipper. Living link with our past." Local radio in the 1940's of ***Lives of Girls and Women*** was a homely affair, but by the later episodes of ***The Beggar Maid,*** it is glossier and more sophisticated: on radio and television, as in social life generally, people are ready to tell intimate details of their lives to complete strangers. Everything is preserved for its entertainment value and presented with a carefully rehearsed spontaneity: "When she talked in public she was frank and charming; she had a puzzled, diffident way of leading into her anecdotes, as if she were just now remembering, had not told them a hundred times already."

Her childhood, and Flo in particular, furnish much of the material for Rose's stories: "She delivered Flo and the store in bold strokes." Later visits to Flo provide such cameos as the trifle story (which demolishes Rose's vision of herself returning to West Hanratty and patiently looking after Flo in her old age) and the parking story: "That was one of the stories she told about Flo. She did it well; her own exhaustion and sense of virtue; Flo's bark, her waving cane, her fierce unwillingness to be the object of anybody's rescue." Flo's letter protesting at Rose's exposure of a bare breast in a television play is a good talking-point for a dinner party: Rose reads it out "for comic effect, and dramatic effect, to show the gulf that lay behind her." In a characteristic narrative shift, Munro shows Rose's sudden sense, not just of shame at her exposure of Flo, but of the validity of Flo's protests: "they were painfully, truly, meant; they were all a hard life had to offer." Simplified and highlighted, Flo is also betrayed; for the broad outlines of her behavior, the predictable clichés of her speech, are indeed those of a stock figure. The difference is in the motivation of the behavior, the feeling behind the hackneyed "lines." Up from the country for the day, unintentionally making an exhibition of herself at a Toronto reception, "Flo did look like a comic character, except that her bewilderment, her authenticity, were quite daunting."

Fortunately for Rose's integrity as a story-teller, her childhood experience in West Hanratty, while providing her with her stock of anecdotes, also alerts her to the ways fiction may "cheat": "Later on Rose would think of Franny when she came across the figure of an idiotic, saintly whore, in a book or a movie. Men who made books and movies seemed to have a fondness for this figure, though Rose noticed they would clean her up." Rose also realizes that the descriptive techniques of nonfiction can be equally misleading. James Agee, in *Let Us Now Praise Famous Men* (another acknowledged influence on Munro's work), had wrestled with the difficulties of writing about Southern sharecroppers without either making them picturesque or generalizing them into abstract "problems" and social "types"; one of his solutions was to try to record what his subjects said and thought without translating them into blander, more objective terms for the reader. Rose has a similar problem in West Hanratty. How, for instance, can a familiar oddity like Milton Homer be explained to an outsider? "The village idiot" is not how people ever thought of him; they just said "Oh, there's Milton." In ***Lives of Girls and Women,*** Del and her boyfriend Jerry amuse themselves pretending to talk "like sociologists" about the country people from outside Jubilee: "From St. Augustine they are run-of-the-mill. Farm folk. They have big yellow teeth. They look as if they eat a lot of oatmeal porridge." In ***The Beggar Maid,*** Munro lets the subjects talk back; she shows how funny the standard labels sound in West Hanratty: "This is the working-class part of town," says Rose with new-found sophistication; "*Working* class?" said Flo. "Not if the ones around here can help it." The "Stories of Flo and Rose" cut both ways: they are told *by* as well as about both women. When Flo is the author of her own story rather than a character in one of Rose's, it is set down straightforwardly, introduced by a colon—"Here is the sort of story Flo told Rose:." She is not easily deflected and cannot be made to perform to order; Rose's attempt to present Flo and the store to Patrick as interesting material for a local historian soon goes awry, for Flo's forte is boastfully lurid story-telling, not oral history.

Instead of a narrative generosity, a pressure to share and tell, Rose at first feels only the common adolescent desire to name things baldly, to strip away the necessary comforting delusions and prevarications surrounding her father's illness: "She dramatized her own part in it, saw herself clear-eyed and unsurprised, refusing all deceptions, young in years but old in bitter experience of life." Behind this severity is her high-school reading, in particular *Macbeth* and Katherine Mansfield. Memorizing Lady Macbeth's speeches, she dramatizes her own coldness and lack of illusion; despising the well-to-do children of "The Garden Party," she starts to become "a prig about poverty." **"Half a Grapefruit"** is, among other things, a tribute to, and an oblique re-telling of "The Garden Party": another young girl's experience of "how death would slice the day." (pp. 193-95)

In **"Half a Grapefruit"** the images are all of division and contrast, from the informal segregation of the high-school classroom into "town" and "country" to the juxtaposition of death and life exemplified by Billy Pope, who lives in the slaughterhouse but grows geraniums on the window sill. This is in keeping with the psychological geography of ***The Beggar Maid*** as a whole: a town cut in two by a river, linked by the bridge where Rose hears voices mocking her social pretensions: "Half-a-grapefruit!" The narrative proceeds through contrast—home and school, past and present—and through ironic inversion: a "beggar maid" who receives "royal beatings" and who "queens it" over her more privileged friends. There is no meeting of separate worlds: "What Dr. Henshawe's house and Flo's house did best, in Rose's opinion, was discredit each other." The effect is quite different from ***Lives of Girls and Women,*** where the narrative flow matches the pace and direction of the river.

Both books end with a rejection of false ways of writing and the promise of a new fidelity to the past and its inhabitants. Once the spell of her Gothic extravaganza is broken, Del is not tempted to opt instead for the utilitarian realism of documentary or journalistic reporting; even before she has finished her revelatory conversation with Bobby Sherriff, she sees the editor of the local newspaper "come out the back door of the *Herald-Advance* building, empty a wastebasket into an incinerator, and plod back in." "Voracious and misguided" as Uncle Craig writing his local history, she will begin her attempt to recapture Jubilee by compiling lists: "A list of all the stores and businesses going up and down the main street and who owned them, a list of family names, names on the tombstones in the cemetery and any inscriptions underneath." (The stratagem is reminiscent of much nineteenth-century American writing, where nothing can be taken for granted and everything must be painstakingly enumerated before it can be made over into art.) No list, though, can ever be accurate enough or exhaustive enough to contain the details of just one life, and only a story, not a list, can connect and make sense of the details so that they are "held together" as well as "held still." . . . The paradoxical lesson of ***Lives of Girls and Women*** is that fiction can only transcend locality when it is firmly grounded in it.

The challenge at the end of ***The Beggar Maid*** is a similar one: where Del in **"Epilogue: The Photographer"** was faced with the irreducible reality of Jubilee, Rose in **"Who Do You Think You Are?"** finds herself confronting the figure of Ralph Gillespie. Ralph is just not susceptible to Rose's style. Once famous for his imitations, he is himself inimitable. The moment of sympathy he and Rose share is silent, but it does relieve the shame she has felt in broadcasting the "old mythology" of her life story, in "reporting antics, when there was always something further, a tone, a depth, a light, that she couldn't get and wouldn't get." Her change of heart depends on the realization that there are things which cannot be dined out on, feelings which it is "dubious" and even "dangerous" to translate into anecdote. In refusing to make a story out of Ralph's death, in recounting it only as it appears in the local paper, Rose can be "glad that there was one thing at least she wouldn't spoil by telling." (pp. 196-97)

Rowena Fowler, "The Art of Alice Munro: 'The Beggar Maid' and 'Lives of Girls and Women,' " in Critique: Studies in Modern Fiction, *Vol. XXV, No. 4, Summer, 1984, pp. 189-98.*

GEORGE WOODCOCK (essay date 1986)

[*Woodcock is a Canadian educator, editor, and critic best known for his biographies of George Orwell and Thomas Merton. He also founded the important literary journal,* Canadian Literature, *and has written extensively on the literature of Canada. In the following excerpt, Woodcock discusses the varied themes in Munro's works and states that her treatments of adult themes in her later stories lack the intensity and realism she achieves in her explorations of childhood in the volumes* Dance of the Happy Shades *and* Lives of Girls and Women.]

Munro offers the portrait of a distinctively Canadian society and does it in a distinctively Canadian way. Her sense of the interplay of setting and tradition is impeccable, so that there are really two ways of reading Munro, the exoteric one of the reader who knows a good story when he comes upon it, and reads it with enjoyment and not too much concern for authenticity, and the esoteric one of the Canadian who is likely to read it with a special sense of its truth or otherwise to the life and land he knows.

Perhaps because, unlike the later collections of stories, it is gathered from the writings of a relatively long period—at least fifteen years as against three or four—***The Dance of the Happy Shades*** is more varied and tentatively venturesome than the later volumes. It shows the author trying out different modes and approaches. There are stories, like **"The Office,"** that rather self-consciously explore the problems of women setting out as writers in an unsympathetic environment. There are others, like **"The Shining Houses,"** a study of the callousness young property owners can show in defending their "values" (i.e. the selling prices of their homes), that are as ambivalently suburban as anything by John Cheever. **"Sunday Afternoon"** is a little social study, highly class-conscious for a Canadian writer, of the relations between a country girl hired to serve in a rich middle-class home and her brittle-brainless employers. And in **"Thanks for the Ride"** Munro makes a rare foray across the sex line and tells in the voice of an adolescent boy the story of his first lay; in fact, the point of view is deceptive, since the real interest of the story lies in the portrait of his partner Lois, a fragile yet tough working-class girl, much used by men and yet—in her coarse independence—strangely inviolate.

Most of the remaining stories fall into a group of which the main theme is childhood and growing up in the Ontario countryside, with action centred sometimes on the farm operated by the father of the central character and sometimes in the nearby town where the mother at times lives separately and where the girl attends school. The father-dominated farm represents the world of nature and feeling, a world devoid of ambition. The mother-dominated house in town represents the world of social and intellectual ambition, just as the school is the setting where the heroine establishes her relationship with her peers among the small-town children but also develops her desire to escape into a broader world. In some of the stories the mother, living or remembered, is shown advancing into the illness—Parkinson's disease—that will accentuate the oddity which most of her neighbours have already mocked in her.

The three stories of childhood, **"Walker Brothers Cowboy," "Images"** and **"Boys and Girls,"** are perhaps the most important of this group, both for their vivid evocation of the decaying rural life a century after the pioneers of Upper Canada, and for their delineation of the relationships between parents and children in hard times.

"Walker Brothers Cowboy," the opening story of the book, takes us to a time when the silver fox farm has failed and Ben Jordan has taken up peddling the patent medicines, spices and food flavourings distributed by Walker Brothers. The story, told by his daughter who does not name herself, begins by relating this time of stress and need to the slightly better past on the farm. The girl's mother, also unnamed, tries desperately to maintain self-respect in a situation she sees as a demeaning loss of social standing, even though she lives physically better in the town than on the farm.

> Fate has flung us onto a street of poor people (it does not matter that we were poor before, that was

> a different kind of poverty), and the only way to take this, as she sees it, is with dignity, with bitterness, with no reconciliation. No bathroom with claw-footed tub and a flush toilet is going to comfort her, nor water on tap and sidewalks past the house and milk in bottles, nor even the two movie theatres and the Venus Restaurant and Woolworths so marvellous it has live birds singing in its fan-cooled corners and fish as tiny as finger-nails, as bright as moons, swimming in its green tanks. My mother does not care.

The father, more self-contained, more ironic, finds ways to live with Depression conditions and salvage his pride. As the story opens we see him walking with his daughter beside Lake Huron and telling her how the Great Lakes were gouged out of the earth by the ice coming down in great probing fingers from the north. Clearly the girl prefers her father's company to her mother's:

> She walks serenely like a lady shopping, like a *lady* shopping, past the housewives in loose beltless dresses torn under the arms. With me her creation, wretched curls and flaunting hair bow, scrubbed knees and white socks—all I do not want to be. I loathe even my name when she says it in public, in a voice so high, proud and ringing, deliberately different from the voice of any other mother on the street.

Travelling his route of the desperate dusty farmlands, Ben Jordan makes fun of his situation by improvising as he rides a kind of endless ballad of his adventures on the road, and this becomes a kind of *leitmotiv* one day when he sets out with the girl and her brother and, leaving his Walker Brothers territory, takes them to a farmhouse where a woman who was once his sweetheart is living. The clean bare farmhouse with Catholic emblems on the walls and an old woman dozing in a corner becomes a kind of stage on which is revealed to the girl that people we know may have dimensions to their lives of which to this point we have been unaware. The sense of something theatrical and unreal and different from ordinary life is given by the fact that Ben Jordan and his old sweetheart Nora Cronin name each other, but nobody else in the story is named. The strangeness of the hitherto unknown past is framed within the nameless ordinariness of the present.

In **"Images"** a different kind of framing takes place. The story begins with the girl, again unnamed and again mainly a spectator, remembering the coarse cousin, Mary McQuade, who comes in to act as a kind of nurse in family crises and who is now filling the house with her overbearing presence because the mother is ill. The father—once again Ben Jordan but now an unspecified farmer—runs a trapline down by the river, and one day he and the girl go down to harvest the muskrats. On their way they encounter a crazy recluse, Joe Phippen, who patrols the river bank with an axe in search of imagined enemies. They go to the cellar where Joe has been living since his house burnt down; for the girl it seems like an underground playhouse, except for its sinister smells and a mad cat the hermit feeds whisky. As they leave the cellar Ben Jordan cautions the girl when she gets back to tell nobody in the house about the axe. At table with Mary McQuade he relates the story of Joe and his drunken cat, and Mary is filled with indignation.

> "A man that'd do a thing like that ought to be locked up."
>
> "Maybe so," my father said. "Just the same I hope they don't get him for a while yet. Old Joe."
>
> "Eat your supper," Mary said, bending over me. I did not for some time realize that I was no longer afraid of her. "Look at her," she said. "Her eyes dropping out of her head, all she's been and seen. Was he feeding whisky to her too?"
>
> "Not a drop," said my father, and looked steadily down the table at me. Like the children in fairy stories who have seen their parents make pacts with terrifying strangers, who have discovered that our fears are based on nothing but the truth, but who come back from marvellous escapes and take up their knives and forks, with humility and good manners, prepared to live happily ever after—like them, dazed and powerful with secrets, I never said a word.

In this story the filial link is complete. The father puts his trust in his daughter, and she keeps it in a kind of complicity to protect the strange and eccentric and unpopular in human behaviour—a complicity that will re-emerge in Munro's fiction.

But in **"Boys and Girls"** the trust between father and daughter is broken, and that is one of the complex aspects of growing up, involving as it does the girl's gradual realization of the difference between the sexes that in the end, and no matter what Freud may have said, makes fathers see sons as their successors and makes men stand together.

The action of this story takes place entirely on the fox farm. In a passage of admirably clear and restrained description Munro creates the feeling of the place and details the daily tasks the girl performs as she helps her father, keeping the pens supplied with water and spreading grass over them to prevent the foxes' pelts from being darkened by sunlight. Her little brother also helps, but she jealously guards the main tasks for herself, and resents her mother's attempts to trap her into household tasks. The curiously detached centre of all this activity is formed by the foxes which, despite generations of captivity, have not ceased to be wild animals, hostile and intractable:

> Naming them did not make pets out of them, or anything like it. Nobody but my father ever went into the pens, and he had twice had blood-poisoning from bites. When I was bringing them their water they prowled up and down on the paths they had made inside their pens, barking seldom—they saved that for nighttime, when they might get up a chorus of community frenzy—but always watching me, their eyes burning, clear gold, in their pointed malevolent faces. They were beautiful for their delicate legs and heavy, aristocratic tails and the bright fur sprinkled on dark down their backs—which gave them their name—but especially for their faces, drawn exquisitely sharp in pure hostility, and their golden eyes.

One has the sense that although loyalty to her father would never let her admit the thought, these wild captive creatures have earned the girl's sympathy, and what happens shortly afterwards seems to confirm this. She begins all at once to realize that her cherished position in the little world of the farm has become insecure:

> This winter also I began to hear a great deal more on the theme my mother had sounded when she

> had been talking in front of the barn. I no longer felt safe. It seemed that in the minds of the people around me there was a steady undercurrent of thought, not to be deflected, on this one subject. The word *girl* had formerly seemed to me innocent and unburdened, like the word *child;* now it appeared that it was no such thing. A girl was not, as I had supposed, simply what I was; it was what I had to become. It was a definition, always touched with emphasis, with reproach and disappointment. Also it was a joke on me. . . .

The critical point comes shortly afterwards, when her loyalties are all at once tested, and her response is as astonishing to her as it is to anyone else. Her father buys superannuated horses to slaughter for fox food; occasionally there will be a perfectly healthy animal among them for which in these days of increasing mechanization a farmer no longer has any use. A mare of this kind, whom they call Flora, is bought and kept over winter. She is a nervous animal, in some ways almost as proud and intractable as the foxes, and on the day she is being taken out to be shot she breaks away into a meadow where a gate has been left open. The girl and her brother are sent to close it.

> The gate was heavy. I lifted it out of the gravel and carried it across the roadway. I had it half-way across when she came into sight, galloping straight towards me. There was just time to get the chain on. Laird came scrambling through the ditch to help me.
>
> Instead of shutting the gate, I opened it as wide as I could. I did not make any decision to do this, it was just what I did. Flora never slowed down; she galloped straight past me, and Laird jumped up and down, yelling, "Shut it, shut it" even when it was too late. . . .

The mare, of course, is eventually caught and killed. And then, at mid-day dinner, her brother Laird tells on the girl:

> My father made a curt sound of disgust. "What did you do that for?"
>
> I did not answer. I put down my fork and waited to be sent from the table, still not looking up.
>
> But this did not happen. For some time nobody said anything, then Laird said matter-of-factly, "She's crying."
>
> "Never mind," my father said. He spoke with resignation, even good humour, the words that absolved and dismissed me for good. "She's only a girl," he said.
>
> I didn't protest that, even in my heart. Maybe it was true.

Two themes that will recur in Munro's later writing have been introduced; the burden of femininity, and the need to break free. They take on increased importance in her first novel, ***Lives of Girls and Women.*** This appears to have begun as another collection of stories that had enough of a common strain for the publisher to suggest she might turn them into a novel; its origin survives in the episodic and rather discontinuous structure of the work.

Lives of Girls and Women really completes the three stories I have just been discussing. The inconsistencies that existed between them are ironed out. Ben Jordan is still the father and he runs a fox farm. The other characters are now all named, the girl becoming Della (or Del), the mother Ida, the brother changing to Owen, and with this naming everything seems to become more precise in intent. Even the locality is named, for the farm is on Flats Road in the disreputable outskirts of the town of Jubilee, and the action alternates between the farm and the town, where Ida takes a house where she and Del live except in the summer months.

The eight parts (significantly they are named but not numbered, so that they seem as much stories as chapters) really serve two functions. Each is an exemplary episode, self-contained even though its characters spill over into the other episodes, so that it can stand on its own. Yet, in the classic manner of the *Bildungsroman,* each episode builds on the last, revealing another side of Del's education in life, and as the progression is generally chronological, the continuity becomes that of a rather conventional novel, which begins in the heroine's childhood and ends when, as a young woman who has just allowed a love affair to divert her from winning a scholarship, she turns to the world of art and begins her first book.

The general inclination of ***Lives of Girls and Women*** is indeed that of a portrait of the artist, and the first-person voice in which it is told is appropriate. It looks back to the final and title story of ***Dance of the Happy Shades,*** which tells of the last party of an old music teacher who astonishes and annoys her middle-class pupils and their parents by producing a girl from a school for the retarded who is clearly, whatever her intelligence, something near to a musical genius:

> Miss Marsalles sits beside the piano and smiles at everybody in her usual way. Her smile is not triumphant, or modest. She does not look like a magician who is watching people's faces to see the effect of a rather original revelation; nothing like that. You would think, now that at the very end of her life she has found someone she can teach—whom she must teach—to play the piano, she would light up with the importance of this discovery. But it seems that the girl's playing like this is something she always expected, and she finds it natural and satisfying; people who believe in miracles do not make much fuss when they actually encounter one. Nor does it seem that she regards this girl with any more wonder than the other children from Greenhill School, who love her, or the rest of us, who do not. To her no gift is unexpected, no celebration will come as a surprise.

The sense of art as a miracle, and the sense also of some special kind of intelligence that recognizes it recurs in Munro's books, and it is linked with the idea that there are levels of access to truth which have nothing to do with what in the world passes for wisdom or intelligence. (pp. 240-46)

[Munro's] second novel, ***Who Do You Think You Are?,*** is a much less convincing book than ***Lives of Girls and Women,*** in both emotional and aesthetic terms. It too is a *Bildungsroman,* extending well beyond childhood into the darker times of middle age with its failed marriages, humiliating love affairs and mundane careers. The story of Rose, her upbringing in the rural slum of West Hanratty, and her subsequent and doomed marriage to a rich fellow student, develops the theme of social climbing and its perils that is already present in ***Lives of Girls and Women.*** The novel, again a series of loosely connected episodes, is written in the third person, and this shift in point of view accompanies—perhaps even creates—a notable change in tone from the earlier book. In ***Lives of Girls and Women*** the sense of familiar authenticity was sustained by the fact that the aspirant writer as central character was assumed to be both participant and observer. In ***Who Do You Think You Are?*** the participant is observed, and there is a kind of hard objectivity to the book with its relentless social documentation of low life in West Hanratty at the end of the Thirties. Though Munro does make a largely successful attempt to project the inner life of her principal character, the other leading figures in the novel, like Rose's crotchety stepmother Flo, her violent father and her snobbish husband, are shallow projections, almost caricatures, portrayed with none of the feeling and understanding that characterized the presentation of the father and mother, Ben and Ida Jordan, in the earlier novel.

Yet, though the general tone of ***Who Do You Think You Are?*** is at once harsher and more brittle than that of ***Lives of Girls and Women,*** there is a variation of quality within the book, and the first four chapters, which deal with childhood in Ontario, are the most effective. When the action moves into other places, notably the alien realm of British Columbia, the documentary background becomes more uncertain, and as Munro deals with the problems of adults living out their erotic fantasies she seems too near her subject for the special kind of luminous objectivity that characterizes the stories of childhood and adolescence to develop.

A similar criticism applies to the later stories contained in ***Something I've Been Meaning to Tell You*** and ***The Moons of Jupiter.*** Reading them, one becomes aware how little Munro has changed as a writer since the early period of the 1950s and the 1960s when she first attracted the attention of readers. She is still at her best as the magic realist. She has not moved, like so many of her contemporaries, into fantasy, or into an experimental use of memory like that of Margaret Laurence, while the episodic and open-ended form of her so-called novels arises not from any deconstructionist intent, but, I suggest, from the kind of perception that sees life discontinuously, episode by episode.

In making these remarks I do not mean to suggest that the later stories are unimpressive. They are always skillful in their presentation of human situations, and the prose never falters. There is not a sloppily written piece among them. As studies of generational distancing, some of the stories seen from the viewpoint of old people, like **"Walking on Water"** and **"Marrakesh,"** are entirely convincing, while here and there are still marvellously lucid evocations of childhood and adolescence like **"The Found Boat"** and **"The Turkey Season."** Much less satisfying are the stories of middle-aged women with elusive lovers, and here the very impeccability of the writing seems to emphasize the psychological hollowness. At times, in recent years, one feels that Munro has fallen into the trap of virtuosity. She is so good at the kind of story she has always written that she seems never to have felt the need to try anything different. The result has been a certain leaching of character from her writing; some of her later stories are so well made that they seem anonymous, like those *New Yorker* stories which might have been written by any one of a number of North American virtuosi; indeed, the Munro stories of which this seems especially true, like **"Dulse"** and **"Labour Day Dinner"** in ***The Moons of Jupiter,*** in fact appeared in the *New Yorker.*

I am conscious, remembering what I expected of Munro when I first read her early stories and ***Lives of Girls and Women,*** of a disappointment with her career seen as a whole. Most of her early stories and some of the later ones are among the best ever written in Canada. But those whom we think of as major writers, while they do not necessarily evolve in the sense of becoming always better, do tend to metamorphose and so indefinitely to enlarge their scope, as poets like Earle Birney and Dorothy Livesay and novelists like Robertson Davies and Timothy Findley have done. In this respect Alice Munro has remained fundamentally unchanged, applying the same realist techniques with the same impeccable skill and merely varying the human situations. Her potentialities have always been major; her achievements have never quite matched them because she has never mastered those transformations of form with which major writers handle the great climactic shifts of life. She has written of all the ages as she first wrote of childhood, and that is why her lives of girls are so much more convincing than her lives of women. (pp. 248-50)

George Woodcock, "The Plots of Life: The Realism of Alice Munro," in Queen's Quarterly, *Vol. 93, No. 2, Summer, 1986, pp. 235-50.*

JOYCE CAROL OATES (essay date 1986)

[*Oates is an American fiction writer who is perhaps best known for her novel* them, *which won a National Book Award in 1970, and for several novels on Gothic themes written in the 1980s. Her fiction is noted for its exhaustive presentation of realistic detail as well as its striking imaginativeness, especially in the evocation of abnormal psychological states. As a critic, Oates has written on remarkably diverse authors—from Shakespeare to Herman Melville to Samuel Beckett—and is appreciated for the individuality and erudition that characterize her critical work. In the following excerpt, Oates reviews Munro's* The Progress of Love, *noting that the stories in this collection are not as fully developed as those in her earlier works.*]

Like her similarly gifted contemporaries Peter Taylor, William Trevor, Edna O'Brien and some few others, the Canadian short-story writer Alice Munro writes stories that have the density—moral, emotional, sometimes historical—of other writers' novels. As remote from the techniques and ambitions of what is currently known as "minimalist" fiction as it is possible to get and still inhabit the same genre, these writers give us fictitious worlds that are mimetic paradigms of utterly real worlds yet *are* fictions, composed with so assured an art that it might be mistaken for artlessness. They give voice to the voices of their regions, filtering the natural rhythms of speech through a more refined (but not obtrusively refined) writerly speech. They are faithful to the contours of local legend, tall tales, anecdotes, family reminiscences; their material is nearly always realistic—"Realism" being that convention among competing others that swept all before it in the mid and late 19th century—and their characters behave, generally, like real people. That is, they surprise us at every turn, without violating probability. They so resemble ourselves that reading about them, at times, is emotionally risky. Esthetically experimental literature, while evoking our admiration, rarely moves us the way this sort of literature moves us.

From the start of her career in 1968 with the Canadian publication of the short-story collection ***Dance of the Happy Shades*** (published in the United States in 1973) through ***Lives of Girls and Women, Something I've Been Meaning to Tell You, The Beggar Maid, The Moons of Jupiter*** and this new collection, ***The Progress of Love,*** Alice Munro has concentrated on short fiction that explores the lives of fairly undistinguished men and women—but particularly women—who live in southwestern rural Ontario. When her characters move elsewhere to live, to British Columbia, for instance, like the couple whose precarious marriage is explored in **"Miles City, Montana,"** it is still Ontario that is home. (But: "When we said 'home' and meant Ontario, we had very different places in mind.") Though Ms. Munro's tonal palette has darkened considerably over the last 20 years, her fictional technique has not changed greatly, nor has the range of her characters. By degrees, of course, they have grown older. Their living fulfills the prophetic conclusion of a beautiful early story, **"Walker Brothers Cowboy"** (from ***Dance of the Happy Shades***): "I feel my father's life flowing back from our car in the last of the afternoon, darkening and turning strange, like a landscape that has an enchantment on it, making it kindly, ordinary and familiar while you are looking at it, but changing it, once your back is turned, into something you will never know, with all kinds of weathers, and distances you cannot imagine."

The most powerful of the 11 stories collected in ***The Progress of Love*** take on bluntly and without sentiment the themes of mortality, self-delusion, puzzlement over the inexplicable ways of fate. In **"Fits"** it is observed that "people can take a fit like the earth takes a fit" after an unaccountable murder-suicide has been discovered in a small rural town. (Indeed, **"Fits"** would have made an excellent title for this collection.) The story yields its secrets slowly, with admirable craft and suspense: the surprise for the reader is that the "fit" at its core is less the sensational act of violence than a woman's mysteriously untroubled response to it.

"A Queer Streak" is a tragically comic (or comically tragic) tale of an ambitious young woman named Violet, a "holy terror" in her youth, whose life is permanently altered by the bizarre behavior of an emotionally unbalanced younger sister. It is a familiar temptation to which Violet succumbs: she decides, against the very grain of her personality, that the loss of her fiancé is a "golden opportunity" and not a disaster. Henceforth she will give up her own life, live for others: "That was the way Violet saw to leave her pain behind. A weight gone off her. If she would bow down and leave her old self behind as well, and all her ideas of what her life should be, the weight, the pain, the humiliation would all go magically. And she could still be chosen. . . . If she prayed enough and tried enough, that would be possible." But this moment of revelation is the high point of Violet's life, as we see it.

Violet, who takes on, by degrees, the "queer streak" of her family, is one of Ms. Munro's unromantic, independent heroines—country bred, proud, resilient, courageous even in her old age. Her story might have been even more moving if it did not unaccountably accelerate in its second half (where the point of view shifts to Violet's cousin Dan about whom we know virtually nothing and who is merely used as an instrument to observe Violet). Also, Ms. Munro is curiously perfunctory in summarizing Violet's love affair with a married man—the most intense emotional experience of Violet's life, presumably. Like the adulterous love affair at the heart of **"White Dump,"** it is alluded to rather than dramatized: the reader knows very little about it, and consequently feels very little.

Recurring in Alice Munro's fiction is a certain female protagonist, clearly kin to Violet, but generally more capable of establishing a life for herself. She is intelligent, though not intellectual; "superior," though often self-doubting. She has the capacity to extract from frequently sordid experiences moral insights of a very nearly Jamesian subtlety and precision. She tells us what she thinks; tells us, often, what *we* would think. Not conventionally beautiful, she is nonetheless attractive to men: which leads her sometimes, as an adolescent, into dangerous situations—as in the new story **"Jesse and Meribeth"** in which the adolescent Jesse is scolded by a near-seducer, an older man, for what he correctly perceives as her overwrought romantic imagination: "You shouldn't go inside places like this with men just because they ask you. . . . You're hot-blooded. You've got some lessons to learn." In the more complex, multigenerational **"White Dump"** a kindred girl is drawn into marriage with a man who "depended on her to make him a man," and who will prove inadequate to her passionate nature. In **"Lichen,"** one of the bleakest of the new stories, the heroine, middle-aged, cheerful, at last adjusted to a solitary life, achieves a moral triumph over her fatuous ex-husband simply by maturing beyond him. She is fully accepting of the terms of her freedom: "This white-haired woman walking beside him . . . dragged so much weight with her—a weight not just of his sexual secrets but of his middle-of-the-night speculations about God, his psychosomatic chest pains, his digestive sensitivity, his escape plans, which once included her. . . . All his ordinary and extraordinary life—even some things it was unlikely she knew about—seemed stored up in her. He could never feel any lightness, any secret and victorious expansion, with a woman who knew so much. She was bloated with all she knew." She has become, ironically, a kind of mother to him; but she looks so much older than he that he is shamed and frightened at the very sight of her.

In one of the collection's finest stories, **"The Progress of Love,"** the daughter of a woman who sacrificed both herself and her children to presumably Christian ideals of integrity chooses deliberately *not* to believe in those ideals, or to marry conventionally as her mother had done; she becomes, in fact, a real estate agent, selling off the old houses and farms that made up the world of her youth. Long divorced, alone but not really lonely, Euphemia—who calls herself Fame—seeks moments of "kindness and reconciliation" rather than serious love; she wonders "if those moments aren't more valued, and deliberately gone after, in the setups some people like myself have now, than they were in those old marriages, where love and grudges could be growing underground, so confused and stubborn, it must have seemed they had forever." But without the old marriages and all that they yielded of sorrow, repression, loss, romance—what remains? Fame's love affairs are affairs merely, matters of convenience. To celebrate birthdays "or other big events" she goes with friends from work to a place called the Hideaway where male strippers perform.

(While Ms. Munro's Ontario countryside has come to bear a disconcerting resemblance to Andrew Wyeth's stark, bleached-out, clinically detailed landscapes, her small towns have been tawdrily transformed—dignified old country inns recycled as strip joints, convenience stores stocked with video games: "jittery electronic noise and flashing light and menacing, modern-day, oddly shaved and painted children.")

More than ***The Beggar Maid*** and ***The Moons of Jupiter,*** the two story collections preceding this one, ***The Progress of Love*** does contain less fully realized stories. So thinly executed is **"Eskimo"** that it reads like an early draft of a typically rich, layered, provocative Munro story: its male protagonist is offstage, its female protagonist senses, or imagines, a psychic kinship with a young Eskimo girl she tries to befriend on an airplane flight, but their encounter comes to nothing and the story dissolves in a self-consciously symbolic dream. **"Miles City, Montana"** recounts a child's near-drowning but fails to integrate the episode with what precedes and follows it, and ends with a rather forced epiphany: "So we went on, with the two in the back seat trusting us, because of no choice, and we ourselves trusting to be forgiven, in time, for everything that had first to be seen and condemned by those children: whatever was flippant, arbitrary, careless, callous—all our natural, and particular, mistakes." **"Monsieur les Deux Chapeaux"** and **"Circle of Prayer"** are each rather sketchily imagined, though brimming with life; and **"White Dump,"** potentially one of the strongest stories in the collection, suffers from a self-conscious structure in which time is fashionably broken and point of view shifts with disconcerting casualness from character to character. We catch only a glimpse of Isabel and her lover and must take Isabel's word for it, that she feels "rescued, lifted, beheld, and safe"; we are not even certain whether the author means her conviction to be serious, or self-deluded. And the image of the "white dump"—the biscuit factory sugar dump—is rather arbitrarily spliced onto the story, poetically vivid as it is.

Even the weaker stories, however, contain passages of genuinely inspired prose and yield the solid pleasures of a three-dimensional world that has been respectfully, if not always lovingly, recorded. And Ms. Munro's minor characters, though fleetingly glimpsed, are frequently the vehicles for others' gestures of compassion and pity. (As in **"The Moon in the Orange Street Skating Rink,"** where decades are compressed within the space of a few pages, and Edgar, whom we have seen as a bright, attractive boy of 17, emerges as an elderly stroke victim, seated in front of a television screen, indifferent to the visit of his cousin and to his cousin's offer to take him for a walk. His wife says of him, simply: "No. He's happy.")

The Progress of Love is a volume of unflinching, audacious honesty, uncompromisingly downright in its dissection of the ways in which we deceive ourselves in the name of love; the bleakness of its vision is enriched by the author's exquisite eye and ear for detail. Life is heartbreak, but it is also uncharted moments of kindness and reconciliation. (pp. 7, 9)

Joyce Carol Oates, "Characters Dangerously Like Us," in The New York Times Book Review, *September 14, 1986, pp. 7, 9.*

D. A. N. JONES (essay date 1987)

[*In the following excerpt, Jones comments on the female characters' opinions of men in Munro's* The Progress of Love *and claims that the collection is dispiriting. Jones suggests that the stories are more evocative when presented singularly, as in* the New Yorker *and other periodicals, rather than collectively.*]

Let us be sexist. ***The Progress of Love*** is a woman's book, particularly interesting to men who want to know what women think of them and know about them. Alice Munro is a 56-year-old Canadian who has been married twice: she is particularly concerned with the knowingness derived from broken relationships. One of the 11 skilful stories in this book (her sixth collection) is called **"Lichen"**—a fungoid growth or eruption used as an image for the progress of love. A civil servant called David, his grey hair dyed, has come to visit his ex-wife, Stella: he brings with him his new partner, Catherine, but he is already sick of her and obsessed with a third woman, the pleasingly trollopy Dina. David accompanies Stella on a visit to her aged father in the Balm of Gilead home. As they leave, he thinks that this troll-like woman, to whom he was married for 21 years, knows him too well: 'He could never feel any lightness, any secret and victorious expansion with a woman who knew so much. She was bloated with all she knew.' Nevertheless, he embraces Stella in the hospital corridor—and, just then, a pretty nurse passes, pushing a trolley and calling: 'Juice time. Orange. Grape.' David feels a very slight discomfort at being seen by such a young and pretty girl in the embrace of Stella. It is not an important feeling—'It simply brushed him and passed'—but Stella knows about it. She says:

> Never mind, David. I could be your sister. You could be comforting your sister. *Older* sister.

Smiling David replies: 'Madam Stella, the celebrated mind reader.'

Earlier in this compact story, Stella has introduced David to one of her neighbours, a cheery bore called Ron who has retired early and says: 'You wouldn't believe how much we find to do. The day is never long enough.' Stella knows something horrid is going to happen because of the serious voice, 'respectful and attentive', in which David says: 'You have a lot of interests?' He brings out of his pocket something which he keeps cupped in his palm, and he flashes it to the bore with a deprecating smile, saying: 'One of my interests.' It is a photograph and he subsequently shows it to Stella, saying: 'That's my new girl.' Stella says: 'It looks like lichen . . . Like moss on a rock.' He points out Dina's spreading legs, monumental, like fallen columns, and between them is what she called lichen—though it is really more like 'the dark pelt of an animal', de-limbed for the furrier, the 'dark silky pelt of some unlucky rodent'. David is perversely tempted to show this picture to his current partner, Catherine. 'She makes me want to hurt her,' he tells Stella. 'I think the best thing to do would be to give her the big chop. Coup de grâce.' He tries to give the photograph to Stella, to evade the temptation, but she will not accept it. When David and the doomed Catherine have gone, Stella finds the photograph tucked behind the living-room curtains, sun-faded now so that the black pelt really looks like lichen. 'This is David's doing. He left it in the sun.' She had said it looked like lichen, though she knew what it was at once, and now her words have come true.

There are many sharp observations in the dozen pages of this dispiriting story. Stella's house is in an area of remodelled farmhouses or winterised summer cottages by the shores of Lake Huron, plenty of comfortable, retired folk, a weaver and a gay dentist—its sunny bleakness exposed when Stella says: 'It's nice for us pensioned-off wives . . . I'm writing my memoirs. I'll stop for a cash payment.' David remarks casually: 'You know, there's a smell women get. It's when they know you don't want them any more. Stale.' David feels fresh. He tells Stella about the redundant Catherine, nearing forty and dated—'She's a hippie survivor really. She doesn't know those days are gone.' Like a boy, he sneaks off to telephone young Dina, the doomed successor to Catherine and Stella. His freshness pleases Stella's father, as they discuss motor-cars in the Balm of Gilead Home. 'Daddy was so pleased to see you,' says Stella. 'A man just means more, for

Daddy. I suppose if he thought about you and me he'd have to be on my side, but that's all right, he doesn't have to think about it.' The fact is that Stella's tolerant knowingness is a form of complicity with David's wilful selfishness—a complicity not uncommon among women who write skilfully about men.

"Lichen" has been singled out because it is so characteristic of Alice Munro's stories. In **"White Dump"** we read: 'They had found out so much about each other that everything had got cancelled out by something else. That was why the sex between them could seem so shamefaced, merely and drearily lustful, like sex between siblings.' In **"Jesse and Meribeth"** a schoolgirl has a crush on a married man, who offers her a sort of paternal advice: at once patronising and sexy, he urges her to appreciate 'the reality of other people'—and the schoolgirl thinks: 'What do I want with anybody who can know so much about me?' This girl is influenced by certain children's books in which 'girls were bound two by two in fast friendship, in exquisite devotion': with her special friend she plans to change their names, herself taking a boy's name, Jesse, to the displeasure of their schoolmistress. Jesse is not altogether different from Callie, in **"The Moon in the Orange Street Skating Rink,"** a stoical little boarding-house 'slavey', who likes to wear boys' clothes: she attaches herself to two athletic lads, skaters and acrobats, who try out their limited sex-knowledge on her. Callie says: 'It would take a lot more than that stupid business to hurt me.'

Other women are more easily frightened, like Marietta in **"The Progress of Love."** She hated barbers' shops, hated their smell, asked her father not to put any dressing on his hair because the smell reminded her. 'A bunch of men standing out on the street, outside a hotel, seemed to Marietta like a clot of poison. You tried not to hear what they were saying, but you could be sure it was vile.' More confident women have their expectations disappointed—like the liberal-minded old lady who allows hippies to swim in her lake and, as a result, returns from her morning swim naked and disconsolate, after an unfortunate experience. 'Christ, Mother!' says her son, throwing her a tablecloth. Her daughter-in-law 'responds to the story' in strange fashion, embarking on an affair with a handsome airman. These clever, powerful and convincing stories are always satisfying, one at a time, when they appear in *Grand Street* or the *New Yorker:* but to read a collection in a book, one after another, is rather dispiriting. The gentle tolerance is almost nurse-like: some of these characters, one feels, should be denounced.

D. A. N. Jones, "What Women Think about Men," in London Review of Books, *Vol. 9, No. 3, February 5, 1987, p. 23.*

ADDITIONAL BIBLIOGRAPHY

Allentuck, Marcia. "Resolution and Independence in the Work of Alice Munro." *World Literature Written in English* 16, No. 2 (November 1977): 340-43.

Commentary on the problems women face in asserting their independence. Allentuck focuses on the oppressive aspects of womanhood presented in Munro's fiction.

Balakian, Nona. Review of *The Beggar Maid* by Alice Munro. *The New York Times* (13 December 1979): 21.

Brief review focusing on the themes and narrative style in Munro's *The Beggar Maid.*

Carscallen, James. "Three Jokers: The Shape of Alice Munro's Stories." In *Centre and Labyrinth: Essays in Honour of Northrop Frye,* edited by Eleanor Cook et al., pp. 128-46. Toronto: University of Toronto Press, 1983.

Study of the thematic cycles in Munro's work. Carscallen provides extensive consideration of image patterns throughout Munro's fiction.

Daziron, Heliane Catherine. "The Preposterous Oxymoron: A Study of Alice Munro's 'Dance of the Happy Shades.' " *The Literary Half-Yearly* 24, No. 2 (July 1983): 116-24.

Examination of Munro's use of opposing phrases and irony in her short story "Dance of the Happy Shades."

———. "Alice Munro's 'The Flats Road.' " *Canadian Woman Studies* 6, No. 1 (1984): 103-04.

Treatment of Munro's *Lives of Girls and Women* as a collection of short fiction. Daziron approaches this work from a biblical perspective and traces an example of the "Jonah complex" through "The Flats Road."

Dombrowski, Eileen. " 'Down to Death': Alice Munro and Transcience." *University of Windsor Review* 14, No. 1 (Fall-Winter 1978): 21-9.

Analysis of the recurring theme of death in Munro's first three collections. Dombrowski compares various characters' reactions to death and suggests that the underlying tension in Munro's fiction is rooted in the mutable and transient nature of life.

Eldredge, L. M. "A Sense of Ending in *Lives of Girls and Women.*" *Studies in Canadian Literature* 9, No. 1 (1984): 110-15.

Discussion of the unconventional structure of Munro's *Lives of Girls and Women.* Eldredge suggests that the episodic format of Munro's work allows for more realistic depictions of characters.

Fleenor, Juliann E. "Rape Fantasies as Initiation Rite: Female Imagination in *Lives of Girls and Women.*" *Room of One's Own* 4, No. 4 (1979): 35-49.

Detailed argument proposing an underlying "rape myth" as the structure of Munro's *Lives of Girls and Women.* Fleenor suggests that Del Jordan's sexual development and understanding is an outgrowth of gender stereotypes. She further submits that the theme of the story is rooted in classical mythology and compares the work's conclusion with that of James Joyce's *Portrait of the Artist as a Young Man.*

Frye, Joanne S. "Growing Up Female: *Lives of Girls and Women* and *The Bluest Eye.*" In *Living Stories, Telling Lives: Women and the Novel in Contemporary Experience,* pp. 77-108. Ann Arbor: University of Michigan Press, 1989.

Consideration of Munro's *Lives of Girls and Women* and Toni Morrison's *The Bluest Eye* as *Bildungsromans.* Frye discusses the importance of narrative technique in developing character identities.

Hunt, Russell. "What You Get Is What You See." *The Fiddlehead,* No. 102 (Summer 1974): 113-19.

Comparative study of Munro's *Something I've Been Meaning to Tell You* and Annie Dillard's *Pilgrim at Tinker Creek.* Hunt comments on the ability of both authors to capture vividly realistic images of life.

Irvine, Lorna. "Questioning Authority: Alice Munro's Fiction." *The CEA Critic* 50, No. 1 (Fall 1987): 57-66.

Discusses the complex role of gender for the author and the reader of literature. Irvine examines the authoritative presence of Munro's female characters.

Macdonald, Rae McCarthy. "Structure and Detail in *Lives of Girls and Women.*" *Studies in Canadian Literature* 3, No. 2 (Summer 1978): 199-210.

Examination of *Lives of Girls and Women* as a novel in which Macdonald studies the tensions and crises which foster the maturity of the protagonist.

Martin, W. R. "Alice Munro and James Joyce." *Journal of Canadian Fiction,* No. 24 (1979): 120-26.

Comparative analysis of Munro's and James Joyce's short stories. Martin discusses the apparent Joycean influence on the structure, theme, and style of Munro's fiction and parallels passages from Joyce's *Dubliners* and Munro's *Dance of the Happy Shades.*

———. "The Strange and the Familiar in Alice Munro." *Studies in Canadian Literature* 7, No. 2 (1982): 214-26.

Consideration of Munro's use of paradox and irony. Martin suggests the existence of a "universal kinship" in Munro's fiction and comments on her ability to reveal the hidden significance of seemingly trivial events.

Oates, Joyce Carol. "The Canadian Inheritance: Engel, Munro, Moore." *The Ontario Review,* No. 11 (Fall-Winter 1979-80): 87-90.

Discussion of the common concern for self-definition in Canadian literature. Oates approaches Munro's *The Beggar Maid* as a novel and comments on Rose's attempts to establish relationships while maintaining personal freedom.

Perrakis, Phyllis Sternberg. "Portrait of the Artist as a Young Girl: Alice Munro's *Lives of Girls and Women.*" *Atlantis* 7, No. 2 (Spring 1982): 61-7.

Study of the artistic development of the protagonist of *Lives of Girls and Women.* Perrakis examines the relationship between Del Jordan's womanhood and her artistry.

Rasporich, Beverly J. "Child-Women and Primitives in the Fiction of Alice Munro." *Atlantis* 1, No. 2 (Spring 1976): 4-14.

Examination of the "female dilemma" in Munro's fiction. Rasporich focuses on the struggle for female characters to break from past stereotypes and establish their identities.

Slopen, Beverly. "Alice Munro." *Publishers Weekly* 230, No. 8 (22 August 1986): 76-7.

Brief interview focusing on *The Progress of Love* and the relationship between Munro's personal life and her fiction.

Stainsby, Mari. "Alice Munro Talks with Mari Stainsby." *British Columbia Library Quarterly* 35, No. 1 (July 1971): 27-31.

Interview in which Munro discusses the development and preparation of her works, the difficulties and personal conflicts of her profession, and her reputation as a "regional writer."

Stubbs, Andrew. "Fictional Landscape: Mythology and Dialectic in the Fiction of Alice Munro." *World Literature Written in English* 23, No. 1 (Winter 1984): 53-62.

Extensive analysis of Munro's exploration of characteristically Canadian themes in her fiction.

Thacker, Robert. "Connection: Alice Munro and Ontario." *The American Review of Canadian Studies* 14, No. 2 (Summer 1984): 213-26.

Study of the interdependence between setting and character in Munro's fiction. Thacker proposes that Munro uses rural Ontario as a device to identify and define the personalities and lives of her characters.

Wallace, Bronwen. "Men, Women, and Body English in Alice Munro." *Books in Canada* 7, No. 7 (August-September 1978): 13.

Brief excerpt from Wallace's study, which later appeared in *The Human Element.* Wallace discusses sexual identity, power, and male-female relationships in Munro's fiction.

Warwick, Susan J. "Growing Up: The Novels of Alice Munro." *Essays on Canadian Writing,* No. 29 (Summer 1984): 204-25.

Discussion of the various time shifts and narrative techniques in Munro's fiction. Warwick treats *Lives of Girls and Women* and *Who Do You Think You Are?* as "open-form" novels and comments on the sense of loss and the sense of optimism that rise out of Munro's manipulation of time.

Wayne, Joyce. "Huron County Blues." *Books in Canada* 11, No. 8 (October 1982): 9-12.

Interview which focuses on the antagonistic relationship between Munro and the citizens of her hometown, Wingham, Ontario, who feel that she denigrates them in her books. Wayne comments on the role of this tension in Munro's fiction.

York, Lorraine M. "The Rival Bards." *Canadian Literature,* No. 112 (Spring 1987): 211-16.

Analysis of the role of the poetry of Alfred Lord Tennyson and Robert Browning in Munro's *Lives of Girls and Women.* York draws parallels between the conflict of tradition and innovation in Victorian poetry and the mother-daughter conflict of Ida and Del Jordan in Munro's work.

Isaac Bashevis Singer

1904-

(Has also written under the pseudonyms Isaac Warshofsky and Isaac Bashevis) Polish-born American short story writer, novelist, author of books for children, memoirist, dramatist, journalist, and translator.

An internationally renowned literary figure, Singer is widely considered the foremost contemporary Yiddish writer. Although he has lived in the United States since 1935, Singer writes almost exclusively in Yiddish, and his works frequently evoke the history and culture of the Polish-Jewish villages or *shtetls* of his heritage. Yet, Singer's fiction is read primarily in translation, and his themes extend far beyond ethnic or provincial concerns. In 1978, Singer was awarded the Nobel Prize in Literature for his "impassioned narrative art which, with roots in a Polish-Jewish cultural tradition, brings universal human conditions to life." Singer's reputation rests largely upon his short stories—most notably "Gimpel the Fool"—in which he explores the individual's search for faith and guidance in a world that makes belief difficult. Regarded as a consummate storyteller, Singer blends traditional modes of plot, characterization, and language style with a modernist sensibility that emphasizes sexuality and expresses a profound, if often sardonic, interest in the irrational.

Singer was born in the Polish *shtetl* of Leoncin, near Warsaw, to parents of devout rabbinical families who intended for him to become a religious scholar. Singer's interests, however, drew him toward non-religious education, and early in his life he began reading secular literature. This dual exposure to strict religious training and nonecclesiastical ideas is amply demonstrated in Singer's fiction, where faith and skepticism regularly conflict. In 1908, Singer and his family moved to Warsaw, where he spent most of his youth, and in 1921, at his father's insistence, Singer enrolled in a Warsaw rabbinical seminary. Singer remained only a year, and in 1923, he began proofreading for *Literarishe Bletter,* a Yiddish literary magazine, and later worked as a translator, rendering such works as Knut Hamsun's *Pan,* Stefan Zweig's *Romain Rolland,* Thomas Mann's *The Magic Mountain,* and Erich Maria Remarque's *All Quiet on the Western Front* into Yiddish. In 1927, Singer published his first piece of short fiction in *Literarishe Bletter,* and seven years later his first novel, *Satan in Goray,* appeared in serial form in the Yiddish periodical *Globus.* An experimental work that draws extensively upon Singer's experiences in the Jewish *shtetl* of Bilgoray, where he lived for several years with his mother beginning in 1917, *Satan in Goray* is widely considered Singer's best long work and examines many of the themes and subjects of his short stories. Often described as an expansive parable, this work explores conflicts of faith and skepticism by depicting the Eastern European Jews' acceptance of the false messiah Sabbatai Zevi after the Cossacks' raids in 1648 and 1649 had devastated their homelands. In 1935, Singer emigrated from Poland to the United States, following his older brother Israel Joshua, who later achieved prominence as a Yiddish novelist, and leaving behind his wife and son. He settled in New York City, where he launched his career by associating with the *Jewish Daily Forward,* for whom he wrote occasional reviews and journalistic essays. In 1940, Singer married his second wife, moved to Manhattan's Upper West Side, and became a regular staff member on the *Forward.* The death of his brother Israel in 1944 had a profound if ambivalent effect upon Singer. While he has acknowledged his brother as "a spiritual father and master," Singer often felt overshadowed by Israel's achievements, which inhibited his own creativity, and he has admitted, in this context, to feelings of both grief and liberation over his brother's death. Throughout the 1940s, Singer's fiction was serialized in the *Forward,* and his reputation among Yiddish-speaking readers grew steadily. In 1950, *The Family Moskat* appeared in translation, the first of Singer's novels to be published in English, and in 1953 "Gimpel the Fool," Singer's classic tale of innocence and faith, appeared in the *Partisan Review,* as translated by Saul Bellow. Through the efforts of such admirers as Bellow and Irving Howe, one of the first critics to recognize Singer's literary accomplishments, Singer was introduced to the American reading public and literary establishment.

Critics generally regard Singer's short fiction as his best work. Unlike his novels, which often rely on realistic description and detailed narratives written in the expansive mode of nineteenth-century fiction, Singer's short stories blend many narrative styles and feature characters torn between faith in God and earthly temptations. The protagonist of "Gimpel the Fool," for example, is considered one of Singer's most enduring characters. A literary descendent of *dos kleine menshele,* or "the common man" archetype of Yiddish and Western literature, Gimpel represents the long-suffering, wise- or sainted-fool figure whose innocence provides humor but also conveys a simple goodness that combats evil and, in this story, is equated with religious faith. Like Gimpel, many of Singer's characters are symbolic representatives of traditional literary types, and his stories are often considered grotesque parables. The protagonist of "The Spinoza of Market Street" epitomizes the classic rational man of the nineteenth century, eschewing emotion in favor of intellect, until a repulsive spinster awakens him to a life of passion and sexual desire. In some of his tales, however, Singer's meaning is ambiguous. In "The Slaughterer," from his collection *The Séance, and Other Stories,* Singer sympathetically examines a pious man's descent into despair when he is passed over as the village's next rabbi and appointed instead as the town slaughterer. Compelled to cause death, he becomes acutely aware of the sanctity of life and struggles with his conflicting obligations to his religion and his conscience.

Like "Gimpel the Fool," "The Spinoza of Market Street," and "The Slaughterer," Singer's most characteristic tales are set within the somber atmosphere of the decaying East European *shtetls,* yet they explore universal themes. In "The Little Shoemakers," Singer depicts the resettlement of Jews from the *shtetls* of Poland to America during World War II, focusing on a modest shoemaker and his family. Another integral facet of Singer's fiction is the presence of demonic elements. In such works as "Short Friday," "The Destruction of Kreshev," "Blood," and "The Black Wedding," Singer's use of supernatural forces, including imps, *dybbuks,* and the Devil himself, infuses the narratives with vitality and imagination. In these tales, Singer allows Satan access to his characters' most secret desires, and the demon uses them to formulate humanity's demise. Vibrant with mysticism and bizarre hallucinations, these stories often feature themes of sin and redemption that carry broad implications.

Concerned in his early stories with the Jewish past as it extends from ancient times to the present, Singer, in his later volumes, particularly *A Friend of Kafka* and *A Crown of Feathers,* more frequently employs contemporary American settings. Yet, in all his stories, Singer strives to blend tradition, spiritualism, imagination, and reality in order to establish a comprehensive view of life and death. As a result, critics often regard his works as continuous and interconnected, encompassing many modes of experience, and incorporating both belief and skepticism. Critical reaction to Singer's fiction has been largely favorable. He is internationally admired for his powers of evocation, his considerable resources as a stylist, and for his brilliant renderings of the Yiddish language. Within traditional Yiddish literary circles, however, Singer is regarded with suspicion. His fascination with the manners of modernism, specifically his preoccupation with sexuality and his irreverent treatment of *Yiddishkeit,* the traditional Yiddish way of life, has alienated many of his native readers. Although some critics have faulted Singer for occasional sentimentality and for exploring repetitious themes, Irving Howe has noted: "[If] Singer moves along predictable lines, they are clearly his own, and no one can accomplish his kind of story so well as he."

(See also *Contemporary Literary Criticism,* Vols. 1, 3, 6, 9, 11, 15, 23, 38; *Contemporary Authors New Revision Series,* Vol. 1; *Contemporary Authors,* Vols. 1-4, rev. ed.; *Children's Literature Review,* Vol. 1; *Something about the Author,* Vols. 3, 27; and *Dictionary of Literary Biography,* Vols. 6, 28.)

PRINCIPAL WORKS

SHORT FICTION

Gimpel the Fool, and Other Stories 1957
The Spinoza of Market Street, and Other Stories 1961
Short Friday, and Other Stories 1964
Selected Short Stories of Isaac Bashevis Singer 1966
The Séance, and Other Stories 1968
A Friend of Kafka, and Other Stories 1970
An Isaac Bashevis Singer Reader 1971
A Crown of Feathers, and Other Stories 1973
Passions, and Other Stories 1975
Old Love 1979
The Collected Stories of Isaac Bashevis Singer 1982
The Image, and Other Stories 1985
The Death of Methuselah, and Other Stories 1988

OTHER MAJOR WORKS

Shoten an Goray (novel) 1935
[*Satan in Goray,* 1955]
Di familie Mushkat (novel) 1950
[*The Family Moskat,* 1950]
Main tatn's beth-din shtub (autobiography) 1956
[*In My Father's Court,* 1966]
The Magician of Lublin (novel) 1960
The Slave (novel) 1962
Zlateh the Goat, and Other Stories (juvenile) 1966
The Manor (novel) 1967
When Schlemiel Went to Warsaw, and Other Stories (juvenile) 1968
A Day of Pleasure: Stories of a Boy Growing Up in Warsaw (juvenile) 1969
The Estate (novel) 1969
Enemies: A Love Story (novel) 1972
Shosha (novel) 1978
A Young Man in Search of Love (autobiography) 1978
Lost in America (autobiography) 1979

ALFRED KAZIN (essay date 1958)

[*A highly respected American literary critic, Kazin is best known for his essay collections* The Inmost Leaf *(1955),* Contemporaries *(1962), and particularly for* On Native Grounds (1942), *a study of American prose writing since the era of William Dean Howells. In the following excerpt from a review of* Gimpel the Fool, and Other Stories, *Kazin discusses Singer's combination of traditional Jewish and modern literary conventions, focusing particularly on his use of the archetypal fool figure of Jewish literature.*]

When I first read **"Gimpel the Fool"** . . . I felt not only that I was reading an extraordinarily beautiful and witty story, but that I was moving through as many historical levels as an archaeologist at work. This is an experience one often gets from the best Jewish writers. The most "advanced" and sophisticated Jewish writers of our time—Babel, Kafka, Bellow—have assimilated, even conquered, the whole tradition of modern literature while reminding us of the unmistakable historic core of the Jewish experience. Equally, a contemporary Yiddish writer like Isaac Bashevis Singer uses all the old Jewish capital of folklore, popular speech and legendry, yet from within this tradition itself is able to duplicate a good deal of the conscious absurdity, the sauciness, the abandon of modern art—without for a moment losing his obvious personal commitment to the immemorial Jewish vision of the world.

Perhaps it is this ability to incarnate all the different periods that Jews have lived through that makes such writers indefinably fascinating to me. They wear whole epochs on their back; they alone record widely separated centuries in dialogue with each other. Yet all these different periods of history, these many *histories,* represent, if not a single point of view, a common historic character. It is the irony with which ancient dogmas are recorded, the imaginative sympathy with which they are translated and transmuted into contemporary terms, that makes the balance that is art.

Gimpel himself is an example of a legendary Jewish type—the saint as *schlemiel.* The mocked, persecuted and wretched people, who nevertheless are the chosen—chosen to bear a certain knowledge through a hostile world—are portrayed again in the town fool, a baker who is married off to a frightful slut without knowing what everyone else in town knows, that she will bear a child in four months. Gimpel is *the* fool of the Jews: a fool because he is endlessly naïve, a fool because, even when he does learn that he has been had, he ignores his own dignity for the sake of others. His wife's unfaithfulness, her shrewishness—these are not the bourgeois concealment, the "cheating" on one's spouse that it would be in another culture, but a massive, hysterical persecution. The child she already has she passes off as her "brother"; Gimpel believes her. When she gives birth to a child four months after the wedding, Gimpel pays for the circumcision honors and rituals, and names the boy after his own father. When he cries out that his wife has deceived him, she deliberately confuses him, as usual, and persuades him that the child is "premature":

> I said, "Isn't he a little too premature?" She said that she had a grandmother who carried just as short a time and she resembled this grandmother of hers as one drop of water does another. She swore to it with such oaths that you would have believed a peasant at the fair if he had used them. To tell the plain truth, I didn't believe her; but when I talked it over next day with the schoolmaster he told me that the very same thing had happened to Adam and Eve. Two they went up to bed, and four they descended.

The humor of this is always very real, for these people are rough old-fashioned village types who know their own. The town boys are always playing tricks on Gimpel, setting him on false trails; he is mocked at his own wedding—some young men carry in a crib as a present. His wife, Elka, is a living nightmare, a shrew of monumental proportions, a Shakespearean harridan. Yet in Gimpel's obstinate attachment to her we recognize, as in his customary meekness, the perfection of a type: what to the great world is folly, in itself may be wisdom; what the world thinks insane may, under the aspect of eternity, be the only sanity. . . . (pp. 283-84)

One night, Gimpel comes home unexpectedly and finds another man in bed with Elka; this time he has had enough, and he separates from her. But the town mischiefs take her side and persecute him, while Gimpel worries whether he *did* see the man:

> Hallucinations do happen. You see a figure or a manikin or something, but when you come up closer it's nothing, there's not a thing there. And if that's so, I'm doing her an injustice. And when I got so far in my thoughts I started to weep. I sobbed so that I wet the floor where I lay. In the morning I went to the rabbi and told him that I had made a mistake.

Elka has another child and "all Frampol refreshed its spirits because of my trouble and grief. However, I resolved that I would always believe what I was told. What's the good of *not* believing? Today it's your wife you don't believe in; tomorrow it's God Himself you won't take stock in."

Even his superstitions—Singer uses local demons and spirits as dramatic motifs—become symbols of his innocent respect for the world. One night, after covering the dough to let it rise, he takes his share of bread and a little sack of flour and starts homeward. . . . (p. 285)

He returns home to find his wife in bed with the apprentice. Characteristically, he suffers rather than storms; characteristically, "the moon went out all at once. It was utterly black, and I trembled"; characteristically, he obeys his wife when she sends him out of the house to see if the goat is well; characteristically, he identifies himself tenderly with the goat, and when he returns home, the apprentice having fled, the wife denies everything, tells him he has been seeing visions, shrieks prodigious curses. Her "brother" beats him with a stick. And Gimpel: "I felt that something about me was deeply wrong, and I said, 'Don't make a scandal. All that's needed now is that people should accuse me of raising spooks and *dybbuks.*' "

So he makes his peace with her, and they live together for twenty years. "All kinds of things happened, but I neither saw nor heard." When his wife dies, she tells him that none of their children is his, and the look on her dead face seems to say to him—"I deceived Gimpel. That was the meaning of my brief life."

Now Gimpel is tempted by the Spirit of Evil himself, who tells him that it is all nothing. " 'What,' I said, '*is* there, then?' 'A thick mire.' " And, succumbing to the devil, Gimpel urinates into the risen dough. His dead wife comes to him in a dream—and, when he weeps in shame at his act, "It's all your fault," she cries—"You fool! You fool! Because I was false, is everything false, too?"

When the mourning period for his wife ends, he gives up everything to tramp through the world, often telling stories to children—"about devils, magicians, windmills, and the like." He dreams constantly of his wife, asks when he will be with her; in his dreams, she kisses him and promises him that they will be together soon. "When I awaken I feel her lips and taste the salt of her tears."

The last paragraph of the story, Gimpel's serene meditation before death, is of great beauty. It sums up everything that

Jews have ever felt about the divinity that hedges human destiny, and it is indeed one of the most touching avowals of faith that I have ever seen. Yet it is all done with lightness, with wit, with a charming reserve—so that it might almost be read as a tribute to human faithfulness itself. (pp. 285-86)

Singer's story naturally suggests a comparison with I. J. Peretz's famous "Bontsha the Silent," who was offered everything in heaven, and meekly asked for a hot roll with fresh butter every morning for breakfast. One thinks also of Sholem Aleichem's Tevye the dairyman, who recited his prayers even as he ran after his runaway horse. But in his technique of ambiguity Singer speaks for our generation far more usefully than the old ritualistic praise of Jewish goodness. While Bontsha and Tevye are entirely folk images, cherished symbols of a tradition, Gimpel—though he and his wife are no less symbols—significantly has to win back his faith, and he wins it in visions, in dreams, that give a background of playfulness and irony to this marvelously subtle story.

This concern with the dream, this everlasting ambiguity in our relations with the divine—this is a condition that our generation has learned to respect, after rejecting the dogmas first of orthodoxy and then of scientific materialism. This delicacy of conception unites Singer to the rest of imaginative humanity today: Man believes even though he knows his belief to be absurd, but what he believes represents a level of imaginative insight which shades off at one end into art, at the other into Gimpel's occasional self-doubt, the thought that he may be "mad."

It is the integrity of the human imagination that Singer conveys so beautifully. He reveals the advantage that an artist can find in his own orthodox training—unlike so many Jews who in the past became mere copyists and mumblers of the holy word. Singer's work *does* stem from the Jewish village, the Jewish seminary, the compact (not closed) Jewish society of Eastern Europe. He does not use the symbols which so many modern writers pass on to each other. For Singer it is not only his materials that are "Jewish"; the world is so. Yet within this world he has found emancipation and universality—through his faith in imagination. (pp. 286-87)

Alfred Kazin, "The Saint as Schlemiel," in his Contemporaries, *Little, Brown and Company, 1962, pp. 283-88.*

IRVING HOWE (essay date 1966)

[*Howe is one of America's most highly respected literary critics and social historians. He is associated with the "New York Intellectuals" and is widely praised for what F. R. Dulles has termed his "knowledgeable understanding, critical acumen and forthright candor." In the following excerpt from his introduction to* Selected Short Stories of Isaac Bashevis Singer, *Howe conducts a broad survey of Singer's work in the context of both modernist and Yiddish literature.*]

No other living writer has yielded himself so completely and recklessly as has Isaac Bashevis Singer to the claims of the human imagination. Singer writes in Yiddish, a language that no amount of energy or affection seems likely to save from extinction. He writes about a world that is gone, destroyed with a brutality beyond historical comparison. He writes within a culture, the remnant of Yiddish in the Western world, that is more than a little dubious about his purpose and stress. He seems to take entirely for granted his role as a traditional storyteller speaking to an audience attuned to his every hint and nuance, an audience that values storytelling both in its own right and as a binding communal action—but also, as it happens, an audience that keeps fading week by week, shrinking day by day. And he does all this without a sigh or apology, without so much as a Jewish groan. It strikes one as a kind of inspired madness: here is a man living in New York City, a sophisticated and clever writer, who composes stories about Frampol, Bilgoray, Kreshev *as if they were still there.* His work is shot through with the bravado of a performer who enjoys making his listeners gasp, weep, laugh and yearn for more. Above and beyond everything else he is a great performer, in ways that remind one of Twain, Dickens, Sholom Aleichem. (p. vi)

Singer's stories claim attention through their vivacity and strangeness of surface. He is devoted to the grotesque, the demonic, the erotic, the quasi-mystical. He populates his alien subworld with imps, devils, whores, fanatics, charlatans, spirits in seizure, disciples of false messiahs. A young girl is captured by the spirit of a dead woman and goes to live with the mourning husband as if she were actually his wife; a town is courted and then shattered by a lavish stranger who turns out to be the devil; an ancient Jew suffering unspeakable deprivations during the First World War, crawls back to his village of Bilgoray and fathers a son whom, with marvelous aplomb, he names Isaac. Sometimes the action in Singer's stories follows the moral curve of traditional folk tales, with a charming, lightly-phrased "lesson" at the end; sometimes, the spiral of a quizzical modern awareness; at best, the complicated motions of the old and the contemporary yoked together, a kind of narrative double-stop.

Orgiastic lapses from the moral order, pacts with the devil, ascetic self-punishments, distraught sexuality occupy the foreground of Singer's stories. Yet behind this expressionist clamor there is glimpsed the world of the *shtetl,* or East European Jewish village, as it stumbled and slept through the last few centuries. Though Singer seldom portrays it full-face, one must always keep this world in mind while reading his stories: it forms the base from which he wanders, the norm from which he deviates but which controls his deviation. (p. vii)

Isaac Bashevis Singer is the only living Yiddish writer whose translated work has caught the imagination of the American literary public. Though the settings of his stories are frequently strange, the contemporary reader—for whom the determination not to be shocked has become a point of honor—is likely to feel closer to Singer than to most other Yiddish writers. Offhand this may be surprising, for Singer's subjects are decidedly remote and exotic: in *Satan in Goray* the orgiastic consequences of the false messianism of seventeenth-century East European Jewish life; in *The Magician of Lublin* a portrait of a Jewish magician-Don Juan in late-nineteenth-century Poland who exhausts himself in sensuality and ends as a penitent ascetic; in his stories a range of demonic, apocalyptic and perversely sacred moments of *shtetl* life. Yet one feels that, unlike many of the Yiddish writers who treat more familiar and up-to-date subjects, Singer commands a distinctly "modern" sensibility.

Now this is partly true—in the sense that Singer has cut himself off from some of the traditional styles and assumptions of Yiddish writing. But it is also not true—in the sense that any effort to assimilate Singer to literary "modernism" without fully registering his involvement with Jewish faith and history, is almost certain to distort his meanings.

Those meanings, one might as well admit, are often enigmatic and hard to come by. It must be a common experience among Singer's readers to find a quick pleasure in the caustic surfaces of his prose, the nervous tokens of his virtuosity, but then to acknowledge themselves baffled as to his point and purpose. That his fiction does have an insistent point and stringent purpose no one can doubt: Singer is too ruthlessly single-minded a writer to content himself with mere slices of representation or displays of the bizarre. His grotesquerie must be taken seriously, perhaps as a recoil from his perception of how ugly—how irremediably and gratuitously ugly—human life can be. He is a writer completely absorbed by the demands of his vision, a vision gnomic and compulsive but with moments of high exaltation; so that while reading his stories one feels as if one were overhearing bits and snatches of monologue, the impact of which is both notable and disturbing, but the meaning withheld.

Now these are precisely the qualities that the sophisticated reader, trained to docility before the exactions of "modernism," has come to applaud. Singer's stories work, or prey, upon the nerves. They leave one unsettled and anxious, the way a rationalist might feel if, waking at night in the woods, he suddenly found himself surrounded by a swarm of bats. Unlike most Yiddish fiction, Singer's stories neither round out the cycle of their intentions nor posit a coherent and ordered universe. They can be seen as paradigms of the arbitrariness, the grating injustice, at the heart of life. They offer instances of pointless suffering, dead-end exhaustion, inexplicable grace. And sometimes, as in Singer's masterpiece, **"Gimpel the Fool,"** they turn about, refusing to rest with the familiar discomforts of the problematic, and drive toward a prospect of salvation on the other side of despair, beyond soiling by error or will. This prospect does not depend on any belief in the comeliness or lawfulness of the universe; whether God is there or not, He is surely no protector. ("He had worked out his own religion," writes Singer about one of his characters. "There was a Creator, but He revealed himself to no one, gave no indications of what was permitted or forbidden.") Things happen, the probable bad and improbable good, both of them subject to the whim of the fortuitous—and the sacred fools like Gimpel, perhaps they alone, learn to roll with the punch, finding the value of their life in a total passivity and credulousness, a complete openness to suffering.

Singer's stories trace the characteristic motions of human destiny: a heavy climb upward **("The Old Man"),** a rapid tumble downward **("The Fast").** Life forms a journeying to heaven and hell, mostly hell. What determines the direction a man will take? Sometimes the delicate maneuvers between his will and desire, sometimes the heat of his vanity, sometimes the blessing of innocence. But more often than not, it is all a mystery which Singer chooses to present rather than explain. As his figures move upward and downward, aflame with the passion of their ineluctable destiny, they stop for a moment in the *shtetl* world. Singer is not content with the limitations of materiality, yet not at all indifferent to the charms and powers of the phenomenal universe. In his calculus of destiny, however, the world is a resting-place and what happens within it, even within the social enclave of the Jews, is not of lasting significance. Thick, substantial and attractive as it comes to seem in Singer's representation, the world is finally but lure and appearance, a locale between heaven and hell, the shadow of larger possibilities.

In most Yiddish fiction the stress is quite different. There the central "character" is the collective destiny of the Jews in *galut,* or exile; the central theme, the survival of a nation deprived of nationhood; the central ethic, the humane education of men stripped of worldly power yet sustained by the memory of chosenness and the promise of redemption. In Singer the norm of collective life is still present, but mostly in the background, as a tacit assumption; his central actions break away from the limits of the *shtetl* ethic, what has come to be known as *Yiddishkeit,* and then move either backward to the abandon of false messianism or forward to the doubt of modern sensibility. (There is an interesting exception, the story called **"Short Friday,"** which in its stress upon family affection, ritual proprieties and collective faith, approaches rather closely the tones of traditional Yiddish fiction.)

The historical settings of East European Jewish life are richly presented in Singer's stories, often not as orderly sequences in time but as simultaneous perceptions jumbled together in the consciousness of figures for whom Abraham's sacrifice, Chmielnicki's pogroms, the rise and fall of Hasidism and the stirrings of the modern world are all felt with equal force. Yet Singer's ultimate concern is not with the collective experience of a chosen martyred people but with the enigmas of personal fate. Given the slant of his vision, this leads him to place a heavy reliance upon the grotesque as a mode of narration, even as an avenue toward knowledge. But the grotesque carries with it a number of literary and moral dangers, not the least being the temptation for Singer to make it into an end in itself, which is to say, something facile and sensationalistic. In his second-rank stories he falls back a little too comfortably upon the devices of which he is absolute master, like a magician supremely confident his tricks will continue to work. But mainly the grotesque succeeds in Singer's stories because it comes to symbolize meaningful digressions from a cultural norm. An uninstructed reader may absorb Singer's grotesquerie somewhat too easily into the assumptions of modern literature; the reader who grasps the ambivalence of Singer's relation to Yiddish literature will see the grotesquerie as a cultural sign by means of which Singer defines himself against his own past.

It is hardly a secret that in the Yiddish literary world Singer is regarded with a certain suspicion. His powers of evocation, his resources as a stylist are acknowledged, yet many Yiddish literary people, including the serious ones, seem uneasy about him. One reason is that "modernism"—which, as these people regard Singer, signifies a heavy stress upon sexuality, a concern for the irrational, expressionist distortions of character and a seeming indifference to the humane ethic of Yiddishism—has never won so strong a hold in Jewish culture as it has in the cultures of most Western countries. For Yiddish writers, "modernism" has been at best an adornment of manner upon a subject inescapably traditional.

The truly "modern" writer, however, is not quite trustworthy in relation to his culture. He is a shifty character by choice and need, unable to settle into that solid representativeness which would allow him to act as a cultural "spokesman." And to the extent that Singer does share in the modernist outlook he must be regarded with distrust by Yiddish readers brought up on such literary "spokesmen" as Peretz, Abraham Reisen and H. Leivick. There is no lack of admiration among Yiddish readers for Singer's work: anyone with half an ear for the cadence and idiom of that marvelous language must respond to his prose. Still, it is a qualified, a troubled admiration. Singer's moral outlook, which seems to move with equal readiness toward the sensational and the ascetic, is hardly calculated to put Yiddish readers at their ease. So they continue to read him, with pleasure and anxiety.

And as it seems to me, they are not altogether wrong. Their admiring resistance to Singer's work may constitute a more attentive and serious response to his iconoclasm than the gleeful applause of those who read him in English translation and take him to be another writer of "black comedy," or, heaven help us, a mid-twentieth century "swinger." (pp. xii-xvi)

Anyone with even a smattering of Yiddish should try to read Singer's stories in the original. . . . Singer has left behind him the oratorical sententiousness to which Yiddish literature is prone, has abandoned its leisurely meandering pace, what might be called the *shtetl* rhythm, and has developed a style that is both swift and dense, nervous and thick. His sentences are short and abrupt; his rhythms coiled, intense, short-breathed. The impression his prose creates is not of a smooth and equable flow of language but rather a series of staccato advances and withdrawals, with sharp breaks between sentences. Singer seldom qualifies, wanders or circles back; his method is to keep darting forward, impression upon impression, through a series of jabbing declarative sentences. His prose is free of "literary" effects, a frequent weakness among Yiddish writers who wish to display their elegance and cultivation. And at the base of his prose is the oral idiom of Yiddish, seeded with ironic proverbs and apothegms ("Shoulders are from God, and burdens too"); but a speech that has been clipped, wrenched, syncopated.

What is most remarkable about Singer's prose is his ability to combine rich detail with fiercely compressed rhythms. (p. xvii)

By its very nature, pace cannot be illustrated, but the richness of Singer's detail can. As in this characteristic passage from **"The Old Man"**:

> His son had died long before, and Reb Moshe Ber said the memorial prayer, *kaddish,* for him. Now alone in the apartment, he had to feed his stove with paper and wood shavings from garbage cans. In the ashes he baked rotten potatoes, which he carried in his scarf, and in an iron pot, he brewed chicory. He kept house, made his own candles by kneading bits of wax and suet around wicks, laundered his shirt beneath the kitchen faucet, and hung it to dry on a piece of string. He set the mousetraps each night and drowned the mice each morning. When he went out he never forgot to fasten the heavy padlock on the door. No one had to pay rent in Warsaw at that time. . . .
>
> The winter was difficult. There was no coal, and since several tiles were missing from the stove, the apartment was filled with thick black smoke each time the old man made a fire. A crust of blue ice and snow covered the window panes by November, making the rooms constantly dark or dusky. Overnight, the water on his night table froze in the pot. No matter how many clothes he piled over him in bed, he never felt warm; his feet remained stiff, and as soon as he began to doze, the entire pile of clothes would fall off, and he would have to climb out naked to make his bed once more. There was no kerosene, even matches were at a premium. Although he recited chapter upon chapter of the Psalms, he could not fall asleep. The wind, freely roaming about the rooms, banged the doors; even the mice left. . . .

Or, grotesquely, from **"Blood"**:

> Frequently she sang for hours in Yiddish and in Polish. Her voice was harsh and cracked and she invented the songs as she went along, repeating meaningless phrases, uttering sounds that resembled the cackling of fowl, the grunting of pigs, the death-rattles of oxen. . . . At night in her dreams, phantoms tormented her: bulls gored her with their horns; pigs shoved their snouts into her face and bit her; roosters cut her flesh to ribbons with their spurs.
>
> (pp. xviii-xix)

Those of Singer's stories which speed downward into hell are often told by devils and imps, sometimes by Satan himself, marveling at the vanity and paltriness of the human creature. Singer's arch-devil is a figure not so much of evil as of skepticism, a thoroughly modern voice to whose corrosive questions Singer imparts notable force. . . . (p. xx)

Using demons and imps as narrators proves to be a wonderful device for structural economy: they replace the need to enter the "inner life" of the characters, the whole plaguing business of the psychology of motives, for they serve as symbolic equivalents and co-ordinates to human conduct, what Singer calls a "spiritual stenography." In those stories, however, where Singer celebrates the power of human endurance, as in **"The Little Shoemakers"** and **"The Old Man,"** he uses third person narrative in the closest he comes to a "high style," so that the rhetorical elevation will help to create an effect of "epical" sweep.

Within his limits Singer is a genius. He has total command of his imagined world; he is original in his use both of traditional Jewish materials and in his modernist attitude toward them; he provides a serious if enigmatic moral perspective; and he is a master of Yiddish prose. Yet there are times when Singer seems to be mired in his own originality, stories in which he displays a weakness for self-imitation that is disconcerting. Second-rate writers imitate others, first-rate writers themselves, and it is not always clear which is the more dangerous.

Having gone this far, we must now turn again. If Singer's work can be grasped only on the assumption that he is crucially a "modernist" writer, one must add that in other ways he remains profoundly subject to the Jewish tradition. And if the Yiddish reader is inclined to slight the "modernist" side of his work, the American reader is likely to underestimate the traditional side.

One of the elements in the Jewish past that has most fascinated Singer is the recurrent tendency to break loose from the burden of the Mosaic law and, through the urging of will and ecstasy, declare an end to the *galut.* Historically, this has taken the form of a series of messianic movements, one led in the seventeenth century by Sabbatai Zevi and another in the eighteenth by Jacob Frank. The movement of Sabbatai Zevi appeared after the East European Jewish community had been shattered by the rebellion-pogrom of the Cossack chieftain, Chmielnicki. Many of the survivors, caught up in a strange ecstasy that derived all too clearly from their total desperation, began to summon apocalytic fantasies and to indulge themselves in long-repressed religious emotions which, perversely, were stimulated by the pressures of cabalistic asceticism. As if in response to their yearnings, Sabbatai, a pretender rising in the Middle East, offered to release them of everything that rabbinical Judaism had confined or suppressed. He spoke for the tempting doctrine that faith is sufficient for salvation; for the wish to evade the limits of mundane life by forcing a religious transcendence; for the union of erotic with mystical appetites; for the lure of a demonism which the very hopelessness of the Jewish situation rendered plausible. In 1665-66 Sabbatianism came to orgiastic climax, whole communities, out of a conviction that the Messiah was in sight, discarding the moral inhibitions of exile. Their hopes were soon brutally disappointed, for Sabbatai, persecuted by the Turkish Sultan, converted to Mohammedanism. His followers were thrown into confusion and despair, and a resurgent rabbinism again took control over Jewish life. Nevertheless, Sabbatianism continued to lead an underground existence among the East European Jews—even, I have been told by *shtetl* survivors, into the late nineteenth and early twentieth century. It became a secret heretical cult celebrating Sabbatai as the apostate savior who had been required to descend to the depths of the world to achieve the heights of salvation.

To this buried strand of Jewish experience Singer has been drawn in fascination and repulsion, portraying its manifestations with great vividness and its consequences with stern judgment. It is a kind of experience that rarely figures in traditional Yiddish writing, yet is a significant aspect of the Jewish past. Bringing this material to contemporary readers, Singer writes *in* Yiddish but often quite apart from the Yiddish tradition; indeed, he is one of the few Yiddish writers whose relation to the Jewish past is not determined or screened by that body of values we call Yiddishism.

Singer is a writer of both the pre-Enlightenment and the post-Enlightenment: he would be equally at home with a congregation of Medieval Jews and a gathering of twentieth-century intellectuals, perhaps more so than at a meeting of the Yiddish P.E.N. club. He has a strong sense of the mystical and antique, but also a cool awareness of psychoanalytic disenchantment. He has evaded both the religious pieties and the humane rationalism of nineteenth-century East European Judaism. He has skipped over the ideas of the historical epoch which gave rise to Yiddishism, for the truth is, I suppose, that Yiddish literature, in both its writers of acceptance and writers of skepticism, is thoroughly caught up with the Enlightenment. Singer is not. He shares very little in the collective sensibility or the *folkstimlichkeit* of the Yiddish masters; he does not unambiguously celebrate *dos kleine menshele* (the common man) as a paragon of goodness; he is impatient with the sensual deprivations implicit in the values of *edelkeit* (refinement, nobility); and above all he moves away from a central assumption of both Yiddish literature in particular and the nineteenth century in general, the assumption of an immanent fate or end in human existence (what in Yiddish is called *tachlis*).

But again qualifications are needed. It is one thing to decide to break from a tradition in which one has been raised, quite another to make the break completely. For Singer has his ties—slender, subterranean but strong—with the very Yiddish writers from whom he has turned away.

At the center of Yiddish fiction stands the archetypal figures of *dos kleine menshele.* It is he, long-suffering, persistent, lovingly ironic, whom the Yiddish writers celebrate. This poor but proud householder trying to maintain his status in the *shtetl* world even as he keeps sinking deeper and deeper into poverty, appeals to the Yiddish imagination far more than mighty figures like Aeneas or Ahab. And from this representative man of the *shtetl* there emerges a number of significant variations. One extreme variation is the ecstatic wanderer, hopeless in this world because profoundly committed to the other. An equally extreme variation is the wise or sainted fool who has given up the struggle for status and thereby acquired the wry perspective of an outsider. Standing somewhere between *dos kleine menshele* and these offshoots is Peretz's Bontsha Schweig, whose intolerable humbleness makes even the angels in heaven feel guilty and embarrassed. Singer's Gimpel is a literary grandson (perhaps only on one side) of Peretz's Bontsha; and as Gimpel, with the piling up of his foolishness, acquires a halo of comic sadness and comes to seem an epitome of pure spirit, one must keep balancing in one's mind the ways in which he is akin to, yet different from Bontsha.

The Yiddish critic Shlomo Bickel has perceptively remarked that Singer's dominating principle is an "anti-Prometheanism," a disbelief in the efficacy of striving defiance and pride, a doubt as to the sufficiency of knowledge or even wisdom. This seems true, but only if one remembers that in a good many of Singer's fictions the central action does constitute a kind of Promethean ordeal or striving. Singer makes it abundantly clear that his characters have no choice: they must live out their desires, their orgiastic yearnings, their apocalyptic expectations. "Anti-Prometheanism" thus comes to rest upon a belief in the unavoidable recurrence of the Promethean urge.

What finally concerns Singer most is the possibilities for life that remain after the exhaustion of human effort, after failure and despair have come and gone. Singer watches his stricken figures from a certain distance, with enigmatic intent and no great outpouring of sympathy, almost as if to say that before such collapse neither judgment nor sympathy matters very much. Yet in all of his fictions the Promethean effort recurs, obsessional, churning with new energy and delusion. In the knowledge that it will, that it must recur, there may also lie hidden a kind of pity, for that too we would expect, and learn to find, in the writer who created Gimpel. (pp. xx-xxiv)

Irving Howe, in an introduction to Selected Short Stories of Isaac Bashevis Singer, *edited by Irving Howe, The Modern Library, 1966, pp. v-xxiv.*

IRVING H. BUCHEN (essay date 1968)

[*In the following excerpt from a chapter of his book-length study of Singer's life and work, Buchen examines Singer's short fiction in terms of its central themes, commenting on its stylistic and thematic unity.*]

Singer is a master of the short story form because he regards caricature not as an aberration but as a norm. In his hands, the short story is not so much a slice as a twist of life. Not accidentally, his shorter novels—*Satan in Goray, The Magician of Lublin, The Slave*—are, in my judgment, his best. Indeed, *Satan in Goray* is essentially a long short story and, like Singer's best tales, is a gnarled sampling that displays the conventional gothic preference for both terror and brevity. Obviously, this does not mean that all Singer's short works are flawless. Jonathan Baumbach, for example, in his review of ***Short Friday*** (1964) [in *Saturday Review*], found only three stories memorable and one, **"Jachid and Jechidah,"** an "extraordinary clinker." (Not really; it is an overworked metaphor for an essay not a story, just as **"The Warehouse"** (1966) is more a sermon than a tale.) Then, Michael Fixler, complaining of Singer's lamentable tendency to force a "quizzical" effect [in *Kenyon Review;* see Additional Bibliography], rightly questions why

> demonic narrators are used gratuitously to bracket stories compelling in themselves. The demons simply offer a coy point of view where Singer could have done as well or better with some old peasant or beggar. **"The Unseen"** and **"The Destruction of Kreshev"** are good examples of first-rate works with trivial narrators.

But Singer's most serious flaw is his marred endings. . . . The only explanation for the pervasive presence of this structural failure is Singer's resistance to the harsh dictates of his own vision. The same desire to soften tragedy results in the sentimental gesture of concluding works with miraculous happenings. But whereas this flaw characterizes all his novels, many of his short stories are rounded out to a perfect fullness, consistent both with their narrative impulses and those of Singer's vision. On this matter, Singer himself said:

> Actually, I prefer the short story because only in a short story can a writer reach perfection—more than in a novel. When you write a novel, especially a larger novel, you are never the ruler of your writing, because you cannot really make a plan for a novel of say, 500 pages, and keep to the rules, or keep to the plan. While in a short story, there is always the possibility of really being perfect.

Moreover, the short stories are different not just in degree but also in kind from the novels. Singer's longer fiction is dominated by a traditional and masculine point of view (often, the two are synonymous). But a great many of the short stories are dominated by an untraditional and feminine point of view; Singer's first story to be published was **"Women."** Indeed, as a correlation, although there are hardly any evil women in Singer's novels, they abound in the tales. Thus, Singer's tales of the *shtetl,* like Chaucer's *Canterbury Tales,* fall into groups and, initially, the most sensational is that of the evil Amazons.

Part of the traditional cast of Singer's vision appears in his acceptance of the subservience of women. He frequently reminds readers that woman was created second, out of Adam's side, and dependent. In the life of the *shtetl* it was not unusual for a wife to work so that she could boast that her husband is free to study the Torah. In the households of Rabbis Katzenellenbogen and Benish, the wives inhabit the background to their husbands' foreground and serve as the peripheral and occasional objects of their interests. But when she breaks free of that masculine tyranny, woman, Singer reminds us, often recovers her original role as temptress. Indeed, as an evil force she is such a scourge that the Devil appears benevolent by comparison. Thus, in **"The Gentleman from Cracow"** (1957), Hodle, the daughter of a ragpicker and drunken father, is the town witch, wanton, and thief; and her curses are so biting and imaginative that the townspeople proverbially dread to fall into her mouth. Significantly, when evil is unmasked in Frampol, Hodle marries Satan and emerges as her ancient prototype, Lilith. An older, more gnarled version of Hodle is Cunegunde, who appears in a number of stories as well as one in her own right, and who is visited by another shrew, appropriately named Zlateh the Bitch, to cast spells on her husband and enemies in **"The Wife-Killer"** (1955). But the supreme feminine devil, who also stakes out Singer's total spectrum of distorted women, is Risha of **"Blood"** (1964).

"Blood" powerfully weds the familiar theme of the progression of perversion with the notion of bloodlust. Singer begins the story by documenting the fusion:

> The cabalists know that the passion for blood and the passion for flesh have the same origin, and this is the reason "Thou shalt not kill" is followed by "Thou shalt not commit adultery."

Twice widowed and now married to an old pious Jew, Risha, like the Wife of Bath, is still frisky and eager. One day while observing Reuben, the ritual slaughterer, efficiently going about his bloody business, lust rises in her. Singer does not permit the reader to forget the cabalistic connection, for he describes Reuben's seduction of Risha in terms of the former's craft; Risha says, " 'You certainly murdered me that time'." Before long, the identification becomes total, and Risha and Reuben copulate in the midst of the slaughtered animals. . . . Having reduced her human nature to that of an animal, Risha then demands that Reuben allow her to assume the man's role of slaughtering the animals. Finally, she caps her adulterous betrayal of her husband by being unfaithful to the Jewish community: she sells non-kosher meat as pure.

Whatever personal reasons motivate Singer's vegetarianism, the slaughtering of animals and fish serves as his theological metaphor of a fallen world. Prior to the fall, Adam and Eve were vegetarians, and Isaiah's prophecy of the lion lying down with the lamb was accompanied by his vision of the lion once again eating grass. But though fallen, man's further descent to the level of the beasts was arrested by means of moral controls, not the least of which are the laws of *Shehitah* or ritual slaughtering. Specifically, in Judaism detailed ritualistic rules are prescribed, perhaps as an expression of guilt for the slaughtering act itself, which are governed by the principles of mercy and purity. The animals must be killed rapidly and, within a restricted group, those selected must be without blemish.

To be sure, even these redemptive strictures fail to satisfy the pitying soul of Yoineh Meir who, in **"The Slaughterer"** (1967), envisions the entire world as a slaughterhouse. Indeed, in his final madness and blasphemy—to Singer the two are one—Yoineh Meir accuses God of being the supreme slaughterer of all. In **"Cockadoodledoo"** (1964), the narrator, a rooster, claims, as does the hero of **"The Parrot"** (1966), that all animals have souls and "If your human ears could hear our weeping, you would throw away all your slaughtering knives." In other words, Singer, whose preoccupation with the slaughtering of animals begins with *Satan in Goray* and continues in even his most recent stories, regards the killing of animals as the expression of fallen man's potential murderousness. To be sure, there is a world of difference between Yoineh Meir and Risha; for whereas Yoineh's tortured *weltschmerz* is informed by heavenly or paradisical standards, Risha's sexual slaughter is perverted to hellish and bestial ends. Indeed, Singer caps Risha's descent to the level of the beasts she kills by having her sell non-kosher meat to indicate that historically and cosmically there is no such thing as a terminal or minor sin. Every personal indiscretion rapidly gains momentum and swells to a communal and biblical betrayal.

But to Singer the most serious betrayal of all and the one that prepares the way for all the others is the blurring of masculine and feminine clarity. From Singer's point of view, the temptation of Eve is an invitation to violate both the boundaries of obedience and of masculine dominance. Significantly, Risha grows stronger as Reuben grows weaker; increasingly, she becomes the more aggressive of the two. That external exchange mirrors a more basic internal substitution that employs lust as a transitional agent.

Physical sensations by their nature are immediate and short-lived. When accompanied by love in Singer's world, those sensations travel through the fullness of the partners and thus are given a longer, reverberating life. But Risha and Reuben are like animals and they rapidly reach points of satisfaction which require perversions to be extended. In the process, they hurry their lives away and become "prematurely old"; glutting themselves, they become so fat they can hardly come together. Ironically, their bloodlust has involved them in a self-consuming cycle; their sexuality, in truth, has become slaughter. By surrendering his masculinity to Risha, Reuben has essentially turned his soul over to his body. Allowing women, in D. H. Lawrence's terms, to stray outside the bounds of man's beliefs and gods, Reuben has created a sexual Frankenstein—a mannish woman.

Risha serves to establish a crucial nexus for a special group of women in Singer's stories. On the one hand, she provides a more naturalistic base for comprehending Singer's cabalistic and already fully-formed devils like Hodle and Cunegunde. On the other hand, Risha serves as an extreme in her own right to a host of mannish women. They include Hindele of **"The Black Wedding"** (1961); Lise of **"The Destruction of Kreshev"** (1961); Yentl of **"Yentl the Yeshiva Boy"** (1962), who actually dresses and passes herself off as a boy; Mrs. Margolis of **"Caricature"** (1961), who increasingly resembles her husband; and Zeitl and Rickel of **"Zeitl and Rickel"** (1968).

The full arc of the group mirrors the span of Singer's chronology and visionary theology. One extreme is embedded in the past and in demonology—in the Garden of Eden and in Lilith. The other is anchored in the modern world and in emancipated types—in an increasingly nonhierarchial and mobile society and in Madame Bovary, Nora, Sister Carrie, Lady Chatterley, and Temple Drake. Risha is the go-between, just as Satan is Singer's eternal panderer. Like Janus, Risha faces in two directions. On one side, she adjusts the absolute incarnations of evil to recognizable human distortions; on the other, she collects and projects the feminine incursions into traditionally masculine realms to their ultimate cosmic ends. To be sure, the latter group of mannish women is not evil per se. Nor are they grotesque like Risha. Nevertheless, she serves as a warning and terminus for one of Singer's recurrent themes: the dilemma of the intelligent woman in the man-dominated world of traditional Judaism. (pp. 115-22)

In *The Family Moskat* the People of the Book were weaned away from the Torah by books. A reminder of this broader context is important because it reveals that the dilemma is not solely a feminine but essentially a Jewish dilemma. To be sure, Singer adjusts the feminine version: Hindele, Lise, Yentl, and Zeitel read not secular but religious works. Standing behind men so long, they are forced initially to channel their desires for independence and individuality into less dramatic areas of contrast. Nevertheless, by extension the full arc is open to them, and as mannish women they are on the way to making synonomous the acquisition of knowledge and of masculinity. In the process, Singer in the novels often indicates that behind every amazon or mannish woman there often is a barbaric or weak man driving her to it. In the short stories, that notion is given a curious psychological twist: all these young girls have scholarly or rabbinical fathers who do not just pass on their knowledge but like dybbuks appear to deposit their natures in the souls of their daughters. In other words, the weak or barbaric man who invites or compels his wife to become mannish finds his counterpart in a strong father who, through excessive involvement, leads his daughter not only towards masculinity but also by guilt to sexual abstinence or by transference to homosexuality. What finally emerges is Singer's characteristic correlation of the pursuit of forbidden knowledge with the release of forbidden desires. Clearly, therefore, Singer's apparently unreasonable and archaic condemnation of women acquiring learning is merely his Jewish means of examining all ways in which women, in trying to become what they are not, blur their sexual clarity. Thus, Hindele marries an evil man and, like Rechele, is beset by a dybbuk in her womb; Lise engages in a steady series of sexual perversions and even becomes a sanctioned whore; and Yentl, who dresses as a young boy, enters a Yeshivah and marries a girl. (pp. 124-25)

Like Swift and Carlyle, Singer employs clothes as man's second creation. The first was God's, and just as He meant flesh to contain the organs of the body, so appropriate clothes serve to restrain man in the world. To Singer, "a rabbi in a long cloak, a beard and sidelocks, is not likely to dally with a girl on the street corner. . . . Clothes guard a person just as words do." In donning man's clothes, Yentl dislocates her sexuality. Like a dybbuk, the alien clothes perplex and possess her until she becomes what she wears. It is almost as if the real Yentl has been taken over by her shadow. Indeed, clothes and shadows are made metaphorical equivalents of each other in Singer's tale of **"Getzel the Monkey"** (1964).

Getzel, a mild, observant Jew, suddenly decides one day to ape the gay life of Todros, the local man-about-town. But the narrator warns:

> A man should stay what he is. The trouble of our world comes from mimicking. Today they call it fashion. A charlatan in Paris invents a train in front and everybody wears it. They are all apes, the whole lot of them. . . . I am afraid of a shadow. A shadow is an enemy. When it has a chance, it takes revenge.

In the process of mimicking Todros, Getzel, who previously had kept to his Jewishness, becomes an irreligious fop. In other words, the confusion of Yentl's sexuality finds its ultimate equivalent in the surrender of Getzel's Jewishness.

In **"Getzel the Monkey"** Singer presents the notion that all men exist in two forms: in an actual form which its fixed and more or less known; and in a secret form which is unformed and more or less unknown. The former is always specific and an original; the latter mysterious and a shadow. To Singer, a shadow is each personality's intimate dybbuk or secret sharer. Dreams, fantasies, sinful desires—all are the expressions of a shadow and represent what an individual might be if he and his shadow exchanged roles and clothes. (pp. 125-26)

Singer's progression is shrewd. He begins with clothes, extends them to shadows, and finally moves to ghosts. One may be possessed by a transmigrated soul in gothic terms or be taken over by the secret soul of one's shadow in psychological terms. But whatever the form, Singer maintains versimilitude, for the possessed individual does not become what he never could be but potentially what he secretly is. The known and the unknown are held together by a secret continuity which it is the story's aim to reveal. Thus, Yentl disguises himself as a man not so that she can become a Casanova or a rabbi but so that she can remain a scholar. But what Yentl and all transgressors cannot foresee is what happens when a familiar personality resides in an alien body. To guard against such exchanges and confusions of substance and shadow, biblical tradition severely judges homosexuality and other sexual blurrings to be abominations, and biblically inspired custom requires the wearing of appropriate clothing. Characteristically, Singer interprets these prohibitions as another indication of man's slavery. Specifically, man is shackled to one religious identity, one sex, one personality, one God—in short, to singularity. To be sure, Singer is aware that such chains are difficult to bear, especially when one is regularly tempted by the unlived possibilities of one's shadow. And again Singer does not legislate traditional views but instead gives free rein to the playing out of all the secret alternatives. In fact, his presentation of Yentl's plight is initially sympathetic. After all, what is so terrible about a woman pursuing knowledge? But to achieve this good end, Yentl must trangress; she must surrender herself to her shadow or rather to her father who serves as her shadow. As a result, by the end of the story, what first appeared to be reasonable turns out to be insane: Yentl gets married. As Yentl switches sexes, sympathy correspondingly shifts from Yentl to Hadass. Whatever Yentl's needs initially, what about Hadass's now? A single step has been taken but released a "multitude of transgressions." Through the shock of recoil at the end of the story, Singer points to the wisdom of keeping one's shadow in its place.

Yentl also is Risha's counterpart in a curious partnership of extremism. Risha's distortion of her femininity rises to the hysterical, cabalistic pitch of bestiality. In Yentl's case it sinks to the quiet undertones of homosexuality. Together, both stake out the cosmic heights and psychological depths of Singer's vision and, in the process, make religious and psychological distortions, not alternatives but versions of each other. The one through lust, the other by biology, preclude the family and thereby terminate the community. Clearly, the implications of distorted femininity, whatever the cause, are ultimately too serious to be bandied about in terms of masculine dominance and feminine subservience or as the battle of the sexes in which neither party is the victor. Behind the bloodlust of Risha and the homosexually inclined scholarship of Yentl, there lurks the ultimate perversion: the refusal to be dependent and vulnerable. To Singer a man truly achieves his manhood and a woman her womanhood only when both realize such goals are unachievable alone. Singer values the traditional subservience of women not because he is a male chauvinist or wishes to perpetuate the evil image of Eve but because that capacity for dependence and surrender created a model for men. But when men forget to be men and good fathers, the women understandably throw off their yokes and ape the dislocated freedom of their mates. In the process, Risha and Yentl reveal that sexual promiscuity and sexual abstinence meet on the common ground of spiritual virginity, and further, as women increasingly become men, so cosmically Satan becomes God. Indeed, love is such a rarity in Singer's world (and perhaps in the world in general) that when it does appear, it takes such radical forms that another group of his stories accurately might be called gothic love tales.

To Singer man's two most private and powerful worlds are those of love and belief. Man's secret longings, his sexual fantasies, his forbidden desires are of a piece with his private conversations, arguments, and prayers to God. Often, what a man will say to a woman in the intimacy of love is what he would say, if he could enjoy the same intimacy, to God. In such transcendent eulogies to unity as **"Joy"** (1951), **"A Wedding in Brownsville"** (1964), and **"Short Friday"** (1964), it is impossible to tell where love leaves off and belief begins. But when the mutuality of both private worlds is not acknowledged, or harmonized, the result is a discordant yoking of curious opposites. Such fragmentations of man's basic duality find frequent external embodiment in Satan's area of mismatching couples in marriage. In a recent story, **"The Warehouse,"** Singer even heretically suggests that heaven eases the Devil's task of mismatching.

The warehouse is a heavenly clearing station where souls await new bodies. Bad souls are punished in two ways: first, traditionally, in Gehenna or hell; second—and here is Singer's twist—by being given new bodies that are the inverse reminders or matches of their prior sinfulness. Thus, a whore is given the ugly body of a spinster; a miser that of a eunuch, etc. But over and above these individual ironies, there is the general problem that whereas long ago bodies and souls used to fit nicely together, now they do not. All kinds of mistakes are made; genitals are mixed up or not attached properly. In other words, what becomes clear in **"The Warehouse"** is that Singer's theme of mismatching couples builds on and compounds the basic mismatching of body and soul. But, unpredictably, he also counterpoints the theme in a number of love stories that present the surprising power of deflected love and belief.

In all these gothic love tales, love is the dream of one who is awake, or of one's shadow. But like all star-crossed lovers, those in Singer's tales are unaware of the extent to which their deepest conscious desires are in contact with their deepest unconscious desires. It is as if the dreams of love reach down to such a basic core that in Hegelian fashion they release their antitheses. The desire for another unexpectedly releases the unknown otherness of the desirer. Often, he anchors this odd coupling in the occult. Thus, the hero of **"Powers"** (1967) states that "in each great love there is an element of telepathy." Indeed, in an excellent long story, **"The Letter Writer"** (1968), the hero, in fact, does achieve the great love of his life through the benevolent intervention of a departed grandmother. In other words, Singer's occultism functions as his gothically inspired psychology and, as such, represents the secular version of his demonically centered theology. Above all, love offers a double mirror: one clear, the other shadowy. It reflects what the dreamer knows about himself and what he does not. Singer's way of imparting terror to love dreams is not to deny but to grant their fulfillment. Thus, **"Alone"** (1962) opens as follows: "Many times I have wished the impossible to happen—and then it happened. But though my wish came true, it was in such a topsy-turvy way that it appeared the Hidden Powers were trying to show me I didn't understand my needs." The hero of the story wishes that he could be alone, understandably, in Miami Beach. And it happens. Suddenly, the hotels are closed, the tourists leave. Significantly, now without the restraint of "society," the solitary survivor feels free to release what really was behind his first wish—the desire for sexual surrender. And that, too, nearly happens when a grotesque Cuban cripple tries to seduce him. She argues that he can afford to be unfaithful to his wife this one time because no one is around to see. But he replies, " 'God sees.' " (God is the ultimate Jewish version of the one who sees but is not seen.) Whereupon she spits on him and adds that if she were not a cripple he would not speak of God. Indeed, her parting fillip edges the hero's moral triumph with irony and reveals that he has escaped infidelity only by the narrowest and luckiest of margins.

In **"Alone"** the revelation of love strikes a compromise between the unknown and known. First, the hero recognizes that his initial capricious wish to be alone actually masked his real desire to be unfaithful: that revelation surprises him. The second, however, confirms his nature. To Singer, the sign of a devout or moral man is not the absence of desire but rather that the antithetical side of his nature is not beyond his powers of restraint. In consequence, the story concludes neither on a sensational note of absolute discontinuity nor on a moralizing note of total continuity but on an adjustment of what the hero knows and does not know of his nature and dreams. (pp. 127-31)

The most severe test of the power of love, however, appears in stories whose heroes are strong intellectuals or devout believers. Indeed, **"The Spinoza of Market Street"** (1961), **"The Shadow of a Crib"** (1961), and **"The Fast"** (1964) hinge on the perversion of too much strength and self-knowledge. Thus, in the first tale, the sage Spinoza is the sole buttress of the scholarly Dr. Fischelson; in **"The Shadow of a Crib"** the physician Dr. Yaretsky leans heavily on the cynical attitude of Schopenhauer toward sex and propagation; and in **"The Fast"** Reb Nokham, imitating the ascetic sages, tries to deny the power of love through fasting and self-flagellation. But in each case love overwhelms reason and forces a corrective extreme upon the hero's excess as a means of restoring dualistic balance.

Dr. Fischelson of **"The Spinoza of Market Street"** is another of Singer's deflective scholarly Jews who in turning from religious to secular materials, like his idol Spinoza, encounters in his incompleted work the face of his own mortality. But his infatuation with Spinoza finds competition from a most unexpected source. He becomes ill and his next door neighbor, Black Dobbe, an ignorant, swarthy, unattractive spinster, comes to nurse him. They talk and one thing leads to another; they become engaged, to the gossiping delight of the tradespeople of Market Street. But on the wedding night, the copy of Spinoza's *Ethics* falls from Dr. Fischelson's hands as Dobbe embraces him. . . . [The following morning] Dr. Fischelson goes to the window, gazes at the awakening cosmos, and falls into his philosophizing habit. The story concludes with his pathetic apology: " 'Divine Spinoza, forgive me. I have become a fool'."

The perversity of man's strength—that he cannot accept happiness at the hands of another. The perversity of the Faustian intellectual and Ivan Karamazov—that they can love only what they first understand. The perversity of Pangloss' slavery to consistency—that he is shackled to a philosophical identity. Dr. Fischelson undoubtedly will live out his life convinced that he has betrayed Spinoza (whereas the reverse is true) and that his life has been turned off from its proper direction (whereas here, too, the opposite is the case). The corrective power of love is applied gently in this story, for it respects Dr. Fischelson's delusions. That is not the case in either **"The Shadow of a Crib"** or **"The Fast."**

Dr. Yaretsky is a cynic who shares Schopenhauer's dictum that a woman is merely a "wide-hipped vessel of sex, which blind lust has formed . . . to perpetuate the eternal suffering and tedium." Moreover, like Asa Heshel of *The Family Moskat,* Dr. Yaretsky is determined not to add to the cycle of birth and death, and supports the proverb that the "luckiest child is the one not born." A Christian, he cannot understand why the Jews, who have suffered so much, continue to propagate more victims. But Dr. Yaretsky's philosophical security and insularity are shattered one night at a ball, when Helena, a stylish young maiden of the town, startles everyone including the doctor, by kissing his hand. That aggressive act disturbs Yaretsky and gives him bad dreams, including a prophetic one of her being ill. In any case, they become engaged, but before the wedding can take place, Dr. Yaretsky slips out of town and is never seen again. The story concludes many years later with the apparition of Dr. Yaretsky returning to haunt the rabbi of the town and Helena's house. Many swear that in Helena's bedroom there was visible the eerie shadow of a crib on the wall.

The ghost of Dr. Yaretsky represents that half of his nature which, though awakened by Helena's love, was suppressed by Schopenhauer's castrating cynicism. But that capacity comes to life after Dr. Yaretsky is dead to play out its unfulfilled dreams. Every unlived love begets a ghost which waits patiently to be incarnated in a natural or unnatural form. With Dr. Fischelson, Spinoza was pushed to the side so that the stored-up love of Black Dobbe could unite with the unlived youth of the scholar while both were alive. But Dr. Yaretsky's Schopenhauer is too strong to be dislodged and as a result the physician's strength turns out to be a source of inadequacy. The distinction of love is that of reality: it assaults. Dr. Yaretsky would not kiss Helena's hand so she kisses his. But though he resisted being violated while alive, so stirring was that kiss that it imparted life after death; and the ghost of Dr. Yaretsky returns to visit his unborn child.

One additional story which is closely related to those above and also provides a transition to two final gothic tales is **"The Fast."** Itche Nokhum proudly discovers after his wife has divorced him that "a man can curb every desire." Itche's way of triumphing over the lust of the flesh is to overcome the needs of the flesh for food. Like Kafka's Hunger Artist, Itche finds exquisite pleasure in pure bowels. Assailed by dreams of his ex-wife, Roise Genendel, appearing as Eve, he puts pebbles in his shoes, flagellates his chest and arms with nettles, and slaps his face and calls himself wanton. Envying the ascetics of old who fasted from Sabbath to Sabbath, Itche embarks on a week-long fast only to find that as his control gets stronger, so do his evil inclinations. Finally, toward the end of the fast, Itche is visited by Roise, who hysterically accuses him of being a devil and visiting her so that she does not have any peace. (pp. 133-37)

William Blake proverbially remarked, "If a fool persists in his folly he will become wise." Singer seems to believe that if one aspect of man's nature is pushed far enough, although its initial intent was to eliminate the other, it, in fact, recovers duality but in such extreme form that it results in the schizophrenia of becoming a transmigrated soul. Thus, as Itche's capacity to control his desire increases, his lust, which originally was never strong, suddenly acquires a strength it never had. Like a man split in two, Itche embarks on a journey of cross-purposes. All the while he is moving toward ascetic sainthood and away from Roise, his unlived sexual life, like a demon, has been visiting, courting, and tempting her. The shock of the story is not that asceticism to Singer is an evil—that is obvious and already familiar in Itche Mates of *Satan in Goray,* with whom Itche Nokhum has a great deal in common. The surprise is that Itche's asceticism is actually a warped form of love which ironically finds its potency only in transmigrated sexuality. (pp. 137-38)

The punitive love of Itche Nokhum is Singer's version of the eternal fusion of hate and love, a fusion which characterizes the two remaining stories in the group of gothic love tales: **"Under the Knife"** (1964) and **"The Unseen"** (1943). Hate and love exist in inevitable proximity and collusion because they reflect man's basic desire both to be needed and to resent being in need. Indeed, the more dependent the greater the hate, just as Itche's rejection of the body does not consume but feeds its antithetical acceptance. . . . Similarly, in **"Under the Knife,"** Leib's hatred of Rooshke is so intertwined with his love of her that it colors the way he plans to murder her: "In the dark, Leib returned to his cherished vision: Rooshke, deathly pale, lay there, dress up, legs stretched out, the yellow-blonde hair in disorder, the knife in her stomach with only the metal handle sticking out." Indeed, in another recurrent dream of sexual murder he slits her throat and makes love to her at the same time; and wakes up claiming "there were two Rooshkes." Similarly, Nathan of **"The Unseen"** who leaves his wife, Roise, to run away with his whore-servant, Shifra, dreams that they

> were one woman with two faces. . . . He kissed the two-faced female, and she returned his kisses with her doubled lips, pressing against him her two pairs of breasts. . . . In her four arms and two bosoms, all his questions were answered. There was no longer life and death, here nor there, beginning nor end. "The truth is twofold," Nathan exclaimed. "This is the mystery of all mysteries!"

The apocalyptic or Blakeian image of the twofold woman serves in the context of the gothic love tales to establish duality as a permanent condition and norm of human nature. Paradoxically, love alone has the power both to release and to harmonize hate and love, desire and violence, asceticism and sensualism in a partnership of cooperating contraries. Love provides an additional revelation only hinted at in the other stories but fully articulated in **"The Unseen."** The acceptance of the tightrope of duality leads to a vision beyond all duality. For the first time, Nathan is aware that the principle of opposition dictates that there are no ends or beginnings. Every thrust of life partly derives its force and meaning from the counterthrust of death so that nothing in creation is singular or even terminated so long as it remains dualistic. Love, which compels the ultimate relationship of human opposites, man and woman, violates man as a solitary unit so that he may experience unity and cosmic coincidence. As such, Love is an agent of God, for her efforts to have man recognize his double nature culminate in his acceptance of this world as a mirror of that nature. When love fails, man is deflected from the cycle of unity and either falls to the level of an animal that regards this world as everything or ascends to the level of an angel who regards this world as nothing. Singer's gothic love tales define love's wholeness through a refraction of fragments.

The publication of Singer's newest collection of short stories, ***The Séance and Other Stories,*** serves not only to confirm his mastery of the short story, but also to designate what now appears to be his essential stylistic range. A survey of Singer's nearly seventy-five collected and uncollected stories reveals a prose style woven of four main strands: the realistic, the philosophic, the demonic, and the apocalyptic.

The realistic strand is never absent from Singer's works. Even his holiest rabbis suffer from stomach cramps, and his most grandiose devils endure the ignominy of warts. The saintly Rabbi of Marshinov, near death, contemplates heavenly realms and has difficulty passing water. Dr. Fischelson, on his honeymoon, gazes up at the expanse of the universe with the rush of a young man's love while his bride snores in bed. As a result, what is rapidly established is that for all Singer's sensational demonism, religious transcendence, miraculous happenings, and gothic psychology, this world is lodged firmly and permanently in the center of his vision. To be sure, although the realistic style, especially in the historical novels, often stands by itself, more characteristically it is interwoven in tension with the remaining modes. Indeed, in large part, the purpose of the other styles is to tease and tug at the substantiality of this world and to beset with shadows and qualifications its ally, realism. Thus, the philosophical mode, which sustains *The Family Moskat, The Manor,* and many short stories, seeks to turn substance into sand. It supports Singer's characteristic sceptical ambivalence and his favorite theme of the collusion between life and death. It generates and buttresses heroes who, as fools or saints (perhaps one has to be one to be the other), wear the mantle of melancholia and serve as the Jewish versions of Hamlet and Yorick spawned in the grave of the ghetto. The philosophical mode bends the realistic to its *weltschmerz* and heralds Ecclesiastes as Singer's supreme authority on the subject of appearance and reality.

If the philosophical point of view tends to put the world under wraps, the demonic heightens and electrifies even the ordinary. A capricious, buoyant mode, it accounts for much of the freshness and vividness of *The Magician of Lublin* and many of the demonic tales. Indeed, the style is the image of Satan himself. Cocky and brash, Satan wastes no time trying to persuade the reader that he exists. Instead, he disarmingly introduces himself as the Evil One and then promptly sets about proving it. He takes credit for mismatching couples in marriage, for instilling faith in the poor so that their lives may be wretched, for inspiring the pursuit of justice in a world in which the "wicked make history." Above all, Satan's claim that he has access to man's most secret desires appears unchallengable. In one story, the Devil confesses, "Evenings, I watch the women at the ritual bath, or make my way into the bedrooms of pious folk and listen to the forbidden talk between man and wife. . . . So sharp are my ears that I can hear thoughts behind the skull." Combining the voyeurism of the peeping tom with the privileged knowledge of the psychiatrist, Satan is the perfect omniscient narrator, for he is free to go everywhere, and no secrets are safe from his prying curiosity. Indeed, to Singer the world is set up to betray secrets. . . . The demonic mode not only embodies that conspiracy, but also presents the temptation of self-betrayal.

Finally, the apocalyptic mode, which glowingly informs *The Slave* and a number of affirmative short stories, provides the maximum opposition to all the other styles. In the process, this ecstatic style also presents a crucial corrective to the notion that Singer's supernaturalism is exclusively demonic. His supernaturalism is a bridge not only to a permanent past—

seventeenth century Poland and biblical times—but also to a permanent future—the afterlife. The Devil is Singer's means of recovering the terror of the past; postmortal visitations are his means of anticipating the future. Indeed, such visitations in *The Slave,* **"Joy," "A Wedding in Brownsville,"** and **"Short Friday"** dramatically reveal that the present does not really exist in Singer's time scheme. His visionary preoccupations with the past or the future preempt the present and leave it as the exclusive province of Satan: "I speak in the present as for me time stands still." To Singer, if the present has any reality it has so only outside this world as the time of eternity.

The contraries of his style support the contraries of his vision. Each mode opposes, questions, and collides with its alternates: devils are answered by angels, sceptical philosophers by visionaries, rationalists by occultists, the Golden Calf by the Ten Commandments. Stubbornly and defiantly, each mode refuses to yield its ground and its claim to the whole truth. The result is an artistic vision locked in battle with itself. Singer's stylistic world is precariously poised for disintegration, just as many of his protagonists teeter on insanity. But because each mode will not surrender its claim to totality, Singer sets them permanently at odds with each other and ultimately employs unrelieved tension as his only guarantee against excessive or distortive partiality. Or as Gimpel the Fool neatly puts it, "No doubt this world is entirely an imaginary world but it is only once removed from the true world."

Curiously, Gimpel's foolishness ultimately leads to balance. Gimpel believes "everything is possible, as it is written in The Wisdom of the Fathers." As a result, the pivot of this deservedly famous story seems to be that Gimpel's gullibility is actually the overflow of faith. Scepticism, which supports the toughness of Singer's morality, need not harden into cynicism or nihilism. That scepticism may be poised as qualified belief is, in fact, one of Gimpel's conclusions and perhaps Singer's as well:

> the longer I lived the more I understood that there are really no lies. Whatever doesn't really happen is dreamed at night. It happens to one if it doesn't happen to another, tomorrow if not today, or a century hence if not next year.

(pp. 138-43)

The aim of **"Gimpel the Fool"** and many of the other stories is to invest the strange with the familiar and to normalize dislocation. . . . To Singer one need not be insane to harbor madness nor unusual to have a shadow. The day is solid and reassuring; the night murky and threatening. One works and one dreams; one wears clothes and makes love without them. Singer's stylistic interchanges make the apparently separate worlds of realism and demonism continuous. . . . Characteristically, Singer, like Gimpel, seeks the totality of a world continuous with the past and future, originals and shadows. Moreover, that sylistic totality supports a thematic totality. Nothing less than that both the experience of love and belief will fulfill man and woman and impart any justification for the world being created in the first place. That many of the stories dramatize not the fulfillment but the fragmentation of such harmonious ends is perhaps his way of representing the rarity of both love and belief and justifying his use of the short story and demonic narrators as appropriate modes of refraction. If there is one controlling notion that binds all the separate tales and groups of stories together, it is undoubtedly the notion that impotence is the bitter fruit of independence. To Singer impotence is the result of willing what cannot be willed and of seeking wholeness that cannot be achieved alone. The wisdom of Gimpel the Fool dictates that surrender often requires greater strength than self-reliance, and that certain illusions are more real and difficult to sustain than the facts of life. Stylistically, too, Singer resists the independence of any one mode by binding them all together in a textual knot whose tension renders his vision in miniature. (pp. 144-45)

Irving H. Buchen, in his Isaac Bashevis Singer and the Eternal Past, *New York University Press, 1968, 239 p.*

LINDA G. ZATLIN (essay date 1969)

[In the following excerpt, Zatlin analyzes Singer's thematic concern with the individual's struggle to achieve faith in an age of skepticism.]

Of all the critical approaches to I.B. Singer's fiction, the most usual, as one would assume, has been evaluation of his relationship to the mainstream of Yiddish literature. However, an examination of his short stories yields a striking thematic concern, unexpectedly placing Singer squarely in the broader stream of twentieth century literature. While he sensitively recreates a time and place in modern history dead and all but forgotten, and while his stories superficially reflect a preoccupation with Jewish folklore, Singer repetitively and compellingly focuses on the individual's struggle to find a viable faith in an age possessed by this very problem. Thus, the stories, despite their setting in the nineteenth century Eastern European Jewish ghetto and their deceptive mask of simple folk tales, portray and explore this predominant problem of modern man with all its accompanying apprehension and tension. Specifically, Singer predicates his fiction on the idea that the presense or absence of human faith in God is an eternal, omnipresent dilemma which the individual must resolve for himself, and he consistently shows that man's fate after death, to be in Heaven or Hell, is directly correlated with his degree of faith in God. Accordingly, Singer's stories run from unshakeable belief in God to inflexible trust in the Devil. (p. 40)

Within this framework, Singer's characters may be viewed as allegorical figures, all working toward their resolution of the dilemma of faith and, thus, their fates because central to their lives is their relationship to God. That this concern permeates all of Singer's characters may be seen by their probing towards such a relationship during their lives as well as before birth, in **"Jachid and Jachidah,"** and after death, in **"Esther Kreindel the Second."** Their sense that attaining some kind of faith is life's purpose impells them to make the Singerian choice. Further, the necessity of choice accounts for Singer's lack of psychological character probing. He does not choose, except in the case of his demons, to dissect the inner workings of his characters' minds because his artistic purpose is to present soul drama rather than psyche drama. In these allegories of the soul, characters fall into one of three types. The first allegorical type is the God-chooser; he directs his energy toward living consistently within His laws. The second is the God-denier; he has already submitted to the forces of evil by embracing Satan. He lives hedonistically and comes to the end which Singer repeatedly posits for the unfaithful: a desire to be in Hell, seeking punishment. The third type is the doubter; he ruminates at length about God's existence but utilizes his drives in resolving his conflict and arrives ultimately at complete faith in or denial of Him. This last group illustrates most clearly the dilemma of modern man.

Since these stories are allegories of the soul and the characters are allegorical figures, one might assume that within each group all types would be similar. To the contrary, within each category there are further gradations, enabling the reader of the Singer canon to view the gamut of modern belief in a world unrestricted as was the Jewish ghetto. An examination of one character which best exemplifies each category will illustrate.

The God-choosers, being wholeheartedly committed to belief in God's existence, as sustained by their faith as they continuously reinforce it. In **"Short Friday,"** for example, an elderly couple, rich only in their love for each other and for God, adhere to every rite and law through their lives together. Their only fear is that one will outlive the other, leaving a grieving spouse. However, they die together, and it is obvious that their simultaneous deaths have been fated by a higher power. Awakening and realizing what has happened, the two await the Angel of Death who is to lead them to Paradise. As they wait serenely, the husband recalls a verse from the Bible: "Lovely and pleasant in their lives, and in their death they were not divided." Here, God rewards the righteous for devotion to Him, not by admitting them to Heaven, which would be their just lot anyway, but by allowing them to die together that they may share the fruits of their devotion.

As the God-chooser is committed, so is the God-denier, but the Satanic response is always initiated by one of the black host. This is natural because in Singer's fictional world Satan is an aggressive, high-pressure salesman of sin while God refrains from taking a personal role in furthering His cause. As provacateur, Satan's persuasive techniques stem from His knowledge of human frailty: "And although my advice led to the abyss, she did not object, for it is well known that my people are vain and will lay down their lives for their vanity. For what is the pursuit of pleasure but pride and delusion?" His minions are able to transmute His knowledge into a triumph of seduction more often than not, since innate disbelievers eagerly twist their powers of reason to work for the Devil. Having little concern for God's law or their own moral righteousness, those who deny Him are intent solely on self-gratification. They sin, and, before they are transported to Hell, generally wish to be punished as evidence of the Evil One's power.

Accordingly, Risha, the personification of lust in **"Blood,"** catalogues the panorama of the species of lust. Despite her haste to satisfy her tastes, she carefully insults God and worships Satan simultaneously. Moving from adultress to community deceptress, Risha is left wishing for her punishment which, of course, comes from both God and Satan: " 'God, come and punish me! Come Satan! Come Asmodeus! Show me your might. Carry me to the burning desert behind the dark mountains!' " And she is shown the might of both. Risha is turned into a werewolf and axed to death by a villager. Etched, thus, is the Satanic response. We do not need to know the inner workings of her mind to comprehend how Risha operates: and of the "why." Risha is continuously aware. Here sole concern is her pleasure. If it is to be attained by the condemnation of God and the cultivation of Satan, Risha will eagerly comply. And because she sinks so low in her dealings with other people and harms so many, as opposed to the self harm inflicted by Zeidel in **"Pope Zeidlus"** and the young matron in **"The Mirror,"** Risha undergoes a metamorphosis, receiving earthly punishment before her hideous death. Thus does Singer point out that innate disbelievers who ignore ethical demands are subject to punishment. Those who have abrogated belief in God, those who are wholly self-seeking, must align themselves with Satan. They find in Satan their God, and although He sustains them, He also destroys them; this is the sole destiny projected for those who succumb to the Satanic forces.

Neutrality is impossible. The doubters, the third allegorical symbol, who have not been able to crystallize their thoughts regarding God's existence, are nonetheless compelled to find one of two alternatives. Those who begin by vacillating either emerge from their conflict with strong, confident faith in God, or enter into a Satanic alliance. The full tension of the Singerian choice is brought into play by the doubters. Therefore, they form a special and separate category of faith as found in Singer's short stories because they most clearly reveal contemporary man's own apprehension and problems in becoming committed. Through these characters Singer shows that man does not necessarily begin as either a believer or a dis-believer but often as a seeker, a struggler, confronting and grappling with obstacles in his way before achieving his resolution. Because these stories contain the clearest expression of the agony of choice, it is necessary to illustrate using more plot summary than previously.

Sometimes, resolving the conflict is easy enough after the protagonist realizes what is ensuing. For example, in the compelling, surrealistic story, **"Alone,"** a man unwittingly begins toying with demonic forces but recommits himself to God when this terrible realization becomes clear to him. But at other times a character may go through personal anguish sufficiently consuming to make him lose faith near the culmination of a righteous life. In **"Joy,"** a rabbi's sixth and last child dies from the same long and painful illness which has already killed her five brothers and sisters. As a result the rabbi denies the existence of God and stops praying; gradually his congregation disperses. But, after a year goes by, the apparition of his youngest daughter appears to him and implores him to resume prayer, saying that she has come to take him to Heaven after the holidays. He does pray, coming to the realization that "if the pious man loses his faith, the truth is shown to him, and he is recalled." It is apparent that this man's faith, though he declares it gone, is present in a quantity great enough to sustain him throughout his period of apparent disbelief.

In direct contrast to these protagonists are those who do not succeed in winning their confrontation with evil. Their desire and intent towards righteousness, though present, do not combine to strengthen them in overcoming the demands made on them. Accordingly, Itche Nokhum loses his soul to Satan. He is drawn to asceticism after his wife leaves him. Itche divorces her, flogs himself with nettles, fasts, immerses himself in cold water, and believes he has curbed all worldly desires. Yet he cannot rid himself of recurring visions of his former wife. When she finally meets with him, it is revealed that, despite his ascetic exercises, he has consorted with the Devil through his continuing desire for her.

The same end comes to Yoineh Meir, who should become the town rabbi, but who is appointed ritual slaughterer. His melancholy increases as he grows to believe it is his destiny to cause torment. Continuously arguing with himself about the necessity of slaughtering animals, Yoineh suffers more as he tries to force himself to believe that God is not a slaughterer Himself. But, ultimately, he denies God and commits suicide, rebellious and raging against Heaven.

Itche's route of faith is through asceticism, while Yoineh's is through obedience to the community leaders. However, since neither man is able to commit himself sincerely to his chosen profession, both Itche's and Yoineh's faith have weak foundations. Thus, while they expend much energy trying to position themselves on the path leading upward, they find that because of their weak faith their paths lead downward to the abyss. As can be seen then, the agony of the Singerian choice is illustrated by the doubters who spend their lives ruminating at length regarding the viability of their belief in God. Man's moral striving, his own effort to achieve personal righteousness, to be sensitively aware of other humans and to build a righteous society, is seen in Singer's stories to be predicated on faith possessed by the individual.

The existence in each story of the character's struggle to keep or to find faith forms the framework, the narration, the underlying conflict, or the atmosphere of all the stories. Singer's characters, as indeed each of us, have been taught that God exists. On this basis they must then make their personal decisions. But because each individual cares fervently about his relationship to God, he cannot be content merely to act in the prescribed manner; this would be indifference. Instead, he struggles to find perfect faith, realizing that one can be possessed by God or by Satan. The fervor, the agonized struggle to believe becomes a tool for Singer in his exploration of the kinds and qualities of human faith, ennabling him to enrich the texture of his stories and to reveal his characters. By establishing his vision in the allegorical microcosm of his fictional world, Singer has also established it in the macrocosm of the real world.

Beyond Singer's theological assumptions are insights into the nature of man. Singer's fictional vision makes clear that the compulsion to align oneself with God or Satan marks the split in man's nature into the humanistic, concerned, creative individual versus the narrow, egotistical, sterile person. This essence of man's current dilemma is what makes Singer universal. (pp. 41-6)

Linda G. Zatlin, "The Themes of Isaac Bashevis Singer's Short Fiction," in Critique: Studies in Modern Fiction, *Vol. XI, No. 2, 1969, pp. 40-6.*

PAUL N. SIEGEL (essay date 1969)

[Siegel is an American critic who has written extensively on English Renaissance literature and the works of William Shakespeare. In the following excerpt, Siegel views the protagonist and narrator of Singer's short story "Gimpel the Fool" as an ironic example of the archetypal wise- or sainted-fool figure in literature.]

"Gimpel the Fool," perhaps the most widely acclaimed work of Isaac Bashevis Singer, has its roots deep in the soil of Yiddish literature. It is concerned with two of what Irving Howe and Eliezer Greenberg tell us, in their *Treasury of Yiddish Stories,* are "the great themes of Yiddish literature," "the virtue of powerlessness" and "the sanctity of the insulted and the injured," and has as its anti-hero the "wise or sainted fool" who is an "extreme variation" of "the central figure of Yiddish literature," "*dos kleine menschele,* the little man." The wise or sainted fool is, however, not merely a recurring character in Yiddish fiction; he is a centuries-old archetypal figure of western literature. The manner in which Singer handles this archetypal figure, making use of the ideas associated with it, but in his own distinctive way, makes **"Gimpel the Fool"** the masterpiece of irony that it is. (p. 159)

Gimpel differs from the other representatives of the archetype, the Yiddish ones as well as the others, in that he is the expression of his creator's own idiosyncratic mixture of faith and skepticism. It is this mixture which, as we shall see in analyzing the story, is the source of its pervasive irony. Singer stated in a *Commentary* interview on November, 1963 that it would be foolish to believe the purveyors of fantasies about psychic phenomena—just as it was foolish of Gimpel to believe the fantastic lies he was told—yet the universe *is* mysterious, and there is something of truth after all in these fantasies, at least a revelation concerning the depths of the human psyche from which these fantasies emerged and perhaps something more as well. The need to continue to search for the truth, the realization that this search cannot result in the attainment of the truth, the need to choose belief, the realization that, intellectually speaking, such a choice cannot be defended against the unbeliever—all of this lies behind **"Gimpel the Fool."**

In many ways the work dealing with the idea of the wise fool that is closest in spirit to **"Gimpel the Fool"** is Erasmus's *The Praise of Folly.* Although Erasmus accepted Christianity as divinely revealed, he was capable of writing, "I like assertions so little that I would easily take sides with the skeptics wherever it is allowed by the inviolable authority of Holy Scripture and the decrees of the Church." Socrates, the man who was so wise because he knew how little he knew, he regarded as a saint equal to St. Paul. He attended the same school of the Brethren of the Common Life and imbibed there the same philosophy of a simple Christianity devoid of scholastic subtleties as did Nicholas of Cusa, who in his *Of Learned Ignorance* maintained that all human knowledge is only speculation and that wisdom consists of the recognition of man's ignorance and the apprehension of God through intuition. The expression of a fusion of skepticism and faith resembling that which underlies **"Gimpel the Fool."** Erasmus's *The Praise of Folly* is pervaded by a similar complex ironic ambiguity. It will be interesting and illuminating, as we proceed in our discussion of Singer's story, to observe the similarities between these two works.

Gimpel is the butt of his village because of his credulity. But is he the fool that the village takes him to be? Telling his story himself, he affirms his own folly in his very first words: "I am Gimpel the fool." In the very next breath, however, he takes it back: "I don't think myself a fool. On the contrary. But that's what folks call me." As he relates the story of his life, this denial of his foolishness seems to be the pitiful defense of his intellect by an evidently weak-witted person who at times tacitly admits that he is a fool, but a steadily deepening ambiguity plays about his narrative. This ambiguity, present from the beginning, is indicated in the title and the opening sentence of the Yiddish, where the epithet used is "*chochem*" or "sage," which often has the ironic meaning of "fool," the meaning in which the villagers and Gimpel's wife use it.

Singer's device of having Gimpel act as the narrator is similar to Erasmus's device of having the allegorical figure of Folly deliver a mock encomium of folly. Are we to take what she has to say seriously? Her oration is in the form of a mock encomium, that is, it is an ironic praising of folly which, it would seem, should be read as the opposite, as a censuring of folly. But then, it is delivered by Folly herself. If Folly censures folly, then it would seem as if Wisdom should praise it. But if Wisdom praises folly and Folly censures it, how are we to know which is Wisdom and which is Folly? We are lost in a labyrinth of irony similar to that which we shall find in **"Gimpel the Fool."**

Gimpel, looking back upon his childhood, seeks to justify the way in which he would allow himself to be taken in. He once played hookey because he had been told that the rabbi's wife had been brought to childbed. But how was he to know that he was being lied to: he hadn't paid any attention to whether her belly was big or not. So too, when he took a detour because he heard a dog barking, how was he to know that it was a mischievous rogue imitating a dog? These excuses of Gimpel sound plausible enough, the first as well as the second. After all, we don't expect a child to note the advance of pregnancy. Each birth is unexpected and comes as a kind of miracle that may happen to any woman.

But as Gimpel continues to explain that he was not really a fool, we see that he was indeed stupidly credulous, accepting the most fantastic stories which all the villagers conspired together to make him believe. Working as an apprentice in the bakery after he left school, he was subjected to a never ending flow of accounts of alleged wonders, each more silly than the other. Whereas before it was the rabbi's wife who was said to have given birth, now the rabbi was said to have given birth to a calf in the seventh month. But, as outrageously ridiculous as the stories are, there is still some uncertainty about how utterly a fool Gimpel is. He had to believe, he tells us, or else people got angry, exclaiming, "You want to call everyone a liar?" His belief, then, was in part the wise acquiescence of the butt who must play his role, knowing that otherwise he will never be free of his wiseacre tormentors.

Yet it was not merely a pretended belief. For always there would come the thought: maybe it is, after all, true? When he was told that the Messiah had come and that his parents had risen from the grave, he knew very well, he informs us, that nothing of the sort had occurred, but nevertheless he went out. "Maybe something had happened. What did I stand to lose by looking?" The jeering he got on that occasion made him resolve to believe nothing more, but he could not stick to this resolution, his poor wits being no match for those of the villagers, who confused him with their argumentation.

Moreover, he came to believe not merely because he was talked into it but also because he wanted to believe. When he was derisively matched with the village prostitute, he knew very well what she was, that her limp was not, as alleged, a coy affectation and that her supposed little brother was actually her bastard child. But, after having been pushed into marriage with her by the entire village, he grew to love her and the uncertain belief in her virtue to which he had been persuaded became a determinedly held belief against all the evidence.

At this point in his narrative Gimpel, the husband of the sharp-tongued Elka, becomes both a henpecked husband and a cuckold, the two figures who have been objects of mirth through the centuries and have often as here been combined in the same person. With comic repetition each time the truth is revealed to him he is talked out of it or talks himself out of it. (pp. 160-64)

His credulity has no limits. Repetition seems to make it easier for him to believe rather than the reverse. We should laugh at this spectacle of the fool continuing in his folly, but we do not, for we have come to wonder if Gimpel, undoubted fool that he has proven himself to be, is not in reality superior to his deceivers. Early in his torments the rabbi had advised him, "It is written, better to be a fool all your days than for one hour to be evil. You are not a fool. They are the fools. For he who causes his neighbor to feel shame loses Paradise himself." The paradox is that Gimpel, born to be a fool all of his days, is not a fool. It is the smart-aleck villagers, devoting their time to playing games upon him, who are fools. (p. 165)

Just as he made a vow before not to believe anything that he was told, a vow which he was unable to keep, so he now makes a vow to believe whatever he is told. "What's the good of *not* believing? Today it's your wife you don't believe; tomorrow it's God Himself you won't take stock in." It is undoubtedly laughable that Gimpel makes faith in the sluttish Elka equivalent to faith in the divine scheme of things. Yet Singer himself, during the *Commentary* interview in November, 1963, in expounding the philosophy of "as if," the doctrine that all of us must lead our lives in accordance with certain assumptions, such as the assumption that we will go on living, even if these assumptions go contrary to the existing evidence, makes use of faith in one's wife as an illustration.

So too Erasmus's Folly makes delusion in marriage representative of the delusions by which all of us must live if society and human life are to continue. Such delusions, a part of life, are, she says, necessary and natural. They are in Singer's words the "as if" by which life is maintained. Gimpel's equating of faith in Elka with faith in the divine scheme of things may thus be seen as an expression of the wisdom of simple, natural folk who accept the things of this world without thought.

Gimpel's belief in Elka despite the evidence of his own senses springs from his love for her. Where love is great, there must be faith. But Gimpel's love is not confined to Elka. It extends to all living things. This is why his faith in her is related to his faith in the divine order. Faith, hope, and charity—Gimpel has the qualities, the tenderness and the forgiveness, of the fool in Christ. (pp. 166-67)

It is his lovingness, indeed, which makes it possible for him to continue to be deceived. (p. 168)

Before Elka dies, she confesses to Gimpel that she has deceived him all of their married life. The Spirit of Evil comes to Gimpel as he is sleeping and, telling him that God and the judgment in the world to come are fables, persuades him to revenge himself against the deceitful world by urinating in the dough so that the *"chachomim,"* the sages of the village, may be fooled into eating filth. (pp. 168-69)

After he has baked the unclean bread, however, and lies dozing by the oven, Elka appears in a dream. She calls him *"chochem"*—ironically wise man and fool—for believing that because she was false everything else is a lie. She had in reality never deceived anyone but herself, and now she is paying for it in the other world. (p. 169)

The "as if" that Elka is faithful by which Gimpel had lived is now seen by him to give way, after it has sunk under him, to other "as ifs." He buries the bread in the ground, divides his wealth among the children—he had earlier casually mentioned in his unworldly way that he had forgotten to say that he had come to be rich—and goes into the world. Before he had regarded his village as the world. Now he finds out that the world has much more in it than he knew. He grows old and gray in his wanderings. He hears many fantastic tales, but the longer he lives the more he comes to realize that there are no lies. Everything, no matter how fantastic, comes to pass sooner or later. The something that was supposed to have happened that he hears and regards as impossible actually happens at a later time. Or even, he says in a sentence omitted in the Bellow translation, a sentence reminiscent of Singer's comment on the magazines devoted to psychic phenomena, if a story is quite imagined, it also has a significance: why does one person dream up one thing and another person an entirely different thing?

Gimpel thus becomes a representative of that other variant of *dos kleine menschele* in Yiddish fiction, "the ecstatic wanderer, hopeless in this world because so profoundly committed to the other," as Greenberg and Howe have put it. He also becomes reminiscent of the Wandering Jew, who according to the legend transmitted through the centuries was punished for having spat into the face of Christ by being deprived of the power to die. Cursed with unwanted life, imbued with the esoteric knowledge he has acquired through having lived through many civilizations, he is generally an evil figure, but he is also sometimes represented as Christ-like in the sustained agony through which he pays for his sin. Longing to join Elka in death, weary from the years of his wandering, Gimpel is transformed by the realization that has come to him from his varied experiences that "the world is entirely an imaginary world," becoming a personification of the ecstatic wisdom that is attained through the agony of suffering.

Yet the wisdom he has attained is the same that he had when, "like a golem," he "believed everyone," reasoning to himself, "Everything is possible, as it is written in the Wisdom of the Fathers, I've forgotten just how." What had seemed to be one of a number of excuses offered by a fool for his gullibility turns out to be indeed wisdom. The outrageously outlandish stories about miraculous births he had accepted really attested to his perception of the miracle of life. The hallucinations which he told himself he had had really attested to his perception that the world is a dream.

But now he who had listened to stories of marvels is the one who tells them: "Going from place to place, eating at strange tables, it often happens that I spin yarns—improbable things that could never have happened—about devils, magicians, windmills, and the like." Sometimes the children who chase after him tell him the particular story they wish to hear, and he satisfies them with a recital of that tale. For Gimpel, it is implied, has come to understand that each one of us has his own favorite fiction to which he is addicted, his own delusion to which he needs to remain faithful. But a sharp youngster tells him that it is really always the same story that he tells. For all of our delusions derive from the dream that is life in this world. The tales which the aged wanderer relates deal with the folk superstitions to which there have been so many references in **"Gimpel the Fool"**—the windmills, however, seem to be a reminiscence of the illusions of that glorious madman, Don Quixote—but these superstitions, silly as they are, are glimpses of the truth shadowed forth in the dream of life: "No doubt the world is entirely an imaginary world, but it is only once removed from the true world."

Dreams themselves are visions of a higher reality. The moment Gimpel closes his eyes he sees Elka standing over the steaming washtub as he had first seen her, but it is an Elka transfigured, her face shining, her eyes radiant, her words consoling, her talk of strange things which he forgets the instant he awakes. He does, however, remember her promise that they will be reunited in a future time.

Yet Gimpel's ecstatic vision is not without its ambiguity. It is similar in this to the conclusion of *The Praise of Folly.* Folly relates how holy men through their meditations attain a brief glimpse of heavenly bliss. When they come to themselves, they do not know whether they were asleep or awake and do not remember what they experienced except that they were rapturously happy. "And therefore they are sorry they are come to themselves again, and desire nothing more than this kind of madness, to be perpetually mad. And this is a small taste of that future happiness." But Folly does not conclude with this description of the ecstatic vision of the saints. She apologizes for her boldness in dealing with such matters but reminds us of the proverb "Sometimes a fool may speak a word in season." Of course, she adds, she is a woman, and the reader may choose not to apply the proverb to women. Moreover, she does not remember what she has said, "having foolishly bolted out such a hodge podge of words," and she advises the reader not to remember them either. It is up to the individual reader, therefore, whether he is to regard the vision of the saints as mere lunacy, whether he is to regard Folly's assurance that it is a taste of future happiness as the words of wisdom which may come from the lips of a fool and whether he is to regard the advice to forget what he has heard as the advice of Folly.

So with Gimpel the Fool. Can we believe in the transformed Elka? Is the Elka who, suffering the pangs of labor, cried out for forgiveness only to relapse into a life of deception capable of such a transformation? Must not reunion with her after the separation of death be similar to the disillusioning reunion with her after the previous separation? Is Gimpel's vision really a foolish dream?

He awakes to taste the salt of the tears Elka had shed over him as she stroked and kissed him. But on previous occasions he had wept himself asleep or had awakened crying. Is this what he is left with now—his own tears? He awaits death as entrance to the true world: "Whatever may be there, it will be real, without complication, without ridicule, without deception. God be praised: there even Gimpel cannot be deceived." But the first time he had found Elka in bed with a man he had told himself, "Enough of being a donkey. Gimpel isn't going to be a sucker all his life. There's a limit even to the foolishness of a fool like Gimpel," yet he had gone on permitting himself to be duped. Even the world of marvels he discovers as a wanderer may be, it is hinted, merely additional evidence of his credulity. "Often I heard tales of which I said, 'Now this is a thing that cannot happen.' But before a year had elapsed I heard that it had actually come to pass somewhere." He *heard* that it had come to pass *somewhere:* he had not himself witnessed it, therefore, but accepted on trust what it was told him had happened elsewhere. Is Gimpel's foolishness, then, really limitless, and is his final assurance that he will attain the world of reality after death either another self-deception or the continuation of an endless deception practiced upon him by malevolent Higher Powers? Will death, instead of blissful certainty, bring him either nothingness or another world of dreams and deception?

The reader is left with this teasing ambiguity, but the intensity of Gimpel's vision is such that it is consigned to the back of his mind. "I choose to believe," said Singer. It is also the choice of Gimpel, not an intellectual choice but one springing from his innermost need. If Singer makes the same choice, he is still able to look upon Gimpel with the detachment of the doubter. We need not share Singer's philosophy to be moved by the compassion mixed with irony with which he regards Gimpel, the fool who has become representative of poor, bewildered, suffering humanity. (pp. 169-73)

Paul N. Siegel, "Gimpel and the Archetype of the Wise Fool," in The Achievement of Isaac Bashevis Singer, *edited by Marcia Allentuck, Southern Illinois University Press, 1969, pp. 159-74.*

ELAINE GOTTLIEB (essay date 1970)

[*An American essayist, novelist, and short story writer, Gottlieb has cotranslated several of Singer's works from Yiddish, including* The Spinoza of Market Street. *In the following excerpt, Gottlieb notes Singer's designation by some critics as "a Yiddish Hawthorne" and evaluates Hawthorne's and Singer's treatment and characterization of Satan and the forces of evil in their fiction.*]

There are in the works of Isaac Bashevis Singer and Nathaniel Hawthorne . . . great disparities in the treatment of the idea of Satan and/or the evil influences emanating from him. Yet critics have referred to Singer as a Yiddish Hawthorne. There are, of course, obvious similarities: both are tale-tellers interested in fantasy, myth, superstition, guilt, and sin. Both have written about witchcraft and the seventeenth century (although Singer has gone back further and they do not write in the same tone). Finally, Hawthorne is speaking of the artist, the individual in his collision with society, while Singer stresses the need for all individuals to relate to God and to man. Hawthorne, in *The Scarlet Letter,* hints at the presence of Satan, calling him "The Black Man," "The Prince of the Air," but never brings him into view. Frequently, however, Satan is an active participant in Singer's stories. Hawthorne's Satan dwells in the forest of man's imagination, but Satan in Singer's work is an actual character or persona, usually invisible, sometimes in disguise.

When Satan possesses a Singer character the possession is graphic and leaves no doubt that a body has been taken over by an evil spirit. In Hawthorne's stories, however, Satan is often synonymous with a state of mind such as the false joy of the merrymakers in "The Maypole of Merrymount" or the lawless passion of Hester and Dimmesdale in *The Scarlet Letter.* In Singer's earlier stories, Satan is more than a symbol; he exists. (pp. 359-60)

One cannot infer from Singer as from Hawthorne that man must live with evil, that it is part of his nature, that perfection occurs only in death. What Singer implies is that man must always be on his guard against the evil that tries to dominate him. Man's imperfection does not obsess Singer; he and his characters accept it as a kind of divine joke. For after all, the Jewish God has promised redemption. . . .

Both Singer and Hawthorne are concerned with damnation, the Fall, original sin; but they approach it differently. (p. 361)

For Singer, the struggle between man's higher and lower natures is the struggle to remain a Jew and a believer amid worldly follies. In *The Magician of Lublin* only the most absolute faith can restore a man from the depths, but the rabbi in **"Joy,"** who denies God's existence after his children die, returns to religion when he thinks he sees his dead daughter standing before him and rebounds to his original position—that one must live "joyously." In **"Gimpel the Fool,"** only the fact that he is a fool protects Gimpel from life's blows; it is as if his foolish goodness were equated with religious faith. In Hawthorne's novels and stories, characters often lose faith but never regain it, nor is their faith always specifically religious. Religious faith, on the other hand, often leads to a perverse harshness, such as the attitude of the townspeople toward Hester in *The Scarlet Letter,* or toward "The Gentle Boy" because he is a Quaker.

The flaw from which Singer's characters suffer is not so much pride, as with Hawthorne, but sensuality and a lust for material possessions. Zirel, who during her husband's prolonged absences loves to contemplate herself nude, in **"The Mirror,"** is at last sucked into it and absorbed by Satan's imp who lives there. **"The Gentleman from Cracow"** lures the townspeople with gifts of money and jewelry into an orgiastic dance in a muddy street, during which the houses and babies left untended are destroyed by fire. Even **"The Spinoza of Market Street,"** an erudite philosopher, recognizes that he has become a fool when he allows himself to sink into the bliss of marriage. Satan and his various minions are real characters in Singer's works. Hawthorne's forces of evil are implied, rather than personified. Even though "Young Goodman Brown" converses with the devil, the tempter finally vanishes as if he had been an aberrant image in the first place.

Undoubtedly contributing to their differences is the fact that though the literary influences of both Singer and Hawthorne came out of the nineteenth century, for Hawthorne it was the romantics and transcendentalists, while Singer has been impressed by the great social realists. Singer manages to combine the mythical with the real in such a way that the mythic, the supernatural, becomes realistic. For Hawthorne, realism turns into a mythic, romantic experience. Singer's spirits talk like people. Hawthorne's people talk like spirits. (pp. 362-63)

Obviously, Singer treats his spirits humorously, which Hawthorne never does. But then they are not the same kind of spirits.

Singer writes of a folk society wherein the spirits as well as the spiritual belong to the lives of his villagers, but Hawthorne wrote of individuals who were in some way detached or even cast off from their society. Singer's characters reflect their milieu—what they do affects the community, and vice versa—but Hawthorne's characters are in a world of their own from beginning to end. (pp. 363-64)

Generally, redemption is inaccessible to Hawthorne's characters, while for Singer a little prayer goes a long way. In **"A Piece of Advice,"** there is the practical note of compromise: "So also with faith. If you are in despair, act as if you believe. Faith will come afterward."

In Singer's stories, what happens to one person happens to all; the community is emotionally united. One woman is sympathetic to Hester on the scaffold, but when Lise, the disgraced wife in Singer's **"The Destruction of Kreshev,"** receives her bill of divorcement after being shamed by a march through town, women lament and men have tears in their eyes. She is one of them, belongs to them, even though she has erred; they are willing to reclaim her. Throughout the march the women escorting Lise try to comfort her "for this march was her atonement, and by repenting she could gain her decency . . . "—unlike Hester, who must always wear her symbol of sin. But in a way, Lise and Hester resemble each other. Neither of them is truly repentant. Accused of adultery, Lise takes her punishment proudly, says nothing, later commits suicide. Hester, throughout the narrative, remains an idealistic New England woman, a kind of advanced thinker, almost a feminist. But she is a romantic feminist. Her experience with Dimmesdale was "consecrated"; she continues to love him. Lise commits adultery out of intellectual curiosity, boredom, perverseness. It is she who is the modern woman. No one is as romantic as Hester anymore. Singer's women are European but provincial. To break away from the community role, to become intellectual, is enough to damn any of them.

It is perhaps their preoccupation with sin and the fantasies concurrent with it—the supernatural, the satanic forces—that unite Singer and Hawthorne, and for both authors it is the acceptance of the reality of the devil, symbolic or not, that provides the tension within which their characters struggle. But Hawthorne's devil obsesses the individual and sets him off from society, a recluse, a misanthrope, damned by his own introspection. Hawthorne's thinking man is frozen in loneliness. His characters do not so much act as react, or withdraw. Singer's characters are all actors in search of an author, waylaid by their director, Satan, who puts into their mouths words that should never have been spoken. If they are lost it is not because they think, but because they let Satan think for them. But the inhumanity and imperfections of mankind that so plagued Hawthorne are for Singer softened by a Jewish optimism. How can a Jewish world that rejoices in fertility and home-cooked meals, a world in which being alive is a congratulatory condition, believe that God's beneficence will not extend to the other side, despite the devil? And if the devil is to be contended with, it is because he is so attractive. How easy it is not to draw a distinction between the false Messiah and the true one—who was promised but never comes. The Jew cannot stop believing that He will come and that Paradise will include all the pleasures of this world and more. Who can blame the individual whose trust in Paradise leads him to the gates of Hell?

But temptation and Hell permeate one's life, and were one to dissect it, one would find the devil and the hopes of the flesh splintered into our days at every hour. Characters suffering from the foolish hopes that they themselves will be realized within mythical expectations, characters searching for God and the afterlife, searching for the good supernatural and finding the weak, the ineffectual, or the evil, populate Singer's recent book of stories, ***The Séance.*** The mythic has not been lost; rather, it has been expanded, becomes synthesized with reality. As a result, these later stories have a more contemporary tone. They are not so obviously tales as stories about people. And because the world's evil and men's passions and rebuttals have become more closely allied with their actions, rather than set off in dialectical arrangements with the devil, Singer's stories now show a closer resemblance to those of Hawthorne. For while Singer has always been the more contemporary of the two, he now tends to use Satan as an idea or symbol, as Hawthorne did, rather than as an actual adversary.

Singer seems to be asking: How does man live with the destructive elements around him, as well as with his own evil tendencies?

In the title story, **"The Séance,"** Dr. Kalisher, an aging intellectual and refugee in New York in 1946, tries to recover for himself the pivot of intellectual commitment and love from which the Nazis have unhinged him. His family and mistress are gone; the philosophical system he had developed, one of "universal eroticism," seems inappropriate. . . . (pp. 364-66)

Mrs. Kopitzky, a middle-aged widow, is having a séance with Dr. Kalisher, who tolerates her mainly because he is in his sixties and poor and alone (she feeds him vegetarian dinners). But he cannot accept her mediumistic prophecies and manifestations any more than he can believe in his now ineffectual philosophy. A weary man with a mortifying physical disability, he lives a life without meaning or hope, devoid of any connections save this one with a woman wrapped lightly in the occult, a woman who is fundamentally a good Jewish mother type looking for a man to fit her dead husband's clothes. The irony here is that Dr. Kalisher the truth-seeker should dwindle into the role of a comfort-seeker, that though her spiritualism is obviously a game to him, he goes along with it.

Mrs. Kopitzky's transparent séances, her deceptive devices for materializing Kalisher's former mistress, disgust him; he longs to escape her spiritual pretensions. She has not reached the other side any more than he has been able to construct a philosophical system that would convey him through the terrors of bodily degradation and decay. But because of his disability he cannot escape her ministrations and becomes as helpless as an infant. Is this perhaps his punishment for having proceeded from a belief in reason to an involvement with the Cabala and the unconscious? Surely Mrs. Kopitzky's séances represent a vulgarization of his own theme, and when she says, "We live and love forever," she is simplifying and distorting his attempts to find a meaningful pattern in life. The significant thing here is that nothing works. The essence of his life has perished and he cannot restore it. Satan, history, illness, old age—all the adversaries of the spirit—have defeated him. Yet illusions persist, perhaps in the guise of Mrs. Kopitzky herself, who represents the false hopes, the seductions, the easy answers of Satan. (pp. 366-67)

The battle between good and evil persists in **"The Dead Fiddler,"** in which one *dybbuk,* then two, inhabit the body of a beautiful young girl, Liebe Yentl. But Liebe Yentl is not any young girl. Like other doomed heroines of Singer she is interested not in household matters but in reading novels and writing. She also has uncommonly long red hair and loves fine clothes. Such characteristics make her easily accessible to a blasphemous, foul-mouthed dead fiddler who takes over her body—which is later inhabited by a dead whore as well. But then, Liebe Yentl's head has always been "full of whims and fancies."

The irreverent, cursing, brandy-swigging spirits, who not only revile the townspeople but each other as well, mock all attempts at exorcism. Though they go as far as to marry within the girl's body, they will not leave until Liebe Yentl's father promises to pray for their souls—an ironic touch.

Still, the damned are the damned, and long after Liebe Yentl is rid of the *dybbuks,* she withdraws from the society of the town, gives up all religious observances, and plays with cats. Eventually, she is glimpsed walking barefoot in the cemetery, hand in hand with a man carrying a violin case. This is of course an apparition; she has died. But the implications are clear. Her preferences are known. There was no need to designate the presence of Satan. . . . (p. 368)

Those who pursue the mystical, the Cabala, the occult, who

seek forbidden knowledge, are of special interest to Singer, who indicates that they put themselves in jeopardy by looking beyond the façade of reality. (pp. 368-69)

In still another story, **"Henne Fire,"** Singer starts out with, "Yes, there are people who are demons." Here Satan is not even needed in the role of seducer. The inevitable has occurred; a demon lives among mortals and causes destruction through her own fiery nature. Fires spring up spontaneously around her; she is venomous and wishes to be nothing else. Kindness has no effect on her. When she dies it is because an inner fire burns her to a crisp. Here is evil (or is it individuality?) that prefers to remain intact and unrepentant, not misanthropic like the reticent character of Hawthorne, but vivaciously malignant to the end.

Or we can take **"Two Corpses Go Dancing,"** in which Satan, as in other stories of Singer's, is the narrator; but again it is Satan with Singer's sense of humor, the practical joker who plays a grisly game, reviving two corpses who do not know they are corpses, and who go through a macabre charade of courtship and marriage that at the moment of consummation sinks into the grave. If this is allegory, as it seems to be, it marks another resemblance to Hawthorne. (p. 369)

For Singer, evil continues to be a recognizable force in the world and Satan a deft and clever adversary whose tantalizing ways do not even cease when life ceases. Living or dead, men are full of absurd desires that end only in Hell; even virtue itself is a luxury for which man pays. . . .

For Hawthorne, individual integrity, whether inspired by Satan or not, may condemn a man to the hell of isolation, but for Singer the only way to live is through integration with the community. It is Satan who lures one outside, and outside there is only Hell. It is fitting, therefore, that Hawthorne's Satan should arise from within man or remain an imagined tendency, a primitive instinct; but Singer's Satan, though he may have become invisible, is still potent enough to have a voice, the ability to act and confuse. Within man or without, he remains a power to be contended with, an emissary of evil, constantly trapping men and women with evanescent inducements. (p. 370)

Elaine Gottlieb, "Singer and Hawthorne: A Prevalence of Satan," in The Southern Review, *Louisiana State University, n.s. Vol. VII, No. 2, April, 1970, pp. 359-70.*

EDWIN GITTLEMAN (essay date 1973)

[*Gittleman is an American critic specializing in the works of Ralph Waldo Emerson and the Transcendentalists. In the following excerpt, Gittleman traces the parameters of Singer's fictional world and defines his chief mode of narrative as non-dramatic, while identifying "the process of telling" as his fiction's primary motif.*]

Publication of Isaac Bashevis Singer's fifth collection of stories in English, ***A Friend of Kafka,*** makes conveniently available twenty-one recent stories by America's most formidable writer of short fiction. Therefore it is a welcome event. But it is a significant one as well. This book amplifies the displacements of consciousness and sensibility which are to be found in Singer's earlier books, and which more than anything else provide the distinctive literary and personal qualities defining him as a writer. Individually and as a collection, the new stories extend the displacements far beyond the experience of the provincial Jewish village of East Europe (the *shtetl*) and the great East European city (Warsaw) in which they originate. ***A Friend of Kafka*** is Singer's most American book. Consequently it calls attention not only to itself but also the fifty-five other impressive stories Singer has published in book form, beginning with ***Gimpel the Fool*** and followed by ***The Spinoza of Market Street, Short Friday,*** and ***The Séance.*** And thus, as never before the reader is forced to confront the baffling literary intelligence responsible for this entire corpus of short fiction.

Non-dramatic narrative is the characteristic mode Isaac Bashevis Singer has developed for his short stories. It was perfected as early as 1933 while he was writing *Satan in Goray,* the protonovelistic fiction which remains his most impressive single book and the work from which his subsequent art of short story derives. Its usual and most interesting form might well be called that of story-as-information since his narrative strategy requires that stories be a telling of a special fictional kind of fact and for a special fictional purpose. As in *Satan in Goray,* what is told purports to be extracted from memories of the past, understood as communal Yiddish culture of the *shtetl* (even for stories not set in Europe) interacting with private history and psychology, and recoverable by a brooding imagination which swiftly and aggressively structures remembered facts. For this reason the narrative pasttenses in his most powerful writing are not so much conventional or convenient as necessary and accurate. The past itself is a current event. It is alive and accessible, more so than the present moment. For Singer nothing significant is possible in the ill-defined present (or future) except the act of telling; everything significant is possible in the cultural-historical-psychological past.

In these non-dramatic narratives the present has no validity. Nothing actually happens or can happen on the level of present experience except the act of recall. The process of telling therefore is the primary reality which defines Singer's short fiction. The authority of the past is such that it either blocks the present or uses it only as the oral space needed for releasing what has been internalized in consciousness and therefore stands urgently in need of utterance. The single function the present can perform for Singer is thus occasional, providing him with opportunities for in-formed recitation.

Geographical places mentioned in Singer's stories, for example, are invariably authentic and locatable on appropriate maps, usually old maps of Poland. These places, which have no present or future meaning, only a significance which is past, are not so much depicted as they are casually named without further identification: Frampol, Krashnik, Yanev, Turbin, Bilgoray, Malopol, or dozens of other such strange-sounding places turning up in Singer's stories. They are cited as if the confident act of naming is sufficient to make the once-known again familiar. By contrast, however, the specific locale for a story acquires its unique identity in a named town by being painstakingly enumerated. . . . Incantational enumeration is the characteristic act by which a Singer story becomes specifically located in the limited geographical space reserved for it. Contained by the past more than by town limits, the locale too—with its alien vegetation and morbid household staples—becomes a matter of fact, however outrageous it might otherwise seem. The past can make anything comprehensible, especially if it is unnerving and disquieting.

In such regions of detailed finiteness which Singer's imagination for the past penetrates—where space is marginal, nonessentials crowded out, the air claustrophobic, and the mood ominous—it is fitting that shadings of light and dark are not at all visible to the reader, certainly not as qualities glancing off the surfaces of things. Rather, they are precisely recalled and distinguishable absolutes whose values are psychological and eschatological. . . . (pp. 248-51)

Nor are ordinary colors shown; instead, when they occur (which is not often in an essentially chiaroscuro atmosphere), they are specified without subtle gradations of tone: "Although yellow hair does not readily change color, Abba's beard had turned completely white, and the white, staining, had turned yellow again." And consistent with the peculiar nature of space and the erratic conditions of light and color, Singerian time does not elapse or have significant duration. . . . Within such a system of fictional coordinates—where experience as we know it is absent or else distorted by compression—it is natural that characters do not develop under the pressures of experience; rather, like towns, places, shading, color, and time, they are fixed by the very process of being mentioned. . . . Accordingly, while character is controlled, emotions cannot be expressed. . . . (pp. 251-52)

In a fictional system in which experience is structured like this, where the voice telling of the past possesses the only available reality, nothing can happen. Events cannot possibly occur. They can only be reviewed. . . . If human situations are not generated by the interactions between character and circumstance in Singer's fiction, then they are formulated by the act of narration itself. . . . The values of the narrative voice alone determine the directions the story will take.

The world evoked in Singer's short stories is therefore a problematical one. But it was not a world without recurring patterns of fact and circumstance which provide laws natural to it: longsuffering old men who reject Satan's irrefutable arguments against God are miraculously capable of engendering children; ambitious women who undertake work, learning, or forms of piety traditionally reserved for men eventually commit monstrous crimes; yellow-haired men with bulging temples are either simpletons or eunuchs; pretty daughters of wealthy fathers marry unhappily and consort with demons; pious rabbis confirm their faith by temporarily abandoning their faith and their faithful followers; queer old women living alone beyond village limits are malicious daughters of Lilith whose rewards will come in Gehenna; hardworking but impoverished shopkeepers and artisans become saints if they are faithful and uneducated or inept; brilliantly intellectual women acquire sexual passions which prove disastrous; common family tragedies undermine belief in God by those who are most pious; virtuous spinsters who eventually marry risk discovering that their bridegrooms are repulsive demons with webbed feet; scholarly writers and learned rabbis are the men most likely to accept Satan's intellectualized skepticisms; anger may condense into fires literally capable of burning houses; mischievous tricks turn out to have deadly effects; modest women who would repeal the sexual advances of ordinary men accept lovers claiming to be demons; superbly efficient servants destroy the happiness of their prosperous masters; and evil spirits, including Satan, frequently commune with Singer's readers because the agents of darkness (and the Wicked One himself) are not only convincingly articulate but magnificent story-tellers as well.

Because of the persistence of the narrative voice, and the responsibilities assigned it by Singer—rendering the past by naming places, enumerating locales, recalling conditions of light and dark, specifying colors, disconnecting time, determining character, describing emotion, reviewing events, and formulating situations—the narrative voice exercises an authority which subordinates all other voices in the stories. It is, after all, the primary means of control in the fiction. Consequently, conversation is never directly heard by the reader, although in his presence it is recollected for him between quotation marks. . . . Heard in dialogue are therefore actually skillful modulations of the narrative. Similarly, nonverbal sounds are not uttered, they are offered to the reader as a series of reports. . . . (pp. 253-55)

Except for the shifting cadences of the narrative voice which determine and sustain the various components of story, actions do not happen in Singer's short fiction; actions there can only be recalled. . . . And gestures do not have the status of motions but function as indications of the controlling intelligence embodied in the narrative. . . .

Like actions and gestures, objects are never presented with an authenticity or immediacy equal to those of the narrative itself. The characteristic form in which objects are recalled is that of a self-consciously recited catalogue. . . . (p. 256)

As a consequence of the force of the narrative voice and its dominant role in the fiction, life in the Singerian village or city is never dramatized or enacted. It is, however, always recorded as data. . . . Within limits imposed by the manner of telling, the reader may hear (or overhear) Singer's stories, but the lives and experiences with which they concern themselves can never be witnessed or envisioned by the reader. The stories can never transcend their status as verbal constructs. They remain *something told.*

Singer's narrative method is of course anti-mimetic in form and perverse in effect. While the mode of narration increases the formal distance separating the reader-listener from the substance of the narrative, it nevertheless creates an intimacy between narrative voice and reader. Each is engaged in a reciprocal transaction which defines the other's role. But it is a dangerous intimacy. In effect, the narrative voice aggressively invades the consciousness of the reader and struggles to control it. An alien presence whose revelations resist being confirmed by the reader's own experience, the narrative voice nevertheless has succeeded in dramatizing and enacting the one basic experience which makes Singer's aural act of the short story possible: the reader, while reading, is—without understanding it at the time—possessed by a *dybbuk.*

According to Jewish folklore, a dybbuk is an aberrant supernatural being, either a demon (perhaps even Satan himself) or the wicked spirit of a dead person, who wanders about in search of a living human body to inhabit. Finding it, the dybbuk is manifested as a terrible voice speaking what ought not be said and causing its unfortunate victim to act in uncharacteristic ways which others consider shocking. . . . A perverse spirit compulsive about its perversity, the dybbuk relentlessly disorients the victim harboring it, and threatens the stability of the community to which he belongs. Exorcism, which may result in the death of the host, is the only way for this dangerous phenomenon to be dealth with. . . . Dybbuks, in the short stories of Singer, are as folk tradition describes them: unwilling brides are possessed by them on their wedding night; bright young men studying sacred books abandon their faith because of them; sexual frustrations and domestic tensions are explosively released by them; entire communities are destroyed by them; and, on behalf of God and righteousness, pious old rabbis painfully struggle against them. But for Singer they are much more besides.

In addition to being an alien will seizing control of an innocent body—and thus a convenient means of showing how religious faith is lost, present values repudiated, and sins committed—and an obvious demonstration of schizophrenia and paranoia in a pre-Freudian world, the dybbuk is a convention full of meaning. For Singer, it is a complex variety of revenant which discloses itself in many subtle ways. "I am possessed by my demons," he once said, and they are largely responsible for "my vision and my expression."

The dybbuk is the disembodied past recklessly returning and seeking ways of preserving itself. It is memory intent upon being articulated and gaining validation. It is personal assertiveness in conflict with orthodox styles of behavior. It is history depriving the present of its claim to a secret destiny of its own. It is old guilt confirming new guilt. It is the surfacing of dangerous thoughts during solitary moments. It is consciousness in quest of form. It is the demonic vision-giving spirit which is responsible for fiction. And, not least significantly, because it is all of these it is also the expressive story-telling voice which can tolerate neither its own silence nor the talk of others, and which therefore struggles to take possession of the conciousness of Singer's unwary reader.

The narrative voice heard in Singer's five collections of stories—whether the teller is unidentified, an old woman, a male gossip, the young son of a rabbi, an imp whose power admittedly resides in his tongue, a Hasid or Misnagid, a credulous fool, an infernal demon, a self-confessed dybbuk, or even Satan himself—is constant and dybbukian: nervously energetic, short-breathed, obsessed with detail, colloquial, limited in understanding, unanalytical, reluctant to make any but conventional moral assessments, possessing an orthodox Jewish memory derived from the communal experience of East Europe, and totally committed to telling. This dybbuk-narrator, whoever he purports to be, commands the reader's attention, insistently using inscrutable facts as instruments of his sauntering authority. He is determined to make the reader become a victim of his dybbukian beliefs and knowledge, imposing upon the consciousness of the reader customs and events foreign to the reader's experience and sense of possibilities.

The reader is neither encouraged nor permitted to willingly suspend disbelief; instead he is deprived forcibly of his own original memory. He is under compulsion to adopt strange assumptions and new beliefs—those of the dybbuk-narrator—in miracle-working rabbis, the imminence of the end of the world, the ritual need to wear prayer shawls and phylacteries, the reality of imps twisting with iron pincers the nipples of women condemned to spend a year in Gehenna before entering Heaven, the reverence owed members of certain renowned rabbinic dynasties, observing the Sabbath as a ceremonial act of joy, the efficacies of witchcraft, the practice of ritual bathing for purposes of spiritual purification, the values of studying Cabala in addition to Pentateuch and Talmud, the usefulness of learning elaborate demonologies, and belief in other such archaisms associated with so-called unenlightened, pre-modern Jewishness.

The function of the reader-listener is therefore only to receive the detached, self-sustaining will of the dybbuk-narrator. In need of a consciousness to possess which can give it effective form, the voice creates its victim, forcing the reader-listener to surrender his own personality and identity, displacing him and disorienting him, depriving him of the power of choice, causing him to experience (in psychological terms) the control being exercised over him, and forcing him to undergo an abstract equivalent of the suffering which is nearly pervasive in the stories told.

In effect, then, given the values which underlie the fiction—as distinct from those which underlie the telling—this is the means by which the humanity of Singer's audience is directly affirmed. He humanizes his readers. For behind the world of Singer's short stories is the conviction that to be human is to be either possessed by a dybbuk or to be exposed to the threat of such possession. However, to be dybbuk-proof, to be exempt from the risk of being possessed by alien power, is to be de-humanized. It is to *be* a dybbuk. But Singer protects his readers against this possibility. Just as he sees the interactions between victims (realized and potential) and victimizers accounting for all of human history, so he enables his readers to participate as innocents in that universal destiny.

In Singer's short stories characters are functionally defined as victims, conceived for the purpose of being tormented either by men or by demons. Passions move them, madness moves them, custom moves them, obsessions move them, reverence moves them, diabolical urges move them, but never the freedom of their own choosing wills. Says one of the narrators, an old gossip: "It is written somewhere that every man is followed by devils—a thousand on the left and ten thousand on the right." (Singer's readers know where that is written—on the pages of his short stories.) If not all his characters are afflicted, this is not so much a function of special grace as it is of the limitations of art and the measured powers at work in the world. Exemption from suffering, when it occurs, is simply an accident of time. The danger remains. To be human is to risk disaster. Given enough writing space, Singer would eventually, in one story or another as yet unwritten, imaginatively remember one which a dybbuk could tell, of every person's encounter with suffering caused by alien power. In Singer's vision, victimage is the universal human destiny and the narrative voice its agent.

This, after all, is the meaning of Singer's stories, if indeed they have any single meaning: suffering is universal; and when joy exists (as infrequently it does), it exists only by virtue of the belief that suffering—as something endured and experienced as real, even though undeserved—is the ultimate confirmation that God exists; and therefore the memory of it is itself mysteriously meaningful, however irrational.

If to be *possessed* is human, then to be *in possession of* is dybbukian. To be a dybbuk is to appropriate form which is not one's own, and to master it by employing words as instruments of control; it is also to remember so strenuously that repose may be found only by putting the past to present use through force of language. The implications of this are clear: to be a literary artist, and especially a writer of fiction, is morally dangerous.

"When people have extreme power over other people," Singer has said, "it's a terrible thing. I always pray to God . . . don't give me any power over any other human beings. I have always avoided this kind of power like the plague." Therefore the rationale for the mode of non-dramatic narrative: a surrogate voice assumes responsibility for both stories and their effect upon readers. It protects Singer by relieving him of moral responsibility for victimage, while at the same time permitting him to continue exercising the kind of control an artist must. He is possessed by his own demons, Singer has said. Not surprisingly then, since he is a writer of both novels and short stories, he has also been reported to have once said: "In a short work you can concentrate on quality. In a large novel, you give only essentials. In short stories you elaborate. . . . It is true that your control cannot be perfect . . . in a novel, only in a short story." Accordingly, by Singer's own admission, his five collections of stories are the best index of his literary art. There his perfect control is elaborated.

But Isaac Bashevis Singer is not the only one moved by the desire to tell stories and to tell them well. All good stories must end, and by bringing his stories to their necessary conclusions, the dybbuk-narrator repeatedly effects his own exorcism. Since words are the sources of his power, the silence which punctuates the cessation of story-telling devastates him. Or rather, it brings about his release, discharging him to wander without form until Singer's next need to protect himself against his own artistry.

It is not accident that allows terminal silence to drive the dybbuk-narrator out of the reader's consciousness, restoring the reader to a more familiar world. For silence is sacred in Singer's scheme of values. It is sacred because it is understood by him as a Divine quality. God Himself is always silent, remaining outside the limits of narrative (just as He is absent from everyday life) and always invisible. Because it exists, His silence complements human suffering as confirmation of His existence. And Singer, too, creative artist that he also is, remains silent in the stories (as he never does in an everyday life filled with interviews, conferences, and university lectures), standing mute and invisible outside the narrative, while the dybbuk-narrator slowly detaches himself by bringing his story-telling to a reluctant close.

Most, but not all of Singer's stories have distinctive narrative dynamics conforming to the dybbukian *shtetl*-Warsaw model which has been described. The significant variation on these patterns of method and meaning is found in what may be called *new-world* stories, of which fourteen have been collected. Nine are concentrated in ***A Friend of Kafka,*** giving it special status as a Singer book; the rest are scattered casually in two collections, ***Short Friday*** and ***The Séance.***

Although set in the United States (all but one in New York City) except for one each in Canada, Argentina, and Israel, the new-world stories are formally distinguished less by geographical fact or matters of culture than by a relationship to memory and the past which is different from that in Singer's other stories: in them the terms of non-dramatic narrative and story-as-information break down.

In an important sense, all of Singer's stories are American stories, regardless of setting or form. They are American by virtue of having been written in the United States as a response to experience in America. By emigrating to New York City from Poland in 1935, Singer made his perceptions of Jewish life in East Europe available in the United States. Translated into English from Yiddish under his supervision, and in recent years by himself with assistance from others, Singer's stories have appeared in such magazines as *The New Yorker, Esquire, Harper's, Cosmopolitan, Partisan Review, Commentary,* and *Playboy.* Consequently, all of his stories are literally products of his American experience, and have become part of our own. But only the new-world stories, with their meaningful deviations from the narrative structures found in the other stories, betray formal indications of the severe cultural shocks Singer suffered by being detached from the old-world sources of his memory and imagination. In them the dybbuk has wandered off from his customary narrative position.

Self-consciousness gives form to the new-world stories *qua* stories. They are aware of themselves as something to be read, not heard or overheard, and are aware of the presence of the reader as reader, not as listener or eavesdropping victim. Bound to its audience by literacy, the intelligence purporting to be responsible is *scribal.* It is a writerly sensibility which is prepared and eager to be absorbed by a complementary reading intelligence. Story-writing perspicuity therefore makes a narrative voice superfluous. . . . [At times] in new-world stories, the scribal authority is asserted by being suppressed, the narration trying but failing to conceal the figure of the writer who by inference is responsible for the story-as-writing.

But more often than not, the scribal authority is exposed at the outset, substituting for the dybbuk-narrator, trying to embody itself as a presence which will participate in the action rather than control it. . . . (pp. 257-65)

Whether hidden or revealed, this scribal intelligence exists on the same reality-plane as the stories he writes and the situations he writes about. Of course, only a fictional creation which chronicles versions of whatever purports to be witnessed and heard, the putative scribe is a sensation-seeking *persona* distilled from Singer's experience in New York, designed to protect Singer's private sense of himself while he publicly reconstructs memories. Appearing personally interested while actually aloof, inviting confessions for the sake of possible stories, exposing the emotions of others while restraining his own, the scribe takes form and comfort in sharing with a reader the superficial reminiscences and confidences he has received.

The scribal stories are contrived, diffuse, and theatrical rather than dramatic. Nevertheless, when characters speak (even in long operatic monologues), voices are heard. And that is where the missing dybbuk has concealed himself—not in the inscribed confessions but in the confessional urges prompting them. Of this the scribe is seemingly unaware.

They are the as yet unarticulated urges of old-world victims who have been transported into an alien new world: people whose endurance continues to be strained by the unfamiliar pressures of the refuge into which they have escaped; crippled people, impoverished people, and demoralized people; people haunted by recollections of other-worldly experiences; people seeking escape from the past by ignoring the present and imagining the future; extrasensory people convinced that their lives involve astral bodies, telepathy, telekinesis, and other dubious varieties of the supernatural; people scarred by the knowledge of German extermination camps; pathetic old women trying futilely to disguise the past by heavy applications of cosmetic rouge and nail lacquer; hemorrhoidal old men with prostate disorders straining to conceal pain and shame; people who have sacrificed old-world pieties and customs in a feeble attempt to engender new lives; and people so fearful of a strange American culture that they turn inward upon their memories. Singer has identified them all. But the scribal intelligence invariably betrays them.

In them, in their ill-defined consciousness—not in the new-world stories in which they are marginally contained—is located the displaced dybbuk. Too remote from readers to have any humanizing effect upon them, the dybbuk nevertheless continues to work away mysteriously on the old-world victims, outside the stories and independently of the cheap sensationalism of the new-world scribe. But being incapable of honest self-scrutiny, the scribe cannot comprehend this. . . . His heroism is suspect. This scribe need not fear any cosmic disaster befalling him, only self-deception. Believing himself dybbuk-proof, he is less than human and insensitive to the dybbuks in others.

In a universe of suffering, the new world is a life full of the Mystery which is freedom, a life which remains even after victimization and defeats. This Singer understands. However, *Satan in Gotham* (a hypothetical new-world counterpart to *Satan in Goray*) is as yet unwritten; and the authentic new-world stories, which will derive from it, await its publication. Isaac Bashevis Singer may have become his own translator, but so far he has failed to imaginatively remember the new-world forms and new-world vocabulary into which dybbukianism may be translated. (pp. 266-68)

Edwin Gittleman, "Dybbukianism: The Meaning of Method in Singer's Short Stories," in Contemporary American-Jewish Literature: Critical Essays, *edited by Irving Malin, Indiana University Press, 1973, pp. 248-69.*

SYLVIA ROTHCHILD (essay date 1974)

[Rothchild is an American writer and journalist who often focuses in her works on the Jewish experience in America. In the following review of A Crown of Feathers, and Other Stories, *Rothchild assesses Singer's position as a Jewish writer wavering between attitudes of faith and skepticism.]*

The stories [in ***A Crown of Feathers, and Other Stories***] are new variations on old themes, set in the United States as well as in pre-Hitler Poland. A new generation and new cities cannot, however, alter the fate of [Singer's] pietists and charlatans. Singer's obsession with ghosts and demons seems less old-fashioned than it used to. It is easy to share his astonishment at the nature of man. "Things happen in life so fantastic that no imagination could have invented them," is a line from one of his autobiographical sketches in the collection, *In My Father's Court.* In **"The Cabalist Of East Broadway,"** a story in the new volume, the effort to explain the hero's behavior ends with the conclusion that "Man does not live according to reason." **["A Crown of Feathers"]** ends with, "if there is such a thing as truth it is as intricate and hidden as a crown of feathers."

Singer's heroes are often writers, scholars and businessmen who are overwhelmed by a universe that is "one big contradiction." Without inner certainty they move from one folly and temptation to the next. Their efforts to sin beyond their capabilities end in suicide. In **"The Bishop's Robe,"** Jacob Getzelles, ordained rabbi, editor and Hebrew teacher marries a wild woman, gets involved with witchcraft and ends up passively accepting his wife's decision that they turn on the gas. **"The Prodigy,"** another version of the same story, describes the spoiling of a genius. His dabbling with spirits and orgies comes to an end when he puts a bullet through his head. In both stories, the path to the devil includes homosexual episodes and the temptations of demonic women. The demons that lived behind the stove in one generation inhabit the people themselves in the next.

Bashevis Singer's characters live either in that claustrophobic hothouse of East European piety or in extreme alternatives to it. He pits an ascetic student against a brothel keeper in **"The Blizzard."** More often he lets the battles rage in the psyche of a single individual. The totally pure become totally evil. The authentic rabbis turn into opportunistic frauds. Akhsa, the beautiful, wise and diligent heroine of **["A Crown of Feathers"]** is deceived by a crown of feathers. She listens to the spirit of her dead grandmother who urges her to do "Whatever your heart desires." This leads her to conversion, marriage with a dissolute nobleman and ultimately a pact with the devil. Her sins are so great that not even repentence can save her.

Though Singer is modern enough to cope with incest, androgyny, sexual perversion and wild orgies, he is not able to describe a woman who does not "shelter within herself devils, imps and goblins . . . the perversity so characteristic of the female's nature." With such prejudice as his foundation, he creates women who will do anything simply because they are by nature unreliable, devilish and destructive. His men are not much better but they can occasionally resist sin by immersing themselves in prayer and study.

But Singer's great gift as a storyteller entices the reader to suspend judgement and follow wherever he leads. There is a feeling of disappointment, however, when the journey has no purpose and one does not arrive at a destination. His best stories offer insights into the human situation rather than gratuitous magic or violence.

"The Son From America," for example, tells of the chasm that separated the Jews who remained in the sleepy villages of Eastern Europe from their relatives who went to New York or Warsaw. A devoted son who has sent his parents money every month for forty years finds when he comes to visit them that they have not spent a penny of it. They have a store of gold coins in a boot under the floor because there is nothing in the town to buy and not even a bank in which to save their treasure. "Thank God we have everything," says the old mother. A half acre field, a goat, a cow and some chickens provide all their needs. The son's gifts have no value. His plans for their dying village are foolish. Singer's description of the old pair, contented with the one room hut they share with their animals, suggests that they are in some way richer than their restless, striving son.

"Grandfather and Grandson" is a story that explores not only the differences between the generations but also the bonds that connect them. (pp. 110-11)

In, **"The Magazine," "A Day In Coney Island"** and **"The Captive,"** Singer offers portraits of writers who struggle with the fear that life has no meaning and yet fight death with the printed word. Some stories take place in some mythical olden time. Others have dates and places to anchor them. When the stories are read together, however, neither time nor place seem to matter. The anarchists, socialists and communists in the story **"Property"** are startingly like the radicals of the sixties. The certainty that "Property Is Theft," that jealousy is a feudal emotion and that a *ménage à trois* is a solution rather than another problem, recurs like a chronic disease. The young revolutionary who turns into the old Miami Beach landlord is familiar and believable.

Singer's stories remind us that the modern era began long before we were born. "A woman is just as entitled to enjoy herself as a man," says the young woman on the way to Zamosc in **"On A Wagon."** "The middle ages are over. It's the twentieth century and high time humanity became civilized." Her gossip and behavior shock the young husband who is also a passenger in the carriage. Upon learning that his wife is infatuated with a vulgar, uneducated barber, "He felt like a mourner. He had to sit shiva for his illusions." The Enlightenment deceived him. "He had to make a choice between God who may not exist and creatures as loathsome as that lecherous barber."

Singer, as writer, does not choose. He oscillates between his worlds. In some stories, he shows how dangerous it is to have faith in God or man and how those who wish for miracles are punished. In others, he shows how ugly and pointless life is without faith. At a time when everyone assumes that we cannot go home again, he persists in telling us that we have never left. Addresses and disguises change but the follies and contradictions remain. The conflict is presented not between what is old and what is new, but between what is the good and the evil inclination. Modern feminists are likely to take umbrage with Singer's penchant for turning that into the choice between the grandmother who says, "Do as your heart desires" and the grandfather who urges justice and obedience to the law.

Though Singer is no longer writing as the obvious moralist in **"Spinoza Of Market Street"** or **"The Magician,"** he still creates the images of Enlightenment and civilization in terms of false messiahs. Civilization arrives as temptation and disappointment. All striving for pleasure ends in pain, indignity and un-Jewishness. Though Singer seems to revel in tales of evil, it is the kind of wickedness that is measured against goodness. The tension that sustains the best stories come from this conflict. His affection for the fragile, rigid, pietists who cannot be transplanted or seduced persists in spite of his certainty that all faith is illusion and all miracles the work of the devil. He writes about lies but lies can only exist if there is such a thing as truth—which, in turn, he finds hard to discover and understand. But as Mrs. Pupko, the bearded lady in **"The Beard,"** says, "Nu, one mustn't know everything."

A universe full of contradictions and mysteries is likely to provide Isaac Bashevis Singer with variations for his old themes for the rest of his life. (pp. 111-12)

Sylvia Rothchild, "True Feathers," in Midstream, *Vol. XX, No. 7, August-September, 1974, pp. 110-12.*

WILLIAM PEDEN (essay date 1975)

[*Peden is an American critic who has written extensively on the American short story. In the following excerpt, he provides a general overview of Singer's short fiction, focusing on his blending of disparate elements, themes, and modes.*]

Whereas most of the leading American-born Jewish fiction writers share a concern with the role of the American Jew in contemporary American society, Singer, particularly in his earlier collections, was preoccupied with echoes of a Jewish past extending from prehistoric days when "time stands still . . . Adam remains naked, Eve lustful . . . Cain kills Abel, the flea lies with the elephant, the flood falls from heaven, the Jews knead clay in Egypt [and] Job scratches at his sore-covered body" to a European present. In his later collections, particularly ***A Friend of Kafka*** and ***A Crown of Feathers,*** he more frequently employs a contemporary American setting ("I have developed roots here," he says in the Author's Note to his most recent collection, but "just the same, my American stories deal only with Yiddish-speaking immigrants from Poland so as to ensure that I know well not only their present way of life but *their* roots—their culture, history, ways of thinking and expressing themselves.")

Regardless of their time and place, Singer's stories are an unforgettable blending of the old and the new, order and change, the ordinary, the spectral, and the surreal; they are a compound of a wild humor, unearthliness, and verisimilitude that can be as convincing as a Baedeker; they are constantly preoccupied with the gulfs and the bridges between illusions and reality. . . . Individually impressive, his stories in toto constitute a panorama of Jewish folklore, tradition, myth, and manners that on the one hand is haunted by the past, subject to the caprice of the occult, the spectral, and the demonic, and on the other alive with the sights and sounds of the late nineteenth and twentieth centuries, whether they emanate from a Warsaw soup kitchen or a cafeteria in Coney Island.

Among Singer's primarily realistic earlier stories are **"The Spinoza of Market Street,"** with its unforgettable portrayal of Dr. Nahum Fishelson, a Warsaw philosopher, and his marriage to the derelict food vendor, Black Dobbe, and consequent redemption as a human being, a vivid depiction of the contrast between the scientific, completely rational life and the emotional, personal urges of man; **"Caricature,"** another story of an elderly Warsaw philosopher and his wife during Hitler's rise to power; **"Gimpel the Fool,"** the story of the baker of Frampol and his whorish wife; and **"The Little Shoemaker,"** the family saga of Abba Shuster, the best shoemaker in Frampol.

At the other extreme are stories like **"The Black Wedding"** (my own personal favorite), **"A Tale of Two Liars," "The Destruction of Kreshev," "The Mirror," "Taibele and Her Demon," "Jachid and Jachida,"** and **"Blood,"** which range from the ghetto of Warsaw or the village of Krashnik to a region inhabited by incubi and succubi, imps, demons, and the Devil himself. These stories are vibrant with the high, singing poetry of the supernatural and the hallucinatory, piercing in their portrayal of crime and punishment, sin and redemption, and universal in their implications.

Contrast is central to the effect created by these strange and wonderful stories. Satan's comments on the depraved Schloimele (in **"The Destruction of Kreshev"**) sum up this aspect of Singer's esthetic:

> Those who understand the complexities of human nature know that joy and pain, ugliness and beauty, love and hate, mercy and cruelty and other conflicting emotions often blend and cannot be separated from each other. Thus I am able not only to make people turn away from the Creator, but to damage their own bodies, all in the name of some imaginary cause.

This strange world simply *is.* It is real and convincing in the same way that Rousseau's jungle paintings or Chagall's *Arabische Nächte* illustrations are real and convincing. In each case, the creator's vision is so complete, so whole, so harmonious within its own juxtaposition of opposites that only the irremediably literally minded individual questions the appearance of Yadwigha's comfortable bourgeois red sofa in the middle of a leafy jungle, or rejects Chagall's bemused and beautiful gold, pink, blue, and emerald-fleshed women, or bizarre, a-worldly animals, birds, and fish. So one accepts the hallucinated bride-to-be of Singer's **"The Black Wedding."** Hindele *knows* that the "fancy garments" of her attendants

> hid heads grown with elf-locks, goose-feet, unhuman navels, long snouts. The sashes of the young men were snakes in reality, their sable hats were actually hedgehogs, their beards clusters of worms. The men spoke Yiddish and sang familiar songs, but the noise they made was really the bellowing of oxen, the hissing of vipers, the howling of wolves. The musicians had tails, and horns grew from their heads. The maids who attended Hindele had canine paws, hoofs of calves, snouts of pigs. The wedding jester was all beard and tongue. The . . . relatives . . . were lions, bears, boars . . . Alas, this was not a human wedding, but a Black Wedding.

Similar juxtapositions characterize Singer's stories set in America or narrated by a Polish emigré in America from **"A Wedding in Brownsville"** (in ***Short Friday***) to more than half the twenty-four stories of ***A Crown of Feathers.*** The heroine of the title story becomes a pawn in a battle between supernatural forces; a chess prodigy insists on a medical examination to verify his bride's virginity; a once-beautiful and talented dancer is destroyed in the bombing of the Warsaw ghetto after a last mad, macabre dance with her son; the "cabalist of East Broadway" falls into a deadly melancholy after being forced to eat pork while hospitalized in a Colorado sanitarium; a marriage feast turns into an hallucinated nightmare.

For the most part, Singer's narrative method is conventional and traditional. Perhaps his favorite mode is the story within a story, often told by a character who is a projection of the storyteller himself. The narrator meets a friend or acquaintance who tells him a story about another friend or acquaintance. Singer's people are prodigious, insatiable, indomitable talkers; I often have the feeling that if the Big One is finally dropped, perhaps the last sound on our planet will be that of one of Singer's wonderful people, relating a tale of love, lust, betrayal, passion, demonic possession, madness, success, frustration, suicide. As is inevitable with this sort of narrative method, related events flow from past to present, time blurs, fuses, is telescoped or fantastically heightened and lengthened. Few authors can manipulate such sequences and time-wrenchings effectively. Singer can. From his earliest to his most recent fictions he is a masterly technician.

But perhaps the most remarkable element in so many of his stories is the presence—not the intrusion, but a kind of extra dimension, never obtrusive, never articulated, but always there—of the narrator himself: wise, witty, skeptical, compassionate, obsessed, emancipated, a kind of all-seeing I-Eye-Consciousness as old as the hills and as contemporary as today, a kaleidoscopic angle of vision alive with understanding and wisdom that continually illuminates his strange and often terrifying glimpses into the human condition. (pp. 129-32)

William Peden, "Oh, These Jews—These Jews! Their Feelings, Their Hearts!" in his The American Short Story: Continuity and Change, 1940-1975, *second edition, Houghton Mifflin Company, 1975, pp. 115-33.*

ALVIN H. ROSENFELD (essay date 1976)

[An American critic and editor, Rosenfeld has written numerous essays on American poetry, Jewish writers, and literature of the Holocaust. In the following excerpt, he discusses the role of dreams, imagination, illusion, and memory in Singer's work, particularly in his collection Passions, and Other Stories.]

Since Goncharov created his famous sedentary Oblomov, has there, in fact, been another writer as intent as Singer on portraying characters who inevitably drop to the mattress or couch, doze off into dreams or start up abruptly out of them? The question is not meant to imply that the Singer hero is typically a sluggard, for usually the reverse is true, yet in almost half of these stories [in ***Passions, and Other Stories***] we are given some version of life-abed. Here, for instance, from **"Old Love,"** is a representative—and revealing—passage:

> Harry Bendiner awoke at five with the feeling that as far as he was concerned the night was finished and he wouldn't get any more sleep. . . . He leaned his hand on the railing and tried to reconstruct the dream he had been having. . . . He closed his eyes for a moment. Why was it impossible to remember dreams? He could recall every detail of events that had happened seventy and even seventy-five years ago, but tonight's dreams dissolved like foam. Some force made sure that not a trace of them remained. A third of a person's life died before he went to his grave.

A large part of Singer's work might be read as an attempt to recover this lost life of dreams. "Lost is lost," speaks the Demon of Rationalism in the author's ear and, compounding this note of mournfulness and finality, History's Demon whispers fatalistically into the other. "Those who stood at the threshold of death remain dead." Yet a writer such as this one finds his way less with his ears than with his eyes and, as already suggested, Isaac Bashevis Singer's eyes seem to see things that the rest of us know too little of. In **"Sabbath in Portugal,"** a semi-autobiographical story, the author is asked, "Do you believe in the resurrection of the dead?" His reply: "They never died." The answer astonishes, not only us but, more crucially, the respondent. Yet such things happen and, as Singer says, they come "with the suddenness of a dream." He is willing to place considerable trust in these flash appearances of knowledge, so much so that, on one level, his stories might be understood as voyages back into the dream-state, a return to some preternatural gleam of understanding. Why travel that route to knowledge? Because "what a person really is comes out only at night, in the dark." Singer is such a night-time explorer, a prowler into the manifold sources of concealment, into the darker sides of dream, fantasy, passion, and imagination. (p. 59)

Singer, as surely everyone knows by now, is a gnostic writer, and one of the major sources of his *gnosis* is the dream. To emphasize and make unmistakable the relationship he sees between his writings and the dream-state, Singer has added a brief "Author's Note" to his [***Passions, and Other Stories***], in which he states: "In literature, as in our dreams, death does not exist." (p. 60)

Stories and dreams, we begin to see, are to Singer acts of psychic retrieval and restoration, overcomings of the psychology of loss. Not only do they not acknowledge death and dissolution, they gather up former significant experience into a new unity, reasserting for the present the fullest claims of the past.

In such a story as **"Two Markets,"** we witness the metamorphosis of Warsaw's old Krochmalna Street bazaar into Tel Aviv's present-day Carmel *shuk.* The same voices, the same odors, even some of the same merchants re-emerge from their distant Polish past, so that Singer is moved to declare: "I found myself both in old Warsaw and in Eretz Yisrael." The transformation may seem merely fanciful, but stories insist upon their own version of things—especially of *lost* things—and, even at the risk of credulity, these must finally prevail: "The critics would call it melodrama, but the truth is not ashamed of appearing contrived."

A recurring and by now familiar truth of Singer's fiction is that, whether it is set in New York or Miami, Buenos Aires or Tel Aviv, the place is always some version of Poland—that is to say, some version of Poland—that is to say, some version of the author's youth. Dream and memory carry him there; his stories of dream and memory carry *us* there. And lest the going appear too easy or artificial—a flight on the back of a magical goose—we are admonished to remember the major historical hurdle that necessarily must be leaped before any fictive recovery of the past is possible—"The whole Holocaust is tied up with amnesia."

Just how much of Singer's fiction is written to ward off that amnesia we cannot know for certain, but it is clear that the exercise of memory is a basic and continuing function of his work. He has already given us two full-scale novels of the Holocaust (I count *The Slave* as one, for although it is set in the immediate aftermath of the Chmielnicki massacres, it directs attention more readily to Jewish fate in the twentieth century than in the seventeenth; the other novel, of course, is *Enemies; A Love Story*) and several stories in previous collections. To these must now be added **"Hanka," "A Tale of Two Sisters,"** and **"A Pair,"** all of which take their major references from the Holocaust and should be read as part of the still-growing body of literature on that enormous tragedy. In a larger and somewhat more abstract sense, though, almost all of Singer's stories exist within this frame of reference, a fact that most readers implicitly recognize. For why else do we read him if not to renew contact with a life that has all but perished? As Isaac, the writer-protagonist of **"Hanka,"** cries out to the woman who stands as an emblematic figure of that vanished world, we recognize the echoes of a familiar yearning, one that cannot be denied because it is also our own:

> I was calling to Hanka, "Why did you run away? Wherever you are, come back. There can be no world without you. You are an eternal letter in God's scroll."

Hanka, "a fugitive and a wanderer," has her own yearnings—for reattachment to family, a bit of permanence, a measure of peace—all of which were destroyed in the war, when "the whole human culture crumbled like a ruin." Her fate is shared by the half-mad women of **"A Tale of Two Sisters,"** a story written against the Nietzschean theory of the eternal return. Why this philosopher as an antagonist? Because "if Nietzsche's crazy theory is true, . . . there'll be another Hitler, another Stalin, another Holocaust." Given that prospect, Singer passes an emphatically Jewish verdict against historical recurrence and its close corollary, *amor fati,* the affirmative acceptance of one's fate whatever it may be. In this case, and as a strong counterweight to some of Singer's tales of a dreamlike indulgence, it is impossible to hypnotize oneself "into thinking that the whole thing had been only a dream, [for] it really happened."

In both of these stories the women characters are especially prominent and resemble some late, near-exhausted version of *la belle dame sans merci,* the feminine embodiment of an enticing but destructive fatalism. Woman in this role is becoming an increasingly familiar type in recent fiction, where she seems to represent the close association of the ravishments of erotic imagination and a sense of a ravaged history, the spoliation of romance set against the more massive destructions and despoilments of recent history, especially the recent history of the Jews. Do these characters signify the end of the tradition of Romantic love, its dissipation and defeat by an excessive and hostile indulgence? Whatever explains them, and it is still a bit too soon to know, we find such deromanticized, death-chased representations of the feminine in recent books by Herbert Gold, Philip Roth, and Saul Bellow. Singer's version of her is Hanka, as memorable—and disturbing—a presence of the female angel of death as is to be found anywhere:

> I expected that I would have a short affair with Hanka. But when I tried to embrace her she seemed to shrink in my arms. I kissed her and her lips were cold. She said, "I can understand you—you are a man. You will find plenty of women here if you look for them. You will find them even if you don't look. But you are a normal person, not a necrophile. I belong to an exterminated tribe and we are not material for sex."

Bella, the ugly and repulsive girl in **"The Witch,"** does offer herself as material for sex, and although she is at first an unlikely candidate for passion, she proves herself more than a match for her lusting teacher. What is especially interesting about Bella—"a witch drenched in blood and semen, a monster that the rising sun transformed into a beauty"—is that she serves in a kind of Sabbatian mystery play, whose final act carries us through sexual striving to theological speculation: "Bella's face seemed to be bathed in blood. Clusters of fire ignited within her eyes. He stood by her, half naked, and they stared into a mirror. He said: 'If there is such a thing as black magic, maybe there is a God, too.' "

At such a moment we touch Singer's work at one of its most imaginative but also one of its most controversial points. Is it the case that, like Reb Meshulam, the defiler of **"Errors,"** he is in some sense "a secret follower of Sabbatai Zevi"? The question needs to be asked, not to accuse Singer of heresy (in our day the word, with no contemporary reference, has lost almost all of its meaning) but the better to understand the sources and intentions of his art. Clearly, Singer understands sexual passion as another source of *gnosis,* and he continues to explore the erotic life for whatever mysteries it may yet yield. In ***Passions*** (aptly named!) these involve some extraordinary sides of erotica—not only the by-now overly familiar forms of sadism and masochism, adulterous and polygamous love, but even an affair with a kind of female golem constructed with the aid of black magic by a lusting Polish squire (she turns out to be little more than wind and foam and is passed over for the pleasures provided by a gypsy woman of more common but more satisfying flesh and blood). Not far behind many of Singer's women is Lilith, or some similar she-demon from Jewish folklore, to dazzle and lead astray the unlucky quester after forbidden pleasures. The sense of the forbidden, it should be noted, remains strong in Singer's work, and interdictions of various kinds are observed in most of the stories, making Singer more of a shy and frustrated Sabbatian than a fulfilled one. That is as it must be, given the strong rabbinical background of his education but, even more important, that is as it must be given the still-lingering Romantic and gnostic cast of Singer's imagination. Lilith, like any muse, can stimulate only as long as she remains unviolated. To know her too completely would be to deplete her quickly; it is more important to maintain her as a *potential* paramour, seeing in her something that could not really be there, the "something," of course, to be added and savored in story and dream.

What is the *good* of such stories? Partly to show that "everything can become a passion, even serving God." That was Spinoza's proposition, which Singer has personally adopted and vividly transmitted in story after story. Consider Leib Belkes's passion—Leib Belkes (in the title story, **"Passions"**) who yearned so much for the Holy Land that he couldn't bear it any more and followed the running moon one star-lit night in Poland until he arrived in the land of Israel. "On foot?" "Yes, on foot." "But everyone knows that to get to the Holy Land one must travel by ship." "Stubbornness is a power . . .; when a man persists he can do things which one might think can never be done."

Herzl, another dreamer and teller of tales, spoke words similar to these and provoked similar disbelief, yet as a result of his stubborn vision the grandchildren of Leib Belkes can today freely follow their own passions in the land of Israel. One notable good of stories, therefore—*stories: the empowering of dreams by words*—is to implement yearning. Does this mean that one can foresee the future in a dream? Yes, at least certain dreamers can—those gifted enough to wed language to vision, say *and* see the ways of the prospective imagination.

Stories, though, as we know from reading Isaac Bashevis Singer, are also an exercise of the retrospective imagination, a preserver or curator of dreams. Elizabeth (in **"The Admirer"**), an ardent but anxious reader of Isaac's stories, pays him a visit, bringing with her a book—*The Revealer of Profundities*—that she cannot decipher, a book, as it turns out, written by their common ancestor. "What kind of profundities did he reveal?" she asks. "That no love of any kind is lost," Isaac replies, although he has never read a word of this book. "Does he say where all the loves, all the dreams, all the desires go?" "They're somewhere," he replies evasively. And she, persistently and with a note of challenge in her voice, "Where? In the profundities?"

At which point we allow ourselves a reader's privilege of interrupting the narrative to offer an answer, the only one, but the one that Singer himself, as author, cannot give: the lost loves go into *stories,* where they mingle with lost dreams and current desires and re-emerge to reward the yearnings we all have for reattachment and immortality. On the level of passion, then, which has its own logic, Singer is surely right: the dead have not died but merely crossed a threshold that separates life from literature, the waking from the dreaming state. (pp. 60-2)

Another good of stories, therefore, is to remind us of that threshold and, from time to time, to reveal some of its crossing points, both to remember what has perished and to recall what lingers on. If the future is a fiction capable of being dreamed into present truth, the past is no less so. In both instances, stories—at least the stories of a master—point the way.

But who is it, anyway, who demands to know what the good of stories is? Why, Tante Yentl, herself a story-teller, one of the familiar narrators of Singer's own tales. Yentl, like all incorrigible talkers something of a scold and a provocateur, chides the young Isaac (in **"The Gravedigger"**) to leave off stories and to "go and study the Ethics of the Fathers." "Later," he replies, for he would rather hear another story. But Tante Yentl is done, at least for now, and sends him off, although not without first giving him, her youthful apprentice in the arts of satisfying, "a cookie and a Sabbath fruit." And she—where will she go as he goes off with his prize? Why, she will go where story-tellers always go to take calculation of their souls and to replenish themselves: "I am going to lie down. . . ." (pp. 62-3)

Alvin H. Rosenfeld, "I. B. Singer: The Good of Stories," in Midstream, *Vol. XXII, No. 5, May, 1976, pp. 59-63.*

SOL GITTLEMAN (essay date 1978)

[*In the following analysis of Singer's short story "The Little Shoemakers," Gittleman examines Singer's portrait of the waning Jewish way of life in the European* shtetl *and his representation of the Jewish immigrant experience in the United States.*]

"The Little Shoemakers" is a story of the transition of Jews from Europe to America; it is hopelessly sentimental, and at the same time an accurate measurement of the hopes and dreams of the Jew who has created a new *shtetl* for himself on the lower end of Manhattan Island. Even more significant, it clearly shows the disintegration of the European *shtetl* at the very last moment of its existence, as Hitler's hordes were sweeping over Poland.

While a short story, Singer's tale has a distinctly epochal flavor. It is the history of many generations of the Shuster family, shoemakers who came to Frampol at the time of the Chmielnitski massacres of 1648. For two hundred and fifty years, the Shusters of Frampol made good shoes, lived the lives of pious men and women, and bore generations of sturdy children, mostly boys. Toward the end of the nineteenth century, the patriarch of the family is Abba Shuster, named for the founder, a man of tradition, good, kind, and possessing all the nobility of his world. As he grows old, he looks around, sees his seven fine sons, and is satisfied with his life: "No, this was good enough for Abba Shuster. There was nothing to change. Let everything stand as it had stood for ages, until he lived out his allotted time and was buried in the cemetery among his ancestors, who had shod the sacred community and whose good name was preserved not only in Frampol but in the surrounding district."

One can only imagine the shock and disbelief when his eldest son Gimpel announces that he is going to America. Abba's reply perfectly reflects the attitude of his generation. "What happened? Did you rob someone? Did you get into a fight?" For the Jews of Poland, not living under the yoke of Czarist oppression, life could be modestly pleasant, and the Shuster family had made, for them, an acceptable adjustment to centuries in a land which they no longer viewed as adopted. Poland was home, the ancestral country of their origin. Abba could not understand why anyone would want to leave. When Gimpel gives as a reason the fact that he has no future, the father replies: "Why not? You know a trade. God willing, you'll marry someday. You have everything to look forward to." What follows is a totally different perception of *shtetl* life, one seen from the perspective of those willing to go, to pull up roots and leave. There is no hint of romanticism, of the later nostalgia. Gimpel's outburst represents a picture of *shtetl* life stripped of any positive feature:

> The boy spoke up, but Abba couldn't understand a word of it. He laid into synagogue and state with such venom, Abba could only imagine that the poor soul was possessed: the Hebrew teachers beat the children, the women empty their slop pails right outside the door, the shopkeepers loiter in the streets, there are no toilets anywhere and the public relieves itself as it pleases, behind the bathhouse or out in the open, encouraging epidemics and plagues. He made fun of Ezreal the healer and of Mecheles the marriage broker, nor did he spare the rabbinical court and the bath attendant, the washerwoman and the overseer of the poorhouse, the professions and the benevolent societies.

Here is an indictment which leaves no hope of improvement; the only way out is to abandon, and Gimpel leaves home. Abba sees a train for the first time when he takes his son to the station in the next town. "He took the headlights of the locomotive for the eyes of a hideous devil." As the boy leaves, Abba cries after him: "Don't forsake your religion!" Of course, Abba is convinced that his son will now fall away from Judaism, so he is thoroughly relieved when a letter arrives after a few months, chronicling the illegal border crossing, a four-week ocean voyage, and the first sights of New York. In the letter Singer symbolically joins the two worlds for one final moment, the superstition and unchanging medievalism of the past—Gimpel writes that he had seen no mermaids or mermen and had not heard them singing—with the image of the free Jew—"The Gentiles speak English. No one walks with his eyes on the ground, everybody holds his head high." Gimpel is already showing the signs of belonging, of identifying with the pride and energy of the immigrant in America. Furthermore, he is quickly losing the image of "the greenhorn," the newly arrived Jew who still carried with him the sartorial and linguistic baggage of the *shtetl.* He now wears a short coat (unlike the Hassidim), and he informs his father in this letter, written, of course, in Yiddish, that he is working as a shoemaker and is *all right.* The last phrase appears alien to Abba's eyes; it is written with the familiar Yiddish letters, that is, the Hebrew alphabet, but it makes no sense to him: what does *all right* mean in Yiddish? Obviously, it was a new kind of Yiddish, a Yiddish unfamiliar to Abba. Gimpel had become an *allrightnik,* a Jew from the *shtetl* who was making out in America, and who was quickly adding little touches of English to his native Yiddish.

In the next letter Gimpel informs his family that he has met a woman from Rumania named Bessie, and they are engaged. She works *at dresses.* Again the foreign phrase with the familiar alphabet. The third letter contains a picture of the wedding which must have been like thousands of similar photographs in Europe and America, which were placed on bureaus or forgotten in the corners of drawers for generations, to be dug out during the past few years as a wave of nostalgia swept America. "Abba could not believe it. His son was wearing a gentleman's coat and a high hat. The bride was dressed like a countess in a white dress, with train and veil; she held a bouquet of flowers in her hand." Gimpel is a participant in the great wave of immigration which produced similar wedding photographs, a world of two-dollar rentals for tuxedos and wedding gowns, of a new *yichus* and status, in terms that were distinctly American now.

Within a matter of a few months all of Abba's children come to America, and the children beg their father to join them, but his world is still Frampol, and he wishes to end his life there. His wife, the faithful Pesha (the perfect *shtetl* wife once again!) dies, and forty years go by. Abba is now an ancient relic; *shtetl* life has not disintegrated; it simply has been forgotten. He spends his time sitting at his wife's grave, reading letters from the children now grown to manhood. There are grandchildren, even great-grandchildren. The world apparently has passed Abba by, and he is quietly and contentedly waiting for his time.

But Abba did not reckon with Hitler's armies, and the modern world remembers the old man. Dive bombers suddenly (and most unlikely) attack Frampol, and Abba finds himself, with a few of his tools, on the road, a refugee. By the enormous effort of his sons, he is located, taken to Italy via Rumania, and sails on the last ship leaving for the United States. The crossing is a maze of images for the old, confused man, who is barely aware of his destination. As the ship docks at New York he is overwhelmed by boys, girls, men and women, talked to "in a strange language, which was both Yiddish and not Yiddish." In short, he had arrived.

Singer now will create a world of *naches* for the Jew in America, one still measured in terms of status, but a status distinctly of the American-Jewish experience. This is a story which the author writes with a specific audience in mind: that aging generation of Yiddish speakers and readers who want this time not problems, but solutions for their problems, as they see their children beginning to benefit from what is both the blessing and the curse of *shtetl* life in America: freedom. What occurs in Singer's story is as close to real life as these people wish to come; it emphasizes the pleasant and minimizes the unpleasant.

The description of the sons' lives in America is the perfect dream for the immigrant parent. All seven families live together, in seven homes surrounded by gardens, in what for this period of the 1930s and 1940s was the ultimate in *yichus:* Elizabeth, New Jersey. They are the owners of a successful shoe company, live happily together (no family squabbles, a later theme of American-Jewish fiction, in this story). There is to be a welcoming celebration in Gimpel's house, "in full compliance with the dietary laws; the meat was kosher, and a completely new set of dishes and utensils had been provided to prevent the least infraction of these laws." Singer goes out of his way to provide a picture of domestic and ritual perfection. The entire family is present, and, although the great numbers of young people speak a different language, the old man can bask in the warmth of his family. Ironically, Singer includes a "colored maid" in this mosaic, as a further reflection of the status of the Shuster family. This is, of course, the *shvartse,* who, like the Polish or Russian peasant, was a measure of whatever status the Jew might enjoy in relation to the Gentile world. The *Shabbes Goy,* the Sabbath Gentile who came to do the chores forbidden to the Jew, is transposed into the black maid, who becomes in Jewish-American *shtetl* lore an almost standard stereotype of prosperity.

Old Abba, however, does not thrive in this new, strange environment. His senses are disordered, he can barely walk, and in Gimpel's house he often would be found lost in some closet. Singer is going to the heart of the problem of aging for the *shtetl* Jew in America. In Frampol, Abba made shoes; in America, he is superfluous, an old man without a profession, and inevitably one of the daughters-in-law suggests a solution which undoubtedly Singer's readers had encountered all too frequently and which was becoming almost a way of life for the increasingly prosperous American Jew: "It wouldn't be such a bad idea to put him in a home." Singer can employ a theme which simply never existed in the *shtetl* Yiddish literature of, for example, Sholom Aleichem. There was no old age home in the normal sense in the Jewish community, although there might have been a *Moyshev Zkeynim,* literally, a home for the old, but this was generally for those few old people who did not have loved ones or *mishpoche* to care for them. The Jewish extended family was a three-generation structure: grandparents, parents, and children. As long as it was possible for all to live under one roof, it was done. It was a loss of esteem for all if any one of these parts left. The aged and infirm were taken care of within the framework of the family. In America, this eventually changed with the movement away from the confines and self-imposed limitations of *shtetl*-ghetto life. Once the Jews—and Italians, Irish, and other ethnic groups—spilled out into suburbia, as often as not the orthodox old people were not able to adapt: it frequently meant walking miles to the nearest synagogue if they wanted to remain orthodox in spite of their children's often lax observance of Jewish ritual. This is the situation in which we find old Abba. Disoriented in his son's home in suburbia, out of step and out of pace with the life around him, generally "in the way," he is in every sense superfluous, even an embarrassment, no less so than Tevye was to his pompous son-in-law Padhatzur. But Singer will not tolerate such a grim solution in this contrived and delightful story. One day, shortly after the suggestion had been made that they put the old man away, he accidentally walked into a closet to discover his shoemaker's tools from Frampol, which he had taken on his hazardous journeys. He picked up an old shoe and began working:

> That day Abba did not lay in bed dozing. He worked busily till evening, and even ate his usual piece of chicken with greater appetite. He smiled at the grandchildren and they came in to see what he was doing. . . . The activity soon proved to be the old man's salvation. . . . He mended every last pair of shoes in the house. . . . He took on new life and looked fifteen years younger.

Continuing in the best and most direct traditions of Yiddish literature, Singer comes on with a direct message for the Jew growing old in America: keep your hands busy and your mind alert. There is no retirement village or old age home for Abba. He rediscovers the beauty of hand labor, of activity. His repaired shoes become the talk of the neighborhood, and a small hut is built in the backyard by his excited children.

There is still another, even more significant dimension to Abba's rebirth: "He even whittled a stylus and began to instruct them in the elements of Hebrew and piety." He rebuilds the old world connection with his grandchildren and great-grandchildren. The story ends as Abba looks at his middle-aged sons and the host of young ones running around enthusiastically in the gardens, and thinks: "No, praise God, they had not become idolators in Egypt. They had not forgotten their heritage, nor had they lost themselves among the unworthy."

Singer has written the perfect Jewish fairy tale for the Jew growing old in America. Assimilation has taken place only insofar as to provide a new kind of *yichus* (the elegant suburban home in New Jersey and the successful business enterprise in this case); in reality, no different from what the Jew had hoped for in Russia. The threat of total Americanization and loss of Jewish identity has been triumphantly beaten back; the little ones are learning Hebrew, and, indeed, it is the older generation which assumes the responsibility. Finally, old age in America can be beautiful as long as you keep busy and have understanding children. But in his efforts to create the Jewish paradise in America, Singer self-consciously underlines the problems for the former Kasrilevkites, the inhabitants of the *shtetls* of the old world who knew how to survive in a hostile environment, but who must face the challenge of prosperity in America with increasing anxieties. (pp. 108-15)

Sol Gittleman, "A Sociology of Mishpoche Stereotypes," in his From Shtetl to Suburbia: The Family in Jewish Literary Imagination, *Beacon Press, 1978, pp. 86-115.*

ROBERT ALTER (essay date 1979)

[An American scholar, Alter has published highly respected studies of Stendhal, the picaresque novel, and American Jewish writers. In the following review of Old Love, *Alter concurs with those critics who have observed a decline in the quality of Singer's later works.]*

[***Old Love***] unfortunately makes one more conscious of [Singer's] limitations than of his achievement, and in some ways explicitly confirms the judgments . . . of those critics who have seen a certain falling-off in his recent work. . . . The weakest stories are first-person narratives in which the narrator is a thinly fictionalized version of Isaac Bashevis Singer, and the plots would appear to be thinly fictionalized accounts of the author's travels and tribulations, or of his fantasies, chiefly sexual, about himself, without the imaginative weight and formal definition of realized fiction. The only stories in the volume that recall the artful poise of Singer's earlier fiction are **"The Boy Knows the Truth"** and **"Tanhum."** . . .

Another objection to Singer's recent writing substantiated by this collection is that his work has become, as Seymour Kleinberg put it in a review of ***A Crown of Feathers*** [see Additional Bibliography], increasingly "private, idiosyncratic and self-indulgent." There is a peculiar violence of imagination in Singer that in these recent stories seems to break through the narrative surface like the unmediated expression of an obsession, without the artistic distancing provided by the folkloric vehicles of his more traditional tales.

Despite the title of the new collection, the stories are for the most part about lust, not love, and a recurrent sequence of associations links concupiscence with some form of perversion or mental derangement . . . and then inflicts on the lustful parties some hideous variety of violence. . . . It is as though Singer the voluptuary and Singer the guilt-ridden moralist were allowed to collide repeatedly in these fictions without much governing artistic direction. (p. 26)

Singer has often been described as a modernist working with traditional materials, but modernism assumes complexity as a supreme value, both in the formal shaping of the literary work and in the realms of psychology and moral experience with which it deals. Singer, on the other hand, is a simple writer, both formally and thematically; and I think he is at his best when he consciously or intuitively takes advantage of this fact. . . .

[For] all that has been said about Singer's greatness as a storyteller, what chiefly engages us in [the] most striking of his fictions is not the tale told since the plots themselves are secondary and sometimes sketchy or contrived, but rather the performance of the teller, the sure pacing, the wit, the vigor, the timbre of the narrating voice. Singer's vivid fictions of a vanished Polish Jewry are in a sense brilliant acts of ventriloquism. (p. 28)

Robert Alter, "Versions of Singer," in The New York Times Book Review, *October 28, 1979, pp. 1, 26, 28.*

RICHARD BURGIN (essay date 1980)

[*An American critic and editor, Burgin has compiled the widely praised works* Conversations with Jorge Louis Borges *(1969) and* Conversations with Isaac Bashevis Singer *(1986; see Additional Bibliography). In the following excerpt, Burgin offers a resolution to the apparent contradictions in Singer's fiction between his traditional techniques and modernist sensibility.*]

Without being a literary theoretician, or ever wishing to, Isaac Bashevis Singer has found himself embroiled in various controversies concerning the aims of fiction. He is, for instance, aesthetically at odds with those fictionists who feel the urge to impart an "important" social, political, or philosophical message in their work. As he has said, "The moment something becomes an '-ism' it is already false." . . .

Consider his prefatory note to ***Passions*** in which Singer precisely and simply states his aesthetics:

> While obscurity in content and style may now be the fashion, clarity remains the ambition of this writer. This is especially important since I deal with unique characters in unique circumstances, a group of people who are still a riddle to the world and often to themselves—the Jews of Eastern Europe, specifically the Yiddish-speaking Jews who perished in Poland and those who emigrated to the U.S.A. The longer I live with them and write about them the more I am baffled by the richness of their individuality and (since I am one of them) by my own whims and passions.

In Singer's case we are dealing with a writer who adheres religiously to the goals of clarity and specificity, writing about only what he knows through some form of direct experience. This is a seminal reason why there is some degree of confusion on the question of his modernity or his contemporary relevance. For Singer is a writer, in an age of cultivated ambiguity, who *wants* us to perceive the epiphanies, doubts, and ambivalences of his characters. The other key term in his brief statement of aesthetics is "riddle"—for that is finally what the universe is for Singer. What he wants us to understand about his characters are their attempts to comprehend the structure and *modus operandi* of a universe that resists understanding. It is one of his special strengths that his characters are not disembodied creations who merely represent metaphysical problems, or their author's obsessions, but are invariably imbued with exceptional vitality and credibility. . . . The apparent contradiction, then, is of a writer who composes lucid, direct sentences about people and situations he knows, but whose metaphysics like Kafka's and Borges's are rooted and have never escaped from the interminable riddles of the modern world. It is clarity, then, in the service of illuminating our essential riddle of existence. Let us not forget that Kafka and Borges employ very similar techniques.

One . . . reason why Singer has adopted many of the stylistic features of nineteenth century fiction is that he feels the work of that period is vastly superior to that of the twentieth. He therefore adopted as his masters Tolstoy, Dostoyevsky, and Flaubert, who expressed their social, psychological, and philosophical conceits in a "natural" way through their characters' relations to each other, and their particular situations in a concrete social milieu. Yet Singer's sensibility is more "modern" than these writers', to whom he is frequently compared.

To understand this more fully we must return to the notion of social structure, which the avant-garde often treats negatively or else with the assumption that there simply isn't any structure to be negative about. For these writers, the family, society's first structure, is generally fractured and uncommunicative at best, and more often a procession of horrors; a never-to-be-reconciled nightmare. . . . What distinguishes [Singer's] fiction from the work of many experimentalists is that man is always seen in a definite context of family and society that even world war (and Singer has written about both of them) does not destroy. This sense of continuity ultimately forms a basis for the deeper mystery of human character that clarity always provides.

When Singer moves from the family, or from man in society, and considers our cosmic structure, his contradictory attitudes are even more difficult to unravel. Though he has characterized our knowledge of the universe as "a little island in an ocean of non-knowledge," Singer nonetheless affirms his belief in God (here he may differ slightly from Borges for whom this question, like infinity itself, is beyond our attempts at description). But Singer has nonetheless described his God as, "a silent God . . . perhaps a petty God, an amnesiac, perhaps a cruel God." In the last analysis he is certain only that we have too little information to know or even to criticize this God who speaks in a language of incomprehensible deeds.

In ***Old Love*** Singer pursues these concerns while broadening his thematic range, dealing explicitly for the first time with homosexuality and bi-sexuality in **"Two,"** with sadomasochism in **"Not for the Sabbath,"** even with incest in **"The Bus."** Despite his emphasis in ***Old Love*** on the sexually aberrational aspects of his characters, as well as the exotic locations of his stories (Spain, Brazil, Israel, Miami), we are firmly rooted in Singer's fictive world populated by demons and imps, resonating with the author's fascination for detail liable to deliquesce in a moment into other worldly visions.

The darker side of sexuality has always been one of Singer's preoccupations; thus, this current collection is more of an extension of an ongoing investigation than an exploration of completely new terrain. Most importantly, not only are Singer's style and point of view consistent with his life's work, so are his aesthetics. A closer look, for example, at **"The Bus,"** the last, longest, and most fully developed story in ***Old Love,*** may help us understand the sly modernism of Singer I mentioned earlier.

The story begins . . . in the middle; that is we are immediately in a crisis the narrator finds inexplicable. . . . (pp. 61-4)

In these opening lines the reader is confronted with what we might call two fields of tension: the continuity of concrete detail and the world of deception, ambiguity, and misconception. The concrete information given the reader includes chronological time, around three in the afternoon in 1956; a definite place, Spain, and a vivid description of Madame Weyerhofer, one of the story's protagonists. But every time information is given it is immediately undermined. The narrator knows he is on a bus, but does not know why. He is pointed to a seat next to a woman flaunting an ominous sign (the black cross) and everything about this woman's appearance seems elusive, at best, or perhaps completely meretricious (dyed hair, rouged face, a use of German that seems suspect).

Though she wears a cross, Celina Weyerhofer soon discloses that she is Jewish, in fact a former inmate of a concentration camp. Her husband, a Swiss bank director who is sitting across from her, compelled her to convert to Christianity because, as she explains, "He hates me."

Since the rules of the bus require passengers to exchange seats daily, he soon gets to know her husband whom his wife has characterized as a pathological liar and latent homosexual. He, in turn, describes his wife's pathology to the narrator.

As the tale grows more dense, it also becomes more bizarre. We soon realize that **"The Bus"** is not going to be a study of the Weyerhofers, for the narrator meets a Mrs. Metalon from Istanbul whose adolescent son Mark, a genius who could do logarithms at the age of five, is scheming to get her married again, this time to the narrator. With a minimal degree of structural complication, Singer artlessly increases the complexity of his story without sacrificing any of its narrative thrust. (pp. 64-5)

What the narrator is dealing with is a set of truths or realities represented by the Weyerhofers and the Metalons, each of whom denies the other's credibility and assures the narrator that his or her truth is the one in which to believe. This is a recurring, indeed, almost archetypal situation in contemporary fiction from the masters of undermined or contradicted truth; Conrad, Faulkner, Kafka, Borges, Beckett, Calvino—to their numerous disciples. What makes this theme unique in **"The Bus"** is that Singer has built it unpretentiously through the personalities and detailed situations of each of the characters. Like Kafka, the more he elaborates, the more clearly he writes; and the more mysterious his situations become. Even the narrator's own motives and passions are unknown to him. He yearns for Mrs. Metalon one moment, but when he has a chance to sleep with her his passion cools. Effortlessly the bus begins to assume symbolic dimensions, but like Kafka's castle it's a multiple symbol or, one might say, an overdetermined one. The bus is at once a symbol of human desire, consciousness, a search for reality, and also an escape from it. Of course, these categories are hardly mutually exclusive; indeed, a central theme of the story is their interrelationship. Consciousness must always desire and when that fails . . . one begins the inevitable progression of self-doubt, of looking for solace in faith, one becomes in effect like Beckett's Watt who relentlessly tries to rationalize the inexplicable. In just this way Singer's narrator in **"The Bus"** confronts man's essential dilemma here discreetly raised to metaphysical proportions: the problem of not knowing.

As Beckett's characters wait for Godot uncertain if he will ever arrive, Singer's characters, like Kafka's land surveyor in search of the Castle, are always moving. In the case of **"The Bus"** there is a clear destination for the narrator's trip, as there is for the land surveyor, but it is a place Singer treats with far less importance or mystification than Kafka does his Castle. It is, in fact, completely demystified, simply a place one can find on a map. Nevertheless, the narrator never reaches it, for, unable to unravel his own tangled motives, he ultimately gets off the bus and takes a train to Biarritz. (pp. 65-6)

Singer's bus, then, is another "little island in an ocean of non-knowledge." In fact it is far too elusive to constitute even a tiny island, and accordingly the narrator vacates it. Both the theme and its treatment reveal Singer to be spiritually akin to Borges, Kafka, Beckett, and Nabokov, for whom the problem of knowledge itself replaces the essential concerns of Tolstoy, Dostoyevsky, and Flaubert. This theme and its particular kind of modernism, or, if you will, post-modernism, are not unique to **"The Bus."** We find it in the novels *Enemies, A Love Story,* Singer's most recent novel *Shosha,* and to a substantial degree in *The Magician of Lublin.* Moreover, we find it in many of his stories from **"Gimpel the Fool"** to much of ***Old Love.*** Indeed the problem of knowledge, which I believe to be a crucial one for contemporary or avant-garde writers, is literally spelled out in the last sentence of the title story of ***A Crown of Feathers***: ". . . If there is such a thing as truth it is as intricate and hidden as a crown of feathers."

This writer is somewhat baffled by those critics who relentlessly stress Singer's devotion to traditional literary and "moral" values while ignoring the meanings that are apparent behind the surface simplicity of his style, and his natural storyteller's gift. (Remember Joyce and Faulkner, Kafka, Borges, and Nabokov are all good, almost obsessive storytellers.) **"The Bus,"** then, like most of the fiction in ***Old Love,*** reveals a writer who manages to dramatize eternal paradoxes in a wholly contemporary fashion without making us overly aware of it. To my knowledge few fictionists have this gift and have demonstrated it so often. (p. 67)

Richard Burgin, "The Sly Modernism of Isaac Singer," in Chicago Review, *Vol. 31, No. 4, Spring, 1980, pp. 61-7.*

CYNTHIA OZICK (essay date 1982)

[*A celebrated American novelist, short story writer, essayist, and critic, Ozick is best known for her fiction in which she mingles a vast array of elements and explores a variety of subjects, including those related to Judaic history and culture. In the following review of* The Collected Stories of Isaac Bashevis Singer, *Ozick discusses the supernatural elements of Singer's short fiction.*]

On one flank Singer is a trickster, a prankster, a Loki, a Puck. His themes are lust, greed, pride, obsession, misfortune, unreason, the oceanic surprises of the mind's underside, the fiery caldron of the self, the assaults of time and place. His stories offer no "epiphanies" and no pious resolutions; no linguistic circumscriptions or Hemingwayesque self-deprivations. Their plenitudes chiefly serve undefended curiosity, the gossip's lure of what comes next. Singer's stories have plots that unravel not because they are "old-fashioned"—they are mostly originals and have few recognizable modes other than their own—but because they contain the whole human world of affliction, error, quagmire, pain, calamity, catastrophe, woe. Things happen; life is an ambush, a snare; one's fate can never be predicted. His driven mercurial processions of predicaments and transmogrifications are limitless, often stupendous. There are whole fistfuls of masterpieces in [***The Collected Stories of Isaac Bashevis Singer***]: a cornucopia of invention.

Because he cracks open decorum to find lust, because he peers through convention into the pit of fear, Singer has in the past been condemned by other Yiddish writers outraged by his seemingly pagan matter, his superstitious villagers, his daring leaps into gnostic furies. The moral grain of Jewish feeling that irradiates the mainstream aspirations of Yiddish literature has always been a kind of organic extension of Talmudic ethical ideals: family devotion, community probity, *derekh erets*—self-respect and respect for others—the stringent expectations of high public civility and indefatigable integrity, the dream of messianic betterment. In Singer, much of this seems absent or overlooked or simply mocked; it is as if he has willed the crashing down of traditional Jewish sanity and sensibility. As a result, in Yiddish literary circles he is sometimes viewed as—it is the title of one of these stories—**"The Betrayer of Israel."**

In fact, he betrays nothing and no one, least of all Jewish idealism. That is the meaning of his imps and demons: that human character, left to itself, is drawn to cleanliness of heart; that human motivation, on its own, is attracted to clarity and valor. Here is Singer's other flank, and it is the broader one. The goblin cunning leads straight to this; Singer is a moralist. He tells us that it is natural to be good, and unholy to go astray. It is only when Lilith creeps in, or Samael, or Ketev Mriri, or the sons of Asmodeus, that evil and impurity are kindled. It is the inhuman, the antihuman, forces that are to blame for harms and sorrows. Surely these imps must be believed in; they may have the telltale feet of geese, like Satan their sire, but their difficult, shaming, lubricious urges are terrestrially familiar. Yet however lamentably known they are, Singer's demons are intruders, invaders, no true or welcome part of ourselves. They are "psychology"; and history; and terror; above all, obsessive will. If he believes in them, so, unwillingly but genuinely, do we.

And to understand Singer's imps is to correct another misapprehension: that he is the recorder of a lost world, the preserver of a vanished sociology. Singer is an artist and transcendent inventor, not a curator. His tales—though dense with the dailiness of a God-covenanted culture, its folkways, its rounded sufficiency, especially the rich intensities of the yeshiva and its bottomless studies—are in no way documents. The Jewish townlets that truly were are only seeds for his febrile conflagrations: Where, outside of peevish imagination, can one come on the protagonist of **"Henne Fire,"** a living firebrand, a spitfire burning up with spite, who ultimately, through the spontaneous combustion of pure fury, collapses into "one piece of coal"? Though every doorstep might be described, and every feature of a head catalogued (and Singer's portraits are brilliantly particularized), parables and fables are no more tied to real places and faces than Aesop's beasts are beasts.

This is not to say that Singer's stories do not mourn those murdered Jewish townlets of Poland, every single one of which, with nearly every inhabitant, was destroyed by the lords and drones of the Nazi Gehenna. This volume includes a masterly memorial to that destruction, the brokenhearted testimony of **"The Last Demon."** . . .

[Singer's] tenderness for ordinary folk, their superstitions, their folly, their plainness, their lapses, is a classical thread of Yiddish fiction, as well as the tree trunk of Singer's own Hasidic legacy—love and reverence for the down-to-earth. **"The Little Shoemakers"** bountifully celebrates the Fifth Commandment with leather and awl; the hero of **"Gimpel the Fool,"** a humble baker, is endlessly duped and stubbornly drenched in permanent grace; the beautiful story **"Short Friday"** ennobles a childless old couple who, despite privation and barrenness, turn their unscholarly piety into comeliness and virtue. Shmul-Leibele's immaculate happiness in prayer, Shoshe's meticulous Sabbath meal, shine with saintliness; Singer recounts the menu, "chicken soup with noodles and tiny circlets of fat . . . like golden ducats," as if even soup can enter holiness. Through a freakish accident—snow covers their little house, and they are asphyxiated—the loving pair ascend in death together to Paradise. When the demons are stilled, human yearning aspires toward goodness and joy. (Singer fails to note, however, whether God or Samael sent the pure but deadly snow.)

In Singer the demons are rarely stilled, and the luminous serenity of **"Short Friday"** is an anomaly. Otherwise pride furiously rules, and wildhearted imps dispose of human destiny. In **"The Unseen,"** a prosperous and decent husband runs off with a lusty maidservant at the urging of a demon; he ends in destitution, a hidden beggar tended by his remarried wife. **"The Gentleman From Cracow"** corrupts a whole town with gold; he turns out to be Ketev Mriri, Satan himself. In **"The Destruction of Kreshev,"** a scholar who is a secret Sabbatean and devil worshiper induces his wife to commit adultery with a Panlike coachman. Elsewhere, excessive intellectual passion destroys genius. An accomplished young woman is instructed by a demon to go to the priest, convert, and abandon her community; the demon assumes the voice of the girl's grandmother, herself the child of a Sabbatean. A rabbi is "plagued by something new and terrifying: wrath against the Creator," and struggles to fashion himself into an atheist Character and motive are turned inside out at the bidding of imps who shove, snarl, seduce, bribe, cajole. Allure ends in rot; lure becomes punishment.

This phantasmagorical universe of ordeal and mutation and shock is, finally, as intimately persuasive as logic itself. There is no fantasy in it. It is the true world we know, where we have come to expect anguish as the consequence of our own inspirations, where we crash up against the very circumstance from which we had always imagined we were exempt. In this true world, suffering is endemic and few are forgiven. Yet it may be that for Singer the concrete presence of the unholy attests the hovering redemptive holy, whose incandescence can scatter demons. (pp. 14-16)

Not all the stories in this collection emerge from that true world, however. The eerie authority of **"The Cabalist of East Broadway"** is a gripping exception, but in general the narratives set in the American environment are, by contrast, too thin. Even when intentionally spare—as in the marvelous **"Vanvild Kava,"** with its glorious opening: "If a Nobel Prize existed for writing little, Vanvild Kava would have gotten it"—the European settings have a way of turning luxuriantly, thickly coherent. Presumably some of these American locales were undertaken in a period when the fertile seed of the townlets had begun to be exhausted; or else it is the fault of America itself, lacking the centripetal density and identity of a yeshiva society, the idea of community as an emanation of God's gaze. Or perhaps it is because many of these American stories center on Singer as writer and celebrity, or on someone like him. It is as if the predicaments that fly into his hands nowadays arrive because he is himself the centripetal force, the controlling imp. And an imp, to have efficacy, as Singer's genius has shown, must be a kind of dybbuk, moving in powerfully from outside; whereas the American narratives are mainly inside jobs, about the unusual "encounters" a famous writer meets up with.

[Singer's translators] cannot reach the deep mine and wine of Singer's mother tongue, thronged (so it was once explained to me by a Tel Aviv poet accomplished in Hebrew, Yiddish and English) with that unrenderable Hebrew erudition and burnished complexity of which we readers in English have not an inkling, and are permanently deprived. Deprived? Perhaps. ***The Collected Stories,*** when all is said and done, is an American master's "Book of Creation." (p. 17)

Cynthia Ozick, "Fistfuls of Masterpieces," in The New York Times Book Review, *March 21, 1982, pp. 1, 14-17.*

BRUCE ALLEN (essay date 1982)

[*In the following excerpt, Allen offers a generally approving review of* The Collected Stories, *although he faults the autobiographical pieces concerning an elderly writer living in New York City.*]

Singer's preeminent position among the storytellers of our time will be firmly consolidated by the current ***Collected Stories,*** which gathers 47 tales from eight previously published volumes. For narrative drive, color and variety, and sheer suggestive power, they seem to me as superior to most contemporary fiction as they are distant from it. Perhaps the unusual texture results from the compounding of various literary influences—such as Poe, Dostoevsky, Knut Hamsun, and Kafka—with Singer's grounding in apocryphal and cabbalistic literature, and Hasidic folktales.

His typical strategy is to state a plain fact, then bring it to life with a sequence of quick specific details. . . . He can create thickly populated, complex areas of activity and conflict as convincingly as any writer since Dickens. These stories are filled with detail about religious and dietary practices—yet we never feel oppressed by mere information. As one of his narrators says in denying that death exists: "everything lives, everything suffers, struggles, desires."

It's useful, I think, to divide these stories into categories. The earliest and arguably the best record the material or spiritual travail of Polish village people. Demons, or their master the "Evil One," are frequent antagonists in **"The Gentleman from Cracow"** and **"Taibele and Her Demon."** Deviations from orthodox behavior are examined in these early stories. In **"Yentl the Yeshiva Boy,"** a woman who longs to become a scholar pretends she's a man; in **"Henne Fire,"** a Herculean shrew *literally* keeps bursting into flames. Yet the perfectly upright, too, are inexplicably tormented in **"The Unseen"** and **"The Slaughterer."** Singer's range includes boisterous comedy (in **"The Dead Fiddler,"** a pair of quarreling *dybbuks* inhabit a single beleaguered body). It also includes slow, rich, patiently developed chronicles of moral crisis and redemption. These often have the density of novellas, as one sees in **"The Little Shoemakers,"** and **"The Destruction of Kreshev."**

A series of even more ambitious stories dramatizes the relativity, or even failure of various philosophical and religious "truths," or argue in Kantian fashion that if reality is subjective, anything can happen. Thus: a goodhearted simpleton and cuckold (**"Gimpel the Fool"**) bases his limitless credulity on his faith that "all things are possible." An elderly scholar-recluse (**"The Spinoza of Market Street"**) is "deceived" into entering fully into life, and feeling—and bitterly laments his human folly. The ambiguity is breathtaking. Ghosts and spirits crowd these stories. Other "worlds" interpenetrate with this one continuously. **"The Letter Writer,"** lone survivor from a family that perished in the Nazi death camps, find solace—and much more—in his correspondences with total strangers, and his fervent belief in "the world beyond." The story just expands, and expands—it's the ultimate expression of Singer's supernaturalism and, in my opinion, his finest story.

I find fewer successes among the mostly recent stories about elderly writers in New York, musing over their colleagues' surprising fates (**"The Cabalist of East Broadway," "A Friend of Kafka"**). Several are honestly moving (**"Old Love," "Neighbors"**), but some are little more than vignettes, and at least one accomplished comedy—**"The Admirer"**—strikes me as both petulant and boorish on the subject of the aging writer as pursued celebrity.

No more negative remarks, except to protest the omission from this collection of two of Singer's very best stories: **"The Captive"** (from ***A Crown of Feathers***) and **"A Pair"** (from ***Passions***). This is one of those books that I regretted to finish and wished were longer. I can think of no higher praise, nor any recent book more deserving of it.

Bruce Allen, "Nobel Laureate's Superb Stories," in The Christian Science Monitor, *April 9, 1982, p. B4.*

DAVID LEAVITT (essay date 1985)

[*Leavitt is an American writer whose initial collection of short stories,* Family Dancing *(1984), received widespread acclaim. In the following favorable review of* The Image, and Other Stories, *Leavitt discusses the settings, subjects, themes, and styles of Singer's fiction.*]

The stories in ***The Image*** take place almost exclusively in the little pockets of sanity that punctuate Jewish history—those moments between pogrom and plague of which Aunt Yentl speaks when she says: "That's how Jews are. When times are bad they lament. When times improve, if only for a minute, they get out all their finery—and those who despise us grit their teeth." In these brief minutes when things improve, Aunt Yentl (and Mr. Singer) tell us, a Jew's terror turns to desire; it's as if the characters simply can't escape the mood of hysteria that accompanies apocalypse. They live each day in a froth of passion, for they have good reason to doubt whether they will still be alive tomorrow.

"Confused" may well be the consummate achievement of the collection. It's a dizzying nightmare of a story, the tale of an elderly writer, exhausted and jet-lagged after a long lecture tour, who receives a phone call from a middle-aged woman named Pessl, a neighbor and fan, begging to meet him. An alcoholic refugee of the Holocaust whose only daughter is a vicious anti-Semite, Pessl supports herself by baby-sitting. She manages to persuade the beleaguered author to spend the night with her at the apartment of another woman, Mrs. Klapperman, who has left her baby in Pessl's care while she is off with her own lover.

A fire breaks out in a nearby apartment, and the author, Pessl and the baby are locked out and must spend the night with the upstairs neighbor, Terry Bickman. She too is a refugee of sorts, a woman living on the brink of insanity, and also an obsessive fan of the author's. . . . There is a stunning claustrophobia about the story, and about these characters' lives, a suggestion that for them the Holocaust has not ended, can never end. Its madness rules them still, even in their comfortable apartments in New York. The story is Mr. Singer at his very best: bitter, sad, rich in stinging, sensual detail.

Most of the stories in ***The Image*** follow an essentially similar formula. An unnamed writer, young or old, in Poland or (later in his life) in America, is approached by someone with a story to tell. As the visitor talks and talks, the writer nods, and occasionally comments. He is not really a character in his own right; the story within the story is the one that counts. But though the tales told through these conversations are often in and of themselves quite marvelous (particularly **"Miracles"** and **"A Telephone Call on Yom Kippur"**), the formulaic sameness of many of them wears a bit after a while. Such stories as **"The Litigants," "The Conference"** and **"The Secret"** seem like mere fragments, scraps of oral history that need some present event in the narrative to counteract or underscore.

The strength of Mr. Singer's best work explodes out of dialogue and confrontation, the wrestling of rival passions. He is at his best when he turns the story-told-to-the-narrator formula on its head, as in the lovely and haunting **"Why Heisherik Was Born,"** in which a young writer and editor is hounded first by Heisherik, a fool turned religious zealot who wants him to edit his nearly illegible autobiography, and then by Heisherik's starving wife, who blames the writer when her crazed husband decides to abandon her and her children and run off to the Holy Land. Only years later, when he learns of the fool/zealot's surprising and heroic fate, does the writer understand why he felt so mysteriously compelled to involve himself with and support this low-life madman and his unquenchable need to tell the story of his life. Here storytelling, the impulse to share events from one's history, which Mr. Singer's characters universally possess, becomes the subject rather than merely the vehicle, and the relationship between listener and teller is enlivened considerably.

And there are other magnificent achievements. **"Remnants"** is the gutsy, unsentimental story of a pair of unlikely lovers brought together again after surviving hellish years of separation. **"Miracles"** is a funny, rich morality tale about a man blessed by God—until he asks for one thing too many. And **"One Day of Happiness"** is the familiar tragic tale of a girl whose idyllic dream of a meeting with the poet she is in love with ends in sorrow and degradation. Here, more than anywhere else in the collection, Mr. Singer the writer is at his virtuosic best, as in this dazzling passage in which the girl's claustrophobic passion takes on an intense and febrile reality:

> Moreover, she was constantly hungry, as if afflicted with a tapeworm. Sometimes at night, lying awake, she could feel her body beginning to swell up like dough. Her skin burned, her breasts tightened as if filled with milk. And though Fela was a virgin, she was sometimes afraid she might suddenly begin to give birth. She felt fluids coursing through her like saps in a plant before blooming. Her breath grew hot, her insides clutched and twisted, and during the night she constantly had to go to the toilet.

This is stunning prose—so itchy with barely suppressed desire, so compelling in its physicality, that the page itself seems to heat up as you read it. It's also just one of the instances in the book in which a woman's sexual desire for a man becomes a kind of hysterical, all-consuming fervor. Most of Mr. Singer's women, it seems, are veritable slaves to lust, and there's no doubt in my mind that for this reason a number of the stories in ***The Image*** are going to rankle women readers even more than they rankled me.

In **"The Bond,"** for instance, a writer, boasting to the narrator about his sexual prowess, tells the tale of a woman so insanely in love with him that she follows him everywhere, even on lecture tours to distant towns. He has discovered, he explains somewhat apologetically, that the only way to calm his lover's hysterical jealousy is to slap her across the face, after which she becomes pleasant and docile. When the young intellectual woman who is going to introduce him at a lecture sees him slapping his lover, she becomes incensed, raving at him that he is a fake and a monster, until finally he is compelled to slap the young feminist as well. Like his lover, she is instantly pacified. The story ends with the writer explaining that the slap constituted a kind of "bond"—not only between him and the young woman, but between the two slapped women themselves, who, we are told, become friends for life.

Needless to say, there's something vaguely misogynistic about this story, with its sadomasochistic undertone, its hints that rape (or its metaphorical equivalent) is all that women (particularly intellectual women) really want. Here, however, Mr. Singer's technique of having the story told to him rather than by him works in his favor. Though we may loathe the narrator within the story, we can't loathe the narrator of the story, because, of course, he's not telling it. The author thus frees himself from the burden of making a moral judgment; he shrugs his literary shoulders and pleads no contest—I'm merely repeating a story I heard someone else tell. And that, it seems to me, is a bit of a cheat.

Perhaps the best answer to the accusation that some of the stories in ***The Image*** malign women, however, is this remark by the narrator of **"A Telephone Call on Yom Kippur."** "I'm not an anti-feminist," he explains. "All I can say about women is that they are neither better nor worse than men." This sentiment applies to Mr. Singer himself as well. If his women are lust-crazed, his men are schlemiels, easy victims, possessed by weaknesses to which they often fall prey (with dire results). And they are certainly as much, if not more, controlled by their passions as the women about whom they so endlessly complain.

Finally, however, the most important identification for most of these characters is not that of sex, but religion. Both the men and women consider themselves Jews first, Jews last, Jews above all else. Even their yearning for each other, strewn as it is across centuries of murder and persecution, is peculiarly Jewish. Mr. Singer's great achievement in these stories, it seems to me, is that he has managed to articulate brilliantly the extent to which a religious and cultural identity permeates a person's life, often against his will, or without his knowing it. Not even a Jew as lapsed and assimilated as myself can fail to be moved by the author's astonishing faith, or to feel churning up in himself a kinship with his people. "I've long been convinced," the teller of **"Miracles"** argues, "that there is a hidden Messiah in every Jew. The Jew himself is one big miracle. The hatred of the Jew is the hatred of miracles, since the Jew contradicts the laws of nature."

Throughout his long career, Mr. Singer has made it his business to show us what the survival of the Jewish people has meant on a day-to-day basis, and the ways in which that fierce instinct for survival has shaped Jewish history and Jewish identity. ***The Image*** splendidly confirms his achievement; more than perhaps any other Jewish writer, he is the recording angel of the Jewish miracle. (pp. 3, 23)

David Leavitt, "Slaves to Lust and Other Passions," in The New York Times Book Review, *June 30, 1985, pp. 3, 23.*

MICHAEL WILDING (essay date 1986)

[*Wilding is an English-born Australian writer and critic. In the following review of* The Image, and Other Stories, *he summarizes Singer's scope, tenor, and fictional techniques while commenting on the general abundance of sexual, spiritual, and political elements in his short fiction.*]

There is no doubt about the achievement of Isaac Bashevis Singer. He is one of the foremost storytellers of our time. His output has been prolific and now, in his 82nd year, comes [***The Image,***] a collection of a further 22 stories. Gathered from twenty years of magazine publication, translated from the Yiddish sometimes by the author himself, sometimes by or in collaboration with others, they nonetheless have a consistency of tone. It would be hard indeed to speculate which come from the mid-Sixties, which from the mid-Eighties. The same personality runs through all of them, that same love of storytelling.

It is tempting to write 'genial' of the personality, but that would be to disregard the sometimes rebarbative note that reveals itself. Beneath the unpretentious, effortless-seeming surface of these stories is a firm, calculated attitude of mind. . . . Singer has always stood out against the lures of Modernism. The strength of his stories is the strength gathered from a return to the living sources of storytelling—the storytelling that still goes on when people talk to each other. A frequent framing situation here is of someone meeting or phoning the writer and then launching into a narrative. . . . Though the point is never spelled out, it is clear that Singer, the Rabbi's son who trained at the Rabbinical Seminary in Warsaw but became a secular writer for the Yiddish press, is re-enacting the listening, advice-giving role of his father. Many of the stories come from episodes overheard when a child. . . . And then there are the stories of times long past that Aunt Yentl tells, stories that draw on the infinite resources of oral history and that merge into the world of the folk tale. . . .

For all the opening polemic [in the Author's Note] against the Modernism which is without narrative, against that lack of beginning, middle and end, Singer's conservatism is not a blind refusal. He is not in this a reactionary. The self-referential nature of Modernism, art aware of and concerned with its own processes, is not absent from his work. There are frequent stories about stories, stories about writers. The Warsaw Yiddish Writers' club is a frequent setting or departure point in this as in earlier works. Indeed the themes revolve as much around the behaviour and contradictions of writers as around Jewishness. In reaction to that awful authorial confidence of the great 19th-century writers who proclaimed a knowledge of everything, a vast social comprehensiveness, these stories consistently attest their personal authenticity, the directly vouched-for. If not what happened to the narrator, they are what happened to people the narrator has known, or the stories told to the narrator by people he has met. In his memoir *Love and Exile* Singer stressed the importance of suspense. . . . But it is not a naive suspense. The old narrative tricks have become over-familiar to the experienced reader. It was in reaction to that exhaustion of the old techniques that Modernist writers had to look for other strategies: but in abandoning suspense and narrative they lost their readers to television. Singer, for all the seeming simplicity of his narratives, is not unsophisticated. In **"A Telephone Call on Yom Kippur"** there is, as often in these stories, the dual perspective of the writer and of the visitor who tells the writer the story. The initial suspense is the writer's anxiety that the visitor will never get to the point, the suspense of wanting it all over and finished. 'I'm coming to the point,' the visitor assures him on the third page. 'But wait, the story is only beginning,' he says on the fifth. 'Now the real story begins,' he promises at the end of the sixth. The ghostly mystery of the dead woman answering the phone that leaves the visitor wiping his forehead and shaking holds no surprises for the writer. 'He sat there pale, pondering his own tale. I said, "Helena was still alive, eh?" ' These old tricks of suspense are still there, but they take a gentler role, so that the more numinous qualities of what is narrated can be dwelt on. . . . Narrative suspense is now appropriately subordinated, but not elided altogether.

Not that Singer is without the bolder narrative strokes. **"One Day of Happiness"** tells of a young girl who, having given herself to be deflowered by a Polish officer-poet, slits her wrist on her return to her parents: 'Sitting on the toilet bowl in the dark, Fela leaned her head against the wall, ready to die. She could feel the blood running from her wrist and she was bleeding below, too.' **"Strong as Death is Love"** concludes with a man so in love with his dead wife that he exhumes her decayed body and is found in bed with her skeleton. **"The Secret"** tells of a woman who conceived by her husband's apprentice and years later finds the child and the apprentice have met and fallen in love: 'My daughter lives with her father! He is her lover. They are planning to marry!"

The dominant tone is not as sensational as these abstracted plot details might suggest, however. Violent action and physical cruelties he generally avoids. The childhood agonising over nature, God, meaning, suffering, cruelty that Singer describes in his autobiographical memoir runs through these stories, providing the impetus, the wondering why. There is a recoil from the cruelties of man to man and of man to the natural world. (p. 22)

Drawing the reader in is Singer's technique for replication of reality. And this realism has a splendid amplitude. The stories in ***The Image*** range from contemporary New York apartment life to late 19th-century Polish aristocratic estates; from the poorhouse and the gaol to the Rabbi's court; from the Warsaw Yiddish Writers' club of the Twenties and Thirties to modern Israel. But Singer is not confined to a limited material reality. His scope is something that comes with his occult interests. One of the few contemporary writers to offer us a larger world of spirit, he unobtrusively suggests these further dimensions—cosmic reaches, spiritual interminglings, the interface of the spirit world with ours. This spirit world is unaffectedly an aspect of his realism. As real as the slums of Krochmalna Street or the subway system of Manhattan, it is introduced not to shock or surprise, not for the artificial frisson of the ghost story, but as a component of human life. This concern is not restricted to the folklore or arcana of a specific creed or race. Singer's occult not only amplifies the picture of Polish and expatriate Jewry, with an attention, for instance, to cabalistic speculation: it is a subject-matter in itself.

Nor is his occult confined to those stories that deal thematically with dybbuks, astral *bodies and clairvoyance. These themes are* present in his collection, though sometimes problematically. . . . Singer's occultism is not something reducible to psychic phenomena, but part of a larger world view. The stories enact his belief that each individual contains in microcosm the forces and tensions of the macrocosm. No matter how small the object on which we focus—the single community, the couple, the individual, the atom—it embodies the forces of the cosmic whole. There in the focus on the claustrophobic settings of a closed family life, of compacted tenement slums, of the prison cell, is the grandeur of creation and the wretchedness and suffering, too. They open out, these tiny episodes that are never miniatures in the usual dismissive sense. This is a quality of Singer's stories that comes, not from a secular literary art, but from a world view. With their extraordinary accessibility, their open immediacy, their seeming artlessness, the stories are compact, ready to grow and blossom into fulfilment, meaning. They are not overworked jewellery, embroidered artefacts. And there is none of the dissatisfaction many readers feel with story collections, with bundles of discrete episodes: for all their range of settings and historic moments, their moods of comedy and horror, resignation and disillusion, published together they comprise a coherent totality.

It is tempting to say that Singer has in the traditions of Hebraism, the upbringing in the Rabbi's household with its mystical volumes—something which is beautifully evoked in *Love and Exile*—a wonderful source of material. But this is to underestimate Singer's very real achievement in bringing these materials to life. Is his source, in fact, any richer than anyone else's? Isn't all life a rich source? Isn't it a mark of his creativity that he gives the impression of a marvellous fund of material—when it is only from what he has made of his material that such an impression can be received? The creativity is so rich, the storytelling so fertile, that we then postulate a pre-existent source. The genius of the stories is that they imply this rich totality, but it is only brought to life through the stories themselves. The art lay in hearing the stories, in finding them, in capturing a pattern from the circumambient world in such a way that that whole world is then illuminated.

Singer's main subject is sex. Sometimes it is with love, sometimes without; sometimes it is with marriage, sometimes with divorce. As he wrote in *Love and Exile,*

> I had made up my mind a long time ago that the creative powers of literature lie not in the forced originality produced by variations of style and word machinations but in the countless situations life keeps creating, especially in the queer complications between man and woman. For the writer, they are potential treasures that could never be exhausted, while all innovations in language soon become clichés.

This latest collection has tragic tales of young girls seeking yet failing to find the satisfactions of love and sexuality, tales of momentary transgressions or near transgressions that result in cataclysmic religious consequences, recurrent tales of adultery, divorce and remarriage. . . . There is a pattern here of multiple affairs and multiple deceptions that owes as much to the repetition compulsions of biography—the same structure of affairs can be found in *Love and Exile*—as to any fictional imaginings. It is all done comparatively tastefully; there are no four-letter words, none of the remorseless physical detail of Henry Miller's cavortings; Singer's erotic themes are associated with drives and compulsions. And whereas Miller was able with his excess of physical detail to break through to a selfawareness, was able to demystify male delusions for himself and his readers, Singer's decorum holds back from that abyss and effectively endorses these tales of duplicity and the double standard.

It has never been easy to write about sexuality. To present its ambiguous behaviour, the graspings and deceptions and delusions, requires a considerable selflessness in those writers who draw on their own experiences. The danger has always been that the presentation of the problematic, of disturbing behaviour that needs to be displayed in order to be able to be analysed and understood and perhaps corrected in future practice, will be read as somehow endorsing what is shown and advocating its replication. Meanwhile it is all too easy to take a simply censorious attitude to presented incidents, refusing to see that the author has built into the narration an apparatus of criticism and assessment. Singer raises enormous problems in this area. **"The Bond"** is about one of those 'cases when a man is forced to slap a woman'. . . . The story is carefully framed, narrated by Berger to the storyteller: so that any identification with Singer's point of view is prevented. But it remains nonetheless a vicious and dangerous piece, and the strategy of framing it in no way exonerates Singer from the responsibility of reproducing it. This is the sort of story that encourages, and can indeed create, those violent and destructive sexist attitudes in impressionable young, and not so young, males; it offers a confirmation of the notion that the way to deal with a hysterical woman is to slap her.

Literature, of course, rarely records stories which tell us what to do with hysterical men. Hysteria, and responding to being slapped in a positive way, are all part of sexist typology, like 'nymphomania'. In **"Remnants"** Zina's 'first husband, the lawyer, said openly that his ex-wife was a nymphomaniac.' The expression is in reported speech, so is not necessarily endorsed by Singer: yet there are no comparably dismissive terms in his stories for the many males who are presented as sexually active. For all the humanity expressed in these stories, they also show a current of disabling sexism (pp. 22-3)

The sexuality of Singer's fiction is very much a male sexuality. Insofar as this reveals and demystifies male delusion and fantasy, it can be positive and cathartic. But there is an undeniable reactionary edge. Machla Krumbein, the sexually liberated writer in **"The Interview",** is presented as a grotesque, and, the ultimate insult, as a bad writer. Other male writers are presented as irredeemably bad, and are generally disabled in some further way: Heisherik, in **"Why Heisherik was born"** is a peasant, Mark Lenchner, in 'Advice', is 'a well-known writer and a Communist, whose wife had tried suicide three times because of his constant betrayals'. In **"Remnants"**, not only is the philandering Benjamin Rashkes' last novel rated as 'the worst kind of mishmash', but the 'nymphomaniac' Zina, his ex-lover, is promoting it and wants the narrator to write an introduction. Zina is one of a recurrent type in Singer's writing, the Jewish girl who has become a Communist. . . . Politically in implacable opposition to them, Singer is nonetheless fascinated by these women. . . .

[But] political discussions find no place in Singer's stories. **"The Conference"** deals with 'a cultural conference. Actually, it was an attempt by the Party hacks to create a united front with various leftist groups.' But the politics are absent: the manoeuvres of Comrade Flora's fending off sexual propositions is the foregrounded subject. The ideas of Socialism and Communism are never confronted by Singer, though his consistent opposition to them is firmly enough established. Stalin is equated with Hitler, but what Communism involves is left unexplored. That the Cold War parallel between Hitler and Stalin begs more questions than it answers seems not to worry him. His rejection of radical politics goes back to the Twenties. And though there is much about the disillusion of those Polish Communists who went to the Soviet Union in the years after the Revolution, the intellectual debate in question is something that has no place in Singer's fiction. . . .

But if the political is avoided, if the realism that issues in socially meaningful observation and analysis, like Gorki's, is rejected, then something has to take its place. If work cannot be foregrounded—and what experience of the work-place does the professional writer have?—then what remains? The preoccupation with sexuality and the occult in Singer's work is an inevitable consequence of his political exclusions. And the conservative nature of those exclusions and choices inevitably permeates the sexual attitudes.

Despite all this, and, for some readers, that is despite quite a lot, Singer's stories retain their appeal. That there are issues to disagree with its not in itself something to be condemned, but a welcome mark of content. Singer's conservatism, even if contentious, is certainly not evasive. At the point where Late or Post-Modernism has lost its non-professional readers, and has lost confidence, too, in its own processes, when the foregrounded manner fails to allure and seems only an advertisement for the absence of anything to say, Singer's stories endure. (p. 23)

Michael Wilding, "The Slap," in London Review of Books, *Vol. 8, No. 7, April 17, 1986, pp. 22-3.*

JAY CANTOR (essay date 1988)

[*In the following review of* The Death of Methuselah, and Other Stories, *Cantor explores the fragmented quality of Singer's short fiction.*]

Isaac Bashevis Singer's stories are not shapely, not "rounded-off." A Singer story doesn't culminate in a character's "epiphany," the mating of character and history that forces him to acknowledge an irrevocable entrapment, a fate. In fact, Singer's stories rarely have culminating moments at all. A Singer character may wonder over his fate, but then he repeats his damnation, or struggles against it, or is cast by tumultuous history into another, distant locale. By most standards, his stories are badly formed. Yet to my surprise, I found them nourishing.

Singer, one might say, doesn't precisely write short stories. Instead, he makes vivid narrative fragments. He knows pieces of a thousand good tales, like the one about how the Jews of Warsaw fled to Russia, only to watch the Stalinist Jews collaborate in betraying the Trotskyites; or about the young yeshiva student who abandons his wife, only to be discovered by her years later, living as a woman with another man; or the story of Methuselah's last temptation and how the devils created in him a longing for death.

And Singer acquires more stories by the moment. "Please forgive me for taking up so much of your precious time," a character will say. "To whom could I tell a story like this? There are philosophers, psychologists, and even those who consider themselves writers at the university, but to confide in them would be sheer suicide." Singer can be trusted, for he won't round off a story with a psychological "truth." Such bagatelles are "just words, names. . . . What people really are they don't know themselves. The fact is that we are all searching." Singer narratives have lively, if quickly told, plots, a vivid sensual apprehension, and, most crucially, a sense of the world gone awry, of evil.

This disorder is too often, and too sourly, identified with the failings of his women characters, their real, or imagined lack of fidelity. Repeated in many of the stories [in ***The Death of Methuselah***], this obsession seems crabbed, unequal to the metaphysical weight that Singer wants to give it. (p. 1)

In Singer's stories, God is at issue even if He is hated. This gives a deep background to the lives Singer tells and an importance to his characters' actions. Society may either be hallowed or remain in exile. The soul will be atoned with God and the community or it will wander alone.

So one's life could have an order, or a profound disorder. This makes for the startling direct address of Singer's characters, as they recount a life that they urgently feel should have had a coherent shape. They know they failed to attain that shape, but they still believe, angrily, as they turn about, that it might have been. And the narrative they tell may be cut off, but they don't end, for in the law, there is always some action one is called upon to perform. (pp. 1, 12)

Singer's fragmentary quality comes, too, from darker sources than this open-ended sense of narrative. The world is awry because we are endlessly askew to our heart's center. Singer is a divided, vain man, who presents himself fully in these narratives, with his yearning for wider experience, and his reverence for the hedge of the law. **"Logarithms"** tells of a brilliant Yeshiva student who is attracted to a Gentile woman for her intelligence and wider culture. And the young narrator, too, shares that attraction. "I could not understand why I felt a great compassion arise in me for Yossele and something like a desire to know Helena, play chess with her and learn logarithms. I remember my brother Joshua in a quarrel saying to my father, 'The other nations studied and learned, made discoveries in mathematics, physics, chemistry, astronomy, but we Jews remained stuck on a little law of an egg which was laid on a holiday.' I also remembered my father answering, 'this little law contains more wisdom than all the discoveries the idolaters have made since the time of Abraham.' " Singer knows that without law, there is faithlessness. But he knows that our hearts are endlessly discontent; we also want logarithms. We can't simply have one coherent saving story. So Singer only knows fragments of stories. But how many can give even that much? (p. 12)

Jay Cantor, "Stories, Like Lives, That Won't Round Off," in Los Angeles Times Book Review, *May 1, 1988, pp. 1, 12.*

DONNA RIFKIND (essay date 1988)

[*In the following review of* The Death of Methuselah, and Other Stories, *Rifkind notes the prominence of deception as both a central literary theme and technique in Singer's short fiction.*]

In Isaac Bashevis Singer's world, things are seldom what they seem. His stories are full of people who are constantly being deceived: men by women, women by men, men by promises of wealth or of a delusory earthly Paradise after revolution. The story that launched Singer's considerable fame in this country, **"Gimpel the Fool"**—published in *Partisan Review* in 1953, in a translation by Saul Bellow—tells of a simpleton who spends his whole life being tricked for the amusement of his townspeople. Preparing to die, he says of the next world: "Whatever may be there, it will be real, without complication, without ridicule, without deception. God be praised: there even Gimpel cannot be deceived." This is thought by many to be one of Singer's best stories, and is probably his most famous.

The storyteller himself is no stranger to deception. His fictional technique is extremely cunning, full of tricks and traps and escape hatches. Often he will appear to be following dutifully in the tradition of Sholem Aleichem and his other Yiddish forebears, only to veer off wildly in his own direction, as if to remind us that his is the only Yiddish voice most literate Americans recognize. Irving Howe once wrote of Singer that "though a master of Yiddish prose, he has cut himself off from the norms and styles of Yiddish culture, simultaneously moving backward to a pre-Enlightenment sensibility and forward to modernism."

While one could argue that Singer is about as much of a modernist as Geoffrey Chaucer, Howe's statement points to the capricious quality that is to me the most interesting aspect of his writing, and which is evident throughout ***The Death of Methuselah,*** his most recent collection of stories. In this volume Singer is by turns blasphemous and reverent, here comic, there tragic, first spiteful, then gentle. Dichotomies are set up like an elaborate slalom course through which characters are forced to maneuver, between the sacred and the profane, faith and doubt, love and hate, asceticism and hedonism, miracles and ordinary life. In **"The Smuggler,"** a visitor tells the author, "You once wrote that human nature is such that one cannot do anything in a straight line. You always have to maneuver between the powers of wickedness and madness. . . . One must always steal one's way among those who have the power and carry weapons."

This visitor's story is one of exile—the story of all Singer's Jews. Escapees from the malignities of Hitler and Stalin, unwelcome city dwellers in Warsaw, or emigres from dirt-poor *shtetls*: none of the survivors here can claim ever to have had a true home. As the visitor boasts, "My body is my contraband. My coming here to America in 1949 was, I may say, a triumph of my smuggling." One of the collection's comic stories, **"Sabbath in Gehenna,"** is set in hell, the ultimate exile. Even here, the damned are struggling to maneuver better conditions and fewer tortures for themselves.

Many of the tales in ***The Death of Methuselah*** share Singer's most familiar premise: a traveler tells another person (frequently an author who may or may not be I. B. Singer) about an amazing episode in his life—usually one which reveals that things are not what they seem. In **"The Impresario,"** a former deserter from the Austrian army in World War I, now a professor in Rio de Janeiro, tells a Singer-like Yiddish writer the story of his marriage to a promiscuous singer in the Yiddish opera. "I knew that to live with this woman would be permanent hell for me," he tells the writer. "I swore a holy oath to get rid of her once and for all. Two weeks later, we got married."

Before long, to the professor's horror (which begins to feel strangely akin to delight), a Polish charlatan, an "impresario," moves in with him and his wife, and soon is even sleeping in their bed with them. The professor, who was once a believer in free will, now claims that "man has no more freedom than a bedbug"; he is no longer able to distinguish between what he wants and what he dreads. Bewildered, he tells the author that for him "pleasure is a form of suffering." (p. 45)

Singer's most remarkable achievement in this collection is [**"The Death of Methuselah"**]. It is a fable about a biblical character, the grandfather of Noah, but it manages to incorporate many themes of the more mundane tales in this volume. Methuselah, 969 years old, is at last near death. A woman he had once desired named Naamah, who is now a demon, persuades him to go with her to hell, which she claims is the true Paradise, where Satan is the true God. In hell "they called life death and death life. For them right was wrong and wrong right." "He could not tell the difference anymore between laughter and crying, the cheering of female demons and the wild cries of male hobgoblins." Methuselah barely manages to escape from this mirror of confusion, which he comes to understand is a vision of the future. The next morning he is found dead, having realized that, from now on, "Man would manage somehow to crawl upon the surface of the earth, forward and backward, until God's covenant with him ended and man's name in the book of life was erased forever."

For Singer, man's earthly scourge is his readiness to be deceived into not distinguishing between wrong and right. No matter how guilefully his characters operate, all are susceptible to this torment, and for some it signals their destruction. A willingness to believe seems always to be accompanied by a willingness to be deceived. The author himself is able to escape this trap—if only temporarily—by telling tales, an act whereby he is able to become for a tiny moment like God, the prime maneuverer.

Singer's own maneuverings have produced a collection that is quite uneven; four or five of the tales are rather trivial, such as **"The Missing Line"** and **"Gifts,"** and one, **"The Jew from Babylon,"** is unnecessarily obscure. Certainly none of the stories approaches the lucid elegance of **"Gimpel the Fool."** But Singer once again proves himself to be a most interesting contradiction: in some ways defiant of the Yiddish tradition to which he is an heir, he still manages to echo key sentiments from that tradition—sentiments that show to what extent the inevitability of deception has always been on the minds of religious Jews. They are dark sentiments, fostered by dark times, and can be summed up in this quotation from Ecclesiastes: "Fear God and keep his commandments, for that is the whole of man." (pp. 45-6)

Donna Rifkind, in a review of "The Death of Methuselah and Other Stories," in The American Spectator, *Vol. 21, No. 9, September, 1988, pp. 45-6.*

ADDITIONAL BIBLIOGRAPHY

Alexander, Edward. *Isaac Bashevis Singer.* Twayne's World Author Series: A Survey of the World's Literature, No. 582. Boston: Twayne Publishers, 1980, 161 p.

General biographical and critical study of Singer and his works, including a chapter devoted to the short stories.

Fixler, Michael. "The Redeemers: Themes in the Fiction of Isaac Bashevis Singer." *The Kenyon Review* XXVI, No. 2 (Spring 1964): 371-86.

Discusses many of Singer's fundamental themes, portraying Singer as a writer "whose approach is . . . radically different from his [Yiddish] predecessors."

Hughes, Ted. "The Genius of Isaac Bashevis Singer." *The New York Review of Books* (22 April 1965): 8-10.

Approving commentary that centers on Singer's concern for what Hughes terms "the collapse of the Hasidic way of life under the pressure of all that it had been developed to keep out."

Kazin, Alfred. "The Earthly City of the Jews: Bellow to Singer." In his *Bright Book of Life: American Novelists and Storytellers from Hemingway to Mailer,* pp. 157-62. Boston: Little, Brown and Co., 1973.

Depicts Singer as "a skeptic who is hypnotized by the world he grew up in" and states: "Singer shares the orthodox point of view without its belief, and he meticulously describes, without sentimentalizing any Jew whatever, a way of life which was murdered with the millions who lived it."

———. "The Atheist Who Hears God's Voice." *The New York Times Book Review* (4 November 1973): 1, 22.

Praises Singer's collection *A Crown of Feathers,* noting particularly his unsentimental portrayal of Jewish life.

———. Review of *Passions, and Other Stories* by Isaac Bashevis Singer. *The New Republic* 173, No. 17 (25 October 1975): 24-5.

Identifying *Passions* as "certainly an uneven collection," Kazin comments on Singer's emergence as a character in his own fiction and describes some difficulties with the "compressiveness" of Singer's "magazine style" prose.

Kleinberg, Seymour. "The Last To Speak That Tongue." *The Nation* 217, No. 17 (19 November 1973): 538-39.

Review of *A Crown of Feathers, and Other Stories* in which Kleinberg adversely compares this collection with Singer's past achievements.

Kresh, Paul. *Isaac Bashevis Singer: The Magician of West 86th Street.* New York: The Dial Press, 1979, 441 p.

Biography of Singer.

Lee, Grace Farrell. *From Exile to Redemption: The Fiction of Isaac Bashevis Singer.* Carbondale, Ill.: Southern Illinois University Press, 1987, 129 p.

Thematic examination of Singer's fiction, featuring a chapter on the short stories.

Malin, Irving. Review of *Short Friday, and Other Stories,* by Isaac Bashevis Singer. *Studies in Short Fiction* III, No. 3 (Spring 1966): 383-85.

Favorable review in which Malin describes Singer's characteristic theme as "the ambiguous openness of existence."

———. *Isaac Bashevis Singer.* New York: Frederick Ungar, 1972, 126 p.

Introductory exposition demonstrating recurring themes, characters, and symbols in Singer's work, including a chapter surveying the short fiction.

———, ed. *Critical Views of Isaac Bashevis Singer.* New York: New York University Press, 1969, 268 p.

Reprints significant early critical essays on Singer's works, as well as two interviews with the author and a bibliography of works by and about Singer in English. In addition, several pieces appear for the first time in this collection, notably Samuel I. Mintz's "Spinoza and Spinozism in Singer's Shorter Fiction." Mintz writes: "Figuratively, Spinoza is a way of focusing in Singer's work on the tension between rationalism and the spirit-world of demons, or between enlightenment and orthodoxy, or between Spinozist intellectualism and Chassidic emotion."

Miller, Henry. "Magic World of Imps and Villagers." *Life* 57, No. 24 (11 December 1964): 14, 20.

Appreciative sketch of Singer written on the publication of his collection *Short Friday, and Other Stories.*

Morrow, Lance. "The Spirited World of I. B. Singer." *The Atlantic* 243, No. 1 (January 1979): 39-43.

General biographical and critical portrait inspired by Singer's reception of the Nobel Prize for Literature.

Pinsker, Sanford. "The Isolated Schlemiels of Isaac Bashevis Singer." In his *The Schlemiel as Metaphor: Studies in the Yiddish and American Jewish Novel,* pp. 55-86. Crosscurrents: Modern Critiques, edited by Harry T. Moore. Carbondale, Ill.: Southern Illinois University Press, 1971.

Describes Singer as "a Yiddish writer without a Yiddish *takhlis,*" or purpose. Pinsker concentrates on Singer's position outside the realm of both American and Yiddish literature, as well as on his relationship to the *shtetl* heritage and his attempts to recreate it in his fiction.

Pinsky, Robert. "Like Sorcery, Like Sex." *The New York Times Book Review* (17 April 1988): 3, 46.

Favorably reviews *The Death of Methuselah,* emphasizing Singer's use of the act of storytelling as a recurring motif.

Schanfield, Lillian. "Singer's 'Yentl': The Fantastic Case of a Perplexed Soul." In *Spectrum of the Fantastic: Selected Essays from the Sixth International Conference on the Fantastic in the Arts,* edited by Donald Palumbo, pp. 185-92. Contributions to the Study of Science Fiction and Fantasy, edited by Marshall Tymn, no. 31. New York: Greenwood Press, 1988.

Presents Singer's story as a work of fantasy, describing it as "an ambiguous tale of hermaphroditic experience in a world 'where anything can happen.' "

Sherman, Joseph. "Isaac Bashevis Singer: Art Versus Propaganda." *English Studies in Africa* 23, No. 2 (1980): 117-26.

Probes the short story "Yentl the Yeshiva Boy" and defends Singer against charges from some critics that he offers a false portrayal of Jewish life and experience.

Siegel, Ben. "Sacred and Profane: Isaac Bashevis Singer's Embattled Spirits." *Critique* VI, No. 1 (Spring 1963): 24-47.

Examines Singer's "sensitive fusion of Yiddish and Western literary traditions" in the short story collections *Gimpel the Fool* and *The Spinoza of Market Street,* as well as in his early novels.

Singer, Isaac Bashevis, and Burgin, Richard. *Conversations with Isaac Bashevis Singer.* New York: Farrar, Straus & Giroux, 1986, 190 p.

Interviews with Singer.

Dylan (Marlais) Thomas

1914-1953

Welsh poet, dramatist, short story writer, and essayist.

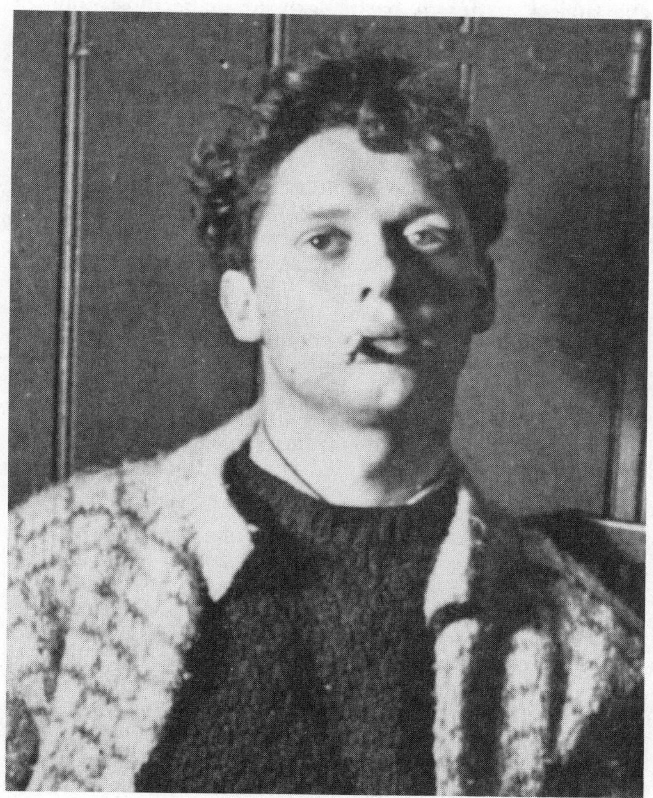

One of the most renowned authors of the twentieth century, Thomas is as well known for his life of excess as for his iconoclastic, critically acclaimed writings. Viewing the act of writing as a process of self-discovery, he sought in both his poetry and his prose to explore the mysteries of his own existence and to communicate his discoveries, asserting: "I do not want to express only what other people have felt. I want to rip something away and show what they have never seen." Thomas's approach resulted in complex, subjective short stories, many of which rely on highly charged imagery rather than narrative exposition for their effect. Critics note that while some of Thomas's stories are obscure, many successfully communicate his personal vision through their powerful, lyrical prose.

Born in a suburb of the port of Swansea, on the southern coast of Wales, Thomas was the second child and only son of middle-class parents. His father, a teacher of English who had a great love for literature, encouraged similar devotion in his son, even going so far as to read the works of Shakespeare aloud to the infant Thomas in his cradle. Such efforts were rewarded when Thomas began writing verses at an early age. He was an otherwise undistinguished student, however, and left school at sixteen to work for the *South Wales Daily Post* in Swansea.

Thomas continued to compose verse while working at the *Post;* following his resignation from the paper early in 1933, poetry became his primary occupation. It was at this time that Thomas began to develop the serious drinking problem that plagued him throughout the remainder of his life and resulted in his death at the age of thirty-nine. His notebooks reveal that many of his most highly regarded poems were either written or drafted during this period and that he had also begun to experiment with short prose pieces. In May of 1933, his poem "And Death Shall Have No Dominion" was published in the *New English Weekly,* marking the first appearance of his work in a London journal, and in December of the following year his first poetry collection, *18 Poems,* was issued. Although this book attracted little attention, Thomas's second volume, *Twenty-Five Poems,* fared somewhat better, and as the decade progressed he gained increasing recognition for both his poetry and his prose.

In the summer of 1937, Thomas married Caitlin Macnamara, an aspiring dancer of Irish descent whose reputation for unconventional behavior rivaled Thomas's own. For the next twelve years the couple led a nomadic existence, staying with friends, relatives, and a series of benefactors. The stories later collected in *Portrait of the Artist as a Young Dog* were written primarily during their stay in the Welsh coastal village of Laugharne in late 1938 and early 1939. Too frail for active military service, Thomas wrote scripts for propaganda films during World War II, at which time he also began to participate in radio dramas and readings for the BBC. Thomas emerged from the war years a respected literary figure and popular performer; however, his gregarious social life and the excessive drinking it encouraged seriously interfered with his writing. Seeking an environment more conducive to poetic production, Thomas and Caitlin returned to Laugharne in 1949.

During this time, Thomas wrote several of his most poignant poems, including "Do Not Go Gentle into That Good Night" and "Lament." He also completed the radio drama *Under Milk Wood* and began work on an autobiographical novel, which was left unfinished at his death and published posthumously as *Adventures in the Skin Trade.* Nevertheless, he feared that his creative powers were rapidly waning, and, partly in an attempt to avoid the pressures of writing, he embarked on a speaking tour of the United States in the spring of 1950. A highly charismatic speaker, Thomas charmed American audiences with his readings and shocked them with his often lascivious, irresponsible behavior. He returned to the United States three times in the next two years; during his final tour, in the fall of 1953, Thomas died from a massive overdose of alcohol.

Critics divide Thomas's short stories into two groups: those written prior to 1939 and described by Jacob Korg as "vigorous fantasies in poetic style," and the more realistic later stories that appeared in the volumes *Portrait of the Artist as a Young Dog* and *Quite Early One Morning.* The stories of the first group are generally static in nature, containing little or no plot in the traditional sense and communicating the author's deepest fears in their images of death, mutilation (particularly castration), sexual passion, and madness. A number of these stories also rely upon dreams as a means of recounting characters' explorations of their own consciousness, reflecting Thomas's search for both his essential self and his poetic subject matter. A particularly dramatic illustration of this technique occurs in the story "The Woman and the Mouse," which begins when a poet dreams of a compellingly attractive woman. After the poet writes about the woman, she assumes an existence independent of his consciousness and becomes so menacing that he kills her by writing "the woman died." The result is that the poet begins to understand his own vulnerability to his creative products, a revelation that robs him of his sanity. The fantastic nature of such stories has led critics to compare Thomas's early prose to that of the Surrealists. Thomas, who associated with members of the Surrealist group during the 1930s, objected to this comparison; he noted that while the Surrealists attempted to create dreamlike visions by randomly selecting and juxtaposing visual elements, he carefully chose his images for their symbolic value and constructed his narratives with painstaking precision. Despite Thomas's skillful use of symbols, critics suggest that his meaning in these stories is often obscure, and they are generally regarded as inferior to his later prose.

The stories Thomas wrote after 1938 depict his personal journey from innocence to experience in a more concrete fashion, focusing on the people and events that shaped his awareness. His relatives and boyhood friends appear thinly or not at all disguised, although many of the events described are telescoped, exaggerated, or entirely fictional. In the first story of *Portrait of the Artist as a Young Dog,* "The Peaches," Thomas lovingly recreates his aunt Ann Jones, illustrating her humility and goodness through a fictional anecdote in which she is rebuffed when she offers some cherished preserved peaches to a haughty woman as a gesture of hospitality. Similarly, in "Who Do You Wish Was with Us," Thomas exaggerates the childhood adversities of a boyhood friend in order to emphasize the tragedy of the boy's existence. While many of Thomas's fictional anecdotes are humorous in nature, critics note that the stories in which they appear are generally infused with a mood of nostalgic longing, and D. C. Muecke has identified the pain of loss as a recurrent motif in Thomas's later prose.

While Thomas is best remembered for his lyric poetry, his short stories are regarded as an important part of his contribution to modern literature. Indeed, his highly accessible later prose is admired by many who find his verse disturbing or unnecessarily recondite. Critics note in particular the evocative power of Thomas's prose and his ability to convey sensory impressions. They further suggest that Thomas, building upon the innovative narrative techniques developed by James Joyce, helped to shape current approaches to short fiction by successfully shifting the emphasis of his stories from action to character, symbol, and mood.

(See also *Twentieth-Century Literary Criticism,* Vols. 1, 8; *Contemporary Authors,* Vols. 104, 120; and *Dictionary of Literary Biography,* Vols. 13, 20.)

PRINCIPAL WORKS

SHORT FICTION

The Map of Love (short stories and poetry) 1939
Portrait of the Artist as a Young Dog 1940
Quite Early One Morning (short stories and essays) 1954
Adventures in the Skin Trade, and Other Stories (short stories and unfinished novel) 1955
Selected Writings of Dylan Thomas 1970
Dylan Thomas: Early Prose Writings (short stories and essays) 1971
Collected Stories 1980

OTHER MAJOR WORKS

18 Poems (poetry) 1934
Twenty-Five Poems (poetry) 1936
New Poems (poetry) 1943
Deaths and Entrances (poetry) 1946
Collected Poems, 1934-1952 (poetry) 1952
In Country Sleep (poetry) 1952
Under Milk Wood (drama) 1954

ANTHONY WEST (essay date 1955)

[*The son of Rebecca West and H. G. Wells, West was an English author whose novels examined the moral, social, psychological, and political disruptions of the twentieth century. He also composed a critical study of D. H. Lawrence, numerous literary essays, and book reviews. In the following excerpt from his review of* Quite Early One Morning, *West discusses the uneven quality of the stories in that volume.*]

Quite Early One Morning is ostensibly a collection of prose pieces by the poet Dylan Thomas, but less than half of the collection was written by the poet, and the rest was composed by what Blake would have called his spectre. The spectre inhabited the world of daily bread and fed the poet with its labors, working as an actor for the British Broadcasting Corporation, as a journalist, a lecturer, and a buffoon to earn the odd guinea and the odder dollar. The spectre worked just as hard, though, at preserving the poet's privacy as it did at keeping him fed, clothed, and housed, and it created an impenetrable barrier between him and the wider public that valued him as a wild, moon-struck bully boy, a joculator and clown, who would perform on demand when paid with a drink. The spectre's work, most of which appears in what is labelled Part II of ***Quite Early One Morning,*** is not worth much; even though there are a number of brilliant jokes and fast pieces of good fooling in it, the stuff was turned out in Satan's mill and is best forgotten. Luckily, Part I, except for two pieces (a British Broadcasting Corporation feature and a film script, both of them bread-and-butter jobs), is by the poet, writing freely, and without any sense of an end in view, about Wales and his childhood. Although the area from which he was writing was near the surface, where poet melts into spectre, he was saying what he wanted to say in these pieces, and they are bright with the reflected radiance of his greater self. Read straight through, they are bracing; the experience is like riding on a roller coaster that racks up to a peak, metaphor by metaphor, and then slides down like lightning through a dozen bizarrely related images, breathtakingly associated. At the end of the trip one wants another ride, to have the excitement all over again. It has all seemed a tremendous lark. It has been, too, but it has also been fundamentally extremely serious. The sketch that gives this collection its name runs from exaggeration to exaggeration, so it is easy to take it for nothing more than a Rabelaisian gasconade. It begins,

> Quite early one morning in the winter in Wales, by the sea that was lying down still and green as grass after a night of tar-black howling and rolling, I went out of the house, where I had come to stay for a cold unseasonable holiday, to see if it was raining still, if the outhouse had been blown away, potatoes, shears, rat-killer, shrimp nets, and tins of rusty nails aloft on the wind, and if all the cliffs were left. It had been such a ferocious night that someone in the smoky ship-pictured bar had said he could feel his tombstone shaking even though he was not dead or, at least, was moving; but the morning shone as clear and calm as one always imagines tomorrow will shine.

It goes on from joke to joke:

> Someone was snoring in one house. I counted ten savagely indignant grunts-and-groans like those of a pig in a model and mudless farm, which ended with a window-rattler, a washbasin-shaker, a trembler of tooth glasses, a waker of dormice. It thundered with me up to the chapel railings, then brassily vanished.
>
> Smoke from another chimney now: they were burning their last night's dreams: up from a chimney came a long-haired wraith, like an old politician; somebody had been dreaming of the Liberal party.

Finally the voices of the wakers under the roofs make themselves heard, one by one, speaking in verse:

> Do you hear that whistling?—It's me, I am Phoebe,
> the maid at the King's Head, and I am whistling like a bird.
> Someone spilt a tin of pepper in the tea.
> There's twenty for breakfast, and I'm not going to say a word.

The sketch ends, in prose again:

> Thus some of the voices of a cliff-perched town at the far end of Wales moved out of sleep and darkness into the newborn, ancient and ageless morning, moved and were lost.

But when one goes over it a second time one discovers the rough notes for a serious poem. In the opening passage, the poet is going out to see if the world-ending storm has blown the dross of potatoes, shears, rat-killer, shrimp nets, and tins of rusty nails away. He finds that the world has been purified, but only visually. The first living things the poet meets are birds, traditional "poetic" symbols of innocence:

> Birds sang in eaves, bushes, trees, on telegraph wires, rails, fences, spars and wet masts, not for love or joy, but to keep other birds away. The landlords in feathers disputed the right of even the flying light to descend and perch.

This looks like merely a simple joke by somebody who knows his ornithology, deriding the sentimentality of ordinary bird lovers, but its references are not as simple as they seem. The phrase "not for love or joy" is a reference to a lyrical passage in one of Blake's prophetic books, presenting the morning chorus of the birds as an act of worship; Thomas is rejecting that view of life. The phrase in the second sentence, "flying light," is a Gnostic Christian phrase describing the divine spirit, which the birds, as representatives of unimaginative life, will not receive. Thomas returns to this idea a few lines further on, when he passes a rooming house called The Cosy and imagines the dreams that its proprietress, Miss Hughes, ought to have if she was a creature of the spiritual realm. But daylight is here element, and it is getting stronger every minute. The realities are becoming more apparent:

> Everywhere there glowed and rayed the colors of the small, slate-grey woman's dreams: purple, magenta, ruby, sapphire, emerald, vermilion, honey. But I could not believe it. She knitted in her tidy sleep-world a beige woollen shroud with "Thou Shalt Not" on the bosom.

This leads to a sequence of let-downs—a grocer dreams flat dreams of accounts, and a sea captain dreams of bar-parlor images of beer and onions instead of dreaming of Circe's island—and ends with the snore that comes up to the chapel railings, roaring like a lion.

> The chapel stood grim and grey, telling the day there was to be no nonsense. The chapel was not asleep; it never catnapped nor nodded nor closed its long cold eye. I left it telling the morning off and a seagull hung, rebuked, above it.

When the people of the town are all finally awake, they declare their dim hopes of a world unlighted by imagination in a deliberately flat verse form:

> I am only Mr. Griffiths, very shortsighted, B.A., Aber.
> As soon as I finish my egg I must shuffle off to school.
> Oh, patron saint of teachers, teach me to keep order,
> and *forget* those words on the blackboard—
> "Griffiths Bat is a fool."

The entire structure is a lament for the living who are enclosed in the world and—since they will never see the light of the morning in which the poet lives—lost.

The whole thing may seem a tedious trampling of a *jeu d'esprit* into the ground. But it was precisely Thomas's tragedy that he lived in an age when it could seem so. He inherited the Welsh poetic tradition of elaborately constructed, elaborately referenced, riddling verse, made to be heard, and thought about, by an audience brought up to respect and understand poetry and its language of image and symbol. He knew his art and craft better than all but a very few of the poets of his time, and he used it more naturally, for industrialism and popular scientific rationalism never took poetry out of life in Wales as they did almost everywhere else in Europe. Because he spoke "as one with authority," having a mastery of his art, and of his culture, behind him, he was rewarded by being thought God's fool, who spouted a stream of half-understood images, not caring whether his listeners followed more than a quarter of what he was saying. His English-speaking admirers were unaware of how often his images drew on medieval and earlier Welsh patterns of association, and of how thoroughly the later Welsh tradition sanctioned what seemed to them to be his own metrical and structural eccentricities. It was his misfortune that he was too big to be provincial and that his largeness of mind and spirit took him out of Wales and into the anti-poetic English-speaking world, where poets are valued not so much for their poetry as for what sort of Byron-Keats-Shelley turn they can put on. The book ends, suitably, with what has become, ironically, the most widely distributed of any of Thomas's writings—the spectre's account of the evisceration and destruction of the poet, "dying of welcome," as one of the poems says. The piece, **"A Visit to America,"** was enormously popular, and it was considered one of his best jokes. It turned out to be his epitaph. (pp. 106-08)

Anthony West, "A Singer and a Spectre," in The New Yorker, *Vol. XXX, No. 49, January 22, 1955, pp. 106-08.*

D. C. MUECKE (essay date 1959)

[*In the following excerpt, Muecke discusses the prevalence of the loss motif in Thomas's prose.*]

No one could accuse Dylan Thomas of triviality. Poem after poem shows him preoccupied with the universal tragedy, the pity and terror of irreversible time, ineluctable death. In this he neighbours Shakespeare, living not next door but, so to speak, over against him; for while in the *Sonnets* alien time lays siege to loveliness, in Thomas beauty and corruption, the green and the dying, are sister and stronger brother of the same birth. (p. 69)

This universal war of life and death, which in his poetry Thomas sees as such, has its particular battles and moreover throws shadows of pathos or terror upon the ordinary chances of life. These incidents and rumours of war are lively or loud in much of Thomas's prose: someone dies, lost childhood is remembered, a daft old man runs away from home to find a more comfortable burying place, a friend or a lover is lost, never to be found again. Peculiarly strong in the prose is the implication or the expression of anguish and heartbreak and this in spite of Thomas's imagination being just as strongly attracted by the comedy of life's incongruities.

A boy on holiday on his uncle's farm encounters a girl who makes love to him and later leaves him. From this plot grew the early story **"A Prospect of the Sea,"** a partly realistic, partly symbolical presentation of the boy's experiences. The girl's going away is represented by her running into the sea, not a sea of water but "a white-faced sea of people, the terrible mortal number of the waves, all the centuries' sea drenched in the hail before Christ."

> "Come back! Come back!" the boy cried to the girl. . . . but she had mingled with the people moving in and out. Their tides were drawn by a grave moon that never lost an arc. Their long, sea gestures were deliberate, the flat hands beckoning, the heads uplifted, the eyes in the mask faces set in one direction. Oh, where was she now in the sea? Among the white, walking, and the coral-eyed. "Come back! Come back! Darling, run out of the sea."

This going into the sea is a symbol of dying, but death may in turn be a symbol for some other kind of loss. There is no mistaking, however, the anguish the boy feels although he had been frightened when she was making him love her. Her going away is the end of his world, the leaving of Eden and the flood of Noah; the old, wicked, innocent, story-book time is over. The title ironically conceals the story's terror behind its seeming innocence.

Nearly all the stories in ***Portrait of the Artist as a Young Dog,*** though filled with comedy, are sad. All are semi-fictional rememberings of Thomas's Swansea days before he went to London. There is no open nostalgia, only a recurring feeling that the world is strangely sad even when you are happy. One story begins: "One afternoon, in a particularly bright and glowing August, some years before I knew I was happy. . . ."

The first story in the book, **"The Peaches,"** has the same actual setting as **"A Prospect of the Sea"** but narrowed, to fit the story's realism, from the timeless hill and field to the everyday farmyard and house. The boy on holiday is Dylan. The uncle is J. Jones and there is an Aunt Annie who is a version of the Ann Jones of "After the Funeral." The farm is here called Gorsehill, but Fern Hill in the poem, where we read:

> And nothing I cared, at my sky blue trades, that time allows
> In all his tuneful turning so few and such morning songs
> Before the children green and golden
> Follow him out of grace,
>
> Nothing I cared, in the lamb white days, that time would take me
> Up to the swallow thronged loft by the shadow of my hand,
> In the moon that is always rising,
> Nor that riding to sleep
> I should hear him fly with the high fields
> And wake to the farm forever fled from the childless land.
> Oh as I was young and easy in the mercy of his means,
> Time held me green and dying
> Though I sang in my chains like the sea.

"The Peaches" ends with the loss of a boyhood friend and a broken holiday.

> Mrs. Williams sent the chauffeur for Jack's luggage. Annie came to the door, trying to smile and curtsy, tidying her hair, wiping her hands on her pinafore.
>
> Mrs. Williams said, "Good afternoon," and sat with Jack in the back of the car and stared at the ruin of Gorsehill.
>
> The chauffeur came back. The car drove off, scattering the hens. I ran out of the stable to wave to Jack. He sat still and stiff by his mother's side. I waved my handkerchief.

The style deliberately is flat to express the emptiness of Dylan's world—a small tragedy perhaps, but to a boy "the weeping end of the world."

In the same volume there are two "lost lover" stories, **"Extraordinary Little Cough"** and **"One Warm Saturday."** The first of these, another story of a broken holiday, has a double plot, the climax of each half reacting upon and intensifying the other. George Hooping, "heavily spectacled, small-paunched," nick-named Little Cough, though passing a test of endurance imposed upon him by two bullies, nonetheless fails to make good his claim to be an ordinary boy. His holiday companions, thoroughly boyish boys, fail too, losing their girls to the handsome ugly bullies.

> We sat by the fire . . . and tried not to listen to the soft voices in the tent. Gwyneth's laughter floated out over the suddenly moonlit field, but Jean, with the beast, was smiling and silent in the covered warmth; I knew her little hand was in Brazell's hand.
>
> "Women!" I said.

> Dan spat in the fire.

"One Warm Saturday" is the best short story Thomas wrote. It is also the fullest treatment of the lost lover theme. Again a shattered holiday, though only a Saturday; again the finding and losing a girl; again the anguish, this time not implied but fully and passionately expressed; again the closing image of universal sadness and hopelessness. Drunk and lost in the rotting tenement where the girl has a room, the young man stumbles up and down stairs, along passages hearing—

> Lou's voice in a fresh fever drive him on, call him to return, speak to him with such passion and abandonment that even in the darkness and the pain of his haste he was dazzled and struck still. She spoke, there on the rotting stairs in the middle of the poor house, a frightening rush of love words; from her mouth, at his ear, endearments were burned out. Hurry! Hurry! Every moment is being killed. Love, adored, dear, run back and whistle to me, open the door, shout my name, lay me down. Mr. O'Brien has his hands on my side.

But he can't find his way back. Lou is lost to Mr. O'Brien as Jean to Brazell.

> He tapped all the doors and whispered her name. He beat on the doors and shouted. . . . For a long time he waited on the stairs. . . . Then he walked out of the house on to the waste space and under the leaning cranes and ladders. The light of the one weak lamp in a rusty circle fell across the brick-heaps and the broken wood and the dust that had been houses once, where the small and hardly-known and never-to-be-forgotten people of the dirty town had lived and loved and died and, always, lost.

In **"Who Do You Wish Was with Us?"** the theme takes the form of a man's remembering his dead brother. Dylan Thomas and Raymond Price, a boy and a young man, go on a walking holiday. Ray's family were all dead except his mother who was crippled with arthritis. Bitterly he remembered a life of cooking and nursing, changing the sheets twice a day for Harry his consumptive brother, holding his father down on the bed when he had fits. His sister died in a sanatorium. Obsessed by memories, a chance word would release him from the actual.

> He stared at his dusty white shoes and I knew what shapes his imagination made of them: they were the feet of a man dead in bed, and he was going to talk about his brother. Sometimes . . . I caught him staring at his own thin hand: he was thinning it more and more, removing the flesh, seeing Harry's hand in front of him, with the bones appearing through the sensitive skin. If he lost the world around him for a moment, if I left him alone, if he cast his eyes down, if his hand lost its grip on the hard, real fence or the hot bowl of his pipe, he would be back in ghastly bedrooms, carrying cloths and basins and listening for handbells.

In spite of knowing this Dylan felt compelled to ask, as they sat alone and remote on a rock at the sea's edge, the world's end, "Who do you wish was with us?" For Ray there could be only one answer, filled with all his love and longing for his dead brother. "I wish my brother was with us," Ray said. "I wish Harry was here. I wish he was here now, at this moment, on this rock." Then alone and cold with Harry's ghost come back and sun gone down, they realize that the sea has cut them off from the mainland.

Terror, in this story, has more weight than grief, but this is only a shift of emphasis; the world inevitably brings both. (pp. 70-3)

Although Vernon Watkins, a close friend of his, speaks of Thomas's "essentially tragic vision" and although this article has laboured to bring into relief an essentially tragic theme that runs through fourteen years of Thomas's prose, I should not wish it thought that the tragic element in Thomas's work was all-important.

In the first place there is, at least equally important and much more obvious, his passionate and total apprehension of the world about him. Again like Shakespeare, his feeling for what was tragic in this world was strong in proportion to what was perhaps largely its cause, his love of the multitudinary world. And as he grew older, so he said, the world became even larger and brighter.

> . . . the closer I move
> To death, one man through his sundered hulks,
> The louder the sun blooms
> And the tusked, ramshackling sea exults;
> And every wave of the way
> And gale I tackle, the whole world then,
> With more triumphant faith
> Than ever was since the world was said,
> Spins its morning of praise,
>
> I hear the bouncing hills
> Grow larked and greener at berry brown
> Fall and the dew larks sing
> Taller this thunderclap spring, and how
> More spanned with angels ride
> The mansouled fiery islands!

In the second place there is some reason to suppose he had found or was trying to find some reconciliation, some philosophy transcending the conflict of life and death. A poem first published in 1939 ("If My Head Hurt a Hair's Foot") he described as "a series of conflicting images which move through pity and violence to an unreconciled acceptance of suffering," but speaking in 1950 of a long "optimistic" poem he had meant to write he said:

> . . . the poem becomes, at last, an affirmation of the beautiful and terrible worth of the Earth. It grows into a praise of what is and what could be on this lump in the skies. It is a poem about happiness.

Perhaps Polly Garter knew what Thomas was after when she sighed: "Oh, isn't life a terrible thing, thank God?" (pp. 75-6)

D. C. Muecke, "Come Back! Come Back!: A Theme in Dylan Thomas's Prose," in Meanjin, *Vol. XVIII, No. 1, April, 1959, pp. 69-76.*

JOHN ACKERMAN (essay date 1964)

[*In the following excerpt, Ackerman discusses elements of humor and nostalgia in* Portrait of the Artist as a Young Dog.]

In ***Portrait of the Artist as a Young Dog*** Thomas for the first time reveals himself as an artist in comedy. Vernon Watkins has described how he

> suddenly abandoned the highly charged, artificial

> yet impulsive symbolism of such stories as **"The Orchards," "The Lemon"** and the unfinished fragment **"In The Direction of the Beginning"** at about the time of his twenty-fourth birthday. . . . Quite suddenly he began to write about people as they actually were and behaved.

Thomas's eye had now turned outward from his own introspective, obsessive emotions to the world about him. It was the varied and many-coloured life of South Wales that attracted his attention; for he was developing a consuming, though generally unjudging, curiosity about other people's lives. The picture that he gives of Wales is an idealized and exuberant one: ***Portrait of the Artist as a Young Dog*** is, on the whole, genial in tone. In these stories Thomas drew extensively upon his memories of childhood:

> Through the exact memory he had of his childhood and an extraordinary power to recreate it he released a spring of comedy, both of character and situation, which had been hidden from himself because it was at first too close to his experience. These were the stories about Swansea and the surroundings of that, his native town; and very Welsh they were, more true to Swansea than Swansea itself. [Vernon Watkins, in his Foreword to ***Adventures in the Skin Trade, and Other Stories*** (1955).]

The story of the Welsh childhood has become a familiar genre. In the short story the reader is usually offered an isolated and semi-autobiographical incident. Most Anglo-Welsh writers of this century show, in their early work, this need to record the experiences of their childhood and adolescence. In so doing they lay particular emphasis upon the community in which they were brought up. ***Portrait of the Artist as a Young Dog*** was among the first of these autobiographical works to blend successfully comedy and nostalgia. The comedy of the book is at once apparent, but its nostalgic mood has received less critical attention. This idealistic looking over the shoulder to a bygone state of innocence and joy is one of Thomas's most characteristic attitudes.

Unlike many other accounts of the Welsh childhood, ***Portrait of the Artist as a Young Dog*** possesses a unity of structure. That unity is the picture it gives of its author, the delineation of a poet's growing consciousness of himself and of the world in which he lives. It is typical of Thomas that he should have chosen to parody the familiar literary mode, the portrait of the artist. There had been a recent modern example of this literary form in Joyce's *Portrait of the Artist as a Young Man.* Thomas, however, hides the real seriousness of his picture behind the mask of comedy. Too many readers, unfortunately, have not seen beyond the mask. Many critics, too, have overemphasized the influence of Joyce. (pp. 104-05)

Thomas's volume of stories is carefully planned. Each story deals with a stage in his childhood, youth, or early manhood and he never repeats a situation or experience. Though all the stories are linked and have a tremendous sense of life and movement, each has its own atmosphere and mood. Always, in these tales, Thomas is the observer and interpreter, a little detached from the rest of the group. He is, for example, ever aware of other people's discomfort, and quick to see the pathos of their situation. Though humorous, and sometimes gently satiric, his attitude is compassionate and, despite all their imperfections and oddities, he accepts and delights in the humanity of his characters. (pp. 105-06)

[The] opening story, **"The Peaches,"** tells of a childhood visit to Ann Jones's farm. He reveals at once an uncanny sympathy for his subject: as in the picture of Uncle Jim, who stops for a drink and is a little guilty about his drinking: " 'I'll be out straight away,' he said fiercely, as though I had contradicted him, 'you stay there quiet'." In true Welsh style: "He sang hymns all the way to Gorsehill in an affectionate bass voice, and conducted the wind with his whip." Thomas records his tendency as a child to dramatize himself:

> There was welcome then. The clock struck twelve as she [his aunt] kissed me, and I stood among the shining and striking like a prince taking off his disguise. One minute I was small and cold, skulking dead-scared down a black passage in my stiff, best suit . . . unfamiliar to myself, a snub-nosed storyteller lost in his own adventures and longing to be home; the next I was a royal nephew in smart town clothes, embraced and welcomed, standing in the snug centre of my stories and listening to the clock announcing me.

In stories such as this Thomas reveals himself as extremely sensitive, both to his own feelings and to the feelings of others. He is far from the tough, happy-go-lucky tomboy, unlettered and insensitive, many critics have imagined:

> I climbed the stairs; each had a different voice. The house smelt of rotten wood and damp and animals. I thought that I had been walking long, damp passages all my life, and climbing stairs in the dark, alone.

Vividly, too, he describes his youthful, imaginative feeling for nature. By imaginative, in this instance, I refer to his tendency to enlarge upon a particular situation:

> On my haunches, eager and alone, casting an ebony shadow, with the Gorsehill jungle swarming, the violent impossible birds and fishes leaping, hidden under four-stemmed flowers the height of horses, in the early evening in a dingle near Carmarthen, my friend Jack Williams invisibly near me, I felt all my young body like an excited animal surrounding me.

Thomas was keenly aware of the way of life peculiar to South Wales. In **"The Peaches,"** for example, he describes a sermon which his cousin Gwilym, who is studying to be a preacher, gives in the barn. It is an effective parody of the *hwyl* that characterizes Welsh preaching:

> I sat on the hay and stared at Gwilym preaching, and heard his voice rise and crack and sink to a whisper and break into singing and Welsh and ring triumphantly and be wild and meek.

Thomas reserves some of his satiric shafts for the well-to-do Mrs. Williams who visits the farm:

> She said: "Please don't put yourself out for me, Mrs. Jones, there's a dear." She dusted the seat of a chair with a lace handkerchief from her bag before sitting down. . . .

Annie prepares tea for her visitor:

> "Now, you must have some peaches, Mrs. Williams, they're lovely . . ."
>
> "No, no, Mrs. Jones, thanks the same," she said. "I don't mind pears or chunks, but I can't bear peaches."

Throughout this scene Thomas effectively exposes Mrs. Williams's snobbish insensitivity. She is a proud, vulgar woman, conscious only of her wealth and her consequent importance, and the reader's sympathy goes out to Annie.

In **"Where Tawe Flows"** Thomas satirizes the excesses of Welsh Nationalism: the scene is a meeting of the literary group to which "young Mr. Thomas" belongs:

> "We're looking for seditious literature," said Mr. Humphries with difficulty, raising his hand in a salute.
>
> "Heil, Saunders Lewis! and we know where to find it," said Mr. Roberts. Mr. Evans turned off his torch, "Come in out of the night air, boys, and have a drop of something. It's only parsnip wine," he added.

Saunders Lewis, the Welsh Nationalist leader, had set fire to an aerodrome in Wales in 1938.

Throughout ***Portrait of the Artist as a Young Dog*** Thomas is anxious to represent himself as an *enfant terrible:*

> I let Edgar Reynolds be whipped because I had taken his homework; I stole from my mother's bag; I stole from Gwyneth's bag; I stole twelve books in three visits from the library, and threw them away in the park; I drank a cup of my water to see what it tasted like; I beat a dog with a stick so that it would roll over and lick my hand afterwards; I looked with Dan Jones through the keyhole while his maid had a bath; I cut my knee with a penknife, and put the blood on my handkerchief and said it had come out of my ears so that I could pretend I was ill and frighten my mother; I pulled my trousers down and showed Jack Williams.

The list of delinquencies need not be taken too seriously and at least saves the account from sentimentality, which is always apt to enter into recollections of childhood. This mischievous desire to shock his more respectable readers gives his writing a certain toughness and honesty.

One of the most delightful scenes in ***Portrait of the Artist as a Young Dog*** occurs in **"A Visit to Grandpa's"** and describes a situation that could only be found in Wales, where, by tradition, much emphasis and concern is given to a person's place of burial. The elderly are usually anxious to be buried in their ancestral churchyard, a feeling which, in its philosophical acceptance of death, would attract Thomas's interest. A coffin was sometimes prepared in advance and highly prized by its prospective occupant, and many a bottom drawer contains the "laying out" clothes. The grandfather in the story one morning disappears. It is soon realized that he has gone to Llangadock—for he has put on his best waistcoat—to be buried. He is discovered, *en route,* in Carmarthen. The final scene has a peculiarly Welsh blend of comedy and high seriousness:

> Mr. Griff pointed his coloured stick at him.
>
> "And what do you think you are doing on Carmarthen bridge in the middle of the afternoon," he said sternly, "with your best waistcoat and your old hat?"
>
> Grandpa did not answer, but inclined his face to the river wind, so that his beard was set dancing and wagging as though he talked, and watched the coracle men move, like turtles, on the shore.
>
> Mr. Griff raised his stunted barber's pole. "And where do you think you are going," he said, "with your old black bag?"
>
> Grandpa said: "I am going to Llangadock to be buried." And he watched the coracle shells slip into the water lightly, and the gulls complain over the fish-filled water as bitterly as Mr. Price complained:
>
> "But you aren't dead yet, Dai Thomas."
>
> For a moment grandpa reflected, then: "There's no sense in lying dead in Llanstephan," he said, "The ground is comfy in Llangadock; you can twitch your legs without putting them in the sea."
>
> His neighbours moved close to him. They said:
>
> "You aren't dead, Mr. Thomas."
>
> "How can you be buried, then?"
>
> "Nobody's going to bury you in Llanstephan."
>
> "Come on home, Mr. Thomas."
>
> "There's strong beer for tea."
>
> "And cake."
>
> But grandpa stood firmly on the bridge, and clutched his bag to his side, and stared at the flowing river and the sky, like a prophet who has no doubt.

Thomas's grandfather, it seems, was reluctant to be buried in Llanstephan and wanted to be laid to rest in his old home,

Thomas in 1933.

Llangadock, where "the ground is comfy." The closing comparison of the old man to "a prophet who has no doubt," with its Biblical and druidic associations, is particularly effective.

It was Thomas's habit to note down phrases, even whole sentences, that occurred to him while drinking in a pub or talking with friends. Often, in the middle of a witty story or a literary argument, he would drag a cigarette packet from his pocket, tear off the end, write a few words, and thrust the piece into another pocket. Some phrase, metaphor, or joke had jostled its way through the tobacco haze in the crowded bar-parlour. This note-making seldom caused a break in his discourse: he continued his drinking, smoking, talking, his pockets crammed with hastily written notes and observations. Perhaps surprisingly, he was a good listener, and the embroidered pub-stories of human foibles remained ready for use in his capacious memory. The wealth of objective detail in his prose writing demonstrates his receptiveness to the life around him.

Sense impressions he conveys with remarkable immediacy: a good example being the description of his first pint of Welsh beer:

> I liked the taste of beer, its live, white lather, its brass-bright depths, the sudden world through the wet-brown walls of the glass, the tilted rush to the lips and the slow swallowing down to the lapping belly, the salt on the tongue, the foam at the corners.

Thomas usually ends his stories on a note of pathos. Often it is a single sentence which strikes this note, as in the story of Little Cough, where he beautifully conveys the child's sense of life's terrible seriousness. George Hooping (nicknamed Little Cough) has been running on Rhossili sands for hours to prove his toughness to the other boys: "And when I stared round at George again he was lying on his back fast asleep in the deep grass and his hair was touching the flames." There is, in each story, a specific, well-defined mood. The Swansea streets are full of emotional connotations for Thomas; a mood of nostalgia always directs the experience.

> I was a lonely nightwalker and a steady stander-at-corners. I liked to walk through the wet town after midnight, when the streets were deserted and the window lights out, alone and alive on the glistening tram-lines in dead and empty High Street under the moon, gigantically sad in the damp streets by ghostly Ebenezer Chapel. And I never felt more a part of the remote and overpressing world, or more full of love and arrogance and pity and humility, not for myself alone, but for the living earth I suffered on. . . . I leant against the wall of a derelict house in the residential areas or wandered in the empty rooms, stood terrified on the stairs or gazing through the smashed windows at the sea or at nothing, and the lights going out one by one in the avenues.

Such a paragraph, for all the bravado, is a portrait of the artist.

Thomas grew up in the Swansea of the depression, and this period of poverty and unemployment left its mark on his memory:

> Mr. Farr hurried down High Street, savagely refusing laces and matches, averting his eyes from the shabby crowds. He knew that the poor the sick and the ugly, unwanted people were so close around him that, with one look of recognition, one gesture of sympathy, he would be lost among them and the evening would be spoilt for ever.

The story **"Who Do You Wish Was with Us?"** shows his concern with pain and bodily suffering. Dylan's friend Ray, who is accompanying him on a day's outing, keeps remembering his brother, a sufferer from tuberculosis:

> I had to change the sheets twice a day for my brother, there was blood on everything. I watched him getting thinner and thinner; in the end you could lift him up with one hand. And his wife wouldn't go to see him because he coughed in her face.

The story which closes the volume, **"One Warm Saturday,"** was Thomas's favourite and is, perhaps, the most complex and personal in the collection. The poet is wandering by himself about Swansea:

> The young man, in his wilderness, saw the holiday Saturday set down before him, false and pretty, as a flat picture under a vulgar sun; the disporting families with paper bags, buckets and spades, parasols and bottles, the happy, hot, and aching girls with sunburn liniments in their bags . . . moved him, he thought dramatically in his isolation, to an old shame and pity; outside all holiday, like a young man doomed for ever to the company of his maggots.

He joins in a game of cricket with a family on the sands, until a dog carries the ball into the sea and swims with it out of reach. He sees Mr. Matthews, a typical Nonconformist "hell-fire preacher": "Boys with pea-shooters sat quietly near him. A ragged man collected nothing in a cap." The day moves to its close: "the evening dull as a chapel. All his friends had vanished into their pleasures." Thomas characteristically compares the dull evening to a chapel. He mocks himself, however, poking fun at his self-pity and despair:

> He thought: Poets live and walk with their poems; a man with visions needs no other company. . . . I must go home and sit in my bedroom by the boiler. But he was not a poet living and walking, he was a young man in a sea town on a warm bank holiday, with two pounds to spend.

He meets a beautiful young woman, and his conflicting emotions are viewed with the irony of the detached observer:

> The young man in the window seat, still bewildered by the first sight of her entering the darkened room, caught the kiss to himself and flushed. He thought to run out of the room and through the miracle-making gardens, to rush into his house and hide his head in the bed-clothes and lie all night there, dressed and trembling, her voice in his ears, her green eyes wide awake under his closed eyelids. But only a sick boy with tossed blood would run from his proper love into a dream, lie down in a bedroom that was full of his shames, and sob against the feathery, fat breast and face of the damp pillow. He remembered his age and poems, and would not move.

Eventually, and inevitably, he gets drunk and goes to a party with the young woman. The story moves to a hazy, dream-like close, as he makes his way home alone. A final, elegiac

paragraph suggests man's continuing need for compassion and fuller understanding:

> For a long time he waited on the stairs, though there was no love now to wait for and no bed but his own too many miles away to lie in, and only the approaching day to remember his discovery. . . . Then he walked out. . . . The light of the one weak lamp in a rusty circle fell across the brick-heaps and the broken wood and the dust that had been houses once, where the small and hardly known and never-to-be-forgotten people of the dirty town had lived and loved and died and, always, lost.

In ***Portrait of the Artist as a Young Dog*** the half-mythical Welsh landscapes of the early stories have been replaced by more closely observed, often indoor, and always specifically Welsh scenes charged with comedy and dramatic life. (pp. 106-13)

John Ackerman, in his Dylan Thomas: His Life and Work, *Oxford University Press, London, 1964, pp. 104-14.*

JACOB KORG (essay date 1965)

[*Korg is an American critic and editor best known for his numerous studies of the works of George Gissing. In the following excerpt from his critical analysis of the work of Dylan Thomas, Korg discusses the development of Thomas's narrative technique.*]

Thomas' fiction may be divided sharply into two classifications: vigorous fantasies in poetic style, a genre he discontinued after 1939; and straightforward, objective narratives. Until 1939 he seems to have thought of the short prose narrative as an alternate poetic form—as a vehicle for recording the action of the imagination in reshaping objective reality according to private desire. Almost every story of this period (the exceptions being **"After the Fair"** and **"The Tree"**) perceives actuality through the screen of an irrational mind. The main characters are madmen, simpletons, fanatics, lechers, and poets in love: people enslaved by the dictates of feeling. Their stories are narrated in a heavily poetic prose reflecting the confusion of actual and imaginary experiences which constitutes their reality, so that the material and psychological intersect without a joint, forming a strange new area of being. For example, as Mr. Davies, the deluded rector of **"The Holy Six,"** is washing the feet of his six colleagues, believing that he is performing a holy deed, we are told that "light brought the inner world to pass," that his misconception was transformed into actuality. Some of the stories seem transitional in style, enabling the reader to witness these transformations as an outsider. In **"The Dress,"** the fleeing madman, who yearns for a chance to sleep, thinks of sleep as personified by another object of desire—a girl. When he breaks into the cottage where the young housewife is sitting, he follows the logic of his delusion, mistakes her for sleep, and puts his head in her lap.

The setting of most of these stories is the seaside Welsh town wickedly called Llareggub (to be read backwards), also the scene of *Under Milk Wood,* with its neighboring countryside, including a valley named after Jarvis, a lecherous nineteenth-century landlord, some farms, and a mountain called Cader Peak. Among the inhabitants of this region are young men obsessed by unfulfilled love, as in **"The Mouse and the Woman"** and **"The Orchards"**; clergymen crazed by lust, as in **"The Holy Six"** and **"The Burning Baby"**; wise men or women who teach some cabalistic magic art, as in **"The Tree," "The Map of Love," "The School for Witches,"** and **"The Lemon"**; and enigmatic girls who rise from the sea or the soil as in **"The Mouse and the Woman"** and **"A Prospect of the Sea."** The fancies of these people, narrated in a manner rendering them indistinguishable from objective reality, fill the town and the countryside with visions, supernatural forces, and fantastic episodes recalling the world of fairy tale and of folklore. People and objects are whisked into new shapes, small and intimate experiences are magnified until they embody fundamental realities—"creation screaming in the steam of the kettle"—and the order of nature is constantly subject to disruption. In this milieu the anomalous is the ordinary; at the end of **"Prologue to an Adventure,"** for example, the barroom where the two friends are standing runs down the drains of the town into the sea.

In one of his letters to Vernon Watkins, Thomas observes that the reader of verse needs an occasional rest but that the poet ought not to give it to him; this sustained intensity is more natural to poetry than to prose. In applying this principle to his stories, Thomas produced complex, involuted narratives with rich surfaces of language and imagery. At first impression they have no depths; but analysis shows that the order of imagination operating in them is the one which produced Thomas' poetry. His stories, unlike his earliest poems, deal with recognizable people and places; but they invest them with the same mythic atmosphere found in the poems. As we have already observed, there are numerous and detailed affinities between the poems and these early, fantastic stories. Common themes, the burning of a child, the "falling" of time, the unity of life, and the verbal capacities of nature provide subjects for both, and are also reflected in rhetorical details. But the most general resemblance is an awareness of the cosmic import of small events, a tendency to develop the significance of experiences by referring them to the absolute limits of the continuum of which they are a part. The lust of Rhys Rhys in **"The Burning Baby"** culminates in incest and in the murder of his child; the desire of the poet in **"The Mouse and the Woman"** raises a beautiful woman for him on the seashore; the vision of heaven the boy sees from the top of his ladder in **"A Prospect of the Sea"** is an endless Eden stretching to meet itself above and below.

In **"The Tree,"** which first appeared in the *Adelphi* in December, 1934, within a week of the publication of *18 Poems,* the style typical of Thomas' fantastic stories is still at an early stage of its development, so that it is possible to distinguish actual events from the delusions going on in the minds of the characters. The story also provides a convenient dramatization of the creative process at work in these stories. The gardener transmits his obsession to the boy; the boy, at the end of the story, tries to transform it into actuality. In writing his fantastic stories, Thomas, the narrator, acted the part of the boy. Borrowing delusions from his characters, Thomas produced in the narrative itself a version of reality corresponding to the delusions.

The gardener in the story is a naïve religious who, by one of those primitive metaphorical associations familiar to us from Thomas' poems, takes all trees as counterparts of the "tree" of the cross. As he tells the boy the story of Jesus, the child fixes on the elder tree in the garden as the scene of the crucifixion. When he is let into the locked tower as a Christmas gift, the boy is bitterly disappointed to find it empty; but he associates the Jarvis hills, which are visible through the window, with Bethlehem; for they, like Bethlehem, are toward the east. The idiot standing under the tree in the garden, exposed to the wind and rain, has already had Christlike intimations of his destiny when the boy finds him in the morning. And when the boy learns that he has come from the eastern hills that he has mistaken for Bethlehem, he fits the tree, the hills, and the idiot into the pattern described by the gardener, and sets about making the story of Jesus a reality. As the story closes, he has put the idiot against the tree and is crucifying him on it. The ultimate point of the story is the idiot's acceptance of his suffering; in the final scene the ignorant piety of the gardener is being transformed, through the imagination of the child and the love and humility of the idiot, into a reality.

The narrative style blending actual and imagined worlds appears for the first time in **"The Visitor,"** whose main character, as he approaches death, perceives the continuity between the living and dead aspects of the cosmos. Because we know the actual world which is the background of his delusion, we can see that the first part of the narrative has a double structure; and we can easily separate Peter's delusions from external reality. His idea that the sheets are shrouds, that his heart is a clock ticking, and that he lacks feelings because he is dead are simply misinterpretations of sensory clues. Only occasionally does his mind drift into clear hallucination, as when he thinks he is looking down at his own dead face in the coffin. Otherwise his thoughts are perfectly intelligible; he recalls that his first wife died seven years earlier in childbirth, and the guilt he experiences is expressed in a remarkable metaphor: "He felt his body turn to vapour, and men who had been light as air walked, metal-hooved, through and beyond him."

In the second part of the story, however, we enter fully into Peter's dying delirium and the basis of fact offered by the external world fades away. In a region of pure fantasy, we are unable, like Peter himself, to distinguish the imaginary from the real or even to detect the moment of division between life and death. In his delirium, Callaghan, the visitor Peter has been expecting, comes and carries him away into a realm of essential being where the pulsations of alternate growth and destruction are perfectly visible in a stripped, transparent landscape. Here a new prose style, the one Thomas adopts as a means of objectifying mystical perception, presents itself. More descriptive than narrative, it is full of grotesque, clearly realized images. Sometimes rhapsodic, sometimes strangely matter of fact, it seeks to capture the disruption imposed upon nature by hallucinatory vision. As in the poems, metaphor ceases to compare, and equates instead, so that "the flowers shot out of the dead," and "the light of the moon . . . pulled the moles and badgers out of their winter."

The journey ends when Peter, suddenly returned to his sickbed again, feels restored to his body and speaks to his wife. But she does not hear him, and he does not realize he is dead until she pulls the sheet over his face. Just as he had the delusion, when he was living, that he was dead, so at the end Peter has the delusion, when he is dead, that he is alive. The division between the two states is slight, and disembodied vitality persists so powerfully that moving from the aspect of being we call life to the one we call death hardly matters to it. As one of the poems concludes, "The heart is sensual, though five eyes break."

In **"The Visitor,"** Peter experiences actual and imaginary realms at different times; the two meet only at the boundary between them, where their edges are not clear. But in the further development of his narrative style, Thomas presented situations where imagined and actual events are superimposed upon one another as single experiences. Two closely related short stories published in 1936, **"The Orchards"** and **"The Mouse and the Woman,"** illustrate this. Both have the same theme as **"The Hunchback in the Park"**: the creation of an imaginary woman by a mind obsessed by the need for love. And both are tragedies of delusion, for they show that the dreamer is pitifully exposed to the demands of the actual world.

The woman loved by Marlais, the poet of **"The Orchards,"** comes to him in a dream in the form of a scarecrow who stands, with her sister, in a landscape of burning orchards. When he wakes up, the memory of this dream persists and distracts him from his writing. Oppressed by the disparity between the passion of his dream thoughts and the dullness of the town outside his window, Marlais makes an effort of the imagination which leads him to mystic perception. What follows is perhaps Thomas' most complete description of mystic vision. The distinction between objective and subjective is canceled: "There was dust in his eyes; there were eyes in the grains of dust. . . ." Individual things seem part of greater wholes, saturated with absolute significance: "His hand before him was five-fingered life." Opposites are reconciled: "It is all one, the loud voice and the still voice striking a common silence. . . ." Intoxicated with the feeling that he commands both spiritual and actual realms, so that he is "man among ghosts, and ghost in clover," Marlais now "moved for the last answer."

A second sleep shows him that the landscape of his dream and the woman he loves are still there; and when he wakes he goes out of the town to find it. The second half of the story, like that of **"The Visitor,"** is the journey of a mental traveler; but Marlais travels on the ground, not in the air, as Peter does. And his imagined world is spread over the real countryside, whose objective features emerge, like peaks rising out of the clouds of his thoughts. The Whippet valley, a part of the real countryside which has been destroyed by mining, is succeeded by a wood whose trees are said to spring from the legend of the Fall. As his walk continues, Marlais enters the realm of myth and becomes a myth himself; when he has penetrated into this imaginary world, he finds the orchards of his dream and the girl in it. An objective observer would probably say that Marlais had been invited to have a picnic tea with an ordinary girl; for the tablecloth, cups, and bread she produces are real enough. But, as Marlais views the scene, the conditions of his dream impose themselves upon this objective reality, and the scene is transformed to correspond with it. The orchards break into fire; the girl is changed into a scarecrow and calls up her sister, as in the dream; and Marlais has his desire.

But we have been warned at the beginning that Marlais' passion was "a story more terrible than the stories of the reverend madmen in the Black Book of Llareggub," and the conclusion tells us why. The fires of Marlais' dream are put out by "the real world's wind," and it becomes a fact, not a dream. The imaginative tide of his obsession recedes, leaving him stranded in actuality, kissing a scarecrow, and exposing his madness.

"The Mouse and the Woman" is a more elaborate treatment of the same theme: the betrayal of a poet by his obsession with love. In this story, as in **"The Orchards,"** the hero creates a dream woman, and he shuttles back and forth between a dream world and a waking world that seem equally real. But Thomas has added to the situation a moral aspect represented by the mouse. The story opens with a remarkable description of the madman in the lunatic asylum, and it then moves back in his memory to trace the steps of his alienation. As in **"The Orchards,"** the woman comes to him in a dream, and her memory persists when he is awake until he is caught between reality and delusion; he does not know whether to believe in her existence or not. He creates her by writing about her, ". . . it was upon the block of paper that she was made absolute," thus surrendering to imagination; he then goes out on the beach to find her and bring her to his cottage. This begins the part of the story where hallucination is perfectly superimposed upon actuality. The girl is, of course, pure imagination; but the mouse, which is associated with evil, and the mousehole the hero nails up to keep it away seem representative of objective actuality. Oddly, within this waking dream the hero has nocturnal dreams containing frightening enigmatic symbols. When he strips the girl and becomes her lover, two related events follow: the mouse emerges from its hole; and the notion of original sin enters the consciousness of the lovers as the man tells the girl the story of the Fall. She realizes that he has felt evil in their relationship.

The mouse and what it represents are the seed of destruction in his euphoric delusion; for the woman leaves him. Though he pursues her, she will not have him back. Her rejection of him is marvelously conveyed in the fairy tale episode where he lights upon her hand, like an insect, pleads with her, and is crushed as she closes her hand over him. Since he has created her by thought, he can kill her by thought. He writes "The woman died" on his writing pad, and we are told that "There was dignity in such a murder." He sees her dead body lying on the beach. But the knowledge that "he had failed . . . to hold his miracle" is too much for him, and he becomes the madman who appears at the beginning of the story.

The story goes a step further than **"The Orchards,"** for it explains why the certainty offered by delusion should disappear. The poet's sense of guilt, emerging from within his mind as the mouse emerges from the walls of the house, poisons his dream. His derangements are no longer orderly and joyful, but confused: "The secret of that alchemy that had turned a little revolution of the unsteady senses into a golden moment was lost as a key is lost in the undergrowth." He has regained some contact with the objective world, but he wants to kill the woman. And, in order to do this, he must return to the world of imagination where she exists. In killing her, he also kills the dream she dominates, on which his happiness depends. The mouse, now fully in possession of the kitchen, silently presides over the grief he feels at this self-destruction. Trapped between two systems of reality and unable to commit himself to either, the poet can only howl at life from behind the bars of the asylum.

In four stories published in 1937 and 1938, the hallucinatory technique advances so far that it is no longer possible—or desirable—to disentangle imagined from actual episodes. External reality responds flexibly to the thoughts and feelings of the characters, so that the narrative amounts to a psychological allegory. This genre, it will be recalled, is the one to which "Ballad of the Long-Legged Bait" belongs, and two of the four stories now under discussion are so closely related to this poem that they seem to be prose sketches for it. The member of this group closest to the earlier stories is **"A Prospect of the Sea."** It has the same elements as **"The Orchards"** and **"The Mouse and the Woman":** a girl who is encountered at the seashore, and who disappears, and a delirious shuttling back and forth between different orders of reality.

In **"A Prospect of the Sea,"** the boy begins by enjoying the summer day and then makes up a story about a drowned princess; but this level of thought is intersected by another—the appearance of a country girl who confronts him in the actual landscape. This siren figure both tempts and terrifies him, for she has the power to make the world swell and shrink. His fantasies of death and disfigurement alternate with the actual events of her erotic advances. As evening comes, he yields himself to another daydream, a mystic's vision of power, piercing sight, and multiplied Edens. But the girl calls him into an actual world that is now strangely insubstantial: ". . . she could make a long crystal of each tree, and turn the house wood into gauze." She leads him on a race through a mystically disrupted realm; and then, in the morning, in spite of his agonized protests, she walks into the sea and disappears. As he turns to walk inland, he confronts the elements of the Noah story: an old man building a boat, the beginning of rainfall, and a stream of animals entering the door. Apparently, then, the episodes of the story belong to the corrupt time God had determined to end by means of the Flood.

But **"A Prospect of the Sea"** is an innocent pastoral in comparison with **"Prologue to an Adventure,"** a chronicle of town sin, a subject that offers a far richer opportunity for Thomas' grotesque metaphoric energies than the country scenes of the earlier stories. There is little action. The speaker wanders through the streets and, with an acquaintance named Daniel Dom (a variant of the name "Domdaniel" appearing in one of Thomas' unpublished poems), visits two bars; then, as in **"A Prospect of the Sea,"** destructive water comes as the scene is immersed by waves.

The interest of this story lies in the remarkable play of scenes and imagery conveying the feverish atmosphere of a night on the town. "Now in the shape of a bald girl smiling, a wailing wanton with handcuffs for earrings, or the lean girls that live on pickings, now in ragged women with a muckrake curtseying in the slime, the tempter of angels whispered over my shoulder." As the speaker says, there is "more than man's meaning" in this torrent of fearsome, Hieronymus Boschlike visions, for holiness is caught up and debased in it. "I have the God of Israel in the image of a painted boy, and Lucifer, in a woman's shirt, pisses from a window in Damaroid Alley."

The two scenes in the bars are incoherent jumbles of fleeing images, glimpses of transcendental visions, and striking expressionistic effects. They look backward in technique and subject to the Circe scene of Joyce's *Ulysses* and forward to Thomas' *Doctor and the Devils* for their atmosphere of pinched debauchery. The speaker and his friend aspire for a moment to reach out of this welter of temptresses, oppressed children, and indifferent city streets to some heavenly goal, but they come instead to a new bar where, after joining the corrupt festivities, they turn to the window and witness the coming of the deluge. There are no alternate realms of reality in this story. It is all an inescapable mental reality, consisting entirely of representations of the desires, fears, suspicions, and other emotions of the narrator; for, as his visions tell him,

"We are all metaphors of the sound of shape, of the shape of sound, break us we take another shape."

"In the Direction of the Beginning" and **"An Adventure from a Work in Progress"** are mythlike tales written in a hallucinatory style. The first, a short account of the creation, tells of the appearance of figures resembling Adam and Eve. Its enchanted, visionary prose presents a dizzying succession of images referring fleetingly to various seasons, ages, and episodes of history and legend. There is almost no physical action; the Fall is suggested as the man becomes entrapped by the woman's siren spell and as his obsession with her is projected through imagery showing that he feels her to be personified in every detail of the universe. The same obsession appears in **"An Adventure from a Work in Progress,"** an account of a man pursuing a shadowy woman through a strangely active archipelago where awesome cataclysms endanger him. At the climax of the story the woman merges with the mountain, just as the Eve in **"In the Direction of the Beginning"** merges with the soil. When the hero ultimately catches her, she undergoes a series of startling metamorphoses and shrinks to a tiny monster in the palm of his hand. After being thus betrayed by his obsession, like the lovers in **"The Orchards"** and **"The Mouse and the Woman,"** the hero returns from the imaginary world to the actual one, and sails away on "the common sea."

The "revolving islands and elastic hills" of this story show that it takes place in the realm that is more fully described in **"The Map of Love."** In the latter, the stages of sexual initiation are represented by a bewitched landscape; a curious animated map or model of this region exhibits its vital sexual properties, so that the children to whom it is being displayed blush at "the copulation in the second mud." The libido-charged landscape represented by the map is the world as it presents itself to the heroes of the last two stories, who find the women they love embodied in cliffs, seas, and mountains. The children in **"The Map of Love"** are guided by Sam Rib, who is named for the origin of love, and are encouraged by the spirit of their lecherous Great-Uncle Jarvis, who speaks to them from the fields where he has lain with ten different mistresses. But they never succeed in swimming up the river to the island of the first beasts of love. Apparently, they are too shy, too lacking in lust; mere "synthetic prodigals" of Sam Rib's laboratory, they are unable to share the dangerous vitality of nature. (pp. 154-64)

Thomas was still working on the last of his fantastic narratives in 1938 when he began to write the realistic stories which were collected in ***Portrait of the Artist as a Young Dog.*** In March, 1938, he wrote to Watkins that the first of "a series of short, straightforward stories about Swansea" had already been published. This statement must refer to **"A Visit to Grandpa's,"** which appeared in the *New English Weekly* on March 10, 1938. The change in narrative style between these two groups of stories is, of course, a radical one; moreover, it paralleled the much more subtle change in Thomas' poetic style that was going on at about the same time. Many of the casual details of these stories are drawn without change from Thomas' Swansea days, and some of the characters are based on actual people: the aunt in **"The Peaches"** is Ann Jones, and Dan Jenkyns in **"The Fight"** is Daniel Jones. In his "Poetic Manifesto," Thomas declared that the title he assigned to the collection was a variant, not of Joyce's title, but of one often given by painters to self-portraits. He admitted that the general influence of *Dubliners* might be felt in his stories, but he added that this was an influence no good writer of short stories could avoid.

The protagonist in all the stories is clearly Thomas himself, though the stories are narrated indifferently in first and third persons and though each presents him at a different age. They are about ordinary experiences: visits with relatives, excursions to the country, adventures with gangs of children, explorations of the town. In some of them the plot is so slight that the story approaches a reminiscence or cluster of impressions. Obviously written with only a loose unity in mind, they have no common theme; but taken as a group, they seem to trace the child's emergence from his domain of imagination and secret pleasures into an adult world where he observes suffering, pathos, and dignity.

Most of the stories are about an observer or witness, one whose experience consists of awakening to the experiences of others. The events are presented in sharp, well-selected impressions. When he is observing a general scene, such as a boy's room or a crowded street, Thomas proceeds by piling up a lively list of the quintessential details or characteristic people. Sometimes his attitude toward people, places, and episodes is affectionate or amused; sometimes he finds grotesque nightmare evocations in them. But he encounters his strongest emotions in moments of solitude when he can hug his general impressions of the external world to himself as personal possessions—while walking down a street late at night, wandering in moody isolation on a noisy beach, or enjoying the atmosphere of an expensive bar.

The first three stories—**"The Peaches," "A Visit to Grandpa's"** and **"Patricia, Edith and Arnold"**—set the idyllic existence of a child side by side with the trials of adults. As the grownups suffer, the child remains indifferent or cruel; yet it appears at the end that he has understood and sympathized more than he knew, thus anticipating the ultimate union of the childish and adult points of view. **"The Peaches"** may be said to have "separateness" as an identifiable theme. Mrs. Williams, who brings her son for a holiday at the farm, is too superior to stay a moment longer than necessary, and refuses the precious canned peaches that have been saved for her visit. Jim curses her snobbery, but he cannot keep himself from drinking up the profits of the farm and distressing his wife. Gwilym, the son, who closely resembles the religious gardener in **"The Tree,"** is occupied with a vision of himself as a preacher, and makes the barn a church for his pretended sermons. To these mutually uncommunicating attitudes toward life is added that of the boys who are busy with their games of wild Indian and indifferent to the concerns of the adults. But even here a division occurs when Jack Williams betrays his playmate by telling his mother an incriminating mixture of truth and falsehood about his treatment at the farm, and is taken away. At the end of **"The Peaches,"** the boy waves his handkerchief at his departing betrayer, innocent that any wrong has been done to him, or to his aunt and uncle.

But in **"Patricia, Edith and Arnold,"** the child, at first cruelly indifferent to the pain felt by the two maidservants who have learned that the same young man has been walking out with both of them, gains some insight into adult sorrows. The story begins with a chaos of irreconcilable interests: the absorption of the girls in their love triangle, and the rambunctious joy of the child who is all-conquering in his imaginary play world. But as the painful comedy of Arnold's entrapment is played out, the boy, uncomfortably cold and wet, feels his own distress and unconsciously comes to sympathize with Patricia. Returning to the shelter to retrieve his cap, he sees Arnold reading the letters he has written to the other girl, but he mercifully spares Patricia this knowledge. And his own experience of pain, a minor counterpart of the adult pain Patricia has suffered, comes when he thaws his cold hands at the fire. Patricia's final remark, "Now we've all had a good cry today," formulates both the similarity of their trials and their capacity to endure them.

Cruel jokes, of the sort that life has played on Arnold, occur in some of the other stories. In **"Just Like Little Dogs,"** the brothers exchange partners with each other in the middle of an evening of casual love. As a result, when the women become pregnant, it is not clear which brother is the father of their respective children. The two forced but loveless marriages take place, and now the two fathers spend their evenings in the street, standing hopelessly in the cold night air. In **"Old Garbo,"** the neighbors take up a collection for Mrs. Prothero, whose daughter is supposed to have died in childbirth; after Mrs. Prothero has drunk up the money, it is learned that the daughter has survived. The mother, ashamed at having taken the money under false pretenses, jumps into the river.

It is significant that in each of these stories the anecdotal nucleus is subordinated to the vehicle which conveys it. The impressive element of **"Just Like Little Dogs"** is the spectacle of the young men sheltering aimlessly from the night under the railway arch; they have no place more interesting to go and nothing more interesting to do. **"Old Garbo"** is, in reality, a story of initiation; the young reporter, eager to share the knowledge and maturity of the older one, follows him into the haunts where Mrs. Prothero's comic tragedy occurs. In this way he exchanges the boyish pastimes of the cinema and the novelty shop in the first part of the story for the more serious experience in the slum pub. He is not a qualified observer, for he becomes drunk, sick, and helpless; and the older reporter tells him, in an odd conclusion, that the story which has just been narrated has certain confused details; but he is still naïvely determined to put all the things the older reporter has shown him into a story.

Some of the stories have a note of personal futility and inadequacy which conspires with their prevailing comic tone to produce penetrating irony. The inferior boy who is the hero of **"Extraordinary Little Cough"** is bullied and mocked. But he turns his shy habit of running away when girls appear into a feat; for, while the other boys are idling with the girls and yielding to romantic illusions, he runs the five miles of beach. As he falls to the ground exhausted at the end of the story, it is clear that he has risen nobly to a challenge while the others have ended in frustration and petty animosities. The two boys who go for a country hike in **"Who Do You Wish Was with Us?"** feel they are escaping their town lives in the freedom of the country and the beach. But Ray, whose life has been full of terrible family misfortunes, is overtaken by sorrow for his dead brother in the middle of his holiday. The sea turns cold and threatening, and both boys feel that they cannot really escape the life they have fled.

The most powerful story about escape, and the most impressive one in the volume is the last, **"One Warm Saturday."** Having rejected invitations to join his friends, the young man wanders despondently among the crowds on the beach, finding solace only in the face of a girl whom he flees shyly at first. Ultimately, he again meets the girl, Lou; and, as the two become involved in an oddly mixed group of drinkers, she promises him that his love for her will be fulfilled when they are alone. The party moves from the pub where it began to Lou's room in a huge ramshackle tenement. The young man's anxiety and Lou's demonstrations of affection are intensified, but the others show no signs of leaving. A grotesque frustration occurs when the young man goes out to the lavatory. He is unable to find his way back to Lou's room to claim the night of love she has promised him. Instead, he loses himself in the squalid maze of the tenement and stumbles into the rooms of other lodgers. Ultimately, he gives up and wanders out into the street, having made the "discovery" during his search that all the obscure people of the town share his experience of loss.

Thomas' uncompleted novel, ***Adventures in the Skin Trade,*** may be considered a continuation of the quasi-autobiography loosely sketched in ***Portrait of the Artist as a Young Dog,*** though it is more broadly comic in style than any of the stories. It takes up the narrative of a life much like Thomas' at the point where the last of the stories ends, and its protagonist, Samuel Bennet, is not inconsistent with the wandering, imaginative youths found in the earlier book, though he is much better defined. Thomas seems to have begun ***Adventures*** in 1940; and, though the first section was published in *Folios of New Writing* in 1941 under the title **"A Fine Beginning"** and though he was encouraged to continue with it, it remained a fragment at the time of his death.

It may be described as a farce based on the fact that Samuel Bennet and his world are excruciatingly uncomfortable with each other. On the night before he leaves his home town for London, Samuel prepares a number of surprises for his family by breaking his mother's china, tearing up his sister's crochet-work, and scribbling on the lessons that his father, a teacher, is correcting. But he does all this in tears, as if it were a painful necessity; and he says an affectionate farewell the next morning. On the other hand, he is not eager to see London; unwilling to make any decisions or to take any actions, he lingers in the station café until a friend forces him to leave.

The London in which Samuel finds himself is a damp, angular, crowded, eccentric world; and it is both surprising and significant that he likes it as well as he does. The chaos he encounters is well represented by his first stop, a warehouse full of furniture piled up in unlikely heaps which nevertheless serves as living quarters for a number of people. The general technique of ***Adventures*** is suggested by the locked bathroom with its bird cages where a strange girl makes an attempt on Samuel's virtue in a tub full of used bathwater after drugging him with a drink of cologne. In the book, as in this scene, violent imaginative force explodes in a narrow enclosure filled with ordinary objects and people, toppling them into ludicrous attitudes and combinations. A mundane paraphernalia of Bass bottles, umbrellas, rubber ducks, bootpolish, Worcestershire sauce, and Coca-Cola is juggled into patterns of uproarious private meaning, sometimes by Samuel's imagination, sometimes by the author's. Realism swims in a whirlpool of uninhibited fancy.

If the atmosphere of ***Adventures*** is found anywhere else, it is in Brinnin's accounts of the social events Thomas attended, where the poet, guided by some motivation of wit or self-dramatization, cunningly introduced chaos. Mr. Allingham observes that the Bass bottle which has become wedged on Samuel's little finger is an enigma. Samuel, noticing that a barmaid looks like a duchess riding a horse, makes the irrelevant reply of "Tantivy" to some remark. But the curious thing is that Samuel, in spite of the hostility and defiance with which he confronts the world, is completely unready for the world's retaliation. As he is pushed and prodded from one place to another, drugged, undressed, bullied, and thrown out of a bar, he experiences terror and confusion. Samuel is too innocent to absorb what he sees. A stumbling, swooning, dreaming source of confusion, he is himself confused, and he seems destined to remain a timid and withdrawn picaro among the sharp and knowing characters who take possession of him. According to Robert Pocock, who discussed ***Adventures*** with Thomas, the novel was to end with Samuel stripped naked (except, no doubt, for the Bass bottle clinging enigmatically to his little finger), and arrested in Paddington Station. (pp. 168-74)

Jacob Korg, in his Dylan Thomas, *Twayne Publishers, Inc., 1965, 205 p.*

WARREN FRENCH (essay date 1967)

[*An American critic and editor, French has written widely on the major authors of the twentieth century, including John Steinbeck and J. D. Salinger. In the following essay, he explores the intent of* A Portrait of the Artist as a Young Dog, *suggesting that Thomas's autobiographical account bears many similarities to James Joyce's* Portrait of the Artist as a Young Man *but presents an essentially romantic vision of the artist which contrasts with Joyce's classicist view.*]

[Though] even early reviewers noted the relationship of Thomas's [***Portrait of the Artist as a Young Dog***] to Joyce's [***Portrait of the Artist as a Young Man***], few critics have perceived its possible extent. Even the kinship of the titles has been denied. Jacob Korg reports that the author declared in a "Poetic Manifesto" that he was using "a variant, not of Joyce's title, but of one often given by painters to self-portraits" [see excerpt above]. Thomas's correspondent Vernon Watkins reports that he suggested the title be scrapped, but that Thomas replied that he had "kept the flippant title for—as publishers advised—moneymaking reasons." Korg also points out that Thomas acknowledged the influence of Joyce's *Dubliners* on his stories, but considered it one that no good writer of short stories could avoid. No one seems to have looked behind these remarks to seek out deep-seated similarities between the superficially quite different books.

The differences are inescapable. Joyce's novel is extremely compressed and tightly unified, distilled out of earlier versions (the fragments we possess of these give some clue to the vast changes he made). The five parts of the final form of the story depict closely related episodes in a young man's maturation from his discovery of his indomitable individualism through his discovery and rejection of the lives of both fleshly pleasure and priestly asceticism to his discovery and at last enthusiastic embracing of the artistic vocation. This choice, he feels, will provide the outlet for his individualism that he could not envision being adequately provided by either the life of "Byron's publichouse" or "Clontarf Chapel." Thomas's book is a collection of ten seemingly unconnected sketches, written from a variety of points of view and often loosely constructed, dealing with a bizarre assortment of comic and tragic episodes in the disorderly growing up of a young "dog" who had apparently while still a schoolboy decided he would be a poet.

Yet one cannot escape the feeling that if the two young men are to mature into different kinds of artists, the portrayal of their development requires quite different approaches.

Then there are specific provocative parallels between the first and last stories in Thomas's collection and materials in Joyce's novel. Thomas's opening story, **"The Peaches,"** contains what could serve as a satirical portrait of Joyce at the time that his fictional counterpart Stephen Dedalus decided upon an artistic career: "Gwilym was a tall young man aged nearly twenty, with a thin stick of a body and spade-shaped face. You could dig the garden with him. He had a deep voice that cracked in half when he was excited, and he sang songs to himself, treble and bass, with the same sad hymn tune, and wrote hymns in the barn."

Gwilym is, of course, not the hero of the narrative, but an older boy who attempts to influence the younger. I find it noteworthy that the detail Gwilym singles out to stress the squalor of the ill-managed farm where he must pursue his dreams of influencing men is that a pig has eaten one of her recent litter. This unpleasant event recalls Stephen Dedalus's famous description of Ireland as "the old sow that eats her farrow." Even a sermon that Gwilym delivers with its rhythmic repetitions—"Thou canst see in everything we do, in the night and the day, in the day and the night, everything, everything"—recalls the languorous artificiality of the villanelle that Joyce offers to us as the sole example of Stephen's youthful art.

Might Thomas have reason to burlesque Joyce? Much as he admired the Irishman's art, the disreputable young Welshman might regard as a bit pompous one who described his budding artist as "a priest of eternal imagination, transmuting the daily bread of experience into the radiant body of ever-living life."

The parallels to the climax of Joyce's novel in Thomas's last stories are a far more serious matter than the younger man's possible digs at his model in launching his analogous tale. In both men's crucial accounts of their recognition of their vocation, the figure that crystallizes their vision is a woman in the water. Stephen Dedalus discovers his artistic calling when he sees a girl standing in the middle of a rivulet. Although he never speaks to her, he feels that "her image had passed into his soul for ever," that she is "an envoy from the fair courts of life." Thomas's **"Old Garbo"** is no such envoy; she has plunged herself into midstream to drown.

She is title character of a curious story that has distressed some critics because it is named for only one of the many sketchy figures that a young reporter encounters during a night of revelry. Jacob Korg indeed thinks that the story is simply about the way in which a young reporter learns to exchange childish pleasure for serious duties by following an older man. Korg comments that the young reporter "is not a qualified observer . . . and the older reporter tells him, in an odd conclusion, that the story which has just been narrated has certain confused details."

Examining the story, however, we find that the corrections the older reporter makes involve inconsequential details: "The boy with the handkerchief danced in the 'Jersey.' Fred Jones was singing in the 'Fishguard.' " It is not such precise accuracy of detail that concerns the younger man; it is rather singling out from the evening's confusion the one incident that is fraught with tragic significance. "I'll put them all in a story by and by," he determinedly tells the older man, after hearing the objections. The old reporter with his scrupulous literal-mindedness will never become the artist who will make not a transient news story but a timeless tale out of the observations of his "dog days." If we consider Thomas's collection as the account of the making of an artist, **"Old Garbo"** is the climactic story, for it records the events that crystallize (like Stephen's seeing the girl in the stream) the young reporter's determination not to follow in the footsteps of an older man, but to write "the story," which the older man with his particular preoccupations does not perceive.

And **"Old Garbo"** is more. I use the term "climactic story," for my principal quarrel is with Jacob Korg's statement that Thomas's stories have "no common theme." I think that I perceive a unifying theme, announced—even as Joyce's is—in the closing words of the book, "The light of the one weak lamp in a rusty circle fell across the brickheaps and the broken wood and the dust that had been houses once, where the small and hardly known and never-to-be-forgotten people of the dirty town had lived and loved and died and, always, lost." "The light of the one weak lamp" is the work of the artist, whose theme is life and love and death, but especially loss—who celebrates "the dirty town."

Looking back over the collection in the light of the last sentence, we see that—despite their hilarity—all these tales focus upon tragic losses. We see further that it is out of his developing perception of these losses and his attempt to put them into "a story" that the artist has developed from the "young dog."

The first tale, **"Peaches,"** describes a young boy's loss through the touchiness of adults of a supposed friend. Although the boy does not understand the reason for the loss at the time it occurs, the artist he has become perceives it and communicates it to the reader. The young boy is still an observer—not fully understanding what he sees—in **"A Visit to Grandpa's,"** which depicts an old man's loss of the desire to live, a loss that has reached the point that the old man is no longer tempted from thoughts of death by even his favorite cake and strong beer.

The small boy's capacity to understand the losses that he witnesses has grown by the time he observes the sad triangle of **"Patricia, Edith, and Arnold."** Although the lad plagues a serving girl by dirtying himself in a coal-hole, he is sensitive enough not to break the girl's heart by telling her of her lover's narcissism when the child learns that the swain has been courting another girl as well and gets pleasure from reading copies of the love letters he has written both young ladies. Instead the young boy finds in the fierce chill of the day an occasion to cry as the two girls have previously from the fierce chill of their disillusionment. Even though the boy weeps for a more superficial reason, he affords his governess the consolation of being able to say at last, "Now we've all had a good cry today."

Thomas on the banks of Carmarthen Bay, Wales.

When this first flickering ability to understand and help assuage loss manifests itself, the experiences of childhood useful in the development of the artist are at an end. The next story plunges us far ahead to the time the teen-aged schoolboy learns something of the losses that will alienate him from his elders' world.

In **"The Fight,"** the aspiring young poet gains the friendship of another extravagant young creator, but at about the same time loses the sympathy of his elders when he reluctantly recites to a minister who loves Tennyson but allows his wife to become lonely to the point of madness a poem about the "unfulfillment of desired force" and a woman's "dead, dark body." **"Extraordinary Little Cough"** records the boy's disillusionment with those nearer his own age when some much admired older boys with idle falsehoods drive the "Little Cough" of the title to his extraordinary but aimless feat while his exploiters dally with some young ladies.

But the pleasure of even such dalliance is fleeting. **"Just Like Little Dogs"** reveals the recognition of a much deeper sense of loss when the young man meets another pair who are slightly older than he and learns that they, as a result of the kind of night of pleasure described in the previous story, find themselves tied to wives they do not love, with nothing left to do but stand beneath a railroad arch silently watching the sands until early next morning.

Having learned of the losses that even pleasures may entail, the adolescent has reached the end of the experiences that will be useful to the artist. We next meet the "young dog" as a prospective journalist attending an extraordinary session of a committee that is attempting collectively to write a novel. **"Where Tawe Flows"** focuses, however, not on this unpromising enterprise, but on one of the group's thinly veiled tale of his wife's loss of the social position that she once held and of his efforts to humor her to compensate for the loss. From one point of view, this story is the high point of the collection, for its Mr. Evans has learned to live with his experiences by transmuting them into art. The young listener will become an artist when he has learned the same lesson; but first—for contrast—he must meet someone who cannot triumph over his experiences as Mr. Evans has.

He does in **"Who Do You Wish Was with Us,"** the story of another young man whose life has been so scarred by personal tragedy—"his father and sister and brother were dead, and his mother sat all day in a wheelchair"—that he cannot long enjoy even "the unaccustomed happiness" of a day's outing without his thoughts returning to the events that have "embittered" his outlook. What the budding artist learns from this companion is reinforced by the following story of **"Old Garbo,"** who couldn't face again the friends who had taken up a collection that she had spent for drink, when it was discovered that the daughter whose death promoted the collection was not dead after all. Even among the most raffish pub-crawlers, loss of face makes life unbearable.

The last story in the collection is the most complicated, for it deals with the young writer's personal experience of an adult sense of loss. Invited after a night's boozing to the tenement bedroom of a desirable girl, he finds after he has been obliged to wander through the house in search of a water closet, he cannot find the girl's room again. When he begins to beat on doors, a woman "dressed in a vest and a hat" drives him out with a walking-stick.

Echoes of Joyce again? At the climax of his novel, Stephen Dedalus has established the contact—though it is not physical—with his "wild angel" that the physically eager young Thomas is denied with his "girl in a million." But can it be purely co-incidental that each girl does accept the boys' voiceless admiration? Although the man succeeds where the "dog" fails, both are moved by their experience to become artists. Stephen responds to the call of the girl's eyes to forge "the uncreated conscience" of his race. Thomas avoids embitterment—like his Mr. Evans—by sublimating through art his sense of loss.

These different culminations of the sequence of experiences recorded in the two books may provide the basis for a comparison that extends beyond the work of the two artists. Joyce's novel may be described as the manifesto of a modern classicism; Thomas's as the example of a modern romanticism.

Too many words have been lavished upon the elusive contrast between these temperaments; but one influential concept of the distinction is clarified by Irving Babbitt's *Rousseau and Romanticism.* In identifying "the final gap that opens between classicist and romanticist," Babbitt says that "to look to a true centre is, . . . according to the classicist, to grasp the abiding human element through all the change in which it is implicated." On the other hand, he considers that "in general a thing is romantic when . . . it is wonderful rather than probable; in other words, when it violates the normal sequence of cause and effect in favor of adventure." The classicist, in short, seeks to escape the fluctuations of life by moving toward a still center; his art is essentially centripetal. The romanticist, on the contrary, seeks to escape the monotonous routine of life by moving centrifugally in quest of adventure.

In his long explanation of his aesthetic, Joyce's Stephen captures Babbitt's concept of the classic vision: "I mean that the tragic emotion is static . . . The esthetic emotion (I used the general term) is therefore static. The mind is arrested and raised above desire and loathing." "The artist," according to this theory, "like the God of the creation, remains within or behind or beyond or above his handiwork, invisible, refined out of existence, indifferent, paring his fingernails." The artist disappears into the work as Joyce himself did by devoting most of his life to trying to embody in two novels the archetypal waking and sleeping experiences of man.

Contrast this vision with Thomas's as expressed most vividly in "Reminiscences of Childhood," which deals like the last section of Joyce's *Portrait* with the making of an early poem. In a closing passage, Thomas expresses the same concern for flight that causes Stephen Dedalus at last to appeal to Icarus, "old father, old artificer"; but what a different flight! In Thomas's vision, the artist is not "refined out of existence," but becomes the highly conspicuous cause of consternation among pedants: "And when they do not believe me, I flap my arms and slowly leave the ground only a few inches at first, then gaining air until I fly waving my cap level with the upper windows of the school, peering in until the mistress at the piano screams and the metronome falls to the ground and stops, and there is no more time."

Both artists seek to destroy time, but what one hopes to achieve by merging invisibly into the still center of the work itself, the other achieves by upsetting the metronome. I do not mean to argue, of course, that Thomas consciously devised his book to stand in the same relationship to the development of a new romanticism that the book whose title it echoes does to the development of a new classicism. Thomas's book thus consciously designed would as surely have failed to embody a romantic vision as Joyce's would to embody an archetypically classic one if it had been less self-consciously designed. I am arguing that intuitively Thomas created a book that stands in the same relation to a movement that exalts intuition that Joyce's intellectual creation does to a movement that exalts the intellect. (pp. 261-66)

Warren French, "Two Portraits of the Artist: James Joyce's 'Young Man'; Dylan Thomas's 'Young Dog'," in The University of Kansas City Review, *Vol. XXXIII, No. 4, Summer, 1967, pp. 261-66.*

ANNIS PRATT (essay date 1970)

[*In the following excerpt, Pratt discusses the style and structure of Thomas's early short stories.*]

[Dylan Thomas regarded] madness, dream, and myth as a fertile source of imagery and narrative material. His tales are concerned with how the storyteller breaks from the bounds of consciousness into the unconscious world, what he experiences there, how he manages to return, and what happens if he does not return (Marlais takes something resembling a psychedelic "trip" in **"The Orchards,"** as does Peter in **"The Visitor"** and Nant in **"The Lemon"**). The inward journey of the poetic imagination, which is usually implicit in the poetry, is more explicit in the prose, where it is *the* adventure by which Thomas self-consciously defines his narrative mode.

Even though the symbolic forms of the unconscious provide both the goal of his heroes and the structure of his tales, he is careful that the unconscious world never usurps control of the narrative. . . . [The] only passages of "automatic writing" in the tales occur when Thomas wants to describe the abrogation of consciousness: he seems to have felt that the further inward the narrative penetrates, the stronger must be the role played by the intellect. "The more subjective a poem," he wrote, "the clearer the narrative line." The intense and often hallucinatory subjectivity of the early tales required an unusual amount of conscious control, and it is probably for this reason that Thomas intruded so often as omniscient narrator. As Jacob Korg has noted, he shapes paranoia and hallucination into "an atmosphere where the mind rules the material world, exercising its powers of creation and distortion over it."

The "progressive line, or theme, or movement" which Thomas insisted upon for every poem is also present in every tale, where it is defined by the progress of the hero from desire through quest to release and renewal. The plots are divided into three or four sections which succeed each other with the rhythm of ritual movements. The tales usually culminate in a sacrament or rite, an act of sexual release, or an archetypal vision. The release may take the form of the loosing of a flood (as in **"A Prospect of the Sea"** and **"The Map of Love"**) or of an apocalyptic event (**"The Holy Six," "An Adventure from a Work in Progress," "The Visitor"**). Often the beginning of a new epoch of search and birth is implicit in the cataclysmic denouement, giving a cyclical shape to the narrative.

William York Tindall includes "landscape and sea, enclosures such as garden, island, and cave, and in addition city and tower" under the category of archetype. He goes on to explain that "uniting the personal and the general and commonly ambivalent, these images, not necessarily symbolic in themselves, become symbolic by context, first in our sleeping minds and then in poems." Thomas' landscapes embody the personal or sexual, the impersonal or mythical, and the poetic aspirations of his heroes. Images of the poetic quest seem to rise up as autonomous entities out of the countryside: words become incarnate in trees, in blood, and in the transforming sea. Often, at the denouement of a tale, they find their final expression in a "voice of thunder" which announces the hero's achievement.

Since Thomas' landscape is not only geographical but anatomical, personal or sexual imagery is latent in the countryside as well as in the bodies of hero and heroine. The hills and valleys of **"A Prospect of the Sea," "The Map of Love,"** the two fragments (**"In the Direction of the Beginning"** and **"An Adventure from a Work in Progress"**), and **"The Holy Six"** are metaphors of the feminine anatomy, the breasts, belly, and so forth, of the earth-mother herself. In **"The Map of Love"** the map which Sam Rib explicates is of sexual intercourse: the island "went in like the skin of lupus to his touch. . . . Here seed, up the tide, broke on the boiling coasts; the sand grains multiplied." In the tales where the cyclical pattern is most pronounced the feminine landscape is itself circular, dominated by a woman who draws the hero into the "mothering middle of the earth." In **"In the Direction of the Beginning," "An Adventure from a Work in Progress," "The Enemies,"** and **"The Holy Six,"** the heroes walk from the rim of an island or valley through ancestral fields into intercourse. Each consummation is analogous to a mythological event, during which the island or circular valley participates in an orgy of division and regeneration. As Dr. Maud has aptly pointed out [in his *Entrances to Dylan's Poetry* (1963)], Thomas' mingling of geographic and sexual imagery is a successful method of "distancing the intimate," a means of describing the act of love so that both its intimate and mythical qualities are dramatically embodied.

Neither the aesthetic imagery, which expresses the poetic quest of the hero, nor the sexual imagery of a given tale predominates. In each case poetic and anatomical metaphors describe a narrative line which is essentially mythological, both in the inward sense ("the union of ritual and dream in the form of verbal communication") and in the outward or historical sense (the use of Welsh, Egyptian, and other folklore for background). The final synthesis is always personal: images describing the heroes' thrust towards sexual and poetic maturity are overlaid by thematic antitheses of unity and division, love and death. (pp. 33-7)

"If ritual is the cradle of language," declares Suzanne Langer, "metaphor is the law of its life." Thomas' narratives depend upon the conflict, mergence, and progression of specific metaphors. Given the analogy of geography and anatomy which underlies most of the early tales, even his descriptive images bear a metaphorical burden. In **"The Burning Baby,"** for example, the relationship between images of gorse, flesh, and fire marks the progression of the plot towards its grim crescendo. At the outset, Thomas describes Rhys Rhys preaching a sermon on "The beauty of the harvest" and explains that in the preacher's mind "it was not the ripeness of God that glistened from the hill. It was the promise and the ripeness of the flesh, the good flesh, the mean flesh, flesh of his daughter, flesh, flesh, the flesh of the voice of thunder howling before the death of man." The biblical metaphor of flesh to grass is the raw material of Rhys' perversion. It embodies both the sensual level ("the flesh of his daughter") and the poetic level ("the flesh of the voice of thunder") of the plot.

Further on in the tale a third element is added to the metaphor: the little brother "saw the high grass at [his sister's] thighs. And the blades of the upgrowing wind, out of the four windsmells of the manuring dead, might drive through the soles of her feet, up the veins of the legs and stomach, into her womb and her pulsing heart." The grass has become an even more explicitly sexual metaphor, each blade being analogous to the father's phallus. The "upgrowing wind" surging through the grass is in turn analogous to the spirit, both as the biblical wind which "bloweth where it listeth" and as the impregnator of Mary. Coming into conjunction with flesh the fiery biblical wind ignites as the elements of gorse, flesh, wind, and fire merge in the burning baby. The denouement is organic, in the sense of propounding a natural, season-oriented or cyclical worldview. Rhys Rhys sets fire to the gorse to burn the incestuously begotten son as the tale concludes, its final scene a variation on Abraham's sacrifice of Isaac, God's sacrifice of Christ, and man's perennial sacrifice of himself. (pp. 37-8)

[In] **"The Mouse and the Woman," "The Lemon,"** and **"The Orchards,"** Thomas uses images from a series of related dreams to underline the narrative. In the tales where there is no dreaming he makes use of a similar mode of metaphorical progression. For each of the three key characters of **"The Enemies"** and **"The Holy Six,"** the world shapes itself into images appropriate to his perception of it. Mr. Owen is a kind of Great-Uncle Jarvis, a lover of the "vegetable world" that "roared under his feet." Endowing his garden with his own virility, he works upon the "brown body of the earth, the green skin of the grass, and the breasts of the Jarvis hills." Mrs. Owen's feminine powers are embodied in her crystal ball, which contains the extremities of hot and cold, clarity and obscurity and is analogous both to her womb and to the round earth whirling outside of the house. Davies, withered with age and insubstantial with sterility, perceives the Jarvis valley as a place of demonic vitality, death, and nausea. Throughout the narrative, it remains a "great grey green earth" that "moved unsteadily beneath him."

Ghostliness, virility, and demonic lust are embodied in Davies' nausea, Owen's garden, and Mrs. Owen's crystal ball. As the narrative moves towards its consummation the action moves entirely indoors to concentrate upon the ball and Mrs. Owen's pregnant womb. The six clergymen are made to share in Davies' nausea, vomiting up their desires under the influence of "mustard and water." At the denouement the conflict centers upon a question of paternity: whose child is in Mrs. Owen's womb? Ghostliness triumphs as Davies is assured that he has not loved Amabel in vain. As Owen, like Callaghan, laughs that there should "be life in the ancient loins," Davies sees "the buried grass shoot through the new night and move on the hill wind." Mr. Owen is revealed as the midwife-gardener to Mrs. Owen and Davies, laboring to bring new life out of a woman who conceives only in the arms of death. The antithetical metaphors of virility and ghostliness are woven into a new synthesis by Mrs. Owen's paradoxical desires. The narrative as a whole is a symbolic representation of an apocalyptic union of spirit and flesh, the dead and the living.

So intensely does Thomas concentrate upon a metaphor to make it render its utmost significance that his figures nearly burst their usual function, no longer representing a similarity but a metamorphosis. It is as if he, like his heroes, could change real objects into their subjective equivalents, and elements of the outer world into his lyric image of them. Thus in **"A Prospect of the Sea"** the boy sees a tree turn into the countryside: "every leaf of the tree that shaded them grew to man-size then, the ribs of the bark were channels and rivers wide as a great ship; and the moss on the tree, and the sharp grass ring round the base, were all the velvet covering of a green country's meadows blown hedge to hedge." By a process similar to hallucination the objects of the landscape become elements of a subjective vision, the tree on the hill becoming a symbolic expression of the boy's own transformation.

"The chief source of obscurity in these stories," remarks Jacob Korg, "is the fact that imagined things are expressed in the language of factual statement instead of the language of metaphor." Thus when Thomas writes of the girl in **"A Prospect of the Sea"** that "the heart in her breast was a small red bell that rang in a wave," one cannot comprehend the metaphor until one accepts the previous statement that the waves not only resemble but *are* a "white-faced sea of people, the terrible mortal number of the waves, all the centuries' sea drenched in the hail before Christ." The girl herself *is* a wave, her heart a meeting place of men and mermen, land and sea. If the sea is a metaphor of the human race, it is what Tindall has termed a "metaphysical metaphor," symbolic in itself and an "element of a symbolic structure."

Thomas' "metaphysical metaphors" are thematic symbols embodying the progression and antitheses upon which such a narrative depends. They are not literary tokens heightening realistic situations in the classic sense, nor are they incorporated into the tales from an external system. Within each story, they are distinguished from minor metaphors by the way that they juxtapose, blend, and contain the several dominant themes. The tree in **"The Tree," "A Prospect of the Sea,"** and **"The Orchards"**; the house in **"The Enemies," "The Holy Six"** and **"The Dress"**; and the tower in **"The Lemon"** and **"The School for Witches"** are such inclusive symbols. None of them is the only major symbol in its context, however. Tree, tower, and house form a symbolic triad in **"The Tree"**; orchard, scarecrow, and maiden are one among several such triads in **"The Orchards,"** while house, hill, and sea contain the thematic meaning of **"The Mouse and the Woman"** and **"A Prospect of the Sea."**

In each tale, objects contract and expand, merge and reshape themselves according to the pressure of the hero's mind. Like a magician, the poet-hero forces the image of a thing to become the thing itself. Although he draws upon the worlds of magic, folk belief, and madness for his material, Thomas exercises careful control over it, subordinating it to the expression of the hero's quest for meaning. Discontented with images and metaphors that are merely literary and decorative, the hero condemns the "dead word," story-princesses, and conventional metaphors, forcing himself into the dangerous world of the unconscious where symbols are live things which devour as they illuminate. Since the stories are about the search for a source of all story the symbolic visions which mark each denouement are ends in themselves. (pp. 39-42)

[Thomas's] texts alternate between lengthy descriptive passages, briefer paragraphs which sum up the descriptions or outline further action, and brief dialogues. Even in the longer descriptive sections there is a great deal of activity, the prose bristling with verbs of action and reaction describing the thematic conflict. Thomas often relies upon a series of clauses or phrases which he builds into a crescendo at the climax of a passage. In **"A Prospect of the Sea"** one paragraph begins with a brief and realistic statement: "It was hot that morning in the unexpected sunshine. A girl dressed in cotton put her mouth to his ear," and continues

> Along the bright wrackline, from the horizon where the vast birds sailed like boats, from the four compass corners, bellying up through the weed-beds, melting from orient and tropic, surging through the ice hills and the whale grounds, through sunset and sunrise corridors, the salt gardens and the herring fields, whirlpool and rock pool, out of the trickle in the mountain, down the waterfalls, a white-faced sea of people. . . .

The participial series, "bellying," "melting," "surging," gives way to a series of adverbial phrases which finally find their subject at the middle of the paragraph. The prose catalogue suggests a sweeping up and down of the earth, a gathering of the "white-faced sea of people" from the north and south, the east and west.

Passages so rich and lengthy generally occur only near the climax of the tales. Thomas leads up to them with shorter paragraphs, composed of a simple sentence at the beginning and end and one or two more complex sentences in between. Brief statement, mounting descriptive rhythms, and brevity of concluding statement are the basic units not only of individual paragraphs but of each story as a whole. Each tale begins and ends with a simplicity which must take its significance from the complex material in between. In nearly every case the plot is rounded out with some such simple statement as

> Hold my hand, he said. And then: Why are you putting the sheet over my face? **("The Visitor")**

or

> Brother, he said. He saw that the child held silver nails in the palm of his hand. **("The Tree")**

or

> Cool rain began to fall. **("A Prospect of the Sea")**

Thomas' dialogues are constructed along similar lines, occurring not as conventional conversations but as catechetical interchanges which usually precede or follow a complex and lengthy description. In **"The Visitor"** the paragraphs describing the arrival of Peter and Callaghan in the land of death are followed by this interchange:

> What is this valley? said Peter's voice.
>
> The Jarvis valley, said Callaghan. Callaghan, too, was dead. Not a bone or a hair stood up under the steadily falling frost.
>
> This is no Jarvis valley.
>
> This is the naked valley.

From this dialogue, resembling that of God and Ezekiel in the valley of dry bones, the reader is flung on into the powerful description of the deluge of blood which causes even the "monstrous nostrils of the moon" to widen in horror. In **"The Tree,"** similarly, the description of the boy's view of the Jarvis valley is followed by his question and the gardener's answer:

> Who are they, who are they?
>
> They are the Jarvis hills, said the gardener, which have been from the beginning.

A variation of the catechetical dialogue appears in the riddling interchanges that summarize the paradoxical themes of **"The Horse's Ha"** and **"In the Direction of the Beginning."** These bring the reader to a stop and make him, like the hero, puzzle over the significance of the adventure, giving him a pause for reflection before he is plunged into ever more complex prose. Thomas possibly derived this technique from the rhetoric of Welsh preachers. (pp. 43-5)

Thomas' early tales, as we have seen, are "poetic" in their dependence upon a balance, progression, and contrast of thematic images and symbols. They differ from the work of Woolf, Lawrence, and Joyce, however, not only in their brevity but in their intense subjectivism. Where the other novelists create a number of distinct characters upon whose minds the outer world registers its impressions, Thomas' tales more often center upon one protagonist. Even when a consort, father-figure or antagonist is present he or she is absorbed, in the end, into an inward or personal vision. (The triad of Mrs. Owen, Mr. Owen, and Davies in **"The Enemies"** is a notable exception to this practice.) When a number of persons are involved, as in **"The Horse's Ha"** and **"The School for Witches,"** they all are absorbed into a demonic or ritual unity at the denouement. Thomas thus pays little heed to Stephen Dedalus' plea for dramatic distancing over lyric subjectivism, for the conflict within each tale is less between separate persons than between the hero's Blakean faculties of imagination, reason, and desire. (pp. 48-9)

Annis Pratt, in his Dylan Thomas' Early Prose: A Study in Creative Mythology, *University of Pittsburgh Press, 1970, 226 p.*

Thomas and Caitlin in their Chelsea studio, 1944.

KENNETH SEIB (essay date 1978)

[*Seib is an American critic and the author of studies concerning the works of twentieth-century writers James Agee and Albert Camus. In the following excerpt, he discusses the thematic unity of the stories in* Portrait of the Artist as a Young Dog.]

Thomas' stories are artful contrivances, as complex as many of his better poems and worthy of careful consideration. They seem to me, after years of teaching and reading them, to be as subtly wrought as those in *Dubliners* by James Joyce, an author from whom Thomas borrowed heavily. What is needed, to begin with, is an overview and a roadmap, a way of seeing Thomas' fiction in coherent patterns. No better place to start than with ***Portrait of the Artist as a Young Dog.*** The earlier stories in ***The Map of Love*** provide no map at all, for the seven tales therein seem present merely to flesh out a volume that otherwise would have contained only sixteen poems. ***Portrait,*** published in 1940, is a book intended to stand by itself.

Thomas himself, his severest critic, gives credence to the notion that the stories in ***Portrait*** are of little worth. "I am hoping to sell some new straight autobiographical stories in America for a whole pile of England-trotting money," he wrote, while working on ***Portrait,*** to Henry Treece in 1939. In a later letter to Bert Trick, he calls the stories "mostly potboilers . . . stories toward a provincial autobiography." The reasons for such denigration, uncommon for Thomas, are not hard to find. A conscientious objector, he was depressed by the war and fearful of conscription—"Prison & the Medical Corps are both disagreeable to me," he wrote to Glyn Jones. Faced at the same time with near poverty, he envisioned the lucrative (though inartistic) possibility of offering his pen for hire: "If there's any profiteering to be done, I in my fashion wish to be in on it." Like Dr. Johnson, he even sought a patron. Poetry was Thomas' highest calling, however, and his continuing patron was Calliope. Both war and poverty caused him to compromise what he felt were his divine gifts. Writing short stories—"potboilers"—was to Thomas a descent from Parnassus, even though the slope was greased with money. The stories in ***Portrait,*** for instance, "may be amusing eventually, but the writing of them means the writing of a number of poems less."

Admittedly the stories in ***Portrait*** are not poetry—but neither are they pot-boilers. That they are "straight autobiographical stories" is equally questionable. For example, the details of **"A Visit to Grandpa's"**—grandpa's middle-of-the-night bedroom ride, "sitting straight up in bed and rocking from side to side as though the bed were on a rough road," as well as his subsequent walk, in best waistcoat and old hat, to be buried—may very well have come from childhood experience. But the final image of the story, not straight autobiography, is clearly artistic shaping: "But grandpa stood firmly on the bridge, and clutched his bag to his side, and stared at the flowing river and the sky, like a prophet who has no doubt." Standing midway between one world and the next, but still firmly clutching the material things of this world, grandpa stares at the Heraclitean flow of time below and the imponderable seat of heaven above, with certain knowledge that he is, like all of us, heading deathward. Grandpa becomes Everyman, and the story becomes clearly more than autobiography and potboiler.

But the stories *are* autobiography, in the same sense that those in Joyce's *Dubliners* are the shaped experiences of the author's life. Thomas admitted the influence of *Dubliners* on ***Portrait of the Artist as a Young Dog,*** but only to the extent that all modern stories are indebted to Joyce's tales composed in a style of scrupulous meanness. But the debt to Joyce goes further than that. Whatever Thomas' disclaimer, the title of his volume points irrefutably to Joyce's *A Portrait of the Artist as a Young Man.* There is no doubt that Thomas was aware of Joyce's earlier work, for he wrote to Pamela Hansford Johnson in 1933 that among the books in his personal library was "most of Joyce, with the exception of *Ulysses.*" And are we really to believe that Thomas, so aware of audience, did not realize that his title would bring inevitable comparison of his book with Joyce's? Surely several similarities exist. Both authors, for instance, disregard clear chronological sequence for the pointillist technique of portraiture, and their narratives abound with color. Both books concentrate on overall unity, each part designed to form a total "portrait" of a young man's growth to maturity. Thomas' title-change from "man" to "dog" suggests that the principal character of ***Portrait of the Artist as a Young Dog,*** like Joyce's Stephen Dedalus, is more failed than successful artist, a fact firmly established as well by Thomas' final story, **"One Warm Saturday,"** in which a youthful Dylan is lost and left in the dark. Finally, Thomas' stories employ much of the same symbolism found in Joyce's *Portrait*: sea, circle, light, dark, sermon, and dog. One even suspects "dog" of being a Joycean anagram for "God"; thus Thomas' title implies that his fictional Dylan is, all told, a young god become one more Welsh whelp fallen into dog days. His ***Portrait,*** like much of his poetry, recapitulates the Fall.

But it is with *Dubliners* that Thomas' ***Portrait*** most strongly compares. Thomas apparently wished to do for Welshmen what Joyce succeeded in doing for Dubliners—write a chapter of their moral history and allow them to have a good look at themselves in the "nicely polished looking-glass" of his art. What an Irishman could do, after all, any decent Welshman could equal, especially the Rimbaud of Cwmdonkin Drive. His stories, he wrote to Bert Trick, "are all about Swansea life: the pubs, clubs, billiard rooms, promenades, adolescence and the suburban nights, friendships, tempers and the humiliations." Like those in *Dubliners,* Thomas' stories reject "well-made" plot and commercial slickness, for controlling theme and rhetorical balance. Take handkerchiefs, for instance. The first story in ***Portrait,*** **"The Peaches,"** concludes with young Dylan waving his handkerchief to departing playmate Jack, whose angry and deceitful behavior is the first sign of Dylan's corrupted innocence. In the second story, **"A Visit to Grandpa's,"** Dylan is in a caravan of concerned citizens seeking wandering Grandpa. With bicycle bells ringing and pony-traps full of passengers, the caravan passes housewives who gawk, point, or flee—and one woman waves a bright handkerchief. In the third story, **"Patricia, Edith, and Arnold,"** the servant-girls' dashing but down-at-the-heels lover, Arnold Matthews, sports a flashy red handkerchief in his breast pocket, while Edith, discovering Arnold's disloyalty, picks "at the edge of her handkerchief." The handkerchief motif recurs elsewhere—the handkerchief-waving shopgirls in **"Old Garbo,"** the young man with "a dazzling handkerchief round his head" in the same story, or the kerchiefed weekend wives in **"One Warm Saturday."** As ubiquitous as wheels in Samuel Beckett's writings or that man in the mackintosh in Joyce's

Ulysses, Thomas' handkerchiefs link part to part, providing overall unity.

Equally omnipresent are circles, cats, and dogs. The circular wheels of Uncle Jim's grass-green cart in **"The Peaches"** and of grandpa's carts (both imaginary and real), the circle of companions around the campfire in **"Extraordinary Little Cough,"** the beer circles drawn by Dylan on the pub table in **"One Warm Saturday,"** all combine in **"Who Do You Wish Was with Us,"** a story of cycles, circles, and wheels. Beginning with "boys on bicycles ringing their bells and pedalling down the slight slope to make the whirrers in their wheels startle the women gabbing on the sunny doorsteps" and small girls "wheeling young brothers and sisters in prams" or watching them "on the circular swing in the public playground," the story involves Dylan and his friend Raymond Price, accompanied by a party of cyclists, enjoying the pleasures of merely circulating. At the seaside, his feet making "circular commotions in the water," Raymond mentally circles back to his arthritically crippled mother—"his mother sat all day in a wheel-chair"—and to his dead brother Harry. The story, about the cycles of birth and death and the omnipresence of death in life, concludes with chilling wind, the destructive element of the sea, and embracing darkness: "A wind, cornering the Head, chilled through our summer shirts, and the sea began to cover our rock quickly, our rock already covered with friends, with living and dead, racing against the darkness."

In eight of the ten stories in ***Portrait,*** dogs are present in one way or another. Only in **"Extraordinary Little Cough"** and **"Where Tawe Flows"** are no dogs visible, though in one story the young lovers behave just like little dogs, and in the other, cats—traditional antagonists of dogs—are prominent. At almost the center of Thomas' collection is **"Just Like Little Dogs,"** a story that not only reinforces the title of the book, but which also emphasizes the animal-level of Welsh young manhood. The narrator, beneath a railway arch and standing alone (like Little Cough of the previous story), stares at "the miles of sands" (like the sands on which Little Cough ran) and encounters two young men in the early dark (darkness ended the story of Little Cough). These three young dogs about town, with nothing better to do, smoke cigarettes, make small talk, and listen to the sounds of wind, rumbling trams, and a howling "chained dog." Lonely and chained in the same way, Walter and Tom tell of their marriage to Norma and Doris—though neither to the woman he loves. Just like little dogs, they were once in heat and are now out in the cold. Unlike little dogs, however, they have lived up to their commitments ("We had to do the right thing by them, didn't we?"), and they feel brotherly attachment to each other. Not really little dogs, they are merely little humans dogged by the failures of their own lives.

No dogs, but cats pervade **"Where Tawe Flows."** This story, Thomas' equivalent of "Ivy Day in the Committee Room," is a witty put-down of Welsh cultural pretension among a group of catty literary aspirants—including Dylan himself, a young man who is "penniless, and hoped, in a vague way, to live on women." Mr. Humphries, a school teacher and failed novelist; Mr. Roberts, an insurance collector; and Mr. Emlyn Evans, "a traveller in rubber, rubber toys and syringes and bathmats," comprise the rest of this artistically indigent group. Socialism, Shavianism, government officials, friends, neighbors, and relatives get a going over here, as the four, soused on home-made wine, gather presumably to discuss their joint-effort novel of provincial life, *Where Tawe Flows,* the first chapter of which is finished. That it will never get much further is a good bet, for neither Mr. Thomas nor Mr. Roberts has written a thing for chapter two, and Humphries and Evans very little. All are more interested in drink, idle chatter, and catty gossip. Only when Sambo, the Evans' family cat, is put out for the night do Evans' three friends leave—perhaps to become little dogs again.

In sum, Thomas, through intricate image, has collected in ***Portrait*** not disparate autobiographical sketches, but rather cunning stories linked by repetitive theme and metaphor. If searching for maps, the reader can best gain entrance by first seeing—as I have tried to show—how each story points to others, and, second, by looking for general thematic patterns that encompass all ten stories. There are many general themes, few of them mentioned by critics. The stories, as Jacob Korg notes, "seem to trace the child's emergence from his domain of imagination and secret pleasures into an adult world where he observes suffering, pathos, and dignity." But Korg finds "loose unity" where I find tight. The narrator not only "observes suffering," he becomes part of that suffering. What Korg and others miss, it seems to me, is irony, like that in the title. The character Dylan is the artist as dog, a worthless youth who falls victim to the mediocrity around him—in short, no artist at all. The stories move from the partially Edenic innocence of childhood, with its pastoral open-spaces and imaginative adventures, to the corruption of adulthood, with its urban slums, pubs, and rotting tenements. That the character Dylan is no artist becomes apparent as the stories progress. In **"The Fight,"** Dylan is aspiring poet, with little to show for it other than Tennyson imitations, poems about bestial remorse, unfulfilled desire, tearing lust, and dark dead bodies. In **"Just Like Little Dogs,"** he is "a lonely nightwalker and a steady stander-at-corners," a vagrant and inactive Welsh youth. **"Where Tawe Flows"** presents Dylan as posing dilettante: "He had been writing, that week, the story of a cat who jumped over a woman the moment she died and turned her into a vampire. He had reached the part of the story where the woman was an undead children's governess, but he could not think how to fit it into the novel." Vampires, lifeless creatures, are now his subject, not living beings; and prose, not poetry, his genre. To Thomas the artist, the artist was poet—not prose writer—and his fictional Dylan has abandoned genuine artistry for supernatural "potboilers."

By the final story, **"One Warm Saturday,"** Dylan's failure is complete. After a brief stint as a newspaper reporter in **"Old Garbo"**—another comedown for an aspiring poet—Dylan has become a lonely vagrant and Romantic poseur, longing for beautiful ladies and drowning his sorrow in drink. The story is filled with images of death, drowning, and destruction. To the barman in the Victoria saloon, Dylan looks like "death warmed up"; empty bottles cover the table like the dead and later, at Lou's apartment, dead bottles are lined on the mantelpiece. All of this takes place at the end of a "dying holiday." Wearing a sailor's jersey, Dylan is linked with a drowning motif throughout the story. At the seaside, young girls scream "as the sea rose to their waists," and a collie dog carries a ball into the sea beyond the reach of his owners. (Later, Dylan associates this scene with his peace, which is "struck away, like a ball, . . . into the sea.") In the pub, the barman sees Dylan as "the only one saved from the wreck and the only wreck saved." Dylan, therefore, is metaphoric ship-wrecked seaman tossed up from the wreckage around him. And others around him are clearly wrecks. Lou, Marjorie, and Mrs. Franklin are seaside floozies who can drink "like a deep-sea diver." The drunk in the Victoria saloon is a physical wreck, with half of his behind missing: "Do you know what I got for losing my bottom? Four and three! Two and three ha'pence a cheek. That's cheaper than a pig!" Like one of Odysseus' mariners, the drunk is later turned into a pig by Circe-like Lou when he lies down at her feet (like a dog as well as a pig) and goes to sleep. Another wreck, the barman, is jesting pilot of this crew, a hardened mariner who steers aimlessly from drink to drink, woman to woman. By the end of the story, Dylan sinks into the polluted sea of this low-life: sick, depressed, and drunk, he is on Lou's bed, which is "pitching like a ship," and later stumbles out the door on "sailor's legs."

That all of this is detrimental to poetry and artists is clear from the story. "Poets live and walk with their poems; a man with visions needs no other company," Dylan meditates. "But he was not a poet living and walking, he was a young man in a sea-town on a warm bank holiday, with two pounds to spend; he had no visions. . . ." Seated in the pub, in "the safe centre of his own identity," he is immured from "the spreading town where everything was happening"—and a poet should be where things are happening. Later, at Lou's, Dylan argues with Marjorie's boyfriend, Harold, about Tennyson, whom Harold's grandfather remembered as "a little man with a hump." This view of Tennyson, the poet deformed, is appropriate for the various cripples gathered at Lou's, though clearly wrong for Dylan. Yet one suspects that Dylan, too, is a deformed poet. Lou calls him "Jack," a confusion of identity, and gives him a Judas-like kiss at the door of her apartment. If Dylan is Jack Christ, it is a kiss of betrayal, for Lou ends up with Mr. O'Brien, who purchases her for the equivalent of thirty pieces of silver. (Furthermore, O'Brien's name suggests that he is an Irishman—to a Welshman, someone only a shade better than an Englishman). All things considered, then, Dylan is crippled poet and sad Jack Christ, betrayed by the shoddy group around him and incapable of finding true identity, so necessary to artists. At the end of the story, he is lost in confusing corridors, wandering blindly in a tunnel, opening all the wrong doors; he is cut off from Lou who, although a whore, is his Beatrice-like vision of beauty, poetry, and the feminine creative principle. But Beatrice is gone, the light (of creativity) is out, there is "no love now to wait for," and Dylan is wandering "across the brick-heaps and the broken wood and the dust that had been houses once, where the small and hardly known and never-to-be-forgotten people of the dirty town had lived and loved and died and, always, lost." Like all woebegotten Welshmen, Dylan is another loser, doomed never to rise above the squalid life around him.

Along with the movement from childhood to adulthood, the principal direction of the stories is from Edenic innocence to Adamic fall. Other movements exist in the book: from the private to the public, from the "safe centre of his own identity" to the exterior world in which identity is either confused or lost; from the narrator's objective witness of life around him to subjective participation in the mean and fallen Welsh world. Essentially, as in Joyce's *Dubliners,* the world of the work is a fallen one of frustration, thwarted ambition, and sterile companionship. For artists, it is a world of death, sterility, and spiritual debasement. The first story, **"The Peaches,"** exemplifies the latter in Gwilym, whose religious hypocrisy and frightening sermons seem meant to represent the Welsh clergy in general. Obsessed with sin and confession, Gwilym couples sexual desire with religious fervor, mistaking his own lust for others' sin. Gwilym's spade-shaped face ("You could dig the garden with him") and black garb suggest the grave; Gwilym's religion is not a living one and contributes only to Dylan's "fall"—from tree-top, Jack's friendship, and innocence. The Adamic fall carries over into **"A Visit to Grandpa's,"** the beginning of which finds Dylan dreaming of painful whips, binding lariats, and serpents in the Garden. Other falls occur in other stories: the man who falls from the bicycle at the beginning of **"Extraordinary Little Cough,"** or the youngsters on swings in **"Who Do You Wish Was with Us"** ("Ooh! I'm falling!").

Modeled after *Dubliners,* ***Portrait of the Artist as a Young Dog*** is a composite picture of Welshmen fallen into physical decay **("A Visit to Grandpa's")**, religious hypocrisy **("The Peaches")**, loveless marriage **("Just Like Little Dogs")**, provincial art **("Where Tawe Flows")**, unrewarding work **("Old Garbo")**, and spiritual torpor **("One Warm Saturday")**. Unrequited love **("Patricia, Edith and Arnold")**, broken friendship **("The Peaches")**, loneliness and humiliation **("Extraordinary Little Cough")**, escape into fantasy **("The Fight")**: all are dominant in the lives of those who people Thomas' stories and all, presumably, were to Thomas dominant among the Welsh. The stories themselves even parallel in subject matter many of the stories in Joyce's *Dubliners.* Joyce's "An Encounter" and Thomas' **"Who Do You Wish Was with Us,"** for instance, both involve two young schoolboys walking seaward toward a jetty, encountering during their journeys significant views of self. **"Extraordinary Little Cough"** (a title that echoes Joyce's "A Little Cloud") is, like the Joyce story, one of isolation from society, insensitivity, and thwarted desire. **"Peaches,"** with its trees and religious hypocrisy, is reminiscent of Joyce's "The Sisters," with its simoniac priest and of "Araby," with its central apple tree. **"Where Tawe Flows"** is a gossipy Welsh version of Joyce's "Ivy Day in the Committee Room," a story in which Irish gossip flows freely. Finally, **"One Warm Saturday"** is Thomas' "The Dead," a story of failed love, life, and passion. ***Portrait,*** in fact, could easily have been called *Swanseans* or *Welshmen.* Why it was not can only be because Thomas, unlike Joyce, remained physically rooted to his birthplace—it was no accident that Thomas suffered his severe breakdowns in America. Wales was both solace and suffering to Thomas, and to write objectively of Welshmen was to distance himself from them. Instead, Thomas placed himself squarely among his countrymen; as he once announced proudly, he was a Welshman, a drunkard, and a heterosexual—in that order. His main character in ***Portrait*** is Dylan—himself—as much a salty dog as any roistering and word-frenzied Welshman, and as susceptible to Welsh sin as the worst among them. But unlike most of his countrymen, Dylan the artist toiled with words toward "the ambush of his wounds," and, falling, achieved dominion over defeat. If the Dylan of ***Portrait*** is different from Dylan the author—well, then, why not? "I, in my intricate image, stride on two levels," he wrote.

Among the papers that Thomas left after his death was this note for a possible poem: "Although he was too proud to die, he *did* die, blind, in the most agonizing way but he did not flinch from death & was brave in his pride." Left as epitaph for his father, it is just as easily an epitaph for the son—as it is perhaps for all the blind and thwarted lives, dogged by doom, that populate the world of Dylan Thomas' ***Portrait.*** (pp. 240-46)

Kenneth Seib, " 'Portrait of the Artist as a Young Dog': Dylan's 'Dubliners'," in Modern Fiction Studies, *Vol. 24, No. 2, Summer, 1978, pp. 239-46.*

ADDITIONAL BIBLIOGRAPHY

Amis, Kingsley. "Thomas the Rhymer." *Spectator* 195, No. 6633 (12 August 1955): 227-28.

Review of *A Prospect of the Sea, and Other Stories and Prose Writings,* an English edition of selected writings by Thomas. Amis praises Thomas's realistic stories but finds little value in his earlier, surrealistic prose pieces.

Bruns, Gerald L. "Daedalus, Orpheus, and Dylan Thomas's Portrait of the Artist." *Renascence* 34, No. 1 (Spring 1973): 147-56.

Contrasts Thomas's view of the function of the artist with that of James Joyce.

Davies, Walford. "Imitation and Invention: The Use of Borrowed Material in Dylan Thomas's Prose." *Essays in Criticism* 18, No. 3 (July 1968): 275-95.

Examines the extent to which Thomas used material taken from the works of others and reused material from his early short stories in later works.

———. *Dylan Thomas.* Aberystwyth: University of Wales Press, 1972, 93 p.

Brief biographical study emphasizing the importance of Welsh culture and geography in Thomas's work.

Dupee, F. W. "Portrait of Dylan Thomas." *New Republic* 103, No. 27 (30 December 1940): 906.

Review of *Portrait of the Artist as a Young Dog.* Dupee states: "There is not a great deal to say of this book except that it is very good. If Thomas' verse is generally baffling in its obscurity, his stories—these stories at any rate—discourage comment by their very transparency."

Ferris, Paul. *Dylan Thomas.* New York: Dial Press, 1977, 399 p.

Comprehensive critical biography.

FitzGibbon, Constantine. *The Life of Dylan Thomas.* Boston: Little, Brown, 1965, 370 p.

Critical biography.

Hauser, Marianne. "Sketches of Youth." *New York Times* (29 December 1940): 4,14.

Positive review of *Portrait of the Artist as a Young Dog.*

Hoffman, Frederick J. "Further Interpretations." In his *Freudianism and the Literary Mind,* pp. 272-96. Baton Rouge: Louisiana State University Press, 1957.

Finds elements of Freudian psychology in Thomas's literary endeavor to penetrate the dark side of human psychology.

Jennings, Elizabeth. "Thomas the Novelist." *Spectator* 195, No. 6641 (7 October 1955): 462-63.

Review of *Adventures in the Skin Trade.* Jennings praises the lyrical, visceral quality of Thomas's prose but doubts that he could have realized the narrative goals he set for himself in the novel.

Jones, T. H. "The Map of Love." In his *Dylan Thomas,* pp. 23-51. New York: Grove, 1963.

Includes a brief discussion of Thomas's short stories.

Kelly, Richard. "The Lost Vision in Dylan Thomas' 'One Warm Saturday'." *Studies in Short Fiction* 6, No. 2 (Winter 1969): 205-09.

Analysis of "One Warm Saturday." Kelly suggests that "Thomas' autobiographical protagonist, like Joyce's Stephen Dedalus, undergoes a strikingly similar process of maturing with one important difference—whereas Joyce's wading girl provides Stephen with aesthetic and emotional autonomy, the girl in the anti-romantic 'One Warm Saturday' fills the young man with anguish and frustration and returns him to an ugly, hostile world."

Morris, Frances. "The Man Who Loved and Haunted Himself." *Times Literary Supplement* (2 March 1984): 227.

Discusses the strong autobiographical element in Thomas's fiction.

Phelps, Robert. "In Country Dylan." *Sewanee Review* 63, No. 3 (July-September 1955): 681-87.

Brief appreciation of Thomas's prose.

Schwartz, Delmore. "With a Deep-Set Romantic Attitude." *New York Times Book Review* 60, No. 21 (22 May 1955): 4, 20.

Review of *Adventures in the Skin Trade, and Other Stories.* Schwartz praises the title piece of the collection but notes that many of the others, written during Thomas's earlier, surrealist period, "require and not always justify a close and heightened attention to language and symbolism, and sometimes read as if the Bible and *A Pilgrim's Progress* had been revised by Poe and Krafft-Ebing to prove the satanic inspiration of both books."

Stanford, Derek. "Part III: Prose and Drama." In his *Dylan Thomas,* pp, 155-88. New York: Citadel Press, 1954.

Includes a brief discussion of Thomas's short stories.

Tritschler, Donald. "The Stories in Dylan Thomas' Red Notebook." *Journal of Modern Literature* 2, No. 1 (September 1971): 33-56.

Compares manuscript versions of nine of Thomas's short stories with published versions.

Short Story Criticism Indexes

Literary Criticism Series
Cumulative Author Index

SSC Cumulative Nationality Index

SSC Cumulative Title Index

This Index Includes References to Entries in These Gale Series

Contemporary Literary Criticism

Presents excerpts of criticism on the works of novelists, poets, dramatists, short story writers, scriptwriters, and other creative writers who are now living or who have died since 1960. Cumulative indexes to authors and nationalities are included, as well as an index to titles discussed in the individual volume. Volumes 1-55 are in print.

Twentieth-Century Literary Criticism

Contains critical excerpts by the most significant commentators on poets, novelists, short story writers, dramatists, and philosophers who died between 1900 and 1960. Cumulative indexes to authors, nationalities, and titles discussed are included in each new volume. Volumes 1-33 are in print.

Nineteenth-Century Literature Criticism

Offers significant passages from criticism on authors who died between 1800 and 1899. Cumulative indexes to authors, nationalities, and titles discussed are included in each new volume. Volumes 1-23 are in print.

Literature Criticism from 1400 to 1800

Compiles significant passages from the most noteworthy criticism on authors of the fifteenth through eighteenth centuries. Cumulative indexes to authors, nationalities, and titles discussed are included in each new volume. Volumes 1-11 are in print.

Classical and Medieval Literature Criticism

Offers excerpts of criticism on the works of world authors from classical antiquity through the fourteenth century. Cumulative indexes to authors, titles, and critics are included in each volume. Volumes 1-3 are in print.

Short Story Criticism

Compiles excerpts of criticism on short fiction by writers of all eras and nationalities. Cumulative indexes to authors, nationalities, and titles discussed are included in each new volume. Volumes 1-3 are in print.

Children's Literature Review

Includes excerpts from reviews, criticism, and commentary on works of authors and illustrators who create books for children. Cumulative indexes to authors, nationalities, and titles discussed are included in each new volume. Volumes 1-18 are in print.

Contemporary Authors Series

Encompasses five related series. *Contemporary Authors* provides biographical and bibliographical information on more than 92,000 writers of fiction, nonfiction, poetry, journalism, drama, motion pictures, and other fields. Each new volume contains sketches on authors not previously covered in the series. Volumes 1-127 are in print. *Contemporary Authors New Revision Series* provides completely updated information on active authors covered in previously published volumes of *CA*. Only entries requiring significant change are revised for *CA New Revision Series.* Volumes 1-27 are in print. *Contemporary Authors Permanent Series* consists of updated listings for deceased and inactive authors removed from the original volumes 9-36 when these volumes were revised. Volumes 1-2 are in print. *Contemporary Authors Autobiography Series* presents specially commissioned autobiographies by leading contemporary writers. Volumes 1-9 are in print. *Contemporary Authors Bibliographical Series* contains primary and secondary bibliographies as well as analytical bibliographical essays by authorities on major modern authors. Volumes 1-2 are in print.

Dictionary of Literary Biography

Encompasses three related series. *Dictionary of Literary Biography* furnishes illustrated overviews of authors' lives and works and places them in the larger perspective of literary history. Volumes 1-81 are in print. *Dictionary of Literary Biography Documentary Series* illuminates the careers of major figures through a selection of literary documents, including letters, notebook and diary entries, interviews, book reviews, and photographs. Volumes 1-6 are in print. *Dictionary of Literary Biography Yearbook* summarizes the past year's literary activity with articles on genres, major prizes, conferences, and other timely subjects and includes updated and new entries on individual authors. Yearbooks for 1980-1988 are in print. A cumulative index to authors and articles is included in each new volume.

Concise Dictionary of American Literary Biography

A six-volume series that collects revised and updated sketches on major American authors that were originally presented in *Dictionary of Literary Biography.* Volumes 1-3 are in print.

Something about the Author Series

Encompasses two related series. *Something about the Author* contains heavily illustrated biographical sketches on juvenile and young adult authors and illustrators from all eras. Volumes 1-54 are in print. *Something about the Author Autobiography Series* presents specially commissioned autobiographies by prominent authors and illustrators of books for children and young adults. Volumes 1-8 are in print.

Yesterday's Authors of Books for Children

Contains heavily illustrated entries on children's writers who died before 1961. Complete in two volumes. Volumes 1-2 are in print.

Literary Criticism Series Cumulative Author Index

This index lists all author entries in the Gale Literary Criticism Series and includes cross-references to other Gale sources. References in the index are identified as follows:

AAYA: *Authors & Artists for Young Adults,* Volume 1
CAAS: *Contemporary Authors Autobiography Series,* Volumes 1-9
CA: *Contemporary Authors* (original series), Volumes 1-127
CABS: *Contemporary Authors Bibliographical Series,* Volumes 1-2
CANR: *Contemporary Authors New Revision Series,* Volumes 1-27
CAP: *Contemporary Authors Permanent Series,* Volumes 1-2
CA-R: *Contemporary Authors* (revised editions), Volumes 1-44
CDALB: *Concise Dictionary of American Literary Biography,* Volume 1-3
CLC: *Contemporary Literary Criticism,* Volumes 1-54
CLR: *Children's Literature Review,* Volumes 1-18
CMLC: *Classical and Medieval Literature Criticism,* Volumes 1-3
DLB: *Dictionary of Literary Biography,* Volumes 1-84
DLB-DS: *Dictionary of Literary Biography Documentary Series,* Volumes 1-6
DLB-Y: *Dictionary of Literary Biography Yearbook,* Volumes 1980-1988
LC: *Literature Criticism from 1400 to 1800,* Volumes 1-11
NCLC: *Nineteenth-Century Literature Criticism,* Volumes 1-22
SAAS: *Something about the Author Autobiography Series,* Volumes 1-8
SATA: *Something about the Author,* Volumes 1-56
SSC: *Short Story Criticism,* Volumes 1-3
TCLC: *Twentieth-Century Literary Criticism,* Volumes 1-33
YABC: *Yesterday's Authors of Books for Children,* Volumes 1-2

A. E. 1867-1935 .... **TCLC 3, 10**
See also Russell, George William
See also DLB 19

Abbey, Edward 1927-............. **CLC 36**
See also CANR 2; CA 45-48

Abbott, Lee K., Jr. 19??........... **CLC 48**

Abé, Kōbō 1924- .... **CLC 8, 22, 53**
See also CANR 24; CA 65-68

Abell, Kjeld 1901-1961............ **CLC 15**
See also obituary CA 111

Abish, Walter 1931-.............. **CLC 22**
See also CA 101

Abrahams, Peter (Henry) 1919- ..... **CLC 4**
See also CA 57-60

Abrams, M(eyer) H(oward) 1912-... **CLC 24**
See also CANR 13; CA 57-60

Abse, Dannie 1923-............. **CLC 7, 29**
See also CAAS 1; CANR 4; CA 53-56; DLB 27

Achebe, (Albert) Chinua(lumogu) 1930- .... **CLC 1, 3, 5, 7, 11, 26, 51**
See also CANR 6; CA 1-4R; SATA 38, 40

Acker, Kathy 1948- .... **CLC 45**
See also CA 117, 122

Ackroyd, Peter 1949-.......... **CLC 34, 52**
See also CA 123, 127

Acorn, Milton 1923-.............. **CLC 15**
See also CA 103; DLB 53

Adamov, Arthur 1908-1970 ...... **CLC 4, 25**
See also CAP 2; CA 17-18; obituary CA 25-28R

Adams, Alice (Boyd) 1926- ... **CLC 6, 13, 46**
See also CA 81-84; DLB-Y 86

Adams, Douglas (Noel) 1952- ...... **CLC 27**
See also CA 106; DLB-Y 83

Adams, Henry (Brooks) 1838-1918 .... **TCLC 4**
See also CA 104; DLB 12, 47

Adams, Richard (George) 1920- .... **CLC 4, 5, 18**
See also CANR 3; CA 49-52; SATA 7

Adamson, Joy(-Friederike Victoria) 1910-1980 .... **CLC 17**
See also CANR 22; CA 69-72; obituary CA 93-96; SATA 11; obituary SATA 22

Adcock, (Kareen) Fleur 1934-...... **CLC 41**
See also CANR 11; CA 25-28R; DLB 40

Addams, Charles (Samuel) 1912-1988 .... **CLC 30**
See also CANR 12; CA 61-64

Adler, C(arole) S(chwerdtfeger) 1932- .... **CLC 35**
See also CANR 19; CA 89-92; SATA 26

Adler, Renata 1938-............ **CLC 8, 31**
See also CANR 5, 22; CA 49-52

Ady, Endre 1877-1919 .... **TCLC 11**
See also CA 107

Agee, James 1909-1955 .... **TCLC 1, 19**
See also CA 108; DLB 2, 26; CDALB 1941-1968

Agnon, S(hmuel) Y(osef Halevi) 1888-1970 .... **CLC 4, 8, 14**
See also CAP 2; CA 17-18; obituary CA 25-28R

Ai 1947-...................... **CLC 4, 14**
See also CA 85-88

Aiken, Conrad (Potter) 1889-1973 .... **CLC 1, 3, 5, 10, 52**
See also CANR 4; CA 5-8R; obituary CA 45-48; SATA 3, 30; DLB 9, 45

Aiken, Joan (Delano) 1924-........ **CLC 35**
See also CLR 1; CANR 4; CA 9-12R; SAAS 1; SATA 2, 30

Ainsworth, William Harrison 1805-1882 .... **NCLC 13**
See also SATA 24; DLB 21

Ajar, Emile 1914-1980
See Gary, Romain

Akhmadulina, Bella (Akhatovna) 1937- . . . . **CLC 53**
See also CA 65-68

Akhmatova, Anna 1888-1966. . . . **CLC 11, 25**
See also CAP 1; CA 19-20; obituary CA 25-28R

Aksakov, Sergei Timofeyvich 1791-1859 . . . . **NCLC 2**

Aksenov, Vassily (Pavlovich) 1932-
See Aksyonov, Vasily (Pavlovich)

Aksyonov, Vasily (Pavlovich) 1932- . . . . **CLC 22, 37**
See also CANR 12; CA 53-56

Akutagawa Ryunosuke 1892-1927 . . . . **TCLC 16**
See also CA 117

Alain-Fournier 1886-1914 . . . . **TCLC 6**
See also Fournier, Henri Alban

Alarcon, Pedro Antonio de 1833-1891 . . . . **NCLC 1**

Alas (y Urena), Leopoldo (Enrique Garcia) 1852-1901 . . . . **TCLC 29**
See also CA 113

Albee, Edward (Franklin,) (III) 1928- . . . **CLC 1, 2, 3, 5, 9, 11, 13, 25, 53**
See also CANR 8; CA 5-8R; DLB 7; CDALB 1941-1968

Alberti, Rafael 1902- . . . . **CLC 7**
See also CA 85-88

Alcott, Amos Bronson 1799-1888 . . **NCLC 1**
See also DLB 1

Alcott, Louisa May 1832-1888 . . . . **NCLC 6**
See also CLR 1; YABC 1; DLB 1, 42; CDALB 1865-1917

Aldanov, Mark 1887-1957 . . . . **TCLC 23**
See also CA 118

Aldington, Richard 1892-1962. . . . . . **CLC 49**
See also CA 85-88; DLB 20, 36

Aldiss, Brian W(ilson) 1925- . . . . **CLC 5, 14, 40**
See also CAAS 2; CANR 5; CA 5-8R; SATA 34; DLB 14

Aleichem, Sholom 1859-1916. . . . . . . **TCLC 1**
See also Rabinovitch, Sholem

Aleixandre, Vicente 1898-1984 . . . **CLC 9, 36**
See also CA 85-88; obituary CA 114

Alepoudelis, Odysseus 1911-
See Elytis, Odysseus

Aleshkovsky, Yuz 1929-. . . . . **CLC 44**
See also CA 121

Alexander, Lloyd (Chudley) 1924- . . **CLC 35**
See also CLR 1, 5; CANR 1; CA 1-4R; SATA 3, 49; DLB 52

Alger, Horatio, Jr. 1832-1899. . . . . **NCLC 8**
See also SATA 16; DLB 42

Algren, Nelson 1909-1981 . . . . **CLC 4, 10, 33**
See also CANR 20; CA 13-16R; obituary CA 103; DLB 9; DLB-Y 81, 82; CDALB 1941-1968

Alighieri, Dante 1265-1321 . . . . **CMLC 3**

Allen, Heywood 1935-
See Allen, Woody
See also CA 33-36R

Allen, Roland 1939-
See Ayckbourn, Alan

Allen, Woody 1935- . . . . **CLC 16, 52**
See also Allen, Heywood
See also CANR 27; CA 33-36R; DLB 44

Allende, Isabel 1942- . . . . **CLC 39**

Allingham, Margery (Louise) 1904-1966 . . . . **CLC 19**
See also CANR 4; CA 5-8R; obituary CA 25-28R

Allston, Washington 1779-1843. . . . **NCLC 2**
See also DLB 1

Almedingen, E. M. 1898-1971 . . . . . . **CLC 12**
See also Almedingen, Martha Edith von
See also SATA 3

Almedingen, Martha Edith von 1898-1971
See Almedingen, E. M.
See also CANR 1; CA 1-4R

Alonso, Damaso 1898- . . . . **CLC 14**
See also CA 110

Alta 1942- . . . . **CLC 19**
See also CA 57-60

Alter, Robert B(ernard) 1935-. . . . . . **CLC 34**
See also CANR 1; CA 49-52

Alther, Lisa 1944-. . . . . **CLC 7, 41**
See also CANR 12; CA 65-68

Altman, Robert 1925-. . . . . **CLC 16**
See also CA 73-76

Alvarez, A(lfred) 1929-. . . . . **CLC 5, 13**
See also CANR 3; CA 1-4R; DLB 14, 40

Alvarez, Alejandro Rodriguez 1903-1965
See Casona, Alejandro
See also obituary CA 93-96

Amado, Jorge 1912- . . . . **CLC 13, 40**
See also CA 77-80

Ambler, Eric 1909-. . . . . **CLC 4, 6, 9**
See also CANR 7; CA 9-12R

Amichai, Yehuda 1924- . . . . **CLC 9, 22**
See also CA 85-88

Amiel, Henri Frederic 1821-1881 . . **NCLC 4**

Amis, Kingsley (William) 1922- . . . . . . **CLC 1, 2, 3, 5, 8, 13, 40, 44**
See also CANR 8; CA 9-12R; DLB 15, 27

Amis, Martin 1949- . . . . **CLC 4, 9, 38**
See also CANR 8; CA 65-68; DLB 14

Ammons, A(rchie) R(andolph) 1926- . . . . **CLC 2, 3, 5, 8, 9, 25**
See also CANR 6; CA 9-12R; DLB 5

Anand, Mulk Raj 1905-. . . . . **CLC 23**
See also CA 65-68

Anaya, Rudolfo A(lfonso) 1937- . . . . **CLC 23**
See also CAAS 4; CANR 1; CA 45-48

Andersen, Hans Christian 1805-1875 . . . . **NCLC 7**
See also CLR 6; YABC 1

Anderson, Jessica (Margaret Queale) 19?? . . . . **CLC 37**
See also CANR 4; CA 9-12R

Anderson, Jon (Victor) 1940- . . . . **CLC 9**
See also CANR 20; CA 25-28R

Anderson, Lindsay 1923-. . . . . **CLC 20**

Anderson, Maxwell 1888-1959 . . . . . **TCLC 2**
See also CA 105; DLB 7

Anderson, Poul (William) 1926- . . . . **CLC 15**
See also CAAS 2; CANR 2, 15; CA 1-4R; SATA 39; DLB 8

Anderson, Robert (Woodruff) 1917- . . . . **CLC 23**
See also CA 21-24R; DLB 7

Anderson, Roberta Joan 1943-
See Mitchell, Joni

Anderson, Sherwood 1876-1941 . . . . . . **TCLC 1, 10, 24; SSC 1**
See also CAAS 3; CA 104, 121; DLB 4, 9; DLB-DS 1

Andrade, Carlos Drummond de 1902- . . . . **CLC 18**

Andrewes, Lancelot 1555-1626 . . . . **LC 5**

Andrews, Cicily Fairfield 1892-1983
See West, Rebecca

Andreyev, Leonid (Nikolaevich) 1871-1919 . . . . **TCLC 3**
See also CA 104

Andrezel, Pierre 1885-1962
See Dinesen, Isak; Blixen, Karen (Christentze Dinesen)

Andric, Ivo 1892-1975 . . . . **CLC 8**
See also CA 81-84; obituary CA 57-60

Angelique, Pierre 1897-1962
See Bataille, Georges

Angell, Roger 1920- . . . . **CLC 26**
See also CANR 13; CA 57-60

Angelou, Maya 1928-. . . . . **CLC 12, 35**
See also CANR 19; CA 65-68; SATA 49; DLB 38

Annensky, Innokenty 1856-1909. . . **TCLC 14**
See also CA 110

Anouilh, Jean (Marie Lucien Pierre) 1910-1987 . . . . . . **CLC 1, 3, 8, 13, 40, 50**
See also CA 17-20R

Anthony, Florence 1947-
See Ai

Anthony (Jacob), Piers 1934- . . . . . . **CLC 35**
See also Jacob, Piers A(nthony) D(illingham)
See also DLB 8

Antoninus, Brother 1912-
See Everson, William (Oliver)

Antonioni, Michelangelo 1912- . . . . . **CLC 20**
See also CA 73-76

Antschel, Paul 1920-1970
See Celan, Paul
See also CA 85-88

Anwar, Chairil 1922-1949 . . . . **TCLC 22**
See also CA 121

Apollinaire, Guillaume 1880-1918 . . . . **TCLC 3, 8**
See also Kostrowitzki, Wilhelm Apollinaris de

Appelfeld, Aharon 1932- . . . . **CLC 23, 47**
See also CA 112

Apple, Max (Isaac) 1941-. . . . . **CLC 9, 33**
See also CANR 19; CA 81-84

Appleman, Philip (Dean) 1926- . . . . . **CLC 51**
See also CANR 6; CA 13-16R

Apuleius, (Lucius) (Madaurensis) 125?175? . . . . **CMLC 1**

Aquin, Hubert 1929-1977 .... **CLC 15**
See also CA 105; DLB 53

Aragon, Louis 1897-1982 .... **CLC 3, 22**
See also CA 69-72; obituary CA 108; DLB 72

Arbuthnot, John 1667-1735 .... **LC 1**

Archer, Jeffrey (Howard) 1940- .... **CLC 28**
See also CANR 22; CA 77-80

Archer, Jules 1915- .... **CLC 12**
See also CANR 6; CA 9-12R; SATA 4

Arden, John 1930- .... **CLC 6, 13, 15**
See also CAAS 4; CA 13-16R; DLB 13

Arenas, Reinaldo 1943- .... **CLC 41**

Arguedas, Jose Maria 1911-1969 .... **CLC 10, 18**
See also CA 89-92

Argueta, Manlio 1936- .... **CLC 31**

Ariosto, Ludovico 1474-1533 .... **LC 6**

Arlt, Roberto 1900-1942 .... **TCLC 29**
See also CA 123

Armah, Ayi Kwei 1939- .... **CLC 5, 33**
See also CANR 21; CA 61-64

Armatrading, Joan 1950- .... **CLC 17**
See also CA 114

Arnim, Achim von (Ludwig Joachim von Arnim) 1781-1831 .... **NCLC 5**

Arnold, Matthew 1822-1888 ...... **NCLC 6**
See also DLB 32, 57

Arnold, Thomas 1795-1842 ...... **NCLC 18**
See also DLB 55

Arnow, Harriette (Louisa Simpson) 1908-1986 .... **CLC 2, 7, 18**
See also CANR 14; CA 9-12R; obituary CA 118; SATA 42, 47; DLB 6

Arp, Jean 1887-1966 .... **CLC 5**
See also CA 81-84; obituary CA 25-28R

Arquette, Lois S(teinmetz) 1934-
See Duncan (Steinmetz Arquette), Lois
See also SATA 1

Arrabal, Fernando 1932- ...... **CLC 2, 9, 18**
See also CANR 15; CA 9-12R

Arrick, Fran 19?? .... **CLC 30**

Artaud, Antonin 1896-1948 .... **TCLC 3**
See also CA 104

Arthur, Ruth M(abel) 1905-1979 .... **CLC 12**
See also CANR 4; CA 9-12R; obituary CA 85-88; SATA 7; obituary SATA 26

Artsybashev, Mikhail Petrarch 1878-1927 .... **TCLC 31**

Arundel, Honor (Morfydd) 1919-1973 .... **CLC 17**
See also CAP 2; CA 21-22; obituary CA 41-44R; SATA 4; obituary SATA 24

Asch, Sholem 1880-1957 .... **TCLC 3**
See also CA 105

Ashbery, John (Lawrence) 1927- ... **CLC 2, 3, 4, 6, 9, 13, 15, 25, 41**
See also CANR 9; CA 5-8R; DLB 5; DLB-Y 81

Ashton-Warner, Sylvia (Constance) 1908-1984 .... **CLC 19**
See also CA 69-72; obituary CA 112

Asimov, Isaac 1920- .... **CLC 1, 3, 9, 19, 26**
See also CLR 12; CANR 2, 19; CA 1-4R; SATA 1, 26; DLB 8

Astley, Thea (Beatrice May) 1925- .... **CLC 41**
See also CANR 11; CA 65-68

Aston, James 1906-1964
See White, T(erence) H(anbury)

Asturias, Miguel Angel 1899-1974 .... **CLC 3, 8, 13**
See also CAP 2; CA 25-28; obituary CA 49-52

Atheling, William, Jr. 1921-1975
See Blish, James (Benjamin)

Atherton, Gertrude (Franklin Horn) 1857-1948 .... **TCLC 2**
See also CA 104; DLB 9

Atwood, Margaret (Eleanor) 1939- .... **CLC 2, 3, 4, 8, 13, 15, 25, 44; SSC 2**
See also CANR 3; CA 49-52; DLB 53

Aubin, Penelope 1685-1731? .... **LC 9**
See also DLB 39

Auchincloss, Louis (Stanton) 1917- .... **CLC 4, 6, 9, 18, 45**
See also CANR 6; CA 1-4R; DLB 2; DLB-Y 80

Auden, W(ystan) H(ugh) 1907-1973 ..... **CLC 1, 2, 3, 4, 6, 9, 11, 14, 43**
See also CANR 5; CA 9-12R; obituary CA 45-48; DLB 10, 20

Audiberti, Jacques 1899-1965 ...... **CLC 38**
See also obituary CA 25-28R

Auel, Jean M(arie) 1936- .... **CLC 31**
See also CANR 21; CA 103

Austen, Jane 1775-1817 .... **NCLC 1, 13, 19**

Auster, Paul 1947- .... **CLC 47**
See also CA 69-72

Austin, Mary (Hunter) 1868-1934 .... **TCLC 25**
See also CA 109; DLB 9

Avison, Margaret 1918- .... **CLC 2, 4**
See also CA 17-20R; DLB 53

Ayckbourn, Alan 1939- .... **CLC 5, 8, 18, 33**
See also CA 21-24R; DLB 13

Aydy, Catherine 1937-
See Tennant, Emma

Ayme, Marcel (Andre) 1902-1967 ... **CLC 11**
See also CA 89-92; DLB 72

Ayrton, Michael 1921-1975 .... **CLC 7**
See also CANR 9, 21; CA 5-8R; obituary CA 61-64

Azorin 1874-1967 .... **CLC 11**
See also Martinez Ruiz, Jose

Azuela, Mariano 1873-1952 .... **TCLC 3**
See also CA 104

"Bab" 1836-1911
See Gilbert, (Sir) W(illiam) S(chwenck)

Babel, Isaak (Emmanuilovich) 1894-1941 .... **TCLC 2, 13**
See also CA 104

Babits, Mihaly 1883-1941 .... **TCLC 14**
See also CA 114

Bacchelli, Riccardo 1891-1985 ..... **CLC 19**
See also CA 29-32R; obituary CA 117

Bach, Richard (David) 1936- .... **CLC 14**
See also CANR 18; CA 9-12R; SATA 13

Bachman, Richard 1947-
See King, Stephen (Edwin)

Bacovia, George 1881-1957 .... **TCLC 24**

Bagehot, Walter 1826-1877 ...... **NCLC 10**
See also DLB 55

Bagnold, Enid 1889-1981 .... **CLC 25**
See also CANR 5; CA 5-8R; obituary CA 103; SATA 1, 25; DLB 13

Bagryana, Elisaveta 1893- .... **CLC 10**

Bailey, Paul 1937- .... **CLC 45**
See also CANR 16; CA 21-24R; DLB 14

Baillie, Joanna 1762-1851 .... **NCLC 2**

Bainbridge, Beryl 1933- .... **CLC 4, 5, 8, 10, 14, 18, 22**
See also CA 21-24R; DLB 14

Baker, Elliott 1922- .... **CLC 8**
See also CANR 2; CA 45-48

Baker, Russell (Wayne) 1925- ...... **CLC 31**
See also CANR 11; CA 57-60

Bakshi, Ralph 1938- .... **CLC 26**
See also CA 112

Baldwin, James (Arthur) 1924-1987 ..... **CLC 1, 2, 3, 4, 5, 8, 13, 15, 17, 42, 50**
See also CANR 3; CA 1-4R; CABS 1; SATA 9; DLB 2, 7, 33; CDALB 1941-1968

Ballard, J(ames) G(raham) 1930- .... **CLC 3, 6, 14, 36; SSC 1**
See also CANR 15; CA 5-8R; DLB 14

Balmont, Konstantin Dmitriyevich 1867-1943 .... **TCLC 11**
See also CA 109

Balzac, Honore de 1799-1850 ..... **NCLC 5**

Bambara, Toni Cade 1939- .... **CLC 19**
See also CA 29-32R; DLB 38

Banim, John 1798-1842 and **Banim, Michael** 1798-1842 .... **NCLC 13**

Banim, John 1798-1842
See Banim, John and Banim, Michael

Banim, Michael 1796-1874
See Banim, John and Banim, Michael

Banim, Michael 1796-1874 and **Banim, John** 1796-1874
See Banim, John and Banim, Michael

Banks, Iain 1954- .... **CLC 34**

Banks, Lynne Reid 1929- .... **CLC 23**
See also Reid Banks, Lynne

Banks, Russell 1940- .... **CLC 37**
See also CANR 19; CA 65-68

Banville, John 1945- .... **CLC 46**
See also CA 117; DLB 14

Banville, Theodore (Faullain) de 1832-1891 .... **NCLC 9**

Baraka, Amiri 1934- . . . . **CLC 1, 2, 3, 5, 10, 14, 33**
See also Baraka, Imamu Amiri; Jones, (Everett) LeRoi
See also DLB 5, 7, 16, 38

Baraka, Imamu Amiri 1934- . . . . **CLC 1, 2, 3, 5, 10, 14, 33**
See also Baraka, Amiri; Jones, (Everett) LeRoi
See also DLB 5, 7, 16, 38; CDALB 1941-1968

Barbellion, W. N. P. 1889-1919 . . . **TCLC 24**

Barbera, Jack 1945- . . . . **CLC 44**
See also CA 110

Barbey d'Aurevilly, Jules Amedee 1808-1889 . . . . **NCLC 1**

Barbusse, Henri 1873-1935 . . . . **TCLC 5**
See also CA 105

Barea, Arturo 1897-1957 . . . . **TCLC 14**
See also CA 111

Barfoot, Joan 1946- . . . . **CLC 18**
See also CA 105

Baring, Maurice 1874-1945 . . . . **TCLC 8**
See also CA 105; DLB 34

Barker, Clive 1952- . . . . **CLC 52**
See also CA 121

Barker, George (Granville) 1913- . . . . **CLC 8, 48**
See also CANR 7; CA 9-12R; DLB 20

Barker, Howard 1946- . . . . **CLC 37**
See also CA 102; DLB 13

Barker, Pat 1943- . . . . **CLC 32**
See also CA 117, 122

Barlow, Joel 1754-1812 . . . . **NCLC 23**
See also DLB 37

Barnard, Mary (Ethel) 1909- . . . . **CLC 48**
See also CAP 2; CA 21-22

Barnes, Djuna (Chappell) 1892-1982 . . . **CLC 3, 4, 8, 11, 29; SSC 3**
See also CANR 16; CA 9-12R; obituary CA 107; DLB 4, 9, 45

Barnes, Julian 1946- . . . . **CLC 42**
See also CANR 19; CA 102

Barnes, Peter 1931- . . . . **CLC 5, 56**
See also CA 65-68; DLB 13

Baroja (y Nessi), Pio 1872-1956 . . . . **TCLC 8**
See also CA 104

Barondess, Sue K(aufman) 1926-1977
See Kaufman, Sue
See also CANR 1; CA 1-4R; obituary CA 69-72

Barrett, (Roger) Syd 1946-
See Pink Floyd

Barrett, William (Christopher) 1913- . . . . **CLC 27**
See also CANR 11; CA 13-16R

Barrie, (Sir) J(ames) M(atthew) 1860-1937 . . . . **TCLC 2**
See also CLR 16; YABC 1; CA 104; DLB 10

Barrol, Grady 1953-
See Bograd, Larry

Barry, Philip (James Quinn) 1896-1949 . . . . **TCLC 11**
See also CA 109; DLB 7

Barth, John (Simmons) 1930- . . . . . . **CLC 1, 2, 3, 5, 7, 9, 10, 14, 27, 51**
See also CANR 5, 23; CA 1-4R; CABS 1; DLB 2

Barthelme, Donald 1931- . . . . . . **CLC 1, 2, 3, 5, 6, 8, 13, 23, 46; SSC 2**
See also CANR 20; CA 21-24R; SATA 7; DLB 2; DLB-Y 80

Barthelme, Frederick 1943- . . . . **CLC 36**
See also CA 114, 122; DLB-Y 85

Barthes, Roland 1915-1980 . . . . **CLC 24**
See also obituary CA 97-100

Barzun, Jacques (Martin) 1907- . . . . **CLC 51**
See also CANR 22; CA 61-64

Bassani, Giorgio 1916- . . . . **CLC 9**
See also CA 65-68

Bataille, Georges 1897-1962 . . . . **CLC 29**
See also CA 101; obituary CA 89-92

Bates, H(erbert) E(rnest) 1905-1974 . . . . **CLC 46**
See also CA 93-96; obituary CA 45-48

Baudelaire, Charles 1821-1867 . . . . **NCLC 6**

Baum, L(yman) Frank 1856-1919 . . . **TCLC 7**
See also CLR 15; CA 108; SATA 18; DLB 22

Baumbach, Jonathan 1933- . . . . . . **CLC 6, 23**
See also CAAS 5; CANR 12; CA 13-16R; DLB-Y 80

Bausch, Richard (Carl) 1945- . . . . . . **CLC 51**
See also CA 101

Baxter, Charles 1947- . . . . **CLC 45**
See also CA 57-60

Baxter, James K(eir) 1926-1972 . . . . **CLC 14**
See also CA 77-80

Bayer, Sylvia 1909-1981
See Glassco, John

Beagle, Peter S(oyer) 1939- . . . . **CLC 7**
See also CANR 4; CA 9-12R; DLB-Y 80

Beard, Charles A(ustin) 1874-1948 . . . . **TCLC 15**
See also CA 115; SATA 18; DLB 17

Beardsley, Aubrey 1872-1898 . . . . . **NCLC 6**

Beattie, Ann 1947- . . . . **CLC 8, 13, 18, 40**
See also CA 81-84; DLB-Y 82

Beauvoir, Simone (Lucie Ernestine Marie Bertrand) de 1908-1986 . . . **CLC 1, 2, 4, 8, 14, 31, 44, 50**
See also CA 9-12R; obituary CA 118; DLB 72; DLB-Y 86

Becker, Jurek 1937- . . . . **CLC 7, 19**
See also CA 85-88

Becker, Walter 1950- and **Fagen, Donald** 1950- . . . . **CLC 26**

Becker, Walter 1950-
See Becker, Walter and Fagen, Donald

Beckett, Samuel (Barclay) 1906- . . . . . . **CLC 1, 2, 3, 4, 6, 9, 10, 11, 14, 18, 29**
See also CA 5-8R; DLB 13, 15

Beckford, William 1760-1844 . . . . **NCLC 16**
See also DLB 39

Beckman, Gunnel 1910- . . . . **CLC 26**
See also CANR 15; CA 33-36R; SATA 6

Becque, Henri 1837-1899 . . . . **NCLC 3**

Beddoes, Thomas Lovell 1803-1849 . . . . **NCLC 3**

Beecher, John 1904-1980 . . . . **CLC 6**
See also CANR 8; CA 5-8R; obituary CA 105

Beer, Johann 1655-1700 . . . . **LC 5**

Beerbohm, (Sir Henry) Max(imilian) 1872-1956 . . . . **TCLC 1, 24**
See also CA 104; DLB 34

Behan, Brendan 1923-1964 . . . . **CLC 1, 8, 11, 15**
See also CA 73-76; DLB 13

Behn, Aphra 1640?1689 . . . . **LC 1**
See also DLB 39

Behrman, S(amuel) N(athaniel) 1893-1973 . . . . **CLC 40**
See also CAP 1; CA 15-16; obituary CA 45-48; DLB 7, 44

Beiswanger, George Edwin 1931-
See Starbuck, George (Edwin)

Belasco, David 1853-1931 . . . . **TCLC 3**
See also CA 104; DLB 7

Belcheva, Elisaveta 1893-
See Bagryana, Elisaveta

Belinski, Vissarion Grigoryevich 1811-1848 . . . . **NCLC 5**

Belitt, Ben 1911- . . . . **CLC 22**
See also CAAS 4; CANR 7; CA 13-16R; DLB 5

Bell, Acton 1820-1849
See Bronte, Anne

Bell, Currer 1816-1855
See Bronte, Charlotte

Bell, Madison Smartt 1957- . . . . **CLC 41**
See also CA 111

Bell, Marvin (Hartley) 1937- . . . . . **CLC 8, 31**
See also CA 21-24R; DLB 5

Bellamy, Edward 1850-1898 . . . . . . **NCLC 4**
See also DLB 12

Belloc, (Joseph) Hilaire (Pierre Sebastien Rene Swanton) 1870-1953 . . . . **TCLC 7, 18**
See also YABC 1; CA 106; DLB 19

Bellow, Saul 1915- . . . . . **CLC 1, 2, 3, 6, 8, 10, 13, 15, 25, 33, 34**
See also CA 5-8R; CABS 1; DLB 2, 28; DLB-Y 82; DLB-DS 3; CDALB 1941-1968

Belser, Reimond Karel Maria de 1929-
See Ruyslinck, Ward

Bely, Andrey 1880-1934 . . . . **TCLC 7**
See also CA 104

Benary-Isbert, Margot 1889-1979 ... **CLC 12**
See also CLR 12; CANR 4; CA 5-8R; obituary CA 89-92; SATA 2; obituary SATA 21

Benavente (y Martinez), Jacinto 1866-1954 ... **TCLC 3**
See also CA 106

Benchley, Peter (Bradford) 1940- ... **CLC 4, 8**
See also CANR 12; CA 17-20R; SATA 3

Benchley, Robert 1889-1945 ... **TCLC 1**
See also CA 105; DLB 11

Benedikt, Michael 1935- ... **CLC 4, 14**
See also CANR 7; CA 13-16R; DLB 5

Benet, Juan 1927- ... **CLC 28**

Benet, Stephen Vincent 1898-1943 ... **TCLC 7**
See also YABC 1; CA 104; DLB 4, 48

Benet, William Rose 1886-1950 ... **TCLC 28**
See also CA 118; DLB 45

Benford, Gregory (Albert) 1941- ... **CLC 52**
See also CANR 12, 24; CA 69-72; DLB-Y 82

Benn, Gottfried 1886-1956 ... **TCLC 3**
See also CA 106; DLB 56

Bennett, Alan 1934- ... **CLC 45**
See also CA 103

Bennett, (Enoch) Arnold 1867-1931 ... **TCLC 5, 20**
See also CA 106; DLB 10, 34

Bennett, George Harold 1930-
See Bennett, Hal
See also CA 97-100

Bennett, Hal 1930- ... **CLC 5**
See also Bennett, George Harold
See also DLB 33

Bennett, Jay 1912- ... **CLC 35**
See also CANR 11; CA 69-72; SAAS 4; SATA 27, 41

Bennett, Louise (Simone) 1919- ... **CLC 28**
See also Bennett-Coverly, Louise Simone

Bennett-Coverly, Louise Simone 1919-
See Bennett, Louise (Simone)
See also CA 97-100

Benson, E(dward) F(rederic) 1867-1940 ... **TCLC 27**
See also CA 114

Benson, Jackson J. 1930- ... **CLC 34**
See also CA 25-28R

Benson, Sally 1900-1972 ... **CLC 17**
See also CAP 1; CA 19-20; obituary CA 37-40R; SATA 1, 35; obituary SATA 27

Benson, Stella 1892-1933 ... **TCLC 17**
See also CA 117; DLB 36

Bentley, E(dmund) C(lerihew) 1875-1956 ... **TCLC 12**
See also CA 108; DLB 70

Bentley, Eric (Russell) 1916- ... **CLC 24**
See also CANR 6; CA 5-8R

Berger, John (Peter) 1926- ... **CLC 2, 19**
See also CA 81-84; DLB 14

Berger, Melvin (H.) 1927- ... **CLC 12**
See also CANR 4; CA 5-8R; SAAS 2; SATA 5

Berger, Thomas (Louis) 1924- ... **CLC 3, 5, 8, 11, 18, 38**
See also CANR 5; CA 1-4R; DLB 2; DLB-Y 80

Bergman, (Ernst) Ingmar 1918- ... **CLC 16**
See also CA 81-84

Bergson, Henri 1859-1941 ... **TCLC 32**

Bergstein, Eleanor 1938- ... **CLC 4**
See also CANR 5; CA 53-56

Berkoff, Steven 1937- ... **CLC 56**
See also CA 104

Bermant, Chaim 1929- ... **CLC 40**
See also CANR 6; CA 57-60

Bernanos, (Paul Louis) Georges 1888-1948 ... **TCLC 3**
See also CA 104; DLB 72

Bernhard, Thomas 1931- ... **CLC 3, 32**
See also CA 85-88

Berriault, Gina 1926- ... **CLC 54**
See also CA 116

Berrigan, Daniel J. 1921- ... **CLC 4**
See also CAAS 1; CANR 11; CA 33-36R; DLB 5

Berrigan, Edmund Joseph Michael, Jr. 1934-1983
See Berrigan, Ted
See also CANR 14; CA 61-64; obituary CA 110

Berrigan, Ted 1934-1983 ... **CLC 37**
See also Berrigan, Edmund Joseph Michael, Jr.
See also DLB 5

Berry, Chuck 1926- ... **CLC 17**

Berry, Wendell (Erdman) 1934- ... **CLC 4, 6, 8, 27, 46**
See also CA 73-76; DLB 5, 6

Berryman, Jerry 1914-1972
See also CDALB 1941-1968

Berryman, John 1914-1972 ... **CLC 1, 2, 3, 4, 6, 8, 10, 13, 25**
See also CAP 1; CA 15-16; obituary CA 33-36R; CABS 2; DLB 48; CDALB 1941-1968

Bertolucci, Bernardo 1940- ... **CLC 16**
See also CA 106

Besant, Annie (Wood) 1847-1933 ... **TCLC 9**
See also CA 105

Bessie, Alvah 1904-1985 ... **CLC 23**
See also CANR 2; CA 5-8R; obituary CA 116; DLB 26

Beti, Mongo 1932- ... **CLC 27**
See also Beyidi, Alexandre

Betjeman, (Sir) John 1906-1984 ... **CLC 2, 6, 10, 34, 43**
See also CA 9-12R; obituary CA 112; DLB 20; DLB-Y 84

Betti, Ugo 1892-1953 ... **TCLC 5**
See also CA 104

Betts, Doris (Waugh) 1932- ... **CLC 3, 6, 28**
See also CANR 9; CA 13-16R; DLB-Y 82

Bialik, Chaim Nachman 1873-1934 ... **TCLC 25**

Bidart, Frank 19?? ... **CLC 33**

Bienek, Horst 1930- ... **CLC 7, 11**
See also CA 73-76

Bierce, Ambrose (Gwinett) 1842-1914? ... **TCLC 1, 7**
See also CA 104; DLB 11, 12, 23, 71; CDALB 1865-1917

Billington, Rachel 1942- ... **CLC 43**
See also CA 33-36R

Binyon, T(imothy) J(ohn) 1936- ... **CLC 34**
See also CA 111

Bioy Casares, Adolfo 1914- ... **CLC 4, 8, 13**
See also CANR 19; CA 29-32R

Bird, Robert Montgomery 1806-1854 ... **NCLC 1**

Birdwell, Cleo 1936-
See DeLillo, Don

Birney (Alfred) Earle 1904- ... **CLC 1, 4, 6, 11**
See also CANR 5, 20; CA 1-4R

Bishop, Elizabeth 1911-1979 ... **CLC 1, 4, 9, 13, 15, 32**
See also CA 5-8R; obituary CA 89-92; CABS 2; obituary SATA 24; DLB 5

Bishop, John 1935- ... **CLC 10**
See also CA 105

Bissett, Bill 1939- ... **CLC 18**
See also CANR 15; CA 69-72; DLB 53

Biyidi, Alexandre 1932-
See Beti, Mongo
See also CA 114

Bjornson, Bjornstjerne (Martinius) 1832-1910 ... **TCLC 7**
See also CA 104

Blackburn, Paul 1926-1971 ... **CLC 9, 43**
See also CA 81-84; obituary CA 33-36R; DLB 16; DLB-Y 81

Black Elk 1863-1950 ... **TCLC 33**

Blackmore, R(ichard) D(oddridge) 1825-1900 ... **TCLC 27**
See also CA 120; DLB 18

Blackmur, R(ichard) P(almer) 1904-1965 ... **CLC 2, 24**
See also CAP 1; CA 11-12; obituary CA 25-28R; DLB 63

Blackwood, Algernon (Henry) 1869-1951 ... **TCLC 5**
See also CA 105

Blackwood, Caroline 1931- ... **CLC 6, 9**
See also CA 85-88; DLB 14

Blair, Eric Arthur 1903-1950
See Orwell, George
See also CA 104; SATA 29

Blais, Marie-Claire 1939- ... **CLC 2, 4, 6, 13, 22**
See also CAAS 4; CA 21-24R; DLB 53

Blaise, Clark 1940- ... **CLC 29**
See also CAAS 3; CANR 5; CA 53-56R; DLB 53

Blake, Nicholas 1904-1972
See Day Lewis, C(ecil)

Author Index

Blake, William 1757-1827 . . . . **NCLC 13**
See also SATA 30

Blasco Ibanez, Vicente
1867-1928 . . . . **TCLC 12**
See also CA 110

Blatty, William Peter 1928-. . . . . **CLC 2**
See also CANR 9; CA 5-8R

Blessing, Lee 1949-. . . . . **CLC 54**

Blish, James (Benjamin)
1921-1975 . . . . **CLC 14**
See also CANR 3; CA 1-4R;
obituary CA 57-60; DLB 8

Blixen, Karen (Christentze Dinesen)
1885-1962
See Dinesen, Isak
See also CAP 2; CA 25-28; SATA 44

Bloch, Robert (Albert) 1917-. . . . . . . **CLC 33**
See also CANR 5; CA 5-8R; SATA 12;
DLB 44

Blok, Aleksandr (Aleksandrovich)
1880-1921 . . . . **TCLC 5**
See also CA 104

Bloom, Harold 1930- . . . . **CLC 24**
See also CA 13-16R

Blount, Roy (Alton), Jr. 1941- . . . . . **CLC 38**
See also CANR 10; CA 53-56

Bloy, Leon 1846-1917. . . . . **TCLC 22**
See also CA 121

Blume, Judy (Sussman Kitchens)
1938- . . . . **CLC 12, 30**
See also CLR 2, 15; CANR 13; CA 29-32R;
SATA 2, 31; DLB 52

Blunden, Edmund (Charles)
1896-1974 . . . . **CLC 2, 56**
See also CAP 2; CA 17-18;
obituary CA 45-48; DLB 20

Bly, Robert (Elwood)
1926- . . . . **CLC 1, 2, 5, 10, 15, 38**
See also CA 5-8R; DLB 5

Bochco, Steven 1944? and **Kozoll, Michael**
1944? . . . . **CLC 35**

Bochco, Steven 1944?
See Bochco, Steven and Kozoll, Michael

Bodker, Cecil 1927- . . . . **CLC 21**
See also CANR 13; CA 73-76; SATA 14

Boell, Heinrich (Theodor) 1917-1985
See Boll, Heinrich
See also CA 21-24R; obituary CA 116

Bogan, Louise 1897-1970. . . . . **CLC 4, 39, 46**
See also CA 73-76; obituary CA 25-28R;
DLB 45

Bogarde, Dirk 1921-. . . . . **CLC 19**
See also Van Den Bogarde, Derek (Jules
Gaspard Ulric) Niven
See also DLB 14

Bogosian, Eric 1953- . . . . **CLC 45**

Bograd, Larry 1953-. . . . . **CLC 35**
See also CA 93-96; SATA 33

Bohl de Faber, Cecilia 1796-1877
See Caballero, Fernan

Boiardo, Matteo Maria 1441-1494 . . . . **LC 6**

Boileau-Despreaux, Nicolas
1636-1711 . . . . **LC 3**

Boland, Eavan (Aisling) 1944-. . . . . . **CLC 40**
See also DLB 40

Boll, Heinrich (Theodor)
1917-1985 . . . **CLC 2, 3, 6, 9, 11, 15, 27, 39**
See also Boell, Heinrich (Theodor)
See also DLB 69; DLB-Y 85

Bolt, Robert (Oxton) 1924- . . . . **CLC 14**
See also CA 17-20R; DLB 13

Bond, Edward 1934-. . . . . . . **CLC 4, 6, 13, 23**
See also CA 25-28R; DLB 13

Bonham, Frank 1914-. . . . . **CLC 12**
See also CANR 4; CA 9-12R; SAAS 3;
SATA 1, 49

Bonnefoy, Yves 1923-. . . . . **CLC 9, 15**
See also CA 85-88

Bontemps, Arna (Wendell)
1902-1973 . . . . **CLC 1, 18**
See also CLR 6; CANR 4; CA 1-4R;
obituary CA 41-44R; SATA 2, 44;
obituary SATA 24; DLB 48, 51

Booth, Martin 1944-. . . . . **CLC 13**
See also CAAS 2; CA 93-96

Booth, Philip 1925-. . . . . **CLC 23**
See also CANR 5; CA 5-8R; DLB-Y 82

Booth, Wayne C(layson) 1921- . . . . . **CLC 24**
See also CAAS 5; CANR 3; CA 1-4R

Borchert, Wolfgang 1921-1947 . . . . . **TCLC 5**
See also CA 104; DLB 69

Borges, Jorge Luis
1899-1986 . . . **CLC 1, 2, 3, 4, 6, 8, 9, 10, 13, 19, 44, 48**
See also CANR 19; CA 21-24R; DLB-Y 86

Borowski, Tadeusz 1922-1951 . . . . . . **TCLC 9**
See also CA 106

Borrow, George (Henry)
1803-1881 . . . . **NCLC 9**
See also DLB 21, 55

Bosschere, Jean de 1878-1953. . . . . **TCLC 19**
See also CA 115

Boswell, James 1740-1795 . . . . **LC 4**

Bottoms, David 1949-. . . . . **CLC 53**
See also CANR 22; CA 105; DLB-Y 83

Boucolon, Maryse 1937-
See Condé, Maryse
See also CA 110

Bourget, Paul (Charles Joseph)
1852-1935 . . . . **TCLC 12**
See also CA 107

Bourjaily, Vance (Nye) 1922- . . . . **CLC 8**
See also CAAS 1; CANR 2; CA 1-4R;
DLB 2

Bourne, Randolph S(illiman)
1886-1918 . . . . **TCLC 16**
See also CA 117; DLB 63

Bova, Ben(jamin William) 1932-. . . . **CLC 45**
See also CLR 3; CANR 11; CA 5-8R;
SATA 6; DLB-Y 81

Bowen, Elizabeth (Dorothea Cole)
1899-1973 . . . . . **CLC 1, 3, 6, 11, 15, 22; SSC 3**
See also CAP 2; CA 17-18;
obituary CA 41-44R; DLB 15

Bowering, George 1935-. . . . . **CLC 15, 47**
See also CANR 10; CA 21-24R; DLB 53

Bowering, Marilyn R(uthe) 1949- . . . **CLC 32**
See also CA 101

Bowers, Edgar 1924- . . . . **CLC 9**
See also CA 5-8R; DLB 5

Bowie, David 1947- . . . . **CLC 17**
See also Jones, David Robert

Bowles, Jane (Sydney) 1917-1973. . . . **CLC 3**
See also CAP 2; CA 19-20;
obituary CA 41-44R

Bowles, Paul (Frederick)
1910- . . . . **CLC 1, 2, 19, 53; SSC 3**
See also CAAS 1; CANR 1, 19; CA 1-4R;
DLB 5, 6

Box, Edgar 1925-
See Vidal, Gore

Boyd, William 1952-. . . . . **CLC 28, 53**
See also CA 114, 120

Boyle, Kay 1903- . . . . **CLC 1, 5, 19**
See also CAAS 1; CA 13-16R; DLB 4, 9, 48

Boyle, Patrick 19??. . . . . **CLC 19**

Boyle, Thomas Coraghessan
1948- . . . . **CLC 36, 55**
See also CA 120; DLB-Y 86

Brackenridge, Hugh Henry
1748-1816 . . . . **NCLC 7**
See also DLB 11, 37

Bradbury, Edward P. 1939-
See Moorcock, Michael

Bradbury, Malcolm (Stanley)
1932- . . . . **CLC 32**
See also CANR 1; CA 1-4R; DLB 14

Bradbury, Ray(mond Douglas)
1920- . . . . **CLC 1, 3, 10, 15, 42**
See also CANR 2; CA 1-4R; SATA 11;
DLB 2, 8

Bradley, David (Henry), Jr. 1950- . . **CLC 23**
See also CA 104; DLB 33

Bradley, John Ed 1959-. . . . . **CLC 55**

Bradley, Marion Zimmer 1930-. . . . . **CLC 30**
See also CANR 7; CA 57-60; DLB 8

Bradstreet, Anne 1612-1672. . . . . **LC 4**
See also DLB 24; CDALB 1640-1865

Bragg, Melvyn 1939- . . . . **CLC 10**
See also CANR 10; CA 57-60; DLB 14

Braine, John (Gerard)
1922-1986 . . . . **CLC 1, 3, 41**
See also CANR 1; CA 1-4R;
obituary CA 120; DLB 15; DLB-Y 86

Brammer, Billy Lee 1930?1978
See Brammer, William

Brammer, William 1930?1978 . . . . . . **CLC 31**
See also obituary CA 77-80

Brancati, Vitaliano 1907-1954. . . . . **TCLC 12**
See also CA 109

Brancato, Robin F(idler) 1936- . . . . . **CLC 35**
See also CANR 11; CA 69-72; SATA 23

Brand, Millen 1906-1980 . . . . **CLC 7**
See also CA 21-24R; obituary CA 97-100

Branden, Barbara 19??. . . . . **CLC 44**

Brandes, Georg (Morris Cohen)
1842-1927 . . . . **TCLC 10**
See also CA 105

Branley, Franklyn M(ansfield) 1915- . . . . **CLC 21**
See also CANR 14; CA 33-36R; SATA 4

Brathwaite, Edward 1930- . . . . **CLC 11**
See also CANR 11; CA 25-28R; DLB 53

Brautigan, Richard (Gary) 1935-1984 . . . . **CLC 1, 3, 5, 9, 12, 34, 42**
See also CA 53-56; obituary CA 113; DLB 2, 5; DLB-Y 80, 84

Brecht, (Eugen) Bertolt (Friedrich) 1898-1956 . . . . **TCLC 1, 6, 13**
See also CA 104; DLB 56

Bremer, Fredrika 1801-1865 . . . . . **NCLC 11**

Brennan, Christopher John 1870-1932 . . . . **TCLC 17**
See also CA 117

Brennan, Maeve 1917- . . . . **CLC 5**
See also CA 81-84

Brentano, Clemens (Maria) 1778-1842 . . . . **NCLC 1**

Brenton, Howard 1942- . . . . **CLC 31**
See also CA 69-72; DLB 13

Breslin, James 1930-
See Breslin, Jimmy
See also CA 73-76

Breslin, Jimmy 1930- . . . . **CLC 4, 43**
See also Breslin, James

Bresson, Robert 1907- . . . . **CLC 16**
See also CA 110

Breton, Andre 1896-1966 . . . **CLC 2, 9, 15, 54**
See also CAP 2; CA 19-20; obituary CA 25-28R; DLB 65

Breytenbach, Breyten 1939- . . . . . **CLC 23, 37**
See also CA 113

Bridgers, Sue Ellen 1942- . . . . **CLC 26**
See also CANR 11; CA 65-68; SAAS 1; SATA 22; DLB 52

Bridges, Robert 1844-1930. . . . . **TCLC 1**
See also CA 104; DLB 19

Bridie, James 1888-1951 . . . . **TCLC 3**
See also Mavor, Osborne Henry
See also DLB 10

Brin, David 1950- . . . . **CLC 34**
See also CA 102

Brink, Andre (Philippus) 1935- . . . . **CLC 18, 36**
See also CA 104

Brinsmead, H(esba) F(ay) 1922- . . . . **CLC 21**
See also CANR 10; CA 21-24R; SATA 18

Brittain, Vera (Mary) 1893?1970 . . . **CLC 23**
See also CAP 1; CA 15-16; obituary CA 25-28R

Broch, Hermann 1886-1951 . . . . **TCLC 20**
See also CA 117

Brock, Rose 1923-
See Hansen, Joseph

Brodkey, Harold 1930- . . . . **CLC 56**
See also CA 111

Brodsky, Iosif Alexandrovich 1940-
See Brodsky, Joseph (Alexandrovich)
See also CA 41-44R

Brodsky, Joseph (Alexandrovich) 1940- . . . . **CLC 4, 6, 13, 36, 50**
See also Brodsky, Iosif Alexandrovich

Brodsky, Michael (Mark) 1948- . . . . **CLC 19**
See also CANR 18; CA 102

Bromell, Henry 1947- . . . . **CLC 5**
See also CANR 9; CA 53-56

Bromfield, Louis (Brucker) 1896-1956 . . . . **TCLC 11**
See also CA 107; DLB 4, 9

Broner, E(sther) M(asserman) 1930- . . . . **CLC 19**
See also CANR 8; CA 17-20R; DLB 28

Bronk, William 1918- . . . . **CLC 10**
See also CA 89-92

Bronte, Anne 1820-1849. . . . . **NCLC 4**
See also DLB 21

Bronte, Charlotte 1816-1855 . . . . **NCLC 3, 8**
See also DLB 21

Bronte, (Jane) Emily 1818-1848 . . **NCLC 16**
See also DLB 21, 32

Brooke, Frances 1724-1789 . . . . **LC 6**
See also DLB 39

Brooke, Henry 1703?1783 . . . . **LC 1**
See also DLB 39

Brooke, Rupert (Chawner) 1887-1915 . . . . **TCLC 2, 7**
See also CA 104; DLB 19

Brooke-Rose, Christine 1926- . . . . . . **CLC 40**
See also CA 13-16R; DLB 14

Brookner, Anita 1928- . . . . . . **CLC 32, 34, 51**
See also CA 114, 120; DLB-Y 87

Brooks, Cleanth 1906- . . . . **CLC 24**
See also CA 17-20R; DLB 63

Brooks, Gwendolyn 1917- . . . . **CLC 1, 2, 4, 5, 15, 49**
See also CANR 1; CA 1-4R; SATA 6; DLB 5; CDALB 1941-1968

Brooks, Mel 1926- . . . . **CLC 12**
See also Kaminsky, Melvin
See also CA 65-68; DLB 26

Brooks, Peter 1938- . . . . **CLC 34**
See also CANR 1; CA 45-48

Brooks, Van Wyck 1886-1963 . . . . . . **CLC 29**
See also CANR 6; CA 1-4R; DLB 45, 63

Brophy, Brigid (Antonia) 1929- . . . . **CLC 6, 11, 29**
See also CAAS 4; CA 5-8R; DLB 14

Brosman, Catharine Savage 1934- . . . . **CLC 9**
See also CANR 21; CA 61-64

Broughton, T(homas) Alan 1936- . . . **CLC 19**
See also CANR 2; CA 45-48

Broumas, Olga 1949- . . . . **CLC 10**
See also CANR 20; CA 85-88

Brown, Charles Brockden 1771-1810 . . . . **NCLC 22**
See also DLB 37, 59; CDALB 1640-1865

Brown, Claude 1937- . . . . **CLC 30**
See also CA 73-76

Brown, Dee (Alexander) 1908- . . **CLC 18, 47**
See also CAAS 6; CANR 11; CA 13-16R; SATA 5; DLB-Y 80

Brown, George Douglas 1869-1902
See Douglas, George

Brown, George Mackay 1921- . . . . **CLC 5, 28**
See also CAAS 6; CANR 12; CA 21-24R; SATA 35; DLB 14, 27

Brown, Rita Mae 1944- . . . . **CLC 18, 43**
See also CANR 2, 11; CA 45-48

Brown, Rosellen 1939- . . . . **CLC 32**
See also CANR 14; CA 77-80

Brown, Sterling A(llen) 1901- . . . . **CLC 1, 23**
See also CA 85-88; DLB 48, 51, 63

Brown, William Wells 1816?1884 . . **NCLC 2**
See also DLB 3, 50

Browne, Jackson 1950- . . . . **CLC 21**

Browning, Elizabeth Barrett 1806-1861 . . . . **NCLC 1, 16**
See also DLB 32

Browning, Robert 1812-1889 . . . . . **NCLC 19**
See also DLB 32

Browning, Tod 1882-1962 . . . . **CLC 16**
See also obituary CA 117

Bruccoli, Matthew J(oseph) 1931- . . **CLC 34**
See also CANR 7; CA 9-12R

Bruce, Lenny 1925-1966 . . . . **CLC 21**
See also Schneider, Leonard Alfred

Brunner, John (Kilian Houston) 1934- . . . . **CLC 8, 10**
See also CANR 2; CA 1-4R

Brutus, Dennis 1924- . . . . **CLC 43**
See also CANR 2; CA 49-52

Bryan, C(ourtlandt) D(ixon) B(arnes) 1936- . . . . **CLC 29**
See also CANR 13; CA 73-76

Bryant, William Cullen 1794-1878 . . . . **NCLC 6**
See also DLB 3, 43; CDALB 1640-1865

Bryusov, Valery (Yakovlevich) 1873-1924 . . . . **TCLC 10**
See also CA 107

Buchanan, George 1506-1582 . . . . **LC 4**

Buchheim, Lothar-Gunther 1918- . . . . **CLC 6**
See also CA 85-88

Buchwald, Art(hur) 1925- . . . . **CLC 33**
See also CANR 21; CA 5-8R; SATA 10

Buck, Pearl S(ydenstricker) 1892-1973 . . . . **CLC 7, 11, 18**
See also CANR 1; CA 1-4R; obituary CA 41-44R; SATA 1, 25; DLB 9

Buckler, Ernest 1908-1984. . . . . **CLC 13**
See also CAP 1; CA 11-12; obituary CA 114; SATA 47

Buckley, William F(rank), Jr. 1925- . . . . **CLC 7, 18, 37**
See also CANR 1; CA 1-4R; DLB-Y 80

Buechner, (Carl) Frederick 1926- . . . . **CLC 2, 4, 6, 9**
See also CANR 11; CA 13-16R; DLB-Y 80

Buell, John (Edward) 1927- . . . . **CLC 10**
See also CA 1-4R; DLB 53

Buero Vallejo, Antonio 1916- . . . **CLC 15, 46**
See also CA 106

Bukowski, Charles 1920- . . . . **CLC 2, 5, 9, 41**
See also CA 17-20R; DLB 5

Bulgakov, Mikhail (Afanas'evich) 1891-1940 . . . . **TCLC 2, 16**
See also CA 105

Bullins, Ed 1935- . . . . **CLC 1, 5, 7**
See also CA 49-52; DLB 7, 38

Author Index

Bulwer-Lytton, (Lord) Edward (George Earle Lytton) 1803-1873 .... **NCLC 1**
See also Lytton, Edward Bulwer
See also DLB 21

Bunin, Ivan (Alexeyevich) 1870-1953 .... **TCLC 6**
See also CA 104

Bunting, Basil 1900-1985 .... **CLC 10, 39, 47**
See also CANR 7; CA 53-56; obituary CA 115; DLB 20

Bunuel, Luis 1900-1983 .... **CLC 16**
See also CA 101; obituary CA 110

Bunyan, John (16281688) .... **LC 4**
See also DLB 39

Burgess (Wilson, John) Anthony 1917- ..... **CLC 1, 2, 4, 5, 8, 10, 13, 15, 22, 40**
See also Wilson, John (Anthony) Burgess
See also DLB 14

Burke, Edmund 1729-1797 .... **LC 7**

Burke, Kenneth (Duva) 1897- .... **CLC 2, 24**
See also CA 5-8R; DLB 45, 63

Burney, Fanny 1752-1840 .... **NCLC 12**
See also DLB 39

Burns, Robert 1759-1796 .... **LC 3**

Burns, Tex 1908?
See L'Amour, Louis (Dearborn)

Burnshaw, Stanley 1906- ..... **CLC 3, 13, 44**
See also CA 9-12R; DLB 48

Burr, Anne 1937- .... **CLC 6**
See also CA 25-28R

Burroughs, Edgar Rice 1875-1950 .... **TCLC 2, 32**
See also CA 104; SATA 41; DLB 8

Burroughs, William S(eward) 1914- .... **CLC 1, 2, 5, 15, 22, 42**
See also CANR 20; CA 9-12R; DLB 2, 8, 16; DLB-Y 81

Busch, Frederick 1941- ... **CLC 7, 10, 18, 47**
See also CAAS 1; CA 33-36R; DLB 6

Bush, Ronald 19?? .... **CLC 34**

Butler, Octavia E(stelle) 1947- ..... **CLC 38**
See also CANR 12; CA 73-76; DLB 33

Butler, Samuel 1835-1902 ...... **TCLC 1, 33**
See also CA 104; DLB 18, 57

Butor, Michel (Marie Francois) 1926- .... **CLC 1, 3, 8, 11, 15**
See also CA 9-12R

Buzzati, Dino 1906-1972 .... **CLC 36**
See also obituary CA 33-36R

Byars, Betsy 1928- .... **CLC 35**
See also CLR 1, 16; CANR 18; CA 33-36R; SAAS 1; SATA 4, 46; DLB 52

Byatt, A(ntonia) S(usan Drabble) 1936- .... **CLC 19**
See also CANR 13; CA 13-16R; DLB 14

Byrne, David 1953? .... **CLC 26**

Byrne, John Keyes 1926-
See Leonard, Hugh
See also CA 102

Byron, George Gordon (Noel), Lord Byron 1788-1824 .... **NCLC 2, 12**

Caballero, Fernan 1796-1877 ..... **NCLC 10**

Cabell, James Branch 1879-1958 ... **TCLC 6**
See also CA 105; DLB 9

Cable, George Washington 1844-1925 .... **TCLC 4**
See also CA 104; DLB 12

Cabrera Infante, G(uillermo) 1929- .... **CLC 5, 25, 45**
See also CA 85-88

Cage, John (Milton, Jr.) 1912- ..... **CLC 41**
See also CANR 9; CA 13-16R

Cain, G. 1929-
See Cabrera Infante, G(uillermo)

Cain, James M(allahan) 1892-1977 .... **CLC 3, 11, 28**
See also CANR 8; CA 17-20R; obituary CA 73-76

Caldwell, Erskine (Preston) 1903-1987 .... **CLC 1, 8, 14, 50**
See also CAAS 1; CANR 2; CA 1-4R; obituary CA 121; DLB 9

Caldwell, (Janet Miriam) Taylor (Holland) 1900-1985 .... **CLC 2, 28, 39**
See also CANR 5; CA 5-8R; obituary CA 116

Calhoun, John Caldwell 1782-1850 .... **NCLC 15**
See also DLB 3

Calisher, Hortense 1911- .... **CLC 2, 4, 8, 38**
See also CANR 1, 22; CA 1-4R; DLB 2

Callaghan, Morley (Edward) 1903- .... **CLC 3, 14, 41**
See also CA 9-12R

Calvino, Italo 1923-1985 .... **CLC 5, 8, 11, 22, 33, 39; SSC 3**
See also CANR 23; CA 85-88; obituary CA 116

Cameron, Peter 1959- .... **CLC 44**

Campana, Dino 1885-1932 .... **TCLC 20**
See also CA 117

Campbell, John W(ood), Jr. 1910-1971 .... **CLC 32**
See also CAP 2; CA 21-22; obituary CA 29-32R; DLB 8

Campbell, (John) Ramsey 1946- .... **CLC 42**
See also CANR 7; CA 57-60

Campbell, (Ignatius) Roy (Dunnachie) 1901-1957 .... **TCLC 5**
See also CA 104; DLB 20

Campbell, Thomas 1777-1844 .... **NCLC 19**

Campbell, (William) Wilfred 1861-1918 .... **TCLC 9**
See also CA 106

Camus, Albert 1913-1960 .... **CLC 1, 2, 4, 9, 11, 14, 32**
See also CA 89-92; DLB 72

Canby, Vincent 1924- .... **CLC 13**
See also CA 81-84

Canetti, Elias 1905- .... **CLC 3, 14, 25**
See also CA 21-24R

Canin, Ethan 1960- .... **CLC 55**

Cape, Judith 1916-
See Page, P(atricia) K(athleen)

Capek, Karel 1890-1938 .... **TCLC 6**
See also CA 104

Capote, Truman 1924-1984 ..... **CLC 1, 3, 8, 13, 19, 34, 38; SSC 2**
See also CANR 18; CA 5-8R; obituary CA 113; DLB 2; DLB-Y 80, 84; CDALB 1941-1968

Capra, Frank 1897- .... **CLC 16**
See also CA 61-64

Caputo, Philip 1941- .... **CLC 32**
See also CA 73-76

Card, Orson Scott 1951- .... **CLC 44, 47, 50**
See also CA 102

Cardenal, Ernesto 1925- .... **CLC 31**
See also CANR 2; CA 49-52

Carducci, Giosué 1835-1907 .... **TCLC 32**

Carey, Ernestine Gilbreth 1908-
See Gilbreth, Frank B(unker), Jr. and Carey, Ernestine Gilbreth
See also CA 5-8R; SATA 2

Carey, Peter 1943- .... **CLC 40, 55**
See also CA 123, 127

Carleton, William 1794-1869 ...... **NCLC 3**

Carlisle, Henry (Coffin) 1926- ...... **CLC 33**
See also CANR 15; CA 13-16R

Carlson, Ron(ald F.) 1947- .... **CLC 54**
See also CA 105

Carlyle, Thomas 1795-1881 ...... **NCLC 22**
See also DLB 55

Carman, (William) Bliss 1861-1929 .... **TCLC 7**
See also CA 104

Carpenter, Don(ald Richard) 1931- .... **CLC 41**
See also CANR 1; CA 45-48

Carpentier (y Valmont), Alejo 1904-1980 .... **CLC 8, 11, 38**
See also CANR 11; CA 65-68; obituary CA 97-100

Carr, Emily 1871-1945 .... **TCLC 32**
See also DLB 68

Carr, John Dickson 1906-1977 ...... **CLC 3**
See also CANR 3; CA 49-52; obituary CA 69-72

Carr, Virginia Spencer 1929- .... **CLC 34**
See also CA 61-64

Carrier, Roch 1937- .... **CLC 13**
See also DLB 53

Carroll, James (P.) 1943- .... **CLC 38**
See also CA 81-84

Carroll, Jim 1951- .... **CLC 35**
See also CA 45-48

Carroll, Lewis 1832-1898 .... **NCLC 2**
See also Dodgson, Charles Lutwidge
See also CLR 2; DLB 18

Carroll, Paul Vincent 1900-1968 .... **CLC 10**
See also CA 9-12R; obituary CA 25-28R; DLB 10

Carruth, Hayden 1921- .... **CLC 4, 7, 10, 18**
See also CANR 4; CA 9-12R; SATA 47; DLB 5

Carter, Angela (Olive) 1940- ..... **CLC 5, 41**
See also CANR 12; CA 53-56; DLB 14

Carver, Raymond 1938-1988 .... **CLC 22, 36, 53, 55**
See also CANR 17; CA 33-36R; obituary CA 126; DLB-Y 84, 88

Cary, (Arthur) Joyce (Lunel) 1888-1957 .... **TCLC 1, 29**
See also CA 104; DLB 15

Casares, Adolfo Bioy 1914-
See Bioy Casares, Adolfo

Casely-Hayford, J(oseph) E(phraim) 1866-1930 .... **TCLC 24**

Casey, John 1880-1964
See O'Casey, Sean

Casey, Michael 1947-.............. **CLC 2**
See also CA 65-68; DLB 5

Casey, Warren 1935-
See Jacobs, Jim and Casey, Warren
See also CA 101

Casona, Alejandro 1903-1965 ...... **CLC 49**
See also Alvarez, Alejandro Rodriguez

Cassavetes, John 1929-............ **CLC 20**
See also CA 85-88

Cassill, R(onald) V(erlin) 1919-... **CLC 4, 23**
See also CAAS 1; CANR 7; CA 9-12R; DLB 6

Cassity, (Allen) Turner 1929- .... **CLC 6, 42**
See also CANR 11; CA 17-20R

Castaneda, Carlos 1935? .... **CLC 12**
See also CA 25-28R

Castro, Rosalia de 1837-1885 ..... **NCLC 3**

Cather, Willa (Sibert) 1873-1947 ...... **TCLC 1, 11, 31; SSC 2**
See also CA 104; SATA 30; DLB 9, 54; DLB-DS 1; CDALB 1865-1917

Catton, (Charles) Bruce 1899-1978 .... **CLC 35**
See also CANR 7; CA 5-8R; obituary CA 81-84; SATA 2; obituary SATA 24; DLB 17

Cauldwell, Frank 1923-
See King, Francis (Henry)

Caunitz, William 1935- .... **CLC 34**

Causley, Charles (Stanley) 1917-..... **CLC 7**
See also CANR 5; CA 9-12R; SATA 3; DLB 27

Caute, (John) David 1936-......... **CLC 29**
See also CAAS 4; CANR 1; CA 1-4R; DLB 14

Cavafy, C(onstantine) P(eter) 1863-1933 .... **TCLC 2, 7**
See also CA 104

Cavanna, Betty 1909-............. **CLC 12**
See also CANR 6; CA 9-12R; SATA 1, 30

Cayrol, Jean 1911-............... **CLC 11**
See also CA 89-92

Cela, Camilo Jose 1916-......... **CLC 4, 13**
See also CANR 21; CA 21-24R

Celan, Paul 1920-1970 ...... **CLC 10, 19, 53**
See also Antschel, Paul
See also DLB 69

Celine, Louis-Ferdinand 1894-1961 ..... **CLC 1, 3, 4, 7, 9, 15, 47**
See also Destouches, Louis-Ferdinand-Auguste
See also DLB 72

Cellini, Benvenuto 1500-1571 .... **LC 7**

Cendrars, Blaise 1887-1961 .... **CLC 18**
See also Sauser-Hall, Frederic

Cernuda, Luis (y Bidon) 1902-1963 .... **CLC 54**
See also CA 89-92

Cervantes (Saavedra), Miguel de 1547-1616 .... **LC 6**

Cesaire, Aime (Fernand) 1913- .. **CLC 19, 32**
See also CA 65-68

Chabon, Michael 1965? .... **CLC 55**

Chabrol, Claude 1930- .... **CLC 16**
See also CA 110

Challans, Mary 1905-1983
See Renault, Mary
See also CA 81-84; obituary CA 111; SATA 23; obituary SATA 36

Chambers, Aidan 1934- .... **CLC 35**
See also CANR 12; CA 25-28R; SATA 1

Chambers, James 1948-
See Cliff, Jimmy

Chandler, Raymond 1888-1959 ... **TCLC 1, 7**
See also CA 104

Channing, William Ellery 1780-1842 .... **NCLC 17**
See also DLB 1, 59

Chaplin, Charles (Spencer) 1889-1977 .... **CLC 16**
See also CA 81-84; obituary CA 73-76; DLB 44

Chapman, Graham 1941?
See Monty Python
See also CA 116

Chapman, John Jay 1862-1933 ..... **TCLC 7**
See also CA 104

Chappell, Fred 1936- .... **CLC 40**
See also CAAS 4; CANR 8; CA 5-8R; DLB 6

Char, Rene (Emile) 1907-1988 .... **CLC 9, 11, 14, 55**
See also CA 13-16R; obituary CA 124

Charyn, Jerome 1937- .... **CLC 5, 8, 18**
See also CAAS 1; CANR 7; CA 5-8R; DLB-Y 83

Chase, Mary Ellen 1887-1973 .... **CLC 2**
See also CAP 1; CA 15-16; obituary CA 41-44R; SATA 10

Chateaubriand, Francois Rene de 1768-1848 .... **NCLC 3**

Chatterji, Bankim Chandra 1838-1894 .... **NCLC 19**

Chatterji, Saratchandra 1876-1938 .... **TCLC 13**
See also CA 109

Chatterton, Thomas 1752-1770 .... **LC 3**

Chatwin, (Charles) Bruce 1940-..... **CLC 28**
See also CA 85-88

Chayefsky, Paddy 1923-1981....... **CLC 23**
See also CA 9-12R; obituary CA 104; DLB 7, 44; DLB-Y 81

Chayefsky, Sidney 1923-1981
See Chayefsky, Paddy
See also CANR 18

Chedid, Andree 1920-............. **CLC 47**

Cheever, John 1912-1982 ..... **CLC 3, 7, 8, 11, 15, 25; SSC 1**
See also CANR 5; CA 5-8R; obituary CA 106; CABS 1; DLB 2; DLB-Y 80, 82; CDALB 1941-1968

Cheever, Susan 1943-.......... **CLC 18, 48**
See also CA 103; DLB-Y 82

Chekhov, Anton (Pavlovich) 1860-1904 ...... **TCLC 3, 10, 31; SSC 2**
See also CA 104, 124

Chernyshevsky, Nikolay Gavrilovich 1828-1889 .... **NCLC 1**

Cherry, Caroline Janice 1942-
See Cherryh, C. J.

Cherryh, C. J. 1942-.............. **CLC 35**
See also DLB-Y 80

Chesnutt, Charles Waddell 1858-1932 .... **TCLC 5**
See also CA 106; DLB 12, 50

Chester, Alfred 1929?1971......... **CLC 49**
See also obituary CA 33-36R

Chesterton, G(ilbert) K(eith) 1874-1936 .... **TCLC 1, 6; SSC 1**
See also CA 104; SATA 27; DLB 10, 19, 34, 70

Ch'ien Chung-shu 1910-........... **CLC 22**

Child, Lydia Maria 1802-1880 .... **NCLC 6**
See also DLB 1

Child, Philip 1898-1978 .... **CLC 19**
See also CAP 1; CA 13-14; SATA 47

Childress, Alice 1920-.......... **CLC 12, 15**
See also CLR 14; CANR 3; CA 45-48; SATA 7, 48; DLB 7, 38

Chislett, (Margaret) Anne 1943?.... **CLC 34**

Chitty, (Sir) Thomas Willes 1926-
See Hinde, Thomas
See also CA 5-8R

Chomette, Rene 1898-1981
See Clair, Rene
See also obituary CA 103

Chopin, Kate (O'Flaherty) 1851-1904 .... **TCLC 5, 14**
See also CA 104, 122; DLB 12; CDALB 1865-1917

Christie, (Dame) Agatha (Mary Clarissa) 1890-1976 ...... **CLC 1, 6, 8, 12, 39, 48**
See also CANR 10; CA 17-20R; obituary CA 61-64; SATA 36; DLB 13

Christie, (Ann) Philippa 1920-
See Pearce, (Ann) Philippa
See also CANR 4

Christine de Pizan 1365?1431? .... **LC 9**

Chulkov, Mikhail Dmitrievich 1743-1792 .... **LC 2**

Churchill, Caryl 1938- .... **CLC 31, 55**
See also CANR 22; CA 102; DLB 13

Churchill, Charles 1731?1764 . . . . **LC 3**

Chute, Carolyn 1947- . . . . **CLC 39**

Ciardi, John (Anthony) 1916-1986 . . . . **CLC 10, 40, 44**
See also CAAS 2; CANR 5; CA 5-8R; obituary CA 118; SATA 1, 46; DLB 5; DLB-Y 86

Cicero, Marcus Tullius 106 B.C.43 B.C. . . . . **CMLC 3**

Cimino, Michael 1943? . . . . **CLC 16**
See also CA 105

Clair, Rene 1898-1981 . . . . **CLC 20**
See also Chomette, Rene

Clampitt, Amy 19?? . . . . **CLC 32**
See also CA 110

Clancy, Tom 1947- . . . . **CLC 45**

Clare, John 1793-1864 . . . . **NCLC 9**
See also DLB 55

Clark, (Robert) Brian 1932- . . . . **CLC 29**
See also CA 41-44R

Clark, Eleanor 1913- . . . . **CLC 5, 19**
See also CA 9-12R; DLB 6

Clark, John Pepper 1935- . . . . **CLC 38**
See also CANR 16; CA 65-68

Clark, Mavis Thorpe 1912? . . . . **CLC 12**
See also CANR 8; CA 57-60; SATA 8

Clark, Walter Van Tilburg 1909-1971 . . . . **CLC 28**
See also CA 9-12R; obituary CA 33-36R; SATA 8; DLB 9

Clarke, Arthur C(harles) 1917- . . . . . . **CLC 1, 4, 13, 18, 35; SSC 3**
See also CANR 2; CA 1-4R; SATA 13

Clarke, Austin 1896-1974 . . . . **CLC 6, 9**
See also CANR 14; CAP 2; CA 29-32; obituary CA 49-52; DLB 10, 20, 53

Clarke, Austin (Ardinel) C(hesterfield) 1934- . . . . **CLC 8, 53**
See also CANR 14; CA 25-28R; DLB 53

Clarke, Marcus (Andrew Hislop) 1846-1881 . . . . **NCLC 19**

Clarke, Shirley 1925- . . . . **CLC 16**

Clash, The . . . . **CLC 30**

Claudel, Paul (Louis Charles Marie) 1868-1955 . . . . **TCLC 2, 10**
See also CA 104

Clavell, James (duMaresq) 1924- . . . . **CLC 6, 25**
See also CA 25-28R

Cleaver, (Leroy) Eldridge 1935- . . . . **CLC 30**
See also CANR 16; CA 21-24R

Cleese, John 1939-
See Monty Python
See also CA 112, 116

Cleland, John 1709-1789 . . . . **LC 2**
See also DLB 39

Clemens, Samuel Langhorne 1835-1910
See Twain, Mark
See also YABC 2; CA 104; DLB 11, 12, 23, 64; CDALB 1865-1917

Cliff, Jimmy 1948- . . . . **CLC 21**

Clifton, Lucille 1936- . . . . **CLC 19**
See also CLR 5; CANR 2; CA 49-52; SATA 20; DLB 5, 41

Clutha, Janet Paterson Frame 1924-
See Frame (Clutha), Janet (Paterson)
See also CANR 2; CA 1-4R

Coburn, D(onald) L(ee) 1938- . . . . . . **CLC 10**
See also CA 89-92

Cocteau, Jean (Maurice Eugene Clement) 1889-1963 . . . . **CLC 1, 8, 15, 16, 43**
See also CAP 2; CA 25-28

Codrescu, Andrei 1946- . . . . **CLC 46**
See also CANR 13; CA 33-36R

Coetzee, J(ohn) M. 1940- . . . . **CLC 23, 33**
See also CA 77-80

Cohen, Arthur A(llen) 1928-1986 . . . . **CLC 7, 31**
See also CANR 1, 17; CA 1-4R; obituary CA 120; DLB 28

Cohen, Leonard (Norman) 1934- . . . . **CLC 3, 38**
See also CANR 14; CA 21-24R; DLB 53

Cohen, Matt 1942- . . . . **CLC 19**
See also CA 61-64; DLB 53

Cohen-Solal, Annie 19?? . . . . **CLC 50**

Colegate, Isabel 1931- . . . . **CLC 36**
See also CANR 8, 22; CA 17-20R; DLB 14

Coleridge, Samuel Taylor 1772-1834 . . . . **NCLC 9**

Coles, Don 1928- . . . . **CLC 46**
See also CA 115

Colette (Sidonie-Gabrielle) 1873-1954 . . . . **TCLC 1, 5, 16**
See also CA 104

Collett, (Jacobine) Camilla (Wergeland) 1813-1895 . . . . **NCLC 22**

Collier, Christopher 1930- and **Collier, James L(incoln)** 1930- . . . . **CLC 30**

Collier, Christopher 1930-
See Collier, Christopher and Collier, James L(incoln)
See also CANR 13; CA 33-36R; SATA 16

Collier, James L(incoln) 1928-
See Collier, Christopher and Collier, James L(incoln)
See also CLR 3; CANR 4; CA 9-12R; SATA 8

Collier, James L(incoln) 1928- and **Collier, Christopher** 1928-
See Collier, Christopher and Collier, James L(incoln)

Collier, Jeremy 1650-1726 . . . . **LC 6**

Collins, Hunt 1926-
See Hunter, Evan

Collins, Linda 19?? . . . . **CLC 44**

Collins, Tom 1843-1912
See Furphy, Joseph

Collins, (William) Wilkie 1824-1889 . . . . **NCLC 1, 18**
See also DLB 18, 70

Collins, William 1721-1759 . . . . **LC 4**

Colman, George 1909-1981
See Glassco, John

Colton, James 1923-
See Hansen, Joseph

Colum, Padraic 1881-1972 . . . . **CLC 28**
See also CA 73-76; obituary CA 33-36R; SATA 15; DLB 19

Colvin, James 1939-
See Moorcock, Michael

Colwin, Laurie 1945- . . . . **CLC 5, 13, 23**
See also CANR 20; CA 89-92; DLB-Y 80

Comfort, Alex(ander) 1920- . . . . **CLC 7**
See also CANR 1; CA 1-4R

Compton-Burnett, Ivy 1892-1969 . . . . **CLC 1, 3, 10, 15, 34**
See also CANR 4; CA 1-4R; obituary CA 25-28R; DLB 36

Comstock, Anthony 1844-1915 . . . . **TCLC 13**
See also CA 110

Condé, Maryse 1937- . . . . **CLC 52**
See also Boucolon, Maryse

Condon, Richard (Thomas) 1915- . . . . **CLC 4, 6, 8, 10, 45**
See also CAAS 1; CANR 2; CA 1-4R

Congreve, William 1670-1729 . . . . **LC 5**
See also DLB 39

Connell, Evan S(helby), Jr. 1924- . . . . **CLC 4, 6, 45**
See also CAAS 2; CANR 2; CA 1-4R; DLB 2; DLB-Y 81

Connelly, Marc(us Cook) 1890-1980 . . . . **CLC 7**
See also CA 85-88; obituary CA 102; obituary SATA 25; DLB 7; DLB-Y 80

Conner, Ralph 1860-1937 . . . . **TCLC 31**

Conrad, Joseph 1857-1924 . . . . **TCLC 1, 6, 13, 25**
See also CA 104; SATA 27; DLB 10, 34

Conroy, Pat 1945- . . . . **CLC 30**
See also CA 85-88; DLB 6

Constant (de Rebecque), (Henri) Benjamin 1767-1830 . . . . **NCLC 6**

Cook, Robin 1940- . . . . **CLC 14**
See also CA 108, 111

Cooke, Elizabeth 1948- . . . . **CLC 55**

Cooke, John Esten 1830-1886 . . . . . **NCLC 5**
See also DLB 3

Cooper, J. California 19?? . . . . **CLC 56**
See also CA 125, 127

Cooper, James Fenimore 1789-1851 . . . . **NCLC 1**
See also SATA 19; DLB 3; CDALB 1640-1865

Coover, Robert (Lowell) 1932- . . . . **CLC 3, 7, 15, 32, 46**
See also CANR 3; CA 45-48; DLB 2; DLB-Y 81

Copeland, Stewart (Armstrong) 1952-
See The Police

Coppard, A(lfred) E(dgar) 1878-1957 . . . . **TCLC 5**
See also YABC 1; CA 114

Coppee, Francois 1842-1908 . . . . . . **TCLC 25**

Coppola, Francis Ford 1939- . . . . **CLC 16**
See also CA 77-80; DLB 44

Corcoran, Barbara 1911- .... **CLC 17**
See also CAAS 2; CANR 11; CA 21-24R; SATA 3; DLB 52

Corman, Cid 1924- .... **CLC 9**
See also Corman, Sidney
See also CAAS 2; DLB 5

Corman, Sidney 1924-
See Corman, Cid
See also CA 85-88

Cormier, Robert (Edmund) 1925- .... **CLC 12, 30**
See also CLR 12; CANR 5; CA 1-4R; SATA 10, 45; DLB 52

Corn, Alfred (Dewitt III) 1943- ..... **CLC 33**
See also CA 104; DLB-Y 80

Cornwell, David (John Moore) 1931-
See le Carre, John
See also CANR 13; CA 5-8R

Corso, (Nunzio) Gregory 1930- ... **CLC 1, 11**
See also CA 5-8R; DLB 5, 16

Cortazar, Julio 1914-1984 ..... **CLC 2, 3, 5, 10, 13, 15, 33, 34**
See also CANR 12; CA 21-24R

Corvo, Baron 1860-1913
See Rolfe, Frederick (William Serafino Austin Lewis Mary)

Cosic, Dobrica 1921- .... **CLC 14**
See also CA 122

Costain, Thomas B(ertram) 1885-1965 .... **CLC 30**
See also CA 5-8R; obituary CA 25-28R; DLB 9

Costantini, Humberto 1924?1987 ... **CLC 49**
See also obituary CA 122

Costello, Elvis 1955- .... **CLC 21**

Cotter, Joseph Seamon, Sr. 1861-1949 .... **TCLC 28**
See also DLB 50

Couperus, Louis (Marie Anne) 1863-1923 .... **TCLC 15**
See also CA 115

Cousteau, Jacques-Yves 1910- ...... **CLC 30**
See also CANR 15; CA 65-68; SATA 38

Coward, (Sir) Noel (Pierce) 1899-1973 .... **CLC 1, 9, 29, 51**
See also CAP 2; CA 17-18; obituary CA 41-44R; DLB 10

Cowley, Malcolm 1898- .... **CLC 39**
See also CANR 3; CA 5-6R; DLB 4, 48; DLB-Y 81

Cowper, William 1731-1800 .... **NCLC 8**

Cox, William Trevor 1928-
See Trevor, William
See also CANR 4; CA 9-12R

Cozzens, James Gould 1903-1978 .... **CLC 1, 4, 11**
See also CANR 19; CA 9-12R; obituary CA 81-84; DLB 9; DLB-Y 84; DLB-DS 2; CDALB 1941-1968

Crane, (Harold) Hart 1899-1932 .... **TCLC 2, 5**
See also CA 104; DLB 4, 48

Crane, R(onald) S(almon) 1886-1967 .... **CLC 27**
See also CA 85-88; DLB 63

Crane, Stephen 1871-1900 .... **TCLC 11, 17, 32**
See also YABC 2; CA 109; DLB 12, 54, 78; CDALB 1865-1917

Craven, Margaret 1901-1980 .... **CLC 17**
See also CA 103

Crawford, F(rancis) Marion 1854-1909 .... **TCLC 10**
See also CA 107; DLB 71

Crawford, Isabella Valancy 1850-1887 .... **NCLC 12**

Crayencour, Marguerite de 1913-
See Yourcenar, Marguerite

Creasey, John 1908-1973 .... **CLC 11**
See also CANR 8; CA 5-8R; obituary CA 41-44R

Crebillon, Claude Prosper Jolyot de (fils) 1707-1777 .... **LC 1**

Creeley, Robert (White) 1926- .... **CLC 1, 2, 4, 8, 11, 15, 36**
See also CA 1-4R; DLB 5, 16

Crews, Harry (Eugene) 1935- .... **CLC 6, 23, 49**
See also CANR 20; CA 25-28R; DLB 6

Crichton, (John) Michael 1942- .... **CLC 2, 6, 54**
See also CANR 13; CA 25-28R; SATA 9; DLB-Y 81

Crispin, Edmund 1921-1978 .... **CLC 22**
See also Montgomery, Robert Bruce

Cristofer, Michael 1946- .... **CLC 28**
See also CA 110; DLB 7

Crockett, David (Davy) 1786-1836 .... **NCLC 8**
See also DLB 3, 11

Croker, John Wilson 1780-1857 .. **NCLC 10**

Cronin, A(rchibald) J(oseph) 1896-1981 .... **CLC 32**
See also CANR 5; CA 1-4R; obituary CA 102; obituary SATA 25, 47

Cross, Amanda 1926-
See Heilbrun, Carolyn G(old)

Crothers, Rachel 1878-1953 .... **TCLC 19**
See also CA 113; DLB 7

Crowley, Aleister 1875-1947 .... **TCLC 7**
See also CA 104

Crumb, Robert 1943- .... **CLC 17**
See also CA 106

Cryer, Gretchen 1936? .... **CLC 21**
See also CA 114

Csath, Geza 1887-1919 .... **TCLC 13**
See also CA 111

Cudlip, David 1933- .... **CLC 34**

Cullen, Countee 1903-1946 .... **TCLC 4**
See also CA 108; SATA 18; DLB 4, 48, 51

Cummings, E(dward) E(stlin) 1894-1962 .... **CLC 1, 3, 8, 12, 15**
See also CA 73-76; DLB 4, 48

Cunha, Euclides (Rodrigues) da 1866-1909 .... **TCLC 24**

Cunningham, Julia (Woolfolk) 1916- .... **CLC 12**
See also CANR 4, 19; CA 9-12R; SAAS 2; SATA 1, 26

Cunningham, J(ames) V(incent) 1911-1985 .... **CLC 3, 31**
See also CANR 1; CA 1-4R; obituary CA 115; DLB 5

Cunningham, Michael 1952- .... **CLC 34**

Currie, Ellen 19?? .... **CLC 44**

Dabrowska, Maria (Szumska) 1889-1965 .... **CLC 15**
See also CA 106

Dabydeen, David 1956? .... **CLC 34**

Dacey, Philip 1939- .... **CLC 51**
See also CANR 14; CA 37-40R

Dagerman, Stig (Halvard) 1923-1954 .... **TCLC 17**
See also CA 117

Dahl, Roald 1916- .... **CLC 1, 6, 18**
See also CLR 1, 7; CANR 6; CA 1-4R; SATA 1, 26

Dahlberg, Edward 1900-1977 ... **CLC 1, 7, 14**
See also CA 9-12R; obituary CA 69-72; DLB 48

Daly, Elizabeth 1878-1967 .... **CLC 52**
See also CAP 2; CA 23-24; obituary CA 25-28R

Daly, Maureen 1921- .... **CLC 17**
See also McGivern, Maureen Daly
See also SAAS 1; SATA 2

Daniken, Erich von 1935-
See Von Daniken, Erich

Dannay, Frederic 1905-1982
See Queen, Ellery
See also CANR 1; CA 1-4R; obituary CA 107

D'Annunzio, Gabriele 1863-1938 .... **TCLC 6**
See also CA 104

Danziger, Paula 1944- .... **CLC 21**
See also CA 112, 115; SATA 30, 36

Dario, Ruben 1867-1916 .... **TCLC 4**
See also Sarmiento, Felix Ruben Garcia
See also CA 104

Darley, George 1795-1846 .... **NCLC 2**

Daryush, Elizabeth 1887-1977 .... **CLC 6, 19**
See also CANR 3; CA 49-52; DLB 20

Daudet, (Louis Marie) Alphonse 1840-1897 .... **NCLC 1**

Daumal, Rene 1908-1944 .... **TCLC 14**
See also CA 114

Davenport, Guy (Mattison, Jr.) 1927- .... **CLC 6, 14, 38**
See also CA 33-36R

Davidson, Donald (Grady) 1893-1968 .... **CLC 2, 13, 19**
See also CANR 4; CA 5-8R; obituary CA 25-28R; DLB 45

Davidson, John 1857-1909 .... **TCLC 24**
See also CA 118; DLB 19

Davidson, Sara 1943- .... **CLC 9**
See also CA 81-84

Author Index

Davie, Donald (Alfred) 1922- ... **CLC 5, 8, 10, 31**
See also CAAS 3; CANR 1; CA 1-4R; DLB 27

Davies, Ray(mond Douglas) 1944- .. **CLC 21**
See also CA 116

Davies, Rhys 1903-1978 ... **CLC 23**
See also CANR 4; CA 9-12R; obituary CA 81-84

Davies, (William) Robertson 1913- ... **CLC 2, 7, 13, 25, 42**
See also CANR 17; CA 33-36R

Davies, W(illiam) H(enry) 1871-1940 ... **TCLC 5**
See also CA 104; DLB 19

Davis, H(arold) L(enoir) 1896-1960 ... **CLC 49**
See also obituary CA 89-92; DLB 9

Davis, Rebecca (Blaine) Harding 1831-1910 ... **TCLC 6**
See also CA 104

Davis, Richard Harding 1864-1916 ... **TCLC 24**
See also CA 114; DLB 12, 23

Davison, Frank Dalby 1893-1970 ... **CLC 15**
See also obituary CA 116

Davison, Peter 1928- ... **CLC 28**
See also CAAS 4; CANR 3; CA 9-12R; DLB 5

Davys, Mary 1674-1732 ... **LC 1**
See also DLB 39

Dawson, Fielding 1930- ... **CLC 6**
See also CA 85-88

Day, Clarence (Shepard, Jr.) 1874-1935 ... **TCLC 25**
See also CA 108; DLB 11

Day, Thomas 1748-1789 ... **LC 1**
See also YABC 1; DLB 39

Day Lewis, C(ecil) 1904-1972 ... **CLC 1, 6, 10**
See also CAP 1; CA 15-16; obituary CA 33-36R; DLB 15, 20

Dazai Osamu 1909-1948 ... **TCLC 11**
See also Tsushima Shuji

De Crayencour, Marguerite 1903-
See Yourcenar, Marguerite

Deer, Sandra 1940- ... **CLC 45**

Defoe, Daniel 1660?1731 ... **LC 1**
See also SATA 22; DLB 39

De Hartog, Jan 1914- ... **CLC 19**
See also CANR 1; CA 1-4R

Deighton, Len 1929- ... **CLC 4, 7, 22, 46**
See also Deighton, Leonard Cyril

Deighton, Leonard Cyril 1929-
See Deighton, Len
See also CANR 19; CA 9-12R

De la Mare, Walter (John) 1873-1956 ... **TCLC 4**
See also CA 110; SATA 16; DLB 19

Delaney, Shelagh 1939- ... **CLC 29**
See also CA 17-20R; DLB 13

Delany, Samuel R(ay, Jr.) 1942- ... **CLC 8, 14, 38**
See also CA 81-84; DLB 8, 33

De la Roche, Mazo 1885-1961 ... **CLC 14**
See also CA 85-88

Delbanco, Nicholas (Franklin) 1942- ... **CLC 6, 13**
See also CAAS 2; CA 17-20R; DLB 6

Del Castillo, Michel 1933- ... **CLC 38**
See also CA 109

Deledda, Grazia 1875-1936 ... **TCLC 23**

Delibes (Setien), Miguel 1920- ... **CLC 8, 18**
See also CANR 1; CA 45-48

DeLillo, Don 1936- ... **CLC 8, 10, 13, 27, 39, 54**
See also CANR 21; CA 81-84; DLB 6

De Lisser, H(erbert) G(eorge) 1878-1944 ... **TCLC 12**
See also CA 109

Deloria, Vine (Victor), Jr. 1933- ... **CLC 21**
See also CANR 5, 20; CA 53-56; SATA 21

Del Vecchio, John M(ichael) 1947- ... **CLC 29**
See also CA 110

de Man, Paul 1919-1983 ... **CLC 55**
See also obituary CA 111; DLB 67

De Marinis, Rick 1934- ... **CLC 54**
See also CANR 9; CA 57-60

Demby, William 1922- ... **CLC 53**
See also CA 81-84; DLB 33

Denby, Edwin (Orr) 1903-1983 ... **CLC 48**
See also obituary CA 110

Dennis, John 1657-1734 ... **LC 11**

Dennis, Nigel (Forbes) 1912- ... **CLC 8**
See also CA 25-28R; DLB 13, 15

De Palma, Brian 1940- ... **CLC 20**
See also CA 109

De Quincey, Thomas 1785-1859 ... **NCLC 4**

Deren, Eleanora 1908-1961
See Deren, Maya
See also obituary CA 111

Deren, Maya 1908-1961 ... **CLC 16**
See also Deren, Eleanora

Derleth, August (William) 1909-1971 ... **CLC 31**
See also CANR 4; CA 1-4R; obituary CA 29-32R; SATA 5; DLB 9

Derrida, Jacques 1930- ... **CLC 24**

Desai, Anita 1937- ... **CLC 19, 37**
See also CA 81-84

De Saint-Luc, Jean 1909-1981
See Glassco, John

De Sica, Vittorio 1902-1974 ... **CLC 20**
See also obituary CA 117

Desnos, Robert 1900-1945 ... **TCLC 22**
See also CA 121

Destouches, Louis-Ferdinand-Auguste 1894-1961
See Celine, Louis-Ferdinand
See also CA 85-88

Deutsch, Babette 1895-1982 ... **CLC 18**
See also CANR 4; CA 1-4R; obituary CA 108; SATA 1; obituary SATA 33; DLB 45

Devkota, Laxmiprasad 1909-1959 ... **TCLC 23**

DeVoto, Bernard (Augustine) 1897-1955 ... **TCLC 29**
See also CA 113; DLB 9

De Vries, Peter 1910- ... **CLC 1, 2, 3, 7, 10, 28, 46**
See also CA 17-20R; DLB 6; DLB-Y 82

Dexter, Pete 1943- ... **CLC 34, 55**
See also CA 127

Diamond, Neil (Leslie) 1941- ... **CLC 30**
See also CA 108

Dick, Philip K(indred) 1928-1982 ... **CLC 10, 30**
See also CANR 2, 16; CA 49-52; obituary CA 106; DLB 8

Dickens, Charles 1812-1870 ... **NCLC 3, 8, 18**
See also SATA 15; DLB 21, 55, 70

Dickey, James (Lafayette) 1923- ... **CLC 1, 2, 4, 7, 10, 15, 47**
See also CANR 10; CA 9-12R; CABS 2; DLB 5; DLB-Y 82

Dickey, William 1928- ... **CLC 3, 28**
See also CA 9-12R; DLB 5

Dickinson, Charles 1952- ... **CLC 49**

Dickinson, Emily (Elizabeth) 1830-1886 ... **NCLC 21**
See also SATA 29; DLB 1; CDALB 1865-1917

Dickinson, Peter (Malcolm de Brissac) 1927- ... **CLC 12, 35**
See also CA 41-44R; SATA 5

Didion, Joan 1934- ... **CLC 1, 3, 8, 14, 32**
See also CANR 14; CA 5-8R; DLB 2; DLB-Y 81, 86

Dillard, Annie 1945- ... **CLC 9**
See also CANR 3; CA 49-52; SATA 10; DLB-Y 80

Dillard, R(ichard) H(enry) W(ilde) 1937- ... **CLC 5**
See also CAAS 7; CANR 10; CA 21-24R; DLB 5

Dillon, Eilis 1920- ... **CLC 17**
See also CAAS 3; CANR 4; CA 9-12R; SATA 2

Dinesen, Isak 1885-1962 ... **CLC 10, 29**
See also Blixen, Karen (Christentze Dinesen)
See also CANR 22

Disch, Thomas M(ichael) 1940- ... **CLC 7, 36**
See also CAAS 4; CANR 17; CA 21-24R; DLB 8

Disraeli, Benjamin 1804-1881 ... **NCLC 2**
See also DLB 21, 55

Dixon, Paige 1911-
See Corcoran, Barbara

Dixon, Stephen 1936- ... **CLC 52**
See also CANR 17; CA 89-92

Doblin, Alfred 1878-1957 ... **TCLC 13**
See also Doeblin, Alfred

Dobrolyubov, Nikolai Alexandrovich 1836-1861 ... **NCLC 5**

Dobyns, Stephen 1941- ... **CLC 37**
See also CANR 2, 18; CA 45-48

Doctorow, E(dgar) L(aurence) 1931- .... **CLC 6, 11, 15, 18, 37, 44**
See also CANR 2; CA 45-48; DLB 2, 28; DLB-Y 80

Dodgson, Charles Lutwidge 1832-1898
See Carroll, Lewis
See also YABC 2

Doeblin, Alfred 1878-1957........ **TCLC 13**
See also CA 110

Doerr, Harriet 1910- .... **CLC 34**
See also CA 117, 122

Donaldson, Stephen R. 1947-....... **CLC 46**
See also CANR 13; CA 89-92

Donleavy, J(ames) P(atrick) 1926- .... **CLC 1, 4, 6, 10, 45**
See also CA 9-12R; DLB 6

Donnadieu, Marguerite 1914-
See Duras, Marguerite

Donne, John 1572?1631............ **LC 10**

Donnell, David 1939?............. **CLC 34**

Donoso, Jose 1924-........ **CLC 4, 8, 11, 32**
See also CA 81-84

Donovan, John 1928-............. **CLC 35**
See also CLR 3; CA 97-100; SATA 29

Doolittle, Hilda 1886-1961
See H(ilda) D(oolittle)
See also CA 97-100; DLB 4, 45

Dorfman, Ariel 1942-............. **CLC 48**

Dorn, Ed(ward Merton) 1929-... **CLC 10, 18**
See also CA 93-96; DLB 5

Dos Passos, John (Roderigo) 1896-1970 ... **CLC 1, 4, 8, 11, 15, 25, 34**
See also CANR 3; CA 1-4R; obituary CA 29-32R; DLB 4, 9; DLB-DS 1

Dostoevski, Fedor Mikhailovich 1821-1881 .... **NCLC 2, 7, 21; SSC 2**

Doughty, Charles (Montagu) 1843-1926 .... **TCLC 27**
See also CA 115; DLB 19, 57

Douglas, George 1869-1902....... **TCLC 28**

Douglass, Frederick 1817-1895.... **NCLC 7**
See also SATA 29; DLB 1, 43, 50; CDALB 1640-1865

Dourado, (Waldomiro Freitas) Autran 1926- .... **CLC 23**
See also CA 25-28R

Dove, Rita 1952-................. **CLC 50**
See also CA 109

Dowson, Ernest (Christopher) 1867-1900 .... **TCLC 4**
See also CA 105; DLB 19

Doyle, (Sir) Arthur Conan 1859-1930 .... **TCLC 7, 26**
See also CA 104, 122; SATA 24; DLB 18, 70

Dr. A 1933-
See Silverstein, Alvin and Virginia B(arbara Opshelor) Silverstein

Drabble, Margaret 1939- .... **CLC 2, 3, 5, 8, 10, 22, 53**
See also CANR 18; CA 13-16R; SATA 48; DLB 14

Drayton, Michael 1563-1631......... **LC 8**

Dreiser, Theodore (Herman Albert) 1871-1945 .... **TCLC 10, 18**
See also CA 106; SATA 48; DLB 9, 12; DLB-DS 1; CDALB 1865-1917

Drexler, Rosalyn 1926- .... **CLC 2, 6**
See also CA 81-84

Dreyer, Carl Theodor 1889-1968.... **CLC 16**
See also obituary CA 116

Drieu La Rochelle, Pierre 1893-1945 .... **TCLC 21**
See also CA 117; DLB 72

Droste-Hulshoff, Annette Freiin von 1797-1848 .... **NCLC 3**

Drummond, William Henry 1854-1907 .... **TCLC 25**

Drummond de Andrade, Carlos 1902-
See Andrade, Carlos Drummond de

Drury, Allen (Stuart) 1918-........ **CLC 37**
See also CANR 18; CA 57-60

Dryden, John 1631-1700 .... **LC 3**

Duberman, Martin 1930-........... **CLC 8**
See also CANR 2; CA 1-4R

Dubie, Norman (Evans, Jr.) 1945- .. **CLC 36**
See also CANR 12; CA 69-72

Du Bois, W(illiam) E(dward) B(urghardt) 1868-1963 .... **CLC 1, 2, 13**
See also CA 85-88; SATA 42; DLB 47, 50; CDALB 1865-1917

Dubus, Andre 1936- .... **CLC 13, 36**
See also CANR 17; CA 21-24R

Ducasse, Isidore Lucien 1846-1870
See Lautreamont, Comte de

Duclos, Charles Pinot 1704-1772 ..... **LC 1**

Dudek, Louis 1918- .... **CLC 11, 19**
See also CANR 1; CA 45-48

Dudevant, Amandine Aurore Lucile Dupin 1804-1876
See Sand, George

Duerrenmatt, Friedrich 1921-
See also CA 17-20R

Duffy, Bruce 19??................ **CLC 50**

Duffy, Maureen 1933- .... **CLC 37**
See also CA 25-28R; DLB 14

Dugan, Alan 1923-............... **CLC 2, 6**
See also CA 81-84; DLB 5

Duhamel, Georges 1884-1966 .... **CLC 8**
See also CA 81-84; obituary CA 25-28R

Dujardin, Edouard (Emile Louis) 1861-1949 .... **TCLC 13**
See also CA 109

Duke, Raoul 1939-
See Thompson, Hunter S(tockton)

Dumas, Alexandre (Davy de la Pailleterie) (pere) 1802-1870........... **NCLC 11**
See also SATA 18

Dumas, Alexandre (fils) 1824-1895 .... **NCLC 9**

Dumas, Henry (L.) 1934-1968....... **CLC 6**
See also CA 85-88; DLB 41

Du Maurier, Daphne 1907-...... **CLC 6, 11**
See also CANR 6; CA 5-8R; SATA 27

Dunbar, Paul Laurence 1872-1906 .... **TCLC 2, 12**
See also CA 104; SATA 34; DLB 50, 54; CDALB 1865-1917

Duncan (Steinmetz Arquette), Lois 1934- .... **CLC 26**
See also Arquette, Lois S(teinmetz)
See also CANR 2; CA 1-4R; SAAS 2; SATA 1, 36

Duncan, Robert (Edward) 1919-1988 .... **CLC 1, 2, 4, 7, 15, 41, 55**
See also CA 9-12R; obituary CA 124; DLB 5, 16

Dunlap, William 1766-1839....... **NCLC 2**
See also DLB 30, 37

Dunn, Douglas (Eaglesham) 1942- .... **CLC 6, 40**
See also CANR 2; CA 45-48; DLB 40

Dunn, Elsie 1893-1963
See Scott, Evelyn

Dunn, Stephen 1939- .... **CLC 36**
See also CANR 12; CA 33-36R

Dunne, Finley Peter 1867-1936.... **TCLC 28**
See also CA 108; DLB 11, 23

Dunne, John Gregory 1932-........ **CLC 28**
See also CANR 14; CA 25-28R; DLB-Y 80

Dunsany, Lord (Edward John Moreton Drax Plunkett) 1878-1957.......... **TCLC 2**
See also CA 104; DLB 10

Durang, Christopher (Ferdinand) 1949- .... **CLC 27, 38**
See also CA 105

Duras, Marguerite 1914- .... **CLC 3, 6, 11, 20, 34, 40**
See also CA 25-28R

Durban, Pam 1947-............... **CLC 39**

Durcan, Paul 1944-............... **CLC 43**

Durrell, Lawrence (George) 1912- .... **CLC 1, 4, 6, 8, 13, 27, 41**
See also CA 9-12R; DLB 15, 27

Durrenmatt, Friedrich 1921- .... **CLC 1, 4, 8, 11, 15, 43**
See also Duerrenmatt, Friedrich
See also DLB 69

Dwight, Timothy 1752-1817...... **NCLC 13**
See also DLB 37

Dworkin, Andrea 1946- .... **CLC 43**
See also CANR 16; CA 77-80

Dylan, Bob 1941- .... **CLC 3, 4, 6, 12**
See also CA 41-44R; DLB 16

East, Michael 1916-
See West, Morris L.

Eastlake, William (Derry) 1917-..... **CLC 8**
See also CAAS 1; CANR 5; CA 5-8R; DLB 6

Eberhart, Richard 1904-... **CLC 3, 11, 19, 56**
See also CANR 2; CA 1-4R; DLB 48; CDALB 1941-1968

Eberstadt, Fernanda 1960-......... **CLC 39**

Echegaray (y Eizaguirre), Jose (Maria Waldo) 1832-1916 .... **TCLC 4**
See also CA 104

Echeverria, (Jose) Esteban (Antonino) 1805-1851 .... **NCLC 18**

Eckert, Allan W. 1931- . . . . **CLC 17**
See also CANR 14; CA 13-16R; SATA 27, 29

Eco, Umberto 1932- . . . . **CLC 28**
See also CANR 12; CA 77-80

Eddison, E(ric) R(ucker) 1882-1945 . . . . **TCLC 15**
See also CA 109

Edel, Leon (Joseph) 1907- . . . . . . **CLC 29, 34**
See also CANR 1, 22; CA 1-4R

Eden, Emily 1797-1869 . . . . **NCLC 10**

Edgar, David 1948- . . . . **CLC 42**
See also CANR 12; CA 57-60; DLB 13

Edgerton, Clyde 1944- . . . . **CLC 39**
See also CA 118

Edgeworth, Maria 1767-1849. . . . . . **NCLC 1**
See also SATA 21

Edmonds, Helen (Woods) 1904-1968
See Kavan, Anna
See also CA 5-8R; obituary CA 25-28R

Edmonds, Walter D(umaux) 1903- . . **CLC 35**
See also CANR 2; CA 5-8R; SAAS 4; SATA 1, 27; DLB 9

Edson, Russell 1905- . . . . **CLC 13**
See also CA 33-36R

Edwards, G(erald) B(asil) 1899-1976 . . . . **CLC 25**
See also obituary CA 110

Edwards, Gus 1939- . . . . **CLC 43**
See also CA 108

Edwards, Jonathan 1703-1758. . . . . **LC 7**
See also DLB 24

Ehle, John (Marsden, Jr.) 1925- . . . . **CLC 27**
See also CA 9-12R

Ehrenbourg, Ilya (Grigoryevich) 1891-1967
See Ehrenburg, Ilya (Grigoryevich)

Ehrenburg, Ilya (Grigoryevich) 1891-1967 . . . . **CLC 18, 34**
See also CA 102; obituary CA 25-28R

Eich, Guenter 1907-1971
See also CA 111; obituary CA 93-96

Eich, Gunter 1907-1971 . . . . **CLC 15**
See also Eich, Guenter
See also DLB 69

Eichendorff, Joseph Freiherr von 1788-1857 . . . . **NCLC 8**

Eigner, Larry 1927- . . . . **CLC 9**
See also Eigner, Laurence (Joel)
See also DLB 5

Eigner, Laurence (Joel) 1927-
See Eigner, Larry
See also CANR 6; CA 9-12R

Eiseley, Loren (Corey) 1907-1977. . . . **CLC 7**
See also CANR 6; CA 1-4R; obituary CA 73-76

Eisenstadt, Jill 1963- . . . . **CLC 50**

Ekeloef, Gunnar (Bengt) 1907-1968
See Ekelof, Gunnar (Bengt)
See also obituary CA 25-28R

Ekelof, Gunnar (Bengt) 1907-1968 . . **CLC 27**
See also Ekeloef, Gunnar (Bengt)

Ekwensi, Cyprian (Odiatu Duaka) 1921- . . . . **CLC 4**
See also CANR 18; CA 29-32R

Eliade, Mircea 1907-1986 . . . . **CLC 19**
See also CA 65-68; obituary CA 119

Eliot, George 1819-1880. . . . **NCLC 4, 13, 23**
See also DLB 21, 35, 55

Eliot, John 1604-1690 . . . . **LC 5**
See also DLB 24

Eliot, T(homas) S(tearns) 1888-1965 . . . . **CLC 1, 2, 3, 6, 9, 10, 13, 15, 24, 34, 41, 55**
See also CA 5-8R; obituary CA 25-28R; DLB 7, 10, 45, 63; DLB-Y 88

Elkin, Stanley (Lawrence) 1930- . . . . **CLC 4, 6, 9, 14, 27, 51**
See also CANR 8; CA 9-12R; DLB 2, 28; DLB-Y 80

Elledge, Scott 19?? . . . . **CLC 34**

Elliott, George P(aul) 1918-1980. . . . . **CLC 2**
See also CANR 2; CA 1-4R; obituary CA 97-100

Elliott, Janice 1931- . . . . **CLC 47**
See also CANR 8; CA 13-16R; DLB 14

Elliott, Sumner Locke 1917- . . . . **CLC 38**
See also CANR 2, 21; CA 5-8R

Ellis, A. E. 19?? . . . . **CLC 7**

Ellis, Alice Thomas 19?? . . . . **CLC 40**

Ellis, Bret Easton 1964- . . . . **CLC 39**
See also CA 118

Ellis, (Henry) Havelock 1859-1939 . . . . **TCLC 14**
See also CA 109

Ellis, Trey 1964- . . . . **CLC 55**

Ellison, Harlan (Jay) 1934- . . . **CLC 1, 13, 42**
See also CANR 5; CA 5-8R; DLB 8

Ellison, Ralph (Waldo) 1914- . . . . **CLC 1, 3, 11, 54**
See also CANR 24; CA 9-12R; DLB 2; CDALB 1941-1968

Ellmann, Richard (David) 1918-1987 . . . . **CLC 50**
See also CANR 2; CA 1-4R; obituary CA 122

Elman, Richard 1934- . . . . **CLC 19**
See also CAAS 3; CA 17-20R

Eluard, Paul 1895-1952 . . . . **TCLC 7**
See also Grindel, Eugene

Elvin, Anne Katharine Stevenson 1933-
See Stevenson, Anne (Katharine)
See also CA 17-20R

Elyot, (Sir) James 1490?1546 . . . . **LC 11**

Elyot, (Sir) Thomas 1490?1546 . . . . . . **LC 11**

Elytis, Odysseus 1911- . . . . **CLC 15, 49**
See also CA 102

Emecheta, (Florence Onye) Buchi 1944- . . . . **CLC 14, 48**
See also CA 81-84

Emerson, Ralph Waldo 1803-1882 . . . . **NCLC 1**
See also DLB 1; CDALB 1640-1865

Empson, William 1906-1984 . . . . **CLC 3, 8, 19, 33, 34**
See also CA 17-20R; obituary CA 112; DLB 20

Enchi, Fumiko (Veda) 1905-1986 . . . **CLC 31**
See also obituary CA 121

Ende, Michael 1930- . . . . **CLC 31**
See also CLR 14; CA 118; SATA 42

Endo, Shusaku 1923- . . . . . **CLC 7, 14, 19, 54**
See also CANR 21; CA 29-32R

Engel, Marian 1933-1985. . . . . **CLC 36**
See also CANR 12; CA 25-28R; DLB 53

Engelhardt, Frederick 1911-1986
See Hubbard, L(afayette) Ron(ald)

Enright, D(ennis) J(oseph) 1920- . . . . **CLC 4, 8, 31**
See also CANR 1; CA 1-4R; SATA 25; DLB 27

Enzensberger, Hans Magnus 1929- . . . . **CLC 43**
See also CA 116, 119

Ephron, Nora 1941- . . . . **CLC 17, 31**
See also CANR 12; CA 65-68

Epstein, Daniel Mark 1948- . . . . **CLC 7**
See also CANR 2; CA 49-52

Epstein, Jacob 1956- . . . . **CLC 19**
See also CA 114

Epstein, Joseph 1937- . . . . **CLC 39**
See also CA 112, 119

Epstein, Leslie 1938- . . . . **CLC 27**
See also CA 73-76

Erdman, Paul E(mil) 1932- . . . . **CLC 25**
See also CANR 13; CA 61-64

Erdrich, Louise 1954- . . . . **CLC 39, 54**
See also CA 114

Erenburg, Ilya (Grigoryevich) 1891-1967
See Ehrenburg, Ilya (Grigoryevich)

Eseki, Bruno 1919-
See Mphahlele, Ezekiel

Esenin, Sergei (Aleksandrovich) 1895-1925 . . . . **TCLC 4**
See also CA 104

Eshleman, Clayton 1935- . . . . **CLC 7**
See also CAAS 6; CA 33-36R; DLB 5

Espriu, Salvador 1913-1985 . . . . **CLC 9**
See also obituary CA 115

Estleman, Loren D. 1952- . . . . **CLC 48**
See also CA 85-88

Evans, Marian 1819-1880
See Eliot, George

Evans, Mary Ann 1819-1880
See Eliot, George

Evarts, Esther 1900-1972
See Benson, Sally

Everson, Ronald G(ilmour) 1903- . . . **CLC 27**
See also CA 17-20R

Everson, William (Oliver) 1912- . . . . **CLC 1, 5, 14**
See also CANR 20; CA 9-12R; DLB 5, 16

Evtushenko, Evgenii (Aleksandrovich) 1933-
See Yevtushenko, Yevgeny

Ewart, Gavin (Buchanan) 1916- . . . . **CLC 13, 46**
See also CANR 17; CA 89-92; DLB 40

Ewers, Hanns Heinz 1871-1943 . . . **TCLC 12**
See also CA 109

Ewing, Frederick R. 1918-
See Sturgeon, Theodore (Hamilton)

Exley, Frederick (Earl) 1929- .... **CLC 6, 11**
See also CA 81-84; DLB-Y 81

Ezekiel, Tish O'Dowd 1943- .... **CLC 34**

Fagen, Donald 1948-
See Becker, Walter and Fagen, Donald

Fagen, Donald 1948- and **Becker, Walter** 1948-
See Becker, Walter and Fagen, Donald

Fair, Ronald L. 1932-............. **CLC 18**
See also CA 69-72; DLB 33

Fairbairns, Zoe (Ann) 1948- .... **CLC 32**
See also CANR 21; CA 103

Fairfield, Cicily Isabel 1892-1983
See West, Rebecca

Fallaci, Oriana 1930-............. **CLC 11**
See also CANR 15; CA 77-80

Faludy, George 1913-............. **CLC 42**
See also CA 21-24R

Fanshaw, Lady Anne 1625-1706 ..... **LC 11**

Fanshawe, Lady Ann 1625-1706 ..... **LC 11**

Farah, Nuruddin 1945-............ **CLC 53**
See also CA 106

Fargue, Leon-Paul 1876-1947 ..... **TCLC 11**
See also CA 109

Farigoule, Louis 1885-1972
See Romains, Jules

Farina, Richard 1937?1966 .... **CLC 9**
See also CA 81-84; obituary CA 25-28R

Farley, Walter 1920- .... **CLC 17**
See also CANR 8; CA 17-20R; SATA 2, 43; DLB 22

Farmer, Philip Jose 1918- .... **CLC 1, 19**
See also CANR 4; CA 1-4R; DLB 8

Farrell, James T(homas) 1904-1979 .... **CLC 1, 4, 8, 11**
See also CANR 9; CA 5-8R; obituary CA 89-92; DLB 4, 9; DLB-DS 2

Farrell, J(ames) G(ordon) 1935-1979 .... **CLC 6**
See also CA 73-76; obituary CA 89-92; DLB 14

Farrell, M. J. 1904-
See Keane, Molly

Fassbinder, Rainer Werner 1946-1982 .... **CLC 20**
See also CA 93-96; obituary CA 106

Fast, Howard (Melvin) 1914- ...... **CLC 23**
See also CANR 1; CA 1-4R; SATA 7; DLB 9

Faulkner, William (Cuthbert) 1897-1962 .... **CLC 1, 3, 6, 8, 9, 11, 14, 18, 28, 52; SSC 1**
See also CA 81-84; DLB 9, 11, 44; DLB-Y 86; DLB-DS 2

Fauset, Jessie Redmon 1884?1961 .... **CLC 19, 54**
See also CA 109; DLB 51

Faust, Irvin 1924-................. **CLC 8**
See also CA 33-36R; DLB 2, 28; DLB-Y 80

Fearing, Kenneth (Flexner) 1902-1961 .... **CLC 51**
See also CA 93-96; DLB 9

Federman, Raymond 1928- ...... **CLC 6, 47**
See also CANR 10; CA 17-20R; DLB-Y 80

Federspiel, J(urg) F. 1931-......... **CLC 42**

Feiffer, Jules 1929-.............. **CLC 2, 8**
See also CA 17-20R; SATA 8; DLB 7, 44

Feinstein, Elaine 1930-............ **CLC 36**
See also CAAS 1; CA 69-72; DLB 14, 40

Feldman, Irving (Mordecai) 1928-.... **CLC 7**
See also CANR 1; CA 1-4R

Fellini, Federico 1920-............ **CLC 16**
See also CA 65-68

Felsen, Gregor 1916-
See Felsen, Henry Gregor

Felsen, Henry Gregor 1916- .... **CLC 17**
See also CANR 1; CA 1-4R; SAAS 2; SATA 1

Fenton, James (Martin) 1949-...... **CLC 32**
See also CA 102; DLB 40

Ferber, Edna 1887-1968.......... **CLC 18**
See also CA 5-8R; obituary CA 25-28R; SATA 7; DLB 9, 28

Ferlinghetti, Lawrence (Monsanto) 1919? .... **CLC 2, 6, 10, 27**
See also CANR 3; CA 5-8R; DLB 5, 16; CDALB 1941-1968

Ferrier, Susan (Edmonstone) 1782-1854 .... **NCLC 8**

Feuchtwanger, Lion 1884-1958 ..... **TCLC 3**
See also CA 104

Feydeau, Georges 1862-1921 ...... **TCLC 22**
See also CA 113

Fiedler, Leslie A(aron) 1917- .... **CLC 4, 13, 24**
See also CANR 7; CA 9-12R; DLB 28

Field, Andrew 1938-.............. **CLC 44**
See also CA 97-100

Field, Eugene 1850-1895 .... **NCLC 3**
See also SATA 16; DLB 21, 23, 42

Fielding, Henry 1707-1754 .... **LC 1**
See also DLB 39

Fielding, Sarah 1710-1768 .... **LC 1**
See also DLB 39

Fierstein, Harvey 1954-........... **CLC 33**

Figes, Eva 1932-................. **CLC 31**
See also CANR 4; CA 53-56; DLB 14

Finch, Robert (Duer Claydon) 1900- .... **CLC 18**
See also CANR 9; CA 57-60

Findley, Timothy 1930- .... **CLC 27**
See also CANR 12; CA 25-28R; DLB 53

Fink, Janis 1951-
See Ian, Janis

Firbank, Louis 1944-
See Reed, Lou

Firbank, (Arthur Annesley) Ronald 1886-1926 .... **TCLC 1**
See also CA 104; DLB 36

Fisher, Roy 1930-................ **CLC 25**
See also CANR 16; CA 81-84; DLB 40

Fisher, Rudolph 1897-1934 .... **TCLC 11**
See also CA 107; DLB 51

Fisher, Vardis (Alvero) 1895-1968.... **CLC 7**
See also CA 5-8R; obituary CA 25-28R; DLB 9

FitzGerald, Edward 1809-1883 .... **NCLC 9**
See also DLB 32

Fitzgerald, F(rancis) Scott (Key) 1896-1940 .... **TCLC 1, 6, 14, 28**
See also CA 110; DLB 4, 9; DLB-Y 81; DLB-DS 1

Fitzgerald, Penelope 1916-...... **CLC 19, 51**
See also CA 85-88; DLB 14

Fitzgerald, Robert (Stuart) 1910-1985 .... **CLC 39**
See also CANR 1; CA 2R; obituary CA 114; DLB-Y 80

FitzGerald, Robert D(avid) 1902-... **CLC 19**
See also CA 17-20R

Flanagan, Thomas (James Bonner) 1923- .... **CLC 25, 52**
See also CA 108; DLB-Y 80

Flaubert, Gustave 1821-1880 .... **NCLC 2, 10, 19**

Fleming, Ian (Lancaster) 1908-1964 .... **CLC 3, 30**
See also CA 5-8R; SATA 9

Fleming, Thomas J(ames) 1927- .... **CLC 37**
See also CANR 10; CA 5-8R; SATA 8

Flieg, Hellmuth
See Heym, Stefan

Flying Officer X 1905-1974
See Bates, H(erbert) E(rnest)

Fo, Dario 1929-.................. **CLC 32**
See also CA 116

Follett, Ken(neth Martin) 1949- .... **CLC 18**
See also CANR 13; CA 81-84; DLB-Y 81

Foote, Horton 1916-.............. **CLC 51**
See also CA 73-76; DLB 26

Forbes, Esther 1891-1967.......... **CLC 12**
See also CAP 1; CA 13-14; obituary CA 25-28R; SATA 2; DLB 22

Forche, Carolyn 1950-............ **CLC 25**
See also CA 109, 117; DLB 5

Ford, Ford Madox 1873-1939 ... **TCLC 1, 15**
See also CA 104; DLB 34

Ford, John 1895-1973............. **CLC 16**
See also obituary CA 45-48

Ford, Richard 1944-.............. **CLC 46**
See also CANR 11; CA 69-72

Foreman, Richard 1937-........... **CLC 50**
See also CA 65-68

Forester, C(ecil) S(cott) 1899-1966 .... **CLC 35**
See also CA 73-76; obituary CA 25-28R; SATA 13

Forman, James D(ouglas) 1932- .... **CLC 21**
See also CANR 4, 19; CA 9-12R; SATA 8, 21

Fornes, Maria Irene 1930-......... **CLC 39**
See also CA 25-28R; DLB 7

Forrest, Leon 1937- .... **CLC 4**
See also CAAS 7; CA 89-92; DLB 33

Forster, E(dward) M(organ) 1879-1970 .... **CLC 1, 2, 3, 4, 9, 10, 13, 15, 22, 45**
See also CAP 1; CA 13-14; obituary CA 25-28R; DLB 34

Forster, John 1812-1876 .... **NCLC 11**

Forsyth, Frederick 1938- . . . . . . **CLC 2, 5, 36**
See also CA 85-88

Forten (Grimke), Charlotte L(ottie)
1837-1914 . . . . **TCLC 16**
See also Grimke, Charlotte L(ottie) Forten
See also DLB 50

Foscolo, Ugo 1778-1827 . . . . **NCLC 8**

Fosse, Bob 1925- . . . . **CLC 20**
See also Fosse, Robert Louis

Fosse, Robert Louis 1925-
See Bob Fosse
See also CA 110

Foucault, Michel 1926-1984 . . . . **CLC 31, 34**
See also CA 105; obituary CA 113

Fouque, Friedrich (Heinrich Karl) de La Motte 1777-1843 . . . . **NCLC 2**

Fournier, Henri Alban 1886-1914
See Alain-Fournier
See also CA 104

Fournier, Pierre 1916-
See Gascar, Pierre
See also CANR 16; CA 89-92

Fowles, John (Robert)
1926- . . . . **CLC 1, 2, 3, 4, 6, 9, 10, 15, 33**
See also CA 5-8R; SATA 22; DLB 14

Fox, Paula 1923- . . . . **CLC 2, 8**
See also CLR 1; CANR 20; CA 73-76; SATA 17; DLB 52

Fox, William Price (Jr.) 1926- . . . . . **CLC 22**
See also CANR 11; CA 17-20R; DLB 2; DLB-Y 81

Frame (Clutha), Janet (Paterson)
1924- . . . . **CLC 2, 3, 6, 22**
See also Clutha, Janet Paterson Frame

France, Anatole 1844-1924 . . . . **TCLC 9**
See also Thibault, Jacques Anatole Francois

Francis, Claude 19??. . . . . **CLC 50**

Francis, Dick 1920- . . . . **CLC 2, 22, 42**
See also CANR 9; CA 5-8R

Francis, Robert (Churchill) 1901- . . . **CLC 15**
See also CANR 1; CA 1-4R

Frank, Anne 1929-1945 . . . . **TCLC 17**
See also CA 113; SATA 42

Frank, Elizabeth 1945- . . . . **CLC 39**
See also CA 121

Franklin, (Stella Maria Sarah) Miles
1879-1954 . . . . **TCLC 7**
See also CA 104

Fraser, Antonia (Pakenham)
1932- . . . . **CLC 32**
See also CA 85-88; SATA 32

Fraser, George MacDonald 1925- . . . . **CLC 7**
See also CANR 2; CA 45-48

Frayn, Michael 1933- . . . . . . **CLC 3, 7, 31, 47**
See also CA 5-8R; DLB 13, 14

Fraze, Candida 19?? . . . . **CLC 50**

Frazer, Sir James George
1854-1941 . . . . **TCLC 32**
See also CA 118

Frazier, Ian 1951- . . . . **CLC 46**

Frederic, Harold 1856-1898 . . . . . . **NCLC 10**
See also DLB 12, 23

Fredro, Aleksander 1793-1876 . . . . . **NCLC 8**

Freeling, Nicolas 1927- . . . . **CLC 38**
See also CANR 1, 17; CA 49-52

Freeman, Douglas Southall
1886-1953 . . . . **TCLC 11**
See also CA 109; DLB 17

Freeman, Judith 1946- . . . . **CLC 55**

Freeman, Mary (Eleanor) Wilkins
1852-1930 . . . . **TCLC 9; SSC 1**
See also CA 106; DLB 12

Freeman, R(ichard) Austin
1862-1943 . . . . **TCLC 21**
See also CA 113; DLB 70

French, Marilyn 1929- . . . . **CLC 10, 18**
See also CANR 3; CA 69-72

Freneau, Philip Morin 1752-1832 . . **NCLC 1**
See also DLB 37, 43

Friedman, B(ernard) H(arper)
1926- . . . . **CLC 7**
See also CANR 3; CA 1-4R

Friedman, Bruce Jay 1930- . . . . **CLC 3, 5, 56**
See also CANR 25; CA 9-12R; DLB 2, 28

Friel, Brian 1929- . . . . **CLC 5, 42**
See also CA 21-24R; DLB 13

Friis-Baastad, Babbis (Ellinor)
1921-1970 . . . . **CLC 12**
See also CA 17-20R; SATA 7

Frisch, Max (Rudolf)
1911- . . . . **CLC 3, 9, 14, 18, 32, 44**
See also CA 85-88; DLB 69

Fromentin, Eugene (Samuel Auguste)
1820-1876 . . . . **NCLC 10**

Frost, Robert (Lee)
1874-1963 . . . **CLC 1, 3, 4, 9, 10, 13, 15, 26, 34, 44**
See also CA 89-92; SATA 14; DLB 54

Fry, Christopher 1907- . . . . **CLC 2, 10, 14**
See also CANR 9; CA 17-20R; DLB 13

Frye, (Herman) Northrop 1912- . . . . **CLC 24**
See also CANR 8; CA 5-8R

Fuchs, Daniel 1909- . . . . **CLC 8, 22**
See also CAAS 5; CA 81-84; DLB 9, 26, 28

Fuchs, Daniel 1934- . . . . **CLC 34**
See also CANR 14; CA 37-40R

Fuentes, Carlos
1928- . . . . **CLC 3, 8, 10, 13, 22, 41**
See also CANR 10; CA 69-72

Fugard, Athol 1932- . . . **CLC 5, 9, 14, 25, 40**
See also CA 85-88

Fugard, Sheila 1932- . . . . **CLC 48**

Fuller, Charles (H., Jr.) 1939- . . . . . . **CLC 25**
See also CA 108, 112; DLB 38

Fuller, (Sarah) Margaret
1810-1850 . . . . **NCLC 5**
See also Ossoli, Sarah Margaret (Fuller marchesa d')
See also DLB 1; CDALB 1640-1865

Fuller, Roy (Broadbent) 1912- . . . . **CLC 4, 28**
See also CA 5-8R; DLB 15, 20

Fulton, Alice 1952- . . . . **CLC 52**
See also CA 116

Furphy, Joseph 1843-1912 . . . . **TCLC 25**

Futrelle, Jacques 1875-1912 . . . . . . **TCLC 19**
See also CA 113

Gaboriau, Emile 1835-1873 . . . . . . **NCLC 14**

Gadda, Carlo Emilio 1893-1973 . . . . **CLC 11**
See also CA 89-92

Gaddis, William
1922- . . . . **CLC 1, 3, 6, 8, 10, 19, 43**
See also CAAS 4; CANR 21; CA 17-20R; DLB 2

Gaines, Ernest J. 1933- . . . . . . **CLC 3, 11, 18**
See also CANR 6; CA 9-12R; DLB 2, 33; DLB-Y 80

Gale, Zona 1874-1938 . . . . **TCLC 7**
See also CA 105; DLB 9

Gallagher, Tess 1943- . . . . **CLC 18**
See also CA 106

Gallant, Mavis 1922- . . . . **CLC 7, 18, 38**
See also CA 69-72; DLB 53

Gallant, Roy A(rthur) 1924- . . . . **CLC 17**
See also CANR 4; CA 5-8R; SATA 4

Gallico, Paul (William) 1897-1976 . . . **CLC 2**
See also CA 5-8R; obituary CA 69-72; SATA 13; DLB 9

Galsworthy, John 1867-1933 . . . . **TCLC 1**
See also CA 104; DLB 10, 34

Galt, John 1779-1839 . . . . **NCLC 1**

Galvin, James 1951- . . . . **CLC 38**
See also CA 108

Gann, Ernest K(ellogg) 1910- . . . . . . **CLC 23**
See also CANR 1; CA 1-4R

Garcia Lorca, Federico
1899-1936 . . . . **TCLC 1, 7**
See also CA 104

Garcia Marquez, Gabriel (Jose)
1928- . . . . **CLC 2, 3, 8, 10, 15, 27, 47, 55**
See also CANR 10; CA 33-36R

Gardam, Jane 1928- . . . . **CLC 43**
See also CLR 12; CANR 2, 18; CA 49-52; SATA 28, 39; DLB 14

Gardner, Herb 1934- . . . . **CLC 44**

Gardner, John (Champlin, Jr.)
1933-1982 . . . . **CLC 2, 3, 5, 7, 8, 10, 18, 28, 34**
See also CA 65-68; obituary CA 107; obituary SATA 31, 40; DLB 2; DLB-Y 82

Gardner, John (Edmund) 1926- . . . . . **CLC 30**
See also CANR 15; CA 103

Garfield, Leon 1921- . . . . **CLC 12**
See also CA 17-20R; SATA 1, 32

Garland, (Hannibal) Hamlin
1860-1940 . . . . **TCLC 3**
See also CA 104; DLB 12, 71

Garneau, Hector (de) Saint Denys
1912-1943 . . . . **TCLC 13**
See also CA 111

Garner, Alan 1935- . . . . **CLC 17**
See also CANR 15; CA 73-76; SATA 18

Garner, Hugh 1913-1979 . . . . **CLC 13**
See also CA 69-72

Garnett, David 1892-1981 . . . . **CLC 3**
See also CANR 17; CA 5-8R; obituary CA 103; DLB 34

Garrett, George (Palmer, Jr.)
1929- . . . . **CLC 3, 11, 51**
See also CAAS 5; CANR 1; CA 1-4R; DLB 2, 5; DLB-Y 83

Garrigue, Jean 1914-1972 .... **CLC 2, 8**
See also CA 5-8R; obituary CA 37-40R

Gary, Romain 1914-1980 .... **CLC 25**
See also Kacew, Romain

Gascar, Pierre 1916-.............. **CLC 11**
See also Fournier, Pierre

Gascoyne, David (Emery) 1916- .... **CLC 45**
See also CANR 10; CA 65-68; DLB 20

Gaskell, Elizabeth Cleghorn
1810-1865 .... **NCLC 5**
See also DLB 21

Gass, William H(oward)
1924- .... **CLC 1, 2, 8, 11, 15, 39**
See also CA 17-20R; DLB 2

Gautier, Theophile 1811-1872 ..... **NCLC 1**

Gaye, Marvin (Pentz) 1939-1984 ... **CLC 26**
See also obituary CA 112

Gebler, Carlo (Ernest) 1954-....... **CLC 39**
See also CA 119

Gee, Maurice (Gough) 1931-....... **CLC 29**
See also CA 97-100; SATA 46

Gelbart, Larry (Simon) 1923- ...... **CLC 21**
See also CA 73-76

Gelber, Jack 1932-........... **CLC 1, 6, 14**
See also CANR 2; CA 1-4R; DLB 7

Gellhorn, Martha (Ellis) 1908- ..... **CLC 14**
See also CA 77-80; DLB-Y 82

Genet, Jean
1910-1986 ... **CLC 1, 2, 5, 10, 14, 44, 46**
See also CANR 18; CA 13-16R; DLB 72;
DLB-Y 86

Gent, Peter 1942-................ **CLC 29**
See also CA 89-92; DLB 72; DLB-Y 82

George, Jean Craighead 1919-...... **CLC 35**
See also CLR 1; CA 5-8R; SATA 2;
DLB 52

George, Stefan (Anton)
1868-1933 .... **TCLC 2, 14**
See also CA 104

Gerhardi, William (Alexander) 1895-1977
See Gerhardie, William (Alexander)

Gerhardie, William (Alexander)
1895-1977 .... **CLC 5**
See also CANR 18; CA 25-28R;
obituary CA 73-76; DLB 36

Gertler, T(rudy) 1946? .... **CLC 34**
See also CA 116

Gessner, Friedrike Victoria 1910-1980
See Adamson, Joy(-Friederike Victoria)

Ghelderode, Michel de
1898-1962 .... **CLC 6, 11**
See also CA 85-88

Ghiselin, Brewster 1903- .... **CLC 23**
See also CANR 13; CA 13-16R

Ghose, Zulfikar 1935-............ **CLC 42**
See also CA 65-68

Ghosh, Amitav 1943- .... **CLC 44**

Giacosa, Giuseppe 1847-1906 ...... **TCLC 7**
See also CA 104

Gibbon, Lewis Grassic 1901-1935 ... **TCLC 4**
See also Mitchell, James Leslie

Gibbons, Kaye 1960- .... **CLC 50**

Gibran, (Gibran) Kahlil
1883-1931 .... **TCLC 1, 9**
See also CA 104

Gibson, William 1914- .... **CLC 23**
See also CANR 9; CA 9-12R; DLB 7

Gibson, William 1948- .... **CLC 39**

Gide, Andre (Paul Guillaume)
1869-1951 .... **TCLC 5, 12**
See also CA 104

Gifford, Barry (Colby) 1946-....... **CLC 34**
See also CANR 9; CA 65-68

Gilbert, (Sir) W(illiam) S(chwenck)
1836-1911 .... **TCLC 3**
See also CA 104; SATA 36

Gilbreth, Ernestine 1908-
See Carey, Ernestine Gilbreth

Gilbreth, Frank B(unker), Jr. 1911- and
Carey, Ernestine Gilbreth
1911- .... **CLC 17**

Gilbreth, Frank B(unker), Jr. 1911-
See Gilbreth, Frank B(unker), Jr. and
Carey, Ernestine Gilbreth
See also CA 9-12R; SATA 2

Gilchrist, Ellen 1935-.......... **CLC 34, 48**
See also CA 113, 116

Giles, Molly 1942- .... **CLC 39**

Gilliam, Terry (Vance) 1940-
See Monty Python
See also CA 108, 113

Gilliatt, Penelope (Ann Douglass)
1932- .... **CLC 2, 10, 13, 53**
See also CA 13-16R; DLB 14

Gilman, Charlotte (Anna) Perkins (Stetson)
1860-1935 .... **TCLC 9**
See also CA 106

Gilmour, David 1944-
See Pink Floyd

Gilroy, Frank D(aniel) 1925-........ **CLC 2**
See also CA 81-84; DLB 7

Ginsberg, Allen
1926- .... **CLC 1, 2, 3, 4, 6, 13, 36**
See also CANR 2; CA 1-4R; DLB 5, 16;
CDALB 1941-1968

Ginzburg, Natalia 1916-...... **CLC 5, 11, 54**
See also CA 85-88

Giono, Jean 1895-1970.......... **CLC 4, 11**
See also CANR 2; CA 45-48;
obituary CA 29-32R; DLB 72

Giovanni, Nikki 1943- .... **CLC 2, 4, 19**
See also CLR 6; CAAS 6; CANR 18;
CA 29-32R; SATA 24; DLB 5, 41

Giovene, Andrea 1904-............. **CLC 7**
See also CA 85-88

Gippius, Zinaida (Nikolayevna) 1869-1945
See Hippius, Zinaida
See also CA 106

Giraudoux, (Hippolyte) Jean
1882-1944 .... **TCLC 2, 7**
See also CA 104

Gironella, Jose Maria 1917- .... **CLC 11**
See also CA 101

Gissing, George (Robert)
1857-1903 .... **TCLC 3, 24**
See also CA 105; DLB 18

Gladkov, Fyodor (Vasilyevich)
1883-1958 .... **TCLC 27**

Glanville, Brian (Lester) 1931- ...... **CLC 6**
See also CANR 3; CA 5-8R; SATA 42;
DLB 15

Glasgow, Ellen (Anderson Gholson)
1873?1945 .... **TCLC 2, 7**
See also CA 104; DLB 9, 12

Glassco, John 1909-1981 .... **CLC 9**
See also CANR 15; CA 13-16R;
obituary CA 102

Glasser, Ronald J. 1940? .... **CLC 37**

Glendinning, Victoria 1937-........ **CLC 50**
See also CA 120

Glissant, Edouard 1928-........... **CLC 10**

Gloag, Julian 1930- .... **CLC 40**
See also CANR 10; CA 65-68

Gluck, Louise (Elisabeth)
1943- .... **CLC 7, 22, 44**
See also CA 33-36R; DLB 5

Gobineau, Joseph Arthur (Comte) de
1816-1882 .... **NCLC 17**

Godard, Jean-Luc 1930-........... **CLC 20**
See also CA 93-96

Godden, (Margaret) Rumer 1907-... **CLC 53**
See also CANR 4, 27; CA 7-8R; SATA 3,
36

Godwin, Gail 1937-........ **CLC 5, 8, 22, 31**
See also CANR 15; CA 29-32R; DLB 6

Godwin, William 1756-1836...... **NCLC 14**
See also DLB 39

Goethe, Johann Wolfgang von
1749-1832 .... **NCLC 4, 22**

Gogarty, Oliver St. John
1878-1957 .... **TCLC 15**
See also CA 109; DLB 15, 19

Gogol, Nikolai (Vasilyevich)
1809-1852 .... **NCLC 5, 15**
See also CAAS 1, 4

Gokceli, Yasar Kemal 1923-
See Kemal, Yashar

Gold, Herbert 1924-....... **CLC 4, 7, 14, 42**
See also CANR 17; CA 9-12R; DLB 2;
DLB-Y 81

Goldbarth, Albert 1948-......... **CLC 5, 38**
See also CANR 6; CA 53-56

Goldberg, Anatol 1910-1982 .... **CLC 34**
See also obituary CA 117

Goldemberg, Isaac 1945- .... **CLC 52**
See also CANR 11; CA 69-72

Golding, William (Gerald)
1911- .... **CLC 1, 2, 3, 8, 10, 17, 27**
See also CANR 13; CA 5-8R; DLB 15

Goldman, Emma 1869-1940....... **TCLC 13**
See also CA 110

Goldman, William (W.) 1931- .... **CLC 1, 48**
See also CA 9-12R; DLB 44

Goldmann, Lucien 1913-1970 ...... **CLC 24**
See also CAP 2; CA 25-28

Goldoni, Carlo 1707-1793 .... **LC 4**

Goldsberry, Steven 1949-.......... **CLC 34**

Goldsmith, Oliver 1728?1774......... **LC 2**
See also SATA 26; DLB 39

Gombrowicz, Witold 1904-1969 . . . . **CLC 4, 7, 11, 49**
See also CAP 2; CA 19-20; obituary CA 25-28R

Gomez de la Serna, Ramon 1888-1963 . . . . **CLC 9**
See also obituary CA 116

Goncharov, Ivan Alexandrovich 1812-1891 . . . . **NCLC 1**

Goncourt, Edmond (Louis Antoine Huot) de 1822-1896 and **Goncourt, Jules (Alfred Huot) de** 1822-1896 . . . . **NCLC 7**

Goncourt, Edmond (Louis Antoine Huot) de 1822-1896
See Goncourt, Edmond (Louis Antoine Huot) de and Goncourt, Jules (Alfred Huot) de

Goncourt, Jules (Alfred Huot) de 1830-1870
See Goncourt, Edmond (Louis Antoine Huot) de and Goncourt, Jules (Alfred Huot) de

Goncourt, Jules (Alfred Huot) de 1830-1870 and **Goncourt, Edmond (Louis Antoine Huot) de** 1830-1870
See Goncourt, Edmond (Louis Antoine Huot) de and Goncourt, Jules (Alfred Huot) de

Gontier, Fernande 19?? . . . . **CLC 50**

Goodman, Paul 1911-1972 . . . . **CLC 1, 2, 4, 7**
See also CAP 2; CA 19-20; obituary CA 37-40R

Gorden, Charles William 1860-1937
See Conner, Ralph

Gordimer, Nadine 1923- . . . . **CLC 3, 5, 7, 10, 18, 33, 51**
See also CANR 3; CA 5-8R

Gordon, Adam Lindsay 1833-1870 . . . . **NCLC 21**

Gordon, Caroline 1895-1981 . . . . **CLC 6, 13, 29**
See also CAP 1; CA 11-12; obituary CA 103; DLB 4, 9; DLB-Y 81

Gordon, Mary (Catherine) 1949- . . . . **CLC 13, 22**
See also CA 102; DLB 6; DLB-Y 81

Gordon, Sol 1923- . . . . **CLC 26**
See also CANR 4; CA 53-56; SATA 11

Gordone, Charles 1925- . . . . **CLC 1, 4**
See also CA 93-96; DLB 7

Gorenko, Anna Andreyevna 1889?1966
See Akhmatova, Anna

Gorky, Maxim 1868-1936 . . . . **TCLC 8**
See also Peshkov, Alexei Maximovich

Goryan, Sirak 1908-1981
See Saroyan, William

Gosse, Edmund (William) 1849-1928 . . . . **TCLC 28**
See also CA 117; DLB 57

Gotlieb, Phyllis (Fay Bloom) 1926- . . . . **CLC 18**
See also CANR 7; CA 13-16R

Gould, Lois 1938? . . . . **CLC 4, 10**
See also CA 77-80

Gourmont, Remy de 1858-1915 . . . . **TCLC 17**
See also CA 109

Govier, Katherine 1948- . . . . **CLC 51**
See also CANR 18; CA 101

Goyen, (Charles) William 1915-1983 . . . . **CLC 5, 8, 14, 40**
See also CANR 6; CA 5-8R; obituary CA 110; DLB 2; DLB-Y 83

Goytisolo, Juan 1931- . . . . **CLC 5, 10, 23**
See also CA 85-88

Gozzi, (Conte) Carlo 1720-1806 . . **NCLC 23**

Grabbe, Christian Dietrich 1801-1836 . . . . **NCLC 2**

Grace, Patricia 1937- . . . . **CLC 56**

Gracq, Julien 1910- . . . . **CLC 11, 48**
See also Poirier, Louis

Grade, Chaim 1910-1982 . . . . **CLC 10**
See also CA 93-96; obituary CA 107

Graham, Jorie 1951- . . . . **CLC 48**
See also CA 111

Graham, R(obert) B(ontine) Cunninghame 1852-1936 . . . . **TCLC 19**

Graham, Winston (Mawdsley) 1910- . . . . **CLC 23**
See also CANR 2; CA 49-52; obituary CA 118

Graham, W(illiam) S(ydney) 1918-1986 . . . . **CLC 29**
See also CA 73-76; obituary CA 118; DLB 20

Granville-Barker, Harley 1877-1946 . . . . **TCLC 2**
See also CA 104

Grass, Gunter (Wilhelm) 1927- . . **CLC 1, 2, 4, 6, 11, 15, 22, 32, 49**
See also CANR 20; CA 13-16R

Grau, Shirley Ann 1929- . . . . **CLC 4, 9**
See also CANR 22; CA 89-92; DLB 2

Graves, Richard Perceval 1945- . . . . **CLC 44**
See also CANR 9; CA 65-68

Graves, Robert (von Ranke) 1895-1985 . . . **CLC 1, 2, 6, 11, 39, 44, 45**
See also CANR 5; CA 5-8R; obituary CA 117; SATA 45; DLB 20; DLB-Y 85

Gray, Alasdair 1934- . . . . **CLC 41**

Gray, Amlin 1946- . . . . **CLC 29**

Gray, Francine du Plessix 1930- . . . . **CLC 22**
See also CAAS 2; CANR 11; CA 61-64

Gray, John (Henry) 1866-1934 . . . . **TCLC 19**
See also CA 119

Gray, Simon (James Holliday) 1936- . . . . **CLC 9, 14, 36**
See also CAAS 3; CA 21-24R; DLB 13

Gray, Spalding 1941- . . . . **CLC 49**

Gray, Thomas 1716-1771 . . . . **LC 4**

Grayson, Richard (A.) 1951- . . . . **CLC 38**
See also CANR 14; CA 85-88

Greeley, Andrew M(oran) 1928- . . . . **CLC 28**
See also CAAS 7; CANR 7; CA 5-8R

Green, Hannah 1932- . . . . **CLC 3, 7, 30**
See also Greenberg, Joanne
See also CA 73-76

Green, Henry 1905-1974 . . . . **CLC 2, 13**
See also Yorke, Henry Vincent
See also DLB 15

Green, Julien (Hartridge) 1900- . . **CLC 3, 11**
See also CA 21-24R; DLB 4, 72

Green, Paul (Eliot) 1894-1981 . . . . . . **CLC 25**
See also CANR 3; CA 5-8R; obituary CA 103; DLB 7, 9; DLB-Y 81

Greenberg, Ivan 1908-1973
See Rahv, Philip
See also CA 85-88

Greenberg, Joanne (Goldenberg) 1932- . . . . **CLC 3, 7, 30**
See also Green, Hannah
See also CANR 14; CA 5-8R; SATA 25

Greene, Bette 1934- . . . . **CLC 30**
See also CLR 2; CANR 4; CA 53-56; SATA 8

Greene, Gael 19?? . . . . **CLC 8**
See also CANR 10; CA 13-16R

Greene, Graham (Henry) 1904- . . . . . **CLC 1, 3, 6, 9, 14, 18, 27, 37**
See also CA 13-16R; SATA 20; DLB 13, 15; DLB-Y 85

Gregor, Arthur 1923- . . . . **CLC 9**
See also CANR 11; CA 25-28R; SATA 36

Gregory, Lady (Isabella Augusta Persse) 1852-1932 . . . . **TCLC 1**
See also CA 104; DLB 10

Grendon, Stephen 1909-1971
See Derleth, August (William)

Greve, Felix Paul Berthold Friedrich 1879-1948
See Grove, Frederick Philip
See also CA 104

Grey, (Pearl) Zane 1872?1939 . . . . . . **TCLC 6**
See also CA 104; DLB 9

Grieg, (Johan) Nordahl (Brun) 1902-1943 . . . . **TCLC 10**
See also CA 107

Grieve, C(hristopher) M(urray) 1892-1978
See MacDiarmid, Hugh
See also CA 5-8R; obituary CA 85-88

Griffin, Gerald 1803-1840 . . . . **NCLC 7**

Griffin, Peter 1942- . . . . **CLC 39**

Griffiths, Trevor 1935- . . . . **CLC 13, 52**
See also CA 97-100; DLB 13

Grigson, Geoffrey (Edward Harvey) 1905-1985 . . . . **CLC 7, 39**
See also CANR 20; CA 25-28R; obituary CA 118; DLB 27

Grillparzer, Franz 1791-1872 . . . . . . **NCLC 1**

Grimke, Charlotte L(ottie) Forten 1837-1914
See Forten (Grimke), Charlotte L(ottie)
See also CA 117

Grimm, Jakob (Ludwig) Karl 1785-1863 and **Grimm, Wilhelm Karl** 1785-1863 . . . . **NCLC 3**
See also SATA 22

Grimm, Jakob (Ludwig) Karl 1785-1863
See Grimm, Jakob (Ludwig) Karl and Grimm, Wilhelm Karl

Grimm, Wilhelm Karl 1786-1859
See Grimm, Jakob (Ludwig) Karl and Grimm, Wilhelm Karl

Grimm, Wilhelm Karl 1786-1859 and **Grimm, Jakob (Ludwig) Karl** 1786-1859
See Grimm, Jakob (Ludwig) Karl and Grimm, Wilhelm Karl

Grimmelshausen, Johann Jakob Christoffel von 1621-1676 .... **LC 6**

Grindel, Eugene 1895-1952
See also CA 104

Grossman, Vasily (Semenovich) 1905-1964 .... **CLC 41**

Grove, Frederick Philip 1879-1948 .... **TCLC 4**
See also Greve, Felix Paul Berthold Friedrich

Grumbach, Doris (Isaac) 1918- .... **CLC 13, 22**
See also CAAS 2; CANR 9; CA 5-8R

Grundtvig, Nicolai Frederik Severin 1783-1872 .... **NCLC 1**

Grunwald, Lisa 1959-............. **CLC 44**
See also CA 120

Guare, John 1938- .... **CLC 8, 14, 29**
See also CANR 21; CA 73-76; DLB 7

Gudjonsson, Halldor Kiljan 1902-
See Laxness, Halldor (Kiljan)
See also CA 103

Guest, Barbara 1920-............. **CLC 34**
See also CANR 11; CA 25-28R; DLB 5

Guest, Judith (Ann) 1936- .... **CLC 8, 30**
See also CANR 15; CA 77-80

Guild, Nicholas M. 1944-.......... **CLC 33**
See also CA 93-96

Guillen, Jorge 1893-1984.......... **CLC 11**
See also CA 89-92; obituary CA 112

Guillen, Nicolas 1902- .... **CLC 48**
See also CA 116

Guillevic, (Eugene) 1907-.......... **CLC 33**
See also CA 93-96

Gunn, Bill 1934-.................. **CLC 5**
See also Gunn, William Harrison
See also DLB 38

Gunn, Thom(son William) 1929-................ **CLC 3, 6, 18, 32**
See also CANR 9; CA 17-20R; DLB 27

Gunn, William Harrison 1934-
See Gunn, Bill
See also CANR 12; CA 13-16R

Gurney, A(lbert) R(amsdell), Jr. 1930- .... **CLC 32, 50, 54**
See also CA 77-80

Gurney, Ivor (Bertie) 1890-1937 ... **TCLC 33**

Gustafson, Ralph (Barker) 1909-.... **CLC 36**
See also CANR 8; CA 21-24R

Guthrie, A(lfred) B(ertram), Jr. 1901- .... **CLC 23**
See also CA 57-60; DLB 6

Guthrie, Woodrow Wilson 1912-1967
See Guthrie, Woody
See also CA 113; obituary CA 93-96

Guthrie, Woody 1912-1967 .... **CLC 35**
See also Guthrie, Woodrow Wilson

Guy, Rosa (Cuthbert) 1928-........ **CLC 26**
See also CANR 14; CA 17-20R; SATA 14; DLB 33

Haavikko, Paavo (Juhani) 1931- .... **CLC 18, 34**
See also CA 106

Hacker, Marilyn 1942- .... **CLC 5, 9, 23**
See also CA 77-80

Haggard, (Sir) H(enry) Rider 1856-1925 .... **TCLC 11**
See also CA 108; SATA 16; DLB 70

Haig-Brown, Roderick L(angmere) 1908-1976 .... **CLC 21**
See also CANR 4; CA 5-8R; obituary CA 69-72; SATA 12

Hailey, Arthur 1920-.............. **CLC 5**
See also CANR 2; CA 1-4R; DLB-Y 82

Hailey, Elizabeth Forsythe 1938-... **CLC 40**
See also CAAS 1; CANR 15; CA 93-96

Haley, Alex (Palmer) 1921-...... **CLC 8, 12**
See also CA 77-80; DLB 38

Haliburton, Thomas Chandler 1796-1865 .... **NCLC 15**
See also DLB 11

Hall, Donald (Andrew, Jr.) 1928- .... **CLC 1, 13, 37**
See also CAAS 7; CANR 2; CA 5-8R; SATA 23; DLB 5

Hall, James Norman 1887-1951 ... **TCLC 23**
See also SATA 21

Hall, (Marguerite) Radclyffe 1886-1943 .... **TCLC 12**
See also CA 110

Hall, Rodney 1935- .... **CLC 51**
See also CA 109

Halpern, Daniel 1945- .... **CLC 14**
See also CA 33-36R

Hamburger, Michael (Peter Leopold) 1924- .... **CLC 5, 14**
See also CAAS 4; CANR 2; CA 5-8R; DLB 27

Hamill, Pete 1935-............... **CLC 10**
See also CANR 18; CA 25-28R

Hamilton, Edmond 1904-1977....... **CLC 1**
See also CANR 3; CA 1-4R; DLB 8

Hamilton, Gail 1911-
See Corcoran, Barbara

Hamilton, Ian 1938-.............. **CLC 55**
See also CA 106; DLB 40

Hamilton, Mollie 1909?
See Kaye, M(ary) M(argaret)

Hamilton, (Anthony Walter) Patrick 1904-1962 .... **CLC 51**
See also obituary CA 113; DLB 10

Hamilton, Virginia (Esther) 1936-... **CLC 26**
See also CLR 1, 11; CANR 20; CA 25-28R; SATA 4; DLB 33, 52

Hammett, (Samuel) Dashiell 1894-1961 .... **CLC 3, 5, 10, 19, 47**
See also CA 81-84

Hammon, Jupiter 1711?1800? ..... **NCLC 5**
See also DLB 31, 50

Hamner, Earl (Henry), Jr. 1923- ... **CLC 12**
See also CA 73-76; DLB 6

Hampton, Christopher (James) 1946- .... **CLC 4**
See also CA 25-28R; DLB 13

Hamsun, Knut 1859-1952....... **TCLC 2, 14**
See also Pedersen, Knut

Handke, Peter 1942- .. **CLC 5, 8, 10, 15, 38**
See also CA 77-80

Hanley, James 1901-1985 ... **CLC 3, 5, 8, 13**
See also CA 73-76; obituary CA 117

Hannah, Barry 1942-.......... **CLC 23, 38**
See also CA 108, 110; DLB 6

Hansberry, Lorraine (Vivian) 1930-1965 .... **CLC 17**
See also CA 109; obituary CA 25-28R; DLB 7, 38; CDALB 1941-1968

Hansen, Joseph 1923-............ **CLC 38**
See also CANR 16; CA 29-32R

Hansen, Martin 1909-1955 .... **TCLC 32**

Hanson, Kenneth O(stlin) 1922- .... **CLC 13**
See also CANR 7; CA 53-56

Hardenberg, Friedrich (Leopold Freiherr) von 1772-1801
See Novalis

Hardwick, Elizabeth 1916- .... **CLC 13**
See also CANR 3; CA 5-8R; DLB 6

Hardy, Thomas 1840-1928 ... **TCLC 4, 10, 18, 32; SSC 2**
See also CA 104, 123; SATA 25; DLB 18, 19

Hare, David 1947- .... **CLC 29**
See also CA 97-100; DLB 13

Harlan, Louis R(udolph) 1922-..... **CLC 34**
See also CA 21-24R

Harling, Robert 1951? .... **CLC 53**

Harmon, William (Ruth) 1938-..... **CLC 38**
See also CANR 14; CA 33-36R

Harper, Frances Ellen Watkins 1825-1911 .... **TCLC 14**
See also CA 111; DLB 50

Harper, Michael S(teven) 1938- .. **CLC 7, 22**
See also CA 33-36R; DLB 41

Harris, Christie (Lucy Irwin) 1907- .... **CLC 12**
See also CANR 6; CA 5-8R; SATA 6

Harris, Frank 1856-1931 .... **TCLC 24**
See also CAAS 1; CA 109

Harris, George Washington 1814-1869 .... **NCLC 23**
See also DLB 3

Harris, Joel Chandler 1848-1908 ... **TCLC 2**
See also YABC 1; CA 104; DLB 11, 23, 42

Harris, John (Wyndham Parkes Lucas) Beynon 1903-1969
See Wyndham, John
See also CA 102; obituary CA 89-92

Harris, MacDonald 1921- .... **CLC 9**
See also Heiney, Donald (William)

Harris, Mark 1922- .... **CLC 19**
See also CAAS 3; CANR 2; CA 5-8R; DLB 2; DLB-Y 80

Harris, (Theodore) Wilson 1921-.... **CLC 25**
See also CANR 11; CA 65-68

Harrison, Harry (Max) 1925-...... **CLC 42**
See also CANR 5, 21; CA 1-4R; SATA 4; DLB 8

Harrison, James (Thomas) 1937-
See Harrison, Jim
See also CANR 8; CA 13-16R

Harrison, Jim 1937- .... **CLC 6, 14, 33**
See also Harrison, James (Thomas)
See also DLB-Y 82

Harrison, Tony 1937- .... **CLC 43**
See also CA 65-68; DLB 40

Harriss, Will(ard Irvin) 1922- .... **CLC 34**
See also CA 111

Harte, (Francis) Bret(t)
1836?1902 .... **TCLC 1, 25**
See also CA 104; SATA 26; DLB 12, 64; CDALB 1865-1917

Hartley, L(eslie) P(oles)
1895-1972 .... **CLC 2, 22**
See also CA 45-48; obituary CA 37-40R; DLB 15

Hartman, Geoffrey H. 1929- .... **CLC 27**
See also CA 117

Haruf, Kent 19?? .... **CLC 34**

Harwood, Ronald 1934- .... **CLC 32**
See also CANR 4; CA 1-4R; DLB 13

Hasek, Jaroslav (Matej Frantisek)
1883-1923 .... **TCLC 4**
See also CA 104

Hass, Robert 1941- .... **CLC 18, 39**
See also CA 111

Hastings, Selina 19?? .... **CLC 44**

Hauptmann, Gerhart (Johann Robert)
1862-1946 .... **TCLC 4**
See also CA 104

Havel, Vaclav 1936- .... **CLC 25**
See also CA 104

Haviaras, Stratis 1935- .... **CLC 33**
See also CA 105

Hawkes, John (Clendennin Burne, Jr.)
1925- .... **CLC 1, 2, 3, 4, 7, 9, 14, 15, 27, 49**
See also CANR 2; CA 1-4R; DLB 2, 7; DLB-Y 80

Hawthorne, Julian 1846-1934 .... **TCLC 25**

Hawthorne, Nathaniel
1804-1864 .... **NCLC 2, 10, 17, 23; SSC 3**
See also YABC 2; DLB 1, 74; CDALB 1640-1865

Hayashi, Fumiko 1904-1951 .... **TCLC 27**

Haycraft, Anna 19??
See Ellis, Alice Thomas

Hayden, Robert (Earl)
1913-1980 .... **CLC 5, 9, 14, 37**
See also CA 69-72; obituary CA 97-100; CABS 2; SATA 19; obituary SATA 26; DLB 5; CDALB 1941-1968

Hayman, Ronald 1932- .... **CLC 44**
See also CANR 18; CA 25-28R

Haywood, Eliza (Fowler) 1693?1756 .... **LC 1**
See also DLB 39

Hazzard, Shirley 1931- .... **CLC 18**
See also CANR 4; CA 9-12R; DLB-Y 82

H(ilda) D(oolittle)
1886-1961 .... **CLC 3, 8, 14, 31, 34**
See also Doolittle, Hilda

Head, Bessie 1937-1986 .... **CLC 25**
See also CA 29-32R; obituary CA 109

Headon, (Nicky) Topper 1956?
See The Clash

Heaney, Seamus (Justin)
1939- .... **CLC 5, 7, 14, 25, 37**
See also CA 85-88; DLB 40

Hearn, (Patricio) Lafcadio (Tessima Carlos)
1850-1904 .... **TCLC 9**
See also CA 105; DLB 12

Hearne, Vicki 1946- .... **CLC 56**

Heat Moon, William Least 1939- .... **CLC 29**

Hebert, Anne 1916- .... **CLC 4, 13, 29**
See also CA 85-88

Hecht, Anthony (Evan)
1923- .... **CLC 8, 13, 19**
See also CANR 6; CA 9-12R; DLB 5

Hecht, Ben 1894-1964 .... **CLC 8**
See also CA 85-88; DLB 7, 9, 25, 26, 28

Hedayat, Sadeq 1903-1951 .... **TCLC 21**
See also CA 120

Heidegger, Martin 1889-1976 .... **CLC 24**
See also CA 81-84; obituary CA 65-68

Heidenstam, (Karl Gustaf) Verner von
1859-1940 .... **TCLC 5**
See also CA 104

Heifner, Jack 1946- .... **CLC 11**
See also CA 105

Heijermans, Herman 1864-1924 .... **TCLC 24**

Heilbrun, Carolyn G(old) 1926- .... **CLC 25**
See also CANR 1; CA 45-48

Heine, Harry 1797-1856
See Heine, Heinrich

Heine, Heinrich 1797-1856 .... **NCLC 4**

Heinemann, Larry C(urtiss) 1944- .... **CLC 50**
See also CA 110

Heiney, Donald (William) 1921-
See Harris, MacDonald
See also CANR 3; CA 1-4R

Heinlein, Robert A(nson)
1907-1988 .... **CLC 1, 3, 8, 14, 26, 55**
See also CANR 1, 20; CA 1-4R; obituary CA 125; SATA 9; DLB 8

Heller, Joseph
1923- .... **CLC 1, 3, 5, 8, 11, 36**
See also CANR 8; CA 5-8R; CABS 1; DLB 2, 28; DLB-Y 80

Hellman, Lillian (Florence)
1905?1984 .... **CLC 2, 4, 8, 14, 18, 34, 44, 52**
See also CA 13-16R; obituary CA 112; DLB 7; DLB-Y 84

Helprin, Mark 1947- .... **CLC 7, 10, 22, 32**
See also CA 81-84; DLB-Y 85

Hemingway, Ernest (Miller)
1899-1961 .... **CLC 1, 3, 6, 8, 10, 13, 19, 30, 34, 39, 41, 44, 50; SSC 1**
See also CA 77-80; DLB 4, 9; DLB-Y 81; DLB-DS 1

Hempel, Amy 1951- .... **CLC 39**
See also CA 118

Henley, Beth 1952- .... **CLC 23**
See also Henley, Elizabeth Becker
See also DLB-Y 86

Henley, Elizabeth Becker 1952-
See Henley, Beth
See also CA 107

Henley, William Ernest
1849-1903 .... **TCLC 8**
See also CA 105; DLB 19

Hennissart, Martha
See Lathen, Emma
See also CA 85-88

Henry 1491-1547 .... **LC 10**

Henry, O. 1862-1910 .... **TCLC 1, 19**
See also Porter, William Sydney

Hentoff, Nat(han Irving) 1925- .... **CLC 26**
See also CLR 1; CAAS 6; CANR 5; CA 1-4R; SATA 27, 42

Heppenstall, (John) Rayner
1911-1981 .... **CLC 10**
See also CA 1-4R; obituary CA 103

Herbert, Frank (Patrick)
1920-1986 .... **CLC 12, 23, 35, 44**
See also CANR 5; CA 53-56; obituary CA 118; SATA 9, 37, 47; DLB 8

Herbert, Zbigniew 1924- .... **CLC 9, 43**
See also CA 89-92

Herbst, Josephine 1897-1969 .... **CLC 34**
See also CA 5-8R; obituary CA 25-28R; DLB 9

Herder, Johann Gottfried von
1744-1803 .... **NCLC 8**

Hergesheimer, Joseph
1880-1954 .... **TCLC 11**
See also CA 109; DLB 9

Herlagnez, Pablo de 1844-1896
See Verlaine, Paul (Marie)

Herlihy, James Leo 1927- .... **CLC 6**
See also CANR 2; CA 1-4R

Hernandez, Jose 1834-1886 .... **NCLC 17**

Herriot, James 1916- .... **CLC 12**
See also Wight, James Alfred

Herrmann, Dorothy 1941- .... **CLC 44**
See also CA 107

Hersey, John (Richard)
1914- .... **CLC 1, 2, 7, 9, 40**
See also CA 17-20R; SATA 25; DLB 6

Herzen, Aleksandr Ivanovich
1812-1870 .... **NCLC 10**

Herzog, Werner 1942- .... **CLC 16**
See also CA 89-92

Hesse, Hermann
1877-1962 .... **CLC 1, 2, 3, 6, 11, 17, 25**
See also CAP 2; CA 17-18

Heyen, William 1940- .... **CLC 13, 18**
See also CA 33-36R; DLB 5

Heyerdahl, Thor 1914- .... **CLC 26**
See also CANR 5, 22; CA 5-8R; SATA 2, 52

Heym, Georg (Theodor Franz Arthur)
1887-1912 .... **TCLC 9**
See also CA 106

Heym, Stefan 1913- .... **CLC 41**
See also CANR 4; CA 9-12R; DLB 69

Heyse, Paul (Johann Ludwig von)
1830-1914 .... **TCLC 8**
See also CA 104

Hibbert, Eleanor (Burford) 1906- .... **CLC 7**
See also CANR 9; CA 17-20R; SATA 2

Higgins, George V(incent)
1939- .... **CLC 4, 7, 10, 18**
See also CAAS 5; CANR 17; CA 77-80; DLB 2; DLB-Y 81

Highsmith, (Mary) Patricia
1921- .... **CLC 2, 4, 14, 42**
See also CANR 1, 20; CA 1-4R

Highwater, Jamake 1942- .... **CLC 12**
See also CAAS 7; CANR 10; CA 65-68; SATA 30, 32; DLB 52; DLB-Y 85

Hikmet (Ran), Nazim 1902-1963.... **CLC 40**
See also obituary CA 93-96

Hildesheimer, Wolfgang 1916- ..... **CLC 49**
See also CA 101; DLB 69

Hill, Geoffrey (William)
1932- .... **CLC 5, 8, 18, 45**
See also CANR 21; CA 81-84; DLB 40

Hill, George Roy 1922- .... **CLC 26**
See also CA 110

Hill, Susan B. 1942- .... **CLC 4**
See also CA 33-36R; DLB 14

Hilliard, Noel (Harvey) 1929- ...... **CLC 15**
See also CANR 7; CA 9-12R

Hilton, James 1900-1954 .... **TCLC 21**
See also CA 108; SATA 34; DLB 34

Himes, Chester (Bomar)
1909-1984 .... **CLC 2, 4, 7, 18**
See also CANR 22; CA 25-28R; obituary CA 114; DLB 2

Hinde, Thomas 1926- .... **CLC 6, 11**
See also Chitty, (Sir) Thomas Willes

Hine, (William) Daryl 1936- .... **CLC 15**
See also CANR 1, 20; CA 1-4R; DLB 60

Hinton, S(usan) E(loise) 1950- ..... **CLC 30**
See also CLR 3; CA 81-84; SATA 19

Hippius (Merezhkovsky), Zinaida (Nikolayevna) 1869-1945...... **TCLC 9**
See also Gippius, Zinaida (Nikolayevna)

Hiraoka, Kimitake 1925-1970
See Mishima, Yukio
See also CA 97-100; obituary CA 29-32R

Hirsch, Edward (Mark) 1950- ... **CLC 31, 50**
See also CANR 20; CA 104

Hitchcock, (Sir) Alfred (Joseph)
1899-1980 .... **CLC 16**
See also obituary CA 97-100; SATA 27; obituary SATA 24

Hoagland, Edward 1932- .... **CLC 28**
See also CANR 2; CA 1-4R; SATA 51; DLB 6

Hoban, Russell C(onwell) 1925- .. **CLC 7, 25**
See also CLR 3; CA 5-8R; SATA 1, 40; DLB 52

Hobson, Laura Z(ametkin)
1900-1986 .... **CLC 7, 25**
See also CA 17-20R; obituary CA 118; SATA 52; DLB 28

Hochhuth, Rolf 1931- .... **CLC 4, 11, 18**
See also CA 5-8R

Hochman, Sandra 1936- .... **CLC 3, 8**
See also CA 5-8R; DLB 5

Hochwalder, Fritz 1911-1986 ...... **CLC 36**
See also CA 29-32R; obituary CA 120

Hocking, Mary (Eunice) 1921- ..... **CLC 13**
See also CANR 18; CA 101

Hodgins, Jack 1938- .... **CLC 23**
See also CA 93-96; DLB 60

Hodgson, William Hope
1877-1918 .... **TCLC 13**
See also CA 111; DLB 70

Hoffman, Alice 1952- .... **CLC 51**
See also CA 77-80

Hoffman, Daniel (Gerard)
1923- .... **CLC 6, 13, 23**
See also CANR 4; CA 1-4R; DLB 5

Hoffman, Stanley 1944- .... **CLC 5**
See also CA 77-80

Hoffman, William M(oses) 1939- ... **CLC 40**
See also CANR 11; CA 57-60

Hoffmann, Ernst Theodor Amadeus
1776-1822 .... **NCLC 2**
See also SATA 27

Hoffmann, Gert 1932- .... **CLC 54**

Hofmannsthal, Hugo (Laurenz August Hofmann Edler) von
1874-1929 .... **TCLC 11**
See also CA 106

Hogg, James 1770-1835 .... **NCLC 4**

Holberg, Ludvig 1684-1754 .... **LC 6**

Holden, Ursula 1921- .... **CLC 18**
See also CANR 22; CA 101

Holderlin, (Johann Christian) Friedrich
1770-1843 .... **NCLC 16**

Holdstock, Robert (P.) 1948- .... **CLC 39**

Holland, Isabelle 1920- .... **CLC 21**
See also CANR 10; CA 21-24R; SATA 8

Holland, Marcus 1900-1985
See Caldwell, (Janet Miriam) Taylor (Holland)

Hollander, John 1929- ...... **CLC 2, 5, 8, 14**
See also CANR 1; CA 1-4R; SATA 13; DLB 5

Holleran, Andrew 1943?........... **CLC 38**

Hollinghurst, Alan 1954- .... **CLC 55**
See also CA 114

Hollis, Jim 1916-
See Summers, Hollis (Spurgeon, Jr.)

Holmes, John Clellon 1926-1988.... **CLC 56**
See also CANR 4; CA 9-10R; obituary CA 125; DLB 16

Holmes, Oliver Wendell
1809-1894 .... **NCLC 14**
See also SATA 34; DLB 1; CDALB 1640-1865

Holt, Victoria 1906-
See Hibbert, Eleanor (Burford)

Holub, Miroslav 1923- .... **CLC 4**
See also CANR 10; CA 21-24R

Homer c. 8th century B.C. .... **CMLC 1**

Honig, Edwin 1919- .... **CLC 33**
See also CANR 4; CA 5-8R; DLB 5

Hood, Hugh (John Blagdon)
1928- .... **CLC 15, 28**
See also CANR 1; CA 49-52; DLB 53

Hood, Thomas 1799-1845......... **NCLC 16**

Hooker, (Peter) Jeremy 1941- ...... **CLC 43**
See also CANR 22; CA 77-80; DLB 40

Hope, A(lec) D(erwent) 1907- .... **CLC 3, 51**
See also CA 21-24R

Hope, Christopher (David Tully)
1944- .... **CLC 52**
See also CA 106

Hopkins, Gerard Manley
1844-1889 .... **NCLC 17**
See also DLB 35, 57

Hopkins, John (Richard) 1931- ...... **CLC 4**
See also CA 85-88

Hopkins, Pauline Elizabeth
1859-1930 .... **TCLC 28**
See also DLB 50

Horgan, Paul 1903- .... **CLC 9, 53**
See also CANR 9; CA 13-16R; SATA 13; DLB-Y 85

Horovitz, Israel 1939- .... **CLC 56**

Horwitz, Julius 1920-1986......... **CLC 14**
See also CANR 12; CA 9-12R; obituary CA 119

Hospital, Janette Turner 1942- ..... **CLC 42**
See also CA 108

Hostos (y Bonilla), Eugenio Maria de
1893-1903 .... **TCLC 24**

Hougan, Carolyn 19?? .... **CLC 34**

Household, Geoffrey (Edward West)
1900- .... **CLC 11**
See also CA 77-80; SATA 14

Housman, A(lfred) E(dward)
1859-1936 .... **TCLC 1, 10**
See also CA 104; DLB 19

Housman, Laurence 1865-1959 ..... **TCLC 7**
See also CA 106; SATA 25; DLB 10

Howard, Elizabeth Jane 1923- ... **CLC 7, 29**
See also CANR 8; CA 5-8R

Howard, Maureen 1930- ..... **CLC 5, 14, 46**
See also CA 53-56; DLB-Y 83

Howard, Richard 1929- ...... **CLC 7, 10, 47**
See also CA 85-88; DLB 5

Howard, Robert E(rvin)
1906-1936 .... **TCLC 8**
See also CA 105

Howe, Fanny 1940- .... **CLC 47**
See also CA 117; SATA 52

Howe, Julia Ward 1819-1910 ..... **TCLC 21**
See also CA 117; DLB 1

Howe, Tina 1937- .... **CLC 48**
See also CA 109

Howells, William Dean
1837-1920 .... **TCLC 7, 17**
See also CA 104; DLB 12, 64; CDALB 1865-1917

Howes, Barbara 1914- .... **CLC 15**
See also CAAS 3; CA 9-12R; SATA 5

Hrabal, Bohumil 1914- .... **CLC 13**
See also CA 106

Hubbard, L(afayette) Ron(ald)
1911-1986 .... **CLC 43**
See also CANR 22; CA 77-80; obituary CA 118

Huch, Ricarda (Octavia)
1864-1947 . . . . **TCLC 13**
See also CA 111

Huddle, David 1942- . . . . **CLC 49**
See also CA 57-60

Hudson, W(illiam) H(enry)
1841-1922 . . . . **TCLC 29**
See also CA 115; SATA 35

Hueffer, Ford Madox 1873-1939
See Ford, Ford Madox

Hughart, Barry 1934- . . . . **CLC 39**

Hughes, David (John) 1930- . . . . **CLC 48**
See also CA 116; DLB 14

Hughes, Edward James 1930-
See Hughes, Ted

Hughes, (James) Langston
1902-1967 . . . . . **CLC 1, 5, 10, 15, 35, 44**
See also CANR 1; CA 1-4R;
obituary CA 25-28R; SATA 4, 33;
DLB 4, 7, 48, 51

Hughes, Richard (Arthur Warren)
1900-1976 . . . . **CLC 1, 11**
See also CANR 4; CA 5-8R;
obituary CA 65-68; SATA 8;
obituary SATA 25; DLB 15

Hughes, Ted 1930- . . . . . **CLC 2, 4, 9, 14, 37**
See also CLR 3; CANR 1; CA 1-4R;
SATA 27, 49; DLB 40

Hugo, Richard F(ranklin)
1923-1982 . . . . **CLC 6, 18, 32**
See also CANR 3; CA 49-52;
obituary CA 108; DLB 5

Hugo, Victor Marie
1802-1885 . . . . **NCLC 3, 10, 21**
See also SATA 47

Huidobro, Vicente 1893-1948 . . . . . **TCLC 31**

Hulme, Keri 1947- . . . . **CLC 39**

Hulme, T(homas) E(rnest)
1883-1917 . . . . **TCLC 21**
See also CA 117; DLB 19

Hume, David 1711-1776. . . . . **LC 7**

Humphrey, William 1924- . . . . **CLC 45**
See also CA 77-80; DLB 6

Humphreys, Emyr (Owen) 1919- . . . . **CLC 47**
See also CANR 3; CA 5-8R; DLB 15

Humphreys, Josephine 1945- . . . . **CLC 34**
See also CA 121

Hunt, E(verette) Howard (Jr.)
1918- . . . . **CLC 3**
See also CANR 2; CA 45-48

Hunt, (James Henry) Leigh
1784-1859 . . . . **NCLC 1**

Hunter, Evan 1926- . . . . **CLC 11, 31**
See also CANR 5; CA 5-8R; SATA 25;
DLB-Y 82

Hunter, Kristin (Eggleston) 1931- . . . **CLC 35**
See also CLR 3; CANR 13; CA 13-16R;
SATA 12; DLB 33

Hunter, Mollie (Maureen McIlwraith)
1922- . . . . **CLC 21**
See also McIlwraith, Maureen Mollie
Hunter

Hunter, Robert (d.?1734 . . . . **LC 7**

Hurston, Zora Neale
1891-1960 . . . . **CLC 7, 30**
See also CA 85-88; DLB 51

Huston, John (Marcellus) 1906- . . . . **CLC 20**
See also CA 73-76; DLB 26

Huxley, Aldous (Leonard)
1894-1963 . . **CLC 1, 3, 4, 5, 8, 11, 18, 35**
See also CA 85-88; DLB 36

Huysmans, Charles Marie Georges
1848-1907
See Huysmans, Joris-Karl
See also CA 104

Huysmans, Joris-Karl 1848-1907 . . **NCLC 7**
See also Huysmans, Charles Marie Georges

Hwang, David Henry 1957- . . . . **CLC 55**
See also CA 127

Hyde, Anthony 1946? . . . . **CLC 42**

Hyde, Margaret O(ldroyd) 1917- . . . **CLC 21**
See also CANR 1; CA 1-4R; SATA 1, 42

Ian, Janis 1951- . . . . **CLC 21**
See also CA 105

Ibarguengoitia, Jorge 1928-1983 . . . . **CLC 37**
See also obituary CA 113

Ibsen, Henrik (Johan)
1828-1906 . . . . **TCLC 2, 8, 16**
See also CA 104

Ibuse, Masuji 1898- . . . . **CLC 22**

Ichikawa, Kon 1915- . . . . **CLC 20**
See also CA 121

Idle, Eric 1943-
See Monty Python
See also CA 116

Ignatow, David 1914- . . . . . . **CLC 4, 7, 14, 40**
See also CAAS 3; CA 9-12R; DLB 5

Ihimaera, Witi (Tame) 1944- . . . . **CLC 46**
See also CA 77-80

Ilf, Ilya 1897-1937 and **Petrov, Evgeny**
1897-1937 . . . . **TCLC 21**

Immermann, Karl (Lebrecht)
1796-1840 . . . . **NCLC 4**

Ingalls, Rachel 19?? . . . . **CLC 42**

Inge, William (Motter)
1913-1973 . . . . **CLC 1, 8, 19**
See also CA 9-12R; DLB 7;
CDALB 1941-1968

Innaurato, Albert 1948- . . . . **CLC 21**
See also CA 115, 122

Innes, Michael 1906-
See Stewart, J(ohn) I(nnes) M(ackintosh)

Ionesco, Eugene
1912- . . . . **CLC 1, 4, 6, 9, 11, 15, 41**
See also CA 9-12R; SATA 7

Iqbal, Muhammad 1877-1938 . . . . . **TCLC 28**

Irving, John (Winslow)
1942- . . . . **CLC 13, 23, 38**
See also CA 25-28R; DLB 6; DLB-Y 82

Irving, Washington
1783-1859 . . . . **NCLC 2, 19; SSC 2**
See also YABC 2; DLB 3, 11, 30;
CDALB 1640-1865

Isaacs, Susan 1943- . . . . **CLC 32**
See also CANR 20; CA 89-92

Isherwood, Christopher (William Bradshaw)
1904-1986 . . . . **CLC 1, 9, 11, 14, 44**
See also CA 13-16R; obituary CA 117;
DLB 15; DLB-Y 86

Ishiguro, Kazuo 1954? . . . . **CLC 27, 56**
See also CA 120

Ishikawa Takuboku 1885-1912 . . . . **TCLC 15**
See also CA 113

Iskander, Fazil (Abdulovich)
1929- . . . . **CLC 47**
See also CA 102

Ivanov, Vyacheslav (Ivanovich)
1866-1949 . . . . **TCLC 33**
See also CA 122

Ivask, Ivar (Vidrik) 1927- . . . . **CLC 14**
See also CA 37-40R

Jackson, Jesse 1908-1983 . . . . **CLC 12**
See also CA 25-28R; obituary CA 109;
SATA 2, 29, 48

Jackson, Laura (Riding) 1901-
See Riding, Laura
See also CA 65-68; DLB 48

Jackson, Shirley 1919-1965 . . . . **CLC 11**
See also CANR 4; CA 1-4R;
obituary CA 25-28R; SATA 2; DLB 6;
CDALB 1941-1968

Jacob, (Cyprien) Max 1876-1944 . . . **TCLC 6**
See also CA 104

Jacob, Piers A(nthony) D(illingham) 1934-
See Anthony (Jacob), Piers
See also CA 21-24R

Jacobs, Jim 1942- and **Casey, Warren**
1942- . . . . **CLC 12**

Jacobs, Jim 1942-
See Jacobs, Jim and Casey, Warren
See also CA 97-100

Jacobs, W(illiam) W(ymark)
1863-1943 . . . . **TCLC 22**
See also CA 121

Jacobsen, Josephine 1908- . . . . **CLC 48**
See also CA 33-36R

Jacobson, Dan 1929- . . . . **CLC 4, 14**
See also CANR 2; CA 1-4R; DLB 14

Jagger, Mick 1944- and **Richard, Keith**
1944- . . . . **CLC 17**

Jagger, Mick 1944-
See Jagger, Mick and Richard, Keith

Jakes, John (William) 1932- . . . . **CLC 29**
See also CANR 10; CA 57-60; DLB-Y 83

James, C(yril) L(ionel) R(obert)
1901- . . . . **CLC 33**
See also CA 117

James, Daniel 1911-
See Santiago, Danny

James, Henry (Jr.)
1843-1916 . . . . **TCLC 2, 11, 24**
See also CA 104; DLB 12, 71;
CDALB 1865-1917

James, M(ontague) R(hodes)
1862-1936 . . . . **TCLC 6**
See also CA 104

James, P(hyllis) D(orothy)
1920- . . . . **CLC 18, 46**
See also CANR 17; CA 21-24R

James, William 1842-1910 ..... **TCLC 15, 32**
See also CA 109

Jami, Nur al-Din 'Abd al-Rahman 1414-1492 ..... **LC 9**

Jandl, Ernst 1925- ..... **CLC 34**

Janowitz, Tama 1957- ..... **CLC 43**
See also CA 106

Jarrell, Randall 1914-1965 ..... **CLC 1, 2, 6, 9, 13, 49**
See also CLR 6; CANR 6; CA 5-8R; obituary CA 25-28R; CABS 2; SATA 7; DLB 48, 52; CDALB 1941-1968

Jarry, Alfred 1873-1907 ..... **TCLC 2, 14**
See also CA 104

Jeake, Samuel, Jr. 1889-1973
See Aiken, Conrad

Jean Paul 1763-1825 ..... **NCLC 7**

Jeffers, (John) Robinson 1887-1962 ..... **CLC 2, 3, 11, 15, 54**
See also CA 85-88; DLB 45

Jefferson, Thomas 1743-1826 ..... **NCLC 11**
See also DLB 31; CDALB 1640-1865

Jellicoe, (Patricia) Ann 1927- ..... **CLC 27**
See also CA 85-88; DLB 13

Jenkins, (John) Robin 1912- ..... **CLC 52**
See also CANR 1; CA 4Rk; DLB 14

Jennings, Elizabeth (Joan) 1926- ..... **CLC 5, 14**
See also CAAS 5; CANR 8; CA 61-64; DLB 27

Jennings, Waylon 1937- ..... **CLC 21**

Jensen, Laura (Linnea) 1948- ..... **CLC 37**
See also CA 103

Jerome, Jerome K. 1859-1927 ..... **TCLC 23**
See also CA 119; DLB 10, 34

Jerrold, Douglas William 1803-1857 ..... **NCLC 2**

Jewett, (Theodora) Sarah Orne 1849-1909 ..... **TCLC 1, 22**
See also CA 108; SATA 15; DLB 12

Jewsbury, Geraldine (Endsor) 1812-1880 ..... **NCLC 22**
See also DLB 21

Jhabvala, Ruth Prawer 1927- ..... **CLC 4, 8, 29**
See also CANR 2; CA 1-4R

Jiles, Paulette 1943- ..... **CLC 13**
See also CA 101

Jimenez (Mantecon), Juan Ramon 1881-1958 ..... **TCLC 4**
See also CA 104

Joel, Billy 1949- ..... **CLC 26**
See also Joel, William Martin

Joel, William Martin 1949-
See Joel, Billy
See also CA 108

Johnson, B(ryan) S(tanley William) 1933-1973 ..... **CLC 6, 9**
See also CANR 9; CA 9-12R; obituary CA 53-56; DLB 14, 40

Johnson, Charles (Richard) 1948- ..... **CLC 7, 51**
See also CA 116; DLB 33

Johnson, Denis 1949- ..... **CLC 52**
See also CA 117, 121

Johnson, Diane 1934- ..... **CLC 5, 13, 48**
See also CANR 17; CA 41-44R; DLB-Y 80

Johnson, Eyvind (Olof Verner) 1900-1976 ..... **CLC 14**
See also CA 73-76; obituary CA 69-72

Johnson, James Weldon 1871-1938 ..... **TCLC 3, 19**
See also Johnson, James William
See also CA 104; DLB 51

Johnson, James William 1871-1938
See Johnson, James Weldon
See also SATA 31

Johnson, Lionel (Pigot) 1867-1902 ..... **TCLC 19**
See also CA 117; DLB 19

Johnson, Marguerita 1928-
See Angelou, Maya

Johnson, Pamela Hansford 1912-1981 ..... **CLC 1, 7, 27**
See also CANR 2; CA 1-4R; obituary CA 104; DLB 15

Johnson, Uwe 1934-1984 ..... **CLC 5, 10, 15, 40**
See also CANR 1; CA 1-4R; obituary CA 112

Johnston, George (Benson) 1913- ..... **CLC 51**
See also CANR 5, 20; CA 1-4R

Johnston, Jennifer 1930- ..... **CLC 7**
See also CA 85-88; DLB 14

Jolley, Elizabeth 1923- ..... **CLC 46**

Jones, David 1895-1974 ..... **CLC 2, 4, 7, 13, 42**
See also CA 9-12R; obituary CA 53-56; DLB 20

Jones, David Robert 1947-
See Bowie, David
See also CA 103

Jones, D(ouglas) G(ordon) 1929- ..... **CLC 10**
See also CANR 13; CA 113; DLB 53

Jones, Diana Wynne 1934- ..... **CLC 26**
See also CANR 4; CA 49-52; SATA 9

Jones, Gayl 1949- ..... **CLC 6, 9**
See also CA 77-80; DLB 33

Jones, James 1921-1977 ..... **CLC 1, 3, 10, 39**
See also CANR 6; CA 1-4R; obituary CA 69-72; DLB 2

Jones, (Everett) LeRoi 1934- ..... **CLC 1, 2, 3, 5, 10, 14, 33**
See also Baraka, Amiri; Baraka, Imamu Amiri
See also CA 21-24R

Jones, Madison (Percy, Jr.) 1925- ..... **CLC 4**
See also CANR 7; CA 13-16R

Jones, Mervyn 1922- ..... **CLC 10, 52**
See also CAAS 5; CANR 1; CA 45-48

Jones, Mick 1956?
See The Clash

Jones, Nettie 19?? ..... **CLC 34**

Jones, Preston 1936-1979 ..... **CLC 10**
See also CA 73-76; obituary CA 89-92; DLB 7

Jones, Robert F(rancis) 1934- ..... **CLC 7**
See also CANR 2; CA 49-52

Jones, Rod 1953- ..... **CLC 50**

Jones, Terry 1942?
See Monty Python
See also CA 112, 116; SATA 51

Jong, Erica 1942- ..... **CLC 4, 6, 8, 18**
See also CA 73-76; DLB 2, 5, 28

Jonson, Ben(jamin) 1572-1637 ..... **LC 6**
See also DLB 62

Jordan, June 1936- ..... **CLC 5, 11, 23**
See also CLR 10; CA 33-36R; SATA 4; DLB 38

Jordan, Pat(rick M.) 1941- ..... **CLC 37**
See also CA 33-36R

Josipovici, Gabriel (David) 1940- ..... **CLC 6, 43**
See also CA 37-40R; DLB 14

Joubert, Joseph 1754-1824 ..... **NCLC 9**

Jouve, Pierre Jean 1887-1976 ..... **CLC 47**
See also obituary CA 65-68

Joyce, James (Augustine Aloysius) 1882-1941 ..... **TCLC 3, 8, 16, 26; SSC 3**
See also CA 104, 126; DLB 10, 19, 36

Jozsef, Attila 1905-1937 ..... **TCLC 22**
See also CA 116

Juana Ines de la Cruz 1651?1695 ..... **LC 5**

Julian of Norwich 1342?1416? ..... **LC 6**

Just, Ward S(wift) 1935- ..... **CLC 4, 27**
See also CA 25-28R

Justice, Donald (Rodney) 1925- ..... **CLC 6, 19**
See also CA 5-8R; DLB-Y 83

Kacew, Romain 1914-1980
See Gary, Romain
See also CA 108; obituary CA 102

Kacewgary, Romain 1914-1980
See Gary, Romain

Kadare, Ismail 1936- ..... **CLC 52**

Kafka, Franz 1883-1924 ..... **TCLC 2, 6, 13, 29**
See also CA 105

Kahn, Roger 1927- ..... **CLC 30**
See also CA 25-28R; SATA 37

Kaiser, (Friedrich Karl) Georg 1878-1945 ..... **TCLC 9**
See also CA 106

Kaletski, Alexander 1946- ..... **CLC 39**
See also CA 118

Kallman, Chester (Simon) 1921-1975 ..... **CLC 2**
See also CANR 3; CA 45-48; obituary CA 53-56

Kaminsky, Melvin 1926-
See Brooks, Mel
See also CANR 16

Kane, Paul 1941-
See Simon, Paul

Kanin, Garson 1912- ..... **CLC 22**
See also CANR 7; CA 5-8R; DLB 7

Kaniuk, Yoram 1930- ..... **CLC 19**

Kantor, MacKinlay 1904-1977 ..... **CLC 7**
See also CA 61-64; obituary CA 73-76; DLB 9

Kaplan, David Michael 1946- . . . . . . **CLC 50**

Karamzin, Nikolai Mikhailovich 1766-1826 . . . . **NCLC 3**

Karapanou, Margarita 1946- . . . . **CLC 13**
See also CA 101

Karl, Frederick R(obert) 1927- . . . . . **CLC 34**
See also CANR 3; CA 5-8R

Kassef, Romain 1914-1980
See Gary, Romain

Katz, Steve 1935- . . . . **CLC 47**
See also CANR 12; CA 25-28R; DLB-Y 83

Kauffman, Janet 1945- . . . . **CLC 42**
See also CA 117; DLB-Y 86

Kaufman, Bob (Garnell) 1925-1986 . . . . **CLC 49**
See also CANR 22; CA 41-44R; obituary CA 118; DLB 16, 41

Kaufman, George S(imon) 1889-1961 . . . . **CLC 38**
See also CA 108; obituary CA 93-96; DLB 7

Kaufman, Sue 1926-1977 . . . . **CLC 3, 8**
See also Barondess, Sue K(aufman)

Kavan, Anna 1904-1968 . . . . **CLC 5, 13**
See also Edmonds, Helen (Woods)
See also CANR 6; CA 5-8R

Kavanagh, Patrick (Joseph Gregory) 1905-1967 . . . . **CLC 22**
See also obituary CA 25-28R; DLB 15, 20

Kawabata, Yasunari 1899-1972 . . . . **CLC 2, 5, 9, 18**
See also CA 93-96; obituary CA 33-36R

Kaye, M(ary) M(argaret) 1909? . . . . **CLC 28**
See also CA 89-92

Kaye, Mollie 1909?
See Kaye, M(ary) M(argaret)

Kaye-Smith, Sheila 1887-1956. . . . . **TCLC 20**
See also CA 118; DLB 36

Kazan, Elia 1909- . . . . **CLC 6, 16**
See also CA 21-24R

Kazantzakis, Nikos 1885?1957 . . . . **TCLC 2, 5, 33**
See also CA 105

Kazin, Alfred 1915- . . . . **CLC 34, 38**
See also CAAS 7; CANR 1; CA 1-4R

Keane, Mary Nesta (Skrine) 1904-
See Keane, Molly
See also CA 108, 114

Keane, Molly 1904- . . . . **CLC 31**
See also Keane, Mary Nesta (Skrine)

Keates, Jonathan 19?? . . . . **CLC 34**

Keaton, Buster 1895-1966 . . . . **CLC 20**

Keaton, Joseph Francis 1895-1966
See Keaton, Buster

Keats, John 1795-1821. . . . . **NCLC 8**

Keene, Donald 1922- . . . . **CLC 34**
See also CANR 5; CA 1-4R

Keillor, Garrison 1942- . . . . **CLC 40**
See also Keillor, Gary (Edward)
See also CA 111

Keillor, Gary (Edward)
See Keillor, Garrison
See also CA 117

Kell, Joseph 1917-
See Burgess (Wilson, John) Anthony

Keller, Gottfried 1819-1890. . . . . . . **NCLC 2**

Kellerman, Jonathan (S.) 1949- . . . . . **CLC 44**
See also CA 106

Kelley, William Melvin 1937- . . . . . . **CLC 22**
See also CA 77-80; DLB 33

Kellogg, Marjorie 1922- . . . . **CLC 2**
See also CA 81-84

Kelly, M. T. 1947- . . . . **CLC 55**
See also CANR 19; CA 97-100

Kemal, Yashar 1922- . . . . **CLC 14, 29**
See also CA 89-92

Kemble, Fanny 1809-1893 . . . . **NCLC 18**
See also DLB 32

Kemelman, Harry 1908- . . . . **CLC 2**
See also CANR 6; CA 9-12R; DLB 28

Kempe, Margery 1373?1440? . . . . **LC 6**

Kempis, Thomas á 1380-1471 . . . . **LC 11**

Kendall, Henry 1839-1882. . . . . . . **NCLC 12**

Keneally, Thomas (Michael) 1935- . . . . . . **CLC 5, 8, 10, 14, 19, 27, 43**
See also CANR 10; CA 85-88

Kennedy, John Pendleton 1795-1870 . . . . **NCLC 2**
See also DLB 3

Kennedy, Joseph Charles 1929-
See Kennedy, X. J.
See also CANR 4; CA 1-4R; SATA 14

Kennedy, William (Joseph) 1928- . . . . **CLC 6, 28, 34, 53**
See also CANR 14; CA 85-88; DLB-Y 85; AAYA 1

Kennedy, X. J. 1929- . . . . **CLC 8, 42**
See also Kennedy, Joseph Charles
See also DLB 5

Kerouac, Jack 1922-1969 . . . . **CLC 1, 2, 3, 5, 14, 29**
See also Kerouac, Jean-Louis Lebrid de
See also DLB 2, 16; DLB-DS 3; CDALB 1941-1968

Kerouac, Jean-Louis Lebrid de 1922-1969
See Kerouac, Jack
See also CA 5-8R; obituary CA 25-28R; CDALB 1941-1968

Kerr, Jean 1923- . . . . **CLC 22**
See also CANR 7; CA 5-8R

Kerr, M. E. 1927- . . . . **CLC 12, 35**
See also Meaker, Marijane
See also SAAS 1

Kerr, Robert 1970? . . . . **CLC 55**

Kerrigan, (Thomas) Anthony 1918- . . . . **CLC 4, 6**
See also CANR 4; CA 49-52

Kesey, Ken (Elton) 1935- . . . . **CLC 1, 3, 6, 11, 46**
See also CANR 22; CA 1-4R; DLB 2, 16

Kesselring, Joseph (Otto) 1902-1967 . . . . **CLC 45**

Kessler, Jascha (Frederick) 1929- . . . . **CLC 4**
See also CANR 8; CA 17-20R

Kettelkamp, Larry 1933- . . . . **CLC 12**
See also CANR 16; CA 29-32R; SAAS 3; SATA 2

Kherdian, David 1931- . . . . **CLC 6, 9**
See also CAAS 2; CA 21-24R; SATA 16

Khlebnikov, Velimir (Vladimirovich) 1885-1922 . . . . **TCLC 20**
See also CA 117

Khodasevich, Vladislav (Felitsianovich) 1886-1939 . . . . **TCLC 15**
See also CA 115

Kielland, Alexander (Lange) 1849-1906 . . . . **TCLC 5**
See also CA 104

Kiely, Benedict 1919- . . . . **CLC 23, 43**
See also CANR 2; CA 1-4R; DLB 15

Kienzle, William X(avier) 1928- . . . . **CLC 25**
See also CAAS 1; CANR 9; CA 93-96

Killens, John Oliver 1916- . . . . **CLC 10**
See also CAAS 2; CA 77-80; DLB 33

Killigrew, Anne 1660-1685. . . . . **LC 4**

Kincaid, Jamaica 1949? . . . . **CLC 43**

King, Francis (Henry) 1923- . . . . . **CLC 8, 53**
See also CANR 1; CA 1-4R; DLB 15

King, Stephen (Edwin) 1947- . . . . **CLC 12, 26, 37**
See also CANR 1; CA 61-64; SATA 9; DLB-Y 80

Kingman, (Mary) Lee 1919-. . . . . **CLC 17**
See also Natti, (Mary) Lee
See also CA 5-8R; SATA 1

Kingsley, Sidney 1906- . . . . **CLC 44**
See also CA 85-88; DLB 7

Kingsolver, Barbara 1955- . . . . **CLC 55**

Kingston, Maxine Hong 1940- . . **CLC 12, 19**
See also CANR 13; CA 69-72; SATA 53; DLB-Y 80

Kinnell, Galway 1927- . . . . **CLC 1, 2, 3, 5, 13, 29**
See also CANR 10; CA 9-12R; DLB 5

Kinsella, Thomas 1928- . . . . . . **CLC 4, 19, 43**
See also CANR 15; CA 17-20R; DLB 27

Kinsella, W(illiam) P(atrick) 1935- . . . . **CLC 27, 43**
See also CAAS 7; CANR 21; CA 97-100

Kipling, (Joseph) Rudyard 1865-1936 . . . . **TCLC 8, 17**
See also YABC 2; CA 20, 105; DLB 19, 34

Kirkup, James 1918- . . . . **CLC 1**
See also CAAS 4; CANR 2; CA 1-4R; SATA 12; DLB 27

Kirkwood, James 1930- . . . . **CLC 9**
See also CANR 6; CA 1-4R

Kizer, Carolyn (Ashley) 1925- . . . **CLC 15, 39**
See also CAAS 5; CA 65-68; DLB 5

Klausner, Amos 1939-
See Oz, Amos

Klein, A(braham) M(oses) 1909-1972 . . . . **CLC 19**
See also CA 101; obituary CA 37-40R

Klein, Norma 1938- . . . . **CLC 30**
See also CLR 2; CANR 15; CA 41-44R; SAAS 1; SATA 7

Klein, T.E.D. 19?? . . . . **CLC 34**
See also CA 119

Kleist, Heinrich von 1777-1811. . . . **NCLC 2**

Klima, Ivan 1931- . . . . **CLC 56**

Klimentev, Andrei Platonovich 1899-1951
See Platonov, Andrei (Platonovich)
See also CA 108

Klinger, Friedrich Maximilian von 1752-1831 . . . . **NCLC 1**

Klopstock, Friedrich Gottlieb 1724-1803 . . . . **NCLC 11**

Knebel, Fletcher 1911- . . . . **CLC 14**
See also CAAS 3; CANR 1; CA 1-4R; SATA 36

Knight, Etheridge 1931- . . . . **CLC 40**
See also CA 21-24R; DLB 41

Knight, Sarah Kemble 1666-1727 . . . . . **LC 7**
See also DLB 24

Knowles, John 1926- . . . . . . **CLC 1, 4, 10, 26**
See also CA 17-20R; SATA 8; DLB 6

Koch, C(hristopher) J(ohn) 1932- . . . **CLC 42**

Koch, Kenneth 1925- . . . . **CLC 5, 8, 44**
See also CANR 6; CA 1-4R; DLB 5

Kochanowski, Jan 1530-1584 . . . . **LC 10**

Kock, Charles Paul de 1794-1871 . . . . **NCLC 16**

Koestler, Arthur 1905-1983 . . . . **CLC 1, 3, 6, 8, 15, 33**
See also CANR 1; CA 1-4R; obituary CA 109; DLB-Y 83

Kohout, Pavel 1928- . . . . **CLC 13**
See also CANR 3; CA 45-48

Konigsberg, Allen Stewart 1935-
See Allen, Woody

Konrad, Gyorgy 1933- . . . . **CLC 4, 10**
See also CA 85-88

Konwicki, Tadeusz 1926- . . . . . **CLC 8, 28, 54**
See also CA 101

Kopit, Arthur (Lee) 1937- . . . . **CLC 1, 18, 33**
See also CA 81-84; DLB 7

Kops, Bernard 1926- . . . . **CLC 4**
See also CA 5-8R; DLB 13

Kornbluth, C(yril) M. 1923-1958 . . . . **TCLC 8**
See also CA 105; DLB 8

Korolenko, Vladimir (Galaktionovich) 1853-1921 . . . . **TCLC 22**
See also CA 121

Kosinski, Jerzy (Nikodem) 1933- . . . . **CLC 1, 2, 3, 6, 10, 15, 53**
See also CANR 9; CA 17-20R; DLB 2; DLB-Y 82

Kostelanetz, Richard (Cory) 1940- . . **CLC 28**
See also CA 13-16R

Kostrowitzki, Wilhelm Apollinaris de 1880-1918
See Apollinaire, Guillaume
See also CA 104

Kotlowitz, Robert 1924- . . . . **CLC 4**
See also CA 33-36R

Kotzwinkle, William 1938- . . . **CLC 5, 14, 35**
See also CLR 6; CANR 3; CA 45-48; SATA 24

Kozol, Jonathan 1936- . . . . **CLC 17**
See also CANR 16; CA 61-64

Kozoll, Michael 1940?
See Bochco, Steven and Kozoll, Michael

Kramer, Kathryn 19?? . . . . **CLC 34**

Kramer, Larry 1935- . . . . **CLC 42**

Krasicki, Ignacy 1735-1801 . . . . **NCLC 8**

Krasinski, Zygmunt 1812-1859 . . . . **NCLC 4**

Kraus, Karl 1874-1936 . . . . **TCLC 5**
See also CA 104

Kreve, Vincas 1882-1959 . . . . **TCLC 27**

Kristofferson, Kris 1936- . . . . **CLC 26**
See also CA 104

Krleza, Miroslav 1893-1981 . . . . **CLC 8**
See also CA 97-100; obituary CA 105

Kroetsch, Robert 1927- . . . . **CLC 5, 23**
See also CANR 8; CA 17-20R; DLB 53

Kroetz, Franz Xaver 1946- . . . . **CLC 41**

Krotkov, Yuri 1917- . . . . **CLC 19**
See also CA 102

Krumgold, Joseph (Quincy) 1908-1980 . . . . **CLC 12**
See also CANR 7; CA 9-12R; obituary CA 101; SATA 48; obituary SATA 23

Krutch, Joseph Wood 1893-1970 . . . . **CLC 24**
See also CANR 4; CA 1-4R; obituary CA 25-28R; DLB 63

Krylov, Ivan Andreevich 1768?1844 . . . . **NCLC 1**

Kubin, Alfred 1877-1959 . . . . **TCLC 23**
See also CA 112

Kubrick, Stanley 1928- . . . . **CLC 16**
See also CA 81-84; DLB 26

Kumin, Maxine (Winokur) 1925- . . . . **CLC 5, 13, 28**
See also CANR 1, 21; CA 1-4R; SATA 12; DLB 5

Kundera, Milan 1929- . . . . . **CLC 4, 9, 19, 32**
See also CANR 19; CA 85-88

Kunitz, Stanley J(asspon) 1905- . . . . **CLC 6, 11, 14**
See also CA 41-44R; DLB 48

Kunze, Reiner 1933- . . . . **CLC 10**
See also CA 93-96

Kuprin, Aleksandr (Ivanovich) 1870-1938 . . . . **TCLC 5**
See also CA 104

Kurosawa, Akira 1910- . . . . **CLC 16**
See also CA 101

Kuttner, Henry 1915-1958 . . . . **TCLC 10**
See also CA 107; DLB 8

Kuzma, Greg 1944- . . . . **CLC 7**
See also CA 33-36R

Labrunie, Gerard 1808-1855
See Nerval, Gerard de

Laclos, Pierre Ambroise Francois Choderlos de 1741-1803 . . . . **NCLC 4**

La Fayette, Marie (Madelaine Pioche de la Vergne, Comtesse) de 1634-1693 . . . . **LC 2**

Lafayette, Rene
See Hubbard, L(afayette) Ron(ald)

Laforgue, Jules 1860-1887 . . . . **NCLC 5**

Lagerkvist, Par (Fabian) 1891-1974 . . . . **CLC 7, 10, 13, 54**
See also CA 85-88; obituary CA 49-52

Lagerlof, Selma (Ottiliana Lovisa) 1858-1940 . . . . **TCLC 4**
See also CLR 7; CA 108; SATA 15

La Guma, (Justin) Alex(ander) 1925-1985 . . . . **CLC 19**
See also CA 49-52; obituary CA 118

Lamartine, Alphonse (Marie Louis Prat) de 1790-1869 . . . . **NCLC 11**

Lamb, Charles 1775-1834 . . . . **NCLC 10**
See also SATA 17

Lamming, George (William) 1927- . . . . **CLC 2, 4**
See also CA 85-88

LaMoore, Louis Dearborn 1908?
See L'Amour, Louis (Dearborn)

L'Amour, Louis (Dearborn) 1908-1988 . . . . **CLC 25, 55**
See also CANR 3; CA 1-4R; obituary CA 125; DLB-Y 80

Lampedusa, (Prince) Giuseppe (Maria Fabrizio) Tomasi di 1896-1957 . . . . **TCLC 13**
See also CA 111

Lancaster, Bruce 1896-1963 . . . . **CLC 36**
See also CAP 1; CA 9-12; SATA 9

Landis, John (David) 1950- . . . . **CLC 26**
See also CA 112

Landolfi, Tommaso 1908-1979 . . . **CLC 11, 49**
See also obituary CA 117

Landon, Letitia Elizabeth 1802-1838 . . . . **NCLC 15**

Landor, Walter Savage 1775-1864 . . . . **NCLC 14**

Landwirth, Heinz 1927-
See Lind, Jakov
See also CANR 7; CA 11-12R

Lane, Patrick 1939- . . . . **CLC 25**
See also CA 97-100; DLB 53

Lang, Andrew 1844-1912 . . . . **TCLC 16**
See also CA 114; SATA 16

Lang, Fritz 1890-1976 . . . . **CLC 20**
See also CA 77-80; obituary CA 69-72

Langer, Elinor 1939- . . . . **CLC 34**

Lanier, Sidney 1842-1881 . . . . **NCLC 6**
See also SATA 18; DLB 64

Lanyer, Aemilia 1569-1645 . . . . **LC 10**

Lapine, James 1949- . . . . **CLC 39**

Larbaud, Valery 1881-1957 . . . . **TCLC 9**
See also CA 106

Lardner, Ring(gold Wilmer) 1885-1933 . . . . **TCLC 2, 14**
See also CA 104; DLB 11, 25

Larkin, Philip (Arthur) 1922-1985 . . . **CLC 3, 5, 8, 9, 13, 18, 33, 39**
See also CA 5-8R; obituary CA 117; DLB 27

Larra (y Sanchez de Castro), Mariano Jose de 1809-1837 . . . . **NCLC 17**

Larsen, Eric 1941- . . . . **CLC 55**

Larsen, Nella 1893-1964 . . . . **CLC 37**

Larson, Charles R(aymond) 1938- . . . **CLC 31**
See also CANR 4; CA 53-56

Latham, Jean Lee 1902- CLC 12
See also CANR 7; CA 5-8R; SATA 2

Lathen, Emma CLC 2
See also Hennissart, Martha; Latsis, Mary J(ane)

Latsis, Mary J(ane)
See Lathen, Emma
See also CA 85-88

Lattimore, Richmond (Alexander) 1906-1984 CLC 3
See also CANR 1; CA 1-4R; obituary CA 112

Laughlin, James 1914- CLC 49
See also CANR 9; CA 21-24R; DLB 48

Laurence, (Jean) Margaret (Wemyss) 1926-1987 CLC 3, 6, 13, 50
See also CA 5-8R; obituary CA 121; DLB 53

Laurent, Antoine 1952- CLC 50

Lautreamont, Comte de 1846-1870 NCLC 12

Lavin, Mary 1912- CLC 4, 18
See also CA 9-12R; DLB 15

Lawrence, D(avid) H(erbert) 1885-1930 TCLC 2, 9, 16, 33
See also CA 104, 121; DLB 10, 19, 36

Lawrence, T(homas) E(dward) 1888-1935 TCLC 18
See also CA 115

Lawson, Henry (Archibald Hertzberg) 1867-1922 TCLC 27
See also CA 120

Laxness, Halldor (Kiljan) 1902- CLC 25
See also Gudjonsson, Halldor Kiljan

Laye, Camara 1928-1980 CLC 4, 38
See also CA 85-88; obituary CA 97-100

Layton, Irving (Peter) 1912- CLC 2, 15
See also CANR 2; CA 1-4R

Lazarus, Emma 1849-1887 NCLC 8

Leacock, Stephen (Butler) 1869-1944 TCLC 2
See also CA 104

Lear, Edward 1812-1888 NCLC 3
See also CLR 1; SATA 18; DLB 32

Lear, Norman (Milton) 1922- CLC 12
See also CA 73-76

Leavis, F(rank) R(aymond) 1895-1978 CLC 24
See also CA 21-24R; obituary CA 77-80

Leavitt, David 1961? CLC 34
See also CA 116, 122

Lebowitz, Fran(ces Ann) 1951? CLC 11, 36
See also CANR 14; CA 81-84

Le Carre, John 1931- CLC 3, 5, 9, 15, 28
See also Cornwell, David (John Moore)

Le Clezio, J(ean) M(arie) G(ustave) 1940- CLC 31
See also CA 116

Leduc, Violette 1907-1972 CLC 22
See also CAP 1; CA 13-14; obituary CA 33-36R

Ledwidge, Francis 1887-1917 TCLC 23
See also DLB 20

Lee, Andrea 1953- CLC 36

Lee, Andrew 1917-
See Auchincloss, Louis (Stanton)

Lee, Don L. 1942- CLC 2
See also Madhubuti, Haki R.
See also CA 73-76

Lee, George Washington 1894-1976 CLC 52
See also CA 125; DLB 51

Lee, (Nelle) Harper 1926- CLC 12
See also CA 13-16R; SATA 11; DLB 6; CDALB 1941-1968

Lee, Lawrence 1903- CLC 34
See also CA 25-28R

Lee, Manfred B(ennington) 1905-1971
See Queen, Ellery
See also CANR 2; CA 1-4R; obituary CA 29-32R

Lee, Stan 1922- CLC 17
See also CA 108, 111

Lee, Tanith 1947- CLC 46
See also CA 37-40R; SATA 8

Lee, Vernon 1856-1935 TCLC 5
See also Paget, Violet
See also DLB 57

Lee-Hamilton, Eugene (Jacob) 1845-1907 TCLC 22

Leet, Judith 1935- CLC 11

Le Fanu, Joseph Sheridan 1814-1873 NCLC 9
See also DLB 21, 70

Leffland, Ella 1931- CLC 19
See also CA 29-32R; DLB-Y 84

Leger, (Marie-Rene) Alexis Saint-Leger 1887-1975
See Perse, St.-John
See also CA 13-16R; obituary CA 61-64

Le Guin, Ursula K(roeber) 1929- CLC 8, 13, 22, 45
See also CLR 3; CANR 9; CA 21-24R; SATA 4, 52; DLB 8, 52

Lehmann, Rosamond (Nina) 1901- CLC 5
See also CANR 8; CA 77-80; DLB 15

Leiber, Fritz (Reuter, Jr.) 1910- CLC 25
See also CANR 2; CA 45-48; SATA 45; DLB 8

Leino, Eino 1878-1926 TCLC 24

Leithauser, Brad 1953- CLC 27
See also CA 107

Lelchuk, Alan 1938- CLC 5
See also CANR 1; CA 45-48

Lem, Stanislaw 1921- CLC 8, 15, 40
See also CAAS 1; CA 105

Lemann, Nancy 1956- CLC 39
See also CA 118

Lemonnier, (Antoine Louis) Camille 1844-1913 TCLC 22

Lenau, Nikolaus 1802-1850 NCLC 16

L'Engle, Madeleine 1918- CLC 12
See also CLR 1, 14; CANR 3, 21; CA 1-4R; SATA 1, 27; DLB 52

Lengyel, Jozsef 1896-1975 CLC 7
See also CA 85-88; obituary CA 57-60

Lennon, John (Ono) 1940-1980 and **McCartney, Paul** 1940-1980 CLC 12

Lennon, John (Ono) 1940-1980 CLC 35
See also Lennon, John (Ono) and McCartney, Paul
See also CA 102

Lennon, John Winston 1940-1980
See Lennon, John (Ono)

Lennox, Charlotte Ramsay 1729 or 17301804 NCLC 23
See also DLB 39, 39

Lennox, Charlotte Ramsay 1729?1804 NCLC 23
See also DLB 39

Lentricchia, Frank (Jr.) 1940- CLC 34
See also CA 25-28R

Lenz, Siegfried 1926- CLC 27
See also CA 89-92

Leonard, Elmore 1925- CLC 28, 34
See also CANR 12; CA 81-84

Leonard, Hugh 1926- CLC 19
See also Byrne, John Keyes
See also DLB 13

Leopardi, (Conte) Giacomo (Talegardo Francesco di Sales Saverio Pietro) 1798-1837 NCLC 22

Lerman, Eleanor 1952- CLC 9
See also CA 85-88

Lerman, Rhoda 1936- CLC 56
See also CA 49-52

Lermontov, Mikhail Yuryevich 1814-1841 NCLC 5

Leroux, Gaston 1868-1927 TCLC 25
See also CA 108

Lesage, Alain-Rene 1668-1747 LC 2

Lessing, Doris (May) 1919- CLC 1, 2, 3, 6, 10, 15, 22, 40
See also CA 9-12R; DLB 15; DLB-Y 85

Lessing, Gotthold Ephraim 1729-1781 LC 8

Lester, Richard 1932- CLC 20

Lever, Charles (James) 1806-1872 NCLC 23
See also DLB 21

Leverson, Ada 1865-1936 TCLC 18
See also CA 117

Levertov, Denise 1923- CLC 1, 2, 3, 5, 8, 15, 28
See also CANR 3; CA 1-4R; DLB 5

Levi, Peter (Chad Tiger) 1931- CLC 41
See also CA 5-8R; DLB 40

Levi, Primo 1919-1987 CLC 37, 50
See also CANR 12; CA 13-16R; obituary CA 122

Levin, Ira 1929- CLC 3, 6
See also CANR 17; CA 21-24R

Levin, Meyer 1905-1981 CLC 7
See also CANR 15; CA 9-12R; obituary CA 104; SATA 21; obituary SATA 27; DLB 9, 28; DLB-Y 81

Levine, Norman 1924- CLC 54
See also CANR 14; CA 73-76

Levine, Philip 1928- CLC 2, 4, 5, 9, 14, 33
See also CANR 9; CA 9-12R; DLB 5

Levinson, Deirdre 1931- . . . . **CLC 49**
See also CA 73-76

Levi-Strauss, Claude 1908- . . . . **CLC 38**
See also CANR 6; CA 1-4R

Levitin, Sonia 1934- . . . . **CLC 17**
See also CANR 14; CA 29-32R; SAAS 2; SATA 4

Levr, Charles James 1806-1872. . . **NCLC 23**
See also DLB 21

Lewis, Alun 1915-1944 . . . . **TCLC 3**
See also CA 104; DLB 20

Lewis, C(ecil) Day 1904-1972
See Day Lewis, C(ecil)

Lewis, C(live) S(taples)
1898-1963 . . . . **CLC 1, 3, 6, 14, 27**
See also CLR 3; CA 81-84; SATA 13; DLB 15

Lewis (Winters), Janet 1899- . . . . **CLC 41**
See also Winters, Janet Lewis

Lewis, Matthew Gregory
1775-1818 . . . . **NCLC 11**
See also DLB 39

Lewis, (Harry) Sinclair
1885-1951 . . . . **TCLC 4, 13, 23**
See also CA 104; DLB 9; DLB-DS 1

Lewis, (Percy) Wyndham
1882?1957 . . . . **TCLC 2, 9**
See also CA 104; DLB 15

Lewisohn, Ludwig 1883-1955 . . . . . . **TCLC 19**
See also CA 73-76; obituary CA 29-32R

L'Heureux, John (Clarke) 1934- . . . . **CLC 52**
See also CANR 23; CA 15-16R

Lieber, Stanley Martin 1922-
See Lee, Stan

Lieberman, Laurence (James)
1935- . . . . **CLC 4, 36**
See also CANR 8; CA 17-20R

Li Fei-kan 1904-
See Pa Chin
See also CA 105

Lightfoot, Gordon (Meredith)
1938- . . . . **CLC 26**
See also CA 109

Ligotti, Thomas 1953- . . . . **CLC 44**

Liliencron, Detlev von
1844-1909 . . . . **TCLC 18**
See also CA 117

Lima, Jose Lezama 1910-1976
See Lezama Lima, Jose

Lima Barreto, (Alfonso Henriques de)
1881-1922 . . . . **TCLC 23**
See also CA 117

Lincoln, Abraham 1809-1865 . . . . . **NCLC 18**

Lind, Jakov 1927- . . . . **CLC 1, 2, 4, 27**
See also Landwirth, Heinz
See also CAAS 4; CA 9-12R

Lindsay, David 1876-1945 . . . . **TCLC 15**
See also CA 113

Lindsay, (Nicholas) Vachel
1879-1931 . . . . **TCLC 17**
See also CA 114; SATA 40; DLB 54; CDALB 1865-1917

Linney, Romulus 1930- . . . . **CLC 51**
See also CA 1-4R

Li Po 701-763 . . . . **CMLC 2**

Lipsyte, Robert (Michael) 1938- . . . . **CLC 21**
See also CANR 8; CA 17-20R; SATA 5

Lish, Gordon (Jay) 1934- . . . . **CLC 45**
See also CA 113, 117

Lispector, Clarice 1925-1977 . . . . **CLC 43**
See also obituary CA 116

Littell, Robert 1935? . . . . **CLC 42**
See also CA 109, 112

Liu E 1857-1909 . . . . **TCLC 15**
See also CA 115

Lively, Penelope 1933- . . . . **CLC 32, 50**
See also CLR 7; CA 41-44R; SATA 7; DLB 14

Livesay, Dorothy 1909- . . . . **CLC 4, 15**
See also CA 25-28R

Llewellyn, Richard 1906-1983 . . . . **CLC 7**
See also Llewellyn Lloyd, Richard (Dafydd Vyvyan)
See also DLB 15

Llewellyn Lloyd, Richard (Dafydd Vyvyan)
1906-1983
See Llewellyn, Richard
See also CANR 7; CA 53-56; obituary CA 111; SATA 11, 37

Llosa, Mario Vargas 1936-
See Vargas Llosa, Mario

Lloyd, Richard Llewellyn 1906-
See Llewellyn, Richard

Locke, John 1632-1704 . . . . **LC 7**
See also DLB 31

Lockhart, John Gibson
1794-1854 . . . . **NCLC 6**

Lodge, David (John) 1935- . . . . **CLC 36**
See also CANR 19; CA 17-20R; DLB 14

Loewinsohn, Ron(ald William)
1937- . . . . **CLC 52**
See also CA 25-28R

Logan, John 1923- . . . . **CLC 5**
See also CA 77-80; DLB 5

Lombino, S. A. 1926-
See Hunter, Evan

London, Jack 1876-1916 . . . . **TCLC 9, 15**
See also London, John Griffith
See also SATA 18; DLB 8, 12; CDALB 1865-1917

London, John Griffith 1876-1916
See London, Jack
See also CA 110, 119

Long, Emmett 1925-
See Leonard, Elmore

Longbaugh, Harry 1931-
See Goldman, William (W.)

Longfellow, Henry Wadsworth
1807-1882 . . . . **NCLC 2**
See also SATA 19; DLB 1; CDALB 1640-1865

Longley, Michael 1939- . . . . **CLC 29**
See also CA 102; DLB 40

Lopate, Phillip 1943- . . . . **CLC 29**
See also CA 97-100; DLB-Y 80

Lopez Portillo (y Pacheco), Jose
1920- . . . . **CLC 46**

Lopez y Fuentes, Gregorio
1897-1966 . . . . **CLC 32**

Lord, Bette Bao 1938- . . . . **CLC 23**
See also CA 107

Lorde, Audre (Geraldine) 1934- . . . . . **CLC 18**
See also CANR 16; CA 25-28R; DLB 41

Loti, Pierre 1850-1923 . . . . **TCLC 11**
See also Viaud, (Louis Marie) Julien

Lovecraft, H(oward) P(hillips)
1890-1937 . . . . **TCLC 4, 22; SSC 3**
See also CA 104

Lovelace, Earl 1935- . . . . **CLC 51**
See also CA 77-80

Lowell, Amy 1874-1925 . . . . **TCLC 1, 8**
See also CA 104; DLB 54

Lowell, James Russell 1819-1891 . . **NCLC 2**
See also DLB 1, 11, 64; CDALB 1640-1865

Lowell, Robert (Traill Spence, Jr.)
1917-1977 . . . **CLC 1, 2, 3, 4, 5, 8, 9, 11, 15, 37**
See also CA 9-12R; obituary CA 73-76; CABS 2; DLB 5

Lowndes, Marie (Adelaide) Belloc
1868-1947 . . . . **TCLC 12**
See also CA 107; DLB 70

Lowry, (Clarence) Malcolm
1909-1957 . . . . **TCLC 6**
See also CA 105; DLB 15

Loy, Mina 1882-1966 . . . . **CLC 28**
See also CA 113; DLB 4, 54

Lucas, George 1944- . . . . **CLC 16**
See also CA 77-80

Lucas, Victoria 1932-1963
See Plath, Sylvia

Ludlam, Charles 1943-1987 . . . . . **CLC 46, 50**
See also CA 85-88; obituary CA 122

Ludlum, Robert 1927- . . . . **CLC 22, 43**
See also CA 33-36R; DLB-Y 82

Ludwig, Otto 1813-1865 . . . . **NCLC 4**

Lugones, Leopoldo 1874-1938 . . . . . **TCLC 15**
See also CA 116

Lu Hsun 1881-1936 . . . . **TCLC 3**

Lukacs, Georg 1885-1971 . . . . **CLC 24**
See also Lukacs, Gyorgy

Lukacs, Gyorgy 1885-1971
See Lukacs, Georg
See also CA 101; obituary CA 29-32R

Luke, Peter (Ambrose Cyprian)
1919- . . . . **CLC 38**
See also CA 81-84; DLB 13

Lurie (Bishop), Alison
1926- . . . . **CLC 4, 5, 18, 39**
See also CANR 2, 17; CA 1-4R; SATA 46; DLB 2

Lustig, Arnost 1926- . . . . **CLC 56**
See also CA 69-72; SATA 56

Luther, Martin 1483-1546 . . . . **LC 9**

Luzi, Mario 1914- . . . . **CLC 13**
See also CANR 9; CA 61-64

Lynn, Kenneth S(chuyler) 1923- . . . . **CLC 50**
See also CANR 3; CA 1-4R

Lytle, Andrew (Nelson) 1902- . . . . . . **CLC 22**
See also CA 9-12R; DLB 6

Lyttelton, George 1709-1773 . . . . **LC 10**

Lytton, Edward Bulwer 1803-1873
See Bulwer-Lytton, (Lord) Edward (George Earle Lytton)
See also SATA 23

Maas, Peter 1929- . . . . **CLC 29**
See also CA 93-96

Macaulay, (Dame Emile) Rose
1881-1958 . . . . **TCLC 7**
See also CA 104; DLB 36

MacBeth, George (Mann)
1932- . . . . **CLC 2, 5, 9**
See also CA 25-28R; SATA 4; DLB 40

MacCaig, Norman (Alexander)
1910- . . . . **CLC 36**
See also CANR 3; CA 9-12R; DLB 27

MacDermot, Thomas H. 1870-1933
See Redcam, Tom

MacDiarmid, Hugh
1892-1978 . . . . **CLC 2, 4, 11, 19**
See also Grieve, C(hristopher) M(urray)
See also DLB 20

Macdonald, Cynthia 1928- . . . . . . **CLC 13, 19**
See also CANR 4; CA 49-52

MacDonald, George 1824-1905 . . . . . **TCLC 9**
See also CA 106; SATA 33; DLB 18

MacDonald, John D(ann)
1916-1986 . . . . **CLC 3, 27, 44**
See also CANR 1, 19; CA 1-4R; obituary CA 121; DLB 8; DLB-Y 86

Macdonald, (John) Ross
1915-1983 . . . . . . **CLC 1, 2, 3, 14, 34, 41**
See also Millar, Kenneth

MacEwen, Gwendolyn (Margaret)
1941-1987 . . . . **CLC 13, 55**
See also CANR 7, 22; CA 9-12R; obituary CA 124; SATA 50; DLB 53

Machado (y Ruiz), Antonio
1875-1939 . . . . **TCLC 3**
See also CA 104

Machado de Assis, (Joaquim Maria)
1839-1908 . . . . **TCLC 10**
See also CA 107

Machen, Arthur (Llewellyn Jones)
1863-1947 . . . . **TCLC 4**
See also CA 104; DLB 36

Machiavelli, Niccolo 1469-1527 . . . . . . **LC 8**

MacInnes, Colin 1914-1976 . . . . . . **CLC 4, 23**
See also CA 69-72; obituary CA 65-68; DLB 14

MacInnes, Helen (Clark)
1907-1985 . . . . **CLC 27, 39**
See also CANR 1; CA 1-4R; obituary CA 65-68, 117; SATA 22, 44

Macintosh, Elizabeth 1897-1952
See Tey, Josephine
See also CA 110

Mackenzie, (Edward Montague) Compton
1883-1972 . . . . **CLC 18**
See also CAP 2; CA 21-22; obituary CA 37-40R; DLB 34

Mac Laverty, Bernard 1942- . . . . **CLC 31**
See also CA 116, 118

MacLean, Alistair (Stuart)
1922-1987 . . . . **CLC 3, 13, 50**
See also CA 57-60; obituary CA 121; SATA 23

MacLeish, Archibald
1892-1982 . . . . **CLC 3, 8, 14**
See also CA 9-12R; obituary CA 106; DLB 4, 7, 45; DLB-Y 82

MacLennan, (John) Hugh
1907- . . . . **CLC 2, 14**
See also CA 5-8R

MacLeod, Alistair 1936- . . . . **CLC 56**
See also CA 123; DLB 60

MacNeice, (Frederick) Louis
1907-1963 . . . . **CLC 1, 4, 10, 53**
See also CA 85-88; DLB 10, 20

Macpherson, (Jean) Jay 1931- . . . . . . **CLC 14**
See also CA 5-8R; DLB 53

MacShane, Frank 1927- . . . . **CLC 39**
See also CANR 3; CA 11-12R

Macumber, Mari 1896-1966
See Sandoz, Mari (Susette)

Madach, Imre 1823-1864 . . . . **NCLC 19**

Madden, (Jerry) David 1933- . . . . **CLC 5, 15**
See also CAAS 3; CANR 4; CA 1-4R; DLB 6

Madhubuti, Haki R. 1942- . . . . **CLC 6**
See also Lee, Don L.
See also DLB 5, 41

Maeterlinck, Maurice 1862-1949 . . . **TCLC 3**
See also CA 104

Mafouz, Naguib 1912-
See Mahfuz, Najib

Maginn, William 1794-1842 . . . . **NCLC 8**

Mahapatra, Jayanta 1928- . . . . **CLC 33**
See also CANR 15; CA 73-76

Mahfūz Najīb 1912- . . . . **CLC 52, 55**
See also DLB-Y 88

Mahon, Derek 1941- . . . . **CLC 27**
See also CA 113; DLB 40

Mailer, Norman
1923- . . . . . . **CLC 1, 2, 3, 4, 5, 8, 11, 14, 28, 39**
See also CA 9-12R; CABS 1; DLB 2, 16, 28; DLB-Y 80, 83; DLB-DS 3

Maillet, Antonine 1929- . . . . **CLC 54**
See also CA 115, 120; DLB 60

Mais, Roger 1905-1955 . . . . **TCLC 8**
See also CA 105

Maitland, Sara (Louise) 1950- . . . . . . **CLC 49**
See also CANR 13; CA 69-72

Major, Clarence 1936- . . . . **CLC 3, 19, 48**
See also CAAS 6; CANR 13; CA 21-24R; DLB 33

Major, Kevin 1949- . . . . **CLC 26**
See also CLR 11; CANR 21; CA 97-100; SATA 32; DLB 60

Malamud, Bernard
1914-1986 . . . . . **CLC 1, 2, 3, 5, 8, 9, 11, 18, 27, 44**
See also CA 5-8R; obituary CA 118; CABS 1; DLB 2, 28; DLB-Y 80, 86; CDALB 1941-1968

Malherbe, Francois de 1555-1628 . . . . . **LC 5**

Mallarme, Stephane 1842-1898 . . . . **NCLC 4**

Mallet-Joris, Francoise 1930- . . . . . . **CLC 11**
See also CANR 17; CA 65-68

Maloff, Saul 1922- . . . . **CLC 5**
See also CA 33-36R

Malone, Louis 1907-1963
See MacNeice, (Frederick) Louis

Malone, Michael (Christopher)
1942- . . . . **CLC 43**
See also CANR 14; CA 77-80

Malory, (Sir) Thomas ?1471 . . . . **LC 11**
See also SATA 33

Malouf, David 1934- . . . . **CLC 28**

Malraux, (Georges-) Andre
1901-1976 . . . . **CLC 1, 4, 9, 13, 15**
See also CAP 2; CA 21-24; obituary CA 69-72; DLB 72

Malzberg, Barry N. 1939- . . . . **CLC 7**
See also CAAS 4; CANR 16; CA 61-64; DLB 8

Mamet, David (Alan)
1947- . . . . **CLC 9, 15, 34, 46**
See also CANR 15; CA 81-84; DLB 7

Mamoulian, Rouben 1898- . . . . **CLC 16**
See also CA 25-28R

Mandelstam, Osip (Emilievich)
1891?1938? . . . . **TCLC 2, 6**
See also CA 104

Mander, Jane 1877-1949 . . . . **TCLC 31**

Mandiargues, Andre Pieyre de
1909- . . . . **CLC 41**
See also CA 103

Manley, (Mary) Delariviere
1672?1724 . . . . **LC 1**
See also DLB 39

Mann, (Luiz) Heinrich 1871-1950 . . . **TCLC 9**
See also CA 106

Mann, Thomas
1875-1955 . . . . **TCLC 2, 8, 14, 21**
See also CA 104

Manning, Frederic 1882-1935 . . . . . **TCLC 25**

Manning, Olivia 1915-1980 . . . . . . **CLC 5, 19**
See also CA 5-8R; obituary CA 101

Mano, D. Keith 1942- . . . . **CLC 2, 10**
See also CAAS 6; CA 25-28R; DLB 6

Mansfield, Katherine
1888-1923 . . . . **TCLC 2, 8**
See also CA 104

Manso, Peter 1940- . . . . **CLC 39**
See also CA 29-32R

Mapu, Abraham (ben Jekutiel)
1808-1867 . . . . **NCLC 18**

Marat, Jean Paul 1743-1793 . . . . **LC 10**

Marcel, Gabriel (Honore)
1889-1973 . . . . **CLC 15**
See also CA 102; obituary CA 45-48

Marchbanks, Samuel 1913-
See Davies, (William) Robertson

Marie de l'Incarnation 1599-1672 . . . . **LC 10**

Marinetti, F(ilippo) T(ommaso)
1876-1944 . . . . **TCLC 10**
See also CA 107

Marivaux, Pierre Carlet de Chamblain de (16881763) .... **LC 4**

Markandaya, Kamala 1924- ...... **CLC 8, 38**
See also Taylor, Kamala (Purnaiya)

Markfield, Wallace (Arthur) 1926- ... **CLC 8**
See also CAAS 3; CA 69-72; DLB 2, 28

Markham, Robert 1922-
See Amis, Kingsley (William)

Marks, J. 1942-
See Highwater, Jamake

Marley, Bob 1945-1981 .... **CLC 17**
See also Marley, Robert Nesta

Marley, Robert Nesta 1945-1981
See Marley, Bob
See also CA 107; obituary CA 103

Marmontel, Jean-Francois 1723-1799 .... **LC 2**

Marquand, John P(hillips) 1893-1960 .... **CLC 2, 10**
See also CA 85-88; DLB 9

Marquez, Gabriel Garcia 1928-
See Garcia Marquez, Gabriel

Marquis, Don(ald Robert Perry) 1878-1937 .... **TCLC 7**
See also CA 104; DLB 11, 25

Marryat, Frederick 1792-1848 .... **NCLC 3**
See also DLB 21

Marsh, (Dame Edith) Ngaio 1899-1982 .... **CLC 7, 53**
See also CANR 6; CA 9-12R; DLB 77

Marshall, Garry 1935? .... **CLC 17**
See also CA 111

Marshall, Paule 1929- ..... **CLC 27; SSC 3**
See also CANR 25; CA 77-80; DLB 33

Marsten, Richard 1926-
See Hunter, Evan

Martin, Steve 1945? .... **CLC 30**
See also CA 97-100

Martin du Gard, Roger 1881-1958 .... **TCLC 24**
See also CA 118

Martinez Ruiz, Jose 1874-1967
See Azorin
See also CA 93-96

Martinez Sierra, Gregorio 1881-1947 and **Martinez Sierra, Maria (de la O'LeJarraga)** 1881-1947 ...... **TCLC 6**

Martinez Sierra, Gregorio 1881-1947
See Martinez Sierra, Gregorio and Martinez Sierra, Maria (de la O'LeJarraga)
See also CA 104, 115

Martinez Sierra, Maria (de la O'LeJarraga) 1880?1974
See Martinez Sierra, Gregorio and Martinez Sierra, Maria (de la O'LeJarraga)
See also obituary CA 115

Martinez Sierra, Maria (de la O'LeJarraga) 1880?1974 and **Martinez Sierra, Gregorio** 1880?1974
See Martinez Sierra, Gregorio and Martinez Sierra, Maria (de la O'LeJarraga)

Martinson, Harry (Edmund) 1904-1978 .... **CLC 14**
See also CA 77-80

Marvell, Andrew 1621-1678 .... **LC 4**

Marx, Karl (Heinrich) 1818-1883 .... **NCLC 17**

Masaoka Shiki 1867-1902 .... **TCLC 18**

Masefield, John (Edward) 1878-1967 .... **CLC 11, 47**
See also CAP 2; CA 19-20; obituary CA 25-28R; SATA 19; DLB 10, 19

Maso, Carole 19?? .... **CLC 44**

Mason, Bobbie Ann 1940- ...... **CLC 28, 43**
See also CANR 11; CA 53-56; SAAS 1

Mason, Nick 1945-
See Pink Floyd

Mason, Tally 1909-1971
See Derleth, August (William)

Masters, Edgar Lee 1868?1950 .... **TCLC 2, 25**
See also CA 104; DLB 54; CDALB 1865-1917

Masters, Hilary 1928- .... **CLC 48**
See also CANR 13; CA 25-28R

Mastrosimone, William 19?? .... **CLC 36**

Matheson, Richard (Burton) 1926- .... **CLC 37**
See also CA 97-100; DLB 8, 44

Mathews, Harry 1930- .... **CLC 6, 52**
See also CAAS 6; CANR 18; CA 21-24R

Mathias, Roland (Glyn) 1915- ...... **CLC 45**
See also CANR 19; CA 97-100; DLB 27

Matthews, Greg 1949- .... **CLC 45**

Matthews, William 1942- .... **CLC 40**
See also CANR 12; CA 29-32R; DLB 5

Matthias, John (Edward) 1941- ...... **CLC 9**
See also CA 33-36R

Matthiessen, Peter 1927- ... **CLC 5, 7, 11, 32**
See also CANR 21; CA 9-12R; SATA 27; DLB 6

Maturin, Charles Robert 1780?1824 .... **NCLC 6**

Matute, Ana Maria 1925- .... **CLC 11**
See also CA 89-92

Maugham, W(illiam) Somerset 1874-1965 .... **CLC 1, 11, 15**
See also CA 5-8R; obituary CA 25-28R; DLB 10, 36

Maupassant, (Henri Rene Albert) Guy de 1850-1893 .... **NCLC 1; SSC 1**

Mauriac, Claude 1914- .... **CLC 9**
See also CA 89-92

Mauriac, François (Charles) 1885-1970 .... **CLC 4, 9, 56**
See also CAP 2; CA 25-28; DLB 65

Mavor, Osborne Henry 1888-1951
See Bridie, James
See also CA 104

Maxwell, William (Keepers, Jr.) 1908- .... **CLC 19**
See also CA 93-96; DLB-Y 80

May, Elaine 1932- .... **CLC 16**
See also DLB 44

Mayakovsky, Vladimir (Vladimirovich) 1893-1930 .... **TCLC 4, 18**
See also CA 104

Maynard, Joyce 1953- .... **CLC 23**
See also CA 111

Mayne, William (James Carter) 1928- .... **CLC 12**
See also CA 9-12R; SATA 6

Mayo, Jim 1908?
See L'Amour, Louis (Dearborn)

Maysles, Albert 1926- and **Maysles, David** 1926- .... **CLC 16**

Maysles, Albert 1926-
See Maysles, Albert and Maysles, David
See also CA 29-32R

Maysles, David 1932-
See Maysles, Albert and Maysles, David

Mazer, Norma Fox 1931- .... **CLC 26**
See also CANR 12; CA 69-72; SAAS 1; SATA 24

McAuley, James (Phillip) 1917-1976 .... **CLC 45**
See also CA 97-100

McBain, Ed 1926-
See Hunter, Evan

McBrien, William 1930- .... **CLC 44**
See also CA 107

McCaffrey, Anne 1926- .... **CLC 17**
See also CANR 15; CA 25-28R; SATA 8; DLB 8

McCarthy, Cormac 1933- .... **CLC 4**
See also CANR 10; CA 13-16R; DLB 6

McCarthy, Mary (Therese) 1912- .... **CLC 1, 3, 5, 14, 24, 39**
See also CANR 16; CA 5-8R; DLB 2; DLB-Y 81

McCartney, (James) Paul 1942- .... **CLC 35**
See also Lennon, John (Ono) and McCartney, Paul

McCauley, Stephen 19?? .... **CLC 50**

McClure, Michael 1932- .... **CLC 6, 10**
See also CANR 17; CA 21-24R; DLB 16

McCorkle, Jill (Collins) 1958- ...... **CLC 51**
See also CA 121; DLB-Y 87

McCourt, James 1941- .... **CLC 5**
See also CA 57-60

McCoy, Horace 1897-1955 .... **TCLC 28**
See also CA 108; DLB 9

McCrae, John 1872-1918 .... **TCLC 12**
See also CA 109

McCullers, (Lula) Carson (Smith) 1917-1967 .... **CLC 1, 4, 10, 12, 48**
See also CANR 18; CA 5-8R; obituary CA 25-28R; CABS 1; SATA 27; DLB 2, 7; CDALB 1941-1968

McCullough, Colleen 1938? .... **CLC 27**
See also CANR 17; CA 81-84

McElroy, Joseph (Prince) 1930- .... **CLC 5, 47**
See also CA 17-20R

McEwan, Ian (Russell) 1948- ...... **CLC 13**
See also CANR 14; CA 61-64; DLB 14

McFadden, David 1940- .... **CLC 48**
See also CA 104; DLB 60

McGahern, John 1934- . . . . **CLC 5, 9, 48**
See also CA 17-20R; DLB 14

McGinley, Patrick 1937- . . . . **CLC 41**
See also CA 120

McGinley, Phyllis 1905-1978 . . . . . . **CLC 14**
See also CANR 19; CA 9-12R; obituary CA 77-80; SATA 2, 44; obituary SATA 24; DLB 11, 48

McGinniss, Joe 1942- . . . . **CLC 32**
See also CA 25-28R

McGivern, Maureen Daly 1921-
See Daly, Maureen
See also CA 9-12R

McGrath, Patrick 1950- . . . . **CLC 55**

McGrath, Thomas 1916- . . . . **CLC 28**
See also CANR 6; CA 9-12R; SATA 41

McGuane, Thomas (Francis III) 1939- . . . . **CLC 3, 7, 18**
See also CANR 5; CA 49-52; DLB 2; DLB-Y 80

McGuckian, Medbh 1950- . . . . **CLC 48**
See also DLB 40

McHale, Tom 1941-1982 . . . . **CLC 3, 5**
See also CA 77-80; obituary CA 106

McIlvanney, William 1936- . . . . **CLC 42**
See also CA 25-28R; DLB 14

McIlwraith, Maureen Mollie Hunter 1922-
See Hunter, Mollie
See also CA 29-32R; SATA 2

McInerney, Jay 1955- . . . . **CLC 34**
See also CA 116

McIntyre, Vonda N(eel) 1948- . . . . . **CLC 18**
See also CANR 17; CA 81-84

McKay, Claude 1890-1948 . . . . **TCLC 7**
See also CA 104; DLB 4, 45

McKuen, Rod 1933- . . . . **CLC 1, 3**
See also CA 41-44R

McLuhan, (Herbert) Marshall 1911-1980 . . . . **CLC 37**
See also CANR 12; CA 9-12R; obituary CA 102

McManus, Declan Patrick 1955-
See Costello, Elvis

McMillan, Terry 19?? . . . . **CLC 50**

McMurtry, Larry (Jeff) 1936- . . . . **CLC 2, 3, 7, 11, 27, 44**
See also CANR 19; CA 5-8R; DLB 2; DLB-Y 80

McNally, Terrence 1939- . . . . . . **CLC 4, 7, 41**
See also CANR 2; CA 45-48; DLB 7

McPhee, John 1931- . . . . **CLC 36**
See also CANR 20; CA 65-68

McPherson, James Alan 1943- . . . . . **CLC 19**
See also CA 25-28R; DLB 38

McPherson, William 1939- . . . . **CLC 34**
See also CA 57-60

McSweeney, Kerry 19?? . . . . **CLC 34**

Mead, Margaret 1901-1978 . . . . **CLC 37**
See also CANR 4; CA 1-4R; obituary CA 81-84; SATA 20

Meaker, M. J. 1927-
See Kerr, M. E.; Meaker, Marijane

Meaker, Marijane 1927-
See Kerr, M. E.
See also CA 107; SATA 20

Medoff, Mark (Howard) 1940- . . . **CLC 6, 23**
See also CANR 5; CA 53-56; DLB 7

Megged, Aharon 1920- . . . . **CLC 9**
See also CANR 1; CA 49-52

Mehta, Ved (Parkash) 1934- . . . . **CLC 37**
See also CANR 2; CA 1-4R

Mellor, John 1953?
See The Clash

Meltzer, Milton 1915- . . . . **CLC 26**
See also CA 13-16R; SAAS 1; SATA 1; DLB 61

Melville, Herman 1819-1891 . . . . **NCLC 3, 12; SSC 1**
See also DLB 3; CDALB 1640-1865

Mencken, H(enry) L(ouis) 1880-1956 . . . . **TCLC 13**
See also CA 105; DLB 11, 29, 63

Mercer, David 1928-1980 . . . . **CLC 5**
See also CA 9-12R; obituary CA 102; DLB 13

Meredith, George 1828-1909 . . . . . . **TCLC 17**
See also CA 117; DLB 18, 35, 57

Meredith, William (Morris) 1919- . . . . **CLC 4, 13, 22, 55**
See also CANR 6; CA 9-12R; DLB 5

Merezhkovsky, Dmitri 1865-1941 . . . . **TCLC 29**

Merimee, Prosper 1803-1870 . . . . . . **NCLC 6**

Merkin, Daphne 1954- . . . . **CLC 44**

Merrill, James (Ingram) 1926- . . . . **CLC 2, 3, 6, 8, 13, 18, 34**
See also CANR 10; CA 13-16R; DLB 5; DLB-Y 85

Merton, Thomas (James) 1915-1968 . . . . **CLC 1, 3, 11, 34**
See also CANR 22; CA 5-8R; obituary CA 25-28R; DLB 48; DLB-Y 81

Merwin, W(illiam) S(tanley) 1927- . . . . . . **CLC 1, 2, 3, 5, 8, 13, 18, 45**
See also CANR 15; CA 13-16R; DLB 5

Metcalf, John 1938- . . . . **CLC 37**
See also CA 113; DLB 60

Mew, Charlotte (Mary) 1870-1928 . . . . **TCLC 8**
See also CA 105; DLB 19

Mewshaw, Michael 1943- . . . . **CLC 9**
See also CANR 7; CA 53-56; DLB-Y 80

Meyer-Meyrink, Gustav 1868-1932
See Meyrink, Gustav
See also CA 117

Meyers, Jeffrey 1939- . . . . **CLC 39**
See also CA 73-76

Meynell, Alice (Christiana Gertrude Thompson) 1847-1922 . . . . **TCLC 6**
See also CA 104; DLB 19

Meyrink, Gustav 1868-1932 . . . . **TCLC 21**
See also Meyer-Meyrink, Gustav

Michaels, Leonard 1933- . . . . **CLC 6, 25**
See also CANR 21; CA 61-64

Michaux, Henri 1899-1984 . . . . . . **CLC 8, 19**
See also CA 85-88; obituary CA 114

Michener, James A(lbert) 1907- . . . . **CLC 1, 5, 11, 29**
See also CANR 21; CA 5-8R; DLB 6

Mickiewicz, Adam 1798-1855 . . . . . **NCLC 3**

Middleton, Christopher 1926- . . . . . . **CLC 13**
See also CA 13-16R; DLB 40

Middleton, Stanley 1919- . . . . **CLC 7, 38**
See also CANR 21; CA 25-28R; DLB 14

Migueis, Jose Rodrigues 1901- . . . . . **CLC 10**

Mikszath, Kalman 1847-1910 . . . . . **TCLC 31**

Miles, Josephine (Louise) 1911-1985 . . . . **CLC 1, 2, 14, 34, 39**
See also CANR 2; CA 1-4R; obituary CA 116; DLB 48

Mill, John Stuart 1806-1873 . . . . . **NCLC 11**

Millar, Kenneth 1915-1983
See Macdonald, Ross
See also CANR 16; CA 9-12R; obituary CA 110; DLB 2; DLB-Y 83

Millay, Edna St. Vincent 1892-1950 . . . . **TCLC 4**
See also CA 104; DLB 45

Miller, Arthur 1915- . . . . **CLC 1, 2, 6, 10, 15, 26, 47**
See also CANR 2; CA 1-4R; DLB 7; CDALB 1941-1968

Miller, Henry (Valentine) 1891-1980 . . . . **CLC 1, 2, 4, 9, 14, 43**
See also CA 9-12R; obituary CA 97-100; DLB 4, 9; DLB-Y 80

Miller, Jason 1939? . . . . **CLC 2**
See also CA 73-76; DLB 7

Miller, Sue 19?? . . . . **CLC 44**

Miller, Walter M(ichael), Jr. 1923- . . . . **CLC 4, 30**
See also CA 85-88; DLB 8

Millhauser, Steven 1943- . . . . **CLC 21, 54**
See also CA 108, 110, 111; DLB 2

Millin, Sarah Gertrude 1889-1968 . . **CLC 49**
See also CA 102; obituary CA 93-96

Milne, A(lan) A(lexander) 1882-1956 . . . . **TCLC 6**
See also CLR 1; YABC 1; CA 104; DLB 10

Milner, Ron(ald) 1938- . . . . **CLC 56**
See also CANR 24; CA 73-76; DLB 38

Millosz Czeslaw 1911- . . . . **CLC 5, 11, 22, 31, 56**
See also CA 81-84

Milton, John 1608-1674 . . . . **LC 9**

Miner, Valerie (Jane) 1947- . . . . **CLC 40**
See also CA 97-100

Minot, Susan 1956- . . . . **CLC 44**

Minus, Ed 1938- . . . . **CLC 39**

Miro (Ferrer), Gabriel (Francisco Victor) 1879-1930 . . . . **TCLC 5**
See also CA 104

Mishima, Yukio 1925-1970 . . . . **CLC 2, 4, 6, 9, 27**
See also Hiraoka, Kimitake

Mistral, Gabriela 1889-1957 . . . . **TCLC 2**
See also CA 104

Mitchell, James Leslie 1901-1935
See Gibbon, Lewis Grassic
See also CA 104; DLB 15

Mitchell, Joni 1943- .... **CLC 12**
See also CA 112

Mitchell (Marsh), Margaret (Munnerlyn)
1900-1949 .... **TCLC 11**
See also CA 109; DLB 9

Mitchell, W(illiam) O(rmond)
1914- .... **CLC 25**
See also CANR 15; CA 77-80

Mitford, Mary Russell 1787-1855.. **NCLC 4**

Mitford, Nancy 1904-1973......... **CLC 44**
See also CA 9-12R

Mo, Timothy 1950-............... **CLC 46**
See also CA 117

Modarressi, Taghi 1931- .... **CLC 44**
See also CA 121

Modiano, Patrick (Jean) 1945- ..... **CLC 18**
See also CANR 17; CA 85-88

Mofolo, Thomas (Mokopu)
1876-1948 .... **TCLC 22**
See also CA 121

Mohr, Nicholasa 1935-............ **CLC 12**
See also CANR 1; CA 49-52; SATA 8

Mojtabai, A(nn) G(race)
1938- .... **CLC 5, 9, 15, 29**
See also CA 85-88

Moliere 1622-1673 .... **LC 10**

Molnar, Ferenc 1878-1952........ **TCLC 20**
See also CA 109

Momaday, N(avarre) Scott
1934- .... **CLC 2, 19**
See also CANR 14; CA 25-28R; SATA 30, 48

Monroe, Harriet 1860-1936....... **TCLC 12**
See also CA 109; DLB 54

Montagu, Elizabeth 1720-1800 .... **NCLC 7**

Montagu, Lady Mary (Pierrepont) Wortley
1689-1762 .... **LC 9**

Montague, John (Patrick)
1929- .... **CLC 13, 46**
See also CANR 9; CA 9-12R; DLB 40

Montaigne, Michel (Eyquem) de
1533-1592 .... **LC 8**

Montale, Eugenio 1896-1981... **CLC 7, 9, 18**
See also CA 17-20R; obituary CA 104

Montgomery, Marion (H., Jr.)
1925- .... **CLC 7**
See also CANR 3; CA 1-4R; DLB 6

Montgomery, Robert Bruce 1921-1978
See Crispin, Edmund
See also CA 104

Montherlant, Henri (Milon) de
1896-1972 .... **CLC 8, 19**
See also CA 85-88; obituary CA 37-40R; DLB 72

Montisquieu, Charles-Louis de Secondat
1689-1755 .... **LC 7**

Monty Python .... **CLC 21**
See also Cleese, John; Gilliam, Terry (Vance); Idle, Eric; Jones, Terry; Palin, Michael

Moodie, Susanna (Strickland)
1803-1885 .... **NCLC 14**

Mooney, Ted 1951-............... **CLC 25**

Moorcock, Michael (John)
1939- .... **CLC 5, 27**
See also CAAS 5; CANR 2, 17; CA 45-48; DLB 14

Moore, Brian
1921- .... **CLC 1, 3, 5, 7, 8, 19, 32**
See also CANR 1; CA 1-4R

Moore, George (Augustus)
1852-1933 .... **TCLC 7**
See also CA 104; DLB 10, 18, 57

Moore, Lorrie 1957-........... **CLC 39, 45**
See also Moore, Marie Lorena

Moore, Marianne (Craig)
1887-1972 ... **CLC 1, 2, 4, 8, 10, 13, 19, 47**
See also CANR 3; CA 1-4R; obituary CA 33-36R; SATA 20; DLB 45

Moore, Marie Lorena 1957-
See Moore, Lorrie
See also CA 116

Moore, Thomas 1779-1852........ **NCLC 6**

Morand, Paul 1888-1976 .... **CLC 41**
See also obituary CA 69-72

Morante, Elsa 1918-1985........ **CLC 8, 47**
See also CA 85-88; obituary CA 117

Moravia, Alberto
1907- .... **CLC 2, 7, 11, 18, 27, 46**
See also Pincherle, Alberto

More, Henry 1614-1687............. **LC 9**

More, Thomas 1478-1573........... **LC 10**

Moreas, Jean 1856-1910 .... **TCLC 18**

Morgan, Berry 1919- .... **CLC 6**
See also CA 49-52; DLB 6

Morgan, Edwin (George) 1920-..... **CLC 31**
See also CANR 3; CA 7-8R; DLB 27

Morgan, (George) Frederick
1922- .... **CLC 23**
See also CANR 21; CA 17-20R

Morgan, Janet 1945- .... **CLC 39**
See also CA 65-68

Morgan, Robin 1941-.............. **CLC 2**
See also CA 69-72

Morgenstern, Christian (Otto Josef Wolfgang)
1871-1914 .... **TCLC 8**
See also CA 105

Moricz, Zsigmond 1879-1942 ..... **TCLC 33**

Morike, Eduard (Friedrich)
1804-1875 .... **NCLC 10**

Mori Ogai 1862-1922............ **TCLC 14**
See also Mori Rintaro

Mori Rintaro 1862-1922
See Mori Ogai
See also CA 110

Moritz, Karl Philipp 1756-1793 ...... **LC 2**

Morris, Julian 1916-
See West, Morris L.

Morris, Steveland Judkins 1950-
See Wonder, Stevie
See also CA 111

Morris, William 1834-1896 .... **NCLC 4**
See also DLB 18, 35, 57

Morris, Wright (Marion)
1910- .... **CLC 1, 3, 7, 18, 37**
See also CA 9-12R; DLB 2; DLB-Y 81

Morrison, James Douglas 1943-1971
See Morrison, Jim
See also CA 73-76

Morrison, Jim 1943-1971.......... **CLC 17**
See also Morrison, James Douglas

Morrison, Toni 1931-..... **CLC 4, 10, 22, 55**
See also CA 29-32R; DLB 6, 33; DLB-Y 81; AAYA 1

Morrison, Van 1945- .... **CLC 21**
See also CA 116

Mortimer, John (Clifford)
1923- .... **CLC 28, 43**
See also CANR 21; CA 13-16R; DLB 13

Mortimer, Penelope (Ruth) 1918-.... **CLC 5**
See also CA 57-60

Mosley, Nicholas 1923- .... **CLC 43**
See also CA 69-72; DLB 14

Moss, Howard
1922-1987 .... **CLC 7, 14, 45, 50**
See also CANR 1; CA 1-4R; DLB 5

Motion, Andrew (Peter) 1952-..... **CLC 47**
See also DLB 40

Motley, Willard (Francis)
1912-1965 .... **CLC 18**
See also CA 117; obituary CA 106

Mott, Michael (Charles Alston)
1930- .... **CLC 15, 34**
See also CAAS 7; CANR 7; CA 5-8R

Mowat, Farley (McGill) 1921- ..... **CLC 26**
See also CANR 4; CA 1-4R; SATA 3

Mphahlele, Es'kia 1919-
See Mphahlele, Ezekiel

Mphahlele, Ezekiel 1919-......... **CLC 25**
See also CA 81-84

Mqhayi, S(amuel) E(dward) K(rune Loliwe)
1875-1945 .... **TCLC 25**

Mrozek, Slawomir 1930- .... **CLC 3, 13**
See also CA 13-16R

Mtwa, Percy 19??............... **CLC 47**

Mueller, Lisel 1924-........... **CLC 13, 51**
See also CA 93-96

Muir, Edwin 1887-1959 .... **TCLC 2**
See also CA 104; DLB 20

Muir, John 1838-1914 .... **TCLC 28**

Mujica Lainez, Manuel
1910-1984 .... **CLC 31**
See also CA 81-84; obituary CA 112

Mukherjee, Bharati 1940- .... **CLC 53**
See also CA 107; DLB 60

Muldoon, Paul 1951- .... **CLC 32**
See also CA 113; DLB 40

Mulisch, Harry (Kurt Victor)
1927- .... **CLC 42**
See also CANR 6; CA 9-12R

Mull, Martin 1943-............... **CLC 17**
See also CA 105

Munford, Robert 1737?1783 .... **LC 5**
See also DLB 31

Munro, Alice (Laidlaw) 1931- . . . . **CLC 6, 10, 19, 50; SSC 3**
See also CA 33-36R; SATA 29; DLB 53

Munro, H(ector) H(ugh) 1870-1916
See Saki
See also CA 104; DLB 34

Murasaki, Lady c. 11th century . . . **CMLC 1**

Murdoch, (Jean) Iris 1919- . . . . . . **CLC 1, 2, 3, 4, 6, 8, 11, 15, 22, 31, 51**
See also CANR 8; CA 13-16R; DLB 14

Murphy, Richard 1927- . . . . **CLC 41**
See also CA 29-32R; DLB 40

Murphy, Sylvia 19??. . . . . **CLC 34**

Murphy, Thomas (Bernard) 1935-. . . **CLC 51**
See also CA 101

Murray, Les(lie) A(llan) 1938- . . . . . **CLC 40**
See also CANR 11; CA 21-24R

Murry, John Middleton 1889-1957 . . . . **TCLC 16**
See also CA 118

Musgrave, Susan 1951- . . . . **CLC 13, 54**
See also CA 69-72

Musil, Robert (Edler von) 1880-1942 . . . . **TCLC 12**
See also CA 109

Musset, (Louis Charles) Alfred de 1810-1857 . . . . **NCLC 7**

Myers, Walter Dean 1937- . . . . **CLC 35**
See also CLR 4, 16; CANR 20; CA 33-36R; SAAS 2; SATA 27, 41; DLB 33

Nabokov, Vladimir (Vladimirovich) 1899-1977 . . . . **CLC 1, 2, 3, 6, 8, 11, 15, 23, 44, 46**
See also CANR 20; CA 5-8R; obituary CA 69-72; DLB 2; DLB-Y 80; DLB-DS 3; CDALB 1941-1968

Nagy, Laszlo 1925-1978. . . . . **CLC 7**
See also obituary CA 112

Naipaul, Shiva(dhar Srinivasa) 1945-1985 . . . . **CLC 32, 39**
See also CA 110, 112; obituary CA 116; DLB-Y 85

Naipaul, V(idiadhar) S(urajprasad) 1932- . . . . **CLC 4, 7, 9, 13, 18, 37**
See also CANR 1; CA 1-4R; DLB-Y 85

Nakos, Ioulia 1899?
See Nakos, Lilika

Nakos, Lilika 1899? . . . . **CLC 29**

Nakou, Lilika 1899?
See Nakos, Lilika

Narayan, R(asipuram) K(rishnaswami) 1906- . . . . **CLC 7, 28, 47**
See also CA 81-84

Nash, (Frediric) Ogden 1902-1971 . . **CLC 23**
See also CAP 1; CA 13-14; obituary CA 29-32R; SATA 2, 46; DLB 11

Nathan, George Jean 1882-1958 . . . **TCLC 18**
See also CA 114

Natsume, Kinnosuke 1867-1916
See Natsume, Soseki
See also CA 104

Natsume, Soseki 1867-1916. . . . . **TCLC 2, 10**
See also Natsume, Kinnosuke

Natti, (Mary) Lee 1919-
See Kingman, (Mary) Lee
See also CANR 2; CA 7-8R

Naylor, Gloria 1950- . . . . **CLC 28, 52**
See also CANR 27; CA 107

Neihardt, John G(neisenau) 1881-1973 . . . . **CLC 32**
See also CAP 1; CA 13-14; DLB 9

Nekrasov, Nikolai Alekseevich 1821-1878 . . . . **NCLC 11**

Nelligan, Emile 1879-1941. . . . . **TCLC 14**
See also CA 114

Nelson, Willie 1933-. . . . . **CLC 17**
See also CA 107

Nemerov, Howard 1920- . . . . **CLC 2, 6, 9, 36**
See also CANR 1; CA 1-4R; CABS 2; DLB 5, 6; DLB-Y 83

Neruda, Pablo 1904-1973 . . . . **CLC 1, 2, 5, 7, 9, 28**
See also CAP 2; CA 19-20; obituary CA 45-48

Nerval, Gerard de 1808-1855. . . . . . **NCLC 1**

Nervo, (Jose) Amado (Ruiz de) 1870-1919 . . . . **TCLC 11**
See also CA 109

Neufeld, John (Arthur) 1938- . . . . . . **CLC 17**
See also CANR 11; CA 25-28R; SAAS 3; SATA 6

Neville, Emily Cheney 1919-. . . . . . . **CLC 12**
See also CANR 3; CA 5-8R; SAAS 2; SATA 1

Newbound, Bernard Slade 1930-
See Slade, Bernard
See also CA 81-84

Newby, P(ercy) H(oward) 1918- . . . . **CLC 2, 13**
See also CA 5-8R; DLB 15

Newlove, Donald 1928- . . . . **CLC 6**
See also CA 29-32R

Newlove, John (Herbert) 1938-. . . . . **CLC 14**
See also CANR 9; CA 21-24R

Newman, Charles 1938-. . . . . **CLC 2, 8**
See also CA 21-24R

Newman, Edwin (Harold) 1919- . . . . **CLC 14**
See also CANR 5; CA 69-72

Newton, Suzanne 1936-. . . . . **CLC 35**
See also CANR 14; CA 41-44R; SATA 5

Ngugi, James (Thiong'o) 1938- . . . . **CLC 3, 7, 13, 36**
See also Ngugi wa Thiong'o; Wa Thiong'o, Ngugi
See also CA 81-84

Ngugi wa Thiong'o 1938-. . . **CLC 3, 7, 13, 36**
See also Ngugi, James (Thiong'o); Wa Thiong'o, Ngugi

Nichol, B(arrie) P(hillip) 1944-. . . . . **CLC 18**
See also CA 53-56; DLB 53

Nichols, John (Treadwell) 1940-. . . . **CLC 38**
See also CAAS 2; CANR 6; CA 9-12R; DLB-Y 82

Nichols, Peter (Richard) 1927- . . . **CLC 5, 36**
See also CA 104; DLB 13

Nicolas, F.R.E. 1927-
See Freeling, Nicolas

Niedecker, Lorine 1903-1970. . . . **CLC 10, 42**
See also CAP 2; CA 25-28; DLB 48

Nietzsche, Friedrich (Wilhelm) 1844-1900 . . . . **TCLC 10, 18**
See also CA 107

Nievo, Ippolito 1831-1861 . . . . **NCLC 22**

Nightingale, Anne Redmon 1943-
See Redmon (Nightingale), Anne
See also CA 103

Nin, Anais 1903-1977. . . **CLC 1, 4, 8, 11, 14**
See also CANR 22; CA 13-16R; obituary CA 69-72; DLB 2, 4

Nissenson, Hugh 1933-. . . . . **CLC 4, 9**
See also CA 17-20R; DLB 28

Niven, Larry 1938-. . . . . **CLC 8**
See also Niven, Laurence Van Cott
See also DLB 8

Niven, Laurence Van Cott 1938-
See Niven, Larry
See also CANR 14; CA 21-24R

Nixon, Agnes Eckhardt 1927-. . . . . . **CLC 21**
See also CA 110

Nkosi, Lewis 1936-. . . . . **CLC 45**
See also CA 65-68

Nodier, (Jean) Charles (Emmanuel) 1780-1844 . . . . **NCLC 19**

Nordhoff, Charles 1887-1947. . . . . . **TCLC 23**
See also CA 108; SATA 23; DLB 9

Norman, Marsha 1947- . . . . **CLC 28**
See also CA 105; DLB-Y 84

Norris, (Benjamin) Frank(lin) 1870-1902 . . . . **TCLC 24**
See also CA 110; DLB 12, 71; CDALB 1865-1917

Norris, Leslie 1921- . . . . **CLC 14**
See also CANR 14; CAP 1; CA 11-12; DLB 27

North, Andrew 1912-
See Norton, Andre

North, Christopher 1785-1854
See Wilson, John

Norton, Alice Mary 1912-
See Norton, Andre
See also CANR 2; CA 1-4R; SATA 1, 43

Norton, Andre 1912- . . . . **CLC 12**
See also Norton, Mary Alice
See also DLB 8, 52

Norway, Nevil Shute 1899-1960
See Shute (Norway), Nevil
See also CA 102; obituary CA 93-96

Norwid, Cyprian Kamil 1821-1883 . . . . **NCLC 17**

Nossack, Hans Erich 1901-1978 . . . . . **CLC 6**
See also CA 93-96; obituary CA 85-88; DLB 69

Nova, Craig 1945-. . . . . **CLC 7, 31**
See also CANR 2; CA 45-48

Novak, Joseph 1933-
See Kosinski, Jerzy (Nikodem)

Novalis 1772-1801 . . . . **NCLC 13**

Nowlan, Alden (Albert) 1933-. . . . . . **CLC 15**
See also CANR 5; CA 9-12R; DLB 53

Noyes, Alfred 1880-1958 .... **TCLC 7**
See also CA 104; DLB 20

Nunn, Kem 19?? .... **CLC 34**

Nye, Robert 1939- .... **CLC 13, 42**
See also CA 33-36R; SATA 6; DLB 14

Nyro, Laura 1947- .... **CLC 17**

Oates, Joyce Carol
1938- ..... **CLC 1, 2, 3, 6, 9, 11, 15, 19, 33, 52**
See also CANR 25; CA 5-8R; DLB 2, 5; DLB-Y 81

O'Brien, Darcy 1939-............ **CLC 11**
See also CANR 8; CA 21-24R

O'Brien, Edna 1932-.... **CLC 3, 5, 8, 13, 36**
See also CANR 6; CA 1-4R; DLB 14

O'Brien, Fitz-James 1828?1862... **NCLC 21**
See also DLB 74

O'Brien, Flann
1911-1966 .... **CLC 1, 4, 5, 7, 10, 47**
See also O Nuallain, Brian

O'Brien, Richard 19?? .... **CLC 17**

O'Brien, (William) Tim(othy)
1946- .... **CLC 7, 19, 40**
See also CA 85-88; DLB-Y 80

Obstfelder, Sigbjorn 1866-1900.... **TCLC 23**

O'Casey, Sean
1880-1964 .... **CLC 1, 5, 9, 11, 15**
See also CA 89-92; DLB 10

Ochs, Phil 1940-1976............. **CLC 17**
See also obituary CA 65-68

O'Connor, Edwin (Greene)
1918-1968 .... **CLC 14**
See also CA 93-96; obituary CA 25-28R

O'Connor, (Mary) Flannery
1925-1964 ... **CLC 1, 2, 3, 6, 10, 13, 15, 21; SSC 1**
See also CANR 3; CA 1-4R; DLB 2; DLB-Y 80; CDALB 1941-1968

O'Connor, Frank 1903-1966 .... **CLC 14, 23**
See also O'Donovan, Michael (John)

O'Dell, Scott 1903-.............. **CLC 30**
See also CLR 1, 16; CANR 12; CA 61-64; SATA 12; DLB 52

Odets, Clifford 1906-1963 .... **CLC 2, 28**
See also CA 85-88; DLB 7, 26

O'Donovan, Michael (John) 1903-1966
See O'Connor, Frank
See also CA 93-96

Oe, Kenzaburo 1935-.......... **CLC 10, 36**
See also CA 97-100

O'Faolain, Julia 1932-....... **CLC 6, 19, 47**
See also CAAS 2; CANR 12; CA 81-84; DLB 14

O'Faolain, Sean 1900-..... **CLC 1, 7, 14, 32**
See also CANR 12; CA 61-64; DLB 15

O'Flaherty, Liam 1896-1984 ..... **CLC 5, 34**
See also CA 101; obituary CA 113; DLB 36; DLB-Y 84

O'Grady, Standish (James)
1846-1928 .... **TCLC 5**
See also CA 104

O'Hara, Frank 1926-1966 ..... **CLC 2, 5, 13**
See also CA 9-12R; obituary CA 25-28R; DLB 5, 16

O'Hara, John (Henry)
1905-1970 .... **CLC 1, 2, 3, 6, 11, 42**
See also CA 5-8R; obituary CA 25-28R; DLB 9; DLB-DS 2

O'Hara Family
See Banim, John and Banim, Michael

O'Hehir, Diana 1922-............. **CLC 41**
See also CA 93-96

Okigbo, Christopher (Ifenayichukwu)
1932-1967 .... **CLC 25**
See also CA 77-80

Olds, Sharon 1942-........... **CLC 32, 39**
See also CANR 18; CA 101

Olesha, Yuri (Karlovich)
1899-1960 .... **CLC 8**
See also CA 85-88

Oliphant, Margaret (Oliphant Wilson)
1828-1897 .... **NCLC 11**
See also DLB 18

Oliver, Mary 1935-........... **CLC 19, 34**
See also CANR 9; CA 21-24R; DLB 5

Olivier, (Baron) Laurence (Kerr)
1907- .... **CLC 20**
See also CA 111

Olsen, Tillie 1913- .... **CLC 4, 13**
See also CANR 1; CA 1-4R; DLB 28; DLB-Y 80

Olson, Charles (John)
1910-1970 ..... **CLC 1, 2, 5, 6, 9, 11, 29**
See also CAP 1; CA 15-16; obituary CA 25-28R; CABS 2; DLB 5, 16

Olson, Theodore 1937-
See Olson, Toby

Olson, Toby 1937- .... **CLC 28**
See also CANR 9; CA 65-68

Ondaatje, (Philip) Michael
1943- .... **CLC 14, 29, 51**
See also CA 77-80; DLB 60

Oneal, Elizabeth 1934-
See Oneal, Zibby
See also CA 106; SATA 30

Oneal, Zibby 1934-.............. **CLC 30**
See also Oneal, Elizabeth

O'Neill, Eugene (Gladstone)
1888-1953 .... **TCLC 1, 6, 27**
See also CA 110; DLB 7

Onetti, Juan Carlos 1909-....... **CLC 7, 10**
See also CA 85-88

O'Nolan, Brian 1911-1966
See O'Brien, Flann

O Nuallain, Brian 1911-1966
See O'Brien, Flann
See also CAP 2; CA 21-22; obituary CA 25-28R

Oppen, George 1908-1984 .... **CLC 7, 13, 34**
See also CANR 8; CA 13-16R; obituary CA 113; DLB 5

Orlovitz, Gil 1918-1973.......... **CLC 22**
See also CA 77-80; obituary CA 45-48; DLB 2, 5

Ortega y Gasset, Jose 1883-1955 ... **TCLC 9**
See also CA 106

Ortiz, Simon J. 1941-............ **CLC 45**

Orton, Joe 1933?1967........ **CLC 4, 13, 43**
See also Orton, John Kingsley
See also DLB 13

Orton, John Kingsley 1933?1967
See Orton, Joe
See also CA 85-88

Orwell, George
1903-1950 .... **TCLC 2, 6, 15, 31**
See also Blair, Eric Arthur
See also DLB 15

Osborne, John (James)
1929- .... **CLC 1, 2, 5, 11, 45**
See also CANR 21; CA 13-16R; DLB 13

Osborne, Lawrence 1958- .... **CLC 50**

Osceola 1885-1962
See Dinesen, Isak; Blixen, Karen (Christentze Dinesen)

Oshima, Nagisa 1932- .... **CLC 20**
See also CA 116

Ossoli, Sarah Margaret (Fuller marchesa d')
1810-1850
See Fuller, (Sarah) Margaret
See also SATA 25

Otero, Blas de 1916- .... **CLC 11**
See also CA 89-92

Owen, Wilfred (Edward Salter)
1893-1918 .... **TCLC 5, 27**
See also CA 104; DLB 20

Owens, Rochelle 1936-............. **CLC 8**
See also CAAS 2; CA 17-20R

Owl, Sebastian 1939-
See Thompson, Hunter S(tockton)

Oz, Amos 1939- ... **CLC 5, 8, 11, 27, 33, 54**
See also CA 53-56

Ozick, Cynthia 1928-......... **CLC 3, 7, 28**
See also CA 17-20R; DLB 28; DLB-Y 82

Ozu, Yasujiro 1903-1963 .... **CLC 16**
See also CA 112

Pa Chin 1904-.................. **CLC 18**
See also Li Fei-kan

Pack, Robert 1929-.............. **CLC 13**
See also CANR 3; CA 1-4R; DLB 5

Padgett, Lewis 1915-1958
See Kuttner, Henry

Padilla, Heberto 1932-............ **CLC 38**

Page, Jimmy 1944- and **Plant, Robert**
1944- .... **CLC 12**

Page, Jimmy 1944-
See Page, Jimmy and Plant, Robert

Page, Louise 1955-............... **CLC 40**

Page, P(atricia) K(athleen)
1916- .... **CLC 7, 18**
See also CANR 4; CA 53-56

Paget, Violet 1856-1935
See Lee, Vernon
See also CA 104

Palamas, Kostes 1859-1943 .... **TCLC 5**
See also CA 105

Palazzeschi, Aldo 1885-1974....... **CLC 11**
See also CA 89-92; obituary CA 53-56

Paley, Grace 1922-........... **CLC 4, 6, 37**
See also CANR 13; CA 25-28R; DLB 28

Palin, Michael 1943-
See Monty Python
See also CA 107

Palma, Ricardo 1833-1919 . . . . **TCLC 29**

Pancake, Breece Dexter 1952-1979
See Pancake, Breece D'J

Pancake, Breece D'J 1952-1979 . . . . **CLC 29**
See also obituary CA 109

Papadiamantis, Alexandros
1851-1911 . . . . **TCLC 29**

Papini, Giovanni 1881-1956 . . . . **TCLC 22**
See also CA 121

Parini, Jay (Lee) 1948- . . . . **CLC 54**
See also CA 97-100

Parker, Dorothy (Rothschild)
1893-1967 . . . . **CLC 15; SSC 2**
See also CAP 2; CA 19-20;
obituary CA 25-28R; DLB 11, 45

Parker, Robert B(rown) 1932- . . . . . . **CLC 27**
See also CANR 1; CA 49-52

Parkin, Frank 1940- . . . . **CLC 43**

Parkman, Francis 1823-1893 . . . . . **NCLC 12**
See also DLB 1, 30

Parks, Gordon (Alexander Buchanan)
1912- . . . . **CLC 1, 16**
See also CA 41-44R; SATA 8; DLB 33

Parnell, Thomas 1679-1718 . . . . **LC 3**

Parra, Nicanor 1914- . . . . **CLC 2**
See also CA 85-88

Pasolini, Pier Paolo
1922-1975 . . . . **CLC 20, 37**
See also CA 93-96; obituary CA 61-64

Pastan, Linda (Olenik) 1932- . . . . . . **CLC 27**
See also CANR 18; CA 61-64; DLB 5

Pasternak, Boris 1890-1960 . . . **CLC 7, 10, 18**
See also obituary CA 116

Patchen, Kenneth 1911-1972 . . . **CLC 1, 2, 18**
See also CANR 3; CA 1-4R;
obituary CA 33-36R; DLB 16, 48

Pater, Walter (Horatio)
1839-1894 . . . . **NCLC 7**
See also DLB 57

Paterson, Andrew Barton
1864-1941 . . . . **TCLC 32**

Paterson, Katherine (Womeldorf)
1932- . . . . **CLC 12, 30**
See also CLR 7; CA 21-24R; SATA 13, 53;
DLB 52

Patmore, Coventry Kersey Dighton
1823-1896 . . . . **NCLC 9**
See also DLB 35

Paton, Alan (Stewart)
1903-1988 . . . . **CLC 4, 10, 25, 55**
See also CANR 22; CAP 1; CA 15-16;
obituary CA 125; SATA 11

Paulding, James Kirke 1778-1860. . **NCLC 2**
See also DLB 3

Paulin, Tom 1949- . . . . **CLC 37**
See also DLB 40

Paustovsky, Konstantin (Georgievich)
1892-1968 . . . . **CLC 40**
See also CA 93-96; obituary CA 25-28R

Paustowsky, Konstantin (Georgievich)
1892-1968
See Paustovsky, Konstantin (Georgievich)

Pavese, Cesare 1908-1950 . . . . **TCLC 3**
See also CA 104

Payne, Alan 1932-
See Jakes, John (William)

Paz, Octavio 1914- . . **CLC 3, 4, 6, 10, 19, 51**
See also CA 73-76

Peacock, Thomas Love
1785-1886 . . . . **NCLC 22**

Peake, Mervyn 1911-1968 . . . . **CLC 7, 54**
See also CANR 3; CA 5-8R;
obituary CA 25-28R; SATA 23; DLB 15

Pearce, (Ann) Philippa 1920- . . . . **CLC 21**
See also Christie, (Ann) Philippa
See also CA 5-8R; SATA 1

Pearl, Eric 1934-
See Elman, Richard

Pearson, T(homas) R(eid) 1956- . . . . **CLC 39**
See also CA 120

Peck, John 1941- . . . . **CLC 3**
See also CANR 3; CA 49-52

Peck, Richard 1934- . . . . **CLC 21**
See also CLR 15; CANR 19; CA 85-88;
SAAS 2; SATA 18

Peck, Robert Newton 1928- . . . . **CLC 17**
See also CA 81-84; SAAS 1; SATA 21

Peckinpah, (David) Sam(uel)
1925-1984 . . . . **CLC 20**
See also CA 109; obituary CA 114

Pedersen, Knut 1859-1952
See Hamsun, Knut
See also CA 104

Peguy, Charles (Pierre)
1873-1914 . . . . **TCLC 10**
See also CA 107

Pepys, Samuel 1633-1703 . . . . **LC 11**

Percy, Walker
1916- . . . . **CLC 2, 3, 6, 8, 14, 18, 47**
See also CANR 1; CA 1-4R; DLB 2;
DLB-Y 80

Perec, Georges 1936-1982 . . . . **CLC 56**

Pereda, Jose Maria de
1833-1906 . . . . **TCLC 16**

Perelman, S(idney) J(oseph)
1904-1979 . . . **CLC 3, 5, 9, 15, 23, 44, 49**
See also CANR 18; CA 73-76;
obituary CA 89-92; DLB 11, 44

Peret, Benjamin 1899-1959 . . . . **TCLC 20**
See also CA 117

Peretz, Isaac Leib 1852?1915 . . . . . **TCLC 16**
See also CA 109

Perez, Galdos Benito 1853-1920 . . . **TCLC 27**

Perrault, Charles 1628-1703 . . . . **LC 2**
See also SATA 25

Perse, St.-John 1887-1975 . . . . **CLC 4, 11, 46**
See also Leger, (Marie-Rene) Alexis
Saint-Leger

Pesetsky, Bette 1932- . . . . **CLC 28**

Peshkov, Alexei Maximovich 1868-1936
See Gorky, Maxim
See also CA 105

Pessoa, Fernando (Antonio Nogueira)
1888-1935 . . . . **TCLC 27**

Peterkin, Julia (Mood) 1880-1961. . . **CLC 31**
See also CA 102; DLB 9

Peters, Joan K. 1945- . . . . **CLC 39**

Peters, Robert L(ouis) 1924- . . . . **CLC 7**
See also CA 13-16R

Petöfi, Sándor 1823-1849 . . . . **NCLC 21**

Petrakis, Harry Mark 1923- . . . . **CLC 3**
See also CANR 4; CA 9-12R

Petrov, Evgeny 1902-1942 and **Ilf, Ilya**
1902-1942
See Ilf, Ilya 1897-1937 and Petrov, Evgeny
1902-1942

Petry, Ann (Lane) 1908- . . . . . . **CLC 1, 7, 18**
See also CLR 12; CAAS 6; CANR 4;
CA 5-8R; SATA 5

Petursson, Halligrimur 1614-1674 . . . . **LC 8**

Philipson, Morris (H.) 1926- . . . . **CLC 53**
See also CANR 4; CA 1-4R

Phillips, Jayne Anne 1952- . . . . . **CLC 15, 33**
See also CA 101; DLB-Y 80

Phillips, Robert (Schaeffer) 1938- . . . **CLC 28**
See also CANR 8; CA 17-20R

Pica, Peter 1925-
See Aldiss, Brian W(ilson)

Piccolo, Lucio 1901-1969 . . . . **CLC 13**
See also CA 97-100

Pickthall, Marjorie (Lowry Christie)
1883-1922 . . . . **TCLC 21**
See also CA 107

Piercy, Marge 1936- . . . **CLC 3, 6, 14, 18, 27**
See also CAAS 1; CANR 13; CA 21-24R

Pilnyak, Boris 1894-1937? . . . . **TCLC 23**

Pincherle, Alberto 1907-
See Moravia, Alberto
See also CA 25-28R

Pineda, Cecile 1942- . . . . **CLC 39**
See also CA 118

Pinero, Miguel (Gomez)
1946-1988 . . . . **CLC 4, 55**
See also CA 61-64; obituary CA 125

Pinero, Sir Arthur Wing
1855-1934 . . . . **TCLC 32**
See also CA 110; DLB 10

Pinget, Robert 1919- . . . . **CLC 7, 13, 37**
See also CA 85-88

Pink Floyd . . . . **CLC 35**

Pinkwater, D(aniel) M(anus)
1941- . . . . **CLC 35**
See also Pinkwater, Manus
See also CLR 4; CANR 12; CA 29-32R;
SAAS 3; SATA 46

Pinkwater, Manus 1941-
See Pinkwater, D(aniel) M(anus)
See also SATA 8

Pinsky, Robert 1940- . . . . **CLC 9, 19, 38**
See also CAAS 4; CA 29-32R; DLB-Y 82

Pinter, Harold
1930- . . . . **CLC 1, 3, 6, 9, 11, 15, 27**
See also CA 5-8R; DLB 13

Pirandello, Luigi 1867-1936 . . . . . **TCLC 4, 29**
See also CA 104

Pirsig, Robert M(aynard) 1928- . . . **CLC 4, 6**
See also CA 53-56; SATA 39

Pix, Mary (Griffith) 1666-1709 . . . . **LC 8**

Plaidy, Jean 1906-
See Hibbert, Eleanor (Burford)

Plant, Robert 1948-
See Page, Jimmy and Plant, Robert

Plante, David (Robert)
1940- . . . . **CLC 7, 23, 38**
See also CANR 12; CA 37-40R; DLB-Y 83

Plath, Sylvia
1932-1963 . . . . **CLC 1, 2, 3, 5, 9, 11, 14, 17, 50, 51**
See also CAP 2; CA 19-20; DLB 5, 6; CDALB 1941-1968

Platonov, Andrei (Platonovich)
1899-1951 . . . . **TCLC 14**
See also Klimentov, Andrei Platonovich

Platt, Kin 1911- . . . . **CLC 26**
See also CANR 11; CA 17-20R; SATA 21

Plimpton, George (Ames) 1927-. . . . . **CLC 36**
See also CA 21-24R; SATA 10

Plomer, William (Charles Franklin)
1903-1973 . . . . **CLC 4, 8**
See also CAP 2; CA 21-22; SATA 24; DLB 20

Plumly, Stanley (Ross) 1939- . . . . . . **CLC 33**
See also CA 108, 110; DLB 5

Poe, Edgar Allan
1809-1849 . . . . **NCLC 1, 16; SSC 1**
See also SATA 23; DLB 3; CDALB 1640-1865

Pohl, Frederik 1919- . . . . **CLC 18**
See also CAAS 1; CANR 11; CA 61-64; SATA 24; DLB 8

Poirier, Louis 1910-
See Gracq, Julien
See also CA 122

Poitier, Sidney 1924? . . . . **CLC 26**
See also CA 117

Polanski, Roman 1933- . . . . **CLC 16**
See also CA 77-80

Poliakoff, Stephen 1952- . . . . **CLC 38**
See also CA 106; DLB 13

Police, The . . . . **CLC 26**

Pollitt, Katha 1949- . . . . **CLC 28**
See also CA 120, 122

Pollock, Sharon 19?? . . . . **CLC 50**

Pomerance, Bernard 1940-. . . . . **CLC 13**
See also CA 101

Ponge, Francis (Jean Gaston Alfred)
1899- . . . . **CLC 6, 18**
See also CA 85-88

Pontoppidan, Henrik 1857-1943 . . . **TCLC 29**

Poole, Josephine 1933-. . . . . **CLC 17**
See also CANR 10; CA 21-24R; SAAS 2; SATA 5

Popa, Vasko 1922- . . . . **CLC 19**
See also CA 112

Pope, Alexander 1688-1744 . . . . **LC 3**

Porter, Gene (va Grace) Stratton
1863-1924 . . . . **TCLC 21**
See also CA 112

Porter, Katherine Anne
1890-1980 . . . **CLC 1, 3, 7, 10, 13, 15, 27**
See also CANR 1; CA 1-4R; obituary CA 101; obituary SATA 23, 39; DLB 4, 9; DLB-Y 80

Porter, Peter (Neville Frederick)
1929- . . . . **CLC 5, 13, 33**
See also CA 85-88; DLB 40

Porter, William Sydney 1862-1910
See Henry, O.
See also YABC 2; CA 104; DLB 12; CDALB 1865-1917

Potok, Chaim 1929- . . . . **CLC 2, 7, 14, 26**
See also CANR 19; CA 17-20R; SATA 33; DLB 28

Pound, Ezra (Loomis)
1885-1972 . . . . . **CLC 1, 2, 3, 4, 5, 7, 10, 13, 18, 34, 48, 50**
See also CA 5-8R; obituary CA 37-40R; DLB 4, 45, 63

Povod, Reinaldo 1959- . . . . **CLC 44**

Powell, Anthony (Dymoke)
1905- . . . . **CLC 1, 3, 7, 9, 10, 31**
See also CANR 1; CA 1-4R; DLB 15

Powell, Padgett 1952-. . . . . **CLC 34**

Powers, J(ames) F(arl) 1917-. . . . **CLC 1, 4, 8**
See also CANR 2; CA 1-4R

Pownall, David 1938-. . . . . **CLC 10**
See also CA 89-92; DLB 14

Powys, John Cowper
1872-1963 . . . . **CLC 7, 9, 15, 46**
See also CA 85-88; DLB 15

Powys, T(heodore) F(rancis)
1875-1953 . . . . **TCLC 9**
See also CA 106; DLB 36

Prager, Emily 1952-. . . . . **CLC 56**

Pratt, E(dwin) J(ohn) 1883-1964 . . . . **CLC 19**
See also obituary CA 93-96

Premchand 1880-1936 . . . . **TCLC 21**

Preussler, Otfried 1923-. . . . . **CLC 17**
See also CA 77-80; SATA 24

Prevert, Jacques (Henri Marie)
1900-1977 . . . . **CLC 15**
See also CA 77-80; obituary CA 69-72; obituary SATA 30

Prevost, Abbe (Antoine Francois)
1697-1763 . . . . **LC 1**

Price, (Edward) Reynolds
1933- . . . . **CLC 3, 6, 13, 43, 50**
See also CANR 1; CA 1-4R; DLB 2

Price, Richard 1949- . . . . **CLC 6, 12**
See also CANR 3; CA 49-52; DLB-Y 81

Prichard, Katharine Susannah
1883-1969 . . . . **CLC 46**
See also CAP 1; CA 11-12

Priestley, J(ohn) B(oynton)
1894-1984 . . . . **CLC 2, 5, 9, 34**
See also CA 9-12R; obituary CA 113; DLB 10, 34; DLB-Y 84

Prince (Rogers Nelson) 1958? . . . . . . **CLC 35**

Prince, F(rank) T(empleton) 1912- . . **CLC 22**
See also CA 101; DLB 20

Prior, Matthew 1664-1721 . . . . **LC 4**

Pritchard, William H(arrison)
1932- . . . . **CLC 34**
See also CA 65-68

Pritchett, V(ictor) S(awdon)
1900- . . . . **CLC 5, 13, 15, 41**
See also CA 61-64; DLB 15

Procaccino, Michael 1946-
See Cristofer, Michael

Prokosch, Frederic 1908-. . . . . **CLC 4, 48**
See also CA 73-76; DLB 48

Prose, Francine 1947-. . . . . **CLC 45**
See also CA 109, 112

Proust, Marcel 1871-1922 . . **TCLC 7, 13, 33**
See also CA 104, 120; DLB 65

Pryor, Richard 1940- . . . . **CLC 26**

Puig, Manuel 1932- . . . . **CLC 3, 5, 10, 28**
See also CANR 2; CA 45-48

Purdy, A(lfred) W(ellington)
1918- . . . . **CLC 3, 6, 14, 50**
See also CA 81-84

Purdy, James (Amos)
1923- . . . . **CLC 2, 4, 10, 28, 52**
See also CAAS 1; CANR 19; CA 33-36R; DLB 2

Pushkin, Alexander (Sergeyevich)
1799-1837 . . . . **NCLC 3**

P'u Sung-ling 1640-1715 . . . . **LC 3**

Puzo, Mario 1920- . . . . **CLC 1, 2, 6, 36**
See also CANR 4; CA 65-68; DLB 6

Pym, Barbara (Mary Crampton)
1913-1980 . . . . **CLC 13, 19, 37**
See also CANR 13; CAP 1; CA 13-14; obituary CA 97-100; DLB 14

Pynchon, Thomas (Ruggles, Jr.)
1937- . . . . **CLC 2, 3, 6, 9, 11, 18, 33**
See also CANR 22; CA 17-20R; DLB 2

Quasimodo, Salvatore 1901-1968 . . . **CLC 10**
See also CAP 1; CA 15-16; obituary CA 25-28R

Queen, Ellery 1905-1982 . . . . **CLC 3, 11**
See also Dannay, Frederic; Lee, Manfred B(ennington)

Queneau, Raymond
1903-1976 . . . . **CLC 2, 5, 10, 42**
See also CA 77-80; obituary CA 69-72; DLB 72

Quin, Ann (Marie) 1936-1973 . . . . **CLC 6**
See also CA 9-12R; obituary CA 45-48; DLB 14

Quinn, Simon 1942-
See Smith, Martin Cruz

Quiroga, Horacio (Sylvestre)
1878-1937 . . . . **TCLC 20**
See also CA 117

Quoirez, Francoise 1935-
See Sagan, Francoise
See also CANR 6; CA 49-52

Rabe, David (William) 1940-. . . **CLC 4, 8, 33**
See also CA 85-88; DLB 7

Rabelais, Francois 1494?1553 . . . . **LC 5**

Rabinovitch, Sholem 1859-1916
See Aleichem, Sholom
See also CA 104

Rachen, Kurt von 1911-1986
See Hubbard, L(afayette) Ron(ald)

Radcliffe, Ann (Ward) 1764-1823 . . **NCLC 6**
See also DLB 39

Radiguet, Raymond 1903-1923 . . . . **TCLC 29**

Radnoti, Miklos 1909-1944 . . . . **TCLC 16**
See also CA 118

Rado, James 1939-
See Ragni, Gerome andRado, James
See also CA 105

Radomski, James 1932-
See Rado, James

Radvanyi, Netty Reiling 1900-1983
See Seghers, Anna
See also CA 85-88; obituary CA 110

Rae, Ben 1935-
See Griffiths, Trevor

Raeburn, John 1941- . . . . **CLC 34**
See also CA 57-60

Ragni, Gerome 1942- and **Rado, James** 1942- . . . . **CLC 17**

Ragni, Gerome 1942-
See Ragni, Gerome and Rado, James
See also CA 105

Rahv, Philip 1908-1973 . . . . **CLC 24**
See also Greenberg, Ivan

Raine, Craig 1944- . . . . **CLC 32**
See also CA 108; DLB 40

Raine, Kathleen (Jessie) 1908- . . . **CLC 7, 45**
See also CA 85-88; DLB 20

Rainis, Janis 1865-1929 . . . . **TCLC 29**

Rakosi, Carl 1903- . . . . **CLC 47**
See also Rawley, Callman
See also CAAS 5

Ramos, Graciliano 1892-1953 . . . . . **TCLC 32**

Rampersad, Arnold 19??. . . . . **CLC 44**

Ramuz, Charles-Ferdinand 1878-1947 . . . . **TCLC 33**

Rand, Ayn 1905-1982. . . . . **CLC 3, 30, 44**
See also CA 13-16R; obituary CA 105

Randall, Dudley (Felker) 1914-. . . . . . **CLC 1**
See also CA 25-28R; DLB 41

Ransom, John Crowe 1888-1974 . . . . **CLC 2, 4, 5, 11, 24**
See also CANR 6; CA 5-8R; obituary CA 49-52; DLB 45, 63

Rao, Raja 1909- . . . . **CLC 25, 56**
See also CA 73-76

Raphael, Frederic (Michael) 1931- . . . . **CLC 2, 14**
See also CANR 1; CA 1-4R; DLB 14

Rathbone, Julian 1935- . . . . **CLC 41**
See also CA 101

Rattigan, Terence (Mervyn) 1911-1977 . . . . **CLC 7**
See also CA 85-88; obituary CA 73-76; DLB 13

Ratushinskaya, Irina 1954- . . . . **CLC 54**

Raven, Simon (Arthur Noel) 1927- . . . . **CLC 14**
See also CA 81-84

Rawley, Callman 1903-
See Rakosi, Carl
See also CANR 12; CA 21-24R

Rawlings, Marjorie Kinnan 1896-1953 . . . . **TCLC 4**
See also YABC 1; CA 104; DLB 9, 22

Ray, Satyajit 1921-. . . . . **CLC 16**
See also CA 114

Read, Herbert (Edward) 1893-1968 . . **CLC 4**
See also CA 85-88; obituary CA 25-28R; DLB 20

Read, Piers Paul 1941- . . . . . . **CLC 4, 10, 25**
See also CA 21-24R; SATA 21; DLB 14

Reade, Charles 1814-1884 . . . . **NCLC 2**
See also DLB 21

Reade, Hamish 1936-
See Gray, Simon (James Holliday)

Reading, Peter 1946- . . . . **CLC 47**
See also CA 103; DLB 40

Reaney, James 1926- . . . . **CLC 13**
See also CA 41-44R; SATA 43

Rebreanu, Liviu 1885-1944 . . . . **TCLC 28**

Rechy, John (Francisco) 1934- . . . . **CLC 1, 7, 14, 18**
See also CAAS 4; CANR 6; CA 5-8R; DLB-Y 82

Redcam, Tom 1870-1933 . . . . **TCLC 25**

Redgrove, Peter (William) 1932- . . . . **CLC 6, 41**
See also CANR 3; CA 1-4R; DLB 40

Redmon (Nightingale), Anne 1943- . . . . **CLC 22**
See also Nightingale, Anne Redmon
See also DLB-Y 86

Reed, Ishmael 1938-. . **CLC 2, 3, 5, 6, 13, 32**
See also CA 21-24R; DLB 2, 5, 33

Reed, John (Silas) 1887-1920 . . . . . . **TCLC 9**
See also CA 106

Reed, Lou 1944- . . . . **CLC 21**

Reeve, Clara 1729-1807 . . . . **NCLC 19**
See also DLB 39

Reid, Christopher 1949-. . . . . **CLC 33**
See also DLB 40

Reid Banks, Lynne 1929-
See Banks, Lynne Reid
See also CANR 6, 22; CA 1-4R; SATA 22

Reiner, Max 1900-
See Caldwell, (Janet Miriam) Taylor (Holland)

Reizenstein, Elmer Leopold 1892-1967
See Rice, Elmer

Remark, Erich Paul 1898-1970
See Remarque, Erich Maria

Remarque, Erich Maria 1898-1970 . . . . **CLC 21**
See also CA 77-80; obituary CA 29-32R

Remizov, Alexey (Mikhailovich) 1877-1957 . . . . **TCLC 27**

Renard, Jules 1864-1910 . . . . **TCLC 17**
See also CA 117

Renault, Mary 1905-1983 . . . . **CLC 3, 11, 17**
See also Challans, Mary
See also DLB-Y 83

Rendell, Ruth 1930- . . . . **CLC 28, 48**
See also Vine, Barbara
See also CA 109

Renoir, Jean 1894-1979 . . . . **CLC 20**
See also obituary CA 85-88

Resnais, Alain 1922-. . . . . **CLC 16**

Reverdy, Pierre 1899-1960 . . . . **CLC 53**
See also CA 97-100; obituary CA 89-92

Rexroth, Kenneth 1905-1982 . . . . . . **CLC 1, 2, 6, 11, 22, 49**
See also CANR 14; CA 5-8R; obituary CA 107; DLB 16, 48; DLB-Y 82; CDALB 1941-1968

Reyes, Alfonso 1889-1959 . . . . **TCLC 33**

Reyes y Basoalto, Ricardo Eliecer Neftali 1904-1973
See Neruda, Pablo

Reymont, Wladyslaw Stanislaw 1867-1925 . . . . **TCLC 5**
See also CA 104

Reynolds, Jonathan 1942? . . . . **CLC 6, 38**
See also CA 65-68

Reynolds, Michael (Shane) 1937- . . . **CLC 44**
See also CANR 9; CA 65-68

Reznikoff, Charles 1894-1976 . . . . **CLC 9**
See also CAP 2; CA 33-36; obituary CA 61-64; DLB 28, 45

Rezzori, Gregor von 1914-. . . . . **CLC 25**

Rhys, Jean 1890-1979 . . . . . . **CLC 2, 4, 6, 14, 19, 51**
See also CA 25-28R; obituary CA 85-88; DLB 36

Ribeiro, Darcy 1922- . . . . **CLC 34**
See also CA 33-36R

Ribeiro, Joao Ubaldo (Osorio Pimentel) 1941- . . . . **CLC 10**
See also CA 81-84

Ribman, Ronald (Burt) 1932- . . . . **CLC 7**
See also CA 21-24R

Rice, Anne 1941- . . . . **CLC 41**
See also CANR 12; CA 65-68

Rice, Elmer 1892-1967. . . . . **CLC 7, 49**
See also CAP 2; CA 21-22; obituary CA 25-28R; DLB 4, 7

Rice, Tim 1944- and **Webber, Andrew Lloyd** 1944- . . . . **CLC 21**

Rice, Tim 1944-
See Rice, Tim and Webber, Andrew Lloyd
See also CA 103

Rich, Adrienne (Cecile) 1929- . . . . **CLC 3, 6, 7, 11, 18, 36**
See also CANR 20; CA 9-12R; DLB 5

Richard, Keith 1943-
See Jagger, Mick and Richard, Keith

Richards, I(vor) A(rmstrong) 1893-1979 . . . . **CLC 14, 24**
See also CA 41-44R; obituary CA 89-92; DLB 27

Richards, Keith 1943-
See Richard, Keith
See also CA 107

Richardson, Dorothy (Miller) 1873-1957 . . . . **TCLC 3**
See also CA 104; DLB 36

Richardson, Ethel 1870-1946
See Richardson, Henry Handel
See also CA 105

Richardson, Henry Handel 1870-1946 . . . . **TCLC 4**
See also Richardson, Ethel

Richardson, Samuel 1689-1761 . . . . **LC 1**
See also DLB 39

Richler, Mordecai 1931- . . . . **CLC 3, 5, 9, 13, 18, 46**
See also CA 65-68; SATA 27, 44; DLB 53

Richter, Conrad (Michael) 1890-1968 . . . . **CLC 30**
See also CA 5-8R; obituary CA 25-28R; SATA 3; DLB 9

Richter, Johann Paul Friedrich 1763-1825
See Jean Paul

Riding, Laura 1901- . . . . **CLC 3, 7**
See also Jackson, Laura (Riding)

Riefenstahl, Berta Helene Amalia 1902-
See Riefenstahl, Leni
See also CA 108

Riefenstahl, Leni 1902- . . . . **CLC 16**
See also Riefenstahl, Berta Helene Amalia

Rilke, Rainer Maria 1875-1926 . . . . **TCLC 1, 6, 19**
See also CA 104

Rimbaud, (Jean Nicolas) Arthur 1854-1891 . . . . **NCLC 4**

Ringwood, Gwen(dolyn Margaret) Pharis 1910-1984 . . . . **CLC 48**
See also obituary CA 112

Rio, Michel 19?? . . . . **CLC 43**

Ritsos, Yannis 1909- . . . . **CLC 6, 13, 31**
See also CA 77-80

Ritter, Erika 1948? . . . . **CLC 52**

Rivers, Conrad Kent 1933-1968 . . . . . . **CLC 1**
See also CA 85-88; DLB 41

Roa Bastos, Augusto 1917- . . . . **CLC 45**

Robbe-Grillet, Alain 1922- . . . . . . **CLC 1, 2, 4, 6, 8, 10, 14, 43**
See also CA 9-12R

Robbins, Harold 1916- . . . . **CLC 5**
See also CA 73-76

Robbins, Thomas Eugene 1936-
See Robbins, Tom
See also CA 81-84

Robbins, Tom 1936- . . . . **CLC 9, 32**
See also Robbins, Thomas Eugene
See also DLB-Y 80

Robbins, Trina 1938- . . . . **CLC 21**

Roberts, (Sir) Charles G(eorge) D(ouglas) 1860-1943 . . . . **TCLC 8**
See also CA 105; SATA 29

Roberts, Kate 1891-1985 . . . . **CLC 15**
See also CA 107; obituary CA 116

Roberts, Keith (John Kingston) 1935- . . . . **CLC 14**
See also CA 25-28R

Roberts, Kenneth 1885-1957 . . . . . . **TCLC 23**
See also CA 109; DLB 9

Roberts, Michele (B.) 1949- . . . . **CLC 48**
See also CA 115

Robinson, Edwin Arlington 1869-1935 . . . . **TCLC 5**
See also CA 104; DLB 54; CDALB 1865-1917

Robinson, Henry Crabb 1775-1867 . . . . **NCLC 15**

Robinson, Jill 1936- . . . . **CLC 10**
See also CA 102

Robinson, Kim Stanley 19?? . . . . **CLC 34**

Robinson, Marilynne 1944- . . . . **CLC 25**
See also CA 116

Robinson, Smokey 1940- . . . . **CLC 21**

Robinson, William 1940-
See Robinson, Smokey
See also CA 116

Robison, Mary 1949- . . . . **CLC 42**
See also CA 113, 116

Roddenberry, Gene 1921- . . . . **CLC 17**

Rodgers, Mary 1931- . . . . **CLC 12**
See also CANR 8; CA 49-52; SATA 8

Rodgers, W(illiam) R(obert) 1909-1969 . . . . **CLC 7**
See also CA 85-88; DLB 20

Rodriguez, Claudio 1934- . . . . **CLC 10**

Roethke, Theodore (Huebner) 1908-1963 . . . . . . **CLC 1, 3, 8, 11, 19, 46**
See also CA 81-84; CABS 2; SAAS 1; DLB 5; CDALB 1941-1968

Rogers, Sam 1943-
See Shepard, Sam

Rogers, Will(iam Penn Adair) 1879-1935 . . . . **TCLC 8**
See also CA 105; DLB 11

Rogin, Gilbert 1929- . . . . **CLC 18**
See also CANR 15; CA 65-68

Rohan, Koda 1867-1947 . . . . **TCLC 22**

Rohmer, Eric 1920- . . . . **CLC 16**
See also Scherer, Jean-Marie Maurice

Rohmer, Sax 1883-1959 . . . . **TCLC 28**
See also Ward, Arthur Henry Sarsfield
See also DLB 70

Roiphe, Anne (Richardson) 1935- . . . . **CLC 3, 9**
See also CA 89-92; DLB-Y 80

Rolfe, Frederick (William Serafino Austin Lewis Mary) 1860-1913 . . . . . . **TCLC 12**
See also CA 107; DLB 34

Rolland, Romain 1866-1944 . . . . **TCLC 23**
See also CA 118

Rolvaag, O(le) E(dvart) 1876-1931 . . . . **TCLC 17**
See also CA 117; DLB 9

Romains, Jules 1885-1972 . . . . **CLC 7**
See also CA 85-88

Romero, Jose Ruben 1890-1952 . . . **TCLC 14**
See also CA 114

Ronsard, Pierre de 1524-1585 . . . . **LC 6**

Rooke, Leon 1934- . . . . **CLC 25, 34**
See also CA 25-28R

Roper, William 1498-1578 . . . . **LC 10**

Rosa, Joao Guimaraes 1908-1967 . . . **CLC 23**
See also obituary CA 89-92

Rosen, Richard (Dean) 1949- . . . . **CLC 39**
See also CA 77-80

Rosenberg, Isaac 1890-1918 . . . . **TCLC 12**
See also CA 107; DLB 20

Rosenblatt, Joe 1933- . . . . **CLC 15**
See also Rosenblatt, Joseph

Rosenblatt, Joseph 1933-
See Rosenblatt, Joe
See also CA 89-92

Rosenfeld, Samuel 1896-1963
See Tzara, Tristan
See also obituary CA 89-92

Rosenthal, M(acha) L(ouis) 1917- . . . **CLC 28**
See also CAAS 6; CANR 4; CA 1-4R; DLB 5

Ross, (James) Sinclair 1908- . . . . **CLC 13**
See also CA 73-76

Rossetti, Christina Georgina 1830-1894 . . . . **NCLC 2**
See also SATA 20; DLB 35

Rossetti, Dante Gabriel 1828-1882 . . . . **NCLC 4**
See also DLB 35

Rossetti, Gabriel Charles Dante 1828-1882
See Rossetti, Dante Gabriel

Rossner, Judith (Perelman) 1935- . . . . **CLC 6, 9, 29**
See also CANR 18; CA 17-20R; DLB 6

Rostand, Edmond (Eugene Alexis) 1868-1918 . . . . **TCLC 6**
See also CA 104

Roth, Henry 1906- . . . . **CLC 2, 6, 11**
See also CAP 1; CA 11-12; DLB 28

Roth, Joseph 1894-1939 . . . . **TCLC 33**

Roth, Philip (Milton) 1933- . . . . . . **CLC 1, 2, 3, 4, 6, 9, 15, 22, 31, 47**
See also CANR 1, 22; CA 1-4R; DLB 2, 28; DLB-Y 82

Rothenberg, Jerome 1931- . . . . **CLC 6**
See also CANR 1; CA 45-48; DLB 5

Roumain, Jacques 1907-1944 . . . . . . **TCLC 19**
See also CA 117

Rourke, Constance (Mayfield) 1885-1941 . . . . **TCLC 12**
See also YABC 1; CA 107

Rousseau, Jean-Baptiste 1671-1741 . . . **LC 9**

Roussel, Raymond 1877-1933 . . . . . **TCLC 20**
See also CA 117

Rovit, Earl (Herbert) 1927- . . . . **CLC 7**
See also CANR 12; CA 5-8R

Rowe, Nicholas 1674-1718 . . . . **LC 8**

Rowson, Susanna Haswell 1762-1824 . . . . **NCLC 5**
See also DLB 37

Roy, Gabrielle 1909-1983 . . . . **CLC 10, 14**
See also CANR 5; CA 53-56; obituary CA 110

Rozewicz, Tadeusz 1921- . . . . **CLC 9, 23**
See also CA 108

Ruark, Gibbons 1941- . . . . **CLC 3**
See also CANR 14; CA 33-36R

Rubens, Bernice 192? . . . . **CLC 19, 31**
See also CA 25-28R; DLB 14

Rudkin, (James) David 1936- ...... **CLC 14**
See also CA 89-92; DLB 13

Rudnik, Raphael 1933-............. **CLC 7**
See also CA 29-32R

Ruiz, Jose Martinez 1874-1967
See Azorin

Rukeyser, Muriel
1913-1980 .... **CLC 6, 10, 15, 27**
See also CA 5-8R; obituary CA 93-96; obituary SATA 22; DLB 48

Rule, Jane (Vance) 1931-.......... **CLC 27**
See also CANR 12; CA 25-28R; DLB 60

Rulfo, Juan 1918-1986............. **CLC 8**
See also CA 85-88; obituary CA 118

Runyon, (Alfred) Damon
1880-1946 .... **TCLC 10**
See also CA 107; DLB 11

Rush, Norman 1933-.............. **CLC 44**
See also CA 121

Rushdie, (Ahmed) Salman
1947- .... **CLC 23, 31, 55**
See also CA 108, 111

Rushforth, Peter (Scott) 1945- ..... **CLC 19**
See also CA 101

Ruskin, John 1819-1900.......... **TCLC 20**
See also CA 114; SATA 24; DLB 55

Russ, Joanna 1937-............... **CLC 15**
See also CANR 11; CA 25-28R; DLB 8

Russell, George William 1867-1935
See A. E.
See also CA 104

Russell, (Henry) Ken(neth Alfred)
1927- .... **CLC 16**
See also CA 105

Rutherford, Mark 1831-1913...... **TCLC 25**
See also DLB 18

Ruyslinck, Ward 1929-........... **CLC 14**

Ryan, Cornelius (John) 1920-1974 ... **CLC 7**
See also CA 69-72; obituary CA 53-56

Rybakov, Anatoli 1911?........ **CLC 23, 53**
See also CA 126

Ryder, Jonathan 1927-
See Ludlum, Robert

Ryga, George 1932- .... **CLC 14**
See also CA 101; DLB 60

Séviné, Marquise de Marie de Rabutin-Chantal 1626-1696..... **LC 11**

Saba, Umberto 1883-1957 .... **TCLC 33**

Sabato, Ernesto 1911- .... **CLC 10, 23**
See also CA 97-100

Sachs, Marilyn (Stickle) 1927- ..... **CLC 35**
See also CLR 2; CANR 13; CA 17-20R; SAAS 2; SATA 3, 52

Sachs, Nelly 1891-1970 .... **CLC 14**
See also CAP 2; CA 17-18; obituary CA 25-28R

Sackler, Howard (Oliver)
1929-1982 .... **CLC 14**
See also CA 61-64; obituary CA 108; DLB 7

Sade, Donatien Alphonse Francois, Comte de
1740-1814 .... **NCLC 3**

Sadoff, Ira 1945-.................. **CLC 9**
See also CANR 5, 21; CA 53-56

Safire, William 1929-............. **CLC 10**
See also CA 17-20R

Sagan, Carl (Edward) 1934-........ **CLC 30**
See also CANR 11; CA 25-28R

Sagan, Francoise
1935- .... **CLC 3, 6, 9, 17, 36**
See also Quoirez, Francoise

Sahgal, Nayantara (Pandit) 1927-... **CLC 41**
See also CANR 11; CA 9-12R

Saint, H(arry) F. 1941- .... **CLC 50**

Sainte-Beuve, Charles Augustin
1804-1869 .... **NCLC 5**

Sainte-Marie, Beverly 1941-
See Sainte-Marie, Buffy
See also CA 107

Sainte-Marie, Buffy 1941-......... **CLC 17**
See also Sainte-Marie, Beverly

Saint-Exupery, Antoine (Jean Baptiste Marie Roger) de 1900-1944 .... **TCLC 2**
See also CLR 10; CA 108; SATA 20; DLB 72

Saintsbury, George 1845-1933..... **TCLC 31**

Sait Faik (Abasiyanik)
1906-1954 .... **TCLC 23**

Saki 1870-1916 .... **TCLC 3**
See also Munro, H(ector) H(ugh)

Salama, Hannu 1936-............. **CLC 18**

Salamanca, J(ack) R(ichard)
1922- .... **CLC 4, 15**
See also CA 25-28R

Salinas, Pedro 1891-1951......... **TCLC 17**
See also CA 117

Salinger, J(erome) D(avid)
1919- .... **CLC 1, 3, 8, 12, 56; SSC 2**
See also CA 5-8R; DLB 2; CDALB 1941-1968

Salter, James 1925- .... **CLC 7, 52**
See also CA 73-76

Saltus, Edgar (Evertson)
1855-1921 .... **TCLC 8**
See also CA 105

Saltykov, Mikhail Evgrafovich
1826-1889 .... **NCLC 16**

Samarakis, Antonis 1919- .... **CLC 5**
See also CA 25-28R

Sanchez, Luis Rafael 1936-........ **CLC 23**

Sanchez, Sonia 1934-.............. **CLC 5**
See also CA 33-36R; SATA 22; DLB 41

Sand, George 1804-1876.......... **NCLC 2**

Sandburg, Carl (August)
1878-1967 .... **CLC 1, 4, 10, 15, 35**
See also CA 5-8R; obituary CA 25-28R; SATA 8; DLB 17, 54; CDALB 1865-1917

Sandburg, Charles August 1878-1967
See Sandburg, Carl (August)

Sanders, (James) Ed(ward) 1939- ... **CLC 53**
See also CANR 13; CA 15-16R; DLB 16

Sanders, Lawrence 1920-.......... **CLC 41**
See also CA 81-84

Sandoz, Mari (Susette) 1896-1966 .. **CLC 28**
See also CANR 17; CA 1-4R; obituary CA 25-28R; SATA 5; DLB 9

Saner, Reg(inald Anthony) 1931- .... **CLC 9**
See also CA 65-68

Sannazaro, Jacopo 1456?1530........ **LC 8**

Sansom, William 1912-1976....... **CLC 2, 6**
See also CA 5-8R; obituary CA 65-68

Santiago, Danny 1911-............ **CLC 33**

Santmyer, Helen Hooven
1895-1986 .... **CLC 33**
See also CANR 15; CA 1-4R; obituary CA 118; DLB-Y 84

Santos, Bienvenido N(uqui) 1911-... **CLC 22**
See also CANR 19; CA 101

Sappho c. 6th-century B.C. .... **CMLC 3**

Sarduy, Severo 1937-.............. **CLC 6**
See also CA 89-92

Sargeson, Frank 1903-1982 .... **CLC 31**
See also CA 106

Sarmiento, Felix Ruben Garcia 1867-1916
See also CA 104

Saroyan, William
1908-1981 ..... **CLC 1, 8, 10, 29, 34, 56**
See also CA 5-8R; obituary CA 103; SATA 23; obituary SATA 24; DLB 7, 9; DLB-Y 81

Sarraute, Nathalie
1902- .... **CLC 1, 2, 4, 8, 10, 31**
See also CA 9-12R

Sarton, Eleanore Marie 1912-
See Sarton, (Eleanor) May

Sarton, (Eleanor) May
1912- .... **CLC 4, 14, 49**
See also CANR 1; CA 1-4R; SATA 36; DLB 48; DLB-Y 81

Sartre, Jean-Paul (Charles Aymard)
1905-1980 ... **CLC 1, 4, 7, 9, 13, 18, 24, 44, 50, 52**
See also CANR 21; CA 9-12R; obituary CA 97-100; DLB 72

Sassoon, Siegfried (Lorraine)
1886-1967 .... **CLC 36**
See also CA 104; obituary CA 25-28R; DLB 20

Saul, John (W. III) 1942- .... **CLC 46**
See also CANR 16; CA 81-84

Saura, Carlos 1932- .... **CLC 20**
See also CA 114

Sauser-Hall, Frederic-Louis 1887-1961
See Cendrars, Blaise
See also CA 102; obituary CA 93-96

Savage, Thomas 1915- .... **CLC 40**

Savan, Glenn 19??................ **CLC 50**

Sayers, Dorothy L(eigh)
1893-1957 .... **TCLC 2, 15**
See also CA 104, 119; DLB 10, 36

Sayers, Valerie 19?? .... **CLC 50**

Sayles, John (Thomas)
1950- .... **CLC 7, 10, 14**
See also CA 57-60; DLB 44

Scammell, Michael 19??........... **CLC 34**

Scannell, Vernon 1922- .... **CLC 49**
See also CANR 8; CA 5-8R; DLB 27

Schaeffer, Susan Fromberg 1941- .... **CLC 6, 11, 22**
See also CANR 18; CA 49-52; SATA 22; DLB 28

Schell, Jonathan 1943-............ **CLC 35**
See also CANR 12; CA 73-76

Scherer, Jean-Marie Maurice 1920-
See Rohmer, Eric
See also CA 110

Schevill, James (Erwin) 1920-....... **CLC 7**
See also CA 5-8R

Schisgal, Murray (Joseph) 1926-..... **CLC 6**
See also CA 21-24R

Schlee, Ann 1934-................ **CLC 35**
See also CA 101; SATA 36, 44

Schlegel, August Wilhelm von 1767-1845 .... **NCLC 15**

Schlegel, Johann Elias (von) 1719?1749 .... **LC 5**

Schmidt, Arno 1914-1979.......... **CLC 56**
See also obituary CA 109; DLB 69

Schmitz, Ettore 1861-1928
See Svevo, Italo
See also CA 104

Schnackenberg, Gjertrud 1953-..... **CLC 40**
See also CA 116

Schneider, Leonard Alfred 1925-1966
See Bruce, Lenny
See also CA 89-92

Schnitzler, Arthur 1862-1931 ...... **TCLC 4**
See also CA 104

Schorer, Mark 1908-1977 .... **CLC 9**
See also CANR 7; CA 5-8R; obituary CA 73-76

Schrader, Paul (Joseph) 1946-...... **CLC 26**
See also CA 37-40R; DLB 44

Schreiner (Cronwright), Olive (Emilie Albertina) 1855-1920......... **TCLC 9**
See also CA 105; DLB 18

Schulberg, Budd (Wilson) 1914- .... **CLC 7, 48**
See also CANR 19; CA 25-28R; DLB 6, 26, 28; DLB-Y 81

Schulz, Bruno 1892-1942.......... **TCLC 5**
See also CA 115

Schulz, Charles M(onroe) 1922- .... **CLC 12**
See also CANR 6; CA 9-12R; SATA 10

Schuyler, James (Marcus) 1923- .... **CLC 5, 23**
See also CA 101; DLB 5

Schwartz, Delmore 1913-1966 .... **CLC 2, 4, 10, 45**
See also CAP 2; CA 17-18; obituary CA 25-28R; DLB 28, 48

Schwartz, Lynne Sharon 1939-..... **CLC 31**
See also CA 103

Schwarz-Bart, Andre 1928-....... **CLC 2, 4**
See also CA 89-92

Schwarz-Bart, Simone 1938-........ **CLC 7**
See also CA 97-100

Schwob, (Mayer Andre) Marcel 1867-1905 .... **TCLC 20**
See also CA 117

Sciascia, Leonardo 1921-...... **CLC 8, 9, 41**
See also CA 85-88

Scoppettone, Sandra 1936-......... **CLC 26**
See also CA 5-8R; SATA 9

Scorsese, Martin 1942- .... **CLC 20**
See also CA 110, 114

Scotland, Jay 1932-
See Jakes, John (William)

Scott, Duncan Campbell 1862-1947 .... **TCLC 6**
See also CA 104

Scott, Evelyn 1893-1963........... **CLC 43**
See also CA 104; obituary CA 112; DLB 9, 48

Scott, F(rancis) R(eginald) 1899-1985 .... **CLC 22**
See also CA 101; obituary CA 114

Scott, Joanna 19?? .... **CLC 50**

Scott, Paul (Mark) 1920-1978....... **CLC 9**
See also CA 81-84; obituary CA 77-80; DLB 14

Scott, Sir Walter 1771-1832 ..... **NCLC 15**
See also YABC 2

Scribe, (Augustin) Eugene 1791-1861 .... **NCLC 16**

Scudery, Madeleine de 1607-1701..... **LC 2**

Sealy, I. Allan 1951- .... **CLC 55**

Seare, Nicholas 1925-
See Trevanian; Whitaker, Rodney

Sebestyen, Igen 1924-
See Sebestyen, Ouida

Sebestyen, Ouida 1924-........... **CLC 30**
See also CA 107; SATA 39

Sedgwick, Catharine Maria 1789-1867 .... **NCLC 19**
See also DLB 1

Seelye, John 1931-................ **CLC 7**
See also CA 97-100

Seferiades, Giorgos Stylianou 1900-1971
See Seferis, George
See also CANR 5; CA 5-8R; obituary CA 33-36R

Seferis, George 1900-1971....... **CLC 5, 11**
See also Seferiades, Giorgos Stylianou

Segal, Erich (Wolf) 1937- .... **CLC 3, 10**
See also CANR 20; CA 25-28R; DLB-Y 86

Seger, Bob 1945-................. **CLC 35**

Seger, Robert Clark 1945-
See Seger, Bob

Seghers, Anna 1900-1983........... **CLC 7**
See also Radvanyi, Netty Reiling
See also DLB 69

Seidel, Frederick (Lewis) 1936-..... **CLC 18**
See also CANR 8; CA 13-16R; DLB-Y 84

Seifert, Jaroslav 1901-1986..... **CLC 34, 44**

Selby, Hubert, Jr. 1928- ..... **CLC 1, 2, 4, 8**
See also CA 13-16R; DLB 2

Senacour, Etienne Pivert de 1770-1846 .... **NCLC 16**

Sender, Ramon (Jose) 1902-1982 .... **CLC 8**
See also CANR 8; CA 5-8R; obituary CA 105

Senghor, Léopold Sédar 1906-...... **CLC 54**
See also CA 116

Serling, (Edward) Rod(man) 1924-1975 .... **CLC 30**
See also CA 65-68; obituary CA 57-60; DLB 26

Serpieres 1907-
See Guillevic, (Eugene)

Service, Robert W(illiam) 1874-1958 .... **TCLC 15**
See also CA 115; SATA 20

Seth, Vikram 1952-............... **CLC 43**

Seton, Cynthia Propper 1926-1982 .... **CLC 27**
See also CANR 7; CA 5-8R; obituary CA 108

Seton, Ernest (Evan) Thompson 1860-1946 .... **TCLC 31**
See also CA 109; SATA 18

Settle, Mary Lee 1918- .... **CLC 19**
See also CAAS 1; CA 89-92; DLB 6

Sévigné, Marquise de Marie de Rabutin-Chantal 1626-1696..... **LC 11**

Sexton, Anne (Harvey) 1928-1974 .... **CLC 2, 4, 6, 8, 10, 15, 53**
See also CANR 3; CA 1-4R; obituary CA 53-56; CABS 2; SATA 10; DLB 5; CDALB 1941-1968

Shaara, Michael (Joseph) 1929- .... **CLC 15**
See also CA 102; DLB-Y 83

Shackleton, C. C. 1925-
See Aldiss, Brian W(ilson)

Shacochis, Bob 1951-............. **CLC 39**
See also CA 119

Shaffer, Anthony 1926- .... **CLC 19**
See also CA 116; DLB 13

Shaffer, Peter (Levin) 1926- ....**CLC 5, 14, 18, 37**
See also CA 25-28R; DLB 13

Shalamov, Varlam (Tikhonovich) 1907?1982 .... **CLC 18**
See also obituary CA 105

Shamlu, Ahmad 1925- .... **CLC 10**

Shammas, Anton 1951-............ **CLC 55**

Shange, Ntozake 1948-....... **CLC 8, 25, 38**
See also CA 85-88; DLB 38

Shapcott, Thomas W(illiam) 1935- .. **CLC 38**
See also CA 69-72

Shapiro, Karl (Jay) 1913- .. **CLC 4, 8, 15, 53**
See also CAAS 6; CANR 1; CA 1-4R; DLB 48

Sharpe, Tom 1928-............... **CLC 36**
See also CA 114; DLB 14

Shaw, (George) Bernard 1856-1950 .... **TCLC 3, 9, 21**
See also CA 104, 109; DLB 10, 57

Shaw, Henry Wheeler 1818-1885 .... **NCLC 15**
See also DLB 11

Shaw, Irwin 1913-1984....... **CLC 7, 23, 34**
See also CANR 21; CA 13-16R; obituary CA 112; DLB 6; DLB-Y 84; CDALB 1941-1968

Shaw, Robert 1927-1978 .... **CLC 5**
See also CANR 4; CA 1-4R; obituary CA 81-84; DLB 13, 14

Shawn, Wallace 1943- .... **CLC 41**
See also CA 112

Sheed, Wilfrid (John Joseph) 1930- .... **CLC 2, 4, 10, 53**
See also CA 65-68; DLB 6

Sheffey, Asa 1913-1980
See Hayden, Robert (Earl)

Sheldon, Alice (Hastings) B(radley) 1915-1987
See Tiptree, James, Jr.
See also CA 108; obituary CA 122

Shelley, Mary Wollstonecraft Godwin 1797-1851 .... **NCLC 14**
See also SATA 29

Shelley, Percy Bysshe 1792-1822 .... **NCLC 18**

Shepard, Jim 19??................ **CLC 36**

Shepard, Lucius 19?? .... **CLC 34**

Shepard, Sam 1943- .... **CLC 4, 6, 17, 34, 41, 44**
See also CANR 22; CA 69-72; DLB 7

Shepherd, Michael 1927-
See Ludlum, Robert

Sherburne, Zoa (Morin) 1912-...... **CLC 30**
See also CANR 3; CA 1-4R; SATA 3

Sheridan, Frances 1724-1766......... **LC 7**
See also DLB 39

Sheridan, Richard Brinsley 1751-1816 .... **NCLC 5**

Sherman, Jonathan Marc 1970? .... **CLC 55**

Sherman, Martin 19?? .... **CLC 19**
See also CA 116

Sherwin, Judith Johnson 1936-... **CLC 7, 15**
See also CA 25-28R

Sherwood, Robert E(mmet) 1896-1955 .... **TCLC 3**
See also CA 104; DLB 7, 26

Shiel, M(atthew) P(hipps) 1865-1947 .... **TCLC 8**
See also CA 106

Shiga, Naoya 1883-1971.......... **CLC 33**
See also CA 101; obituary CA 33-36R

Shimazaki, Haruki 1872-1943
See Shimazaki, Toson
See also CA 105

Shimazaki, Toson 1872-1943....... **TCLC 5**
See also Shimazaki, Haruki

Sholokhov, Mikhail (Aleksandrovich) 1905-1984 .... **CLC 7, 15**
See also CA 101; obituary CA 112; SATA 36

Shreve, Susan Richards 1939-...... **CLC 23**
See also CAAS 5; CANR 5; CA 49-52; SATA 41, 46

Shue, Larry 1946-1985........... **CLC 52**
See also obituary CA 117

Shulman, Alix Kates 1932- ...... **CLC 2, 10**
See also CA 29-32R; SATA 7

Shuster, Joe 1914-
See Siegel, Jerome and Shuster, Joe

Shute (Norway), Nevil 1899-1960... **CLC 30**
See also Norway, Nevil Shute

Shuttle, Penelope (Diane) 1947- ..... **CLC 7**
See also CA 93-96; DLB 14, 40

Siegel, Jerome 1914- and **Shuster, Joe** 1914- .... **CLC 21**

Siegel, Jerome 1914-
See Siegel, Jerome and Shuster, Joe
See also CA 116

Sienkiewicz, Henryk (Adam Aleksander Pius) 1846-1916 .... **TCLC 3**
See also CA 104

Sigal, Clancy 1926-............... **CLC 7**
See also CA 1-4R

Sigourney, Lydia (Howard Huntley) 1791-1865 .... **NCLC 21**
See also DLB 1, 42, 73

Siguenza y Gongora, Carlos de 1645-1700 .... **LC 8**

Sigurjonsson, Johann 1880-1919... **TCLC 27**

Silkin, Jon 1930- .... **CLC 2, 6, 43**
See also CAAS 5; CA 5-8R; DLB 27

Silko, Leslie Marmon 1948- .... **CLC 23**
See also CA 115, 122

Sillanpaa, Franz Eemil 1888-1964... **CLC 19**
See also obituary CA 93-96

Sillitoe, Alan 1928-..... **CLC 1, 3, 6, 10, 19**
See also CAAS 2; CANR 8; CA 9-12R; DLB 14

Silone, Ignazio 1900-1978 .... **CLC 4**
See also CAP 2; CA 25-28; obituary CA 81-84

Silver, Joan Micklin 1935- .... **CLC 20**
See also CA 114

Silverberg, Robert 1935- .... **CLC 7**
See also CAAS 3; CANR 1, 20; CA 1-4R; SATA 13; DLB 8

Silverstein, Alvin 1933- and **Silverstein, Virginia B(arbara Opshelor)** 1933- .... **CLC 17**

Silverstein, Alvin 1933-
See Silverstein, Alvinand Silverstein, Virginia B(arbara Opshelor)
See also CANR 2; CA 49-52; SATA 8

Silverstein, Virginia B(arbara Opshelor) 1937-
See Silverstein, Alvin and Silverstein, Virginia B(arbara Opshelor)
See also CANR 2; CA 49-52; SATA 8

Simak, Clifford D(onald) 1904-1988 .... **CLC 1, 55**
See also CANR 1; CA 1-4R; obituary CA 125; DLB 8

Simenon, Georges (Jacques Christian) 1903- .... **CLC 1, 2, 3, 8, 18, 47**
See also CA 85-88; DLB 72

Simenon, Paul 1956?
See The Clash

Simic, Charles 1938-....... **CLC 6, 9, 22, 49**
See also CAAS 4; CANR 12; CA 29-32R

Simmons, Dan 1948-............. **CLC 44**

Simmons, James (Stewart Alexander) 1933- .... **CLC 43**
See also CA 105; DLB 40

Simms, William Gilmore 1806-1870 .... **NCLC 3**
See also DLB 3, 30

Simon, Carly 1945-............... **CLC 26**
See also CA 105

Simon, Claude (Henri Eugene) 1913- .... **CLC 4, 9, 15, 39**
See also CA 89-92

Simon, (Marvin) Neil 1927- .... **CLC 6, 11, 31, 39**
See also CA 21-24R; DLB 7

Simon, Paul 1941- .... **CLC 17**
See also CA 116

Simonon, Paul 1956?
See The Clash

Simpson, Louis (Aston Marantz) 1923- .... **CLC 4, 7, 9, 32**
See also CAAS 4; CANR 1; CA 1-4R; DLB 5

Simpson, Mona (Elizabeth) 1957-... **CLC 44**

Simpson, N(orman) F(rederick) 1919- .... **CLC 29**
See also CA 11-14R; DLB 13

Sinclair, Andrew (Annandale) 1935- .... **CLC 2, 14**
See also CAAS 5; CANR 14; CA 9-12R; DLB 14

Sinclair, Mary Amelia St. Clair 1865?1946
See Sinclair, May
See also CA 104

Sinclair, May 1865?1946 .... **TCLC 3, 11**
See also Sinclair, Mary Amelia St. Clair
See also DLB 36

Sinclair, Upton (Beall) 1878-1968 .... **CLC 1, 11, 15**
See also CANR 7; CA 5-8R; obituary CA 25-28R; SATA 9; DLB 9

Singer, Isaac Bashevis 1904- .... **CLC 1, 3, 6, 9, 11, 15, 23, 38; SSC 3**
See also CLR 1; CANR 1; CA 1-4R; SATA 3, 27; DLB 6, 28, 52; CDALB 1941-1968

Singer, Israel Joshua 1893-1944... **TCLC 33**

Singh, Khushwant 1915-........... **CLC 11**
See also CANR 6; CA 9-12R

Sinyavsky, Andrei (Donatevich) 1925- .... **CLC 8**
See also CA 85-88

Sirin, V.
See Nabokov, Vladimir (Vladimirovich)

Sissman, L(ouis) E(dward) 1928-1976 .... **CLC 9, 18**
See also CANR 13; CA 21-24R; obituary CA 65-68; DLB 5

Sisson, C(harles) H(ubert) 1914-..... **CLC 8**
See also CAAS 3; CANR 3; CA 1-4R; DLB 27

Sitwell, (Dame) Edith 1887-1964... **CLC 2, 9**
See also CA 9-12R; DLB 20

Sjoewall, Maj 1935-
See Wahloo, Per
See also CA 65-68

Sjowall, Maj 1935-
See Wahloo, Per

Skelton, Robin 1925- . . . . **CLC 13**
See also CAAS 5; CA 5-8R; DLB 27, 53

Skolimowski, Jerzy 1938- . . . . **CLC 20**

Skolimowski, Yurek 1938-
See Skolimowski, Jerzy

Skram, Amalie (Bertha)
1847-1905 . . . . **TCLC 25**

Skrine, Mary Nesta 1904-
See Keane, Molly

Skvorecky, Josef (Vaclav)
1924- . . . . **CLC 15, 39**
See also CAAS 1; CANR 10; CA 61-64

Slade, Bernard 1930- . . . . **CLC 11, 46**
See also Newbound, Bernard Slade
See also DLB 53

Slaughter, Carolyn 1946- . . . . **CLC 56**
See also CA 85-88

Slaughter, Frank G(ill) 1908- . . . . . . **CLC 29**
See also CANR 5; CA 5-8R

Slavitt, David (R.) 1935- . . . . **CLC 5, 14**
See also CAAS 3; CA 21-24R; DLB 5, 6

Slesinger, Tess 1905-1945 . . . . **TCLC 10**
See also CA 107

Slessor, Kenneth 1901-1971. . . . . **CLC 14**
See also CA 102; obituary CA 89-92

Slowacki, Juliusz 1809-1849 . . . . . **NCLC 15**

Smart, Christopher 1722-1771. . . . . **LC 3**

Smart, Elizabeth 1913-1986. . . . . **CLC 54**
See also CA 81-84; obituary CA 118

Smiley, Jane (Graves) 1949- . . . . **CLC 53**
See also CA 104

Smith, A(rthur) J(ames) M(arshall)
1902-1980 . . . . **CLC 15**
See also CANR 4; CA 1-4R;
obituary CA 102

Smith, Betty (Wehner) 1896-1972. . . **CLC 19**
See also CA 5-8R; obituary CA 33-36R;
SATA 6; DLB-Y 82

Smith, Cecil Lewis Troughton 1899-1966
See Forester, C(ecil) S(cott)

Smith, Charlotte (Turner)
1749-1806 . . . . **NCLC 23**
See also DLB 39

Smith, Clark Ashton 1893-1961 . . . . **CLC 43**

Smith, Dave 1942- . . . . **CLC 22, 42**
See also Smith, David (Jeddie)
See also CAAS 7; DLB 5

Smith, David (Jeddie) 1942-
See Smith, Dave
See also CANR 1; CA 49-52

Smith, Florence Margaret 1902-1971
See Smith, Stevie
See also CAP 2; CA 17-18;
obituary CA 29-32R

Smith, John 1580?1631 . . . . **LC 9**
See also DLB 24, 30

Smith, Lee 1944-. . . . . **CLC 25**
See also CA 114, 119; DLB-Y 83

Smith, Martin Cruz 1942- . . . . **CLC 25**
See also CANR 6; CA 85-88

Smith, Martin William 1942-
See Smith, Martin Cruz

Smith, Mary-Ann Tirone 1944-. . . . . **CLC 39**
See also CA 118

Smith, Patti 1946- . . . . **CLC 12**
See also CA 93-96

Smith, Pauline (Urmson)
1882-1959 . . . . **TCLC 25**
See also CA 29-32R; SATA 27

Smith, Rosamond 1938-
See Oates, Joyce Carol

Smith, Sara Mahala Redway 1900-1972
See Benson, Sally

Smith, Stevie 1902-1971. . . . **CLC 3, 8, 25, 44**
See also Smith, Florence Margaret
See also DLB 20

Smith, Wilbur (Addison) 1933- . . . . . **CLC 33**
See also CANR 7; CA 13-16R

Smith, William Jay 1918- . . . . **CLC 6**
See also CA 5-8R; SATA 2; DLB 5

Smollett, Tobias (George) 1721-1771 . . **LC 2**
See also DLB 39

Snodgrass, W(illiam) D(e Witt)
1926- . . . . **CLC 2, 6, 10, 18**
See also CANR 6; CA 1-4R; DLB 5

Snow, C(harles) P(ercy)
1905-1980 . . . . **CLC 1, 4, 6, 9, 13, 19**
See also CA 5-8R; obituary CA 101;
DLB 15

Snyder, Gary (Sherman)
1930- . . . . **CLC 1, 2, 5, 9, 32**
See also CA 17-20R; DLB 5, 16

Snyder, Zilpha Keatley 1927- . . . . . . **CLC 17**
See also CA 9-12R; SAAS 2; SATA 1, 28

Sodergran, Edith 1892-1923. . . . . . **TCLC 31**

Sokolov, Raymond 1941- . . . . **CLC 7**
See also CA 85-88

Sologub, Fyodor 1863-1927 . . . . **TCLC 9**
See also Teternikov, Fyodor Kuzmich

Solomos, Dionysios 1798-1857 . . . **NCLC 15**

Solwoska, Mara 1929-
See French, Marilyn

Solzhenitsyn, Aleksandr I(sayevich)
1918- . . . **CLC 1, 2, 4, 7, 9, 10, 18, 26, 34**
See also CA 69-72

Somers, Jane 1919-
See Lessing, Doris (May)

Sommer, Scott 1951- . . . . **CLC 25**
See also CA 106

Sondheim, Stephen (Joshua)
1930- . . . . **CLC 30, 39**
See also CA 103

Sontag, Susan 1933-. . . **CLC 1, 2, 10, 13, 31**
See also CA 17-20R; DLB 2

Sophocles c. 496?c. 406? . . . . **CMLC 2**

Sorrentino, Gilbert
1929- . . . . **CLC 3, 7, 14, 22, 40**
See also CANR 14; CA 77-80; DLB 5;
DLB-Y 80

Soto, Gary 1952-. . . . . **CLC 32**
See also CA 119

Souster, (Holmes) Raymond
1921- . . . . **CLC 5, 14**
See also CANR 13; CA 13-16R

Southern, Terry 1926- . . . . **CLC 7**
See also CANR 1; CA 1-4R; DLB 2

Southey, Robert 1774-1843 . . . . **NCLC 8**

Soyinka, Akinwande Oluwole 1934-
See Soyinka, Wole

Soyinka, Wole 1934- . . **CLC 3, 5, 14, 36, 44**
See also CA 13-16R; DLB-Y 86

Spackman, W(illiam) M(ode)
1905- . . . . **CLC 46**
See also CA 81-84

Spacks, Barry 1931-. . . . . **CLC 14**
See also CA 29-32R

Spanidou, Irini 1946- . . . . **CLC 44**

Spark, Muriel (Sarah)
1918- . . . . **CLC 2, 3, 5, 8, 13, 18, 40**
See also CANR 12; CA 5-8R; DLB 15

Spencer, Elizabeth 1921- . . . . **CLC 22**
See also CA 13-16R; SATA 14; DLB 6

Spencer, Scott 1945-. . . . . **CLC 30**
See also CA 113; DLB-Y 86

Spender, Stephen (Harold)
1909- . . . . **CLC 1, 2, 5, 10, 41**
See also CA 9-12R; DLB 20

Spengler, Oswald 1880-1936 . . . . . . **TCLC 25**
See also CA 118

Spenser, Edmund 1552?1599 . . . . **LC 5**

Spicer, Jack 1925-1965 . . . . **CLC 8, 18**
See also CA 85-88; DLB 5, 16

Spielberg, Peter 1929- . . . . **CLC 6**
See also CANR 4; CA 5-8R; DLB-Y 81

Spielberg, Steven 1947- . . . . **CLC 20**
See also CA 77-80; SATA 32

Spillane, Frank Morrison 1918-
See Spillane, Mickey
See also CA 25-28R

Spillane, Mickey 1918- . . . . **CLC 3, 13**
See also Spillane, Frank Morrison

Spinoza, Benedictus de 1632-1677 . . . . **LC 9**

Spinrad, Norman (Richard) 1940- . . . **CLC 46**
See also CANR 20; CA 37-40R; DLB 8

Spitteler, Carl (Friedrich Georg)
1845-1924 . . . . **TCLC 12**
See also CA 109

Spivack, Kathleen (Romola Drucker)
1938- . . . . **CLC 6**
See also CA 49-52

Spoto, Donald 1941-. . . . . **CLC 39**
See also CANR 11; CA 65-68

Springsteen, Bruce 1949- . . . . **CLC 17**
See also CA 111

Spurling, Hilary 1940- . . . . **CLC 34**
See also CA 104

Squires, (James) Radcliffe 1917-. . . . **CLC 51**
See also CANR 6, 21; CA 1-4R

Stael-Holstein, Anne Louise Germaine Necker, Baronne de 1766-1817 . . . . **NCLC 3**

Stafford, Jean 1915-1979 . . . . . . **CLC 4, 7, 19**
See also CANR 3; CA 1-4R;
obituary CA 85-88; obituary SATA 22;
DLB 2

Stafford, William (Edgar) 1914- .... **CLC 4, 7, 29**
See also CAAS 3; CANR 5, 22; CA 5-8R; DLB 5

Stannard, Martin 1947- .... **CLC 44**

Stanton, Maura 1946- .... **CLC 9**
See also CANR 15; CA 89-92

Stapledon, (William) Olaf 1886-1950 .... **TCLC 22**
See also CA 111; DLB 15

Starbuck, George (Edwin) 1931- .... **CLC 53**
See also CANR 23; CA 21-22R

Stark, Richard 1933-
See Westlake, Donald E(dwin)

Stead, Christina (Ellen) 1902-1983 .... **CLC 2, 5, 8, 32**
See also CA 13-16R; obituary CA 109

Steele, Timothy (Reid) 1948- .... **CLC 45**
See also CANR 16; CA 93-96

Steffens, (Joseph) Lincoln 1866-1936 .... **TCLC 20**
See also CA 117; SAAS 1

Stegner, Wallace (Earle) 1909- .... **CLC 9, 49**
See also CANR 1, 21; CA 1-4R; DLB 9

Stein, Gertrude 1874-1946 .... **TCLC 1, 6, 28**
See also CA 104; DLB 4, 54

Steinbeck, John (Ernst) 1902-1968 ... **CLC 1, 5, 9, 13, 21, 34, 45**
See also CANR 1; CA 1-4R; obituary CA 25-28R; SATA 9; DLB 7, 9; DLB-DS 2

Steiner, George 1929- .... **CLC 24**
See also CA 73-76

Steiner, Rudolf(us Josephus Laurentius) 1861-1925 .... **TCLC 13**
See also CA 107

Stendhal 1783-1842 .... **NCLC 23**

Stephen, Leslie 1832-1904 .... **TCLC 23**
See also CANR 9; CA 21-24R; DLB 57

Stephens, James 1882?1950 .... **TCLC 4**
See also CA 104; DLB 19

Stephens, Reed
See Donaldson, Stephen R.

Steptoe, Lydia 1892-1982
See Barnes, Djuna

Sterling, George 1869-1926 .... **TCLC 20**
See also CA 117; DLB 54

Stern, Gerald 1925- .... **CLC 40**
See also CA 81-84

Stern, Richard G(ustave) 1928- .... **CLC 4, 39**
See also CANR 1; CA 1-4R

Sternberg, Jonas 1894-1969
See Sternberg, Josef von

Sternberg, Josef von 1894-1969 .... **CLC 20**
See also CA 81-84

Sterne, Laurence 1713-1768 .... **LC 2**
See also DLB 39

Sternheim, (William Adolf) Carl 1878-1942 .... **TCLC 8**
See also CA 105

Stevens, Mark 19?? .... **CLC 34**

Stevens, Wallace 1879-1955 .... **TCLC 3, 12**
See also CA 104; DLB 54

Stevenson, Anne (Katharine) 1933- .... **CLC 7, 33**
See also Elvin, Anne Katharine Stevenson
See also CANR 9; CA 17-18R; DLB 40

Stevenson, Robert Louis 1850-1894 .... **NCLC 5, 14**
See also CLR 10, 11; YABC 2; DLB 18, 57

Stewart, J(ohn) I(nnes) M(ackintosh) 1906- .... **CLC 7, 14, 32**
See also CAAS 3; CA 85-88

Stewart, Mary (Florence Elinor) 1916- .... **CLC 7, 35**
See also CANR 1; CA 1-4R; SATA 12

Stewart, Will 1908-
See Williamson, Jack

Still, James 1906- .... **CLC 49**
See also CANR 10; CA 65-68; SATA 29; DLB 9

Sting 1951-
See The Police

Stitt, Milan 1941- .... **CLC 29**
See also CA 69-72

Stoker, Abraham
See Stoker, Bram
See also CA 105

Stoker, Bram 1847-1912 .... **TCLC 8**
See also Stoker, Abraham
See also SATA 29; DLB 36, 70

Stolz, Mary (Slattery) 1920- .... **CLC 12**
See also CANR 13; CA 5-8R; SAAS 3; SATA 10

Stone, Irving 1903- .... **CLC 7**
See also CAAS 3; CANR 1; CA 1-4R; SATA 3

Stone, Robert (Anthony) 1937? .... **CLC 5, 23, 42**
See also CA 85-88

Stoppard, Tom 1937- ...... **CLC 1, 3, 4, 5, 8, 15, 29, 34**
See also CA 81-84; DLB 13; DLB-Y 85

Storey, David (Malcolm) 1933- .... **CLC 2, 4, 5, 8**
See also CA 81-84; DLB 13, 14

Storm, Hyemeyohsts 1935- .... **CLC 3**
See also CA 81-84

Storm, (Hans) Theodor (Woldsen) 1817-1888 .... **NCLC 1**

Storni, Alfonsina 1892-1938 .... **TCLC 5**
See also CA 104

Stout, Rex (Todhunter) 1886-1975 ... **CLC 3**
See also CA 61-64

Stow, (Julian) Randolph 1935- .. **CLC 23, 48**
See also CA 13-16R

Stowe, Harriet (Elizabeth) Beecher 1811-1896 .... **NCLC 3**
See also YABC 1; DLB 1, 12, 42; CDALB 1865-1917

Strachey, (Giles) Lytton 1880-1932 .... **TCLC 12**
See also CA 110

Strand, Mark 1934- .... **CLC 6, 18, 41**
See also CA 21-24R; SATA 41; DLB 5

Straub, Peter (Francis) 1943- .... **CLC 28**
See also CA 85-88; DLB-Y 84

Strauss, Botho 1944- .... **CLC 22**

Straussler, Tomas 1937-
See Stoppard, Tom

Streatfeild, (Mary) Noel 1897- .... **CLC 21**
See also CA 81-84; obituary CA 120; SATA 20, 48

Stribling, T(homas) S(igismund) 1881-1965 .... **CLC 23**
See also obituary CA 107; DLB 9

Strindberg, (Johan) August 1849-1912 .... **TCLC 1, 8, 21**
See also CA 104

Strugatskii, Arkadii (Natanovich) 1925- and **Strugatskii, Boris(Natanovich)** 1925- .... **CLC 27**

Strugatskii, Arkadii (Natanovich) 1925-
See Strugatskii, Arkadii (Natanovich) and Strugatskii, Boris (Natanovich)
See also CA 106

Strugatskii, Boris (Natanovich) 1933-
See Strugatskii, Arkadii (Natanovich) and Strugatskii, Boris (Natanovich)
See also CA 106

Strugatskii, Boris (Natanovich) 1933- and **Strugatskii, Arkadii (Natanovich)** 1933-
See Strugatskii, Arkadii (Natanovich) and Strugatskii, Boris (Natanovich)

Strummer, Joe 1953?
See The Clash

Stuart, (Hilton) Jesse 1906-1984 .... **CLC 1, 8, 11, 14, 34**
See also CA 5-8R; obituary CA 112; SATA 2; obituary SATA 36; DLB 9, 48; DLB-Y 84

Sturgeon, Theodore (Hamilton) 1918-1985 .... **CLC 22, 39**
See also CA 81-84; obituary CA 116; DLB 8; DLB-Y 85

Styron, William 1925- .. **CLC 1, 3, 5, 11, 15**
See also CANR 6; CA 5-8R; DLB 2; DLB-Y 80

Sudermann, Hermann 1857-1928 .. **TCLC 15**
See also CA 107

Sue, Eugene 1804-1857 .... **NCLC 1**

Sukenick, Ronald 1932- .... **CLC 3, 4, 6, 48**
See also CA 25-28R; DLB-Y 81

Suknaski, Andrew 1942- .... **CLC 19**
See also CA 101; DLB 53

Sully-Prudhomme, Rene 1839-1907 .... **TCLC 31**

Su Man-shu 1884-1918 .... **TCLC 24**

Summers, Andrew James 1942-
See The Police

Summers, Andy 1942-
See The Police

Summers, Hollis (Spurgeon, Jr.) 1916- .... **CLC 10**
See also CANR 3; CA 5-8R; DLB 6

Summers, (Alphonsus Joseph-Mary Augustus) Montague 1880-1948 .... **TCLC 16**

Sumner, Gordon Matthew 1951-
See The Police

Surtees, Robert Smith 1805-1864 .... **NCLC 14**
See also DLB 21

Susann, Jacqueline 1921-1974 .... **CLC 3**
See also CA 65-68; obituary CA 53-56

Suskind, Patrick 1949- .... **CLC 44**

Sutcliff, Rosemary 1920- .... **CLC 26**
See also CLR 1; CA 5-8R; SATA 6, 44

Sutro, Alfred 1863-1933 .... **TCLC 6**
See also CA 105; DLB 10

Sutton, Henry 1935-
See Slavitt, David (R.)

Svevo, Italo 1861-1928 .... **TCLC 2**
See also Schmitz, Ettore

Swados, Elizabeth 1951- .... **CLC 12**
See also CA 97-100

Swados, Harvey 1920-1972 .... **CLC 5**
See also CANR 6; CA 5-8R; obituary CA 37-40R; DLB 2

Swarthout, Glendon (Fred) 1918- ... **CLC 35**
See also CANR 1; CA 1-4R; SATA 26

Swenson, May 1919- .... **CLC 4, 14**
See also CA 5-8R; SATA 15; DLB 5

Swift, Graham 1949- .... **CLC 41**
See also CA 117

Swift, Jonathan 1667-1745 .... **LC 1**
See also SATA 19; DLB 39

Swinburne, Algernon Charles 1837-1909 .... **TCLC 8**
See also CA 105; DLB 35, 57

Swinfen, Ann 19?? .... **CLC 34**

Swinnerton, Frank (Arthur) 1884-1982 .... **CLC 31**
See also obituary CA 108; DLB 34

Symons, Arthur (William) 1865-1945 .... **TCLC 11**
See also CA 107; DLB 19, 57

Symons, Julian (Gustave) 1912- .... **CLC 2, 14, 32**
See also CAAS 3; CANR 3; CA 49-52

Synge, (Edmund) John Millington 1871-1909 .... **TCLC 6**
See also CA 104; DLB 10, 19

Syruc, J. 1911-
See Milosz, Czeslaw

Szirtes, George 1948- .... **CLC 46**
See also CA 109

Tabori, George 1914- .... **CLC 19**
See also CANR 4; CA 49-52

Tagore, (Sir) Rabindranath 1861-1941 .... **TCLC 3**
See also Thakura, Ravindranatha

Taine, Hippolyte Adolphe 1828-1893 .... **NCLC 15**

Talese, Gaetano 1932-
See Talese, Gay

Talese, Gay 1932- .... **CLC 37**
See also CANR 9; CA 1-4R

Tallent, Elizabeth (Ann) 1954- ..... **CLC 45**
See also CA 117

Tally, Ted 1952- .... **CLC 42**
See also CA 120

Tamayo y Baus, Manuel 1829-1898 .... **NCLC 1**

Tammsaare, A(nton) H(ansen) 1878-1940 .... **TCLC 27**

Tanizaki, Jun'ichiro 1886-1965 .... **CLC 8, 14, 28**
See also CA 93-96; obituary CA 25-28R

Tarkington, (Newton) Booth 1869-1946 .... **TCLC 9**
See also CA 110; SATA 17; DLB 9

Tasso, Torquato 1544-1595 .... **LC 5**

Tate, (John Orley) Allen 1899-1979 .... **CLC 2, 4, 6, 9, 11, 14, 24**
See also CA 5-8R; obituary CA 85-88; DLB 4, 45, 63

Tate, James 1943- .... **CLC 2, 6, 25**
See also CA 21-24R; DLB 5

Tavel, Ronald 1940- .... **CLC 6**
See also CA 21-24R

Taylor, C(ecil) P(hillip) 1929-1981 .. **CLC 27**
See also CA 25-28R; obituary CA 105

Taylor, Edward 1644?1729 .... **LC 11**
See also DLB 24

Taylor, Eleanor Ross 1920- .... **CLC 5**
See also CA 81-84

Taylor, Elizabeth 1912-1975 ... **CLC 2, 4, 29**
See also CANR 9; CA 13-16R; SATA 13

Taylor, Henry (Splawn) 1917- ...... **CLC 44**

Taylor, Kamala (Purnaiya) 1924-
See Markandaya, Kamala
See also CA 77-80

Taylor, Mildred D(elois) 1943- ..... **CLC 21**
See also CLR 9; CA 85-88; SATA 15; DLB 52

Taylor, Peter (Hillsman) 1917- .... **CLC 1, 4, 18, 37, 44, 50**
See also CANR 9; CA 13-16R; DLB-Y 81

Taylor, Robert Lewis 1912- .... **CLC 14**
See also CANR 3; CA 1-4R; SATA 10

Teasdale, Sara 1884-1933 .... **TCLC 4**
See also CA 104; SATA 32; DLB 45

Tegner, Esaias 1782-1846 .... **NCLC 2**

Teilhard de Chardin, (Marie Joseph) Pierre 1881-1955 .... **TCLC 9**
See also CA 105

Tennant, Emma 1937- .... **CLC 13, 52**
See also CAAS 9; CANR 10; CA 65-68; DLB 14

Teran, Lisa St. Aubin de 19?? ...... **CLC 36**

Terkel, Louis 1912-
See Terkel, Studs
See also CANR 18; CA 57-60

Terkel, Studs 1912- .... **CLC 38**
See also Terkel, Louis

Terry, Megan 1932- .... **CLC 19**
See also CA 77-80; DLB 7

Tertz, Abram 1925-
See Sinyavsky, Andrei (Donatevich)

Tesich, Steve 1943? .... **CLC 40**
See also CA 105; DLB-Y 83

Tesich, Stoyan 1943?
See Tesich, Steve

Teternikov, Fyodor Kuzmich 1863-1927
See Sologub, Fyodor
See also CA 104

Tevis, Walter 1928-1984 .... **CLC 42**
See also CA 113

Tey, Josephine 1897-1952 .... **TCLC 14**
See also Mackintosh, Elizabeth

Thackeray, William Makepeace 1811-1863 .... **NCLC 5, 14, 22**
See also SATA 23; DLB 21, 55

Thakura, Ravindranatha 1861-1941
See Tagore, (Sir) Rabindranath
See also CA 104

Thelwell, Michael (Miles) 1939- .... **CLC 22**
See also CA 101

Theroux, Alexander (Louis) 1939- .... **CLC 2, 25**
See also CANR 20; CA 85-88

Theroux, Paul 1941- .... **CLC 5, 8, 11, 15, 28, 46**
See also CANR 20; CA 33-36R; SATA 44; DLB 2

Thesen, Sharon 1946- .... **CLC 56**

Thibault, Jacques Anatole Francois 1844-1924
See France, Anatole
See also CA 106

Thiele, Colin (Milton) 1920- .... **CLC 17**
See also CANR 12; CA 29-32R; SAAS 2; SATA 14

Thomas, Audrey (Grace) 1935- .... **CLC 7, 13, 37**
See also CA 21-24R; DLB 60

Thomas, D(onald) M(ichael) 1935- .... **CLC 13, 22, 31**
See also CANR 17; CA 61-64; DLB 40

Thomas, Dylan (Marlais) 1914-1953 .... **TCLC 1, 8; SSC 3**
See also CA 104, 120; DLB 13, 20

Thomas, Edward (Philip) 1878-1917 .... **TCLC 10**
See also CA 106; DLB 19

Thomas, John Peter 1928-
See Thomas, Piri

Thomas, Joyce Carol 1938- .... **CLC 35**
See also CA 113, 116; SATA 40; DLB 33

Thomas, Lewis 1913- .... **CLC 35**
See also CA 85-88

Thomas, Piri 1928- .... **CLC 17**
See also CA 73-76

Thomas, Ross (Elmore) 1926- ...... **CLC 39**
See also CANR 22; CA 33-36R

Thomas, R(onald) S(tuart) 1913- .... **CLC 6, 13, 48**
See also CAAS 4; CA 89-92; DLB 27

Thompson, Ernest 1860-1946
See Seton, Ernest (Evan) Thompson

Thompson, Francis (Joseph) 1859-1907 .... **TCLC 4**
See also CA 104; DLB 19

Thompson, Hunter S(tockton) 1939- .... **CLC 9, 17, 40**
See also CA 17-20R

Thompson, Judith 1954- .... **CLC 39**

Thomson, James 1834-1882...... **NCLC 18**
See also DLB 35

Thoreau, Henry David 1817-1862............... **NCLC 7, 21**
See also DLB 1; CDALB 1640-1865

Thurber, James (Grover) 1894-1961....... **CLC 5, 11, 25; SSC 1**
See also CANR 17; CA 73-76; SATA 13; DLB 4, 11, 22

Thurman, Wallace 1902-1934...... **TCLC 6**
See also CA 104; DLB 51

Tieck, (Johann) Ludwig 1773-1853.................. **NCLC 5**

Tillinghast, Richard 1940-......... **CLC 29**
See also CA 29-32R

Tindall, Gillian 1938-.............. **CLC 7**
See also CANR 11; CA 21-24R

Tiptree, James, Jr. 1915-1987... **CLC 48, 50**
See also Sheldon, Alice (Hastings) B(radley)
See also DLB 8

Tocqueville, Alexis (Charles Henri Maurice Clerel, Comte) de 1805-1859.. **NCLC 7**

Tolkien, J(ohn) R(onald) R(euel) 1892-1973....... **CLC 1, 2, 3, 8, 12, 38**
See also CAP 2; CA 17-18; obituary CA 45-48; SATA 2, 32; obituary SATA 24; DLB 15

Toller, Ernst 1893-1939.......... **TCLC 10**
See also CA 107

Tolson, Melvin B(eaunorus) 1900?1966................... **CLC 36**
See also obituary CA 89-92; DLB 48

Tolstoy, (Count) Alexey Nikolayevich 1883-1945.................. **TCLC 18**
See also CA 107

Tolstoy, (Count) Leo (Lev Nikolaevich) 1828-1910......... **TCLC 4, 11, 17, 28**
See also CA 104; SATA 26

Tomlin, Lily 1939-............... **CLC 17**

Tomlin, Mary Jean 1939-
See Tomlin, Lily

Tomlinson, (Alfred) Charles 1927-............ **CLC 2, 4, 6, 13, 45**
See also CA 5-8R; DLB 40

Toole, John Kennedy 1937-1969.... **CLC 19**
See also CA 104; DLB-Y 81

Toomer, Jean 1894-1967...... **CLC 1, 4, 13, 22; SSC 1**
See also CA 85-88; DLB 45, 51

Torrey, E. Fuller 19??............ **CLC 34**

Tournier, Michel 1924-...... **CLC 6, 23, 36**
See also CANR 3; CA 49-52; SATA 23

Townshend, Peter (Dennis Blandford) 1945-.................... **CLC 17, 42**
See also CA 107

Tozzi, Federigo 1883-1920........ **TCLC 31**

Trakl, Georg 1887-1914........... **TCLC 5**
See also CA 104

Tranströmer, Tomas (Gösta) 1931-........................ **CLC 52**
See also CA 117

Traven, B. 1890-1969........... **CLC 8, 11**
See also CAP 2; CA 19-20; obituary CA 25-28R; DLB 9, 56

Tremain, Rose 1943-.............. **CLC 42**
See also CA 97-100; DLB 14

Tremblay, Michel 1942-........... **CLC 29**
See also CA 116; DLB 60

Trevanian 1925-................. **CLC 29**
See also CA 108

Trevor, William 1928-..... **CLC 7, 9, 14, 25**
See also Cox, William Trevor
See also DLB 14

Trifonov, Yuri (Valentinovich) 1925-1981................... **CLC 45**
See also obituary CA 103

Trilling, Lionel 1905-1975.... **CLC 9, 11, 24**
See also CANR 10; CA 9-12R; obituary CA 61-64; DLB 28, 63

Trogdon, William 1939-
See Heat Moon, William Least
See also CA 115

Trollope, Anthony 1815-1882..... **NCLC 6**
See also SATA 22; DLB 21, 57

Trotsky, Leon (Davidovich) 1879-1940.................. **TCLC 22**
See also CA 118

Trotter (Cockburn), Catharine 1679-1749..................... **LC 8**

Trow, George W. S. 1943-......... **CLC 52**
See also CA 126

Troyat, Henri 1911-.............. **CLC 23**
See also CANR 2; CA 45-48

Trudeau, Garry 1948-............ **CLC 12**
See also Trudeau, G(arretson) B(eekman)

Trudeau, G(arretson) B(eekman) 1948-
See Trudeau, Garry
See also CA 81-84; SATA 35

Truffaut, Francois 1932-1984....... **CLC 20**
See also CA 81-84; obituary CA 113

Trumbo, Dalton 1905-1976........ **CLC 19**
See also CANR 10; CA 21-24R; obituary CA 69-72; DLB 26

Tryon, Thomas 1926-........... **CLC 3, 11**
See also CA 29-32R

Ts'ao Hsueh-ch'in 1715?1763......... **LC 1**

Tsushima Shuji 1909-1948
See Dazai Osamu
See also CA 107

Tsvetaeva (Efron), Marina (Ivanovna) 1892-1941................... **TCLC 7**
See also CA 104

Tunis, John R(oberts) 1889-1975... **CLC 12**
See also CA 61-64; SATA 30, 37; DLB 22

Tuohy, Frank 1925-.............. **CLC 37**
See also DLB 14

Tuohy, John Francis 1925-
See Tuohy, Frank
See also CANR 3; CA 5-8R

Turco, Lewis (Putnam) 1934-...... **CLC 11**
See also CA 13-16R; DLB-Y 84

Turgenev, Ivan 1818-1883....... **NCLC 21**

Turner, Frederick 1943-........... **CLC 48**
See also CANR 12; CA 73-76; DLB 40

Tutuola, Amos 1920-........ **CLC 5, 14, 29**
See also CA 9-12R

Twain, Mark 1835-1910.... **TCLC 6, 12, 19**
See also Clemens, Samuel Langhorne
See also DLB 11, 12, 23

Tyler, Anne 1941-.... **CLC 7, 11, 18, 28, 44**
See also CANR 11; CA 9-12R; SATA 7; DLB 6; DLB-Y 82

Tyler, Royall 1757-1826.......... **NCLC 3**
See also DLB 37

Tynan (Hinkson), Katharine 1861-1931.................. **TCLC 3**
See also CA 104

Tytell, John 1939-............... **CLC 50**
See also CA 29-32R

Tzara, Tristan 1896-1963.......... **CLC 47**
See also Rosenfeld, Samuel

Uhry, Alfred 1947?............... **CLC 55**
See also CA 127

Unamuno (y Jugo), Miguel de 1864-1936................. **TCLC 2, 9**
See also CA 104

Underwood, Miles 1909-1981
See Glassco, John

Undset, Sigrid 1882-1949.......... **TCLC 3**
See also CA 104

Ungaretti, Giuseppe 1888-1970.............. **CLC 7, 11, 15**
See also CAP 2; CA 19-20; obituary CA 25-28R

Unger, Douglas 1952-............. **CLC 34**

Unger, Eva 1932-
See Figes, Eva

Updike, John (Hoyer) 1932-...... **CLC 1, 2, 3, 5, 7, 9, 13, 15, 23, 34, 43**
See also CANR 4; CA 1-4R; CABS 2; DLB 2, 5; DLB-Y 80, 82; DLB-DS 3

Urdang, Constance (Henriette) 1922-....................... **CLC 47**
See also CANR 9; CA 21-24R

Uris, Leon (Marcus) 1924-....... **CLC 7, 32**
See also CANR 1; CA 1-4R; SATA 49

Ustinov, Peter (Alexander) 1921-.... **CLC 1**
See also CA 13-16R; DLB 13

Vaculik, Ludvik 1926-............. **CLC 7**
See also CA 53-56

Valenzuela, Luisa 1938-........... **CLC 31**
See also CA 101

Valera (y Acala-Galiano), Juan 1824-1905................. **TCLC 10**
See also CA 106

Valery, Paul (Ambroise Toussaint Jules) 1871-1945................ **TCLC 4, 15**
See also CA 104, 122

Valle-Inclan (y Montenegro), Ramon (Maria) del 1866-1936............... **TCLC 5**
See also CA 106

Vallejo, Cesar (Abraham) 1892-1938................... **TCLC 3**
See also CA 105

Van Ash, Cay 1918-.............. **CLC 34**

Vance, Jack 1916?............... **CLC 35**
See also DLB 8

Vance, John Holbrook 1916?
See Vance, Jack
See also CANR 17; CA 29-32R

Van Den Bogarde, Derek (Jules Gaspard Ulric) Niven 1921-
See Bogarde, Dirk
See also CA 77-80

Vanderhaeghe, Guy 1951- . . . . **CLC 41**
See also CA 113

Van der Post, Laurens (Jan) 1906- . . . **CLC 5**
See also CA 5-8R

Van de Wetering, Janwillem 1931- . . . . **CLC 47**
See also CANR 4; CA 49-52

Van Dine, S. S. 1888-1939. . . . . **TCLC 23**

Van Doren, Carl (Clinton) 1885-1950 . . . . **TCLC 18**
See also CA 111

Van Doren, Mark 1894-1972. . . . . **CLC 6, 10**
See also CANR 3; CA 1-4R;
obituary CA 37-40R; DLB 45

Van Druten, John (William) 1901-1957 . . . . **TCLC 2**
See also CA 104; DLB 10

Van Duyn, Mona 1921- . . . . **CLC 3, 7**
See also CANR 7; CA 9-12R; DLB 5

Van Itallie, Jean-Claude 1936- . . . . . . **CLC 3**
See also CAAS 2; CANR 1; CA 45-48;
DLB 7

Van Ostaijen, Paul 1896-1928. . . . . **TCLC 33**

Van Peebles, Melvin 1932- . . . . . . **CLC 2, 20**
See also CA 85-88

Vansittart, Peter 1920-. . . . . **CLC 42**
See also CANR 3; CA 1-4R

Van Vechten, Carl 1880-1964 . . . . . . **CLC 33**
See also obituary CA 89-92; DLB 4, 9, 51

Van Vogt, A(lfred) E(lton) 1912-. . . . . **CLC 1**
See also CA 21-24R; SATA 14; DLB 8

Varda, Agnes 1928- . . . . **CLC 16**
See also CA 116

Vargas Llosa, (Jorge) Mario (Pedro) 1936- . . . . **CLC 3, 6, 9, 10, 15, 31, 42**
See also CANR 18; CA 73-76

Vassilikos, Vassilis 1933-. . . . . **CLC 4, 8**
See also CA 81-84

Vazov, Ivan 1850-1921. . . . . **TCLC 25**
See also CA 121

Veblen, Thorstein Bunde 1857-1929 . . . . **TCLC 31**
See also CA 115

Verga, Giovanni 1840-1922 . . . . **TCLC 3**
See also CA 104

Verhaeren, Emile (Adolphe Gustave) 1855-1916 . . . . **TCLC 12**
See also CA 109

Verlaine, Paul (Marie) 1844-1896. . **NCLC 2**

Verne, Jules (Gabriel) 1828-1905 . . . **TCLC 6**
See also CA 110; SATA 21

Very, Jones 1813-1880. . . . . **NCLC 9**
See also DLB 1

Vesaas, Tarjei 1897-1970. . . . . **CLC 48**
See also obituary CA 29-32R

Vian, Boris 1920-1959 . . . . **TCLC 9**
See also CA 106; DLB 72

Viaud, (Louis Marie) Julien 1850-1923
See Loti, Pierre
See also CA 107

Vicker, Angus 1916-
See Felsen, Henry Gregor

Vidal, Eugene Luther, Jr. 1925-
See Vidal, Gore

Vidal, Gore 1925- . . . . **CLC 2, 4, 6, 8, 10, 22, 33**
See also CANR 13; CA 5-8R; DLB 6

Viereck, Peter (Robert Edwin) 1916- . . . . **CLC 4**
See also CANR 1; CA 1-4R; DLB 5

Vigny, Alfred (Victor) de 1797-1863 . . . . **NCLC 7**

Villiers de l'Isle Adam, Jean Marie Mathias Philippe Auguste, Comte de, 1838-1889 . . . . **NCLC 3**

Vine, Barbara 1930-. . . . . **CLC 50**
See also Rendell, Ruth

Vinge, Joan (Carol) D(ennison) 1948- . . . . **CLC 30**
See also CA 93-96; SATA 36

Visconti, Luchino 1906-1976 . . . . **CLC 16**
See also CA 81-84; obituary CA 65-68

Vittorini, Elio 1908-1966 . . . . . . **CLC 6, 9, 14**
See also obituary CA 25-28R

Vizinczey, Stephen 1933-. . . . . **CLC 40**

Vliet, R(ussell) G(ordon) 1929-1984 . . . . **CLC 22**
See also CANR 18; CA 37-40R;
obituary CA 112

Voight, Ellen Bryant 1943- . . . . **CLC 54**
See also CANR 11; CA 69-72

Voigt, Cynthia 1942- . . . . **CLC 30**
See also CANR 18; CA 106; SATA 33, 48

Voinovich, Vladimir (Nikolaevich) 1932- . . . . **CLC 10, 49**
See also CA 81-84

Von Daeniken, Erich 1935-
See Von Daniken, Erich
See also CANR 17; CA 37-40R

Von Daniken, Erich 1935- . . . . **CLC 30**
See also Von Daeniken, Erich

Vonnegut, Kurt, Jr. 1922- . . . . **CLC 1, 2, 3, 4, 5, 8, 12, 22, 40**
See also CANR 1; CA 1-4R; DLB 2, 8;
DLB-Y 80; DLB-DS 3

Vorster, Gordon 1924- . . . . **CLC 34**

Voznesensky, Andrei 1933- . . . . . . **CLC 1, 15**
See also CA 89-92

Waddington, Miriam 1917- . . . . **CLC 28**
See also CANR 12; CA 21-24R

Wagman, Fredrica 1937- . . . . **CLC 7**
See also CA 97-100

Wagner, Richard 1813-1883. . . . . . . **NCLC 9**

Wagner-Martin, Linda 1936-. . . . . . . **CLC 50**

Wagoner, David (Russell) 1926- . . . . **CLC 3, 5, 15**
See also CAAS 3; CANR 2; CA 1-4R;
SATA 14; DLB 5

Wah, Fred(erick James) 1939-. . . . . . **CLC 44**
See also CA 107; DLB 60

Wahloo, Per 1926-1975 . . . . **CLC 7**
See also CA 61-64

Wahloo, Peter 1926-1975
See Wahloo, Per

Wain, John (Barrington) 1925- . . . . **CLC 2, 11, 15, 46**
See also CAAS 4; CA 5-8R; DLB 15, 27

Wajda, Andrzej 1926-. . . . . **CLC 16**
See also CA 102

Wakefield, Dan 1932-. . . . . **CLC 7**
See also CAAS 7; CA 21-24R

Wakoski, Diane 1937- . . . . **CLC 2, 4, 7, 9, 11, 40**
See also CAAS 1; CANR 9; CA 13-16R;
DLB 5

Walcott, Derek (Alton) 1930- . . . . **CLC 2, 4, 9, 14, 25, 42**
See also CA 89-92; DLB-Y 81

Waldman, Anne 1945- . . . . **CLC 7**
See also CA 37-40R; DLB 16

Waldo, Edward Hamilton 1918-
See Sturgeon, Theodore (Hamilton)

Walker, Alice 1944- . . . . **CLC 5, 6, 9, 19, 27, 46**
See also CANR 9; CA 37-40R; SATA 31;
DLB 6, 33

Walker, David Harry 1911-. . . . . **CLC 14**
See also CANR 1; CA 1-4R; SATA 8

Walker, Edward Joseph 1934-
See Walker, Ted
See also CANR 12; CA 21-24R

Walker, George F. 1947- . . . . **CLC 44**
See also CANR 21; CA 103; DLB 60

Walker, Joseph A. 1935- . . . . **CLC 19**
See also CA 89-92; DLB 38

Walker, Margaret (Abigail) 1915- . . . . **CLC 1, 6**
See also CA 73-76

Walker, Ted 1934- . . . . **CLC 13**
See also Walker, Edward Joseph
See also DLB 40

Wallace, David Foster 1962-. . . . . . . **CLC 50**

Wallace, Irving 1916-. . . . . **CLC 7, 13**
See also CAAS 1; CANR 1; CA 1-4R

Wallant, Edward Lewis 1926-1962 . . . . **CLC 5, 10**
See also CANR 22; CA 1-4R; DLB 2, 28

Walpole, Horace 1717-1797. . . . . **LC 2**
See also DLB 39

Walpole, (Sir) Hugh (Seymour) 1884-1941 . . . . **TCLC 5**
See also CA 104; DLB 34

Walser, Martin 1927-. . . . . **CLC 27**
See also CANR 8; CA 57-60

Walser, Robert 1878-1956 . . . . **TCLC 18**
See also CA 118

Walsh, Gillian Paton 1939-
See Walsh, Jill Paton
See also CA 37-40R; SATA 4

Walsh, Jill Paton 1939- . . . . **CLC 35**
See also CLR 2; SAAS 3

Wambaugh, Joseph (Aloysius, Jr.) 1937- .... **CLC 3, 18**
See also CA 33-36R; DLB 6; DLB-Y 83

Ward, Arthur Henry Sarsfield 1883-1959
See Rohmer, Sax
See also CA 108

Ward, Douglas Turner 1930-....... **CLC 19**
See also CA 81-84; DLB 7, 38

Warhol, Andy 1928-1987.......... **CLC 20**
See also CA 89-92; obituary CA 121

Warner, Francis (Robert le Plastrier) 1937- .... **CLC 14**
See also CANR 11; CA 53-56

Warner, Rex (Ernest) 1905-1986.... **CLC 45**
See also CA 89-92; obituary CA 119; DLB 15

Warner, Sylvia Townsend 1893-1978 .... **CLC 7, 19**
See also CANR 16; CA 61-64; obituary CA 77-80; DLB 34

Warren, Mercy Otis 1728-1814... **NCLC 13**
See also DLB 31

Warren, Robert Penn 1905- .. **CLC 1, 4, 6, 8, 10, 13, 18, 39, 53**
See also CANR 10; CA 13-16R; SATA 46; DLB 2, 48; DLB-Y 80

Washington, Booker T(aliaferro) 1856-1915 .... **CLC 34**
See also CA 114; SATA 28

Wassermann, Jakob 1873-1934..... **TCLC 6**
See also CA 104

Wasserstein, Wendy 1950-......... **CLC 32**
See also CA 121

Waterhouse, Keith (Spencer) 1929- .... **CLC 47**
See also CA 5-8R; DLB 13, 15

Waters, Roger 1944-
See Pink Floyd

Wa Thiong'o, Ngugi 1938- .... **CLC 3, 7, 13, 36**
See also Ngugi, James (Thiong'o); Ngugi wa Thiong'o

Watkins, Paul 1964-.............. **CLC 55**

Watkins, Vernon (Phillips) 1906-1967 .... **CLC 43**
See also CAP 1; CA 9-10; obituary CA 25-28R; DLB 20

Waugh, Auberon (Alexander) 1939- .. **CLC 7**
See also CANR 6, 22; CA 45-48; DLB 14

Waugh, Evelyn (Arthur St. John) 1903-1966 ... **CLC 1, 3, 8, 13, 19, 27, 44**
See also CANR 22; CA 85-88; obituary CA 25-28R; DLB 15

Waugh, Harriet 1944- .... **CLC 6**
See also CANR 22; CA 85-88

Webb, Beatrice (Potter) 1858-1943 and **Webb, Sidney (James)** 1858-1943 .... **TCLC 22**

Webb, Beatrice (Potter) 1858-1943
See Webb, Beatrice (Potter) and Webb, Sidney (James)
See also CA 117

Webb, Charles (Richard) 1939-...... **CLC 7**
See also CA 25-28R

Webb, James H(enry), Jr. 1946-.... **CLC 22**
See also CA 81-84

Webb, Mary (Gladys Meredith) 1881-1927 .... **TCLC 24**
See also DLB 34

Webb, Phyllis 1927-.............. **CLC 18**
See also CA 104; DLB 53

Webb, Sidney (James) 1859-1947
See Webb, Beatrice (Potter) and Webb, Sidney (James)
See also CA 117

Webb, Sidney (James) 1859-1947 and **Webb, Beatrice (Potter)** 1859-1947
See Webb, Beatrice (Potter) and Webb, Sidney (James)

Webber, Andrew Lloyd 1948-
See Rice, Tim and Webber, Andrew Lloyd

Weber, Lenora Mattingly 1895-1971 .... **CLC 12**
See also CAP 1; CA 19-20; obituary CA 29-32R; SATA 2; obituary SATA 26

Wedekind, (Benjamin) Frank(lin) 1864-1918 .... **TCLC 7**
See also CA 104

Weidman, Jerome 1913-............ **CLC 7**
See also CANR 1; CA 1-4R; DLB 28

Weil, Simone 1909-1943.......... **TCLC 23**
See also CA 117

Weinstein, Nathan Wallenstein 1903?1940
See West, Nathanael
See also CA 104

Weir, Peter 1944-................ **CLC 20**
See also CA 113

Weiss, Peter (Ulrich) 1916-1982 .... **CLC 3, 15, 51**
See also CANR 3; CA 45-48; obituary CA 106; DLB 69

Weiss, Theodore (Russell) 1916- .... **CLC 3, 8, 14**
See also CAAS 2; CA 9-12R; DLB 5

Welch, (Maurice) Denton 1915-1948 .... **TCLC 22**
See also CA 121

Welch, James 1940-......... **CLC 6, 14, 52**
See also CA 85-88

Weldon, Fay 1933-.... **CLC 6, 9, 11, 19, 36**
See also CANR 16; CA 21-24R; DLB 14

Wellek, Rene 1903- .... **CLC 28**
See also CAAS 7; CANR 8; CA 5-8R; DLB 63

Weller, Michael 1942-......... **CLC 10, 53**
See also CA 85-88

Weller, Paul 1958-............... **CLC 26**

Wellershoff, Dieter 1925-.......... **CLC 46**
See also CANR 16; CA 89-92

Welles, (George) Orson 1915-1985 .... **CLC 20**
See also CA 93-96; obituary CA 117

Wellman, Manly Wade 1903-1986 .. **CLC 49**
See also CANR 6, 16; CA 1-4R; obituary CA 118; SATA 6, 47

Wells, H(erbert) G(eorge) 1866-1946 .... **TCLC 6, 12, 19**
See also CA 110; SATA 20; DLB 34, 70

Wells, Rosemary 1943-........... **CLC 12**
See also CLR 16; CA 85-88; SAAS 1; SATA 18

Welty, Eudora (Alice) 1909- .... **CLC 1, 2, 5, 14, 22, 33; SSC 1**
See also CA 9-12R; CABS 1; DLB 2; CDALB 1941-1968

Wen I-to 1899-1946 .... **TCLC 28**

Werfel, Franz (V.) 1890-1945 ...... **TCLC 8**
See also CA 104

Wergeland, Henrik Arnold 1808-1845 .... **NCLC 5**

Wersba, Barbara 1932-........... **CLC 30**
See also CLR 3; CANR 16; CA 29-32R; SAAS 2; SATA 1; DLB 52

Wertmuller, Lina 1928- .... **CLC 16**
See also CA 97-100

Wescott, Glenway 1901-1987....... **CLC 13**
See also CA 13-16R; obituary CA 121; DLB 4, 9

Wesker, Arnold 1932- .... **CLC 3, 5, 42**
See also CAAS 7; CANR 1; CA 1-4R; DLB 13

Wesley, Richard (Errol) 1945-....... **CLC 7**
See also CA 57-60; DLB 38

Wessel, Johan Herman 1742-1785 .... **LC 7**

West, Anthony (Panther) 1914-1987 .... **CLC 50**
See also CANR 3, 19; CA 45-48; DLB 15

West, Jessamyn 1907-1984 ...... **CLC 7, 17**
See also CA 9-12R; obituary CA 112; obituary SATA 37; DLB 6; DLB-Y 84

West, Morris L(anglo) 1916-..... **CLC 6, 33**
See also CA 5-8R

West, Nathanael 1903?1940..... **TCLC 1, 14**
See also Weinstein, Nathan Wallenstein
See also DLB 4, 9, 28

West, Paul 1930- .... **CLC 7, 14**
See also CAAS 7; CANR 22; CA 13-16R; DLB 14

West, Rebecca 1892-1983 .. **CLC 7, 9, 31, 50**
See also CA 5-8R; obituary CA 109; DLB 36; DLB-Y 83

Westall, Robert (Atkinson) 1929-... **CLC 17**
See also CANR 18; CA 69-72; SAAS 2; SATA 23

Westlake, Donald E(dwin) 1933- .... **CLC 7, 33**
See also CANR 16; CA 17-20R

Westmacott, Mary 1890-1976
See Christie, (Dame) Agatha (Mary Clarissa)

Whalen, Philip 1923-........... **CLC 6, 29**
See also CANR 5; CA 9-12R; DLB 16

Wharton, Edith (Newbold Jones) 1862-1937 .... **TCLC 3, 9, 27**
See also CA 104; DLB 4, 9, 12; CDALB 1865-1917

Wharton, William 1925-........ **CLC 18, 37**
See also CA 93-96; DLB-Y 80

Wheatley (Peters), Phillis 1753?1784 .. **LC 3**
See also DLB 31, 50; CDALB 1640-1865

Wheelock, John Hall 1886-1978 .... **CLC 14**
See also CANR 14; CA 13-16R; obituary CA 77-80; DLB 45

Whelan, John 1900-
See O'Faolain, Sean

Whitaker, Rodney 1925-
See Trevanian

White, E(lwyn) B(rooks) 1899-1985 .... **CLC 10, 34, 39**
See also CLR 1; CANR 16; CA 13-16R; obituary CA 116; SATA 2, 29; obituary SATA 44; DLB 11, 22

White, Edmund III 1940-.......... **CLC 27**
See also CANR 3, 19; CA 45-48

White, Patrick (Victor Martindale) 1912-............ **CLC 3, 4, 5, 7, 9, 18**
See also CA 81-84

White, Terence de Vere 1912-...... **CLC 49**
See also CANR 3; CA 49-52

White, T(erence) H(anbury) 1906-1964 .... **CLC 30**
See also CA 73-76; SATA 12

White, Walter (Francis) 1893-1955 .... **TCLC 15**
See also CA 115; DLB 51

White, William Hale 1831-1913
See Rutherford, Mark

Whitehead, E(dward) A(nthony) 1933-......................... **CLC 5**
See also CA 65-68

Whitemore, Hugh 1936-........... **CLC 37**

Whitman, Sarah Helen 1803-1878 .... **NCLC 19**
See also DLB 1

Whitman, Walt 1819-1892........ **NCLC 4**
See also SATA 20; DLB 3, 64; CDALB 1640-1865

Whitney, Phyllis A(yame) 1903-.... **CLC 42**
See also CANR 3; CA 1-4R; SATA 1, 30

Whittemore, (Edward) Reed (Jr.) 1919-......................... **CLC 4**
See also CANR 4; CA 9-12R; DLB 5

Whittier, John Greenleaf 1807-1892 .... **NCLC 8**
See also DLB 1; CDALB 1640-1865

Wicker, Thomas Grey 1926-
See Wicker, Tom
See also CANR 21; CA 65-68

Wicker, Tom 1926-................ **CLC 7**
See also Wicker, Thomas Grey

Wideman, John Edgar 1941-.................. **CLC 5, 34, 36**
See also CANR 14; CA 85-88; DLB 33

Wiebe, Rudy (H.) 1934-...... **CLC 6, 11, 14**
See also CA 37-40R; DLB 60

Wieland, Christoph Martin 1733-1813 .... **NCLC 17**

Wieners, John 1934-............... **CLC 7**
See also CA 13-16R; DLB 16

Wiesel, Elie(zer) 1928-..... **CLC 3, 5, 11, 37**
See also CAAS 4; CANR 8; CA 5-8R; DLB-Y 1986

Wight, James Alfred 1916-
See Herriot, James
See also CA 77-80; SATA 44

Wilbur, Richard (Purdy) 1921-............ **CLC 3, 6, 9, 14, 53**
See also CANR 2; CA 1-4R; CABS 2; SATA 9; DLB 5

Wild, Peter 1940-................ **CLC 14**
See also CA 37-40R; DLB 5

Wilde, Oscar (Fingal O'Flahertie Wills) 1854-1900 .... **TCLC 1, 8, 23**
See also CA 104; SATA 24; DLB 10, 19, 34, 57

Wilder, Billy 1906-............... **CLC 20**
See also Wilder, Samuel
See also DLB 26

Wilder, Samuel 1906-
See Wilder, Billy
See also CA 89-92

Wilder, Thornton (Niven) 1897-1975 ...... **CLC 1, 5, 6, 10, 15, 35**
See also CA 13-16R; obituary CA 61-64; DLB 4, 7, 9

Wiley, Richard 1944-............. **CLC 44**
See also CA 121

Wilhelm, Kate 1928-............... **CLC 7**
See also CAAS 5; CANR 17; CA 37-40R; DLB 8

Willard, Nancy 1936-........... **CLC 7, 37**
See also CLR 5; CANR 10; CA 89-92; SATA 30, 37; DLB 5, 52

Williams, Charles (Walter Stansby) 1886-1945 .... **TCLC 1, 11**
See also CA 104

Williams, C(harles) K(enneth) 1936-.................... **CLC 33, 56**
See also CA 37-40R; DLB 5

Williams, Ella Gwendolen Rees 1890-1979
See Rhys, Jean

Williams, (George) Emlyn 1905-.... **CLC 15**
See also CA 104; DLB 10

Williams, Hugo 1942-............. **CLC 42**
See also CA 17-20R; DLB 40

Williams, John A(lfred) 1925-.... **CLC 5, 13**
See also CAAS 3; CANR 6; CA 53-56; DLB 2, 33

Williams, Jonathan (Chamberlain) 1929-...................... **CLC 13**
See also CANR 8; CA 9-12R; DLB 5

Williams, Joy 1944-.............. **CLC 31**
See also CANR 22; CA 41-44R

Williams, Norman 1952-.......... **CLC 39**
See also CA 118

Williams, Paulette 1948-
See Shange, Ntozake

Williams, Tennessee 1911-1983 .... **CLC 1, 2, 5, 7, 8, 11, 15, 19, 30, 39, 45**
See also CA 5-8R; obituary CA 108; DLB 7; DLB-Y 83; DLB-DS 4; CDALB 1941-1968

Williams, Thomas (Alonzo) 1926-... **CLC 14**
See also CANR 2; CA 1-4R

Williams, Thomas Lanier 1911-1983
See Williams, Tennessee

Williams, William Carlos 1883-1963 .... **CLC 1, 2, 5, 9, 13, 22, 42**
See also CA 89-92; DLB 4, 16, 54

Williamson, David 1932-.......... **CLC 56**

Williamson, Jack 1908-........... **CLC 29**
See also Williamson, John Stewart
See also DLB 8

Williamson, John Stewart 1908-
See Williamson, Jack
See also CA 17-20R

Willingham, Calder (Baynard, Jr.) 1922-..................... **CLC 5, 51**
See also CANR 3; CA 5-8R; DLB 2, 44

Wilson, A(ndrew) N(orman) 1950- .. **CLC 33**
See also CA 112; DLB 14

Wilson, Andrew 1948-
See Wilson, Snoo

Wilson, Angus (Frank Johnstone) 1913-............. **CLC 2, 3, 5, 25, 34**
See also CA 5-8R; DLB 15

Wilson, August 1945-.......... **CLC 39, 50**
See also CA 115, 122

Wilson, Brian 1942-.............. **CLC 12**

Wilson, Colin 1931-............ **CLC 3, 14**
See also CAAS 5; CANR 1; CA 1-4R; DLB 14

Wilson, Edmund 1895-1972 .... **CLC 1, 2, 3, 8, 24**
See also CANR 1; CA 1-4R; obituary CA 37-40R; DLB 63

Wilson, Ethel Davis (Bryant) 1888-1980 .... **CLC 13**
See also CA 102

Wilson, John 1785-1854.......... **NCLC 5**

Wilson, John (Anthony) Burgess 1917-
See Burgess, Anthony
See also CANR 2; CA 1-4R

Wilson, Lanford 1937-....... **CLC 7, 14, 36**
See also CA 17-20R; DLB 7

Wilson, Robert (M.) 1944-........ **CLC 7, 9**
See also CANR 2; CA 49-52

Wilson, Sloan 1920-.............. **CLC 32**
See also CANR 1; CA 1-4R

Wilson, Snoo 1948-............... **CLC 33**
See also CA 69-72

Wilson, William S(mith) 1932- ..... **CLC 49**
See also CA 81-84

Winchilsea, Anne (Kingsmill) Finch, Countess of 1661-1720.................. **LC 3**

Winters, Janet Lewis 1899-
See Lewis (Winters), Janet
See also CAP 1; CA 9-10

Winters, (Arthur) Yvor 1900-1968 .... **CLC 4, 8, 32**
See also CAP 1; CA 11-12; obituary CA 25-28R; DLB 48

Wiseman, Frederick 1930-......... **CLC 20**

Wister, Owen 1860-1938 .... **TCLC 21**
See also CA 108; DLB 9

Witkiewicz, Stanislaw Ignacy 1885-1939 .... **TCLC 8**
See also CA 105

Wittig, Monique 1935?........... **CLC 22**
See also CA 116

Author Index

Wittlin, Joseph 1896-1976 . . . . **CLC 25**
See also Wittlin, Jozef

Wittlin, Jozef 1896-1976
See Wittlin, Joseph
See also CANR 3; CA 49-52; obituary CA 65-68

Wodehouse, (Sir) P(elham) G(renville) 1881-1975 . . . **CLC 1, 2, 5, 10, 22; SSC 2**
See also CANR 3; CA 45-48; obituary CA 57-60; SATA 22; DLB 34

Woiwode, Larry (Alfred) 1941- . . . **CLC 6, 10**
See also CANR 16; CA 73-76; DLB 6

Wojciechowska, Maia (Teresa) 1927- . . . . **CLC 26**
See also CLR 1; CANR 4; CA 9-12R; SAAS 1; SATA 1, 28

Wolf, Christa 1929- . . . . **CLC 14, 29**
See also CA 85-88

Wolfe, Gene (Rodman) 1931- . . . . **CLC 25**
See also CANR 6; CA 57-60; DLB 8

Wolfe, George C. 1954- . . . . **CLC 49**

Wolfe, Thomas (Clayton) 1900-1938 . . . . **TCLC 4, 13, 29**
See also CA 104; DLB 9; DLB-Y 85; DLB-DS 2

Wolfe, Thomas Kennerly, Jr. 1931-
See Wolfe, Tom
See also CANR 9; CA 13-16R

Wolfe, Tom 1931- . . . **CLC 1, 2, 9, 15, 35, 51**
See also Wolfe, Thomas Kennerly, Jr.

Wolff, Geoffrey (Ansell) 1937- . . . . . **CLC 41**
See also CA 29-32R

Wolff, Tobias (Jonathan Ansell) 1945- . . . . **CLC 39**
See also CA 114, 117

Wolitzer, Hilma 1930- . . . . **CLC 17**
See also CANR 18; CA 65-68; SATA 31

Wollstonecraft (Godwin), Mary 1759-1797 . . . . **LC 5**
See also DLB 39

Wonder, Stevie 1950- . . . . **CLC 12**
See also Morris, Steveland Judkins

Wong, Jade Snow 1922- . . . . **CLC 17**
See also CA 109

Woodcott, Keith 1934-
See Brunner, John (Kilian Houston)

Woolf, (Adeline) Virginia 1882-1941 . . . . **TCLC 1, 5, 20**
See also CA 104; DLB 36

Woollcott, Alexander (Humphreys) 1887-1943 . . . . **TCLC 5**
See also CA 105; DLB 29

Wordsworth, William 1770-1850 . . **NCLC 12**

Wouk, Herman 1915- . . . . **CLC 1, 9, 38**
See also CANR 6; CA 5-8R; DLB-Y 82

Wright, Charles 1935- . . . . **CLC 6, 13, 28**
See also CAAS 7; CA 29-32R; DLB-Y 82

Wright, Charles (Stevenson) 1932- . . **CLC 49**
See also CA 9-12R; DLB 33

Wright, James (Arlington) 1927-1980 . . . . **CLC 3, 5, 10, 28**
See also CANR 4; CA 49-52; obituary CA 97-100; DLB 5

Wright, Judith 1915- . . . . **CLC 11, 53**
See also CA 13-16R; SATA 14

Wright, L(aurali) R. 1939- . . . . **CLC 44**

Wright, Richard (Nathaniel) 1908-1960 . . . **CLC 1, 3, 4, 9, 14, 21, 48; SSC 2**
See also CA 108; DLB-DS 2

Wright, Richard B(ruce) 1937- . . . . . . **CLC 6**
See also CA 85-88; DLB 53

Wright, Rick 1945-
See Pink Floyd

Wright, Stephen 1946- . . . . **CLC 33**

Wright, Willard Huntington 1888-1939
See Van Dine, S. S.
See also CA 115

Wright, William 1930- . . . . **CLC 44**
See also CANR 7; CA 53-56

Wu Ch'eng-en 1500?1582? . . . . **LC 7**

Wu Ching-tzu 1701-1754 . . . . **LC 2**

Wurlitzer, Rudolph 1938? . . . . . **CLC 2, 4, 15**
See also CA 85-88

Wycherley, William 1640?1716 . . . . **LC 8**

Wylie (Benet), Elinor (Morton Hoyt) 1885-1928 . . . . **TCLC 8**
See also CA 105; DLB 9, 45

Wylie, Philip (Gordon) 1902-1971 . . . **CLC 43**
See also CAP 2; CA 21-22; obituary CA 33-36R; DLB 9

Wyndham, John 1903-1969 . . . . **CLC 19**
See also Harris, John (Wyndham Parkes Lucas) Beynon

Wyss, Johann David 1743-1818 . . **NCLC 10**
See also SATA 27, 29

Yanovsky, Vassily S(emenovich) 1906- . . . . **CLC 2, 18**
See also CA 97-100

Yates, Richard 1926- . . . . **CLC 7, 8, 23**
See also CANR 10; CA 5-8R; DLB 2; DLB-Y 81

Yeats, William Butler 1865-1939 . . . . **TCLC 1, 11, 18, 31**
See also CANR 10; CA 104; DLB 10, 19

Yehoshua, A(braham) B. 1936- . . . . **CLC 13, 31**
See also CA 33-36R

Yep, Laurence (Michael) 1948- . . . . . **CLC 35**
See also CLR 3; CANR 1; CA 49-52; SATA 7; DLB 52

Yerby, Frank G(arvin) 1916- . . . **CLC 1, 7, 22**
See also CANR 16; CA 9-12R

Yevtushenko, Yevgeny (Alexandrovich) 1933- . . . . **CLC 1, 3, 13, 26, 51**
See also CA 81-84

Yezierska, Anzia 1885?1970 . . . . **CLC 46**
See also obituary CA 89-92; DLB 28

Yglesias, Helen 1915- . . . . **CLC 7, 22**
See also CANR 15; CA 37-40R

Yorke, Henry Vincent 1905-1974
See Green, Henry
See also CA 85-88; obituary CA 49-52

Young, Al 1939- . . . . **CLC 19**
See also CA 29-32R; DLB 33

Young, Andrew 1885-1971 . . . . **CLC 5**
See also CANR 7; CA 5-8R

Young, Edward 1683-1765 . . . . **LC 3**

Young, Neil 1945- . . . . **CLC 17**
See also CA 110

Yourcenar, Marguerite 1903-1987 . . . . **CLC 19, 38, 50**
See also CA 69-72; DLB 72

Yurick, Sol 1925- . . . . **CLC 6**
See also CA 13-16R

Zamyatin, Yevgeny Ivanovich 1884-1937 . . . . **TCLC 8**
See also CA 105

Zangwill, Israel 1864-1926 . . . . **TCLC 16**
See also CA 109; DLB 10

Zappa, Francis Vincent, Jr. 1940-
See Zappa, Frank
See also CA 108

Zappa, Frank 1940- . . . . **CLC 17**
See also Zappa, Francis Vincent, Jr.

Zaturenska, Marya 1902-1982 . . . . **CLC 6, 11**
See also CA 13-16R; obituary CA 105

Zelazny, Roger 1937- . . . . **CLC 21**
See also CA 21-24R; SATA 39; DLB 8

Zhdanov, Andrei A(lexandrovich) 1896-1948 . . . . **TCLC 18**
See also CA 117

Ziegenhagen, Eric 1970- . . . . **CLC 55**

Ziegenhagen, Eric 1970? . . . . **CLC 55**

Zimmerman, Robert 1941-
See Dylan, Bob

Zindel, Paul 1936- . . . . **CLC 6, 26**
See also CLR 3; CA 73-76; SATA 16; DLB 7, 52

Zinoviev, Alexander 1922- . . . . **CLC 19**
See also CA 116

Zola, Emile 1840-1902 . . . . . . **TCLC 1, 6, 21**
See also CA 104

Zorrilla y Moral, Jose 1817-1893 . . **NCLC 6**

Zoshchenko, Mikhail (Mikhailovich) 1895-1958 . . . . **TCLC 15**
See also CA 115

Zuckmayer, Carl 1896-1977 . . . . **CLC 18**
See also CA 69-72; DLB 56

Zukofsky, Louis 1904-1978 . . . . **CLC 1, 2, 4, 7, 11, 18**
See also CA 9-12R; obituary CA 77-80; DLB 5

Zweig, Paul 1935-1984 . . . . **CLC 34, 42**
See also CA 85-88; obituary CA 113

Zweig, Stefan 1881-1942 . . . . **TCLC 17**
See also CA 112

SSC Cumulative Nationality Index

AMERICAN
Anderson, Sherwood 1
Barnes, Djuna 3
Barthelme, Donald 2
Bowles, Paul 3
Capote, Truman 2
Cather, Willa 2
Cheever, John 1
Faulkner, William 1
Freeman, Mary Wilkins 1
Hawthorne, Nathaniel 3
Hemingway, Ernest 1
Irving, Washington 2
Marshall, Paule 3
Melville, Herman 1
O'Connor, Flannery 1
Parker, Dorothy 2
Poe, Edgar Allan 1
Salinger, J. D. 2
Singer, Isaac Bashevis 3
Thurber, James 1
Toomer, Jean 1
Welty, Eudora 1
Wright, Richard 2

CANADIAN
Atwood, Margaret 2
Munro, Alice 3

ENGLISH
Ballard, J. G. 1
Bowen, Elizabeth 3
Chesterton, G. K. 1
Clarke, Arthur C. 3
Hardy, Thomas 2
Lovecraft, H. P. 3
Wodehouse, P. G. 2

FRENCH
Maupassant, Guy de 1

IRISH
Bowen, Elizabeth 3
Joyce, James 3

ITALIAN
Calvino, Italo 3

RUSSIAN
Chekhov, Anton 2
Dostoevski, Fedor 2

WELSH
Thomas, Dylan 3

SSC Cumulative Title Index

"À sale" (Maupassant) **1**:262
"L'abandonné" (Maupassant) **1**:259
"The Abduction From the Seraglio" (Barthelme) **2**:46, 51-2
"About Love" (Chekhov) **2**:139, 141, 143, 157
"The Absence of Mr. Glass" (Chesterton) **1**:131
"Absent-Mindedness in a Parish Choir" (Hardy) **2**:206, 215, 217
"The Actor and the Alibi" (Chesterton) **1**:138
"Ad Astra" (Faulkner) **1**:147
"Adam, One Afternoon" (Calvino) **3**:112
Adam, One Afternoon, and Other Stories (Calvino)
See *Ultimo viene il corvo*
"The Admirer" (Singer) **3**:378, 384
"Adventure" (Anderson) **1**:18, 58
"An Adventure from a Work in Progress" (Thomas) **3**:402, 407
"The Adventure of a Clerk" (Calvino) **3**:116
"Adventure of a Photographer" (Calvino) **3**:111
"Adventure of a Poet" (Calvino) **3**:111, 116
"The Adventure of a Reader" (Calvino) **3**:112
"Adventure of a Traveller" (Calvino) **3**:111
"The Adventure of the Black Fisherman" (Irving) **2**:241, 247
"The Adventure of the Englishman" (Irving) **2**:262
"The Adventure of the German Student" (Irving) **2**:241, 256-57, 261
"The Adventure of the Mason" (Irving) **2**:266
"Adventure of the Mysterious Picture" (Irving) **2**:261, 265
"Adventure of the Mysterious Stranger" (Irving) **2**:261
Adventures in the Skin Trade, and Other Stories (Thomas) **3**:396, 403-04
"The Affair at Grover Station" (Cather) **2**:102
After Such Pleasures (Parker) **2**:273-74
"After the Fair" (Thomas) **3**:399
"After the Race" (Joyce) **3**:205, 208-09, 226, 231, 234, 247-48
"After the Storm" (Hemingway) **1**:216, 234
"Afternoon of a Playwright" (Thurber) **1**:424
"Agafia" (Chekhov) **2**:155
The Alhambra (Irving) **2**:242-46, 251, 254, 265, 268
"Alicia's Diary" (Hardy) **2**:211, 214
"All at One Point" (Calvino) **3**:103, 108
"All Saints" (Bowen) **3**:40, 42
"All That Glitters" (Clarke) **3**:134
"All the Dead Pilots" (Faulkner) **1**:147
"All the Other Stories" (Calvino) **3**:101
"All the Time in the World" (Clarke) **3**:135
"Allal" (Bowles) **3**:69
"Aller et Retour" (Barnes) **3**:7-8, 10, 14-17, 24
"Alone" (Singer) **3**:360-61, 364
"An Alpine Idyll" (Hemingway) **1**:210, 217
"Am I Not Your Rosalind?" (Thurber) **1**:420, 425
"Amateurs" (Barthelme) **2**:47
"The Ambitious Guest" (Hawthorne) **3**:182, 186-87
"Ambuscade" (Faulkner) **1**:170, 177
"Among the Paths to Eden" (Capote) **2**:74-5
Gli amori difficili (*Difficult Loves*) (Calvino) **3**:111-13, 116-18
"Amour" (Maupassant) **1**:278, 280
"And Then" (Barthelme) **2**:47
"Andrey Satchel and the Parson and Clerk" (Hardy) **2**:215
"L'âne" (Maupassant) **1**:259
"The Angel of the Bridge" (Cheever) **1**:96, 100, 110
"The Angel of the Odd" (Poe) **1**:407-08
"Ann Lee's" (Bowen) **3**:54
"Anna on the Neck" (Chekhov) **2**:131, 157
"Annette Delarbre" (Irving) **2**:241, 251, 259
"Gli anni-lucci" (Calvino) **3**:92
"An Anonymous Story" ("A Story without a Title") (Chekhov) **2**:130-31, 157-58
"An Anonymous Story" (Chekhov)
See "A Story without a Title"
"Another Man's Wife" (Anderson) **1**:39
"Another Story" (Cheever) **1**:112
"Another Wife" (Anderson) **1**:31, 50-1
"The Antique Ring" (Hawthorne) **3**:189, 191
"Apparition" (Maupassant) **1**:265, 281
"The Apple Tree" (Bowen) **3**:33, 41
"The Apple-Tree Table" (Melville) **1**:294-95, 298
"Apropos of the Wet Snow" ("Concerning Wet Snow") (Dostoevski) **2**:187
"Apropos of the Wet Snow" (Dostoevski)
See "Concerning Wet Snow"
"The Aquatic Uncle" (Calvino)
See "Lo zio acquativo"
"Araby" (Joyce) **3**:202-03, 205, 208, 217-18, 225, 231, 234, 237, 242, 245-46, 249
"Ardessa" (Cather) **2**:99, 110-11
The Argentine Ant (Calvino)
See *La formica argentina*
"Ariadna" (Chekhov)
See "Ariadne"
"Ariadne" ("Ariadna") (Chekhov) **2**:131-32, 157
"Ariadne" (Chekhov)
See "Ariadna"

"Arrangement in Black and White" (Parker) **2**:274-75, 278, 280, 283, 286
"The Arrow of Heaven" (Chesterton) **1**:128
"The Art of Bookmaking" (Irving) **2**:254
"Artemis, the Honest Well-Digger" (Cheever) **1**:107-08
"Arthur Jermyn" (Lovecraft) **3**:258, 264
"The Artificial Nigger" (O'Connor) **1**:343, 345, 347, 353
"The Artist of the Beautiful" (Hawthorne) **3**:169-71, 174, 183-84
"The Artistic Career of Corky" (Wodehouse) **2**:342
"An Artist's Story" (Chekhov) See "The House with a Mezzanine"
"An Artist's Story" (Chekhov) See "The House with an Attic"
"An Artist's Story" ("The House with the Maisonette") (Chekhov) **2**:131, 139, 157
"An Artist's Story" (Chekhov) See "The House with the Maisonette"
"Asphodel" (Welty) **1**:467-69, 472
"The Assassination of John Fitzgerald Kennedy Considered as a Downhill Motor Race" (Ballard) **1**:70-1, 75
"The Assignation" (Poe) **1**:394
"At Christmas-time" (Chekhov) **2**:130-31
"At Daybreak" (Calvino) **3**:109
"At Geisenheimer's" (Wodehouse) **2**:355
"At Home" (Chekhov) **2**:139, 142, 155, 157-58
"At Paso Rojo" (Bowles) **3**:59, 61-2, 66, 79
"At the End of the Mechanical Age" (Barthelme) **2**:47
"At the Krungthep Plaza" (Bowles) **3**:80
"At the Landing" (Welty) **1**:468
"At the Tolstoy Museum" (Barthelme) **2**:31, 35, 40, 48, 56
"The Atrocity Exhibition" (Ballard) **1**:75
The Atrocity Exhibition (Ballard) See *Love and Napalm: Export U.S.A.*
"An Attack of Nerves" ("A Nervous Breakdown") (Chekhov) **2**:153, 155-56
"An Attack of Nerves" (Chekhov) See "A Nervous Breakdown"
"Attractive Modern Homes" (Bowen) **3**:54
"L'auberge" (Maupassant) **1**:265
"Auprès d'un mort" (Maupassant) **1**:281
"The Author's Chamber" (Irving) **2**:265
"Autobiography" (Atwood) **2**:15
"Gli avangnardisti a Mentone" (Calvino) **3**:97
"L'aventure de Walter Schnafs" (Maupassant) **1**:263
"L'aveu" (Maupassant) **1**:263, 274
"Avey" (Toomer) **1**:441, 443-45, 451, 453, 458-59
"An Awakening" (Anderson) **1**:34, 44-5
"The Awakening" (Clarke) **3**:143, 148
"The Awakening of Rollo Podmarsh" (Wodehouse) **2**:344
"The Awful Gladness of the Mate" (Wodehouse) **2**:356
"Azathoth" (Lovecraft) **3**:273
"The Back Drawing-Room" (Bowen) **3**:40, 54
"The Balcony" (Irving) **2**:266
"The Balloon" (Barthelme) **2**:31, 33, 36, 42
"The Balloon Hoax" (Poe) **1**:406
"The Banquet of Crow" (Parker) **2**:280, 285
"Un baptême" (Maupassant) **1**:256, 259, 284
"Baptizing" (Munro) **3**:331, 339-40
"Barbados" (Marshall) **3**:299-300, 302-04, 306-08, 316-17
"Barbara of the House of Grebe" (Hardy) **2**:204, 209, 214-15, 221
"Barn Burning" (Faulkner) **1**:163, 165
The Baron in the Trees (Calvino) See *Il barone rampante*
Il barone rampante (*The Baron in the Trees*) (Calvino) **3**:89-91, 93-95, 99, 117-18
"The Barrel" (Maupassant) **1**:269
"The Barricade" (Hemingway) **1**:208
"Bartleby, the Scrivener: A Story of Wall-Street" (Melville) **1**:293, 295, 297-98, 303-04, 311, 317, 322-23, 325, 328, 331
"The Battler" (Hemingway) **1**:242, 244-45, 247
"The Beach Murders" (Ballard) **1**:72-4
"The Bear" (Faulkner) **1**:148, 152-58, 167, 172-74, 182
"A Bear Hunt" (Faulkner) **1**:177
"The Beard" (Singer) **3**:375
The Beast in Me, and Other Animals: A New Collection of Pieces and Drawings about Human Beings and Less Alarming Creatures (Thurber) **1**:425
"The Beauties" (Chekhov) **2**:156
"A Beautiful Child" (Capote) **2**:81
"Becky" (Toomer) **1**:445, 456-58
"Before Breakfast" (Cather) **2**:93-4
"Before Eden" (Clarke) **3**:127
"Before the War" (Atwood) **2**:16
The Beggar Maid: Stories of Flo and Rose (Munro) See *Who Do You Think You Are?*
"Behind the Singer Tower" (Cather) **2**:99, 103-04, 111
"Un bel gioco dura poco" (Calvino) **3**:97
"The Belated Travellers" (Irving) **2**:262
"The Bella Lingua" (Cheever) **1**:93, 106, 112
"The Bell-Tower" (Melville) **1**:298, 303
"Benito Cereno" (Melville) **1**:293, 295-300, 303-04, 310-12, 320-23, 328, 330
"Berenice" (Poe) **1**:396, 398
"Bertie Changes His Mind" (Wodehouse) **2**:356
The Best of Arthur C. Clarke: 1937-1971 (Clarke) **3**:149
The Best Short Stories of J. G. Ballard (Ballard) **1**:74
"The Best Years" (Cather) **2**:93-4, 105
"The Bet" (Chekhov) **2**:130
"La bête à Maître Belhomme" (Maupassant) **1**:259, 273, 281
"The Betrayer of Israel" (Singer) **3**:383
"Betrothed" ("The Betrothed") (Chekhov) **2**:131, 139, 143, 149, 151
"Betrothed" (Chekhov) See "The Betrothed"
"The Betrothed" (Chekhov) See "Betrothed"
"Betty" (Atwood) **2**:14, 22
"Beyond" (Faulkner) **1**:162
"Beyond the End" (Barnes) See "Spillway"
"Beyond the Wall of Sleep" (Lovecraft) **3**:258, 268
"Big Black Good Man" (Wright) **2**:364
"Big Blonde" (Parker) **2**:273-74, 276, 278-81, 284
"Big Boy Leaves Home" (Wright) **2**:360-61, 363, 365, 367-69, 371-76, 379-81, 386-90
"The Big Broadcast of 1938" (Barthelme) **2**:26
"Big Game Hunt" (Clarke) **3**:133-34
"Big Two-Hearted River" (Hemingway) **1**:208, 214, 220, 231, 234, 240, 243-48
"Les bijoux" (Maupassant) **1**:273, 286, 288
"Billenium" (Ballard) **1**:68-9, 75
Billy Budd, Foretopman (Melville) See *Billy Budd, Sailor: An Inside Narrative*
Billy Budd, Sailor: An Inside Narrative (*Billy Budd, Foretopman*) (Melville) **1**:294-303, 305-16, 318, 321, 329
Billy Budd, Sailor: An Inside Narrative (Melville) See *Billy Budd, Foretopman*
"The Birds and the Foxes" (Thurber) **1**:426, 431
"The Birthmark" (Hawthorne) **3**:159, 168-70, 178, 183-84, 189, 191-94
"The Bishop" (Chekhov) **2**:131, 148-49, 157-58
"The Bishop's Robe" (Singer) **3**:374
"The Black Cat" (Poe) **1**:389-90, 406, 408
"The Black Friar" (Chekhov) See "The Black Monk"
"The Black Magic of Barney Haller" (Thurber) **1**:415
"The Black Monk" ("The Black Friar") (Chekhov) **2**:126, 131-32, 143, 147-48
"The Black Monk" (Chekhov) See "The Black Friar"
"The Black Wedding" (Singer) **3**:359, 375-76
Blandings Castle (Wodehouse) **2**:346-47, 353
"The Blast of the Book" (Chesterton) **1**:131
"The Blizzard" (Singer) **3**:374
"Blood" (Singer) **3**:356, 358, 364, 375
"Blood, Sea" (Calvino) **3**:109-10
"Blood-Burning Moon" (Toomer) **1**:443, 445, 450, 452-53, 458
"The Blue Cross" (Chesterton) **1**:119, 123, 133, 135, 138
"Bluebeard's Egg" (Atwood) **2**:17, 21
"The Boarding House" (Joyce) **3**:201, 205-07, 234, 237, 247-48
"The Bohemian Girl" (Cather) **2**:96-7, 101, 103-05, 108
"Boitelle" (Maupassant) **1**:263
"The Bold Dragoon" (Irving) **2**:256
"Bombard" (Maupassant) **1**:263
"Bona and Paul" (Toomer) **1**:444, 446, 450, 452-54, 458-62
"The Bond" (Singer) **3**:385, 387
"Bone Bubbles" (Barthelme) **2**:31
A Book (Barnes) **3**:3-4, 14, 22, 26
"The Book of the Grotesque" (Anderson) **1**:57
"The Bookkeeper's Wife" (Cather) **2**:99, 110
"The Bottomless Well" (Chesterton) **1**:122
"Boule de suif" (Maupassant) **1**:255-57, 259, 263, 266, 269, 271-76, 281-83, 286-88, 290
"Box Seat" (Toomer) **1**:440, 443, 445-48, 450-53, 458
"A Box to Hide In" (Thurber) **1**:414, 417
"A Boy Asks a Question of a Lady" (Barnes) **3**:10-11
"Boy in Rome" (Cheever) **1**:100
"The Boy Knows the Truth" (Singer) **3**:380
"Boys and Girls" (Munro) **3**:321, 343-44
Bracebridge Hall (Irving) **2**:240, 244-46, 251, 254-55, 258-59, 265
"Brain Damage" (Barthelme) **2**:32-3, 39-40, 42, 47, 55

"Brazil" (Marshall) 3:299, 300, 302-04, 306, 317
"Bread" (Atwood) 2:19-20
"Breakfast" (Bowen) 3:54
Breakfast at Tiffany's (Capote) 2:67-76, 78-9, 81
"Breaking Strain" (Clarke) 3:144, 150
"The Breaking Up of the Winships" (Thurber) 1:419, 435
"The Bride of the Innisfallen" (Welty) 1:476, 479, 484, 495
The Brigadier and the Golf Widow (Cheever) 1:94-5, 100
"Bright and Morning Star" (Wright) 2:363, 368, 373, 375, 377, 379-83, 387-88, 391-92
"British Guiana" (Marshall) 3:299-300, 302, 305, 317
"The Broken Heart" (Irving) 2:243, 245
"Broken Sword" (Chesterton)
See "The Sign of the Broken Sword"
"The Brooch" (Faulkner) 1:165
"Brooklyn" (Marshall) 3:300, 302, 304-05, 307-08, 314-17
"Brother Death" (Anderson) 1:32, 37, 39, 50-1, 56-7
"Brother Earl" (Anderson) 1:52
"Brothers" (Anderson) 1:52
"La bûche" (Maupassant) 1:274
"Buckthorne and His Friends" (Irving) 2:241, 251, 261-62
"Build-Up" (Ballard) 1:68, 76-7
"The Burglar's Christmas" (Cather) 2:100
"The Burning" (Welty) 1:476, 479, 484
"The Burning Baby" (Thomas) 3:399, 407
"The Bus" (Singer) 3:381-82
"The Bus to St. James's" (Cheever) 1:100, 106
"The Business Man" (Poe) 1:407
"The Butterfly" (Chekhov) 2:126
"By the People" (Faulkner) 1:178
"By the Water" (Bowles) 3:71-2
"The Cabalist of East Broadway" (Singer) 3:374, 383-84
"Call at Corazón" (Bowles) 3:59, 61-2, 66, 69, 77, 79
"The Call of Cthulhu" (Lovecraft) 3:258, 261, 263-64, 269-70, 274, 278, 280, 283, 290
"A Call on Mrs. Forrester" (Thurber) 1:431
"Calling Jesus" (Toomer) 1:445, 447, 450
"A Canary for One" (Hemingway) 1:209, 217, 232, 237
Cane (Toomer) 1:439-55, 458-60, 462
"The Cane in the Corridor" (Thurber) 1:420, 422
"The Canterbury Pilgrims" (Hawthorne) 3:185-86
"The Capital of the World" (Hemingway) 1:217, 232, 234, 245
"The Captive" (Singer) 3:374, 384
"The Captured Woman" (Barthelme) 2:46
"The Car We Had to Push" (Thurber) 1:431
"Carcassonne" (Faulkner) 1:181
"Careless Talk" (Bowen) 3:31
"Caricature" (Singer) 3:359, 375
"Carma" (Toomer) 1:456-57
"Carpe Noctem, If You Can" (Thurber) 1:424
Carry on, Jeeves (Wodehouse) 2:337, 346
"Un cas de divorce" (Maupassant) 1:286
"Le cas de Madame Luneau" (Maupassant) 1:259, 286
"The Cask of Amontillado" (Poe) 1:378, 394, 407-08
"Cassation" ("A Little Girl Tells a Story to a Lady") (Barnes) 3:6, 10, 16, 24-5
"The Cassowary" (Bowen) 3:33
"Castaway" (Clarke) 3:125, 135-36, 149
"The Castle of Crossed Destinies" (Calvino) 3:101-02
"Cat in the Rain" (Hemingway) 1:244-45
"The Cat Jumps" (Bowen) 3:41, 53
"The Catbird Seat" (Thurber) 1:422, 425, 431-32, 435
"The Catechist" (Barthelme) 2:37, 39, 55
"The Cats of Ulthar" (Lovecraft) 3:262
"The Cattle Dealers" (Chekhov) 2:128
Il cavaliere inesistente (*The Nonexistent Knight*; *The Invisible Knight*; *The Nonexistent Knight and the Cloven Viscount*) (Calvino) 3:90-1, 99, 106-07, 117
"The Celestial Railroad" (Hawthorne) 3:178, 181, 183
"Centaur in Brass" (Faulkner) 1:177
"Châli" (Maupassant) 1:259
"La chambre 11" (Maupassant) 1:288
"Le champ d'Oliviers" (Maupassant) 1:273, 283
"A Changed Man" (Hardy) 2:211, 220
A Changed Man, The Waiting Supper, and Other Tales (Hardy) 2:210-11, 214-15, 221
"Che ti dice la patria?" (Hemingway) 1:232
"The Cheery Soul" (Bowen) 3:32, 54
"À Cheval" (Maupassant) 1:278, 280
"The Chief Mourner of Marne" (Chesterton) 1:128, 138
"Le chien" (Maupassant) 1:259
"Children on Their Birthdays" (Capote) 2:61, 63-6, 70, 72-3, 75-8
"The Chimera" (Cheever) 1:97, 105
"The Chorus Girl" (Chekhov) 2:130, 137, 139
"The Christmas Banquet" (Hawthorne) 3:181, 183
"Christmas Is a Sad Season for the Poor" (Cheever) 1:107
"Christmas Jenny" (Freeman) 1:191
"A Christmas Memory" (Capote) 2:67, 72-3, 75-6
"A Christmas Party and a Wedding" ("A Christmas Tree and a Wedding") (Dostoevski) 2:190, 194-95, 197
"A Christmas Party and a Wedding" (Dostoevski)
See "A Christmas Tree and a Wedding"
"A Christmas Tree and a Wedding" ("A Christmas Party and a Wedding") (Dostoevski) 2:171, 193
"A Christmas Tree and a Wedding" (Dostoevski)
See "A Christmas Party and a Wedding"
"Chronopolis" (Ballard) 1:69, 84
Chronopolis, and Other Stories (Ballard) 1:71
"The Cigarstore Robbery" (Hemingway) 1:208
"A Circle in the Fire" (O'Connor) 1:343-44, 347, 356
"Circle of Prayer" (Munro) 3:348
"The Circular Valley" (Bowles) 3:66, 69-71, 79
"City Life" (Barthelme) 2:40
"A City of Churches" (Barthelme) 2:37, 39, 41, 54
"Clancy in the Tower of Babel" (Cheever) 1:107
"Clay" (Joyce) 3:205, 209, 211, 221-22, 226, 233-34, 237, 247
"A Clean, Well-Lighted Place" (Hemingway) 1:216, 230, 232, 237-38
"The Clemency of the Court" (Cather) 2:96, 100, 103, 105
"Clementina" (Cheever) 1:100, 107
The Clicking of Cuthbert (Wodehouse) 2:344, 354
"Clothe the Naked" (Parker) 2:275, 280-81, 286
The Cloven Viscount (Calvino)
See *Il visconte dimezzato*
The Club of Queer Trades (Chesterton) 1:120, 122, 139
"Clytie" (Welty) 1:466, 468, 471, 481, 495
"The Coach House" (Chekhov) 2:128
"Cock-a-Doodle-Doo!" (Melville) 1:295, 298, 303, 305, 322
"Cockadoodledoo" (Singer) 3:358
"Coco" (Maupassant) 1:275
"Un coeur simple" (Maupassant) 1:286
Collected Stories: 1939-1976 (Bowles) 3:65, 68-9
The Collected Stories of Dorothy Parker (*Here Lies*) (Parker) 2:276
The Collected Stories of Dorothy Parker (Parker)
See *Here Lies*
The Collected Stories of Isaac Bashevis Singer (Singer) 3:383-84
Collected Stories of William Faulkner (Faulkner) 1:151, 161-62, 177, 181
"Le collier" (Maupassant) 1:259
"The Colloquy of Monos and Una" (Poe) 1:401-02
"The Colour out of Space" (Lovecraft) 3:261, 263, 267-69, 274, 281, 290-91
Come Back, Dr. Caligari (Barthelme) 2:26-9, 31, 37-9, 46, 49, 51
"The Comforts of Home" (O'Connor) 1:343-44, 351, 353, 365
"Coming, Aphrodite!" (Cather) 2:91-2, 95, 104, 111-12
"Coming, Eden Bower!" (Cather) 2:111-12, 114
"Coming Home" (Bowen) 3:40
"A Committee-Man of 'The Terror'" (Hardy) 2:220
"Company for Gertrude" (Wodehouse) 2:346
"The Complaint Ledger" (Chekhov) 2:130
"Concerning the Bodyguard" (Barthelme) 2:44
"Concerning Wet Snow" ("Apropos of the Wet Snow") (Dostoevski) 2:169
"Concerning Wet Snow" (Dostoevski)
See "Apropos of the Wet Snow"
"The Conference" (Singer) 3:385, 388
"A Conflict Ended" (Freeman) 1:196-97, 199
"Confused" (Singer) 3:384
"A Conquest of Humility" (Freeman) 1:198
"Consequences" (Cather) 2:110-11, 115
"Conservatory" (Barthelme) 2:51
Contes de la Bécasse (Maupassant) 1:257
"The Contessina" (Bowen) 3:40
"The Contract" (Anderson) 1:52
"The Conversation of Eiron and Charmion" (Poe) 1:402
"Conversations with Goethe" (Barthelme) 2:51

"The Conversion of Sum Loo" (Cather) **2**:102
"Cool Air" (Lovecraft) **3**:258, 262, 274
"Un coq chanta" (Maupassant) **1**:272
"The Corn Planting" (Anderson) **1**:37
"Cosmic Casanova" (Clarke) **3**:133
Le cosmicomiche (*Cosmicomics*) (Calvino) **3**:92-6, 98-100, 103-04, 106-07, 110, 112, 116-17
Cosmicomics (Calvino)
See *Le cosmicomiche*
"The Count of Crow's Nest" (Cather) **2**:100, 102
"The Count of Monte Cristo" (Calvino) **3**:93, 95-6
"Counterparts" (Joyce) **3**:200-01, 205, 209, 226, 231, 234, 246, 249
"Country Church" (Irving) **2**:244
"The Country Husband" (Cheever) **1**:90, 100-02
"A Couple of Hamburgers" (Thurber) **1**:418-19
"A Courtship" (Faulkner) **1**:151, 178
"Cousin Larry" (Parker) **2**:280, 283
"The Coward" (Barnes) **3**:18-22
Credos and Curios (Thurber) **1**:424
"Crevasse" (Faulkner) **1**:147
"Le crime au père Boniface" (Maupassant) **1**:274
"The Crime of Gabriel Gale" (Chesterton) **1**:124
"The Crime Wave at Blandings" (Wodehouse) **2**:344, 346, 349
"Critical Mass" (Clarke) **3**:134
"Critique de la vie quotidienne" (Barthelme) **2**:39-40, 42, 55
"Cross-Country Snow" (Hemingway) **1**:217, 244
"A Crown of Feathers" (Singer) **3**:374
A Crown of Feathers, and Other Stories (Singer) **3**:374-76, 380, 382, 384
"Crystals" (Calvino) **3**:108-09
"The Curb in the Sky" (Thurber) **1**:418, 425
"The Cure" (Cheever) **1**:89
"The Curse" (Clarke) **3**:124, 143-44
"A Curtain of Green" (Welty) **1**:487
"The Custard Heart" (Parker) **2**:275, 280-81, 286
"The Custody of the Pumpkin" (Wodehouse) **2**:346-47
"The Dagger with Wings" (Chesterton) **1**:130-31
"Dagon" (Lovecraft) **3**:258, 262, 268, 272-73, 282, 285, 289
"The Dance at Chevalier's" (Cather) **2**:101, 105, 107
"Dance of the Happy Shades" (Munro) **3**:321, 328-30, 335, 346
"Dancing Girls" (Atwood) **2**:6-8, 10, 12
Dancing Girls and Other Stories (Atwood) **2**:3-7, 10, 13-16, 20-2
"The Dancing Mistress" (Bowen) **3**:30, 43, 54
"The Danger in the House" (Thurber) **1**:429
"The Darling" (Chekhov) **2**:131-32, 135
"Daughter of Albion" (Chekhov) **2**:126
"Daughters" (Anderson) **1**:52
"Daumier" (Barthelme) **2**:39, 42, 49, 55
"De Daumier-Smith's Blue Period" (Salinger) **2**:293, 301, 315
"David Swan" (Hawthorne) **3**:160
"A Day in Coney Island" (Singer) **3**:374
"Day of the Butterfly" (Munro) **3**:329-30, 337
"The Day the Dam Broke" (Thurber) **1**:426, 428, 432
"The Day the Pig Fell into the Well" (Cheever) **1**:100
Daylight and Nightmare (Chesterton) **1**:140
"A Day's Work" (Capote) **2**:81
"The Dead" (Joyce) **3**:202-06, 208, 210-11, 214-15, 217, 223-26, 228, 232-40, 242-45, 247, 249
"The Dead Fiddler" (Singer) **3**:369, 384
"Dead Mabelle" (Bowen) **3**:30, 44, 54
"Death" (Anderson) **1**:30, 42
"Death" (Calvino) **3**:110
"Death and the Senator" (Clarke) **3**:147
"A Death in the Desert" (Cather) **2**:90-1, 98, 103, 105, 113
"Death in the Woods" (Anderson) **1**:31, 37-8, 40, 50-2, 56, 58-62
"Death of a Traveling Salesman" (Welty) **1**:466, 472, 481, 493, 497
"The Death of Edward Lear" (Barthelme) **2**:49, 52
"The Death of Justina" (Cheever) **1**:100
"The Death of Methuselah" (Singer) **3**:389
The Death of Methuselah, and Other Stories (Singer) **3**:389
"Décoré" (Maupassant) **1**:256, 263
"Découverte" (Maupassant) **1**:259
"Deep End" (Ballard) **1**:69
"The Defenestration of Ermintrude Inch" (Clarke) **3**:134
"The Delicate Prey" (Bowles) **3**:59-63, 66, 72, 77
The Delicate Prey, and Other Stories (Bowles) **3**:58-65, 67, 70-2, 76-7, 79-80
"The Delta at Sunset" (Ballard) **1**:69
"Delta Autumn" (Faulkner) **1**:166
"The Demon Lover" (Bowen) **3**:31-2, 41, 50-2, 54
The Demon Lover, and Other Stories (*Ivy Gripped the Steps, and Other Stories*) (Bowen) **3**:30-3, 41, 44, 48, 50-2
"The Demonstrators" (Welty) **1**:488
"Departure" (Anderson) **1**:31, 42, 45-6
"Derring-Do" (Capote) **2**:81
"A Descent into the Maelström" (Poe) **1**:385, 400, 402
"Desire in November" (Calvino) **3**:112
"The Destruction of Kreshev" (Singer) **3**:358-59, 368, 375, 383-84
"Deux amis" (Maupassant) **1**:275
"The Devil and Tom Walker" (Irving) **2**:241, 247-48, 250-51, 254, 262
"The Devil in the Belfry" (Poe) **1**:407
"Le diable" (Maupassant) **1**:270, 284
"Dial F for Frankenstein" (Clarke) **3**:145
"A Diamond Guitar" (Capote) **2**:67
"The Diamond Mine" (Cather) **2**:91-2
"Diddling Considered as One of the Exact Sciences" (Poe) **1**:407
Difficult Loves (Calvino)
See *Gli amori difficili*
"Difficult People" (Chekhov) **2**:155
"The Dinosaurs" (Calvino) **3**:103, 109
"The Disinherited" (Bowen) **3**:33, 41, 45, 48-9, 51
"The Dismissal" (Bowles) **3**:75, 80
"The Displaced Person" (O'Connor) **1**:335-36, 338, 343-45, 347, 359
"The Distance of the Moon" (Calvino)
See "La distanza della luna"
"A Distant Episode" (Bowles) **3**:59, 61-2, 66-9, 72, 78
"La distanza della luna" ("The Distance of the Moon") (Calvino) **3**:92, 103, 107, 109
"The Distracted Preacher" (Hardy) **2**:203, 205, 208, 213-15, 219-21
"Do You Want to Make Something Out of It?" (Thurber) **1**:428
"Doc Marlowe" (Thurber) **1**:414
"The Doctor and the Doctor's Wife" (Hemingway) **1**:208, 217, 234, 241, 245
"Dr. Bullivant" (Hawthorne) **3**:164
"Dr. Heidegger's Experiment" (Hawthorne) **3**:154, 178, 186-87
Doctor Martino, and Other Stories (Faulkner) **1**:180
"The Doctors" (Barnes) **3**:9-10
"A Doctor's Visit" (Chekhov) **2**:127, 156-58
Dollari e vecchie mondane (*Dollars and the Demi-Mondaine*) (Calvino) **3**:91
Dollars and the Demi-Mondaine (Calvino)
See *Dollari e vecchie mondane*
"Dolph Heyliger" (Irving) **2**:241, 247-48, 251, 254, 256, 259-60
"The Dolt" (Barthelme) **2**:38, 52
"Doña Faustina" (Bowles) **3**:64, 66, 80, 83
"Le donneur d'eau bénite" (Maupassant) **1**:281
"The Doom of the Darnaways" (Chesterton) **1**:131, 138
"The Door of the Trap" (Anderson) **1**:27, 39, 52
"El Dorado: A Kansas Recessional" (Cather) **2**:101, 105
"Double Birthday" (Cather) **2**:99, 113-15
"Down at the Dinghy" (Salinger) **2**:290-91, 295-96, 298-300, 314
"Down by the Riverside" (Wright) **2**:360-61, 363, 365-69, 371, 374-75, 379-81, 387, 390-91
"The Dragon at Hide and Seek" (Chesterton) **1**:140
"The Dream of a Queer Fellow" ("The Dream of a Ridiculous Man") (Dostoevski) **2**:166
"The Dream of a Queer Fellow" (Dostoevski)
See "The Dream of a Ridiculous Man"
"The Dream of a Ridiculous Man" (Dostoevski) **2**:183, 185
"The Dream of a Ridiculous Man" (Dostoevski)
See "The Dream of a Queer Fellow"
"Dreams" (Chekhov) **2**:156
"The Dreams in the Witch-House" (Lovecraft) **3**:258, 260, 263, 268, 272, 274-76, 282
"A Dreary Story" ("A Dull Story") (Chekhov) **2**:126, 131, 143, 150, 156
"A Dreary Story" (Chekhov)
See "A Dull Story"
"The Dress" (Thomas) **3**:399, 408
"The Drowned Giant" (Ballard) **1**:68, 74
"Drowne's Wooden Image" (Hawthorne) **3**:185
"Dry September" (Faulkner) **1**:148, 180-81
Dubliners (Joyce) **3**:201-03, 205-07, 210, 213-14, 216-18, 224-26, 228-30, 233-35, 237-39, 244-45, 247-49
"The Duchess" (Cheever) **1**:106
"The Duchess and the Bugs" (Thurber) **1**:430
"The Duchess of Hamptonshire" (Hardy) **2**:204

"The Duel" (Chekhov) **2**:131, 143, 145, 150-51, 155, 157
"The Duel of Dr. Hirsch" (Chesterton) **1**:138
"A Duel without Seconds" (Barnes) **3**:13
"The Duke's Reappearance" (Hardy) **2**:210
"A Dull Story" (Chekhov)
See "A Dreary Story"
"Dulse" (Munro) **3**:346
"The Dunwich Horror" (Lovecraft) **3**:258-59, 263, 269-70, 274-76, 290-92, 294
"Dusie" (Barnes) **3**:10, 16
"Dusk before Fireworks" (Parker) **2**:273-74, 281, 284-85
Early Stories (Bowen) **3**:40
"Earth's Holocaust" (Hawthorne) **3**:162, 181-82, 189
"The Easter Egg Party" (Bowen) **3**:43, 47
"Easter Eve" (Chekhov) **2**:130
"The Eccentric Seclusion of the Old Lady" (Chesterton) **1**:120
"The Echo" (Bowles) **3**:59, 61-2, 66, 72, 77, 79
"The Edge of the World" (Cheever) **1**:88
"The Educational Experience" (Barthelme) **2**:53
"Edward and Pia" (Barthelme) **2**:30
"Edward Randolph's Portrait" (Hawthorne) **3**:179, 182
"The Egg" (Anderson)
See "The Triumph of the Egg"
"Egotism; or, the Bosom Serpent" (Hawthorne) **3**:159, 178, 183, 189
Eight Men (Wright) **2**:364, 366, 370, 386, 388
"Eleanor's House" (Cather) **2**:99, 103
"The Embarkment for Cythera" (Cheever) **1**:93
"The Empty Amulet" (Bowles) **3**:76
"En famille" (Maupassant) **1**:259-60, 263, 272, 274, 278
"En voyage" (Maupassant) **1**:280
"En wagon" (Maupassant) **1**:263
"The Encantadas; or, The Enchanted Isles" (Melville)
See "Hood's Isle and the Hermit Oberlus"
"The Encantadas; or, The Enchanted Isles" ("Two Sides to a Tortoise") (Melville) **1**:293, 297-99, 303-04, 308, 310-11, 321-22, 329
"The Encantadas; or, The Enchanted Isles" (Melville)
See "Two Sides to a Tortoise"
"The Enchanted Bluff" (Cather) **2**:97, 102, 104-05, 108
"An Enchanted Garden" (Calvino)
See "Un giardino incantato"
"The Enchanted Garden" (Calvino)
See "Un giardino incantato"
"An Encounter" (Joyce) **3**:201, 205, 208, 217-18, 225-26, 230, 232, 234, 237, 247
"Encounter at Dawn" (Clarke) **3**:127, 135, 143
Encounters (Bowen) **3**:29, 40
"The End of Something" (Hemingway) **1**:208, 234, 244-45
"The End of Wisdom" (Chesterton) **1**:140
"Endicott and the Red Cross" (Hawthorne) **3**:175-76
"L'endormeuse" (Maupassant) **1**:284
"The Enduring Chill" (O'Connor) **1**:342-43, 356, 365
"Enemies" (Chekhov) **2**:158
"The Enemies" (Thomas) **3**:407-09
"Engineer-Private Paul Klee Misplaces an Aircraft between Milbertschofen and Cambrai, March 1916" (Barthelme) **2**:49, 54
"English Writers on America" (Irving) **2**:244, 254
"The Enormous Radio" (Cheever) **1**:106, 109
The Enormous Radio, and Other Stories (Cheever) **1**:89, 92, 95, 98-100
"Enragée" (Maupassant) **1**:274
"Enter a Dragoon" (Hardy) **2**:215
L'entrata in guerra (Calvino) **3**:97, 116
"Epilogue: The Photographer" (Munro) **3**:332, 338, 340, 343
"Les epingles" (Maupassant) **1**:263, 286
"Eric Hermannson's Soul" (Cather) **2**:96, 100-01, 105, 107
"Error" (Singer) **3**:377
"An Error in Chemistry" (Faulkner) **1**:179
"Escapement" (Ballard) **1**:68
"Eskimo" (Munro) **3**:347
"Esther" (Toomer) **1**:445, 450-51, 457, 459
"Esther Kreindel the Second" (Singer) **3**:363
"The Eternal Husband" (Dostoevski) **2**:166-67, 175-77, 184-85
"Ethan Brand" (Hawthorne) **3**:159, 179-80, 182
"Eugénie Grandet" (Barthelme) **2**:40
"Eveline" (Joyce) **3**:205, 226, 231, 234, 247-48
"The Evening's at Seven" (Thurber) **1**:417, 425
"Events of That Easter" (Cheever) **1**:93
"Everything That Rises Must Converge" (O'Connor) **1**:341, 363
"Excellent People" (Chekhov) **2**:155
"Exile of Eons" (Clarke) **3**:144
"Expedition to Earth" (Clarke) **3**:150
"The Explanation" (Barthelme) **2**:35, 40-1, 55
"Extraordinary Little Cough" (Thomas) **3**:394, 403, 406, 411-12
"Extricating Young Gussie" (Wodehouse) **2**:342
"The Eye" (Bowles) **3**:75, 80
"The Eye of Apollo" (Chesterton) **1**:121, 136
Fables for Our Time and Famous Poems Illustrated (Thurber) **1**:415, 417, 422, 424, 426-27
"The Face in the Target" (Chesterton) **1**:122
"The Facts in the Case of M. Valdemar" (Poe) **1**:379, 385, 400
"The Fad of the Fisherman" (Chesterton) **1**:122
"A Faint Heart" ("A Weak Heart") (Dostoevski) **2**:170-72, 191-92
"A Faint Heart" (Dostoevski)
See "A Weak Heart"
"Fairy Tale" (Chesterton) **1**:136
"The Fall of the House of Usher" (Poe) **1**:377, 379-80, 383, 385-86, 391, 398-99, 403-07
"The Falling Dog" (Barthelme) **2**:55
"The Falling Sleet" (Dostoevski) **2**:165
"Fancy's Show Box" (Hawthorne) **3**:160, 190-91
"A Far-Away Melody" (Freeman) **1**:191
"Farce Normande" (Maupassant) **1**:272
"Farewell" (Barthelme) **2**:51
"Farewell to Earth" (Clarke) **3**:128
"The Fast" (Singer) **3**:355, 361
"Fathers and Sons" (Hemingway) **1**:212, 216, 230, 240-42
"The Fear That Walks by Noonday" (Cather) **2**:100
"The Feast of Crispian" (Ballard) **1**:72
"Feathertop" (Hawthorne) **3**:158, 179
"Fellow-Townsmen" (Hardy) **2**:202-03, 207, 215-16, 228-31
"La femme de Paul" (Maupassant) **1**:259, 261
"Le fermier" (Maupassant) **1**:274, 285
"Fern" (Toomer) **1**:441, 444, 457-58, 460
"The Festival" (Lovecraft) **3**:263, 269, 274, 292, 294-95
"A Few Crusted Characters" (Hardy) **2**:206, 209, 214-15, 217, 219-20
"La ficelle" ("A Piece of String") (Maupassant) **1**:259, 262, 284, 286, 288
"La ficelle" (Maupassant)
See "A Piece of String"
"The Fiddler" (Melville) **1**:304
"The Fiddler of the Reels" (Hardy) **2**:216-22, 224-25
"Fifty Grand" (Hemingway) **1**:209, 211, 218, 232, 234-35, 248
"The Fight" (Anderson) **1**:31, 50
"The Fight" (Thomas) **3**:402, 406, 411-12
"Un fils" (Maupassant) **1**:275
"A Final Note on Chanda Bell" (Thurber) **1**:421
"A Fine Beginning" (Thomas) **3**:403
"Fire and Cloud" (Wright) **2**:361, 363, 365, 368, 371, 373, 375, 379-81, 383-84, 387
"The Fire and the Hearth" (Faulkner) **1**:182
"Fire Worship" (Hawthorne) **3**:182
"The Fires Within" (Clarke) **3**:125, 129, 135, 143, 149
"The First Countess of Wessex" (Hardy) **2**:204, 208-09
"First Encounter" (Clarke) **3**:128
The First Forty-Nine Stories (Hemingway) **1**:230, 240
"First Love" (Welty) **1**:467-69, 482
"The First of April" (Barnes) **3**:13
"The First-Class Passenger" (Chekhov) **2**:130
"Fits" (Munro) **3**:347
"The Five-Forty-Eight" (Cheever) **1**:100
"The Flats Road" (Munro) **3**:331-32
"Flavia and Her Artists" (Cather) **2**:98, 103
"The Flight of Pigeons from the Palace" (Barthelme) **2**:37, 40, 55-6
"The Flight of the Israelites" (Ballard) **1**:72
"The Flood" (Anderson) **1**:51
"Florence Green is 81" (Barthelme) **2**:27
"Flowers for Marjorie" (Welty) **1**:466, 487-88
"The Flying Stars" (Chesterton) **1**:119, 127, 129
"The Food of the Gods" (Clarke) **3**:133-34
"Fool about a Horse" (Faulkner) **1**:177
"Foothold" (Bowen) **3**:40, 44
"For Conscience' Sake" (Hardy) **2**:207, 212, 214-15, 220
"For Esmé" ("For Esmé--with Love and Squalor") (Salinger) **2**:293, 316-18
"For Esmé" (Salinger)
See "For Esmé--with Love and Squalor"
"For Esmé--with Love and Squalor" ("For Esmé") (Salinger) **2**:289, 293-97, 299-300, 303-05, 314, 316-18
"For Esmé--with Love and Squalor" (Salinger)
See "For Esmé"
"Forgiveness in Families" (Munro) **3**:331
"The Forgotten Enemy" (Clarke) **3**:124
"The Form of Space" (Calvino)

Title Index

See "La forma dello spazio"
"La forma dello spazio" ("The Form of Space") (Calvino) **3**:92, 109
La formica argentina (*The Argentine Ant*) (Calvino) **3**:91-2, 98, 117
"Forty Stories" (Barthelme) **2**:56
"The Found Boat" (Munro) **3**:346
Four Faultless Felons (Chesterton) **1**:126, 132
The Four-Dimensional Nightmare (Ballard) **1**:68
"The Fourth Alarm" (Cheever) **1**:101, 110
"The Fourth Day Out from Santa Cruz" (Bowles) **3**:61-2, 72
"The Fqih" (Bowles) **3**:68
"Franny" (Salinger) **2**:291, 293, 297, 302-03, 305
Franny and Zooey (Salinger) **2**:297, 304, 318
"A Friend of Kafka" (Singer) **3**:384
A Friend of Kafka, and Other Stories (Singer) **3**:370, 373, 375
"A Friend of the Earth" (Thurber) **1**:422, 427
"The Friend of the Family" ("The Village of Stepanchikovo") (Dostoevski) **2**:172
"A Friend of the World" (Bowles) **3**:64, 83
"From the Diary of a New York Lady" (Parker) **2**:278, 286
"The Frozen Fields" (Bowles) **3**:65-6, 79, 84
Further Fables for Our Time (Thurber) **1**:426-28
"The Future, If Any, of Comedy; or, Where Do We Not-Go from Here?" (Thurber) **1**:424
G. K. Chesterton: Selected Short Stories (Chesterton) **1**:135
"A Gala Dress" (Freeman) **1**:196, 201
"La gallina di reparto" (Calvino) **3**:98
"The Gambler, the Nun, and the Radio" (Hemingway) **1**:218, 234
"The Game" (Barthelme) **2**:40
"Games without End" (Calvino) **3**:109
"The Garden" (Bowles) **3**:64, 68, 80
"The Garden at Mons" (Hemingway) **1**:208, 236
"The Garden Lodge" (Cather) **2**:90, 98, 103
"The Garden of Time" (Ballard) **1**:71, 74, 77
"Le gâteau" (Maupassant) **1**:274, 286
"The Generations of America" (Ballard) **1**:82
"Gentian" (Freeman) **1**:197
"The Gentle Boy" (Hawthorne) **3**:164, 167, 181, 185-87
"The Gentleman from Cracow" (Singer) **3**:358, 368, 383-84
"A Gentleman's Friend" (Chekhov) **2**:137-39
"The Geometry of Love" (Cheever) **1**:97, 101
"The Geranium" (O'Connor) **1**:364
"Get Thee to a Monastery" (Thurber) **1**:429
"Getzel the Monkey" (Singer) **3**:359
"Un giardino incantato" ("An Enchanted Garden"; "The Enchanted Garden") (Calvino) **3**:90, 97, 112
"Gift from the Stars" (Clarke) **3**:128
"Gifts" (Singer) **3**:389
"Gimpel the Fool" (Singer) **3**:352, 355, 363, 365-68, 375, 382-84, 389
Gimpel the Fool, and Other Stories (Singer) **3**:370
"The Gioconda of the Twilight Noon" (Ballard) **1**:69
"La giornata d'uno scrutatore" ("The Watcher") (Calvino) **3**:98-9, 116-19
"The Girl with the Stoop" (Bowen) **3**:54
"Giving Birth" (Atwood) **2**:3-4, 6-10, 12, 14, 16
"The Glass Mountain" (Barthelme) **2**:34, 40
Gloomy People (Chekhov) **2**:146
"Glory in the Daytime" (Parker) **2**:273-74, 280, 283
"Go Down, Moses" (Faulkner) **1**:182-83
"A Goatherd at Luncheon" (Calvino) **3**:116
"The God of the Gongs" (Chesterton) **1**:127
"God Rest You Merry, Gentlemen" (Hemingway) **1**:216
"Godliness" (Anderson) **1**:18, 42, 57
"The Go-Getter" (Wodehouse) **2**:346
"Going to Naples" (Welty) **1**:476, 484
"The Gold Bug" (Poe) **1**:378, 390
"Gold Is Not Always" (Faulkner) **1**:177
"A Gold Slipper" (Cather) **2**:91
"The Golden Age" (Cheever) **1**:106
The Golden Apples (Welty) **1**:473-74, 479, 483-85, 492, 494, 497
"Golden Land" (Faulkner) **1**:167
"Gone Away" (Bowen) **3**:53
"Good Country People" (O'Connor) **1**:335, 343-45, 350, 356, 359-60
"The Good Girl" (Bowen) **3**:33
"A Good Man Is Hard to Find" (O'Connor) **1**:339, 344, 347-48, 356, 358, 360-63, 371
"Goodbye, My Brother" (Cheever) **1**:89, 99, 103-05, 108
"Gooseberries" (Chekhov) **2**:136-37, 139, 141-43, 155-57
"Grace" (Joyce) **3**:202, 205-06, 208, 210-11, 214-15, 225-26, 232-235, 237, 247-48
"The Grande Malade" ("The Little Girl Continues") (Barnes) **3**:5-6, 9-10, 16, 24-6
"Grandfather and Grandson" (Singer) **3**:374
"The Grasshopper" (Chekhov) **2**:155
"The Grave by the Handpost" (Hardy) **2**:210
"The Grave of the Famous Poet" (Atwood) **2**:3-5, 7, 10-11, 16
"The Gravedigger" (Singer) **3**:378
"The Gray Champion" (Hawthorne) **3**:164, 167, 171, 175-76, 178, 186-87
"The Great Carbuncle" (Hawthorne) **3**:157, 159, 181-82, 184, 185, 188
Great Days (Barthelme) **2**:44, 46
"The Great Stone Face" (Hawthorne) **3**:159, 178, 182, 184
"The Greatest Man in the World" (Thurber) **1**:420, 431
"The Greatest Television Show on Earth" (Ballard) **1**:71
"Green Holly" (Bowen) 32, 54
"The Green Isle in the Sea" (Thurber) **1**:417
"The Green Man" (Chesterton) **1**:129
"Greenleaf" (O'Connor) **1**:343, 358, 360
A Group of Noble Dames (Hardy) **2**:203-07, 209, 212-13, 220-21
"Guardian Angel" (Clarke) **3**:149
"Guests from Gibbet Island" (Irving) **2**:241, 247-48
Guilty Pleasures (Barthelme) **2**:39, 41
"Gusev" (Chekhov) **2**:128-29, 143, 147
"Hair" (Faulkner) **1**:147, 151
"Hair Jewellery" (Atwood) **2**:3, 5-7, 10-11, 14, 16
"Half a Grapefruit" (Munro) **3**:334, 342
"The Hall of Fantasy" (Hawthorne) **3**:181
"The Hamlet of Stepanchikovo" ("The Village of Stepanchikovo") (Dostoevski) **2**:176
"The Hammer of God" (Chesterton) **1**:124, 130, 136
"Hand" (Atwood) **2**:20
"Hand in Glove" (Bowen) **3**:54
"Hand Upon the Waters" (Faulkner) **1**:179
"Handcarved Coffins: A Nonfiction Account of an American Crime" (Capote) **2**:80-2
"Hands" (Anderson) **1**:32-3, 42, 44, 57
"Hanka" (Singer) **3**:377
"Happiness" (Chekhov) **2**:130, 156
"The Happy Autumn Fields" (Bowen) **3**:31-2, 50-1
"Happy Endings" (Atwood) **2**:15, 19-20
"The Happy Failure" (Melville) **1**:303
"Hapworth 16, 1924" (Salinger) **2**:308, 314
"The Haunted Mind" (Hawthorne) **3**:181
"The Haunter of the Dark" (Lovecraft) **3**:259, 263, 273-75, 279, 284
"Hautot père et fils" (Maupassant) **1**:270, 280, 285, 288
"Having a Wonderful Time" (Ballard) **1**:79
"He" (Lovecraft) **3**:259, 262, 283, 289
"He of the Assembly" (Bowles) **3**:68, 83-4
"The Head of Babylon" (Barnes) **3**:19-20
"The Head of the Family" (Chekhov) **2**:127
"The Headless Hawk" (Capote) **2**:61-3, 66, 69, 72, 75-6
The Heart of a Goof (Wodehouse) **2**:329, 350
"Henne Fire" (Singer) **3**:370, 383-84
"Her Boss" (Cather) **2**:111
"Her Table Spread" (Bowen) **3**:34-6, 38, 41, 51
"Herbert West--Reanimator" (Lovecraft) **3**:282, 293-94
"Here Come the Tigers" (Thurber) **1**:429
Here Lies (*The Collected Stories of Dorothy Parker*) (Parker) **2**:274-75
Here Lies (Parker)
See *The Collected Stories of Dorothy Parker*
"Here to Learn" (Bowles) **3**:75, 79-80
"Here We Are" (Parker) **2**:273-74, 281, 283
"L'heritage" (Maupassant) **1**:256, 259-60, 263, 270, 276, 283
"Hide and Seek" (Clarke) **3**:124-26, 133, 150
"Hiding Man" (Barthelme) **2**:26, 41-2, 54
"Hills Like White Elephants" (Hemingway) **1**:210, 217, 232, 234
"Him" (Atwood) **2**:20
"His Chest of Drawers" (Anderson) **1**:52
"L'histoire d'une fille de ferme" (Maupassant) **1**:257, 259, 261, 272, 274-75
"History Lesson" (Clarke) **3**:124, 133, 143-44
"The History of the Hardcomes" (Hardy) **2**:215
"The Hitch-Hikers" (Welty) **1**:466, 468, 481, 487-88, 494
"Hog Pawn" (Faulkner) **1**:178
"The Hole in the Wall" (Chesterton) **1**:122
"The Hollow of the Three Hills" (Hawthorne) **3**:154, 157, 180-81
"The Holy Six" (Thomas) **3**:399, 407-08
"Homage to Switzerland" (Hemingway) **1**:211
"The Honest Quack" (Chesterton) **1**:133
"An Honest Soul" (Freeman) **1**:198, 201
"An Honest Thief" (Dostoevski) **2**:166, 171, 193
"The Honour of Israel Gow" (Chesterton) **1**:134, 137
"Hopeless" (Atwood) **2**:20
"Hop-Frog" (Poe) **1**:408
"Le horla" (Maupassant) **1**:259, 262, 265, 269, 273, 283-84, 286-88

"The Horror at Red Hook" (Lovecraft) **3**:258, 262, 289
"The Horror in the Museum" (Lovecraft) **3**:279
Horses and Men (Anderson) **1**:23, 25, 27, 30, 46, 50
"The Horse's Ha" (Thomas) **3**:409
"A Horse's Name" (Chekhov) **2**:130
"The Horse-Stealers" (Chekhov) **2**:130
"Horsie" (Parker) **2**:273-75, 280, 283-84
"A Host of Furious Fancies" (Ballard) **1**:79
"The Hound" (Faulkner) **1**:177
"The Hound" (Lovecraft) **3**:258, 262, 274, 276, 282
"The Hours after Noon" (Bowles) **3**:64-6, 80, 82
"House of Flowers" (Capote) **2**:67, 69, 72, 75
"The House with the Maisonette" (Chekhov) See "An Artist's Story"
"The Housebreaker of Shady Hill" (Cheever) **1**:111
The Housebreaker of Shady Hill, and Other Stories (Cheever) **1**:89-92, 95, 100
"The Household" (Irving) **2**:265
"How I Write My Songs" (Barthelme) **2**:52
"How Many Midnights" (Bowles) **3**:60, 69, 72, 79
"How Much Shall We Bet?" (Calvino) **3**:104
"How to Write a" *Blackwood* "Articl" (Poe) **1**:405
"Howe's Masquerade" (Hawthorne) **3**:154, 187
"The Human Being and the Dinosaur" (Thurber) **1**:426, 430
"Human Habitation" (Bowen) **3**:55
"A Humble Romance" (Freeman) **1**:196
A Humble Romance, and Other Stories (Freeman) **1**:191, 194-95, 197, 201
"The Hunchback in the Park" (Thomas) **3**:400
A Hundred Camels in the Courtyard (Bowles) **3**:68
"The Huntsman" (Chekhov) **2**:155
"Hurricane Hazel" (Atwood) **2**:21-3
"The Husband" (Bowles) **3**:80
"The Hyena" (Bowles) **3**:64-5, 68, 80
"I and My Chimney" (Melville) **1**:298, 304, 322, 326-27
"I Live on Your Visits" (Parker) **2**:283
I nostri antenati (*Our Ancestors*) (Calvino) **3**:91-2, 106, 117
I racconti (Calvino) **3**:96-7, 116
"I Remember Babylon" (Clarke) **3**:131
"I Want to Know Why" (Anderson) **1**:20, 23, 27, 35, 37-8, 40, 48-9, 62
"Iconography" (Atwood) **2**:15, 20
"Une idylle" (Maupassant) **1**:256, 270
"'If I Forget Thee, O Earth'" (Clarke) **3**:124, 126, 143
"If I Should Open My Mouth" (Bowles) **3**:64, 68-9, 80, 83, 85
"The Illuminated Man" (Ballard) **1**:69
"I'm a Fool" (Anderson) **1**:23, 25, 27, 30, 37-8, 40, 48-50
The Image, and Other Stories (Singer) **3**:384-86
"Images" (Munro) **3**:326, 338, 343-44
"An Imaginative Woman" (Hardy) **2**:215, 220, 223, 225
"The Impossible Man" (Ballard) **1**:75-7
"The Impresario" (Singer) **3**:389
"In a Strange Town" (Anderson) **1**:50
"In Another Country" (Hemingway) **1**:209, 230-32, 234
"In Exile" (Chekhov) **2**:157
In Our Time (Hemingway) **1**:207-08, 212, 214-15, 234, 236, 238, 243-45
in our time (Hemingway) **1**:206-07, 235, 241, 243
"In the Cart" (Chekhov) **2**:156-58
"In the Direction of the Beginning" (Thomas) **3**:396, 402, 407, 409
"In the Ravine" ("In the River") (Chekhov) **2**:128, 131-32, 145, 156-57
"In the Ravine" (Chekhov) See "In the River"
"In the River" (Chekhov) See "In the Ravine"
"In the Square" (Bowen) **3**:31
"In the Vault" (Lovecraft) **3**:262
The Incredulity of Father Brown (Chesterton) **1**:128
"An Independent Thinker" (Freeman) **1**:196
"Indian Camp" (Hemingway) **1**:214, 219, 234, 240-41, 244-45
"The Indian Sign" (Thurber) **1**:425
"Indian Summer" (Barnes) **3**:12, 22
"The Indian Uprising" (Barthelme) **2**:35-6, 38, 42, 46, 53
"The Inherited Clock" (Bowen) **3**:31-2
The Innocence of Father Brown (Chesterton) **1**:119-21, 124-25
"The Insoluble Problem" (Chesterton) **1**:128
"Instructions for the Third Eye" (Atwood) **2**:16-17
"Intensive Care Unit" (Ballard) **1**:79
"Interlopers at the Knap" (Hardy) **2**:203, 205, 207, 216, 229-31
"The Interview" (Singer) **3**:387
"The Interview" (Thurber) **1**:420
"Interview with a Lemming" (Thurber) **1**:417
"Into the Comet" (Clarke) **3**:147
"L'inutile beauté" (Maupassant) **1**:273, 275, 286-87
"The Inverted Forest" (Salinger) **2**:309
The Invisible Knight (Calvino) See *Il cavaliere inesistente*
"The Invisible Man" (Chesterton) **1**:130, 134, 136, 142
"Ionych" (Chekhov) See "Ionitch"
"Ionych" ("Iónych") (Chekhov) **2**:128, 131-32, 155
"Ionych" (Chekhov) See "Iónych"
"Iónych" (Chekhov) See "Ionych"
"The Italian Banditti" (Irving) **2**:251, 261
Italian Folktales (Calvino) **3**:105, 119
"Italian Robber" (Irving) **2**:255
"Ivory, Apes, and People" (Thurber) **1**:426
"L'ivrogne" (Maupassant) **1**:274
"Ivy Day in the Committee Room" (Joyce) **3**:201, 205-06, 210-11, 214, 218-21, 225-26, 228, 231, 234, 237, 240, 242, 248
"Ivy Gripped the Steps" (Bowen) **3**:31-2, 38, 41, 48, 51
Ivy Gripped the Steps, and Other Stories (Bowen) See *The Demon Lover, and Other Stories*
"Jachid and Jechidah" (Singer) **3**:357, 363, 375
"Jeeves and the Dog MacIntosh" (Wodehouse) **2**:355-56
"Jeeves and the Greasy Bird" (Wodehouse) **2**:344
"Jeeves and the Yuletide Spirit" (Wodehouse) **2**:356
"Jesse and Meribeth" (Munro) **3**:347, 349
"The Jest of Jests" (Barnes) **3**:18
"The Jew from Babylon" (Singer) **3**:389
"The Jewels of the Cabots" (Cheever) **1**:101
"Jimmy Rose" (Melville) **1**:303-04, 325-26
"John Bull" (Irving) **2**:244, 251, 253
"John Inglefield's Thanksgiving" (Hawthorne) **3**:189
"Joining Charles" (Bowen) **3**:30, 47
"The Joker's Greatest Triumph" (Barthelme) **2**:28, 34
"The Journey" (Irving) **2**:244, 265
"Joy" (Singer) **3**:360, 363-64, 368
"The Joy of Nelly Deane" (Cather) **2**:98, 104
"Judgement Day" (O'Connor) **1**:343, 365
"Jug of Silver" (Capote) **2**:63, 65-6, 70
"June Recital" (Welty) **1**:474, 480, 483, 485, 495, 497
"The Jungle" (Bowen) **3**:30, 33, 49
"Jupiter Five" (Clarke) **3**:124, 129, 134-35, 149
"A Jury Case" (Anderson) **1**:50
"Just a Little One" (Parker) **2**:281
"Just Before the War with the Eskimos" (Salinger) **2**:300
"Just Like Little Dogs" (Thomas) **3**:403, 406, 411-12
"Just One More Time" (Cheever) **1**:100
"Just Tell Me Who It Was" (Cheever) **1**:90
"A Justice" (Faulkner) **1**:147, 177, 181
"Kabnis" (Toomer) **1**:440, 442-44, 446-48, 451-54, 457, 459-60
"Karintha" (Toomer) **1**:441, 452, 455-56, 459
"Kashtánka" (Chekhov) **2**:130
"Keela, the Outcast Indian Maiden" (Welty) **1**:468, 470, 497
"The Key" (Welty) **1**:468
"Kierkegaard Unfair to Schlegel" (Barthelme) **2**:31, 38-9, 54
"The Killers" (Hemingway) **1**:211, 218-19, 234-36, 242
"The Killing Ground" (Ballard) **1**:76
"Kin" (Welty) **1**:475-76, 487
"A King Listens" (Calvino) **3**:119
"The King of Greece's Tea Party" (Hemingway) **1**:208
"King Pest" (Poe) **1**:406
"The Kiss" (Chekhov) **2**:126, 156
"Kitty" (Bowles) **3**:76, 80
"Knight's Gambit" (Faulkner) **1**:178-81
"Labour Day Dinner" (Munro) **3**:346
"Lady Eleanore's Mantle" (Hawthorne) **3**:184
"The Lady from the Land" (Thurber) **1**:424
"The Lady Icenway" (Hardy) **2**:205
"Lady Mottisfont" (Hardy) **2**:208
"The Lady Penelope" (Hardy) **2**:209
"Lady with a Lamp" (Parker) **2**:273-74, 280, 285
"The Lady with the Dog" (Chekhov) See "The Lady with a Lapdog"
"The Lady with the Dog" ("The Lady with the Pet Dog") (Chekhov) **2**:127-28, 131-33, 135, 150, 155, 157
"The Lady with the Dog" (Chekhov) See "The Lady with the Pet Dog"
"The Lady with the Pet Dog" (Chekhov) See "The Lady with the Dog"

Title Index

"The Lame Shall Enter First" (O'Connor) **1**:343-45, 356, 365
"Laments for the Living" (Parker) **2**:272, 274
"Lamp in a Window" (Capote) **2**:80
"Landing in Luck" (Faulkner) **1**:177
"The Landlady" (Dostoevski) **2**:163, 170-71, 173-74, 181, 191, 193
"Le lapin" (Maupassant) **1**:263, 274
"L'Lapse" (Barthelme) **2**:40
"The Last Demon" (Singer) **3**:383
"The Last Night in the Old Home" (Bowen) **3**:41
"The Last Tea" (Parker) **2**:274, 285
"A Late Encounter with the Enemy" (O'Connor) **1**:356
"The Laughing Man" (Salinger) **2**:293, 296, 299, 313-14, 316
"The Law of the Jungle" (Cheever) **1**:99
"Lazy Sons" (Calvino) **3**:112
"The Leap" (Barthelme) **2**:45, 55
"Learning to Be Dead" (Calvino) **3**:113
"Legend of Prince Ahmed Al Kemel, or The Pilgrim of Love" (Irving) **2**:267
"The Legend of Sleepy Hollow" (Irving) **2**:239, 241, 243-51, 253, 255, 259-60
"Legend of the Arabian Astrologer" (Irving) **2**:267
"The Legend of the Moor's Legacy" (Irving) **2**:246, 254, 268
"Legend of the Rose of Alhambra" (Irving) **2**:246, 268
"Legend of the Three Beautiful Princesses" (Irving) **2**:267
"La Légende du Mont-Saint-Michel" (Maupassant) **1**:285, 288
"The Lemon" (Thomas) **3**:396, 399, 407-08
"Let There Be Light" (Clarke) **3**:130
Let Your Mind Alone! and Other More or Less Inspirational Pieces (Thurber) **1**:414, 422-23, 426
"The Letter That Was Never Mailed" (Barnes) **3**:13
"The Letter Writer" (Singer) **3**:360, 384
Letters from the Underworld (*Notes from the Underground*) (Dostoevski) **2**:164-65
Letters from the Underworld (Dostoevski) See *Notes from the Underground*
"Letters to the Editore" (Barthelme) **2**:40
"The Liar" (Faulkner) **1**:177
"Lichen" (Munro) **3**:347-49
"Life Everlastin'" (Freeman) **1**:192, 195
"Life with Freddie" (Wodehouse) **2**:344
"The Life You Save May Be Your Own" (O'Connor) **1**:343-44, 348-49, 356, 359-60
Life's Little Ironies (Hardy) **2**:205-08, 210, 212, 214-16, 220, 222-23
"Ligeia" (Poe) **1**:377, 379-80, 385, 393-97, 399
"The Light of the World" (Hemingway) **1**:242, 245
"Lightning" (Barthelme) **2**:51
"The Lightning-Rod Man" (Melville) **1**:298, 303-04
"The Light-Years" (Calvino) **3**:104
"Like a Queen" (Anderson) **1**:31, 52-3
"Liking Men" (Atwood) **2**:20
"Lily Daw and the Three Ladies" (Welty) **1**:470, 482, 497
"The Lily's Quest" (Hawthorne) **3**:181
"Lion" (Faulkner) **1**:182
"The Lion of Comarre" (Clarke) **3**:145, 148
"Le lit 29" (Maupassant) **1**:274
"The Litigants" (Singer) **3**:385
"A Little Cloud" (Joyce) **3**:205, 209-10, 226, 231, 234, 245, 248
"Little Curtis" (Parker) **2**:274, 280-81, 283
"The Little Girl Continues" (Barnes) See "The Grande Malade"
"A Little Girl Tells a Story to a Lady" (Barnes) See "Cassation"
"The Little Girl's Room" (Bowen) **3**:33, 43
"The Little Hero" (Dostoevski) **2**:171, 189-90
"The Little Hours" (Parker) **2**:274, 281
"The Little House" (Bowles) **3**:76
"The Little Man in Black" (Irving) **2**:242
"The Little Shoemakers" (Singer) **3**:356, 375, 378, 383-84
Lives of Girls and Women (Munro) **3**:323, 325-28, 330-33, 335-36, 338-46
"Lives of the Poets" (Atwood) **2**:3-4, 6, 10-11
"Livvie" (Welty) **1**:467, 469, 471
"Lizards in Jamshyd's Courtyard" (Faulkner) **1**:177
"Logarithms" (Singer) **3**:388
"Loneliness" (Anderson) **1**:30, 44
"Long Black Song" (Wright) **2**:360-63, 365, 367, 369, 371, 374, 376, 379-81, 387
"The Longest Science Fiction Story Ever Told" (Clarke) **3**:133
"Look at All Those Roses" (Bowen) **3**:55
"Loophole" (Clarke) **3**:125, 148-50
"Lord Emsworth Acts for the Best" (Wodehouse) **2**:346, 348
"Lord Emsworth and the Girl Friend" (Wodehouse) **2**:346-49
"Loss of Breath" (Poe) **1**:407
"The Lost Novel" (Anderson) **1**:31
"Lou, the Prophet" (Cather) **2**:96, 100, 105
"Louisa" (Freeman) **1**:196
"Loulou; or, The Domestic Life of the Language" (Atwood) **2**:18, 21, 23
"Love" (Bowen) **3**:33, 41
Love and Napalm: Export U.S.A. (Ballard) See *The Atrocity Exhibition*
"A Love Story" (Bowen) **3**:41, 54
"The Lovely Leave" (Parker) **2**:277, 280, 285-86
"The Lover" (Bowen) **3**:40
"The Lowboy" (Cheever) **1**:112
"Low-Flying Aircraft" (Ballard) **1**:73-4, 83
Low-Flying Aircraft, and Other Stories (Ballard) **1**:71-3
"Lui?" (Maupassant) **1**:265-66, 281
"Luna e G N A C" (Calvino) **3**:97
"Lunch" (Bowen) **3**:40
"The Lurking Fear" (Lovecraft) **3**:258, 260, 281
"Ma femme" (Maupassant) **1**:280
"The Macbeth Murder Mystery" (Thurber) **1**:426
"Mademoiselle Fifi" (Maupassant) **1**:256, 259, 274, 287
"Maelstrom II" (Clarke) **3**:129, 147
"The Magazine" (Singer) **3**:374
"The Magician" (Singer) **3**:375
"La main" (Maupassant) **1**:281
"La main d'ecorché" (Maupassant) **1**:281
"La maison Tellier" (Maupassant) **1**:271-72, 274, 287
"Making Arrangements" (Bowen) **3**:54
"Making Poison" (Atwood) **2**:17
"The Man from Mars" (Atwood) **2**:3, 5-7, 10-11, 14, 21
"The Man in a Case" (Chekhov) See "The Man in a Shell"
"The Man in a Shell" ("The Man in a Case") (Chekhov) **2**:139, 141, 143, 155, 157
"The Man in a Shell" (Chekhov) See "The Man in a Case"
"The Man in the Brown Coat" (Anderson) **1**:21, 27
"The Man in the Passage" (Chesterton) **1**:136
"The Man of Adamant" (Hawthorne) **3**:171, 185
"Man of All Work" (Wright) **2**:388
"The Man of the Crowd" (Poe) **1**:379
"The Man of the Family" (Bowen) **3**:45
"The Man That Was Used Up" (Poe) **1**:407-08
The Man Upstairs, and Other Stories (Wodehouse) **2**:347
"The Man Who Became a Woman" (Anderson) **1**:30, 37, 48-50
"The Man Who Killed a Shadow" (Wright) **2**:366, 385-86
The Man Who Knew Too Much (Chesterton) **1**:121-22, 125-26
"The Man Who Lived Underground" (Wright) **2**:364, 366, 370, 373-74, 377, 379, 387-88
"The Man Who Ploughed the Sea" (Clarke) **3**:134
"The Man Who Saw the Flood" (Wright) **2**:366
"The Man Who Was Almos' a Man" ("The Man Who Was Almost a Man") (Wright) **2**:376
"The Man Who Was Almos' a Man" (Wright) See "The Man Who Was Almost a Man"
"The Man Who Was Almost a Man" ("The Man Who Was Almos' a Man") (Wright) **2**:366, 388
"The Man Who Was Almost a Man" (Wright) See "The Man Who Was Almos' a Man"
The Man with Two Left Feet (Wodehouse) **2**:327
"Manhole 69" (Ballard) **1**:68
"The Manor of Stepanchikovo" ("The Village of Stepanchikovo") (Dostoevski) **2**:172
"The Manor of Stepanchikovo" (Dostoevski) See "The Village of Stepanchikovo"
"The Man's Story" (Anderson) **1**:39, 52
"The Mantle of Whistler" (Parker) **2**:273, 283
"The Map of Love" (Thomas) **3**:399, 402, 407
"The Marchioness of Stonehenge" (Hardy) **2**:204, 217
Marcovaldo; or, the Seasons in the City (Calvino) **3**:106-07
"Marie, Marie, Hold on Tight" (Barthelme) **2**:34, 40
"Marrakesh" (Munro) **3**:346
"The Marriage of Phaedra" (Cather) **2**:98, 103
"Marroca" (Maupassant) **1**:257
"Le masque" (Maupassant) **1**:274, 286
"The Masque of the Red Death" (Poe) **1**:379, 389-90, 398, 406
"Master John Horseleigh, Knight" (Hardy) **2**:210
"Master Misery" (Capote) **2**:63-5, 72-3, 75, 78
"The Maypole of Merry Mount" (Hawthorne) **3**:164-67, 180-81, 183-84, 187, 188

"Me and Miss Mandible" (Barthelme) **2**:26-7, 35, 47, 49, 53
Meet Mr. Mulliner (Wodehouse) **2**:325, 338
"A Meeting South" (Anderson) **1**:37, 52-3
"A Meeting with Medusa" (Clarke) **3**:128, 130, 132, 135-36, 138-40, 146
"Meiosis" (Calvino) **3**:109
"Mejdoub" (Bowles) **3**:68
"The Melancholy Hussar of the German Legion" (Hardy) **2**:214-15, 220
"Mellonta Tauta" (Poe) **1**:401, 406
"Memorial" (Munro) **3**:331
"Memories of D. H. Lawrence" (Thurber) **1**:414
"A Memory" (Welty) **1**:466, 469-70, 472
Men without Women (Hemingway) **1**:209-12, 214, 216-17
"Menuet" (Maupassant) **1**:278
"A Mere Interlude" (Hardy) **2**:211, 215
"La mère sauvage" (Maupassant) **1**:277-78
"Merle" (Marshall) **3**:317
Merle: A Novella, and Other Stories (Marshall)
See *Reena, and Other Stories*
"Mes vingt-cinq jours" (Maupassant) **1**:274
"Mesmeric Revelation" (Poe) **1**:401
"Metamorphoses" (Cheever) **1**:94, 100
"Metzengerstein" (Poe) **1**:379
The Middle-Aged Man on the Flying Trapeze: A Collection of Short Pieces (Thurber) **1**:413, 420, 423
"Midnight at Tim's Place" (Thurber) **1**:429
"Midnight Mass" (Bowles) **3**:75, 80
"Miles City, Montana" (Munro) **3**:347-48
"The Minister's Black Veil" (Hawthorne) **3**:154, 159--60, 164, 171, 177-78, 184, 186-87
"Miracles" (Singer) **3**:385-86
"Miriam" (Capote) **2**:61-2, 64, 66, 69, 73-5, 78-9, 83
"The Mirror" (Singer) **3**:364, 368, 375
"A Miscellany of Characters That Will Not Appear" (Cheever) **1**:93, 100
"Misery" (Chekhov) **2**:128, 130, 155
"Miss Harriet" (Maupassant) **1**:259, 271, 274, 280, 285-87
"The Missing Line" (Singer) **3**:389
"Mrs. Bullfrog" (Hawthorne) **3**:180
"Mrs. Moysey" (Bowen) **3**:30, 33, 40, 42
"Mrs. Windermere" (Bowen) **3**:40, 54
"The Mistake of the Machine" (Chesterton) **1**:131
"Mr. and Mrs. Elliot" (Hemingway) **1**:208
"Mr. Durant" (Parker) **2**:274
"Mr. Foolfarm's Journal" (Barthelme) **2**:40
"Mr. Higginbotham's Catastrophe" (Hawthorne) **3**:154
Mr. Mulliner Speaking (Wodehouse) **2**:338
Mister Palomar (Calvino) **3**:113-18
"Mister Palomar in the City" (Calvino) **3**:113, 115
"Mister Palomar's Vacation" (Calvino) **3**:113
"Mr. Potter Takes a Rest Cure" (Wodehouse) **2**:355-56
"Mr. Preble Gets Rid of His Wife" (Thurber) **1**:418
"Mr. Prokharchin" (Dostoevski) **2**:170, 191-94
"Mrs. Hofstadter on Josephine Street" (Parker) **2**:283
"Mitosis" (Calvino) **3**:109-10
"Mobile" (Ballard) **1**:68
"The Moderate Murderer" (Chesterton) **1**:132
"Mohammed Fripouille" (Maupassant) **1**:275
"Mojave" (Capote) **2**:79-80
"Mon oncle Jules" (Maupassant) **1**:277
"Mon oncle Sosthène" (Maupassant) **1**:263, 272
"The Money Diggers" (Irving) **2**:251, 261-62
"Monk" (Faulkner) **1**:165, 179
"Monsieur les deux chapeux" (Munro) **3**:348
"Monsieur Parent" (Maupassant) **1**:259-60, 283
"The Moon in the Orange Street Skating Rink" (Munro) **3**:348-49
"Moon Lake" (Welty) **1**:474, 486
The Moons of Jupiter (Munro) **3**:346-47
"Moon-Watcher" (Clarke) **3**:127-28
"More Alarms at Night" (Thurber) **1**:428
"Morning" (Barthelme) **2**:45, 55
Mosses from an Old Manse (Hawthorne) **3**:155, 160, 174, 180, 185
"Motel Architecture" (Ballard) **1**:79
"Mother" (Anderson) **1**:33, 44
"Mother" (Barnes) **3**:22, 26
"A Mother" (Joyce) **3**:205, 210-11, 234, 237, 245, 247, 249
"The Mother of a Queen" (Hemingway) **1**:211
"Motherhood" (Anderson) **1**:27
"Mouche" (Maupassant) **1**:273, 284
"The Mound" (Lovecraft) **3**:270-71, 274, 279
"Mountjoy" (Irving) **2**:242
"The Mouse and the Woman" (Thomas) **3**:399-402, 408
"La moustache" (Maupassant) **1**:274
"Moving Spirit" (Clarke) **3**:134
"MS. Found in a Bottle" (Poe) **1**:379, 391-92, 398
"Mule in the Yard" (Faulkner) **1**:177
Mulliner Nights (Wodehouse) **2**:338
"The Murder" (Chekhov) **2**:150
"Murder in the Dark" (Atwood) **2**:15, 17, 19-20
"The Murders in the Rue Morgue" (Poe) **1**:378, 387, 389, 395, 406
"Music for Chameleons" (Capote) **2**:80
"Music from Spain" (Welty) **1**:474, 495
"The Music Lesson" (Cheever) **1**:100
"The Music of Erich Zann" (Lovecraft) **3**:269
"The Music Teacher" (Cheever) **1**:106
"The Mutability of Literature" (Irving) **2**:251, 254
"Mute" (Atwood) **2**:16
"My Aunt" (Irving) **2**:242
"My Kinsman, Major Molineux" (Hawthorne) **3**:164-65, 167, 171, 175-76, 179-80, 182-83, 186-87, 189
"My Life" (Chekhov) **2**:128, 130-32, 135-36, 145, 155, 157
My Life and Hard Times (Thurber) **1**:413-14, 419, 421-24, 426-28, 435
"My Old Man" (Hemingway) **1**:208, 219, 234, 245
"My Side of the Matter" (Capote) **2**:61-2, 65, 70, 83-5
"My Uncle John" (Irving) **2**:242
My World--And Welcome to It (Thurber) **1**:420
"Mysterious Kôr" (Bowen) **3**:31-2, 39, 41-2, 44, 53
"The Mystery of Marie Rogêt" (Poe) **1**:386, 388, 400, 406
"Myths of the Near Future" (Ballard) **1**:78-9
"The Name, the Nose" (Calvino) **3**:119
"The Name-Day Party" (Chekhov)
See "Name-Day"
"The Name-Day Party" ("The Party") (Chekhov) **2**:128, 130-31, 133, 149, 155-56
"The Name-Day Party" (Chekhov)
See "The Party"
"The Nameless City" (Lovecraft) **3**:262-63, 269, 274, 276
"The Namesake" (Cather) **2**:97, 103-04, 113
"Nanette: An Aside" (Cather) **2**:101
"A Nation of Wheels" (Barthelme) **2**:40
"The National Pastime" (Cheever) **1**:100
"A Natural History of the Dead" (Hemingway) **1**:211
"The Necklace" (Maupassant)
See "La parure"
"The Needlecase" (Bowen) **3**:41
"Neighbors" (Singer) **3**:384
"Neighbour Rosicky" (Cather) **2**:105, 115-17
"A Nervous Breakdown" (Chekhov)
See "An Attack of Nerves"
"Neutron Tide" (Clarke) **3**:133
"Never Bet the Devil Your Head" (Poe) **1**:407
"The New Country House" (Chekhov)
See "The New Villa"
"A New England Nun" (Freeman) **1**:192, 197, 199
A New England Nun, and Other Stories (Freeman) **1**:191, 194-95, 197
"A New England Prophet" (Freeman) **1**:197
"The New Englander" (Anderson) **1**:27, 30, 39, 46-7, 53, 55
"The New House" (Bowen) **3**:40, 54
"The New Music" (Barthelme) **2**:55
"The New Villa" ("The New Country House") (Chekhov) **2**:131, 156
"The New Villa" (Chekhov)
See "The New Country House"
"New York to Detroit" (Parker) **2**:274, 280, 285
"News from the Sun" (Ballard) **1**:78-9
"The Next Tenants" (Clarke) **3**:135
"Nice Girl" (Anderson) **1**:52
The Nick Adams Stories (Hemingway) **1**:240
"The Nigger" (Barnes) **3**:5, 10-11, 14, 22
"A Night among the Horses" (Barnes) **3**:5-7, 10, 14, 16, 22-4
"A Night at Greenway Court" (Cather) **2**:100
"Night Driver" (Calvino) **3**:109
"A Night in the Woods" (Barnes) **3**:18
"Night Sketches" (Hawthorne) **3**:189, 191
"The Night the Bed Fell" (Thurber) **1**:428
"The Night the Ghost Got In" (Thurber) **1**:428, 432
"The Nine Billion Names of God" (Clarke) **3**:134-35, 137, 145
Nine Stories (Salinger) **2**:289-91, 299, 312-13, 316, 318-19
"No Morning After" (Clarke) **3**:149
"No Place for You, My Love" (Welty) **1**:476, 479, 484, 493
"Nobody Knows" (Anderson) **1**:34, 45
"No-Man's-Mare" (Barnes) **3**:11-2, 22
The Nonexistent Knight (Calvino)
See *Il cavaliere inesistente*
The Nonexistent Knight and the Cloven Viscount (Calvino)
See *Il cavaliere inesistente*
The Nonexistent Knight and the Cloven Viscount (Calvino)

Title Index

See *Il visconte dimezzato*
"Un normand" (Maupassant) **1**:288
"Nos Anglais" (Maupassant) **1**:263
"Not for the Sabbath" (Singer) **3**:381
"Not Sixteen" (Anderson) **1**:52
Notes from the Underground (*Letters from the Underworld*) (Dostoevski) **2**:168, 172-73, 178-83, 186, 188-89
Notes from the Underground (Dostoevski)
See *Letters from the Underworld*
Nothing Serious (Wodehouse) **2**:345
"A Novel in Nine Letters" (Dostoevski) **2**:170
"Now I Lay Me" (Hemingway) **1**:220, 241, 247
"Now: Zero" (Ballard) **1**:68
"No. 16" (Bowen) **3**:41
La nuvola di smog (*Smog*) (Calvino) **3**:98, 111-12, 117
"Nyarlathotep" (Lovecraft) **3**:269, 273
"O City of Broken Dreams" (Cheever) **1**:89, 107
"O Youth and Beauty!" (Cheever) **1**:90, 110
Obscure Destinies (Cather) **2**:92, 115, 117-18
"L'occhio del padrone" (Calvino) **3**:97
"The Ocean" (Cheever) **1**:94, 111
"An Odor of Verbena" (Faulkner) **1**:171
"Of Love: A Testimony" (Cheever) **1**:88, 99
"The Office" (Munro) **3**:322, 325, 340, 343
Oh What a Paradise It Seems (Cheever) **1**:108, 113-15
"An Ohio Pagan" (Anderson) **1**:27, 30, 39
"The Old Apple Dealer" (Hawthorne) **3**:189
"The Old Beauty" (Cather) **2**:93-4
The Old Beauty and Others (Cather) **2**:93
"Old Esther Dudley" (Hawthorne) **3**:186
"Old Garbo" (Thomas) **3**:403-06, 410-12
"Old Love" (Singer) **3**:376, 384
"Old Man" (Faulkner) **1**:159-61, 167-68
"The Old Man" (Singer) **3**:355-56
The Old Man and the Sea (Hemingway) **1**:222-24, 226-28, 238-39, 247-50
"Old Man at the Bridge" (Hemingway) **1**:234
"The Old Manse" (Hawthorne) **3**:159, 174, 184
"Old Mr. Marblehall" (Welty) **1**:466, 471, 498
"Old Mrs. Harris" (Cather) **2**:97, 102, 115-17
"Old News" (Hawthorne) **3**:174
"Old Ticonderoga" (Hawthorne) **3**:174
"On A Wagon" (Singer) **3**:375
"On Angels" (Barthelme) **2**:32, 38
"On Official Duty" (Chekhov) **2**:128
"On the Divide" (Cather) **2**:96-7, 100-01, 105-07
"On the Gulls' Road" (Cather) **2**:99, 104
"On the Quai at Smyrna" (Hemingway) **1**:244
"On the Walpole Road" (Freeman) **1**:201
"On the Western Circuit" (Hardy) **2**:206-07, 214, 220, 222-23
"On Writing" (Hemingway) **1**:240, 243
"One Day of Happiness" (Singer) **3**:385-86
"One Good Time" (Freeman) **1**:198
"One is a Wanderer" (Thurber) **1**:417, 420, 425, 427, 435
"One Reader Writes" (Hemingway) **1**:211
"One Warm Saturday" (Thomas) **3**:394-95, 398, 403, 410-12
"The Oracle of the Dog" (Chesterton) **1**:133-34, 136
"The Orchards" (Thomas) **3**:396, 399-402, 407-08
"The Origin of the Birds" (Calvino) **3**:108-10
"Oscar" (Barnes) **3**:2-4
"The Other Gods" (Lovecraft) **3**:274
The Other Side of the Sky (Clarke) **3**:125, 131-32
"The Other Woman" (Anderson) **1**:30
"The Ottawa Valley" (Munro) **3**:337
Our Ancestors (Calvino)
See *I nostri antenati*
"Our Exploits at West Poley" (Hardy) **2**:214, 216, 221
"Out of Nowhere into Nothing" (Anderson) **1**:21, 27, 30, 39, 46-7, 53
"Out of Season" (Hemingway) **1**:245
"Out of the Eons" (Lovecraft) **3**:279
"Out of the Sun" (Clarke) **3**:132, 135-36
"The Outsider" (Lovecraft) **3**:258, 260, 262, 264, 274
"The Oval Portrait" (Poe) **1**:392
"The Overloaded Man" (Ballard) **1**:74-7
Overnight to Many Distant Cities (Barthelme) **2**:50-1, 56
"The Page" (Atwood) **2**:15, 17
"Pages from Cold Point" (Bowles) **3**:59, 61-2, 66, 69, 73, 76-7, 85
"Pain maudit" (Maupassant) **1**:263
"A Painful Case" (Joyce) **3**:203, 205, 209-11, 234-35, 246, 249
"The Painter's Adventure" (Irving) **2**:262
"A Pair" (Singer) **3**:377, 384
"La panchina" (Calvino) **3**:97
"Pantaloon in Black" (Faulkner) **1**:148, 174, 183
"Le Papa de Simon" (Maupassant) **1**:261, 271
"The Paradise of Bachelors and the Tartarus of Maids" (Melville)
See "The Paradise of Bachelors"
"The Paradise of Bachelors and the Tartarus of Maids" ("The Tartarus of Maids") (Melville) **1**:298, 303-05, 323
"The Paradise of Bachelors and the Tartarus of Maids" (Melville)
See "The Tartarus of Maids"
The Paradoxes of Mr. Pond (Chesterton) **1**:125, 139
"Paraguay" (Barthelme) **2**:35, 38, 41
"Le parapluie" (Maupassant) **1**:286
"Parker's Back" (O'Connor) **1**:344-45, 357, 359, 368-70
"The Parrot" (Bowen) **3**:37, 55
"The Parrot" (Singer) **3**:358
Parti-colored Stories (Chekhov) **2**:130
"Une partie de campagne" (Maupassant) **1**:260-61
"The Partridge Festival" (O'Connor) **1**:356
"The Party" (Barthelme) **2**:39, 55
"The Party" (Chekhov)
See "The Name-Day Party"
"La parure" ("The Necklace") (Maupassant) **1**:273, 278, 280, 284, 286, 288
"La parure" (Maupassant)
See "The Necklace"
"Passer-by" (Clarke) **3**:134
"The Passing of Ambrose" (Wodehouse) **2**:356
"The Passion" (Barnes) **3**:5, 24-7
"Une passion" (Maupassant) **1**:274
"Passions" (Singer) **3**:378
Passions, and Other Stories (Singer) **3**:376-77, 381, 384
"Pastor Dowe at Tacaté" (Bowles) **3**:59, 61-3, 66-7, 69, 79
"Pastoral" (Anderson) **1**:52
"Patent Pending" (Clarke) **3**:133-34
"A Patient Waiter" (Freeman) **1**:201
"Patricia, Edith, and Arnold" (Thomas) **3**:402, 405, 410, 412
"La patronne" (Maupassant) **1**:256
"Paul's Case" (Cather) **2**:90-1, 94, 103, 113, 118, 121-22
"The Peace of Utrecht" (Munro) **3**:321, 326
"The Peacelike Mongoose" (Thurber) **1**:426
"The Peaches" (Thomas) **3**:394, 396, 402, 404-05, 410-12
"The Peasant Marey" (Dostoevski) **2**:166
"Peasant Women" (Chekhov) **2**:155
"Peasants" ("The Peasants") (Chekhov) **2**:126, 131, 156
"The Peasants" (Chekhov)
See "Peasants"
"Peasants" (Chekhov)
See "The Peasants"
"Pecheneg" (Chekhov) **2**:155
"Le père" (Maupassant) **1**:275
"Le père amable" (Maupassant) **1**:259, 284
"A Perfect Day for Bananafish" (Salinger) **2**:290-93, 295, 297-99, 303, 305, 308, 312, 314, 318
"The Perfect Murder" (Barnes) **3**:13
"The Peril in the Streets" (Cheever) **1**:99
"The Perishing of the Pendragons" (Chesterton) **1**:131, 138
"Perpetua" (Barthelme) **2**:55
"Pesci grossi, pesci piccoli" (Calvino) **3**:96
"Peter" (Cather) **2**:96-7, 100, 105
"Peter Goldthwaite's Treasure" (Hawthorne) **3**:183, 185
"Le petit fût" (Maupassant) **1**:259, 284
"Petit soldat" (Maupassant) **1**:259
"La petite rogue" (Maupassant) **1**:275, 283, 288
"Petrified Man" (Welty) **1**:465, 467, 469, 471, 482, 490, 493-95, 497
"La peur" (Maupassant) **1**:265, 288
"The Phantom of the Opera's Friend" (Barthelme) **2**:31, 35, 52, 54
"The Piazza" (Melville) **1**:303
The Piazza Tales (Melville) **1**:295-97
"Pickman's Model" (Lovecraft) **3**:261-62
"The Picture in the House" (Lovecraft) **3**:262, 275-76, 292-95
"A Piece of Advice" (Singer) **3**:368
"A Piece of News" (Welty) **1**:468, 478, 487, 496
"A Piece of String" (Maupassant)
See "La ficelle"
"Pierrot" (Maupassant) **1**:277-78
"Pig Hoo-o-o-o-ey!" (Wodehouse) **2**:346, 348
"Pink May" (Bowen) **3**:31-2, 41
"The Pit and the Pendulum" (Poe) **1**:405-06
"The Pleasures of Solitude" (Cheever) **1**:88
"A Plunge into Real Estate" (Calvino)
See "La speculazione edilizia"
The Poet and the Lunatics (Chesterton) **1**:124-26, 132
"A Point of Law" (Faulkner) **1**:177
"Polaris" (Lovecraft) **3**:288
"Polarities" (Atwood) **2**:2-5, 7-8, 10, 13-14
"The Policeman's Ball" (Barthelme) **2**:31, 45
"Polzunkov" (Dostoevski) **2**:170, 192-93

"Un pomeriggio Adamo" (Calvino) **3**:97
The Ponder Heart (Welty) **1**:474, 477, 483, 494-95, 497
"Poor Man's Pudding and Rich Man's Crumbs" (Melville)
See "Poor Man's Pudding"
"Poor Man's Pudding and Rich Man's Crumbs" ("Rich Man's Crumbs") (Melville) **1**:303, 323
"Poor Man's Pudding and Rich Man's Crumbs" (Melville)
See "Rich Man's Crumbs"
"Pope Zeidlus" (Singer) **3**:364
"Porcupines at the University" (Barthelme) **2**:56
"Le port" (Maupassant) **1**:264
Portrait of the Artist as a Young Dog (Thomas) **3**:394-97, 399, 402-04, 410-13
"The Possessed" (Clarke) **3**:132, 135, 143-44, 148
"The Post" (Chekhov) **2**:130, 156
"Postcard" (Munro) **3**:322
"The Pot of Gold" (Cheever) **1**:89, 99
"Powerhouse" (Welty) **1**:466, 488, 494
"Powers" (Singer) **3**:360
"Pranzo con un pastore" (Calvino) **3**:97
"A Predicament" (Poe) **1**:405-06
"The Premature Burial" (Poe) **1**:407
"The President" (Barthelme) **2**:31
"Pretty Mouth and Green My Eyes" (Salinger) **2**:290, 293, 298, 300
"The Pride of the Village" (Irving) **2**:240-41, 245, 251
"Prima Belladonna" (Ballard) **1**:68
"The Princess" (Chekhov) **2**:130, 144
"The Princess Baladina--Her Adventure" (Cather) **2**:100
"Priscilla" (Calvino) **3**:95-6
"The Private Life of Mr. Bidwell" (Thurber) **1**:419
"Privilege" (Munro) **3**:334
"The Privy Counsilor" (Chekhov) **2**:130
"Problem No. 4" (Cheever) **1**:99
"The Procession of Life" (Hawthorne) **3**:181, 190
"The Prodigy" (Singer) **3**:374
"The Professor's Commencement" (Cather) **2**:99, 103, 113
"The Profile" (Cather) **2**:98, 103-04
"The Progress of Love" (Munro) **3**:347, 349
"Prologue to an Adventure" (Thomas) **3**:399, 401
"Promenade" (Maupassant) **1**:260, 274
"Property" (Singer) **3**:374
"The Prophetic Pictures" (Hawthorne) **3**:158, 181, 185-86, 190-91
"A Prospect of the Sea" (Thomas) **3**:394, 399, 401, 407-09
"Le protecteur" (Maupassant) **1**:280
"Publicity Campaign" (Clarke) **3**:134, 150
"The Purloined Letter" (Poe) **1**:387-88
"The Purple Hat" (Welty) **1**:468-69, 471, 479
"The Purple Wig" (Chesterton) **1**:131
"A Pursuit Race" (Hemingway) **1**:216, 219
"Quanto scommettiamo" (Calvino) **3**:92
"The Queer Feet" (Chesterton) **1**:119, 125, 127, 130
"A Queer Heart" (Bowen) **3**:33, 41, 43, 49-50
"The Queer Streak" (Munro) **3**:347
"The Quest of Iranon" (Lovecraft) 274
"A Question of Re-Entry" (Ballard) **1**:68
"Qui sait?" (Maupassant) **1**:273
Quite Early One Morning (Thomas) **3**:392
"The Rabbit" (Barnes) **3**:6-7, 22-4
"The Rabbit-Pen" (Anderson) **1**:52
"The Rabbits Who Caused All the Trouble" (Thurber) **1**:431
"Raid" (Faulkner) **1**:170
"Raise High the Roofbeam, Carpenters" (Salinger) **2**:291-93, 298, 307, 314
"Raise High the Roofbeam, Carpenters and Seymour: An Introduction" (Salinger) **2**:318
"Ralph Ringwood" (Irving) **2**:241
"A Ramble Among the Hills" (Irving) **2**:266
"Rape Fantasies" (Atwood) **2**:3-4, 6-8, 10-12
"Rappaccini's Daughter" (Hawthorne) **3**:159, 171, 173-74, 179-80, 189, 191-92
"The Rats in the Walls" (Lovecraft) **3**:258, 262, 267, 269, 275, 277
"Rattlesnake Creek" (Cather) **2**:106
"Raw Materials" (Atwood) **2**:17-19
Reach for Tomorrow (Clarke) **3**:124, 129
"Reading a Wave" (Calvino) **3**:113
"A Real Discovery" (Chesterton) **1**:140
"Recent Photograph" (Bowen) **3**:40
"Recollections of the Gas Buggy" (Thurber) **1**:431
"Red Leaves" (Faulkner) **1**:147, 162, 168-70, 180
"The Red Moon of Meru" (Chesterton) **1**:129
"Reduced" (Bowen) **3**:33
"Re" e"n" (Marshall) **3**:300, 303, 308, 310, 313, 315, 317
Reena, and Other Stories (Merle: A Novella, and Other Stories) (Marshall) **3**:*313, 315-17*
"The Reference" (Barthelme) **2**:55
"The Reluctant Orchid" (Clarke) **3**:133-34
"Remainders at Bouselham" (Bowles) **3**:66
"Remnants" (Singer) **3**:385, 387
"Le remplacant" (Maupassant) **1**:256
"Renunciation" (Barnes) **3**:16
"The Reptile Enclosure" (Ballard) **1**:68-9
"The Requiem" (Chekhov) **2**:155
"Requiescat" (Bowen) **3**:40
"Rescue Party" (Clarke) **3**:124-26, 135-36, 148-49
"Respectability" (Anderson) **1**:18, 53, 58
"The Resplendent Quetzal" (Atwood) **2**:3, 5, 7, 10-11, 15-16, 19, 22
"The Resurrection of Father Brown" (Chesterton) **1**:129, 137-38
"Le retour" (Maupassant) **1**:285
"Retreat" (Faulkner) **1**:170-71
"Retreat from Earth" (Clarke) **3**:148
"The Return" (Anderson) **1**:31, 39, 50
"The Return" (Bowen) **3**:40, 53
"Return of the Native" (Thurber) **1**:424
"Reunion" (Cheever) **1**:100
"Reunion" (Clarke) **3**:133
"Rêveil" (Maupassant) **1**:274
"Revelation" (O'Connor) **1**:341-42, 344
"The Reversed Man" (Clarke)
See "Technical Error"
"The Revolt of 'Mother'" (Freeman) **1**:192, 196-97, 200
"The Revolutionist" (Hemingway) **1**:244
"Rhobert" (Toomer) **1**:445, 450, 458-59
"Rich Man's Crumbs" (Melville)
See "Poor Man's Pudding and Rich Man's Crumbs"
"A Ride with Olympy" (Thurber) **1**:431
"Rip Van Winkle" (Irving) **2**:239-51, 253, 256-60, 262-64
"The Rise of Capitalism" (Barthelme) **2**:37, 39, 47
"The River" (O'Connor) **1**:344-45, 356
"The Road to the Sea" (Clarke) **3**:135-36
The Robber Bridegroom (Welty) **1**:471-72, 483, 489-90, 496
"Robert Kennedy Saved from Drowning" (Barthelme) **2**:31, 36, 42, 46-7
"The Robin's House" (Barnes) **3**:12
"Roger Melvin's Burial" (Hawthorne) **3**:157, 164, 166-67, 171, 185-86, 189
Rolling All the Time (Ballard) **1**:72
"The Romantic Adventures of a Milkmaid" (Hardy) **2**:211, 215-18, 221, 224
"Rosalie Prudent" (Maupassant) **1**:286
"A Rose for Emily" (Faulkner) **1**:147-52, 158, 162, 165, 180-81
"Le rosier de Madame Husson" (Maupassant) **1**:280
"Rothschild's Fiddle" (Chekhov)
See "Rothschild's Violin"
"Rothschild's Violin" ("Rothschild's Fiddle") (Chekhov) **2**:157-58
"Rothschild's Violin" (Chekhov)
See "Rothschild's Fiddle"
"La rouille" (Maupassant) **1**:256, 272, 274
"Rural Life in England" (Irving) **2**:244
"Sabbath in Gehenna" (Singer) **3**:389
"Sabbath in Portugal" (Singer) **3**:376
"The Sad Horn Blowers" (Anderson) **1**:23, 27, 30
Sadness (Barthelme) **2**:37-40, 46-7, 49
"The Salad of Colonel Cray" (Chesterton) **1**:131
Salmagundi (Irving) **2**:241, 250-53
"The Salt Garden" (Atwood) **2**:21
"The Sandman" (Barthelme) **2**:52
"Saturn Rising" (Clarke) **3**:132
The Scandal of Father Brown (Chesterton) **1**:128, 139
"Scarlet Ibis" (Atwood) **2**:18, 22
"The School" (Barthelme) **2**:53
"The School for Witches" (Thomas) **3**:399, 408-09
"The Schoolmistress" (Chekhov) **2**:128
"The Scorpion" (Bowles) **3**:59, 61, 68, 70-2, 79
"The Sculptor's Funeral" (Cather) **2**:90, 94-5, 98, 100, 103, 105
"The Sea of Hesitation" (Barthelme) **2**:51
"The Séance" (Singer) **3**:369
The Séance, and Other Stories (Singer) **3**:362, 369-70, 373
"The Seaside Houses" (Cheever) **1**:100, 105
"The Season of Divorce" (Cheever) **1**:99
"The Secession" (Bowen) **3**:40
"Second Dawn" (Clarke) **3**:131, 135, 144, 150
"The Secret" (Singer) **3**:385-86
"The Secret Garden" (Chesterton) **1**:119, 134, 137
"The Secret Life of Walter Mitty" (Thurber) **1**:420, 422, 424, 427, 431-32, 435
The Secret of Father Brown (Chesterton) **1**:128, 131
"The Secret of Flambeau" (Chesterton) **1**:126
"See the Moon?" (Barthelme) **2**:35, 42-3, 53
"Seeds" (Anderson) **1**:20, 27, 46
"Un segno" (Calvino) **3**:92
"A Select Party" (Hawthorne) **3**:181
Selected Works of Djuna Barnes (Barnes) **3**:5, 7, 13, 20, 22

Selected Writings of Truman Capote (Capote) **2**:72, 74
"Señor Ong and Señor Ha" (Bowles) **3**:59, 61, 69, 79
"The Sentence" (Barthelme) **2**:38, 41, 44
"Sentiment" (Parker) **2**:273-74, 280, 285
"The Sentimentality of William Tavener" (Cather) **2**:101
"The Sentinel" (Clarke) **3**:124, 127, 135, 145-46, 149-50
"Senza colori" (Calvino) **3**:92
"The Sergeant" (Barthelme) **2**:53
"Sergeant Prishibeev" (Chekhov) **2**:155
"Seventh Street" (Toomer) **1**:443, 450, 458
"Sex Ex Machina" (Thurber) **1**:431
"The Sexes" (Parker) **2**:273, 281, 283
"Seymour: An Introduction" (Salinger) **2**:296, 307-09
"Shadow, a Parable" (Poe) **1**:379
"The Shadow of a Crib" (Singer) **3**:361
"The Shadow of the Shark" (Chesterton) **1**:124
"The Shadow out of Time" (Lovecraft) **3**:258-61, 263, 266, 268, 271-72, 274-75, 279, 290
"The Shadow over Innsmouth" (Lovecraft) **3**:259. 263, 271-77, 291
"The Shadowy Third" (Bowen) **3**:54
"The Shaker Bridal" (Hawthorne) **3**:185-86
"The Shape of Things" (Capote) **2**:65
"The Shepherd's Pipe" (Chekhov) **2**:130, 156
"Shingles for the Lord" (Faulkner) **1**:178
"The Shining Houses" (Munro) **3**:321, 336, 343
"The Shining Ones" (Clarke) **3**:132
"A Shipload of Crabs" (Calvino) **3**:116
"Shoes: An International Episode" (Bowen) **3**:30, 49
"The Shooting of the Cabinet Ministers" (Hemingway) **1**:208, 238
"The Shore and the Sea" (Thurber) **1**:430
"Short Friday" (Singer) **3**:355, 360, 363-64, 383
Short Friday, and Other Stories (Singer) **3**:357, 370, 373, 376
"The Short Happy Life of Francis Macomber" (Hemingway) **1**:217, 230, 232, 234
The Short Stories of Thomas Hardy (Hardy) **2**:212
"A Shower of Gold" (Barthelme) **2**:27-8, 38, 42, 52, 55
"Shower of Gold" (Welty) **1**:483, 485, 493
"The Shunned House" (Lovecraft) **3**:262, 276, 282
"Shut a Final Door" (Capote) **2**:61-2, 64, 66, 69, 72-6, 83
"A Sign in Space" (Calvino)
See "Sign of Space"
"Sign of Space" ("A Sign in Space") (Calvino) **3**:104, 109
"The Sign of the Broken Sword" ("Broken Sword") (Chesterton) **1**:127, 136-37, 142
"The Sign of the Broken Sword" (Chesterton)
See "Broken Sword"
"Significant Moments in the Life of My Mother" (Atwood) **2**:17, 21-3
"Silence, a Fable" (Poe) **1**:379
"Silence Please" (Clarke) **3**:133
"The Silences of Mr. Palomar" (Calvino) **3**:113
"The Silver Key" (Lovecraft) **3**:258, 262, 276, 286
"Simmering" (Atwood) **2**:19-20
"A Simple Enquiry" (Hemingway) **1**:216
"The Sin Eater" (Atwood) **2**:15, 18, 22
"A Singer's Romance" (Cather) **2**:101
"Sir Rabbit" (Welty) **1**:474, 480, 486, 495
"Sister Liddy" (Freeman) **1**:199-200
"The Sisters" (Joyce) **3**:201, 205-06, 208, 211-12, 216-17, 225, 230, 232, 234-35, 237, 244-47, 249
Six Trees (Freeman) **1**:194
Sixty Stories (Barthelme) **2**:46, 51, 56
The Sketch Book (*The Sketch Book of Geoffrey Crayon, Gent.*) (Irving) **2**:238-46, 250-51, 253-55, 257-59, 262, 265, 267
The Sketch Book (Irving)
See *The Sketch Book of Geoffrey Crayon,* Gent.
The Sketch Book of Geoffrey Crayon, Gent. (*The Sketch Book*) (Irving) **2**:252
The Sketch Book of Geoffrey Crayon, Gent. (Irving)
See *The Sketch Book*
"Sketches from Memory" (Hawthorne) **3**:157
"A Sketching Trip" (Welty) **1**:480
"Skirmish at Sartoris" (Faulkner) **1**:170-71
"The Slaughterer" (Singer) **3**:358, 384
"Sleeping Beauty" (Clarke) **3**:134
"Sleeping like Dogs" (Calvino) **3**:112
"Sleepy" (Chekhov) **2**:130, 146-49
"A Slice of Life" (Wodehouse) **2**:347
"The Smile" (Ballard) **1**:79
Smog (Calvino)
See *La nuvola di smog*
"Smoke" (Barnes) **3**:18
"Smoke" (Faulkner) **1**:178-80
Smoke, and Other Early Stories (Barnes) **3**:17, 19
"The Smuggler" (Singer) **3**:389
"The Snow Image" (Hawthorne) **3**:159, 177, 183
The Snow Image, and Other Twice-Told Tales (Hawthorne) **3**:184
"The Snows of Kilimanjaro" (Hemingway) **1**:214-15, 217-18, 229, 234
"Les soeurs Rondoli" (Maupassant) **1**:256, 259, 270, 274, 283, 288
"The Soft Moon" (Calvino) **3**:94, 108-09
"Un soir" (Maupassant) **1**:274, 280
"Soldier's Home" (Hemingway) **1**:208, 244
"Soldiers of the Republic" (Parker) **2**:276, 281-82
"A Solitary" (Freeman) **1**:197
"Solitude" (Maupassant) **1**:262
"Some Get Wasted" (Marshall) **3**:303
Some People, Places, and Things That Will Not Appear in My Next Novel (Cheever) **1**:92, 100
"Some Words with a Mummy" (Poe) **1**:402
Something I've Been Meaning to Tell You (Munro) **3**:328, 331, 335, 339, 346
"Something Squishy" (Wodehouse) **2**:355-56
"The Son From America" (Singer) **3**:374
"A Son of the Celestial" (Cather) **2**:100, 102
"The Song of the Flying Fish" (Chesterton) **1**:129, 138
"Song of the Shirt, 1941" (Parker) **2**:277, 280-81, 285-86
"Songs My Father Sang Me" (Bowen) **3**:41
"The Songs of Distant Earth" (Clarke) **3**:135-36
"The Son's Veto" (Hardy) **2**:215-16, 223
"Sophistication" (Anderson) **1**:30, 42, 44-5
"Sorrow" (Chekhov) **2**:128
"The Sorrows of Gin" (Cheever) **1**:100
Soul Clap Hands and Sing (Marshall) **3**:299-304, 307-08, 316-17
"Sound Sweep" (Ballard) **1**:68
"The Spanish Lady" (Munro) **3**:339
"The Spectacles" (Poe) **1**:407-08
"The Spectre Bridegroom" (Irving) **2**:240-41, 246, 251, 255-56
"The Speculation of the Building Constructors" (Calvino)
See "La speculazione edilizia"
"La speculazione edilizia" ("A Plunge into Real Estate"; "The Speculation of the Building Constructors") (Calvino) **3**:91, 111-12, 117-18
"Spelling" (Munro) **3**:339
Spillway (Barnes) **3**:4-5, 12-4, 16, 22
"The Spinoza of Market Street" (Singer) **3**:361, 368, 375, 384
The Spinoza of Market Street, and Other Stories (Singer) **3**:370
"The Spiral" (Calvino)
See "La spirale"
"La spirale" ("The Spiral") (Calvino) **3**:92, 103-04, 108-09
"Spotted Horses" (Faulkner) **1**:167, 177
"Spring Song of the Frogs" (Atwood) **2**:22
"A Sprinkle of Comedy" (Barnes) **3**:18
"The Stage Coach" (Irving) **2**:245
"The Standard of Living" (Parker) **2**:278, 281, 283
"The Star" (Clarke) **3**:125-27, 130, 136-38, 141-42
"The Statement of Randolph Carter" (Lovecraft) **3**:258-60, 262, 282
"The Steppe" (Chekhov) **2**:129-30, 143, 146, 151, 156
"A Still Moment" (Welty) **1**:467-69, 482
Stories (Bowen) **3**:39
The Stories of John Cheever (Cheever) **1**:105-06, 108-09
"The Storm" (Bowen) **3**:38-9
"The Storm Ship" (Irving) **2**:254
"The Story of Lahcen and Idir" (Bowles) **3**:80
"The Story of the Young Italian" ("The Young Italian") (Irving) **2**:261
"The Story of the Young Italian" (Irving)
See "The Young Italian"
"The Story of the Young Robber" ("The Young Robber") (Irving) **2**:255, 262
"The Story of the Young Robber" (Irving)
See "The Young Robber"
"A Story without a Title" (Chekhov)
See "An Anonymous Story"
"The Stout Gentleman" (Irving) **2**:250-51, 254, 259
"La strada di San Giovanni" (Calvino) **3**:97
"The Strange Crime of John Boulais" (Chesterton) **1**:138
"The Strange High House in the Mist" (Lovecraft) **3**:262, 277
"Strange Stories by a Nervous Gentleman" (Irving) **2**:251, 261
"The Strategy of the Were-Wolf Dog" (Cather) **2**:100
"Stratford-on-Avon" (Irving) **2**:245
"The Street" (Lovecraft) 292
"The Strength of God" (Anderson) **1**:18
"Strong as Death is Love" (Singer) **3**:386
"The Student" (Chekhov) **2**:158

"The Student of Salamanca" (Irving) **2**:251, 254, 259
"The Subliminal Man" (Ballard) **1**:68-9, 77-8
"Subpoena" (Barthelme) **2**:37, 39
"The Successor" (Bowles) **3**:64-5, 80, 83
"The Summer Farmer" (Cheever) **1**:99, 106
"Summer Night" (Bowen) **3**:39, 41, 46, 51
"Summer Theatre" (Cheever) **1**:99
"Summertime on Icarus" (Clarke) **3**:130, 138, 147
"Sunday Afternoon" (Bowen) **3**:41, 53
"Sunday Afternoon" (Munro) **3**:343
"Sunday at Home" (Hawthorne) **3**:189
"Sunday Evening" (Bowen) **3**:53
"Sunjammer" (Clarke) **3**:132
"The Sunrise" (Atwood) **2**:17-18, 21-2
"Sunset" (Faulkner) **1**:177
"The Superintendent" (Cheever) **1**:99, 107
"Superiority" (Clarke) **3**:126, 150
"The Superstitious Man's Story" (Hardy) **2**:217
"Sur l'eau" (Maupassant) **1**:261-62, 265, 278
"Surgery" (Chekhov) **2**:130
"The Swimmer" (Cheever) **1**:94, 100, 102, 106, 108
"A Symphony in Lavender" (Freeman) **1**:199
"The System of Doctor Tarr and Professor Fether" (Poe) **1**:407
"t zero" (Calvino) **3**:93
t zero (Calvino)
See *Ti con zero*
"Taibele and Her Demon" (Singer) **3**:375, 384
"The Tale of Astolpho on the Moon" (Calvino) **3**:101
"A Tale of Jerusalem" (Poe) **1**:407
"The Tale of the Ingrate and His Punishment" (Calvino) **3**:101-02
"A Tale of the Ragged Mountains" (Poe) **1**:400, 402
"A Tale of the White Pyramid" (Cather) **2**:100
"A Tale of Two Liars" (Singer) **3**:375
"A Tale of Two Sisters" (Singer) **3**:377
Tales by Edgar A. Poe (Poe) **1**:388
Tales from the White Hart (Clarke) **3**:131, 133
Tales of a Traveller (Irving) **2**:241, 244, 246, 250-51, 254-55, 258-62, 268
Tales of the Grotesque and Arabesque (Poe) **1**:389-90
Tales of the Long Bow (Chesterton) **1**:133
"The Tall Men" (Faulkner) **1**:151, 162
"The Taming of the Nightmare" (Chesterton) **1**:140
"Tanhum" (Singer) **3**:380
"Tapiama" (Bowles) **3**:64-5, 80, 83
"The Tartarus of Maids" (Melville)
See "The Paradise of Bachelors and the Tartarus of Maids"
"A Taste of Honey" (Freeman) **1**:196
"Tea on the Mountain" (Bowles) **3**:61, 72, 79
"The Teacher" (Anderson) **1**:18, 45, 52
"The Teacher of Literature" ("A Teacher of Literature") (Chekhov) **2**:128, 131-32, 155
"A Teacher of Literature" (Chekhov)
See "The Teacher of Literature"
"The Teacher of Literature" (Chekhov)
See "A Teacher of Literature"
"Teacher's Pet" (Thurber) **1**:422-23
"The Teachings of Don B.: A Yankee Way of Knowledge" (Barthelme) **2**:40
"Tears, Idle Tears" (Bowen) **3**:33, 41, 47
"Technical Error" ("The Reversed Man") (Clarke) **3**:124-25, 129
"Teddy" (Salinger) **2**:293, 295, 300-01, 307, 309, 311-12, 316
"A Telephone Call" (Parker) **2**:274, 278, 280, 285
"A Telephone Call on Yom Kippur" (Singer) **3**:385-86
"Tell Me Yes or No" (Munro) **3**:335
"Telling" (Bowen) **3**:30, 33, 40
"The Tell-Tale Heart" (Poe) **1**:384, 393-94, 408
"The Temple" (Lovecraft) **3**:282, 289
"A Temple of the Holy Ghost" (O'Connor) **1**:343
"Temptation of St. Anthony" (Barthelme) **2**:37, 54
"The Terminal Beach" (Ballard) **1**:69, 76, 80
The Terminal Beach, and Other Stories (Ballard) **1**:68-70, 73
"The Terrible Old Man" (Lovecraft) **3**:292
"Terror" (Anderson) **1**:30
"The Terrorists" (Barnes) **3**:19
"Th Whisperer in Darkness" (Lovecraft) **3**:258-60, 263, 269-71, 274-75, 278-80, 284, 291, 294
"Thanks for the Ride" (Munro) **3**:322, 329, 331, 336, 343
"That Evening Sun" (Faulkner) **1**:147, 162, 181, 183
"That Sophistication" (Anderson) **1**:50
"Theater" (Toomer) **1**:441, 443-45, 450, 452, 458, 460-61
"Theatre of War" (Ballard) **1**:79, 82
"Then It All Came Down" (Capote) **2**:81
"There She Is--She Is Taking Her Bath" (Anderson) **1**:50
These Thirteen (Faulkner) **1**:180-81, 184
"These Walls Are Cold" (Capote) **2**:65
"They called for more structure" (Barthelme) **2**:50
"The Thing on the Doorstep" (Lovecraft) **3**:259, 263, 272, 274-75, 283
"The Thinker" (Anderson) **1**:43-5
"Thou Art the Man" (Poe) **1**:406
Three Stories and Ten Poems (Hemingway) **1**:206
"The Three Strangers" (Hardy) **2**:202-03, 205, 208, 212-15, 218, 220, 223, 226-27
"Three Tools" (Chesterton) **1**:136
"Three Years" (Chekhov) **2**:131, 155-57
"The Three-Day Blow" (Hemingway) **1**:208, 219, 244
"The Three-Fold Destiny" (Hawthorne) **3**:160, 177-78, 182-83, 189
"Through the Gates of the Silver Key" (Lovecraft) **3**:262, 267, 272-73, 286, 294
The Thurber Carnival (Thurber) **1**:416, 426
Ti con zero (*t zero*) (Calvino) **3**:92, 94-6, 98-9, 107, 117
"The Time of Death" (Munro) **3**:329-30
"The Time of Friendship" (Bowles) **3**:63-7, 81-2
"Time's Arrow" (Clarke) **3**:133-34, 142
"To Da-duh, in Memoriam" (Marshall) **3**:301, 303, 307, 313-15, 317
"Today is Friday" (Hemingway) **1**:228-29
"The Toll-Gatherer's Day" (Hawthorne) **3**:158
"Les tombales" (Maupassant) **1**:263
"The Tommy Crans" (Bowen) **3**:33, 41
"Tommy, the Unsentimental" (Cather) **2**:100, 105
"Tomorrow" (Faulkner) **1**:165, 179, 181
"Tony Kytes, the Arch Deceiver" (Hardy) **2**:206-07
"Too Bad" (Parker) **2**:274, 280, 285
"Torch Song" (Cheever) **1**:89, 99, 106, 109-10
A Tour of the Prairies (Irving) **2**:244
"Track 12" (Ballard) **1**:68
"A Tradition of 1804" (Hardy) **2**:215, 220-21
"A Tragedy of Two Ambitions" (Hardy) **2**:205-06, 214-17, 223
"Training" (Atwood) **2**:3-4, 7-8, 10, 12-13, 16
"Transience" (Clarke) **3**:127, 135, 142
"Transit Bed" (Calvino) **3**:112
"Transit of Earth" (Clarke) **3**:147
"A Travel Piece" (Atwood) **2**:3-4, 6-7, 10, 12, 15-16
"The Tree" (Thomas) **3**:399, 402, 408-09
"A Tree of Night" (Capote) **2**:61-3, 66, 69, 72-5
A Tree of Night, and Other Stories (Capote) **2**:61-4, 72, 74, 83
"The Trees of Pride" (Chesterton) **1**:122
"The Trial of the Old Watchdog" (Thurber) **1**:426
"Tribuneaux rustiques" (Maupassant) **1**:259, 286
The Triumph of the Egg (Anderson) **1**:19-20, 22, 26-7, 30, 32, 34, 46-7, 50
"The Triumph of the Egg" (Anderson)
See "The Egg"
The Troll Garden (Cather) **2**:90, 93, 96, 103, 113
"The Trouble of Marcie Flint" (Cheever) **1**:90
"Trouble with the Natives" (Clarke) **3**:124, 149
"The Truant" (Irving) **2**:265
"A Tryst at an Ancient Earthwork" (Hardy) **2**:210, 214-15
"The Turkey Season" (Munro) **3**:346
"Tutto in un punto" (Calvino) **3**:92
Twice-Told Tales (Hawthorne) **3**:154-55, 157-61, 180, 184-85, 190
"Two" (Singer) **3**:381
"Two Corpses Go Dancing" (Singer) **3**:370
"Two Friends" (Cather) **2**:100, 109, 115, 117-18
"Two Gallants" (Joyce) **3**:200-01, 205-06, 209, 214, 220-21, 225, 231-34, 237, 246
"Two Markets" (Singer) **3**:377
"Two Old Lovers" (Freeman) **1**:197, 200-01
"Two Sides to a Tortoise" (Melville)
See "The Encantadas; or, The Enchanted Isles"
"Two Soldiers" (Faulkner) **1**:151
"The Two Temples" (Melville) **1**:303, 323
"Uglypuss" (Atwood) **2**:18, 22
"Ukridge Sees Her Through" (Wodehouse) **2**:354
The Ultimate City (Ballard) **1**:72, 74, 83-4
"The Ultimate Melody" (Clarke) **3**:133-34
Ultimo viene il corvo (*Adam, One Afternoon, and Other Stories*) (Calvino) **3**:106, 116
Uncle Tom's Children (Wright) **2**:360-61, 363, 365-68, 370-71, 373-75, 379, 381-84, 386-88
"Uncle Valentine" (Cather) **2**:98, 113-15
"Uncle Wiggily in Connecticut" (Salinger) **2**:290, 292, 295, 299, 305-06, 313-14
"Uncle Willy" (Faulkner) **1**:151

Title Index

"Uncle's Dream" (Dostoevski) **2**:164, 172, 184
The Uncollected Wodehouse (Wodehouse) **2**:343
"The Undefeated" (Hemingway) **1**:209, 216, 218-19, 224, 230, 234
"Under Glass" (Atwood) **2**:3, 6, 10, 13, 16
"Under the Jaguar Sun" (Calvino) **3**:118-19
"Under the Knife" (Singer) **3**:362
"Under the Sky" (Bowles) **3**:59, 61-2, 67, 79
"The Underground" (Dostoevski) **2**:187
"Unearthing Suite" (Atwood) **2**:17, 22
"An Unfinished Collection" (Wodehouse) **2**:343
"The Unicorn in the Garden" (Thurber) **1**:427-28, 431
"Unlighted Lamps" (Anderson) **1**:27, 30, 39, 46-7, 53, 55
"The Unnameable" (Lovecraft) **3**:262, 276, 293-94
"The Unparalleled Adventure of One Hans Pfaall" (Poe) **1**:400, 402, 406
"An Unpleasant Predicament" (Dostoevski) **2**:166, 184
"The Unseen" (Singer) **3**:358, 362, 383-84
Unspeakable Practices, Unnatural Acts (Barthelme) **2**:29-31, 35, 37-8, 51
"The Untold Lie" (Anderson) **1**:21, 34, 39, 41-2, 44, 52
"'Unused'" (Anderson) **1**:23, 27, 30, 39-40, 46-7, 53, 55
The Unvanquished (Faulkner) **1**:151, 170, 177, 180
"Unwelcome Words" (Bowles) **3**:85-6
Unwelcome Words: Seven Stories (Bowles) **3**:85
"Uomo nei gerbidi" (Calvino) **3**:96
"Up, Aloft in the Air" (Barthelme) **2**:38
"Up in Michigan" (Hemingway) **1**:207, 219
"Uprooted" (Chekhov) **2**:130
"The Valet" (Barnes) **3**:22-4
"The Valley Between" (Marshall) **3**:303, 308-09, 312, 315, 317
"The Vanishing of Vaudrey" (Chesterton) **1**:131
"The Vanishing Prince" (Chesterton) **1**:122
"Vánka" (Chekhov) **2**:130
"The Vanvild Kava" (Singer) **3**:383
"Vendée" (Faulkner) **1**:171
"Une vendetta" (Maupassant) **1**:277
"The Vengeance of 3902090" (Thurber) **1**:419
Vermilion Sands (Ballard) **1**:78
Very Good, Jeeves (Wodehouse) **2**:346
"The Very Proper Gander" (Thurber) **1**:431
"Veteran of the Private Evacuations" (Ballard) **1**:70
"Victory" (Faulkner) **1**:148
"The Victory Burlesk" (Atwood) **2**:19
"The Viennese Opera Ball" (Barthelme) **2**:28
"A View of the Woods" (O'Connor) **1**:342-45, 356
"Views of My Father Weeping" (Barthelme) **2**:31, 42, 46, 48, 55
The Viking Portable Library Dorothy Parker (Parker) **2**:276, 278
"The Village of Stepanchikovo" (Dostoevski) See "The Friend of the Family"
"The Village of Stepanchikovo" (Dostoevski) See "The Hamlet of Stepanchikovo"
"The Village of Stepanchikovo" ("The Manor of Stepanchikovo") (Dostoevski) **2**:164, 175
"The Village of Stepanchikovo" (Dostoevski) See "The Manor of Stepanchikovo"
"A Village Singer" (Freeman) **1**:197, 200
"A Virtuoso's Collection" (Hawthorne) **3**:171
Il visconte dimezzato (*The Cloven Viscount*; *The Nonexistent Knight and the Cloven Viscount*) (Calvino) **3**:90-1, 94, 99, 106, 117
"The Vision of the Fountain" (Hawthorne) **3**:178, 182
"A Vision of the World" (Cheever) **1**:93-6, 105
"A Visit of Charity" (Welty) **1**:470
"A Visit to America" (Thomas) **3**:393
"A Visit to Grandpa's" (Thomas) **3**:397, 402, 405, 410, 412
"The Visitor" (Bowen) **3**:40
"The Visitor" (Thomas) **3**:400, 407, 409
"Visitors" (Barthelme) **2**:56
"The Voices of Time" (Ballard) **1**:71, 80
"Von Kempelen and His Discovery" (Poe) **1**:402
"A Wagner Matinée" (Cather) **2**:90-1, 96, 103, 105, 108
"The Waiting Grounds" (Ballard) **1**:68, 76
"The Waiting Supper" (Hardy) **2**:211, 215-16, 219, 223
"Wakefield" (Hawthorne) **3**:154, 159, 161-62, 178, 189, 191
"A Walk in the Dark" (Clarke) **3**:124, 147-49
"A Walk in the Woods" (Bowen) **3**:54
"Walker Brothers Cowboy" (Munro) **3**:321, 329, 343, 347
"Walking on Water" (Munro) **3**:331, 346
"The Wall of Darkness" (Clarke) **3**:125, 129, 147
"The Waltz" (Parker) **2**:274, 281, 283, 285-86
"The Wanderers" (Welty) **1**:479, 493
"The War in the Bathroom" (Atwood) **2**:4, 6-8, 10
"Ward No. 6" ("Ward Number Six") (Chekhov) **2**:126, 131-32, 143, 152, 157
"Ward No. 6" (Chekhov) See "Ward Number Six"
"Ward Number Six" (Chekhov) See "Ward No. 6"
"The Warehouse" (Singer) **3**:358, 360
"Was" (Faulkner) **1**:148, 173-74, 182
"Wash" (Faulkner) **1**:166, 180
"Watch This Space" (Clarke) **3**:133
"The Watcher" (Calvino) See "La giornata d'uno scrutatore"
The Watcher, and Other Stories (Calvino) **3**:98-9
"The Water of Izli" (Bowles) **3**:68
"The Way of the World" (Cather) **2**:102-03
The Way Some People Live (Cheever) **1**:87-8, 92, 98-100
"A Way You'll Never Be" (Hemingway) **1**:218, 245, 247
"A Weak Heart" ("A Faint Heart") (Dostoevski) **2**:195
"A Weak Heart" (Dostoevski) See "A Faint Heart"
"The Weaver and the Worm" (Thurber) **1**:428
"A Wedding in Brownsville" (Singer) **3**:360, 363, 376
"The Wedding Knell" (Hawthorne) **3**:154
Wessex Tales (Hardy) **2**:202-03, 205, 212, 214-15, 220, 223, 225-26, 229
"The Westbound Train" (Cather) **2**:102
"Westminster Abbey" (Irving) **2**:244-45, 250-51
"Whacky" (Clarke) **3**:134
"What Do You Mean It Was Brillig?" (Thurber) **1**:428
"What Do You See, Madam?" (Barnes) **3**:18
"What Goes Up" (Clarke) **3**:134
"What the Shepherd Saw" (Hardy) **2**:210
"When It Happens" (Atwood) **2**:4, 6-7, 10, 13, 16
"Where Tawe Flows" (Thomas) **3**:397, 406, 411-12
"The Whip-Poor-Will" (Thurber) **1**:422
"The Whistle" (Welty) **1**:468
"White Dump" (Munro) **3**:347-49
"White Nights" (Dostoevski) **2**:171-72
"The White Old Maid" (Hawthorne) **3**:154, 159, 180-81
"The White Rabbit Caper" (Thurber) **1**:431
"White Spot" (Anderson) **1**:52
"Who Do You Think You Are?" (Munro) **3**:343
"Who Do You Wish Was With Us" (Thomas) **3**:395, 398, 403, 406, 411-12
"Who Is This Tom Scarlett?" (Barnes) **3**:18
"The Whole World Knows" (Welty) **1**:474, 479-80, 483
"Who's There" (Clarke) **3**:134
"Why Heisherik Was Born" (Singer) **3**:385, 387
"Why I Live at the P. O." (Welty) **1**:465, 468-69, 471, 476-79, 482, 489, 494, 497
"Why I Want to Fuck Ronald Reagan" (Ballard) **1**:70, 75, 82
"Why the Little Frenchman Wears His Arm in a Sling" (Poe) **1**:407
"The Wide Net" (Welty) **1**:467, 469, 471, 494
"The Widow and Her Son" (Irving) **2**:240-41, 251
"The Widow's Ordeal" (Irving) **2**:241
"The Wife" (Irving) **2**:240-41, 243, 245, 251
"The Wife of Another and the Husband under the Bed" (Dostoevski) **2**:171, 193
"The Wife-Killer" (Singer) **3**:358
"The Wild Palms" (Faulkner) **1**:159-61
"Will You Tell Me" (Barthelme) **2**:27
Willa Cather's Collected Short Fiction (Cather) **2**:103, 105
"William Wilson" (Poe) **1**:378, 385-86, 394-97, 407
"The Willing Muse" (Cather) **2**:98, 103
"The Wind at Beni Midar" (Bowles) **3**:64, 85
"The Winds" (Welty) **1**:472
Winesburg, Ohio (Anderson) **1**:17-19, 22, 24-35, 38-46, 48, 51-2, 55, 57-8
Winner Take Nothing (Hemingway) **1**:211, 216-17
"Winter Wind" (Munro) **3**:331
"The Winters and the Palmeys" (Hardy) **2**:207, 209
The Wisdom of Father Brown (Chesterton) **1**:120-21, 124
"The Witch" (Singer) **3**:377
"The Withered Arm" (Hardy) **2**:202-03, 205, 208, 213-14, 217-20, 227-28, 231-34
"Without Colors" (Calvino) **3**:104, 108-09
"The Wives of the Dead" (Hawthorne) **3**:159, 164, 186
Wodehouse on Crime (Wodehouse) **2**:352
"Wolfert Webber" (Irving) **2**:241, 247, 249, 251-52, 262, 266, 268
"Wolfert's Roost" (Irving) **2**:246
"A Woman without a Country" (Cheever) **1**:95, 100

"A Woman's Kingdom" (Chekhov) **2**:156-57
"Women" (Singer) **3**:358
"The Wonderful Old Gentleman" (Parker) **2**:274, 281, 283
"The Wood Duck" (Thurber) **1**:414, 422
"The Working Party" (Bowen) **3**:30, 40, 49
"The World of Apples" (Cheever) **1**:112
"A Worn Path" (Welty) **1**:466, 470, 491-92, 494
"Worship" (Atwood) **2**:20
"The Worst Crime in the World" (Chesterton) **1**:129, 138
"The Wrong Shape" (Chesterton) **1**:121, 129-30, 136
"The Yellow Bird" (Chesterton) **1**:124-25, 133
"The Yellow Gown" (Anderson) **1**:52
"Yentl the Yeshiva Boy" (Singer) **3**:359, 384
"You Are Not I" (Bowles) **3**:59-61, 66, 68-9, 72, 76-7
"You Have Left Your Lotus Pods on the Bus" (Bowles) **3**:69
"You Were Perfectly Fine" (Parker) **2**:272, 278, 281
"Young Goodman Brown" (Hawthorne) **3**:164-68, 171-74, 177-78, 180, 182-83, 185-87, 189, 191-93
"The Young Italian" ("The Story of the Young Italian") (Irving) **2**:260, 268
"The Young Italian" (Irving) See "The Story of the Young Italian"
Young Men in Spats (Wodehouse) **2**:325, 328
"The Young Robber" ("The Story of the Young Robber") (Irving) **2**:257, 262
"The Young Robber" (Irving) See "The Story of the Young Robber"
"A Young Woman in Green Lace" (Parker) **2**:273, 283
Youth and the Bright Medusa (Cather) **2**:91-2, 94, 98, 103, 111-13
"Yveline Samoris" (Maupassant) **1**:283
"Yvette" (Maupassant) **1**:263, 275, 283
"Zeitl and Rickel" (Singer) **3**:359
"Lo zio acquativo" ("The Aquatic Uncle") (Calvino) **3**:92-3, 109
"Zodiac 2000" (Ballard) **1**:79
"Zone of Terror" (Ballard) **1**:68
"Zooey" (Salinger) **2**:291, 293-94, 296-97, 302-05, 308